NORMAN MAILER

A DOUBLE LIFE

ALSO BY J. MICHAEL LENNON

On God: An Uncommon Conversation (with Norman Mailer)

Norman Mailer: Works and Days (with Donna Pedro Lennon)

Conversations with Norman Mailer (editor)

Critical Essays on Norman Mailer (editor)

NORMAN MAILER
A DOUBLE LIFE

J MICHAEL LENNON

SIMON &
SCHUSTER

London · New York · Sydney · Toronto · New Delhi

A CBS COMPANY

First published in Great Britain by Simon & Schuster UK Ltd, 2013
A CBS COMPANY

Designed by Esther Paradelo

1 3 5 7 9 10 8 6 4 2

Simon & Schuster UK Ltd
1st Floor
222 Gray's Inn Road
London WC1X 8HB

www.simonandschuster.co.uk

Simon & Schuster Australia, Sydney
Simon & Schuster India, New Delhi

A CIP catalogue record for this book
is available from the British Library

ISBN: 978-1-84737-672-5
ISBN: 978-1-47111-488-5 (ebook)

Printed and bound by CPI Group (UK) Ltd, Croydon, CR0 4YY

To my wife, Donna Pedro Lennon,
and
Barbara Mailer Wasserman,
with love and gratitude

and to the memory of Robert F. Lucid

"There are two sides to me, and
the side that is the observer is paramount."

—Norman Mailer

CONTENTS

NORMAN MAILER
A DOUBLE LIFE

PROLOGUE
THE RIPTIDES OF FAME: JUNE 1948

After delivering the manuscript of his war novel *The Naked and the Dead* to his publisher, Norman Mailer sailed to Europe with his wife, Beatrice, on October 3, 1947. Having for most of his life known only the Depression and the war in the Pacific, he had always viewed with romantic envy the expatriate pasts of the Lost Generation writers he admired: Hemingway, Fitzgerald, Dos Passos, and Henry Miller. So to go to Europe on the GI Bill as he now could seemed like a miraculous opportunity. Paris was the bull's-eye destination for aspiring writers, including Stanley Karnow, a Harvard graduate and veteran who arrived there a few months before Mailer. His memoir, *Paris in the Fifties*, opens with the question: "*Porquoi Paris?* Its name alone was magic. The city, the legendary *Ville Lumière*, promised something for everyone—beauty, sophistication, culture, cuisine, sex, escape and that indefinable called ambience." Mailer partook of all of these pleasures during his ten-month stay there. He differed from most of his countrymen, however, in one respect: he *was* a writer when he arrived: besides *Naked*, he had written two unpublished novels in college. While enjoying Paris and taking trips to other countries, he was trying to get a new novel going. It was one of the happiest seasons of his life, shadowed only by his anxiety about the future.

In the spring of 1948 he drove to Italy in a small Peugeot, accompanied by his wife, younger sister, and mother—Beatrice, Barbara, and Fanny. They left Paris on June 1, drove east to Switzerland and then south to Italy. It began to rain as they drove through the foothills of the Alps, and turned to snow when they reached higher elevations. Mailer had to keep downshifting on the hairpin turns because the Peugeot didn't have much horsepower. By the time they reached the St. Gotthard Pass, they were in a blizzard. At the peak they had to back up to let another car pass, coming perilously close to the edge. Mailer relished the experience. They spent a few days in the villages and resorts of the northern lake country, and then moved on to Florence and Venice. In mid-June they arrived in Rome, where they hoped to pick up their mail, forwarded by Mailer's father, Barney, an accountant working for a post-war relief organization in Paris.

Rinehart and Co., Mailer's publisher, had mounted a major publicity campaign for *The Naked and the Dead*, and he and his family (his mother and sister had come over in April) were eager for news of its reception. The mail in Rome contained several reviews, all positive, even glowing. After two or three days of sightseeing, Fan left them and took the train back to Paris to join Barney. Mailer, Bea, and Barbara drove down to Naples, then on the morning of June 23 they began the long drive back to France. Mailer was preoccupied, thinking about the reviews, the return trip to the United States, and a cable he had just received from Lillian Hellman, who wanted to write a dramatic adaptation of his novel. He had seen her play *The Little Foxes* on Broadway when he was in college, and had "a lot of respect for her as a playwright," as he told his editor. In Paris, he had begun a new novel, but it was a fragment, and he didn't know if he wanted to continue with it. He had the feeling that he'd be busy when he got home in August. They drove on, and after a long ride arrived in the late afternoon at the American Express office in Nice. Barney had forwarded the next batch of mail from the States.

A month earlier, Mailer recorded his anticipations in his journal. He had seen "batches of reviews" by May 12—the novel came out on May 6—and realized its prospects were excellent.

> The thing I've got to get down here is my reactions to the book's success. The depression to start with—I feel trapped. My anonymity is lost, and the book I wrote to avoid having to expose my mediocre talents in harsher market places has ended in this psychological sense by betraying me; I dread the return to America where every word I say will have too much importance, too much misinterpretation. And of course I am sensitive to the hatreds my name is going to evoke.
>
> But across from that is the other phenomenon. I feel myself more

> empty than I ever have, and to fill the vacuum, to prime the motor, I need praise. Each good review gives fuel, each warm letter, but as time goes by I need more and more for less and less effect. This kind of praise-opium could best be treated in fiction through the publicity mad actress who has to see her face and name more and more to believe in her reality, and of course loses the line between her own personality, and the one created for her by the papers.

Mailer's desire for fame, and his distaste for it, never abated over his long career. Nor did his ability to determine how he might write about his current situation, whatever it might be. It became a reflex.

Hot and dusty and sweaty from the ride to Nice, Barbara and Bea sat in the Peugeot while Mailer went in for the mail. He returned with an enormous packet of clippings, cables, reviews, and letters. "The reviews were mostly marvelous," Barbara wrote. "Our friends were all excited and writing to us (I remember my Progressive Party lover wrote, 'What kind of book is this that both the *Times* and the *Daily Worker* praise?')" The atmosphere in the car got "somewhat frenetic and hysterical."

> I don't think we finished reading any letter or review because it was always interrupted by word of a comment on what someone else was reading. Finally Norman said, in a rather small voice which I will never forget the sound of because it so totally captured the feeling that none of this was quite real, "Gee, I'm first on the best seller list." We laughed. And laughed. And I thought of all this excitement going on 3,000 miles away, and Norman was the cause of it, but it didn't seem to have any relation to "Us."

Looking back on that day almost sixty years later, Mailer said, "It was a great shock." He had been hoping he would earn enough money from *Naked and the Dead* to write his next book. Now the novel was number one on the *New York Times* bestseller list, where it stayed for eleven consecutive weeks. All told, it remained on the list for sixty-two weeks. "I knew I'd be a celebrity when I came back to America and I felt very funny towards it, totally unprepared," he said. "I'd always seen myself as an observer. And now I knew, realized, that I was going to be an actor. An actor on the American stage, so to speak. I don't mean I knew it all at once. But there were certainly intimations of that."

Shortly after leaving the army, Mailer had been told by a New York editor that no one was interested in war novels. Everyone was tired of the war. But by 1948, readers were eager to remember and explore the experience, and Mailer's novel, which looked at World War II from both the battlefields of the Pacific and the home front, was perfectly suited. "It was the luckiest timing of my career," he said later. Even so, he was concerned that the publicity surrounding the novel, and its huge sales, would alienate the readers of the leading literary journal in the United States, the *Partisan Review.* Success as a writer, he said, was like getting "caught in a riptide. Two waves coming in from different directions. You get more attention in one place and less in the other. The ego is on a jumping jack." He and Bea believed *PR*'s readers were mainly snobs, but he still wanted to see his name on its front cover.

But the largest drawback of fame was that it cut him off from real experience, as he called it, the kind he'd had in the army, experience that was thrust on you, as opposed to the kind one sought. "I used to feel that I didn't know anything because I got rich too soon," he said. "I used to feel sorry for myself." But after some years of demeaning his fame, he started to enjoy it. It was "an acquired appetite." He agreed with the Marquis de Sade that "there is no pleasure greater than that obtained from a conquered repugnance." When he reached that point he wanted more and more of it, recognizing that being famous at an early age was a genuine, if unusual, experience. If he was unable to enjoy normal life, he now had "a sense of how . . . not tenuous, not fragile . . . how delicate, perhaps, is identity." Success had brought on an identity crisis. After that, he said, "It was as if there was somebody named Norman Mailer, but to meet him people had to meet me first." Then, as his fame waxed and waned over the next decade, he saw that "I could now write about the identity of people who had a certain amount of power." One of Mailer's most important subjects is power, and how it is gained, lost, regained, or dwindled away, and the conflicted, intricate psyches of those who exercise it.

His literary career had a significant foreground—in Brooklyn, Harvard, and combat in the Philippines—but it began officially, one might say, on that hot day in Nice. Before they opened the mail and saw the magnitude of the novel's reception, Barbara said, "was the last time

Norman could feel he was himself and not Norman Mailer." He said that he "felt kind of blue" after reading the mail in Nice. When they returned to Paris a few days later, he told his sister, "I think the book may be better than I am." He had turned twenty-five only a few months earlier.

ONE
LONG BRANCH AND BROOKLYN

Norman Mailer knew little about his grandparents' lives in Lithuania, then part of Russia. The Mailers and the Schneiders lived in three towns, not more than sixty miles apart, in central and northeastern Lithuania: Panevezys, Anyksciai, and Utena. Unknown to each other in Russia, the two families emigrated at the end of the nineteenth century to escape economic hardship or persecution, or both, the Mailers settling in Johannesburg, South Africa, and the Schneiders in New Jersey.

Mailer's maternal grandfather, Hyman (Chaim) Jehuda Schneider, was a precocious child who studied the Torah and Talmud from a very early age. Mailer's mother, Fan, said that he was "sent at the age of seven to the yeshiva in Wolozin [Volozhin], Russia, which was comparable to Columbia [University] in the U.S." Commonly referred to as "the Mother of Yeshivas," the Volozhin Yeshiva was the home of the *Misnagdim*, the opponents of Hasidism, the rambunctious, anti-formalist movement that developed among European Jews in the latter part of the eighteenth century. "My father," Fan wrote, "was a staunch follower of the *Misnagdim*. He felt the Hasidim were not so learned; they depended too much on the rabbi and his blessings." There is more than a slight irony in the fact that her son would become fascinated by the mysticism of the Hasidim. In the early 1960s, he wrote six columns for *Commentary*, reflections on folk stories collected by Martin Buber that centered on the Hasidim's dialectic, which, Mailer said, "placed madness next to practicality, illumination side by side with duty, and arrogance in bed with humility." Early and late, Mailer gravitated to incompatibles.

Born in 1859, Schneider was a rabbi by sixteen and, at about the same age, married Ida Kamrass. They had six children, in order: Joseph, Rebecca (Beck), Jennie, a son who died at childbirth, Rose, and the youngest, Fanny or Fan. At the end of the century, the Jews in the Pale of Settlement (comprised of the bulk of Poland, Ukraine, Lithuania, Latvia, and Belarus) were being driven abroad by double taxation and forced enlistments in the czar's army. Parlous conditions from 1881 to 1914 forced over two million to emigrate. Sometime in early 1891, Schneider left for the United States with his half-sister, Lena, his half-brother, Morris, and his wife's youngest sister, Minnie. Ida, pregnant with Fan, stayed behind. The Schneiders were separated for three years. Ida, her sixty-two-year-old mother, Leah Sacks, and the five children arrived in New York in October 1894, sailing from Rotterdam on the SS *Veendam*.

When Hyman Schneider arrived in 1891, he was advised to set up a soda water and newspaper stand on the Lower East Side. He and Lena opened the stand at four A.M. and worked shifts until late at night. Irish gangs, operating with impunity, dominated the area and took what they wanted. Sixty years later, Mailer had an apartment not far from where his grandfather had once toiled. After six months, Schneider left the city and became a peddler in rural New Jersey. He also taught Hebrew to Jewish families in Belmar before finally settling in the resort town of Long Branch, where, according to Fan, he was "induced" by the small local Jewish community to start a kosher grocery store.

In *The Naked and the Dead*, Mailer drew on his earliest memories for a description of the store run by Joey Goldstein's grandfather, a learned Jew who quotes the medieval Jewish poet and scholar Yehuda Halevi:

> Inside there is a narrow marble counter and an aisle about two feet wide for the customers who stand on the eroded oil cloth. In the summer it is sticky, and the pitch comes off on one's shoes. On the counter are two glass jars with metal covers and a bent ladling spoon containing essence of cherry, essence of orange. (Coca-Cola is not yet in vogue.) Beside them is a tan moist cube of halvah on a block of wood. The flies are sluggish, and one has to prod them before they fly away.

The Schneider store catered to the Jewish population, which burgeoned each summer with the arrival of middle-class visitors and a few wealthy New Yorkers. Preoccupied by his studies, Rabbi Schneider played a relatively small role in the store; the women and older girls did most of the work with the two younger girls helping after school. Only Rose and Fan were able to graduate from high school.

Along with recent arrivals from the Pale, itinerant rabbis, cantors, and others were put up for days at a time at their home, often staying until enough money could be collected for them to move on to the next town. Hyman was their informal counselor, an independent scholar who was glad to learn and teach. Over tea and sweets, he regaled the household with stories from the Talmud or read accounts of the life of his hero, Baruch Spinoza, a freethinking Portuguese Jew who was excommunicated by the Orthodox Jewish community of Amsterdam. Rabbi Schneider's intellectual ability is an article of faith in the Mailer family. Fan's husband, Barney, said the source of his son's talent was "his maternal grandfather. A Talmudic scholar." Fan added, "three of his grandsons went to Harvard." Marjorie "Osie" Radin, the eldest of Mailer's American cousins, who was nineteen when the rabbi died, said, "That's where all the brains and talent came from." In a memoir, Mailer's sister, Barbara, answers the question "Who was Grandpa?"

> Certainly, in one view, the archetype of the timid Jew, the one who whispers in front of the firing squad, "Don't make waves." But also the saintly, kindly man, the revered intellectual, brave enough to come to a foreign land and work at menial entrepreneurship, too afraid of violence to stay in New York (a gang of thugs once overturned his peddler's cart), but too proud to be a rabbi who takes orders from others, orthodox in his rituals, but on the edge of apostasy in thought.

In 1913 the Schneiders established a boardinghouse with sixty rooms in three adjacent houses on Morris Avenue, naming it the Maple Hotel and Cottages. Beck and her husband, Louis Shapiro, partnered with her parents in the operation of the Maple for two years before it burned to the ground in the winter of 1915, one of many such fires in Long Branch. The family remained in the hotel business, however, especially since it was easy to provide the guests with kosher food from the store. From 1916 to 1918, again with Beck and her husband, they leased the Scarboro Hotel on Ocean Avenue, built in 1882 and catering to an almost exclusively Jewish clientele. Beck and Louis later bought the hotel, expanded it, and added a coat of white stucco; eventually it became the largest hotel (two hundred rooms) in Long Branch and was a source of family pride until it too burned down in 1941.

Although the Schneider girls worked twelve-hour days in the family business, they had a passionate interest in culture. At age twelve Fan read *Anna Karenina* (her son's favorite novel) and, later in high school, Dickens and George Eliot. On Saturday nights, they went to the movies and, in the summers saw Broadway tryout plays and Gilbert and Sullivan operettas at Riverside Park.

BY THE SUMMER of 1919, Fan would go into the hotel business full-time with her parents. She and her father went to Lakewood, New Jersey, in October of 1919 to lease a place as a winter resort. The fifteen-bedroom house was called Lakeview Lodge, although Fan noted bluntly, "I assure you there was no view." New visitors were sought by placing ads in the New York Yiddish newspaper, the *Tageblatt*.

One of the ads was read by a twenty-eight-year-old veteran of World War I, Isaac Barnett Mailer. Barney, as he was generally known, had studied accounting at Transvaal University in Johannesburg and then joined the South African army. Stationed in London from 1917 to 1919, he was mustered out in the summer of 1919 and decided to travel to the United States rather than return home. His parents, Benjamin and Celia Mailer, had lived in Johannesburg since emigrating from Lithuania in 1900, when Barney, the second of eleven surviving children, was nine. The Mailers had established themselves solidly there, operating various businesses. Barney arrived from Liverpool on the White Star liner SS *Baltic* in November 1919, and moved in with his sister Anne and her husband, David Kessler, who were then living in the Flatbush section of Brooklyn.

The favorite child of his mother, Barney was a compulsive gambler whose debts had caused his family considerable anguish. According to Barbara, the family finally gave her father "an ultimatum: go in the army or we will wash our hands of you." World War I forced Barney to give up or at least curtail his betting in London; the United States was to be where he would redeem himself. The plan was simple: live with Anne and Dave (who were childless) until he found a professional position and a wife, then settle down. Shortly after Barney's arrival, Anne caught the flu at the tail end of the pandemic of 1918–19. Reservations were made at Lakeview Lodge for her recuperation and in January 1920, Barney and the Kesslers took the train to Lakewood. Fan recounts the various circumstances of their first meeting three separate times in her memoir, written at the request of her son.

> The rug was rolled back, so we could have dancing Saturday night. Sunday afternoon we all took a walk to the Lake, and Monday morning just before leaving, Dad [Barney] and I found we were all alone in the living room. We were both shy, there was a pack of playing cards on the table and Dad said, "Let me show you some card tricks." I thought he was very nice, polite and really handsome.

Barney Mailer was also a fashion plate. His dress, if somewhat conservative, was tasteful. He wore pearl gray spats, carried gloves, an umbrella or cane, and wore a felt hat. In his photographs, he seems always to be dressed in a three-piece suit. His manners were refined, his accent intriguing, and his handwriting spidery and graceful. Unlike his son, whose unruly hair became a trademark, Barney's hair was always neatly combed. He had a strong, slightly cleft chin and good features, and looked a bit like Donald Rumsfeld, his son said. With his round spectacles, he appeared slightly owlish. He did not look uneasy holding a martini or a deck of cards. Women found him attractive and he reciprocated; he had a roving eye. Mailer used words like "dapper," "fussy," and "punctilious" to describe his father; he also called him "an elegant, impoverished figure out of Chekhov," who "was very English as only a South African can be."

Barney and Fan immediately struck up a correspondence. Barney wrote the first letter, as propriety dictated. His letters are courtly, self-conscious, and somewhat reserved; Fan's are warmer, bolder; her infatuation was obvious. In June 1920, she told him that she loved him and he replied that she was too young to make this sort of statement. Without revealing his gambling addiction, he warned her of it obliquely, writing that she didn't really know who he was. Fan was ready to take the next step; Barney was not ready. But in September he arranged for a visit to Long Branch. It was during this visit or shortly afterward that Barney brought up his vice. Mailer recalled his mother telling him the story: "Before they were married, he said to her, 'I gamble.' 'Oh,' she said, 'well, you won't gamble after we're married, I'm sure.' And he said, 'I guess not.' " When Barney met the extended family, they were impressed with him, although his Beau Brummel appearance and British accent puzzled them slightly. "I think it always pleased him," Barbara wrote, "that he wasn't readily taken for Jewish." He had long ceased using his Jewish name, Yitzhak Benjamin, and in New York gambling circles his code name was "I. B. from Brooklyn," as his son learned from his bookie decades later.

Before Barney left in October 1920 for Milwaukee and a new accounting job with a large firm, he and Fan were unofficially engaged. The following spring, he was back in New York and the engagement became official. Barney found a job in the city, commuting from Long Branch, where they lived temporarily with her parents. Decades later, after Barney had died, she said that he "seemed to pick up gambling friends in New York. I was so naïve about gambling, I couldn't understand why anyone would want to lose hard earned money, money that was needed for daily life, money that furnished freedom to give one hope and ambition to climb the ladder of success." But as a young woman (not as young as she pretended), Fan was elated for having made "a very favorable match," as she described it, with a professional man. They were married by two rabbis on February 14, 1922, in Manhattan, with a hundred guests in attendance. After a week in Atlantic City, they returned to Long Branch. Barbara noted in her memoir, "Dad once confided to Norman that of all the women he'd known, Mother was the best." By the beginning of May, Fan was pregnant.

Each had a secret: Barney gambled and Fan lied about her age. Sometime after they were out of school and looking for husbands, Fan and her sisters lowered their ages. Prompted by the desire, if not the necessity, to find a suitable husband, they availed themselves of the once-in-a-lifetime opportunity afforded to immigrants from faraway places. Aware that birth records in Russia were inaccessible, they felt secure in erasing a few years. Fan went so far as to claim in her memoir that she and Rose were born in this country. According to Barbara, Fan's likely birth date is December 1891. She told Barney that she had been born in 1901. He probably never knew her true age. Fan gave a number of birth years, but never relented on her fundamental story that she was several years younger than Barney (born January 1891), even long after he died. Born within months of him, she outlived him by almost thirteen years. Her gravestone and the family Bible record the false dates.

Fan's deception was common in that era. Barney's secret compulsion, one he clung to his entire life, was deeply hurtful. His gambling destroyed Fan's blithe hopes for a carefree life, forced her to become the chief breadwinner, and caused severe tensions with the Kesslers. Mailer said that "the Kesslers felt guilty. They knew that they hadn't really leveled; they had not warned her off. They were happy to get him married to her." In retrospect, the only member of his family who was not completely appalled by Barney's gambling was his son. In 1944, while undergoing basic training, Mailer ended a letter to his father, as follows: "As time goes by, I feel more and more like you, more and more your son. On outward things we are very different, but I think I understand and sympathize with you, better than any person I know."

He concluded that he was "lucky that my parents are so different, that I have had such a range of personality to draw on." Shortly after his mother died, he described his parents. "My mother," he said,

> was, if you will, the motor in the family, and without her I don't know what would have happened to us. My mother had an iron heart. My mother was not unlike many other devoted, loving Jewish mothers. She had circles of loyalty. The first loyalty was her children. The second was her sisters, her family. The third loyalty was her husband. The fourth her cousins, the fifth, neighbors she'd known for 20 years. It was a nuclear family. And my mother was the center of it and my father was one of the electrons. I must say he was a most dapper electron. And women adored him because he had the gift of speaking to each woman as if she was the most important woman he'd ever spoken to. And he didn't fake it. He adored women.

In the early evening of January 30, 1923, Fan felt labor pains and was admitted to Monmouth Memorial Hospital. Dr. Slocum, the Schneider family physician, was summoned. A son was born at 7:04 A.M. on January 31, after Fan had been in labor for twelve hours. It was a difficult, breech birth. The baby's Hebrew name, Nachum Melech, came from his grandmother Mailer's brother, Nachum Melech Shapiro, who arrived in the United States in 1900. "Melech" means king in Hebrew, but his birth certificate says "Norman Kingsley Mailer." Because Barney had not applied for citizenship when he married Fan, their son was legally a British citizen at birth. He chuckled when he learned of this circumstance many years later, joking that it might allow him to become "Sir Norman." His parents became citizens in 1926.

The Schneiders began to prosper in the hotel business during the boom-year summers of 1920–23. They purchased three large "cottages" on Ocean Avenue. The complex, overlooking the beach, was named "Kingsley Court" in honor of Norman. This success encouraged Fan and Barney to try their hand at what was now a burgeoning family business. Barney was still working in an accounting position in New York, but in 1924 he and Fan rented Kingsley Court from her parents for $4,000 and operated it as a small hotel. They did the same the following summer and made a good profit.

Norman was the darling of the clan, catered to by his parents, grandparents, three aunts, and three older female cousins, Osie, Adele, and Sylvia, plus Dave and Anne Kessler, who visited often. One summer day in 1925 when Norman was two and a half, Adele remembered, he locked himself in the bathroom and called out the third floor window, "Goodbye everybody forever." Fan went into hysterics and called the fire department, but he let himself out before the firemen came. During the summers of the mid-1920s, he often left home in a huff. Adele said, "He'd get angry; he'd leave a note for his mother, 'Goodbye forever,' and he'd walk around the block. His temper would abate and he'd come back." These tantrums are the first recorded instances of Mailer's lifelong and pronounced impetuosity, and his impulse to dramatize.

Nearly every year one or another member of the family leased a new hotel, trying to find the right combination of variables for a windfall season. But profits were meager and Fan got discouraged. She became pregnant in the summer of 1926 and by the end of the season was drained. "I had no heart for the hotel business," she wrote. "It was just devouring all my strength for nothing." The birth of Barbara Jane on April 6, 1927, increased the load, as did her aging parents, whose health was declining rapidly. The stress of running a busy resort hotel and taking care of her small children made Fan "very, very upset," according to Barbara. "Her parents were dying, and she realized my father was a gambler; she went to her doctor and told him, 'I think I'm going to have a nervous breakdown.' Dr. Slocum said, 'Fanny, there's nothing I can do for you. You're going to have to pull yourself together.' My mother said, 'So I pulled myself together.' " Fan's mother died on May 29, 1928, at the age of seventy. Shortly afterward, when Barbara was eighteen months old, and her brother five and a half, the Mailers moved to Brooklyn, while Rabbi Schneider moved in with his son Joe. In late November, the beloved patriarch died of heart disease and was eulogized at the synagogue he had helped to found.

THE MAILERS SETTLED on Cortelyou Road, a few blocks from Flatbush Avenue. Norman, not yet six, began school in September at P.S. 181, a few blocks from their four-room apartment. Barney left early for work in Manhattan and Fan walked Norman the half mile through the lower-middle-class Jewish neighborhood to school, leaving Barbara with a nurse, Agnes. As always, Fan was anxious about the goyim—many second-generation Irish and Italians lived nearby. Mailer completed grades one through four at P.S. 181 and his grades were uniformly excellent. His mother was the leader of a tribe of women who, throughout his childhood, coddled and praised him, catered to his whims and encouraged his individuality. His cousin Adele remembered that for Fan, "it was always Norman." Barbara quickly recognized this reality but never showed any animosity or jealousy. There were no gaps in the circle of female affection surrounding the young prince.

With the passing of her parents, Fan and Barney began living a different kind of life. They ceased observing Jewish dietary laws. Mailer recalled that his mother was not deeply religious. "She was observant," he said. "There's a difference." Barney, he continued, "was pro-forma observant." Barbara remembers her mother lighting the candles on the eve of the Sabbath. "I still have the image of Mother, her back to me, lighting the candles that sat on the antique cabinet and whispering a prayer in Hebrew. It was one more element in that adult world which baffled but protected me." Her brother remembered his mother telling him that the Shekinah, a divine female embodiment of the spiritual, passed over the candles when they were lit. Often, he said, Fan had tears in her eyes.

When he was seven or eight, with Fan's encouragement, he began writing stories. One of the earliest surviving pieces, in six chapters of three to four hundred words each, is "The Adventures of Bob and Paul," the story of twin brothers who survive perilous adventures. Another notable piece among the early juvenilia is a three-page how-to booklet, "Boxing Lessons." It consists of a series of tips and observations about Mailer's favorite sport. "When I land," it begins, "every ounce of my weight goes into the punch. The timing of it I get by humming a tune and crashing in when I see an opening." Boxing was a sport that he engaged in and wrote about for several decades, producing what are, arguably, some of the finest boxing narratives written by an American.

The culmination, and the conclusion, of Mailer's early writing career came early. During the winter of 1933–34, he finished reading the Princess of Mars books of Edgar Rice Burroughs and also became a devoted fan of the Buck Rogers show on the radio. Encouraged by his mother, he wrote a 35,000-word novel, "The Martian Invasion, A Story in Two Parts," and dedicated it to "My mother, who always wanted me to write a good story." "This novel filled two and a half paper notebooks," he recalled. "You know the type, about 7 x 10. They had shiny blue covers, and they were, oh, only ten cents in those days, or a nickel. They ran to perhaps 100 pages each and I used to write on both sides." The novel was written in a disciplined spurt during the summer of 1934 at one of the family's hotels in Long Branch. Mailer's bottomless fascination with war, violence, and suffering is on display in this adventure novel.

On his application to Harvard Mailer noted that as a boy, encouraged by Fan and his aunts and cousins, he "used to write stories at the 'drop-of-a-hat,' " but he also engaged in the usual activities of stickball, marbles, and roller skating. In the late fall of 1932, the family moved a couple of miles north to the mainly Jewish neighborhood of Crown Heights, where Norman finished fifth grade at P.S. 161. They lived in a four-story, ornamental brick apartment building at the corner of Albany and Crown Streets. Mailer described the neighborhood as "a quiet section of two-family houses and trees, a mile from Ebbets Field and Prospect Park." He recalled that "in those days there was so little traffic we used to play touch football and roller hockey in the streets." The houses had "small lawns in front, so small that when you were playing roller hockey, if you bodychecked somebody hard they'd go flying across the sidewalk, and you had to go scrambling up a lawn that was banked. If that ever happened to you you'd come out with fire in your eyes and your skates full of dirt."

Roller hockey was as physical as the somewhat delicate young Mailer ever got. Late in life, he told Christopher Hitchens that Jews "had to make certain basic distinctions very early in life. Would you fight if someone called you a dirty Jew, or wouldn't you?" In the interview's context, his question is rhetorical and unanswered, but other statements make it clear that the young Mailer shied away from violence. "I was a physical coward as a child," he said in 1959, a statement supported by the recollections of childhood chums who said Mailer never got into fistfights and stayed close to home. One of them, Arnold Epstein, said, "He seemed to be on a shorter leash, more obedient, kind of quiet." Epstein added that Mailer's family "was very proper." More testimony comes from Aaron Goldman, a summer chum of Mailer's older cousin Cy Rembar, Beck's son. He remembers Mailer during the summers of the early 1930s as a tearful, bookish momma's boy who watched Cy play baseball and tennis in the recreation area behind the Scarboro Hotel. While the Crown Heights neighborhood was not particularly rough, it was not without hazard, as Mailer explained in 1980. "I grew up in a world where really I was cultivated. I was cultivated in the sense that my mother and father treated my sister and myself as very important people. We were the center of their universe and so it was the outside world that was difficult. You know, go out in the street and you know if you didn't have friends you get beaten up. It was as simple as that. And so I was always terribly alert to the outside world. I took the inside world for granted. And I was free to indulge myself too, to change from one personality to another." Barbara confirms the affirmation she and her brother felt: "Not only did we know that we were expected to be better and smarter than everyone else, we pretty much thought we were." Fan was insistent on her children's exceptionalism, but the unintended consequence was that Mailer had, as he later explained, "an ego that was lopsided."

The Crown Street apartment was a bastion where Mailer was spoiled and protected. Fan kept out most of the neighborhood boys, but another kind of trouble came home regularly with Barney. On rare occasions he would win at cards or on horse races. But more often, he would run up a debt with the bookies and try to win it back. When this failed, he would write a string of bad checks or embezzle from his employer (General Motors, for example) in an effort to recoup his losses. The crises accelerated when Barney lost his job and the debts—$5,000 to $10,000, vast sums during the Depression—soared. The bookies would begin calling on the telephone and Fan would become frantic. Invariably, the Kesslers would be summoned. "I've got criminal blood in me," Mailer said later, adding that his father "would have gone to jail if it hadn't been for my uncle, who would always bail him out and my father knew it." He first became aware of Barney's gambling because of his parents' "terrible fights." A day or so after a bad one, "Dave would come over with Anne and Anne would be crying. Everybody was stiff and tense all through the meal. Barbara and myself would be packed off to bed after dinner. I'd lie awake for hours listening to them argue." Barney was cool in these clinches, Mailer said, and it was a bit of a comedy, but "a comedy on the edge of a cliff. Dave would get apoplectic. Dave died of asthma, finally, and I think my father was one of the people who gave it to him because Dave would blow gaskets in his brain to keep from strangling my father." When Dave would verbally assault his brother-in-law, Barney would reply in his clipped British accent, " 'I don't know Dave how you can speak to me in that fashion.' At which point Dave's asthma would deepen."

After one particularly bad confrontation just before Norman's bar mitzvah in February 1936, a distraught Fan contemplated leaving Barney and confided in her son. He said, "How can you do that to us, when we're kids?" Fan then gave him a blunt report of the extent of Barney's gambling. "I knew my father was an irresponsible gambler," Mailer said. "I always heard it from her side, never from his." But Fan never spoke again of a divorce because, Mailer said, it "went against every tradition in her. In those days, you got married and took what you got and didn't complain. To her, a divorced woman was a whore."

> She had a great anger at my father—it was almost implacable—for not being a provider. But at the same time, she loved him in her way. After that one attempt, she gave it up. If the children didn't want it, then she was not about to do it against our will. Years later, I used to think, "Gee, maybe I did her a terrible injustice and cut off her life and her possibilities." On the other hand, when I think of a stepfather and how it would have torn her. I didn't brood about it . . . except for those awful nights which went on until I went away to college; those dreadful nights when my uncle came to the door and I could see by his face: "Uh-oh, one of those nights."

At some point, he told his sister that Barney was a gambler. She "resented it more. And so she was cool toward him; she stayed cool and angry toward him. Which broke his heart. He *adored* her." Barbara was "closer to my mother," he said. "It was that feminist business: my mother was working so hard and this man's not responsible." From the mid-1930s on, Fan ran a small oil service and delivery firm, the Sunlight Oil Corporation, which Dave Kessler had set up, partly to provide oil to his candy company and partly to help out the Mailers. Initially, Barney worked there, but after he began tipping the till, he was out and Fan took over entirely, working with one driver. "She really lived and breathed for that business," Mailer said, taking late night calls from customers with broken furnaces and empty tanks while earning a quarter of a cent per gallon profit.

Barbara explained that her mother's hard work and financial anxiety, combined with her loathing of Barney's addiction to games of chance, "leached the complexities out of her and made her monolithic." No surprise that she referred to herself, as did her children, as the Rock of Gibraltar, "deep and large, and all there to see. The metaphor for Dad, on the other hand, could be a tidal pool—charming on the surface, and teeming with a secret life in the shallows beneath." Barney gambled when he could and worked when he could, but usually lost his bets and was rarely employed. "One of my recollections in the depth of the Depression," Mailer recalled, "is my father coming home after looking for work all day and Barbara and myself running to the door and saying, 'Did you get a job today, Dad?' And he sadly shaking his head no. . . . How sad we all were about that. 'Brother, Can You Spare a Dime' is one of my favorite songs."

In addition to his parents' precarious financial situation and the possibility of a divorce, he was buffeted by a cross-hatch of other pressures. On the one hand, there was his mother's unshakable belief in his talents, buttressed by the approval of his tight-knit extended family, with Anne and Dave Kessler acting as a second set of parents. He was also enthralled by the gangster films of the 1930s (especially the brash energies of James Cagney) and the romantic novels of Rafael Sabatini and Jeffery Farnol, which he had begun to devour. On the other side of the ledger were his fear of the Irish toughs a few blocks outside the Jewish cocoon and a sharp sense of his puny physicality ("We also had a sense," he remarked decades later, "of not being as tough as the Irish"). Vying for primacy with Fan in defining his emerging ego was his father's "prodigious double life," as he later described it, a life he pondered with awe.

Nine months before he died, he told a friend about Barney's influence: "Everything that is adventurous in me came from him." These opposed pressures opened a fissure in the adolescent Mailer's personality that widened as time passed until it became a gaping divide.

"Very intense" is how his sister remembers him as a boy; their older cousin Osie, she said, called him "Desperate Ambrose," after the comic strip character. His friend Robert F. Lucid compared the young Mailer to Alexander Portnoy, "the most fabulous kid who ever lived," but one who had been given a "tremendous sense of mission." Mailer put it this way: "I'd been frightened in the womb by my mother's dream of having a little Einstein in her belly." His sister recalls that his family regularly referred to him as a genius from the time he took the Stanford-Binet IQ exam in third grade. He excelled in all his classes and even skipped the latter halves of grades seven and eight. Fan's hopes were confirmed when, according to Barbara's friend Rhoda Lazare, the principal announced at his eighth grade graduation that Norman Mailer had an IQ of 170, the highest ever recorded at P.S. 161.

If on the lip of puberty his inner life was a narcissistic moil, his pursuits were ordinary. After school, he spent most of his time studying, attending Hebrew School (through eighth grade), reading, playing stickball and Monopoly, building model airplanes and experimenting with his chemistry set. He also went to see gangster movies at Loew's Kameo and the Savoy on Eastern Parkway, often bringing his sister along. He often said that he felt he knew Humphrey Bogart as well as a favorite uncle. Summers were spent in Long Branch, where he observed the feats of his cousin Cy, eight years his senior.

> I worshipped him (with enormous funds of love and envy) because he was a hero. He was one of the few people I've ever known who had a happy look on his face when he came to bat in the late innings with men on base, his side behind, and the need for a homer prominent in everyone's head. Indeed he had his smile because it was slightly better than even money he was going to hit that homer. In fact, he would. This is not hyperbole. If I saw him in a hundred baseball games, there must have been fifty late-inning spots of exactly the sort I describe: he probably hit thirty-six homers out of fifty. . . . These were Depression years. Much gloom abounded in everyone, but he was the bright spot.

Cy Rembar remained Mailer's hero (later becoming his lawyer) and one of his most important role models. His cousin's string of victories on the playing fields contrasted glaringly with his father's run of defeats at the poker table.

In a memoir written just before he died, Barbara described her brother as generous, encouraging, and always interesting. "He loved to teach," she said, and often recommended books to her. She remembers that in high school he got a book that diagrammed the fox trot and they practiced together. "I learned to dance," she said. "I'm afraid he did not." Mailer recalled going with his father, who cared little for baseball, to see the Dodgers play. Mailer was not a recluse, but as a friend recalled, he did not hang around much at the candy store on the corner of Crown Street and Kingston Avenue with the other boys. By the time of his bar mitzvah in February 1936 at the Temple Shaari Zedek in Brooklyn, Fan had long since transferred her hopes from Barney to her brilliant son. She guarded him like a mother hawk.

Coached by his Hebrew teacher, who had leftist sympathies, Mailer wrote, memorized, and delivered a five-hundred-word bar mitzvah speech that was, with two exceptions, conventional. He began by thanking his family, citing the commandments, and stating his joy at becoming "a member of the people of Israel." He lauded some great Jews—Moses Maimonides, Albert Einstein, Baruch Spinoza, and Karl Marx. Naming these last two—a freethinking excommunicant and an atheist radical—raised a few eyebrows and "the rabbi looked very pale" after his speech, Mailer remembered. In the second notable remark in his speech, he said, "Yes, my friends! From now on I become a Jew, but not a MAYOFIS JEW, with a bent back to receive innocently the inhuman Nazis. I become a Jew to uphold the ideals and strengths of Judaism, and the rights of my country." In an interview he gave in connection with his final novel, about Hitler's youth, *The Castle in the Forest*, Mailer remembered his mother's warnings about the Nazis from three quarters of a century earlier.

> Hitler has been in my mind since I was nine years old. By 1932, my mother was already sensitive, and intensely so, to the dangers he presented. After Hitler came to power in 1933, everything that happened in Nazi Germany used to cause my mother pain. It was as if she knew in advance what was going to occur. She'd grown up

> with the knowledge of the anti-Semitism her father had had to face in Lithuania. Then, as a child going to school in Long Branch, New Jersey, kids on the street would call her "Christ killer"—no surprise, then, if Hitler was immensely real to her.

His bar mitzvah speech, including the reference to the Nazis, pleased the family, most of whom had come up from Long Branch despite a storm that left more than a foot of snow. Millionaire Uncle Louis in South Africa sent a $500 gift, which enabled Fan to put out a fine buffet at 555 Crown Street after the ceremony. But Barney's secret life again intruded. His bookie sent the gift of a watch. Fan didn't hesitate to reply: "I phoned his home, his wife answered. I did not spare either of them, I cursed him out of existence. She begged me not to say those things, that her husband had a weak heart, so I followed it up by saying he could drop dead that minute and I hung up." Fan took no prisoners.

LESS IS KNOWN of Mailer's high school years than any other period of his life. He had stopped writing stories the year before he entered and wrote few letters before going away to college. We do know that like most of the Crown Heights boys, he took the Tompkins Avenue trolley to Boys High in the Bedford-Stuyvesant section of Brooklyn, or walked to save a nickel. We also know that because he had skipped a primary school grade, he was one of the youngest boys in his class, entering his freshman year at age 12. He later recalled, "I felt straddled between my friends who were my age at home and were two years behind me at school. So I didn't feel I belonged particularly in one life or another." His interest in his chemistry set and sports waned, but his passion for model airplanes, some with tiny gasoline engines, burgeoned during his high school years, 1935–39. He was a devoted member of the aviation club in high school and his first piece in print, "Model Airplanes," appeared in a mimeographed school publication, *Physical Scientist*, in December 1938, when he was a senior. Occasionally, on weekends, his parents would drive him out to the open fields in Canarsie where he could launch his fragile creations. The largest of these, which took him six months to build, had an amazing six-foot wingspan. "When launched," he recalled, "it soared briefly, but then its wings suddenly folded up—like an umbrella."

Mailer seldom wrote about his childhood. In 2004, he said that he had avoided writing about Long Branch and Brooklyn because "too many crystals are there" and "you don't want to write about the material. . . . Preserve it because it's endlessly fruitful." Crystals, as he explained several times, are memories of wrenching or exhilarating experiences, epiphanies in one's past that, properly considered, are illuminating. When a crystal is aligned just so, it casts an imaginative beam that clarifies a new experience, acting as a kind of emotional spectrometer. We can only speculate on his childhood crystals, but given the instances of childhood fear and timidity already noted, it seems quite possible that he was referring to moments of ignominious humiliation. Late in life, he said, "I don't feel joy going back to the old streets in Brooklyn."

Mailer was an outstanding student at Boys High, graduating near the top of his 650-member class. His grades were nearly as high as those of valedictorian Martin Lubin, a boy he knew slightly and later roomed with at Harvard. But Mailer's lack of involvement in athletics and student government—indeed, his lack of involvement in any school activity except for the aviation club—left him out of the running for valedictorian. Overall, his best grades were in math and science (a 99.5 in Algebra and a 99 in Chemistry), but his English, French, and History grades were only a few points lower. His lowest academic grade was in drawing, an 80; his grades in physical training were dismal. Beatrice Silverman, his first wife, said he had trouble vaulting over the horse in gym class. His report cards gained plaudits at home, especially the math and science grades, but not in the neighborhood, where he was just another skinny kid. "In Brooklyn I was always a little ashamed of being smart," he said. "Somehow you weren't manly if you were smart." He did have some success with the opposite sex, however. Barbara's friend Rhoda Wolf had a crush on him and his girlfriend, Phyllis Bradman, according to his sister, was the prettiest girl in the neighborhood, although they never got beyond kissing and light petting. The summer before he died, he remembered his situation.

> I was 13; it was 1936. The New Deal was on; a great deal was happening. But we, in Brooklyn, in my end of Brooklyn, weren't thinking about anything but sex. We wanted to get laid. We wanted to muzzle a girl as they called it, and put our hands on their breasts. We wanted to be able to neck with them. And none of us were. The girls

> were nice Jewish girls who were loath and we were inhibited—the Jews were very inhibited about sex. . . . And I remember that in all those years of adolescence, I was absolutely focused on girls and pornography. There used to be little magazines like *Spicy Detective* in those days, where the women had huge tits poking through gossamer scraps of torn blouse. And that was a huge turn-on.

One scheme dreamed up by Mailer and two other boys, Arnold Epstein and another friend, Harold Kiesel, was to form a musical trio and get a summer job at a Catskills resort where they might seduce some Jewish women. He convinced his parents to buy him a clarinet; Kiesel played the trumpet and Epstein the drums. On afternoons after school, they practiced at the apartment of Epstein, who remembered their sessions: "I could keep beat with anything. But Kiesel and Norman had to get tunes out of their instruments, and I think they were equally bad. We'd laugh and giggle and fall on the floor." The project soon collapsed. Mailer never learned to play an instrument and had trouble carrying a tune. He remembered going to a few dances in high school, but was "a wallflower . . . a terrible dancer, very stiff-legged." At the Scarboro Hotel one summer there was a flirtation with a pretty girl named Bunny Schwab, but nothing sexual came of it. Decades later, he still vividly remembered his humiliation when Bunny described his large, sunburned ears as "red sails in the sunset."

"High school's that place, that country," he reflected later, "where you get laid for the first time; you have marvelous memories and you go around with a girl, you go to the prom." But for him high school was studying and he was bitter because his social life was so dull. People who knew him in high school, he said, thought he was "quiet, studious and inconsequential." His work paid off, however. His grades got him accepted to both MIT and Harvard. He knew that he was more likely to realize his dream of becoming an aeronautical engineer at MIT, as it had a program in this specialty, something Harvard lacked. But because of his age, MIT wanted him to go to prep school for a year. This circumstance led him to Harvard. What clinched it, he often said, was the reaction of girls on Crown Street. MIT's name didn't impress them, but "when I said I might go to Harvard, they lit up and they saw me with new eyes." Choosing Harvard, for reasons he could not have guessed at the time, was one of the luckiest things he ever did.

TWO
HARVARD

The distinguished historian and journalist Theodore H. White, who graduated from Harvard in 1938, came up with a system of classifying prewar Harvard students. They were divided, he wrote, into three groups, "white men, gray men, and meatballs." The first group was comprised of wealthy WASPs from New England who graduated from private prep schools. The gray men were middle-class boys from public schools, mainly outside New England. The meatballs were non-WASP students who commuted and/or were on scholarship. White, a Jew whose father was born in Russia, claimed meatball status. He didn't attend Harvard "to enjoy the games, the girls, the burlesque shows of the Old Howard, the companionship, the elms, the turning leaves of fall, the grassy banks of the Charles." He was there to gobble up cultural riches from learned professors, from the libraries, museums, poetry readings, tutorials—all of this under a dome of reverence for intellectual and scholarly pursuits. Mailer and his friend Marty Lubin, both of whom received scholarships (sophomore year for Mailer), were classic meatballs, although such was the subtlety of condescension at Harvard that they probably never heard the term. Mailer was also there for the culture, although it took him the better part of a year to find it. Unlike White, he was profoundly interested in girls, although the kind he sought were as difficult to find as were the right professors.

He was assigned to Grays Hall, a five-story freshman dorm on Massachusetts Avenue accommodating about sixty men. They lived in comparative luxury in two- or three-person suites, cleaned by "biddies," with a shared bathroom and a working fireplace. Like the Oxbridge house system that it mimicked, Harvard's houses and halls had a master living on the first floor who regularly invited students for tea and dinner. The administration more or less randomly assigned the approximately eight hundred resident members of his class (about a hundred more commuted) to approximately fifteen freshman dorms. Most nationalities, states, and several foreign countries were represented in the class. WASPs, German-Americans, and Irish-Americans dominated, although more than 10 percent of the class was Jewish. Mailer shared his second-floor suite with Richard Weinberg from Memphis and Maxwell Kaufer from Kingston, Pennsylvania. Looking back, he said that he noticed no discrimination. Harvard, he said, "had solved more delicate social situations than any other institution . . . of the establishment." He estimated that during his first year four out of five of his friends were middle-class Jews and they socialized in the same way black students would a generation later. In his second semester, he would become friendly with several non-Jewish men, most of whom he later associated with on the college literary magazine, the *Advocate*, or the Signet Society, an intellectual luncheon club. But for his first semester, his group included three other Grays men, Seymour Breslow, Myron Kaufmann, and Stanley Lampert. Marty Lubin, Harold Katz, Douglas Woolf, Peter Ruderman, and Harold Marantz, who lived in other dorms, made it nine. All Jews, all meatballs.

Mailer's and Lubin's parents had gotten to know each other a bit in Brooklyn and Mr. Lubin drove the boys up to Cambridge on September 16, 1939. Later, Fan Mailer and Eva Lubin would occasionally take Saturday night train trips to Cambridge bringing cookies and clean laundry to their sons, returning late Sunday and arriving in Brooklyn as the sun came up. For his college wardrobe, Mailer had purchased an outlandish set of clothes that could have been worn with Charles Bovary's infamous hat: green and blue vertical striped trousers, a gold jacket, and saddle shoes. These garments were quickly discarded once he observed the narrow-lapeled tweed jackets and gray flannel trousers of the other students. Mailer said later that in going from Brooklyn to Harvard he felt like "a young man going from a small town in the Caucasus to Moscow for advanced studies."

"Unformed" is the word Mailer used to describe himself as a first semester freshman. We can add unprepared; Harvard was a shock and at first he drew inward. Kaufer later said that his new roommate was quiet, pleasant, "a smiler" who didn't venture out much during his first semester, unlike his gregarious roommates. One thing that his classmates all seem to remember about Mailer as a freshman is the collage of pinups over his desk. We know that one of them was a George Petty centerfold from *Esquire*, signed salaciously by his buddies, because Mailer wrote home to give his parents fair warning of its placement before their first visit. Betty Grable's legs were probably included and there was also a photograph of Amy Arnell, a vocalist in the Tommy Tucker big band; her big hit was "I Don't Want to Set the World on Fire." When the band had appeared in Long Branch in the summer of 1939, Mailer was much taken by a large, framed photo of Arnell in the lobby of the West End Hotel. Wearing a tool belt and work clothes, he brazenly unscrewed the entire frame containing Arnell's photo and walked out with it. A friend from Long Branch remembers seeing it in his Harvard room. There were bull sessions about sex, of course, and he discovered that he had "a bunch of roommates who also hadn't been laid. . . . We'd heard of working-class kids who got laid when they were 13 or 14. Here we were, good middle-class kids, and we weren't able to get laid. . . . You bore a standard of shame."

The required courses for his first semester were an engineering drafting course, physics, and the first halves of math and English courses. His sole elective was French. The English course, English A, was a composition course, required of all students who did not turn in an outstanding performance on the English exam taken by new freshmen. In Mailer's time, students in English A had to write a variety of descriptive and argumentative themes, often in response to assigned readings in collections of essays and short stories and, later, novels. At first, he did not like the course, writing home on October 25 that the course was "about the dullest." But when he read the contemporary novels assigned, his interest not only sharpened, he said, the novels changed his life.

> Before I was seventeen I had formed the desire to be a major writer, and this desire came upon me rather suddenly in the last two months of my sixteeth year, a time I remember well enough because it was my first semester at Harvard. All through December 1939 and January 1940 I was discovering modern American literature. In those sixty days I read and reread *Studs Lonigan, U.S.A.*, and *The Grapes of Wrath*. Later I would add Wolfe, Hemingway and Faulkner, and to a small measure, Fitzgerald; but Farrell, Dos Passos and Steinbeck were the novel for me in that sixty days before I turned seventeen.

Of the three books that Mailer names, James T. Farrell's *Studs Lonigan* trilogy, set on the South Side of Chicago in the early part of the twentieth century, was at first the most influential. For the rest of his life he said that Farrell had awakened him to his vocation. What Farrell provided was the recognition that the social atmosphere of Brooklyn was similar to that enveloping the lower-middle-class Irish toughs that Farrell chronicled. It was liberating, Mailer wrote, to find a novelist who could write about "the monotony and the boredom, and the killing deadness of the average simple life among many people who were not well educated." Until he read Farrell, Dos Passos, and Steinbeck, the novels he prized were stories of the romantic past or the imagined future; he had no sense that the stumblings and longings of his pals at the candy store and the burlesque house were the stuff of fiction. "Suddenly," he said, "I realized you could write about your own life."

During his first semester, the struggle to keep up with his courses was wearing him down. Several weeks into the semester, he was cut from the 150-pound crew team. It was, he said, "the bitterest blow freshman year," salved only slightly when he learned from a friend that the coach never had the slightest interest in him because his arms were too short. The other disappointment was women: he had no dates until he returned home for the Christmas holiday and saw Phyllis Bradman, taking her to a New York Rangers hockey game. But on New Year's Eve he had no date, and went skating in the afternoon and to a burlesque show. Back at Harvard for semester exams in late January, he realized that physics was too much for him and he dropped it early in the second semester. He was maintaining As and Bs in his other courses, including English A, where the instructor had informed the class that short stories could be submitted in lieu of topical essays. Mailer, who once said, "I threw down my pen at 11," began writing fiction again.

He also looked into the possibility of getting on *The Harvard Lampoon*, but he was rejected. The *Lampoon* was dominated by students with prep school pedigrees. "I can't write humorously," he told his parents, and also noted the *Lampoon*'s $100 initiation fee. Then, on February 12, 1940, he attended an open house put on by the *Advocate,* the college's venerable literary magazine, founded in 1866, among whose contributors were T. S. Eliot, Wallace Stevens, Marianne Moore, and Henry Miller. At the meeting, he met Bruce "Pete" Barton, also a freshman and the son of a prominent advertising executive and congressman from Manhattan's Silk Stocking district. Mailer was attracted to the quiet, well-mannered young Barton. "He was the first man I met who was the son of a very powerful man, a tycoon. And he was also very much a gentleman," he said. Barton was drawn to Mailer not only for his literary interests but because he felt the Brooklynite could tell him about life outside his pampered existence. The next day, Mailer wrote to his parents to say he was trying out for the magazine and ask if they would pay the $40 initiation fee. They gave their enthusiastic assent in a telephone call and he began assembling the required three-piece application packet.

Also in February, he took two additional steps in pursuit of his ambition: he accepted an invitation to join a weekly, extracurricular writing seminar, and he began keeping a notebook, the first of innumerable such records he kept for the rest of his life. Not much is known about the seminar save an anecdote from his friend Larry Weiss, a sophomore transfer student, who had considerable influence on him. Weiss recalls that Mailer argued for the importance of writers describing every bodily function, including bowel movements. Weiss said he had no problem with such descriptions, but it was wrong to call them literature. Mailer responded by reading aloud from the "Calypso" chapter of *Ulysses,* Joyce's account of Leopold Bloom in the outhouse.

The pocket-sized notebook of thirty-odd pages contains one-sentence character sketches and two-sentence plot ideas, memorable people, places, and moments, a list of his dates with girls in Brooklyn, with telephone numbers and a letter grade next to each (Phyllis Bradman got a B, the highest), snippets of conversation and quotations from several writers, including Hemingway ("Everybody was drunk"). Some of the ideas are the usual freshman theme fodder: tearing down the goalposts after a football game. But others are more ambitious: a boy with a castration complex, based on a line from Havelock Ellis's *Studies in the Psychology of Sex*; a young white man dancing with a black woman for "altruistic reasons" who gets sexually aroused; "fellow meeting mother long lost and finding she is a prostitute[;] you know that's crap have him lay her first then find out it's mother—don't give it away but have it sharp dialogue piece"; "a homosexual who has an otherwise fine character . . . have it from an accident." A significant number are pensées about the writing life: "It is only when an author reproduces some personal experiences of ours that we can fully understand his meaning."

The most impressive thing about the notebook is how it functioned as a wellspring. The examples of his literary trinity of Farrell, Dos Passos, and Steinbeck, encouragement in English A, and interaction with other aspiring writers in the seminar, generated writing momentum. He wrote fifteen stories based on the notebook jottings over the second semester of his freshman year and the following summer. His desire to write was also whet by the possibility of getting on the *Advocate*. When his Uncle Dave found out about his hopes for the magazine, he offered to speak to Bruce Barton Sr., whom he knew from New York business circles, but Mailer nixed the idea, writing home, "There's no use making it, if I can't do it on my own." A week later he wrote home with the bad news that the *Advocate* had rejected his application, saying the stories he submitted were deemed fluid but deficient in plot. The editors, he admitted, were probably right.

His first semester papers for English A are on garden-variety topics, for example, freedom of speech and a discussion of Malthus's Law. But second semester he turned in six short stories, including the two he submitted to the *Advocate*. Never the minimalist, he wrote one that was almost six thousand words. His grades ranged from C+ to B+. For the last paper of the year, Mailer asked if he could submit one more story, and his instructor, after some discussion, agreed. Originally titled "Now I Lay Me Down to Sleep," he concluded that this too blatantly echoed a Hemingway story title and settled on "Prelude to Sleep." Submitted on May 21, the story is a first person psychological account of the loss of virginity by Mark, a Brooklyn youth, before he goes off to college, an event preceded by months of frustrated petting with his girlfriend, Susan, punctuated by his self-serving theories on free love, true love, the family, and society. After Mark convinces Susan to have sex, he concludes that the "long, terrifying, childish period of sexual self-analysis and shame" was finally over only to find the consummation tainted. He discovers that "even at the height of coitus, his analytical mind was working and it annoyed him." The story received an A−, his highest grade of the year, and brought his final grade up to B. Harvard was stingy with grades, especially for freshmen.

AS MAILER WAS forging his literary vocation in the smithy of English A, isolationists and interventionists were lining up against each other on campus. Poet Archibald MacLeish, in a welcoming address to his class, compared it with the class of 1918. The earlier generation saw World War I "as a finality," he said, but they were wrong. "The last war was not an end but a beginning." Harvard's students were not at all pleased with this news. The *Crimson* came out four-square against the war, saying in an editorial, "We are frankly determined to have peace at any price." But President James B. Conant told the first chapel service of the year, "The forces of violence must be beaten by superior violence." Mailer's first response to the war, made while MacLeish was giving his importuning speech, was to jot down a very brief story, titled "It," which follows:

> We were going through the barbed-wire when a machine gun started. I kept walking until I saw my head lying on the ground. "My God, I'm dead," my head said. And my body fell over.

If his mini-story demonstrates his awareness of the war, it should be said that it was impossible to ignore. The newspapers, newsreels, and radio were saturated with reports of the events in Europe—the German-Italian alliance, the German-Soviet pact, the invasion of Poland, speeches by Hitler and Churchill, and general mobilizations in England and France. Harvard's 3,500 undergraduates knew that if the United States entered the war they would be among the first to go and, compensatorily, they partied a lot. Swing bands were the rage and Glenn Miller's "Moonlight Serenade" was the big hit of the year. A member of the class of 1942, one Lothrop Withington Jr., started a nationwide craze by swallowing a live goldfish, just months before Congress began discussing the first-ever peacetime draft. In his letters home Mailer made no mention of anything but grades, football games, laundry, allowance checks, and, more and more as time went on, literary activities. In avoiding the topic of war, he was not much different from his fellow Harvard students. In a May 1940 poll, 91 percent of them opposed going to war. In 1939 and early 1940, Harvard wanted it to go away.

A good part of student reluctance to accept the inevitability of war came from the widespread sympathy for leftist ideas and principles. The leader of Harvard noninterventionists was the grave, revered F. O. Matthiessen, an avowed socialist and author of *American Renaissance: Art and Expression in the Age of Emerson and Whitman*. Mailer heard him lecture more than once and was deeply impressed. Arthur Schlesinger Jr. (Harvard '38) visited Matthiessen at a time when England was beleaguered. During their discussion of the war situation, Schlesinger said that Churchill was the only hope. "Matty said with great intensity, 'Winston Churchill is the epitome of everything I have hated all my life.' " But when Germany invaded Russia in June 1941, Matthiessen endorsed the war. He even wrote an essay for the 1943 yearbook, "The Humanities in a Time of War," in which he praised the engaged humanism of André Malraux, who would soon become one of Mailer's heroes.

Mailer's sentiments changed in about the same time frame as Matthiessen's. John Crockett, with whom Mailer would later be associated on the *Advocate*, remembers talking to him after MacLeish's welcoming address. Mailer, he said, called the speech "crap" and argued that there would be no war. Although he did not remember meeting Crockett until February 1940, he could very well have been antiwar in September 1939. In his "Harvard Journal" he recalls that after reading Farrell, Dos Passos, and Steinbeck, he became "a leftist & an advocate of free love. The leftism came from the books; I can't remember that the problem bothered me before then." He adds that by his sophomore year, "I was violently leftist, & almost joined the YCL [Young Communist League]." Support for U.S. involvement in the war began to grow with the fall of France in June 1940, but Mailer showed no real interest in world events until later. He had something else on his mind: sex.

During his sophomore year, Mailer went to the Treasure Room of the Widener Library and there read D. H. Lawrence's novel *Lady Chatterley's Lover*, unpublished in the United States at that time. It was one of the perks of the Harvard experience and deeply moving, he said. "It changed my sex life, or rather, accelerated it." He read Henry Miller's *Tropic of Cancer* at about the same time and later paid homage to Lawrence and Miller in his work. From the very beginning of his writing career, Mailer wanted to jump into the ocean of sex and plumb its secrets. He admired the resistance to anti-obscenity laws and prudery in general by Lawrence, Joyce, and Miller, and was eager to explore sex from A to Z. From one perspective, his sixty years of writing can be seen as an untrammeled examination of all things sexual—a long list. He would grapple with everything from the funky odors of lovemaking to the inalienable joys of marriage and children, from promiscuity and free love to abortion, masturbation, and orgies. He examined the humor in obscene speech and writing, as well as the problems of contraception and the mysteries of conception and pregnancy. He wrote about homosexuality, bisexuality, sadism, masochism, pornography, AIDS, and incandescent one-night stands. Sometimes he seemed ahead of the times, as when he was called the prophet-seer of the 1960s sexual revolution; sometimes he appeared to be deeply regressive, as in opposing contraception, but he was always a passionate responder to the conundrums of sexuality and identity. In Henry James's era, he would have expired of frustration. In 1941, when he read the unexpurgated *Lady Chatterley*, the Depression was ending, life was opening up, and the Victorian ark of sexual repression was sinking. But it was going down too slowly. Mailer wanted to torpedo it.

One of the last stories he wrote his freshman year, "Life Is Where You Find It," concerns an eighteen-year-old Harvard student, Hal Stewart, a would-be writer who wants to go hitchhiking in the summer to find "some cheap tail." When he returns to school, Hal realizes that he will have to face a choice: "whether he'd be a writer or an engineer." Mailer was not ready to tell his family that he was approaching this same crossroad. That announcement would have to wait until such a time as he could produce some literary bona fides. It was still understood by the family that he was preparing for a career designing airplanes, although shortly after he arrived at Harvard he must have recognized that his degree would be in a general engineering program (engineering sciences), as Harvard did not have an aeronautical engineering program, merely a few courses. Further complicating matters was the fact that he had not taken high school Latin, which was required for a bachelor of arts degree at Harvard, and so could not change his major to English, although he talked to his friends about doing so.

Another issue was money. He had entered Harvard with the understanding that his parents would, by whatever means (including help from Uncle Dave and Aunt Anne), find the money for his first year's college expenses, $1,200, a huge sum for a family with a sporadically employed father. On his application he had put down $3,000 as total family income for the year, supplemented by the $60 he claimed he would earn as a summer counselor at the Scarboro Hotel. For his part, he agreed to apply himself to his studies so as to be eligible for a scholarship in his sophomore year. This meant getting on the dean's list, which he accomplished by getting three Bs and an A (in Mathematics, the subject in which he always scored highest). His family was happy with his performance but, apparently, these grades weren't high enough, for in July he was informed that his scholarship application had been turned down. Another disappointment was not getting into one of Harvard's residential houses for his sophomore year. He and Sy Breslow applied for a suite in Dunster House, with Adams as a backup, and were rejected for both. Marty Lubin was also turned down, and the three friends decided to share a suite in one of the dormitories, Claverly Hall.

Mailer went to Long Branch for the summer to write. Over the next ten weeks, holed up with his portable Remington in the Scarboro Hotel room provided by Aunt Beck, he wrote eight short stories, all of which he would submit the following year. This would be the pattern for three successive summers: write during the summer and bank the work for the fall, a routine that enabled him to tackle ever more ambitious projects. He also wanted to roam and gain experience, especially sexual experience, something that was hard to obtain in Long Branch where there were too many sharp-eyed cousins. In August he and a summer friend decided to hitchhike 125 miles to Scranton where, they had learned from college chums, there was an entire street of brothels. Mailer anticipated this experience in "Love Is Where You Find It" and captured it retrospectively in another short story, titled "Love-Buds," written his senior year but never submitted as class work. In 2007 he referred to the experience as "the disaster of Scranton." In the short story Eppy is Mailer.

They set off with toothbrushes, clean underwear, chocolate bars and some apples, more like Huck and Tom than red-eyed Lotharios. Both are seventeen-year-old virgins and "privately, they were each convinced they would die without having known a woman." The story ends this way:

> "How was it?" Eppy asked tentatively.
>
> "It was wonderful," said Al.
>
> "Yeah, just wonderful."
>
> "Were you able to do it?" Al squeeked.
>
> "No. Were you?"
>
> "No."
>
> By the admission, each had somehow saved the honor of the other. Al let out a whoop of laughter, and Eppy pummeled him on the back. They laughed, they hugged one another, they jumped up

and down on the city street beneath the light of a street lamp, and roared with laughter at themselves and each other.

IN THE FALL of 1940, Mailer signed up for required courses in engineering, math, and physics and one full-year elective: English 1-A, a creative writing course taught by Robert Gorham Davis. An active communist and a member of Matthiessen's clique, the WASPish Davis later wrote short stories for *The New Yorker.* Armed with his cache of stories written over the summer, Mailer impressed Davis, who was exactly the mentor he needed at this stage of his life, although their relationship almost foundered at its start. He submitted "He Was Her Man," a 1,400-word story, and Davis selected it to read in part to the class of approximately fifty students. A businessman and his wife are staying at a resort hotel and when he leaves on a trip, she invites a bellboy to her room. The man returns unexpectedly and finds his wife in bed with him and shoots her in the back of her head. When another bellboy gets to the room, the first one having fled, he finds blood and brains splattered everywhere. After shooting his wife, the man shot himself. "I could make out where her eyes and mouth had been, but I wondered what had happened to her nose. I couldn't guess whether it was smashed into the carpet, or if it was still floating around. I hoped it was in the ground, because stepping on it was certainly better than breathing it in."

At this point, the class broke up. "I can't tell you how my back was scalded by the laughter," Mailer said. But the next day Davis apologized to him, and the relationship was repaired and strengthened. He got a C− on the story, which Davis said in his written comments was "just a mash of brains and nausea." Mailer remembered the grade to be an A−, but his error is clearly a tribute to the man who helped launch his writing career.

In his sophomore year he read Thomas Wolfe and said that Wolfe "made the biggest dent," although his influence was not apparent until later. He also read Saroyan, Faulkner, Fitzgerald, and Hemingway. Sy Breslow said that Mailer kept a gin bottle on his mantel because he read that Hemingway drank it. Papa's macho athleticism and his adventures in the Spanish Civil War were well known and he tried to emulate him. Friends remember the skinny kid from Brooklyn shadow boxing and pretending to be Rocky Graziano. His shyness began to fall away. Along with his friend Larry Weiss, who also lived in Claverly Hall, he tried out for the house football team. Mailer, who was a fan of contact sports, but not much of a participant, made the team, while Weiss did not. The team wore pads and uniforms, but only fourteen or fifteen players showed up for any one game and, except for the running backs, everyone played both offense and defense for the full forty-eight minutes. "I weighed 135 pounds then and played the line: running guard on offense, cannon fodder on defense. And I had fun." Mailer talked proudly about playing house football at Harvard many times over the years; it was a significant milestone.

His virginity weighed heavy, especially after the Scranton disaster. As he wrote later, he had "accepted Lawrence's thesis about untrammeled and illimitable rights and liberties and pleasures of sexual love," but alas, alack, no partner was to be found. Phyllis Bradman came up to Cambridge once each semester, but he never progressed beyond first or second base with her, in Brooklyn parlance. At the end of his freshman year Harold Marantz had introduced him to a young woman who might solve his problem, as she had solved Marantz's. Mailer began seeing her and resumed the seduction when he returned for sophomore year, traveling once a week to her home in Cambridge. "She was too plain to take out," he said, "I would have been embarrassed." After a few visits, he got to third base. "I remember I had not washed my hands, purposely. And I walked by one of my sleeping roommates, put my fingers under his nose and said, 'Whiff that.' That was exactly the level of our social discourse in those days."

The seduction went slowly. The woman's mother hovered in the kitchen, listening and breaking in on their petting. Finally, one evening after several hours on the couch, it happened. "And now I was a man. And I paid a hell of a price because I didn't like the girl. I felt for her, but I didn't like her." During the course of his visits, he had mentioned his literary interests and she reciprocated by giving him a novel she had written. He read it and saw that she had copied it, word for word, from a recent bestseller by Robert Nathan, *Portrait of Jennie*, a treacly fantasy. Asked for his opinion of her manuscript at their next meeting, he said, "Robert Nathan couldn't have done better." She replied, "Who's he," and said it so convincingly that he concluded she was a great actress. "That gave me a sense," he said, "then limited—much greater now—of the depth of that poor girl's need."

The second semester of his sophomore year began well. His grades improved, even in physics; he continued his friendly relationship with Robert Gorham Davis; and he was awarded a $150 scholarship for the term beginning in January, which took some pressure off the family's finances. He made new non-Jewish friends, and began dating girls from the local colleges. He was also producing longer and more sophisticated stories, most of them revealing the influence of Hemingway. Over the weekend of February 8–9, he wrote a five-thousand-word story, "The Greatest Thing in the World." The *Advocate* informed Mailer that the story was a suitable submission for his application, but probably would not be published. Davis also liked the story, saying it was the best he had received all year. Mailer relayed this information home with the announcement, "I simply can't stand any of my engineering courses," adding that he would discuss his dissatisfaction when he came home later in the month. But then his hopes dimmed. He wrote home to say that although the *Advocate* editors liked the story, "they're a bunch of snobs, and Brooklyn may go against me." He had reason to believe this; not many Jews had ever been selected for the magazine. Ultimately, however, his raw talent appealed to a majority of the *Advocate* board, especially those who deplored the cape-and-walking-stick crowd who had long dominated the magazine. Pete Barton led the new faction. (John Crockett and Bowden Broadwater, a "supernova of eccentricity" who later married Mary McCarthy, were the leaders of the aesthetes.) A week later Mailer was invited to be an editor on the magazine.

As was customary, the new associates were told to write and present a sketch at the Advocate House initiation, where heavy drinking was de rigueur. Mailer and George Washington Goethals, one of his new WASP friends, wrote a lewd parody of Hemingway's latest novel, titled "For Whom the Balls Squall: Farewell to Qualms," with a cast of four: Goethals as Martha Gets-Horned, David Roberts as Ernie the Hernia Kid, Mailer as I. Ram Soreloins, and John Elliott Jr. as Ariscrofules. The script is lost; only a playbill survives. It lists the players and notes that the play is "a little piece probing into copulation without population, or safety first." Goethals recalled that he was wearing high heels and a snood and got "horned" with a large sausage wielded by I. Ram Soreloins.

A few days after the April 9 initiation he wrote home with the news that "The Greatest Thing" would be in the lead position in the April magazine. He also reported that he'd written eight thousand words of a "novelette." The most important news was that "The Greatest Thing" had also been chosen to be submitted to the nationwide college contest sponsored by *Story,* a magazine of short fiction founded in 1931 by Whit Burnett and his wife, Martha Foley. The magazine published the early work of a number of Mailer's contemporaries, including J. D. Salinger, Truman Capote, and Joseph Heller. Mailer felt his chances of winning were slight, but was nevertheless happy that his was one of two stories selected out of forty-five submitted by Harvard students. Davis, he learned, was one of the judges, along with two other professors, Mark Schorer and Howard Baker. A week after the April magazine's publication, an editorial appeared in *The Harvard Crimson*—Mailer's first review, in effect—praising the story for having "the emotional conviction of a nightmare." It ended with an endorsement of the *Advocate*'s new direction, realism replacing the "artificialities and the polished sophistications" of the old *Advocate*. He sent a copy of the editorial home and Fan pasted it in the scrapbook of Harvard memorabilia she proudly kept. "It's all happening too easy," he wrote to his parents.

Millie Brower, a friend from Long Branch, read the editorial when she came up for a weekend in early May 1941. Apparently she also read some of his writing because in a letter to her written after her visit, Mailer comments on "The Greatest Thing in the World," which Millie passed on to a college friend, an editor at a college student newspaper. The friend criticized the story's grammar and Mailer did not take the criticism well. "Please tell your friend to go take a hot-running fuck," he wrote, and went on angrily for a full page, calling her "immature" and "a bore." He links her with Bowden Broadwater, the Pegasus, or literary editor of the *Advocate*, whose picture had just appeared in a major story on Harvard in *Life* magazine. "Very cordially dislike him," he wrote. "He writes very well, and bores me so much I can't finish his stories. His grammar is perfect." Mailer's string of victories was stocking the medicine chest of his psyche with energy and frankness, as well as some angry defensiveness. "The nice Jewish boy from Brooklyn" who he later found to be "absolutely insupportable" would never entirely fade, but at this point he was in decline.

On May 7, he was informed that he had been elected to the Signet Society, which unlike the *Advocate*, had its own building at 46 Dunster Street. The society's members, now as then, are chosen on merit, unlike

Harvard's "final clubs," which selected their members based on family ties and prep school affiliations. For the Signet, members of the college's various publications were often chosen for some of the twenty-eight seats given to each class. Mailer ate lunches regularly at the society over the next two years and returned several times after graduation for reunions. For his initiation on May 20, he produced a second sketch parodying Hemingway. For this one, he borrowed from a recent *Life* article on the novelist that was accompanied by Robert Capa photographs of Papa in Sun Valley and Spain. The heavily illustrated, buttery piece notes that Hemingway rewrote some passages in *For Whom the Bell Tolls* sixty to seventy times "to achieve the precise feeling." Mailer's five-minute piece, which he delivered in a borrowed tuxedo, purports to contain excerpts from some of these rewrites; for example: "She was bare and nude and clear and cold and clear and tight and warm and hot, rich inside and richer insider . . . her breasts were square." He always had great admiration for Hemingway as writer and man, and some reservations—his snobbery and his anti-intellectualism—but Papa, even after his 1961 suicide, was the measure Mailer used to gauge himself for nearly seventy years.

Good news continued to pour in. As a new *Advocate* editor, he attended the magazine's seventy-fifth anniversary dinner on April 10 at the Harvard Club. That night he met Roy E. Larsen, the executive editor of *Time*, who had read "The Greatest Thing in the World." He told Mailer he was impressed. Larsen then sent the story to a young editor at Rinehart, Theodore Amussen, who immediately sent his own congratulatory comments. He said he'd like to see more material, especially a novel, and Mailer wrote back saying he'd have one soon. He was working hard on a novella that would eventually be a full-length novel titled "No Percentage."

This praise certainly encouraged him, but nothing fortified him more than the thunderbolts that arrived at the beginning of June. First, Professor Davis wrote to him to congratulate him for winning the national *Story* magazine contest. Then, a telegram from Whit Burnett arrived at the *Advocate* with the same news. It was followed a few days later by a formal letter from Burnett to Mailer at the *Advocate* offices, forwarded by a nonplussed John Crockett, stating that the story was the unanimous choice of the judges. It would be published by *Story* in the fall, Burnett told him, adding that the Story Press, affiliated with publisher J. B. Lippincott, would be eager to consider any novel he might submit. "Probably nothing has happened in the years I've been writing which changed my life as much," Mailer wrote in 1959. "The far-away, all-powerful and fabulous world of New York publishing—which, of course, I saw through Thomas Wolfe's eyes—had said 'yes' to me." That summer the $100 prize money from *Story* arrived, proof positive to Fan and Barney of the genius of their son. The airplane models that hung in the apartment on Crown Street were no longer the preamble to his life's work. Now he was a writer.

BY LATE JUNE Mailer had set up shop at the Scarboro. Before he arrived, he had written 45,000 words of "No Percentage" and was no longer referring to it as a novelette. The Schneider clan, of course, was aware of all that had happened at Harvard and gave their prodigy even more deference. Fan and Barney came down on weekends, and in between she wrote encouraging notes: "How is the writing coming along, honey? Put all the feeling you possess into it and it has to be good. When you were a tiny infant every time I nursed you, I would whisper a little prayer in your ear, 'Please God, make him a great man some day.' This is a secret between you and me, sonny. Take care of yourself. Love, Mother." Word came to Long Branch a few weeks later that Fan had to go in the hospital in Brooklyn for an undisclosed operation, which turned out to be a hysterectomy. No details were mentioned in the flurry of notes and letters among the family, and when he wrote to his mother at the end of July he merely said that he hoped she was feeling better (she recovered quickly). But this comes at the end of his letter; he leads off by announcing that he has written another fourteen thousand words of "No Percentage."

Initially, he had intended the novel to be set entirely in Brooklyn and the Jersey Shore. His plan was to focus on the romantic problems of Robert Branstein, a twenty-one-year-old arts graduate of the University of Pennsylvania. But after winning the *Story* contest, and with Amussen eager to see a full-length work, he decided to expand it by one third and add an additional setting. As recast, the novel opens with Branstein back home in Crown Heights. He has a wealthy blond girlfriend, Sheila Wexler, who lives with her parents in the penthouse of the tallest building in the neighborhood. Her father, Sherman, a powerful and devious figure, has links to organized crime, much like Barney Kelly in Mailer's 1965 novel, *An American Dream*. The gorgeous, vacuous Sheila satisfies all of Branstein's sexual needs, but he yearns for involvement in some altruistic cause. Her father attempts to blackmail him into the marriage, using some incriminating evidence he has on Branstein's father. There is a good deal of violence, including the most striking scene in the entire novel, a bloody altercation between Sherman Wexler and Branstein's grandfather Abram. At this point, Mailer broke off, recognizing Robert had to get away again and undergo a testing. Around the beginning of August, he mailed off part one to Theodore Amussen at Rinehart and then set off on a hitchhiking trip.

Going on the road was a crucial experience for Mailer, a leap from the family safety net. He said the idea came from Dos Passos, whose *U.S.A.* has many stories of bumming around the country. He also hoped his trip would give him the wherewithal to make his protagonist more dynamic. In two weeks he hitchhiked over 1,200 miles, slept almost every night outside, and pushed himself to his limits. He got as far south as New Bern, North Carolina, before turning back. He hitch-hiked through numerous sleepy southern towns. In Danville, Virginia, he went to a whorehouse. This time he was up for the occasion, but found it unsatisfying. He told his friends how he lost his virginity to an old prostitute named Lila, protecting the identity of the Cambridge woman. Two days later he arrived home hungry, dirty, and broke. After a few days of rest and Fan's cooking, he returned to the Scarboro to finish the novel.

Part three centers on Branstein's attempt to hop a moving freight car, something he has never attempted. He tells himself that a successful attempt will be the equivalent of his grandfather's escape from Russia. But he misses the ladder, and this failure presages another defeat, with which the novel concludes. Branstein crawls back to Sheila and his "past life of indecision and fear." The novel ends with a gloomy coda describing their honeymoon in California. Sheila is pleased with her catch; he is beaten down and morose.

Bristling with adjectives, thin on motivation and clogged with dialogue, Mailer's first novel is nevertheless an amazing feat for a nineteen-year-old. He was teaching himself how to write an extended narrative with a dozen or fifteen major characters, all seen from an omniscient point of view, a practice run that would help him in depicting the thoughts of as many GIs in *The Naked and the Dead*. With some gaps here and some repetitions there, he was still able to maintain a narrative line for ninety thousand words, pacing it with various set pieces, some of them containing sharply observed evocations of place. The novel also recycles, sometimes awkwardly, previously written short stories. He was learning to marshal his resources. While the novel shows promise, and some of his one-dimensional characters are sharply drawn, the background of a world at war—save for a few references to the Civil War in Spain—is completely ignored. The novel is a revilement of hedonism and corruption. Robert Branstein sells out to the power nexus but is not entirely despicable because he has learned some lessons, the first being to dislike himself. Shortly after Mailer finished the novel, there was a fire at the Scarboro, a major tragedy for the family. The Schneider clan was distressed; the retreat where he had learned to write burned to the ground.

The completed novel went off to Amussen at about the same time that Mailer arrived at Harvard in mid-September 1941, driving up in a 1936 Chevy convertible given to him by Uncle Dave. He and Marty Lubin had been accepted the previous spring into Dunster House, home of the "Dunster Funsters," and had moved into a fifth floor suite overlooking the Charles River. The Dunster suite, the car (equipped with a mattress in the trunk), not to mention his *Advocate* and Signet sinecures, gave him for the first time the sense of being fully vested at Harvard. He was again playing house football and was co-captain for a time. His family had let him keep the $100 from *Story* and he had a student job drafting a schematic of Harvard's gas and water mains. The only fly in the ointment was his major, now that his avocation had become his vocation. He wrote home that he hated his sole engineering course. His other courses were Philosophy, Sociology, and English 2-A, the second in Harvard's series of creative writing courses. As in his sophomore writing class, he submitted portions of his summer's work—excerpts from "No Percentage"—as well as six new stories.

Amussen arranged to meet Mailer in Cambridge and came by on October 4 to tell him that John Farrar liked "No Percentage" and was going to show it to his partner, Stanley Rinehart. Anne and Dave Kessler, whose support of their nephew seemed overly proprietary to Fan, visited twice during the fall semester to congratulate him. "The Greatest Thing in the World" came out in *Story* on October 15 and within days Mailer had received letters expressing interest in his work, one from a literary agent and another from an editor. They were followed by a letter from Burnett, who wrote to say he hoped Mailer would give him right of first refusal for future work. Two weeks later Amussen wrote to say that he had given the novel to an agent, Monte Stein, for an outside opinion. Stein said it "shows brilliance," and Amussen agreed. Whit Burnett, who had been sent one of several copies of the typescript, came to the same conclusion, telling Mailer that "the writing and psychology are brilliant."

ON DECEMBER 7 the Japanese attacked Pearl Harbor, and the next day the United States declared war. President Conant called a mass meeting at Sanders Theatre. Mailer probably attended, but if not he certainly heard the gist of Conant's message: the time of uncertainty about the U.S. war role is over and Harvard men will be called on to serve. The campus was transformed within weeks and graduation was accelerated for many students. Mailer's response was to begin a new journal of observations, plans, and sketches. Sy Breslow said that Mailer felt the war "would feed the novel he wanted to write afterward. He was desperately searching for experience," an observation confirmed by what Mailer later wrote about the moment his generation would never forget:

> I may as well confess that by December 8th or 9th of 1941, in the forty-eight hours after Pearl Harbor, while worthy young man were wondering where they could be of aid to the war effort, and practical young men were deciding which branch of the service was the surest for landing a safe commission, I was worrying darkly whether it would be more likely that a great war novel would be written about Europe or the Pacific.

Mailer's journal was also used for a running commentary on his relationship with Beatrice Silverman, a Boston University student from nearby Chelsea whom he met just after the Pearl Harbor attack, and with whom he had his first mature sexual relationship. Larry Weiss, now one of his closest friends, introduced him to Bea, as everyone called her. The plan was for the two Harvard men to meet Bea and another BU woman at a Boston Symphony concert. While waiting to see if tickets were available, they talked and Bea saw that Mailer "didn't know his ass from his elbow about music." He suggested that they return to his room at Dunster for a drink. Necking followed and when the others left, they went to bed. Bea was not a sexual novice. "She was very helpful, put it that way," Mailer recalled, "and it worked."

> And so we were off to the races for a year and a half. We were together all the time. But I had to be the best she'd ever had, which started a crazy theme in my head, which I didn't get rid of for many, many, many years, because I always had a fear that I wasn't the best lover with any woman I was with, that I was serious about, and if it didn't take, that was the end of it. And if it did take, then I had to be the best. And if I couldn't be, that was probably the end of it, too. So, you know, you can get a woman to tell you anything.

Physically, they were an odd couple. Bea was five foot two, and slightly zaftig. She had long brown hair and an attractive heart-shaped face. Mailer was a few pounds lighter than Bea and six or seven inches taller. He described himself in his journal as having a "triangular face, oily, too much hair, glasses too big, chin too small." No matter, they were in love and were soon a well-known couple at Harvard, where Bea spent a lot of time. Women were not allowed in the houses in the evening, but she flouted the rules and stayed overnight on many a weekend and their adventures in the sack became notorious; they were "setting records," he said, and were proud of it.

Bea used profanity regularly and this offended some of their friends, but Mailer admired Bea's use of crude language, which surpassed his own. Her favorite expression, meant to convey *tempus fugit*, was "Meanwhile, the foetus is growing." But she was also kind and maternal, he said. They were both leftist in their politics but Bea was a step ahead, having read a lot of left-wing literature as well as Havelock Ellis and some Freud. In a psychological profile of her, written as a term paper his senior year, Mailer noted that "to her any concept of absolutes or static custom is absurd." She was a feminist thirty years ahead of the wave, he said later, and was both intellectually honest and candid. He believed that he was brighter than she was and liked that because it gave him a "comfort zone," but he admitted that she was more knowledgeable and was a better student. A musicology major, she also took courses in social psychology. Lacking much financial support from her parents, she paid for her final two years of college by waitressing and giving lessons on the piano, an instrument she had played from an early age. Her relations with her parents were sour and she looked forward to being out of the house and independent. Within a few months, they were talking about marriage.

At the start of the spring semester Mailer's *Advocate* friend Pete Barton invited Mailer for dinner at Lowell House, where they discussed Mailer's writing, specifically, "The Schedule Breaker," which Barton liked. This story of seduction led Barton, in a halting manner, to ask Mailer how many times he had had sex. Mailer told him everything and they went on to speak of Barton's fears of disease and pregnancy. The contrast between the reserved Barton and the uninhibited Mailer can be seen in another entry in his journal. At first titled "Exit Blues," but later known (by its chorus line) as "The Bodily Function Blues," it was to be sung to the tune of "St. Louis Blues." The fact that Mailer was classed as a "listener" or "monotone" in grade school music classes did not deter him from delivering it with gusto from his college days until well into his eighties. A sample:

Ah can't piss, Ah can't urinate
Ah can't bleed, Ah can't even menstruate
Ah can't talk, Ah can't elucidate
Ah can't shit, Ah can't defecate
Ah can't gargle, Ah can't salivate
But worst of all, the worst of all
Ah can't fuck, Ah just can't copulate
Ah got those bodily function blues.

In addition to the exaggerated carnality of the lyrics, the contrast between the Anglo-Saxon and Latinate synonyms is worth noting. The juxtaposition of the two lexical streams, which would become one of the hallmarks of his prose, came in great measure from what he termed a "triangle" of influence—Hemingway, Faulkner, and Farrell. From Hemingway there was "the power of restraint" deriving in part from the sparing use of Latinate words; from Faulkner, "the power of excess" that came from the expansive use of multisyllabic words. Farrell was powerful because he "gave you the sense that reality is what you had to obey more than anything. I think I learned more from those three writers than any other American writers."

The influence of the three was heightened because Mailer never took any courses in English or continental literature except for a drama course his senior year. Because of the courses required for his major, and the six writing courses he took, his program of study was tight. Besides a year of French, his only other electives were one course each in philosophy, psychology, sociology, and fine arts. Mailer's lopsided curriculum, coupled with his early loss of interest in engineering, was a boon. With little opportunity to be seduced by liberal arts courses, much of his energy went into mastering fictional techniques and reading contemporary writers. His curriculum, or lack of one, allowed him to look at the world without disciplinary glasses, much as another Harvard man, William James, had, and do so fearlessly.

In the second semester of his junior year, he took "Modern American Literature" with Howard Mumford Jones. It was in this course, which he later said meant a lot to him, that he first encountered the writing of Dreiser and Faulkner. During his four years at Harvard, the only contact he had with European literature came when he sat in on some of Harry Levin's course on Proust, Mann, and Joyce. Mailer had scant interest in eighteenth-century British poetry and this was another reason (the lack of high school Latin being the other) he didn't change majors. Temperamentally, he was never much in sympathy with the British literary tradition, especially poetry, although he came to admire Milton. In later years he did favor continental writers, especially the French, an admiration that began when he read *Man's Fate* in his senior year. Shortly after graduation he told a friend, "I'd like to be another Malraux."

At the same time as he was reading Faulkner, he was enrolled in his fourth writing course, English 3-A, with Theodore Morrison, a poet, novelist, and Chaucer scholar, who said he was "struck at once by the unmistakable presence of talent in Mailer's undergraduate work." The story that impressed him was "Right Shoe on Left Foot," a taut seven thousand words about racial injustice in the South in which he attempted, with some success, to present the dialects of both southern blacks and whites. Pete Barton, Mailer wrote home, was crazy about the story and it was immediately accepted by the editors of the *Advocate*. The *Crimson* praised the new story, calling it a welcome departure from the "haunted degeneracy" of the aesthetes who had earlier dominated the magazine. Mailer was turning out stories at a rapid rate now, and Fan and a coworker at Sunlight Oil had some difficulty keeping up with his requests for clean, typed copies for his submissions and competitions. Another of his stories for Morrison, "Maybe Next Year," was also accepted by the *Advocate*. Mailer thought enough of it to reprint it in *Advertisements for Myself* with a prefatory note explaining that the inspiration was Faulkner's *The Sound and the Fury*.

When he learned that MGM was running a college contest to identify fledgling screenwriters, he bundled five stories he had written for Morrison, added "The Greatest Thing," and submitted them. At the same time, he sent "Maybe Next Year" to Amussen, who sent it on to *The New Yorker*. He was also corresponding with Whit Burnett and planned to see him in New York. In his regular letters home, he often devoted a page to comments on the short stories of his sister, the beginning of his lifelong mentoring of other writers. As the star of the *Advocate*, he spent a great deal of time in the boardroom reading old copies of the magazine, although he found time to drop condoms filled with water out a third story window. Goethals found Mailer to be "incredibly self-disciplined," but not at all starry-eyed about writing. "To him it was work. He used to say, 'George, this business of inspiration is shit.' "

When Barton took over as president of the magazine, Crockett replaced Broadwater as Pegasus. Mailer was a senior editor. It was the job of Pegasus to gather up all the manuscripts, supervise the layout, and get the magazine printed. The April '42 issue was the first effort of the new team and each staff member had a story or poem in it. The issue was delayed, however, and delayed again. Crockett reported problems with the printers in Vermont and cautioned patience. Barton, Mailer wrote in "Our Man at Harvard," "had suspended himself into a state of forbearance worthy of a Zen warrior considering the immense agitation the late appearance of the magazine had caused." When it finally appeared, the contributions of almost all the new editorial team were gone. Crockett had boldly replaced the planned magazine with an entirely new one, a seventy-fifth anniversary double issue containing essays, poems, and stories from the likes of Wallace Stevens, Marianne Moore, William Carlos Williams, and many others. Crockett told Hilary Mills, Mailer's first biographer, that his motive was to publish material of high quality rather than the "smart-alecky undergraduate juvenilia" that Barton and

Mailer wanted to publish. In "Our Man at Harvard," Mailer described Crockett's coup as "a mammoth virtuoso literary crypto-CIA affair." Barton, whom he likened to Billy Budd, took the blame for the entire situation, which was not a total fiasco in that Crockett's assemblage, the last crack of the aesthetes' whip, was acclaimed in the Boston papers. To keep everyone happy, Barton decreed that the planned issue would come out in May, containing the material that Crockett had suppressed. As a result, the *Advocate* fell into a financial slough and remained there until well after World War II.

"Right Shoe on Left Foot" appeared in the May issue and "Maybe Next Year" in June, which lessened any pain Mailer may have felt when he learned that the story Amussen submitted to *The New Yorker* was turned down. He was also disappointed to learn that he was not selected in the MGM competition for young screenwriters, which, on the basis of his *Story* feat, he thought he had a chance to win. MGM had asked about his military obligation, but he didn't want to think about it, although he knew he would have to sign up for the draft. His parents were getting concerned as millions of young men were enlisting or being drafted. There was a family discussion toward the end of his junior year in which a graduate school deferment in engineering was considered. When classes ended, Mailer told his family he wanted to remain in Boston, ostensibly to work on his latest literary interest—writing plays—but Bea, of course, was the magnet. The family knew about her by now and wanted to meet her as much as Bea wanted to meet them. He recorded a vignette in his journal that says a lot about their besotted state in early 1942.

> Bea and I were eating at McBride's tonight. We were sitting next to each other, alone, sitting very close. When the waitress came for the dessert & handed us *two* menus, Bea looked at them, smiling. "Two?" she said. "Two? Do we look like two people?"

One unhappy by-product of their romance was a drop in his grades. For the second semester, he had only one A (from Theodore Morrison in English), two Cs, and a B. This slippage caused him to lose the scholarship he had had for two years and would crimp the family's finances.

Before final exams, Mailer nursed the Chevy back to Brooklyn to be junked. When he returned and the school year was over, he and Douglas

Woolf, a Dunster friend, got jobs as attendants at the Boston State Hospital (formerly called the Lunatic Asylum) in nearby Mattapan. They were paid $15 a week plus room and board. He wrote home to say that the inmates were not dangerous and the grounds looked like a college campus. Fan was upset and Mailer tried to calm her down by telling her he was working mainly with shell-shocked veterans and that he was collecting material for his writing. They were assigned to the violent ward, where there were sixty inmates. Woolf was exhausted by the workload—mainly herding the unruly inmates—and the sixty-five-hour week and quit. Mailer hung on but after eight days left because of the pervasive brutality. When a black inmate went berserk, swinging two table legs, the attendants moved in with mattresses and Mailer tackled him. Then they beat him into unconsciousness. Mailer did not take part in the beating, but he sensed that he eventually might and, in revulsion, quit. He wrote home that the job had been "very hard, very horrible." The systematic and heartless use of violence as an instrument of control marked him deeply.

His parents and Uncle Dave sent him money to stay afloat and he sought work at the navy shipyard, newspapers, theaters, and at Harvard. He had written a one-act play, "The Darndest Thing Happened on Mars," and made friends with members of the Harvard Dramatic Society. Within three days of leaving the hospital, he landed a soda fountain job for $18 a week and meals at a big department store, the C. F. Hovey Company in the Savin Hill section of Boston, not far from where he was sharing a room with friends. He had nights and weekends off and of course spent as much time as possible with Bea, mainly at her home on Cary Avenue in Chelsea, as neither the Chevy nor the Dunster suite were available. This threw him into contact with Bea's mother, Jenny, who was annoyed by the couple's petting.

> She used to wrinkle her nose and looked on the sex like it was smelly, which was a big thing among most of those middle-class women at that point, that sex was something you didn't talk about; it was kind of a smelly activity and let's not get into it. And of course, I was all for the smells. For me, that was the most positive thing about sex, precisely, that it was a smelly activity. So there we are, and we'd neck on the couch. And Jenny would come marching in, making enough noise so that we could disengage if it was getting that far. And she'd

> say, "Norman, I just wish you knew how many times I've come in here and seen Bea necking with one of you or another." And I'd say, "Just getting ready for me." I was very sassy with her.

Fan, unaccompanied by Barney, came up for a visit in mid-July at about the same time that Mailer quit his job making sandwiches and sundaes. It is likely that it was during this trip that she met Bea, although there is no record of it. He started work as a press agent for the Joy Street Playhouse, a carriage house theater on Beacon Hill. There was no pay, but he got some free meals. He wrote releases, distributed posters, performed short walk-on roles, and schmoozed drama critics. "The work is congenial," he wrote home at the end of July, "everyone is poor." In mid-August he went to a reception where he met the cast of *Othello*—Paul Robeson, Uta Hagen, and José Ferrer—who were trying out the play in Boston before its two-year run on Broadway. This foray into the dramatic world sparked an interest that would last a lifetime. It also gave him a sufficient sense of stagecraft to recast his experience at the state hospital in dramatic form.

To write the play, he decided, quite naturally, to go to the Jersey Shore. The Scarboro was now a vacant lot so he went to Monmouth Beach, where Aunt Beck was running a hotel. It had been decided that it was time for Bea to meet the clan and she traveled, separately (and thus appropriately), to Monmouth Beach sometime during the last week of August. The round of visits with the aunts and cousins apparently went smoothly because Mailer sent his mother a postcard on the last day of August saying that Beck, the senior sister, liked Bea very much. Bea returned to Chelsea and he got to work on the play, using as the inciting incident the beating of the black inmate. He called the play "The Naked and the Dead." Mailer scholar Robert F. Lucid, in his commentary on the unpublished play, noted that "Fear, for Norman, had probably always been the most authentic emotion," and "the administration of fear as a public policy" that he encountered at the hospital "penetrated to the deepest center of his imagination." He would return again and again to the ways powerful regimes and administrations at all levels of American society created what he called in his first published novel a "fear ladder," whereby blandishments, threats, favors, and physical harm were increased or decreased as necessary for the maintenance of control, much as the water temperature (euphemized as hydrotherapy) was modulated at the state hospital to pacify unruly mental patients.

It took him fifteen days to complete the three-act, eight-scene play, all of which takes place in a mental institution. In more than one way it seems to anticipate Ken Kesey's 1962 novel, *One Flew Over the Cuckoo's Nest.* The combined and disorienting use of both harsh and sophisticated control methods by a despotic head nurse, the slow corruption of well-meaning staff members in an atmosphere of spying and informing, and the eventual revolt and escape of some of the tyrannized can be found in both works. The play has a number of redundant scenes and the line of action is sometimes difficult to follow, yet it has the force of its "fear ladder" thesis as well as the most believable dialogue he had yet written. After the rebellious black inmate is subdued and sent to hydrotherapy, the two young orderlies in the play realize they cannot change the institution's deeply embedded methods of control. They quit and go on a fishing trip to regain their equilibrium, much as Nick Adams does in Hemingway's "Big Two-Hearted River." But before they go, one has an epiphany, which he blurts out to the other during an argument: "This all happened on a bigger scale in Germany. Germany is like an attendant!" Shortly after finishing the play, Mailer returned to Cambridge, where he submitted the play to the Harvard Dramatic Society and prepared for his senior year.

BY THE FALL of 1942, Harvard had gone to year-round instruction and thousands of army and navy officer candidates were housed on campus. Mailer returned to Dunster, sharing a fourth floor suite with Harold Katz, a mathematics and philosophy major from Indiana. Many of the class of '43 had gone into an accelerated program and graduated a year early. In late September, he began talking with the Harvard draft advisor about joining the enlisted reserve. He also began checking on graduate school requirements in engineering, but was told that no course could keep him from being drafted.

Harvard had gone to war and Mailer was eager to engage war in his writing, not as background as in several of his previous year's stories, but head-on. He had been reading Malraux and Hemingway and began planning a new narrative, to be set in the South Pacific, where American soldiers were fighting. Like everyone else, he was getting the dispiriting news from the war front. In April 1942, shortly after General Douglas MacArthur left the Philippines for Australia, the American-Philippine army surrendered to the Japanese on the Bataan Peninsula. The battle for Guadalcanal in the Solomon Islands dragged on though the last half of 1942, causing dismay. The Japanese were on the offensive. This cheerless mood would be reflected in Mailer's writing. He was not taking a writing course but worked on the novella with his usual focus. His courses that semester were two required engineering courses, a drama survey course, and Henry Murray's course in abnormal psychology. And, for the length of the fall semester, he awaited word from the Harvard Dramatic Society on the fate of his play. Because of wartime limitations, the society was only mounting plays that could be handled with small stage crews. A note in the *Crimson* said his play, now retitled "Man Chasm," was "a dark horse among the plays considered." Ultimately, the play was turned down and he focused on completing the war novella, which carried a title, "The Foundation," plucked from a passage in *Man's Fate*:

> All that men are willing to die for, beyond self-interest, tends more or less obscurely to justify that fate by giving it a foundation in dignity: Christianity for the slave, the nation for the citizen, Communism for the worker.

There was one additional influence: the horrendous fire and pandemonium at the Cocoanut Grove supper club in Boston. On the night of November 28, 492 people, including many servicemen and their companions, were burned, asphyxiated, or trampled to death when flammable paper decorations caught fire. For identification purposes, the morgue where most of the bodies were sent, the Southern Mortuary, was opened to the public. Mailer wrote home to say he was safe in Dunster when the fire occurred, not mentioning that he and Bea had gone to view the bodies. Afterward, he transposed his memory of one of the victims to the memory of the key figure in the novella, Captain Bowen Hilliard, a Harvard graduate:

> He remembered the burnt body of a man that he had looked at for quite a time. It had seemed a terrible degradation, as if the man in burning to death had reverted to a prehistoric type. He had been

> blackened all over, his flesh in shriveling had given the appearance of black fur, and his features, almost burned off, had been snubbed and shrunken, so that the man's face in death had only registered a black circle of mouth with the teeth grimacing whitely and out of place in the blackness of the ape.

The novella is a kind of prospective dirge in which five Americans inwardly grieve and ponder their all but certain deaths as a force of invading Japanese surround them on the fictional island of Tinde in April 1942. Only brief and tentative descriptions of combat are provided; Mailer is much more at home in giving the texture of American life in capsule biographies of his characters. The novella winds down quickly after the five realize they are completely cut off. It ends with a Hemingway flourish. As they smoke their final cigarettes, one character notes that it is going to be a sunny day. "Yes," says another, "sometimes you want to look pretty carefully at it." Later retitled *A Calculus at Heaven*, the novella strongly prefigures *The Naked and the Dead*, especially in the use of a hovering, brooding, sympathetic narrative consciousness. He completed the novella over semester break in Brooklyn in preparation for submitting it in Professor Robert Hillyer's English 5-A course the upcoming semester, his last at Harvard. In the middle of his senior year, he wrote in his journal that he wanted to do "a little philosophical accounting." What is most striking about this nine-page entry is his effort to tell the worst, to probe and pinch his weaknesses as if they were lice on his body. He starts by casting back to his arrival at Harvard, saying he came with little self-knowledge.

> I lived completely (and my moods depended on) in the impressions of others. I would lie, boast, exaggerate so that they would think more of me, & so that I by some rather difficult rationalization might believe it too. This deception did not always work with me, & I went through periods of extreme realization & unhappiness. To myself I was no good.

He continues with a description of the stair steps of his growth as a reader, writer, and lover, commenting on his failure in the Scranton brothel, his success in the one in Virginia, and the seduction in Cambridge. He examines his political awakening and discusses hitting "the jackpot" with "The Greatest Thing." At the end of his sophomore year, he writes, "My egoism was extreme, & the fact of it bothered me." In his junior year, lacking any belief in God, he constructed a sensualist philosophy. Then he met Bea and "I've been loving–not loving her ever since. The sex-ego business is laid to rest. I'm a good lover without being as great as Bea thinks I am." He ends with a reflection that augured well for a writer who would later examine sympathetically the psyches of moral monsters such as Gary Gilmore, Lee Harvey Oswald, and Adolf Hitler: "Every villain in a melodrama considers himself as the hero. That is one of the fundamental things to learn about life. It is one of the milestones of intelligence."

Amussen wrote at the end of March 1943 to say that *A Calculus at Heaven* was the best piece of writing he had yet produced and offered to help him find a publisher for the twenty-thousand-word novella. Mailer's friends, who he said were his toughest critics, agreed with Amussen's evaluation as Mailer reported to Millie Brower in an April letter. He also told her that he expected to be in the army by July 1, and that he'd like to see her in New York in June if she would be there. His relationship with Bea is still very much alive, he continued, but it had been through many evolutions. "It's been wonderful, & exciting, & maturing for me, (and her) but it won't survive the next five years of war, I fear. Nothing could."

He wrote to his parents the same day to discuss what was on everyone's mind as graduation approached—the army. He was both resigned to being drafted and eager to seize the experiential possibilities of life in the army melting pot.

> You say, Mother (and I'll include you dad) that you will worry if I'm in the army, and that therefore, I should reconsider it. If you only knew how much I've thought about this, and how many my temptations have been. (Don't forget, I have much besides Harvard to keep me in Boston.) And yet, as a writer, and you must believe me since I can't explain it to you, I feel it necessary to enter a private, to get the feel of the nation, to *know* what [servicemen] think about, rather than guessing.

Uncle Dave came up to Cambridge in April to discuss his nephew's plans—no family member came more often. As a graduation present, he offered to underwrite Mailer's participation in a trip to Mexico with several of his friends, and Mailer seemed eager to go. His friends planned to leave on May 20, a week before graduation, but he decided to go through the ceremony with the family in the audience. "Lord knows you've waited long enough for it," he wrote to them. He had already told them that he was planning to start a new work, another novel, which he would base on his play about the insane asylum. He had a title: *A Transit to Narcissus*.

For the remainder of the semester, he worked on the novel and did sufficient work in his final, required engineering course to get a passing grade. He told his parents he might get only a C, which was not impressive, "but what importance do my masks have now anyway." He was also engaged in deep conversations with Bea. Earlier in the semester, she had asked him if he wanted to get married and he replied that their commitment would persist without marriage, even if one or both of them were unfaithful. There was no sense, therefore, in getting married just "so we can participate in the great American custom," he wrote in his journal. "Bea loves me as a vase now, something valuable to her because it's clever and sensitive." The romance was obviously a work in progress because when the time came to make a decision about going to Mexico, Mailer opted out. He told his parents he'd prefer to take his vacation in a small town on the tip of Cape Cod, Provincetown, with which he would be associated for the remainder of his life. He didn't tell them that Bea would be going too, or how serious their relationship had become.

He got a B in his engineering course and As in his other three courses, which enabled him to graduate cum laude. With his parents, Barbara, and the Kesslers in the audience, he received his SB degree in Engineering Sciences on May 27. Winston Churchill was to have been the graduation speaker and receive an honorary degree, but his meetings in Washington with President Roosevelt forced him to cancel. Bea also did not attend—the number of tickets was limited—but Barbara stayed with her in Chelsea and Barney met her for the first time. After a reception at Dunster House, the family returned to Brooklyn and Mailer awaited greetings from the army.

THREE
THE ARMY

Two weeks after his graduation, Mailer and Bea took the ferry from Boston to Provincetown. A fishing village on the tip of Cape Cod, P-Town, as it is often called, is encircled by ocean, tidal flats, and sand dunes. During the week they vacationed there, the town had an "unearthly" beauty at night, Mailer said. A wartime blackout had been imposed on the East Coast a year earlier and when the couple walked along Commercial Street fronting the harbor, a gibbous moon gave the town's colonial architecture "the feel of 1790," Mailer said. They stayed at an inn on Standish Street where their marital status went unquestioned by the landlady or anyone else, and enjoyed an idyllic week in each other's arms and at the beach. Provincetown has never been a starchy place and the two free love advocates promised that they would return if and when he returned safely. He was certain that a draft notice awaited him at his parents' new residence in Brooklyn Heights, an apartment at 102 Pierrepont Street. Bea had a final semester to complete in Boston and they went their separate ways on June 15.

Ambivalence is the only word to describe Mailer's attitude about the army during that summer. Right after graduation, he told George Goethals that he planned to enlist and get it over with, but in July he asked Amussen to request that Stanley Rinehart write a letter to his draft board seeking a deferment so he could finish *A Transit to Narcissus*. Rinehart was interested in his writing but counseled that such a request would be unwise. "I was a little frightened of going to war, and a great deal ashamed of not going to war, and terrified of my audacity in writing so ambitious a novel," Mailer wrote in the introduction to *Transit* when it was finally published in 1978. Every day the draft notice was expected and every day it failed to appear. He pushed on with the first draft of *Transit* and then began the second. Occasionally, he took the train to see Bea in Chelsea, or she visited Brooklyn. For both, it was an anxious period and Mailer's state of mind—"I was as lonely as I have ever been"—is reflected in the mood of the novel, a mix of the febrile and the lugubrious.

There was some cheer that summer. Amussen's efforts to find a publisher for *A Calculus at Heaven* were successful. Edwin Seaver wrote at the end of August to say that he was accepting the novella, with only minor changes, for publication the following spring in *Cross-Section: A Collection of New American Writing*, the first of a series of anthologies of new work by young writers. It would be Mailer's first appearance in a book. Published with him were several important young writers whose careers were also given a boost: Jane Bowles, Richard Wright, Shirley Jackson, Ralph Ellison, and two others whom Mailer came to know well in Brooklyn after the war, Arthur Miller and poet Norman Rosten.

Set in the summer of 1938 in an unnamed city, *A Transit to Narcissus* focuses on a college senior, Paul Scarr, who works at what is called "the insane asylum," where he is a ward attendant. As in Mailer's own experience and his play, "The Naked and the Dead," a troublesome black inmate is punched and kicked into unconsciousness by the attendants. Scarr is distraught but also strangely exhilarated by the regular and condoned brutality.

The novel's overarching struggle is between the Syndicate that controls the asylum and a crusading newspaper run by an idealistic publisher. During a ruckus with inmates, Scarr kicks one in the stomach, and the inmate later dies. Because the Syndicate controls the D.A.'s office, Scarr is offered a lighter sentence by the Syndicate's consigliere, a Mephistophelean lawyer named Riorden, if he does not reveal the horrors and graft at the asylum. He agrees but later reneges.

As the novel proceeds, Scarr becomes emotionally calloused and finds that violence beguiles him more and more. The methods employed to cow the inmates eventually turn nearly all of the employees into little fascists. The hospital scenes and routines (including an elaborate, fiendish system of distributing discarded cigarette butts among the inmates), based on Mailer's experience, ring true. The depiction of the newspaper and its staff and the Syndicate thugs is thin, and Scarr's bizarre suicide (with which the novel ends) is unconvincing. The sex scenes, written shortly after he completed Henry A. Murray's abnormal psychology course, are slavishly Freudian. Plot strings are left dangling, nothing is resolved. The ending gives every sign of authorial haste and confusion. As Mailer biographer Carl Rollyson notes, *Transit* "was a devastating novel to write, for Mailer deliberately turned in on himself before he had the experience to develop the shields of the various personae who would appear in his later work."

THE NOVEL MAY have ground to such an abrupt ending because the size of Mailer's ambitions finally overpowered him. He was worn out by what he called the novel's "ponderosities" and the tensions between Marxist and Freudian themes. Bea was also a large factor. He took the manuscript with him when he went on a ski trip with her to North Conway, New Hampshire, for a week in late December. The real purpose of the trip was a serious discussion of their future now that she was about to graduate and his army service was looming. Both of them were somewhat uncertain because they prized their freedom, but since Bea's mother knew they were sleeping together she was nagging her to get married and not bring great shame on the family.

> Yeah, and suddenly I felt very bad. Like: I do love her, she's so lovely, why am I so mean to her and so I said, "Let's get married." She smiled, looked a tiny bit, nodded her head. Years later, she told me she felt a moment of gloom when I asked her. (laughs). In any event, gloom, doom and happiness, whatever.

On January 7, 1944, he and Bea were secretly married in a civil ceremony in Yonkers, New York. He gave her a twenty-five-cent silver Mexican ring. There was no honeymoon, no guests, no reception; she returned shortly afterward for graduation from Boston University.

He was encouraged by a meeting at this time with a literary agent, Berta Kaslow of the William Morris Agency, who had written to him at the suggestion of Seaver. She became an enthusiastic admirer of *Transit* and after he went into the service sent it to a dozen publishers, albeit unsuccessfully. Still ambivalent, he again sought respite from his draft board. At his request, Seaver wrote a "To Whom It May Concern" letter attesting to Mailer's talent and seeking an extension. He wrote to Seaver to thank him, adding that seeking a delay "occasions [in] me a great deal of soulsearching for I feel guilty when I think of some candy store owner torn from his loving children." Sometime around the middle of the month, the draft notice arrived. Mailer responded on January 19 by submitting a formal request for a thirty- to forty-day delay, arguing that he was trying to finish "an important literary work" that contained "an attempt on my part to analyze some of the fundamental differences between the Fascist and democratic minds" that had "some relevance to the war effort." His appeal was rejected and he was ordered to report for induction on March 27.

According to Bea, Fan wanted the marriage annulled. "Fanny," she said, "just didn't want her little genius to be married." Bea's mother, Jenny Silverman, wasn't entirely happy either; she had hoped Bea would marry a doctor. The opinion of the two fathers is not recorded; Fan and Jenny ruled their households. Ultimately, everyone came around when it was clear that the couple was committed, and on March 18 they were married again at her home in Chelsea. The families wanted, and got, a full Jewish service: a rabbi, a service under a *chuppah*, the reading of the *Sheva Brachot* (Seven Blessings), and the ceremonial breaking of the wineglass. Mailer despised the ritual. Writing to his mother months later to defend his sister's relationship with a non-Jewish man, he said:

> Neither Barbara nor I feel very strongly about being Jews—I am neither proud nor ashamed. But what I am ashamed of, and to this day my face flushes when I think of it, was that disgraceful exhibition—my marriage ceremony. Ughh. And you insisted on it, and were wrong, as I think you realized that night. Certainly, it was hardly an encouragement for Barbara to marry a Jew; she was as nauseated by it as I.

AFTER A WEEK at Camp Upton, where he took an army IQ test and scored 145, Mailer reported for basic training at Fort Bragg, North Carolina, arriving in early April. Before he departed, Berta Kaslow sent him a telegram informing him that Robert N. Linscott, the top editor at Random House, felt after reading *Transit* that Mailer was a "potentially very important writer." Mailer's family, especially Fan, wrote to him weekly and he and Bea wrote to each other several times a week for the next two years. They had an extraordinary correspondence, over four hundred letters, erotic and literary, full of plans for the future. Shortly after he had departed, she joined the WAVES, went though officer training, was commissioned an ensign and assigned to Norfolk, Virginia. When the men in his unit learned of her rank, he was asked over and over whether he had to salute before they had sex. He grew weary of the joke.

As a Harvard graduate, Mailer could easily have obtained a commission and a desk job, perhaps in intelligence, but he decided that being in the enlisted ranks would give him a far greater chance to observe. Although he told Columbia University professor Steven Marcus in 1963 that he was burned out after the dispiriting effort of writing *Transit*, he quickly recovered and began pondering the shape of his next novel. Before he departed, he told Bea that he intended to write "THE war novel" and shortly after he arrived at Fort Bragg on April 8, he wrote home to say that instead of keeping a journal, he would send home regular observations to Bea, a plan he kept to for the duration of his time in the army.

Because of his engineering degree he was assigned to training for an assignment in artillery fire control. He found the math to be elementary. Even with calisthenics, rifle practice, and marching in addition to his artillery training, he found time to compile a lexicon of military slang for his parents. He provided detailed explanations for "goldbricker," "chow," "snafu," and his favorite, "t.s.," the army's blunt, unsympathetic response to GI complaints. The obscene humor of the army resonated happily in Mailer and would be a staple in *The Naked and the Dead*. Twenty years later in *The Armies of the Night*, he recalled (writing about himself in the third person) the humor he discovered in the army.

> Mailer never felt more like an American than when he was naturally obscene—all the gifts of the American language came out in the happy play of obscenity upon concept, which enabled one to go back to concept again. What was magnificent about the word shit is that it enabled you to use the word noble: a skinny Southern cracker with a beatific smile on his face saying in the dawn in a Filipino rice paddy, "Man, I just managed to take me a noble shit." Yeah, that was Mailer's America.

His platoon sergeant, Donald Mann, was a southerner (and later his physical model for Sergeant Croft in *Naked*), but most of his friends in basic training were New York Jews. One of his closest friends was Clifford Maskovsky. He kept an eye on Mailer because, as Maskovsky recalled, "He wasn't that good at physical things." Nor was he adept at inspections. A few weeks into basic, he was "gigged" for some infraction and his entire unit lost their weekend passes. "When it came to taking care of myself," Mailer said, "I had little to offer next to the practical sense of an illiterate sharecropper." One of his distractions was reading; another was taking notes on the sex lives of the other soldiers. Everyone knew he was a Harvard graduate, but he didn't reveal his literary aspirations. A copy of *Cross-Section* arrived in late May, along with reviews of it in *The New York Times Book Review* and the *New York Herald Tribune Weekly Book Review*, but he doesn't seem to have shown these around the barracks. Maskovsky said he never saw Mailer in an argument with an officer during basic, and Mailer recalled that he got through the war "with my lip buttoned." There would be a notable blow up just before he was discharged, but for most of his twenty-five months of active duty, his reputation was that of a detached, quiet observer.

In late May, he sent Bea his first extended piece of writing for later use, a description of a fierce rainstorm that hit his unit when they were on the firing range. The most notable detail that he used later is a tableaux of sodden GIs huddled in the uncertain lee of a truck singing "Buddy, Can You Spare a Dime?" Every other letter to Bea contained some patch of observation—the rhythms of insect life on the square foot of ground before your face as you lay prone with your rifle, the "phaWhom" sound of dynamite exploding in the water, a comparison of the sound of a passing artillery shell with the slithering noise a snake makes in dry grass. His letters also contained comments on his reading. He praised Arthur Koestler's *Darkness at Noon*, calling its author "one of the best novelists living today"; and found John Hersey's *A Bell for Adano* to be a "stinker." Kaslow continued to pepper him with letters about *Transit*'s chances with various publishers and her enthusiasm deterred him from abandoning the novel. As late as April 1945, he wrote to Bea that he wanted to make a pile of money so that he could write "a twenty volume Transit that would out-Joyce James."

His letters also contained speculations about the nature of combat and, as the summer approached, eager anticipation of Bea's visit to Fayetteville July 29–30. He scheduled the reunion to the minute. On the weekend before her visit he inspected the room, and checked to see if her train would be on time. All went according to plan. Bea arrived with a silver chain for his dog tags and they had a lusty thirty-two hours together.

Mailer did not yet have a plan for the war novel. All he knew was that it would be a combat novel. When he learned of the D-Day invasion in France, he wrote to Bea, "my first reaction was of disappointment—I wanted to be on the beach. Secretly and selfishly I had wanted the invasion to wait for me." Later on, he recognized that being sent to the Pacific, as would happen, was fortunate in that the American hunger for power was palpable in places like the Philippines, but not in Europe. More important, to write about the war in France and Germany, it was necessary to have "a feeling for the culture of Europe and the collision of America upon it." Irwin Shaw did this in *The Young Lions,* an ambitious novel that looked at the experience of both the German and American soldiers. Mailer wrote in 1959 that this novel's "considerable merits" were flawed by Shaw's lack of feeling for the continent's past, a comment that reflects Mailer's competitive nature in that period more than the shortcomings of Shaw's novel, which was based on his war experience. Shaw landed at Normandy and a few days later greeted a chagrined Ernest Hemingway as he waded ashore.

After completing his artillery training in early August, he had a ten-day furlough. He divided it between Brooklyn and Norfolk, and then boarded a train at Penn Station with his friend Clifford Maskovsky for the five-day trip to the West Coast and his next assignment at Fort Ord, California. The train took the northern route, via Chicago, which gave him the opportunity to feel insignificant in the great empty spaces of the prairie, the foothills, and finally the mountains. Writing from the King George Hotel in San Francisco, he recalled a conversation with his sister about William James's observation that the fundamental human emotions come from nature:

> I can understand that—in the cities God is a reactionary, an anarchic & perverted symbol. In the west, in the heart of the prairie and the foothills and the sky God seems to be everywhere, he is the hills and the sky and the battle between light and darkness, he is all the thundering vast music ever written, and in the city he is nothing. He is the frenetic beat of tension, anxiety, city jazz. Nerves snapping, all the time.

Mailer is often described as an urban writer. This is glib. From *Naked* and *Why Are We in Vietnam?* to *The Executioner's Song* and *Tough Guys Don't Dance* (not to mention his matchless renderings of the craters and pockmarks of the moonscape in *Of a Fire on the Moon*), his landscape descriptions crackle and pulse with energy and must be ranked among the best of postwar American writers. Diana Trilling observed, "The most dramatic moments in *The Naked and the Dead* are precipitated by intensities in nature," which is to say that Mailer's terrain is often an externalization of the thoughts, moods, and sometimes the unconscious promptings of his characters. Later on, his responses to nature will be filled with heartache at the Faustian destruction of the American wilderness, "that sad deep sweet beauteous mystery land of purple forests, and pink rock, and blue water, Indian haunts from Maine to the shore of Californ, all gutted, shit on, used and blasted." Although he grew up in cities, his sensitivity to nature's resonances must be counted as one of his most commanding skills.

After spending a few days in San Francisco at the end of August, Mailer and Maskovsky took the bus to Fort Ord, some ninety miles south. He told his ever anxious mother that his artillery assignment would keep him well behind the front lines. Knowing Fan's detestation of Hitler, he told her he was reading one of the first major biographies, Konrad Heiden's *The Führer: Hitler's Rise to Power*, which he found to be difficult but exciting (sixty years later, he reread it when researching his novel of young Hitler, *The Castle in the Forest*). Shortly after finishing the book, he began reading Oswald Spengler's *The Decline of the West* and right away wrote to his sister to say it would become one of the most important books of his life. Spengler's "immense thundering insight which takes all of history as its meat and rechops it as no man has ever done" excited him, gave him a sense of historical scope and flux that he had not encountered before. He was astonished by Spengler's ability to seize the relationships among developments in widely separated fields—warfare, astronomy, architecture, medicine, agriculture, the arts, statecraft—and align them to reveal a culture's tendencies, to show its movement in the inevitable cycle of development and decline, as well as to identify parallel cycles in other cultures. Always seeking the distinctive characteristics of a culture that were manifestations of its deep structure, its morphology, Spengler ranged with apparent ease through Egyptian, classical, Chinese, Hindu, Arab, and Western civilizations, commenting on, for example, the arcana of Egyptian breastplates, the nature of the tribunate in Rome, the advent of infinitesimal calculus, and the discovery of the circulation of the blood.

Diana Trilling once observed that Mailer's "mind is peculiarly violable by idea, even by ideology." Spengler's study is perhaps the clearest instance of this susceptibility. In 1944, not yet having read Nietzsche, nor much Marx, he was ravished by Spengler's ideas about the Faustian desire in the West to achieve the Godhead, to strive for the divine, even if it led to death. Spengler saw the past as an organism. Every culture moved through stages of flowering, decadence, ossification, death, and rebirth. Mailer's pronounced preference for the organic over the analytic, for metaphor over measure, has its origin in *The Decline of the West.* An invincible dualist, Spengler based many of his arguments on the superiority of the second term in a set of paired opposites—causality-destiny, space-time, nature-history, thought-will. He distrusted the rational scientist (Darwin was his negative hero), while admiring the forceful, intuitive artist (Goethe was his positive hero). Whatever the roots of Mailer's own dichotomous thinking, Spengler deepened the cleft. Within two weeks of his letter to his sister, he was writing to Bea about a new idea for a novella with "a ridge or peak as symbol" of "the higher aspirations of man, the craving for the secret, the core of life, (or as Spengler might say—the Faustian need) for power and particularly for Godhead and the vanquishing of death."

ON NOVEMBER 7 he cast his first vote, an absentee ballot for FDR. A week later he completed his fire control training and after three weeks at Camp Stoneman, the West Coast embarkation center, shipped out on the USS *Sea Barb.* He sailed under the Golden Gate Bridge on December 6, almost three years to the day after Pearl Harbor. In October, the Japanese had experienced catastrophic naval losses in the Battle of Leyte Gulf and were about to be defeated on Leyte Island. Southern Europe had fallen to the Allies, who had invaded France and were pushing into Germany. The Battle of the Bulge was being fought as Mailer's ship crossed the Pacific, and planning was under way for the invasion of Luzon, the main island of the Philippine archipelago, where the capital of Manila was located. On all fronts, the tide was finally starting to turn, although the Axis Powers were offering ferocious resistance.

He spent most of his time on deck writing letters and watching the water and sky. It was a quiet crossing. He wrote Bea that he was at peace with himself and believed that he would survive the war—a soothing lie he repeated many times—in part because of his artillery assignment. "Without you," he wrote, "I should have been an insolent unhappy youth forever jousting with the dark shadows of my vanity." As he sunned himself during the long transparent days, he went over the "ridge novella" in his mind and began to populate it with soldiers he had known, although except for Sergeant Mann, none of them would be used in *Naked and the Dead.* Instead, he would draw on the men from a unit as yet unknown to him: the 112th Cavalry Regiment, a National Guard unit out of Fort Bliss, Texas.

Created in 1921 mainly with men from North Texas, the 112th was federalized in November 1940 and served over five years on active duty, with 434 days of combat. After a hot, gloomy Christmas anchored in Hollandia Bay, New Guinea, on the *Sea Barb*, Mailer joined the unit on Leyte on December 29, 1944. It had received many replacements, but as he remembered much later, "the aristocracy of the outfit were these old Texas boys, most of them privates who had been busted down a number of times." He continued:

> They'd been overseas for three years at this point; they'd been allowed to keep their own sidearms. They had handkerchiefs tied around their heads, and they all had jungle rot, these open ulcers on the skin the size of fingernails that they had been painting with iodine. They just stared at us and sharpened their knives. It was like *Deliverance*. I didn't open my mouth for six months in that outfit. They were all crazy.

All the Texans could ride, as the unit had originally been a horse cavalry unit with a reconnaissance mission and roots going back to engagements against Pancho Villa. For its first overseas assignment on the French island of New Caledonia, the troopers still had their horses, making it one of the last U.S. Army units to be deployed as a mounted force. A Texas historian described them as "a Texas regiment defending a French island from a Japanese aggressor while mounted on Australian horses." The horses were impractical for jungle fighting, however, and the 112th became an infantry unit after it left New Caledonia, but the reconnaissance mission continued. When Mailer and twenty other replacements arrived, they learned that the 112th Cavalry was now part of the 112th Regimental Combat Team (RCT), along with the 148th Field Artillery. Because of his advanced training, he expected to be assigned to the 148th. But several weeks earlier, the 148th had received a group of infantrymen, trained them as artillerymen, and wasn't about to give them up. As he put it, "So, the infantry replacements had been retrained as artillerymen, and we artillerymen found ourselves in the infantry. Typical Army SNAFU." Disappointed at the time, he soon recognized how fortunate his happenstance infantry assignment had been.

The invasion of Luzon began on January 9, 1945. The 112th arrived at Lingayen Gulf, Luzon, on the USS *Monrovia* (APA 31) and went ashore on January 27. The Sixth Army, under General Walter Krueger, was already on its way south to Manila, and the job of the 112th was to cover the left flank of the advance, which had bypassed many Japanese units, and guard supply lines from the beachhead. The 112th Mailer said, was a "trip-wire," assigned to slow down any Japanese forces that attempted to attack the Sixth Army from the rear. The 1,200 men of the 112th were stretched out to the east of a north–south highway eighty miles long, as well as in observation posts in the hills beyond. Other units were involved in fighting on the outskirts of Manila with the 1st Cavalry Division, which entered Manila in early February. The Luzon campaign was huge. The Americans and the Japanese committed more troops than in any previous campaign. Each army had over a quarter million troops stationed on Luzon. But the Japanese were ill equipped and by the end, sick and starving. After Manila fell in early March, the fighting diminished throughout the spring and by July was all but over.

In his first letter to Bea after arriving on Luzon, Mailer told her not to fret about his safety as he would always be between two and twenty miles behind the front lines, a disingenuous assurance in that there was no discernible front line for the 112th. But regimental headquarters company, where he had a typing assignment in the Intelligence and Operations section of Headquarters Troop (the Harvard pedigree), was of necessity removed from immediate danger, although the men assigned there kept their rifles next to their typewriters. His assignment was to type daily intelligence reports. For the moment, he was happy with the work because he had an inside view of how the campaign was unfolding. He was also for the first time working closely with officers. At one point, he was present when the commanding general of the RCT, Julian W. Cunningham, was discussing operations with a colonel.

A self-taught typist, Mailer made many errors. He took pains to improve but to no avail, and he was reassigned to read manuals on interpreting aerial photographs with the possibility of getting a permanent assignment, but nothing came of it. He told Bea that it was "galling at times to be so utterly insignificant," but the experience deepened his novelistic commitment. Then he was given the lowly job of building a shower for officers. He was, apparently, of little value where he was and toward the end of March was transferred to a communications platoon unrolling and repairing wire between outlying units and HQ.

The advantage of the assignment was getting to observe small units of the 112th in villages, rice paddies, and on hilltops. There were large tracts of uncontested territory—no-man's-land—and he rode far afield in a jeep laying wire and repairing breaks. As junior man in the platoon, Mailer had to squat on the fender with his carbine ready. The downside of the assignment was that occasionally the enemy would cut the wire and ambush the repair team. "Variety, darling," he wrote to Bea, "is the only spice in army life, so I cannot gripe. And look at the training I'm getting for being a general. I'll *know* my army." He took copious notes and sent them to Bea four or five times a week. Perhaps a third of his letters are love letters, filled with erotic fantasies and plans, but the rest are experiential logs. His unflagging belief in his future greatness as a writer compensated in his mind for his serious lacks as a soldier.

While he was still in HQ Troop, the 112th engaged the Japanese in a small town on the highway to Manila. He went with some staff officers to see the aftermath. "It had a little bit of the spirit of an outing," he wrote to Bea, "almost to the packing of sandwiches." After a half hour ride, they neared the front and he noticed an odor that was "a good deal like faeces leavened with ripe garbage." When he saw the dead Japanese, he was immediately reminded of "the ape-like charred bodies" in the Boston morgue after the gruesome Cocoanut Grove fire. The description he gave to Bea, which follows, was later used in Chapter 7 of Part Two of *Naked and the Dead*, an account of the search for enemy souvenirs on a battlefield by soldiers in a reconnaissance platoon. These were the first war dead that Mailer encountered.

> Another Japanese lay on his back a short distance away with a great hole in his intestines which bunched out in a thick white cluster like a coiled white garden hose. They were surrounded by the very red flesh of his belly, and it seemed curiously like the jettison of some excrement by a red flower. He had an anonymous pleasant face with small snubbed features, and he seemed quite rested in death. His legs had swollen and his buttocks so that they filled his pants tightly as if they were full stockings. Somehow he looked like a little ballet dancer with those curiously full perfect legs, but more like a doll whose stuffing had broken forth.

The army on Luzon could not always come up with hot chow, but books seem to have been available, even new titles. In his early months, he read widely: Spengler in short bursts, each of which occasioned some reflection in a letter; Walter Benton's anthology of love poems *This Is My Beloved*, which Bea also read; Robert Graves's *I, Claudius*; and Lytton Strachey's *Eminent Victorians*. He savored Strachey's portrait of Cardinal Manning for its dissection of papal diplomacy and intrigue. The Catholic Church would continue to fascinate Mailer but, excepting Spengler, it was the work of Somerset Maugham that elicited the most commentary in his letters.

He found Maugham's 1941 novella *Up at the Villa* to be "an unguent for the psyche." Set in Florence in the late 1930s, it is the story of Mary Panton, a young British widow juggling the attentions of three men. She has a one-night stand with one of them, a young Austrian fiddle player, who kills himself with her pistol when she rejects him. Complications ensue. One of the other suitors, a rich "waster" named Rowley Flint, is described as someone who is not "any better than he should be," a remark that caused Mailer to reflect on the "perpetual oscillation" in himself between the kind of live-and-let-live attitude that would wink at Flint's conduct and a countervailing view that saw

> man only as tragic and of large dimensions and universality; when all of his acts of love, so magnificent at the instant, do have permanence and dignity, an individuality as perfect as he believes. But curiously, somewhere in all the twisted crannies of my nature, the two have become mixed, for my good spirits come always from the cyni-

> cal view, the abstention of judgment, and my depressions are deepest when I take the tragic view.

Maugham's tolerant cynicism made Mailer question his belief that everything was the product of inner drives and outer forces. Perhaps some people were demonstrably better and some obviously worse than they ought to be. Perhaps he could stretch himself. He later referred to Maugham's line about Rowley in *The Deer Park,* where Sergius O'Shaugnessy derides it as equivalent to a view of the universe as "an elaborate clock." Mailer's Spinozan determinism, buttressed by Spengler's sense of historic destiny, would persist, however, through the writing of *The Naked and the Dead.*

Barney was working in Washington, D.C., at the Office of Price Administration and Mailer wrote to him occasionally. But he wrote his mother and sister about once a week, knowing that Fan would start calling her congressman if she didn't hear from him regularly. In one letter from Luzon, he told her that "there's a wonderful quality in you like that of an unspoiled young girl who's always looking eagerly and zestfully for what's going to happen next." Barbara has the same quality, he added, but it is "a more timid rather breathless facsimile." When he had returned safely after the war and was sorting through his correspondence while writing *Naked*, he wrote a note on the letter: "At the time, I was in Luzon and probably believed my bullet was being made in some Japanese factory so thought I'd give the old girl something to keep." Men in the 112th were being killed. The unit had 192 casualties during the Luzon campaign, including forty-one killed. In early February, he was awarded the Combat Infantryman's Badge and began receiving combat pay.

In early April, he wrote Bea that he'd "been in a little combat, nothing very tremendous, but still one of the three or four 'first experiences' a man has." While searching for a wire break in no-man's-land, his unit of twenty soldiers ran into a Japanese patrol. Mailer stood guard with a few others at a creek crossing while the bulk of the patrol went ahead. Shots were fired in their direction and a tommy gun returned fire. Then the largest part of the American patrol returned and reported that ten Japanese had been killed. The American lieutenant in command brought back a shiny, bloody Samurai sword. Mailer reported that when the firing started what he felt was "not exactly fear—it was more, well, 'awareness.' But an awareness so acute that it approached pain and fear." He became adept at carefully unpacking and recording his emotions in every circumstance while in the Philippines, and was able to harvest the nuances when he did the same for a dozen soldiers in *Naked*.

During his time on Luzon, Barbara's romance with his college buddy Jack Maher was percolating. Jack had joined the army but kept writing to her at Radcliffe. Mailer wrote to his mother more than once about their romance, which Fan still ferociously opposed. In late April Mailer wrote to Bea, who was now asked to intercede with Barney, who heretofore had sided with Fan on the unhappiness that would ensue if the romance continued. "You must make him realize," he told Bea, "that he'll have no intimacy with his daughter" if he tries to block her life decisions. Fan's opposition to Barbara marrying a goy was granitic; she believed she was saving her love-struck daughter's life by her interference. The romance continued long-distance, and shortly after Mailer returned from the war Fan overheard Barbara talking to him about Maher. With great bravura, Fan fell to the floor with a heart attack and would not get up to get help until Barbara agreed to break it off. Barbara caved in and except for a few meetings did not see Maher again for over fifty years. She remained angry with her mother—whose attack almost certainly was feigned—and their relations were strained for years. Fan's victory, which marked the high-water mark of her control over the family, was Pyrrhic. Mailer told Barbara that she acted nobly.

UPPERMOST IN HIS mind during this period, however, now that he had seen some combat, were plans for the "ridge novella." Ideas for revising *A Transit to Narcissus* still came up in his letters, but as the spring wore on, the new project moved to the fore. He had heard about the mythic eight-day patrol undertaken by a 112th platoon across the upper Angat River in Leyte and his imagination, exercised by the veterans' tales, began to see the novella structured around a long patrol. He thought about beginning it with soldiers on a boat watching a sunset, followed by a "birth allegory," with the patrol moving through thick jungle brush to "emerge into sentience and then fear" as they glimpse the mountain, "ineffable ridge beyond ridge." On April 24, a week after writing Bea of his plans for the novella, Mailer asked for a transfer to the Reconnaissance Platoon of HQ Troop.

The next day, he explained to Bea that he had felt humiliated in his previous assignments. His transfer decision might be seen as "quixotic," he said, but it was the only way to maintain his dignity. "You're doing something when you go out on a patrol that you don't do when you lay a mile of wire." To allay her fears he said that Recon was no more dangerous than the wire job because the platoon's job, some of it in enemy territory, was to gather information, not to fight. General Cunningham used Recon as his intelligence arm. Yes, he told Bea, the unit had lost men in previous campaigns, but on Luzon, it had so far experienced no casualties. He had already been on two patrols and the landscape, the heat, and the sweat added up to a good feeling, he said. Over the next three months, he would make at least twenty-five patrols, mainly in the area around the town of Antipolo, twenty miles south of Manila.

He had read John Hersey's *Into the Valley* and Harry Brown's *A Walk in the Sun* before he arrived in the Philippines, and the idea for writing about a patrol originated with these books. But it was his time in Recon that solidified it. The patrols gave him time to think and plan. "A part of me was working on this long patrol. I even ended up in a reconnaissance outfit which I had asked to get into. A reconnaissance outfit, after all, tends to take long patrols. Art kept traducing life." It was clear that the Japanese were going to be defeated and "none of us had the slightest desire to be killed in an action which could not even give a good marble of fact to the ponderous idiots who directed our fate." Most platoon leaders, therefore, would not push into potentially dangerous areas unnecessarily. His sergeant asked his men if they saw any activity through field glasses and if the answer was no, he'd say, "Good, I don't see none either. Let's go back." The platoon would report no enemy activity in the area and a red pin would go into the map. Mailer had already read *War and Peace* and remembered Tolstoy's observation that every army moves on waves of ignorance and misinformation. Recon's troopers often walked miles with their heads down. They would traverse rice paddies, walk through streambeds, climb over hills, and return at night "fifteen miles older in the feet, wet twice with rain and sweat." It was grueling, but the novelistic gleanings were rich.

Sometimes patrols were accompanied by communist partisans, the Hukbalahap or Huks, who had fought the Japanese from the start.

One day they found a dead Huk with a Japanese light machine gun in his arms. His Filipino comrades carried him away to their village and the Recon platoon went along. Mailer volunteered to carry the twenty-pound gun and, as he wrote Bea, immediately regretted it. He consulted his letter for the following, taken from a 1952 short story, "The Dead Gook."

> The gun had a detestable odor. There was the smell of Japanese fish oil, and the smell of Luiz who had acquired the gun, the smell of a Filipino peasant which to Brody meant carabao flop and Philippine dust and Filipino food, an amalgam not unlike stale soya sauce. Worst of all, there was the odor of Luiz' blood, a particularly sweet and intimate smell, fetid and suggesting to his nostrils that it was not completely dry. It was the smell of a man who had died, and it mingled with the fish oil and the soya sauce and the considerable stench of Brody's own body and Brody's own work-sweated clothes, until he thought he would gag.

His most memorable patrol took place in mid-May. Colonel Philip Hooper, the CO of the 112th Cavalry and one of the few officers he admired, gave Recon an important assignment. According to an intelligence report, a unit of "crack Japanese marines," perhaps as many as seventy, had infiltrated American lines. Recon, with its thirty men, was to find and destroy them. Most of the platoon carried a rifle, two bandoliers of ammunition, a cartridge belt of ammunition, two grenades, two canteens, C rations, and a helmet, about forty pounds. At 130 pounds, Mailer was in good shape at the time, although he was recovering from jaundice. Other men carried the machine gun, ammunition boxes containing 250 rounds, and the radio.

The platoon was dropped off by jeeps and began walking. Soon they had to climb a five-hundred-foot hill. The footing was miserable; they ascended a steep, slimy staircase of waist-high rocks covered with vegetation and surrounded by bamboo thickets with vicious thorns. Quickly, everyone was exhausted. "The most intense ecstasy I could imagine," he said, "would have been to *stop* climbing." The radio operator was gasping and nauseated. The machine gun crew fell behind. The remaining men, led by Lieutenant Horton, pushed on. Mailer discovered that "you can never plumb the last agony of exertion, there seems always a worse one beneath it." Pride kept him from quitting. The men at the front of the column had the worst of it because they anticipated an ambush at every turn of the trail. After an hour of climbing, at the edge of total collapse, they were attacked. Someone in the front of the column kicked over a nest of hornets and the enraged insects buzzed and stung the entire line. The thrashing, frenzied platoon was cut in half. Mailer and the men in the lead made it to the top; the rest, including those with the machine gun, stumbled down to the valley.

He ended his description of the ordeal to Bea by saying that the hornet patrol was "the kind of experience I never want to become a connoisseur of." But, in fact, it is precisely what he became: a discriminating observer of war's pains, pangs, fears, and throes. As one commentator on *Naked and the Dead* observed, "No other writer on war has so devastatingly caught the depths of physical tiredness." The climactic chapter in which Sergeant Croft attempts to drive his platoon over Mount Anaka becomes an odyssey of fear, exhaustion, and death. Croft kicks the football-sized hornet's nest, derailing Recon's mission to determine if the Japanese could be attacked from the rear. Driven off the mountain, Croft's platoon, like Horton's, collapsed on the muddy ground, twitching. As they rested, it began raining, which brought some relief. Horton radioed back to HQ saying the platoon had hit a hornet's nest and was returning. The duty officer who got the message said, "What the hell did Horton mean by all of that? Is he speaking of a literal or a metaphorical hornet's nest?" Like other great naturalistic writers—Zola, Crane, Steinbeck—Mailer in *Naked and the Dead* presents a natural world that is uncaring, unyielding, implacable, and, occasionally, beautiful.

His erotic letters could be as long and elaborate as his descriptions of patrols. They often had dramatic elements—costumes, props, scene changes—and resemble Jacobean masques as much as pornography. In one letter he describes a small room, heavily curtained and lit by candles. He is dressed only in a robe and Bea has a "black halo, black stockings and shoes and flimsy-like short black panties with no seat, and of course some wisp across your paps." They drink wine and he places an olive in her navel and then lettuce leaves on her breasts, which he nibbles. They eat off the same plate, taking bites between embraces.

> We go back to finish the raspberry ice, and you straddle me in the chair and my hot hard pride slips into your lubricious embrace. We fuck very gently, and finish the ice, and light cigarettes, and drink more wine, until we glow and become tumescent so that I must lay you out on the divan, and fuck the shit out of you. Do you like my French mind, darling? Do you love the thought of alternating food nibbles and love nibbles? Am I heating your snatch from 10,000 miles?

Bea's letters, while ardent, were more restrained. They were long, supportive, and full of plans for the future. Her duty was considerably easier than his and her belief in his potential as a writer was rock steady. She told him about her friends, family news, and sent him portions of the novel that she was writing about life in the WAVES. Mailer sent back supportive critiques, but her novel was turned down after the war and she didn't have the desire to continue. "I gave up writing," she said in 1948. "I found out how hard it was."

When Bea wrote to him about being heartsick and confused by photographs of war atrocities, asking what it all meant, he gave her two possibilities. Perhaps God was the supreme artist, he said, detached but curious about how the situations and oppositions put in motion would play out. This deity would resemble "a very intense Somerset Maugham," but one utterly without compassion. Another possibility was that everything was chaos, meaningless, and men killed each other in the same savage way that ants did. Years later, he said to an interviewer, "Remember that awful priest who said, 'There are no atheists in foxholes'? It was a remark to turn people into atheists for 25 years. I remember every time I got into a foxhole I said to myself, 'This is one man who's an atheist in a foxhole!'"

By late June, the 112th began to relax a bit. The invasion of Japan was at the back of everyone's mind, but it was many months away. Patrols continued, with only occasional contact with the dispirited enemy. Mailer was able to focus more on the novel, especially after he learned that Seaver was turning down an excerpt from *A Transit to Narcissus* for the 1945 *Cross-Section.* He knew the men in Recon well by now and had begun the culling process, choosing his models. He told Bea that this novel would differ from his earlier ones in two respects: he wanted it to grow out of the interaction of his characters with the natural environment, and he intended to pick his characters before he had the plot.

In June, Mailer met Francis Irby Gwaltney, or "Fig," a tall, red-haired soldier from Arkansas, who transferred into the 112th. He had not been to college but had literary interests and the night they met the two sat up all night in a foxhole talking about the novels of Thomas Wolfe. He admired Fig's nasal drawl and his irreverence. They soon became buddies and their friendship deepened when a soldier said something negative about Jews. Fig shouted, "You can't talk that way—I'm Jewish!" The soldier said Gwaltney was no Jew and Fig yelled back, "I am a fuckin' Jew." Fig, Mailer later said, was about as Jewish as George W. Bush. Assigned to Recon, Fig made patrols with Mailer, whom he later described as "a brave soldier, but not a good one. He couldn't see worth a damn. Nearsighted." Mailer told Fig about his plans for the novel. He would use him as the model for Wilson, one of the key characters of *Naked*. Fig was the only member of the 112th Mailer stayed in regular contact with after the war.

In addition to Fig, Sergeant Mann, and General Cunningham, Mailer selected four other soldiers as models: Red Matthiesen, Ysidro Martinez, Isadore Feldman, and Roy Gallagher, soldiers whose ancestry was, respectively, Swedish, Mexican, Jewish, and Irish. He sent Bea a few comments on Feldman, a Brooklyn welder who was the model for Joey Goldstein, but never mentioned Gallagher, the sullen Bostonian whose name he retained. Martinez (Julio in the novel) and Red (Valsen in the novel) were described at length because they were the principals in incidents that would be plot turns in the novel. Martinez was one of a half dozen sergeants in Recon, and led Mailer's squad. The contradictions in his character attracted Mailer. He was "soft-spoken, sly, deceitful, like an animal in the brush, and demonstrated more courage than any man I've ever known." Terribly fearful and certain he was going to be killed, Martinez nevertheless volunteered repeatedly to lead patrols. He had huge qualms about killing, yet slit the throat of a Japanese soldier in the dead of night, as does his namesake in *Naked*.

He had even more to say about Red, and borrowed more of his actual words than from any other soldier. An itinerant worker who rode the rails around the country from 1931 to 1937, Red was often only a few dollars away from hunger. He was in his late thirties when Mailer met him. Uneducated but intelligent, he impressed Mailer with his theology: "If there is a God, He sure must be a son of a bitch." They became friends, and the reticent Red eventually told him his life story. He had no allegiances to any individual but huge sympathy for every underdog, including blacks. Fearless and ready to fight anyone who gave him any trouble, he recognized that his kidneys were going and he would soon have to compromise. In *Naked,* a weakened Red is forced to back down, crawfish, by the platoon sergeant, who is based—physically, not psychologically—on Sergeant Mann. His name is Sam Croft.

In selecting a soldier as a character mold, Mailer looked for traits that would enable him to put that individual in dramatic situations with others. Obviously, he combined some characters and sculpted the personalities of others. But he began with real soldiers. Thus, the framework of the novel grew by accretion as he sorted through the hundreds of GIs he had known. Later, he constructed charts showing which soldiers had scenes with others to ensure that all characters had been used sufficiently and appropriately. "I studied engineering at Harvard, and I suppose it was the book of a young engineer," he said. The last two major characters (who would not be delineated or given major roles until much later), were the commanding general, eventually called Edward Cummings, and a young second lieutenant, perhaps based in part on Horton, but definitely owing something to Lieutenant Hilliard in *A Calculus at Heaven.* At first he was just called "the second looey" and then later, Robert Hearn. He is the novel's titular hero and he is murdered by Croft, the novel's secret hero.

BY MID-JULY, FIGHTING on Luzon was effectively over and Mailer was in garrison learning for the umpteenth time the manual of arms, reading Spengler, and discussing books with Fig. He was excited about the new GI Bill and the 52-20 Club, which would provide veterans with $20 a week for fifty-two weeks or until they got a job. He calculated that the two programs would give him and Bea a combined income of about $300 a month, plus tuition money. In addition, they had already saved $2,000. She was able to increase her savings rate because she was living with Fan, having transferred to New York. Barney was still in Washington and Barbara in Cambridge. Mailer and Bea discussed living in Boston and taking graduate courses at Harvard. Influenced by Spengler, he was interested in studying comparative religion and history.

There was but one obstacle, but it was stupendous, and studiously avoided in Mailer's letters: the pending invasion of Japan, which was to be the largest amphibious assault in history. Operation Olympic would land fourteen divisions on the southern Japanese island of Kyushu on November 1, 1945. Four months later, using Kyushu as a base, Operation Coronet would land twenty-five divisions on the southern shore of the main Japanese island of Honshu and push north a hundred miles to Tokyo. His outfit, Mailer learned later, was scheduled to land at Tateyama Naval Airdrome on Honshu, which was surrounded by gun emplacements embedded in cliffs surrounding the base on three sides. "We would have been massacred," he said.

The invasion plans became moot when atomic bombs were dropped on Hiroshima and Nagasaki three days apart in early August. The Japanese surrendered on August 15. On August 8 Mailer wrote to Bea that he approved of anything that got Americans home sooner, but he found the prospects for the future horrifying. He went on to condemn the sentimental adulation for machines that he had observed, especially among men in the air corps and the navy, saying that he felt "pathological" about machines. He ends the letter on a Spenglerian note: "*We have come to the age when we love machines and hate women.*" Mailer's suspicion of all things mechanical and electronic, which would become one of the hallmarks of his worldview, was irreversible by August 1945. Twelve years later, he would begin his most famous essay, "The White Negro," by pointing to the ongoing, immeasurable "psychic havoc" created by the combination of the atomic bomb and the concentration camps. He was perhaps the first writer to link these horrors in an integral way with the suffering and discrimination felt by African Americans, the aftermath of slavery.

The invasion force was transformed into an occupation force. He was eager to see Japan and curious about the people, having only seen "starved, grinning, irritatingly polite and friendly prisoners." But his comments on Japan, indeed his comments on all topics (save his novel), were outweighed for some time by speculation about and plans for his homecoming. Using the military's point system, he calculated that he would have sufficient credits to be discharged in about a year. He wrote Bea that he could now think of the months ahead as "milestones instead of a chasm." The knowledge that he was going to survive and that there would be no more campaigns made him think of all the dead, and of the "many summers that had gone by while they had hopes to go home. I could have wept for them."

At the end of August, the 112th sailed on the USS *Lavaca* (APA 180) for Japan. His ship was with the assembled fleet when the Japanese signed the surrender documents aboard the USS *Missouri* (BB 63) on September 2. There was a radio hook-up that allowed everyone to hear the ceremony. The 112th was given a place of honor, the fifty-yard line, as one trooper put it. All eyes were trained on the *Missouri*'s main deck. Mailer wrote to his parents, "The commentator said, 'The sun has come out and is shining on Tokyo Bay as the surrender is signed and peace is with us.' " This, he said, "was one of the largest, bare-assed lies I'd ever heard." The day was cloudy, with rain threatening. That afternoon the 112th landed at Tateyama, across the bay from Yokohama.

His unit was now a constabulary force charged with demobilizing Japanese combat units. Tateyama was on the lip of a mountainous peninsula honeycombed with caves and bunkers connected underground by roads wide enough to accommodate jeeps. For a month, the soldiers detonated munitions and destroyed weapons. As they did their work, they saw the big guns that rolled on rails through tunnels cut to the back side of the mountain. The Japanese planned to elevate the guns and fire over the mountains into the harbor, while remaining unseen and impervious. The troopers shook their heads when they realized how deadly Operation Coronet would have been.

Boredom set in and Mailer volunteered to be a cook. Now that the fighting was over, he was unemployed as a rifleman, so to speak, and had little to do but stand inspections. He hated the arrogance of army cooks, but liked the idea of learning to cook. The real incentive, however, was getting every other day off. He captured the raspy relationship between cooks and soldiers in "Chorus: The Chow Line," one of the comic interludes in *Naked and the Dead*:

> *The troops file by in an irregular line. . . . As they go by they sniff at the main course which has been dumped into a big square pan. It is canned Meat and Vegetable Stew heated slightly. The second cook, a fat red-faced man with a bald spot and a perpetual scowl, slaps a large spoonful in each of their mess plates.*
>
> *Red:* What the fug is that swill?
>
> *Cook:* It's owl shit. Wha'd you think it was?

Red: Okay, I just thought it was somethin' I couldn't eat. . . .

Wilson: Ah swear, don't you ration destroyers know another way to fug up this stew?

Cook: "When it's smokin', it's cookin'; when it's burnin', it's done." That's our motto.

Wilson: (chuckling) Ah figgered you all had a system.

Mailer was still a private first class (having been promoted a few months earlier), and the chances for further promotion in Recon Platoon were slim. As much as he disliked the army, the idea of a sergeant's stripes on his sleeve—which would come if he became a first cook—was attractive. The mess sergeant liked him, he told Bea, and that augured well.

Despite his exasperation at the delay in getting home, his time in Tateyama, and later in Choshi, one hundred miles north of Tateyama on the Pacific coast, was his happiest time in the military. He quickly mastered the army cooking routine and took pride in his work. Off duty, he explored the cliffs overlooking the ocean and made many notes for what he now referred to as "the jungle novel." And he read widely. For the last half of 1945, a partial list includes Eric Ambler's spy novels, Maugham's *The Razor's Edge*, and Arthur Koestler's collection of essays, *The Yogi and the Commissar*. He praised Lillian Smith's novel about the lynching of blacks, *Strange Fruit*, but said it would have been better if it also explored the poor whites who committed the lynching. Her novel ends, he says, with the old question, "Why evil, why, why, why?" His answer: "Evil is not hard to understand. It is difficult only when the explanation tries to establish that it is not fundamental to the nature of man." Charles Jackson's novel of alcoholic abandon, *The Lost Weekend*, terrified him "because I have so much in common with the hero." He found French novelist Georges Simenon's *Home Town* to be magnificent. Over the years, Mailer read and reread hundreds of books by the prolific Simenon, praised his ability to construct tight, believable plots and gave copies of the Inspector Maigret novels to friends. But after Spengler, he had the most to say about Tolstoy and Dostoyevsky.

He tackled *The Brothers Karamazov* first, reading it at the same time as Bea. He wasn't at all impressed, he said, with the saintliness of Dostoyevsky's Alyosha or by any of Tolstoy's peasants in *War and Peace*. The men he had liked in the army because of their goodness struck him even more because of their lack of force. "Their goodness had no radiation," he said. For the "jungle novel," he planned to present each character in the manner of Tolstoy, that is, in "the self-beloved circle of his own mind." He rhapsodized about *Anna Karenina*, finding it to be much greater than *War and Peace*. Throughout his life, he remarked on Tolstoy's deep knowledge of humanity, his severe and unsentimental compassion, which he said later "reminds us that life is like a gladiator's arena for the soul and so we feel strengthened by those who endure, and feel awe and pity for those who do not."

Tolstoy's Kitty reminded him of Bea, and he pictured Anna with Bea's face and body. He recalled their meals at Petitpas, a table d'hôte restaurant on West 29th Street where they engaged in "the language of knee against knee." While he aimed for Tolstoyan scope and severity in his writing, his letters to Bea, now that their reunion was certain and near, often gushed with tenderness: "I adore thee sweets. Ever. I miss you as hard and clearly now as I did ten months ago. I shall never learn to live without you." He would, of course, but he could hardly have foreseen it at the time.

Cooking for 160 men in Tateyama was hard physical work. He liked it, felt useful. He put on some weight and hiked on off-days. He was now one of the senior men in the 112th, as most of the Texans had rotated home. The unit itself was due to return to Texas in January 1946 and be deactivated. Mailer was suspicious that he might be kept overseas because the military wanted to maintain troops in the Far East to counter Russian expansionism. In the meantime, cooking increased his self-confidence. "I feel very strong," he told Bea. "I feel perfectly capable of telling a guy to blow it out his asshole if I don't like what he says." At the end of December 1945, he was transferred to the 649th Ordnance Ammunition Company in Choshi, and when the first cook was sent home, he was made acting first cook. A month later he was promoted to sergeant, Tech-4. Although he told his parents that he felt like "a peon in a fascist organization," he had his photo taken in his dress uniform, with his three stripes and combat infantryman's badge, and sent it home to the family.

Around the time he was transferred, one of the key characters of the jungle novel, Sergeant Croft, began to emerge. Mailer called him the "vision sergeant," because of his deep yet inchoate desire to conquer the mountain that loomed over the jungle, and thus attain some deeper vision of the Godhead. Like Moby Dick, the mountain is real and symbolic, and he explicitly compares Croft to Ahab in the same letter in which he describes his sergeant as "an archetype of all the dark, bitter, inarticulate, capable and brooding men that America spawns." He had already told Bea the story he had heard about a sergeant and a private in the 112th who captured a starving Japanese soldier. They gave him water, a K ration, and a cigarette, and when he closed his eyes, a bullet in the temple. "He died happy," the sergeant said. He now decided that his vision sergeant would be the one to pull the trigger and Red (based on Matthieson) would be the private. Life was again traducing art; the incident would become one of the episodes that define Croft in *Naked and the Dead.* Except for a tense change, the description of Croft in "The Time Machine" chapter comes verbatim from Mailer's letter:

> He was efficient and strong and usually empty and his main cast of mind was a superior contempt toward nearly all men. He hated weakness and he loved practically nothing. There was a crude unformed vision in his soul but he was rarely conscious of it.

Mailer's buddies had discovered geisha houses and learned the distinction between a geisha—a woman who entertained, poured sake, and in some instances had sex with visitors—and a *joro*, or common whore, who lacked the social graces. Before he was transferred to Choshi, he was taken by his friend Nat Ellis to a geisha house, where he made what he called "the time-honored American purchase—a piece of ass." It was the first time he had had sex since he last saw Bea in the United States a year earlier. He went to geisha houses three more times, including once during one of his two visits to Tokyo the following March. He remembered his troubled feelings six decades later:

> I had very mixed feelings about fidelity. I thought we should be faithful; I wanted her [Bea] to be faithful to me, I'd go crazy at the thought she might be having an affair. As it turned out later, I think she did have a few unhappy, little affairs—unhappy in the sense that they were to her in her mind not quite right—I was having the same with the geisha girls. Just one or two, and it wasn't right and I didn't feel very virile because I was violating my own standards of, oaths of fidelity. And what I discovered is that an oath has a great influence upon a hard-on. You know, don't give an oath and think your

hard-on can ignore it. It can't. That I learned early and never really learned it.

Unfaithful in all of his marriages, Mailer was a serial philanderer. His affairs caused him and his family much misery over the next fifty years. But that night in Tateyama, when he returned to the barracks, he felt guilty and empty, as he told Bea when he confessed the next day.

FROM SEPTEMBER OF 1945 to February of 1946, his discharge date changed almost weekly. He followed the changing promises of the War Department and watched the news as servicemen all over the world complained and demonstrated for early release. Mailer encouraged his mother and mother-in-law, two formidable Jewish matrons, to lobby on his behalf, and they did. By the beginning of March, he was all but certain that he would be home sometime in April.

Planning the logistics for writing the novel was already under way. He wrote to Fan and gave her instructions on the kind of portable typewriter he wanted, and asked Bea to separate out all his letters dealing with the novel. Given the centrality of the mountain to his novel, he said it would be important to do some mountain climbing, perhaps in North Conway, where they had skied. Provincetown in the summer would be the perfect place to write, and Bea (who would be discharged shortly) began to look for a suitable place. All the while, plans for the novel spilled out in profusion. He sketched an outline of the events leading to the war and Roosevelt's brilliance in mobilizing the country. With the passing of the president—"a great humanist"—Mailer feared there would be "a fascist backwash" in America after the war, given America's victories and enormous power. He wanted this perspective to be the novel's geopolitical backdrop.

He wrote out the names of 161 soldiers he had known since he had been in the army. He had already selected eight of his principal characters, but needed more and wanted the largest possible pool from which to draw. He wanted his Recon platoon to have thirty to forty soldiers in it, but worried about the number he could include without confusion, and began counting the number of significant characters in novels at hand. When he found that there were only sixteen in a novel he admired, Liam O'Flaherty's *The Informer*, he concluded that he would limit his roster to fifteen. He ended up with a total of fourteen enlisted men as significant characters in *Naked*'s Recon platoon. Only three officers—General Cummings, Lieutenant Hearn, and Major Dalleson—have important roles.

Looking back over his reading of the past year, he selected four books as models. He said he wanted to reread them before he started writing what he thought would be a novel of 90,000 to 100,000 words, a huge underestimation—*Naked and the Dead* is over 300,000 words. First on his list was *The Informer*, a tightly written story of betrayal and animalistic fear in the aftermath of the Irish Civil War. He prized it for its deft one- or two-paragraph character portraits. Simenon's *Home Town* was next, admired for its "insights into the weakly Evil, the men who are small of soul & afraid rather than malign." Albert Maltz's 1944 novel, *The Cross and the Arrow*, set in wartime Germany, is the story of a factory worker who perseveres as the Nazi regime begins to devour its own. He wanted to study Maltz's presentation of stubborn nobility. Finally, he planned to read *Anna Karenina* again in order "to steep myself in a good humanistic mood."

Mailer was sent to Onahama, another hundred miles up the Pacific coast, in late January on temporary assignment as mess sergeant for twenty-five men. At the end of February, he returned to Choshi, where he reported to the top mess sergeant. He had excellent relations with his Japanese KPs in all of his cooking assignments. "I don't know if it's Harvard or Aunt Anne's instruction in table manners," he told Bea, "but I cannot treat a person as a servant." The KPs worked twelve-hour days, seven days a week but they considered themselves fortunate because they ate well. He was a kindly boss. The spokesman of one KP group said to him: "Sair, there are much joyness in the hearts of the kitchen boys since you have come to be cook here." Mailer enjoyed joking with them in Japanese, which he had learned a bit of. He also enjoyed writing "Sgt." before his name on the return address of his letters. He kept thinking how nice his stripes would look when he returned to Brooklyn.

On the night of April 3, he was awakened by the top mess sergeant. The KPs had left the kitchen in a mess, and he ordered Mailer to clean it up. Mailer wrote to Bea that he called him a "chickenshit son-of-a-bitch" and the sergeant stomped out. Mailer was summoned to the captain's office. Drunk and angry, the captain ordered Mailer to apologize to the mess sergeant and threatened to court-martial him when he argued back. Mailer apologized and, throbbing with self-loathing, walked out. "I hated him [the captain] enough to kill him then," he said. After a sleepless night, he decided he'd turn in his stripes, which made him feel better. But the next day when he told the captain he was turning in his stripes, the captain replied with some heat, "You're not turning them in, I'm taking them." Later, the mess sergeant told him the captain had no intention of demoting him until Mailer opened his mouth. He told Bea that his only solace was to feel the joy of complete renunciation. "Sweet Sarge is Poor Private again," he said. He told Bea that he had gotten too proud of his sergeant's stripes. He left the army the way he came in, as a buck private.

The moment when the captain took away his sergeantcy, he said later, "was when the keel was laid for *The Naked and the Dead.*" He transformed the crawfishing incident into the pivotal confrontation between General Cummings and Lieutenant Hearn, which leads indirectly to Hearn's death. But this came much later, in the final draft of *Naked.* His immediate response to the event was to write Bea a letter outlining an episode in which Red Valsen commits an offense similar to his own and is court-martialed. Valsen's hatred of officers is so intense that it becomes a blind spot in his otherwise fair-minded outlook. Mailer was not much different in this regard. Even in his old age, he would snap at some slight by saying, "You sound like an officer!"

In this last letter home in April, he announced to Bea that he had received travel orders. A week later he was on his way to the 4th Replacement Depot in Yokohama. When he arrived there, he ran into his buddy from basic training and Fort Ord, Clifford Maskovsky, who now was a master sergeant. When Mailer saw his rank, he said, "Whose ass did you kiss to get those stripes?" The two friends were both aboard the USS *U.S. Grant* (AP 29) when it left with a thousand-plus GIs for the United States on April 26, arriving at Fort Lawton, near Seattle, a week later. Maskovsky was sergeant of the guard on the crossing and Mailer asked him for a good detail so he could avoid guard duty. Maskovsky put him in charge of candy distribution, a soft job. He read *Anna Karenina* for the third time on the voyage.

By the time they arrived, Mailer had given away all his medals, even his Combat Infantryman's Badge. He was the only buck private on the train from Seattle to Fort Dix. There was a final ignominy; everyone on the train was drinking and horsing around, and he got into a fight with a much bigger GI who broke his nose. On May 2, having served two years, one month, and six days, he was given an honorable discharge and mustering-out pay of $117.91. He got on the train and "went home like a stripped duck."

Mailer often said that the army had been the worst experience of his life, and the most valuable. Trained as a fire control operator, he served consecutively as a clerk, aerial photography trainee, shower builder, wire lineman, rifleman, laundryman, cook, and mess sergeant. Shot at several times, he shot back but probably killed no one. He was demeaned, ignored, humiliated, busted, and tested to a fare-thee-well. By his own admission, he was "the third lousiest guy in a platoon of 12." But he survived twenty-five reconnaissance patrols and grew as a man and an artist. He knew his army. He summed up his situation concisely in a letter to Bea halfway through his tour: "You know really my only decent function as a man is to be a lover and/or an author." Sustained by his wife, his family, and a sturdy belief in his vocation, he was now prepared to become a full-time writer, the only line of work, besides soldiering, he ever followed for more than a couple of months. "Through most of the Great Wet Boot which was World War II for me," he wrote,

> I kept a cold maniacal thing in my heart, sharp as a shiv. I would listen to other G.I.s beating their gums about how when they got out they were going to write a fugging book which would expose the fugging army, and I would think in my fatigue-slowed brain that if they only knew what I was going to do, they would elect me sergeant on the spot.

THE NIGHT OF his homecoming, Bea and Mailer went to a Brooklyn Heights hotel. The "unguent" of Bea's breasts, as he said in his letters, was all he needed to heal his ego bruises. The hotel was expensive, however, and after a week they moved into the family's apartment down the street. The clan laved out solicitude. After a few weeks, he was eager to begin writing, but before they left for Provincetown, Mailer made an appointment with the senior editor at Random House, Robert Linscott, who had found some merit in *A Transit to Narcissus*. He told the white-haired editor his idea for the novel, and the kindly Linscott said, "Oh, dear boy, don't, don't, write a war novel. We've over-published war novels and you won't be able to get a publisher." Mailer was unsettled by this advice, but knew he had no choice. "It was the only book I had in me, and I had to write it." He had support from Adeline (née Lubell) Naiman.

Adeline was the former Radcliffe roommate of Bea's sister, Phyllis, and had become a good friend of Mailer's sister, Barbara. She, the Silverman sisters, her friend Rhoda Lazare, and Adeline had created what Mailer called "the Norman legend" during the war. After Adeline was hired as a junior editor at Little, Brown, she began corresponding with Mailer in Japan and asked if she could see *Transit*, adding that she believed he was going to be a great writer. By then, he had decided it was a badly flawed work, and replied he would only consent to publication if no changes were requested and it appeared under a nom de plume. There the matter rested until mid-June when he, Bea, and Fan went to visit the Silvermans in Chelsea, and a luncheon meeting with Adeline and her mother at the Oxford Grill in Cambridge was arranged. Adeline remembers being disappointed by a slight, short young man "who wasn't dashingly articulate." Mailer was knocked back by her cultivation; he estimated she had read three times as much as he had. "She was a real name dropper, culturally speaking . . . very sure of herself. Full of stuff, full of vitamins," he recalled. Although he was uncharacteristically reserved at the luncheon, he did tell her about the new novel and they agreed to stay in touch. She became a lifelong friend.

After the luncheon, he and Bea took the train to Provincetown. Bea had arranged to rent a cottage. The Mailers thought that the Crow's Nest Cottages, as the double row of beachfront cottages were called, were in Provincetown, but they were actually a half mile over the line in North Truro. They had no car and pedaled bikes into Provincetown to go shopping. He immediately fell into a routine, writing from eleven to six on Mondays, Tuesdays, Thursdays, and Fridays. Fan, Barney, and Barbara came up for a week in July, and the Silvermans also visited, but the young couple didn't socialize much. By the end of August, he had a 184-page typescript.

It had always been Mailer's baseline assumption that there would be no hero in *The Naked and the Dead*. This is clear from the sheaf of letters Bea had pulled together, close to a hundred from his overseas correspondence. There were as many comments on Martinez, Red, and Wilson as on Croft, but fewer on General Cummings and Lieutenant

Hearn. Mailer was writing an ensemble novel about an understrength reconnaissance platoon. Each soldier would have his time in the spotlight and would interact, more or less, with every other soldier. He also intended to write about officers, drawing on his experience as a regimental clerk. By the time he reached Provincetown, he had a four-by-six card for each major character, the front side giving a baker's dozen of the soldier's traits and the back outlining his history. For example, the front of General Cummings's card lists: "love of planning & chess, ambition, love of wife, weight of responsibility, love of ease and luxury, maintenance of manner (bonhomie), wise hard knowledge of men, fear (pressure from the top), love of army ethical system, snobbery." The back of Red's card gives his year of birth (1912) and his jobs: "coal miner 1927–1930; hobo, 1930–31—sporadic, 1931–41; short order cook, shingler, plumber, harvester, flop house keeper, painter, truck driver, tailor." All of these occupations are mentioned in Red's "Time Machine" episode; he doesn't change markedly from Mailer's first conception of him. Cummings, on the other hand, while retaining some of the traits listed, underwent a major transformation. He becomes more intellectual, spartan, sadistic, and, most important, more reactionary. And, by the final draft, he has no love for his wife. He tells Hearn, "The truth is, Robert, my wife is a bitch." Mailer makes Cummings a homosexual, as he later stated.

In addition to the cards, which contain the names of the men on whom they are based, he drew up various charts detailing the interactions of the men in Croft's platoon. It is comprised largely of men from all around the country, lower- and middle-class who have been beaten down, first by the Depression, and next by the army. Eight of the platoon (Croft, Valsen, Martinez, Gallagher, Wilson, Brown, Stanley, and Toglio) are veterans of the disastrous preceding campaign at the (fictional) island of Motome, where the Japanese blasted them out of their rubber assault rafts with antiaircraft guns. The other six members of the platoon are green replacements: Ridges, a dirt farmer from Arkansas; Roth, an unathletic Jew from New York who falls to his death climbing Mount Anaka, the peak that dominates the island; Goldstein, a welder from Brooklyn; Wyman, another midwesterner; Minetta, a malingerer from New Jersey; and Czienwicz, a petty criminal from Chicago known to all as "Polack." Mailer was careful in how he allotted space to his characters. The backgrounds of eight of the fourteen enlisted men

(Martinez, Croft, Valsen, Gallagher, Wilson, Goldstein, Brown, Polack), and two officers (Cummings and Hearn), are given in "Time Machine" flashbacks, a device adapted from the biographical chapters in John Dos Passos's *U.S.A.* The others are revealed in conversation or via his omniscient narrator, who presents the thoughts of nearly every named character in the novel, more than two dozen. Critics have argued, with some justice, that some of the profiles (Brown and Polack, in particular) are stereotypical, although Mailer has been praised for others, generally those that his own background enabled him to handle more surely (Roth, Goldstein, Gallagher, Hearn). On the other hand, most readers agree that the "Time Machine" device is helpful in understanding the actions of the men under duress. They are sociosexual in nature, again revealing the influence of D. H. Lawrence. The soldiers carry their carnal fears and desires with them, another weight in their backpacks. Mailer saw the biographies as "bi-functional": they illumine motivation and provide pace. He explained one of his guiding beliefs for *Naked and the Dead*: "One was the product of one's milieu, one's parents, one's food, one's conversations, one's dearest and/or most odious human relations. One was the sum of one's own history as it was cradled in the larger history of one's time." So while there is justice in saying that some of the characters are stock and predictable, it is not true of Cummings and Hearn; their heavily worked intellectual conversations "show something of the turn my later writing would take," he said. The two officers and, arguably, Croft and Goldstein, are dynamic characters who change in unforeseen ways in the crucible of jungle warfare.

Roth's original name was Frankenheim. Mailer changed it to Rothberg and finally to Roth. He is a graduate of City College of New York, and worked in the city's real estate tax office. The only enlisted man in his outfit with a college education, he is also the only character with a four-by-six card that has no "Time Machine" episode. Sensitive, lazy, and depressed, Roth is the martyred Jew in the novel. Like Mailer, he is recently married. One reason, it can be surmised, why Mailer eschewed a "Time Machine" biography for Roth is to avoid having two New York Jews profiled. The other, perhaps, is so comparisons to his creator would not be as easy to make. There is no mention of a Roth, a Rothberg, or a Frankenheim in his master list of soldiers, in his letters, or the recollections of others in the 112th. But Mailer was not drawing a self-portrait. As with characters in several of his later novels—Stephen

Rojack in *An American Dream,* most notably—Roth is a fictional first cousin at best.

A meeting with Adeline was arranged for early September, and he and Bea took the morning ferry across the bay to Boston. He brought his first draft and Adeline sequestered herself to read it, finishing in the late afternoon. Her brief report, written that same day, stated boldly that the novel "is going to be the greatest novel to come out of World War II and we must publish it." Mailer remembered it as an "incredible document." She followed her spontaneous encomium about ten days later with a formal assessment, in which she outlined the novel's loose plot and lauded "the author's marvelous sense of spoken language rhythms and the colloquial idiom." In her conclusion she warns that if the novel is not accepted, "we are passing up the first really important novel to come out of the war and a potentially tremendous author." She predicted that the novel could sell as many as 7,300 copies, a large number for a first novel, but far below its actual sales figures. She was the first professional to see the importance of the novel.

When Little, Brown senior editor Angus Cameron read it, he was impressed but troubled by the strong language. Raymond Everitt, executive vice president, had the same response. It went to the president, Alfred McIntyre, and he was insistent: a major expurgation would be required. It was decided to get an outside opinion from Bernard DeVoto, Pulitzer Prize–winning historian of the American West and a Mark Twain scholar. Adeline had heard that the literary guru had a foul mouth and she happily agreed to the choice.

Mailer also went along with De Voto, but offered more arguments for the novel. He was irritated. He wrote a long letter to Adeline pointing to the patrol's attempt to climb Mount Anaka as the novel's spine, and stating that it would first and foremost be "a piece of realism." He made two more key points. First, the novel would be antiwar, although indirectly: "The terrible subtle evil of war on men is in every page." Second, it would be "a romantic novel concerned with the extraordinary." He continued.

> There are going to be troubling terrifying glimpses of order in disorder, of a horror which may or may not lurk beneath the surface of things. Remember when Hennessey is killed, and Croft and Red and Martinez all have primitive glimpses of a structure behind things?

> That emotion will be recurrent although warped into the style of each man's perceptions. It's the old business of man constructing little tag-ends of a God for himself in his moral wilderness. In war, it's more direct, more impacting on the senses—there is always a familiar unreality to everything you see and do, except for the occasional chilling moments when you feel as if you're on the edge of a deeper knowledge.

His comment about the structure behind the Anopopei campaign, his rough-hewn sense that there was intentionality behind the pasteboard masks of things, was ignored by everyone at the time, and not really noticed by readers or critics after it was published. He told *New York Times* columnist Harvey Breit in 1951 that he was on "a mystic kick" when he wrote *Naked and the Dead*; the primary influence on the novel was *Moby-Dick,* he said. But the novel's thick, textured realism, and the awesome power of nature, overwhelmed any recognition of the subtle intimations felt by Croft and others. Mailer did not forget, however, the transcendentalism he first encountered in Matthiessen's *American Renaissance*. It would come to the fore a decade later.

DeVoto's six-page critique, which Mailer received at the end of October, echoed what everyone at Little, Brown, including Adeline, had said. DeVoto did not question the verisimilitude of the obscenity; he questioned its effectiveness. He found the vernacular offensive and boring and said it would undercut any real consideration of the novel as a work of art. If published without severe pruning, he said, "it is certain to be prosecuted and suppressed in Massachusetts." He allowed that it would be a mistake not to make an investment in Mailer, but that was all the enthusiasm he could muster. DeVoto made one further criticism: the general and his aide were the "least live characters" in the manuscript and needed to be reconceived, individualized.

In the face of these criticisms, all Little, Brown was willing to discuss was an option contract for a few hundred dollars. This meant that they could still reject the book out of hand after changes were made. Mailer wasn't ready yet to break off negotiations, however, and told Adeline that he was definitely willing to write a new draft. In regard to Cummings and Hearn, he said, "DeVoto's criticism is essentially sound." He added that the option offered was a miserly hedging of the firm's bet. Although he felt "weak and battered" by the rain of negative comments, he ended by saying that "the best part of the book is to come. There's a chapter I've written since I've come home [from Massachusetts] which has about forty of the best pages ever written by an American. Sayonara, Norman."

He was almost certainly referring to the longest, most vivid episode in the first third of the novel, the Japanese night attack at the river. Recon withstands a lengthy and intense assault, with Croft rallying his platoon each time it falters. Before the first wave attacks, the Japanese call, again and again, across the river:

> "We you *coming-to-get,* Yank."
>
> He shivered terribly for a moment, and his hands seemed congealed on the machine gun. He could not bear the intense pressure in his head.
>
> "We you coming-to-get Yank," the voice screamed.
>
> "COME AND GET ME YOU SONSOFBITCHES," Croft roared. He shouted with every fiber of his body as though he plunged at an oaken door. There was no sound at all for perhaps ten seconds, nothing but the moonlight on the river and the taut rapt buzzing of the crickets. Then the voice spoke again. "Oh, we come, Yank, we come."
>
> Croft pulled back the bolt on the machine gun, and rammed it home. His heart was still beating with frenzy. "Recon . . . RECON, UP ON THE LINE," he shouted with all his strength. . . .
>
> In the light of the flare the Japanese had the stark frozen quality of men revealed by a shaft of lightning. Croft no longer saw anything clearly; he could not have said at that moment where his hands ended and the machine gun began; he was lost in a vast moil of noise out of which individual screams and shouts etched in his mind for an instant. He could never have counted the Japanese who charged across the river; he knew only that his finger was rigid on the trigger bar. He could not have loosened it. In those few moments he felt no sense of danger. He just kept firing.

Mailer probed more deeply into the psyches of Sergeant Croft and General Cummings than he did with any of his other characters. DeVoto's critique made him realize that his initial depiction of them was trammeled by their predetermined traits. They are the only two characters in the novel who believe that they can affect events, the only two who feel they have the inner sanction to act. Croft is best seen as Cummings's demonic underling—what Fedallah is to Ahab—although the two never interact, or even meet.

Mailer was educated by Croft, much as Shakespeare drew on Brutus for Hamlet. Marion Faye, Mailer's hipster hero for a post-Hiroshima world in *The Deer Park*, derives from Croft, as do Rojack in *An American Dream* and Gary Gilmore in *The Executioner's Song*, among others. He was profoundly fascinated by Croft because his Texas sergeant was trying to get to the bottom of his own violent and divided nature. "I hate everything which is not in myself," Croft says at the end of his "Time Machine" episode. He despises everyone who is weak, phony, lazy, or undisciplined. Close to psychotic, he is the finest soldier in the outfit. Critic Robert Ehrlich points out that Croft's portrait is in line with D. H. Lawrence's description of the American psyche: "hard, isolate, stoic, and a killer."

Intellectually, Mailer disapproved of Croft's violence but on another level found him to be the character for whom he had "the most secret admiration." Croft is a test case; he wanted to see how he might channel his violence, and whether he could plumb it or sate it or even transcend it. As Alfred Kazin noted of the novel, "Killing and being killed become forms of intoxication that get people out of their usual selves—always a prime motive in Mailer." Ostensibly, the assault on Mount Anaka is to determine whether there is a way to outflank the Japanese, but it soon becomes apparent that Croft's crazy attempt is a way of satisfying the "crude unformed vision in his soul." When he is driven off the mountain by the hornets, he is relieved to have found "a limit to his hunger," but nevertheless feels that he has "missed some tantalizing revelation of himself. Of himself and much more. Of life. Everything."

Except for the "Time Machine" episodes, the novel's action is confined to the island. This locus provides tremendous narrative concentration. The reader knows that the island will eventually be taken. It must, historically, because the Japanese were defeated on one island before the Americans jumped to the next and the next. This focus also imposes a constrained time scheme; we know that Cummings's island campaign will not stretch on endlessly. As on Prospero's magical isle, the characters will arrive, be transformed, and depart.

Major General Edward Cummings invades Anopopei with a six-thousand-man force. Shaped like an ocarina, the island is 150 miles long by fifty miles wide, tapering at the ends. The ocarina's mouthpiece, a peninsula where Cummings lands his troops after naval and air bombardment, juts out about twenty miles from the northwest quadrant of the island, as depicted on the line drawing in every edition of the novel. Following the book's title pages, this drawing is the first thing that readers encounter, which is Mailer's way of emphasizing landscape as a defining circumstance in the novel. When we have finished *Naked and the Dead*, we know Mailer's island as intimately as Prospero's or Crusoe's.

Anopopei, for Cummings, is a stepping-stone to the apex of political power in the semi-fascistic state he envisions the United States becoming. Such a state was Mailer's nightmare; like many ex-GIs he worried that World War II would be followed by war with Russia. "General Cummings," he said shortly after *Naked* was published, "articulates a kind of unconscious bent in the thinking of the Army brass and top rank politicians. He's an archetype of the new man, the coming man, the one who's really dangerous." Winston Churchill gave his "Iron Curtain" speech the month before Mailer left Japan, and during the fifteen months he was writing the novel the Soviets were seizing power in Eastern Europe. The Cold War was under way. Mailer felt that "people in our government were leading us into war again. The last half [of *Naked*] was written on this nerve right in the pit of my stomach."

THE MAILERS RETURNED to Brooklyn in September and rented an apartment at 49 Remsen Street, just around the corner from his parents' place on Pierrepont. During the negotiations with Little, Brown, Bea mentioned a Brooklyn Heights poet she had met during the war; his name was Norman Rosten and she thought he might be able to help get the novel published. Mailer met him on the street one day in October and they connected. Rosten had published two books with Rinehart, but didn't take on any airs. Mailer described what he learned from Rosten: "You could be a published writer and still be comfortable." It turned out that they both knew Arthur Miller. He lived in the same brownstone as Fan and Barney, and was writing a new play—*The Death of a Salesman.* When Miller and Mailer would bump into each other, Mailer said, "We would talk and then we'd go away, and I know he was thinking what I was, which was, 'That other guy is never going to amount to anything.' " The paths of the three Brooklyn writers crossed many times in later years, and all three would become involved with Marilyn Monroe: Miller married her; Rosten became a confidant; Mailer wrote her biography.

Rosten suggested that Mailer meet his editor at Rinehart, Ted Amussen. Mailer, of course, knew Amussen from before the war, but had lost contact. In early November, the two Normans took the subway to Rinehart's Manhattan offices, and Mailer gave Amussen his manuscript, now at least a hundred pages longer and including the firefight at the river. He also gave him a copy of Adeline's ecstatic editorial report and told him, somewhat angrily, "If you give me a contract, you can have it." Amussen ran into some opposition, but got the contract. It was Stanley Rinehart, the president and cofounder (with John Farrar) of the firm, who made the final decision, overriding his editor in chief, John Selby. Amussen told Rinehart that he'd be a "damn fool if you don't sign it up." A young editor named William Raney was supportive of Amussen, and became the editor that Mailer worked with most at the publishing house. Rinehart's advance was $1,250, on the high side for a first novel.

Before the contract was signed, he had to attend a profanity conference. Amussen and Raney were there and the two Johns—as Mailer called them—Selby and Farrar. It is possible that Stanley Rinehart also attended. Mailer agreed to reduce the profanity to "the irreducible minimum," which meant that an estimated one fifth of the obscene language would be cut, and the remaining, unwritten part of the novel would use "fug" and "shit" and "cock" and "pussy" in the same proportions. This reduction was deemed sufficient to placate Rinehart's mother, the celebrated mystery writer Mary Roberts Rinehart, who was on the firm's board. Amussen left Rinehart to work at another publishing firm soon after the manuscript had been accepted and William Raney took over as Mailer's chief contact.

In the summer of 1947, Mailer rented Rosten's one-room garret studio at 20 Remsen Street. Bea was writing her novel in their apartment and he needed a quiet place to revise his, based in part on Raney's critique. He also received feedback from family members—his sister, Cy Rembar and his sister, Osie, Dave and Anne, his parents, and, of course, Bea. Living at 20 Remsen was another literary man, Charles Devlin, who became the model for McLeod, one of the chief characters of Mailer's second novel, *Barbary Shore*. "A saturnine Irishman," as Mailer described him, Devlin had long, literary conversations with Mailer, who remembered him as "a dear friend." Devlin read the manuscript of the novel when it was done and criticized it severely. "It's a better book than I thought it would be, but you have no gift for metaphor," he said. "Metaphor reveals a man's character, and his true grasp of life. To the degree that you have no metaphor, you are an impoverished writer, and have lived no life." He never forgot Devlin's lecture and worked hard on his tropes ever after.

An unpublished, impecunious writer of the James T. Farrell school, Devlin was a good editor. Mailer hired him for a month at $50 a week to edit *Naked* because he was running up against a deadline. The manuscript was originally due in August, now had to be turned in by the end of September to meet Rinehart's publication date of May 1948, and Mailer and Bea planned to go to Europe as soon as the manuscript was submitted. Devlin was "sometimes cruel in his criticism," Mailer said, yet they got along. When Mailer was in the throes of writing *The Deer Park* in 1953, he wrote to Devlin and recalled their back-and-forth: "Oh, for the good old days of *Naked* when Bob Hope Devlin used to say to Mailer Colonna, 'You can't use that four hundred pages—they're no good,' and Norman Colonna would say cheerfully, 'I can't?' (Quick look at his watch.) 'I have three days before I go to Europe. Okay, boys, tear her down.' Thrommmp!" Mailer's confidence was such, he said, that if the novel needed "the Shah of Brat-mah-phur to make an entrance, I'd run to the library, read fifty pages on Hindu philosophy, and come back ready to enter the Shah's mind." Unlike his next two novels, *Naked* was easy to write.

Buttressed by his letters to Bea, his four-by-six cards, his charts, and vivid memories of Luzon, Mailer surged along, completing one draft and starting on another. This last draft, which he said was "a bonus," was almost a hundred pages longer and included the nuanced ideological debates between the general and his aide. His style shifted in these scenes, became "less forceful and more articulated." The last thing he wrote was the scene in which a humiliated Lieutenant Hearn is ordered to pick up a crushed cigarette the general has thrown down. He does but is still reassigned to take over Recon platoon from Croft. Without these additions, he said, *Naked and the Dead* "would have been considered an interesting war novel, with some good scenes." He wrote four days a week, five hours a day, producing about thirty typed pages a week. In the mornings, he would usually read a few pages of *Anna Karenina* before starting; in the afternoons, he would prime himself with a can of beer.

Mailer's family was around the corner and he was able to take days off to go to the beach or to a baseball game. Jackie Robinson was playing his first season as a Dodger, and Mailer said it was the most exciting year Brooklyn fans could remember. Occasionally, he would meet with a group of writers at the Manhattan apartment of Millie Brower, his old friend from Long Branch, where works in progress were read aloud. He hired Millie's husband, Harvey Anhalt, to type a clean copy of the *Naked* manuscript, after the changes suggested by Devlin had been made, paying him $150 for the nine-hundred-plus-page monster. On New Year's Eve, Barbara gave a party at her parents' apartment. Among those attending were Alison Lurie, her college classmate. She was amazed to see how jolly Mailer was; most of the writers she knew were anxious and unhappy. Barbara said that her brother's success "seemed to me at the time both miraculous *and* totally expected."

Sometime in the weeks before the party, he took a break from writing to make a film. He had seen two of Fritz Lang's classic films, *M* and *The Testament of Dr. Mabuse*, before he was drafted, and after the war he saw a number of surrealist films, such as Jean Cocteau's *Blood of the Poet*, at the Museum of Modern Art. Over the course of a week, Mailer and Harvey Anhalt made an eleven-minute, silent, experimental film, shot with a camera bought by Dave Kessler. According to film critic Michael Chaiken, who helped restore the untitled film, it is quite well done for an amateur effort. Chaiken says Mailer makes use of "several in-camera tricks: lap dissolves, stop motion, irising of the lens. Also, thematically, it's fairly bold for its time. A young, middle class girl, played by Millie Brower, is held in a trance state of dread over an unwanted pregnancy as she contemplates abortion. The repressive atmosphere of her domestic life is brought into relief by her inability to connect to her family who sit at the dinner table and eat robotically." It was the beginning of a filmmaking career that would resume in 1967, when Mailer made the first of three more experimental films.

At some point in the writing of *Naked and the Dead*, he and Bea attended an adult education class that discussed all the major theories of history. The professor said at one point, "I think we Jews have a separate theory of history which I would call the catastrophic theory of history." It was a form of history, he said, "that the Jews knew all too well." While Mailer was long past the point of specifically applying the theory to *Naked*, it definitely resonated with him, as he wrote in a 1997 letter. The conclusion of *Naked* might be seen as a manifestation of this theory, although the endurance and sacrifice shown by the men in the platoon qualifies the impact of the suffering in the last quarter of the novel.

In response to criticism that that novel paints a bleak picture of humanity, he made the following comment shortly after publication.

> Actually, it offers a good deal of hope. I intended it to be a parable about the movement of man through history. I tried to explore the outrageous proportions of cause and effect, of effort and recompense, in a sick society. The book finds man corrupted, confused to the point of helplessness, but it also finds that there are limits beyond which he cannot be pushed, and it finds that even in his corruption and sickness there are yearnings for a better world.

At the end, the men move off to a new island campaign. Soon they will be in the Philippines and six months later the war will be over. The reader gets the sense that while the campaign and the novel have been conclusive, and the men tested in the harshest ways without succumbing, they will now face new challenges. The Japanese on Anopopei have been vanquished, and American casualties have been comparatively light, but what lies ahead in the peacetime world is uncertain. The experience of being at war and writing about it led Mailer to develop a corollary to his antiwar belief, as Alfred Kazin has pointed out, one that would plague him ever after: "War may be the ultimate purpose of technological society." This corollary would become the chief premise of his next novel.

Mailer made changes to the novel right to the end of September, when it was submitted to Raney at Rinehart. Both novelist and editor would continue working on it long-distance, as Mailer and Bea were leaving for Paris. On October 3, after a bon voyage party at 102 Pierrepont, they boarded the RMS *Queen Elizabeth* for the crossing.

FOUR
PARIS AND HOLLYWOOD: PROMINENT AND EMPTY

The Mailers shivered through their first few weeks in Paris. They were staying at the Hôtel de l'Avenir, at 65 Rue Madam, on the Left Bank, not far from the Luxembourg Gardens. Their room, with a Murphy bed and a bathroom down the hall, cost one dollar a day. About the time that they began French classes at the Sorbonne, they moved a short distance to a three-room apartment at 11 Rue Bréa, a few blocks from the intersection of the Boulevard Montparnasse and the Boulevard Raspail—a part of Paris that Hemingway knew well. The three-room apartment, for which they paid *less* than a dollar a day, had red wallpaper, an orange rug, and a bathtub in the kitchen. It was small, but warmer than the hotel, and the Sorbonne, where they began classes in early November, was only a short walk. His most vivid memory of his early months in Paris was walking the streets conjugating subjunctive verbs.

Along with several hundred other ex-GIs, the Mailers were enrolled in the *Cours de Civilisation Française*, concocted to garner American tuition dollars. It was essentially an introductory language course and attendance was not always taken. Nonetheless, the couple worked with moderate diligence on their French skills with the knowledge that the combined $180 a month from the GI Bill they received would cease if they flunked. They also had the Rinehart advance and a remnant of their wartime savings. They were comparatively well off in a city still exhausted from the war. There were electricity shortages and strikes, and everything was restrained and gloomy, as he wrote to Fig. "You get to longing pretty hard for America and its ballsy kind of noise and excitement," he said. Lonely at first, they soon met several Americans: Mitchell Goodman and his English wife, the poet Denise Levertov, and a friend from Dunster House and the *Advocate*, Mark Linenthal, and his wife, Alice Adams, who later became a well-known *New Yorker* writer. Linenthal and Adams remained friends with Mailer over the years. They also met Stanley and Eileen Geist, expatriates who hosted an American salon. Geist graduated from Harvard the year Mailer entered, and had written a critical study of Melville while working as F. O. Matthiessen's research assistant on *American Renaissance*, which of course interested Mailer. Geist read the manuscript of *Naked* and told him it wasn't bad, perhaps the first comment he received on the novel from a professional critic. Mailer said he felt "ennobled" by this response.

There was no way to share his manuscript with Fig Gwaltney, who was in Arkansas attending college and trying to write novels. But they wrote to each other regularly during the ten months the Mailers were in Europe. Mailer always needed correspondents with whom he could be frank about his projects and problems. Fig was the first of these. Writing to him from the ship on October 7, he gave an unvarnished summary of his political views, which were exacerbated by his detestation of the red-baiting that was going on in the United States. Grossly inflated fears of communist influence and infiltration had prompted President Harry Truman, on March 21, 1947, to institute a Loyalty Program, which required all federal employees to swear they had never advocated or approved "the commission of acts of force or violence" that would "alter the form of the United States government." Mailer wrote:

> I've gone quite a bit to the Left since I've gotten out of the army. I'm a Jew Radical from New York now. And one of the areas of disagreement would be or perhaps would be—you may agree with me for all I know—that (1) we, that is, the leaders of the United States (I'm including the whole scurvy lot from the industrialists & state dept. to muff divers like Uncle Harry) want to go to war, and are doing everything in their power to bring us to war. And (2) I don't think Russia is the villain it's made out to be. I don't know what the hell they're like but when I find the worst fucking scum in the country (American Legion, Hearst press, etc.) going all out against them, I begin to doubt the whole works.

A few months after he got to Paris, in early 1948, he met someone who would school him in the quintessence of revolutionary socialism.

Through the Geists, he was introduced to Jean Malaquais, a Polish Jew from Warsaw (born Wladimir Malacki) whose parents had presumably perished in the Holocaust. Fifteen years older than Mailer, he had fought with the Lenin International Column of POUM, an anti-Stalinist Communist Party, against Franco in the Spanish Civil War, was almost captured by the Germans as a French soldier, escaped and fled to Mexico in 1943, where he participated in the political debates of the émigré circle there. A short, wiry man who looked a bit like Picasso, Malaquais had left Warsaw in 1925 and after many travels found himself in France in the depths of the Depression. He was able to find work in the lead and silver mines of La Londe-les-Maures in Provence, where a polyglot crew of Europeans and Russians fleeing from totalitarian oppression worked as day laborers. Malaquais' first book, *Men from Nowhere* (1939), described the workers' horrific working conditions and rough camaraderie. It won the Prix Renaudot. Like another Polish emigrant, Joseph Conrad, Malaquais had taught himself to write with elegance in a nonnative language. He had moved to Paris in the mid-1930s and immersed himself in French literature at the Bibliothéque Saint-Geneviéve while working nights unloading crates in the marketplace, Les Halles, the "belly of Paris."

"Morally and intellectually I was a tramp," Malaquais said, "a companion of the dispossessed." But he was also a sophisticated radical thinker who had been associated with writers such as André Gide and with Leon Trotsky (who praised *Men from Nowhere*). Proud and severe as only a stateless, formidably cultured Marxist intellectual could be, he had worked for years as a manual laborer. In a Preface to a reissue of Malaquais' 1954 novel, *The Joker*, Mailer summed up his acumen:

> Malaquais loathed formula, propaganda, or any variety of thinking which deprived a situation of its nuance. So he was capable of advancing a new thesis, anticipating your objections, stating them with clarity (like Freud disarming his critics) and then would overtake his own verification of your position in the return swing of the dialectic. He would do this with such power that when he argued, the veins in his forehead would throb as though to demonstrate that the human head was obliged to be the natural site if not the very phallus of Mind.

Malaquais, Mailer said, "had more influence upon my mind than anyone I ever knew from the time we had gotten well acquainted while he was translating *The Naked and the Dead.*" Mailer later recommended Malaquais for the year-long task—he had a good command of written English—and added $1,000 to the paltry $2,000 paid to Malaquais by Mailer's French publisher, Albin Michel. By the time that the translation was completed in 1950, the two men had become fast friends. But their meetings the year before in Paris were sometimes testy. Mailer told Malaquais about his hopes for Henry Wallace's presidential campaign as the Progressive Party nominee. Malaquais said that Mailer's voluble comments resembled those of "a boy scout or a young Kibbutznik," and proceeded to demolish Mailer's notion that Wallace represented a legitimate peace movement, or "any kind of . . . incipient revolutionary starting point." Malaquais told him that the communists would "exploit him and then they would drop him and cover him with dirt." Mailer "disliked me very strongly," according to Malaquais, especially when he told him that the Wallace campaign had been infiltrated by Stalinists. Unable to refute Malaquais, Mailer was yet unwilling to desert Wallace. At first he thought Malaquais was "an arrogant bastard. He was a little guy, very, very well knit and very determined and very superior, very haughty." Things were cool between them until they met again in Brooklyn in the fall of 1948.

Through a "long leaky French winter," he waited anxiously for reports on how *Naked* was faring at Rinehart. He was particularly concerned that Stanley Rinehart might want to cut the novel's profanity. Finally, near the end of 1947, he heard from editor William Raney that Rinehart was in love with the novel. He relayed the good news to Barney in Warsaw, where his father had a position with the American Joint Distribution Committee, a Jewish charity. "I have never heard such hosannas," Mailer wrote. Rinehart intended to write a letter praising the novel to the book trade, a tactic he used only rarely. Much relieved, Mailer told his father that he planned to start a new novel immediately, and hoped to get a lot written "so that I won't be scared if Naked and Dead gets a big reception."

Before he began, he and Bea went on a skiing trip over the holidays in Saint-Cergue, Switzerland, and visited the cities of Ouchy, Geneva, and Lausanne. He came back with two ideas: one a novel about a rich young California man who spends a year abroad, supporting himself by carrying money between France and Switzerland for black marketers; the second about Jews in Europe, focusing on an American Jewish couple who work for the Marshall Plan. He also kicked around the possibility of writing what he called "a collective novel" about people he knew in New York. None of these ideas gained traction, and he began to fret. "Maybe I'm not scared," he wrote to Barney. His inability to decide on a new novel, one that could take several years to complete, is understandable given the choices before him. He summed up his choices: "If my past had become empty as a theme, was I to write about Brooklyn streets, or my mother and father, or another war novel (*The Naked and the Dead Go to Japan*), or was I to do the book of the returning veteran when I had lived like a mole writing and rewriting seven hundred pages in those fifteen months?" So through the wet winter of 1947–48 he worked on his French verbs and waited to hear from Rinehart.

While waiting, he decided to read some non-American novels, although they jangled him as much as they inspired. Right after he had submitted *Naked,* he started reading E. M. Forster's novels; in Paris he tackled *Passage to India.* He also read an unnamed work by Jean-Paul Sartre as well as Stendhal's classic *The Red and the Black*, a novel that would have a large influence on him. He also read something by Evelyn Waugh, about which he wrote to Fig, grudgingly: "That English fairy can write, much as I hate to admit it." The book that affected him most was Christopher Isherwood's *Goodbye to Berlin*, especially Sally Bowles, Isherwood's charming, decadent floozy, who is oblivious to the rise of the Nazis. She would become the model for Mailer's first memorable female character, Mrs. Guinevere, in his next novel.

When he did hear from Raney, the letter was vague about possible cuts. Mailer wrote back on January 23, and again the next day, saying he anticipated "emasculation" and, worse, that he would have no recourse because changes would be expensive to make after the galleys went to the printer. If that was the case, he would "have a shit hemorrhage." Most distressing to him was his fear that Polack's reply to Wyman's question about whether there was a God ("If there is, he sure is a sonofabitch"), which he linked to Croft kicking over the hornet's nest as manifestations of divine meddling, had been cut. "Without that line, it is no longer my book as far as I am concerned," he said. He was willing to be overridden on the design of the book jacket, with its line drawing of a shell-shocked infantryman, and he was prepared to make other concessions, but he drew the line on Polack's remark. He ended the second letter by noting that he wanted to rewrite a few passages and asked what revisions would cost, closing with "I remain suspended, Norman."

Apparently, his volley of "howls and sulks," as he called them, acted as a purge because over the next two weeks he wrote the first fifty pages of "Mrs. Guinevere," the beginning of which centered on an ex-burlesque queen of the same name who runs a boardinghouse in Brooklyn Heights. In her self-absorption and flirtatiousness, she resembles Sally Bowles. Bea was writing a new novel about Russian immigrants, but she spent more time playing the piano in their apartment and enjoying Paris. The Mailers now had a fairly wide range of acquaintances, including some poor French artists. One was so destitute that Mailer and Bea, and Barbara when she arrived, took painting lessons from him. In early February, Raney wrote again to say he was coming to Paris, but did not say when the galleys would arrive. Mailer wrote him back a single-spaced, three-page, margin-less letter in which he went through all of his concerns. He made his points reasonably, emphasizing that he is burning no bridges and hopes to maintain his friendship with Raney, and includes tips on things to see during Raney's upcoming visit. After recounting the history of the manuscript in regard to obscenity at both Little, Brown and Rinehart, he got to the heart of his argument about why profanity was integral to *Naked*, saying it was not merely for authenticity;

> It is a tone which creates a sub-stratum of mood for the whole thing, and there is a limit to how much can be cut out without altering its context completely, and making the dialogue cute and "tough," and placing the most disgusting kind of emphasis on it. I refer you to abortions like "A Walk in the Sun," or any number of unmentionable plays where a laugh is aroused because someone roars, "Damn" or "Hell" or "Bastard." There is a psychological process to reading where the reader's attention sinks to a second cruising level, and there profanity does not strike him directly providing attention is

> not called to it by its spacing. He will notice it in time no more than articles and prepositions, and it will affect him the way it should affect him, an element in war experience.

He also questioned the decision-making process at Rinehart, and asks for a full list of profanity changes. He also wants to know if any substitutions for "fug" have been made. Finally, he complained about the infantryman drawing on the jacket, which he described as a sentimental, Ernie Pyle version of combat fatigue (Mailer missed entirely the appeal of the now iconic sketch of a GI by Joseph Karov, riddled with what appear to be bullet holes). His insistence on authentic speech—vocabulary and cadence—and the details of book design, both of which he belabors mightily to Raney, would become abiding concerns over the course of his career.

As his sister later pointed out, even as Mailer was agonizing over his next book and Rinehart's actions, he "always had an aura that projected a love of life." In all but the worst circumstances, "he had an ability to have a good time, and good times meshed with everything else." During the ski trips, she said, he was especially animated and full of play. "We took ourselves very seriously while we were there, but we were really playing." This European sojourn may have been the longest vacation of Mailer's life.

On February 26 page proofs arrived. He found to his great relief that there were no significant deletions or changes. He wrote back to Raney on March 1 that he had "no bitch" and apologized for all his complaining. The number of swear words dropped was not great and in one place at least, he said, the change, "crap" for "shit," was for the better. He included a list of over a hundred small corrections and a few changes and offered to pay for them. Considerably relieved, he and Bea left on March 6 for a week's skiing in the French Alps, near the town of Valloire. Upon their return to Paris, Mailer wrote letters on St. Patrick's Day to Barney in Poland and Fan and Barbara in Brooklyn about the family reunion planned for the end of April. Barney was to join Norman and Bea in Paris and they would drive to the port of Cherbourg to pick up Barbara and Fan. They would be driving a 6 *chevaux* Peugeot, purchased for $1,100 with a loan from Fan to be paid out of anticipated royalties. Both letters were as sunny as Paris, which had warmed up considerably. "Around dusk, with everyone in the outdoor cafes," he said, "you get some awful happy feelings." All was well at Rinehart, he informed them, and the first printing of *Naked* would be 25,000 copies, a big press run for a first novel. The date of publication was set for May 13 at a price of $4.50 (changed later to May 6 and $4, considered high). He and Bea were planning to drive to Barcelona and Madrid in April, and later to Italy. The winter of discontent was over.

In her memoir of her first visit to Europe, Mailer's sister explains that the trip to Spain came as a result of the contacts her brother and Bea had made with a group of anti-Franco Spanish students and refugees. The Spaniards convinced the Mailers to assist them in extracting a couple of their friends from a prison work camp in Spain.

> An American-owned car could prove a formidable weapon. Particularly persuasive was Paco Benet-Goitia. A bright twenty-one-year-old, very intellectual and passionately anti-Franco, he was the only one of the Spanish students who was not a refugee and could therefore travel back and forth. He also had a network of contacts in the small world of anti-Franco resistance that still simmered inside Spain. He would accompany Norman and Bea. They decided to go.

With a stash of antifascist leaflets hidden in the Peugeot, they drove with the Linenthals to Barcelona, where they passed on the leaflets to Paco's friends. Mailer was asked if he wanted to see the brothels in the Barrio Chino. As a young man, Picasso had been a customer. In *Portrait of Picasso as a Young Man* (1995), Mailer recalled his visit to the most famous whorehouse in the quarter, one which he surmised the painter had visited.

> In a large bare room, along a dais some sixty or seventy feet in length, forty or more women in bras and panties were bellowing out the catalogue of their specialties before a near mob of a couple hundred men, just about all of these putative customers puffing away on cigarettes as if to raise a wall of smoke between themselves and the cacophony of sexual advertisement bombarding them. The density of smoke in that room cannot be exaggerated.

From Barcelona they drove to Madrid, but the situation had changed and they were unable to help Paco's friends. After a few days and their first bullfight, they drove back to Paris. Later, after his family arrived on April 21, Mailer learned that an escape was now possible. He was getting preoccupied with prepublication activity and so asked his sister, who didn't know how to drive, if she wanted to go to Spain, to try again with Paco. Barbara, who had been having an affair with a Marxist in the States, was "thrilled" by the prospect of a romantic adventure to assist leftists. Mailer, never a proficient driver himself, gave her some driving lessons. A young woman named Barbara Probst (later married to Mailer's Harvard classmate Howard Solomon), whom Fan and Barbara met on the boat from the United States, was enlisted to go along. Probst, who had a driver's license, was eager. Mailer thought he should first test her driving skills, and his sister's, so they took a trip to Chartres. Barbara Probst Solomon recalled:

> What pleased me was that he treated me like an adult. He was awestruck by Chartres yet at the same time juggled with other thoughts, other ideas. He wondered—what would my Spanish experience be? How would it affect me? There we were, two Americans suddenly stunned by the Rose Window. Architecture, when it's amazing and has soul, affected Norman (he was enthralled by the visual) as profoundly as politics and literature, and in that magical golden spring afternoon, he talked and talked, telling me tons of stuff about Chartres.

The mission was scary but successful, and the two Barbaras rescued Paco's friends.

Mailer was in good spirits that spring, and enjoyed alternating between family gatherings and dealing with a wave of publishing correspondence. To Adelaide Scherer of the Sam Jaffe Agency in Hollywood, who contacted him, he said he would consider having them represent him and was willing to work on a screen treatment of the novel. He also asked for Scherer's advice on hiring a literary agent. After he parted company, amicably, with Berta Kaslow, his cousin Cy Rembar began representing him, but professional help was now needed. He also agreed to hire a clipping service and asked that all reviews be sent to him at Rue Bréa. From Rinehart, a copy of a letter from John Dos Passos arrived. Mailer's literary hero had read an advance copy of *Naked and the Dead* and written to Stan Rinehart to praise the book as "a courageous piece of publishing," calling the author "a first rate novelist." Mailer was immensely pleased. When asked years later what American novels affected him the most as a young man, Mailer said, "*U.S.A.* meant more than them all."

In early May, around the time of publication, the Mailers drove with Barbara and the Linenthals to Mont St. Michel, built on a tidal island in the eighth century after St. Michael the Archangel, it is said, burned a hole with his finger in the skull of the dilatory local bishop whom he had instructed to build a church there. They spent the night and the following day admiring the architecture of the church. "Norman was flush with success, and he was doing a southern accent," Linenthal recalled. They played a game called "The Naked and the Dead," with Bea as Wilson and Mailer as Croft. It was a role that he always enjoyed, especially after a few drinks.

Gore Vidal and Tennessee Williams were in Paris in April 1948. Mailer did not meet them or Truman Capote, who visited Vidal and Williams at the Hôtel de l'Université. Over the next four decades, he would have rocky relationships with all three. Vidal recalled that the publicity about Mailer's 721-page novel reached them in Paris. He wrote, "I remember thinking meanly: So somebody did it. Each previous war had had its big novel, yet so far there had been none for our war, though I knew that a dozen busy friends and acquaintances were grimly taking out tickets in the Grand War Novel Lottery." Mailer was by no means certain that he had, indeed, *done it*, not so far, but the first reviews that crossed the Atlantic certainly augured well. In mid-May, before his month-long trip to Italy began, they began arriving. He was restrained when he wrote to Fig in late May, saying that while the reviews were good enough, only one in five understood the novel. "All they could do was choke over the profanity and while that gave me a bang in the beginning it ended by boring the shit out of me." He was eager to leave the city with Bea, Barbara, and his mother, even though he told Fig that he loved it as never before. It was too easy to do nothing in Paris and "drown in inertia."

While Mailer was traveling he learned that Lillian Hellman wanted to adapt *Naked* into a play on Broadway to be produced by Kermit Bloomgarden (the following year he would present Arthur Miller's *Death of a Salesman*). Excited by the prospect, he wrote to Raney from Venice that he was empowering Rinehart, working with Dave Kessler (who had his power of attorney), and Cy Rembar, to make whatever financial arrangements they saw fit. "I have no worries [about] a flop hurting a movie sale because I don't see it selling to the movies anyway," he wrote. The chance to collaborate with one of the country's most important playwrights clearly excited him.

Mailer had planned to return to the States in mid-August, but after he and Bea returned to Paris from their trip to Italy at the end of June, he decided to leave a few weeks earlier. He wanted to meet with Hellman, see friends, and play a role in the Wallace presidential campaign. Most of all, he wanted to celebrate. He and Bea flew back to the United States, arriving on July 21.

HE DID NOT tell anyone at Rinehart about his early return; he wanted time to take Hellman's measure before being caught up in promoting *Naked and the Dead*. He met with her within a few days of arrival and found her to be "a tough baby, but very pleasant and direct." He would later describe her as being "what the French would call *joli-laide*, that is, she was not at all pretty or beautiful, but she was attractive, and there was a vitality . . . an intensity." Hellman liked him as well; he was young, handsome, and energetic. When he went to her Manhattan apartment, she received him in her bedroom. She was in a sexy nightgown and showed him a "truly formidable bare breast." When someone called from downstairs, Hellman answered, "Come on up. What did you think we were doing? Fucking?" There was always a bit of sexual electricity between them.

Hellman knew next to nothing about army life and had a long list of questions: "What is a carbine?" "What is a squad tent?" "How do you dig a latrine?" Mailer drew sketches of weapons and tents and explained the rank structure and army organization from division to platoon. Hellman had done a twenty-three-page outline of the novel before they met, and had begun identifying scenes. He drew maps of Anopopei to show General Cummings's tactical options. The Cummings-Hearn debates were inherently dramatic, but they saw no easy way to stage the ascent of Mount Anaka. Hellman didn't want Hearn to die, and Mailer agreed to this significant change. Then he and Bea made arrangements to go to Maine for a week with the Linenthals, now returned from Paris. On August 5, the day before they left, Mailer went to visit with

Sinclair Lewis in Williamstown, Massachusetts, at the elder novelist's invitation. The visit went well and two months later Lewis praised him to an interviewer: "Speaking of newcomers in the field—one of the greatest writers today is young Norman Mailer—author of *The Naked and the Dead*—an amazing bit of writing. That boy has talent worth preserving. There's nothing petty about Mailer—he's the author of the hour—the greatest writer to come out of his generation." Mailer's books carried this last phrase for many years.

The Naked and the Dead reached first place on *The New York Times* bestseller list on June 20, and Rinehart wanted Mailer to meet with the press. He submitted to interviews with the *Times, Cue,* the *New York Star*, and *The New Yorker*'s Lillian Ross, with whom he remained friendly. But at Bea's urging, he had turned down a request from *Life* for a photo at the airport, saying, "Getting your mug in the papers is one of the shameful ways of making a living," a remark that drew chuckles in later years. It appears that *Life* wanted the photograph to accompany a full-page editorial on August 16 calling for "a novelist to re-create American values instead of wallowing in the literary slums." The piece was unsigned but had Henry R. Luce's imprimatur. The core complaint is that

> Both Anopopei and Mr. Mailer's stateside U.S. teem with riotous, essentially meaningless life. But does Mr. Mailer really mean that life is meaningless? What he seems to tell us is that such purposes as marrying and procreating and raising a family or mastering an art or a profession or building a business or beating the Japs are without value to anybody now living.

This attack was the beginning of decades of predominantly negative reviews and commentary from the Time-Life organization. Three years later, *Life* referred to *Naked and the Dead* as "insidious slime." Among national publications, only William F. Buckley's *National Review* had a higher batting average in berating Mailer.

In late August, the Mailers flew to Arkansas for a two-week visit with Fig and his new wife, Ecey. The foursome went on picnics, swam, and relaxed. The Gwaltneys liked Bea, who was her usual frank, earthy self. Fig remembered that when the Mailers were ready for bed, Bea would ask if she needed to install a birth control device, hollering out in a voice "both vulgar and innocent, 'Norm, do you want to fuck me tonight?' "

Rinehart's extremely effective marketing campaign was aided by strong word-of-mouth support and generally superlative reviews. A postcard went to top editors and publicity staff at all the major publishers heralding the novel's publication and stating that "all but the tough-skinned" will turn from the book's "unrestrained accuracy of detail in speech and thought"—code for plenty of profanity and sex. Posters with Karov's drawing of the infantryman were displayed in bookstores. Initially, they carried no information, just the face of the soldier with a thousand-yard stare and nine bullet holes. According to Adeline, "Everyone was both startled and shocked," but the tactic worked and "by the time the book was published, the jacket had become famous." As reviews appeared, snippets from them were added to the poster: *The New Yorker*: "closer to Tolstoy . . . than to Crane or Remarque"; *The New York Times*: "its total effect is overwhelming"; *Newsweek*: "powerful . . . brutal . . . astonishingly thoughtful"; *New York Herald Tribune Book Review*: "a prodigal and brilliant talent." Within two weeks of publication Rinehart had ordered two more printings, bringing the total to 65,000; the Book Find Club chose it as their July selection and printed 35,000 copies. When reviewers found anything to complain about, it was usually the profanity. Orville Prescott, in his *Times* column, said it contained "more explicitly vile speech . . . than I have ever seen printed in a work of serious literature before." But the vast majority of reviewers believed Mailer's language was an accurate reflection of the way GIs in barracks and battles had actually spoken. The preponderant view was that he was a pioneer of free speech, although the book was banned by many local libraries and in several foreign countries.

The negative reviews troubled him. "I think I suffered more over the reviews of *The Naked and the Dead*, even the good ones, than over the reviews for any other book. I wanted to sit down and write a letter to every critic—they had misinterpreted something I said even though they liked the book." But he had no time for rejoinders. He was busy making speeches for Wallace. In September and October, he made over thirty, mainly in the New York area, but also in Hollywood. Bea also worked on the campaign and both of them became associated with the Progressive Party's unofficial newspaper, the *National Guardian*. At the end of September, Mailer traveled to Evansville, Indiana, on assignment from the *New York Post*, a liberal paper that gave extensive coverage to the Wallace campaign. A young instructor at Evansville College had recently been fired for heading the local Wallace committee. Mailer spent four days there, interviewed about twenty people, and then wrote a 2,500-word feature article built around a devastating interview with the college's president. It was his first piece of professional journalism. The strong feelings and occasional violence against the Wallace campaign indicated the depth of anticommunism in the United States at this time.

In mid-October, he flew to Hollywood to enlist movie stars as Wallace supporters. At a party at the home of Gene Kelly and his wife, Betsy Blair, Mailer gave a speech to a large crowd that included Montgomery Clift, Farley Granger, Edward G. Robinson, and Shelley Winters, who later said, "Everyone who was anyone was at this party, AND I MEAN EVERYONE, in Hollywood." Mailer, reflecting the influence of Malaquais, whom he had been meeting with regularly, said that America's huge institutions—the government, corporations, and labor unions—were commensurate with Russia's equally large and oppressive bureaucracies. The Progressive Party, he argued, was the only way to prevent the drift toward war with Russia. He recalled that he had been "unintentionally eloquent," although it was clear that many in attendance weren't going to endorse Wallace. At one point, Robinson stood up and said, "See here—who do you think you are, you little punk? You know, I'm known all over the world, I'm world famous, and you're telling me how to vote? I'll keep my vote to myself, if you don't mind."

A second purpose of the event was to raise money for the Hollywood Ten, a group of current or former communist producers, writers, and directors who refused to tell a congressional committee whether they were or had been members of the party. All ten were eventually sent to prison. Mailer asked those present to sign an amicus curiae brief to be used when the convictions were appealed to the U.S. Supreme Court. Many at the event responded by giving cash, but only two—Winters and Granger—signed the brief. They also gave Mailer checks for $100. Granger recalled that Mailer, "unbeknownst to us . . . probably saved Shelley and me from bringing our careers to an early end." The Hollywood blacklist was now in force and Mailer, fearing that their checks could be traced, returned them. He also tore up the brief containing their signatures. A month earlier, he had signed another such brief, along with two hundred other writers and film industry figures, including Charlie Chaplin, John Garfield, John Huston, Dorothy Parker, and Burt Lancaster.

On October 17, he was the keynote speaker at a fundraiser at the El Patio Theatre on Hollywood Boulevard. His speech, titled "Ballots vs. Book Burning," hammered on the point that the Progressive Party was the only way to oppose a third world war. He gave the same speech several more times after he returned east, and may have garnered some support in New York, where Wallace received almost half of his 1.1 million votes, a total slightly less than Strom Thurmond's Dixiecrat Party. Truman, against all expectations, soundly defeated Wallace, Thurmond, and the GOP candidate, Thomas E. Dewey. Wallace, who was mocked for allowing communists to infiltrate his party's ranks, was quoted as saying, "Communists are the closest thing to the early Christian martyrs." He retired after the election. Mailer became disenchanted with electoral politics and didn't vote again until 1960.

JUST BEFORE THE election, the Mailers were living in a furnished apartment at 49 Remsen Street, the same address where they had lived when he was writing *Naked and the Dead.* Malaquais had moved to New York and was lecturing at the New School for Social Research. One of his students was a man named Dan Wolf, who was a friend of Mailer's. (Later, with Edwin Fancher, Wolf, Mailer, and a few others would found *The Village Voice.*) Through Wolf, Mailer reconnected with Malaquais, who lived around the corner on Montague Street. They met often and Mailer now found Malaquais' ideas more appealing. It was at this time that Mailer asked him to translate *Naked.* At Mailer's request, Malaquais drew up a reading list for him. "When I met Norman in Paris, he knew nothing about the history of the Russian Revolution, of the Russian movement going back to the 1880s. In Western Europe all students are political animals but in America a writer is a writer is a writer," Malaquais said. "But that curiosity began in Paris, and he became very interested. Being young and perturbed on an intellectual level by the Cold War, he was open-minded to a degree. He was willing at least to confront and combat." One of the books Malaquais suggested was *Report of Court Proceedings in the Case of the Anti-Soviet "Bloc of Right" and Trotskyites* (1938), a verbatim transcript of the Moscow show trials of Stalin's enemies, real and perceived. The show trials and the executions that followed led many Communist sympathizers to turn against Russia. Another title Malaquais recommended was *Stalin: A Critical Survey of Bolshevism* (1939), which traced the tumultuous history of Marxism in Russia up to the outbreak of World War II. It was written by Boris Souvarine, a fervent anti-Stalinist Malaquais knew in Paris. These two books and several others on Malaquais' list obliterated what remained of Mailer's belief in the Soviet Union as the foundation of a new world culture. For the rest of his life he referred to Russian history, including the history of Russian Jews, with familiarity.

Malaquais' flinty geopolitical analyses impressed Mailer, but not his friends. Irving Howe, the founding editor of *Dissent* and a longtime flag bearer for socialism, admired Malaquais' *War Diary* (1944), but found the man to be "opinionated, cocksure, and dogmatic." He thought Malaquais was joking when he said there were only two genuine Marxists left: himself and Marc Chirik, a key figure in Malaquais' 1948 novel, *World Without Visa.* When Mailer brought Hellman and Malaquais together, "it was a disaster," Mailer said. "They couldn't bear each other." Cy Rembar didn't much care for Malaquais, and Mickey Knox, a young Hollywood actor who would become Mailer's close friend, found Malaquais to be "unrelenting." Before Mailer met Malaquais, his guide to Marxism had been Charles Devlin, and back in Brooklyn after the election, he arranged for Devlin to meet Malaquais. He said that Devlin was a specialist on the Russian economy, but Malaquais found him to be "a thoroughly constipated Stalinist hack." It was "child's play," Malaquais said, "to destroy him." The meeting with Devlin reinforced Mailer's recognition that he had been used by the communists who had infiltrated the Wallace campaign.

Wallace's horrendous showing, coupled with the ongoing popularity of *Naked and the Dead* (nineteen weeks in first place on the *New York Times* bestseller list, through November 19) led to a period of self-reflection. When he went out in public admirers surrounded him, and given the wonderful reviews *Naked* had received, he felt like a champ, bulging with self-esteem. "There were times," he said, when *Naked and the Dead* seemed like "the greatest book written since *War and Peace.*" But in his sessions with Malaquais, he was painfully reminded of the limitations of his knowledge, and when he looked in the mirror, he saw someone who, he said, was "a bit of an imposter," as much a fraud as a champ. Many times over the years, Mailer looked back at that young man who felt unworthy. For example, in 1979: "You're 25 and you've written one good book that you wrote on a streak that was a natural book, and then you don't know what you want to do with yourself after that. It was a terribly tricky time." He began to examine the assets and liabilities of fame. Two things were certain: First, women were attracted to him as never before. "Celebrity," he said, "was great for one-night stands." Second, fame "cauterizes a lot of your past." It was, he said, using another medical term, "a lobotomy to my past." There were two Norman Mailers. One enjoyed the attention and savored what he called the "ego-gobblings" of celebrity, while the other suspected that the compliments he received were ploys of phonies. "Once I had been a young man whom many did not notice," but after the success of *Naked*, "I was prominent but empty."

> I was a dependable pain in the ass to a great many people, because all through the first year I'd keep saying, "Oh, now I will never know the experience of other people." . . . I kept wanting to go back to what seemed like a sweet past when only a few people knew that I had talent. A young writer, if he is unknown, can be at a party and watch what everyone is doing. If he has a marvelous ear for dialogue, he can wake up the next morning and remember all that was said and how it was said. He is a bird on a branch. Sees like a bird and writes books that can be extraordinarily well observed. But once you are successful, especially if it happens quickly, it's as if the bird is now an emu. It cannot fly. It's big and it grows haunches and fore shoulders and a mane: Lo and behold, it is a lion. And everyone is looking at the lion, including the birds. But it is a lion with the heart of a bird and the mind of a bird.

He wrote to Sinclair Lewis in mid-November and told him he was getting started on a new novel, "a big fat one." But it does not appear that he began until after he and Bea moved to Jamaica, Vermont, near several ski resorts, where they leased a house from January to May of 1949. Mailer spent November and December in Brooklyn reading and meeting with Malaquais, who later came for long visits in Vermont. After six weeks of research and outlining, he began a new novel in mid-February. The idea came from the week in October that he had spent in

Indiana gathering information on the case of the college professor who was fired. The working title was "The Devil's Advocate," but he also referred to it as the "strike novel." For raw material, he relied on notes and clippings referring to a contested strike and subsequent blacklisting of Indiana union workers. Cy Rembar sent him material on the 1947 Taft-Hartley Act, which labor leaders viewed as unfairly restricting the right to organize and strike. Mailer struggled to embody the strike in narrative form, but finally, realizing that he didn't know "a damn thing about labor unions," abandoned it. The twenty-one pages he eked out tell the story of the death of the matriarch of a Ukrainian union family, and the visit of a labor organizer. His name is William McLeod, the same name Mailer would use for the central character of his second novel, *Barbary Shore*, which would grow out of "Mrs. Guinevere," begun in Paris. "Full of second-novel panic," he worked on the manuscript through April, interrupting it only for a brief visit to New York at the end of March to participate in an international peace conference, sponsored by the National Council of Arts, Sciences and the Professions. It was called the Waldorf Conference, after the Waldorf-Astoria Hotel, where it was held.

The conference, which ran March 25–27, brought together close to three thousand delegates from around the world to discuss ways to promote peace. Although this sounds benign, America's attitude toward Russia at this moment was one of fear and loathing, and all the newspapers and magazines of the day, with few exceptions (most notably *The New York Times*), attacked the gathering as a communist front designed to alter American foreign policy. The hotel was literally surrounded by right-wing groups such as the American Legion and Catholic War Veterans, but also by refugees from Eastern Europe protesting Russian-backed takeovers of Eastern European countries.

The right-wing protesters had come, Mailer wrote, "out of the dream that the doors of the Waldorf might open to them, and they could smash some motherfucking Reds, loot the silk of that overrich hotel and perhaps drag back to Queens or Staten Island a real live Russian to char over a slow fire on their barbecue pit." The Russian delegation included the world-famous composer Dmitri Shostakovich, who was pale and nervous in all his appearances. It was reported that he agreed to attend only after Stalin told him to. The American delegates and sponsors, many of whom Mailer knew, were well-known Russian sympathizers, "Stalinoids," as anti-Stalin literary critic Dwight Macdonald referred to them: Henry Wallace, Langston Hughes, Arthur Miller, Lillian Hellman, Dashiell Hammett, Dorothy Parker, Charlie Chaplin, Frank Lloyd Wright, and many others. Several Harvard professors attended, including his psychology instructor, Henry A. Murray, and F. O. Matthiessen, with whom Mailer had campaigned for Wallace. *Life* magazine, rabidly anti-Soviet, ran a five-page story about the conference that included a double-page spread, "Dupes and Fellow Travelers Dress Up Communist Fronts," consisting of photographs of fifty prominent conferees. A smiling Mailer, in a white T-shirt, was one of them.

Mailer's ten-member panel on writing and publishing in the Starlight Roof Room drew a packed audience of over eight hundred. It was chaired by poet Louis Untermeyer, who had been involved in a public debate with political philosopher Sidney Hook, a strident anti-Stalinist and head of a new organization, the Congress for Cultural Freedom, secretly backed by the CIA. Some CCF members—Robert Lowell, Mary McCarthy, Elizabeth Hardwick, and Dwight Macdonald—were in the audience and challenged the Russians on the panel. Malaquais was also there. When Untermeyer made a comment about Hook being a dirty four-letter word, Lowell objected strenuously. As each speaker was introduced, including Matthiessen, there were cries for Mailer. When he did speak, he said that he was at the conference as a Trojan Horse and had been uncertain about whether to come at all. Immediately after the conference, he called his speech a "melancholy debauch" and recalled that he was almost weeping. In his speech, he said that "both Russia and America are moving radically towards state capitalism, and that the differences between them finally will be cultural differences, minor deviations, and that actually there is no future in fighting for one side or the other." He concluded by warning that if the movement continued, "we would be put in concentration camps." The only thing writers can do, he said, is to tell the truth and perhaps what is written will affect "the next turmoils of world history."

Norman Podhoretz, a writer and editor who later became Mailer's friend, wrote that Mailer "must always work everything out for himself and by himself, as though it were up to him to create the world anew over and over again in his own experience." Podhoretz's insight is generally accurate. Mailer was a lifelong autodidact. But the exception that proves the rule was the political tutorial Malaquais conducted for Mailer from October 1948 through March 1950. Their conversations and the books Malaquais gave him to read, convinced Mailer that Stalin was a monster and—the central point—that the Russian and American economic systems were implicitly geared for war. He was now ready for immersion in the bible of revolutionary socialism. At Malaquais's urging, he began reading *Das Kapital* after the Waldorf Conference. By his own accounting, he spent a year "living more closely in the history of Russia from 1917 to 1937 than in the events of my own life." It should be remembered that Mailer never took a history course in college, and until he met Malaquais, Spengler was his chief historical guide. The model of cultural growth, blossoming, and decay that he absorbed from *Decline of the West* was amply confirmed by Malaquais' interpretation of the revolutions, wars, and catastrophes of the twentieth century.

Mailer said that he "felt like a rodent" at the conference because he was leaving the Progressive Party. Indeed, he was booed at the end of his speech just as vigorously as he had been cheered before he began. He was unsure if he had spoken "out of a new and deep political conviction," or if he was "afraid of the final wrath of those psychically starved hoodlums on the street outside." When Irving Howe praised his bravery and candor, therefore, he was quite pleased. "I was immediately able to recognize the intellectual fingerprint of who was behind that speech—Jean Malaquais," Howe said. When Mailer went outside, Dwight Macdonald came up to him on the street and told him he liked his speech. As Malaquais's influence waned in the mid-1950s, Macdonald would become one of his intellectual godfathers. Mary McCarthy, Robert Lowell, and especially Howe also became close to him after the conference.

Back in Vermont, he tried to work on *Barbary Shore*. There were no money worries. *Naked* had sold 197,000 copies in eight months, earning him about $80,000 in royalties. Only Lloyd C. Douglas's book about St. Peter, *The Big Fisherman*, sold more copies that year. The Mailers banked most of the royalty money. Hellman was still working on the play, but said she wouldn't have anything ready until the fall. The plan was to ski, write, and watch Bea grow larger; she was about three months pregnant by the end of March. Mailer had written to Fig requesting him to address mail to him as Kingsley Mailer so he could "stay incognito to avoid all the literary teas." Progress on the novel was slow; he was having difficulty finding the right tone. As he had explained in a letter to a Harvard friend, Larry Weiss, his approach alternated between "the theoretical and empirical," or between the realistic methods employed so successfully in *Naked and the Dead* and the abstractions delivered to him by Malaquais. He had also been stirred by Kafka's *The Castle* and told Fig he saw it as "an adult fairy tale." He would attempt to meld all of these elements in *Barbary Shore*.

There was something else on his mind: Hollywood. He had been lionized there and had met celebrities like Hedy Lamarr, Burt Lancaster, and John Garfield, as well as up-and-coming actors like Shelley Winters, Farley Granger, and Marlon Brando. Winters always claimed that she introduced Mailer to her roommate, Marilyn Monroe, in 1948, but he could not remember meeting her. He did remember another woman, Lois Mayfield Wilson, a blond graduate student from Kentucky whom he met at a Stanford party given by the Linenthals. She recalled that she left the party with him, and they had an erotic wrestling match in the car, which became the basis for Sergius O'Shaugnessy's tussle with Lulu Meyers in *The Deer Park*. He gave her the pseudonym of "Junebug" in his letters to her. They were deeply attracted to each other and would have a very lengthy long-distance affair.

Mailer decided to spend some time in Hollywood and asked Malaquais, who had worked as a screenwriter in Mexico and France, and his wife, Galy, to join him and Bea in California. Bea, who loved films as much as her husband did, and was equally gregarious, was eager to go. His desire to sell *Naked and the Dead* to a film studio was another consideration in relocating. In late April, he wrote to Rembar about sale possibilities and also asked for help getting screenwriting jobs, noting that Malaquais had "a good flair for plots which I do not." His conditions were $2,000 a week and a start date of September so that he could finish *Barbary Shore*. Because of Bea's pregnancy, she would fly and he would drive.

Barbara Probst Solomon recalled that one night in Paris after *Naked*'s extraordinary success was known, she was present when Barney said to Bea, somewhat bluntly, "You're going back to America, Norman's going to be famous, and you're going to have a lot of competition." He advised her to dress well and look attractive if she wanted the marriage to work. Bea blanched. But Barney was a bit of a womanizer himself and knew what he was talking about. After they returned from France, their marriage became "iffy," Mailer recalled. When Bea got pregnant, he said, "I thought maybe that would improve the marriage, and it didn't, of course. In fact, the marriage probably was worse afterward, because I hated having a baby; I felt trapped. I wanted freedom, I wanted to be screwing a lot of girls and here I am stuck. So it was all of that. So we ended up with this . . . and then after she [daughter Susan] was born, it just kept getting worse and worse. And I kept having more and more affairs on the side, whenever and wherever I could." One of them was with Lois Wilson, whom he contacted when they reached California.

MAILER LEFT IN early June 1949 for California, driving via Chicago. His sister was working in Chicago and, for a few days, he visited with her and Adeline, now married. After a week's visit with Fig and Ecey in Arkansas, he drove through Texas, New Mexico, and Arizona to Los Angeles. In late June, he arrived in "the ugliest city in the whole world," as he described it to Fig. He rented an apartment at the Chateau Marmont, the castlelike hotel overlooking Sunset Boulevard where celebrities have acted up since 1931. When Bea joined him, she was more than seven months pregnant. Mailer wrote a cheerful letter to Malaquais in early July saying that he thought they had a chance to "reap the wind yet, the golden wind." He had been seeing Montgomery Clift and interested him in the idea of making Stendhal's *The Red and the Black* into a film, with Clift as Julien Sorel. Malaquais would not arrive for a couple of months; he was only at page 380 in his translation of *Naked*.

Shortly after the Mailers left Vermont, the British edition of *Naked and the Dead* was published by Allan Wingate. There was immediate criticism, led by the *Sunday Times*. On May 1, in a front-page editorial, the paper said that the novel was "incredibly foul and beastly." It should be suppressed, the editorial continued, adding that "no decent man could leave it lying about the house without shame that his womenfolk were reading it." Mailer responded in a telephone interview with the Associated Press by saying that the London paper was entitled to its opinion, but that the obscenity in the novel "is like a bell ringing in the background while you work. Before long you don't notice it." The British attorney general, Sir Hartley Shawcross, speaking on the floor of Parliament, called the book "foul, lewd and revolting," but declined to prosecute it. Many British reviewers called the book brilliant, and the attention generated by indignant condemnation and unqualified praise led to tremendous sales. By the end of 1949, eighty thousand copies had been sold. Mailer took note of how the controversy sold the book. The fight against suppressing *Naked* was led by his Wingate editor, André Deutsch, a Hungarian Jew. Mailer said winning the fight to publish *Naked and the Dead* was "the biggest move" of Deutsch's life. The novel's success encouraged Deutsch and another Wingate editor, Diana Athill, to form their own firm, the eponymous André Deutsch, with which Mailer would later affiliate.

Perhaps the shrewdest British reviewer was V. S. Pritchett, the eminent short story writer and critic. He found the obscenity flap overblown, noting that "respectable society cannot expect to indulge in two major wars in one generation without getting a flood of raw documents about what goes on in the minds and comes out of the mouths of ordinary men who are sent out punctually to these slaughters." Pritchett praised the novel, especially the long patrol, which he said was done perfectly. But he found the book too long and thought the "Time Machine" episodes could have been cut entirely. Criticism of Mailer's verbosity would be heard again.

The length of *Naked* did not trouble George Orwell, who called the novel in a 1950 letter "the best war book of the last war yet." Mailer admired Orwell's work and praised his "profoundly prophetic" vision of the future in his 1949 novel, *1984*. Mailer said that Orwell had accomplished what he was trying to do in *Barbary Shore*: "combine the political essay with fiction." Mailer worked hard on the new novel for his first two months in "Lotus Land," as he called it, and finished the first draft on August 16 as Bea approached term. Hellman was visiting Hollywood scouting for male leads in the play and met with Mailer several times. Most of his time, however, was spent trying to work out a final agreement with Norma Productions, which had optioned the film rights of *Naked*. The company was a joint effort of Burt Lancaster, whom Mailer liked, and Harold Hecht, who handled the business side of the partnership. Hecht wouldn't give Mailer the level of script oversight that he wanted and the haggling went on for weeks. Lancaster was slated to play Lieutenant Hearn. Mailer finally got the approval he wanted, but when he saw the script, written by two Hollywood veterans, he didn't like it. The deal ultimately fell apart, hastened in part by war clouds over Korea, where fighting broke out in June 1950.

Sometime shortly after the Mailers arrived, Shelley Winters asked for his help. She wanted desperately to get a role in an upcoming film, *A Place in the Sun*, based on Theodore Dreiser's *An American Tragedy*, which George Stevens was directing and producing for Paramount. According to Winters, after a dinner at a Mexican restaurant with Mailer and Burt Lancaster (with whom she was having an affair), she asked Mailer to explain the novel to her, especially the character Roberta Alden, a factory girl who is murdered by the protagonist, Clyde Griffiths (played by Montgomery Clift in the film). After Lancaster left, Winters asked him to come to her apartment. Mailer remembered that he had his "own little agenda tucked into the middle of it. Hey, I'll be alone with this blonde actress and maybe good things will come of it," but Winters was "totally unsexy" that night. She was very worried and looked "ready to go in for a strong case of the weeps," he said. Winters was impressed by his blue eyes, and for several hours, she said, "the young handsome Norman Mailer talked to me about the inner workings of that girl's mind and what Dreiser wanted the reader to feel about the whole American syndrome of success at any price. Norman knew so much about Dreiser that I got the feeling he had been his protégé." Mailer gave her the key character trait: Alden is "a girl completely without artifice." Winters used the line with Stevens, got the role, and did a magnificent job in it. The film won seven Academy Awards, including best director, and Clift and Winters were nominated for Oscars. She told and retold the story of how he coached her many times, always acknowledging with gratitude his role in launching her career.

The Mailers moved to a seven-room house at 1601 Marlay Drive in the foothills just beyond Sunset Boulevard. Jean and Galy Malaquais moved into the small apartment over the garage. On August 28, Bea gave birth to a daughter, Susan. Malaquais was named godfather. Mailer told his parents that the six-pound baby "looked like a prize fighter at the end of a fight," but the swelling quickly disappeared and now she looked "astonishingly like you, mother." Writing to Fig a few weeks later to announce the birth, his tone was different. He said he had been "running to the hospital, dicking around, getting bawled out by my wife who acts infinitely superior to me now, and just generally suffering." No scriptwriting jobs had turned up; negotiations with Hecht were inching; *Barbary Shore* needed more work; and the new father was, temporarily, a satellite. He continued reading *Kapital* and discussing it with Malaquais, who was still laboring on his translation of *Naked*.

When he was at Harvard he had dreamed of being a screenwriter and now he had his chance. Sometime around mid-October, Cy and Mailer's new agent, George Landy, arranged a meeting with Samuel Goldwyn at MGM. Malaquais said that the first meeting with the legendary producer was "high comedy." Goldwyn met them in his bathrobe in a huge living room with dummy books on the walls. Malaquais gave an overview of the script they wanted to write and Goldwyn asked for a two-page outline, which they refused, knowing it could be stolen. Shortly afterward, they got a $50,000 contract—a $5,000 advance and $15,000 for each of three revisions. They were also given offices and secretaries. "The day after the contract was signed," Malaquais said, "a notice appeared in *Variety*, and I became overnight a VIP of sorts, trailing in Norman's shadow." The working title of the script was "The Character of the Victim."

Inspired by *Miss Lonelyhearts*, Nathanael West's novel about a depressed advice columnist, the Mailer-Malaquais script is the story of two disc jockeys, Peter Pity and Victor Vision. By happenstance, the two receive a record from someone seeking advice. Eventually, they solicit records on the air, and their show becomes a tremendous success—anticipating the reality television shows of the 2000s. Pity, the Good Samaritan, is eventually killed by a guest on the show. They worked on the script for a month and produced ninety pages. When they showed it to Goldwyn, he had already begun conversations with Montgomery Clift and Charles Boyer about playing the lead roles. But as Malaquais recalled, "He wanted it changed so that good sentiments would be rewarded and bad sentiments would be punished." Mailer remonstrated with Goldwyn, telling him that he was a professional writer and would not have his work tampered with by hacks. He harrumphed on for a good while until Goldwyn said, "Mailer, please stop this professional writer shit, and start writing," a comment Mailer came to relish. Then Goldwyn offered to buy the script. They refused and retained the rights. In retrospect, Mailer said that the script "stank. It was half-art, half-commercial, the sort of thing you can delude yourself about for a long time." After Goldwyn's death, Mailer said that he "treated me well—if eccentrically—hurrah!—and I remain outrageously fond of his memory." The same week in late November that the break with Goldwyn occurred, he got a letter from his father.

Given his huge royalties and his father's unquenchable gambling habit, Mailer had been half expecting the letter. Barney's opening line was: "I want you to give me a *loan* of $3,000.00! OUCH!!" He went on to say that he knew he was putting his request "rather brusquely and this carries with it the appropriate sense of alarm. Well, there is no alarm, and if I put it this way, it's only that I want to get around that old characteristic of mine of being timid when it comes to asking a favor of my son—or anyone else. Call it false pride—or what you will, but I always seem to go through a sense of shameful emotions when I have to ask you for a monetary favor." He drops his indirections only once, and that is in a doubly underlined and vehement injunction not to tell Fan of this request. The reason for his loan is never mentioned. Mailer answered immediately, on Thanksgiving Day 1949:

> If I ever had any doubt as to where I got my writing ability from, I know now finally that it comes from you. Your last letter was a masterpiece in which every line and every word is perfect—I doubt whether I have ever written two pages as good as that myself.
>
> However, being a practitioner of the written word myself, I have come to understand a little about the emotional processes that go into writing, and so I find that I cannot accept your letter completely. For while it is a masterful document of the English colonel writing to his son about one of those bagatelles—a gambling debt—I finish it by reminding myself that you are not an English colonel but a Jewish accountant in Brooklyn, and that it is time you grew up.
>
> I must confess that I have little hope in this direction. If I had I'd probably spend a great deal of time upbraiding you—I would scream about the three thousand dollars, would appeal to you as a grandfather (the money represents two years of college for Susan) would complain as a son (I figured out today that when I work in Hollywood for a thousand dollars a week, it represents after paying agent's and lawyer's fees, income tax, and subtracting living expenses, no more than three hundred dollars each seven days are saved. Thus this sum represents ten weeks of very unpleasant work to me.) But actually, I've always understood you better than Mother. There's no use upbraiding you because your eyes look away, your mind wanders, and your mouth gets sullen. One's a fool to nag a little boy.

Mailer tells his father he will pay the $3,000 but insists that Barney tell the bookies that this is the last time he will pay. He adds that if Barney tries to invade any of the accounts of the customers of Mailer and Troll, Barney's new accounting firm, "I shall probably let you go to prison, but in any case I shall never speak to you again. And I shall tell Barbara everything." He ends by noting that "my own vices are quite the equal of yours—but because the situation is intolerable, and I do not intend to be burdened with it for the rest of my life." The letter infuriated Barney and he promptly ran up his debt to the bookie to $5,000. Dave Kessler had written Barney off after years of backstopping him and now Mailer, with his new wealth, became Barney's guarantor. He paid his father's debt.

Barney was adamant about keeping Fan in the dark because he had avoided any significant gambling debts during the war years and hoped to establish that he had beaten his addiction. Fan was still vigilant, but whenever she tried to ferret out evidence of Barney playing poker or betting on the ponies, he would parry her probes. On one occasion, Mailer, in a pseudo-British accent, imitated his father's feigned irritation: "Oh Fan, are you going to bring that up again? What's the use of us being together if you are always referring to that former problem?" Mailer used a similarly indignant tone when he was questioned about his infidelities by Norris, his last wife, as she recounts in her memoir, *A Ticket to the Circus*. His infidelities are, in fact, the vices to which he refers in his letter. They are also the reason he believed that he was exactly like his father: he was also a secret addict, not to gambling, but to women.

A few months before his death, he told his biographer, "When in doubt about my motivation, *cherchez la femme*." Barney's double life gave Mailer a model and even sanction for his own. His infidelities were numerous, but they were not motivated solely, or even mainly, by his desire for sex, although it was always strong. His thirst for new experience was the final cause of his duplicities. If risk was involved, so much the better; it added sauce. Lust partnered with curiosity. In his mind, the veins that novelists had been mining for over a century were petering out. Sex and violence were the last lodes. This meant exploring every kind of sexual activity and every sort of violence. There were countervailing factors, of course, and his children and wives (Norris especially); his sister, Barbara; and Fan, the rock of family solidarity, would have a moderating influence on his philandering. Barney played an emblematic role, one not incongruent, as Mailer might have put it, with a comment he made toward the end of his life: "Whatever value my works have comes from my Dad going against the tide. My mother was in the center of the current."

Barney and Fan came to Hollywood in the late fall to see their granddaughter. Mailer squired them around and introduced them to Chaplin, which pleased Fan greatly. But their visit marked the beginning of the Hollywood experiment going sour. Barney pinched a few girls, according to Mickey Knox, including his wife, Georgette, which raised hackles. Malaquais's self-importance and his influence on her son angered Fan. She said he was "a sponger" who was taking advantage of him. But Bea, who didn't like Malaquais at first, finding him to be pompous, came to admire his intellectual qualities. "I even fell a little bit in love with him," she remembered. At the same time, she seemed to be falling out of love with her husband. Fan believed Bea "was the unhappiest woman in the world" because of the adulation her husband received.

At Christmas, the Mailers threw a party and invited a large crowd. "It was," Mailer said, "the nearest I ever came to having a Hollywood celebrity party." He sent telegrams to anyone he thought might want to meet the author of *Naked and the Dead.* Humphrey Bogart was there, as were Chaplin, Goldwyn, Clift, Ginger Rogers, Cecil B. DeMille, Elizabeth Taylor, Adolphe Menjou, Fredric March, John Huston, Jean and Galy, Mickey Knox, John Ford, Victor McLaglen, Gene Kelly and Betsy Blair, and Winters, who came with Marlon Brando. Before the night was over Malaquais had gotten into an argument with Chaplin about the United States and Russia. Chaplin's position was that each country should have its own sphere of influence, which Malaquais found laughable. "Look, Mr. Chaplin," Malaquais said, "as far as being an actor, you are [a] genius, but when it comes to politics, you are a nincompoop." Malaquais' candor seems to have endeared him to Chaplin, who later invited him to dinner. Accounts of the party do not entirely agree, but one incident, reported by Winters, points to the ambiguous position that Mailer now occupied in Hollywood. When Brando started to leave, Mailer came up to him and encouraged him to stay. Brando responded, "Norman, what the fuck are you doing here? You're not a screenwriter. Why aren't you on a farm in Vermont writing your next novel? What kind of shit is this?" But he did not immediately take Brando's advice.

He still wanted to see *Naked* made into a film. Shortly after the party, the Mailers rented a fourteen-room house at 7475 Hillside Drive, in the Hollywood Hills, where the parties continued.

"Norman had an enormous reputation in that town," Knox said, "as the first young writer to come out of the war." In poker terms, his reputation was his stack, and he was prepared to bet it. After Mailer returned Goldwyn's advance, he planned to sell the screenplay elsewhere. But word got around that things had soured with Goldwyn, and its appeal diminished. When the deal with Lancaster and Hecht disintegrated, he tried to sell *Naked* to the big studios or independent producers, but had no success. He and Malaquais looked for more screenwriting work and almost landed a job at Twentieth Century-Fox, but that also fell through. There were daily meetings and lunches with actors, executives, and producers, all to no avail. When Hellman told him in late 1949 that she was abandoning her effort to turn *Naked and the Dead* into a Broadway play, it was just one more disappointment. Mailer was learning that reputation was a bubble.

He knew he had to finish *Barbary Shore* (the title refers to the oncoming barbarism of totalitarianism) and got back to work on it in mid-March. Malaquais had finished translating *Naked* by then and in early April he and Galy left town, hastened perhaps by the sour mood in the house. The Mailers knew their time in Lotus Land was coming to an end. At the end of March, he told his parents that "the whole Hollywood venture has turned out to be a fairly sad mistake." To Fig, he was more direct: "Hollywood stinks," he said, and then opened up about his deteriorating relationship with Bea. She has become "the Mother," he said. "Never sleeps at night, pushes me around. I just carry a fucking guilt complex all the time." The baby, however, gave him cheer. Susan is cute, he said, and laughs a lot. They left California in early May, driving to Chicago, where Mailer was introduced to Nelson Algren, who took him to see a police lineup. He wrote to Barbara that Algren's *The Man with the Golden Arm* "is the best novel written in America" since *Naked*, and he and Algren saw each other more than once when Mailer visited Chicago. After a brief stay in Brooklyn, the Mailers went to Provincetown from June 1 through the end of September.

OVER THE NEXT six decades, he would summer on Cape Cod all but a handful of years. The house where he stayed in 1950, and again in 1960, the Joseph Hawthorne house on Miller Hill Road, stands at one of the highest points in Provincetown. He described it in "Advertisements for Myself on the Way Out," the prologue to a novel about a hipster named Marion Faye that he never finished.

> The house Marion purchased was on a sand dune behind the last hill overlooking the town, and it was isolated, especially in fall and winter, reached by a sandy road that dipped down one dune and up another to give a view of rolling furze, rain water ponds, and the ocean and beach of the back shore. In bad weather the wind was a phenomenon, a New England wind of the lost narrow faiths that slashed through open doors, tempted shutters loose from their catch and banged them through the night, vibrated every small pane in every Cape Cod window and came soughing out of the sky with the cries of storm water in its vaults—on such nights the hundred years of the house were alive with every murderous sleep it had ever suffered: it was the kind of house in which the dogs barked insanely in bad weather, and the nurse could not rest, and the baby awoke in hysterical terror at one in the morning while the mother would feel dread at the hundred rages of her husband beside her in marriage sleep, and the house shifted and swayed to the wind like a ship in the north Atlantic seas, yes it seemed to contain every emotion that had died a frustrated death in its rooms and walls through a hundred New England winters.

The passage reflects the pain and regret Mailer remembered from those months in Provincetown in 1950. When he went into the Old Colony Bar, he was surrounded by admirers, young women among them, who were as interested in one-night stands as was the handsome young author with a wife and a baby waiting for him in the house on the hill. Bea, having abandoned novel writing, was working seriously on piano playing, and was also translating a long political document, "Socialism and Barbary," written by Malaquais and some Trotskyite associates.

He pushed ahead on the novel, working in the mornings and producing three pages of typescript a day. When Fan and Barney came for a visit in July, they "almost drove me nuts," he wrote to Adeline in Chicago, "and I acted like a complete bastard, almost incapable of being civil to either of them." In a letter to his sister he castigates her for spending time reading Henry Miller, who, he said, "fulfills none of the qualifications of the serious writer." This is precisely what Mailer was straining to be in the summer of 1950: a class-conscious, committed-to-social-change writer. As he told Harvey Breit in 1951, "If a writer really wants to be serious he has to become intellectual, and yet nothing is harder." Henry Miller was a serious writer and social critic with a prose style that Mailer would come to envy, but Miller loathed politics. When Mailer rediscovered him in the 1970s, he would elevate him to the high plateau of literary eminence occupied by his literary heroes: Farrell, Dos Passos, Hemingway, and Melville. But in 1950 he saw Miller's Rabelaisian adventures as frivolous.

He finished the second draft of *Barbary Shore* on August 15, and in October they moved to Putney, Vermont, not far from where they had lived in 1949. It was a last attempt to salvage the marriage. For $9,000, they bought a 150-year-old farmhouse with a dozen rooms and a big barn. But it put the left-wing couple into a guilty mood: "To own something! Oh, Christ. We'll probably have to be psychoanalyzed." (Undergoing psychoanalysis was something that Mailer began to consider during this period.) His absorption in the failure of the Russian Revolution and its aftermath is reflected in the novel's lengthy debates between McLeod, an ex-Soviet agent now to the left of Trotsky, and a sadistic FBI agent, Leroy Hollingsworth, in a Brooklyn boardinghouse. Hollingsworth's protracted effort to gain McLeod's confession finally succeeds. But Mailer felt, as he said later, as if he was "not writing the book myself," but that it was being written by his unconscious, which "was much more interested in other matters: murder, suicide, orgy, psychosis, all the themes I discuss in *Advertisements* [*for Myself*]. Since the gulf between these conscious and unconscious themes was vast and quite resistant to any quick literary coupling, the tension to get a bridge across resulted in the peculiar feverish hothouse atmosphere of the book."

The gulf was hardly bridged and even Mailer's most enthusiastic readers were disappointed. The novel is set in Brooklyn Heights and the narrator, Mickey Lovett, an amnesiac war veteran, whose roots are as cauterized as Mailer's, lives in an attic room identical to the one where he wrote *Naked and the Dead.* Mrs. Guinevere, described by critic Philip Bufithis as "brazen, touchy, touching, trifling, pathetic and gamey . . . bewildered and bewildering," is modeled on Mailer's buxom, redheaded Irish landlady, whose curves, according to Norman Rosten, were hard to miss. McLeod's political philosophy is derived root and branch from Malaquais, but his self-lacerating Irish wit, obsessive neatness, and "quinine tongue" came from Charlie Devlin. He later said that he put "Malaquais' philosophy in Devlin's body." McLeod's long-windedness also belongs to Malaquais, who could hold the floor for hours in debate. What completely destroyed any small chance the novel had for a sympathetic reception was timing: it was published on May 24, 1951, less than a year after the start of the Korean War, a period when anything that offered a socialistic alternative was abominated.

The anticommunist fervor of the time, and the novel's mash-up of a plot, combined to produce the worst reviews he would ever receive. Consider: three ex-Trotskyites (Lovett, McLeod, and Lannie Madison, a mad Cassandra still in mourning for the murder of "the man with a beard"—Trotsky—by "the man with a pipe"—Stalin) and Hollingsworth, are all sexually and/or romantically linked with Mrs. Guinevere, who writes hilarious movie treatments about a doctor with "the biggest whang on him in the whole town, and maybe he don't know it." The five chief characters visit each other's rooms at all hours to smoke countless cigarettes and talk about politics and history until the last third of the novel, where McLeod makes an interminable, polemical-hortatory confession speech, after which Hollingsworth offers him a slot in a protection program if he will surrender the unnamed but priceless object—Guinevere calls it a "thingamajig"—that he stole from the FBI office where he worked after giving up his job as one of Stalin's hangmen. After much back-and-forth and gnashing of teeth, McLeod refuses, passes the revolutionary torch and the object to Lovett, and is shot by agents.

The uniformly strong praise that Mailer had received for the debates between Hearn and Cummings in *Naked and the Dead* led him to build his second novel around another debate, albeit a far more protracted one, between McLeod and Hollingsworth. One need only compare the symbolic power of the objects on which the respective plots turn—the hornet's nest and the thingamajig—to see how Mailer, honorably and in places brilliantly, stumbled in his second outing. Nevertheless, *Barbary Shore* was an advance in one important way. He had begun to use language differently. In *Naked*, there are masterful descriptions of physical action, but there are also turgid and repetitive stretches, and his style is greatly dependent on Dos Passos, Farrell, and Thomas Wolfe. In his second novel, style became more important and he began to see prose as more than a conveyor of content. While he would always have reservations about style for its own sake, he now saw that style as a considered reflection of self was a great, if elusive, good. He would not fully achieve his characteristic style until several years later.

The completion of the final draft of the novel in January 1951 coincided with the breakup of the marriage. Bea was reading Simone de Beauvoir's *Second Sex* and trying to write a book that Mailer said "would have been a precursor of Women's Liberation" if she had finished it. She tried painting and gave it up. They had visitors but Bea was miserable. "Here I was with this darling little girl, the house was so gorgeous, and we had very interesting friends—writers and artists," she said, but "I was a very depressed woman. It just wasn't my bag to be the wife of a famous man without a life of my own." At Mailer's suggestion, she began to think about a career as a doctor, and eventually became a psychiatrist. He was similarly miserable. Later, he said that one reason the marriage fell apart was that Bea "was a very strong woman."

> She was perfectly prepared to go out and work for years in order to make enough money for me to stay at home and write a good many books. And if that happened, we probably would have been a happy couple of that sort, she the strong one, I the gentle one. Then what happened? I became successful so suddenly I got much more macho. My God, nothing like success for increasing the size of your muscle! I literally went from 140 to 180 pounds in one year—it wasn't all fat, it was muscle. I suddenly felt like a strong man. That altered everything between us.

THERE WERE SEVERAL meetings at Rinehart about *Barbary Shore*. They were not happy occasions, but trips were an excuse to leave Putney. Sometimes he brought Susan with him and stayed with his parents in Brooklyn. One evening in February 1951, he and Dan Wolf were deep into a bottle at the East 64th Street apartment that Mailer had borrowed. "Norman was making one of his big moves," Wolf said. The breakup with Bea was impending and he could smell freedom. Wolf told him about a beautiful Spanish-Peruvian woman he knew named Adele Morales, an aspiring painter who made her living constructing papier-mâché displays for department store windows. She and Wolf had been lovers for a short time and Wolf's friend Ed Fancher had more or less lived with her for three years. She was just coming off a brief affair with Jack Kerouac. Mailer was intrigued. It was late, but Wolf called her and invited her over for a drink. Mailer got on the phone and read her a quotation from Fitzgerald's unfinished novel, *The Last Tycoon*. Monroe Stahr, the novel's protagonist, is beginning an affair with Kathleen Moore, the ex-mistress of a king. He feels something stirring: "He listened inside himself as if something by an unknown composer, powerful and strange and strong, was about to be played for the first time." Adele was moved and agreed to take a cab and meet him. "How could I know that Scott Fitzgerald, Norman Mailer, and that cab ride would change my life forever?" she later wrote.

Because he was thinking about writing his next novel about Hollywood, it is almost impossible to imagine that *The Last Tycoon* did not give Mailer a push in that direction. His portrait of Charles Francis Eitel, the movie director protagonist of *The Deer Park*, clearly owes a debt to Fitzgerald's Stahr. Several weeks earlier, he had written to George Landy, his agent, about getting him a screenwriting job in Hollywood. He would prefer something light, not a war film, he wrote. "A thriller, a western (Sam Croft is my credentials) and preferably a polish job, although I don't care. Actually, I'll take anything." What he really wanted was a chance to get more material for the novel.

Experience for Mailer and many of his contemporaries—James Jones, Saul Bellow, William Styron, and Jack Kerouac, certainly—had a talismanic quality. Dust jackets of American novels from the 1930s to the early 1960s typically bragged about the author's experiences as a short-order cook, reporter, fisherman, hobo, farmworker, and, after World War II, veteran. A college education wasn't a drawback, but a working knowledge of Crane, London, Lewis, Steinbeck, Hemingway, Dos Passos, and—the key figure—Thomas Wolfe was much more important. Coming from Boston or Philadelphia was suspect. Brooklyn or Chicago or Middletown, U.S.A., was much better. The idea was to rebel against mean-spirited Puritanism, do a hitch in the service and then bum around the country, working here and there, loafing and observing your soul, reading tattered copies of the Viking portable authors and writing lyrical but realistic prose about the view from boxcars as you rumbled through the great, mysterious American night. Then, as a matter of course, came discovery, publication, white-hot fame, Hollywood, and a long happily-ever-after. If no writer ever had such a storybook experience, Mailer and James Jones came closer than anyone else.

Mailer learned that a first novel by Jones was receiving the kind of intense publicity from Scribner's that *Naked and the Dead* had received from Rinehart—the kind that *Barbary Shore* was not getting, as he ruefully noted. When he read the galleys of Jones's *From Here to Eternity*, he was more than routinely impressed. "It knocked me down, almost knocked me out," he said. "All the while I was reading it, I had a sinking feeling, 'Well, you're no longer the most talented writer to come out of World War II. You've been replaced.' " He gave it a blurb.

> It's a big fist of a book with powerful virtues and serious faults, but if the very good is mixed with the sometimes bad, those qualities are inseparable from the author. Jones writes with a wry compassionate anger which is individual and borrows from no writer I know. I think his book is one of the best of the "war novels," and in certain facets is perhaps the best.

They met soon afterward in New York and enjoyed each other's company. "It always gave me a boost to know that Jim was in town," Mailer said. They almost had to become friends, he said, because they shared unique experiences. Both were young and had written war novels set in the Pacific; both books enjoyed fantastic sales and reviews; both writers became famous overnight. "So in a certain sense," Mailer said, "we felt like the touchdown twins." Although it would be brief, his relationship with Jones would be the most intense male friendship of his life.

HE AND ADELE were immediately attracted when they met that first night. After Dan Wolf went to sleep, they made love. In the morning, Adele had an impulse to leave, but then she recalled the "incredible explosion" of the night before, and wanted "this half-stranger all over again, his sweet-smelling body and his beautiful cock inside me." She decided it was not a one-night stand. "What I gave and took was not to be discarded with last night's drinks. He was happy, I could see it in his face, and so was I." His recollection was much the same: "It was intense on the first night, very. Very. It was a memorable first night."

> I'd had a few affairs while I was with Bea, but almost always these affairs, the sexuality was sort of analogous to my own, in other words, you could pump it up, you could tone it down, you could control it. It was very much under one's control. With Adele, there was this feeling that it was never under her control. There was a power that took her over. And so it was the first passion I'd really encountered. And mind you, a lot of people [would] say, "What? There he was, what was his age?" Most people don't realize there's very few passionate women in the world. Especially in modern times, I don't know about ancient times, or medieval times or the Renaissance, or the Enlightenment. But by now, given the double impact of religious orthodoxy and civilization itself, a great many women see sex as something that is best controlled. And so that was the startling element in the relationship with Adele.

The affair was headlong; his marriage was over. By the end of March, he and Bea had agreed to separate and sell the house in Putney. He sublet the 64th Street apartment and was spending the majority of his time there, with Adele sleeping over regularly.

All during this time, he was mulling his idea for a Hollywood novel, but didn't want to begin it until *Barbary Shore* came out and he had absorbed the blows that he was anticipating. In the meantime, he needed to work. In January, he had done a longish piece, "The Meaning of Western Defense," written in "the third-rate Eighteenth Brumaire style" of Marx, for an English symposium on the West's military preparedness against a possible Soviet attack. Mounting a strong defense would only enrage the Russians, he argued, ergo, "Western Defense has the ultimate and abominable meaning of Western annihilation." A month later, he again confirmed his anti-Stalinist Marxism when, in answer to a question about the nature of his humanism, he said he was an atheistic humanist, and added that "the particular equipment of writers like myself, to wit, Marx and Freud, are more of a cross than a crutch when it comes to embodying what one has learned from them in one's work," a point made less gently in the reviews of *Barbary Shore*.

The Mailer and Silverman families learned of the split in April when Mailer wrote to Dave and Anne to announce it. "We had a good marriage," he said, "but now it is best we part." They divided the money in the bank, and Bea went to Mexico with a new boyfriend, Steve Sánchez, a student at the New School she had met through Dan Wolf. Susan, who was not yet two, would remain for a time in Brooklyn with Fan and Barney. While Mailer was absorbed with Adele, he still had time to answer a letter from Lois Wilson, who had asked him to come to San Francisco for a visit. He said that he found himself "liking you immensely, maybe even loving you a little," and would "love to have your round sweet ass under my hands." But, he concluded, "I find it not possible to love two or three girls at once." Adele had captured him.

Neither Mailer nor his editors at Rinehart were prepared for the almost unrelieved nastiness of the reviews, which ran ten to one unfavorable. *Time* labeled the novel "small-beer *Nineteen Eighty-Four*" and called the novel "paceless, tasteless and graceless," a phrase that became etched on the tablets of Mailer's memory. Anthony West in *The New Yorker* said that the novel had "a monolithic, flawless badness, like Mussolini's play about Napoleon." Even the tepid praise of leftist critics like Irving Howe and Harvey Swados was mixed with negatives. The novel's overelaborated political debate and dithering plot pleased no one, although some of the characters—Mrs. Guinevere, especially—were found to be imaginatively drawn. The British reviews, coming after the book's publication by Jonathan Cape in January 1952, were slightly better. V. S. Pritchett praised it, saying that Mailer was "the most interesting American novelist to appear since the war." In some of the reviews, in both the United States and England, there was some tentative cheering for a novelist trying to break new ground. Trying to make lemonade out of lemons, someone at Rinehart had the idea of running excerpts from the best and the worst reviews side by side. It was a technique that Mailer would rely on for the remainder of his career, usually with excerpts that he personally chose. In the case of *Barbary Shore*, it may have helped a bit: the novel did make the bestseller list for three weeks after it was published on May 24. Jones's *From Here to Eternity* had made number one two months earlier and remained in first place for a month after Mailer's novel had disappeared. The success of *From*

Here to Eternity would give Mailer the desire to write a new novel that would top Jones.

Mailer had hoped that Malaquais, to whom the novel is dedicated, would find some merit in the book. After all, he and Malaquais belonged to "a party of two," on the left wing of Trotskyism. "I took up that position with great relief because it was an island," Mailer said. "You really could be against everything, but with an inner purity of soul." But his mentor was also a critic of exacting standards, and he found fault. "It's a political tract, not a novel," Malaquais said. "You don't make a novel with political themes or you have to be a genius. I didn't like the book and I told Norman so." But he did not give his opinion until almost two months after the book and the reviews appeared. Malaquais said he had not written earlier because he didn't know what address to use. Mailer responded by noting that Malaquais could have found it easily enough: "But I rather suspect that your most infuriating vice—the pomp and false dignity of a third rate Central American diplomat came to the fore—and you probably thought, 'I, Jean Malaquais, do not write a letter to be forwarded like a common beggar.' " The reviews angered and depressed him, he told Malaquais. He called the reviewers "first-rate cocksuckers," and ended defiantly, "Fuck them. If I'm any good, I'll last no matter what they write, and if I'm not any good, it doesn't matter." He began to wonder for the first time since his sophomore year at Harvard if he was really a writer, and if he shouldn't consider other occupations. He signed his letter, "The Misunderstood Genius." The fall of 1951 was one of the low points of his life.

He had recently rented a loft at 85 Monroe Street between the Brooklyn Bridge and Grand Street on the Lower East Side. It was a tough neighborhood and he used to carry a roll of quarters in each hand when walking home at night, his version of brass knuckles. One hundred feet long, twenty-five wide, and four flights up, the loft cost $30 a month. Such a loft, with rows of windows overlooking the East River, would be where Sergius O'Shaugnessy lives and runs his bullfighting school in his 1958 short story "The Time of Her Time." From March to mid-June, Mailer divided his time between the loft and the sublet apartment on 64th Street. Until the Putney house sold the following spring, he let Jean and Galy use it. Adele thought Mailer handled the reviews well, but saw "an underlying anger and depression." He bought her new clothes, a lot of black velvet, she recalled, and took her to a party where she met Charlie Chaplin, who told her she was beautiful. She said she got a good idea of what Bea had gone through at parties. "Women flirted with him, boldly," Adele said, "as if I wasn't there."

To prepare for the Hollywood novel, he decided he needed to go there again. Mickey Knox was driving to Hollywood to see his girlfriend, Lois Andrews, and Mailer joined him, planning to see Lois Wilson. Years later, he said he had another reason for going. He wasn't ready to commit to Adele and was "looking for action"—women. When they got close to California, Mailer asked if they could detour so he could see the resort town of Palm Springs, where Hollywood stars and moguls often vacationed. Knox said that they spent only about twenty minutes in the town and then got back on the highway. When he read *The Deer Park* a few years later, he saw that Mailer had caught the town's architecture, landscape, and character with amazing accuracy.

In Hollywood, he and Knox rented an apartment on North Vine, where Mailer saw old friends. Knox introduced him to Andrews, whom he used as a model for Dorothea O'Faye in *The Deer Park*. He took notes, and soaked up all he could over the two weeks he was there, but was unable to find any studio work. Shortly after he arrived, he spent a night in bed with two women and told Adele about it in a letter. She was upset and retaliated by going to bed with a man and his wife. She wrote to Mailer about it and when he returned in mid-July, they fought. She told him that she had done it out of jealousy. As so often happened, they made up in bed. "Later," she said, "he told me he had walked around for so many years feeling dead inside, feeling nothing, but I had changed that." Within two weeks of his return, they decided to have a party in the Monroe Street loft so Adele could meet all his friends.

According to Malaquais, about fifty people came to the party. He and Galy had driven down from Vermont, and Fig and Ecey had come all the way from Arkansas. Dan Wolf was there and several actors attended, including Montgomery Clift, Kevin McCarthy, Marlon Brando, and Rita Moreno, who came with Brando. Lillian Hellman came, and also a young southern novelist named Calder Willingham, art dealer Richard Bellamy, and other of Adele's friends from her painting classes. Adele said the party was "a mingling of personalities, painters, beat poets, writers, actors, critics, a lot of brains, sex appeal, beautiful women, and extra men, good talk against a background of laughter, the clinking of ice cubes in glasses and jazz on the radio." The party went well until about two A.M. when four or five local thugs crashed in. They were looking for a woman who had said something negative to them on the street, a guest at the party. Mailer tried to reason with them to no avail; one of them had a hammer and Mailer took two whacks to the head. He was staggering and bleeding, but still able to fight, he said later. Adele screamed and chased the gang out. Mailer wore a bandage on his head for a time and told his mother he'd gotten hurt in a taxicab accident. After that night, Adele was terrified of the neighborhood and wanted to give up the Monroe Street loft.

In August, they went to Provincetown and stayed in a seaside apartment on Commercial Street. Because of her painter friends, Adele was as well known as Mailer. He took part in a Provincetown Art Association panel on censorship with Dwight Macdonald, Willem de Kooning, and Edmund Wilson, the esteemed literary critic and friend of F. Scott Fitzgerald's, who summered in nearby Truro. At the time, Mailer said, Wilson "was the nearest thing to Jehovah" in his mind. Dwight Macdonald had nude beach parties in Truro (later satirized by Saul Bellow in his 1975 novel, *Humboldt's Gift*), and Adele remembers "the sight of paunchy, aging bodies, sipping martinis, engaged in conversations as if they were fully dressed." Macdonald, she said, "with his white goatee, a long string bean of a body, and his cute little pot belly," was a sight. For a month, Adele painted and he worked on *The Deer Park*. After Labor Day, they returned to New York and moved to a "grim apartment, renovated in battleship grey" at 14 Pitt Street in Manhattan, not far from the Williamsburg Bridge. For his living space, Mailer alternated between beat-up bohemian lofts and handsome country houses.

Shortly after moving in, he was cheered by a letter from a young novelist, Vance Bourjaily, who wrote to him with praise for *Barbary Shore* and comments about the difficulties of writing second novels. Mailer had read about Bourjaily's 1947 novel, *The End of My Life*, in John Aldridge's 1951 book, *After the Lost Generation: A Critical Study of the Writers of Two Wars*, in which he and Bourjaily had been affirmed as important writers, along with Gore Vidal; expatriate Paul Bowles, author of *The Sheltering Sky*; and Truman Capote, whose slim gothic novel, *Other Voices, Other Rooms*, was published just a few months before *Naked and the Dead*. Aldridge's study had been praised by Mailer's Harvard mentor, Robert Gorham Davis, on the front page of the same issue of *The New York Times Book Review* that contained a surly review of *Barbary Shore*. When Aldridge's work was reprinted in 1985, Mailer wrote an introduction in which he said that Aldridge's study had given him a much needed sense of identity at the time. Aldridge soon became a friend—introduced by Bourjaily—and Mailer's most important admirer in the critical world for over forty years.

Mailer wrote back to Bourjaily with thanks for his kind words on *Barbary Shore*, adding, "The reviews were depressing, economically as well as psychically," and that he made himself go through his novel again "to remind myself that it's not all bad." A few months later when James Jones was in New York, Bourjaily telephoned him and said that Jones was visiting him. Mailer invited them over to his cold-water flat on Pitt Street for a drink. He recalled their first meeting: "In those days," Mailer recalled, "Jones was an avatar of energy."

> His presence could certainly fill any small room. The variety of his small-town personality was not only canny and overbearing, but also as warm as your best buddy. It felt like a great new kid had just moved onto the block. How rich was his simplicity—his was the wisdom of a good redneck. No doubt about it, he made Vance and me feel pale, establishmentarian, and much too modest by comparison.
>
> But we all got drunk. That equaled us out. By twilight, we were the best of friends. And on the rise of this good musketeer spirit, three good writers ready to tackle all the ugly asinine powers above, we got candid with each other. Finally, Jones asked, "Vance, do you ever cheat on your wife?"
>
> Now you had to know how cool Vance was in those days. He never showed his hand. . . . We had, however, forged a mood. Vance's belief in those days (it may still be active) was that there were few things as unattractive and dispiriting as being the man to kill a good mood. So he looked up, and a glint of divine or diabolical light came into his eye, and he said, "Yes! Whenever and wherever I can," and these being the lost years of rampant male authority (it feels like a millennium ago!) we all roared and hit another belt of booze and felt for a godly half-hour like the swashbucklers we were not, not quite.

A few weeks later, Mailer introduced Jones to Montgomery Clift at a party at Bourjaily's apartment in Greenwich Village. Clift always claimed that it was at that party that he and Jones talked about making a film of *From Here to Eternity*. The film's huge success—it won eight Oscars including Best Picture—undoubtedly helped reignite Mailer's desire to see *Naked* made into a film.

By October he had 240 pages of the new novel, but he was dissatisfied with the draft, which he later said was "the worst writing I had ever done." He then turned "dispiritedly" to short stories. The easiest topic for him was the army, and by the end of 1951 he had turned out three stories, "The Paper House" (based on a story about a geisha house told to him by Bourjaily), "The Dead Gook," for which he drew on his memory of the Filipino Huks he had fought with in Luzon, and "The Language of Men," a story about an army cook, his most autobiographical short story. He wrote all three in a day or two each, his idea being that if he couldn't finish a story in one day, it wasn't meant to be written. If one made a bad bet on the direction of one's plot, he said, it would mean the wastebasket and new beginning. Therefore, when writing a novel, he said, "I move ahead like a banker, careful not to lose the investment of my work." Cy Rembar tried unsuccessfully to sell the stories to some of the most prestigious fictional outlets of that time: *The New Yorker, Harper's Bazaar, Vogue,* and *Mademoiselle.*

Mailer turned a small contretemps with Adele into another story, "The Notebook." They had exchanged angry words after an old friend of hers paid too much attention in a restaurant. When he began recording the incident in the small notebook he always carried, Adele became more upset and told him, "You were just watching yourself be angry, taking notes on your emotional condition." She sulked for the rest of the walk home. He turned the situation into a gem, the narrative equivalent of a mirror held up to a mirror. The story's narrator is castigated by his girlfriend, much as Adele snapped at Mailer, for being "nothing but a notebook," after which she stomps off, "her high heels mocking her misery in their bright tattoo upon the sidewalk." He asks himself if he started the fight so he could record it, and then "considers this, priding himself on the fact that he would conceal no motive from himself, no matter how unpleasant." As he runs after her, he rehearses how he will justify his incessant notebook jottings, and then asks himself if his explanation is for her or for the notebook. He stops and makes another entry. The story also underlines one clause in his credo, traceable all the way back to the notebooks he kept at

Harvard: a promise never to hide his motives from himself, no matter how ignoble.

AFTER A WEEK-LONG ski trip with Adele in early January 1952 to Stowe, Vermont, he started a brief untitled journal. He was still working on the short stories, and Lillian Ross had promised him a reading by a top editor at *The New Yorker*, but he devalued the stories to Ross. He always believed he was a "journeyman" in the form. He was experimenting with marijuana a bit, the beginning of a long love affair with the drug, and the journal has some entries about his experiences while smoking it. His actions puzzle him: "I will be so nice to people, so desperately determined to make them like me, and yet will be driven to give false romantic pictures of my own degeneration. How deeply I must be convinced of how uninteresting I am." The journal is studious in detailing what he called his "irrationality." The two chief topics of the journal, however, are his relationship with Adele and his ideas for a new novel. The two are more than just temporally linked, as the following excerpts from the journal demonstrate. He interrogates his feelings about Adele the day after asking her to stand naked before him.

> She is so beautiful, her pointed breasts, her firm buttocks, her long back, her dark skin which does look golden even though I always feel as if I'm lying when I use the word to her. And yet she's beautiful as a Gauguin and all fuck. It is the adolescent hungers which never die, the idea that I am making love to a woman who is all fuck, who exists only to deploy herself sensually for me which furnishes such excitement. I suppose always we make love in obeisance to our adolescent archetypes. Certainly Adele does. She enjoys sex so much because it is dirty to her, because she is raped, ravished, taken, ground into nothing, and repaid with the sweetest kind of pleasure. It is probably the nature of women when all superstructure and complexity is cut away to be naturally, amoral whore and tender mother. It is why Adele is so womanly.

In the next paragraph, he says that what he has written is false to a degree because he has left out something: "I hate her often for her social inadequacies which make me feel bound (how romantic!) to a lower level of the world than I aspire to—dinner parties in the East Sixties which I give?" After this admission, he says that "even if I hurt her often, I like her, I wish her well, I feel tender toward her." Through several more long entries through the end of March, when the journal ceases, Mailer traces the sinuousities of their relationship. He never mentions Pygmalion, although in her memoir, *The Last Party*, Adele says that he had "an intense need to play Pygmalion" but that she "resisted the role of Galatea." From Mailer's journal:

> *January 14:* As a writer, these have been the worst months of my life. Nothing breaks through, no ideas with any fluency, nothing seems to develop. I'm living in a vacuum. How long can it possibly continue.
>
> *January 15: Idea for a novel.* About Adele written in first or third person, somewhat in the manner of [Alberto Moravia's 1949 novel] The Woman of Rome, about a Greenwich Village girl, and what happens to her, the milieu she passes through, the qualities and lacks she feels in her life.
>
> *January 16:* Adele told me last night that she's been having fantasies of going into a convent, i.e., getting religious first and then convent—probably from [Graham Greene's 1951 novel] The End of the Affair. Also of dropping everything, job and all, and going to a strange city. Also, of murdering me, and then committing suicide.
>
> *January 17:* In comfort station in subway, a man taking a piss wonders if the man next to him is a homosexual, then wonders if the man next to him suspects him in turn. Then has a moment of interest in the fate of poor driven subway homosexuals, remembers an episode from his childhood when a man had sat next to him, and had wanted to suck his cock.
>
> *February 5:* For the omnibus novel: One of the lives—the life of crime. The end of the novel might be found in the life of resistant action to the powers that be—take the quote from Zola—but the problem is to find the definite action. Always the problem for today's novels. The quote: "Ah, to live indignant, to live enraged at treacherous arts, at false honor, at universal mediocrity! To be unable to read a newspaper without paling in anger! To feel the continual and irresistible need of crying aloud what one thinks, above all when one is alone in thinking it, and to be ready to abandon all the sweets of life for it."

Toward the end of February he rented a studio in the Ovington Building on Fulton Street in Brooklyn and he took the subway from Pitt Street most days to work there. He was seeing James Jones a lot and had recently met William Styron. Dan Wolf was someone else he saw often during this difficult period. Mailer admired Wolf and confided in him. They also did a fair amount of drinking and carousing together. The new novel still had not come into focus and his affair with Adele was reaching a critical juncture.

> *February 22:* Right now, today, the thing with Adele seems hopeless, with no future. I cannot conceive of myself as married to her. We drag upon each other so, we exhaust each other like leeches turned sucker to sucker. Without sex, I wonder if there would be anything at all in the relationship other than need. Yet a week ago, I felt very much in love with her (for me), I felt no sense of loss in emptying the house in Vermont, I felt warm and close to Adele. Was it only because Jim Jones obviously admired her?
>
> I'm always so afraid of stops on a train, afraid someone will sit next to me, and I shall be forced to talk. It is even more irrational than that—I just don't want a body next to me. This hasn't changed in all the years. In social life I have a crutch, I am Norman Mailer, and I get a false sense of ego, but to be alone on a train, eat in a train diner, and everything intimidates me, including the hostess, the waitress and the other passengers. Once again I am little and ugly.
>
> *March 3:* It's ironic. I sit here and plan a novel or at least the beginning of one, so vast, so comprehensive, that the amount of energy, invention and determination to see it through would be staggering. Yet, never have I felt as lackadaisical, flat, and spiritless. From such beginning could a book come? I note this, only for the odd chance that I may follow it through.
>
> Am I fucking too much? Can this account partially for my washed-out dispirit?

Mailer was not a huge admirer of the women's magazines where Cy was peddling his stories. In 1947, when he was writing *Naked and the Dead*, Adeline had introduced him to Pearl Kazin (Alfred's sister), an editor at *Harper's Bazaar.* "She irritated the hell out of me. She was so super-superior," he recalled. "She read more books; she was more on top of things." When Kazin later wrote to ask if he would care to submit something to the magazine, he wrote back: "Dear Pearl Kazin, I'm still too young and too arrogant to care to write the kind of high-grade horseshit you print in *Harper's Bazaar.*" He was "very happy" to mail that letter, he said. But in early 1952, his arrogance was on a leash. At a cocktail party in early March that he hosted, he met Cyrilly Abels, the managing editor of *Mademoiselle*, where his stories were being considered. A close friend of Katherine Anne Porter's, she was responsible for publishing new young writers such as James Baldwin, Capote, Carson McCullers, and Flannery O'Connor. But she was not immediately taken by his stories. "What a horror she was. I felt like screaming Shit while talking to her about my stories which [she said] were very interesting but not quite right for them," he said. "At one point I had to say something about, 'I know editors always want blood, but what color blood do you want?' " He got drunk after the party and his stories were later turned down. He ends his account of the failure to connect with Abels by saying that he wished he could "forget all this shit connected with short stories." What he really wanted was "to get my teeth into a novel."

FIVE
THE DEER PARK

The next day, a Sunday, he woke with a hangover. Dan Wolf had been at the party and he too was hung over, as he informed Mailer when he called to tell him that he had obtained "a dirty film" from Ed Fancher. Mailer went to Brooklyn to borrow his mother's projector as Adele, her friend Irene Fornes, Dan Wolf, and Rhoda Lazare (whom he would later marry), gathered in Wolf's Village apartment. The DC current in the building blew out the motor and when they put new fuses in the projector, it blew out the power in the entire building. "Just Kafkan," Mailer wrote in the journal. Adele remembered that Norman Rosten had a projector and Mailer rushed back to Brooklyn Heights to borrow it while the rest of the party went to the Pitt Street apartment, which had AC current. They ate, drank, and watched the film several times, and after the others had left, he and Adele watched it again while making love. But the film had "depersonalized us," Mailer said, and the lovemaking was "without personal heat."

After confiding these "hilarious" events to his journal the next day, he had a thought. Perhaps what happened the night before could be recast as a comic prologue to the omnibus novel he was trying to conceptualize. He began making notes. It would be told from the point of view of a novelist thinking about the nature of his profession:

> How the novelist must be paranoid and therefore seeks to fuse with the entire world, how he must have a feminine component to his nature and be obsessed with his masculinity; how he must be terrified of experience and intensely hungry for it; how inferiority and megalomania must alternate in his conception of himself. Is this sufficient to project the novel? Also he must want power, and have no capacity to gain it. Be a narcissist, too.

The vast ambition of this novelist character (who, it must be said, has a good deal in common with his creator) would be realized in a sequence of eight interlocking novels that would explore the following worlds, in this order: pleasure, business, communism, church, the working class, crime, homosexuality, and end with mysticism. The narrator, he wrote in the prologue, "dreams or conceives of himself in many milieu, and traces out his adventures in each milieu with the same set of characters." This scheme, which he said would require "the seat of Zola and the mind of Joyce," was one of the ways Mailer fought off the depression that followed the failure of *Barbary Shore*. Several times over the next half century, including his final years, he came up with ambitious, skeletal plans for multinovel projects as a way of getting started on the next one. The projects were huge, daunting, but not to him; he was energized by their scope and complexity. Robert Lucid called Mailer's bootstrapping efforts "exercises in imagination-isometrics"; they are also reminiscent of Baron Munchausen pulling himself out of the swamp by his own hair.

Mailer plunged in. He retained the novelist as the unidentified narrator, but he is a step removed. The protagonist of the prologue is "a small frustrated man, a minor artist manqué," one Sam Slovoda, who makes his living writing continuity for comic strips, but toys with the idea of writing a novel. The eight novels, in Mailer's conception, were to be stages of the dream he has after watching a pornographic film with his wife and friends. With encouragement from Adele, his sister, Lillian Ross, and Dan Wolf, he wrote "The Man Who Studied Yoga" in a month of hard work, finishing it in early April (the title refers to the old joke about the man who goes to India to study yoga and is told to unscrew his navel whereupon his ass falls off). The 29-page story, perhaps his finest, that grew out of the abandoned prologue, opens with his ghostly narrator speaking: "I would introduce myself if it were not useless. The name I had last night will not be the same as I have tonight. For the moment, then, let me say that I am thinking of Sam Slovoda." We soon see that Sam is nothing close to a heroic figure, but he has one redeeming virtue: he doesn't like himself; he wants to grow.

Overstimulated by the film, Slovoda is displeased with himself for wasting another day. His vision for the enormous novel he hopes to write "lies foundered, rotting on a beach of purposeless effort." As he dozes off, the narrator, who seems to be the shade of a novelist now turned muse, gives Sam an idea: "Destroy time, and chaos may be ordered." Inflamed by this idea, Sam will now dream the first novel of the sequence, which will be devoted to pleasure. He remembers reading about a garden of Louis XV where beautiful virgins were brought to be despoiled by the king. It was called the Deer Park, and Sam's meditation on it in "The Man Who Studied Yoga" reappears as the epigraph to Mailer's pleasure novel of the same name.

Adele will serve as the model for the female protagonist, Elena Esposito, who has affairs with two friends of Charles Eitel's, the male protagonist, before settling into a complicated affair with him. Mailer may have drawn on the director John Huston—beholden to the studio system, but with a deep maverick streak—for some of Eitel's traits. Whatever the case, he now had all he needed to make a new start on *The Deer Park*: a prologue, a vast narrative scheme, and a first novel that would draw on his time in Hollywood, his current Latina lover, and his twenty-minute visit to Palm Springs with Knox. As he was finishing "The Man Who Studied Yoga," he wrote in his journal that he had the strength and optimism to work on the project for years to come, "going into obscurity if that is necessary, indeed even looking forward to that." Most of his energy for the next three and a half years would be expended on *The Deer Park*.

In April 1952 Bea married Steve "Chavo" Sánchez in Mexico, and when Mailer wrote to congratulate her, he said that he had not been in touch earlier because he was revamping the novel. The effort was "agony," he wrote to Fig, but by early May he had established a foothold of thirty pages. He was determined not to go back to the 240-page draft he had shelved; he wanted the new version to be markedly different. Writing to Adeline in late May, he described its style as "quiet, witty, sad." He mentioned to her that he had an article in the May-June *Partisan Review*, his first contribution to what was then considered one of the most significant literary-political journals in the United States. Founded by William Phillips and Philip Rahv in 1934 as a platform for what was sometimes called the "independent left," it became anti-Soviet in the late 1930s. With a circulation never much above ten thousand, it was nonetheless a major force in American intellectual life until the late 1960s when it was overshadowed by *The New York Review of Books*. *Partisan Review*'s notable contributors (most of whom migrated to *The New York Review of Books*), included a number who became friends and/or sparring partners with Mailer: Macdonald, Howe, Rahv, Lowell, Mary McCarthy, Bellow, Baldwin, Diana Trilling, Leslie Fiedler, Cynthia Ozick, Susan Sontag, and Norman Podhoretz.

His inaugural contribution was part of a symposium titled "Our Country and Our Culture." The twenty-five participants were asked by the editors to expound on the current role of writers and whether the old American tradition of nonconformism could or should be maintained, as exemplified by exiles like Henry James and Ezra Pound, whose hostile statements about the barrenness of American life preface the editorial statement. Mailer stated boldly: "I think I ought to declare straightaway that I am in almost total disagreement with the assumptions of this symposium." He derided American intellectuals for moving from social protest to writing uplifting pieces for *Time* and *Life*. The American writer, he said, "is being dunned to become healthy, to grow up, to accept the American reality." Mailer was having none of it. The writer works best in "opposition," he said, and integration into society was "more conducive to propaganda than art."

Of the twenty-five participants on the panel, which included Howe, Margaret Mead, Delmore Schwartz, Arthur Schlesinger Jr., Louise Bogan, Leslie Fiedler, and Lionel Trilling, only Howe was as truculent as Mailer. Howe contacted him after seeing the symposium in print, and asked him to write something for a new left-wing magazine that he and some others were founding. Howe and his colleagues recognized that a mass socialist labor party modeled after those in Europe could not compete with the Democrats or Republicans in the United States, not in the 1950s. *Dissent*, therefore, would try to work within the Democratic Party for some of the goals of socialism, while standing firmly against totalitarian regimes. The first issue appeared in winter 1954 and Mailer's name was on the masthead as a contributing editor. He published three pieces there in 1954, and in 1955 became a member of the editorial board.

In early 1952, Mailer saw Jones and Styron several times. Mickey Knox often joined them, making it a quartet. They hit the bars of the Village and Eighth Avenue in Manhattan, boozing and playing liar's poker for dollars. "We did a prodigious amount of drinking, and there were always flocks of girls around," Styron later wrote. Given his continuing doubts about his writing, Mailer got a kick out of these outings with his peers. Styron said later that there seemed to be "a moratorium on envy" among writers at the time, and much camaraderie, "as if there were glory enough to go around for all the novelists trying to fit themselves into Apollonian niches alongside the earlier masters." Envy may have been absent, but not competition. Knox described a contest Mailer had with Jones: "At the last bar one night, the match finally took place. They sat in a booth facing each other. Their forearms held the middle position for endless seconds." The look on Jones's face "was concentrated determination. He was not going to be put down. He wasn't. He slowly pushed Norman's arm up until they reached the middle position again and it was over: a tie. They unclasped at the same time without a word being said."

One night walking in the Village, Knox recalled, Styron put his arms around the shoulders of his two novelist friends, "joyously announcing, 'Here we are, the three best young writers in America!' Neither Norman nor Jim objected, but let it be noted that they did appear both pleased and embarrassed." "Moving about at night with Jim," Styron said of the writer who would become one of his closest friends, "was like keeping company with a Roman emperor." When the partying wound down, the group would settle into a corner of the bar with their drinks and talk about writers and books, often until the sun came up.

HE WROTE TO Bea, with whom he still had warm relations, about his slow progress. "I seem unable to recapture the kind of simple humanity I had in the best parts of Naked," he said, and characterized his new style as "a kind of lush gargoyle." The root problem, he continued, was that for most of the previous year, "I was convinced that I was through as a writer," which, in turn, made him reflect on the pain Bea had felt at the time of their breakup when she didn't know what to do with her life. Now she was in medical school and committed to a career while he was "irritable, gloomy and feeling quite hopeless in my distaste for myself." He was, however, able to keep the same schedule he had kept for *Naked*: four days a week, seven hours a day.

In early July, he had his appendix removed. He told Bea that he was "seriously fagged" by the operation, and needed time in Provincetown to recuperate. "I need this vacation physically, emotionally, spiritually, and what have you," he said. He and Bea had promised to state frankly in their correspondence any gripes they had, and he ended his sour letter by laying into Bea for telling Fan that "Danny Wolf is a procurer," which was, apparently, her interpretation of Wolf's role in introducing Adele to him. Bea's comment was turning Fan against Adele about whom she already had a low estimate. "I felt very antagonistic to Adele" Fan wrote in 1971. "To me she was an interloper, a plain ignorant girl ready to satisfy Norman's physical needs. How could she ever measure up to my son, a Harvard graduate, a famous author." Mailer's love of his mother was unshakable; he revered her always but ignored her judgments about his male friends and female companions. Fan called the former "bums" and "spongers"; for the women she had harsher language. Adele "was just a plain common sucker," and his relationship with her, she said, was the first big mistake of her son's life.

After his vacation, he learned that his three war stories had been accepted: "The Paper House" by *New World Writing* and "The Language of Men" by *Esquire*, the magazine that Mailer would write more words for than any other over the next half century. The third story, "The Dead Gook," after being rejected by *The New Yorker*, was taken by a new periodical, *Discovery*. Its coeditors, Vance Bourjaily and John Aldridge, sent out a statement of the periodical's goals that tweaked the nose of Time-Life publications by saying that the editors would reject the sort of material that appeared in large-circulation magazines, writing that was "inoffensively general, meeting the romantic needs of the pablum set at both ends of the human life span." The inaugural issue of *Discovery* was printed as a three-hundred-page paperback, and distributed by Pocket Books. Styron had the longest piece in the collection, a novella titled *The Long March,* an account of the killing of eight Marine recruits by misdirected mortar fire during basic training at Camp Lejeune. Mailer admired the story extravagantly and wrote to Styron to tell him so: "I've been meaning to write ever since I read *Long March* about a month ago. I think it's just terrific, how good I'm almost embarrassed to say, but as a modest estimate it's certainly as good an eighty pages as any American has written since the war, and really I think it's much better than that." Styron wrote back a warm letter thanking him and said that he had been influenced by *The Naked and the Dead*, although not revealing where or how. The friendship of the Brooklyn Jew and the Tidewater WASP took a leap after this exchange and would grow even stronger until it blew up in another exchange of letters exactly five years later.

Lillian Ross had continued to encourage Mailer, and he wrote her with praise for her controversial "Portrait of Hemingway," which *The New Yorker* had published two years earlier. He knew she would be aware of *Life* magazine's recent publication of Hemingway's short novel *The Old Man and the Sea*. He liked Hemingway's idea of the old Cuban fisherman's Homeric struggle to land a huge fish, "but I just can't bear his prose," which he said was ripe with "affectation." But what really bothered him was that Hemingway was always implying the following: "I am a great man who happens incidentally to be a great writer. I know that all of you will be interested in my noble, strong, and beautiful attempts to exercise myself as a great man, and will be happy when I succeed except for professors, other writers, and assorted cocksuckers." This was the first time he had put his feelings about the elder writer into words since his Harvard parodies. The earlier work, especially the short stories, *A Farewell to Arms*, and *Death in the Afternoon*, were close to sacred texts, but he had reservations about Hemingway's later books and distaste for his enormous public presence.

By the late 1950s he would reverse himself, however, and praise Hemingway for struggling to "make his personality enrich his works." Looking back at the time when he was rewriting *The Deer Park,* Mailer realized that he was now "one of the few writers of my generation who was concerned with living in Hemingway's discipline, by which I do not mean I was interested in trying for some second-rate imitation of his style, but rather that I shared with Papa the notion, arrived at slowly in my case, that even if one dulled one's talent in the punishment of becoming a man, it was more important to be a man than to be a good writer." A good deal of Mailer's self-reflective writing from *Advertisements for Myself* to *The Fight* would explore the web of relations between personal valor and virtue and literary growth and mastery. In regard to Hemingway, he was inconsistent, lauding him here and socking him there.

In September, he and Adele moved from Pitt Street, but only a few blocks away, to 41 First Avenue, between 2nd and 3rd Streets. The rear windows of the apartment overlooked the New York Marble Cemetery, the oldest public cemetery in the city. The apartment was near Dan Wolf's and next door to Adele's—she had kept her place there even though she was spending most of her nights with Mailer. The First Avenue apartments were sixty feet long and eight to eleven feet wide, what were known as "railroad flats." He and Adele knocked down some interior walls between the apartments, added bookshelves, and painted the walls white. Then he borrowed plumbing tools and with the help of Mickey Knox ran forty feet of gas pipe through three walls, hooked the pipe to a heater, and installed a hot water line and a bathtub. When Lillian Hellman came to a party there one night, climbing six flights to the apartment, he proudly showed off his handiwork. She told him that it was "more impressive than *The Naked and the Dead*," a remark he never forgot. Having learned the skills of carpentry, wiring, and plumbing, he now believed he could make a living with his hands, if necessary. "I don't think Norman was ever happier than he was in that cold-water flat," Adele said. When he wasn't improving the apartment, he was in his Fulton Street studio writing. He still saw *The Deer Park* as the first of eight connected novels, and he intended to start on the second one—devoted to the business world—before polishing the manuscript of the first, leapfrogging in this manner through all eight in the series. The "overall scheme is so grandiose," he wrote to Graham Watson, his British agent, that it was possible he would "steal away from it in terror." By October 1952, he passed the two-hundred-page mark in the manuscript.

He pushed on through November and at the end of the month turned in to Rinehart a manuscript of approximately three hundred pages. It carried a subtitle—"The Search for the Obscene"—crossed out on the title page. He accomplished this while entertaining Susan, who had been visiting for a month. The three-year-old enjoyed her time with her father and Adele and visits with both sets of grandparents. Mailer flew her home to Mexico on December 1—Adele remained in New York—and he enjoyed his first visit with Bea and Steve (as did they) for a week, and then stopping off for a weekend with the Gwaltneys in Little Rock. When he returned, he found out that the Rinehart editors had some large reservations about his manuscript. He pushed back, asking for another reading by an outsider. John Selby, his editor, accepted his recommendation of John Aldridge, who Mailer thought would naturally side with him. Aldridge agreed to do an objective report, despite his friendly relations with Mailer. He was writing as critic, not novel doctor.

The editors approved, Aldridge recalled, "So I wrote the report in that way, and then with great glee they went waving it in Mailer's face." The frank sexual scenes in the book—it was after all a novel about pleasure—didn't bother Aldridge. He wrote that there was nothing in *The Deer Park* that would trouble "anyone above the level of 16-year-old daughters and 70-year-old grandmothers." But the episodes of casual fornication in the novel did bother Rinehart's top editors, and partly because of his mother, they bothered Stanley Rinehart even more. Mailer always believed that behind the scenes, Mary Roberts Rinehart had much to do with her son's intense dislike of the novel. A seventy-six-year-old grandmother of six, and also a director of Rinehart, Inc., Mrs. Rinehart, it can be surmised, detested the idea of seeing her last name on the title page of *The Deer Park*. Aldridge assumed that the crossed-out subtitle revealed the real theme of the book. "Mailer is careful never to deviate" from his search for the obscene, he wrote. "The result of his singlemindedness is that the experience he presents is precisely as dull, mechanical, monotonous, passionless and unobscene to the reader as it is to the characters." Aldridge also said that Mailer had made a terrible mistake in sharing the manuscript with twenty friends and relatives. The fact that he sought such extensive feedback made Aldridge conclude that Mailer "felt an uncertainty and insecurity." These criticisms angered Mailer.

He wrote back to Aldridge that "The Search for the Obscene" was meant to refer to all eight interlocking novels, not merely the first one, which was about the disasters and corruption that flow from a search for mere pleasure. Thus, the strikeover of the words. "You have hardly acted toward me like a friend," he said. In fact, you act "like a sort of literary General MacArthur [Aldridge had a similar profile] delivering harsh pronunciamentos from your high and lonely peak, deriving your pleasure I suspect from the bitter notion that you have been true to yourself, and hang the consequences. The worst of it is that like the good General it gives you such pleasure." Mailer argued vociferously, and defensively, that it was a writer's sole prerogative to show or not show early work in progress. It was none of the critic's business and "Jehovah" Aldridge was unfair to object. But he didn't forget what Aldridge had said, and by the late 1950s had come around to the idea that it was a mistake to let anyone see his manuscripts at an early stage. When work jelled—polished first draft—he would share it with his family, editors, agents, and secretaries, most notably Judith McNally, who worked for him for almost three decades. In later years, he shared his manuscripts with some of his older children and friends, most notably Jean Malaquais; Mickey Knox; scholar-critic Bob Lucid; his lawyer, Ivan Fisher; writer and filmmaker Richard Stratton; and Walter Anderson, editor of *Parade*. His last wife, Norris, saw all of his first drafts from the time they met in 1975 until his death. His sister is the only person who read every one of his major books before publication.

While he was mulling over what revisions he would make, he learned that his father had been contacted by the Civil Service Commission and told that there was a "reasonable doubt" about his, Barney's, loyalty to the country. This allegation was made because his father, an accountant at the War Department, was said to have a "continuing close association" with a person who was a "concealed Communist, that is, his son." This allegation occurred at the height of Senator Joseph McCarthy's campaign to expose and punish secret communists and fellow travelers. Cy Rembar was brought in, and with his counsel Mailer drafted an affidavit in response. It began by addressing the question of whether the son had influenced the father.

> My father is a man of conservative stable temperament, and though we have many of the relations proper to a father and a son, I think I may say with assurance that he has never had any political influence on me nor I upon him, nor for that matter have I ever made any attempt to influence him. He is not in the habit of ever speaking about the details of his work, nor have I ever had any interest in asking him about his work. Our political ideas are in great disagreement, and I should like to submit to the members of the Loyalty Board the notion that disagreement between fathers and sons is a human phenomenon which has been long remarked.

The second allegation, that he was a "concealed Communist," Mailer dealt with by pointing out that for years the communists "have been calling me a Trotskyist; the Trotskyists call me a 'so-called splinter Socialist'; the splinter socialists call me an anarchist; the anarchists call me a capitalist," and now the Loyalty Board has brought it full circle by calling me a "concealed Communist." In actuality, he continued, he was "admittedly and openly a dissident from the conventional and generally accepted attitudes about America and its position in the world today" and "had influenced exactly no one." He ended with a dramatic fragment, the Mailer family at dinner arguing:

> THE TIME: (one of those rare times when politics is discussed.)
>
> NORMAN MAILER: I think the whole thing in Korea is hopeless. It's a pilot-light war. Ignorant Americans and ignorant Orientals are just butchering each other.
>
> I. B. MAILER: I don't know where an intelligent boy like you picks up such idiotic rubbish.
>
> FAN MAILER (the mother): Don't call him an idiot.
>
> NORMAN MAILER: Well, he's not so smart himself.
>
> I. B. MAILER: I never talked to my father the way you talk to me.

The charge was dropped without a hearing and Barney continued his position with the War Department.

A few weeks later on his thirtieth birthday, January 31, 1953, Mailer was in a black mood. He and Adele had just returned from two weeks of skiing in Canada. He was unsure how to respond to the calls for revision from Rinehart. He had written his General MacArthur letter to Aldridge before the trip, but had many afterthoughts during the vacation. Bernard DeVoto's evaluation of *Naked and the Dead* had convinced him to fill out the characterizations of General Cummings and Lieutenant Hearn, and now Aldridge's critique was making him reconsider the lineaments of Eitel, the novel's protagonist. In a flurry of letters to friends and family over the next few months, he laid out the problems: Eitel verged on being a flat character; his narrator was somewhat unfocused; the story was too tightly focused on sex. The eight-novel scheme, he concluded, would have to be scrapped because he wished to add material planned for the later novels in the first one, material about business, corruption, the media, and the blacklisting and red-baiting rife in Hollywood. To accomplish this, he would have to write a new draft, not just improve the old one. That, he told Bea, was something that required "precisely the courage I could never get up on Barbary." *The Deer Park* would have to be redone from "top to bottom, made much bigger, much rounder, more story." He also felt an inner pressure to introduce "some sort of evil genius," as he later put it, who could challenge Eitel, and bring him into greater relief.

The idea for such a character came to him when he read the reports of the Manhattan trial of twenty-two-year-old Minot "Mickey" Jelke, a high-society procurer, which dominated the New York media during the first half of the year. Jelke was the son of John Faris Jelke, whose family had become enormously wealthy selling Good Luck Dutch Girl Oleomargarine. Short of ready money until he inherited a fortune on his twenty-fifth birthday, the younger Jelke turned to pandering and was tried as a "common pimp." What intrigued Mailer was that Jelke took up his line of work not merely for the income and the pretty girls, but because he liked the excitement. He was tried twice. The first conviction was thrown out because the judge had cleared the court at the start of the proceedings, saying it would be "steeped in filth." A higher court ordered a new trial after virtually every newspaper in New York City joined in a brief protesting the abridgement of the defendant's constitutional right to an open trial.

Like everyone else, Mailer was eager to get a glimpse of the café society pimp, as the press called him. He could not attend the first trial, because the courtroom was sealed. Two years later, Jelke was convicted at a new trial and served twenty-one months in Sing Sing. Mailer kept a clip file on the story, and Jelke became the rough model for the philosopher pimp Marion Faye, the "evil genius" of *The Deer Park*. Faye, however, would prove to be much more complex. He makes his living the same way Jelke did, but he also detests sham, false piety, and knee-jerk patriotism. Before he plunges into near-terminal sadomasochism, Faye's chief purpose in the novel is to serve as Eitel's conscience, shaming him into not naming names when he is called before a House of Representatives red-hunting committee. He tells Eitel that giving the names of former or current communists to the House Un-American Activities Committee would only grant him the license to make more trashy sentimental movies. Like most of the dark characters in Mailer's fiction, there is an enclave of virtue in his evil, and future redemption is possible.

Finding his "evil genius" was an important advance, but he had a more fundamental problem: should Sergius O'Shaugnessy, a former air force pilot in Korea, be a first-person narrator, similar in many ways to Nick Carraway in *The Great Gatsby*, or should he be depicted by an omniscient, anonymous narrator, such as he used in *Naked and the Dead*? All through April, as he explained to Styron, "I've been rushing virtually on alternate days from third person and back again, disgusted in first person by the artificial barriers I set up on a book which shouldn't have them." With Sergius telling the story, there was no way to detail the complex affair between Eitel and Elena Esposito, the fiery flamenco dancer modeled on Adele. Eitel is a "boudoir Pygmalion" and his fascinating affair with her is at the heart of the novel. Yet when Mailer switched to the third person to gain access to their thoughts and their bedroom, another problem arose: "I find that when I write in the third person," he told Styron, "I'm so bound, so constipated, that I can't seem to enter people's heads—I write as if the damn thing were a play, scene, dialogue, entrance, exit."

Hobbled by both perspectives, he told Styron that the third person had the additional misery of possibly revealing what he feared might be a "fundamental poverty of imagination." The impasse persisted until the summer, when he returned to the first person draft that Rinehart and Aldridge so disliked. For the length of his career, Mailer would be hypersensitive to the challenges and opportunities of point of view. In 1963 he said, "The most powerful leverage in fiction comes from point of view." He wrestled with how to employ this leverage for over a decade before finding a way, in *The Armies of the Night*, to escape from the subjective-objective dilemma, to gain the advantages of first-person immediacy without relinquishing the detachment, the aesthetic distance, provided by the third. But in the spring and early summer of 1953, he was nearly paralyzed by the problem. He wrote the first chapter of *The Deer Park* over and over and over.

A SUMMER TRIP to Mexico to see Susan had been planned for some time; the break from writing would be a boon. He and Adele made the long drive in a new Studebaker convertible, stopping in Marshall, Illinois, where James Jones lived. Jones and his mentor and lover, Lowney Handy, ran a writers colony in the small town not far from the Indiana border. She and her husband, Harry, had supported Jones while he wrote *From Here to Eternity*, and he had repaid them by putting the lion's share of his earnings into the colony. The colonists lived in small cabins and earned their keep by doing manual labor under the supervision of Lowney, who was a tough taskmaster. Everyone had to copy, word for word, passages from Hemingway, Dos Passos, Fitzgerald, and other writers in the morning before turning to their own work, a pump-priming technique that Mailer thought might have some benefits. Jones had invited him to see the colony, meet the Handys, and talk shop. Jones was now embarked on writing a novel about a returning GI and a postwar society moving into commercial overdrive. It was titled *Some Came Running*, and when it appeared in 1958, it was, at 1,266 pages, perhaps the longest novel by a major U.S. novelist ever published.

The film version of *From Here to Eternity*, starring Montgomery Clift, Deborah Kerr, Frank Sinatra, Burt Lancaster, and Donna Reed, was due to be released in the fall. Jones had been paid $85,000 for the rights to his novel by MGM, and had learned just before Mailer's visit that he would receive $100,000 from New American Library for the paperback rights, a larger sum than Mailer had received from the same publisher for *Naked*. Mailer was slightly in awe of all this, as he wrote to Styron.

> Lowney Handy and Jones are people whom one can satirize so easily, and yet one's missed it all, for both of them are such extraordinarily passionate people, that their errors as well as their successes have a kind of grotesque to them. Lowney Handy burns—I kept thinking of fanatics like John Brown when I looked into her eyes. Jones like all of us is having his troubles with the second book, but everything that happens to Jonesie [is] on so big a scale that his troubles are flamboyant next to ours, and involve money, movie scripts, gymnastics, obscenities, raw insecurity, triumphant phallicism, and wham, wham, wham, it's all explosion. With it all, I like him tremendously. I suppose I have a kind of friendship with him that I had when I was a kid with other kids on the block. He's really worth knowing. I've never come across anyone so intelligent and stupid, so penetrating and insensitive all in one.

The young, unpublished writers at the colony were also dazzled by Jones, who lived in a silver Airstream trailer. He did flips on a trampoline, boxed, and drank martinis at lunch to loosen up. When Mailer arrived and then was joined by Montgomery Clift, the colonists were agog. John Bowers, in his wry memoir, *The Colony*, described his reactions when he witnessed the arrival of Mailer and, at his elbow, "the beautiful, raven-haired woman introduced as Adele." When no one was looking, Bowers returned to the Studebaker and took a quick look.

> There was still an indentation in the front seat. By God and Christ, his ass had sat on that veritable spot. The steering wheel showed palm prints, and I pictured the dark-haired man on the book jacket tooling along with an intelligent, Harvard-grad countenance. I couldn't imagine him stopping along the highway for an Eskimo pie; and when he got gas somewhere, it must have been in such a holy manner that the attendants were left faint. At the *ramada* entrance I caught a glimpse of dark curls, a sharp boyish profile, and someone with hands confidently on hips like a general. He was talking to Jones—not listening, *talking*.

Adele and Jones, who had met in New York, had uneasy relations; Adele sensed that they were competing for Mailer's attention. Lowney and Jones were polite enough, but she felt ignored. It was hot and she remembered walking around in "as little as possible, a tiny bra and a pair of brief shorts. I don't think Lowney was too pleased by my seminakedness tempting her monks." Mailer and Jones got drunk every night and then arm-wrestled and had push-up contests. Jones, in better shape than Mailer, won the latter. During the day, they spent long hours talking about writing and the pluses and minuses of celebrity.

After three days, they left and drove to New Orleans, where they fell in with some local literary bohemians. One night at a party they both drank peyotl, made from peyote cactus buttons and used in religious ceremonies by southwestern Indians. Afterward, they went to hear Max Roach and Charlie Parker play at a jazz club. Adele got nauseated and vomited violently. She had a synesthesia experience and saw beautiful colors as "the music ripped into my open mouth, down my throat through my stomach to my groin pressing against the silken crotch of my panties, pressing against the fabric of my dress, and against the chair seat. I felt like the cat, I thought, who nibbled the cheese that was on the plate that lay on the table that was in the house that Norman built." Mailer, who remembers getting very sick, had a vision of an Aztec sacrifice with Indians atop a pyramid holding ceremonial knives, followed by visions of hallucinogenic Disney cartoons. The drugs took a long while to wear off.

They arrived in Mexico City in early July. Susan was happy to see them and Mailer wrote to Dan Wolf that "deep down, I feel that in ten years I'll love her more than anyone or anything else. Except perhaps

Adele. There were difficult moments on the trip," he continued, times when "I could have murdered her for infantile relapses," but "she's in my flesh, and to be extravagant I've got my cross and my salvation—for she keeps me alive, dumb little Mo [Adele] with her amoeba heart that pushes like a tentacle into everything I say, and feel." By the end of the month, they were settled in a place just outside Mexico City called the Turf Club, a former country club that wealthy Mexicans, he told Styron, used "as boffing huts for their mistresses." Here he settled down for the next ten weeks to revise the novel.

He worked steadily, with breaks to tour Cuernavaca, see some bullfights, and watch jai-alai matches. Jones's successful sale of *From Here to Eternity* to Hollywood remained on his mind and he wrote Cy at the end of August that he wanted to restart the process of selling *Naked and the Dead*, even though he thought that advance publicity for *The Deer Park* might have put him on the blacklist. Cy was instructed to ask for $200,000, but be willing to accept $85,000, the amount paid for *Eternity.* Selling it for less, "what with the income tax and other deductions, plus Dad's go-ahead to gamble a little more will mean that I'll be very little richer a year or two from now." If the novel was going to be "crapped up" by Hollywood, then a big paycheck and financial independence would be requisite compensation. "It's the old business of if you're going to be a whore, you ought to be the most expensive one in the land." He also expressed concern about Stan Rinehart trying to get out of the contract for *The Deer Park* and the necessity of a lawsuit to get the $10,000 advance. His apprehensions were correct.

As he was preparing to leave Mexico at the end of September, feeling somewhat relieved at having made some progress, he answered a letter from Vance Bourjaily in which he looked back at his career to date and gave what amounted to his novelistic credo at age thirty. He adhered to it, more or less, for the rest of his life.

> My experience with all three novels now has been one of starting with characters, finding things for them to do, and then sometimes after I've finished, as with Naked, or else at the 3/4 point as with Barbary and Deer Park, I discover what my damn theme is. And to hell with the theme in a way, for I always know even before I start something what the connected theme is between all the books, the thing which makes us write I suppose, and for me it's probably never

> been anything more profound than, "Itch, you bastards, I hope I make you uncomfortable to the death." In that sense, perhaps all I write is political (short stories excepted) and my themes are political.

In his letter, Bourjaily had made the point that he wrote from a set of well-considered principles. Mailer countered with the primacy of experience.

> Maybe you're right, probably you're right—I've had the argument with Malaquais many times—but to me the fact remains that the more experience the better the chance to come up with something fortunate. I don't even know quite how, but at its best experience can give you ideas for other things, so that maybe working as a stevedore for a year might help one write a novel about priests. There's something somewhere about the idea of proportion, and seeing everything in its place. Besides, one can go after experience consciously, determinedly, and in a funny way not disqualify oneself for writing about the material. . . . I think it can almost be put that one feels the need to say certain large things and takes for the purpose whatever world one is capable of throwing up at the moment, and the theme rides as a kind of bridge, *an afterthought*, between the two. Therefore, the better the world one can throw up at the moment, the better the book. I didn't write Naked because I wanted to say war was horrible, or that history is complex, resistant, and almost inscrutable, or because I wanted to say that the coming battle between the naked fanatics and the dead mass was approaching, but because really what I wanted to say was, "Look at me, Norman Mailer, I'm alive, I'm a genius, I want people to know that; I'm a cripple, I want to hide that," and so forth.

While he felt some disquiet about what Stan Rinehart and his mother might say about the next draft of *Deer Park*, he knew that Ted Amussen, who had returned to Rinehart as vice president, was on his side. Mailer had charmed and cajoled Rinehart's editors into approving his first two novels without making any major concessions, and felt fairly confident he could do it again, although he was certainly upping the ante with his description of his Hollywood producer, Herman Teppis, getting a blowjob. But the publishing world was now less prudish than in 1948; the walls had cracked with "fug" and were breached three years later when Jones used "fuck" repeatedly in *Eternity.* Trailblazing writers and wily editors could usually find ways to undercut the last bulwarks of Comstockery. Mailer was feeling something close to these sentiments when he returned to New York with Adele and Susan in mid-October. He was anxious to get back to work and the last day on the road, they arose at three A.M. and drove eight hundred miles. Susan remembers sitting in her little car seat in the front, peering at the stars, watching the sun come up, and then stopping for breakfast at a diner.

For the next eight months, he regularly predicted that he was close to finishing the novel, only to find that there was more to be done. A rewrite of one section created problems elsewhere; change begat change and the manuscript began to resemble Penelope's shroud: finished here, unraveled there, always in progress, never completed. When Howe asked him for a contribution to *Dissent*, he replied that he was no socialist scholar and had time only for *The Deer Park*. "I'm sick of writing it, I want to be quit of the thing," he told him. Writing to Styron, he reported that *New World Writing* had put out a new issue that contained a piece by Gore Vidal written under the pseudonym "Libra." Titled "Ladders to Heaven: Novelists and Critics," the essay names and praises the greatest living U.S. writers: Paul Bowles, Tennessee Williams, and Carson McCullers. "We don't even get mentioned," he told Styron. "Another small delicious victory for the fag axis," Mailer concluded, "but I boiled that they get away with it by pseudonyms." In reply, Styron called Vidal "that talentless, self-promoting, spineless slob."

Styron had met Vidal in 1951, but had little contact with him over the years. Mailer and Vidal intersected regularly, not only because they were East Coast novelists of the same generation, but also because they were gregarious, ambitious, ornery, and permanently critical of the imperialistic streak in American foreign policy. The two met at Millie Brower's apartment on East 27th Street in 1952. In slightly different ways, they both recalled that at their first meeting Vidal was eager to know at what age Mailer's grandparents had died. Mailer said around seventy. Vidal announced that his grandparents had died much older and, therefore, he told Mailer, "I've got you." He went on, saying that the one who lived the longest would have the best purchase on literary fame. Brower remembered that Mailer told her that Vidal was "gornisht," the Yiddish word for nothing. According to Vidal, years later

Mailer told him that when they first met he thought Vidal was the devil. Mailer apparently remembered what he had said because in 1993, and again in 2002, Mailer directed and acted in George Bernard Shaw's *Don Juan in Hell.* Mailer was the Commodore in the first performance and Don Juan in the second. Vidal, wearing a wine-red vest, played the Devil and stole the show both times.

As 1953 drew to a close his unfinished novel and his relationship with Adele were on Mailer's mind. He was telling everyone that the novel was done, but that he needed to redo "fifty pages in the middle (the central chapters on Eitel and Elena) which are fairly tepid and too expository." He knew that delineating their intense, guilt-ridden relationship from the inside was imperative, even if he had to temporarily resort to omniscience and marginalize Sergius as a narrator. He called this work the "half third draft" and thought it would take him the first three or four months of 1954 to complete. Susan was living with his mother now, and he and Adele saw her every day. Susan and Adele got along well and this temporarily reconciled Fan to Adele. Mailer expected that he and Adele would probably marry in a few months. He went on about the marriage situation in a letter to Charlie Devlin, saying he was definitely getting domesticated. Although he was ready to tie the knot, he had reservations. "I go off dreaming of all the women I will never enter," he said, "all the adventures I will never have, all the . . . ah, we were meant to end by cutting the family turkey." Adele, he adds, is leery about getting married after pressuring him earlier. "She knows that the guilt which holds me so faithful will change to the gallant bucko the moment we're legally stitched." It is a prescient statement, for henceforth Mailer would swing irregularly between sexual adventuring and family responsibilities, the gallant bucko alternating with the family man carving the bird at Thanksgiving.

Mailer got involved that fall in a literary group that Vance Bourjaily established. It met on Sunday afternoons at the White Horse Tavern on the corner of Hudson and West 11th Streets in the West Village. According to Dan Wolf, "Norman found that if you invited people to your house, it was not that easy to get rid of them," a problem avoided by going to the White Horse, which was a quiet neighborhood bar frequented by local Irish. Aldridge, who was coediting *Discovery* with Bourjaily, attended some of the meetings, as did Herman Wouk, whose novel of the U.S. Navy in the South Pacific, *The Caine Mutiny*, along with Jones's *Eternity*, was one of the leading bestsellers of 1951. Calder Willingham, whose southern accent Mailer would sometimes imitate, came, as did Styron. Dan Wolf attended, and Lewis Allen, a film producer whom Mailer later saw a lot of in Mexico. Bourjaily brought his wife, Tina, but Mailer—who generally presided—always came alone.

Louis Auchincloss, a Wall Street lawyer who published a string of bestselling novels about the legal world in the 1960s, as well as the archetypal prep school novel *The Rector of Justin*, came to several of the gatherings, although he said he felt somewhat uncomfortable at first because of his Wall Street and Republican affiliations. Mailer welcomed him, however, and then told him that he admired a story, "The Gem-like Flame," that Auchincloss had recently published, saying he would have been happy to have written the story. "I was so pleased," Auchincloss said, "that I went right home. I wanted to leave one such assembly with a happy impression." Part of Mailer's welcoming attitude toward Auchincloss was his refusal to stereotype people; part of it was his curiosity about the wealthy. He said more than once that he agreed with F. Scott Fitzgerald that the rich are indeed different from the other classes. The White Horse group lasted through the early spring of 1955.

EXCEPTING JONES, MAILER'S most important friendship during this period was with Robert Lindner, a psychoanalyst who had written a sharp critique of psychoanalytic practice, *Prescription for Rebellion*. After their initial exchange of letters, they got together in New York after Mailer returned from Mexico. Three months before Mailer died, he remembered his first meeting with Lindner, a tall, handsome man with a "rusty, soft moustache." He was "a guy I could *talk* to. His head was fertile, full of ideas. I was full of ideas. We just yakked, which I needed." They continued their correspondence and for a time talked almost every day on the telephone. Initially drawn together by their disgust with Senator McCarthy's hunt for communists in government, and the dull fog of conformity rolling over the country, as well as mutual distaste for President Dwight Eisenhower, their relationship deepened when they recognized each other's ambition and how they might help each other. Both recognized Freud's genius but chafed under the yoke of repression, renunciation, and compromise that he believed made civilization possible. Lindner was an establishmentarian and worked from within;

Mailer was a rebel with a cause: the spontaneous expression of feelings, including the violent and the sexual. Kindred spirits, they were joined by their belief that people could transform themselves, become bolder and more creative, and that society itself could be renovated. Both were tremendously ambitious and competitive, but their spheres of interest were adjacent, only partially overlapping, and thus neither had to worry about being outshined.

Mailer had read Lindner's *Prescription for Rebellion.* Lindner was convinced that most of Freud's theories were sound, but he parted company with his peers on the merits of getting along by conforming. It has "become axiomatic with our culture and in our society that adjustment is the highest good and the absolute right," he said. "A way has to be found to unbind the Prometheus within each one of us, to unloose the rebelliousness of our natures, and to give full sway to that instinct upon which our survival as free individuals depends." Lindner made this same point a variety of ways in several other books: *Rebel Without a Cause; Fifty-Minute Hour; Must You Conform?* The gist of his argument is simple: "The alternative to adjustment is rebellion." Although Mailer was eight years younger than Lindner, his relationship with him was nothing like the one he had with Malaquais, whose views were secure and settled. Mailer and Lindner were both more open to new ideas.

Mailer had also been reading the work of Wilhelm Reich and was much taken with his ideas about the pernicious effects of repression on sexual potency. The following passage, taken from Charles Rycroft's brief study of Reich, is apposite, if not identical with Mailer's ideas. Reich was "surely right," Rycroft states, "in asserting that no neurotics are orgastically potent and that the great majority of human beings suffer from a character neurosis. His theories of character armor and orgasm constitute, therefore, a sweeping indictment of the sexual life of civilized man, an indictment similar in many ways to that made by D. H. Lawrence." Mailer's infatuation with Reich would grow throughout the 1950s, and he would later build his own version of Reich's infamous "orgone box," a telephone-booth-sized chamber where one repaired to replenish or accumulate orgonic, or life energy, but also rumored to promote erections. At this point, Reich was only one of several theorists that interested Mailer.

His friendship with Lindner grew to the point where they discussed their own sexuality. Lindner, like Mailer, had had extramarital affairs and was sympathetic to Mailer's mixed feelings about Adele, which he described many years later.

> He thought she was very sexy. He understood that entirely. He also thought she was kind of—how to put it—that spiritually speaking she was a very expensive wife for me. Not because she cost me money, but because—he understood my social ambitions, which were high. I wanted to be feted as the number one writer in America, and there were new sprouts coming up all over the place. The torch was being handed over in other places and that had me irritated. And Adele was no help socially to me. In fact, she was a drawback. She knew it and I knew it and there was a tension between us.

He confided his most private feelings to Lindner and although he believed that undergoing psychoanalysis would harm his work, he asked Lindner if he would take him on. Lindner said it would ruin their friendship. That was the end of it. Mailer later said that one of the things he was most proud of in his life was that he had never gone into analysis. Nevertheless, he still talked to Lindner about his problems. "One of them," Mailer said, "was a buried fear that under everything I'm a homosexual. That was always a fear. He would just say, 'Look, on the basis of my experience, you're not. What you're suffering is latent homosexual anxiety, which is common to all of us.' And so forth and so forth. Occasionally, I had an episode when I couldn't get it up and that bothered me." Lindner listened and told him to shrug it off.

Another matter he brought up with Lindner was his friend "Bernard" (his pseudonym for Barney), a compulsive gambler. Lindner responded by sending his article "The Psychodynamics of Gambling." It argues that gamblers are compelled to both win and lose, suffering either way. Mailer told Lindner that he was struck by how well it explained his father's addiction. "While I read your monograph a fund of rare compassion for him began to form in me—I understood how terribly compulsively neurotic Bernard is, how helpless he is, and I felt more tender toward him." Recalling Barney's 1949 English colonel letter, he went on to recount how "Bernard" had asked to borrow $3,000 and how after Mailer had chastised him, "Bernard succeeded in punishing me by running the debt up to five thousand dollars" and then wrote him a highly abusive letter, the only one of its kind he had ever received from his "friend."

Chipping away at the novel four days a week, Mailer also found time to demonstrate bullfighting in his loft. Writing to Lew Allen in Mexico, he announced that he had become a "renowned *toreros de salon*" with sufficient dexterity "to pass a young lady carrying the horns without sweeping a single highball glass from the coffee table which serves as barrera." He also began experimenting, quite seriously, with the Tarot deck, and came up with his own interpretations. He wrote them out, giving plus and minus characteristics for each of the twenty-one trump cards or "Major Arcana" (the oppositions intrigued him), and noting that the meanings were dynamic and "always dependent upon the constellation of the cards." He revamped the rules slightly—as he was wont to do with all the games he played.

Jonathan Cape, whose firm of the same name had published *Barbary Shore*, wrote to Mailer in January 1954 for a progress report on *The Deer Park*. Mailer replied that he was only four or five weeks away from finishing the new draft, but didn't want to rush the conclusion. He had done that on his first two novels, he said, and now regretted it. He also said that no one had seen the new draft. That changed on the weekend of January 16–17, when Mailer took the train to see Lindner in Baltimore. Adele did not join him; there was friction between her and Lindner's wife, Johnnie. Mailer described Johnnie as "a sort of pepper pot blonde, pepper pot fire. WASP, very strong in a breakable way, in other words vulnerable, vulnerable as hell. She was in the best sense of the word, a dame. She was full of strong feelings, full of love, full of lust, full of fire, full of the inability to pardon." Mailer brought the manuscript along and Lindner read it, as did Johnnie. They both gave him warm feedback. Lindner was intrigued with Marion Faye, whom he called the novel's "evil principle," a description that Mailer said was close to his own feelings about the pimp.

Lindner was the staff psychologist at the local women's prison and had a collateral interest in criminology. He and Mailer discussed the gamut of mental illnesses, especially schizophrenia and the range of behaviors linked with criminal psychopaths. Lindner was the adept and Mailer the catechumen, questioning, parsing his answers, and challenging Lindner, who for Mailer was to psychology what Malaquais had been to politics. But Mailer was more willing to challenge Lindner—he had after all studied abnormal psychology at Harvard under the redoubtable Professor Murray, read Freud, Reich, and two figures in the early psychoanalytic movement, Karen Horney, and Theodore Reik, and spent most of his adult life observing and writing about human personality, its structure and fault lines, how it cohered, developed, and disintegrated. Creating memorable characters was the raison d'être of his writing life. With Marion Faye, he had opened up a new line of inquiry. He had begun reading Kierkegaard's *Fear and Trembling*, which helped him decide that the psychopath and the saint were more alike than different. Dostoyevsky had charted the path from sinner to saint, and Marion Faye, after plumbing the depths of sadomasochism, could become as selfless as Catholic social reformer Dorothy Day. Sin was not an end, but a beginning, a cathartic experience. This emerging belief was sharpened when he accompanied Lindner to the prison during his visit to Baltimore.

He sat in on Lindner's brief interviews with fifteen inmates and took notes. "The experience was just fantastic," he said. "I left there boiling with rage at the injustice of a sort I haven't felt since I was eighteen," referring to his experience at Boston State Hospital. Observing the women inmates, Mailer said, was one of the great discoveries of his life during this period. They were, he said in an interview in his final year, "not only much like you and me, but in a certain sense had a little touch of intensity that was more than you and me, because they'd been through the prison experience." He asked one woman what she was in for, and she said she almost killed her husband with a knife, and went on to tell him about it. Her statements, he said, gave him a profound sense of

> how deep, *how deep* were the roots of what was commonly called crime. And how human they were, and how *natural*. And for people who were not living as I was, gussied by all sorts of protection, ah, crime was very easy, it was instinctive; it was something you did, it was one of the arrows in your quiver; it was one of your answers to your environment; it was a way of continuing to live. And so very early in life, my thinking life was shaped by the notion that no crime is ever too bad not to be explored, that no judgment is to be made on a criminal for too little. And that stayed with me always, and it was invaluable, absolutely invaluable.

The whole idea of prison, he concluded, was "absolute idiocy." His visit and subsequent conversations with Lindner reawakened the idea of getting a nonliterary job after *The Deer Park* was published, a job in a prison. He thought he would like to write a book on convicts and prison life.

Adele accompanied him to see the Lindners only every third time because of her lack of ease in social situations, Mailer said.

> Adele could never have entertained the people, at that point—later Adele could—that Johnnie had over for dinner. So Adele stood out like a sore thumb. You know, "There's Mailer with his slum kid," was almost the attitude. But Adele wasn't from the slums; she was from the lower middle class, working class, but she was seen that way. It was awkward. You know, "You've brought the wrong person into the room," sort of. And she was very aware of that and Adele's worst fault was that when things got bad, she got worse. She did not respond to crises; she fell apart. And so if somebody handed her a drink and she received it with the wrong hand or something—I'm making this up—it would be something of that sort, whatever the code was, she'd broken it. Sure enough, she'd drop the glass a minute later.

Lindner and his wife had two young children and for this reason rarely came to visit the Mailers in New York. They did, however, attend the Mailers' wedding reception a week after the April 19 ceremony at City Hall.

According to Adele, "I didn't exactly nag Norman about getting married, but I would introduce the subject at every opportunity." But Mailer felt she had reservations, as did he. Similar in age, New York City backgrounds, and hair-trigger tempers, they were different in education, and worlds apart in ambition. Before their children were born, sex was the strongest bond. Finally, they took the leap. He arose late on the morning of his wedding and then sat naked on the bed writing in his notebook. She stifled her annoyance, thinking, "after all, I was in love with a great writer, and living with genius had its price." At the City Hall ceremony, witnessed by Barney and Fan, Mailer gave Adele a $13 ring, later replaced by a gold band. After the wedding, he carried Adele over the threshold, and said: "Well, Mrs. Mailer, it's the beginning of a new chapter." The next day he went to work at his studio in Brooklyn.

Several days later, Dan Wolf and another First Avenue neighbor, Toby Schneebaum, planned a party back at the flat. Besides the Lindners, a number of literary friends came: the Rinehart crowd, Lillian Hellman, Harvey Breit, who wrote about literary matters for *The New York Times* and summered in Provincetown, Ed Fancher, Rhoda Lazare, and James Jones. Jones got drunk, as did Toby, who took a bath in the tub Mailer had installed in the kitchen. Adele, "happy because I was Mrs. Norman Mailer," cut the cake with Toby's machete.

At the time of the wedding, *The Caine Mutiny Court-Martial*, adapted from Herman Wouk's novel, was an enormous hit on Broadway. It was directed by Charles Laughton and produced by Paul Gregory and starred Henry Fonda. Tickets for the show, which ran for over a year, were difficult to obtain. Hoping to capitalize on its success, Gregory got in touch with Mailer to see if he would be interested in dramatizing *Naked and the Dead*. Mailer was dubious for three reasons: Lillian Hellman had taken him down this road, and it had gone nowhere; he didn't want to take the time to work on the adaptation; and Gregory had praised *Naked* as "an extraordinary story of the Marines," adding that he'd read it five times. Lying was bad enough, but mixing up the two service branches nearly destroyed Gregory's credibility. But the opportunity to work with Laughton, whose acting skills Mailer admired, was tempting. If the deal went forward and made anything close to the huge sums Wouk was earning from *The Caine Mutiny*, that would be splendid, but whatever happened, he wanted to try another line of work, perhaps as some sort of factotum in prison administration. But first, he had to finish *The Deer Park*.

WRITING ON APRIL 30, he told a Hollywood friend, Chester Aaron, that "by dint of pushing, nudging, sandpapering, worrying, and as my ex mother in law used to say—gidgying," the novel would be ready in two weeks for final typing, which he planned to do himself. Aaron was thinking about getting married and Mailer gave his friend some advice on what he called "a monster of an institution." Live together, not just sleep together, for at least six months, he said, because a good part of marriage is "the whole business of congenial room-mates." He went on to fault himself for being "old Polonius Mailer," especially because "I'm often convinced I'll be married six times in my life." Adele didn't like to hear her new husband talk about future marriages, he said. Neither of them could have known that his prediction would prove accurate.

By this time, he had shown the novel in near-final form to someone at Rinehart, probably Amussen, because he told Fig that "they" liked it, but it is clear that the manuscript had not yet reached Stan Rinehart's desk. He repeated his news to Lew Allen and for the first time in months sounded upbeat, in part because Jones was back in town. Mailer was unequivocal: "Life with Jonesie has been great," he wrote; "with that loud brawling animal quality of his which loves life so instinctively and so warmly, I begin to feel a little warmer myself." When Jones is around, he continued, "you have the feeling that things are going to happen, as indeed often they do." He gave this example:

> There was a party at Styron's last night, and we all got drunk and decided to send a telegram to [Senator] Joe McCarthy. So here's how it went:
>
> DEAR JOE, WE DIG YOU, BUT GET THE BROWN OUT OF YOUR NOSE! VANCE BOURJAILY, JAMES JONES, NORMAN MAILER, JOHN PHILLIPS, WILLIAM STYRON.
>
> Despite our mirth and our drunkenness, I think deep down we were a little aghast. It's exactly the sort of thing you go to a concentration camp for three years later.

The Jewish catastrophe theory of history, learned first at his mother's knee, was never far from his mind, especially when things were going well.

The Mailers had hoped to leave for Mexico on June 1, as soon as he typed and submitted the final manuscript to Rinehart for copyediting. But before he began, he learned that the rough manuscript submitted earlier, and carrying the unambiguously glowing endorsement of Amussen, had been read by his boss. "Something in the sex has gotten a neurotic hair up Stan Rinehart's ass," Mailer wrote to Charles Devlin. He met with Stan and they had an argument, but a decision on the novel's fate was postponed until Rinehart saw how Mailer had handled his objections. Mailer figured it would take him about two weeks. By May 28 he had starting typing, about the same time he learned that he had "a lousy liver," an after-effect of his wartime jaundice. The doctor said no alcohol—he had been drinking too much anyway—or fried foods for thirty days. No prohibition against marijuana was mentioned, and it became his substitute for Scotch. It would soon become his drug of choice and, within two years, his secret weapon in his war against "the shits" running the country.

As the struggle with Rinehart was unfolding, Mailer heard from Lois Wilson. She would be passing through New York in early June. Could he suggest places and methods for "fancy indiscretions"? She was eager to see him again because "when I think of quality I think of Norman," adding that among her colleagues "there's not a decent piece of ass." He wrote back immediately to say that he was borrowing a friend's apartment for their reunion. Bring along the Polaroid photos you took last time, he said, because "as the years go by, I just get dirtier and dirtier." At loggerheads with his publisher, weakened by a bad liver, and preparing for a four-month trip to Mexico with his bride of a month, Mailer was nevertheless eager to "put both my arms around your big white moon." As he had foreseen, marriage would not interfere with the desires of this "gallant bucko."

Around June 10, Mailer placed the novel in the hands of Amussen. It had taken him thirteen consecutive days to type, and was the last time he would type a long manuscript. The fellatio scene remained intact but, as he explained to Lindner, "I took the descriptive edge off it so the reader will have no more than a sense that something perverted happened." Even a few years later, certainly by 1960, the description (taken from the Rinehart proofs) would hardly arch an eyebrow.

> Tentatively, she reached out a hand to caress his hair, and at that moment Herman Teppis opened his legs and let Bobby slip to the floor. At the expression of surprise on her face, he began to laugh. "Just like this sweetie," he said, and down he looked at that frightened female mouth, facsimile of all those smiling lips he had seen so ready to be nourished at the fount of power and with a shudder he started to talk. "That's a good girlie, that's a good girlie, that's a good girlie," he said in a mild little voice, "you're just an angel darling, and I like you, and you understand, you're my darling darling, oh, that's the ticket," said Teppis.

Mailer had his reunion with Lois Wilson on June 13, and four days later left for Mexico. "Things at Rinehart turned out beautifully," as he wrote to Lindner in mid-July. All the young editors had given enthusiastic reports on the manuscript, and there was no showdown with Stan, who apparently did not want to buck the entire editorial department. Instead, he "retired into sulky silence." *The Deer Park* was accepted as submitted. A publication date of February 1955 was set. Except for reading galleys, nothing remained to do on the novel, and he again asked Lindner about helping him get a prison job. He was looking ahead and feeling good enough to have a few drinks and relax the strict diet he had been on for six weeks. He was smoking "tea," as he referred to it, almost every day. In Mexico he and Adele settled in a fortress-like colonial house surrounded by three-hundred-year-old trees. There was an interior garden with orchards and a large patio. He wrote his Japanese translator, Eiichi Yamanishi, that Adele painted and he studied Spanish and read books about crime and prison. Bea dropped off Susan regularly to visit and she was "a bright spot" in his day, although he worried that his anxieties might make her neurotic.

Stan Rinehart's distaste for the novel was mildly unsettling, but the silence of friends was painful. He had yet to receive any response from Adeline, Malaquais, Styron, Jones, or Devlin, all of whom had been sent copies, nor from his publishers in England, Germany, or Japan. In an anxious mid-July letter to Styron and his new wife, Rose, he said he had "an uneasy feeling" that they had not commented because they surmised that doing so "would alter our friendship." A few days later, a four-page, handwritten letter from Styron arrived. After stating straightaway that the novel was "honest and brilliant," and agreeing with Robert Loomis, his own editor, that it had "a deep sense of morality," Styron shifted gears and worked his way painstakingly through a run of qualifications and small praise, noting, for example, that the novel was "depressing in its magnificent candor," and that it was brimming with "unalleviated and leaden anxiety." He concluded: "I don't like the book, but I admire the hell out of it." Styron also thought that O'Shaughnessy didn't come off well as a narrator.

When Mailer replied, he said that he "truly appreciated" the critique, and that his own reaction would probably be the same "if hypothetically someone else had written it." His tone in a number of letters during this period was muted and agreeable; he would raise no passionate defense of the novel. I was attempting to write a great novel, he said to Styron, one that had the same kind of dry irony found in Stendahl's *The Red and the Black*, but "my imagination and my daring and my day to day improvisation dried up." Nevertheless, he said, his vocation as a writer has been confirmed by surviving the "progressively more depressing" process of writing his second and third novels over the previous five years.

Besides his parents and sister, his main supports were Lindner, Wolf, and Adele. The Gwaltneys read the manuscript when the Mailers stopped on the way to Mexico, and were enthusiastic in their praise. Wolf was a staunch admirer. Lindner—the first person outside the family to read it—offered to write a preface and later wrote a glowing review in *The Village Voice*. Until his untimely death in 1956 at age forty-one of congestive heart disease, he maintained a rich dialogue with Mailer and deeply influenced his emerging conception of the rebel hipster Mailer would call "the white negro." Adele, Mailer recalled, read everything that he wrote. "Because I loved him," she wrote in her memoir, "I handed everything over, my heart, my body, and my talent." He said that she was a sensitive reader and he always valued her opinion. "She had instinctive good taste and she could spot all that was phony in a novel as fast as I could." The novel is dedicated to her and Dan Wolf.

In August, reports appeared noting that *Naked and the Dead* had been sold to Paul Gregory's film company, and that filming would begin in July 1955. Robert Mitchum was slated for a starring role, the articles stated. In fact, the contract for the sale was not signed for another three months, and when the film was finally made in 1958, Mitchum was committed elsewhere. Mailer communicated with Cy Rembar about the contract while he was in Mexico, but with scant enthusiasm. His hunch was that the film would be much less powerful than the magnificent film version of *From Here to Eternity*, and he was right. Nevertheless, he wanted the sale to go through because his income from *Naked* was noticeably diminishing and, if Stan Rinehart's gorge rose again, he said, he might have to publish *The Deer Park* privately at his own expense. A part of him almost hoped this would be the case.

One of the things he had put off for the previous two years was reading the work of his contemporaries. So, in addition to reading crime books and going to bullfights, he began reading books "by the cartload." He found little to admire. The only book that he liked was Saul Bellow's *The Adventures of Augie March*, which had just won the National Book Award. "I found it impressive but somehow unexciting. Really the damndest book—I have to admire his courage, his ambition, his 'openness' to try anything and everything, but the pieces are more exciting than the whole, and nothing in it really disturbs one." For the next thirty years, Mailer had good and bad things to say about Bellow. The negative comments usually echoed what he said here, namely, that Bellow did not make his readers itch, and was too easily pleased by his ability to elegantly repeat the pieties and paradoxes of high culture figures such as Freud, Proust, and Henry James.

HE DID SOME writing in Mexico, namely a short piece he had agreed to write for *One: The Homosexual Magazine*, after a telephone conversation with the New York secretary for the sponsoring organization. He turned him down at first, and the man countered by asking if Mr. Mailer would prefer to write anonymously, shielding his reputation, but still showing support for the aims of the magazine. Mailer wrote, "My pride was that I would say in print anything that I believed, but I was not ready to say a word in public defense of homosexuals." He feared that his article would not be read widely, he said in a letter to the secretary, and that gossip columnist "maggots like [Walter] Winchell and [Lee] Mortimer will print a line—'Norman Mailer writing articles for the limp-wrist set magazine One.' " It would then be taken for granted that he was homosexual, a disagreeable prospect. But he agreed to write the essay. The secretary clinched his approval by saying that if he did, perhaps he could be the movement's first congressman. The man knew "the way to me," Mailer wrote in a preface to the piece when he reprinted it: "Mate the absurd with the apocalyptic, and I was a captive." In mid-September, after approving the galleys of *The Deer Park* with only a few minor corrections, he sat down to write the essay.

The turning point in his views on gays had come after he read Toby Schneebaum's copy of *The Homosexual in America: A Subjective Approach* by Donald Webster Cory. He resisted it as he read, but could not escape the recognition of his bias it provided. In his essay, which he titled "The Homosexual Villain," he wrote, "I had been acting as a bigot in this matter." As a libertarian socialist, he had always insisted that "sexual relations, above everything else, demand their liberty." But he had been unwilling to grant this freedom to homosexuals. Wilhelm Reich in *The Sexual Revolution: Toward a Self-Governing Character Structure*, had first shown him the link, he said, between political and sexual repression, and now he was "properly ashamed." He explained that he had consciously attributed "unpleasant, ridiculous, or sinister connotations" to gay or bisexual characters in his novels, most notably, General Cummings in *Naked and the Dead* and Leroy Hollingsworth in *Barbary Shore*. "I had no conscious homosexual desires," Mailer wrote, but he was suspicious about his dislike of gays, wondering if it might be an unconscious cover for such feelings. Once he had admitted, and corrected, his bias, and begun to enjoy his friendships with men like Schneebaum, he found he was no longer worried about latent homosexuality. Lindner's assurances also played a role.

Dotson Rader, a writer and antiwar activist, met Mailer in 1967 and became a close friend. They had many conversations about homosexuality over the years. Rader said Capote thought Mailer was a latent homosexual, and told Rader, with fingers crossed, that he was afraid Mailer would rape him. "So when I was first with Norman," Rader recalled,

> I would sort of bait him. And he never responded in a way that was negative. He always responded with humor. By baiting him, I mean, I'd lean over and say to him, "Did anyone ever tell you that you have beautiful blue eyes." That kind of stuff; I would tease him as if I was coming on to him. Most homophobes would say, "Keep your hands to yourself," which was kind of funny because bigots, when they react instinctively, in a bigoted way, usually get angry, but they're really angry at themselves because they reveal their cards. Norman was never that way.

A little over a week after he sent off the essay to *One*, Mailer heard from Amussen: Production was about to begin. There was nothing to fret about, he said, everything was "under control." Mailer wrote to Styron the same day to congratulate him on buying a house in Connecticut and thank him for the invitation to visit. In all of his correspondence during his last few weeks in Mexico, he recites his uncertainty about selling *Naked and the Dead* to Hollywood. Being poor and having new experience foisted on him was his preference, yet the prospect of cashing his biggest paycheck since *Naked* was published—$110,000 plus a cut of the profits—had obvious appeal; he thought he could write three or four more books on the proceeds. Nothing was said about *The Deer Park*. It was finished, Mailer thought, and time to move on.

Before he and Adele left Mexico, he had an extraordinary experience on marijuana. He told the story more than once in his later years.

> When the marijuana really hit, I went to the bathroom—I remember this—and vomited. Some of the most incredible vomiting I ever had. It was like an apocalyptic purge, the most unbelievable orgasm of your life except it wasn't agreeable because it was vomiting. But it had the power of an apocalyptic orgasm. And when I came out of it, I was on pot for the first time of my life, really on. Up to that point, I just had intimations of what was on. Now I *was* on. Light deepened, things changed. I remember lying down, getting dizzy, looking at Adele who was sleeping off her pot on another couch; there were two parallel couches, and I could seem to make her face whoever I wanted her to be, just lying there. Her face would change from this person to that person. Probably could change her into an animal if I wished. And that was just the beginning. After that every night for a few weeks, I went down to the car, turned on the radio, listened to it, smoked pot, breathed it in in the car and got into jazz for the first time. For the first time in my life, I could really understand jazz.

He began buying bags of marijuana at a dollar apiece and carefully removing the stems and seeds. Anticipating his luggage being searched when he and Adele and Susan reached the border, he hid his cache with Adele's tampons, which were then put in condoms.

> I had the feeling that this was the way to get it through customs. And sure enough, when the time came and we were crossing the border—I remember Susie, by then, was about five and turned to me and said, "Daddy,"—she had a wonderful sort of Spanish accent—"Why are you so nervous?" I was ready to clout the kid—anyway, the customs

guy sort of went through our bags very carefully and when he got to Adele's bag and he opened it, I had put some black lace panties on top of the Kotex box. He lifted them very gingerly, saw the Kotex box, slapped back the panties, closed her bag and that was it.

Mailer had the supplies he needed for his upcoming campaign.

SIX
GENERAL MARIJUANA AND THE NAVIGATOR

"Calculation never made a hero."
—John Henry Cardinal Newman

Feeling financially secure from the sale of *Naked* to Gregory and Laughton in November 1954, and perhaps weary of looking out their bathroom window on a cemetery, the Mailers decided to move out of the railroad flat on First Avenue. They rented a duplex in a four-story brownstone at 320 East 55th Street, not far from Sutton Place, one of the wealthiest enclaves in New York, where they would remain for the next two years. Susan, who was spending the fall with them, had her own bedroom. Speaking of the move, Mailer told Vance and Tina Bourjaily that he wanted his gravestone to read, "He wished to live only at the bottom or the top." Adele bought new modern furniture and hung her paintings on the wall; he busied himself catching up on his correspondence and trying to place "The Man Who Studied Yoga." He purchased hi-fi equipment but felt guilty about the expense. "When the revolution comes," he wrote to the Bourjailys, "the workers will put me on a spit." He wrote to Gregory to say that Robert Mitchum was too big physically to play Sergeant Croft in the film version of *Naked*. He wanted Brando, whose recent performance in *The Wild One* as the leader of a motorcycle gang impressed him for its subtle combination of repressed violence and "a certain spirituality." In several letters to friends, he cited continental writers who had influenced *The Deer Park*: Stendhal, Gide, Proust, Moravia. Writing to his Uncle Louis in South Africa on November 17, he said that "it meant something to me to get off the floor" after the failure of *Barbary Shore*. A day or two later, with a *Publishers Weekly* advertisement for the novel already in print, Stan Rinehart insisted on deletion of the fellatio scene. Mailer refused; Rinehart halted production. *The Deer Park* was adrift, and although Mailer didn't know it, unfinished.

The story of what happened over the next two months as the novel moved from publisher to publisher, picking up rejection slips like barnacles, is told in his long essay "The Mind of an Outlaw," published in *Esquire* four years later. It is, Mailer later said, "the most accurate account I've ever written of myself," as well his declaration of independence from the New York literary world of "cliques, fashions, vogues, snobs, snots, and fools, not to mention a dozen bureaucracies of criticism." The era of magisterial editors and publishers like Maxwell Perkins and Charles Scribner was gone, he lamented, and "there was no room for the old literary idea of oneself as a major writer, a figure in the landscape." From November 1954 to January 1955 *The Deer Park* was considered and rejected by Random House, Knopf, Simon & Schuster, Harper's, Scribner's, and Harcourt Brace. Styron was enlisted to help at Random House, although he told Hiram Haydn, the top editor there, that he had mixed feelings about it, something Mailer already knew. Haydn also didn't like it, finding it to be "gray and dreary." Mailer was always urging his friends who had reservations about the novel to read it a second time, and when Haydn did, he reversed himself and saw a "convincing strain of compassion for his unlovely and unhappy characters." But this reversal came too late to help him at Random House. Jones may have tried to help at Scribner's, his (and Hemingway's) publisher, but the editors there detested it. Mailer soon learned that Jones felt the same way. He wrote to Mailer that the novel was "a pretty bad book," and compared it unfavorably to *Barbary Shore*. He added, "I still believe there are great books in you. *Great* books. If you can ever get them out." On some days, Mailer thought that *The Deer Park* was, if not great, close to it, and Jones's dismissal of it, on top of Styron's lukewarm praise, dealt a blow to the esprit of the trio.

The novel got the lengthiest consideration from the firm of Alfred A. Knopf. Mailer would have been elated to see its elegant Borzoi wolfhound logo on its title page, given the firm's commitment to high literary endeavor, and several of his literary heroes—Spengler, Mann, Maugham, and Pound—on its rolls. Working with the firm's lawyers for three weeks, he said, "I took out sentence after sentence which might be construed as sexually gratuitous," agreeing to these excisions because they were willing to leave the fellatio scene intact. But when the lawyers pressed for still more cuts, he bridled and negotiations ceased. He blamed Blanche Knopf, the founder's wife, for being "almost irrationally terrified" about the book being prosecuted. But he was wrong; she was "eager" for the firm to take it, as her husband explained in his memoirs. It was Knopf himself, and his top lawyer, Harry Buchman, who were opposed. Shortly after it was turned down, the Knopfs invited the Mailers to a cocktail party. When they were leaving, Alfred went to the door with them. Mailer, he recalled, "immediately offered to bet me that the book would sell over a hundred thousand copies." Mailer repeated the offer a day or two later in a letter, saying he would wager "hard cash" on his instinct, and that if Knopf did not reply, "the impression I obtained of your character when we exchanged 40 words at Blanche's party will be confirmed." Knopf wrote back a terse note, declining the bet and saying he had "no reason to care one whit whether your book sells 250 or 250,000 copies."

Adele remembers that during this period he would "just sit staring at nothing," all the while drinking Scotch and chewing the ice cubes. "Sometimes in the middle of a conversation, he would seem to be distracted. It was as if he was out of his body. He would smile to himself, as if I weren't there, his lips moving soundlessly, having a dialogue with himself." As the rejections piled up, he recounted, he stayed as close to the manuscript "as a stage-struck mother pushing her child forward at every producer's office. I was amateur agent for it, messenger boy, editorial consultant, Machiavelli of the luncheon table, fool of the five o'clock drinks, I was learning the publishing business in a hurry, and I made a hundred mistakes and paid for each one by wasting a new bout of energy." His exposure to the manners and mores of the publishing world was the kind of experience, he said, that "was likely to return some day as good work."

"The Mind of an Outlaw" is that good work. It can be compared, with some justice, to F. Scott Fitzgerald's essay "The Crack-Up," an anguished account of his descent from renown to obscurity. Arresting as it is, Fitzgerald's piece (also published in *Esquire*) reeks of self-pity. Mailer's essay is not without it, but he is considerably feistier, funnier, caustic in some places, self-lacerating in others, and captures perfectly his jangled mood after Rinehart's rejection. Exaggerated descriptions of his novel's obscenity were sloshing around publishers row in New York, and each new rumor, Mailer believed, narrowed the novel's chances at the next house it was sent. To get the payment due him from Rinehart for accepting the manuscript, he had to mount a costly legal effort. The novel he had started about a concentration camp, "The City of God," was another casualty, he said. Given his sea of troubles, beginning a new novel was inconceivable. Finally, the sum of his frustrations "drove a spike into my cast-iron mind," forcing the recognition that he had become "the sort of comic figure I would have cooked to a turn in one of my books, a radical who had the nineteenth-century naïveté to believe that the people with whom he did business were 1) gentlemen, 2) fond of him, and 3) respectful of his ideas even if in disagreement with them." The man who ultimately took the novel, Walter Minton, the new president of Putnam's, was more to Mailer's liking; he reminded him of a general. Minton paid Mailer $10,000, the highest advance in the history of Putnam's. Minton would live up to his reputation a few years later when he would publish another controversial novel, Vladimir Nabokov's *Lolita*. Ted Purdy, editor in chief, was also high on the novel, and Minton later said that *The Deer Park* was "the best novel that's ever been written about Hollywood." Minton asked for no changes, yet Mailer was still unhappy, savoring his anger and half disappointed that he would not be self-publishing *The Deer Park*.

His use of marijuana had accelerated in Mexico; he was also drinking again, his liver having recovered, but "tea" was his drug of choice, opening his senses and his passion for jazz, "intricate music that spoke of the complexity of life," as he later described it. The Mailers went to clubs in Harlem and the Village where they heard Dizzy Gillespie, Sonny Rollins, and Miles Davis. He continued his regular, energetic discussions with Lindner. The combined effects of this stimulation—colloquies with Lindner, jazz, marijuana (and the liquor and sleeping pills with which he tempered it), the raucous, disenthralled culture of Harlem, and the adrenaline that Rinehart's betrayal pumped into his system—led to something bursting within his deepest self.

> I do not know if it was so much a loving heart, as a cyst of the weak, the unreal and the needy, and I was finally open to my anger. I turned within my psyche I can almost believe, for I felt something shift to murder in me. I finally had the simple sense to understand that if I wanted my work to travel further than others, the life of my talent depended on fighting a little more, and looking for help a

> little less. But I deny the sequence in putting it this way, for it took me years to come to this fine point. All I felt then was that I was an outlaw, a psychic outlaw, and I liked it, I liked it a good night better than trying to be a gentleman.

ON DECEMBER 1, 1954, Mailer began setting down the ideas that came in wake of the Rinehart rupture. He called it "Lipton's Journal," a not-so-veiled reference to the "tea" he smoked before he sat at his typewriter. He wrote fast, in bursts of ten or more pages every few days, and over the course of three months, until March 4, 1955, typed 248 pages containing approximately 110,000 words. The entries are numbered, 1 to 689; each is a stand-alone pensée. As he proceeded, he entertained the possibility that his insights could challenge some of the dominant ideas of Western thought, specifically, Freud's theories on the merits of sublimation and repression.

But at a dozen points he faltered, questioning the wisdom of naked soul bearing, much as Walt Whitman did in *Song of Myself.*

> As was evident in the notes yesterday, I was moving toward a depression, and it came on me during the evening. I felt very tired, and rather disgusted with myself. It seemed to me as if I'd been indulging in mental masturbation for quite a few days, playing word games, playing at being a genius, playing at being at the edge of psychotic. . . .
>
> Last night taking my seconals I thought—"A pill for the swill." And I was flat (stunned) by the recognition. How I hate this journal, hate myself, hate Adele, hate my wild kick, hate the garbage I release, how I cling to society to knock me out, to stun my rebellion. If I ever go insane I'll not be a schizo. I'll be manic depressive.

His recoveries are just as fervent; he sometimes sounds like Kerouac.

> I am manic, alive, filled every day with the excitement and revelation of everything I see. . . .
>
> I'm a synthesizer, just as a crook is. I cannot make the original discovery, but I can add the fabulous jewel to it at my best. So I dip into other books and other men's styles, take the ideas I wish, throw

> away the others, understand one facet of a person to the exclusion of the rest because what I want is the jewel in the suitcase—fuck the rest, fuck the furs and the bonds. . . .
>
> My mind is like a tiger.

The journal jumps over a wide arc of heterogeneous material, making it hard at times to find a filament of continuity, yet it hangs together. One reason is that "Lipton's Journal" is a psychoanalytic act. Lindner wouldn't analyze him, so he does the job himself. He looks at his childhood, his wives, his family and friends, his ambitions and his failures, his writings, all with an eye to clarifying the basic lineaments and conflicts of his psyche so that he can move forward and claim his genius, which he boldly asserts. Another claim to coherence is that the journal is a dictionary of dualisms. The indubitable doubleness of all nature, all phenomena, is the centrifugal belief that supports every exploration in the journal. All the antinomies that he had pondered since his youth come tumbling out. He works through a range of commonplace oppositions such as sun-moon, conscious-unconscious, heaven-hell, as well as bodily functions—orgasms and vomiting, weeping and laughter, intercourse as giving and taking—and dozens of others: choice-habit, antacid-analgesic (which he proposes as the title of a one-thousand-page novel), and energetic repetitions of the saint-psychopath dualism. He considers his sexuality, his addictions, and like Nathaniel Hawthorne's Reverend Dimmesdale, practices vigils of self-examination.

> Looking at myself in the mirror, high on Lipton's, I saw myself as follows: The left side of my face is comparatively heavy, sensual, possessor of hard masculine knowledge, strong, proud, and vain. Seen front-face I appear nervous, irresolute, tender, anxious, vulnerable, earnest, and Jewish middle-class. The right side of my face is boyish, saintly, bisexual, psychopathic, and suggests the victim.

For Mailer it was incontestable that two people—not two halves of one—lived inside every human. As he put it, "*Every man is a marriage within himself.*" The two people inhabiting him, referred to over and over as the saint and the psychopath, are linked by "the apparently silly compromise of an over-friendly anxious boyish Jewish intellectual, 'seductive' and inhibited by turns." This front-face construct, a "social image," is close to being a "despised image," he says, but one necessary for fruitful relations with those he is too much in awe of to disclose his real self, or selves. He names as authority figures Ted Amussen, Stan Rinehart, and John Aldridge, but says there are many others. Lindner is not one of them. He is Mailer's audience of one, a source of psychoanalytic practice and insight and, in a real way, his collaborator on the journal. They are utterly candid.

> The inter-fecundation is starting. A letter from Bob [Lindner] says, "Occasionally . . . I find myself leaping ahead in my mind—or arguing fiercely as if you were present." It has to be. So many of my ideas are expansions of Bob's ideas—in turn many of mine will be expanded by Bob. Yet, I'm ashamed to say that I was not entirely pleased when I read the above. There's a part of me which is such a *holder.* I really hate to give with a part of me, and I usually give best when I will not be totally accepted. (Bob was right about this.) I'm so afraid things will be stolen—which of course is the way of saying things will be improved. What causes the rich man so much anguish when his joint is looted is that deep in him he suspects that the thief will enjoy his property more than he did. There is one other fear about Bob which is justifiable perhaps. I'm not at all sure he's the revolutionary—he is so capable of turning back to be the mere reformer.

When Mailer became rampant and arrogant during a December visit to Baltimore, Lindner called him "a pint-sized Hitler." "It's so true," Mailer acknowledged in the journal. He could be just as frank: "Lindner gave me a pain in the ass last weekend," he wrote. "He acted like a shy sexy teasing society bitch who gave you the sexual come-on when you'd given up, and threw her manners at you when you advanced." When Lindner said that Mailer was "blindly paranoid," Mailer countered with a list of his friend's lacks: "his shlumperness, his sly (but heavy) manipulations, his hang-dogness, his fear of authority, his half-works, his games with [his wife] Johnn[ie], his guilt about it, his guilt about every fucking thing." Yet they were close enough for Mailer to compare their relationship to that of Marx and Engels, and concluded, "If I didn't like him so much, if I didn't feel so psychicly [sic] close, as if we were the two talented Jewish sons of the same family, the older brother I never had, I really would be tempted to slug that sly stealing cocksucker." As he completed portions of the journal, he would mail the carbon to Lindner, who responded with long letters.

Mailer knew the writings of Marx better than he did those of Freud; the converse was true of Lindner, but both felt the ideas of the two great thinkers needed irrigation. Mailer laid it out:

> So, modestly, I see my mission. It is to put Freud into Marx, and Marx into Freud. Put Tolstoy into Dostoyevsky and Dostoyevsky into Tolstoy. Open anarchism with its soul-sense to the understanding of complexity, and infuse complex gloom with the radiance of anarchism. As Jenny Silverman [Bea's mother] said of me once, "The little pisherke with the big ideas." Pint-sized Hitler. Yes.

In another entry, he fleshed out the reciprocal, developing nature of their missions.

> I who was one of the worst soldiers ever to go into an Army, one of the people who had the least feeling for Army life, nonetheless was the one who had to capture the psychology inside and out of the Army. I, who am timid, cowardly, and wish only friendship and security, am the one who must take on the whole world. I, whose sexual nature is to cling to one woman like a child embracing the universe, am driven by my destiny to be the orgiast, or at least the intellectual mentor of orgiasm. I, who find it essentially easier to love than to hate; I who could probably find more people to love in the world than anyone I know, am destined to write about characters who are conventionally "unlovable."

Mailer's Marxist mentor, Malaquais, receives a few comments and it is clear that their friendship will continue, although slightly altered. Mailer is grateful to Malaquais, but no longer stands in awe of him. This can be seen in an early entry, a reflection on the "square blunt building-brick quality" that Mailer found to characterize most socialist analyses. His emerging style can be seen in the extended metaphor with which he reveals the evolution of their relationship.

> His thought of course has the nobility of a cathedral, but he's filled every square inch of the cathedral with a tile, and so his new thought

> can consist merely of improving the total design. He can replace one tile by another. But he will never build a cathedral which dissolves into light. For all the beauty of his conceptions, a dank oppressive gloom breathes out of the doors and no one wants to enter Malaquais' cathedral. He is left the gloomy caretaker of it. One reason he cannot chase me away entirely is that I'm the village boy who wandered in one evening and stayed to admire the cathedral for many years, asking the caretaker every day, "Don Malaquais, tell me about the saints, and why this stone is this color?" I was a naughty boy and I was forever quitting his lessons to throw stones at the bats, but what he cannot bear, dear Malaquais, is the silence now that I am gone. Timidly, terrified, like a shy old miser, he is making endless preparations necessary to go out and buy a new hat. He has no real hope he'll be detained in the village and find a place to build a new cathedral, he knows he'll go back to the old one and watch the bats multiply.

If there is any doubt about the shift in his feelings, his list of desired literary executors in the journal makes it clear. He names his sister, Cy Rembar, Dan Wolf, and, as chief executor, Lindner. Malaquais is not on the list. Barney is.

In late January 1955, Mailer spent most of the day with his father. It was, he wrote, the first real talk they had ever had, and he told his father that he loved him, "instead of hitting him with all kinds of shit and making him feel like a piece of dirt," as he wrote in "Lipton's Journal." For the first time, he had the conviction that he understood Barney from Barney's perspective. He saw that his father's gambling was not just a neurotic condition, but also "an expression of his artistry," not only an aberration but also a source of deep pleasure for Barney, however much it aggrieved the conventional sensibilities of his mother. He repeated that Barney understood him better than his mother, and what appeared to be his father's pompousness was really a burlesque of Fan's bourgeois sentiments.

> He overdid it. Unconsciously, he made her sound ridiculous. It was his private way of encouraging me to be a rebel. Her dictums made a certain practical common-sense. To rebel against them would have made me feel too guilty. But there was my father, repeating what she

> said, exaggerating it, multiplying it, until the sheer human nonsense of bourgeois human values rang in my head. . . . From deep within him, he was warning me, he was saying, "Go out, son, be a rebel, because if you're not a rebel you'll end up a pompous fool, ignored, and the subject of people's contempt." So I loved him today.

He would soon enough overtop his father's transgressions, although he would never cut himself off from his mother's family values. If Fan was a bourgeois "saint," Barney, as Mailer's sister put it, "was probably a bit psychopathic."

On his thirty-second birthday, Mailer wrote over ten thousand words in "Lipton's Journal," a record. He was preparing himself, anointing himself. In his thirty-third, Christological year, he would begin his public mission as prophet and culture hero. The journal's ruminations and meditations, the postscripts to his first three novels, the brutally honest self-analysis, and the candid portraits of family members and friends comprise a web of carefully considered calibrations of his relationships with people, events, and ideas, set down in preparation for this mission. We can in fairness call the journal an examination of conscience and consciousness (reminiscent of that practiced by William James), but perhaps more than anything else it is an urgent summoning of his powers. He called his introspections a "great adventure," adding "I don't think I have ever been so frightened in my life."

He wrote long passages in the journal exploring the relations between the saint and the psychopath, often sounding like D. H. Lawrence, whose continuing influence on Mailer cannot be gainsaid. Here is Lawrence, commenting on Tolstoy's espousal of Christianity in his late works, followed by Mailer.

> And this is Tolstoi, the philosopher with a very nauseating Christian-brotherhood idea of himself. Why limit man to a Christian brotherhood? I myself, I could belong to the sweetest Christian-brotherhood one day, and ride after Attila with a raw beefsteak for my saddle-cloth, to see the red cock crow in flame over all Christendom, next day.

> One must love disorder and love order, hate order and hate disorder. Yet, here is where I disagree with the Greeks and all the other

> Golden Meaners—there is no such thing as a Golden Mean in Life. It is only by welcoming the extremes of one's personality, tempering those extremes only—assuming of which I'm not certain that life here is better than life-after-death—tempering those extremes only by the knowledge that one must not be destroyed by them, that one goes on, one grows, one finds creative-destroying fulfillment.

The journal is also a testament of his love for Adele.

> Adele's qualities. She hated the portrait of Elena [Esposito, in *The Deer Park*], it hurt her terribly, she felt it was the way I saw her, yet she accepted it, she loves the book. Part of it of course is her despised image of herself, but more important still is the terrific woman in her who accepts my work no matter how painful it is to her, who is even capable of wishing only the best for it.

Near the end of the journal, he states explicitly what until then he had held back: "Today I can know that I love her because the thought of losing her, through death, through the army [he feared being recalled if war with the Soviet Union broke out], through jail, through whatever, is unbearable to me. A void opens. I know that without her I would be a cripple." Their relationship was far from settled; there was rough ground ahead. But they had reached a plateau.

ADELE RECALLED HIS mood swings in early 1955, and the extremes of his personality. At parties, she said, he took pains to include her in conversations, while holding her hand and smiling. "I never felt pushed into the background," she said, "because I was essentially not competitive with him. If anything, I was proud of my darling when he was at his sober, intelligent, funny, best in public." But when he was drinking heavily, he flirted with other women, and got into arguments. Adele says she began to find telephone numbers written down on matchbooks, and wondered why he had to prove to himself that women liked him. Once, she wrote, when they had an argument in the presence of Dan Wolf, he slapped her. She often drank heavily at parties, trying to drown the "nagging voice in my head that whispered, 'You're an imposter. You're not this cool, beautiful wife of a famous writer.' " The booze freed her, she said, to play opposite Mailer's repertoire of roles, including "Rocky Marciano, Jesse James, Miles Davis the Cool and Scott Fitzgerald the Drunk."

His experimentation with personas in "Lipton's Journal" contains extended characterological theories and ruminations arising from his new identity as saint-psychopath. He planned to deploy his ideas in at least three novels: the recently aborted concentration camp novel, "The City of God"; "Antacid-Analgesic," a mammoth novel about sex; a third is a continuation of the stories of Marion Faye and Sergius O'Shaugnessy. None of these came to pass, but their themes would be examined in the essay that established Mailer's reputation as a philosopher of hip, "The White Negro." The first idea is recorded in his entry for December 31, 1954: "Wild thought. The atom bomb may naturally have kicked off hipsterism." The link persisted in memory, and in the early spring of 1957 he wrote the first sentence of the essay: "Probably, we will never be able to determine the psychic havoc of the concentration camps and the atom bomb upon the unconscious mind of almost everyone alive in these years." The hipster, the American existentialist, he wrote, appeared on "this bleak scene," determined to live in the "enormous present" under the overhang of past totalitarian liquidation and potential nuclear destruction. The prime model for the hipster, Mailer avers, is the urban Negro ("Black" was not an accepted term until the mid-1960s and "African American" until even later). He may have been the first writer to link the restless energies and suffering of American blacks, the atom bomb, and the German crematoria.

On January 27, 1955, he introduced a new topic in the journal: the sexual potency of blacks. He says that "Southern rage" at Negro progress is due to the "unconscious belief in the myth—which may well be right—that the nigger has a happy sex life, happier than the white, and the Negro is recompensed for his low state in society by his high state in the fuck. The scales are balanced." Two years later, he told his idea to a journalist, Lyle Stuart, and Stuart sent it to William Faulkner, Eleanor Roosevelt, and several others for comment. The mainly negative responses that came back, and Faulkner's curt dismissal, prompted Mailer to begin "The White Negro." "Lipton's Journal" would be his source book for the essay, and many passages have their origin there. The idea of the existential "enormous present," for example, is found in the journal, and the following passage, written on February 1, undergirds the entire essay.

> Generally speaking we have come to the point in history—in this country anyway—where the middle class and upper middle class is composed primarily of the neurotic-conformists, and the saint-psychos are found in some of the activities of the workingclass (as opposed to the workingclass itself), in the Negro people, in Bohemians, in the illiterates, among the reactionaries, a few of the radicals, some of the prison population, and of course in the mass communication media.

When he realized that he would have to immerse himself in the Putnam's galleys of *The Deer Park*, he knew that he would have to end the journal, and this led to several final recognitions. The regular use of marijuana, followed by sleeping pills and/or Scotch and then a lot of coffee would have to stop. If he wanted to write another long work—the journal being "quite unpublishable in its present form"—he would have to plod along without drugs. "Now," he wrote, "I have to take an enormous step, and my capacities may not be equal to it. Still, I don't regret the too-quick opening, the great take of these past few months. I had to, for my health, and besides one should also try for more, not for less. That's the only real health."

Although he was still focused on the novel, for the first time he began to see that he wanted to try other genres and forms. "I must desert my old obsession" about only writing one thing at a time and take on a variety of projects, "and whenever I feel bored or worn out with one, I must leave it for the next." For the remainder of his career, he would move with little strain from the novel to the essay, newspaper and magazine columns to poetry, plays to biographies, and also glide effortlessly from private labor to public activity—rotating his crops, as he once put it.

Toward the end of the journal, Mailer reflects on several of his salient mental faculties, which, as they developed, resembled Emerson's.

> My capacity to do something exceptional comes from the peculiar combination of powerful instincts face to face with my exceptional

> detachment. I am one of the few people I know who can feel a genuinely powerful emotion, and yet be able to observe it. That is what I must depend on, instead of violating my capacities by trying to make the rational scholarly effort to illumine my understanding of other men's jargons. Instead of poring (pouring) over all the relevant books, and there are five hundred I "ought" to start studying tomorrow, I do better to "waste" time and discover things for myself. The only things I've ever learned have been the things I've discovered for myself.

An exception to his rule of self-discovery happened one night in June 1953 when he was at the Handy Colony in Illinois. Jones had just given him a brief tutorial in Eastern religions, karma, and reincarnation. Mailer, then a hard-shell atheist, was somewhat incredulous. "You *believe* in that?" Mailer asked. Jones answered, "Oh, sure. That's the only thing that makes sense." Jones's answer, he said, "rang in my head for years." It opened a shaft to deep waters, and may have been the foundation for what happened on February 25, 1955. In a long entry at the very end of "Lipton's Journal," he describes how on that night he smoked marijuana when he was "already in a state of super-excitation,"

> I had nothing less than a vision of the universe which it would take me forever to explain. I also knew I was smack on the edge of insanity, that I was wandering through all the mountain craters of schizophrenia. I knew I could come back, I was like an explorer who still had a life-line out of the caverns, but I understood also that it would not be all that difficult to cut the life line. Insanity comes from obeying a hunch—it is a premature freezing of perceptions—one takes off into cloud seven before one has properly prepared the ground, and one gives all to an "unrealistic" appreciation of one's genius.

This was Mailer's road to Damascus experience. His atheism withered and belief took hold, belief in a God who was not all-powerful, an existential God. Writing in 1970, he remembered being "terrified" in that hour when he "first encountered the thought around one of the bends of marijuana fifteen years ago." All of his later ideas had their roots in that moment, he said, although it would be three years before he was able to fully articulate his beliefs.

THE PUTNAM'S GALLEYS arrived in early February, but the novel had a June publication date and Mailer doesn't seem to have looked at them except in a cursory way. Accompanying the galleys was Ted Purdy's letter with some suggestions for improving the novel, but ruling out a major rewrite. The new deadline for turning in the corrected galleys was April 15, but Mailer had given one of his sets with marginal notes to Charles Laughton with the hope of interesting him in a film version of *The Deer Park*. Laughton had been in New York in connection with his film *The Night of the Hunter*, and from February 23 to March 2, they met daily at the St. Moritz Hotel to discuss *Naked*, which Laughton was still interested in producing. He remembered the experience fondly in a 1968 letter to Laughton's widow, Elsa Lanchester. He told her that he had never met a more intelligent or learned actor. "He gave me a marvelous brief education in the problems of a movie director," he said, "as he would explain to me, sometimes patiently, sometimes at the edge of his monumental impatience, how certain scenes which worked in the book just weren't feasible for the movie." When Laughton was having trouble visualizing the characters, he asked Mailer to draw pictures of them. Mailer protested that he lacked the skill, whereupon Laughton said, "Nonsense, Mailer, anybody can draw. You go ahead and do it and that will give me some idea of what you have in your mind that you can't express." Laughton was correct, and Mailer got many new insights about his characters. After a week of work, Laughton said, " 'Mailer, let's get the hell out of here, I feel like seeing some art.' And we went over to the Oriental Room of the Metropolitan where he was, of course, well known, and I was introduced that day to [the Japanese artists] Hiroshige and Hokusai, a pleasure for which I'm still in debt."

Mailer wrote to Laughton at the end of March asking for the return of the galleys. Laughton replied by telephone and promised that they would be sent shortly. When the galleys arrived nearly three weeks later, Mailer went to work, assuming he would have them done in a few weeks. He dearly wanted to put *The Deer Park* behind him. But what he discovered as he began was that the voice of his narrator, Sergius O'Shaugnessy, did not match his experience. He sounded more like Fitzgerald's Nick Carraway, a Princeton graduate, than a young man who had been brought up in an orphan asylum, scuffled through adolescence and early manhood, and earned his first lieutenant's silver bars flying a score of combat missions over Korea. The only course was to begin "ripping up the silk of the original syntax" and give O'Shaugnessy a more aggressive tone, a more colloquial voice, one that matched his hardscrabble background.

When planning *The Deer Park* four years earlier, Mailer had been a different person. At that time, before suffering through the reviews of *Barbary Shore* and the ensuing doubts about his vocation; before meeting Adele and Lindner; before beginning to seriously smoke marijuana while conducting a self-analysis in "Lipton's Journal"; before jettisoning lingering pieties about the literary establishment and catching a glimpse of a vertiginous universe; before identifying more closely with his father's rebellious ways; prior, in short, to his rebirth as a psychic outlaw, Mailer resembled in more ways than one a sensitive young man. Now he was stronger, more cynical and belligerent, and his new narrator, as he came into focus, was not only a shrewder, more credible observer of Elena's love affair with Eitel and his slow, tragic corruption by Hollywood, he was, Mailer recognized, "an implicit portrait of myself as well." He didn't like the notion of using his own divided psyche as the armature for O'Shaugnessy's. Doing so, he wrote, "was a psychological violation." But there was no alternative. His editors were getting anxious. They were not happy when he asked that his delivery date for the galley proofs be pushed back to June 1.

Without drugs, he couldn't write; he needed more than in the past. Along with marijuana, Seconal, booze, coffee, and two packs of cigarettes a day, he began taking a tranquilizer, Miltown, and a type of amphetamine with the trade name of Benzedrine. Bennies, long used by long-haul truckers and pilots, were a favorite of various Beat Generation figures, Jack Kerouac and Allen Ginsberg most notably. The trick was to find the point at which the drugs balanced out and he could write for an hour or two. "Bombed and sapped and charged and stoned," he lurched forward through May, feeling as tired as he had when on patrols in Luzon. He missed the June submission date and negotiated a final, drop-dead date of August 1, which pushed publication to mid-October. He knew that further delay would destroy any chance of good fall sales.

Working through a very hot summer in New York, he managed to meet the deadline. Then he drove up to Provincetown with Adele to unwind. There he slept, swam, and shed some of the drugs while waiting for further proofs. He also began reading Thomas Mann's multilayered symbolic novel, *The Magic Mountain*, which, he said, "lowered *The Deer Park* down to modest size in my brain." He finished final revisions and sent them off on August 15. A week later, back in New York, he took one more look and decided on one more change. With the addition of still another drug—mescaline—to his pharmacopeia, he rewrote the last page of the novel, the conclusion of O'Shaugnessy's imagined conversation with God about the relationship of sex and time. The cryptic lines continue to puzzle readers: God tells him to "think of Sex as Time, and Time as the connection of new circuits." He wrote to Lindner about the mystical effects of using mescaline. "Truly Bob," he said, "it was a little like entering paradise." In "The Mind of an Outlaw," Mailer says that the novel's ending is the only good writing he had ever done while stoned, although it has bewildered readers for fifty years.

IN A PATTERN that he would follow for the rest of his life, Mailer wrote to almost no one during the final sprint. But as soon as the novel was finished, he sent out a stream of letters to family and friends. Writing to Uncle Dave and Aunt Anne, he announced that the book would be published on October 14. He added that he and Adele had purchased two standard poodles, Tibo (who "looks like the black sheep") and Zsa Zsa (who would be the mother of their thirty-four pups). He became inordinately fond of Tibo's intelligence and verve. He once said that the variety of intelligent sounds made by Tibo convinced him that the dog was close to speaking. He included one more piece of information: he was a silent partner in a new weekly newspaper in Greenwich Village, *The Village Voice*. Ed Fancher was to be the publisher and Dan Wolf the editor.

It became clear by the end of August that Laughton had lost interest in the film version of *Naked and the Dead*, and Paul Gregory would now be the lead producer. Mailer suspected that the script was already written. With time on his hands, and feeling somewhat rested, he began dropping in at the *Voice*'s offices on Greenwich Avenue. Because of the sale of *Naked*, he was comparatively wealthy at the time. According to the 1955 financial statement prepared by Barney (the *Voice*'s first accountant), Mailer's net worth at the end of 1955 was $108,270, most of it invested in stocks and bonds. He had put $5,000 into the paper for a 30 percent share. Wolf and Fancher also had 30 percent shares; the remaining 10 percent was owned by Cy Rembar, who drew up the corporation papers. Mailer took credit for inventing the name, although others remembered that he had selected it from a list of proposed titles.

His focus in the early fall of that year was not *The Village Voice*, however. Advancing the fortunes of *The Deer Park* was his first priority. Around the beginning of September he began sending out inscribed copies in the hope of reaping some responses that could be used, if not for the jacket, then for advertisements. He mailed off copies to Philip Rahv and Alberto Moravia, whom he knew fairly well, and to Graham Greene, Cyril Connolly, and Ernest Hemingway, whom he didn't know at all. Brando got a copy and a note saying Mailer had learned from his work and thought Brando could learn from the novel. Others went to friends: Malaquais, Jones, and Styron, Dan and Rhoda (née Lazare) Wolf and Fancher, Howe, Hellman, Lillian Ross, Harvey Breit, Dwight Macdonald, Vance Bourjaily, and perhaps Vidal. He asked Mickey Knox, pointedly, to give his best wishes to Vidal in Hollywood.

He pinned his highest hopes on Hemingway, as he later wrote: "I could not keep myself from thinking that twenty good words from Ernest Hemingway would make the difference between half-success and a breakthrough. He would like the book, he would have to—it would be impossible for him not to see how much there was in it." But Mailer was angry at himself for begging, "for stealing a trick from the Hollywood I knew so well," and undercut himself with the inscription on the copy he mailed to Hemingway in Cuba. In *Advertisements for Myself*, he gives the disastrously qualified inscription.

> To Ernest Hemingway
>
> —because finally after all these years I am deeply curious to know what you think of this.
>
> —but if you do not answer, or if you answer with the kind of crap you use to answer unprofessional writers, sycophants, brown-nosers, etc., then fuck you, and I will never attempt to communicate with you again.
>
> —and since I suspect that you're even more vain than I am, I might as well warn you that there is a reference to you on page 353 which you may or may not like.
>
> Norman Mailer

The reference concerns a bullfighting novel that O'Shaugnessy, having left California and now teaching bullfighting in the Village, is trying to write. The novel wasn't very good, he admits, because it "was inevitably imitative of that excellently exiguous mathematician, Mr. Ernest Hemingway." The book came back ten days later, apparently unopened. He pondered the various possibilities: that it was a bad address; that all unsolicited books were returned; that Hemingway's wife Mary interceded; that Hemingway read the novel but was uncertain what to say and punted; or that he had read the inscription and said to himself, "If you want to come on that hard, Buster, don't write words like 'deeply curious,' " mailed it back, in its original wrappings, "and started to drink fifteen minutes early that day." Four years later, probably at the urging of George Plimpton, Hemingway sent a handwritten letter to Mailer, thanking him for sending the novel. He said he had later bought a copy and read it while laid up from an illness or injury and had liked it, even though it had "shitty reviews." He went on to encourage Mailer and gave him this advice on reviews: "Try for Christ sake not to worry about it so much. All that is poison. Remember only suckers worry. You can't write, fuck or fight if you worry. That doesn't mean not to think. This [is] all that I can tell you that might be any use." Hemingway's encouragement would have been welcome in 1955; Mailer was indeed worried. His effort to gain encomia from established novelists and critics, and from Brando, "ended in fiasco," he said.

The only one who answered him was Moravia, who said that it had Mailer's "usual qualities of vitality, aggressiveness, sincerity and naiveness," but it was too long. O'Shaugnessy, he said, "has no function (I mean dramatic function) and therefore one feels that he is not necessary." The novel, he says, would have been much improved if he had written the book in the third person and focused on the affair of Elena and Eitel. Mailer's narrator—"a duplicate of yourself," he correctly concludes—could be cut out entirely.

MAILER WAS NOT the first American writer to be interviewed on the occasion of a book's publication. But few sought or embraced such publicity with his avidity. Over the course of his career, he was interviewed over seven hundred times, surely a record for a writer. In 1955, however, interviews with writers were far less common than in the years following the revamping, by the editors of *The Paris Review*, of the form into a well-edited collaboration, rather than a confrontation, or a search for authorial gaffes. For *The Deer Park*, he appears to have set up interviews with Martha MacGregor, the book editor of the *New York Post*, and with Lyle Stuart, editor of the muckraking monthly *Exposé* (later called *The Independent*). He struck back at Stan Rinehart in the MacGregor interview, telling the story of how he responded when the publisher said he didn't feel he could put his name on *The Deer Park*. "I said, 'Why Stanley, I'm deeply shocked. How dare you say something like that after publishing *A House Is Not a Home*,' " a reference to Polly Adler's bestselling 1953 memoir about her career running Mafia-connected brothels in Manhattan and elsewhere. The Stuart interview, which Mailer gave "with a couple of drinks in me and a good drag or two of pot," appeared in late November when *The Deer Park* had climbed to number six on the bestseller list, is his first major interview, and his first conscious attempt to shape his public image. He states that he believes in God, "but it is a very personal faith," and he wants no connection with religious institutions; he defines himself as a "Marxian anarchist, a contradiction in terms," but one which gives breathing space to both extremes of his personality; he says he thinks "once in a while of becoming the president," but says that "politics as politics interests me less today than politics as part of everything else." He is also blunt about his ambition to be "a really great writer," an artist whose role is "to be as disturbing, as adventurous, as penetrating as his energy and courage make possible," a line which would be quoted many times over the decades. Mailer qualified, but never backed away from any of these aspirations, except running for president. He settled for mayor of New York.

By publication day, the novel was in its third printing. Mailer began sending advertising copy to Putnam's, quoting from the MacGregor interview and the early reviews. He suggested the same technique used for *Barbary Shore*: alternating positive reviews with negative ones, raves with stink bombs. The *New York Times*'s Orville Prescott called it "a thoroughly nasty book," but Malcolm Cowley, a friend of Hemingway's and chronicler of the "Lost Generation," said it was "the serious and reckless novel on the movie colony that we have been waiting for since Scott Fitzgerald failed to finish *The Last Tycoon*." Several newspaper ads and bookstore flyers quoted this comment, and the novel went into its fourth and fifth printings. As expected, *Time* panned it, comparing it to the sleazy scandal magazine *Confidential*. Putnam's spent $10,000 on advertising, a very high sum for the period. Overall, the reviews leaned toward the negative, especially outside the biggest cities.

The most important advertisement for the novel, however, was not paid out of this budget. Appearing in the fourth weekly issue of *The Village Voice* on November 16 was a half-page ad designed and paid for ($127.50) by Mailer. Under the headline: "All over America 'THE DEER PARK' is getting nothing but RAVES," he arrayed fifteen negative blasts, all attributed. A sample: "The year's worst snake pit in fiction," "sordid and crummy," "moronic mindlessness," "nasty," "unsavory," "dull," and in large letters at the bottom: "A BUNCH OF BUMS." It was his way of announcing, he said, "that I no longer gave a dog's drop for the wisdom, the reliability, and the authority of the public's literary mind, those creeps and old ladies of vested reviewing." He thought the ad might sell some books, and it may have, as the novel remained in sixth place on the bestseller list through the end of November. In the end, however, he would have lost his bet with Alfred Knopf. When all the returns were in, the novel had sold just under fifty thousand copies, an estimable number, but an order of magnitude less than the number *The Naked and the Dead* eventually sold.

IN HIS MEMOIR *New York in the Fifties*, Dan Wakefield recalled the mood of the Village during that decade. "Our generation," he said,

> needed the Village and all it stood for as much as the artists, writers, and rebels of preceding generations—maybe even more. If the mood of the country was to force everyone to conform, to look and dress like the man in the gray flannel suit, surely it was all the more important to have at least one haven where people were not only allowed but expected to dress, speak, and behave differently from the herd. This was a time when a beard might be regarded as a sign of subversion.

When he saw that *The Deer Park* was not going to have extraordinary sales, Mailer began "to feel the empty winds of a post-partum gloom." He was in no condition for the kind of monastic seclusion needed to write a thousand-page novel. His self-analysis was still under way and the ideas of his journal were still percolating. He wanted to vent, preach, and howl. "At heart," he said, "I wanted a war." The members of the generation described by Wakefield would be the recruits for his army. Mailer gave himself a new name: "General Marijuana," and for the first time began referring to himself in the third person:

> Drawing upon hash, lush, Harlem, Spanish wife, Marxist culture, three novels, victory, defeat, and draw, the General looked over his terrain and found it a fair one, the Village a seed-ground for the opinions of America, a crossroads between the small town and the mass-media. Since the General was nothing if not Hip (in the self-estimation of his brain) he was of course aware that the mind of the Village was a tight sphincter, ringed with snobbery, failure, hatred and spleen.

He made many suggestions about how the *Voice* should develop, but Fancher and Wolf rejected them. In a late interview, Mailer drew quick portraits of his partners. He had met Wolf first, through Malaquais, in 1948.

> He was everybody's guru. We'd all go to him with our problems, our thoughts and so forth. One of his best friends [Ed Fancher] was a psychoanalyst, and I had a hunch that the psychoanalyst even listened to Dan because he had a huge knowledge of psychoanalysis, and a huge sense of people and could have been a psychoanalyst, but hated the profession and considered himself in a funny way superior to it. . . . He was very private; he was very dissatisfied with his life. He wanted power; he had none. He was this quiet man with this wise sad smile, who was an absolute intensity of unsatisfied desires within. It had to do with prominence and prestige. He knew that he was brighter than anyone around and he wasn't getting enough for it.

Fancher, whom Mailer met through Wolf, had one quality that was "extraordinary."

> He was like a lineman in football who could take fifty hits in a game and still be standing at the end of the game, still ready to tackle anybody who was trying to come through his hole. And so he had that kind of strength. Dan had the wiliness of a great quarterback who never wanted to be intercepted, never wanted to hand the ball off to anyone wrong, who never wanted to call a play that wasn't going to work. Very cautious, but occasionally daring. So the two of them had skills that complemented one another.

Wolf and Fancher had much to learn about running a newspaper, although they recognized that for it to succeed they needed advertising, and to get that the paper had to appeal to several publics. For the old-time Irish and Italian residents of the Village, there had to be copy about church, social, and political organizations. For the younger crowd, stories were needed about the cultural scene—poetry readings, foreign films, jazz, and folk music. And there had to be some hard news. The headline of the lead story of the first issue on October 26 was "Village Trucker Sues Columbia"; there was little in the early issues to distinguish the *Voice* from its competitor, *The Villager.* In its first four months, the paper was quite bland. It was also hemorrhaging money, $1,000 a week. At the end of the year, Mailer loaned the paper $10,000.

Fancher and Wolf could hardly refuse Mailer when he proposed himself as a weekly columnist. They expected his column, "Quickly: A Column for Slow Readers," to be "radical and abrasive," Fancher said, and generate controversy. They had no inkling of how deliberately abusive it would be. Writing to Hollywood chum Chester Aaron shortly after starting the column, Mailer said that he should have lived in the previous century, "what with *épater le bourgeois* being the dominant passion of my life." In his notes for *Advertisements for Myself*, written in 1958, he recalled his motives for the column: "I really had the notion that the Village was going to dig what I did—that the results would be apocalyptic—we would see that a hero had appeared in the breach, any one of us (myself of course), but that the swindle was finally to be made apparent." The first column, accompanied by his photograph in the kind of lumberjack shirt that Kerouac would later wear in public, with tousled hair and a surly look, appeared on January 11, 1956.

He begins by stating baldly that the column will not be well written. To do so would require the expenditure of too much effort on a lost cause: trying to please the snobs and critics that abound in the Village, ambitious people whose lack of fulfillment only makes them "more venomous. Quite rightly. If I found myself in your position, I would not be charitable either. Nevertheless, given your general animus to those more talented than yourselves, the only way I see myself becoming one of the more cherished institutions of the Village is to be actively disliked each week." The column, he notes, took him an "unprofitable fifty-two minutes" to write.

His maiden effort brought a handful of irritated letters, including a sarcastic one from Joe Jensen of Bank Street stating his hope that "Quickly" would keep Mailer from writing another novel. Mailer now recognized that his task was to divert the anger onto "more deserving subjects." In the next column, he attacked the hypocrisy of the mass media. Much of the column was a redaction of reflections in "Lipton's Journal" on these topics. He called himself a "dialectical idealist," one who sought to improve society by attacking shibboleths like the abhorrence of obscenity. "For what are obscenities finally," he asked, "but our poor debased gutturals for the magical parts of the human body." The column might have gone down fairly smoothly, but he undercut it by adding a preface telling slow readers to skip the column and urging those who did read it to "have the courtesy to concentrate. The art of careful writing is beginning to disappear before the mental impotence of such lazy audiences as the present one."

After this column, the number of angry and dismissive letters from readers increased. Jensen attacked Mailer for imitating Dos Passos in "your ONE & ONLY BOOK," and comparing the column to "the very overworked, tired, boring, creaky, mimeographed Henry Miller." The tone of the rest of the letters is captured in one from Phyllis Lind: "This guy Mailer. He's a hostile, narcissistic pest. Lose him." He's the kind of character, she said, "who moves into a nice neighborhood and can't stand the warmth and harmony, so he does all in his power to disrupt it." Reading this, Mailer must have said, "Exactly!" It was, as he said later in *Advertisements for Myself*, "blitzkrieg."

The column went on for seventeen weeks. Mailer tried everything. He parodied the major gossip columnists and turned the column over to a Village wag for a parody of "Quickly" titled "Burp: A Column for People Who Can Read by Normal Failure." He celebrated three iconoclastic comedians—Steve Allen, George Gobel, and Ernie Kovacs—and debated the merits of psychoanalysis with a practitioner. About halfway through the run, Mailer began including letters from readers and his responses. When someone complained about his egotism, he replied: "Let others profit by my unseemly absorption, and so look to improve their own characters." He ran a contest, offering $20 to anyone who could guess his candidate for president in the 1956 election (Hemingway, one reader did). In his next column, he elaborated on Hemingway's credentials: physical courage, a good war record, and the charm of appearing to have had "a good time now and again." He also replied at length to another nasty letter from Jensen, who had complained about his "congenital or rigged up ostentation."

In late February, Robert Lindner died. He was forty-one. Mailer lauded his boldness and intelligence in his March 7 column, and also called him "one of the warmest people I have ever known." But he said that Lindner would have hated a "facile eulogy," and so devoted the rest of the column to quotations from his work, including one from Lindner's final book, *Must You Conform?*, published a few weeks before his death. Lindner's study reflects his collaboration with Mailer on "Lipton's Journal," as well as his own long-standing belief that current psychology practice falsely held that "human development is linked to human passivity." He ends the column with his own comment on Lindner's legacy: "Because of the instinct of rebellion, man has never been content, finally, with the limits of his life: it has caused him to deny death and to war with mortality. Man is a rebel. He is committed by his biology *not* to conform, and herein lies the paramount reason for the awful tension he experiences today in relation to Society."

Mailer was obviously saddened by Lindner's death. But he felt something else, as he explained when he neared his own death.

> I talked to him on the phone one day and he said "There's nothing they can do; I'm going to die." And he burst into tears. And I was so cold and so full of anger at where we'd gotten, and when I look back, it was one of the most unpleasant moments in my life. I didn't feel a fucking thing for him. I felt contempt that he was weakened. You see, my feeling was: "We're soldiers and if we die, we die." I have that feeling now; it's a lot easier now, I can assure you. But I remember not being sympathetic. Going through the dull motions of being sympathetic, the way one does when one's not there with a

> friend, but not really giving him what he needed. And I didn't believe he was going to die. And then, some weeks later, he died. And that was one of the great blows of my life because I couldn't believe it. And then I felt woe, and then I felt contrition. And then I remember at his funeral, his memorial service, I remember speaking and talking about him, and creating a sensation at the memorial service because I was talking about all his many wonderful qualities, and I said, "And on top of all that, he was a rogue." "Whohooohoo" went through the audience at the memorial service. There's his wife, his widow and all. But it was true.

A line from "The White Negro" may help us to understand what prompted him to blurt out what he did at the memorial: "The psychopath knows instinctively that to express a hidden impulse actively is far more beneficial to him than to confess the desire in the safety of a doctor's room." Truth telling would always be paramount for Mailer, whatever the cost. By his logic, he was honoring Lindner with his candor.

He changed the title of his column to "The Hip and the Square" not long after Lindner's death. The passing of his friend drove him back to his journal where he found the materials to begin creating a philosophy of Hip. He was also seriously reading Sartre for the first time, and exploring in his column what he felt were the profound differences between European and American existentialism. Both were the products of alienation from the conditions of twentieth-century existence. Both were premised on the inalienable freedom of the self and rejected tradition and authority. Both had leftist inclinations. Both were concerned with decoding the involutions of consciousness—sensory perceptions, intuitions, motives, and frissons. As Mailer put it a few years later, Sartre "had a dialectical mind good as a machine for cybernetics, immense in its way, he could peel a nuance like an onion." But Sartre and his followers were "alienated beyond alienation from their unconscious" and "its enormous teleological sense." Hip, he wrote in his penultimate column, "is based on a mysticism of the flesh." According to Mailer, Hip had faith in the possibility of personal spiritual transcendence, as yet undefined; most continental existentialists dismissed the idea of an afterlife.

Throughout his tenure as a columnist, Mailer's relations with the staff were tense at best. He berated them for a lack of boldness and for missing opportunities. For example, he wanted to run interviews with criminals, a murderer, perhaps. He was particularly incensed at proofreading and typesetting errors in his column, and when an editor substituted "nuisance" for "nuance" in a column that he, as usual, had turned in late, Mailer screamed at him over the telephone: "WHY DON'T YOU GET YOUR FINGER OUT OF YOUR ASS?" At one point, Wolf, who was usually quiet and detached, yelled back at him: "For a socialist you're acting like the worst capitalist in the world."

The shouting matches intensified and Mailer resigned. The final straw, he said in his farewell, were the typos in all but two of his columns. But the deeper cause, he argued, was that Wolf and Fancher wanted the *Voice* to be "more conservative, more Square," and he wanted it to be more hip. Wolf and Fancher were working long days just to get the paper out and had no desire to revamp it. Mailer thought the newspaper "should be very radical, full of sex and drugs," Wolf recalled. Mailer didn't think the paper would make it, Wolf said, "so it should go out in a blaze of glory like a big firecracker." Wolf and Fancher believed that there was room for two community newspapers in the Village, while Mailer scorned the idea. He thought the *Voice* should distinguish itself from *The Villager* by publishing sharp critiques of a society that was smothering creativity instead of civilized commentary on New York politics, cheery neighborhood vignettes, and listings of French films. He noted, however, that his column had never been edited or censored. He retained a minority shareholder stake in the *Voice* for over a decade, and after a three-year hiatus began writing occasional pieces for it.

Letters of regret poured in when Mailer resigned. The *Voice* printed eight of them. Seven were positive. The negative letter said the *Voice* was "richer for the loss of the castrated bellow of N. Mailer." The final letter was from a reader who had changed his mind.

> To Mr. Mailer:
>
> Let me say that I am extremely sorry your May 2 column is your final one. In all your columns, while some were damned aggravating (and why shouldn't they have been), what you did say, in essence, when the decorations were dismissed, and when the chips were down, was true and truly strong and original to read.
>
> Sincerely,
>
> Joe Jensen, Bank Street

A half century later, reflecting on his first stint as a columnist, Mailer said that once Wolf realized that the Village was on the edge of social change,

> that it was open and angry and wanted stuff, once he saw that my notion of it had not been incorrect, he went with it, and probably proceeded with vastly more wisdom than I would have. I would have wrecked it all over again in a few months because I was a wild man. I wanted the revolution to come; I wanted blood in the streets; I wanted the whole thing to start, and of course Dan would have been opposed and we would have been fighting all over again.

AS HIS ACTIVE involvement with the *Voice* began to wind down, Mailer took the advice he had given himself in his journal, and cast about for new projects. "I had mad ideas," he said later, and became "very curious" about the next stage of his own development. "You start making all sorts of experiments. I put myself in a laboratory." There were times, he wrote to Mickey Knox, "when I have to crack up a little or else I'll crack up big." He and Adele had discussed a trip to Europe for some time, and he wrote to Malaquais to make arrangements for what would be a ten-week trip that summer.

Although he was dismayed by the idea of starting a novel before he had recovered from the strains of *The Deer Park*, he began thinking about a short story that would eventually become part of "the big novel," as he would soon refer to it. Sergius O'Shaugnessy was by now a comfortable avatar, and "The Time of Her Time" is an account of his orgasmic struggles with a young woman, Denise Gondelman, set in the Village loft where he runs a bullfighting school by day and offers sexual therapy by night. He planned to include the story in a paperback collection consisting of his *Dissent* essays, *Voice* columns, plus some new material. His most momentous idea is first noted in a letter to Irving Howe. He asked if *Dissent* might be interested in an essay "on the philosophy of the hipster, because I think there are certain things in the ambiance of hipsters which should be interesting to radicals since the hipster, after all, is a new kind of underground proletariat and one which does cut across classes." He said that the idea was "most provisional," but given the conscientious probing of his psyche over the previous eighteen months, his heroic aspirations, and the coalescing of his new theology, writing "The White Negro" in this season of his life now seems to have been inevitable.

Just before they left for Paris on May 15, he and Adele went to see the acclaimed Broadway production of Samuel Beckett's *Waiting for Godot.* In his May 2 column where he announced he was leaving the paper, he had dismissed the play, while admitting that he had neither read nor seen it. The reviews of *Godot* had led him to conclude that Beckett, unlike his friend and countryman James Joyce, saw humanity as hapless, powerless. "So I doubt if I will like it," Mailer had written, "because finally not everyone is impotent, nor is our final fate, our human condition, necessarily doomed to impotence, as old Joyce knew, and Beckett I suspect does not." Then he read the play, and he and Adele went to see it. The power of Beckett's vision was clear. On the ride home from the theater, he was depressed and made more so when Adele said, "Baby, you fucked up." He got up the next morning, and "finally putting together what he had learned in seventeen weeks," wrote a three-thousand-word mea culpa, and paid the *Voice* to publish it.

His essay, "A Public Notice on Waiting for Godot," printed partially in tiny agate font, and taking up one full page of the *Voice*'s May 9 issue, is more than just an apology, however. He gives a very competent summary and analysis of the play, and then, toward the end, amplifies the theological ideas he had been mulling since encountering them "in the bends of marijuana" a year earlier. Either "consciously or unconsciously," Mailer says, Beckett is saying that "God's destiny is flesh and blood with ours," that the deity is not a distant, all-powerful Jehovah, but a God who is "determined by man's efforts, man who has free will and can no longer exercise it and God therefore in bondage to the result of man's efforts." Mailer wished to recruit and lead an army that would storm the redoubts of liberal caution and bourgeois prudishness to free God.

From the time Mailer began "Lipton's Journal," he had been dipping into Martin Buber's *Tales of the Hasidim*, reading snippets as he was "riding the electric rail of long nights on marijuana." In the two-volume collection, Buber, an internationally known philosopher, scholar, and religious existentialist, clarified and organized the oral teachings of the Hasidic movement, beginning with the founder Rabbi Israel ben Eliezer (1700–60). The Hasidim, it will be remembered, were opposed by a more scholarly sect, the *Misgnagdim,* children of the *Haskalah,* the Jewish Enlightenment, favored by Mailer's grandfather. Buber "hulled" the most telling anecdotes of the Hasidic masters "from the mass of the irrelevant" for his collection. The Rabbi ben Eliezer, known as the Baal Shem Tov, or Master of the Good Name (for his knowledge of how to employ the secret names of God), and his followers over several generations were revered as charismatic teachers, or *zaddikim.* These spiritual masters claimed to the power to discern, intermittently, the divine emanations surrounding humanity and, in indirect ways, to communicate with God. The *zaddikim* taught with parables and metaphors of the homeliest sort, but leavened with humor, as in the following, which Mailer quoted.

> The Fear of God: Once Zusya prayed to God: "Lord, I love you so much, but I do not fear you enough! Lord, I love you so much, but I do not fear you enough! Let me stand in awe of you like your angels, who are penetrated by your awe-inspiring name." And God heard his prayer, and his name penetrated the hidden heart of Zusya as it does those of the angels. But Zusya crawled under the bed like a little dog, and animal fear shook him until he howled: "Lord, let me love you like Zusya again!" and God heard him this time also.

He did not write about Buber's collection until 1962, but its influence is apparent in the Beckett essay. The *Tales*, he said, became his vehicle in the mid-1950s "for a small intellectual raid into the corporate aisles of modern theology," and a point of departure for his opposition to Sartrean existentialism. Henceforth, Mailer's apprehension of the invisible universe would be a subtle but steady presence in his thinking and writing, although it was rarely taken seriously by his readers, or barely noticed, for several years.

He ended his essay on *Godot* by arguing that Beckett's work could mark the end of ten years of "angry impotence," referring to the anxieties of the postwar period. While he was not a great admirer of the likely Democratic presidential candidate, Adlai Stevenson, he had significantly less regard for President Eisenhower, who he thought might not be reelected. His guarded optimism in the summer of 1956 led him to hear "the whispers of a new time coming. There is a universal rebellion in the air, and the power of the two colossal super-states may be, yes, may be ebbing." If that proved true, then "the creative nihilism of the Hip" might usher in a revolution, "the sexual revolution one senses everywhere"—from the suggestive jokes of TV comedians to the "growing power of the Negro." Thus, in his final piece in the *Voice*, he links black power with sexual emancipation at a time when both were only dimly perceived—and not in tandem—on the cultural horizon. Mailer's essay on *Waiting for Godot* is the prologue to "The White Negro," and his advertisement for himself as the philosopher-general of Hipsterism.

ACCORDING TO ADELE, Mailer was somewhat relaxed on the crossing on the SS *United States of America*. They drank and fought less than they had during the previous few months. Once in Paris, they regularly visited the Montparnasse apartment of Jean Malaquais. It was there that Mailer met James Baldwin, a writer who would influence and later challenge his ideas about black sexuality. The Harlem native was already acclaimed and, with Ralph Ellison, considered to be one of the most talented and promising postwar African American writers. In 1953, he published a novel, *Go Tell It on the Mountain*, about the role of religion in black America, based on his own experience as a teenage preacher in a revivalist church in Harlem. He followed this with a collection of autobiographical essays, *Notes of a Native Son* (1955), that solidified his reputation as a leading commentator on racial issues. One of the essays sharply criticizes *Native Son*, the masterwork of another African American Paris expatriate, Richard Wright. Baldwin was seen to be clearing a place for himself.

Meeting Mailer gave Baldwin the opportunity to measure himself against a writer whose ambition matched his own. "Jimmy had an absolutely wonderful personality in those years," Mailer told James Campbell, Baldwin's biographer. "I don't think there was anyone in the literary world who was more beloved than Jimmy. He had the loveliest manners." Baldwin remembered it this way: "Two lean cats, one white and one black, met in a French living room. I had heard of him, he had heard of me. And here we were, suddenly, circling around each other. We liked each other at once, but each was frightened that the other would pull rank." They were about the same age, both were New Yorkers, both had published three books. Mailer was more famous and considerably wealthier. Baldwin said his chief credentials were being black and knowing more about the "periphery," the mean streets of Harlem. He didn't know that Mailer was already thinking about an essay premised, in part, on the superior sexual prowess of blacks, but Baldwin did know that "to be an American Negro male is also to be a kind of walking phallic symbol."

Baldwin, who was gay, had come to Paris to escape prejudice against blacks and homosexuality. Mailer, deeply curious as usual, wanted to discuss both, as well as jazz, Harlem, criminals, books, everything. When they met, Baldwin had just concluded an unhappy affair with a Swiss man, and was in no mood to discuss intimate matters. He also saw that Mailer accepted the "myth of the sexuality of Negroes," and so he "chickened out" of what he thought would be an excruciating attempt to challenge Mailer's ideas. Instead, he socialized with the Mailers—he could drink as much as Mailer—and after a few weeks left for Corsica. He had no inkling of his new friend's roiled state, his addictions, and career anxieties. Mailer's public visage prevailed, and Baldwin's chief memory of that time in Paris was of "Norman—confident, boastful, exuberant, and loving, striding through the soft Paris nights like a gladiator."

Baldwin hid his despair over his failed affair from the Mailers. He was working on a novel, *Giovanni's Room*, a bold study of violence and homosexuality set in Paris, but was having difficulty finishing it. Nights after leaving the Mailers at the Hôtel Palais Royal, he "wandered through Paris, the underside of Paris, drinking, screwing, fighting—it's a wonder I wasn't killed," he said. Mailer had insomnia and left the hotel in the early morning hours. It would not have been surprising if they had bumped into each other. In a poem about that summer, "A Wandering in Prose: For Hemingway," Mailer begins with the memory of Adele's face "powder which smells like Paris when / I was kicking seconal and used to / get up at four in the morning and / walk the streets into the long wait / for dawn." He would find himself "at five in an Algerian / bar watching the workers take a / swallow of wine for breakfast, the / city tender in its light even to me / and I sicker than I'd ever been, / weak with loathing at all I had not done." He then recalls Adele's "detestation" of him for not being "nearly brave enough for you." Adele's memory is that Mailer, in withdrawal and "still reeling from *The Deer Park* disaster," was both angry and scared and often took it out on her. "In my own way," she said, "I could fling a lot of shit right back at his face." Mailer, however, put on a good face for Baldwin,

Jean and Galy Malaquais, and they didn't grasp the tense state of the Mailers' marriage.

They rented a car and drove to Munich to meet his German publisher. As they approached the German border, Adele told her husband that her heart was pounding. "Norman laughed, 'Baby, mine is pounding harder. I'm a Jew, you aren't.' " The men in Munich "made much of my dark good looks," she said. "I would overhear words like 'schoene mädchen' in restaurants and elevators. Norman looked pleased." They went from Munich to Buchenwald, which Mailer said he felt obliged to visit. They saw all the horrors. The small oven for children, Adele said, was "most graphic and heartbreaking." He never recorded his immediate response to viewing the camp, but his memories of the visit, deeply lodged, surfaced when he wrote "The White Negro." Back in Paris, Adele found she was pregnant. Mailer told her he knew what night the baby was conceived. They were very happy. Adele said that she "never learned to disentangle myself from his moods," but the pregnancy necessarily changed her focus. She found that the odor of alcohol made her ill. The distaste would continue for her pregnancy and through the period that she nursed the baby. "How I wish it had stayed that way for the rest of my life," she wrote, referring to her later alcoholism. They left a few weeks later, again on the *United States*. Mailer, sometimes unfeeling about the illnesses of others, was thoughtful and tended her as the morning sickness continued during the crossing.

He had promised Baldwin that he would do all he could to aid the reception of *Giovanni's Room*, which he had read in manuscript. He sent a blurb for the novel to Baldwin's publisher, and on August 16, before heading to Provincetown, he wrote a letter to Francis Brown, editor of *The New York Times Book Review*, offering to review the novel. Brown politely turned him down. Mailer mailed a carbon of his letter to Brown to Baldwin with a note asking him to let them know when he would be back in New York, and Baldwin wrote a warm note from Corsica thanking Mailer for the "very sweet thing" he'd done. His personal life, he said, "has gone all to pieces. But I imagine I'll recover this winter, if I work hard." They did not see each other for six months, but then their paths crossed often in New York.

Recalling his first meeting, Baldwin said he was "aware of a new and warm presence in my life." Campbell believes that he saw Mailer as "a partner, an equal, and therefore a lover," and this seems quite possible. Baldwin's preference for sexual relationships with bisexual and straight males was well known. He would not be the only gay man who was attracted to Mailer. Their relationship was complex. Campbell summed it up.

> What did exist, on both sides and in plentiful supply, was petulance, ego, vanity, impatience with the other's direction and aspirations. There was a considerable amount of mutual respect, but also a feeling on Mailer's side that Baldwin had wasted his substance in Europe, and on Baldwin's that Mailer's much-vaunted theories about Negroes' superior sexuality and elegance amounted to nothing more than a portrait of the noble savage re-drawn. They mirrored, after all, the kind of stereotypes he had been fighting for years. "Next thing you'll be telling me is that all coloured folks have rhythm!" was one of his favorite rebuffs, borrowed from Richard Wright.

IN SEPTEMBER THE Mailers visited their friends from Mexico Lew and Jay Allen in rural Connecticut, where they had recently moved. They liked the area—rolling hills, horse farms, rambling colonial houses, and lots of green. With a new baby on the way, the 55th Street apartment seemed small and they decided to move to the country. The presence of the Styrons and John Aldridge and his wife, Leslie, was another factor. The Mailers bought a large house and barn on fifty acres of woods and meadow in Bridgewater, about four miles from the Styrons, and not far from the New York state border. "The house is old," he wrote to Malaquais, "and it smells good as a house, the cellar has the odor of a warm bird's wing." It was bracketed by ancient elms.

One night two weeks before they moved, he took Tibo and Zsa Zsa for a walk at one A.M. When he paused near some doorsteps where three young men—"hoodlums" Mailer called them—were sitting, one of them made a crack about the dogs being queer. Mailer said something back and the man called him queer, which led to a fight. Mailer thought he would win, as he was older and heavier, but the hoodlum gouged his eye in a clinch, "very professionally, I may say," Mailer wrote to Malaquais. They clinched again and the man gouged Mailer's other eye.

> At that point a whole crowd of people—a gang—poured out of a house (we were fighting on the sidewalk) and some tremendous brute of a character clouted me, and said "Have you had it?" Well I had had it. I could hardly see, my eyes were bleeding, and I could see myself being beaten to death. So I nodded hopelessly, muttered several times over, "Yes, I've had it, I've had it," picked up the dogs from another hoodlum who ironically enough had been holding them during the fight and shambled off.

For a week, he had to stay in a darkened room because of a blind spot in one eye. He told his family that he had an infection. He was pleased with himself for not backing down, and happy that they had bought the Connecticut house before the fight, he told Malaquais, "or else I would always have felt that I was fleeing New York in a panic." He gave a briefer version of the story to Baldwin, adding that what was worse than the injury was working up the nerve to walk that street again, which he did.

In his letter to Malaquais, Mailer said he was losing many friends in New York because of his radicalism. "Phone calls don't come in any longer from one's elevated social friends." Mailer was obstreperous when he drank, and he was drinking a lot, bourbon mainly. The booze sanctioned crazy behavior. He took on accents—an Irish brogue, a British one that resembled Barney's, and the Texas drawl he had learned in the army, his favorite. When Dwight Macdonald asked why he put on these antic dispositions, he said that he lived "in a perpetual stagefright, going to so many parties," and therefore "assumed the accents as a kind of mask." His *Voice* column, his boozing, and his sexual freedom platform had checkered his reputation. When he went to parties in the Village, he said, the attitude was that "Satan and his wife had come into the room." With the move to Connecticut his lifelong pattern was firmly established: immersion in the "inhuman city with its violence, its coldness, its electric assault on the nerves," and then retreat to the country or Cape Cod.

In the spring of 1956, Mailer's and Jones's relationship was souring; Jones wrote to him that *The Deer Park* was a mistake. He added that "writing a fucking column for the *Village Voice*" was "another serious mistake in judgment." Mailer didn't reply, but when he was in Paris, he drafted a note to Jones.

> Dear Jim—this is just to let you know that this is the last line you will get from me until I have read your 1500 page novel [*Some Came Running*]. On which my congratulations. But, if as I fear, you have turned a little chicken since you've written Eternity, and this book, for all its size, and I suspect growing skill, is the color yellow, then I will feel obliged to tell you so. Mailer

Having rebuked Jones for being craven without even having seen his novel, Mailer thought better of it and decided not to send the note. Jones had the same impulse. The six-page letter he actually had sent to Mailer was a second, toned-down draft. The touchdown twins were disappointed with each other, but enough love remained for them to pull their punches. When he was unpacking in the new house in early November, Mailer dropped a note to Styron asking him to remember him to Jones.

Mailer had also had a serious argument with his old friend Adeline Naiman, and got "boiling mad" at her. At a party at the 55th Street apartment, he accused her of believing Adele to be "intellectually shallow and inferior." Perhaps because Mailer saw Adeline as a "brilliant intellectual," as she speculated, he projected his own views about Adele on her. Her insight was on the mark. The truth, Adeline said, was that she had little in common with Adele but had no ill feelings toward her, just the opposite. His harsh words drove her from the party, and they did not speak for some time. He also fought with Fig about Adele. Undoubtedly entwined with Mailer's intuitions about how his friends felt about Adele was their response to *The Deer Park*. Adeline, Aldridge, Malaquais, Fig, and Jones all disliked it. The novel's admirers were the ever-loyal Knox, Dan Wolf (from whom he was estranged because of the *Voice*), and Lindner, who was dead. Mailer's friendship with Styron was still intact, however, perhaps because Styron had sugared his criticisms of the novel.

Fifty years after the sexual revolution, court cases overturning anti-obscenity laws, and the fading of facades erected before Hollywood's workaday exploitation and sordidness, the merits of *The Deer Park* are more obvious. It was published at a time of knee-jerk prudishness when even metaphoric descriptions of sexual acts were considered bad taste. As Gay Talese noted in his memoir, *A Writer's Life*, a *New York Times* picture editor lost his job in 1954 "because he permitted the publication of a wedding-day photograph showing Marilyn Monroe and Joe DiMaggio revealing their physical attraction to each other while standing in front of City Hall in San Francisco—she with her head back and her mouth slightly open, and he with his lips puckered and his eyes closed." When Dan Wakefield, speaking with Mailer many years later, noted that *The Deer Park* was the most controversial novel of 1955, he replied, "Anything that dealt openly with sex back then was controversial. The issue of sex was the cutting edge of the new novel of exploration in the fifties. It was the way of going beyond the frontier." Looking at the novel sixty years later, Walter Minton's estimate seems on the mark: there is no better novel of Hollywood in the postwar period, or perhaps any period since.

ONCE SETTLED IN Bridgewater, he set up a gym of sorts in the barn, including a boxing ring. He also had a workshop there. He created a studio with a picture window for Adele in the attic, among other projects. In New York he had built a version of Wilhelm Reich's orgone box, a place where he could "scream and snort and bellow and growl and even pipsqueak." In Connecticut, he constructed a variation: a large, polished wooden egg large enough to hold a person in the fetal position. The idea, Adele explained, was to get inside, curl up, and be rocked by someone outside. A bongo board was another project, a fat wooden cylinder with a board on top on which he could balance, roll, and swivel. One day when Lew Allen was visiting and Mailer was demonstrating his agility on his customized version, Mailer fell and got a bloody nose. He convinced Allen to go along with the story that the blood came from a punch as they boxed. "Norman was ready to take offense at anything," Allen recalled. "His whole nervous system was exposed, and his nerve ends were out on stalks. He was on pot all the time and primed."

Adele's parents visited them in Connecticut. Her father, Al, a printer at the New York *Daily News*, in his earlier years had been an amateur fighter. He turned professional briefly and lost half of his twenty matches before retiring. The majority of his fights ended in knockouts. After he gave up boxing, he turned to handball, and played well into his eighties. When Al and Mae Morales arrived, Mailer greeted Al with, "Hiya champ," and they would trade fake punches like old sparring partners. Mailer had again quit smoking and was feeling healthy, although he had ballooned to 175 pounds. He and Al often put on the gloves and boxed a few rounds. Mailer was twenty years younger, so it is not too surprising that in one of their first matches he knocked Al down twice. The next time they visited, Al wanted to box right away. Al landed one on Mailer's chin and knocked him out. As Adele remembers it,

> Norman sat up almost immediately shaking his head, rubbing his jaw. He was still groggy as my father helped him up.
>
> "Jesus, young feller, sorry about that."
>
> Norman was a good sport about the whole thing, and instead of being angry, he admired my father. "Not bad, Al, for a fifty-four-year-old." He touched his chin. "That was some punch you landed."
>
> "Well, Norm," Daddy said, "you've got to be on your toes. You should've seen it coming. But that's the way ya learn."

Mailer did learn and became noticeably better as a boxer over the years. He continued sparring until he was almost sixty, and was quietly proud of the bruises he gave and took in his grandfatherly years.

He probably had not heard of club fighters before he got to know his father-in-law. In any case, the club fighter's attributes—a consistent level of performance, the capacity to absorb punishment, and the ability to learn from mistakes—coalesced into a touchstone metaphor for Mailer. Those who got to know him fairly well, or read his interviews, became accustomed to what he called his "all-purpose expression": "I'm an old club fighter; I get mad when you miss." The compensation for being a club fighter, that is, a fighter whose duty and pride is to spar with superior fighters, is that you not only enable your opponents to sharpen their skills, you might also learn how to slip a punch by taking one on the chin. Also, by taking certain blows, a boxer (now feeling more combative) can counterpunch, something that Mailer learned to do very well inside and outside the ring. Everyone gains, and sometimes the loser learns the most. Two years later, in the opening essay of *Advertisements for Myself*, he used the trope in a capsule autobiography, one he never relinquished: "I started as a generous but very spoiled boy, and I seem to have turned into a slightly punch-drunk and ugly club fighter, who can fight clean and fight dirty, but likes to fight." The literary world, as Mailer defined it, was a place of fierce struggle. Painful experience was the soundest guide.

Mailer was now in a fever to fight. Perhaps it was the memory of his eye gouging in New York or Al Morales's instruction, or the emerging ideas of "The White Negro"—all of these, no doubt, played a role—but what is clear is that in 1957, he was itching for fisticuffs, with or without gloves. One night at the Styrons', Mailer told Random House publisher Bennett Cerf, who had turned down *The Deer Park*, "You're not a publisher, you're a dentist." They went outside, but Styron broke it up. When novelist Chandler Brossard, whom Mailer had met in Mexico, visited, Mailer wanted to box with him. Brossard, who had fought semiprofessionally and been trained by the same man who trained Hemingway—another inducement for Mailer—wisely declined, saying someone (meaning Mailer) could get seriously hurt. "Violence and pain are a form of engagement to Norman, of reality," Brossard said. In 1952, Brossard had published one of the first novels about hipsters, *Who Walks in Darkness*, set in Greenwich Village. On the dust jacket, a question is asked: "What is a hipster? The name derives from the jazz term 'hip' and denotes a person who possesses 'superior awareness.' " The lead character is an African American who passes for white. Mailer read the novel and liked it; it most certainly enriched the essay that was percolating in him.

The memories of Mailer fighting and acting out are what many friends and acquaintances of the period remember, but it wasn't all fireworks. For one thing, Susan had joined them for her annual visit shortly before they moved, and she spent a lot of time with her father. She was also fond of Adele and, like any six-year-old, deeply interested in the pregnancy. Mailer wrote to a friend that he was "beginning to see himself as the patriarch of a vast family," a premonitory remark. As the birth approached, he started writing. He began taking notes for "The White Negro" and also working on a dramatic version of *The Deer Park*. The growing extent of his literary operation can be gauged by the fact that he now had an answering service in New York. Further help came from the Miss Baltimore Agency, a domestic help service that Fan had taken over from her sister Beck in the early 1950s. She supplied maids to her son and his wives for years to come.

TWO WEEKS BEFORE Adele was due, Mailer appeared on a local late night television program, *Night Beat*, hosted by Mike Wallace. Adele accompanied him in a low-cut black velvet dress. "She looked splendid," Mailer recalled, "and sent out the beauty of her pregnancy like a promulgation of status." He was excited to be on live, "the virgin air," he called it, and believed he might be able to move the million or more people who would watch the show by saying the unsayable with "wit, conviction, and passion." His ideas about the repression in American life might catch fire, "buried sentiments could take life." But to do this he had to hold his ground against Wallace, whose "straight black hair and craggy face gave off a presence as formidable as an Indian in a gray flannel suit." And given his own "massive incapacity to stay cool," this would not be easy. Just before airtime, Mailer took out a flask of gin and poured it into his glass, clearly annoying Wallace.

Wallace asked if he was obsessed with sex in his novels and Mailer answered, yes, most definitely. I see myself, he said, continuing the work of pioneering novelists such as Henry Miller. When Wallace quoted *Life* magazine's attack on *The Deer Park* for "immorality, alcoholism, perversion, and political terror," Mailer replied that "only hypocrisy and insincerity are dirty. *Life* magazine is a dirty magazine." He decided to raise the ante. When Wallace quoted a line from one of his columns about the country being run "by men who were essentially women, which indeed is good for neither men nor women," and then pressed for an example, Mailer replied, "Well, I think President Eisenhower is a bit of a woman." He was certain he had scored and "the heart of a million TV sets missed a beat." Wallace's eyes, he recalled, "grew as flat as the eyes of a movie Apache who has just taken a rifle bullet to the stomach." Mailer recalled the moment, writing about himself in the third person.

> In the elevator, going down to the street, his wife said, "Maybe we'll be dead tomorrow, but it was worth it." It is possible they never had a better moment together. They had been with each other for years, yet always fought in the animal rage of never comprehending one another. On this night, however, with the baby two weeks away, they were ready for one hour, at least, to die together. For once Mailer felt like a hero. In those days saying something bad about Dwight D.

> Eisenhower was not a great deal less atrocious than deciding Jesus Christ has something wrong with Him.

In 1957, linking timidity with the female gender was a commonplace and didn't elicit the opprobrium it would a dozen years later, as he would learn. The immediate fallout came several weeks later when he learned that Eisenhower's press secretary, James Haggerty, called Wallace's office to request a transcript of the program. For the first but not the last time, Mailer had gained the attention of a sitting president.

The baby was born in New York on the evening of March 16. Attesting to their continued friendship, the Mailers asked Jean and Galy to be the godparents. Mailer was certain it would be a boy, but was wrong. Susan suggested the name, Danielle. The middle name, Leslie, according to Danielle, came from the French actress and dancer Leslie Caron. Mailer made a fuss in the delivery room when the nurse began shaving Adele's pubic hair, saying it was unnatural to do so, but relented when her contractions got strong. He also tried, and succeeded, in convincing the obstetrician to allow him to stay in the delivery room, something that was considered bizarre in that era. He wrote to Knox to say that he had remained until fifteen minutes before the end, and had "a fantastic experience." The baby had a full head of black hair, he said, and resembled him a bit.

After the birth, around midnight, he showed up at the apartment of his former sister-in-law, Phyllis Silverman-Ott, who had remained in contact with him after he and Bea had divorced. In her 2006 memoir, she says that "Norman always loomed like the North Star over me." He was off-center when he arrived, she recalled, because of his "awe at the power of a woman to endure and create, a glorious humiliation that left him feeling unloved." She had told him earlier that she loved him, and he spent the night in her bed. Being Mailer's lover, she said, made her feel "like I was walking on stilts." A few days later, the Mailers drove back to Connecticut "to begin" as Adele put it, "what I thought would be a new life."

In his letter to Knox about Danielle's birth, Mailer gives a clear sense of his now heightened feelings about personal violence in the wake of the eye-gouging incident. Knox had been threatened by a man in Rome, a rival for a woman's affection, and asked for advice. Mailer told him he had to make a stand, even if "he smashes the living shit out of you":

> Hit him where the hair meets the neck, kick him in the balls, kick his shins, stick your fingers in his eyes, jab your fingertips against the base of his nose, but don't run, and don't just take it. Now I know this sounds easy to say, but I'm talking from experience because I've had a couple of ugly fights as you know in the last year and I know the difference it makes between fighting and quitting. If you fight, even if you take a bad beating it 1) does not hurt that fucking much while it's going on, and 2) you're left with some fucking dignity—you can actually feel good after a bad losing fight.

VIOLENCE WAS MUCH on his mind when he sat down at the beginning of April to write "The White Negro." What is sometimes overlooked is the distinction Mailer makes in the essay between the kind of personal violence he describes in his letter to Knox, and collective violence, the violence of the state, which at its most malign leads to concentration camps and the elimination by hideous means of millions of human beings. In Mailer's mind—Reich's influence is apparent—the hipster stood opposed to the repression of instinctual urges that are noble and natural, a suppression that seemed likely to lead, under the threat of nuclear warfare, to a new epoch of Faustian regimes that would wield technology to eliminate opponents, regimes so efficient that Hitler and Stalin would resemble crude bully boys in comparison. Against the emergence of such regimes stands the hipster. This Adamic figure is patterned, in part, after the Negro, who must often choose between subservience and rebellion; the psychopath, who is in more direct contact with his unconscious than ordinary neurotics; the drug addict, who seeks ecstasy in the absence of community; the jazz musician, whose riffs and glides mimic the rhythms of sex; and the mystic, who lives in "the enormous present." Transcendental spontaneity is the quality they all share. One commentator on Mailer's writing, Joseph Wenke, describes how the hipster's sense of time differs from ordinary clock time.

> Each moment fills, becomes more resonant and complex. Correspondingly, one's experience of time slows down. Such an alteration in one's sense of time is a key element of the Hip quest for freedom. It means that one is now able to control the rhythms of one's own experience and live out of what is really a transcendentalist sense

> that one can recreate one's own identity out of the eternity of the present moment and so escape temporarily from the limits of history. From this subjective standpoint, the future exists only as vision, a romantic vision of ever-expanding possibilities merging with one's experience of freedom in the present.

Because the essay soars and swoops through such imponderables as time, sex, love, God, courage, extermination, and revolution, and is rife with qualifications, extended appositions, and restrictive clauses, it is not an easy read. Mailer later admitted that it was "too elliptic." As literary critic Morris Dickstein has commented, Mailer "rarely bothers to distinguish lurid metaphor from literal prescription," and writes a prose that "mingles fact and fiction, social criticism and confession, cultural prophecy and personal therapy." Nevertheless, one cannot help but feel the seductive energy of the essay—energy, in fact, is its pith and marrow. "The White Negro" is a dithyrambic hymn to energy which pulses in a universe that is not a fact, but "a changing reality whose laws are remade each instant by everything living, but most particularly man." "God," he says, is "energy, life, sex, force, the Yoga's *prana*, the Reichian's orgone, Lawrence's 'blood,' Hemingway's 'good,' the Shavian life-force." This is not the God of organized religion, but the God within "the paradise of limitless energy and perception just beyond the next wave of the next orgasm." How to achieve it? First, one has to be "ready to go, ready to gamble." "Movement is always to be preferred to inaction. In motion a man has a chance, his body is warm, his instincts are quick, and when the crisis comes, whether of love or violence, he can make it, he can win, he can release a little more energy for himself since he hates himself a little less, he can make a little better nervous system, make it a little more possible to go again, to go faster next time."

The essay's promise of escape from Eisenhower's wet blanket helped make it the most discussed American essay in the quarter century after World War II. Maligned as much for its obscurity—Baldwin said it was "downright impenetrable"—as it was celebrated for its orphic verve, it is also the most reprinted essay of the era. A generation of young people proudly carried their copies of the City Lights edition of the essay, a pamphlet whose cover depicts a reverse negative head shot of an archetypal hipster (rumored at the time to be Paul Newman) with them when they migrated to the awakening cities of the nation. Bored with the timidities of the middle class, the new generation saw the essay as a blast on the trumpet of defiance, a call to radical self-assertion and the fullest sexual experience, even though the hipster milieu that it celebrated was not yet real. As Alfred Kazin astutely pointed out, "The White Negro" "is an attempt to impose a dramatic and even noble significance on events that have not genuinely brought it forth." Mailer was trying to imaginatively will into being an army of hipster revolutionaries who could bring about an urban utopia.

From its initial publication in *Dissent* in the summer of 1957, through its reprinting in 1959 by City Lights and the same year in *Advertisements for Myself*, the essay's most controversial passage drew vigorous rejoinders. It comes after a long peroration on the therapeutic benefits of expressing forbidden impulses, even violent ones, a necessary prelude to self-discipline, community, and love. He gives the example of "two strong eighteen-year-old hoodlums" who assault and kill a candy store keeper. Not much gain here, he says, because the victim is not a physical equal. But, he counterargues, "courage of a sort is necessary" because the hoodlums are "daring the unknown, and so no matter how brutal the act, it is not altogether cowardly." Numerous commentators on the passage have expressed revulsion for the notion that even a smidgen of approval is given for such a vicious act, even though it was hypothetical. Mailer was never able to satisfactorily answer such objections, yet he never relinquished his belief that there were morsels of redemptive gain in all risk-taking acts, even when they were criminal. "If one wants a better world," the essay warns, "one does well to hold one's breath, for a worse world is bound to come first." Barbarism, he argued, was preferable to "the cold murderous liquidations of the totalitarian state." He would continue to find things to admire in unsavory individuals, even one who assassinated a president. The essay was a turning point for Mailer, and also, as Dickstein says, "a momentous shift in American literary culture, a turn toward the dark side, the rebellious and the demonic." The 1960s were coming.

MAILER DISCUSSED THE essay with several friends in Connecticut in early 1957. These included Lew and Jay Allen and John Aldridge, who had rented the nearby home of Arthur Miller and Marilyn Monroe, who were in England making a film. Aldridge's wife, Leslie, recently divorced from a young *Esquire* editor, Clay Felker, had known Styron at Duke. That set up what Mailer called "an odd three-way community." Aldridge lived halfway between the two writers and, initially, got along well with both. Aldridge, Mailer recalled, wanted to start "a new Athens in America. It was his idea to get a bunch of intellectuals living out there about 70 miles from New York." Adele remembers thinking that New York was a hard-drinking town, but it was "a kindergarten," she said, compared to the Connecticut scene.

Mailer later recalled the social situation. Styron, he said, was considered by some to be the most talented writer in America. "You can imagine how that hit me." Aldridge was close to Styron, but wanted to get even closer. But Styron "was sort of unhappy about sharing. You know, he was a true southerner—'What I've earned, I've earned, and I'm not eager to deal it out to other people.' " Styron commanded the social scene, Mailer said, "and I began to realize what it is to be a social inferior." Leslie Aldridge "was not a social gift altogether, certainly not in the eyes of Styron." "She was on the make, and obvious. She was never a lady the way Rose [Styron] was, naturally. But compared to Adele, she was pretty slick." Rose, on the other hand,

> had great social gifts. She could make anyone feel good in a hurry who came to her house, that kind of thing. Adele was still awkward, doing her best, but rough at the edges whereas Rose just could move and negotiate. All girl, pick up things, pick up the mood here, quiet the mood there. They had a very good social life, a lot of big literary parties. Well scripted. So there was Styron and I, very competitive as literary men, but he was having a big social life and I was having a small one.

Adele said that for the first year, her husband and Styron got on well, "swapping stories, talking about writing, each being as charming as the other and as drunk as the other. I never saw Bill without a drink in his hand." Adele thought he projected "an air of smug superiority," and that Rose's manner "had a hint of condescension—that is, when she could tear her attention away from my husband." Styron's biographer, James L. W. West III, writes that the evenings the three couples got together "were intense and stimulating, but not especially pleasant." Aldridge spoke with "a ponderous authority" that irritated the others; Styron had "a tendency to stick to superficialities in conversation"; Mailer "was raffish, funny and charming, but he could also be belligerent and confrontational." The men were "ambitious and competitive, all three women were good-looking and sexy." Aldridge's memory is that while Styron "was originally king of the roost," Mailer "quite quickly became the center of energy."

One evening, Adele recalled, "Styron was going on and on about the colored people this and the colored people that" in a smug manner. She called out to him, banged her fist on the table and said, "I happen to be passing for white, so keep your fucking comments to yourself." After a pause, "someone snickered, and my remark was ignored as the conversation resumed. My husband just grinned at me, raising his glass in a half toast." Mailer said this about his relationship with Adele: "I had a situation where I was Pygmalion; I was someone who could develop someone, and I certainly could develop her, develop her into someone quite special. I had a romance with the idea that she was a member, finally, of the working class and here was I, this leftist intellectual (via Jean Malaquais), and now finally I had someone from the working class that I, as a middle-class, guarded, sheltered, spoiled individual, could work for and develop." It was a complex marriage: they drank, they experimented sexually, they became parents, they struggled with their art, they had fierce battles, and maintained a tenuous solidarity through all the difficulties of the next year.

"The White Negro" was by far the most extraordinary piece that had appeared in *Dissent*, and brought the journal needed attention, although the editors had problems with parts of it. Howe was excited to have the piece, but regretted not asking Mailer to cut out the hoodlum-storekeeper passage. Mailer said years later that the essay "made me one of the spokesmen for the Beat Generation," even if the more pacific Beats had their reservations. The *Partisan Review* crowd—William Phillips, Dwight Macdonald, Lionel and Diana Trilling—especially Macdonald—didn't like the antinomian emphasis of the essay, but as Phillips explained, it was still "acceptable," just "as with Lawrence," because "the thinking of a man who's wild was interesting." James Jones had no use for the essay, telling Mailer it was "a good illustration of a swiftly accelerating decadence." Mailer read the essay aloud to Styron, and told him writing it was "like coughing up blood." Styron, always the formalist, didn't admire its rhetoric or agree with its conclusions, yet was "fascinated by it nonetheless." The division of opinion on the essay continues; it is regularly used as a club in the continuing race-gender-power debates of academics. It rasps, it elates, it confuses, but it is unforgettable.

Mailer told Knox the nine-thousand-word essay was the best thing he had ever written. It will be important over the years, he said, because it points to "a new way to think." In addition to the essay's long-term influence, he saw two immediate results: "I was now the intermediary," he said, between the Beats and the intellectuals, between, say, William Burroughs and Dwight Macdonald, and this satisfied his two psyches. It also "emboldened" him later, he said, to write *Advertisements for Myself*, where he planned to take on issues that no one else would. The first new piece he wrote for inclusion in this planned collection for Putnam's was a fragment from the dramatic version of *The Deer Park*. He expected to have a first draft completed soon, as he said in a letter to Chandler Brossard in which he also turned down his request for an interview in a girlie magazine, *Nugget*. He liked the magazine, he said, but felt that appearing in it would show his literary enemies that "my writing about sex is not the act of a serious writer but one who is looking for notoriety."

MAILER FINISHED A draft of the four-act play in early August. It was over three hours long. He wrote to Bea, Knox, and Malaquais on the same day to announce its completion. He told Knox that it was "one of the four or five best plays that have been written since the war," and said to Bea that "it's better than Death of a Salesman and Streetcar Named Desire put together." Mailer had seen both plays on Broadway and admired them extravagantly, so he may have swallowed hard when making this claim. Getting it produced, he told Malaquais, would be difficult because it was "so bold that it could really cause an explosion." Knox wanted to direct it, and Mailer told him choosing a director was the prerogative of the producer. If he ever produced it off-Broadway with his own money, however, Knox would certainly get a role. Ten years later, this is exactly what happened. Knox was the star of the production, playing the comic role of Collie Munshin, Herman Teppis's opportunistic son-in-law, who introduces Eitel and Elena.

Mailer had lunch in New York with a well-known literary agent,

Monica McCall, and got her interested in the play, sight unseen. He mailed her a copy with a cover note saying the play was a bit shorter than Eugene O'Neill's *Long Day's Journey into Night*, which he had also seen. He appended a note with his "dream cast":

Eitel	Charles Boyer or Laurence Olivier
Elena	Marilyn Monroe (if her voice is loud enough)
Marion Faye	Marlon Brando or Ben Gazzara or Monty Clift
Collie Munshin	Jackie Gleason or Jules Munshin
Lulu Meyers	Elizabeth Taylor

It is notable that Sergius O'Shaugnessy is not mentioned. In the dramatic version, his presence is diminished (which suggests his marginality in the novel); he is a sort of impresario, a hip version of the stage manager in *Our Town*. The play, Mailer suggests, is a product of O'Shaugnessy's memory; one that takes place in "a rather incredible hell," a metaphysical perdition. Marion Faye becomes a more important figure, and some of the action occurs after he and Eitel have both served time in prison. The Elena-Eitel affair and Eitel's subtle corruption remain the central actions. McCall began showing the play to producers.

Almost three years had passed since the completion of the novel version of *The Deer Park*, and he wanted to begin the leviathan novel about "the mysteries of murder, suicide, incest, orgy, orgasm, and Time," as he later described it. He had no real excuse not to begin. His play was being considered, but he conceded to Malaquais that it might be "a bad play—enough people are turning it down." A retrospective collection of his work was still on his mind, but he wasn't sure how to proceed with it, especially since Walter Minton was eager to have another novel from him. He wrote to Knox that he was going to put off "side work" and finally, after Thanksgiving 1957, he started on the novel. Over the next month "with a medium gruesome effort," he wrote twenty-seven pages. Then he stalled again. He told Malaquais that with the exception of "The White Negro" and his *Voice* columns, nothing he had done for years had been successful and the thought of "this enormous novel I'm now starting which could well take ten years" was simply too daunting. He read Baudelaire's *Intimate Journals*, an excruciatingly bitter account of his drug- and alcohol-soaked final years, and thought, "Now there's a man who's exactly like me." By the end of the year, he had reached an impasse. He told Malaquais what he needed to write again: "If I had twice the youthful energy which wrote The Naked and the Dead, and had your powers of reasoning, and Meyer Schapiro's retention and culture, and five good friends who supported me, took care of me, even wiped my ass—why then, by God, I could write the book which would create a new radical movement." One side of Mailer desired earnestly to get to work on the leviathan; the other subscribed to David Stacton's aphorism: "An artist exists only in the work he has not yet written, which to others remains unobtainable."

In early 1958, Knox suggested that Mailer bring the play to Actors Studio, a New York City theatrical organization founded by Elia Kazan and a few others in 1947, and subsequently run for over thirty years by Lee Strasberg, the guru of Method acting. The organization's guiding principle is that actors, playwrights, and directors be allowed to develop their skills without commercial pressure; the productions are read or staged on simple sets. Many talented actors have been affiliated over the years, and it was there that Mailer met Rip Torn, Anne Bancroft, Kevin McCarthy, and several others. The camaraderie revived him somewhat. He maintained a membership in the organization for the rest of his life. A friend of Knox's, the director Frank Corsaro, staged some readings of Mailer's script, with Mailer kibitzing. Knox played Munshin, Torn was Faye, McCarthy was Eitel, and Elena was played by Bancroft. But she and Mailer had disagreements and, art following life, Adele took over the role, performing well after some instruction from Corsaro. Mailer had gifts for characterization, but the play in its initial version lacked a dramatic arc, and he withdrew it after several months. He would return with a new version in the fall of 1960, and then tinker with it for several years before its off-Broadway run in 1967. At the time of his death, he was working on still another revision. The Actors Studio involvement heightened his interest in theater, and he later attempted to recast several of his novels into plays or films.

WHILE IN CONNECTICUT, he spent a lot of time in his carpentry shop. Adele remembers hearing "Norman's anger in the piercing whine of the buzz saw." He was "becoming more detached and more depressed," she said. But he spent a lot time with Danielle, whom they called Dandy. Every few weeks they would drive to a party in New York, returning drunk after harrowing drives in winter weather. One night on the way home they got into a mean fight about flirtations at the party. "I handled it in my predictably alcoholic, out-of-control way, hating him, wanting to pull his curly hair out by the roots," Adele recalled. Her mother was visiting them, but they continued to scream at each other and then, in the early hours, took swipes at each other. In the morning, her mother asked her what happened and Adele mentioned divorce. But later they talked it out. "Believe it or not," she told her mother, "we love each other, and he loves the baby. Don't worry, we'll work it out."

On one of their trips to New York in early 1958, at a dinner party at Lillian Hellman's apartment, the Mailers met Norman Podhoretz and his wife, Midge Decter. Just before they met, Podhoretz had published an essay, "The Know-Nothing Barbarians," attacking the Beats, especially Ginsberg and Kerouac, in *Partisan Review.* A Columbia protégé of Lionel Trilling's who had also studied under F. R. Leavis at Cambridge, Podhoretz made some sharp remarks in the piece about Mailer's views on violence in "The White Negro." Like many others, Podhoretz was appalled by what he saw as the hipster's psychopathy. Nevertheless, he was taken with the essay's "sheer intellectual and moral brazenness." Mailer, down in the boxer's crouch he adopted for such occasions, confronted Podhoretz, telling him he had misunderstood "The White Negro." "Like me," Podhoretz said, and "practically every Brooklyn boy I had ever known, he was direct and pugnacious and immensely preoccupied with the issue of manly courage." He parried Mailer's attack by telling him that he should withhold criticism until he had seen a long essay he was writing about him for *Partisan Review.* Within a short time, Podhoretz showed him the galleys of the essay, titled "Norman Mailer: The Embattled Vision." It is the first major examination of Mailer's work, and contains a cogent summary of his strengths and aspirations. Podhoretz doesn't say whether their conversations are reflected in the twenty-five-page essay, but it is a warm, generous appraisal, and the opening accurately captures Mailer's self-estimate. Mailer, he says, is one of the few postwar writers whose qualities "suggest a major novelist in the making." What is most remarkable, he continues, is that

> his work has responded to the largest problems of this period with a directness and an assurance that we rarely find in the novels of his contemporaries. Mailer is very much an American, but he appears to

> be endowed with the capacity for seeing himself as a battleground of history—a capacity that is usually associated with the French and that American writers are thought never to have. He is a man given to ideologies, a holder of extreme positions, and in this too he differs from the general run of his literary contemporaries.

Mailer had to be pleased with his new friend's endorsement of his desire to address complex questions, especially since he did so in the *Partisan Review*, the flagship publication of the mandarin New York literary world. Their friendship was cemented.

He met another couple at the Hellman party who would also play a major role in his acceptance by "The Family," as the political columnist Murray Kempton called the *Partisan Review–Commentary*–Columbia University intellectuals and critics who dominated high culture in New York from the 1940s to the 1960s. Lionel and Diana Trilling were key members, and their approval meant a good deal to Mailer during the next decade. He was seated next to Diana at the table and turned to her with a comment not recommended for establishing a friendship: "And how about you, smart cunt." In her memoir, Trilling said, "I am usually addressed with appalling respect: he got my attention. We became good friends." She would also write a major essay about Mailer, and engage in an important correspondence with him. Steven Marcus, another Columbia professor, also met Mailer at the dinner party. Marcus's 1963 *Paris Review* interview with him became a major document in establishing Mailer as a serious writer. The dinner party confirmed Mailer's long-held belief that the right mixture of liquor and daring at parties could sometimes dramatically change people's lives.

He had written a number of pieces for *Dissent*, and had done his *Village Voice* column, but beginning in the late 1950s he began to move adroitly between highbrow, popular, and Beat publications. He had decided to plow more than one field, and *Partisan Review, Esquire*, and *Big Table*, a Beat publication out of Chicago, demonstrate the spread. In the 1960s, he would add *Paris Review, Commentary*, and *Playboy*, continue with the *Voice*, appear occasionally in girlie magazines such as *Rogue, Stag*, and *Nugget*, as well as in oddball publications such as *Way Out* and *Fuck You: A Magazine of the Arts*. "The White Negro" opened doors. Not only was he invited to the homes of The Family, and asked to speak on college campuses and appear on TV, he began being noticed by important literary critics. Podhoretz was the first, but then came a clutch of essays, some of praise, some of dismay, but all recognizing that Mailer was one of the most important postwar writers. Charles Fenton, writing in *Saturday Review*, said Mailer was a "conspicuous success." Edmund Fuller, who would review his work for decades, wrote in *American Scholar* that "the promising talent of Norman Mailer has collapsed utterly" in his second and third novels. Bridging the gap between Fenton and Fuller was Dwight Macdonald, who had become quite friendly with Mailer. Macdonald named him and Baldwin as the best young novelists. He praised Baldwin for writing successfully about the "homosexual dilemma" in *Giovanni's Room*, but was more expansive about Mailer: "I value Mailer because he is 'a born writer,' whose failures (of which there are plenty) are more interesting than the successes of less-talented writers, but chiefly because he is always experimenting, changing, developing, and, naturally, making a fool of himself." Macdonald also praised his enthusiasm for ideas, saying that if he could bring his intellectual qualities together with his literary skills, "the result may be a masterpiece."

In mid-March, relations with the Styrons, and with James Jones and his wife, Gloria (née Mosolino, whom he had married a year earlier), took a turn. Mailer wrote to his Hollywood friend Chester Aaron to tell him they were returning to New York, as their social life in Connecticut had dissolved. "Lousy people these country gentry," he wrote. "Beneath the manners they don't even have the humanity of slum hoods." Mailer's handwritten, two-page list of twenty-four grievances, titled "Styron's Style," explain some of the circumstances of the breakup. The first complaint, "Hiram Haydn and The Deer Park," indicates Mailer's vexation about the lack of Styron's support for his novel. There are three other literary complaints: that Styron would not freely comment on his work; that he had suggested that Howard Fertig (who did some secretarial work for Mailer) was the real author of Mailer's play; and the "bitchery" with Jones. One notation states that Styron had told him that Jones's 1957 novel, *Some Came Running*, which had been badly hammered by reviewers, "wouldn't be written by a 15-year-old." Mailer wrote later that when Styron would read aloud the worst passages of Jones's novel, he "would laugh along with the rest, but I was a touch sick with myself for doing so."

The majority of the items on the list concern what the Mailers perceived as Styron's high-handedness—cutting them off from Lew and Jay

Allen, dismissing Aldridge's idea for a literary conference, calling Leslie Aldridge "the slut"; and, most irritating, inviting Adele's parents to visit them after Adele had "obviously demurred." When the Styrons visited, Bill would "snoop" and "poke around" on detours from trips to the bathroom. One night he found some of Mailer's pornography and told all the dinner guests about his discovery. Some of the slights seem minor or misinterpreted: the Styrons gave them expensive Christmas gifts and always left some of Adele's food on their plates, "including dessert."

The core of the ill feelings centered, however, on the Mailers' perception of how the Styrons were treating Adele. She was upset because Styron gave her "clumsily patronizing pats on the shoulder" and called her "sweetie," and that they refused to look seriously at any of her paintings. The Mailers also noted Styron's "Adele-go-back-to-Brooklyn remark." But there is no mention of a comment Styron reputedly made that resulted in an angry letter from Mailer, suggesting that this list was drawn up before the comment was made. The Mailers had engaged in various intimacies with another woman on several occasions, and a few times with another couple. His marriage to Adele, Mailer said, was "very free."

> We had a lot of orgies. Mostly with women because Adele was very attracted to other women. And she was attractive to women, so we'd pair her up with another girl and then we had a lot of—and very occasionally, we'd have a four-way orgy but I couldn't stand it, I couldn't stand a man making love to her. That would wipe me out. It was very painful, so those were fewer, but there were a lot of orgies on the other side. Very selfish from my point of view; those were the years I was having two women and that gave me a feeling of great superiority. I'd feel, "Oh well, these other literary lights, they had their social superiority, but I had my sexual superiority," and that was what was feeding me.

Someone told Mailer that Styron was making remarks about Adele being a lesbian. On March 12, he wrote to Styron.

> Bill,
>
> I've been told by a reliable source—closer to you than one might expect—that you have been passing a few atrocious remarks

about Adele. Normally, I would hesitate to believe the story, but my memory of slanderous remarks you've made about other women leaves me not at all in doubt. So I tell you this, Billy-boy. You have got to learn to keep your mouth shut about my wife, for if you do not, and I hear of it again, I will invite you to a fight in which I expect to stomp out of you a fat amount of your yellow and treacherous shit.

What you choose to do about this letter is of course your own affair, but I suggest you do no more than button your lip. The majority of things you do come back to me, and my patience with your cowardly and infantile viciousness—*so demeaning and disgraceful to your talent*—is at an end.

Norman

According to his biographer, Styron was "astonished" by this letter and one that followed two weeks later. Lew Allen, whom Styron showed it to, said, "Bill was scared, really scared." He immediately wrote a point-by-point refutation, one of which accused Mailer's source of having a "warped and perverted imagination." He denied making any remarks about Adele. But he did not mail the letter, and the next day when visiting his wife in the hospital where she had just given birth to their second child, he met Jim and Gloria Jones and informed them of the situation. They concluded that something other than the alleged remarks must be bothering Mailer.

Years Later, Styron said that the letters from Mailer were "profoundly upsetting and depressing." He called the first one "a lightning bolt." But he went on to say the following:

A lot of people didn't like Adele. She was aggressive. She was out of her—you know—I think a lot of people thought she wasn't a lady. I liked her, but she'd get drunk. I think a lot of people regarded her as common—or whatever the word is, and she just didn't fit in, a big aggressive broad . . . and people were put off by her. It may have been indeed—I suspect it was true—that I probably uttered something about her like a lot of other people did and it got back to Norman.

Adele's version divided the blame between the two men. Norman, she speculates, "probably bragged about the few times we'd indulged in a three-way." Styron, "employing one of his sneaky tactics" out of his envy of Mailer's status, "seized on the stories as an excuse to get Norman." In Mailer's recollection, he was partly to blame:

> Yeah, I wrote him a letter and told him to stop bad-mouthing my wife. Because stuff had come back to me and I think looking back on it, I provoked the fight. I didn't have hard evidence of what he'd been bad-mouthing—I was certain he had been bad-mouthing Adele. You could tell almost by the way he looked at her. And of course, Adele in turn, what she had in relation to all these people—most of them WASPs—was she had her sexual intensity and she was letting them know it, so there was a certain hostility basic to the whole thing. And that was very much there in these relationships. You know, her attitude was well, "Styron may be superior in this way, this way, this way, but I have the best sexuality and as a result, Norman does too, and you, poor Bill Styron will never know."

A few weeks earlier, Mailer had written to Jones giving him a critique of his recently published novella, *The Pistol*, which he said, "contains a perfect short novel buried within what was for me, very frankly, a slipshod presentation." He felt it was too didactic, and it needed a "touch of mystery." He ended by saying, "Let's get together soon, you clunkhead. You're the only man I know who has an outside chance of ever understanding me." They did get together more than once in New York, and the Joneses also visited them once in Connecticut. At one of their nights out in New York, Adele got into an argument with Gloria and, distressed at what her husband called "emotional sword-twirling," they left early in the evening. In a March 18 letter, which begins with Jones's response to Mailer's comments on *The Pistol*, Jones said he was sorry about their departure, but still felt that Adele "was pretty much out of line" with both him and Gloria. She tried "to get my goat," he said, "telling me about a conversation (unflattering in the extreme) which she had heard in the hall about me, and did I want to know what people *really* thought about me?" She went on in this vein, Jones said, and so they departed. Apparently, the possibility of a fistfight came up, because Jones said he didn't intend to engage in one because "it would give Adele too much happiness." He and Gloria liked Adele and thought she was "a remarkably sweet gal when she's sober," but they didn't like to be around her when she wasn't. Jones left it up to Mailer about getting together again, but said he was getting too old for "perpetual hassling. If that's what you call living out at the furthest edges of danger, then I'm not for it, and will never make a hipster." Mailer found Jones's letter in his mail when he returned from a trip to Florida.

A letter from Styron was also there when he returned.

> Norman:
>
> . . . Your letter was so mean and contemptible, so revealing of some other attitude toward me aside from my alleged slander, but more importantly so utterly false, that it does not deserve even this much of a reply.
>
> B.S.

Mailer replied first to Jones, painfully. "Parasites," he said, seem to have undermined Jones's ability to "trust the notion that somebody just wants to see you to make friends."

> Well, I'm an old enough clubfighter in New York's social eliminations to have known, even as I was doing it, that it was a big mistake to make it so obvious that I wanted to get together with you, but I kept telling myself to drop the guard just once, that you weren't a shithead snob like all the others I know, and so Mailer takes a chance, you're going to be dead one of these days. Well, buddy, you proved that my sour instincts were more reliable than my few remaining generous ones, and so you did me a damage and I don't like you a hell of a lot for it.
>
> Nor do I like this business of giving Adele the rap. I don't know what the hell she said to Mos [Gloria], but it couldn't have been so godawful because 1) she liked Mos, and 2) she wanted to make friends—she was damn bewildered when the two of you took your powder. My guess—from the kind of stuff you reported as flipping you—was that she went in for some heavy kidding which she saw as teasing, and both of you chose to see as deliberate insult. Well, stow that bullshit. If Adele had come to me doing a burn because Gloria had said this or that unforgivable thing to her, I would have told her

> to stick it up her ass, she was a big enough girl to take a little crap rather than jam up a possible friendship. It just isn't nice of you, Jim, and it isn't of Gloria, either, because you don't tear an evening over a couple of remarks unless you really want to—which is the way I read it, that both of you were not interested in doing much else but tearing the evening. If you saw a fight in the air, I didn't. I wouldn't get into a fight with you unless I were ready to kill you, and I always instinctively assumed that was true for you.

Jones had ended his letter by saying if Mailer wanted to see him, he could come to New York. Mailer ended his by saying he'd meet only in Connecticut, and if Jones didn't want to do that, there was no need "starting a farce of letters back and forth." Jones agreed, apparently, and they did not see each other for several years. Their friendship was all but destroyed. The Joneses left for Paris near the end of March and lived there for the next sixteen years.

A week after writing to Jones, he wrote to Styron:

> I just got back from a few days in Florida, and found this billet-doux. So I invite you to get together with me face-to-face and repeat that my letter is mean, contemptible, and false—if you feel up to it. If you don't, recognize your reply for what it is—a crock of shit.
>
> Mailer

Styron did not reply, and they did not communicate for many years. Styron and the Joneses drew closer after their split with Mailer, and would become even better friends after Mailer published a searing appraisal of their work eighteen months later. Within a few days, Mailer had lost two of his best friends, partly if not largely of his own doing. He believed them to be the only two of his contemporaries, save Baldwin, whose ambition and talent matched his own.

THE SAME DAY that he wrote his last letter to Jones, he wrote to Baldwin. Almost reflexively, it seems, he tried to build a bridge to replace the two that had collapsed. Baldwin was also moving back to New York, and Mailer promised him a big party after the Bridgewater house was sold and they found a place in New York. He said he had just read *Notes* *of a Native Son*, Baldwin's second book, the one that established his reputation as an essayist of the first rank and on which his continuing reputation rests. Mailer said that he thought it to be "beautifully written and intellectually alive. Of how many other things can I say that?" Another letter written that day went to Knox, who along with Malaquais invariably received frank letters about Mailer's inner states. Mailer said he was exhausted and had written only sixty pages of his new work in four months. "Writing ties me into knots which only liquor releases at the expense of my fucked up brains." He was feeling middle-aged, he said, and had grown a mustache and beard.

The new work he referred to consisted of two long stories, one about Marion Faye, "Advertisements for Myself on the Way Out: The Prologue to a Long Novel," and "The Time of Her Time," about O'Shaugnessy cutting a sexual swath through the Village. There was also a fragment about Faye being raped in prison, and after his release showing up at O'Shaugnessy's loft, but it was clearly unfinished and remains unpublished. A few weeks earlier, Mailer had written to Philip Rahv at *Partisan Review* to see if he was interested in either of the stories, which he said were "on the edge between the serious and the pornographic." Rahv wrote back saying that while publishing anything too raw might endanger the magazine's nonprofit status, he nevertheless felt that *PR*'s readers "need to be shocked out of their complacent regard for us," and that he would be glad to look at anything Mailer would send. Mailer replied by saying that he liked this "damn-the-torpedoes invitation," and sent Rahv the two stories. He was also planning to include both pieces in his new collection, which he hoped would generate interest, and give him the prod he needed to proceed. In the end, Rahv selected "Way Out."

Described as "awkward," "muddled," and "cloying" by critics, the story has received little comment. It is all of these things, but it is also a tale, like some of Poe's, that emphasizes the perilous, confused, or mutable condition of its teller. From this point on in his career, Mailer's narrators will inevitably point to the harrowing difficulties of telling their stories, a circumstance that becomes as important as the story itself. Like the narrator of "The Man Who Studied Yoga," whose name changes from day to day, the narrator of "Way Out" is a disembodied figure who says, Ishmael-like, "my name eludes me." He admits to being one or more of the following: "ghost, *geist*, demiurge, dog, bud, flower, tree, house, or some lost way-station of the divine," perhaps a participant in the "fluid conscious of a God." Humans, he says, partake in the deity's struggle to forge an extraordinary destiny, "yes, God is like me, only more so."

He hints that he may even be an old house in Provincetown, one similar to the one on Miller Hill Road where Mailer spent the summer of 1950 with Bea. A "climactic party" of several days duration took place there during a gloomy stretch of fall weather. The narrator says that "in the history of our republic there has never been a party equal in montage." Marion Faye, the ex-con host, is now a fabulously wealthy "master pimp." He has chartered two planes to fly in thirty powerful, prestigious, and/or infamous figures, one each of the following: prostitute, boxer, psychoanalyst, athlete, jazz musician, actor, cop, spy, queer, transsexual, grande dame, crook, mother, taxi driver, TV entertainer, physicist, war hero, bullfighter, etc., etc.—pilgrims all. The *Canterbury Tales* could have served as a model. The party's program: first an orgy, followed by a suicide and a murder. Faye intends to kill someone—a "Brave murder"—and so reverse the process of his corruption. The act will, reciprocally, advance God's program by getting the dialectic working again, helping to blast the twentieth century out of the caution and propriety that is smothering everything artful, brave, and good in life. The one-thousand-page novel that is to follow would then explore the trajectories of the guests and their interactions after this very hip, potentially history-altering party. Mailer was setting a high bar.

At the end, the narrator admits that he is the spirit of the dead man—perhaps Faye himself—and the list of potential identities given at the outset might represent possible stages in his reincarnation, should the embattled God who makes karmic decisions determine that the murder was justified and has aided His cause. On a functional level, Mailer was trying to surmount the point of view difficulties of *The Deer Park*. He was fumbling for a way to retain a first person voice, while remaining free to explore the minds and hearts of a huge cast of characters in a novel of Proustian scope and ambition—a balancing act he worked to perfect all of his writing life. If the murdered man is judged to have been a true warrior of God, he will be reincarnated after he has told the story. The entire mammoth novel will be told in the instant "between the stirrup and the ground." The project was so vast that he never found a way to move forward from the prologue. The victim would have to have been as historically pivotal as Rasputin—someone Mailer planned to write about in his final years—and therein was his problem: he needed a half-heroic, half-malign figure of consequence and at the time couldn't conceive one. We have, therefore, only the assurance of a nameless, irritatingly evanescent narrator that the party is of epochal dimensions. Mailer was unable to come up with a good plot, his inveterate weakness. There was another reason: he was about to be distracted by invitations too alluring to be ignored. The story, therefore, is a curiosity, but one that contains the germ of much of his future fiction.

THE ENGLISH DEPARTMENT of the University of Chicago invited Mailer to speak, and he accepted. He was to meet formally and informally with creative writing students. His host for a week in May 1958 was novelist Richard G. Stern, who would remain friendly with Mailer. Assisting him was Robert Lucid, a graduate student, whose job was to show their guest around town. Lucid became one of his closest friends and vied with Aldridge for the informal title, Dean of Mailer Studies.

Mailer spoke in two of Stern's classes and "enjoyed the sheer hell out of it." He liked the give-and-take with students and told Knox that he could make a living teaching if necessary. In his letter accepting the invitation, he said that he would like to explore a "series of questions on the relations between one's own experience and the experience one writes about." In the event, these questions turned into a recitation of "horror tales" about *The Deer Park*, which no doubt cranked him up to write his essay about its composition, "The Mind of an Outlaw." When he thanked Stern upon his return to Connecticut, he emphasized that his tales had not been exaggerated. The serial rejections of the novel still burned. Mailer enjoyed Chicago immensely. Stern and his wife took him to a nightclub to hear Lenny Bruce, and he did some late night carousing with Lucid and a young poet, Paul Carroll. After the visit, he said Chicago was "the only big city I ever felt comfortable in," largely because it reminded him of Brooklyn, that is, "if Brooklyn ever made it." But the major outcome of the visit—apart from meeting Stern, Lucid, and Carroll—was a published interview he did with Stern.

He had not had much sleep for several days, and in the interview found himself "rushing into a confession of ideas I had never really talked about with anyone before." In his brief preface to the interview,

"Hip, Hell, and the Navigator," Stern says that Mailer's speech rose to "a pitch of excited engagement" as the interview progressed, the words tumbling out with "urgency" and "authenticity." The discussion takes off from "The White Negro," which Stern puts down as a product of "anti-expressionism." Mailer patiently explains that when he was younger, he might have agreed, but "I started as one kind of a writer, and I've been evolving into another kind of writer," moving from Marxist rationalism to mysticism. It has been a hard journey, he says, and "consists of losing all the friends that one's found in the past." Then Mailer made what Stern called "a fantastic assertion."

> I think there is one single burning pinpoint of the vision in Hip: it's that God is in danger of dying. In my very limited knowledge of theology, this never really has been expressed before. I believe Hip conceives of Man's fate being tied up with God's fate. God is no longer all-powerful. (Here a phrase was lost to static on the tape.) The moral consequences of this are not only staggering, but they're thrilling; because moral experience is intensified rather than diminished.

Human beings, Mailer continues, "are the seed-carriers, the voyagers, the explorers, the embodiment of that embattled vision; maybe we are engaged in a heroic activity and not a mean one."

> STERN: This is really something.
>
> MAILER: Well, I would say it is far more noble in its conception, far more arduous as a religious conception than the notion of the all-powerful God who takes care of us.
>
> STERN: And do you take to this conception for its perilous nobility, or do you take to it because you believe in it?
>
> MAILER: I believe in it.
>
> STERN: You believe in it.
>
> MAILER: It's the only thing that makes any sense to me.

Mailer's reply echoes the one that Jones had given him about karma in Illinois five years earlier, before he had begun his evolution, or his transmogrification, into another kind of writer.

Toward the end of the interview Lucid breaks in to say that what bothers him about Mailer's comments is that while the novelist "consciously makes decisions and accepts the moral consequences," the hipster is "unconscious of risks of this kind." Mailer responds by saying that tacit in his comments is the belief that the unconscious "has an enormous teleological sense," that it is always measuring to what degree the actions of individuals are conducive or destructive to growth. Hour by hour, minute by minute, it asks, am I growing or shrinking? "It is with this thing that they move, that they grope forward—this navigator at the seat of their being." He had discovered someone new at the rudder of his psyche. The "anxious boyish Jewish intellectual" who had been the link between the saint and the psychopath has given up his place to a helmsman from the lower depths, a guide and connection to the mysteries of Being and becoming.

AFTER RAHV HAD formally accepted "Way Out" for the fall 1958 issue of *PR*, Mailer wrote to his mother, who was visiting Susan in Mexico, with the news. "*Partisan* is the most important (*by far*) literary magazine in this country," he said, "and to print a long piece by me will do an awful lot of subtle good. I'm really pleased." He was also happy, as he told his Japanese translator, Eiichi Yamanishi, that "The White Negro" was "much discussed," and that he was being touted as "one of the very few reliable guides to the mysteries of the American nihilism which is coming into being." To be accepted by the opposed wings of America's literary culture—the Beats and The Family—put Mailer in the catbird seat he had aspired to since falling from the heights with *Barbary Shore*. His timing couldn't have been better. *On the Road* was published in September 1957, three months after "The White Negro." Kerouac's novel had produced a hunger for insights into the origins and meaning of the Beat movement, and Mailer's essay was often seen as its intellectual manifesto. There were condemnations and celebrations of beatniks in all the major publications, and *Life* did a photo essay.

The first chronicler of the Beat generation, John Clellon Holmes, said that Mailer brought to an understanding of Beatness "the most venturesome intellect (not to mention nerves) currently at work in American literature." He called "The White Negro" a document "fully as important to the secret history of this age as *Notes from the Under-*

ground was to the Europe of its time." The movement wanted intellectual approbation from a celebrated writer, and Mailer wanted attention and the circulation of his ideas. His essay, considered notorious by some, gave him credibility with the Beats. By late 1958, he was at least an associate member of The Family, and the only one to rise above a condescending or angry dismissal of the Beats. While he did not care for the Beats' beatific passivity, or for Kerouac's characterization of the Beats as "solitary Bartlebies staring out at the dead wall window of our civilization," he admired the "ecstatic flux" of his language. Mailer was angry not passive, engaged not withdrawn, and much preferred "American nihilism" to the "Beat Generation." He said that the difference between Beat and Hip was the same as that between rebellion and revolution. "Beat still has no center to its rage, and so is sentimental enough to assume that the world can be saved with words. It is going to take more than that." He never changed his mind on this distinction.

At a party in August, Mailer told his neighbor, novelist Dawn Powell, that he wanted to move to New York. "All that green makes him sick," she recorded in her diary, a remark that brings to mind Woody Allen's line about living in Connecticut: "I am at two with nature." That same month, he saw the film version of *Naked and the Dead* with Adele and his sister during one of their regular trips to the city. Barbara said he was appalled by the production, and she just sank lower and lower in her seat. Mailer wrote up a response a short time later, detailing "the disembowelling naked greed which gutted this movie of its promise." The casting bothered him the most. Aldo Ray, "a big fattish bull of a man with a gravel voice," played Sergeant Croft, "a small, lean man" with "a soft murderous Texas voice." In the novel, he said, "Croft was the hunter, the killer, the horn of the platoon, an icy will-driven phallus of a man, a mountain-climber—one cannot substitute a raw-voiced weightlifter." Added to the casting problems was the inclusion of a big scene in a Hawaii nightclub—no one in the novel ever sets foot in Hawaii—where a stripper, played by a genuine ecdysiast, Lili St. Cyr, is pawed by drunken soldiers. He ends the diatribe by saying that if it seems he has been hard on the producer and director, "I can tell you, friends and foes, dear family, there is no one I feel harder on at the moment than the real villain, that stupid idiot—Norman Mailer." He later called the film "the worst movie I've ever seen," but he did not publish his angry comments on it, as he had originally planned.

There was one more disappointment before the Mailers left Connecticut. He had been hoping that Arthur Miller and Marilyn Monroe, now back from England, would invite them for dinner. They lived only five miles apart, and while not notably friendly, they were both Brooklyn boys who had begun their careers high on the mountain. But Mailer said that the invitation never came, as he remembered in his biography of Monroe (referring to himself as the "novelist"):

> Nor could the novelist in conscience condemn the playwright for such avoidance of drama. The secret ambition, after all, had been to steal Marilyn; in all his vanity he thought no one was so well suited to bring out the best in her as himself, a conceit which fifty million other men may also have held—he was still too untested to recognize that the foundation of her art might be to speak to each man as if he were all of male existence available to her. It was only a few marriages (which is to say a few failures) later that he could recognize how he would have done no better than Miller and probably have been damaged further in the process.

Adele's memory is that Miller did invite them for drinks, and then mentioned casually that Marilyn was not at home, that she had gone to Hollywood on business. Mailer was angry on the drive home. "The bastard waited till she was away to invite us over," he said. Mailer wrote his account fifteen years after the event; Adele's was written nearly forty years later. Either could have misremembered. Miller's memory, however, supports Mailer's. In his autobiography, he says that Mailer "might make good company for an evening," but Monroe "rejected the idea," saying she " 'knew these types,' " that is, "people obsessed with images." Miller wrote his account while still angry about what he felt was an unfair portrait of his marriage in *Marilyn.* He speculated that Mailer might have treated Monroe and him differently "had we fed him one evening and allowed him time to confront her humanity, not merely her publicity." Monroe was aware of Mailer's writing, according to her friend W. J. Weatherby. At some point, she read his copy of *The Deer Park*. Her response: Mailer was "too impressed by power." While this may seem to be a simplistic response to Mailer's hard-won insights into the complexities of how power is wielded in Hollywood, her intuition wasn't all wrong. In a later interview, Mailer said that his plan during his time in Connecticut had been to write a play in which she would star, but in hindsight it would have been a "terrible tragedy" to play Pygmalion with Monroe, admitting that he was just another of the many men who wanted to make the most of this "sweet child of life," but in his own way, not hers.

THE MAILERS MOVED back to New York in December 1958 and rented an apartment at 73 Perry Street in the Village. Mailer had known Allen Ginsberg since the days of his loft parties, but had met Jack Kerouac only in passing. Sometime after they returned, Kerouac and Ginsberg visited. Ginsberg later said that the meeting was friendly, and that the other two writers weren't competitive even though each considered himself the best writer in the country. Mailer liked Kerouac "more than I would have thought," but found him to be tired. "In Buddhist terms," Ginsberg said, Kerouac "was already sick of the world." Mailer, however, was engaged in what Jews call *tikkun olam*, or repairing the world. There may not have been any discussion of "The White Negro," as both Ginsberg and Kerouac had reservations about its positions on violence. On the other hand, Ginsberg said that he felt "a sense of brotherhood" with Mailer, because they were both trying to undermine the nation's pervasive social conformity. For Ginsberg, Mailer's essay was "the most intelligent statement I'd ever seen by any literary-critical person, anyone acquainted with the great world of literature." Over the years, they would have many contacts with each other, especially in the 1960s when they were involved in a number of antiwar protests. But Mailer saw Kerouac at least once more, at a party the Mailers gave in mid-1959, most of which Kerouac spent under the kitchen table, dead drunk.

All through the fall and winter of 1958 and into the spring of the next year, he labored on the collection, still unnamed. Heretofore, he had never worried a great deal about his nonfiction prose style. His forte, he felt, was to deliver unsettling hypotheses and blockbuster theories that would "influence the history of my time," and not engage in the kind of fancy-pants writing he despised when he was writing for the *Advocate*. With "Lipton's Journal" and "The White Negro," his style had become more colloquial, and the prefaces he was writing for each selection reflected this shift. The problem he faced was that to accurately contextualize the pieces in the collection—fiction, nonfiction, a few poems and dramatic fragments—he had to talk about himself more than he cared to. He had always implicitly accepted Flaubert's dictum that "the artist should be in his work, like God's creation, invisible and all-powerful; he should be felt everywhere and seen nowhere," a view he was parroting when he told Lillian Ross in 1948 that it was "much better when people who have read your book don't know anything about you, even what you look like." Writing the prefaces in the face of his growing awareness of the difficulty and doubtful wisdom of separating his personal and artistic worlds had made him "a little desperate," especially since he had quit smoking, again. Yet, he still felt that the prefaces, as he told a friend, were "shit work."

> I got sick of myself, sick of saying I felt this, I knew that, I wondered whether, I induced, and I and one and almost a he or two. It's weird, it's a little like self-analysis before you realize it, and your style dips into your own shitbag so fast it's staggering. So now I'm facing whether to throw all this crap away, and put the book out without the prefaces, three months of work shot, and a less readable book or maybe keep on with the gamble and waste another three months on what may not be writable for me.

But he continued, encouraged by the reception of "Way Out." He told William Phillips, Rahv's coeditor at *PR*, that he had received all good comments on the story, except from Macdonald, who "detested" it. By the end of 1958, he had a provisional plan for the collection, which he sent to Walter Minton, promising he would have everything to Putnam's by February 1. He had already completed some of the prefaces, the brief ones that introduced his short stories, the longer ones—introducing "The White Negro," the *Voice* columns, excerpts from *The Deer Park* and the big novel—remained to be written. He was considering a three-part, chronological division of the material: "Square," "Transitional," and "Hip," with an appendix for his college stories and early journalism. The final shape of the collection owed something to this arrangement, but was more subtle. The only thing he was sure about at this point was that all the prefaces would be in italics.

He began "to jiggle his Self for a style" that would reflect his emerging personality, while feeling "the yaws of conscience" about such concerted and public introspection. This anxious, delicate process, he said, sent his writing "through a circus of variations and postures, a fireworks of virtuosity designed to achieve . . . I do not even know what. Leave it that I become an actor, a quick-change artist, as if I believe I can trap the Prince of Truth in the act of switching a style." He inched along, still worried about tabling the big novel. He told Yamanishi that he had written only seventy pages, and that the final product would take "five or ten years" and be a thousand pages long. Finishing the collection—its working title was now "Advertisements"—stood in the way of getting back to the novel. In a letter to Mickey Knox, he said that he had spent a half year trying to improve "my half-vanished techniques in writing," which gives a hint about his slow progress. Going without cigarettes for nine months, he said, had left him with "less drive and better health." What he needed now was "a stick of dynamite up my ass."

HE DID GET a small jolt when "Hip, Hell, and the Navigator" appeared in February 1959. Lionel Trilling, the informal head of The Family, described it in a TV interview as an "important theological document," and this had created "a little stir" in the *PR* crowd. Just before this happened, Mailer was invited to appear on his second TV program, David Susskind's *Open End*, along with Truman Capote and Dorothy Parker. He had met Parker in Hollywood several times, but knew Capote only by reputation, which by then was growing by leaps and bounds, based on the warm reception for his 1958 novella, *Breakfast at Tiffany*'s. Mailer was "intensely curious" about Capote, he recalled, and enjoyed the limousine ride to the studio with him and Adele. With the Mike Wallace program under his belt, he felt confident about appearing, while Capote, "in a dry little voice that seemed to issue from an unmoistened reed in his nostril," said that he wasn't. "When it comes to personality," Capote said, "I have something small and precise to offer, and it's wrong for such a medium." When the two-hour program was over, Mailer thought he had been forceful and articulate, while Capote had seemed "a hint bewildered." After a celebratory dinner at El Morocco with Capote (who repeatedly insisted that he had been awful), Mailer went to bed happy. The next day, he made a few calls to friends to garner their praises.

Mailer's family loved the show, but most of his friends told him,

"Oh man, did Truman take you." He was getting a lesson, not only of Capote's one-upmanship, but also of the medium's distortions. The diminutive Capote loomed large in the many close-ups of his "young-old face," while the bearded Mailer appeared intense and pious in the medium shots he was accorded. Capote's voice, he realized, was an asset.

> Nothing like it had been heard in New York before. Such presence over the camera. Such homosexual hauteur. He seemed to be certain of every word he was saying even if they were few words. Oh, that voice!—a cross between an adenoidal prince and a telephone operator. Whereas I was a verbose young intellectual spewing more ideas than anyone cared to hear in an over-friendly tone. Ugh! I had my first lesson in the transpositions of reality which come by way of television.

The key moment came when the discussion turned to the Beats. After noting emphatically that he was not a Beat but a hipster, Mailer gave an endorsement of Beat writing, saying that it was "entirely new," and had "broken clean away from the Judeo-Christian tradition." Parker disagreed, saying that it was nothing more than reheated bohemianism. "None of these people have anything interesting to say," Capote added, "and none of them can write, not even Mr. Kerouac." What they do, Capote said, "isn't writing at all—*it's typing.*" Mailer disagreed but his defense of Kerouac was "limp," he recalled, because he was only "two-thirds for Jack's virtues and one-third against Jack's vices." A *New Republic* reviewer said that Capote "demolished Mr. Mailer's arguments at every turn." Capote's putdown of Kerouac has become legendary; Mailer's comments are forgotten. He learned that television viewers prefer terse retorts to three-minute syllogisms. The experience on *Open End* gave him an appreciation for the epigrammatic, and he worked to refine his television style.

Through the early spring of 1959, Mailer continued work on the prefaces. Barbara lived around the corner at 395 Bleecker Street and had begun doing regular secretarial work for him. He missed the February 1 deadline he had given Minton, and got little accomplished the entire month. In one sour letter he said that he needed to get the prefaces "out of the way and fast—I'm sick of fucking around with it, and the novel is not calling me right—seems to be fading as I goof off more and more of my time." He and Adele were going to jazz clubs, especially the Five Spot, on Third Avenue. He was drinking as much as ever, but Adele wasn't drinking at all because she was two months pregnant; they hoped for a boy.

It was a curious period. He was trying "to make the scene," as he put it, at Village parties and events, all the while fiddling with the prefaces, adding confessional material and then drawing back out of his fear that the collection would become "a thoroughgoing autobiography." Some of them were brief, clear, and functional. In others, he was going for something deeper. In one of his drafts, he calls himself "the only writer of my generation who has the particular passion to be great," and finds that his "ridiculous, dreary, narcissistic and noble" self has come to resemble a man he does not admire: Charles de Gaulle. Finally, he began to get some traction on how to handle his contradictions:

> Begin with declaration that my overriding passion for years—from 17 on—has been to be a great writer, and I've written hardly a word which hasn't been seen for how it would look today, and how it would read a hundred years from now. This type of Gaullist narcissism runs through every turn of my ungracious prose—muscular, blunt, brutal, bullying, shrill, mean, pompous, totalitarian, timid, arrogant, clumsy—and be it said—passionate. Because for anyone who knows anything about writing, it will be evident through all the gnarled harsh turns of my prose expression, the graceless dogged determinations of my honest ideas, that I am a man obsessed with the urgency to be great, to be a great writer, leader, philosopher, seer, a God—what! And this humorless heavyweight clubbing toward so ineluctable a goal will appear by turns to anyone concerned with the spirit of the cool, the graceful, and the elegant, as the ludicrous thrashings of a man so impossibly gauche that one can envision him in Parnassus only as the archetype of the hippopotamus, the baboon and the pig. All right. Heavy I am and graceful I would be, and in the distance between the two lies the rhetoric of this work.

By the end of March he was working more successfully, perhaps because he had—"assassin to myself"—gone back to smoking. He finished "The Mind of an Outlaw," and continued working on an estimate of the work of his contemporaries, which would eventually be titled "Evaluation: Quick and Expensive Comments on the Talent in the Room." He also came up with the final sequencing of the pieces, and decided to include two tables of contents: the first follows the actual order of the book, and is more or less chronological; the second is generic—fiction, essays, journalism, interviews, poetry, plays, and "Biography of a Style," which lists the advertisements and postscripts, thirty-four all told, written expressly for the collection. *Advertisements for Myself* was finally coming into focus. Putnam's rescheduled the collection to come out in November.

The rationale for "Biography of a Style" was to encourage readers to swallow the advertisements whole, read them apart from the selections that they frame, for the purpose of revealing the new kind of writer Mailer was becoming. He wanted the agonies of creating the book to bleed through, yet sparingly, in the manner of Yeats, who wanted his readers to "know about the intense and unremitting labor required to create an apparently spontaneous line." For example, he concludes "Sixth Advertisement for Myself" with this tease: "The confession is over—I sense that to give any more of what happened to me in the last few years might make for five thousand good words, but could also strip me of fifty thousand better ones." But the confession is far from over; subsequent advertisements continue to offer glimpses of his life in progress. Many long passages are suffused with the rhetoric of revealing and then shrouding the writer and the process of composition. In addition to being a genre-conflating work—part confession, part tirade, part visionary testament—*Advertisements for Myself* is a great work because Mailer is adept at what we might call confession interruptus. Just when we think he is done baring his battered psyche, he returns with more revelations, laced with witty revilements and cranky pontifications.

MAILER'S SISTER, WHO was typing the manuscript, had reservations about some of the writing in the collection, but said nothing at first. But finally, she recalled, she told him what she felt about "Quick and Expensive Comments."

> "Norman you're not serious about publishing this thing." I was appalled by it. "You don't do this to your fellow writers." I said, "You

don't expect to publish this until after everybody's dead." He said, "Of course I do." And I said, "I really think you shouldn't"—he got so angry at me. He said, "You're wrong, you're always wrong!" And he never got over it, I mean, for years he teased me about how I'd been wrong about it. However, he did change it, a lot. He went over it pretty carefully. Some things he really toned down. I also said, "I think some of it's marvelous."

None of the early drafts of the essay have survived, but even in the softened published version most of the writers he comments on receive a mixture of positive and negative comments, sometimes in two sentences, sometimes in a page, no more. What immediately sets off the piece from the abstracted literary criticism of the day is that mixed in with the usual commentary are surmises and hunches on the characters of the writers themselves—their vanities, virtues, and quirks—based on Mailer's interaction with them, even if it consisted of one meeting. The prose is obscene and prickly, but conversational, as if you were drinking with him over a long winter evening in some snug Provincetown bar. The praise given is grudging as often as not; and the criticisms are a mixture of shrewd insight based on careful reading and ad hominem jibes.

He makes comments on twenty-one writers, in the following order: Jones, Styron, Capote, Kerouac, Bellow, Algren, Salinger, Paul Bowles, Bourjaily, Chandler Brossard, Vidal, Anatole Broyard, Myron Kaufmann, Calder Willingham, Ralph Ellison, Baldwin, Herbert Gold, Mary McCarthy, Jean Stafford, Carson McCullers, and William Burroughs. He had met at least two thirds of the group. Some samples:

Saul Bellow's National Book Award–winning novel, *The Adventures of Augie March*: "at its worst it was a travelogue for timid intellectuals and so to tell the truth I cannot take him seriously as a major novelist." He goes on to call *Seize the Day* "the first of the cancer novels," although he calls the ending "beautiful," and says it is "the first indication for me that Bellow is not altogether hopeless on the highest level." To reach that level, "he must first give evidence, as must Styron, that he can write about men who have the lust to struggle with the history about them."

Nelson Algren: "Of all the writers I know, he is the Grand Odd-Ball. Once he took me to a line-up in Chicago and I could have sworn the police and the talent on the line had read *The Man with the Golden Arm* for they caught the book perfectly, those cops and crooks, they were imitating Algren."

J. D. Salinger, author of *Catcher in the Rye*, "is everyone's favorite. I seem to be alone in finding him no more than the greatest mind ever to stay in prep school."

Kerouac is "the first figure for a new generation," possessed of "a large talent. His literary energy is enormous." But "his rhythms are erratic, his sense of character is nil, and he is as pretentious as a rich whore, sentimental as a lollypop."

"Truman Capote I do not know well, but I like him. He is tart as a grand aunt, but in his way he is a ballsy little guy, and he is the most perfect writer of my generation, he writes the best sentences, word for word, rhythm upon rhythm." But "he has less to say than any good writer I know" because of his "attractions to Society."

Ralph Ellison, the author of *Invisible Man*, "is essentially a hateful writer: when the line of his satire is pure, he writes so perfectly that one can never forget the experience of reading him—it is like holding a live electric wire in one's hand."

"The early work of Mary McCarthy, Jean Stafford and Carson McCullers gave me pleasure," he says near the end of the piece, noting that he was unable to read other women novelists "out of what is no doubt a fault in me." Later, he would enjoy the work of Iris Murdoch, Joan Didion, and Erica Jong, among others, but in 1959 he was genderbound. "At the risk of making a dozen devoted enemies for life," he continues, "the sniffs I get from the ink of the women are always fey, old-hat, Quaintsy Goysy, tiny, too dykily psychotic, crippled, creepish, fashionable, frigid, outer-Baroque, *maquillé* in mannequin's whimsy, or else bright and stillborn." He concluded by saying that "a good novelist can do without everything but the remnant of his balls," a line that would come back to haunt him. When asked about his comment on women writers a few years before his death, he said, "I happened to grow up in a family with a lot of wonderful, adoring women—a marvelous, strong mother and a lot of terrific aunts. So I took it for granted that I could say anything I wanted about women because they knew I loved them." His dismissal of female writers would not only be remembered, it would be bitterly *intoned* by women for decades. This mention is sometimes seen as the first indication of the misogyny he would be accused of in the 1970s.

His comments on Jones and Styron destroyed whatever shreds of comity persisted after their recent quarrels. He begins his comments on Jones generously, saying that *From Here to Eternity* was the best American novel since the end of World War II, despite being "ridden with faults, ignorances, and a smudge of the sentimental." He was unique, Mailer said, because "he had come out of nowhere, self-taught, a clunk in his lacks, but the only one of us who had the beer-guts of a broken glass brawl." But his early success "handcuffed the rebel in him." He concluded that if Jones "dares not to castrate his hatred of society with a literary politician's assy cultivation of it, then I would have to root for him because he may have been born to write a great novel."

Styron, Mailer said, wrote "the prettiest novel of our generation. *Lie Down in Darkness* has beauty at its best, is almost never sentimental, even has whispers of near-genius," although it had three defects: "Styron was not near to creating a man who could move on his feet, his mind was uncorrupted by a new idea, and his book was without evil." Without having read a word of Styron's second novel, *Set This House on Fire*, Mailer speculates that it will be "a cornucopia of fangless perceptions which will please the conservative power and delight the liberal power," because "the mass media is aching for such a novel." The book's reception "will be a study in the art of literary advancement. For Styron has spent years oiling every literary lever and power which could help him on his way, and there are medals waiting for him in the mass-media."

On Baldwin he is no less severe. After lauding *Notes of a Native Son* for its "sense of moral nuance," he says that many paragraphs "are sprayed with perfume. Baldwin seems incapable of saying 'Fuck you' to the reader." But he has one large advantage: his personal experience has been "as fantastic and varied as the life of any of my fellow racketeers," and if he is bold enough "we will have a testament, and not a noble toilet water."

The last writer he discusses is William Burroughs, who had recently published a fragment of his unpublished novel *Naked Lunch*. Mailer saw in him exactly what was lacking in most of his contemporaries: an unflinching assault on the torpor-producing forces of the culture. He found the excerpt to be "more arresting, I thought, than anything I've read by an American in years," and if the rest of the novel were as good,

"Burroughs will deserve rank as one of the most important novelists in America."

He submitted the manuscript of the collection in late April. *Advertisements for Myself* came in at 200,000 words, one third of which was new work. When it was in the hands of the editors at Putnam's, he made arrangements to publish three of the four pieces in magazines just before or at the same time as the collection, which was now scheduled to appear on November 6. "The Mind of an Outlaw" appeared in *Esquire*, "Buddies" in the *Village Voice*, and "Quick and Expensive" in *Big Table*. Finally, two scenes from the dramatic version of *The Deer Park* came out in *Partisan Review,* giving Mailer close to simultaneous exposure in four very different publications, two hip and two "overground," as *Esquire* editor Harold Hayes called his magazine. While prepublication excerpting was nothing new, no one in 1959 was doing it quite so shrewdly or widely. He continued the practice for the rest of his career, and must be considered the leading "magazinist" (a name applied to Poe) of his era.

In "Last Advertisement for Myself Before the Way Out," which concludes the collection, he is nearly as rough on himself as on his peers. Comparing himself to Scott Fitzgerald, "an indifferent caretaker of his talent," he says that he has been "a cheap gambler" with his. He goes on to describe himself as "cowardly," "stupid," and guilty of "fear and vanity," winding up with a flourish that recalls the bold, mythical gesture of Babe Ruth, a passage that would be regularly quoted in the future by detractors and admirers alike. The big novel, he says,

> will be fired to its fuse by the rumor that once I pointed to the farthest fence and said that within ten years I would try to hit the longest ball ever to go up into the accelerated hurricane air of our American letters. For if I have one ambition above all others, it is to write a novel which Dostoyevsky and Marx; Joyce and Freud, Stendhal, Tolstoy, Proust and Spengler; Faulkner, and even old moldering Hemingway might come to read, for it would carry what they had to tell another part of the way.

Mailer didn't hit this "longest ball," but considering what he did produce in the ten years after *Advertisements for Myself*, he had some solid hits. In addition to challenging himself, another motive for his prediction—corroborated by the taunts and dares that he leveled at his "fellow racketeers"—was to stimulate them. He genuinely believed that a great achievement by any of them would be the keenest spur for the rest—which is not to say that he did not feel envy. He explained in a 2007 interview with Andrew O'Hagan how he felt about his contemporaries: "I remember I received a copy of *From Here to Eternity*, which I think I'd asked for, and Jones inscribed it: 'To Norman—my most feared friend; my dearest rival.' That's the nature of friendship among writers. Gore Vidal—who has never been at a loss to see the negative side of human nature—pointed out that 'Whenever a friend succeeds, a little something in me dies.' That's an exaggeration of this notion of competition. But in time we may get to the point where, although something of you does die, some other part of you is encouraged. You say, 'Well if he's doing it, I can do it.'"

MINTON WAS UNCERTAIN about including "The Time of Her Time" because of its detailed sexual descriptions. To this end, Mailer wrote identical letters to thirteen literary critics, stating that a majority of those polled would have to approve of the story for Putnam's to go ahead. If opinion was seriously divided, the story would be cut. Accompanied by a copy of the story, the letter went to: Irving Howe and Norman Podhoretz; F. W. Dupee, Diana and Lionel Trilling, and Richard Chase at Columbia; Leslie Fiedler at the University of Montana; Philip Rahv, William Phillips, and William Barrett at *PR*; two important independent critics, Alfred Kazin and Dwight Macdonald; and Mailer's former professor Robert Gorham Davis. He said he did not like to ask for an appraisal of unpublished work, "but I believe this piece may be important enough to justify the act." He asked for a reply by mid-July 1959. His plan was clever; he not only garnered twelve positive endorsements—Davis demurred—and convinced Minton of the story's merits, he also gained advance support for his collection from a group of influential figures. Four of them went on to write supportive reviews of *Advertisements*, including two that were highly favorable.

The story, a comic masterpiece and perhaps Mailer's finest short story, is a first-person recounting of the Herculean efforts of Sergius O'Shaugnessy, a Village stud who calls his penis "the avenger," to bring Denise Gondelman, a "proud, aggressive, vulgar, tense, stiff and arrogant Jewess" to her first orgasm. As critic Andrew Gordon has explained, "Sergius is the hipster battling Denise the Square, determined to liberate her from her dead-ass sexual repressions, her intellectual priggishness, and her obsession with psychoanalytic jargon, or as Mailer would say, from her totalitarianism. On another level, it is both "a glorification of the power of sex and a *reductio ad absurdum.* The controlling metaphor is sex as war, and sexual intercourse takes on the qualities of a championship boxing match, an encounter between a matador and bull or an epic struggle for survival between two savage beasts in a jungle clearing." O'Shaugnessy, Gordon says, "sees himself, and only half in jest, as a sexual messiah" carrying the gospel of Lawrence and Reich to uptight pagans in Greenwich Village. After several near-victories, she ultimately achieves "the time of her time," an obvious reference to God's whispered words to O'Shaugnessy at the end of *The Deer Park.* Far from being grateful for pushing her over the top after many long nights of phallic endeavor (achieved when he whispers in her ear, "You dirty little Jew"), Denise tells him the following morning that his "whole life is a lie, and you do nothing but run away from the homosexual that is you." Then she departs and is "out the door before I could rise to tell her that she was a hero fit for me." As Gordon points out, the story is a rehearsal for an even more detailed and symbol-laden (if less exhausting) series of sexual bouts in Mailer's 1965 novel, *An American Dream.* O'Shaugnessy, he notes accurately, is "the first of Mailer's *active* narrators" in a fictional work, and a precursor to Stephen Rojack, the narrator-protagonist of that novel.

After he sent the story to the thirteen critics, he gently encouraged them to respond and thanked them when they did. Kazin was one of the first to respond, praising the story's "literary seriousness and power," and calling Mailer "immensely talented." Then this reservation: "You are the Rabbi of screwing, the Talmudist of fucking, the writer who has managed to be so solemn about sex as to make it grim." He argued for more passion, and ended by saying that the "characters make love with a stop-watch in each hand. For *this* I should make love?" Mailer wrote back immediately to say that being called "the Rabbi of screwing" gave him a laugh, and agreeing that the grimness of some of his descriptions was "the single most unattractive feature" of his writing. There was a reason, however: "I am more or less obsessed with the idea that sex is dying in a new ice-age of the psyche, and I think the only way to change one's readers and warm them—for yes, I am guilty of a messianic lust—is to make them set up camp on the ice for a while." In the big novel, he would depict "characters who are monsters of self-consciousness and try for the more difficult and perhaps impossible trip into a terrain where emotion becomes real again." Over the years, Kazin would continue to chide him in reviews and essays about taking his obsessions too seriously, and urging him to distance himself from his characters (a reflection, perhaps, of the Henry James revival then under way).

Kazin was not the only member of The Family pushing Mailer to be more Jamesian. Diana Trilling and Mailer liked each other from the start, and her positive vetting of the story brought them even closer. The fact that she also praised *The Deer Park* in the same letter, calling it "a fantastically courageous book, intelligent book, noble book," was further uplifting, especially since she said that her husband shared her enthusiasm. She began to see him as her personal project, and her letters over the next few years mixed praise, joshing, and advice. Besides giving him her counsel, she said his work was an advance on Hemingway's. He said in reply that *Advertisements for Myself* "is a bit obsessed with Hemingway—I'm afraid he crops up in the book the way an old lover appears in the conversation of a woman who insists the man could now not mean less to her." *Advertisements* is the high-water mark of Mailer's interest in Hemingway, although after his suicide in 1961, his ghost would often return. In his reply to Trilling, written after his return from Provincetown, he did not remark on the concern Trilling expressed at the end of her letter: "I hope to God you're not falling into the trap of explaining yourself. Like seeing yourself in history, self-explanation is one of the new and most elegant ways for a writer to cut his own throat." Like Kazin, she wanted Mailer to put some aesthetic distance between himself and his creations, something he was less and less prone to do. In fact, before the next decade was over, he would do precisely what she wanted him not to, exactly what Henry James had avoided. Podhoretz said Mailer saw himself as "a battleground of history," but Mailer had bigger ideas: he wanted to intervene in history, and dramatize his intervention.

He also sent "The Time of Her Time" to Lois Wilson. She shared it with her husband, Graham Wilson, also an English professor, who knew of and sanctioned their relationship from the beginning. He responded by saying that the Sergius-Denise affair seemed to parallel hers with Mailer, but in reverse. Mailer wrote to her in early May about a tryst they were planning. "A man is nothing without his greed," he said. A couple of weeks later, he wrote to a New York hotel to make a reservation for her, enclosing a money order and signing the letter "Marion Faye." Reflecting on their time together, which both enjoyed greatly, he said:

> once in a while I think we're ripening for one another, that in five years we'll be very good for one another, even be able to restore the nerves of love to one another that the others (some of them) deadened away. Anyway, phony schizophrenic, Junebug Daisy DeSade, have your good time in Europe. I'll be envying you except that I've got the galleys of the book that may change my life again, and I'm working on them for the next five or six weeks. Everything has to be handed in by August First so you will either catch me either exhausted or full of myself depending on what I think of the book. And of myself.

He added that he now had a green sports car, a Triumph, and signed the letter "J. Kafka Hemingway."

As he was making plans for a trip to Germany to meet with his German publisher, Adele gave birth to a girl after ten hours of labor. Elizabeth Ann (soon referred to as Betsy), was born on September 28. He wrote to his Uncle Dave, now a widower, to announce the birth. Unlike Danielle, who looked like Adele, Betsy "was very much a Mailer. She has a most definite chin, and a thin, determined, and quite beautiful mouth." He told Dave that a copy of *Advertisements for Myself* (dedicated to Dave, the memory of Anne, and Barney), would be sent to him shortly. He added that there had been "a boom in my literary stock lately." A week later, he left for Germany.

MAILER LANDED IN Munich on October 11. He gave a reading there, went on to Berlin, and then flew home on the 20th. Almost all that is known of the visit is contained in a November 6 letter to Lois Wilson:

Dear Lady (with the light)

Your letter was nice. First nice letter I've gotten from you since my last work. I am at the moment empty. There was almost too much of a good time in Berlin where I stayed for six days after planning only two, and I fell in love with a bar girl (a tall tough sharp mean and rather honest lady) who fell first in love with me, and would take no further money from me after the first night (as the clean proof of her love) which act unmanned me a bit, for the dream of all whoremongers like myself is to get that hard dikey man-hating pussy for nothing, and at last I had succeeded. So you were right. It was good for me to go to Europe, and it would have been better with a month.

But there is one thing awful about falling in love in Europe. Once one is back it all slips away, inexorable bit by bit, and now the lady is no longer real to me—instead I sit around wondering whether my new rocket is going to break through that most critical smog. It'll be depressing if it doesn't, although not fatal I suspect, but I can't quite keep from thinking that it'll be nice if it does.

At any rate I would rather try to answer the question you half asked me in the letter, but I hesitate because I never have a good sense of when the words we use are the same and when we're no help to each other at all. But when you wrote that you never know what goes on inside me because I do not know myself which way I'll go next, I can only say you're right but hurrah! It's the one part of me I wouldn't want to change.

The German barmaid, Regina, gave Mailer a pocket photograph of herself, inscribed to "Der Dick." He never saw her again, and it appears that they did not correspond. Years later, he identified her as the model for Ruta, Barney Kelly's lubricious maid in *An American Dream.* The letter also shows that the division in his psyche remained. As for his "new rocket," it went into orbit.

Advertisements for Myself had modest sales, less than ten thousand copies in the Putnam's edition, but it was a *succès d'estime*, receiving notably strong reviews in *The New York Times Book Review, Partisan Review*, and the *Village Voice. Time*, unsurprisingly, panned the collection, saying that judging from the excerpts offered from the big novel, its title should be "*The Nude and the Stewed.*" Two of the most positive and perceptive reviews were from prominent members of The Family, Irving Howe and Alfred Kazin. Both had caveats, as might be expected from men who finely sliced their discriminations, but overall they left no doubt about the fact that Mailer had arrived. Howe criticized him for getting carried away with his own metaphors, "using cancer as a synecdoche for the spread of social rot." But he praised the "bouncy" advertisements that held the collection together as being "done with bravado and good humor with an utter willingness to risk full exposure." Howe, a deeply committed socialist, gave his highest praise to Mailer's "devotion to restlessness," and his "fear of stasis" in the culture. This is a new Mailer, he said, a "post-depressive Mailer."

Kazin, one of the most intelligent critics writing in the late 1950s, was Edmund Wilson's heir apparent. As a Brooklyn Jew with leftist inclinations and Family membership, he was comfortable in appraising Mailer's status and prospects. He states unequivocally that his first three books, while interesting, were uneven. He expresses concern that Mailer's "over-intense need to dominate, to succeed, to grasp, to win" may interfere with his artistic development. Nevertheless, he finds *Advertisements for Myself* to be a clear advance, a book that shows "how exciting, yet tragic, America can be for a gifted writer." Tragic because the country "hungrily welcomes any talent that challenges it interestingly—but then holds this talent in the mold of its own shapelessness." Exciting, because Mailer seems to have found a way to be "an honest and intransigent spirit," while remaining thoroughly American. The collection, he says, contains "more penetrating comment on the America of Eisenhower, television, suburbia, and J. D. Salinger than anything I have seen in years." He possesses "a remarkable intelligence," and yet is "one of the most variable, unstable, and on the whole unpredictable writers I have ever read."

The insight Mailer remembered is Kazin's comment on the "marvelously forceful and inventive style" of the advertisements. "His intelligence," he continues, "though muscular, has no real ease or quietly reflective power; he is as fond of his style as an Italian tenor of his vocal cords." Previously, Mailer had doubts about whether he had a style worth discussing. Now he knew that his advertisements were not "crap," as he had called them a few months earlier. As he said in a preface to a later edition, *Advertisements for Myself* "was forged out of a continuing recognition of how difficult it was to put words together when writing about oneself." Nicotine deprivation, he explained, dulled his ability to locate the needed word, and "in compensation I was granted a sensitivity to the rhythm of what I wrote." He moved from "the hegemony of the word to the resonance of the prose rhythm." The collection, he wrote, was assembled after the "slowest and most morale-disrupting" period of his career, the ten years after *Naked and the Dead*. "I suffered prodigies of brain-curdling, and educated myself all over again how to write, write without cigarettes, and found the beginnings of a style which might begin to express the way my mind (as opposed to other writers' minds) was ready to work." The struggle to write *Advertisements* "changed my life," he said, and gave him "a style I thought I might be able to call my own." Kazin's review was confirmation.

SOMETIME NOT LONG after *Advertisements for Myself* was published, Baldwin, Styron, and Knox were drinking at Jones's Paris apartment. Jones had a copy of the book and they began discussing Mailer's comments on their work. "It wasn't a fun evening," Knox recalled. They read passages from the essay, Baldwin said, "in a kind of drunken, masochistic fascination." Then they attacked Knox as "a surrogate for Norman." Jones ignored the complimentary remarks in the piece on Styron, and instead kept reading the same line over and over: "Styron wrote the prettiest novel of our generation," causing Styron "great discomfort," according to Knox. He "started twitching and said, 'Okay, Jim, that's enough, Jim!' "

Gloria Jones said that her husband "kept a copy of *Advertisements*" in their Paris apartment. "Whenever any of the authors Mailer had attacked came through Paris for a visit, Jones would have them write their comments in the margin of the book." Mailer and Jones did not meet again until a 1965 party in novelist John Marquand Jr.'s New York apartment. Marquand thought they might try to kill each other, but they went off into a room and were gone for quite a while. "First Mailer came out by himself," Marquand said, "and he was obviously quite moved. He didn't seem angry; he seemed purged, almost as if there were tears in his eyes." Jones told Marquand that they had worked things out, and said, "I love him, but I don't like him." When Baldwin returned to the United States, he sought out Mailer and they went for a drink. Baldwin asked why he had criticized him, and Mailer replied, "Well, if this was going to break up our friendship, something else would come along to break it up just as fast." But he added that Baldwin was the only one whom he had misgivings about hitting in the essay. "I think I—probably—wouldn't say it quite that way now." Their friendship held.

Aldridge liked the collection. He saw *Advertisements for Myself* as a breakthrough "because it dramatizes the range of your mind, the variety, even the maze, of your temper" in a way that his fiction could not. The advertisements, he says, allowed Mailer "to get in all the as yet unnovelized materials of your being—all the agony, the suspicion, self-love and self-hate, all that terrible supervising conscience which fiction hasn't allowed you to get in." Mailer was pleased and praised "the particular lucidity" of Aldridge's approach to understanding the nature of the relationship between the writer and the world. Then he turned to Styron:

> I could tell you a lot about noble old Bill and how he cut off your roots, stripped your leaves, pulled your bark, scorched your lawn, and didn't even show you a face until you had gotten to the point where it was all you could do to say, "Look, man, I'm dying a little." Then his manners came to the fore and he could say, "I'm sorry to hear that," and Rose could chime in, "Yes, isn't it awful when someone is dying a little." Since I know that the same acts of surgical gardening were performed upon me and that you probably hold the details of my operation as I hold the details of yours, an exchange of intelligence might be mutually fortifying.

The rapprochement with Styron would take many years. Aldridge also broke with Styron and became one of his most persistent detractors. Over the next thirty-five years, Aldridge would have nothing but praise for Mailer, especially for his risk taking, and few qualifications.

SHORTLY AFTER *ADVERTISEMENTS* *for Myself* was published, George Plimpton tried to get Mailer and Hemingway together during Papa's visit to New York in January 1960. Plimpton told him stories of Mailer's thumb wrestling and got Hemingway interested. "You call him," Hemingway told Plimpton. But A. E. Hotchner, a close friend of Hemingway's, advised against it and Papa said, "Oh, well, forget it." Thumb wrestling intrigued him though, and he went at it with Plimpton. When he couldn't get the hang of it, he began to squeeze Plimpton's hand in his powerful grip, leaving marks that lasted a week. When someone asked what they were doing, Hemingway replied, "We're pretending we're a pair of Norman Mailers." Mailer waited in vain for the call from Plimpton, "both scared and excited," he told Plimpton, "and then both disappointed and even a bit relieved when the call never came through." This was as close as they came to meeting. Eighteen months later Hemingway would be dead.

Around this time, Bob Lucid invited him to speak at Wesleyan, where he was teaching, but Mailer declined "because I've been talking much in public lately and will never get to work on the novel if I don't stop." He did, however, continue to accept almost every invitation to read, debate, lecture, and be interviewed, and began to create a relationship with his admirers not seen since Mark Twain's barnstorming days a half century earlier. From 1960 on, Mailer was more and more in the public eye.

He grew closer to Lucid and Aldridge in the next decade, as his friendships with other writers, with few exceptions, waned. He increased his contact with aspiring writers, reading their manuscripts, writing blurbs, and offering advice generously, but was out of sorts with his peers. More and more he saw himself in the company of major writers of the past than with Jones, Baldwin, Styron, Capote, and Kerouac, or with the Jewish writers who came into ascendancy in the 1960s: Bellow, Salinger, I. B. Singer, Susan Sontag, Bernard Malamud, Philip Roth, Joseph Heller, Grace Paley, Cynthia Ozick, and Bruce Jay Friedman, to name the most prominent. He had occasional contact with most of these writers, Salinger being the notable exception, but generally downplayed any suggested commonalities. He wanted his own pedestal, and a few years later Kazin acknowledged his preeminence. It was "entirely possible," he wrote in an essay on Jewish writers, "that Norman Mailer had become the representative American novelist," a Jew who had "mastered the complex resources of the modern novel, who wrote English lovingly, possessively, masterfully, for whom the language and the form, the intelligence of art, had become as natural a way of living as the Law had been" to previous generations of Jews. Mailer may have given a nod to the shade of Rabbi Schneider when he read this, even as he was wrestling with the implications of retaining his novelistic credentials at the same time that his reputation was becoming anchored in his new role of public intellectual.

SEVEN
A FELONIOUS ASSAULT AND *AN AMERICAN DREAM*

Two of the most important events in Mailer's life took place in 1960: he wrote an essay on the presidential candidacy of Senator John F. Kennedy, based in part on two meetings with him and his wife, Jacqueline, and three months later, after a black night of drinking and fighting, he stabbed Adele. Writing "Superman Comes to the Supermarket," a new kind of political commentary, and then observing its extraordinary reception, affected him profoundly and led, indirectly but certainly, to the assault on Adele in the early morning of November 20. Two unexpected upheavals—the Cuban Revolution and the political ascent of Kennedy, an Irish American Catholic—also contributed to the calamity, but the wretched state of the Mailers' marriage and his "Napoleonic" ambition were the chief causes. There were other factors—alcohol, drugs, and the dissolution of friendships—but these were effects as much as causes. Chance also played a part, and had the last featuring blow at the event his friends called "The Trouble."

Gore Vidal's review of *Advertisements for Myself*, which appeared earlier that year, focused on Mailer's burgeoning ambition. Writing in *The Nation*, Vidal discussed in a collegial way Mailer's achievements as a writer—he especially admired *Barbary Shore*—and praised his "honorable" efforts to vex the "Great Golfer," Eisenhower. He called Mailer "a Bolingbroke, a born usurper. He will raise an army anywhere, live off the country as best he can, helped by a devoted underground, even assisted at brief moments by rival claimants like myself." Vidal had some criticisms, of course. Pointing to the barrier erected by Flaubert between his private woes and public face, he suggested that Mailer needed such a wall; writers "create not arguments but worlds," and Mailer "is a born cocktail-party orator" whose prose sometimes shifted into "a swelling, throbbing rhetoric which is not easy to read." As far as Mailer's "preoccupation with actual political power" was concerned, Vidal called it a waste of time in that the possibility of "the American president, any American president, reading a work by a serious contemporary American writer" was unimaginable. Within a year, President Kennedy would prove Vidal wrong.

Vidal's most insightful comment concerned Mailer's sense of mission, which Vidal was among the first to perceive clearly: "His drive seems to be toward power of a religio-political kind. He is a messiah without real hope of paradise on earth or in heaven, and with no precise mission except that dictated by his ever-changing temperament, I am not sure that he should be a novelist at all, or even a writer, despite formidable gifts." Vidal found all these tendencies to be "very dangerous" for "an artist not yet full grown." Mailer read the review and wrote a letter with some mild rejoinders to *The Nation*, but Vidal's analysis was prescient. Eight months later, Mailer would be ready to abandon his literary career and become a full-time politician.

Barbara, who was still doing some work for her brother in 1960, was deeply troubled by his behavior. He had told her that he wouldn't cry at her funeral and she found him to be "violent, full of hate." He hit his wife at a New Year's Eve party, and Adele told Barbara that she feared he might hurt her seriously. "Yet," Barbara wrote in her journal, "she continually provokes his cruelty because she dislikes it less than his neglect." Both women thought that he needed psychological treatment and, in a moment of lucidity, he told his sister that he was also worried about himself. Adele says little in her memoir about Mailer's interest in politics, and nothing about his difficulties in forging a new style, except her passing comment: "I think he was having a lot of trouble writing." She does note, however, his ability to work almost every day in his Brooklyn studio, no matter how drunk and disorderly the night before. For Adele's thirty-fourth birthday, June 12, he gave her a garnet crucifix, a momentary lull in their increasingly nasty public arguments. She preferred parties to hitting the bars, and often did not accompany him when he went to the White Horse or jazz clubs in the Village, although she was with him at the Village Vanguard when Lenny Bruce performed. Mailer was thrilled by Bruce's mix of political irreverence and crass obscenity, a comic version of William Burroughs's riffs in *Naked Lunch*. He saw them as allies in the struggles ahead. Both employed shock techniques and, like Mailer, were happiest when their audiences were uncomfortable.

Parties, Adele wrote, gave her an excuse to drink, which she did soon after Betsy's birth. Her drinking led to flirting, "since I came on with everybody when I was drunk." On a few occasions, she went home with another man, once with an *Esquire* editor, which led to a bad fight with Mailer. He had several one-night stands, and at least one serious affair. We were "steadily digging the grave for our marriage," she recalled. One night they went to the Copacabana nightclub with Knox and Sammy Davis Jr. After three martinis, Adele began talking with Davis's bodyguard. She asked to see his gun.

> Norman glared at me, a silent signal for me to shut up, but my martinis had gotten there first. The bodyguard politely refused. "Come on," I insisted, "let me see your gun." He took it out and passed it around the table. It was the first time I'd held a gun in my hand. I had a strange feeling of power as I pointed it at Norman. I grinned when I said, "I'm gonna kill you, you son of a bitch." My finger was on that trigger, and my husband wouldn't have to worry about his next novel anymore. That's how much rage I had inside me.

IN A MARCH letter to Yamanishi, Mailer answered his translator's question about Trotskyism in the United States. He said that the movement had dwindled, and that *Dissent* might be the last outpost of its influence. While no longer a Trotskyite himself, he was pleased that Trotsky's ideas were still alive in Japan because that could "lead in the direction of something new, something radical, and something better in the same way as Castro's Barbudos in Cuba." This is his first written reference to Fidel Castro, although like everyone else he had followed Castro's overthrow of the Cuban dictatorship in January 1959.

Shortly after writing to Yamanishi, Mailer's name appeared at the end of a full-page advertisement in *The New York Times* for the Fair Play for Cuba Committee, an international group challenging reports that Castro was a communist who would ruthlessly confiscate property and execute his opponents. All of these charges would ultimately prove correct, but Castro's sins were peccadilloes when measured against the hideously cruel and corrupt regime of General Fulgencio Batista, who ruled the country for twenty-five years before being overthrown by Castro's band of bearded—the Barbudos—guerrillas. Besides Mailer, there were thirty signatories, including Baldwin, Capote, Simone de Beauvoir, and Jean-Paul Sartre. Over the next forty years, Mailer would sign scores of open letters in the company of famous writers, academics, and activists.

Mailer called Castro "the first and greatest hero to appear in the world since the Second War," and compared him to Emiliano Zapata, a hero of the Mexican Revolution. Over the years, his belief in Castro's greatness never flagged and was strengthened when they met in Cuba decades later. Asked late in life to list the geniuses he had met in person, Mailer named Ezra Pound, Charlie Chaplin, Muhammad Ali, and Fidel Castro. In November 1960, he anguished over "An Open Letter to Fidel Castro," in which he panegyrized the Cuban, and challenged him to invite Hemingway to write a firsthand report on the Cuban situation. He finished it after three weeks of intense work, but it became a casualty of "The Trouble," and was not published until the following April. His estimate of Castro's stature can be seen in the following passage.

> Back in December, 1956, you landed near Niquero in the Oriente of Cuba with 82 men and a few arms. Your plan was to ignite an insurrection which would rid Cuba of Batista in a few weeks. Instead, you were to lose all but 12 of these men in the first few days, you were to wander through fields and forests in the dark, without real food or water, living on sugar-cane for five days and five nights. In the depths of this disaster, you were to announce to the few men who were still with you: "The days of the dictatorship are numbered."

Castro's confidence was unshakable. A legend began to grow about the Barbudos in the mountains, and the idea of revolution spread across the island. Mailer's golden opinion of Castro's vision and tenacity in the face of great odds invigorated his desire to mount his own revolution in the United States—not political, but moral and sexual. Che Guevara, Castro's chief lieutenant, elicited similar admiration. They met briefly when Guevara came to New York to address the U.N. General Assembly. Mailer wrote, "I met him once. He had a great devil in his eye. I had rarely liked anyone as much."

In mid-1960, Mailer stood high in the regard of *Esquire*'s editors.

Harold Hayes found him to be "very astute" in recommending "The Mind of an Outlaw" for publication in the magazine a few weeks before *Advertisements* was published. "I think he gained immensely by that intersection at that moment—that is, his arrival in our magazine when it was trying to become what it later became." One night in April, Mailer bumped into another young *Esquire* editor he knew, Clay Felker, at the Five Spot. Felker ended up at a table with Mailer and Adele, Mickey Knox, and Joan Morales, Adele's sister. Felker recalled that Adele was attacking Mailer, "exploding all over the place, saying things like, 'We're all shit; we don't add up to anything. You guys think you're significant, but it's all shit.' " Mailer said nothing, just smiled, which increased her anger. Finally, she left and Felker began talking to him about writing a piece on the upcoming Democratic National Convention. "I had read his pronouncement in *Advertisements* that he had been running for president in his mind and wanted to create a revolution in the consciousness of our times. Pundits were going around saying the upcoming election would mark a turning point in American history and usher in a revolutionary age, so I thought, 'What is more natural than turning loose the revolutionary mind on a revolutionary event?' " It was an editor's gamble, a brilliant one. Mailer accepted the assignment but said he didn't know much about politicians and political writing, so Felker agreed to accompany him to the convention, which was to be held in Los Angeles, July 11–15.

Adlai Stevenson, a former governor of Illinois, had been the Democratic candidate for president in 1952 and 1956, and was defeated both times by Eisenhower. He wanted a third chance but did not actively campaign, saying he would accept a draft. He was the sentimental favorite of many Democrats, but several other candidates, most of them U.S. senators, were actively challenging him. Lyndon B. Johnson of Texas, the Senate majority leader, seemed at first the most likely to succeed, based on his experience and connections. But it was the youngest senator in the pack, John F. Kennedy of Massachusetts, who would gain the nomination, and do so, in part, because of the qualities Mailer saw in him. He had neither the jowls of old wheeler-dealers like Johnson (Mailer said he looked like "a well-to-do small-town mortician"), nor the baggage of stout trade union supporters like Senator Hubert H. Humphrey of Minnesota. Kennedy was different. He was a glamorous figure, rich and handsome, with a sharp wit and great self-assurance.

His most "characteristic quality," Mailer said, was "the remote and private air of a man who has traversed some lonely terrain of experience, of loss and gain, of nearness to death." It was Kennedy's boldness that most attracted him.

The Mailers leased the house on Miller Hill Road for the summer of 1960, where he planned to work on the Kennedy piece. On June 1, they drove to Provincetown with Danielle, Betsy, and the two poodles. Zsa Zsa got pregnant easily and Mailer, always dubious about any form of birth control, was not interested in having her spayed. Over more than a dozen years, she and Tibo produced thirty-four puppies. He enjoyed observing them and found much to ponder in Zsa Zsa's habit of nipping at Tibo's genitals, forcing him to sit until she regained her composure. In later years, he loved to tell what he called his "veterinarian story." One winter day in Connecticut when it was snowing, Tibo and Zsa Zsa were outside, and he watched them as they engaged in the procreative act. He saw that they had seized up. Tibo couldn't withdraw, and Adele was afraid they would freeze. With some difficulty, Mailer lifted up both dogs and carried them indoors where they were still "unable to disconnect," as he put it. After a few futile efforts to separate them, he touched Zsa Zsa gently on her bunghole and, open sesame, they came unglued. He told the story with pleasure, and it always drew a big laugh. His jokes and stories were inveterately carnal, as was the store of similes and tropes he employed in table talk.

He continued working on his play and followed Kennedy's campaign. Baldwin came for a visit, and they drank regularly in town with various local characters. Bill Walker and Lester Blackiston, two writers from Washington, D.C., were part of the group, as was Bill Ward, the editor of the *Provincetown Annual*, where Mailer had just published a short essay on Picasso. Seymour Krim, a Beat fellow traveler and scaled-down version of Mailer, came to Provincetown to see the writer that he so admired. Mailer remembered the summers of the early 1960s as "wild, absolutely wild. There were fights. It was an absolutely extraordinary period." Bikers would come roaring into town on weekends, and there were parties on the beach. "At least ten times a summer," he said, "you'd see the sun come up over the flats. The town had a sometimes rich and sometimes sinister sense of impermanence to it, too." Liaisons started up and marriages broke down. Mailer's own was on the brink.

Roger Donoghue, whom Mailer had met the previous year by way of Knox, also spent time at the Miller Hill house, where there were many parties. A former middleweight boxer, Donoghue retired from the ring after a fighter he knocked out in a 1951 Madison Square Garden bout died a few days later. The Mailers introduced him to Fay Mowery, a painter, who was visiting her brother Eldred in Provincetown. Soon after, they married. Donoghue gave Mailer some boxing lessons and Mailer helped him with a book he was trying to write. Donoghue knew Marlon Brando, and told stories about teaching him to box for his Oscar-winning role as Terry Malloy in *On the Waterfront*. Mailer was fascinated by Donoghue's stories and easy Irish humor. He admired the Irish, Adele said. "I sometimes thought he really wanted to be Irish."

A few years later he explained why he had so many Irish friends: "I've always loved the Irish and felt very close to them," he said, because "The Irish have what the Jews didn't have, and the Jews always had what the Irish didn't have. The Jews have this *funny knowledge* that if you respect life enough, it's going to respect you back. The Irish have never understood that. On the other hand the Irish have this *great bravura*, a *style*, an *elegance*." One side of Mailer was drawn to the dutiful Jews; the other, more daring side, took pleasure in Irish characters like Donoghue and, a couple of years later, Brendan Behan, the dramatist and memoirist. Behan, who described himself as "a drinker with writing problems," represented Mailer's Dionysian side. His radical IRA past and rumbustious escapades were enormously appealing to Mailer, who later "blessed" Behan for teaching him to perform in public. Susan, then an adolescent, remembers her father arriving at the apartment with Behan and his girlfriend, Valerie Danby-Smith, a former intimate of Hemingway's. It was seven or eight in the morning, and they were drunk and happy after a night of revelry.

One night that summer, Mailer and Adele were walking home after having drinks at the Atlantic House. It was a little after one in the morning, and when he saw a police car driving slowly by, he called out, impulsively, "taxi, taxi." The two policemen in the cruiser were not amused, words were exchanged, and Mailer was arrested. At the station house, when they put hands of escort on him, he resisted. He described it in a letter to the *New York Post* a few weeks later: "I was afraid of a flip, afraid I would begin to hit a uniform. I had the sustained image of a summer or a year in cellular, and so I did no more; let us say that

I was reduced by this caution to ducking, spinning, blocking and sidestepping." This passive-aggressive behavior inflamed the two officers, and one of them, allegedly, hit him in the back of the head with his billy. It took thirteen stitches to close the cut. He was charged with public drunkenness and disorderly conduct and, rather than pay a fine and admit his guilt, opted for a June 23 bench trial, at which he represented himself. Disproving the canard that nonlawyers are unable to defend themselves in relatively straightforward trials, Mailer won a dismissal of the disorderly charge, but was found guilty of drunkenness. The judge said that Mailer "had enough to drink to act like a fool," and reprimanded the police for being "thin-skinned." Mailer was satisfied with the draw.

RIGHT AFTER THE July 4th holiday, he flew to Los Angeles. He wanted to get the feel of the city before the convention. Driving with Felker from the airport, Mailer said, "The only political writing I know anything about is Marx. I'm not exactly sure how to go about it." Felker introduced him to some reporters, and Mailer found that he already knew some people there, including Arthur Schlesinger Jr., the historian, who would later join the Kennedy administration. Mailer's name, of course, was well known. "The Democrats fascinated him, and they in turn were fascinated by him," Felker recalled. When the convention was under way, he came up to Felker and said, "I know how to do this now." "I had an epiphany," Mailer recalled, "the day I saw Jack Kennedy arrive at the convention. He was in the back seat of an open car, his face suntanned, and there was a crowd of gays on the other side of Pershing Park, all applauding, going crazy, while the convention itself was filled with the whole corrupt trade-union Mafia Democratic machine. And I could feel these two worlds come together."

Mailer (smoking again) had seventeen days to write his essay. Kennedy's "prefabricated politics" bothered him, however, and he did not immediately decide on the stance he would take. Recalling the moment much later, he said, "I never saw Kennedy as a politician I was in agreement with. I saw him as an active agent, as a catalyst, if you will, who would accelerate a great many trends in American life." Subsequently, Mailer was able to override his doubts and produce, for the first time in his life, a piece written with "deliberate political intention; I wanted to get a man elected." He also feared that Kennedy might lose. If party workers "had eased up a little bit," he said, "Nixon might have won." The 1960 presidential election was one of the closest in history, with Kennedy defeating Richard Nixon in the popular vote by just over 100,000 votes.

When Mailer was in the middle of writing what turned out to be a thirteen-thousand-word essay, Felker flew up to Provincetown to get an early look at it. "It was much better than I expected," Felker recalled. When it was all but finished, Mailer got a bonus: Kennedy was in Hyannis Port for a few days, about an hour from Provincetown, and had agreed to an interview. On the appointed day, before meeting privately with Kennedy, he spoke with some of the others gathered in the living room of the senator's waterfront home, including Schlesinger; Prince Radziwill, the husband of Lee Radziwill (Jacqueline Kennedy's sister); Peter Maas, a writer who knew Mailer; and Kennedy's press secretary, Pierre Salinger. Everyone was dressed casually, but Mailer had worn a suit and tie and was uncomfortable in the heat. "Sweating like a goat, tense at the pit of my stomach for I would be interviewing Kennedy in a half hour, I was feeling not a little jangled," and when introduced to Mrs. Kennedy, "I felt like a drunk marine who knows in all clarity that if he doesn't have a fight soon it'll be good for his character but terrible for his constitution." She offered him some iced tea, and they chatted about Provincetown, which she had never seen.

> She must, I assured her. It was one of the few fishing villages in America which still had beauty. Besides it was the Wild West of the East. The local police were the Indians and the beatniks were the poor hard-working settlers. Her eyes turned merry. "Oh, I'd love to see it," she said. But how did one go? In three black limousines and fifty police for escort, or in a sports car at four A.M. with dark glasses? "I suppose now I'll never get to see it," she said wistfully.

(A year later Mrs. Kennedy, now the first lady, got her wish. Accompanied by Gore Vidal, whose stepfather had been married at different times to her mother and to Vidal's, she spent a couple of days in Provincetown with a small Secret Service escort. She wore a blond wig and dark glasses but was still identified by the locals.)

In their conversation, what struck Mailer was something Kennedy said at the outset, which he found to be "altogether meaningful" to him, but otherwise irrelevant. Kennedy said that he had read his books, paused and continued, "I've read *The Deer Park* and . . . the others," a remark that startled Mailer. In countless similar situations, the book invariably mentioned was *The Naked and the Dead.* "If one is to take the worst and assume that Kennedy was briefed for this interview (which is most doubtful), it still speaks well for the striking instincts of his advisors." As it turns out, Kennedy was briefed by Salinger, who, in turn, had been prompted by Maas. According to Maas, there had been some reluctance to grant the interview in the first place, because "at that time in his life Norman was not viewed as Mr. Stability." So Maas told Salinger that "if you really want him eating out of your hand," tell Kennedy to refer to *The Deer Park*. "But string it out a little. The timing has to be just right." Salinger, who was present for the interview, saw his boss deliver the line perfectly, and "Norman just melted." They got along well enough for Kennedy to invite him to come back the next day with his wife, which he did. Mailer wrote later, "After I saw the Kennedys I added a few paragraphs to my piece about the convention, secretly relieved to have liked them, for my piece was most favorable to the Senator."

Three weeks before the election, on October 18, the November issue of *Esquire* appeared, and "Superman Comes to the Supermarket" was given wide attention. Pete Hamill, another Irish-American who became friendly with Mailer, was a young journalist at that time. Looking back, he said, "When it came out, it went through journalism like a wave. Something changed. Everyone said, 'Uh. oh. Here's another way to do it.' " Mailer had taken "political journalism beyond what the best guys—Mencken, Teddy White, Richard Rovere—had done. Rather than just a political sense there was a moral sense that came out of the piece." Felker and Hayes also were impressed: "It made an enormous impact and caused a lot of young writers to begin to think about politics," Felker said. Hayes added that the essay "set the tone for many, many things to come for him, and for us."

Arthur Schlesinger said he had "a vague memory that Kennedy was rather pleased" with the profile. Mailer only learned of Kennedy's reaction much later, but shortly after the piece appeared, he received a four-page handwritten letter from Jacqueline Kennedy expressing gratitude for his essay. "I never dreamed that American Politics could be written about that way—why don't more people have the imagination to do so," she asks, and then answers by saying, "I know why—the poor things don't have the talent." She then assured him that her husband had indeed read *The Deer Park*; she remembered clearly the room where he finished it on a rainy day the previous fall, as well as her own reading of it. Perhaps he and his wife could visit them at the Kennedy compound next summer, she added. Reading this, Mailer began to imagine a role he might play in the new administration.

In her letter, Mrs. Kennedy does not refer to any specific passages in "Superman Comes to the Supermarket," but the following scene could certainly have been one of those that elicited the wonder she felt. It is a description of Kennedy's arrival at the Hotel Biltmore, seen from Mailer's vantage point on an outdoor balcony of the hotel.

> The Kennedy cortege came into sight, circled Pershing Square, the men in the open and leading convertibles sitting backwards to look at their leader, and finally came to a halt in the space cleared for them by the police in the crowd. The television cameras were out, and a Kennedy band was playing some circus music. One saw him immediately. He had the deep orange-brown suntan of a ski instructor, and when he smiled at the crowd his teeth were amazingly white and clearly visible at a distance of fifty yards. For one moment he saluted Pershing Square, and Pershing Square saluted him back, the prince and the beggars of glamour staring at one another across a city street, one of those very special moments in the underground history of the world, and then with a quick move he was out of the car and by choice headed in to the crowd instead of the lane cleared for him into the hotel by the police, so that he made his way inside surrounded by a mob, and one expected at any moment to see him lifted to his shoulders like a matador being carried back to the city after a triumph in the plaza.

"Superman" is a classic piece of reportage and a foundation stone of the New Journalism not least because of Mailer's skill with long periodic sentences. They take us through the scene as if we are watching an overhead tracking shot in a film, while giving hints of the emotions felt not only by the writer (here designated by the indefinite pronoun "one" to emphasize his shared identity with the crowd), but by the crowd, the police, the TV camera operators, the "beggars," the senator's handlers, and Kennedy himself, the ski-instructor-prince-matador-movie-star who spontaneously elects to wade into the crowd. The consequences of the Democrats nominating "a great box-office actor," he continued, "were staggering and not at all easy to calculate." The fact that Kennedy was Irish-American did him no harm in Mailer's eyes. When Kennedy came on the stage at the convention, a writer friend said to Mailer, "Sergius O'Shaugnessy born rich," a remark that struck Mailer. Years later Mailer said that the reason he had "a great many Irish friends" was that he felt "some kind of instinctive link with them." An oft quoted passage in the essay, which comes shortly after the description of Kennedy's triumphant arrival, demonstrates the accuracy of Hamill's comment about a new kind of political journalism:

> Since the First World War Americans have been leading a double life, and our history has moved on two rivers, one visible, the other underground; there has been the history of politics which is concrete, factual, practical and unbelievably dull if not for the consequences of the actions of some of these men; and there is a subterranean river of untapped, ferocious, lonely and romantic desires, that concentration of ecstasy and violence which is the dream life of the nation.

The two rivers came together in Kennedy, a canny, bold political operative ready to shake a thousand hands a day and spend his father's money to win (with the help of his family) a string of nine primaries, but also a war hero with a vision for the future, funds of imperturbability, and looks as heart-piercing as the matinee idols whom Americans had loved and envied in the darkened movie palaces of the Depression and World War II.

Even after receiving Mrs. Kennedy's letter and reaping congratulations all around on "Superman," Mailer still had last-minute pangs. "The night Kennedy was elected," he wrote, "I felt a sense of woe." By presenting Kennedy as an archetype, a young King Arthur, Mailer felt he was "bending reality like a field of space to curve the time I wished to create." He didn't know if he was enabling an opportunist or bringing a hero into his own. Would Kennedy be the first hipster president, or just another politician? "Victory has a thousand fathers, but defeat is an orphan," Kennedy once said, and after he won the White House a number of people claimed paternity. Mailer listed several—Chicago mayor Richard Daley, J. Edgar Hoover, Lyndon Johnson, and Frank Sinatra, a strong supporter of JFK. Mailer said his "cool conclusion" that "Superman Comes to the Supermarket" had been one of the deciding factors "might be high presumption but it was not unique." His contribution, he argued, had been to dramatize the race between the Republican candidate, Richard Nixon—"sober, the apotheosis of opportunistic lead"—and JFK, "a prince in the unstated aristocracy of the American dream." He didn't claim to have shifted 100,000 votes directly, but "a million people might have read my piece and some of them talked to other people." His essay sparked the energies of Kennedy volunteers, "enough to make a clean critical difference through the country."

Shortly after he finished "Superman," he heard that Capote was working on a new book about the savage murder of a family on a Kansas farm the previous fall. *In Cold Blood*, published first in 1965 in *The New Yorker*, and the following year as a book, would have a strong influence on Mailer. "I hate you for writing about murder," he wrote to Capote, "I thought that was my province." He didn't say that the big novel he was preparing himself to write was also about a murder. All he said was that it was too late in the summer to make a big push on it. He added that he was trying to close a deal on a three-story brownstone in Brooklyn Heights not far from Capote's apartment, and if it happened, "the possibility suggests itself to light a candle every night for Senor Capote, our peripatetic Truman." The Brooklyn house didn't work out at that time. Instead, the Mailers began renting a fairly large apartment at 250 West 94th Street, thirteenth floor.

They learned about the apartment from Harold L. "Doc" Humes, who lived in the same building. A writer, activist, provocateur, and devoted marijuana smoker, Humes was one of the founders of *The Paris Review*, and a legendary figure in the hip world. He had written a brilliant novel, *The Underground City*, and in the fall of 1960 founded the Citizens' Emergency Committee in response to the plight of an eccentric comic, Richard "Lord" Buckley, whose permit to perform had been rescinded. Billie Holiday, Charles Mingus, Thelonious Monk, among many others, had also been denied permits. Mailer, who was still involved with the Fair Play for Cuba Committee, signed on with Humes's committee, whose efforts ultimately led to the resignation of the police commissioner, and several years later the dismantling of the cabaret permit system. He began spending a lot of time with Humes, whom he later described as "one of the few people I have ever met, who was essentially, at bottom, more vain, more intellectually arrogant than I am." The success of "Superman" made him fantasize about becoming a member of Kennedy's kitchen cabinet. "I wanted to be an advisor," he said in 1999. "I felt that, you know, I might have a certain talent for it." At that time, he said,

> I realized that life, in its imminence, in its presence, in its resonance, once you could feel it, was extraordinary, and that we were all living like cockroaches, scurrying here and there and not having that life. And so that became, if you will, my sermon. That was what I was preaching for the next 10-15-20 years: let's get back to the instinctive life. Let's get back to where we can feel what's going on in ourselves. And I felt that President Kennedy, and his wife, precisely because of their youth and their good looks, were going to encourage—willy-nilly, whether they chose to or not—an opening in America, a return more to the pagan, to the sense of oneself as an animal who lived in a field of senses.

Kennedy owed him some gratitude, Mailer felt, and in recompense, he wanted "some drinks and dinner and a chance to preach to the President." He was certain he could help Kennedy understand the country better, and perhaps he could become his confidant.

Mailer had his own confidant—Doc Humes—and that fall they were discussing the possibility of Mailer running for mayor of New York on "the existentialist ticket." Humes would be his campaign manager. Humes recalled that Mailer "was grim-faced every day. He wasn't sleeping well, he was using a lot of Demerol and alcohol, and he had collateral worries about his work." He wanted to lead New York, while calling it "this insane, cruel, rapacious, avid, cancerous and alas—in the end—cowardly city." New York was certainly having an effect on him, according to Humes: "I think he even described it once as a Dr. Jekyll–Mr. Hyde type of thing, with the city driving him mad." Others noticed how he changed when he returned from the country or Provincetown. Pleased as he was about his piece in *Esquire*, he was infuriated when the magazine's publisher, Arnold Gingrich, decided to change the final word of the title from "Supermarket" to "Supermart." When Mailer saw the change on his contract, he told Felker to make the restoration, and Felker said he would, but didn't. Consequently, Mailer instructed Rembar to ensure that his future contracts specify that no changes could be made to magazine pieces, including titles, without his permission. Then he wrote a letter to the editors at *Esquire*, detailing his complaints and ended, "You print nice stuff, but you gotta treat the hot writer right or you lose him like you just lost me. When I'm mayor, I'll pay you a visit and see if you've cleaned the stable." In later years, whenever he autographed copies of the essay in the magazine, he always carefully restored the original title by hand. Reasonable people can debate which title is slightly more euphonious.

AFTER DISCUSSIONS WITH friends and family in late October, Mailer began his public campaign for mayor with a flurry of letters. He asked for the support of comedian, writer, and musician Steve Allen, with whom he had become friendly; liberal columnist Murray Kempton, whose idiosyncratic style he admired; Seymour Krim, who had written him about reaching out to New York Catholics and Jews; and Karl Edd, the author of a banned book, *The Tenement Kid*. He asked Edd for the names of "some very hard hip kids" to work in the campaign, and told Krim that he needed public relations professionals who would work for nothing. The kind of people he hoped to attract, he explained to Allen, were people who had "evolved a private philosophy which will have perhaps some point of possible communion with my own." He told his German publisher he had no time to answer questions because "it is necessary to start a new political party in America," and agreed to do an interview with *Mademoiselle* on the condition that it be a discussion of politics. He did respond positively, however, to Allen Ginsberg's request for a testimonial for William Burroughs's *Naked Lunch*, which he had now read. For the Grove Press edition, he wrote, "*Naked Lunch* is a book of great beauty, great difficulty, and maniacally exquisite insight. I think William Burroughs is the only American novelist living today who may conceivably be possessed by genius. And I make these remarks in sourness and without enthusiasm, since Mr. Burroughs, after all, is one of my fellow racketeers. But I don't know that we belong to the same part of the literary Mafia." The second sentence of the blurb continues to appear on editions of Burroughs's novel.

On the campaign trail, Kennedy was talking about the possibility of sending a volunteer force to Cuba to challenge Castro, and Mailer was sufficiently disturbed to write a note to Schlesinger saying that such an operation would be "tragic," and Kennedy might "lose more than he will gain from this" in the election. He also said no to a request to use his name on a national advertisement sent to him from the National Committee of Arts, Letters and Sciences for John F. Kennedy for President. "Kennedy's Wagnerian vision of a new American expeditionary force captained by Saint Grottlesexers and soldiered by some yet undefined Marine corps lumpen proletariat for the invasion of Cuba," he wrote, was "chilling" and he hoped it was only "a perhaps forgivable mistake due to the excesses of campaigning."

NOT ALL OF his letters were as reasonable as these. In undated letters written around election day to four writers, there are signs, at least in retrospect, that the fears of his wife and sister about his mental state were justified. The letters are to pitcher Jim Brosnan, author of professional baseball's first unsanitized memoir, *The Long Season*; John Cheever, who had a fine story, "The Death of Justina," in the same issue of *Esquire* as "Superman"; Stephen Spender, the literary editor of *Encounter*, a highbrow British magazine, where Mailer had sent "Superman" in the hopes of publication; and T. S. Eliot. Spender was the only one that Mailer knew personally. Following are a few lines from the first three, and the whole of his letter to Eliot:

To Brosnan: "I can't pitch worth a fuck, and you write like a dull whore with an honest streak, but if you ain't afraid of a grand slam, which you is, come around when you get to the New York, and we'll have a drink or two—you to beer and small Martinis, me to . . . B, not Bourbon, but blended Bellows, if that's not bragging too hard. Your new pal Fan letter Mailer (First name Norm)"

To Cheever: "For its length it's an extraordinary story, not altogether alienated (?) from a great literature but . . . you did . . . cowardly thing—you kept the children from seeing the dead woman—thus depriving me of their reactions. Yet one does write a letter. Your tablemate, Norman Mailer"

To Spender: "I have a hide like a Bantu flunky but you might recognize the subtle bit that I found you one of the few people who were at bottom not wholly detestable. So not hearing from you it was sad to think that Mailer, the punch-drunk clunk is wrong again. Norman"

Mailer was trying to convince André Deutsch, his publisher in England, to include "The Time of Her Time" in the edition of *Advertisements for Myself* to be published there. He hoped that Eliot, after reading that Denise Gondelman believed that the poet "was the apotheosis of manner" would endorse its inclusion. To Eliot:

> If he [Eliot] comes out with words for The Time of Her Time, I will force my publisher to print or have nothing further to do with him. Self educated gentleman, I will swear a vow on what is important to me that I will not use his letter in any way without the perfectionist permission of his ecclesiastical Name.
>
> Prince Mailer the Norman of Principath to T. S. Lord King of Eliot, Impervious to Compassion, Blind by Pride, Timid as Temerity, Royal as a Royal Roach who has Earned his Place which is High. Spirit of Denial and Quick Withdrawal I, hereby, as Norman, do challenge your inflexible taste by presenting the fruits of my orchard and the war of my castle. Do answer. No answer is war, and one would detest that. Mailer.

It is unlikely that these letters were sent, but it is clear that he was less and less able to bridle his irrationality. The struggle between the saint and the psychopath was challenging the navigator's abilities.

In his reply to Mrs. Kennedy before the election, he responded to her comment about how incredible it would be if he could somehow visit earlier centuries and write reports in the manner of "Superman." Mailer said he would enjoy talking with her in Hyannis Port about his interest in the late-eighteenth-century France. Specifically, he would like to discuss the works of the Marquis de Sade. "There's a man I'd like to do a biography of when I'm dead beyond repair. I might be able to throw a hint or two on the odd strong honor of the man." His balance can be gauged by his feeling that Mrs. Kennedy would naturally be delighted to discuss de Sade's thought as "a fair climax to the Age of Reason." Not surprisingly, she did not reply. Much later, he deduced that he had "smashed the limits of such letter-writing," and trod "as close to the edge as I have ever come." But at the time, "I saw it somewhat differently. The odds were against a reply, I decided, three-to-one against, or eight-to-one against. I did not glean that they were eight-hundred-to-one against. It is the small inability to handicap odds which is family to the romantic, the desperate and the insane."

Two days after he wrote to Mrs. Kennedy, Mailer called a meeting to discuss his candidacy with Irving Howe and a half dozen *Dissent* writers and editors. Mailer opened it by saying he wanted to be mayor "to establish New York as the West Berlin of the world." He called for an existential campaign. He then read his "Open Letter to Fidel Castro" and said that if it was published and Castro responded positively and Hemingway agreed to write an assessment of the Cuban Revolution, voters would get the sense that "New York can be a force in the world." Howe said that the Cuban situation was no way to start a New York mayoral campaign, especially a third party campaign. The meeting ended after a desultory discussion of a name for the new party.

According to his sister, he was surly and difficult in the fall of 1960. One afternoon she came to the 94th Street apartment to deliver something she had typed for him in connection with the mayoral campaign. He found fault with it and said she was trying to sabotage him. They argued and, then, she recalled, "He actually hit me across the side of my face. Broke my glasses. He was very upset. Oh, God, it was a terrible time." Adele was present and remembers Barbara crying and saying to her brother, "What's the matter with you? Are you crazy?" and then leaving. Barbara now believes that Mailer had gotten fascinated with political power when he went to the Democratic convention. "I think he really felt that if I can't change the world with my writing, I can change it if I get some power, some political power." He wasn't merely angry with her, she said, he was angry with his entire family: "He felt that the Kennedys all pulled together, and his family wasn't doing this for him. I wasn't happy at all about his running for mayor. Thought it was a terrible idea." A decade later, Mailer said he was in complete earnest at the time. "I thought I was unique; that I had a unique mission. I had something to do in the world." When the two women spoke the next day, Barbara said, "I've never seen him like this." Adele replied, "Well I have, and it's getting worse."

His descent began to accelerate. On November 14, he was arrested at Birdland, a fancy jazz club in Midtown Manhattan. He insisted on paying a bar bill with a credit card, although the law forbade alcohol purchases on credit at the time. He spent the night in jail. The next afternoon he was cordial during his interview with two young women from *Mademoiselle*. Most of their discussion was given over to the issues raised in "The White Negro" and "Superman." Mailer said Kennedy was a hipster, and that he was as well, but a "terribly philosophical" one. He wasn't about to recommend hipsterism to everyone, he said. "I just ask that the hipster be considered at least as interesting and serious as a young congressman." Mailer admitted to still taking an occasional toke, but found that it was affecting his short-term memory. When the discussion turned to writers, he praised Burroughs. "I think he's going to last a long time after me because he's more intense. He's got a quality I don't have. I mean, I write sentences that embrace people. But he writes sentences that stab people and you never forget the man who stabs you." Indeed.

Mailer was tired after spending the previous night in jail, but nevertheless spent the evening drinking with his Provincetown friends, Lester Blackiston and Bill Ward, at the Cedar Tavern in the Village. He got to bed at six A.M. (We know the specifics of his life for the next three weeks because of a rough diary he kept from November 15 through December 8.) The next afternoon he had a mayoral planning meeting at Downey's Steakhouse in Manhattan with some friends, including Seymour Krim, who along with Allen Ginsberg and Noel Parmentel Jr. (credited with coming up with the famous line about Nixon, "Would you buy a used car from this man?"), were named informal press secretaries for the campaign. He returned to 94th Street for a meeting with Doc Humes and the Citizens' Emergency Committee.

The following day, November 17, Mailer took the train to Providence to give a reading at Brown University. According to an account by Brown student reporter Richard Holbrooke, he began his presentation announcing, "I come to bring you the existentialist word" (five years later, Mailer said that at the time, "I thought I had God's message"). Another reporter, Ellen Shaffer, wrote: "The audiences were at once alienated by this brusque man, and having lost his audience, Mailer never regained it." He read from his work, and "his voice swelled with each obscenity, and he made lewd gestures to aid his re-enactment of the scene." A few members of the audience walked out; others applauded. She concluded: "Norman Mailer is an egocentric, malcontent genius, who has courageously, indignantly come to blows with the world around him." Holbrooke ends his report with Mailer in quiet dialogue about various writers after the reading. "Fitzgerald," Mailer said, "pissed away his talent," and Farrell is "as great as Beckett." Mailer's notes sketch the rest of the evening: "Drinks at Ginger Chivvies (?), Freddy candy (?) man and punch he caught for me, going outside—Chinnie Thibault looking for WPRO, splitting with him and Reis, car-ride out for girl, no-find, eating in a spade joint, near rumble, split-out onto street, back to hotel, chinfest with Reis, sleep."

The next day he met his sister at his apartment. They had a fight about the preparations for the thirtieth birthday party he was giving Roger Donoghue on November 19. Mailer planned to make an informal statement at the party that he was running for mayor; a formal announcement would be made a few days later at a press conference. The Donoghues came by for drinks in the late afternoon, and then they all went to the Stork Club for more. After dinner, he went home and took Tibo for a walk, and the dog ran away. Chasing him, Mailer got into a fight with a "prep school type." He went to bed in the early morning hours.

In the morning, he was "ego-dampened by fatigue." Mickey Knox and Doc Humes's wife, Anna Lou, came by for campaign assignments. After they left, he had an argument with Adele. Then he got on the telephone to invite last-minute guests. George Plimpton, who was helping him, later said that Mailer called him several times that day. His idea, Plimpton said, was that "he was truly suited to represent the disenfranchised of the city . . . and if he could convince this marginal if large group that he had solid connections with the 'power structure' of New York City, he'd get their support." Dutifully, all afternoon, Plimpton made calls to various dignitaries, including the fire commissioner, police commissioner, David Rockefeller of Chase Manhattan Bank, and Sadruddin Aga Khan, the publisher of *The Paris Review.* But the only society representative Plimpton convinced to attend was Peter Duchin, the bandleader.

A heavy load of booze was delivered in the late afternoon and Adele, with the help of their maid, Nettie Biddle, was busy preparing food. C. Wright Mills, the sociologist, came early, as did various street people Mailer had invited. There were many crashers. The party was roaring by ten P.M. Plimpton remembered seeing a man wrapped in bandages and was told he was a victim of police brutality. Tony Franciosa, a film star, was at the party. Mailer knew him through his old friend Shelley

Winters, who had divorced Franciosa the day before. He was the closest thing to a major celebrity who attended. Several close friends and family members were there. Estimates of the number of guests average around two hundred.

Mickey Knox, who thought he had seen the full spectrum of his friend's moods, said that Mailer "was in a strange zone." He paced through the apartment, "taut as a cat," giving his greetings. He had drunk a lot and smoked marijuana, and soon got into arguments about the campaign. He also tried to stare people down. "It was a spooky evening," Doc Humes recalled. "It was exactly the kind of atmosphere that Norman in his state should have avoided." Allen Ginsberg, usually the mildest of men, got into a shouting match with Norman Podhoretz. According to Ginsberg, Podhoretz was patronizing, telling him the only way he could gain entrée into the larger literary world was by breaking with the Beats. "To my eternal shame," Ginsberg recalled, "I lost my temper" and began screaming at Podhoretz. Mailer was called and Ginsberg assured him that he wasn't going to get violent. Ginsberg saw that he was making a scary party worse, so he left, riding down in the elevator with C. Wright Mills.

Scuffles kept breaking out as the party wore on. Larry Alson, Barbara's first husband, remembers that people kept challenging Mailer to a fight. When book editor Jason Epstein arrived, Mailer tried to box with him. "I don't know anything about boxing," Epstein said, "so I just held out my hand as if to make him go away. I didn't touch him, and he fell over." Mailer went down to the street several times for fights, according to his notes, once with a man named Curran: "Punch at Plimpton's belly—P's counter to chin, chasing Duchin and P to cab. Fighting Curran. Taking punishment—holding on—draw. Curran getting into cab—ask him to tell accurate version—gets out, new fight, lands on ground, me astride—he squeezing, me up—finally wanes—goes home. Puerto Rican wants to fight. I shame him." Podhoretz summed it up: "There was a lot of bad feelings in the air, most of it emanating from Norman."

Around three A.M. there were about twenty people left. In his drunken state, Mailer announced he was dividing them into two groups: supporters and enemies. He judged each person; most were found wanting, including Adele. Nettie the maid, he kept saying, was the only person who had remained loyal. As gossip columnist Leonard Lyons wrote the following day, "It has been quite apparent, for more than a year, that the gifted writer needed psychiatric help." Mailer was barely standing, but he went back down to the street. He walked north to Podhoretz's apartment on 106th Street, and called for him to come out. Neither Podhoretz nor his wife heard anything. On the way back, he saw Donoghue and a friend. Mailer tried to fight the friend and then, according to his diary, Donoghue. Although Donoghue was as drunk as Mailer, he knew better and left. Later, Mailer told Donoghue, "I wish you'd hit me." Around 4:30, he went upstairs. His face and bullfighter's shirt were bloody, and he had a black eye.

Only a few people were left. When Adele saw her husband, she taunted him, as she recalled in her memoir: "*Aja toro, aja*, come on you little faggot, where's your *cojones*, did your ugly whore of a mistress cut them off, you son of a bitch." Mailer's diary reads as follows:

> Head upstairs and have trouble getting in. Adele mocks me (fag crack)—I rush the door, others try to push me out, I flail, fight, succeed in getting in, Adele looks away in scorn, I hit her, then order others out. Mannix offers resistance, and I rumble with him, am too weak, and Lester bops him. Then go back in. There is Neddie, Clint, Les, & Adele—Back to the hall with Adele??? We come out, after while she leaves with others. I start to go to sleep, Les comes back, they are over at Humes—glass tale. Humes comes by—I abuse him, drive him away, as he flees, he drops bottle behind him on floor thus stopping my exit.

Several months before he died, Mailer looked back on the worst night of his life.

> Well, Adele and I had been getting into bigger and bigger games when I ran for mayor in '60 that got her, it absolutely got her, in a state of suppressed hysteria because she thought it was going to shatter our lives. What does she know about being a mayor, a mayor's wife, what if I got elected? Like, you know, we had our children by then, we had Danielle, we had Betsy. Those were very important events for me in the '50s, Danielle and Betsy being born. And, so, we were getting along very badly, and we were getting into a kind of gotcha routine where each of us was doing something that was superior to the other. And so finally I had this big party at which I was

> going to announce my coming out for mayor, and Adele was going nuts at the party, from my point of view. And, finally, in a rage I took out my penknife and stuck it into her with the idea of, "Here, you think you're tough, I'm tougher." It was madness. I was pretty drunk at the time and probably on pot. The idea was not to do her any damage, just give her a nick or two, you see? Damn it, if I didn't nick her heart. She could have died from it. And, of course, they took her to the emergency hospital, cut her open from the sternum virtually down to below the navel. So for years afterwards, she had this huge scar and she'd sometimes show it at parties. This would give people the idea that I'd used a butcher knife, which is why Gore Vidal mentions a butcher knife.

Vidal's reference to a butcher knife has not been located, but if he made it, he was not alone in getting things wrong. Evelyn Waugh—no friend of Mailer's—wrote that he had cut his wife's throat, and George Plimpton—always a friend—said that Mailer had used a kitchen knife. Another alleged that scissors had been used, and one claimed Mailer had shot her. In point of fact, the instrument was a slender black penknife or pocketknife with a two-and-a-half-inch blade that he used to clean his nails. He stabbed her twice, once in the back, which proved to be a superficial wound, and once in the upper abdomen. This thrust penetrated the pericardium, the tough, fibrous, conical sac that envelops the heart and the roots of the great blood vessels. By great luck, he missed his wife's heart by a fraction of an inch.

Adele remembers someone named Mannix helping her to Humes's apartment, and then disappearing. Humes says she was pale and in shock. He dragged a mattress from a bed and with his wife's help got Adele to lie down and remain still. Anna Lou Humes held her hand and tried to comfort her as Adele kept repeating that this sort of thing didn't happen to people like her, they only happened to Puerto Ricans. Humes, "always a take-charge guy," according to Anna Lou, got on the telephone and called a doctor he knew, Conrad Rosenberg, who said he would come immediately. Humes also tried to find a psychiatrist because he believed that Mailer would fare better if hospitalized for a mental breakdown than being arrested for assault. Humes also called Barbara and Larry Alson and told them what had happened, and they immediately left for 94th Street to get Betsy, who was alone in the apartment with her father. Fan was notified and she took a cab, leaving Barney home with Danielle, who was visiting for the weekend. Shortly after they all arrived, an ambulance took Adele to University Hospital on 20th Street and Eighth Avenue, where she was admitted at eight A.M. Nettie rode with her.

Doc Humes said that when he saw Mailer in the apartment after the stabbing, he was in a "zombielike" state. "I don't think he was fully aware of having stabbed her," he said. But while Mailer's diary says nothing about a knife or a wound, he later recognized what he had done. Humes had convinced Adele to tell the police and doctors that she had fallen on broken glass, and that was the cause of the wounds to her back and abdomen. That was her first explanation, but later she told the truth: "He didn't say anything. He just looked at me. He didn't say a word. He stabbed me."

Barbara knew a psychiatrist, Dr. Emmanuel Ghent, and had called him before she left for Humes's apartment on 94th Street. She asked him to go to her brother's apartment and examine him. Mailer was awakened by Ghent ringing his bell, but refused to let him in. When Fan and the Alsons arrived, Ghent told them what had happened and offered to see Mailer later. At some point, he told Barbara that Fan reminded him of "a Mafia mother." Before she left for the hospital, Barbara called her brother and told him the situation. He roused himself and was gone by the time Fan arrived to pick up Betsy, who was then fourteen months old.

Mailer and the Alsons arrived at the hospital at about the same time. They found the surgeon attending Adele, Dr. Macklin, and according to Larry Alson, Mailer began talking with him, carefully describing the nature of the incision. The doctor listened patiently and then left, telling them that the operation would take an hour. Mailer was able to get a glimpse of Adele and her sister Joan through a window. He and the Alsons were sent to a lower floor to wait. Mailer's diary: "Descent into Hell on elevator." They were all exhausted and distraught. "Oh, God," Barbara recalled, "that was a terrible time." She told her brother that he had to recognize that he had "flipped," which angered him. For four hours, they waited in silence. Dr. Macklin finally came down in the early afternoon to say that she would make it. Dr. Rosenberg was also there and had a brief opportunity to observe Mailer, as he later testified.

The family and friends began closing ranks. After they left the hospital, there was a conference back at the 94th Street apartment. Attending were Fan and Barney, Cy Rembar and his wife, Billie, Doc Humes, Knox, Lester Blackiston, Podhoretz, a lawyer friend, John Cox, the Donoghues and a friend of theirs, Dick Devine, who advised Mailer to put on a suit. He did and left with Knox and Blackiston. They had drinks at Joey's Bar and then went to the hospital, where he was allowed to see Adele.

Mailer's diary record of the visit is brief: "Descent downtown to hosp. Knife. Adele's fear." In her memoir, she goes into more detail. "He looked haggard and strained, with dark circles under his eyes," she wrote. She was fearful and tried to make him go away. He said, "Do you know that I watched you being wheeled into the operating room, and I'd never seen you look so beautiful. Do you understand why I did it? I love you and I had to save you from cancer." She thought he was "hopelessly crazy," but felt sorry for him. "He cried, and yes, I held him, and we wept together, but even in my grief, I knew his were tears of self-pity. It was all gone between us." Mailer stayed the night at the Donoghues' apartment. He recalled that he had "crazy ideas about going down to Cuba or something, joining Castro," perhaps by renting a fishing boat in Provincetown. But the next morning, he called the hospital and left word he would be there.

Before he left, Fan arrived, and pressed her son to see Dr. Ghent. Mailer wrote about it later in a poem, "A Wandering in Prose: For Hemingway, November, 1960": "That first unmanageable cell to / stifle his existence arrived / on a morning when by / an extreme act of the will / he chose not to strike his / mother." The poem dates the moment as coming two days after he had stabbed his wife. By his reasoning, if it can be called that, he had saved Adele from cancer by stabbing her. And, by not throttling the woman who loved him more than anyone else ever would, he had allowed a cell in his own body to take the leap into cancer. He left with Knox. Mailer asked him to go into the 94th Street apartment and retrieve the open letter to Castro that he had been working on for the past three weeks. "Christ, I thought, he stabbed his wife the night before and what was uppermost in his mind? Getting the letter published. It did not surprise me. The foundation of Norman's being is the sum of his writing, and that letter to Castro was a building block in that foundation." Knox said he would get the letter if Mailer gave him the penknife. "Reluctantly," Mailer agreed, but after Knox gave him the letter Mailer changed his mind and wanted the knife back "for personal reasons." Knox relinquished it.

From there, Mailer left Knox to see Dr. Ghent and had a conversation with him. He then kept a two P.M. appointment with Mike Wallace to tape an interview for WNTA-TV. He told Wallace that he intended to run for mayor on the Existentialist ticket. He also said that disarming young gang members was probably impossible. "The knife to a juvenile delinquent is very meaningful," he said. "You see, it's his sword—his manhood." Mailer met Podhoretz for dinner and asked him to do everything possible to keep him from being sent to a mental institution. Then they went to the hospital, where he planned to be arrested. A nurse told them to wait for five minutes, and then three detectives arrested him and took the knife. Detective Francis J. Burns told him that his wife had admitted he had stabbed her. Mailer denied it. Adele also said that she did not wish to see him. Mailer was handcuffed and taken to the West 100th Street police station. Podhoretz was allowed to go with him, and said the police were polite. Mailer told the police, "I refuse to answer your questions." The lawyer John Cox arrived and, in his presence, Mailer was photographed and booked.

Early the next morning, he was taken to felony court on Centre Street in Lower Manhattan. Reporters were waiting. All Mailer said was that he loved his wife. He was again photographed, and then put in a lineup with other detainees. At the hearing a report from Dr. Rosenberg was read by Assistant District Attorney William Reilly: "In my opinion Norman Mailer is having an acute paranoid breakdown with delusional thinking and is both homicidal and suicidal. His admission to a hospital is urgently advised." According to wire service reports, Mailer challenged the report as "gratuitous and presumptuous." The *Times* carried the rest of his statement: "Naturally I have been a little upset but I have never been out of my mental faculties. I only saw Dr. Rosenberg for thirty seconds or a minute. It is important to me not to be sent to a mental hospital because my work in the future will be considered that of a disordered mind. My pride is that I can explore areas of experience that other men are afraid of. I insist that I am sane." Magistrate Rueben Levy told Mailer, "Your recent history indicates that you cannot distinguish fiction from reality," and committed him to Bellevue Hospital for observation.

Levy's judgment was wise. Mailer was incensed and intoxicated when he stabbed the mother of two of his children, but the next day, sober, he told Mike Wallace and a television audience of his intention to run for mayor of the nation's largest city on the ticket of a political party that did not exist. But if he was unhinged, he was mad north-north-west. His diary detailing the events of the three-week period during which he was detained in Bellevue shows a mind alert to the uniqueness of his experience and eager to garner biographical shards from the men in the violent ward where he was confined. The early part of the diary is retrospective, while the rest was written day by day in the hospital. In the manner of the Puritan fathers, Emerson, and Whitman, Mailer knew the extraordinary benefit of having a written record of a bad time. Emerson turned his diary entries into lectures and essays; Mailer saw his as ore for his fiction. He not only recorded events and his responses to them, he also noted, as he had in the army, marbles of fact that could be used in his fiction. He notes, for example, the "head-sweat on cop" who arrested him; a "Negro being beaten up" at the 100th Street precinct; and the story of Fred W., a murderer who confessed to detectives, in exchange for a pack of cigarettes and a pint of sherry, how he cut the throat of a lover with a broken beer bottle. He wanted to get out of Bellevue, but while there his novelist's instincts never waned. Three years later he would draw on these experiences for *An American Dream*.

The inmates in the violent ward passed their time betting cigarettes in a card game called Bordertown, a variant of pinochle, which Mailer called "my tranquillizer." Forty-five years later, he remembered the rules taught to him by Fred W. He had visitors—his mother and father, Barbara, Cy Rembar, Joseph Brill, a criminal lawyer, and Knox, who Mailer told that he feared getting electric shock treatments. Rev. Steve Chinlund, who Mailer knew slightly, visited and told him about his visits to Adele in the hospital. Mailer was jealous and told his sister to tell Adele not to fall in love with Chinlund. The three men he spent the most time with in Bellevue were Fred W., Harry G., and Arnold Kemp. Fred W., a jailhouse character and con artist, was given a long sentence for his crimes. Kemp, a young man from Harlem who spent almost a decade in prison for armed robbery, later got a graduate degree from Harvard, and wrote a novel that Mailer blurbed. They corresponded for years. Harry G. was in Bellevue for stabbing his brother, and Mailer was eager to hear his story. He had "rabbinical" discussions with Harry, who was highly intelligent but seriously disturbed. Harry "let slip that he is not altogether unconvinced he is the Second Coming." After he was released, he wrote a poem about Harry's assault on his brother: "So long / as / you / use / a knife / there's / some / love left." It is invariably and incorrectly regarded as referring to his assault on Adele.

Dr. Jordan Lachmann was his psychiatrist, and they met daily. Mailer recited his biography to him as he probed his resistance to treatment. He told him the story of Castro in the jungle and "made the argument of existential psychosis." For a time, it was touch-and-go as to whether he would be released, and when Lachmann told him he could be sent to a sanitarium for an extended period, Mailer called it "a Kafkan nightmare." Much later, he remembered telling "the doctors who were quizzing me: 'Didn't you guys ever hear of a crime of passion?' From their point of view, there I was a Jewish intellectual. Jewish intellectuals don't have crimes of passion, they just go crazy." Finally, Mailer said, Lachmann "had the guts to let me out." His diary ends with this entry for December 8.

> At 4:30, the guard who had a writer for wife, took me aside and whispered, "Today," after querying me on when I would get out. A few minutes later I was called, "Mailer, get your belongings." So I said my goodbyes and moved to the door, feeling quite moved at leaving them, and then getting dressed, Captain Kennedy, the trip in the Black Maria with Burns, the Tombs and the Bellevue workers, out to the interview with reporters and trip home with Brill. Kids at the door and then greeting Adele.

Having been declared "not psychotic" by Dr. Lachmann, Mailer appeared on January 12, 1961, in court to learn if there was sufficient evidence for felonious assault charges to be sent to a grand jury. Adele accompanied him and testified. "My husband and I are perfectly happy together," she said, and declined to sign a complaint against him. When asked whether she had seen the penknife, she said she didn't remember because she had been drinking. A few weeks later, a reporter went to the Mailers' apartment to inform him he had been indicted. As Adele cooked dinner and Danielle and Betsy read a picture book, Mailer said that he couldn't say anything about the case. Asked if the charges, which could have led to a five- to ten-year prison term, had affected his writing, he said, "I really couldn't say if this is affecting the writing. I don't think about it—except on certain days." He had spent eight hours that day in his Brooklyn studio.

At first, he pled not guilty, which meant he would have to stand trial. A short time later he decided to change his plea to guilty "because he feared a trial would bring harmful publicity to his wife and two children." When he appeared in court for sentencing, Judge Mitchell D. Schweitzer said, "I gamble on human beings and I intend to gamble on you." Mailer said in response, "I feel I did a lousy, dirty, cowardly thing." Six months later, having kept out of trouble, he was given a suspended sentence and three years' probation.

With few exceptions, he lived quietly during the first few months of 1961. Friends and family rallied around him. A letter appeared in *Time* shortly after he was released in response to the magazine's conclusion that Mailer's critical reputation had declined since *Naked and the Dead.* Signed by eight writers—Baldwin, Jason Epstein, Hellman, Kazin, Robert Lowell, Podhoretz, Lionel Trilling, and William Phillips—the letter said that *Time*'s recent estimate of Mailer needed "correction." His "work is of continuing brilliance and significance." Vidal did not sign the letter, but he did reach out, inviting him and Adele to Edgewater, his home on the Hudson River a hundred miles north of New York. Mailer, who was awaiting trial at the time, never forgot the gesture, calling it "a fine thing to do at that point because it was his way of saying, 'I'm not afraid of you, you're first a literary man and second someone who got into criminal trouble," and that was bold and decent. If our relations had stayed that way, we'd be dear friends today." Podhoretz and Decter were similarly generous, and invited him to a party a couple of weeks after he was released, as Mailer recalled:

> I walked into the room and the reactions were subtle as hell. Five degrees less warmth than I was accustomed to. Not fifteen degrees less—five. I guess that once you bring a violent man to a party, people are generally polite to him. Looking back on it, the stabbing was not altogether the turning point. I mean it was terribly shocking and things could never be the same. If any of us does something like that, people just don't look at them in quite the same way. I think ten years went by before people forgot about it. Once in a while they would get a reminder and they would say, "Oh my God,

> yes." I think the real separation came after Adele and I split up and Jeanne [Campbell] and I started going around together, because then I started traveling in another world.

Mailer met Lady Jeanne Campbell, a New York–based reporter for the *London Evening Standard*, at a party in March 1961. Adele was not at the party. She was out of bed and her incision was healing well, but she was unable to do anything strenuous. She said that there was no letup in his social life, that he was welcomed back to "the bosom of his sympathetic literary friends." Some of them blamed Adele as much if not more than Mailer for "The Trouble." James Jones, for one, said that the stabbing was partly the result of Adele being "a lousy wife." Mailer's army buddy Fig Gwaltney wrote on the envelope of a letter Mailer had written to him from Bellevue: "Letter written in psycho ward after he finally did to Adele what should've been done years earlier." Fan Mailer, who on the day her son was committed to Bellevue told reporters, "My boy's a genius," wrote in her memoir: "Whatever happened with the stabbing she goaded him into it."

Others saw Adele as being noble for not pressing charges. Judy Feiffer, then married to cartoonist and writer Jules Feiffer, said Adele's "behavior towards Norman was admirable and loyal." If Adele had turned against him, if she had revealed the harshest details of their marriage, he probably would have gone to prison. "I saved his neck," Adele wrote in her memoir. "I could have put him away for fifteen years if I had chosen to testify." But she didn't. She wanted to keep the marriage going. "He was the man in her life," Feiffer said, "and she's a passionate woman." After Mailer's release, their relationship began to recover, and then in late March collapsed entirely. According to Adele, the decisive moment came when he returned home the day after a party. She accused him, correctly, of spending the night with another woman and threw him out. The next day she called a divorce lawyer.

"The Trouble" reverberated throughout the family. Even a half century later, Mailer's sister found the event difficult to discuss. "I remember being terribly disappointed in him," she said, "very angry about it." At the time, she thought, "We'd never be the same, sort of like the end of everything." Susan said, "It affected me very much. I wasn't so little; I was eleven when it happened so I understood what was going on. I was very close to Adele, very fond of her." Prior to the stabbing, she felt as if she had two sets of parents—Adele and her father and Chavo and her mother—but when her father was committed, her mother would no longer let her visit New York. This angered Mailer. "I happen to think that she was right," Susan said. "You know, if I had a kid and something like this happened I would have reacted in the same way." Her mother never fully trusted her father after the stabbing, Susan said, adding that the stabbing was "the single most painful thing in my childhood." Danielle, asked when she realized that her father was the famous writer, Norman Mailer, replied, "I was maybe four or five, and thought something like: 'My hair is brown; I'm Norman Mailer's daughter; my father stabbed my mother.' Throughout my childhood, to survive this piece of history, and navigate, I remained stubbornly neutral. Whenever it came to light that he was my father, invariably the person would remark, 'Oh, you're Norman's kid.' Pause. 'Was your mother the one who he . . . ' I have no memory of the post-stabbing events, only my mother's ribbon scar dissecting her stomach. But I was fiercely loyal to my father, never allowed anger or disappointment to enter into our relationship. Only in recent years have I had a chance to reflect on the event in my art: I frequently focus on the female torso."

Two years before her father's death, Betsy repeated to a family friend what her father had said to her about the assault: "I let God down." He had tears in his eyes, she said. The dynamic of the Mailer family was permanently altered. Reflecting on her parents' relationship, she said:

> I think there was so much antipathy at times, and so much guilt at times, and so much remorse and great passion and a depth of connection. It was so much all that all the time. And I think there were times when they loathed each other and there were times when they remembered how passionately they were in love. They both felt poignant and sad about what they had that was gone. I think, at times, there was a desire on both their parts to recover what they had.

"The Trouble" became one of Mailer's memory crystals, an experience to be harvested, via refraction, for his fiction, but never to be delineated autobiographically. When questioned about it, he was usually guarded. In a 1997 interview, he said that his children paid a big price for his crime, and that much of the animosity toward him "comes from the fact of people saying, 'That son of a bitch—he got away with it. He doesn't deserve anything after that.' I say leave it to heaven." He did, however, make two considered statements in his books. The first was in his 1963 miscellany, *The Presidential Papers*: "One got out of Bellevue, one did a little work again. The marriage broke up. The man wasn't good enough. The woman wasn't good enough. A set of psychic stabbings took place." The second, a brief recollection titled "The Shadow of the Crime," came in his 1998 collection, an omnibus volume titled *The Time of Our Time*.

> Through the years a shadow of the crime would accompany many hours. I could never write about it. Not all woe is kin to prose. It was one matter to be guilty—by inner measure, irredeemably guilty—it was another to present some literary manifest of what was lost and what was wasted, what was given to remorse and what was finally resistant to remorse. Violence is the child of the iron in one's heart, and decomposes by its own laws.

The remainder of the piece is for the most part given over to a statement of regret about the collateral damage the stabbing inflicted on his "Open Letter to Fidel Castro," a piece of writing he felt might have had "its effect on history," but appeared too late to be of any consequence. He ended by noting the "incalculable" damage done to his daughters. "Murder and its sibling, assault," he concluded, "are the most wanton of the crimes, for they mangle the possibilities and expectations open to others."

Perhaps his most frank statement about his blighted role as an unfrocked prophet came in a 1965 interview: "I lost any central purchase I had on the right to say what is happening. I'm *parti pris.* Now when I argue the times are violent, they can say, well, look what he did. I destroyed forever the possibility of being the Jeremiah of our time." Not entirely, however. A comeback was not far off. After his release from Bellevue, "a good deal of the sweetness came back," Barbara said. "It's as if he really let go of something." The fact that "he was pretty appalled at himself" made a "big difference" to the family. Years after the stabbing, he said, "A decade's anger made me do it. After that, I felt better." It would take two years for him to fully resume his literary career, but then he had it all his own way, in large part, for the next dozen years.

Adele, after she had recovered, became an alcoholic for twenty years until joining Alcoholics Anonymous, and then quit drinking entirely.

"The Trouble" clouded her life. She became permanently bitter, according to Danielle, and "damaged in a lot of ways. Profoundly. And obsessed—as if symbolically she was never able to cut the tie with him." Betsy said, "You know, my mother never stopped loving him, never. And she's still obsessed with him; she still loves him." At the end of her memoir, Adele wrote, "I was trapped in my purgatory of hatred." Asked why she had written it, she replied, "I want my book to make Mailer suffer." Over the decades, her relationship with him became progressively more distant and troubled.

At the legal proceeding where he was given his suspended sentence, his lawyer told the judge that he would make a contribution to society. He also said that Mailer had "reduced his drinking to a minimum," which was not the case. Mailer wrote little during the months before and after the stabbing, but he drank heavily. Before the event, he drank "explosively"; afterward he drank "steadily—most nights I went to bed with all the vats loaded." His hangovers were "steeped in dread" and he feared becoming an alcoholic. To avoid drinking too early in the day, he sorted through the notes in his pockets, his record of whiskey moments when some bar conversation or insight crystallized.

Cold War

The Lady / was / quite a queen / in her / own right /

You're a great man / you're a / very / great / man / only please / why can't / you be / considerate / of others / as well? /

Heh heh, / can't do two things / at once / said Rasputin. /

The poems, which were published as *Deaths for the Ladies (and Other Disasters)* in 1962, are by turns observant—"Drinker / with a / problem said: I'll drink / to that / even if / it's not / quite / true"; angry—"Rip / the prisons open / Put / the convicts / on / television"; nuanced (and reflecting Lady Jeanne's influence)—"The English / have a sense / of ambush / about vulgarity / it is: / do you / descend / the steps / properly?"; blunt—"In the first week / of their life / male jews / are crucified." There is irony—"I want to / be a / fine / woman / and a / great / mother / to my / children / and / oh yes / you / she said"; and revealing:

"If / Harry Golden / is the gentile's / Jew / can I be / the Golden Goy?" Some are impressionistic, revealing the influence of Ezra Pound, whom Mailer had long admired: "the remembered musk / of wood-smoke at dusk / in Cambridge / and New Haven."

The poetry volume sank quietly with few reviews, most of them late. *Time* was predictably nasty. John Simon, in the first of his long run of negative reviews of Mailer's work, classified him with "the various anti- and non poets, whose tribe, regrettably, increases." Writing in *Poetry*, May Swenson said that Mailer "longs to be a true primitive, a child making figurines out of his excrement," but had praise for two poems, both titled "A Wandering in Prose: for Hemingway." Only Richard Lanham in *The Village Voice*, who praised Mailer's satirical powers, and Selden Rodman in *The New York Times Book Review*, were positive. Rodman, a friend of Mailer's, compared the poems to those of e. e. cummings, and praised his "fast footwork and low blows." Dwight Macdonald, writing in *Commentary*, found the poems to be "slangy" and "ironic," but called the book "a triumph of bad taste." The only reason it was not a trivial collection, he said, is that Mailer "seems to be trying to find out how much weight his ideas (or better, his attitudes) will bear." He advised Mailer to move on, get back to prose. In the only interview given when the book was published, Mailer said that writing poems was an interlude between long stretches of disciplined novel writing. But there was another reason, which he later revealed: poetry was a "way of digging myself out of the hole I had dug for myself." Poetry was "the first rung." He was mending.

AT THE PARTY where Mailer met Jeanne Campbell (Vidal's apartment on East 55th Street), they went off to a separate room to talk, had a long staring match, and were besotted. "The night I met him," she said, "I knew I was going to marry him and have his child." She didn't become pregnant that night but, as with Bea and Adele, the first night was spent in bed. He recalled their meeting eighteen months before he died: "I went to a party and met Jeanne Campbell and we spent a day and a half in the sack. That was the last straw, that and the fact that Adele wanted me to quit drinking because her psychoanalyst said I had to. I said I couldn't quit drinking then or I'd get cancer, but offered to drink outside the house a couple of nights a week. She wouldn't accept this, and so I moved out." He moved into his sister's apartment in the Village, but spent much of his time at Jeanne's.

If Adele lacked self-confidence, Jeanne Louise Campbell was brimming with it. On one side, she was the daughter of Ian Campbell, the 11th Duke of Argyll and head of the Clan Campbell, one of the great families in Scotland. On the other, she was the daughter of Janet Gladys Aitken, whose father, William "Max" Aitken, Lord Beaverbrook, was one of the most powerful press barons in England. A confidant of both Winston Churchill and President Franklin Roosevelt, he headed the British delegation that met with Joseph Stalin after the German invasion of Russia. Beaverbrook's daughter and son-in-law were divorced in 1934, but Beaverbrook had taken over the job of raising Jeanne Louise several years earlier. She was named after Jeanne Marie, Lady Malcolm, the illegitimate daughter of American actress Lily Langtry and Prince Louis of Battenberg, and Princess Louise, the sixth child of Queen Victoria and Prince Albert. Through Jeanne's family connections, and her own moxie, she became acquainted with many of the most influential and accomplished people in Great Britain. Randolph Churchill, son of Winston, was a particular friend.

In the late 1950s, she had a fairly lengthy affair with a man thirty years her senior, Henry Luce, the founder of the Time-Life empire, who met her at La Capponcina, Beaverbrook's villa on the French Riviera. He offered her a job at *Time*; she accepted and came to New York in 1956. Luce thought of marrying the statuesque young woman with a wild mass of curly hair, but his wife, the politician and diplomat Clare Boothe Luce, convinced him otherwise. Campbell had left *Time* and was working for one of her grandfather's papers, the *London Evening Standard*, when she met Mailer at Vidal's party. Vidal found her to be "very attractive, very bright," and Mailer thought he had "some idea of possibly having some sort of liaison with her." When Vidal asked Campbell what had attracted her to Mailer, she said, "I had never gone to bed with a Jew before." Mailer had never slept with the daughter of a duke before, and was similarly curious. Besides the personal attraction he felt, he thought that Lady Jeanne's social ties and acumen could be a great literary resource. That she was leaving the man whose magazines had attacked and ridiculed him for the past decade made her irresistible. He learned that Luce "suffered a bit" when he heard of Jeanne's affair. "I loved the idea," he said.

Jeanne's voice was the first thing that Mailer noticed. "She had this incredibly beautiful voice and was capable of putting on numerous airs, a voice which was as lovely as Mozart. It had an absolute range. If she'd been able to move as well as she spoke, she would have been a great actress." She was thirty-one when they met, he recalled,

> but she looked a little older, maybe 35. And she was slightly . . . almost plump. And she had fiery eyes, these pale green eyes, full of spite and vigor and venom and wit. How to put it? They had their power. Combative, and I was just in the mood for that. She was wearing white pearls and I thought, "She's a very wealthy woman from Westchester." She was wearing a gray outfit with white pearls, and gloves, perhaps. I didn't know it was Lady Jeanne—all I knew was here's this dame who's attractive to me because of some sort of special social—I don't know—upper class about it. Having been with Adele for years, I was in the mood for a woman who was in the upper class.

She was poised, he said, and "very proud to be Lady Jeanne, but never said a word about it." Their dissimilar backgrounds added to their initial attraction, as Mailer recalled: "There I am, from a middle class Jewish family, and I'm in sort of an indefinable position. Because I'm a well-known author, in a certain sense I'm part of the establishment. But I'm a criminal, a felon on parole. There she is, Lady Jeanne, her father is a duke." His situation made him think of how Jones and Styron "would be eating their fucking hearts out" to be in his position. He was having great fun, he said, but more important, "I was learning about things. The novelist in me was absolutely on fire. I loved it." The people who had shaped his thinking the most, he said, were Jean Malaquais (Lindner was second) and Jeanne Campbell, the former on intellectual matters and the latter on social ones. Jeanne's influence on *An American Dream* was especially pronounced, although she got no pleasure from being the model for the protagonist's wife, Deborah Caughlin Mangaravidi Kelly. She called the novel "the hate book of all time." Deborah is murdered in chapter one.

Kate Mailer adds that her parents were drawn to each other not only because of his fascination with Jeanne's background, but also by "her reaction to her background and her refusal to be done down by it, or to be hemmed in by it. A reaction which made her curious about all people in life, everyone. The most ordinary of people could capture her imagination and interest, and this was something that I think he was drawn to, as he could not at first understand it. 'How could you find that person interesting at all,' he told me he would ask her. 'But yes, they are fascinating,' she would answer, 'if you only probe a little below the surface.' He was also charmed by her across-the-board, unflagging gusto for life, and pleased that she shared two of his own obsessions: politics and spies."

In May 1961 he wrote to Knox to say the affair was blossoming: "The Lady and I are making the scene and it is not at all uninteresting." He was still writing poems and had begun sending them for consideration at a dozen different magazines. He also continued his correspondence with his Bellevue friends, enclosing books, cigarettes, and money. "Some of the best people I've come across since the Army were in Bellevue," he wrote to Don Carpenter, a West Coast novelist with whom he frequently corresponded. "It was just simply that for the last six months my little old navigator didn't know whether to get set for a year or less above ground or below ground and I suppose the psychotic sensation is a little like trying to hit a baseball when you are standing on a turntable." When his navigator got its bearings, it sanctioned, we might even say *urged*, a liaison with Jeanne. Always unable to live alone for long, Mailer was hungry for something beyond one-night stands, and Jeanne seemed perfect. It was a fiery, intense affair. Jeanne said of their marriage: "We had both been extremists who knew no limits; and such an alliance takes you a breath from heaven and a sob from hell." Jeanne was more than simply another rung on the ladder out of the pit of depression and nascent alcoholism. She was both the ladder and the prize at the top; she was his new mate. In June, she accompanied him to Provincetown, where they spent a few days in a dune shack, and then to Mexico, where she first met Susan. It was there that they got the news that Hemingway had committed suicide in Ketchum, Idaho, on July 2, 1961.

OFTEN MENTIONED AS Hemingway's successor, a role he had openly sought, Mailer expected to be contacted for a statement after Papa blew his brains out with a double-barreled shotgun. When he read the statements of regret by various celebrities and politicians in the *New York Times* (including President Kennedy's), he said he experienced "one full heart-clot of outraged vanity that the *Times* never thought to ask *his* opinion. In fact, he was not certain he could have given it. He was sick in that miasmal and not quite discoverable region between the liver and the soul." Finally, he gave a statement to Jeanne for her grandfather's newspapers in London, which he paraphrased in *Of a Fire on the Moon*. Papa's suicide, he wrote, would strengthen the hearts of ignoble bureaucrats because "Hemingway constituted the walls of the fort: Hemingway had given the power to believe you could still shout down the corridor of the hospital, live next to the breath of the beast, accept your portion of dread each day. Now the greatest living romantic was dead." He said later that Hemingway is "the father of modern American literature, at least for men."

> I keep thinking of [novelist] John Gardner's unforgettable remark that when a father commits suicide, he condemns his son to the same end. Well, of course, you can go to suicide by more ways than killing yourself. You can rot yourself out with too much drink, too many failures, too much talk, too many wild and unachieved alliances—Hemingway was a great cautioning influence on all of us. One learned not to live on one's airs, and to do one's best to avoid many nights when—thanks to Scott Fitzgerald's work—one knew it was three o'clock in the morning.

What was "doubly depressing," Mailer said shortly after the suicide, "was that he died in silence." Absent any valedictory message, he called his hero's suicide "the most difficult death in America since Roosevelt." Until the end of his own life Mailer ruminated on Hemingway's. He examined every aspect of his life and work—his Midwest childhood, his characters (Jake Barnes, Frederick Henry, and Robert Jordan, mainly), his mistakes (taking the literary world too seriously, and establishing "a royal court of followers"), his sense of identity (as strong as Muhammad Ali's), his narcissism (which he compared to Henry Miller's), his moral vision (comparing it to that of Saint Thomas Aquinas), the inability of biographers to put his character in focus and, several times, his style: "Hemingway's style affected whole generations of us, the way a roomful of men are affected when a beautiful woman walks through—

their night is turned for better or for worse. His style has the ability to hit young writers in the gut."

He derided Papa for posturing, and also for not heeding his call to comment on the Cuban Revolution. He found it to be "damn depressing" that Hemingway didn't "come to the rescue when us Indians were about to burn one of *Life*'s forts" (an ironic comment in light of Mailer's own association with *Life* a decade later). And he worried the bone of the suicide, even to the construction of a scenario.

> There is a no-man's land in each trigger. For the dull hand it is a quarter of an inch. A professional hunter can feel to the division of a millimeter the point where the gun can go off. He can move the trigger up to that point and yet not fire the gun. Hemingway was not too old to test this skill. Perhaps he was trying the deed a first time, perhaps he had tried just such a reconnaissance one hundred times before, and felt the touch of health return ninety times.

Then, with a leap of empathy, Mailer gives a simulacrum of Hemingway's conversation with himself on that particular morning in July.

> Look, we can go in further. It's going to be tricky and we may not get out, but it will be good for us if we go in just a little further, so we will have to try, and now we will, it is the answer to the brothers Mayo, ergo now we go in, damn the critics and this Fiedler fellow, all will be denied if papa gets good again, write about Monroe, and Jimmy Durante, God bless, umbriago, hose down the deck, do it clean, no sweat, no sweat in the palm, let's do it clean, gung ho, a little more, let's go in a little gung ho more ho. No! Oh no! Goddamn it to Hell.

The rendering of Papa's final moments is a run of associations: Mayo refers to the clinic where Hemingway received psychiatric treatment. Marilyn Monroe was a suicide a year after Hemingway (Mailer discussed their deaths in *Esquire*). Umbriago was an imaginary companion of comedian Jimmy Durante, an Italian folklore version of Zorba the Greek. Whether Hemingway actually had any feeling for Umbriago or Durante is unknown, but the comedian did visit Havana in the 1950s when Hemingway was in residence. Leslie Fiedler wrote what can only be called a ghoulish piece, "Hemingway in Ketchum," about his November 1960 visit to the much diminished writer. It came out in *Partisan Review* in September 1962, just before Mailer published his thoughts about Hemingway's final reconnaissance. Hemingway told Fiedler to tell Mailer, whom he called "so articulate," that he had not received the copy of *The Deer Park* sent to him in Cuba. Fiedler's profile may have led Mailer to try to find a happier explanation for Hemingway blasting off the top of his head in his *Esquire* column, which he called "The Big Bite."

Mailer's speculations are outcroppings from a longer examination of Hemingway's psychology in his philosophical self-interview, "The Metaphysics of the Belly," written in the summer of 1962. It was intended to be part of the big novel, which he was then referring to as both "The Saint and the Psychopath" and "The Psychology of the Orgy." One can wonder how this nonnarrative material would fit in, and it is quite possible that the problem of integrating this and two other self-interviews contributed to the slow death of the big novel. But, as so often happened in the course of Mailer's headlong compositional process, the interviews became part of a new project: a study of Picasso. They were to be "an introductory chapter on questions of form and function," he said later. He went so far as to sign a contract for the study with Macmillan in the early spring of 1962, but soon abandoned the project, and did not return to it for decades. In 1995 he published *Portrait of Picasso as a Young Man.*

Hemingway's death was clearly one of the factors that led him—quite naturally given Hemingway's acquaintance with Picasso—to think of a book about the painter. When the self-interviews, which veer far afield from Picasso, were finally published as a whole in his 1966 collection, *Cannibals and Christians*, they came to 135 pages. There is no simple way to describe the catechetical ebb and flow of the dialogues, but his description of the growth and diminution of Being as it moves from state to state, from a molecule in the sea to a piece of driftwood, near-extinction to rebirth—it could be subtitled "The Progress of Souls"—is close to the core of Mailer's concerns, and it could be argued, Picasso's. Mailer's method can be glimpsed in the following conversation of Mailer with himself about the division in Hemingway's psyche.

> MAILER: Postulate a modern soul marooned in constipation, emptiness, boredom and a flat dull terror of death. A soul which

takes antibiotics when ill, smokes filter cigarettes, drinks proteins, minerals, and vitamins in a liquid diet, takes seconal to go to sleep, benzedrine to awake, and tranquilizers for poise. It is a deadened existence, afraid precisely of violence, cannibalism, loneliness, insanity, libidinousness, hell, perversion, and mess, because these are the states that must be passed through, digested, transcended, if one is to make one's way back to life.

INTERVIEWER: *Why must they be passed through, transcended?*

MAILER: . . . These states, these morbid states, as the old-fashioned psychologists used to say, can obtain relief only by coming to life in the psyche. But they can come to life only if they are ignited by an experience outside themselves. . . . A dramatic encounter with death, an automobile accident from which I escape, a violent fight I win or lose decently, these all call forth my crossed impulses which love death and fear it. They give air to it. So these internal and deadly experiences are given life. In some cases, satisfied by the experience, they will subside a bit, give room to easier and more sensuous desires.

INTERVIEWER: *Not always?*

MAILER: Not always. Hemingway, it seems, was never able to tame his dirty ape.

INTERVIEWER: *His dirty ape?*

MAILER: It's a better word than id or anti-social impulse.

INTERVIEWER: *I think it is.*

MAILER: Once we may have had a fine clean brave upstanding ape inside ourselves. It's just gotten dirty over the years.

INTERVIEWER: *Why couldn't Hemingway tame his ape?*

MAILER: . . . An artist is usually such an incredible balance of opposites and incompatibles that the wonder is he can even remain alive. Hemingway was on the one hand a man of magnificent senses. There was a quick lithe animal in him. He was also shackled to a stunted ape, a cripple, a particularly wild dirty little dwarf within himself who wanted only to kill Hemingway. Life as a compromise was impossible. So long as Hemingway did not test himself, push himself beyond his own dares, flirt with, engage, and finally embrace death, in other words so long as he did not propitiate the dwarf, give the dwarf its chance to live and feel emotion, an emotion which could come to life only when one was close to death, Hemingway

> and the dwarf were doomed to dull and deaden one another in the dungeons of the psyche. Everyday life in such circumstances is a plague. The proper comment on Hemingway's style of life may be not that he dared death too much, but too little, that brave as he was, he was not brave enough, and the dwarf finally won.

The discussion is as much an exercise in self-analysis as commentary on Hemingway. The references to Seconal and Benzedrine, the demarcations between timidity and boldness, the predilection to explore extreme states such as cannibalism, libidinousness, violence, and insanity, not to mention the need to propitiate a monster that inhabits one's psyche, point as much to Mailer's psychic states as to Papa's. Mailer's suggestion that "we" may all have our own dirty ape supports this idea. A few years later, Mailer would come to call his ape "the Beast," noting that the monster was "witty in his own way and absolutely fearless," and required a "breath of air" about once a month. Papa's death, like the death of many fathers, liberated something in Mailer, and despite his immediate woe, anger, and disappointment, can be seen as the symbolic beginning of the decade of his greatest achievement.

ADVERTISEMENTS FOR MYSELF was scheduled for publication in England in September and Mailer had been invited by André Deutsch to fly over for a round of publicity events and public appearances. He was peeved with Deutsch for convincing him to accept the evisceration of "The Time of Her Time" (twenty of twenty-six pages cut) in the British edition, and said he did not think that "this draping of breasts and covering of asses will solve very much at all," but he had given Deutsch his word that he would accept the verdict of the lawyers. So he accepted the invitation, and was happy to have Jeanne on his arm during his visit to London. "England was absolutely abuzz with this affair," Mailer recalled. "Each of us loved it, because each of us loved being the center of attention." They arrived in mid-September for a month-long visit, with a week in Paris toward the end. Deutsch had set up a press conference at his editorial offices, and Mailer answered questions for two hours while sipping Scotch and smoking English cigarettes.

Press reports on Mailer's problems preceded him, and the reporters "half-expected," as one of them put it, "a combination of Brendan Behan, De Quincey, Rimbaud, Hemingway and Kerouac." The reporters didn't know what to make of *Advertisements for Myself*, which they called a "hotch-potch," but were clearly charmed by his American candor as well as his statement that "sentence for sentence" English novelists such as Kingsley Amis, Evelyn Waugh, and Graham Greene "write better than we do." It was a relatively subdued event and, it seems, a successful one. He had spoken at political press conferences when he campaigned for Henry Wallace, but this was his first literary press conference. There would be many more.

At some point in his visit, the British philosopher Richard Wollheim interviewed Mailer on the subject of violence. Hemingway was still on his mind, as was Adolf Eichmann, the Nazi death camp bureaucrat who had recently been captured by Israeli agents. In a discussion of the nature of a free act, Mailer distinguished his definition of a free act from Sartre's idea of a willed action by which a person "can literally recreate himself." For Mailer, as for Hemingway, "the life of the day has become more complex than the morality that covers it." His assumption, he said, "is that life always advances far ahead of morality. Morality is the quartermaster corps bringing up supplies to starving soldiers." One acts and then one decides on the morality based on whether the act felt good or not. This sensation was "what Hemingway was writing about all the time," he continued, and the hipster also "follows his unconscious, he acts on the basis of his id," although Mailer didn't like the word "id" preferring "it," as in "get with it." Mailer used Eichmann to distinguish between personal and collective violence. If Eichmann, responsible for uncountable deaths, "had killed 500,000 victims with his bare hands, he would have been a monster," but he would have "worn the scar of his own moral wound," and thus gained "our unconscious respect." He was not to relent on this point; he would continue to seek merit, even a smudge, in the psyches of evil people.

He ended his conversation with Wollheim by saying New York City seemed to be dying slowly. "There's a psychic poverty in the city today, perhaps in the whole country. The thing that distresses me about America is that for all the country's done, I don't think it's done one quarter of what it should. I believe it was destined, by history if you will, to be the greatest country that ever existed. I don't think it's come near it."

For the rest of his life he would harp on his disappointment with the United States for failing to achieve its millennial promise, the Puritan idea of a "city on the hill," a beacon of hope for humankind. The advent of totalitarianism in all its forms—and few writers have identified as many of its subtle variations—was the tocsin he pealed, much as Jonathan Edwards had warned sinners in the hands of an angry God two centuries earlier. Mailer's God was not so much angry as disappointed, tired, and overextended. Humankind was a disappointment. The desire to be a Jeremiah lingered.

He and Jeanne were in England for at least three weeks and socialized with her friends between interviews for his book. We know that he did not visit Lord Beaverbrook during this trip, his first to England since 1947, but there is a record of his visit to the Somerset home of Janet Gladys Kidd, Jeanne's mother. She threw a huge party for the couple, one that Evelyn Waugh attended, as Waugh noted in a letter to a friend.

> Mrs. Kidd's ball was very lavish—nothing remarkable if it had been in Surrey but sensational in Somerset. Two bands, one of niggers & one of buggers, a cabaret, an oyster bar in the harness room, stables flood lit, much to the discomfort of the horses. One bit an American pornographer who tried to give it vodka.
>
> I had never before met Lady Jeanne Campbell and was fascinated. She came to us next day bringing the bitten pornographer. He might have stepped straight from your salon—a swarthy gangster straight out of a madhouse where he had been sent after the attempt to cut his wife's throat. It is his first visit to England.

In 1978, the editor of Waugh's letters wrote Mailer asking about Waugh's comments. Mailer replied.

> The horse did bite me on the finger, but I was not feeding him vodka, just petting him on the nose. Maybe it was my breath that enflamed the animal, or maybe he was fond of Evelyn Waugh. I also thought I could point to the inaccuracy that I did not cut my wife's throat but realized on reflection that throat-cutting is only a general term of description when used by Mr. Waugh. Otherwise, his account is

accurate and his description of me adequate, and will doubtless enhance my status.

Mailer's forbearance is not as unusual as it might seem, and might perhaps be attributed to his admiration for Waugh's facility with sentences.

Colin MacInnes, a novelist and social activist, interviewed Mailer when he was in London. MacInnes, sometimes called the English Norman Mailer, had a long discussion with him on BBC radio, covering a range of issues, including the ways in which mood is undermined by modern life, God and the Devil, hip, and *Time* magazine. *Time* has "a detestation of all the younger and more adventurous American writers," Mailer said, "and willy nilly I'm considered the figurehead." Shortly after they returned to the United States, *Time* reported that Mailer was doing the Twist with Lady Jeanne Campbell at the Peppermint Lounge on 45th Street in New York. An unflattering photograph of a perspiring Mailer accompanied the story. He was upset and wrote to his California friend, Don Carpenter, that the magazine had done "a nice knife job" on him. The piece said he had "a dazed look on my face which my probation officer will naturally read as drugged. In the dreams of Walter Neo-Mitty there is one recurring fantasy. He comes to power like Fidel Castro and enters TIME MAGAZINE with a burp gun."

He decided to make a push on the big novel and in the fall of 1962 rented a house in Bucks County, Pennsylvania, about an hour north of Philadelphia. He and Jeanne spent most of each week there and weekends in New York. The work did not go well. He wrote to Carpenter to complain: "I always suffer from the same thing you suffer from: to wit, I start a novel and immediately I'm getting all my best ideas on the excursions and departures from it." He had never found a way to avoid this, he said, and his only working principle was to "let the unconscious have complete dominion." He wrote to the still incarcerated Harry G. to say how "lucky" he, Mailer, had been to avoid prison, and to say he was sending him a pile of books and a subscription to the *Voice*. Being holed up in the country and writing every day was a "depressing activity," he said to Harry, "sometimes after two hours of writing I feel as if I've done six or seven hours of manual labor." In December, they gave up on country living. "I suppose I suffer from some no doubt misguided notion that New York is the big leagues," he said, "and so when I get away from it for too long I begin to miss the feeling that history is being made around me." Jeanne, now pregnant, was also ready to move. Until the final decade of his life, Mailer shuttled regularly from city to country and back.

Just before Christmas, Jeanne got an assignment to cover the two-day summit meeting in Bermuda between President Kennedy and British prime minister Harold Macmillan. The meeting was to discuss the Berlin Wall, which had recently been constructed by the East Germans to separate the Russian zone from those of the British, French, and Americans. At one of their meetings, Kennedy famously told Macmillan, "I wonder how it is with you, Harold. If I don't have a woman for three days, I get terrible headaches." Campbell's contact with the president was no doubt restricted to press meetings, but she had had a brief affair with him before she met Mailer, rendezvousing with him at her Georgetown town house. Mailer wrote to Knox about Jeanne's trip, adding that she would be flying from Bermuda to her grandfather's villa on the Riviera for a week. "I'll be a bachelor during Christmas. How could this happen to *me*?" he asked.

Emile "Mike" Capouya of Macmillan wrote to Mailer offering $10,000 for a book on Castro. He was tempted but wanted a larger advance, as well as an assurance that he could travel around Cuba with Castro, as Sartre had done. While waiting to hear, he plugged away at the novel, writing only a few pages at a time. On New Year's Eve he missed Jeanne and cabled Randolph Churchill, whom he had met in England, asking him to please call Jeanne at her grandfather's villa and ask his "old honey bun, dearest alley cat," to come home. She flew back almost immediately. Divorce proceedings with Adele were dragging on, he told Knox, and he and Jeanne "are still together, sometimes in and out." But with a child on the way, he was eager to get married. When Clay Felker contacted him about writing a long piece on the first lady and the upcoming televised tour of the White House she was conducting, he agreed instantly, happy to end his feud with *Esquire* and have a paying reason to shelve the big novel.

THE WINTER 1962 issue of *Dissent* contained a fairly harsh critique of the Kennedy administration by left-wing social critic Paul Goodman, whose 1960 book on the disaffection of young people, *Growing Up Absurd*, made him well known. Mailer knew him casually; both contributed regularly to *Dissent*. In the course of his essay, Goodman criticized Mailer for describing Kennedy as a hipster, calling Mailer "a chump" for missing Kennedy's true intentions. Mailer fired off a brilliantly ad hominem letter to the editor that began by saying that he did not read Goodman often "because his style reminds me of the gray unfortunate odor in a prison laundry." He continued:

> I do not know that the cause of pacifism, anarchism, socialism, radicalism, existentialism, Goodmanism, Mailerism, priapism, or the breath of a new underground is going to be enlivened much by Goodman calling me a chump. The insult is not powerful nor accurate enough to touch a creative sore and so sharpen my appetite to work, it is not on the other hand insignificant enough to be ignored. The result has the unhappy effect of an old creep's fart. It seeps into the air and dulls the mood at an office party. *Time* which takes such gas for sneaks of oxygen will end no doubt by quoting Goodman on Mailer.

His letter, "delivered exactly to the jugular," as he later put it, made *Dissent*'s editors unhappy; they wished to avoid unpleasantness, and Mailer agreed, reluctantly, to withdraw it. He liked his association with the journal, "although his private mixture of Marxism, conservatism, nihilism, and large parts of existentialism could no longer produce any polemical gravies for the digestive apparatus of scholarly Socialist minds." Mailer remained on *Dissent*'s board for twenty more years, but never wrote anything for it again. It was another sign that the 1950s were over. For the next decade, the bulk of his magazine work would appear in *Esquire*, the *Voice*, and, at the end of the 1960s, *Harper's* and *Life*.

Something close to 75 percent of the national television audience watched the first lady give a tour of the White House on February 14, 1962. All three networks showed the program, *A Tour of the White House with Mrs. John F. Kennedy*. Unhappy with the lack of authentic furnishings, she had led an ambitious restoration effort and proudly displayed the results during the program. Earlier, Mailer met with press secretary Pierre Salinger in Washington to ask for an interview with the first lady. A few days later, it was denied. Mailer was piqued, as he said in the essay: "One's presence was not required. Which irritated the vanity. The vanity was no doubt outsize, but one thought of oneself as one of the few writers in the country." If she was going to be the nation's muse, or "queen of the arts," he felt she should be willing to stand for an interview. His letter to her about the honor of the Marquis de Sade had not been forgotten, and he would have to write the essay, "An Evening with Jackie Kennedy," from a distance. He was critical of Mrs. Kennedy and the program as stultifying. Mailer's essay was a last yelp of anger against the decorous tedium of the Eisenhower era, one he feared had not yet ended.

Mailer made a comment about the first lady's "surprisingly thin, not unfeverish" legs in the piece, comparing them to the legs of southern girls walking down the street when he was stationed at Fort Bragg. This remark was seen by conservative readers, he said, "as an attack on the flag." Not long after, Mrs. Kennedy came to one of George Plimpton's parties. Gay Talese recalled that as she was escorted in by Plimpton, the host surveyed the large crowd, pausing to decide which of his hundred-odd guests he would introduce to her. "And I could see that the long guest list suddenly got very short. I remember one guy he wouldn't introduce Jackie to, and didn't, was Norman Mailer, who was probably the most famous writer in New York at the time." Mailer's memory coincides with Talese's: "It was a pretty mean piece, actually. Anyway, Jackie walked into George's party, and I remember she made a point of talking to Styron for the longest damn time. I was dying." It didn't end there.

In 1965 or 1966, Mrs. Kennedy asked Richard Goodwin, who had been one of her husband's speechwriters and an important figure in his and the succeeding administration, to help Norman Podhoretz put together a party where she could meet a group of prominent New York writers and editors. Mailer, of course, would have been at the top of any such list, but one of the conditions given to Podhoretz was that he not be included. "So," Mailer said, "Norman, my good friend, didn't invite me." Styron, "who was then my dire rival," was invited, another blow. Styron's star receded somewhat in the next decade, and Mrs. Kennedy broke off her relations with Podhoretz in the late 1960s. In the 1970s, she would become friendly again with Mailer.

In late February 1962, he flew alone to Mexico to finalize his divorce from Adele, and then took a two-week trip to France with Jeanne to inform her father and grandfather of her pregnancy. They visited her father at the ducal seat, Inveraray Castle in western Scotland. Jeanne recalled the visit: "Because my father is really almost out of medieval times, for Norman that was like being put down in the middle of . . . a Japanese court." Mailer remembered the duke as "one of the coldest, nastiest men I've ever known." At dinner, Mailer was seated at the opposite end of a long table from Argyll, with Jeanne in the middle. "He talked to her throughout the entire meal; I was out of it," Mailer said. "It was the stuff of a novel, a comic novel, on a very high level." The visit to Beaverbrook was easier, Jeanne said, "Grandfather and Norman had a meeting ground. Both were intellectuals, they were both very interested in politics, both men of action." Mailer described the visit to La Capponcina at Cap d'Ail, across the bay from Monte Carlo:

> As I was saying goodbye to Beaverbrook at the end of a surprise visit Jeannie and I afforded him (for we did land without warning), I said to him in parting, "Well, sir, under the circumstances you've been gracious," at which point the, I suspect, famous gleam came into his eyes and he repeated in an evaluative voice, half statement, half question, "Under the circumstances." I would like to think it amused him but I can't bet on it.

They were married on May 4, as Jeanne remembered, "by a Black woman Methodist minister in the Maryland Woods." No friends or relatives were present. Later that month, they took possession of the three-story brownstone in Brooklyn that Mailer had first seen two years earlier. The building at 142 Columbia Heights overlooks the East River's Buttermilk Channel, with a matchless triptych of the Statue of Liberty on the left, the lower Manhattan skyline in the center, and the Brooklyn Bridge to the right. Several famous writers have lived in the Heights, including Walt Whitman, Thomas Wolfe, Hart Crane, Carson McCullers, W. H. Auden, and Mailer's erstwhile neighbor Arthur Miller. Fan and Barney, and Truman Capote, lived around the corner on Willow Street. Mailer used to tell friends that Irish politicians favored the Heights as a place to ensconce their mistresses, who then looked longingly across the river to Manhattan. He lived there for the rest of his life.

With the help of a carpenter, Mailer redesigned the third floor to give it the feel of a yacht, with rope and wooden ladders, hanging lines and catwalks. The ceiling was teak, and bowed downward like the side of a ship. He also purchased a brass engine order telegraph and compass binnacle, which remained for decades. To get to his small writing room eighteen feet up, he had to climb a rope ladder and then walk across a ten-inch catwalk. He explained to Yamanishi that to get all the way up to the ridgepole and skylight, twenty-five feet up via the rope ladder, was "so arduous that I have been able to climb successfully to the top only a few times, and then during periods when I'm not smoking." He purposely did not attach the bottom of the ladder to the floor so that it swung and twisted with the exertions of climbing, giving him exercise without "the monotony of calisthenics." Coming down was even more difficult because "one is tired and devils seem to get into the rope." The children enjoyed the rigging and played on it all the time. The chief reason for installing it, he said, was that "Jews have a bad head for heights," and the setup "keeps a small sense of danger present so that it can, I suspect, serve as a tonic for my much-abused liver." The nautical setup (and his memory of walking narrow ledges in San Francisco in 1963) would also help him imagine what negotiating the narrow stone parapet in the Waldorf Towers was like for Stephen Rojack in *An American Dream*.

Jeanne's pregnancy proceeded well while he worked uneasily on the big novel. He wrote Fig (with whom he had reconciled after receiving his glowing review of *Deaths for the Ladies*) that he was not so much moving ahead as "making separate starts" on different versions. One of these would continue the account of Marion Faye's Provincetown party, "Advertisements for Myself on the Way Out," and then alternate, as Mailer wrote in his notes: "The novel sits in two periods, the present and the future. Present is O'Shaugnessy in Monroe St. [the long whitewashed apartment where Mailer had been attacked with a hammer], Marion out of jail, Joyce [Dr. Sandy Joyce, Denise Gondelman's shrink] with Elena, etc. The future is O'Shaugnessy as a TV star, Marion as a millionaire and President-maker, and Joyce as a great intellectual who is dying of cancer." The most important—and final—piece of the big novel to be published is a meditative-fantastical short story worthy of Borges, "Truth and Being; Nothing and Time: A Broken Fragment from a Long Novel," which he wrote in December 1960 after being released from Bellevue. It appeared in *Evergreen Review* in September 1962.

Mailer called it "an odd, even exceptional, essay about: shit. Literally." It appears to be narrated by Dr. Joyce, the "archbishop of the New

Royal Scatological Society," as he is dying of "a rebellion of the cells." He explains the nature of his disease with Spenglerian élan, noting that the rate of his cancer's growth bears a relationship to "the rate of increase in the decomposition of radium to lead." He describes the anus as "the final executor of that will within us to assign value to all which passes through," and ponders the digestive process by which we "expel the exquisite in time with the despised"; out of the asshole "pour the riches of Satan." We are not brave enough to extract the best nutrients from the food we eat, not anymore. The piece can be better appreciated if understood in the larger context of Mailer's cosmic war between good and evil. He concludes that "the state of Being in the Twentieth Century was close to extinction of itself because of the diseases and disasters of soul over the centuries." Totalitarianism, in its subtle and blatant forms, and its handmaiden, technology, were seeking to extinguish civilization. Feces was one battleground.

He was in complete earnest. As the British novelist Anthony Burgess noted in a review of Mailer's 1983 novel of pharaohs, sex, war, magic, odors, and excrement, *Ancient Evenings*, Mailer understood that "Egypt is fertile because of Nile mud, and mud is a form of faeces." Thus, he continues, "The sorcery of the anal passage is the source of power." And odor is one of the keys to the meanings of excrement, as Mailer concluded in "Truth and Being": "It is characteristic," he said, "of revolutionaries, passionate lovers, the very ambitious, the greedy, the stingy, and dogs, to fix on what is excreted by others." Most commentators passed over his fecal interests holding their noses. He didn't care. His navigator told him to keep probing. Burgess was one of a small number who did not mock or dismiss Mailer's hypotheses about shit, but even he could not resist a joke about the matter. The only occasion he met Mailer, Burgess said in his review, was at one of those "fabulous New York parties (literally because the big modern sources of fable were there—Lowell, Warhol, Ginsberg, *et al.*)—he said: 'Burgess, your last book was shit.' I can see now that he was paying me a compliment." Burgess may have been correct. Dung was of inexhaustible interest to Mailer. As Mailer wrote in his essay, "Some of the best and some of the worst of us are drawn to worship at the congregation of the lost cells." In later years when the subject came up, he invariably enjoined: "Never ignore shit."

The Mailers spent the summer of 1962 in Provincetown. The previous months had been turbulent, with the couple sometimes fighting in public. Jeanne wrote later that "we could empty a room quicker than any couple in New York." But the baby was due in August and their lives, perforce, were quieter for a time. He was still working, somewhat fitfully, on various parts of the big novel. Before he left for Cape Cod, he had written to his Bellevue friend, Harry G., with avuncular advice that had personal resonance. He told him to read and "immerse yourself in the past" as a way of confronting his key problem: "your mind is three times more powerful than your culture." Mailer said that for the first time in many years "there is a small chance I am going out of my particular madness which has been like your elephantiasis of the ego." The Mailers spent July and the beginning of August in relative tranquillity.

MAILER WAS AMONG the many novelists from around the world who had been invited to Edinburgh for a five-day conference, "The Novel Today," in late August. He wrote to Sonia Brownell, George Orwell's widow and one of the organizers, saying he wanted to come, especially because there would be no speeches, just unrehearsed exchanges among the assembled novelists. He could not be definitive, however, as Jeanne was due close to the dates of the conference. They were thinking of calling the child "Christmas," Mailer said, which Brownell thought was a marvelous idea. Jeanne's mother came to New York for the birth and was charmed by Mailer. When she wasn't with her daughter, Mrs. Kidd found herself being "whirled round the nightspots" by her son-in-law. He was a "mercurial character, loaded with talent, and someone you either loved or loathed. I loved him." Mailer said he got along "famously" with her. When the baby arrived on August 18, she was named Kate Cailean. He intended to remain home, but both Jeanne and her mother urged him to go to the conference. He flew to Edinburgh on August 21, arriving on the second day. His first statement to the conferees was an announcement of Kate's birth.

Over two thousand attended the conference in McEwan Hall, a massive amphitheater that Mailer likened to a Roman circus. There was much banter from the audience, and the session leaders, Mailer and Mary McCarthy among them, were not totally surprised to learn that someone had filled the water carafes with whisky. "A nice touch, don't you think?" said one of the organizers. No one was allowed to speak for more than five minutes, so the discussion of aspects of the novel was spirited and easy to follow. Besides Mailer and McCarthy, those given a speaking slot included Lawrence Durrell, Muriel Spark, Stephen Spender, Rebecca West, Alex Trocchi, and two writers Mailer was to meet for the first time: William Burroughs and Henry Miller. The French delegation, which was supposed to include Jean-Paul Sartre and Albert Camus, failed to appear, as did the Russian delegation. While the British and Americans dominated, there were representatives from nearly every European country, and some from Asia and Africa. Mailer said that he came to the conclusion that he had to be "a bit of a public figure" at the conference, as the audience would "listen more carefully to Behan than Dos Passos." By some estimates, he was the star of the conference.

When Mary McCarthy lamented that it was difficult to have a real debate about censorship without the presence of a genuine practitioner, Mailer took on the role of devil's advocate, one he always relished. "This man Mailer," one reporter wrote, "stocky, curly-headed, almost cherubic at times (like a Rubens) has the reputation of being so far out as to be almost inarticulate," but when he spoke in favor of censorship, he did so with "quite brilliant articulateness." He began by saying that "a profound argument can be advanced that sexual literature, you see, does weaken warlike potential because it tends to drain it." He elaborated on his hypothesis and drew rejoinders from several speakers, including McCarthy, Burroughs, and Miller. McCarthy cited Sparta where sex "was felt to be the pap of war," and Mailer responded with the example of Stalin using sexual censorship to make Russia into a warlike nation in the 1930s. Burroughs noted tersely that censorship of sexual material was an adjunct to capitalism's desire to "channel the sexual instinct into production and purchase of consumer's goods." Henry Miller held fire until near the end, and then spoke briefly. "It's all very much more simple than it sounds," he began.

> The whole world today is in my mind strangled. We have no freedom of action really, we are all talking nonsense. Well, we all would like to do when we see a good interesting woman is to sleep with her. We should not make any bones about that. There is nothing wrong with lust or with obscenity, we all have impure desires. We should have the pure and the impure, they exist together. Good

and evil belong together. You can't separate them. Let's stop talking about censorship; let's do it, think it, talk it, act it. Thank you.

Miller's remarks (which recall D. H. Lawrence) neatly reinforced Mailer's ideas about the existential life. Remembering his first meeting with Miller, Mailer said he not only admired his work; he admired his personality. "It is all of a piece," he wrote, "no neurotic push-pull, no maggots in the smile, no envies, no nervousness." Miller, wearing knickers and a cap in Edinburgh, had "a good tough face, big nose, near bald head, looking for all the world like Marx's noble proletarian, like some bricklayer, let us say, you started talking to on the train, and then it turned out he had eighty-two kids and worked at his hobby in his spare time—it was translating Sophocles." Mailer recalled that Miller "leaned over and said, 'Where are you from, Norman?' I said, 'Brooklyn.' He said, 'Yeah, I'm from Brooklyn too.' " That cemented things.

His admiration for Burroughs was also burnished by their interaction. At one point, Burroughs was describing his cut-up/fold-in method of composition, whereby he cut typed pages in half vertically, and then folded one half into another cut-up section. "The method," he said, "could also lead to collaboration by writers on an unprecedented scale to produce works that were the composite effort of any number of writers, living or dead." He had used fold-ins, he explained, from Shakespeare, Rimbaud, Saint-John Perse, along with passages from magazines, newspapers, and letters, to produce composite novels whose authorship he shared. When the novelist Khushwant Singh, sitting near him on the speakers' platform, asked if he was really serious, Burroughs, looking for all the world like Buster Keaton, answered, "Yes, of course." Remembering Burroughs at the conference, Mailer said that "he spoke to his friends exactly the same way he spoke to his enemies, which was somewhat remotely." Burroughs remained undemonstrative.

Edinburgh was still a bit Calvinist in 1962, and it was hard to get a drink in a bar after ten. Consequently, there were private drinking parties every night of the conference. "Edinburgh had very many evil spirits loose for those few days." Mailer recalled, "there was madness in the air." At a celebratory party after the final day, he was drinking with Sonia Brownell and John Calder, the two chief conference organizers. Burroughs was also there. They were joined by Max Hayward, the translator of *Doctor Zhivago*, who was quite drunk. Calder says that Hayward made a clumsy pass at Brownell; Mailer remembers him complaining about being roughed up by some Edinburgh hoodlums. Hayward went on interminably, Mailer said, in a whining, self-pitying manner about this unmerited cruelty. Angry or disgusted or both, Mailer picked Hayward off the ground, and with some help from Calder carried him out to the landing. "He told me to let go," Calder said. "When I did, he heaved Hayward over his shoulder and on to the stone stairs, whereupon he rolled down all the four or five flights to the bottom. Five minutes later, he reappeared, blood flowing from several places, and quietly resumed drinking." Many years later, Mailer recalled that crazy night and shook his head. "I could have killed him," he said.

MAILER RETURNED TO a full plate. He had agreed to a September 22 debate in Chicago with William F. Buckley, whom he had called "the most important conservative in the public eye after Barry Goldwater." Two days later, he would go to Comiskey Park to watch the heavyweight boxing match between champion Floyd Patterson and Sonny Liston, which he planned to write about in his new *Esquire* column. He stayed at Hugh Hefner's Playboy mansion overlooking Lake Michigan. Hefner was clearly cultivating Mailer, and Mailer liked "Hef," and looked forward to mingling with the fight crowd and a bevy of playmates at his sybaritic mansion. His first concern upon his return, however, was his wife and the new baby. He found that Jeanne was recovering nicely, and that the "frighteningly bright" Kate had the admirable ability of "staring one hard in the eye." Now the father of four girls, he wondered if he possessed "some exceptional virtue or vice to be so curiously blessed." He was feeling better about himself than he had for some time. Graham Greene's recent letter saying he had been "moved and excited" by the "magnificent" *Advertisements for Myself*, was also encouraging. His literary correspondence had now grown to the point where he needed a full-time secretary.

He hired a young woman named Anne Barry, a WASP from New Hampshire who had just graduated from Radcliffe. She had spent a day with Mailer in Manhattan several months earlier, discussing a paper she was writing on *Advertisements*. Her thesis was that Mailer was having an identity crisis in the late 1950s, and although they laughed about this, she was correct. Shortly after they met, she wrote "First Meeting with Norman, March, 1962."

> He was a particularly intense man. I was, of course, impressed because a famous or rather notorious writer asked me to have a drink with him. I saw that rather square face, that broadshouldered frame now slightly paunchy, those eyes so sharp, in a soft tough too old face, and I knew that every word counted, that I would be judged not unfairly but strictly by this man.
>
> We walked out on the street; we went to Dorgene's; there was a piano, and we couldn't hear ourselves talk, so we went to a bar across the street. "I don't know what it is about you. You interest me." And then, after he said this, "I just thought I'd tell you that now. It's something to take home with you." I thanked him, sarcastically, knowing that I would need this to take home with me—and this made me bitter. So trapped, I am in pettiness. "You can't take a compliment, can you?" (Suddenly he was frighteningly ingenuous.) "You look like a girl who can hold her liquor. I like that." And, later, "When I first saw you, Barry, I thought you were Boston Irish. I came down the stairs, and saw you standing there, with your chin set, looking me over, and I knew right then you were a monster." (His eyes sparkle, his face crinkles into a smile, imp-like, suddenly.) Two bars, four scotches. I must live up to my hard drinking reputation. He walks away from the table: "Get me another drink," and I must, somehow, fight my way past the drunks at the bar, and order him I can't remember what, not paying for it. "I knew you'd get me that drink," he said, and our eyes met, and I knew I'd passed another test. Always testing his friends, his enemies, never relaxing.

Barry typed up whatever he was working on—columns for *Esquire* and *Commentary,* stories, poems, and speeches—he would edit them, and she would retype, sometimes several times. It was a routine he maintained with all his subsequent secretaries. Writing poems on scraps of paper for a couple of years had convinced him of the merits of longhand, and he wrote in pencil on white unlined paper from then on. His relationship with Barry was open and friendly; they joshed and joked. She found him to be "a very funny man," and corrected his punctuation. He called her "Mrs. Mark Twain," and in a letter to Don Carpenter that she typed, "a stuck-up little New Hampshire cunt whom you may have met." She also made him breakfast and lunch, walked Tibo and Zsa Zsa, and later helped him take care of Sadie, Jeanne's maid, who was left with him when Jeanne moved out. Barry said she admired his "freedom, his humor, his willingness to look things that are unpleasant in the eye—a reluctance to make things look nice—these are Jewish qualities, and they come through in his work as well as in the man." They had a warm relationship and remained in contact until his death.

The Chicago debate with Buckley was billed as "The Real Meaning of the Right Wing in America," but the context was the intensifying arms race with Russia—the Cuban Missile Crisis occurred in October 1962—and the emergence of an energized conservative movement led by the GOP senator from Arizona, Barry Goldwater. Buckley's magazine, *National Review*, was Goldwater's cheerleader and applauded his plan to spend more on nuclear weapons. Mailer wanted to end the Cold War, arguing that the United States was demonizing the communist state. "Let communism come to those countries it will come to," he argued before the audience of nearly four thousand. The Cold War, he said, has become "an instrument of megalomaniacal delusion," and had turned the nation's attention away from the true plague, which Mailer defined in more specific ways than he had in the past, a reflection, in part, of his embrace of existential philosophy, especially that of Heidegger. He pointed, for example, to the blandness of modern architecture, the way it masked the functions of buildings: "The airports look like luxury hotels, the luxury hotels are indistinguishable from a modern corporation's home office, and the home office looks like an air-conditioned underground city on the moon." New drugs proliferate to treat "small epidemics with no name," but are ineffective. "Nature is wounded in her fisheries, her forests. Airplanes spray insecticides. Species of insects are removed from the chain of life. Crops are poisoned just slightly. We grow enormous tomatoes which have no taste." Five days after his speech, Rachel Carson's *Silent Spring*, an indictment of environmental pollution that led to the banning of DDT, was published.

Their speeches were published in *Playboy*, Buckley's with the subtitle, "A Conservative's View," Mailer's "A Liberal's View." Mailer took umbrage. "I don't care," he said in a letter to the editor, "if people call me a radical, a rebel, a red, a revolutionary, an outsider, an outlaw, a Bolshevik, an anarchist, a nihilist, or even a left conservative, but please don't ever call me a liberal." Few called him a liberal again, but left conservative or, eventually, Left-conservative, stuck, despite his never-ending difficulty in explaining exactly what he meant by it. For Mailer, a liberal was a knee-jerk, unthinking incrementalist on social issues, a helpful, smiling, reverent, grown-up scout who opposed nothing but discourtesy. Mailer opposed much and wanted to be sure that the world knew it.

In his speech and some of his framing comments for it in *The Presidential Papers*, he added a brief preface of the same kind found in *Advertisements for Myself.* He says that Americans are afraid of something besides the communists. "Dread," he continues, "has been loose in the twentieth century, and America has shivered in its horror since the Depression." Besides the more tangible manifestations of dread, he notes with alarm that philosophy itself may be dying. "Metaphysics disappears, logical positivism arises," and "soon a discussion of death will be considered a betrayal of philosophy," a remark reflecting Heidegger's adjuration to humans to stand "in the openness of Being, of enduring . . . and of out-braving the utmost (Being toward death)." Mailer notes ruefully that the logical positivists are displacing the existentialists in Anglo-American philosophy, and goes on to attack psychologists (excluding Reichians and Jungians) for treating dread as "a repetition of infantile experiences of helplessness." The dread and anxiety felt by humanity, he believes, should be seen as something more primitive and authentic, namely, the danger of "losing some part or quality of our soul unless we act and act dangerously."

There is no way to determine how much influence his reading had on his debate speech. But we do know that during his seventeen-day stay in Bellevue, he had read an anthology edited by Walter Kaufmann, *Existentialism from Dostoevsky to Sartre,* which contained excerpts from the writings of ten existential writers, including Nietzsche, Kierkegaard, and Heidegger. It is no weak supposition to conclude that the title of the Nietzsche chapter, "Live Dangerously," and the Nietzsche quote from which it was taken, rang a big bell for Mailer: "For believe me, the secret of the greatest fruitfulness and the greatest enjoyment of existence is: to *live dangerously!* Build your cities under Vesuvius! Send your ships into uncharted seas! Live at war with your peers and yourselves!"

An excerpt from Kierkegaard's influential work *The Concept of*

Dread, "Dread and Freedom," is included in the anthology. It appears to be the source of Mailer's oft stated notion that "the saint and the psychopath were united to one another, and different from the mass of men," and that this "paradox" had "driven Kierkegaard near to mad for he had the courage to see that his criminal impulses were also his most religious." But it is the Heidegger chapter that may have been uppermost in his mind when he decided to explore the concept of dread in his speech. Dread, for Heidegger, is felt in the face of Nothingness, and courage is the essential virtue that opposes dread and sustains Being (which Heidegger called *Da-sein*, or human existence or presence). Heidegger says the dread felt by courageous persons is no simple joy, but stands "in secret union with the serenity and gentleness of creative longing," which can be taken as certifying the high valor of the artist. The extent to which Mailer's conception of the artist's role was invigorated by the writings in the Kaufmann collection is uncertain, but the force of his belief in the heroic mission of the artist is indisputable. The last line of his 1971 introduction to a new edition of *Deaths for the Ladies* captures it best: *Time*'s dismissive review of his poetry, he says, "put iron into my heart again, and rage, and the feeling that the enemy was more alive than ever, and dirtier in the alley, and so one had to mend, and put on the armor, and go to war, go out to war again, and try to hew huge strokes with the only broadsword God ever gave you, a glimpse of something like Almighty prose."

Gay Talese, who had met Mailer a few years earlier at a prizefight at the St. Nicholas Arena in Manhattan, covered the debate for *The New York Times*. He described it as a contest between the conservative Buckley ("a clever jabber with a tiptoe stance"), and Mailer the hipster ("who hooked with his fists as he spoke"). In his lead, he said the match was considered to have ended in a draw. Talese's story ran on September 24, the day before the Patterson-Liston fight. Mailer read it, and then saw the reporter at one of the prefight receptions for the press. Talese, who remembers wearing "a summer weight suit, a tan, gabardine, three-piece suit," saw Mailer walking his way. "I sensed that he wasn't happy, he wasn't smiling, and he was carrying a drink. I remember him walking over, and he said, 'It wasn't a draw.' " Talese tried to make light of it, but Mailer "continued to be serious and looked at me in a very hostile way. And I did see his drink in his right hand and I thought, 'He's going to throw that drink at me,' because I had a recollection of

Mailer's public image as a guy who could be volatile and throw a drink at someone, or a punch. I thought, 'It is early in the evening, I'm wearing this suit, there are people here who will see this guy throw this drink at me.' " Talese said Mailer looked menacing, and Talese said, "Don't throw that drink at me." Mailer said he had no intention of doing so. "Then there was a smile, and then there was a casual reflection on the article. That little moment passed, but it was my one moment."

Mailer was adamant that he had won the debate. Buckley had used most of his thirty minutes attacking various prominent people on the left—Murray Kempton, Mailer, and Castro—while Mailer had analyzed the nature of the right wing. "The crowd was high partisan that night and cheered separately for us with the kind of excitement one expects in a crowd at a high school football game," he wrote, and "I had succeeded in pushing a salient into the intellectual territory of the Right." Therefore, he argued, the laurels should go to him. Coming after his nimble-footed performance in Edinburgh, the Chicago debate gave him another reason to feel cocky about his extemporaneous speaking abilities. Roger Donoghue, Mailer's second, scored it in the manner of a ten-round boxing match: six, three, one for Mailer.

"I was full of myself," is how Mailer described his state of mind on the eve of the championship bout. He was certain that Patterson would defeat the heavier contender, Sonny Liston, who was favored by the oddsmakers. Patterson was agile and experienced, but Liston's weight and reach proved too much, and Patterson was down and out at two minutes and six seconds into the first round. Some fans hadn't even found their seats when the fight ended. Mailer published his report as his February 1963 "Big Bite" column in *Esquire*. Titled "Ten Thousand Words a Minute," the twenty thousand-word essay (10K per minute) is to sports writing what "Superman Comes to the Supermarket" is to political reportage—a revamping of the genre. Its power resides not only in his extended slow-motion analyses of the action, but in his stunning similes, as in his description of another fight, in which Emile Griffith pounded Benny Paret to death.

> Paret got trapped in a corner. Trying to duck away, his left arm and his head became tangled on the wrong side of the top rope. Griffith was in like a cat ready to rip the life out of a huge boxed rat. He hit him eighteen right hands in a row, an act which took perhaps three

> or four seconds. Griffith made a pent-up whimpering sound all the while he attacked, the right hand whipping like a piston rod which has broken through the crankcase, or like a baseball bat demolishing a pumpkin. I was sitting in the second row in the corner—they were not ten feet away from me, and like everyone else, I was hypnotized.

What further distinguishes the essay from other first-rate sports writing is the way Mailer opens his focus to include portraits of the fight crowd, the celebrities, the dignitaries, the hangers-on, and the reporters who covered the fight: "Have any of you ever been through the smoking car of an old coach early in the morning when the smokers sleep and the stale air settles into congelations of gloom? Well that is a little like the scent of Press Headquarters."

> It is like being at a vast party in Limbo—there is tremendous excitement, much movement and no sex at all. Just talk. Talk fed by cigarettes. One thousand to two thousand cigarettes are smoked every hour. The mind must keep functioning fast enough to offer up stories. (Reporters meet in a marketplace to trade their stories—they barter an anecdote they cannot use about one of the people in the event in order to pick up a different piece which is usable by their paper. It does not matter if the story is true or altogether not true, it must merely be suitable and not too mechanically libelous.) So they char the inside of their bodies in order to scrape up news which can go out to the machine.

The Mob is at the fight—Liston had connections to the underworld—and Mailer devotes a thousand words to a group portrait. A sample: "Heavy types, bouncers, plug-uglies, flatteners, one or two speedy, swishing, Negro ex-boxers, for example, now blown up to the size of fat middleweights, slinky in their walk, eyes fulfilling the operative definition of razor slits, murder coming off them like scent comes off a skunk." His metaphors are surprising but precise: "If a clam had a muscle as large as a man, and the muscle grew eyes, you would get the mood." The Mob bosses are "hawks and falcons and crows, Italian dons looking like little old shrunken eagles, gulls, pelicans, condors." The essay expands the scope of the sports essay, reshapes it, then transcends it.

But it is Mailer's inclusion of himself in the piece that most sharply distinguishes it from the writing of fight reporters of the quality of Red Smith and A. J. Liebling, writers saturated in fight lore, but men (there were no female fight scribes yet) who bowed so deeply to the canons of objectivity that they could not conceive of making themselves major characters in their own work. Mailer, on the other hand, is present from the beginning, depicting his exchanges with other reporters and with handlers, trainers, and managers, including Patterson's, the legendary Cus D'Amato: "He had stopped drinking years ago and so had enormous pent-up vitality. As a talker, he was one of the world's great weight-lifters, not brilliant, but powerful, nonstop, and very solid. Talk was muscle. If you wanted to interrupt, you had to bend his arm off." Toward the end of the piece, Mailer moves to the center of the action.

Drinking all night at Hefner's mansion, he convinced himself and several reporters that he knew how to publicize the inevitable rematch of Liston and Patterson so as to make it ten times more profitable. His plan is to present the idea the following morning before Liston's press conference. He explains how in the "plot-ridden, romantic dungeons of my mind" he has reconceived Norman Mailer as a version of Castro, a man who *knows* the impossible may be accomplished. He drinks until seven A.M., washes up, and goes to the hotel where he learns that Liston had moved his press conference up a half hour, thus stealing Mailer's crowd. He walks into Liston's meeting with reporters, plops himself down on the dais, and tries to insinuate himself into the event. He fails. Removed physically by house detectives, his caper is over, although later he does shake Liston's hand, and they agree they are both bums.

Mailer's drunken behavior was widely reported. His probation officer read about his stunt. He was called in and told that his probation, about to end, would be continued until June 1963. He had paid a high price for his actions, and so reflected at the close of the essay that "some ghost of Don Quixote was laid to rest in me." Once more, after a notable victory, Mailer overreached. It was now a confirmed pattern. He called his essay "a *mélange de genres*," but it is one of the glories of sports writing, and ample recompense for his embarrassing ejection from the press conference. Remembering his story "The Notebook," one can wonder if Mailer staged the stunt in order to write about it. He invariably had two motives for his actions. Although he never revealed his idea, which died aborning, for staging the rematch (beyond billing it as a struggle between Good and Evil), Mailer genuinely believed he was on a mission to crown Floyd Patterson as a genius for the nation to admire. He had yet to meet Muhammad Ali.

A FEW DAYS after the boxing match, Mailer sent a telegram to Attorney General Robert F. Kennedy: "Go to Oxford, Mississippi, or arrange a way for me to go down. I can talk to those students." He was referring to the situation of James Meredith, the first black to enroll in the University of Mississippi. Robert Kennedy had sent federal marshals that President Kennedy backed up by army troops to quell violence and compel his admission. The civil rights movement had grown hugely since the federal desegregation of the Little Rock, Arkansas, public schools in the fall of 1957, and by the fall of 1962 there were outbreaks of violence all over the South arising from the actions of thousands of black and white "freedom riders" who flouted Jim Crow laws by riding on buses and trains, and eating in segregated terminal restaurants. Mailer wanted to get involved, but there was trouble on the home front, and he stayed in New York to try to save his marriage, already in jeopardy.

His relations with Jeanne had frayed since Kate was born. He was traveling a lot, and when he wasn't, attended meetings in Manhattan or wrote in his studio. Jeanne lived on the first floor of the brownstone for a time and then moved out. She had her own journalistic career. Much was left to Anne Barry and Jeanne Johnson, a twenty-year-old woman Mailer had met at Bellevue, who became his ward and helped with chores at the apartment. Mailer had assumed that he and his wife would agree to some sort of household routine. "Having grown up in the middle class, life and background," he said, "I was very responsible to appointments, habits, agreements. For her it was just will-o'-the-wisp. So we could agree to be doing something, and she would change her mind at the last moment. That used to drive me nuts because I thought we couldn't get along without structure."

Jeanne also didn't like living in Brooklyn. "She had a feeling that her social life was swallowed up. I don't know how powerful a factor that was because she was never someone who said, 'I'm giving up more than I'm prepared to give up.' She wouldn't have talked that way," he said. Another factor was Jeanne's strained relations with Fan. "My mother was prepared to accept any woman I was married to, but I'd never pretend they liked each other," he said. Barney, however, with his British manners, got along well with her. Mailer said that infidelities weren't the largest problem: "There may have been a few en route, but that was hardly part of it—I mean, I was screwing everybody I could—she certainly had the right. It was more, that we never could build anything. It got worse and worse. And she was a dreadful cook. I remember she'd invite people over for dinner and it was comic to watch them eating and screwing their mouths—it was awful swill—and they'd say, 'Oh, it's delicious, Jeanne.' Then they'd leave and I'd say, 'You've no idea what an awful cook you are.' " By late fall, the marriage had begun to splinter.

Whatever his domestic problems, he continued to write a lot, mainly essays and book reviews, while making no progress on the big novel. After more than seven years of work, albeit interrupted work, all he had to show was a handful of fragments. But he couldn't interrupt the flow of shorter pieces; he needed income. The reputation of *Advertisements for Myself* and "The White Negro," the debate with Buckley, and his "Big Bite" column in *Esquire* led to many requests for interviews and paid speaking engagements, and he accepted virtually all of them. In 1963, he agreed to give talks at Harvard, the universities of Connecticut, Michigan, Chicago, and Wesleyan University. He also rented Carnegie Hall for a May 31 performance titled "An Existential Evening," and drew a paying crowd of 1,200. *Playboy* and *Esquire* wanted more material from him, and *Cosmopolitan* interviewed him for a profile. But the big novel went begging and debts accumulated. Besides household expenses and the large mortgage payment for 142 Columbia Heights, he was responsible for support payments for several of his children plus alimony for Adele, Anne Barry's salary, and Jeanne Johnson's expenses. Royalties from *The Naked and the Dead* helped, but his lectures and columns for *Esquire* and *Commentary* paid little, and both his U.S. and British publishers wanted him to deliver his promised novel.

Jeanne Campbell moved to Manhattan in early 1963. Mailer wrote to Adeline Naiman about the situation. "Jeanne and I are apart, yet not apart. We see each other almost every night, come together a bit, go away a little—it's deadening in the extreme. Limbo." Desirous of family stability, but eager for affairs, he was torn: "When I was young I was always married and rotting my liver with envy that I was not free. Now that I am almost middle-aged I am of course free, and see for the first time that there can be something rich in a large family and lots of responsible detail." The breakup was prolonged, and even as late as mid-June he wrote to Knox saying there were "indications" that they might patch things up. "She's the toughest babe I've ever known," he wrote, but "most of her friends I find intolerable and sickening, and of course that's a fundamental division in my psyche when I as a radical am traveling around with upper-class types." He had learned all he cared to about these "types." But to *New York Times* columnist Harvey Breit, he spoke of the relationship in the past tense, and bemoaned the losses incurred when his marriages had ended.

> Part of the absolute funk is that one ties one's creativity to one's mate, and when they start grinding you into dry goatball powder and there's nothing left but to split or become a whining piteous concentration camp victim, well there one splits if there's one sperm cell left, but there's a near mortal anguish which consists of even more than the awful execution of the love that's left. For one's killing part of the creativity in oneself—all those delicate habits and projects which were built up around the half-ass life one had with the beloved. And I think it's almost as bad as a woman losing a baby. I've lost three wives, and there was something large to lose in each of them, but I also lost three large chambers of the talent.

A few days later in a letter to his Aunt Moos (married to Barney Mailer's brother Louis), one meant for family consumption, he made it clear that the marriage was over: "She's got a will at least as strong as mine and was no more ready to become a Brooklyn housewife (of the grandest sort, I assure you) than I was ready to become Mr. Lady Jeanne."

There was one bright spot: collecting his recent journalism, interviews, essays, and a few pieces of the big novel for a new collection. He had over 200,000 words, which Putnam's wanted him to cut in half, a task he savored. Initially, he planned to call the miscellany "The Devil Revisited," but the title was changed to *The Presidential Papers* shortly before it was published in November 1963. The focus was to be on Kennedy's administration, for which he had much pointed advice, all of it unheeded. The work was satisfying, but it was only a holding action. Sometime in the winter or early spring of 1963, he came to the conclusion that he needed to write a short novel, one that would amount to a down payment on his large promise that he would "hit the longest ball ever to go up into the accelerated hurricane air of our American letters." If he wasn't ready to hit a home run, perhaps he could belt a double, "dare a bold stroke," one that would give him a big paycheck and enable him, as he wrote to his army buddy, Fig Gwaltney, "to do my big book in relative calm."

After "10,000 Words a Minute," the most ambitious piece of this period is "Norman Mailer Versus Nine Writers," subtitled "Further Evaluations of the Talent in the Room," which establishes it as a continuation of his earlier essay that had so exasperated Jones, Styron, and Baldwin. In the new essay, begun in early March, he discusses the latest novels by these three—respectively, *The Thin Red Line, Set This House on Fire,* and *Another Country*—and recent novels by Burroughs (*Naked Lunch*), Heller (*Catch-22*), Updike (*Rabbit, Run*), Roth (*Letting Go*), Salinger (*Franny and Zooey* and *Raise High the Roof Beam, Carpenters and Seymour: An Introduction*), and Bellow (*Henderson the Rain King*). When it appeared in the July issue of *Esquire*, it was preceded by a full-page photo of a truculent-looking Mailer in suit and tie standing in the corner of a boxing ring at the Gramercy Park Gym. Mailer was deeply impressed by how the photographer, Diane Arbus, caught his mood that day, and had great admiration for her work. Mailer's insights are as unflinching as in the earlier essay, but less rebarbative, and slightly more self-deprecatory, as in his opening comments on *Henderson the Rain King*: "Well, one might as well eat the crow right here. Henderson is an exceptional character, almost worthy of Gulliver or Huckleberry Finn." He goes on for two paragraphs.

> Bellow's main character, Henderson, is a legendary giant American, an eccentric millionaire, six-foot four in height, with a huge battered face, an enormous chest, a prodigious potbelly, a wild crank's gusto for life, and a childlike impulse to say what he thinks. He is a magical hybrid of Jim Thorpe and Dwight Macdonald. And he is tormented by an inner voice which gives him no rest and poisons his marriages and pushes him to go forth. So he chooses to go to Africa (after first contemplating a visit to the Eskimos) and finds a native guide to take him deep into the interior.
>
> The style gallops like Henderson, full of excess, full of light, loaded with irritating effusions, but it is a style which moves along. *The Adventures of Augie March* was written in a way which could

> only be called *all writing*. That was one of the troubles with the book. Everything was mothered by the style. But Henderson talks in a free-swinging easy bang-away monologue which puts your eye in the center of the action.

But Bellow falters, Mailer says, perhaps revealing that he is "too timid to become a great writer." James Jones "or myself," he concludes, "would have been ready to urinate blood" rather than give up "the possibilities of a demonically great ending," as does Bellow in Mailer's shrewd judgment.

He was working on the essay in early March when one evening he went with Roger Donoghue to P. J. Clarke's, a Midtown saloon frequented by Frank Sinatra and other celebrities. Mailer was nursing his wounds over Jeanne Campbell. A sexy blonde, Beverly Bentley, who knew Donoghue, was sitting nearby and motioned them to join her. Sitting with Bentley was a girlfriend and "the Raging Bull," former middleweight boxing champ Jake LaMotta. She got Mailer's attention immediately: "Hey, Norman Motherfuck Mailer, come on over!" An actress from Georgia who broke into show business on Arthur Godfrey's television show, Bentley (formerly Rentz) had appeared in several films and had had roles in television shows (*Naked City*) and Broadway plays (*Romanoff and Juliet*). In the summer of 1959, she had been part of the *quadrilla* at Hemingway's birthday party in Málaga, along with several Spanish bullfighters and Valerie Danby-Smith. Papa told her that she reminded him of Marlene Dietrich. The Hemingway connection impressed Mailer. Shortly before he died, Mailer recalled that night at P. J. Clarke's.

> So I come over and there's this attractive blonde who was full of pep and vigor. And we're chatting away and LaMotta turns to me and says, "Hey, get lost." And I did maybe the single bravest thing—second bravest thing—I've ever done in my life. I looked back at him and I said, "I'll leave when the lady tells me to." And you know something came off him that was enough to give you pause. But I held my ground and then she came through. I figured, "This bitch, she brought me over here and I could be destroyed, then fuck it, I'll be destroyed." In those days, I was hell-bent for destruction. And she said, "No, Jake, Mr. Mailer is my date for tonight." So he left and

> she and me just started talking—yakking and chatting. And ended up in bed. Of course. Every one of my wives—one common denominator in all of them is that we all ended up in bed the first night. Which I'm proud of in a way. I think it's as good a way of deciding something as any.

"I wanted a home and children desperately," Beverly said, recalling their meeting. "I was attracted to the vulnerability underneath the tough act. He walked me to my apartment. That night he was wonderful in bed." Mailer later learned that a few years earlier, when she had been working as a hostess on television quiz shows, she had been in a long-term relationship with jazz trumpeter Miles Davis, a man Mailer admired. Davis would become the model for Shago Martin, a brilliant jazz vocalist who was one of the major figures in his next novel, *An American Dream.*

Mailer was still in touch with Jeanne, but their contacts had diminished. When Randolph Churchill flew to the U.S. to accept honorary citizenship for his father from Congress in April, he stopped in New York and visited with Jeanne, a dear friend. Mailer saved an Associated Press photo of them that appeared in the *New York Post.* Jeanne, wearing a wide brim hat, is smiling and holding Churchill's toy pug, Oswald, in her lap. The dog's name seems to have stuck with Mailer: he used it in *Dream* as Barney Kelly's middle name. His first name came from I. B. Mailer.

By spring, Beverly had moved into 142 Columbia Heights. Mailer wrote to Knox in early June to say that he had been thinking about traveling around the country and "seeing what the mood is." A Broadway play in which Beverly had a leading role, *The Heroine*, had folded and she was eager to join him. First, they would drive to Fayetteville, Arkansas, to see Fig and Ecey, and then on to Las Vegas for the Patterson-Liston rematch on July 22. After the fight, which he considered writing about for *Esquire* as a bookend to "Ten Thousand Words a Minute," they planned to drive to San Francisco for a couple of weeks, and then take the long drive back via Georgia, where he would meet Beverly's family. His idea was to get out of New York, range about the country with his new woman, and see what plot prompts for new work came his way. He had a wisp of a situation in mind, and he told his new agent, Scott Meredith, to leak word that he was working on a novel about "a man who takes a 21-year old girl to Las Vegas." He was thinking of Beverly, although she was thirty-three. He said later, "I wanted a blond American girl; it was really as simple as that. A shiksa. And she was perfect; she fitted perfectly because she was adventurous. She came from a relatively—if you want to get down to it—a quite unremarkable southern family. She had risen in the world through her own efforts." Shortly before they left for Arkansas, Jeanne sent Mailer a telegram saying that her lawyer would telephone him to ask for an immediate Mexican divorce. "My darling let us now be pragmatic," she said. Mailer agreed. On July 9, he and Beverly drove off in his Triumph convertible with Tibo in the backseat. Mailer had given away Zsa Zsa and the last of the pups.

During their four days in Fayetteville, two important things happened: Beverly was tested for pregnancy and Mailer observed an autopsy. Beverly asked a pathologist friend of Fig's if he would give her a pregnancy test, and he agreed to do so. The same doctor invited Mailer to watch him perform an autopsy he was doing the next day. Mailer used the experience in *An American Dream.* In the novel, Rojack's doctor friend opens up an old man whose face was "lustful and proud, much hate in it, but disciplined." He had cancer, but died of peritoneal gangrene when his appendix burst. It is all that Rojack can do not to retch when the odor hits his nostrils.

> I remember I breathed it in to the top of the lung, and drew no further. Pinched it off in the windpipe. After half an hour of such breathing, my lungs were to ache for the rest of the day, but it was impossible to accept the old man's odor all the way in. . . . I kept getting a whiff of the smell for the next two days, all along the trip through the dried hard-up lands of Oklahoma, northern Texas, New Mexico, on into the deserts of Arizona and southern Nevada where Las Vegas sits in the mirror of the moon. Then for weeks I never lost the smell. In the beginning the dead man came back at every turn, he came back from phosphate fertilizer in every farmer's field, he rose up out of every bump of a dead rabbit on the road, from each rotting ghost in the stump of a tree, he chose to come back later at every hint of a hole in emotion or a pit of decay. . . .
>
> In some, madness must come in with breath, mill through the blood and be breathed out again. In some it goes up to the mind.

> Some take the madness and stop it with discipline. Madness is locked beneath. It goes into tissues, is swallowed by the cells. The cells go mad. Cancer is their flag. Cancer is the growth of madness denied. In that corpse I saw, madness went down to the blood—leucocytes gorged the liver, the spleen, the enlarged heart and violet-black lungs, dug into the intestines, germinated stench.

The hypothesis that cancer and schizophrenia were mutually exclusive cohered here, and Mailer's intuition, gained on patrols in Luzon, that smell is the primal sense was further confirmed.

He explored his hunch in *An American Dream* and further elaborated it in later work, especially his 1984 mystery novel, *Tough Guys Don't Dance*. He also spelled it out in a one-page, handwritten note, probably written in late 1963. Titled "Cancer," it begins by hypothesizing that cancer results from "impotent emotion," which "cannot find the situation for its life." An ugly woman who waits for a handsome lover is a slave to this emotion, as is a poor young man who wishes ill on his wealthy relatives but sees them continue to prosper. So too is "any over-civilized person who carries murder within" but represses it. Without relief, the emotion is "visited upon the cells" of the body, and "when such inner tension becomes acute, the cells live at the edge of rebellion—they may dare to secede from the body." This Mailer calls a "psychosis of the cells" in his "Cancer" note; this is the madness Rojack saw in the organs of the old man. "When the weight of impossible desire becomes intolerable, either the mind or the body must divide itself from the whole." Twenty years later, in 1981, neurobiologists conclusively established the hardwired link between the body's immune system and the central nervous system. That mind affects body as much as the reverse was an article of faith for Mailer.

After leaving Arkansas, the couple drove to Las Vegas via the baked landscape of the high plains desert. Mailer thought about beginning the new novel with a description of the autopsy, but used it in the final chapter of *An American Dream*, which covers Rojack's drive on the same route to Las Vegas. Encountering extraordinary bodily corruption by way of his nostrils opened new reaches in his imagination, an experience no doubt heightened by his struggle, all through 1963 and early 1964, to quit smoking two and a half packs of Camels a day. "I used the sense of smell," he said shortly after finishing the novel, "because it's the closest to the dream." In addition, "it is the most shocking sense. All bourgeois society seems to be built on that one abstention. You never mention odors." In *Dream*, he explored these off-limits olfactory lodes more thoroughly than any other American novelist before him or since.

They arrived in Las Vegas on July 20. Meeting them there was Harold Conrad, a fight promoter, and his wife, Mara Lynn, both of whom later appeared in Mailer's films. A good deal of drinking took place and Mailer got into at least two fistfights. The championship fight two days later was a letdown. Mailer had privately concluded that it would be a fifteen-round draw, but Liston again defeated Patterson. His plan had been for the novel's protagonist to drive to Las Vegas with a young woman to see the fight. But the boxing match was a repeat of the first one. Liston again knocked Patterson out in the first round and Mailer didn't know how to proceed.

A telegram from Arkansas was delivered to their hotel: Beverly was pregnant. Because of his already weighty commitments, Mailer was distraught at first. He and Beverly fought, but during a late night drive into the desert were reconciled. The extravagant contrasts of this artificial city in the desert—drunks and millionaires, showgirls and grandmas, winners and losers, icy air-conditioning and baking sun—imprinted themselves on Mailer, always fascinated by opposites at close quarters. He would use Las Vegas as a touchstone for the contradictions of America more than once in books to come. Toward the end of July, with the new novel gestating, they left for San Francisco, where they had made arrangements to meet his *Harvard Advocate* friend Mark Linenthal and his now ex-wife, Alice Adams.

San Francisco was an oasis after Las Vegas. They announced that they were getting married and there was some quiet celebration and outings with Linenthal, Adams, and Don Carpenter. They also spent time with the Beat crowd, including Lawrence Ferlinghetti and Michael McClure. Mailer liked to ramble alone around the city. During several of these walks, he walked on narrow ledges, testing his nerve, probably in the Telegraph Hill area, as he later remembered. Mailer's hand-eye coordination was poor, and he did not excel at sports such as baseball and basketball. At one point, he bought a pool table in an attempt to develop his skills, practiced hard, but had no aptitude for the game. But he prided himself on his balance, and later was able to walk the catenary of a thick hawser (aided by a balance pole) on the decks of his various homes in Provincetown and his Brooklyn apartment. When he awoke in the morning in San Francisco, he knew, as he later recalled, that he would feel a compulsion to walk on narrow ledges. He drew on these daily tests of balance for his description of Rojack's harrowing minutes on the parapet of a penthouse balcony atop the Waldorf Towers.

After two weeks they got back on the road, driving to Arkansas, and then on to Columbus, Georgia, where they visited for two days with Beverly's mother and stepfather, Brownie. In a letter to Fig, Mailer described him as "an ex-Southern master-sergeant, lick lips, blue lightning farter—one of the boys. He's really like so many guys we used to know—the kind that you'd like if you went out on a drunk with him and would dislike if he picked your ass to chew." (They also met Beverly's half-brother, Charlie Brown, who two years later helped Mailer and Provincetown friend Eldred Mowery assemble a model, "Vertical City," out of thousands of Lego blocks.) After a quick stop in Atlanta to meet Beverly's stepmother, "a real crazy Southern-Georgia rich town lady," they returned to New York in late August. With no trace of irony, he told Fig, "It was so nice not to have worries for six weeks."

EXACTLY WHEN HE signed off on the arrangements for the publication of *An American Dream* is uncertain. His agent Scott Meredith was involved in lengthy discussions with Cy Rembar and various publishers while he and Beverly were away. By mid-September the deal was done. Mailer had left much of the bargaining to Meredith, but personally convinced Walter Minton to release him from his Putnam's contract for one book. Mailer also sold the idea of writing the novel as a serial to *Esquire* editor Harold Hayes, who recalled that there was "great interest in the suicidal nature" of Mailer's project. As much of an editorial gambler as Felker (who had moved to the *New York Herald Tribune*), Hayes offered a payment of $20,000. Shortly before or after this, in a forty-eight-hour wheeling-and-dealing session that Mailer said "was much like Hollywood," Meredith sold the hard and soft cover rights to Dial and its paperback subsidiary Dell for what Mailer called "a fantastic advance royalty" of $125,000. "It seems," he wrote to Adeline Naiman, "that I am finally hot again as a property. For the next year I'm in the soup because this novel's got to be fairly good or I'll be ambushed by more crossfire than anybody I can think of in recent years, and indeed will deserve the worst, so I'm off and writing." He had worked against deadlines before, most notably on the weekly *Village Voice* columns and "The Big Bite" in *Esquire*. But now he had agreed to write a novel at the rate of ten to twelve thousand words a month for eight months, "one hundred thousand finished words," as he wrote to Fig. The gamble was the boldest of his life to date.

He had already written the first and most of the second installment of the serial when *The Presidential Papers* came out in early November. It was not reviewed widely or enthusiastically and was all but forgotten in the blur that followed the assassination of the president two weeks later. His plan for writing the serial of the novel, which he pretty much adhered to, was to stay sixty days, or two installments, ahead of *Esquire*'s monthly publication date. The nation was still reeling from the president's death and that of his assassin, Lee Harvey Oswald, when the issue containing the first installment appeared.

The previous issue of *Esquire* (December), contained the last short story Mailer would write, "The Last Night," a science fiction fantasy about the end of the world, and his fourteenth and final "Big Bite" column, in which he announced the serial. "The early installments," he wrote, "will be in print long before I go to work on the later ones. Indeed it is likely I will be working on each installment up to the day Esquire goes to press. It's been a long time since anything of this sort has been tried by an author who takes himself seriously." He distinguished his effort from those of writers—Dreiser, Hemingway, and Fitzgerald—whose serialized novels had been completed before serialization. Dickens and Dostoyevsky were his models, he continued, "novelists of the first rank who put their books together under the exigency of meeting a magazine's publication date each month." He said that "no comparison is intended to Dickens and Dostoevsky," noting that *The Idiot* was written when the Russian was "suffering from epileptic fits, two days past the date he had promised to deliver the manuscript," writing only at night "when his mind could function between each epileptic fit." But the strain Mailer was under, arguably, was somewhat commensurate. When he was only a third of the way done, he wrote to Carpenter that the serial "has me more or less pissing blood." He also called *An American Dream* "one of the more Dostoevskian novels of the last hundred years."

As the following passage from the opening installment in *Esquire* suggests, he intended to use Kennedy, in ways undetermined, in later chapters.

> I met Jack Kennedy, for instance, in 1946. We were both war heroes and were both Freshmen in Congress. Congressman John Fitzgerald Kennedy, Democrat from Massachusetts, and Congressman Stephen Richards Rojack, Democrat from New York. We even spent one night together on a long double date and it promised to be a good night for me. I stole his girl.

The assassination not only smothered the reception of *The Presidential Papers*, it also destroyed whatever plans he had for using Kennedy in the novel. Mailer had intended to set the novel in 1965, but was forced to move Rojack's narration back to an earlier time so that lack of comment on the assassination would not seem intentionally disrespectful. For the novel to be credible, Kennedy had to be president and he had to be alive. Furthermore, because the October 1962 Cuban Missile Crisis was mentioned, and the novel was firmly set late in March, Rojack's retelling of events could take place only in March 1963, approximately nine months before the dark day in Dallas.

But these complications came later. Immediately after the assassination, he seemed ready to abandon the project. He wrote to Mickey Knox on December 17.

> The Kennedy thing hit very hard here. Women were crying in the streets (mainly good-looking women), a lot of middle-aged Negroes looked sad and very worried, and then we all sat around in gloom and watched the television set for the next seventy-two hours [Mailer watched it with Podhoretz]. Altogether it was one of the three events having something profoundly in common: Pearl Harbor Day and the death of Roosevelt being the other two. And the Ruby-Oswald stuff was just too much on top of it. I haven't felt like writing a word about the whole thing, I've been too fucking depressed every which way. The main loss I think was a cultural one. Whether

> he wanted to or not Kennedy was giving a great boost to the arts, not because Jackie Kennedy was inviting Richard Wilbur to the White House, but somehow the lid was off, and now I fear it's going to be clamped on tight again. . . . With Kennedy alive it was a good book, but with him dead, it's just a curiosity, and somehow irritating in tone. I don't even mind the loss of it in a funny way.

He also elaborated on his feelings about Kennedy in a letter to Yamanishi.

> At any rate, I have no desire to write more now because the event is not only deeply depressing but enormous in its ramifications. Kennedy had personal charm—one misses him certainly that way—he was also nothing exceptional as a politician, rather a conventional middle-of-the-road leader of the Democratic Party. What was lost was an intangible good. There was a particular magic or let us say liberty surrounding Kennedy which enabled one to be critical of him in a way that had been impossible in America since the War, and all sorts of subtle but exciting changes were occurring in America's culture.

Mailer said that Kennedy's presidency had affected him personally: "My function has shifted in these few years from some sort of mysterious half-notorious leader of the Beat Generation, a sort of psychic guerilla leader, in fact, to something quite other, a respected if somewhat feared leader of the literary Establishment."

Before Kennedy's rise, he had considered himself a literary outlaw who was pleased to be seen as a contrarian and outsider. But Kennedy's charisma, political ruthlessness, and movie-star looks, not to mention his war hero status and beautiful, artistic wife, galvanized Mailer's imagination and drew him to the power nexus. He wanted a ticket into the new establishment; he wanted to influence it, push it in various adventurous ways; he wanted more energy, more power. He aspired to be the U.S. equivalent of what André Malraux was in de Gaulle's France: minister of culture. But he also wanted to maintain his ties to the demimonde—to Greenwich Village hipsters, Harlem jazz joints, and Provincetown artists. The Kennedy clique seemed to understand his ambitions; one of them told Jeanne Campbell that Mailer was "an intellectual adventurer," a remark Mailer said was accurate, if spiteful. Only such an adventurer, Mailer wrote, would write an open poem to the president, as he had done earlier. His interaction with the Kennedys made him understand the advantages accruing to someone who is both in and out of the game, participant and observer. Within two years of the assassination, Mailer would become the preeminent insider-outsider of American culture. While there were other rival claimants over the next forty years—Gore Vidal, most notably—and periods of partial eclipse, it was a position he never entirely relinquished.

In a 1965 interview, Mailer said it was important to understand Kennedy's nature "because his nature once understood helped to point toward a way of understanding America. So, on a vastly smaller scale, I think some people may be interested in me because something of the same process may be present." After the assassination, he thought and wrote about Kennedy as much as he did Hemingway, returning again and again in works of fiction and nonfiction to the assassination and what might have been. Near the end of his life, he said that no public event in his lifetime had affected him as powerfully. Although he says that a comparison with Kennedy is unfair, he was willing to make it, willing to propose the personality of insider-outsider-left-conservative Norman Mailer as a replacement for the slain president's, and a new key to the deeper meanings of the nation, and would do so for the remainder of the decade. Noting that a comparison was inappropriate, but then making it anyway was one of Mailer's characteristic rhetorical gambits.

In December, he flew to Juárez, Mexico, to finalize his divorce from Jeanne. They disagreed on custody provisions, and Mailer saw their daughter only rarely for the first four or five years of her life, until they came to a new understanding and he saw Kate more regularly, especially in the summer. A few years later, Jeanne recalled her marriage to Mailer: "A holocaust of a love affair in many countries and many rounds of mind," a marriage that produced "a daughter Kate who grows in beauty with hayseed speckling her yellow-green eyes. A bad divorce and a long term of silence, then years of close friendship and some good work together." The collaboration she refers to is his 1968 experimental film, *Maidstone*, in which she played an important role. Mailer's summation: "A remarkable girl, almost as interesting, complex and Machiavellian" as himself. "I was crazy about her," he said, but "our two worlds were pretty far apart."

Matters were much improved with Beverly (whom he called "my Georgia peach") running the household. She developed a warm relationship with Fan, who shared her son's favorite recipes. Beverly and Anne Barry organized Mailer's schedule and visits from the children—Danielle and Betsy came almost every weekend. On December 29, shortly after his divorce was final, he married Beverly, now six months pregnant, in the living room of his Brooklyn Heights apartment. His gloom over Kennedy's death retreated somewhat, and he submitted the fourth installment of the novel on schedule in mid-January 1964. Novel writing on demand was getting interesting, as he wrote to Fig, comparing it to "playing ten-second chess. You have to take the bold choice each time." He was full of metaphors for the effort; perhaps the best was embodied in a story he told Vance Bourjaily.

> Years ago, Theodore Reik was being analyzed by Freud, and as a talented young man he was naturally interested not only in being a superb analyst but a musician, a writer, a lover, a boulevardier, a vigilante, even a mad genius. Freud listened and got angrier and angrier. Finally, he said, "Reik, you want to be a big man? Piss in one spot." So that is what the serial business puts you up to.

The serial may have given Mailer more focus, but writing ten thousand words a month did not completely occupy him. In addition to his college lectures, he wrote a tribute to Kennedy for the *New York Review of Books'* memorial issue; revised his answers to a long interview with Steven Marcus published in *The Paris Review*; engaged in a debate with Yale professor Vincent Scully on modern architecture in *Architectural Forum*; published a short story he had written in 1960, "The Killer," in *Evergreen Review*; and debated Bill Buckley again, this time on David Susskind's television program, *Open End*. At one point, Mailer asked Buckley why he agreed to go on television with him if he disapproved of him. Buckley answered, because "you are a magnetic field in this country." Mailer also flew to Miami to watch a young heavyweight he had met during his Las Vegas trip, Cassius Clay, defeat Sonny Liston for the title, a bout that so intrigued him that he asked Hayes if he could postpone an installment to write about it. Hayes said no, and he went back to work.

The novel's protagonist, Stephen Richards Rojack, a forty-four-year-old Harvard graduate, World War II veteran and New York intellectual, might easily be confused with Norman Kingsley Mailer, who was forty-two when he addressed these similarities in 1965: "Rojack is still considerably different from me—he's more elegant, more witty, more heroic, his physical strength is considerable, and at the same time he is more corrupt than me." Even so, Rojack, who is half Jewish, half WASP, must be considered Mailer's stand-in. The resemblances, Mailer knew, would do the novel no harm. But those between Rojack's wife, Deborah, who has "a huge mass of black hair and striking green eyes," and Jeanne Campbell were another matter, potentially libelous. In the first chapter of the novel, after Rojack strangles Deborah and then pushes her body out the window onto the FDR East River Drive, it is clear that he had brazenly modeled her on his third wife. Both are tall, strong, intelligent, and self-assured women who come from privileged cosmopolitan backgrounds. Like Jeanne, Deborah "could not utter a sentence for giving a tinkle of value to some innocent word," as Rojack says of his wife, although Mailer took the precaution of making Deborah Irish and Italian. There was a more worrisome problem. *Esquire* publisher Arnold Gingrich told Harold Hayes to kill the serial after he read the graphic description of anal intercourse—a first in mainstream American publishing—between Rojack and his wife's German maid, the carnal Ruta. Mailer's description of the "high private pleasure in plugging a Nazi" was based, at least in part, on the five days he had spent with Regina, the German barmaid in 1959. Only after "a pruning job as delicate as any in the annals of magazine editing" by *Esquire*'s fiction editor, Rust Hills, did Gingrich allow the serial to go forward.

Almost every month there was a new problem: Hayes left a chapter in a taxicab (later retrieved); the retrospective plot summaries accompanying the later chapters had errors and imprecisions; the magazine's lawyers peppered Mailer with queries and requests about the explicit sexual descriptions; and monthly copy came in at the last possible minute. He wrote to Harvey Breit on February 11, "I've been down in the mines working on my novel, five installments now done, three to go—mortal terror all around that I will run out of gas." But he didn't, and interest grew as the installments appeared. The magazine's circulation jumped to over 900,000, a record, the first month the serial appeared. To capitalize on the buzz, *Esquire* purchased an ad in *The New York Times* announcing that Dial Press would publish the book in hardcover, Dell would do the paperback, and Warner Brothers would make the movie.

As Beverly came closer to term, Mailer struggled to tie the plot threads together neatly, always difficult for him. He was also distracted by two major cultural events in February 1964: the arrival of the Beatles in America (he approved of their performance on *The Ed Sullivan Show*), and the premiere of Stanley Kubrick's film *Dr. Strangelove, or: How I Learned to Stop Worrying and Love the Bomb*. He wrote to Knox about the latter: "It's the only great movie I know which is great not because it's great as a movie but because it's sociologically great that the thing was made." While he was "banging away now in the pits of the sixth installment," and "feeling wrung out, dull, and smoking too many cigarettes," his first son, Michael Burks, was born on St. Patrick's Day. Mailer reported to his Aunt Moos that the baby "looks more like his mother than like me," and that his ears were "benevolently close to his head." After four daughters, he was enormously pleased.

He was unhappy, however, about the shape of the last half of the novel. He wrote to Knox on April 19 that the fifth, sixth, and seventh installments were "not up to the first four, and I've lost the chance I had to write a really major novel." He continued: "It's been an incredible push because I've had to write figuratively with a locked wrist, since there was no time to explore and follow the kind of incidental bent which two times out of three leads you up a blind alley and then discovers a bigger book within the book." The inclusion of Rojack's intuitions about the cosmic war between good and evil was also weighing on him. When the serial was nearing its close, he told an interviewer of his fears: "A good writer feels he is dealing with secrets about the nature of things, which inspires an almost biological fear." He was referring to the fact that two months before Kennedy's assassination, Mailer had given Deborah's father (and Rojack's antagonist) the middle name Oswald, a spooky circumstance that enhanced his belief in divine and/or demonic meddling. "If psychic coincidences give pleasure to some," he wrote of the coincidence, "I do not know that they give them to me."

In retrospect, it was fortunate that the book was written under deadlines. Mailer was forced to create a novel with an ending that grew organically from what preceded it. Given the wherewithal to wander leisurely through the alleyways of plot possibility, he might have written a novel twice as long but perhaps only half as good. The first seven chapters of *An American Dream* came in at just over 77,000 words, roughly the number desired by *Esquire*. The much foreshadowed climax of the novel, the meeting between Rojack and Kelly, was by now conceived, but Mailer was late in completing it. The presses were literally held waiting for the final pages, which came in at 22,000 words. *Esquire*'s editors were forced to print part of it in six-point type.

Until Mailer wrote *Dream*, his most sensually evocative and lyrical novel, his narrators were not his protagonists (excepting Sam Slovoda in "The Man Who Studied Yoga"). Nor had he invested his heroes with his own deepest beliefs, namely a distrust of pure reason, faith in the authority of the senses, psychic growth achieved by risk taking, courage as the cardinal virtue, anger at the greed and corruption of American life, and fear that fascism might be rooting. Underlying these beliefs was the vision of a heroic but limited God locked in a struggle with a powerful and wily Devil. The fate of the world, perhaps of the universe, hinges on this struggle, one in which humans stood on both sides. Rojack shares these beliefs. A near-alcoholic talk show host and author of a popular book, *The Psychology of the Hangman* (Mailer published a poem, "The Executioner's Song," the month after completing the serial), Rojack, like Mailer, is susceptible to omens and portents. He hears voices, studies the phases of the moon, and waits for either cancer or madness to strike his person.

The operatic plot is easily summarized: Rojack's wife, Deborah, taunts him with her infidelities (he has his share), and attacks his manhood in nasty ways, goading him into a physical attack (which recalls Mailer's assault on Adele) that ends with her strangulation. Rojack then throws her body out of her apartment window ten stories down to the pavement below. He claims that her fall was suicide and the brunt of the story is devoted to his attempts to convince his and her friends and associates, the police, and her father, Barney Oswald Kelly, of his innocence. No one believes him, but the voices he hears and the balm derived from his night in bed with Cherry Melanie, a former jazz singer (modeled on Beverly and Carol Stevens, who would become his fifth wife), plus Kelly's indirect manipulations, keep him from being arrested, but just barely. As he overhears the beating of a black man in another room of the station, the police press him hard, but he is able to sidestep their questions. We learn that Cherry had been Kelly's mistress, and that she also had an affair with an extraordinarily talented African-American jazz vocalist, Shago Martin. He begins to feel the possibility of expiation for his crime, and the end of his moral odyssey. Barry H. Leeds, one of the most perceptive of Mailer critics, says that Rojack moves "from imminent alcoholism, damnation and madness to salvation and sanity. In a modern analogue of *Pilgrim's Progress*, Rojack confronts a series of adversaries, defeating them and the weaknesses in himself that they represent, and in the process absorbing their strengths." Rojack defeats Martin in a fight at Cherry's apartment and carries off his talismanic umbrella as a victory token. She tells him that she is pregnant with his child, and they pledge their love.

The novel shows Mailer at the height of his metaphoric power. The mood of the novel, which takes place over thirty-two hours, is haunted; it swarms with malign and beneficent presences, especially in Kelly's apartment. As Rojack enters the lobby close to midnight, Mrs. Kennedy is about to come down from her Waldorf Towers apartment, further heightening the tense mise-en-scène. As he waits, Rojack imagines that he has

> died and was in the antechamber of hell. I had long had a vision of Hell: not of its details; of its first moment. A giant chandelier of crystal above one's head, red flock on the walls, red carpet, granite pillars (as I proceeded) now a high ceiling, was it gold foil? A floor of white and black, and then a room of blue and green in whose center stood a nineteenth-century clock, eight feet high with a bas relief of faces: Franklin, Jackson, Lincoln, Cleveland, Washington, Grant, Harrison, and Victoria; 1888 the year: in a ring around the clock was a bed of tulips which so looked like plastic I bent to touch and discovered they were real.

This is a description of the actual Waldorf Towers lobby. But, in this as well as in countless other passages in the novel, the reader is uncertain as to which reality is being presented: imagined, remembered, or presently experienced. Subtly shifting states of consciousness, punctuated by the corporal, the sensuous, the bloody, became Mailer's hallmark with *An American Dream*. In December 2005, after reading a portion of the novel, he closed the book, which he was signing for a friend, and said, "I'll never write that well again."

In a conversation in Kelly's bedroom, which resembles a sixteenth-century Italian chapel, replete with a massive gold-framed mirror and a Lucchese bed with "a canopy encrusted in blood-velvet," Kelly, who suggests he may be "a solicitor for the Devil," admits he had been in an incestuous relationship with Deborah since she was fifteen; Rojack confesses that he killed her. They speak a little longer and then Rojack picks up Shago's umbrella, now quivering ominously, and with Kelly following, goes out to the balcony of the thirty-eighth-floor apartment. It is raining with strong gusts, but he knows that he must walk the three-sided parapet of the balcony to propitiate Deborah's spirit. Kelly approves of the test, and Rojack gives him the umbrella before clambering up to the ledge. Sodden with fear, he walks all three sides, and then turns to Kelly, who attempts to push him off with the umbrella. Rojack turns like a bullfighter, seizes the umbrella, jumps down and gives Kelly one fierce retributive whack across the face. Then he heaves the umbrella, its magic expired, over the parapet. He rushes out of the apartment and goes to Cherry's, arriving just in time to see her briefly before she dies, beaten to death by a friend of Shago's, who has also been mistakenly murdered. In the denouement, Rojack drives to Missouri, where he observes the autopsy, and then pushes on to Las Vegas, where he wins $24,000 and pays his debts. Before leaving Vegas, he makes a hallucinated telephone call to Cherry in some chamber of the afterlife. She tells him that Marilyn Monroe sends greetings. Rojack, "something like sane again," leaves the next morning to work out his destiny in Guatemala and Yucatán.

The stir created by the serialization was strong and before Mailer had completed it, Warner Brothers optioned the novel, ultimately paying $200,000 for it. This brought his total income for the novel to $345,000, a tremendous sum at that time. With the last installment completed, he wrote to Knox, "What a murderous fucking installment this last one has been. I'm in pretty good shape, but of course tense as hell, and all burned out from smoking. I feel just the way a wire must feel after a short circuit." In mid-June, he and Beverly left for Provincetown, where he would be joined by all of his children save Kate. Assuming there were no major interruptions, he planned to carefully revise the novel over the summer.

UNTIL THE EARLY 1970s, literary projects dropped into Mailer's lap just in time, all the time. On July 12, after catching up on correspondence and getting the family settled in Provincetown, he flew to San Francisco to cover the GOP convention, on assignment from *Esquire*. He expected that Barry Goldwater, a conservative senator from Arizona, would get the nomination. The right wing of the GOP had grown strong and was ready to wrest control of the party from the old middle-of-the-road gang—retired President Eisenhower, Governor William Scranton of Pennsylvania, Governor George Romney of Michigan, and their ilk. Part of Mailer wanted Goldwater not only to win the nomination, but to defeat the presumptive Democratic candidate, President Johnson, whom he distrusted if not despised. His conjecture was that a Goldwater victory might invigorate the left wing of the Democratic Party. Feeling more confident writing about a convention than he had in 1960, he used the same technique as in the earlier essay: slowly delineate an overarching theme while moving from portrait to portrait of the politicians.

His sketches are acerbic, unforgiving, and hit the mark. Ike, the grand old man of the party, who "usually fought a speech to a draw," comes on like "a cross between a boy and an old retainer." Romney "looked like a handsome version of Boris Karloff, all honesty, big-jawed, soft-eyed, eighty days at sea on a cockeyed passion." Scranton, the favorite of the Eastern Establishment, "a pleasant urbane man, so self-satisfied, so civilized, so reasonable, so innocent of butchers' tubs and spleens and guts." And Goldwater, who won the nomination easily: "Talking in a soft modest voice, he radiated at this moment the skinny boyish sincerity of a fellow who wears glasses but is determined nevertheless to have a good time. Against all odds. It was not unreminiscent of Arthur Miller: that same mixture of vast solemnity and unspoiled boyhood, a sort of shucks and aw shit in the voice."

Mailer was convinced that the nation was in terrible shape, gorging itself on frozen food, sappy television, antibiotics, and cut off from nature by technology and the most insidious of substances, one that was becoming ubiquitous: plastic. He never stopped raging against plastic's lack of any direct organic connection. (In 1981 he had a horrific argument with Norris, his sixth wife, about her purchase of a plastic dishwasher that "smelled like formaldehyde," and said that if it didn't go, he would. It went.) That hardly anyone took him seriously about plastic only enraged him more. The prospect of a Goldwater victory, therefore, made him think, almost hope, that it might produce an underground movement rising against the soft totalitarianism Goldwater's administration might impose. Always disposed to volatilization, Mailer came to this state of happy-warrior-hood at the convention after hearing, day after day, and once at four A.M. in his hotel room, a band of bagpipers, "giving off the barbaric evocation of the Scots, all valor, wrath, firmitude and treachery," a sound that seemed "to pass through all the protective gates in the ear and reach into some nerve where the eschatology is stored." "Acute disease is cure," Mailer had written, and so the idea of a conservative victory was not just exciting, but even necessary, because "like millions of other whites, I had been leading a life which was a trifle too pointless and a trifle full of guilt and my gullet was close to nausea with the needless compromises of an empty liberal center." As he put it in one of his "Big Bite" columns, "If we are ill and yet want to go on, we must put up the ante. If we lose, it does not mean we wished to die." After a decade of being an outsider, he began to think closely about the state of the nation. "One worried," he said, "about it for the first time the way you worried about family or work, a good friend or the future." He would continue to brood, and for a time became Dr. Mailer, diagnostician of America's diseases. Their etiology would be explored in all of his books through 1972.

The finished essay, titled "In the Red Light: A History of the Republican Convention in 1964," went to Harold Hayes for the November *Esquire*. Mailer wrote to his Bellevue friend, Arnold Kemp, still in prison, to say he was pleased with it, and that if Goldwater wasn't so negative about civil rights, he might vote for him. He went on to say he was still working on *An American Dream*, and compared his editing method to adjusting a slack drum, tightening it all around, little by little. You have to do this, he said, "until you can't stand it any more, and then go over it twenty times more. If you're left with nothing by the end of that time, that's probably just as well. There may have been nothing there." André Deutsch hoped to publish the British edition at the same time as the American, and had been pestering him for the final manuscript. Mailer told him he was still tightening the drum and hoped to have it completed by October 15. In the end, he needed until almost the end of the year.

Deutsch was in a dither about Mailer's new agent and his "hard stick-'em-up methods." Meredith had gotten $125,000 up front for *Dream*, which impressed Mailer, especially since before Meredith took over from Rembar, Minton had given him only $50,000, half up front, for a still unwritten novel. Mailer told Deutsch to stop calling Meredith a pirate and recognize that he had good credentials: he was one of the most hated agents in New York. He said he didn't care "to hear about the less agreeable methods of people who work for me, but back them up eventually I must, until they fail to do their job, which is to get me the best publisher and the largest royalty available in every country." Deutsch had already paid $70,000 for the rights to *Dream*, the highest price ever paid in England for the hardcover rights to an American novel, but he would be outbid on later Mailer books.

Twice more before the year ended, Mailer put aside his revisions to *Dream*. Robert Kennedy, formerly his brother's and President Johnson's attorney general, was running in New York against the incumbent Republican senator, Kenneth Keating. His entry in the race came after Johnson had turned aside Kennedy's effort to be named his running mate in the 1964 election. Previously, Mailer had had reservations about Kennedy, but Kennedy's civil rights activism led him to write a piece in *The Village Voice* endorsing him for senator. His logic was this: while both were equally liberal, Keating was dull and "had a face like the plastic dough children play with." Kennedy was an "active principle," he said, who had come "a pilgrim's distance" since his brother's assassination, and "something compassionate, something witty, has come into the face." Kennedy won easily and Mailer became his ardent supporter.

President Johnson incited Mailer's ire more than any politician of the era. He sided with the Kennedy clique in distrusting LBJ, and only grudgingly congratulated him for pushing through the Civil Rights Act. Vietnam was just becoming a major issue—Congress passed the Tonkin Gulf Resolution in August 1964, which led to a military buildup—and Johnson's war policies would soon enrage Mailer, but at the end of 1964 it was the president's prose that riled him. Johnson had written a campaign book, and Mailer agreed to review it. JFK's prose, he wrote, is to LBJ's as Tocqueville's is to Ayn Rand's. "It is even not impossible," he said, "that *My Hope for America* is the worst book ever written by any political leader anywhere." Mailer also disliked Johnson's face, which reminded him of a medieval Italian warlord's, a member of the *condottieri*, with its "hard, greedy, exceptionally intelligent eyes whose cynicism is spiked by a fierce pride, big fleshy (and acquisitive) nose, thin curved mouth." Johnson won the election decisively and got Mailer's vote.

Mailer delivered his revisions of *An American Dream* just before Christmas. Then he began building "a city of the future" out of Lego blocks with Beverly's half-brother, Charlie Brown, and Eldred Mowery, a friend from Provincetown. When completed, it would be a scale model of a fantastical half-mile-high city of fifteen thousand apartments housing sixty thousand people. Mailer was proud of it. In January, "Cities Higher than Mountains" appeared in the Sunday *Times* accompanied by a photo of the assemblage, now called "Vertical City." The project gave him a much needed break from writing. He enjoyed planning Vertical City (which he based on his memory of Mont St. Michel), but given his aversion to plastic, pressing together ten-thousand-plus Legos made him "feel flat and dead." The construction—seven feet by five feet by three feet—stood in a corner of Mailer's Brooklyn apartment for the next forty years. "It was a bitch to dust," Norris often said. It finally began to crumble as the glue they had applied disintegrated. Members of the family and friends kept a few pieces as souvenirs of the structure, a color photo of which graced the cover of his 1966 collection, *Cannibals and Christians*.

MAILER WAS ASKED to help William Burroughs and his publisher, Barney Rosset of Grove Press, who were being prosecuted for obscenity in Boston. On January 12, 1965, along with Allen Ginsberg and poet John Ciardi, he testified to the merits of *Naked Lunch*, specifically about Burroughs's language: "He catches the beauty and, at the same time, the viciousness and the meanness and the excitement, of ordinary talk—the talk of criminals, of soldiers, athletes, junkies. There is a kind of speech, gutter talk, that often has a fine, incisive, dramatic line to it; and Burroughs captures the speech like no other American writer I know." The prosecution won the case, but it was reversed by the Massachusetts Supreme Court, and as Mailer said later, the decision "changed the literary history of America." The banning of books for obscenity in the United States was drawing to an end. Looking back on the decision, Mailer was somewhat nostalgic "for the days of oppression, because in those days you were ready to become a martyr, you had a sense of importance, you could take yourself seriously, and you were fighting the good fight." More than a few times, he humorously fantasized about dying a literary warrior's death, one that would carry his boat to what he called "the golden islands of posthumous investiture."

A POET-PROFESSOR FRIEND, Edmund Skellings, who taught at the University of Alaska, invited Mailer to come for a visit. He replied, somewhat outrageously, that he would come if he could be met by the governor at the airport, address a joint session of the Alaska legislature, and meet with the Democratic Party caucus. The speaker of the Alaska House of Representatives, and later U.S. senator, Mike Gravel, was a friend of Skellings's and an admirer of Mailer, and he arranged for the legislative address and the caucus meeting. Governor William Egan was also willing and invited Mailer to dinner. With all conditions met, Mailer cheerfully agreed to the visit, beginning on April 1. The Alaskans had wanted him to come the previous week, but Mailer's friend José Torres, a light heavyweight boxer from Puerto Rico, was fighting against the champion, Willie Pastrano, at Madison Square Garden. He had been introduced to Torres by Pete Hamill at the Liston-Patterson fight in 1962. They became lifelong friends.

Another invitation came, one that indicated that the literary establishment had changed its views on Mailer. He was asked by the Publishers' Publicity Association to participate in a Manhattan press conference as part of the annual National Book Award events. On March 10, he spoke and answered questions for an hour. The first question concerned Saul Bellow, who the day before had been awarded the National Book Award for his novel *Herzog*. In his acceptance speech, Bellow stated that "our rebels" attribute the low quality of current American literature to "the horrible squareness of our institutions, the debasement of sexual instincts, and the failure of writers to be alienated enough." Not so, he said, adding that it was "evident that polymorphous sexuality and vehement declarations of alienation are not going to produce great works of art." Bellow may still have been smarting over Mailer's comments about him in *Esquire*. In an interview a few months earlier, Bellow had sharply disassociated himself from "the apocalyptic romanticism" of twentieth-century writers who believed "the world is evil, that it must be destroyed and rise again," writers such as D. H. Lawrence. When the interviewer asked his response to Mailer's comment about his timidity, he answered: "I'm sure I'm not a great writer in Norman Mailer's light, but then I don't want to be."

Asked about Bellow's speech, Mailer acknowledged that he was one of the writers (along with Ginsberg and Terry Southern, among others) that Bellow had attacked. "But we moral nihilists," he said, "are responsible for all the real developments in literature. We are the adventurous ones. Conventional morality attacks violence, he said, but better to commit an act of violence against one person than "to curb that impulse and spend 20 years poisoning the lives of everyone around you." Then he turned to Bellow: "I admire the novel 'Herzog' very much. But it is not a book of ideas. There is nothing intellectually new in it. Bellow is mindless. There is depth of feeling in his novel. His humanity gets to you. But his mind is that of a college professor who has read all the good books and absorbed none of them." He concluded by calling Bellow a "hostess of the intellectual canapé table." Mailer's widely quoted remarks understandably poisoned his relations with Bellow.

The publication party for *An American Dream* took place at the Village Vanguard on March 15. The booze was plentiful as were copies of the book with its distinctive dust jacket showing a stylized American flag with an inset photograph of Beverly Bentley, the model for Cherry. James Jones and Irwin Shaw were there, as were Richard Baron, the publisher of Dial Press, and Christopher Lehmann-Haupt, the editor who had worked with Mailer on the novel. Miles Davis also came and began "flirting with Beverly." José Torres saw Mailer getting tense as he watched, and it appeared that he might get into a fight with Davis. Torres was afraid that he might have to step in. "I didn't want to hit Miles Davis," Torres recalled, "but I didn't want him to punch out Norman first. Luckily, Davis just walked away."

Mailer was surly. Lehmann-Haupt remembered that he was "fairly drunk and moody and deep in some funk. I've only seen him that one time in that degree of withdrawn moodiness." Earlier, he had tried to spar with James Jones, and when Lehmann-Haupt stopped at his table to say goodbye, he threw or spilled his drink when Lehmann-Haupt put out his hand. John Aldridge also attended and recalled that Mailer "was absolutely catatonic." As he was leaving, he went up to Mailer, "and he looked as though he was completely out on his feet. He was standing, but propped up against the wall," he said. "I think he was simply plastered." But the next day when he visited Mailer in Brooklyn, he looked no worse for wear. The jazz musicians who played at the party were at the apartment, Beverly was there, and Anne Barry, whom Aldridge remembered as "a small round girl with chubby cheeks and huge horn-rimmed glasses. There were also two black maids in white uniforms. It seemed distinctly a ménage and very much a Mailer ménage—crowded, busy, vital." Mailer had put on weight, twenty pounds, Aldridge estimated, and was sharp and alert. Styron's name came up, and Mailer noted that Styron had been invited to the White House by both Kennedy and Johnson; neither had invited him. He said that Styron's social ambitions might prevent him from being a great writer. He was aware, certainly, that he faced the same problem, but to him divided loyalties were catnip, irresistible.

After lunch, Mailer walked Aldridge to his Brooklyn hotel, "wearing an old trench coat and looking like Harpo Marx. He shook my hand with real warmth and feeling, as if we had some affinity. I felt we had and felt sad to say good-bye to him. He's a very lovable and remarkable man, a genuine creative force, undoubtedly the very best we have." Aldridge's review of *Dream* appeared in *Life* a few days later. Mailer liked it well enough to pay for the reprinting of the heart of it in the same issue of *PR* containing Elizabeth Hardwick's negative review. *PR*'s editor, William Phillips, sent the review to him before publication, and after reading it, Mailer sent him the excerpt from Aldridge's review and this statement:

> *An American Dream* has received the best and worst reviews of any book I've written. Now it is rumored that Elizabeth Hardwick has written a bad review for *Partisan.* I hasten to shudder. She is such a good writer. I also hasten to furnish for her company a review by John Aldridge which appeared in *Life.* I cannot pretend I was displeased to see it there, but I'm nearly as pleased to see it here even if I have to pay for the pleasure.

As Mailer noted, the division of opinion on the novel was nearly absolute. There were few mixed reviews. In addition to Hardwick, who called it "a fantasy of vengeful murder, callous copulations and an assortment of dull cruelties," leading critics and literary figures such as

Granville Hicks, Philip Rahv, Roger Shattuck, Stanley Edgar Hyman, and Tom Wolfe said the novel was a conspicuous failure. On the other side of the chasm, in addition to Aldridge, who called it "a religious book" that "dramatizes the various ways a man may sin in order to be saved, consort with Satan in order to attain to God," was a cadre of enthusiasts: Leo Bersani, Richard Rhodes, Joan Didion, Paul Pickrel, and Richard Poirier, a young academic who would become one of Mailer's most discerning critics.

Perhaps the most significant thing about the book's reception is that his erstwhile admirers at *Partisan Review, The New York Review of Books*, and *The Village Voice* were negative, while stuffy *Harper's*, conservative *National Review*, flag-waving *Chicago Tribune*, and, most surprising of all, Henry Luce's *Life*, applauded the novel, evidence of the new openness to the outrageous in the country. Even *Time* had a few good words (*Newsweek* called it "noxious"). William Buckley sent Mailer an advance copy of the review of Joan Didion, then a young editor at *Vogue*. He added a note: "Congratulations on a nearly near-perfect novel." Didion thought it even better, "a novel in many ways as good as *The Deer Park*, and *The Deer Park* is in many ways a perfect novel." As sensitive to social fragmentation as Mailer, she thought the novel caught the mood of the country, which was going through the same kind of change that it had in the 1920s. *Dream* is "the only serious New York novel since *The Great Gatsby*," she said, adding that Mailer and Fitzgerald shared several things: "The notoriety, the devastating celebrity which is probably in the end as nourishing as it is destructive. The immense technical skill, the passion for realizing the gift. The deep romanticism. And perhaps above all the unfashionableness, the final refusal to sail with the prevailing winds." Mailer wrote to Buckley that it was the "nicest" review he had received. "What a marvelous girl Joan Didion must be." They met soon after and became friendly. In the 1980s, she and her husband, John Gregory Dunne, wrote a screenplay based on *The Deer Park*, but it was never produced.

Mailer himself was, not uncharacteristically, two-headed about the novel. In a letter to Diana Trilling, he said it was either "an extraordinary piece of crap," or "the first novel to come along since The Sun Also Rises which has anything really new in it." He was planning to visit her and Lionel, who was teaching at Oxford for a semester, when he went to England, and had begun anticipating the British reaction to

An American Dream. He was secretly enjoying the argument over the novel's merits, he said, "because no vice of mine could be greater than my desire to create a sensation and be forever talked about. Sometimes I wonder, beloved, if I am the ghost of some long-dead London beauty. Well, well I expect the British will give me a good whipping with the thinnest strings of leather for the outrages I've committed in the name of literature."

The novel sold quite well in the United States and spent several weeks on the *New York Times* bestseller list, reaching number eight in late April. It was his first bestseller (and first novel) in ten years. At this moment in mid-1965, as the country was sliding into carnival and revolt, Mailer's situation can perhaps best be summed up by the title of Aldridge's review—"The Big Comeback of Norman Mailer"—which ended by saying that *Dream* "may well represent the first significant step the current American novel has taken into fresh territories of the imagination." The country was undergoing profound change and Mailer was poised to become its chief chronicler and interpreter. Over the next decade, he would write sixteen books, create three experimental films, produce an off-Broadway play, and in 1969, before appearing on the cover of *Life*, would run for (and lose) the Democratic nomination for mayor of New York City. Five consecutive books during this period, beginning with *The Armies of the Night*, would be nominated for the National Book Award. *Armies* won it, and also a Pulitzer. This would be the most productive, celebrated, and accomplished period of his life.

EIGHT
THIRD PERSON PERSONAL: *ARMIES* AND AFTER

Norman Mailer, professional writer and amateur boxer, climbed in the ring to congratulate José Torres, professional boxer and amateur writer, a moment after he defeated Willie Pastrano for the light heavyweight championship of the world at Madison Square Garden, March 30, 1965. Mailer was as jubilant as Torres. He would soon trade writing lessons for boxing instruction from Torres, the first Latin American to win this championship, and a heroic figure among Puerto Ricans. When financing for the fight seemed in doubt, Mailer had offered to lend him money to guarantee it, a considerable sum, but ultimately the original backers came through. The gesture endeared him to Torres. After the bout, there was a victory party at 142 Columbia Heights. Harry G., Mailer's Bellevue friend, was the bartender for the large crowd, which included Gay Talese and Pete Hamill—both good friends of Torres's—and also Truman Capote and James Baldwin. Barney was there—but not Fan—and enjoyed himself thoroughly as he always did at his son's parties. Torres, in a tuxedo, arrived late with his wife, Ramona, and Mailer "greeted the new champ in the lambency of a triumphant party, and they embraced like two new-born orphans," as another writer present, Brock Brower, recalled. A day later, Mailer flew to Alaska for his five-day visit.

Mailer received enthusiastic applause for his off-the-cuff speech to a joint session of the Alaska legislature in Juneau. Then he flew to Anchorage, where he appeared on local television with Senator Gravel and the two professors who hosted his visit, Edmund Skellings and Donald Kaufmann. At a reception in a downtown hotel, locals came to meet Mailer. As Kaufmann recalled, they glared at Mailer and said things like "Where's that tough guy?" and "Where's that wife-knifer?" At one point, he got into a fight, but security personnel broke it up. Early the next day, he and the two professors flew on a small plane to Fairbanks, the second largest city.

When they arrived, Mailer took a breath of the crystalline air of the city and was ecstatic. "I can breathe here. You can see for miles with clear vision," he said. Ralph Ellison met them at the university, and for the next three days the two writers met with students and addressed audiences assembled for a festival of the arts. As he usually did, Mailer threw himself into meetings with students. He nicknamed the state "God's Attic," and said it had an extraordinary characteristic: "The future of this state is totally unknown. But it is an unknown in extremes, for the end result will be one of two opposites, the best or the worst." He was aware that the hawkish state was generally in favor of the Vietnam War, and that Fairbanks was Alaska's "Sin City," where military personnel came on R&R. He also knew that he was close to the magnetic North Pole, especially after he saw a display of the aurora borealis. In words that anticipated his next novel, he told the university audience: "All the messages of North America go up to the Brooks Range. That land above the circle, man, is the land of icy wilderness and the lost peaks and the unseen deeps and spires, the crystal receiver of the continent." On the return trip to Anchorage, Mailer asked the pilot of the small plane if he could buzz the top of Mount McKinley. The Indians call it Denali, "The Big One." The pilot agreed and told them the altitude would require them to breathe oxygen through small mouth inhalers. "For twenty long minutes," Kaufmann wrote, the pilot "made low passes around the peak, and with each pass, buzz, or mind-skimming on Denali's top, I looked down and wondered what Mailer was imagining or seeing as he sucked oxygen." Nearsighted and vain about wearing glasses, Mailer nevertheless put on a pair for a better look. "I lost myself," Kaufmann wrote, "in simultaneous images of Papa Hemingway peering down on Kilimanjaro, seeing a frozen leopard, and Mailer (on Alaskan oxygen plus magic) peering down on Denali." Would Mailer have written his novel about Alaska, *Why Are We in Vietnam?,* without these loops around the highest point (20,320 feet) on the continent? Kaufmann, with some justice, thinks not.

Upon his return, he wrote to Diana Trilling to nail down the dates of his and Beverly's April 28 visit to Oxford. She suggested that they dine in the Oxford faculty dining room, but Mailer had a different idea.

> Now what I'd like ideally is a dinner for eight at your house and then perhaps a few more people in afterward. One can't possibly get to talk to sixteen or twenty people at dinner by any method known to man, and the Senior Common Room, while appealing to the novelist in me, and very suitable and exciting if it should come to pass promises still less in the way of a delight than dinner for eight in that charming small house you seem to possess. Surely even at Oxford people have been known to drop in after dinner. Isn't that remotely possible.

Trilling wrote to Mailer that the dinner was a great success. Her guests "adored" Mailer and "celebrated you both most shamelessly."

Dinner parties for Mailer were, ideally, a happy combination of pleasure and diplomacy, good food, plenty of drink, laughter, gossip, debate, flirtation, and the exchange of intelligence. He was a careful social planner and personally assembled his guest lists and seating plans. Lunch and dinner guests were sometimes struck by the semiformal arrangements and the solicitous manner of their host. Steven Marcus remembers Mailer preparing and serving lunch in Brooklyn "in what must be called a lordly fashion," with the host conducting himself "without affectation as a kind of secular prince." He drew his guests out in conversation, and was ever eager to hear about their roots, passions, opinions on the events of the day, and the occasional glimpse of an Achilles' heel. Everyone was expected to contribute. In later years, he sat at the head of the table with a woman on either side, often newcomers, while Norris sat at the opposite end with their male partners. He also made it a point, even at large, loud, and crowded parties to try to speak with each guest for a few minutes. His manners were "exquisite," Marcus said.

Family dinners were a bit different. Peter Alson (Barbara's son) recalled his self-consciousness as an adolescent at Uncle Norman's table.

> Being around Norman exacerbated the intensity of the feeling, because he was so fucking brilliant himself that it was impossible to try and share the stage with him. And there's no question that there was a certain amount of theater in those dinners, an aspect of performance art. And of course Norman was always the red-hot center; he dominated in a way that's almost impossible to describe except that it was both incredibly fun but at the same time scary and in-

> timidating, especially if you actually dared to take part. There were two things that characterized him: he always listened very intently when someone else spoke, but he also had an extremely short attention span. If you didn't grab him in the first few sentences you were done. I remember a few times when I started to say something, and ended up trailing off pathetically because I could see that I hadn't grabbed him.

His uncle liked to be provocative, Alson said, but you "could usually see the twinkle in his eye." He enjoyed verbal sparring, and "it could be very tough." But Alson always looked forward to the family dinners "because I knew, *knew*, I was going to be dazzled in the best possible way. I was going to learn things." For many people, a family dinner is something to be endured, he said. "In our family it was something to look forward to with glee and excitement."

Upon his return from England, Mailer flew to California, because he had agreed to speak at a teach-in at Berkeley, part of "Vietnam Days," May 21–22. The event ran for thirty-six hours with an aggregate live audience of thirty thousand, and was also broadcast on radio station KPFA. There were fifty speakers and entertainers, mainly antiwar, although not because the organizers failed to invite administration officials. The State Department and the South Vietnamese embassy declined invitations, as did pro-war members of the Berkeley faculty. Old Left figures were invited, but they posed so many restrictions—X wouldn't come if Y was there, So-and-So didn't like the setup, etc.—that they were excluded. The New Left had replaced the Old. Mailer told Yamanishi it was "the largest audience" he had ever addressed, approximately 10,000.

On May 21, Mailer began by noting that the citizenry's "buried unvoiced faith that the nature of America was finally good, and not evil" had over the past months "taken a pistol whipping." The cause: the most advanced nation in the world was "shedding the blood and burning the flesh of Asian peasants it has never seen." This was being done, officially, to keep the nations of the Far East from falling one after another—the Domino Theory—under the communist yoke. The communists could only flounder in the nations they conquered, he argued. The real reason for the Vietnam War, he continued, was that the president needed to get the country's mind off the civil rights movement at home. His fear, he said, is that this "bully with an Air Force" was "close to insanity" brought on by "his need for action." And so, he said, we stand at a crossroads: "Is this country extraordinary or accursed?" He ended his one-hour speech by urging everyone to attach photos and drawings of Johnson's face on every surface, on walls and phone booths and billboards. "You, Lyndon Johnson, will see those pictures everywhere upside down, four inches high and forty feet high; you, Lyndon Baines Johnson, will be coming up for air everywhere upside down. Everywhere, upside down. Everywhere. Everywhere." *Realist* editor Paul Krassner published the speech in the June issue with an upside-down photo of the president on the cover. Mailer wrote to Yamanishi after the teach-in and said that for the first time in his life he had received "a standing ovation which went on for many minutes." It was most welcome, he said, because that at this stage of his career he was caught between "counter-waves," of approval and disapproval, and "I am being bounced like a cork at the confluence."

FIG AND ECEY and their children joined the Mailers in Provincetown that summer. Barbara, now divorced from Larry Alson, joined them. Her new boyfriend, Al Wasserman, a documentary filmmaker (they married in 1968), was also there. Mailer had hoped to do some new writing, but he was mainly enjoying the summer and starting to put together a new collection, consisting mainly of material written after *The Presidential Papers*. And he was distracted by two of his passions: boxing and protesting the war. In mid-July, before two thousand at Harvard's Sanders Theatre, he gave the same speech he had at Berkeley. Martin Peretz, the Harvard instructor who chaired the teach-in, said the crowd was more than twice as large as the turnout for McGeorge Bundy, President Johnson's national security advisor. Mailer also produced an entirely new antiwar essay for *PR*, where it appeared with those of thirteen other intellectuals, including Irving Howe, Dwight Macdonald, and Susan Sontag. He began the essay by mocking the moderation of the editors: "Three cheers, lads. Your words read like they were written in milk and milk of magnesia. Still your committee didn't close shop until close after this extraordinary remark: 'The time has come for new thinking.' Cha cha cha." Mailer was all for pouring oil on the fires of antiwar protest, and was now the unappointed spokesman for The Family in this regard.

At the end of July, Mailer made a quick trip to San Juan to see Torres successfully defend his light heavyweight title against a strong contender, Tom McNeely. Muhammad Ali fought in an exhibition match before the main event, and the next day Mailer arm wrestled with him on the balcony of the San Jerónimo Hilton. The photo of the mock contest, with Mailer smiling and Ali appearing to strain mightily, has been reprinted endlessly. Henceforth, Mailer would be identified with Ali, even more so than with Torres. Mailer encouraged the connection and while in San Juan called himself Ali's "intellectual precursor."

Also that summer, Mailer was interviewed several times by Brock Brower, a regular contributor to *Esquire*, who was writing a profile of Mailer for *Life*. He also interviewed Beverly, Mailer's parents and sister, and a number of his friends. Mailer was uneasy about the piece, and wondered if *Life* would actually publish it. If it didn't, he told Brower, "We would each become quietly famous as a result, and quiet fame is always, repeat always, superior to public renown. How else account for the happy progress of John Updike." On September 24, *Life* published "In This Corner, Norman Mailer, Never the Champion, Always the Challenger." It is now hard to imagine an American writer receiving this kind of attention—Oprah Winfrey notwithstanding—and, with the exception of Hemingway, it was rare enough at the time. William Buckley was impressed enough to devote his *National Review* column to Brower's piece, stating that it was "final confirmation" of Mailer's status. "He is probably," Buckley said, "the single best-known living American writer." Two things make him interesting, he said. First, "he makes the most beautiful metaphors in the business," and second, "he represents present-day America. He expresses their feelings that America today is shivering in desolation and hopelessness, is looking for her identity after a period of self-alienation." Although Buckley said he would pay "a week's wages" to avoid listening to anyone who spoke "more predictable nonsense" than Mailer on foreign policy, he nevertheless believed him to be "in his own fashion, a conservative." He based this judgment on Mailer's disdain for big government and liberal ideology. Buckley concluded by noting that there was a good deal of hope in Mailer's "turbulent emotions" although he had scant regard for "the emunctory noises of psychic or physical human excesses" in his novels.

Mailer responded immediately, "What the hell does emunctory mean?" and then turning to Buckley's comment about a week's wages:

"Sailor Bill, I come close to loving you here. When the hell did you ever earn a week's wages, you bleeding plutocrat." Buckley, who was independently wealthy, was then running for mayor of New York on the Conservative Party ticket, and Mailer said he'd consider voting for his old debating partner if he wasn't such "a hopeless ass on foreign policy." Buckley wasn't given much of a chance, but "his flair for arch phrasemaking" helped enliven what would have been a dull race for a position that had belonged to Democrats for decades. Asked what he would do if he won, Buckley said, "Demand a recount." His quixotic campaign rekindled Mailer's own desire to be mayor. But Mailer was supporting Republican John Lindsay over both Buckley and the Democratic candidate, Abe Beame.

A week before the election, Mailer's article extolling Lindsay and chiding Buckley appeared on the front page of *The Village Voice*. Buckley is "majestically unsuited" for the position "since it is possible Old Bill has never been in a subway in his life." But he was also "majestically suited for spoiling Lindsay's campaign. Buckley's personality is the highest Camp we are ever going to find in a mayoralty. No other actor on earth can project simultaneous hints that he is in the act of playing Commodore of the Yacht Club, Joseph Goebbels, Robert Mitchum, Maverick, Savonarola, the nice prep-school kid next door, and the snows of yesteryear." Mailer was correct about Buckley's strength. He drew 13 percent of the vote and is given credit by many political observers for nudging Lindsay into a victory over Beame. The two men relished opportunities to tweak each other for perceived errors and vanities. A few years later, Buckley sent a copy of a collection of his columns to Mailer, but did not inscribe it. Knowing that Mailer would look up his name in the index, Buckley wrote next to it, "Hi Norman."

Another marker of Mailer's stature at the end of 1965 came in a poll conducted by the *New York Herald Tribune Book Week*. Richard Kluger, the editor, had written to Mailer and two hundred other leading literary figures, asking them to fill out a form noting the most important works of fiction by Americans in the twenty years after World War II. In his letter, Kluger said that President Johnson "was genuinely pissed off by your piece on him for us," referring to Mailer's review of Johnson's *My Hope for America*. Douglass Cater, the president's special assistant, called *Book Week* and "bawled the hell" out of a staff member for publishing the review two days before the presidential election. "Lady Bird was particularly pissed," Kluger said. Mailer had again gained the attention of a sitting president and his wife.

When the results of the poll, based on the comments of 117 respondents, were published, Mailer was one of the most mentioned writers, ahead of Hemingway, Flannery O'Connor, Styron and Updike, but behind Bellow, Nabokov, Salinger, and Ellison. Kluger sent Mailer the results before publication, and he wrote back to say that there were no surprises. "Just think when Time magazine gets a hold of all this, just think when they start making All-Star teams out of us, just think when they start having mass polls, just think of how James Jones feels to come in behind John Updike, just think how fat Saul's ass is now (fat as his head) just think of all the needless enemies Ellison has made with no desire at all. You are a warlock, Richard."

THE MAILERS REMAINED in Provincetown until the beginning of October. Beverly learned she was pregnant several weeks before they returned to Brooklyn. Mailer was calling his new miscellany *Cannibals and Christians*, his names for two mutant forces in contemporary life arising from the political right and left, respectively. The former stretch from the Republican Party to "the ghosts of the Nazis," he wrote, and the left covers a spectrum from LBJ to Mao Tse-tung. Mailer's dualisms are rarely simple and invariably contain vigorous tinctures of their opposite, "the minority within," to borrow the astute phrase of critic Richard Poirier. A number of reviewers had difficulty understanding the Cannibal-Christian opposition. But, as Poirier noted, the first key to understanding Mailer's mind (and his life) is to realize that he "is quite unable to imagine anything except in oppositions, unable even to imagine one side of the opposition without proposing that it has yet another opposition within itself" that needs to be discovered and illumined. The collection examines Cannibals and Christians, these "two huge types" and the historical whirlpools from whence, like sea monsters, they have emerged. It contains Mailer's latest political and Vietnam pieces, his book reviews and literary criticism, three long self-interviews (two of them reprinted from *Presidential Papers*), and fifty-four poems. The only fictional pieces he could find to include were two previously published short stories.

He was however working on a piece of fiction begun in 1962, perhaps earlier, and then set aside. Known initially as "The Fisher Novel," and then "The Book of the First-Born," it was completely separate from the long-delayed big novel, and like Laurence Sterne's *Tristram Shandy*, begins with the protagonist Stephen Merrill in utero. Over the next decade, he would occasionally read "First-Born" aloud to friends and family, who found its half-stately, half-mock-heroic descriptions of Merrill's earliest days—his breech birth delivery ("the contractions of birth came with the panic of convicts who discovered their dynamite is not sufficient to blow the doors"), his circumcision ("an animal wounded wantonly"), and his breast feeding ("the infant's mouth flew like a hawk to the nipple")—to be riveting. Barbara remembered her brother reading it to her in Provincetown during the summer of 1963; Carol Stevens recalled him reading it to her in the early 1970s. Mailer signed a contract with Walter Minton for the novel and received an advance, but never got beyond eighty pages.

Merrill is born on Mailer's natal day. His head is wrenched by the forceps of Dr. Blucher (much as Tristram Shandy's nose is injured by those of Dr. Slop), although it recovers its shape nicely. He has a big head and will eventually wear a size 7⅜ hat (Mailer's size). Merrill also has Mailer's large red ears. His parents, Jenny (née Fisher) and Archibald "Archie" Merrill (born Mirilovicz), are Jews whose families emigrated to the United States from Lithuania, Archie's via South Africa. Their portraits instantly call to mind Fan and Barney. Jenny "a woman with the courage of a lioness and the innocence in 1923 of a nineteenth century heroine," goes into the hospital with little knowledge of the difficulties of childbirth. She resembled, he wrote, "those healthy women with large pleasant features one sees in photographs put out by the offices of propaganda for Soviet womanhood, strong, direct, free of perversion and the imagination for it."

Archie has Barney's barrel chest, spats, and silver-rimmed eyeglasses; they both look a bit like F. Scott Fitzgerald, "except that Archie's mouth was narrower, his nose was shorter, he looked even more like a Goy than Scott (which is one of the reasons—let us not make Jenny too much of a heroine—that she had been drawn to him) and indeed Archie's speech was English, a touch fraudulent, and stuffy as phumpherdom." Called by his future father-in-law "the strangest Jew I've ever seen," Archie has aspirations for his unborn child (he senses it will be a male), and while he doesn't pray much, his dreams "searched high places."

Jenny, the daughter of a rabbi, prayed to Solomon ("in order that her child take its place among the brightest who ever lived"), King David, the Bal Shem Tov, Abraham Lincoln, Thomas Jefferson, and to England's only Jewish prime minister, Benjamin Disraeli. The narrator explains that the high hopes of mother and father are not just matters to be inculcated as the child grows under their tutelage, no, "the contract was already in his flesh as he was being conceived." Jenny, sentenced to be "a duchess in her family and a small little woman in the world," produced an egg that sought to incorporate "qualities in herself a little opposite to herself." She did not love herself, and "so she wanted a warrior," a son who would "go to places she had never gone and he would change life rather than be shaped by it." This is fiction, and the novelist has license to speculate on the concerted powers of will and aspiration transforming and uniting sperm and egg, but Mailer's personal beliefs, in fact, varied little from his narrator's. When mind, body, and spirit were in special accord—not balance, but a mystical configuration—then remarkable children could be conceived, or as he put it a few years later, "Good fucks make good babies." This is the crudest distillation of his long essay on gender, sexuality, and feminism, *The Prisoner of Sex*, published in 1971. "The Book of the First-Born" prefigures the polemical essay.

As late as the fall of 1974 Mailer was fiddling with this fragment (and he spoke of reviving it through the early 1980s), but always stalled. Besides a need for family history, that he never obtained to his satisfaction, Mailer gave two additional reasons for not continuing with "First-Born," which he described in 1992 as "the saga of the Mailer family back in Russia with my grandfather as I imagined him." The first is that after he had read the work of Isaac Bashevis Singer, the Nobel Prize–winning writer whose stories of life in the shtetls of Poland are depicted with Chekhovian finesse, he thought, "Oh Lord, there is absolutely no need for my book." He gave a second reason in a 2006 interview, where he explained that he intended that "First-Born" would be stored on the computers of a fictional Noah's Ark spaceship that leaves earth sometime in the distant future. The information that the ship's eighty survivors have about human history before its destruction in a nuclear holocaust (he planned to use his short story "The Last Night" to depict the end of the world) is fragmentary. The chief source for the post–World War II world, he explained, was the biography of "a writer of the period in the second half of the 20th century named

Norman Mailer." The heat of the third novel in the trilogy was going to be the story of Merrill-Mailer as told in "First-Born." "The scheme was wonderful! The architectonics were exquisite," he said. Using his American life as an exemplum, a repository of essential cultural memory for unborn generations voyaging to the stars, aligned perfectly with his deepest ambitions. But he was forced to abandon the idea not because he feared sliding into the sloughs of hubris—this troubled him not—but because mastering the scientific-technological physics of spaceships and space travel needed to make the novel credible was beyond him. "My brain power had passed the point where I could retain that kind of information and digest it," he said.

Yamanishi wrote in December to ask if he still planned to use his 1962 story, "Truth and Being, Nothing and Time: A Broken Fragment from a Long Novel," as part of the big novel. Mailer responded by saying that "so many years have gone by, and I have changed so much, that I think the long novel will never be written in its original form." After ten years of stunted efforts, Mailer had finally given up on the narrative adventures of Eitel and Elena, Sergius and Denise, Dr. Sandy Joyce and Marion Faye. Some of these characters would appear in the dramatic version of *The Deer Park* that would be staged in 1967, but nowhere else. The big novel was dead. At least this one.

WITH MAILER'S BLESSING, his friend Bob Lucid had organized an event at the 1965 Chicago conference of the Modern Language Association, and convinced Ralph Ellison and John Cheever to join Mailer in addressing a session entitled "The Modern American Writer and the Cultural Experience." An overflow audience of approximately two thousand filled the Red Lacquer Room of the Palmer House to hear the three novelists speak. Cheever led off and spoke against Podhoretz's idea of the novel as documentary, and also lauded the powers of unfettered imagination. Ellison, speaking without notes, castigated sociologists for obscuring the painful realities of urban life with statistics, and invoked the alienated lives of Harlem. Richard Stern, a friend from the University of Chicago, gave the following summary of Mailer's talk.

> Mailer, in a fine blue suit, vest lapped in black silk, took the microphone like a bulldog and in a voice which gripped every throat in

> the room, read a corrosive, brilliant, hit-and-run analysis of the failure of American novelists to keep up with a whirling country, their division into opposed camps of those who fed titillating pap to the genteel and those, like Dreiser, who pointed American Julien Sorels to the doors of power (though *his* clumsiness could not open them). Down the road were "the metaphorical novelists," Hemingway and Faulkner, one of whom described the paw, the other the dreams of the social beast.

One reason that American writers had been unable to keep pace, Mailer argued, was that American culture changed ten times faster than other cultures, "a phenomenon never before described." The country, he said, grew "like a weed and a monster and a beauty and a pig. And the task of explaining America was taken over by Luce magazines." America had not produced a twentieth-century writer who could "clarify a nation's vision of itself as Tolstoy had done perhaps with *War and Peace* or *Anna Karenina.*" Mailer ended his talk about the failings of the nation's current novelists by saying that the communication "of the deepest and most unrecoverable human experience must yet take place if we are to survive." Although he didn't say so, it was the job he wanted, as must have been obvious to the audience. In this grand setting, a month before his forty-third birthday, Mailer, full of beans, and wearing his blue pinstripe banker's suit (now his public uniform), described the idiosyncratic strengths and weaknesses of novelists as dissimilar as Henry James, Theodore Dreiser, Edith Wharton, Elinor Wylie, Bellow, Capote, James Jones, and Terry Southern, noting the precise location of each in a dynamic artistic constellation of his own creation. Mailer's speeches were not always successful, but Stern said that for this speech the academics "thundered applause," their thirst for affirmation of literature's noble mission "slaked by a master." It was Mailer's second major speech of the year and the professors responded to him as enthusiastically as had Berkeley students. When Mailer first began making public speeches, he had tried to make his audiences itch; now he was making them cheer.

He stayed close to home in the first months of 1966. Beverly was due in early March. He worked on *Cannibals and Christians*, which he hoped would be published in June, and appeared at several antiwar events in Manhattan. As protests against the war increased, President Johnson in February authorized Operation Rolling Thunder, a devastating B-52 bombing campaign against North Vietnamese targets. The expansion incited the protesters, now joined by returning Vietnam vets. That same month Mailer spoke at the Poetry Center at the 92nd Street Y with Howe, Podhoretz, and Columbia's Steven Marcus; a week later he took part in a read-in at Town Hall in Manhattan with twenty-eight other writers and performers, including Hellman, Kazin, Sontag, and Lowell. Mailer and Lowell enjoyed each other's company and began discussing the possibility of traveling to Japan in the summer to speak against the war, and the ominous possibility that the United States would enter into a nuclear war with China. He wrote to Yamanishi to tell him of the possible visit, and also to inform him that he might write a nonfiction book "to explain the country to itself." He said, "America will soon divide, an underground will form, and there must be a few works whose existence will help keep alive some morale in that underground." He finished with some good news: "We had a son last week, whom we named Stephen McLeod (yes, after the characters in An American Dream and Barbary Shore) and he's a handsome boy with calm features and a deep nature, I suspect. Beverly is fine." Now he was the father of six, and his expenses were mushrooming.

Never much of a financial planner, Mailer knew nevertheless that he could not shoulder his obligations on royalties from his earlier work and the relatively small amounts he received for magazine work and college speaking gigs. He needed to produce new work. When he was asked to write an essay for a volume on the American dream, he declined, saying that his load made him feel like "a 19th century novelist most of the time, Dickens, dare I say it, Balzac, Dostoevsky, you know." Despite his commitments, in April he bought a waterfront house at 565 Commercial Street in P-town, next to the one where John Dos Passos had lived for over two decades. Before leaving the city from Provincetown in early May 1966 to take possession, he wrote to Eldridge Cleaver, who was in prison for rape and assault. Cleaver was seeking parole, and Mailer wrote a testimonial to his talent. Later that year, Cleaver, who later became a leader of the Black Panther Party, was released. Writing in *Ramparts* while still imprisoned, Cleaver praised Mailer's essay "The White Negro" for being "prophetic and penetrating in its understanding of the psychology involved in the accelerating confrontation of black and white in America."

ONCE IN PROVINCETOWN, Mailer reconsidered the dramatic version of *The Deer Park*. Beverly was involved in a small theater group there, and they began discussing the idea of presenting the play to a summer audience. He began revising, and it took on a new structure. At the same time, he was thinking about writing a short novel for Walter Minton. He had parted company with Putnam's but still owed them a book, having accepted, and spent, an advance. He began to think about his trip the previous year to Alaska, and came up with a tentative plan. For several years, he had mulled over a story about a group of violent bikers and their women living in the scrub oak thickets of Provincetown's dunes. The novel was "so odd and so horrible" that he kept putting it off.

> I was, as I say, in fear of the book. I loved Provincetown and did not think it was a good way to write about it. The town is so naturally spooky in mid-winter and provides such a sense of omens waiting to be magnetized into lines of force that the novel in my mind seemed more of a magical object than a fiction, a black magic. Nonetheless, I began the book in the spring of '66. It attracted me too much not to begin. Yet because I could not thrust Provincetown into such literary horrors without preparation, I thought I would start with a chapter about hunting bear in Alaska. A prelude.

His plan had been to send "two tough rich boys"—Texans, based on memories of the men he served with in the 112th Cavalry—the father of one boy and a couple of the father's cronies to Alaska to hunt, and then transfer the action to Provincetown. But what was to be a few introductory chapters turned into a complete novel about the savage slaughter of big game with huge caliber guns, fired in some cases from a helicopter (no one missed the parallels with Vietnam), and climaxing when the two young men, D.J. and Tex, go unarmed into the wilderness. By the time they had returned to Dallas, Mailer realized that he was done with them.

His story about the two southern lads was written in an entirely different style—frantic, slangy, and obscene. Marrying a southern woman and becoming the father of two sons also had an influence on *Vietnam*.

He was also writing much more quickly. It is an oversimplification but nevertheless roughly accurate to say that from the mid-1960s on, Mailer had two compositional modalities: fast and slow. When he was in the groove, he could turn out fifteen thousand words a week. When he wasn't, he could stretch a book over a decade, shuffling, revising, and further revising. His 1967 Alaska novel, *Why Are We in Vietnam?*, is the same length as *An American Dream*, but was written in less than half the time. He called these books "bonuses, gifts. You do not have to kill some little part of your flesh to dredge them up." *Vietnam* wrote itself, he said, and "I was full of energy when I was done," which is to say nothing like the shape he was in after completing his previous books.

Anne Barry had left Mailer's employ in the spring of 1966. She was replaced by Madeline Belkin in Brooklyn and Sandy Charlebois Thomas in Provincetown. He kept them both busy, Belkin with his correspondence and New York projects, and Thomas with typing *Vietnam* and the script for *The Deer Park*. The Mailers had a lot of other help—maids and cooks—and the house was usually overflowing with family and guests, including Buzz Farbar, a young editor Mailer met a few years earlier who would become one of his closest friends. When Vance and Tina Bourjaily visited they saw that the house was full of ropewalking equipment. He said that there was "a mystique" about it for Mailer. "It's a feat of balancing that has religious import in some societies and is a circus act in others and a kids' showoff trick in still others. Norman has a capacity not only to get totally absorbed by something like that but also to communicate his enthusiasm for it to everybody else. We hadn't been there an hour before we were trying to find the right rope-walking shoes and Norman was showing us the basic technique. This remarkable enthusiasm for odd things seems to be an important part of his considerable magnetism."

After Mailer stayed with the Trillings in England, Diana Trilling had become his best female friend, vying with Lillian Hellman. The closeness of their relationship is reflected in the number and length of the letters they exchanged over more than two decades. While in Provincetown, he received a long letter from her, and answered at even greater length. She had asked what he said was "an unhappy question." Did they have a real sense of each other? Did he address *"the real Diana Trilling,"* or some construct? His answer explains what he thought about friendship.

> I don't make friends with people because they satisfy my idea of them. I am friends with people because they make me feel good when I talk to them and since everything on earth is extraordinarily limited I often don't want even to have too good an idea of them. I don't want to have too much of a hypothesis to be proved or disproved—rather there's an animal pleasure in friends. One feels a little safer or a little merrier, one shores up a small bulkhead against the large dread that always waits outside the door.

He went on to say that there was a new mood afoot in the country, and he didn't know if he understood it better than anyone else. "These McLuhans, these Pinchens [*sic*] and Jeremy Larners and this love of electronics and plastics and folk/rock makes me feel like Plekhanov scolding the Soviets in 1917. Sometimes I think we are at the tail end of something which soon may be gone forever, so that in 50 years, for instance, there may not be anyone alive who's read all of Remembrance of Things Past." Mailer had already decided that the Twist was evil, and he had limited interest in rock 'n' roll, although he would later allow that Bob Dylan did know how to write a lyric.

These sentiments are explored at great length in *Cannibals and Christians*. It is a difficult book, he told Yamanishi, because "I carry my ideas further than they have ever gone before, including for instance an attack upon the scientific method." The brunt of this attack derives from his assertion that metaphor had partnered with science for centuries in exploring and presenting life. The scientists of the Renaissance and the Enlightenment, Mailer wrote in *Cannibals*, were also "adventurers, rebels, courtiers, painters, diplomats, churchmen." No more, he said. Because the best metaphorical thinking arose from the profoundest experiences of humankind, he argued, destroying art's collaboration with scientific vision meant that our expanding knowledge of nature, of the universe, was not truly grounded. In the mid-twentieth century, science progressed mainly through experimentation and laboratory work; "Science has built a wall across the route of metaphor: poets whine before experts." And what had twentieth-century science produced? The gasoline engine, airplanes, modern architecture, antibiotics, psychoanalysis, the atom bomb, plastics, and the exploration of space. Mailer had reservations about some of these achievements, and deplored the rest. "Modern science may prove to be the final poisoned fruit of the rich European tree, and plague may disclose itself as the most characteristic invention of our time." The plague in all its social, architectural, and technological manifestations is one of the collection's three foci; the other two are literature and politics. Much of the book's political discourse is antiwar argument; it is dedicated to "Lyndon B. Johnson, whose name inspired young men to cheer for me in public."

His polemics, coming at a time when the nation was increasingly roiled about the Vietnam War and uneasy about some of the advances of technology, brought raves from reviewers when *Cannibals and Christians* was published in August. The *New York Times* reviewer, Eliot Fremont-Smith, proposed Mailer for the Nobel Prize in his review. A British reviewer, A. Alvarez, noted that on one page Mailer writes "with the speed and rawness of insight of Dostoievsky," and on the next, when giving an "existential analysis of the bowel-movements," sounds like General Jack D. Ripper, "the bodyfluids man in *Dr. Strangelove.*" He went on to say that "Dr. Mailer" was a diagnostician with "an almost extra-sensory perception for the faintest signs and vibrations which show where the sickness lies" in America. The British poet and novelist John Wain, whose work had appeared with Mailer's in an anthology devoted to the Beats and their English counterparts, the "Angry Young Men," said in his review that Mailer was attempting "to position himself so as to stand face to face with the true identity of our time, our time in America." Written in what Wain called "a time of panic and mortal illness," *Cannibals and Christians* can now be seen as a rehearsal for what many believe to be his greatest work, *The Armies of the Night*, preparing the ground for it much as *Julius Caesar* did for *Hamlet.*

Act IV, the Provincetown theater Beverly was involved in with director Leo Garen, was a small operation, but it put on some ambitious productions, including plays by Pirandello and LeRoi Jones (Amiri Baraka). Mailer cast Beverly as Lulu in Act IV's production of *The Deer Park*, which opened on August 16, 1966. She and Mailer had begun to quarrel, however, and while they would continue to collaborate on dramatic and film projects for two more years, the marriage was beginning to come apart. José Torres recalled one dinner party that summer when they got into a fierce argument. When she made a comment about Mailer's mother, Torres said, Mailer was "white with fury." He said, "Beverly, I am going to get up and throw you out the window," but Torres interceded and he and Mailer went for a walk to defuse the situation. His extramarital flings were one of the chief causes of their difficulties. Over a decade later Beverly said that Mailer was seeing other women not long after they were together. "When I was pregnant, he had an airline stewardess. Three days after bringing home our baby, he began an affair." Beverly may have been referring to Carol Stevens, whom Mailer had met when he was still with Jeanne Campbell.

An accomplished jazz singer from Philadelphia who worked with major artists such as the Modern Jazz Quartet, Coleman Hawkins, and Bill Evans, Stevens was on a date with Clay Felker at Small's Paradise, a jazz nightclub in Harlem, sometime in late 1962, when Mailer walked in. Felker invited him to join them. Mailer danced with Carol and they drank and talked. When it was time to leave, Mailer said, "Let's go" to her. To his surprise, she replied that she was going home with the gentleman who brought her. As they stood on the sidewalk talking, Mailer picked her up and whirled her around over his head, as he once did with his sister. "Sheer exuberance," Stevens recalled. A year later, more or less, he called her on the phone. "Did you finally get down to 'S' in your address book?" she asked. They went out and ended up in bed. Not long after this, she went to the party celebrating his engagement to Beverly and met several members of his family. Barney impressed her, she said. She continued to see Mailer after he married Beverly.

Beverly's acting career was a major cause of friction: she was unhappy about being cast as Lulu in the play, first in Provincetown, and again five months later when the play opened in New York. She wanted to play Elena and believed Mailer had given the part to someone else to hold her down. Mickey Knox disagreed: "Norman never held her down," he said. "In fact, one of the reasons he did *Deer Park* was to put his wives into it" (Adele was the understudy for the role of Elena). Beverly said that he put her down because "he doesn't want to share the limelight. He enjoys humiliating me." Her interpretation is both strengthened and weakened by Mailer's report on the play at the end of the summer to Uncle Louis and Aunt Moos: "We did it up here in Provincetown in a theater Beverly helped to start up (she is, by the way, a superb actress—woe is me—I'm not used to other talent in the family)." Beverly told Mailer biographer Mary Dearborn that she had devoted herself "to running the (at times enormous) Mailer household. Norman's children from his previous marriages came and went, and there were always staffers and Norman's friends underfoot, waiting to be fed." Mailer said later that the marriage to Beverly had "begun to wallow, then had sunk: his fourth wife, an actress, had seen her career drown in the rigors of managing so large a home." Although Beverly told an interviewer in the spring of 1967 that "Norman's career is the most important to me," she said later that his criticisms of her acting troubled her so much that "I began to feel I had no career." After they separated, Beverly went on to a long, successful acting career, mainly on the stage, well into her eighties.

Mailer had cut the play from five hours to two and a half; he told Knox he had gotten rid of "all the lard." He now planned to mount the play the coming winter off-Broadway at the Theatre De Lys in the Village. As he said in another letter, "At least I'll be done finally with the play. Clear and shut after eight years. God." In addition to revising the play and writing *Why Are We in Vietnam?* that summer, he had written a book review of *Rush to Judgment*, Mark Lane's long critique of the Warren Commission Report. Lane argued that the commission "had no intention of trying to find any other assassin than Oswald." Mailer didn't quibble with the commission's massive assemblage of fact, nor did he accuse it of suppressing information. Rather, he faulted it for presenting the evidence so that it "fitted a bed of Procrustes." His suspicion was that the Soviets had made Oswald their minion as the price of allowing him to return home after two years in Minsk. He proposed that a "literary commission supported by public subscription" and headed by someone of the stature of Edmund Wilson or Dwight Macdonald be formed to resift the material in the twenty-six volumes, as well as follow untouched leads. As he said at the end of his review, "The game is not over. Nor the echo of muffled drums. Nor the memory of the riderless horse." His proposal found no backers. But Mailer persisted, and became, with some help from Jean Malaquais, his own commission of investigation. It would take him thirty years to reach the end of his obsession.

The Mailers were back in New York just in time to attend the social event of the year, perhaps the decade, Truman Capote's Black and White Ball. Capote sponsored the event to introduce the *Washington Post*'s new publisher, Katharine Graham, to New York.

Capote chose the Plaza Hotel for the event because he thought it had the most elegant ballroom in the city. He invited 540 people (about four hundred came), including a score of titled European nobility, neighbors from Long Island, and his New York doorman. Writers who attended the November 28 event included Hellman, Plimpton, Harper Lee, Baldwin, Arthur Miller, Buckley, Elizabeth Hardwick and Robert Lowell, Marianne Moore, and John Steinbeck. Lauren Bacall, Henry Fonda, Frank Sinatra and Mia Farrow were there, and many other Hollywood stars. The daughters of three presidents—Alice Roosevelt Longworth, Margaret Truman Daniel, and Lynda Bird Johnson—came, as did several Kennedys, including the late president's mother, his two brothers, Ted and Robert, and two of his sisters, Jean Kennedy Smith and Pat Kennedy Lawford, with whom Mailer began a long friendship that night. President Johnson was not invited, nor was Gore Vidal.

According to his biographer, after the tremendous success earlier that year of *In Cold Blood*, his nonfiction novel about the murder of a family in Kansas, Capote was cockier than Napoleon after Austerlitz. He drew great pleasure from deciding who would come and who not, and said he made five hundred friends and fifteen thousand enemies. Formally, the event was a *bal masqué*, which required men to come in black tie with black masks, while women wore either black or white gowns and masks. Masks were supposed to remain in place until midnight, but this rule was honored as much in the breach as the observance. The guest of honor and Capote greeted guests at the door after they were announced.

Over his tux, Mailer recalled, he was wearing a "dirty gabardine raincoat." Beverly wore a white fur wrap over a black dress. He enjoyed himself tremendously, and called it one of the best parties of all time. Looking back on it, he said, "Everything felt anointed that night. Truman had certainly brought it off. It certainly was his greatest coup. For some, and I might be one of them, that party was even greater than any particular one of his books." McGeorge Bundy, President Johnson's national security advisor, was present, and Mailer could not resist inserting the Vietnam War into a conversation Bundy was having with Hellman. Harsh words were exchanged and Mailer invited him to step outside. "I was dissolute and full of drink. But I'd have killed him that night, I was so angry," he said. "I had a terrible argument with Lillian Hellman as a result. Because she overheard it, she stopped it. She was always such a celebrity fucker. It must be said of Lillian that when the chips were down she'd always go for the guy who had the most clout."

The argument drove a wedge between them and they didn't speak for over a year. *Women's Wear Daily* gave Mailer the Worst-Dressed Award because of his rumpled raincoat. When asked about the award many years later, he laughed and said, "How little they knew about how to murder me."

The ball was held on the same day that preparations for the play (published by Dial Press in mid-1967) began. Dial had paid him $20,000, a high price for a play that had not yet had a full-scale production. After casting and "ten stunning maniacally depressive days of rehearsal" under director Leo Garen, the play opened on January 31, 1967. In his introduction to the published version, Mailer said that the play was "perhaps the dearest work of all my work," even more so than the novel from which it grew. It was, he hoped, funnier, sadder, more tragic, and possessed of more layers. "If the compass was obligatorily more narrow, the well was being dug to a deeper water." He now had a play with thirteen characters and eighty-eight brief scenes (a huge electronic tote board displayed the scene number, counting down to zero) in two acts. Continuity was spotty in a play that went, Mailer said, "from explosion to explosion," as rapid as the cuts in a film. The play was a bastard, he wrote, the offspring of a "realistic play and that electric sense of transition which lives in the interruptions and symbols of The Theatre of the Absurd." The cast was solid, not dazzling. Mailer, who did the casting, had some pros: Hugh Marlow as Eitel, Will Lee as the Hollywood magnate Herman Teppis, and, as Marion Faye, Rip Torn, an impressive young actor who would win an Obie for his role. Beverly continued as Lulu, and Buzz Farbar as the orgiast Don Beda. A relative unknown, Rosemary Tory, played Elena, the female lead, and Knox was Collie Munshin, Teppis's comically unprincipled son-in-law. Mailer thought the play as staged could not be immediately understood, and was worried, therefore, about the critics.

The first reviews were generous, if not superlative, with praise, especially of Lee as the marvelously fraudulent Teppis, "a twin tower of sentimentality and ruthlessness" who is such a shameless vice figure, Walter Kerr wrote in the *Times*, that the audience is happy to see him return. Later notices were not as good, even though Mailer gave lengthy interviews to *The Village Voice* and the *New York Post*. He also published "A Statement of Aims by the Playwright" in the *Voice* and, ten days before the premiere, a long essay on the front page of the arts section of the Sunday *New York Times* explaining the difficulties of hammering it into shape through four rewrites over ten years. He said the play's fate will be decided in "the electric hour when the drama reviewer sprints from the theater, snatches his opening lead from the well-tuned bag of his wit, and is off to his desk, say, his guillotine." He ends his piece, titled "Mr. Mailer Hands Out the Cigars," by saying that the cigar's band reads: "Be advised the actors speak so clearly you need not miss a line." Walt Whitman wrote anonymous reviews of *Leaves of Grass*; Mailer didn't go this far, but he did provide all the leads, prompts, nudges, and background information—a fully packed press kit—needed to make the work of reviewers easier, as well as implying that those of taste and sagacity would appreciate his play. "I wanted the critics to feel self-conscious at the opening," he said. "You have to hustle."

On opening night, he threw a huge party. Over five hundred people crowded into the Mailers' Brooklyn apartment, where a rock 'n' roll band played from a perch under the skylight. He did brief interviews with several invited newspaper columnists. One of them, Dick Schaap of the *New York Post*, quoted Mailer as saying that while it was too early to tell, "I think we've got a hit." At the end of February, he purchased a full-page ad in the *Times*, and to celebrate the show's one hundredth performance at the end of April, he persuaded Dial Press to host a Village block party, with free food, drink, music, and a pep talk from Mailer. By this time, however, the three-hundred-seat Theatre De Lys was only half full for most performances.

He did everything possible to promote the play, beating "his own drum to shreds" as one reviewer put it, but finally it was only a middling success. Why? First, the play has thirteen characters each of whom has a rich history, so "the complicated story needs vast quantities of exposition." Second, the play is set during the Korean War and the characters, now residing in some antechamber of hell, are remembering everything. The action is over; the inmates are serving their sentences. Third, while the evil characters are vividly imagined, those with virtue are stale. As Walter Kerr put it, "Mailer is a moralist and concerned with unmasking evil wherever he finds it, which is everywhere." So there is a great deal of laughter because "unmitigated evil invariably creates in the viewer a happy impulse to hilarity." But Eitel, the director who bewails his lost integrity, is "pompous and more than a bit foolish," Kerr says. Finally, several of the characters are philosophers and "spout philosophy and assorted Mailerisms." Faithful to his vision even as the audiences dwindled, he continued to pump in money. "I hold on because . . . I don't know why—I just don't want to close it," he wrote to Knox. On May 21, after 127 performances, the play closed. He had lost $60,000.

Offsetting this money drain was income from four books he published in 1967. The first was a collection of all nineteen of his previously published short stories for a Dell paperback. The play's script, with a long introduction on the state of American theater (he spent two weeks seeing about a dozen plays in New York), came out in August, followed a month later by *Why Are We in Vietnam?* Finally, in November, CBS/Macmillan published *The Bullfight*, an ill-conceived project worked up in collaboration with his young friend, Buzz Farbar. It consists of Mailer's 8,500-word profile of an iconoclastic Mexican *torero* known as "El Loco," a fine essay (and his first original piece in *Playboy*) that captures the magic of the Sunday bullfight, with ninety-one photographs of a bullfight. Accompanying the book is an LP record of Mailer reading part of the essay, and Hugh Marlow and Rosemary Tory reading Federico García Lorca's famous bullfighting poem "Lament for Sánchez Mejías," which Mailer and his bilingual daughter, Susan, translated. The photos are small, often confusing, and do not follow one particular fight, but several (not El Loco's), making for a jerky presentation. The book and record came packed in a bulky, ugly plastic container that he must have hated; the book was so poorly made that the front cover tended to split at the hinge. The few reviews were bad and the book, perhaps his worst, disappeared quickly.

THAT SPRING, THE National Institute of Arts and Letters invited Mailer to become a member, but he had reservations. Letters went back and forth with Mailer expressing "reluctance" to accept. He said he was troubled that Henry Miller, Algren, Jones, Burroughs, and Ginsberg were not members. Feeling, however, that it would be "ungracious" to his nominators to decline, he accepted membership. He later learned that Miller had been a member since 1957; Algren, Burroughs, and Ginsberg were later elected. Mailer couldn't attend the welcoming dinner; he was giving antiwar speeches at several universities.

His exchange with the institute occurred when the play was still selling out every night. Having seen it fifty times and watched the director make the necessary adjustments, he was getting bored talking to the actors about the nuts and bolts of stagecraft. Instead, he huddled with Farbar and Knox at a table in Casey's, a Village bar. They began creating characters: Mailer, "The Prince," was the leader of a Mafia gang; Knox was "Twenty Years," reflecting his two decades as an actor; Farbar was "Buzz Cameo" a reference to his brief role in the play. "We had absolutely fantastic stuff going as we were drinking," Mailer recalled. As Knox remembers it, "Norman suggested to Buzz and me that since we were so brilliantly witty during our nightly razzle-dazzle repartée, we should make a movie. He conceived of the premise: Three hoods go to the mattresses (hood-talk for hiding out). That was it, leaving the field of action open for us to improvise, be funny, wild, crazy, or inventive." Farbar knew an accomplished young filmmaker, Donn Pennebaker, who had made *Don't Look Back*, a documentary about Bob Dylan, and he agreed to film the action for $10 an hour; he also supplied a room in a Brooklyn office building for the shoot. Mailer put up an initial $1,600 and, in mid-March over four consecutive evenings from midnight until dawn, they made a film called *Wild 90*. There was no script.

Film historian Michael Chaiken described the result as "a gestalt of galoot poetics, direct cinema, and lowbrow comedy with three drunkards launching a barrage of profanity-laced repartee and virulent put-downs." None of the three principals could claim a drop of Italian blood, but they knew how to curse creatively. "Mailer," Chaiken wrote, "sounding like Paul Muni trying to pass a kidney stone" is central to all that transpires in the ninety-minute film (thus the title). He harangues his pals for forty-five minutes, which soon becomes tedious. It revives somewhat in the second half when visitors come to the hideout. Beverly Bentley, playing the Prince's wife, drops in, as do José Torres and his wife, Ramona, and other members of the cast of *The Deer Park*. Torres brings his German shepherd and the film reaches its climax when Mailer gets down on all fours and barks face-to-face with the dog.

Film critic Jonas Mekas convinced Mailer to watch several experimental films at the Filmmakers' Cinémathèque. He and Beverly saw Kenneth Anger's 1964 film about bikers, *Scorpio Rising*, and Andy Warhol's 1965 film, *Kitchen*. Mailer admired Warhol's courage in dramatically slowing the action, but otherwise found it to be "horrible." He said that Warhol's film "had the horror of the twentieth century in it. The refrigerator was making too much noise. The beautiful heroine, Edie Sedgwick, has the sniffles. She keeps blowing her nose while the hero keeps trying to rustle a sandwich together out of wax paper." The film is "almost unendurable," he said. *Wild 90* may be worse. Mailer, operating in what he once referred to as his "usual narcissistic fog," paid no attention to warnings about recording the sound properly, resulting in a film which "sounds," he said, "as if *everybody* is talking through a *jock strap.*"

He began editing the film almost immediately. "I just loved cutting," he said. "I loved the sort of—if you will—the metaphysical problems involved." The film premiered on January 7, 1968, at the New Cinema Playhouse in Manhattan. The reviews were abysmal. Pauline Kael, writing in *The New Yorker*, said that she had seen movies that were worse, but *Wild 90* was "the worst movie that I've stayed to see all the way through. It's terrible in ways that are portentous." Mailer said that the reviews were good for him. "I thought I was going to get a very pleasant reception," he said. "Instead, I got cockamamied in the alley. *Bam! Boom! Boy*, those *mothers*! I found out it was a tough racket." He had an idea for a second film dealing with the relationship of the police and criminals, an idea that grew out of being interrogated at the West 100th Street police station after the stabbing. But he had to take a break from filmmaking. He had another commitment.

When he left for Provincetown in mid-May, his plan was to return to "First-Born." The previous summer Scott Meredith had gotten him a $450,000 advance from New American Library for a novel. It was an enormous sum that strengthened his faith in Meredith's abilities. Mailer had been spending the advance freely, but had produced nothing. He had provided NAL neither an outline nor a sample chapter, only a line in the contract describing a novel about the "Jewish experience." According to Meredith, Mailer "was going to follow a Jewish family like the Mailer family from ancient times to the future." But he was unable to write. Bill Walker, his old drinking buddy, wrote from prison, and Mailer wrote back to send him a check; he added that he usually had trouble getting anything done while waiting for the appearance of a new book (*Why Are We in Vietnam?*). Another reason, he told Carpenter, was that he had gotten "far too concerned" with his movies: "It's such *fun* making movies." And it kept him away from his wife. He and Beverly had "fallen on dull, chilly days," and he kept slipping away to New York to edit the film. Even the news that Styron was publishing a major new novel, *The Confessions of Nat Turner*, failed to put him in a competitive mood. He told Knox that Styron was "putting out peace feelers to him," but he was not receptive. He was concerned about Jones, however. His new novel, *Go to the Widow-Maker*, had been pummeled in the reviews. Mailer asked Knox to tell Jones that he planned to read the novel and to ignore the reviews. He added that he had a hunch that the reason the critics had been so hard on Jones was because he had praised him so highly in *Cannibals and Christians*. He knew this sounded like "paranoia, megalomania," but he sensed that "all those little fucks out there" were dying to prove Norman Mailer wrong.

Even as he was trying and failing to extend "First-Born," and sporadically editing the film, he had several other projects percolating. The first concerned Malaquais. A few weeks before leaving for Cape Cod, he had awakened one morning with "an extraordinary idea." On the spot, he wrote to his friend in France and offered him $6,000 for a year's full-time work. He outlined the job: a reexamination of the Kennedy assassination based on a careful rereading of the Warren Commission Report. His hunch was that the murder had been committed by one or more petty conspirators, and Oswald, probably an agent for the FBI and the CIA, as well as a couple of foreign countries, was one of them. The commission's proceedings, therefore, were "a series of attempts to conceal by multitudinous layers of meaningless evidence the simple contradictions attaching to the embarrassments of the various secret policemen when lo and behold one of their boys seemed to be at the gun." In addition to the $6,000, he offered him the profits of any book that might come of his "detective" work, as he called it. It was Malaquais, he reminded him, who had recited Trotsky's dictum: find the truth by comparing the lies. Malaquais accepted and Mailer mailed him his review of *Rush to Judgment*, the first time he called the work of the commission a cover-up.

Mailer had done the *Playboy* interview with Paul Carroll, and in July one of the magazine's top editors sent him the edited version for his approval, saying that Mailer was too "metaphorical" and "elliptical" in places. In his reply, he said that, yes, it was true that he was "far from crystal-clear." He was not disposed to elaborate, however, merely to please the readers of the magazine. He had avoided writing for *Playboy* until recently, he said, because of "the literality, blandness, and overdedicated organizational exposition of the magazine's style." He preferred to write pieces that made readers work a bit to understand; he wanted them to be "slightly puzzled and slightly nettled" at certain points. *Playboy* backed off and the interview, one of his most important, with extended comments on Vietnam, appeared in January 1968. He was also asked to review a new book by Norman Podhoretz, a memoir titled *Making It.* Shortly afterward, Podhoretz, who was now, along with Cy Rembar and Steven Marcus, one of Mailer's literary executors, brought a copy to Provincetown. Mailer read it forthwith and told Podhoretz that he liked it, but also had some criticisms. But, with other projects pending, he would not write his review for several months.

The first reviews of *Why Are We in Vietnam?* began to appear just as the Mailers returned to New York in fall 1967. They were almost as good as for *Cannibals and Christians*, with John Aldridge in *Harper's* and reviewers in the *Voice, New York Times, Newsweek*, and *The New York Review of Books* proclaiming the novel to be a near-masterpiece. Favorable comparisons with Joyce were made, but there were the usual detractors. *Saturday Review*'s Granville Hicks was grave in his disapprobation of "the proportion of the once forbidden Anglo-Saxon monosyllables to other and more conventional words." *National Review* was outraged, and *Time*'s anonymous reviewer found the book to be "a wildly turgid monologorrhea" narrated by D.J. The novel, however, has two narrators, D.J., or Ranald David Jethroe, a white teenager from Dallas who claims to be "Disc Jockey to the world," and his alter ego, a crippled black "genius brain from Harlem pretending to write a white man's fink fuck book." The chapters alternate between the two. Both use a superabundance of scatological humor, and we never learn which narrator is wearing the mask, or if both are. "The fact of the matter," D.J. says, "is that you're up tight with a mystery, me, and this mystery can't be solved because I'm in the center of it, and I don't comprehend, not necessarily, I could be traducing myself." The two narrators relish the mixup.

But what many reviewers found more compelling than his scatological ventriloquisms was what Denis Donoghue called Mailer's "remarkable feeling for the sensory event." One such passage comes after Tex has shot a wolf and Big Ollie, the Indian guide, gives him and D.J. a cup of blood to drink. It had "a taste of fish, odd enough, and salt, near to oyster sauce and then the taste of wild meat like an eye looking at you in the center of a midnight fire." Big Ollie takes a taste of the blood, and then cuts the head off and turns it for them to see.

> There were two eyes open on El Lobo, both yellow coals of light, but one eye was Signor Lupo, the crazy magician in the wolf, and his eye had the pain of the madman who knows there's a better world but he is excluded, and then the other eye, Willie Wolf, like a fox's eye, full of sunlight and peace, a harvest sun on late afternoon field, shit! it was just an animal eye like the glass they use for an eye in a trophy, no expression, hollow peace maybe, and Big Ollie dug a shallow pan of a hole with his knife in the crust bog tundra, whatever that dry shit moss was, and set the wolf's head in it, muzzle pointing to the north, and covered it over. Then he took a broken twig and laid it in a line with the end of the muzzle, but pointing further North, then got down on his hands and knees and touched his nose to the stick.

Ollie has paid his respects to the wolf. How Mailer was able to imagine this scene after only five days in Alaska two years earlier is a mystery and a marvel. As Henry James said when asked for advice to novelists, "Write from experience, and experience only, I should feel that this was a rather tantalizing monition if I were not careful immediately to add, Try to be one of the people on whom nothing is lost!" *Why Are We in Vietnam?* was later nominated for the National Book Award, a reflection not only of its moving depiction of the Alaska wilderness, but also its implicit antiwar message which was beginning to be heard. Vietnam is mentioned on the novel's last page, when we learn that Tex and D.J. have enlisted and are going to Vietnam.

In early October he started work on the new film, *Beyond the Law.* He coproduced it with Farbar (although Mailer put up all the money), and is listed in the credits as the director, although there was no script and almost no direction given. Actors were given an identity and told to wing it. Joining Pennebaker were two new filmmakers, Jan Welt and Nicholas Proferes. As with *Wild 90*, it was shot over four nights, but this time Mailer used three film crews and reliable sound equipment. The lead, played by Mailer, is an Irish-American vice squad lieutenant, Francis Xavier Pope, and one camera crew moves with him as he makes his station house rounds on a weekend evening. The other two crews worked simultaneously in other parts of the building, meaning that interrogations going on in one part of the precinct were interrupted by loud interactions in other parts. "The intensity of this process," Mailer wrote, "camera, actors, and scenes working simultaneously on the same floor (which is about the way matters proceed in a police station) conceivably worked a magic on the actors." He thought that he had "divined and/or blundered onto the making of the best American movie about the police he had ever seen." His fundamental idea, which grows out of his existentialism, was that "people who were able to talk themselves in and out of trouble," if allowed to speak naturally in certain situations, and not required to memorize anything, could turn in unusual performances.

The cast included several professionals—Rip Torn (a freaked-out Hells Angel), Beverly (Pope's wife), and Knox (another detective)—and two dozen more, all amateurs. Buzz Farbar also played a detective; George Plimpton was the mayor of New York, inspecting the precinct; playwright Jack Richardson was impressive as an icy gambler; and Mailer's Provincetown friend poet Eddie Bonetti was a convincing ax murderer. Michael McClure was another Hells Angel, and a stockbroker, Tom Quinn, was the station sergeant. A young woman named Lee Roscoe, who would work closely with Mailer on his next film and with whom he had an affair, played a college girl who was a weekend dominatrix. Hal Conrad and his wife, Mara Lynn, had parts, as did Torres and two other boxers, Roger Donoghue and Joe Shaw, a rising welterweight. Tom Quinn, along with Mailer, Pete Hamill, Plimpton, and a few others, were for a time Shaw's financial backers, although his career was brief. The cast, therefore, was a haphazard olio of writers, actors, lovers, poets, gamblers, and boxers. Mailer drew on Brendan Behan's persona for his role. In his review, Roger Ebert said, "He's not only convinced that he can act, but that he can play an Irish cop named Francis Xavier Pope and do it with an Irish accent. He can do none of the three," but watching him try is a "hilarious spectacle." Vincent Canby found Mailer to be "slightly manic" in a film that was "good and tough and entertaining" in its presentation of "the existential relationship between cop and crook," and compared it favorably to recent Hollywood detective films. Pennebaker said that the film influenced scriptwriters for television dramas (*Hill Street Blues* and *Law and Order* come to mind), and that it was "a real course in filmmaking for Hollywood" because it demonstrated how the cops "are sort of a counterpart to the crooks. Both sides are both good and bad."

WILD 90 WAS more or less finished by the time *Beyond the Law* was shot, and Mailer was eager to begin editing the new film. He had reduced the eleven hours of raw footage by half when he got a call from Mitchell Goodman, an old friend from Paris with a "lugubrious conscience." Goodman wanted him to take part in an antiwar protest in Washington in October. When Mailer said he had no desire to stand around listening to dull speeches by pacifists, Goodman said this protest would be different. The plan was to "invade the corridors of the Pentagon" to try to shut it down. In the opening of his account of the March on the Pentagon, *The Armies of the Night*, Mailer wrote that Goodman's words gave him no pleasure; he sensed "one little bubble of fear tilt somewhere about the solar plexus." Despite his reservations, he agreed to participate.

Edward de Grazia, a lawyer he had met in Boston when testifying for *Naked Lunch*, was also involved in the March. He picked up Mailer at the airport on October 19, two days before the March, and while driving him to his Washington hotel, the Hay-Adams, explained the situation. There was no central organizing committee, no hierarchy, and relations among the participating groups were strained. Communication was spotty, although there was agreement on a kickoff rally for the March at the Lincoln Memorial, similar to the gathering four years earlier where Martin Luther King had given his famous "I Have a Dream" speech. Negotiations with the various governmental units on all aspects of the protest were ongoing, but meanwhile fifty thousand or more marchers were en route to the city. Also on their way were U.S. marshals, the National Guard, and regular army units, all to reinforce Washington police. At this point, de Grazia said, things "are not in focus."

Neither was Mailer. On the one hand, he was being compared to Joyce as a literary artist and called a sage for his subtle intimations of the nation's fears, follies, and enervating addictions. On the other, he was thought to be a loose cannon, vulgar, violent, and weird, spouting ideas about orgasms and existentialism that resembled the most outrageous theories of Wilhelm Reich. While there was some consistency to his jeremiads, there was little among his novels, which appeared to have been written by five different novelists, and his poems by some mutant offspring of William Burroughs and Ogden Nash. He counted Bill Buckley as one of his best friends, but he was also close to Jerry Rubin and later Abbie Hoffman, although he was critical of some of the actions of the Yippies (Youth International Party), an anarchist group that Rubin and Hoffman helped found at the end of 1967. A convicted felon and multiply divorced, he was the devoted father of six. He had irreproachable antiwar credentials that made him a hero among the young, but he wore three-piece suits made in London. He was "modestly promiscuous" in his drinking and use of marijuana, but made his daughter Susan, now a freshman at Barnard, promise she would use no drugs until she graduated. The jacket of *Why Are We in Vietnam?* showed two photos of him, one with a terrific shiner, and the other with his hair as neatly coiffed as his father's. Beneath was a question, "Will the Real Norman Mailer Please Stand Up?" One of Mailer's ancillary purposes in writing *The Armies of the Night* was to do something about his image, not smooth the wrinkles—he loved his contradictions too much—but give his audience a few metaphors for appreciating what he called his "endless blendings of virtue and corruption."

In the opening pages of *Armies of the Night*, after a quick sketch of the rival factions of his psyche, he describes his attempts to shape the way he is seen by the media.

> He had in fact learned to live in the sarcophagus of his image—at night, in his sleep, he might dart out and paint improvements on the sarcophagus. During the day, while he was helpless, newspapermen and other assorted bravos of the media and the literary world would carve ugly pictures on the living tomb of his legend. Of necessity, part of Mailer's remaining funds of sensitivity went right into the war of supporting his image and working for it.

The passage captures his testy relations with the media, but also reveals that the health of his self-image relied to some extent on blandishments from his dreaming self, his unconscious.

In the "leisurely twilight," as Ed de Grazia drives him to the Hay-Adams, Mailer observed the "tender Southern city" and sighed, for "like most New Yorkers, he usually felt small in Washington." There was no thought in his head about his centrality to the upcoming events, nor that he would write the definitive account of them, and none whatsoever that to do so he would borrow a form used by Emerson and Thoreau, described by critic Warner Berthoff as "the exploratory personal testament in which the writer describes how he has turned his life into a practical moral experiment and put it out at wager according to the chances, and against the odds, peculiar to the public character of his time." Mailer merely wanted to do his bit in D.C., get arrested for the cause, pay his fine, and fly back to New York on Saturday night for an important party.

Again and again, for the greater part of his account of the March, Mailer the writer wheels into frame Mailer the Marcher (aka the Participant, the Novelist, the Ruminant, the Beast), and then comments humorously, obscenely, resignedly, unsparingly, and (rarely) solemnly on many salient aspects of his character and history, using, for example, his troubled marriage, timid youth in Brooklyn, army service, shifting political affiliations, and his relations with various literary figures—Paul Goodman, Robert Lowell, and Dwight Macdonald, principally—as a means of presenting the drama of his three days in Washington. There is a problem, of course, with unbridled self-presentation in memoirs: readers get irritated, or bored. Mailer addressed the matter by changing "I" to "he," or one of the names just noted, and by this simple shift giving himself sanction to talk about Norman Mailer all the more. The device is unsettling at first, but soon works beautifully. He had dabbled with the third person personal, as it might be called, in his *Village Voice* columns and a few other places, but he said that the idea came from editing *Wild 90*. Watching the film made him see himself "as a piece of material, as a piece of yard goods. I'd say: 'Where am I going to cut myself?' " Mailer's evolution as a writer follows step by step, from *The Naked and the Dead* to *Armies of the Night*, his slowly growing awareness of the merits of desegregating his personal and his creative lives.

At the outset of the narrative, he uses a cathedral to describe himself. Architectural metaphors abound in *Armies*, a reflection of Mailer's interests and the unusual shape of the building the protesters hope to engage—at one point, he compares the Pentagon to the colossal architecture of ancient Egypt. His boldness, his fits of shyness, his good manners, and the fact that he is often brusque, make him conclude that "the architecture of his personality bore resemblance to some provincial cathedral which warring orders of the church might have designed separately over several centuries, the particular cathedral falling into the hands of one architect, then his enemy." Not much further on, he extends the architectural imagery by stating that his complex personality "serves willy-nilly as the bridge—many will say the *pons asinorium*—into the crazy house, the crazy mansion" of that historic moment when American citizens marched on a bastion of the nation's military might in order to "wound it *symbolically.*"

> So if the event took place in one of the crazy mansions, or indeed *the* crazy house of history, it is fitting that any ambiguous comic hero of such a history should be not only off very much to the side of the history, but that he should be an egotist of the most startling misproportions, outrageously and often unhappily self-assertive, yet in command of a detachment classic in severity (for he was a novelist and so in need of studying every last lineament of the fine, the noble, the frantic, and the foolish in others and in himself). Such egotism being two-headed, thrusting itself forward the better to study itself, finds itself therefore at home in a house of mirrors, since it has habits, even the talent, to regard itself.

Mailer-now, the writer, observes Mailer-then, the marcher. Although they share the same name and antecedents, they have slightly different sensibilities—Mailer-now has done a bit more, and is in a position to appreciate the small-mindedness and misapprehensions, as well as the generosity and acuity of vision, of his former self, a protagonist, as Mailer said later, who was "half-heroic and three quarters comic." Mailer-then fumbles and fulminates; he is in flux; but he also sees clearly and acts boldly. Mailer-then took no notes, but remembered well, as Robert Lowell later told Dwight Macdonald: "Curious, when you're with X [another novelist], you think he's so sensitive and alert and then you find later he wasn't taking in anything, while Norman seems not to pay much attention but now it seems he didn't miss a trick—and what a memory!"

A scene between Mailer and Lowell at a party before the March will illustrate. Lowell has just finished telling Mailer that he and his wife think Mailer is the "finest journalist in America." Having received a postcard from Lowell to this effect, he is aware of the poet's high opinion. He suspects, however, that Lowell sends out many postcards.

> The first card he'd ever received from Lowell was on a book of poems, *Deaths for the Ladies and other disasters* it had been called, and many people had thought the book a joke which whatever its endless demerits, it was not. Not to the novice poet at least. When Lowell had written that he liked the book, Mailer next waited for some word in print to canonize his thin tome; of course, it never came. If Lowell were to begin to award living American poets in critical print, two hundred starving worthies could in fairness hold out their bowl before the escaped Novelist would deserve his turn. Still, Mailer was irked. He felt he had been part of a literary game. When the second card came a few years later telling him he was the best journalist in America, he did not answer. Elizabeth Hardwick, Lowell's wife, had just published a review of *An American Dream* in *Partisan Review* which had done its best to disembowel the novel. Lowell's card might have arrived with the best of motives, but its timing suggested to Mailer an exercise in neutralmanship—neutralize the maximum of possible future risks. Mailer was not critically equipped for the task, but there was always the distant danger that some bright and not unauthoritative voice, irked at Lowell's enduring hegemony, might come along with a long lance and presume to tell America that posterity would judge Allen Ginsberg to be the greater poet.
>
> This was all doubtless desperately unfair to Lowell who, on the basis of two kind cards, was now judged by Mailer to possess an undue unchristian talent for literary logrolling. But then Mailer was prickly.

When Mailer and Lowell meet in Washington, the poet repeated his remark. "Yes, Norman, I really think you are the best journalist in

America." Mailer replied that he sometimes thought he was "the best writer in America." Lowell, now on the defensive, replied, "Oh, Norman, oh, certainly," he said, "I didn't mean to imply, heavens no, it's just that I have such *respect* for good journalism." Mailer answered with "false graceousness" that writing a good poem was much more difficult.

Despite the unusual, even eccentric, nature of Mailer's point of view in the book, its assumptions and purposes are apparent. Anyone familiar with the modern novel recognizes that the double perspective used by the best writers show us the world through the eyes of their characters without effacing themselves as narrators. A fictional character, one who is changing before our eyes, is presented. The third person personal allowed Mailer to present his sometimes brave, sometimes clownish, sometimes earnest, often peckish, invariably opinionated, regularly comic, and usually honest self without necessarily sounding as if he is preaching for his own saint. By writing about himself instead of a fictional look-alike, Mailer is nevertheless obliged by his point of view to write about some aspects of the real world of events, in this case, a large civil protest with an uncertain outcome. Half of the genius of the book resides in the fact that Mailer's sight extends so clearly to the circumference of his awareness. "The eye is the first circle," says Emerson, "the horizon which it forms is the second." In *Armies of the Night*, we see, as it were, the structure of Mailer's eye and the angles of his vision on various aspects of the March, extending to its periphery with glimpses beyond. He is an intrepid explorer of his own psyche, but his explorations in this narrative (and the five that follow it through 1975), lead us closer to, not further away from, the problems of the republic.

Mailer depicts himself clearly while also tackling a variety of reportorial and analytic tasks—for example, presenting an authoritative analysis of the near-final demise of the Old Left and its "sound-as-brickwork logic of the next step" polemical abstractions, and the rise of the New Left with its focus on the most immediate injustices in the nation. As one of the youngest of the Old Left figures, and godfather to the New, Mailer weighs the assets and liabilities of both, firing commentary from his existential Gatling gun at a long line of emerging or revitalized causes, beginning with poverty and civil rights and ending with sexual freedom, free speech, and environmentalism. The New Left's alphabet soup of groups, he notes, shares these causes almost randomly except for a fierce opposition to the war, the common cause of all the constituent groups.

As one scholar, Sandy Vogelgesang, has noted, the March on the Pentagon was the symbolic event that "marked the move from dissent to resistance." Before the March, many leftist intellectuals questioned whether such actions could result in any real change; Mailer himself wondered about the effectiveness of the March when he spoke to Mitchell Goodman at the beginning of *Armies*. But the March became a firebrand that ignited other acts of resistance, and while tracing its influence with precision may be impossible, it was and is written about and cited repeatedly. Most of the major figures who marched with Mailer—Noam Chomsky, Dr. Benjamin Spock, Paul Goodman, Lowell, Macdonald, and Yale chaplain Rev. William Sloane Coffin Jr.—continued to participate in various antiwar activities. Nothing written about the March (and arguably nothing written about resistance to the Vietnam War) had a more forceful impact on turning the tide of opinion against the war. As the same scholar puts it, "Future historians must consult Norman Mailer's *The Armies of the Night* to understand how and why the American Intellectual Left moved to 'resistance' against Johnson's Vietnam War and, in fact, to comprehend the radicalized intellectual consciousness of the 1960s."

One theme of *Armies* is his ruminations on the March as the beginning of a long war. He draws on memories of his combat experience as a guide to the struggle he foresees, hopes for, and dreads, as well as his awareness of the nearby battlefields of Bull Run, Chancellorsville, and Gettysburg. Walking together on the morning of the March, he and Lowell and Macdonald are in good spirits, "for the war spoke of future redemptions." The day is clear, "and the thin air! wine of Civil War apples in the October air! edge of excitement and awe—how would this day end? No one could know." Mailer is forty-four years old and it has taken him all of his years "to be able to enjoy his pleasures where he found them, rather than worry about those pleasures which eluded him," and yet now he might face imprisonment for civil disobedience. If he was too old to be a revolutionary à la Castro, living in a mountain camp as a guerrilla, he was also "too incompetent" and "too showboat, too lacking in essential judgment—besides, he was too well known!"

> He would pay for the pleasures of his notoriety in the impossibility of disguise. No gun in the hills, no taste for organization, no, he was a figurehead, and therefore he was expendable, said the new modesty—not a future leader, but a future victim: *there* would be his real value. He could go to jail for protest, and spend some years if it came to it, possibly his life, for if the war went on, and America put its hot martial tongue across the Chinese border, well, jail was the probable perspective, detention camps, disassociation centers, liquidation alleys, that would be his portion, and it would come about the time he had learned how to live.

The three men agree on their expendability and conclude that after leading the March, they should get arrested as soon as practicable. After much frustration in crossing the bridge into Virginia in some semblance of orderly rows and files, the unruly army of protesters debouches into a road leading to the Pentagon. The column disintegrates as it arrives. Mailer feels ennobled and happy "as if finally one stood under some mythical arch in the great vault of history." The sense of a nation divided liberated "some undiscovered patriotism in Mailer so that he felt a sharp searing love for his country in this moment, and on this day, crossing some divide in his own mind wider than the Potomac, a love so lacerated he felt as if a marriage were being torn and children lost." He is ready to act and reflects on why soldiers in the front line of battle are ready to die: "there is a promise of some swift transit; one's soul feels clean." He steps over a low rope ("It was as if the air had changed, or light had altered; he felt immediately much more alive—yes, bathed in air—and yet disembodied from himself, as if indeed he were watching himself in a film"), and within minutes is arrested. Lowell and Macdonald hesitate, miss their opportunity, and fly back to New York. Mailer goes to jail.

The remainder of the first part of the narrative, "History as a Novel," is given over to his adventures while incarcerated. The next morning, unshaved, unkempt, and "feeling like the people's choice between Victor McLaglen and Harpo Marx," he appears before a magistrate who fines him $50, gives him a thirty-day sentence (twenty-five days suspended), and releases him on $500 bail. He will appeal the decision. He has missed a dinner party—hosted we finally learn, by Lowell and Elizabeth Hardwick—which "had every promise of being wicked, tasty, and rich."

Mailer's time in the federal workhouse in Occoquan, Virginia, was none of these things, but it enabled him to meet a variety of fellow protesters, guards, and minor officials; he gives quick intaglio portraits of several, and a longer one of a member of the American Nazi Party, with whom he nearly comes to blows. None of these match his high-relief depiction of Lowell, one of the narrative's greatest assets.

In 1969, when a friend asked him if he was embarrassed by Mailer's description of him, Lowell replied, "No, in fact I was quite flattered. Norman didn't have to say all that about me." Writing to Mailer right after he had read the first part of *Armies*, Lowell said, "I've been trying to shake off mannerisms etc. you note. Of course one can't. Probably I am more sharply outlined, Bostonish, noble, sorrowful in Mailer than in life." Mailer's account—which Lowell pointedly says is *not* journalism, but comedy and history, "seems as true as one could ask." Two years later, he said that while Mailer had made him "a Quixote in the retinue of Sancho Panza," it was still "the best, almost the only thing written about me as a living person." He goes on to say that he and Mailer were not close before the March, but became so afterward, and that he had written to Mailer to say he hoped that they would "remain as good friends in life as in fiction." Lowell later published a collection of brief poems, *Notebook, 1967–68*, which includes two on the March, and another, "For Norman Mailer." It begins with a jibe at the corporation man whose heart is a watch. Mailer is the counter figure at the end of the poem: a man in a blue suit who "disproves the many false faces I see as one." The inscription on Mailer's copy reads, "For Norman, This brief though true return for your kind portrait, from Cal" (Lowell's nickname from youth was Caligula).

Lowell had another observation on *Armies of the Night*. He said it was possible that "the form of the book came from me. Not from anything I said but from contrasting me symbolically with himself." This contrast starts in the opening pages and continues right up until Mailer is arrested. After the party where they jousted, Mailer and Lowell move on to the Ambassador Theater, where they speak at a fundraiser. Mailer, the "Prince of Bourbon," drinking from a borrowed mug, observes his friend as they wait to go on. Lowell had "the expression on his face of a dues payer who is just about keeping up with the interest on some enormous debt." He looked most unhappy with the bad acoustics, the unruly crowd, and the cold floor and with the "fatally vulgar" Mailer.

Lowell is perceived as possessing a mixture of strength and weakness, "a blending so dramatic in its visible sign of conflict that one had to assume he would be sensationally attractive to women." He was a man who would fight to the death for some causes, "with an axe in his hand and a Cromwellian light in his eye."

> It was even possible that physically he was very strong—one couldn't tell at all—he might be fragile, he might have the sort of farm mechanic's strength which could manhandle the rear axle and differential off a car and into the back of a pickup. But physical strength or no, his nerves were all too apparently delicate. Obviously spoiled by everyone for years, he seemed nonetheless to need the spoiling.

He looks over and gives what Mailer reads as a look of dismay, one which says, "Every single bad thing I have ever heard about you is not exaggerated." Mailer looks back, and thinks ruefully:

> "You, Lowell, beloved poet of many, what do you know of the dirt and the dark deliveries of the necessary? What do you know of dignity hard-achieved, and dignity lost through innocence, and dignity lost by sacrifice for a cause one cannot name. What do you know about getting fat against your will, and turning into a clown of an arriviste baron when you would rather be an eagle or a count, or rarest of all, some natural aristocrat from these damned democratic states?"

Mailer didn't participate in the March with the idea of writing about it. The event, therefore, unrolled naturally with no imaginative forcing, which, like his time in the army and in Bellevue, was the kind of experience he found most valuable. When the March was over, his first thought was, "What a good short story I've got." He called Scott Meredith and told him about what he had seen and done, and the ever-enterprising Meredith negotiated a $10,000 fee for an article in *Harper's*, which the magazine's editor, Willie Morris, said "was an astronomical figure" for that time. Morris, who had met Mailer in Austin in 1963 through Mailer's old friend Barbara Probst Solomon, moved in 1963 from the editorship of the *Texas Observer* to *Harper's*, and in

1967 published an acclaimed memoir, *North Toward Home*. As an associate editor, Morris had tried to get Mailer into *Harper's*, but his superiors rejected his recommendation. But Mailer's new stature changed things, and Morris arranged the deal with Meredith—twenty thousand words to be written in a month. Later that day, walking up Sixth Avenue, he ran into Mailer and Farbar. He told Mailer that he had spoken with Meredith. Immediately, Morris recalled, Mailer "crouched like a boxer—he used to do that a lot in those days, like he was shadowboxing with me—and he said, 'I know you did; I've just talked to him. I'm going to Provincetown tomorrow, and I will have a great twenty thousand words in one month from today.' "

He wrote at breakneck speed, over ten thousand words a week, but not at first; he had difficulty getting started. He became gloomy. "No book I wrote kept me in a more sustained bad mood (while doing it) than *The Armies of the Night*," he said. His deteriorating relationship with Beverly was one reason. Podhoretz's wife, Midge Decter, a *Harper's* editor at the time, visited Provincetown while he was writing *Armies*. She said that Beverly, who loved Provincetown, felt "isolated and bored" that winter. "She wasn't very happy with that month she put in; that was very clear." After a week or more of false starts, Mailer remembered that when Picasso began a new project, he had a way of "going off in a new direction. He was telling us a secret, which was that style is a tool by which you explore reality." *Time* magazine's brief piece on Mailer and the March, "A Shaky Start," gave him a handhold. Accompanied by a photo of him holding a coffee cup of bourbon, and mocking him for "mumbling and spewing obscenities" at the "scruffy Ambassador Theater," during the rally before the March, the piece made him sound like an incoherent fool, passing over entirely his humor and badinage with the audience, which "really tied the thing together," as de Grazia recalled. He praised Mailer's "excitement and his energy" that night, and "this particular genius he has when he's drunk," something the *Time* stringer missed. "The average reporter," Mailer wrote, "could not get a sentence straight if it were phrased more subtly than his own mind could make phrases. Nuances were forever being munched like peanuts." He began his narrative with *Time*'s three-hundred-word squib followed by: "Now we may leave *Time* in order to find out what happened."

In his freshman English course at Harvard, Mailer read a long chapter from Adams's *The Education of Henry Adams* ("The Virgin and the Dynamo," probably) and, like most readers, was slightly puzzled by the perspective, but he had no memory of thinking of the book afterward. Anyone who reads *Armies of the Night* and knows Adams's masterpiece, however, immediately sees the influence. "It's as if I were the great-grandson," Mailer wrote later. "Adams must have remained in my mind as a possibility, the way a painter might look at a particular Picasso or Cézanne and say to himself, 'That's the way to do it.' Yet the influence might not pop forth for twenty or thirty years. In effect, that's what happened with Henry Adams." But even after he was well into the account, he found that it took an effort of will to write every day. The point of view was "damned odd," he said, and he wrote half the book before he adjusted psychologically to this "dislocating way to regard oneself." Finally, he got used to it, and relished employing that "part of the ego that is superior to ourselves—that person who observes us carefully even as we are doing bizarre things, that special persona, possessed of immaculate detachment." By mid-November, the handwritten pages were accumulating, and his secretary, Sandy Charlebois Thomas, had difficulty keeping up.

As Mailer worked in his third floor study looking out at Long Point and the Provincetown harbor, Morris and Decter waited and worried in New York, while Meredith tried to sell the book version of a narrative he was hard pressed to describe. The New American Library finally purchased it, but the advance was only $25,000. Robert Gutwillig, editor-in-chief, said this was because NAL had "already laid out so much for the novel which wasn't being written"—"First-Born"—and "nobody, including Norman, had any idea what kind of book it [*Armies*] was going to be." On November 20, Mailer wrote to Yamanishi that he thought his account might reach forty thousand words. Sometime after this, Morris, who hoped to get the piece in the March issue of *Harper's*, asked for a progress report. Mailer invited him and Decter to Provincetown. When they arrived in early January, the manuscript, some of it still on yellow legal pads, had grown enormously. "I was stunned," Morris said. "He had gone up there and hadn't had anything to drink for a month, leading a Spartan life with Beverly, and he had turned out this incredible ninety thousand words." Morris telephoned his managing editor, Robert Kotlowitz, to tell him and when Kotlowitz asked him how many words he wanted to run in March, he said, "I think we should run all of it at once." Morris made the decision on the spot to run the longest piece ever published in an American magazine.

Working twelve and fourteen hours a day, Mailer finished writing "The Novel as History" soon after they arrived. The manuscript all but completed, Beverly cooked a celebration dinner to which Mailer contributed his signature dish, mushrooms stuffed with *duxelles*. Morris, who was known to take a drink, brought out a bottle of Wild Turkey bourbon. After dinner, Mailer took Morris and Decter on a drive around Provincetown in his jeep. It was snowing lightly and few lights were visible in the almost deserted town. He drove down narrow, winding Commercial Street along the harbor to the town's center, past the gothic town hall and the tall stone memorial to the Pilgrims, and then to where they had first landed before sailing to Plymouth, a spot occupied then and now by a huge, ghostly motel. From there, he drove to the state highway that separates the town from the towering dunes of the Cape Cod National Seashore, as Morris recalled in his memoir, *New York Days*. It was snowing more as they turned off the highway.

> On one especially precarious dune the vehicle stalled momentarily in the sand, and we had to push it. Mobile again, as we took turns with draws on the bottle, he began talking in the redneck Texas accent he said he had acquired from back-country Texans in the Army. He rolled out in prefaces to sentences a lot of twangy "little ol's" while gesturing sharply with his arms. He said he liked southerners. "Why did you say I had frizzy hair in that book [*North Toward Home*] you wrote?" he asked. "Well," I replied, "because you do." The motor of our conveyance began to buzz and hum a little, and the driver put his wary ear to the dashboard and said, "I think this thing has tuberculosis."

The only open bar in the town was at the local VFW post, and Mailer took Decter and Morris there for a drink. Morris offered a toast to the manuscript, which would be called "The Steps of the Pentagon" when it appeared in *Harper's*. Mailer said, "Look, I wish you'd stop praising it. It makes me edgy"—his unwillingness to welcome good luck too lavishly always hovered in the wings. Some months later, when Fan Mailer heard that *Armies of the Night* had won the Pulitzer Prize, she recalled, "I said, '*Umbashrien Got tsu danken*!' "—God protect us from the evil eye. She said that her father had done the same when good things happened. "I had hoped he would win the prize, and then when he got two prizes, the National Book Award too, I said it again, a double *Umbashrien*!" As they drank, Mailer pushed Morris to publish the still-unfinished second part of *Armies*, "History as a Novel," which recapitulates the entire story of the March in an objective, factual fashion. Morris told him that this thirty-thousand-word piece would work well in book form, but would be "only an afterthought" to the dramatic first part. Mailer disagreed, but was unable to convince him. He subsequently turned to his "old dear great and good friend Norman Podhoretz," who agreed to publish it in *Commentary*'s April issue as "The Battle of the Pentagon." When the threesome returned to the house, Beverly was searching for the needle of her stereo. She told Mailer that he had worked voodoo on the record player because he hated it. Mailer said nothing. He dedicated *Armies of the Night* to Beverly, but by then the marriage had taken another step toward its conclusion.

SHORTLY AFTER HE finished the second part of *Armies*, he began his review of Podhoretz's *Making It*. He found that his initial estimate had changed for the worse. He had also read the reviews. Podhoretz's thesis is that sexual lust, the "dirty little secret" of Victorian times (according to D. H. Lawrence), had been replaced by lust for success in society, most certainly among his colleagues in The Family. He admits his own unqualified desire to be rich, famous, and powerful in the memoir's opening pages, and then goes on to relate his life story as it pertains to his career up to the age of thirty-five (he was born in 1930). The response of reviewers to Podhoretz's revelation of his ambition, and his final admission—thought to be candid by him, considered crass by others—that the book itself was a "Mailer-like bid for literary distinction, fame, and money all in one package" was, he said later, "very nasty indeed." Mailer's review, which appeared in *Partisan Review* just before the second half of *Armies* appeared in *Commentary*, contained some positive comments about his friend's "agreeable variety of aperçus on matters such as status, class, privilege and clan." While it was not "a great or major book," he wrote, it was for the most part "very well written for much of its length." But after these tentative plaudits, Mailer decimated the memoir.

Podhoretz felt betrayed. He knew that Mailer was reviewing the book and thought that it would be positive, even a rave. A rave in *PR*, even one that appeared, as Mailer's did, three months after the book's publication, could offset the damage done by the book's early reviewers, that "squalid yard of humpty-beaters and hard-ons," as Mailer referred to them. "Here I was," Podhoretz told Mailer biographer Peter Manso, "being beaten up all over the place, and instead of helping me when I was down, my great friend was giving me another kick in the ribs." Mailer's critique is two-fold, and depends to some extent on his own view of how The Family had all but abandoned its critical responsibilities in favor of an adoring but unspoken appreciation for the waves of Camp and Pop rolling across the country. His first point, however, is that Podhoretz had failed to see that in writing about himself in the motions of mid-career, he was, in effect, writing a novel. His obligation, therefore, had been to present "himself as a *literary* character, fully so much as any literary character in a work of undisputed fiction." Mailer does not say—nor does Podhoretz seem to have noticed in his scab-picking rejoinders to the review—that Mailer is also referring, implicitly, to the protagonist of *Armies of the Night*, his own just completed work of self-portrayal, clearly labeled as a hybrid of the novel and history. Such an amalgam is tricky, he said, because readers will respond to such a character much the same way they react to characters in a novel. "One is advancing and endangering one's career" by taking on such a challenge.

> The book is now a protagonist in the progress of one's success. Self-interest naturally slants a word here, literary honesty bends it back there. One does not know whether to tell the little lie or shrive oneself. An overload of choices descends on the brain of any ambitious man engaged in giving a contentious portrait of himself. Yet that is not even the worst of the difficulty. The real woe is that one is forced to examine oneself existentially, perceive oneself in the act of perceiving (but worse, far worse—through the act of perceiving, perceive a Self who may manage to represent the separate warring selves by a Style).

The connection is not made and Podhoretz fails to present himself as an American Julien Sorel, a young man from the provinces possessed of a frenzy for riches and renown, and the audacity to seize them. Instead, the reader is "forced to jog along on the washboard road of a memoir," and consequently loses all interest as Podhoretz provides the dreary bureaucratic details of his climb to the editorship of *Commontary.* All that remains are "sketchy anecdotes, abortive essays, isolated insights, and note of the drone—repetitions." The potential of presenting "interplay between ambitious perception and society" is lost, and Podhoretz's "dirty little secret" loses its force in what becomes a "muted limited account of a young provincial."

"Podhoretz apes Mailer, but he is no Mailer. He is, in the end, a small bore," says one reviewer. He lacked the narrative sophistication to write his memoir as Mailer wished him to, but this is not surprising. He was a critic, not a novelist, and it seems somewhat unreasonable to have asked him to write his book according to the specifications of an accomplished novelist who has discovered after twenty years of assiduous effort an innovative way to present himself in nonfiction. But Mailer's other major criticism is quite fair, and devastating. Podhoretz displays a fatal weakness in the book: he flatters The Family instead of revealing the byzantine contours of its envious and brilliant self-aggrandizements. Mailer lists thirty-three Family members and notes that references to each are "invariably as attractive as the sort of remark one makes when giving a reference to a Foundation for a friend." His portraits are "full of sugar"; he depicts "an Establishment composed of the kindest folk: into their ranks enters an ambitious Provincial—what a novel!" Podhoretz, he concludes, "deserted his possibilities as thoroughly as if Stendhal had presented the family of Mademoiselle de la Mole as charming." Years later, Mailer said his review "was probably too cruel." Perhaps it was, but it cast invaluable light on the involuted perspective he used to depict himself in *Armies*.

Eventually Podhoretz recovered from Mailer's review, abandoned his earlier radical-liberal politics, and went on to become a major figure in the neoconservative movement. After the review, their relationship slowly dissolved, but they saw each other occasionally. In 1979, Mailer invited Podhoretz to his home for dinner and told him that he would like his new book, *The Executioner's Song*. Podhoretz answered by saying that Mailer "probably would dislike what I had written about him in my new book, *Breaking Ranks*. 'Well,' he said, 'you owe me one,' and I laughed and replied, 'Yes, I do.' " Afterward Podhoretz told his wife,

Midge Decter, who had helped edit *Armies of the Night*, that Mailer would never forgive him for *Breaking Ranks*. They did not speak again for almost twenty years.

The quarrel was soon lost in the roar of acclaim for *Armies*. It won the Pulitzer and the National Book Award, and a George Polk Award for magazine reporting. Among the major reviews, only John Simon and Mario Puzo were negative—even *Time* was mildly approving—and when Willie Morris wrote to him about the honors for which it was being considered, he replied, "Willie, if I ever get the Pulitzer Prize you realize that the cows are going to come home." Alfred Kazin's front-page review in *The New York Times Book Review*, perhaps the most important and intelligent of the book's notices, described it as a "diary-essay-tract-sermon," and compared Mailer's self-presentation with that of "the best American writers of the 19th century [who] talked about themselves all the time—but, in the Romantic American line, saw the self as the prime condition of democracy." Kazin concluded with this thought: "Mailer's intuition is that the times demand a new form. He has found it." Published twenty years to the day after *The Naked and the Dead, The Armies of the Night* disarmed the literary world and reaffirmed Mailer's genius. The paradox of his achievement is that in a narrative that sundered the protagonist into Mailer-now and Mailer-then, he was able to unite all the actors, currents, and rich particularities of the March, seeing them through the oppositions of his psyche. This division of self by fiat, the resolution of twenty years of point of view uncertainties, was a masterstroke and the most significant aesthetic decision of Mailer's career.

Armies' triumph was a succès d'estime. The book did not make the bestseller list, although it has remained in print since publication and appears on most lists of the greatest nonfiction books of the twentieth century. Mailer's parents saw it as a happy endorsement of their son's talents. Barney and Fan came to the ceremony when he was awarded the National Book Award in March of 1969. Robert J. Lifton, also from Brooklyn, received a National Book Award in the sciences for his moving study *Death in Life: Survivors of Hiroshima* the same night that Mailer received his in the arts and letters category. Lifton and his wife, Betty Jean, knew Mailer and Beverly from summers on Cape Cod. Lifton recalled the ceremony, where they met Mailer's parents: "He immediately took BJ and me over to meet them, and by then they were elderly and they came across as nice Jewish older people. Norman said, 'This is Bob Lifton; he also won a National Book Award.' And she looked at me and said, 'It's so nice that you both won it.' I'm sure what she meant was it was so nice that another nice Jewish boy from Brooklyn also won it. That was my translation." There was a bar backstage and a certain amount of drinking took place before the ceremony. The crowd, Lifton said, "was terrified that Norman was going to misbehave because of his reputation for doing that. He got up and gave a choirboy speech." Mailer said he disagreed with Sartre about turning down the Nobel Prize and, referring to himself in the third person, said, "Your speaker is here to state that he likes prizes," seeing them as "measures of the degree to which an Establishment meets that talent it has hindered and helped." This was especially true, he implied, in a time when society was "poised on the lip, no, the main of a spiritual revolution which will wash the roots of every national institution out to sea." For the next few years, he would alternately warn of and welcome this revolution brought on by American hubris, and what he called in the speech the "Armageddons of technology."

WRITING TO KNOX a week after *Armies* appeared in *Harper's*, Mailer said he was happy with its "pleasant" reception, and had "a few small hopes for the book." Completing the editing of *Beyond the Law*, however, was his immediate concern. With Farbar's help, he had cut it to 110 minutes, but there was more work to be done before its April 2 premiere at the University of Notre Dame. His interest in *Wild 90* had all but disappeared. He had considered entering into the competition at the Cannes Film Festival, but he had already spent $10,000 on theater rentals and advertising. Very few people went to see the film, mainly because of the hideous reviews, but also because Farbar had rented a room in the bowels of a Manhattan office building that lacked a marquee. Mailer was advised by unnamed friends, he told Knox, to forgo Cannes, "because the odds against gaining anything would be very great and the perils of being wiped out enormous." His hopes were now pinned on *Beyond the Law*, and between antiwar speaking engagements he worked steadily on completing the editing.

Despite an imperfect sound system, the premiere at Notre Dame was a success. It held an audience of 3,500, mainly undergraduate students, to the end and boosted Mailer's cinematic ambitions. But a few months later when the film was shown at the New York Film Festival, a significant number of people walked out of Philharmonic Hall, reacting to its violence and obscenity. One critic said in his review that Mailer didn't understand the movies. Unlike novels, the unnamed critic said, "the movies are not there to hit people where they live. The movies are there to keep people alive." Mailer said that this was true in the past, but in the late 1960s "the horror of life has become so completely pervasive" that this sort of emotional nourishment was beside the point; filmgoers needed to be jolted. Nevertheless, he learned something from his first two films, namely, that he hadn't given himself utterly to filmmaking. "Making movies is a religious act," he said, and up to now, "I've just been having an affair with movies." At some point, he said, he was going to have to choose between writing and marrying the movies.

Beyond the Law lost money just as handily as *Wild 90*—over $70,000—although it continued to play to receptive audiences on the college circuit. Its appeal, Mailer felt, lay in his vision of getting "below the reality, beneath the reality, within the reality of an evening in the police station." The relationship of cops and criminals is incredible, he said. "No one's ever begun to deal with how fantastic they are in their love-hate relationship." According to Michael Chaiken, *Beyond the Law* worked because the film had a baseline premise: "people were pegged either a cop or a criminal." *Wild 90*, on the other hand, was less successful because of its "anything-goes-bottomless quality." Mailer's cast in *Beyond the Law*, however, "could easily tap into the cops-and-crooks scenario because in personal moments we're all questioning our own kind of morals and integrity. Mailer found a group of people who were able to draw out things that were very truthful for them." Chaiken added that he thinks that Mailer's experience at Actors Studio enabled him to do a superb job of casting.

All told, he spent nearly eight months editing *Beyond the Law*, four times as long as he had spent writing *Armies of the Night*. Between editing stints, he continued to give time to the antiwar effort, but he had much else on his agenda. Jack Newfield wrote a piece for *The Village Voice* about a day in the life of "Norman Mailer, novelist, counterpuncher, filmmaker, mayoral candidate, stud, essayist, egomaniac, and successor to Whitman and Henry James as American Zeitgeist." On the day in question, May 24, 1968, after several hours of editing, he met with Tom Hayden, one of the founders of Students for a Democratic Society, and asked for his help in meeting Castro. "I want a guarantee," he said, "man to man, that I can see Fidel." Then Mailer went to a cocktail party at Dwight Macdonald's apartment, where he met Mark Rudd and other members of SDS. He said he didn't agree with everything SDS was doing, but he gave them a check because "they are an active principle. They are taking chances." From Macdonald's, he went to a taping of *The Merv Griffin Show*, where Griffin announced him by saying, "Norman Mailer is one of the leading spectator sports in America." He walked on stage, Newfield wrote, "hunching up his shoulders like Carmen Basilio coming to Ray Robinson." Afterward, he attended the light heavyweight championship match at Madison Square Garden between Bob Foster and Dick Tiger (who had taken away José Torres's title in December 1966), which Foster won. After midnight, Mailer climbed over a fifteen-foot fence to confer with Mark Rudd and the other students who had recently taken over the administrative offices of Columbia University, an event that reverberated at campuses across the nation.

Preoccupied as he was with *Beyond the Law*, Mailer got an idea for a new film in June. The nation was still in mourning for Martin Luther King, shot to death on April 4, when Robert Kennedy was assassinated shortly after midnight on June 5, just after he won the Democratic presidential primary in California. Two days earlier Andy Warhol had been shot four times at his studio and almost died. Over the next few days, as the country fell into a state of horror and confusion, Mailer conceived of *Maidstone*. The new film, he wrote, was calling to him "with every stimulus and every fear." Named after a fictional estate on Long Island where the events unfold, the film focuses on a famous-infamous director. Norman T. Kingsley is "one of fifty men who America in her bewilderment and profound demoralization might be contemplating as a possible President." In *Armies of the Night* Mailer admitted that except for JFK, "there had not been a President of the United States nor even a candidate since the Second World War whom Mailer secretly considered more suitable than himself." Kingsley's ambition is similarly large, but the chain of assassinations had unnerved the country, and he believed he could be next. To guard against attack, he is watched by a super-secret police agency called Protection Against Assassination Experiments-Control (PAX-C). We soon learn, however, that some of the agency's operatives seem just as interested in assassinating Kingsley as protecting him. This could be paranoia or it could be genuine—there are contradictory hints. Mailer himself did not know. Carol Stevens, who had a role in the film, said that the mood on the set was "unbelievably paranoiac." Again, there was no script, just a situation.

The situation within the situation is a film Kingsley plans to make about a male brothel located at Maidstone; much of the action—there isn't much—consists of the director interviewing young actresses to play the role of brothel customers. There is another shadowy group of men at Maidstone, the Cashbox, consisting of male prostitutes who are almost as portentous as PAX-C. The two groups overlap. Kingsley's half-brother, Raoul Rey O'Houlihan (played by Rip Torn), is either completely loyal to Kingsley or tempted to kill him. He runs the Cashbox (Buzz Farbar and Eddie Bonetti play the roles of key members). The rest of the cast of fifty to sixty—the numbers change as people drop in and out over the week—include Beverly Bentley, who plays Kingsley's estranged wife; two women Mailer was having affairs with, Lee Roscoe and Shari Rothe, who are two of the "belles"; Grove Press publisher Barney Rosset, who plays a member of the local gentry; and Robert David Lion Gardiner, who owned one of the estates. Jeanne Campbell plays a major role as a British television reporter, and Adeline Naiman is a college president. A number of other friends, including Anne Barry, Paul Carroll, Michael McClure, Torres, Lucid, and Noel Parmentel Jr. have roles, as do Hervé, the dwarf from *Fantasy Island*, and Ultra Violet, a Warhol "superstar." Several film crews, led by Pennebaker, Nick Proferes, Jan Welt, and one of Mailer's Harvard classmates, Richard Leacock, filmed the action using handheld cameras and color film over five days in late July on four different estates in or around East Hampton, Long Island.

James Toback, who later made a number of important films and was influenced by Mailer, wrote a long piece about the making of the film for *Esquire*. He described what he saw when he visited the set.

> There was a fair amount of tension all through the whole shoot and I would say that he was never in control in the way a director is normally in control of a set. First of all, the set was all sprawled out; things were being shot all over the place. People were inventing things at the last minute. So it wasn't subject to any of the normal protections that a director has if in fact he wants to keep control of

> a set. I don't think Norman minded it at all, I think that was part of the idea. But there was, I would say without sounding too melodramatic about it, there was a danger in the air.

Mailer had deliberately created this mood, and made it "tacitly understood" that O'Houlihan was free to threaten or attack Kingsley if the situation called for it. Mailer had told the cast, after all, that they were "a bunch of enforced existentialists." Torn plays his role perfectly and never looks less than ominous, especially on the last night of shooting when he and Mailer, dressed in formal clothes and top hats, attend "The Assassination Ball," along with most of the cast. Torn-O'Houlihan debates whether to strike; it seems imminent. But the moment passes.

The next day, the last day of shooting, Torn struck. Most of the cast and camera crews had departed, and Mailer and Beverly are walking with four of their children, Betsy, Kate, Michael, and Stephen, through a field on Gardiners Island, an actual island owned by the Gardiner family. The children were eight, five, four, and two, respectively. Pennebaker is following them, recording what appears to be a summer idyll. With no warning, Torn, who had been off in the distance, comes running at them, full tilt, with a hammer in his hand. He strikes Mailer in the head twice and blood flows. Beverly screams; Mailer bellows, "You crazy fool cocksucker"; the children cry in terror. Torn-O'Houlihan, still holding the hammer, comes forward and speaks: "You're supposed to die, Mr. Kingsley. You must die, not Mailer, I don't want to kill Mailer, but I must kill Kingsley in this picture." The real and the fictional merge. The two men wrestle and roll on the ground. Mailer bites Torn's ear. More blood, more screams; Beverly cries like a wolverine. Finally, with her help, the two men are separated, and after mutual recriminations, they part. Mailer tells Torn he is taking the scene out of the film.

But on reflection, he changes his mind, realizing that he was complicit, if not directly responsible, for what happened. Through the fall of 1968 and into the first half of 1969, he watched the forty-five hours of film shot by the five crews. To his dismay, he discovers that only six or seven hours are usable. He has given too much autonomy to the camera crews and casts, and most of the good material, "all too unhappily," centers on Kingsley. When he realizes that there is too much Kingsley in the raw footage, he concludes, reluctantly at first, but then unequivocally, that "Torn had therefore been right to make his attack." He proceeds to make the fight the violent culmination of all the whispering and plotting and knowing looks that precede it.

For the next three years, working with two professionals, Jan Welt and Lana Jokel, Mailer devoted more time to editing *Maidstone* than to anything else. He continued to write and produced three books—two of them major works, *Miami and the Siege of Chicago* and *Of a Fire on the Moon*—and also ran for mayor of New York in the 1969 Democratic primary. Film became his passion, however. Just as Henry James, discouraged after years of novel writing, sought in the 1890s to begin a more lucrative, exciting career in the theater, Mailer in the late 1960s considered shelving, or even giving up, the solitary work of a writer to become a producer-director. He imagined himself about to join the company of the period's great directors—Jean-Luc Godard, Federico Fellini, and Michelangelo Antonioni, among them. When he read Toback's *Esquire* article about the filming of *Maidstone*, "At Play in the Fields of the Bored," he was unhappy with it. "When we discussed it," Toback recalled, "he said that he thought that I had taken him too lightly, that it was the first thing to appear in print about him as a director and the result of the article was to encourage that part of the journalistic community that was always ready to make fun of Norman, always ready to take him with a grain of salt, to ridicule him, to mock him. He felt that ideally I would have been writing about him as the American Godard. Instead, I gave ammunition to his enemies." Mailer later saw the merit of the article and got Toback's permission to reprint it as a preface to *Maidstone: A Mystery.*

Another reason for Mailer's fascination with film is that it was challenging the dominant narrative mode, the novel. His films are of continuing interest, Chaiken said, because "they're part of a certain conversation that was happening in New York City at that time about direct cinema and the new American cinema of Shirley Clarke and John Cassavetes. His films are in there with the stuff Andy Warhol was doing, the stuff Jonas Mekas was showing at the Filmmakers' Cinémathèque—Norman's films are absolutely part of that conversation. He was throwing his hat into that ring and was going for something that was unique. He was turning direct cinema on its head. He was using documentary techniques to film quasi-fictitious situations." By the 1960s, film was challenging the novel and Mailer wanted to be a player, Chaiken said. His reputation, coupled with New York City's position as a filmmaking incubator, generated tremendous media interest in *Maidstone*. An early version of it was shown in Provincetown in August 1970, and at the Venice Film Festival later the same month. When Mailer arrived in Italy with Carol Stevens—he and Beverly separated in the fall of 1969—he said, "We came here to try to pick up the marbles." The film did not win a prize, however.

At its showing two months later at the London Film Festival, billed as its world premiere, there were huge crowds. He told Knox that he "drew more than anybody in the whole festival, including the personal appearances of Taylor and Burton. (Which last gives me delight, I confess it.)" But the acoustics were bad and the audience was restless, and when it was over, Mailer appeared on stage, much as Henry James had after the premiere of *Guy Domville* seventy-five years earlier. James was hooted off the stage and subsequently gave up the theater. Mailer said the dialogue with his crowd "came under the head[ing] of free swinging." One voice from the dark asked, "With all this money to throw around, couldn't you make a film with some content?" Mailer retorted, "I'd rather make a movie to agitate than fortify the far recesses of your leaden brain." *Maidstone*, he said, had "an esthetic coherence of a new order," and demonstrated "new modes of perceiving reality." But the audience's comments stung him, and when he returned to the United States, he reedited the film. On September 22, 1971, the film had its American premiere at the Whitney Museum. It ran for ten days, three showings a day, in a small theater and drew seven thousand, a record attendance. But when it was shown commercially the next month, the audiences were tiny, and it folded. Mailer was confounded and asked a good friend to explain what had gone wrong. The friend said that there were seven thousand people in New York who were eager to see *Maidstone*, and they all saw it at the Whitney. Mailer later called it "my failed cinematic masterpiece."

Within days of the end of shooting *Maidstone*, Mailer left to cover the Republican National Convention, August 5–8, in Miami, on assignment from *Harper's*. Morris had promised him the same kind of space given to *Armies*, and Mailer needed income after spending $125,000 on the film. To raise this sum, he had sold a majority of his shares in *The Village Voice*. After Miami, he would have a two-week break, after which he planned to travel to Chicago to cover the Democratic National Convention, August 26–29. The summer of 1968, he wrote at the beginning of *Miami and Siege of Chicago*, was a time when "the Republic hovered on the edge of revolution, nihilism, and lines of police on file to the horizon." John Updike, who at the time resided in the suburbs of Mailer's esteem, provided him with a line about the nation's throes, made after Robert Kennedy was killed: "God may have withdrawn his blessing from America," he said.

The two conventions could not have been more different. The Republicans were united and optimistic about their chances of winning the White House; the Democrats were bitter and divided over the Vietnam War. Richard Nixon had returned from the political graveyard after losing the race for governor of California in 1962, and had traveled the country for five years building support. Neither Governor Nelson Rockefeller of New York nor Governor Ronald Reagan, both relative latecomers to the race, had sufficient backing to mount a real challenge to him. President Johnson's decision not to seek renomination after only narrowly defeating Senator Eugene McCarthy of Minnesota—an early and eloquent opponent of the war—in the New Hampshire primary, and Robert Kennedy's assassination had fractured the Democrats and weakened their eventual, equivocating nominee, Johnson's vice president, Hubert Humphrey. Mailer's report on the Miami convention contains the same sharp-etched character sketches as in *Armies of the Night*, and the same sure grasp of the currents of a large, multifaceted event. The currents, however, were turgid. There were no real surprises at the convention. One of the two most memorable patches of writing in part one, "Nixon in Miami," is the examination of Nixon redux. Referring to himself as "the reporter," Mailer admits he has never written anything favorable about him. "There had never been anyone in American life so resolutely phony as Richard Nixon, nor anyone so transcendentally successful by such means," he wrote. And yet, "Tricky Dick" seemed to have changed. His dark-jowled face now revealed a hint of "inner debate about his value before eternity." His appearance had shifted

> from looking like an undertaker's assistant to looking like an old con seriously determined to go respectable. The Old Nixon, which is to say the young Nixon, used to look, on clasping his hands before him, like a church usher (of the variety who would twist a boy's ear after removing him from church). The older Nixon before the Press

> now—the *new* Nixon—had finally acquired some of the dignity of the old athlete and the old con—he had taken punishment, that was on his face now, he knew the detailed schedule of pain in a real loss.

The press was not admitted to the grand gala dinner at the Fontainebleau Hotel the night before the convention at which Nixon and his wife, Pat, received the guests, but by luck Mailer got into the room before it began. Seeing no place to stand unobserved, he took up a position before the main doors, standing at parade rest, as some two thousand delegates and their spouses strolled in. Posing as a security man, he scrutinized faces for thirty minutes. What he saw helped him understand why the new Nixon had such stout support.

> Most of them were ill-proportioned in some part of their physique. Half must have been, of course, men and women over fifty and their bodies reflected the pull of their character. The dowager's hump was common, and many a man had a flaccid paunch, but the collective tension was rather in the shoulders, in the girdling of the shoulders against anticipated lashings on the back, in the thrust forward of the neck, in the maintenance of the muscles of the mouth forever locked in readiness to bite the tough meat of resistance, in a posture forward from the hip since the small of the back was dependably stiff, loins and mind cut away from each other by some abyss between navel and hip.

Lacking kindred feeling for these stolid, immaculately neat people, he nevertheless "felt a sad sorrowful respect." He saw "in the heavy sturdy moves so many demonstrated of bodies in life's harness . . . the muted tragedy of the Wasp—they were not here on earth to enjoy or even perhaps to love so very much, they were here to serve, and serve they had in public functions and public charities (while recipients of their charity might vomit in rage and laugh in scorn)."

Nixon's landslide in the voting for the nomination is dutifully described. But except for Mailer's miniature of Reagan, then fifty-seven years of age ("he had the presence of a man of thirty, the deferential enthusiasm, the bright but dependably unoriginal mind," coupled with another personality, "very young, boyish, maybe thirteen or fourteen, freckles, cowlick, I tripped-on-my-sneaker-lace aw shucks variety of confusion"), the Miami narrative offers little more than high reportorial professionalism and, in his elaborations of WASPish rectitude, a shrewd application of Wilhelm Reich's theories of psychological "body armoring."

Upon his return, he spent ten days writing the 25,000-word Miami narrative, working rapidly so he had a few days to spend with Jan Welt and Lana Jokel as they worked on *Maidstone*. On August 24, he flew to Chicago. He loved the city, and his opening paean has been quoted by boosters of the Windy City for decades. "The reporter was sentimental about Chicago," he states at the outset of part two, "The Siege of Chicago," because Chicagoans "were like the good people of Brooklyn."

> They were simple, strong, warm-spirited, sly, rough, compassionate, jostling, tricky and extraordinarily good-natured because they had sex in their pockets, muscles on their back, hot eats around the corner, neighborhoods which dripped with the sauce of local legend, and real city architecture, brownstones with different windows on every floor, vistas for miles of red-brick and two-family wood-frame houses with balconies and porches, runty stunted trees rich as farmland in their promise of tenderness the first city evenings of spring, streets where kids played stick-ball and roller-hockey, lots of smoke and iron twilight.

The evocation becomes all the more powerful in memory as the narrative unfolds, culminating in a wrenching description of the "police riot" that besmirched the Democratic convention. Thousands of protesters and many innocent bystanders were beaten bloody by twelve thousand Chicago policemen backed up by 7,500 members of the Illinois National Guard. Some of the violence was seen on national television and helped to insure Nixon's election. Chicago's reputation was badly injured, and Mayor Richard Daley, whose constituency was made up of "people whose ancestors were at home with rude instruments in Polish forests, Ukrainian marshes, Irish bogs," lost a portion of his national clout. When Senator Abraham Ribicoff of Connecticut, in a speech nominating Senator George McGovern, accused Daley of "Gestapo tactics," Mailer wrote, "Daley was on his feet, Daley was shaking his fist at the podium, Daley was mouthing words. One could not hear the words, but his lips were clear. Daley seemed to be telling Ribicoff to go have carnal relations with himself." Mailer faithfully records all the violence on Michigan Avenue and in Lincoln Park, and all the hypocrisy inside the convention hall, including the falsely enthusiastic nomination of Humphrey.

Unlike the March on the Pentagon, Mailer was not a central figure at the convention. He knew his chief function was to record the event, yet he felt waves of shame for not being on the front line with the protesters. Instead, he drank in the Hilton and contemplated his fear. "It seemed to him that he had been afraid all his life, but in recent years, or so it seemed, he had learned how to take a step into his fear." But now he was hesitating. He was reluctant to lose his place, even in a country that was going mad. His country "had allowed him to write—it had even not deprived him entirely of honors, certainly not of an income. He had lived well enough to have six children, a house on the water, a good apartment, good meals, good booze, he had even come to enjoy wine. A revolutionary with taste in wine has come already half the distance from Marx to [Edmund] Burke." Mailer's sympathies were on the side of the Hippies and Yippies and the SDS, but he hated to see the country fall into "the nihilistic maw of a national disorder." He wanted his life to continue as it was going—making films and writing books and enjoying his growing family—but not if that meant being silent about an unjust war. After World War II, he said, he lived for a decade or more with the "potential militancy of a real revolutionary," but "the timing in his soul was apocalyptically maladroit." But when the time came, he did walk across Michigan Avenue to Grant Park and, after listening to Ginsberg and Burroughs he got up and gave a brief speech to the crowd about how long the struggle might continue, perhaps twenty years. He ended by explaining that he would not be with them the next day because he had a deadline and didn't want to chance getting arrested. When he had finished, someone in the crowd yelled, "Write good, baby."

Willie Morris planned to run Mailer's account of the conventions in the November *Harper's*, which would be on the newsstands three weeks before the election. New American Library would publish hardcover and paperback editions at the same time. The hope was that *Miami and the Siege of Chicago* would have the same kind of influence that "Superman Comes to the Supermarket" and "In the Red Light" had on the 1960 and 1964 elections, respectively. He went to work shortly after he returned from Chicago, writing if anything slightly faster than he had on *Armies of the Night*. By August 21, Morris and Robert Gutwillig at NAL had the 75,000-word manuscript in hand. He had written the fifty thousand words of part two in eighteen days. The book's reviews were positive, but somewhat less rapturous than those received by *Armies*. Most reviewers agreed with Eliot Fremont-Smith, the *New York Times* reviewer, that it was "more conventional" than *Armies*. Jack Richardson, for example, in a highly complimentary essay in *The New York Review of Books* noted that Mailer had allowed the conventions "to unfold for the most part unchallenged by his imagination." *Miami* stands in the shadow of *Armies*, and has suffered for it, but in the introduction to a 2008 reprint, Frank Rich said that it "holds up better than most political journalism written last week, let alone four decades ago." Rich argues that Mailer's genuine ambivalence about the events, coupled with his "literary energy and intellectual independence" transcends the "small-bore pack mentality" of what passes for much of today's political journalism, in print and on line. How much *Miami* affected vote totals cannot be gauged. Nixon, as we know, defeated Humphrey by less than one percent of the popular vote, although the ten million votes, mainly in southern states, received by third-party candidate George C. Wallace may have cost the Democrats the election.

NINE
POLITICIAN TO PRISONER

Mailer's campaign for mayor of New York City in 1969 was considerably different from the one he had envisioned in 1960. He made clear to his backers that he intended to run a real campaign, filing nominating papers for the Democratic primary and hiring a professional staff. Nevertheless, the campaign was the operative definition of quixotic. While the literary intelligentsia saw it as intellectually provocative and slightly heroic, the mainstream media considered it to be somewhat nutty and eminently newsworthy. Both were correct. He made his decision to run in early March at almost exactly the same time that he agreed to write a series of articles for *Life* magazine on the upcoming Apollo 11 mission to put a man on the moon, achieving the goal announced by President Kennedy in May 1961. A major factor in his decision was that his stature as a writer was higher than it had been in twenty years, and few intellectuals came close to him as a construer of the tumultuous events of the period, a time when, as he said, "the real had become more fantastic than the imagined." The offer from *Life* and suggestions from three writer friends—Jack Newfield, Noel Parmentel, and Gloria Steinem—that he run for mayor reinforced each other, and satisfied both sides, or all sides, of his nature. He saw that he had reached a critical juncture in his life, and it seemed incumbent on him, as he put it when referring to the March on the Pentagon, to take his recent victories and "bring them whole, intact, in sum, as they stood now, to cast—nay—shades of Henry James—to *fling* [them] on the gaming tables of life resumed in New York, and there amass a doubling and trebling again." What were these victories?

His two most recent books had both been better received than any since *The Naked and the Dead*. Written nine months apart, both were nominated for the 1969 National Book Award. *The Armies of the*

Night, in which he foregrounds his presence, was an arts and letters nominee; *Miami and the Siege of Chicago*, in which he steps back several paces from events, was nominated in the history and biography category. After watching Mailer discuss politics on the *Today* show shortly after *Armies* was published, Pulitzer Prize–winning playwright William Inge wrote to him to say that he admired his work and thought he was handsome enough to run for office. Inge urged him, however, to remember that the artist's concern should be "with the heart and human sensibilities." In his response, Mailer admitted he wanted to do just what Inge suggested, but had concluded that "the disease of the 20th century is that politics had invaded the heart and polluted our sensibilities and there is no real way out—that one must write about politics as endemically as love." As Emerson notes in "Fate," "One key, one solution to the mysteries of the human condition, one solution to the old knots of fate, freedom and foreknowledge, exists: the propounding, namely, of the double consciousness. A man must ride alternately on the horses of his private and his public nature, as the equestrians in the circus throw themselves nimbly from horse to horse, or plant one foot on the back of one and the other foot on the back of the other." Like Emerson's equestrians, Mailer made such leaps with great skill during these years.

There were other indications of how brightly Mailer's reputation shone at the time: in June 1968, the Kennedy family asked him to be a member of the honor guard during the memorial for the slain senator. His new British publisher, Weidenfeld and Nicolson, planned to rush *Armies* into print shortly after its American publication. Thomas Nagel, a Harvard alumnus, asked to nominate him for a position on the Harvard Board of Overseers. Mailer's first impulse was to say no, but after reflecting on the "comic, philosophical, spiritual, existential" possibilities of having a voice in governing his alma mater, he gave his permission. Perhaps the most striking evidence of his standing came from *Time* magazine: the editor proposed him for a cover story. Henry Luce had died in the spring of 1967 and the magazine was moving closer to the political center, but it was Mailer's achievements that forced the decision. The new managing editor, Henry Grunwald, wrote to him to say it was "an auspicious moment to achieve a truce." They had lunch and the story was scheduled for late October, right after the publication of *Miami and the Siege of Chicago*. *Newsweek* also contacted him to propose a fall cover story.

Not all of these possibilities worked out, but his three-day trip to London to publicize *Armies of the Night* was a success, and he was nominated for the Harvard post. He and the other "insurgent" nominee, Herbert R. Norr, a member of the SDS, were not elected, however, and *Time* dropped its plans to do a cover story on him when *Newsweek* beat it to the punch, publishing a head shot of Mailer, looking lean and hungry, on the cover of its December 9, 1968, issue. He agreed, of course, to the Kennedy family request, and watched a huge crowd wait up to six hours to pass by the senator's body as it lay in state in St. Patrick's Cathedral. Watching "the poorest part of the working-class of New York" file by and touch the flag-covered coffin led Mailer to recall "the awful cry of the wounded pig in his throat" the night he learned that the senator had been shot. He had for years believed that one must "balance every moment between the angel in oneself and the swine," and the sound of his cry shocked him. He had spent the afternoon before the senator was shot in Los Angeles "enjoying a dalliance," which led him to conclude that his infidelities had provided "one less piton of mooring for Senator Kennedy in his lonely ascent," a conclusion that demonstrated, once again, Mailer's belief in the concordance of human and divine endeavors and his egotism concerning the signal importance of his own actions. His urge at that moment had been to confess to Beverly, but he lacked the courage to confront "his wife's illimitable funds of untempered redneck wrath." So he remained silent as the marriage worsened.

At the start of 1969, he had intended to devote himself entirely to editing *Maidstone*, and had written a form letter of regret to be sent to the many colleges and universities that asked him to speak. (He did agree to accept an honorary degree from Rutgers University, however, an honor recommended by English professor Richard Poirier, a stalwart admirer.) In the form letter, he said he wanted time to think and edit *Maidstone*, adding that he was "feeling a little tired of the sound of my voice," a remark that in retrospect seems comic considering his daily speaking chores during the mayoral campaign. During the eight-week mayoral campaign, his work on the film ceased entirely, and he wrote only speeches and campaign policy papers. Shortly after making the decision to run, he had his new secretary, Carolyn Mason, invite about twenty potential supporters to a March 31 meeting at his apartment. Campaign manager Joe Flaherty begins his hilarious campaign biography, *Managing Mailer*, with an account of this meeting. In addition to the three writers who had urged him to run, three close friends—Torres, Hamill, and Farbar—were there, as well as Flaherty, Jerry Rubin, and several former workers in Eugene McCarthy's campaign. Columnist Jimmy Breslin, a tribune for working-class readers of New York tabloid newspapers, was also invited. Some of the group thought he should run on the ticket with Mailer and give the campaign some "street smarts," as Gloria Steinem put it. With some arm-twisting, Breslin agreed to run for president of the City Council.

Mailer asked the group for their opinions of his candidacy, and the dialogue that ensued, Flaherty wrote, "could be matched only by the construction crew who worked on the Tower of Babel." It got no better when Mailer said he intended to forge "a hip left-right coalition." When he said he intended to run as a Democrat, Rubin said: "Electoral politics is not relevant." Mailer replied:

> "What do you believe in, Jerry—spirituality?"
>
> "Yes. Spirituality, Norman."
>
> "Then what about the spirituality of the machine? To make it hum, hum, hum . . ."
>
> Suddenly, Rubin looked like a convert as the "hums" graced the air like so many Kyrie Eleisons.

The meeting broke up soon after, and when the group got to the street, Breslin shouted, "Do you know something—that fuckin' bum is serious!" A day later Mailer went to Provincetown for two weeks to think.

While he was away, a full-page ad appeared in *The Village Voice* asking "Do you want Norman Mailer for Mayor and Jimmy Breslin for President of the City Council?" The ad asked for volunteers and contributions and listed some of those who supported the ticket. Steinem agreed to raise money and to run on the ticket as comptroller. She skillfully accomplished the former but, pleading fiscal ignorance, dropped off the ticket almost immediately. Mailer had pursued her romantically, and they had a one-night stand during the campaign. Steinem's biographer says that she went to bed with him "either because of fatigue or because of the nonfeminist kindness that gives out 'mercy fucks.'" Whatever the case, she stuck with the campaign to the end. After he returned from Provincetown in mid-April, he went to a meeting at her apartment. When Flaherty arrived, a noticeably slimmer and rested Mailer snapped at him, "You're a half hour late. Let's make it on time in the future." He was ready to campaign.

A staff was hired, volunteers poured in, nominating petitions were printed, and an office was rented in Midtown Manhattan, near Columbus Circle. Alice Krakauer, a former McCarthy staffer, was put in charge of scheduling. Jack Newfield and Peter Maas were appointed press co-secretaries. A young Rutgers professor, Peter Manso, and Susan Harmon, an urban affairs expert, were assigned to draft position papers. Shortly before the official announcement on May 1, Mailer adopted what would be the campaign's most appealing if controversial plank: make New York City the fifty-first state. He got the idea from either Clay Felker, then editor of *New York* magazine, or Hamill, then a *New York Post* columnist, although the idea may go all the way back to William Randolph Hearst. As late as 1995, New York mayor Rudolph Giuliani was quoted as saying that if the city was the fifty-first state, it would not have a budget deficit. It was one of several ideas from the campaign that are still discussed.

It took Mailer time to learn how to speak to political audiences. Early on, he met with the memberships of several so-called reform clubs whose members opposed the Democratic machine. At the Lexington Democratic Club on East 86th Street, he was challenged on the idea of the fifty-first state. Why would the legislature in the state capital, Albany, give the city its freedom, especially if it would result in the loss of city tax dollars—Mailer had pointed out that the city residents paid out much more than they received back from the state government. He replied that if he won, a constitutional convention would be called, followed by approval by the state assembly, and then by the U.S. Congress. The club's members were unconvinced. At this point Mailer shifted gears and took on what he thought were the folksy tones of an Albany farmer. "Well," he said, "those farmers up there might want to get rid of all us evil Jews and niggers." His impersonation brought groans from the crowd. As the campaign unfolded, he improved.

At the Union Theological Seminary in upper Manhattan, he and Breslin presented another key position of the campaign: neighborhood power. Every part of the city would be allowed, within yet undefined limits, to live in its own way. If Harlem wanted a statue of Martin Luther King, fine; if Staten Island wanted one of John Birch, that was okay too. Breslin spoke first, and said how impressed he was to appear before such an educated group. As for his own education, he went to John Adams High School in Queens—"for five years." Adams High was located near Aqueduct Racetrack, he continued and "The first English sentence I ever learned was 'It is now post time.' " Peals of laughter followed; Breslin knew how to warm up a crowd.

It wasn't his partner's style. As Flaherty pointed out, "Mailer was after all still middle class, Jewish, and Harvard, a reader of Blake, Lowell, and Kierkegaard." He told the assembled academics that the biggest issue facing the city was race relations, and former mayor Robert Wagner, who had just entered the race, was not equipped to deal with this. Then he quietly explained that it was "a spiritual necessity" to give all races, nationalities and interest groups, left and right, the chance to express themselves. "People are healthier if they live out their prejudices rather than suppressing them in uniformity," he said. The audience sat "in ecclesiastical reverence as he did that of which only he was capable—convincing a collective body that the sadness in his soul was symbolic of the sadness in the land." Flaherty was as moved as the audience and, ignoring the political odds, "swore to Christ Mailer was going to become the mayor of New York City."

Besides the city's becoming the fifty-first state, several other campaign ideas took root: free bicycles at city parks, a central farmers market offering fresh vegetables and fruit, citywide stickball competitions. A monorail around Manhattan, an old idea revived by Mailer and campaign associate Peter Manso, was refurbished and became one of the most discussed proposals of the campaign. One impossible scheme continues to be discussed. Mailer articulated it at Menora Temple in Brooklyn, where he said he felt at home among "real people," rather than "phony liberals in Manhattan." The idea was Sweet Sunday, based on a description that he had written in Provincetown: "One Sunday a month, all traffic would stop, all airplanes, all trains. It would be known all over the world that one could not enter or leave New York on that day. With luck, New Yorkers could get a hint of fields or sea in the breeze on Sweet Sunday." He upped the ante by saying that electricity would be shut off, except at hospitals. Not everyone liked the concept. "What about refrigerators and air conditioning?" he was asked. "On the first hot day the populace would impeach me," he said. As the campaign went on, Mailer developed a knack for disarming one-liners. One day at Brooklyn College when talking about the Brooklyn Dodgers, he was interrupted by a questioner who wanted to know what he would do if faced by a snowstorm like the monster that had tied up traffic in Queens for several days the previous winter. He shouted back, "I'd piss on it." He began to get his share of laughs, and Breslin began to talk about issues.

There were lost opportunities and blunders. At Sarah Lawrence College before a notably feminist audience, Mailer described his power-to-the-neighborhoods plan. A young woman spoke up: "Where are the pigs going to live?" Mailer, Flaherty wrote, "made the mistake of putting on his whisky baritone Rhett Butler accent to reply. 'Look, sugar,' he began, and got no further as a chorus attacked him for the endearment." As for Breslin, the campaign staff wasn't worried as much about what he would say, but they were uncertain whether he would continue at all. Whenever he threatened to drop out, he was cajoled back by staff members, as well as Flaherty and Mailer. In response to the announcement that Mailer had won the Pulitzer for *The Armies of the Night*, Breslin was adamant about leaving, saying he couldn't carry Mailer's shoes, and only much handholding brought him around. At the formal announcement of candidacy at the Overseas Press Club, Breslin failed to show up at the appointed hour. Mailer, accompanied by Beverly, started without him. He began by saying that recently "candidates had become a little like the products put out by corporations."

> Well, Breslin and myself were not manufactured in large corporations. We were, in fact, put together by piecework. And if you wish to look at us as products, then think of us as antiques. Because we are sentimental about the past. We want New York to thrive again. We want New York to be a city famous around the world again for the charm, ferocity, elegance, strength, calm, and racy character of our separate neighborhoods.

When the television camera operators asked Mailer to stand on something so he could be seen over the cluster of microphones on the podium, he refused, saying that the city would have to learn to appreciate a man of his stature. Then he told them that he "would not deal in any deceptions, since his campaign slogan was 'No More Bullshit.' " At that moment, Breslin, who "obviously had been on guard duty all night in some saloon," showed up, and after some opening remarks castigated the reporters present for not giving the Mailer-Breslin ticket sufficient coverage.

In truth, the campaign received a disproportionate amount of coverage. "The press was horny with expectation," Flaherty wrote. All five New York dailies, including *The Wall Street Journal*, wrote regular stories, so did the weeklies—the *Voice, New York* magazine, and *Brooklyn Heights Press*. National magazines—*Look, Life*, and *Time*—published features, and *Women's Wear Daily* described Mailer as having "the grace of the Doge and the depth of Dante." But the *Times* outdid all of them, devoting at least a dozen news stories entirely to the Mailer-Breslin ticket. At the height of the campaign, the *Times* Sunday magazine published Mailer's most considered statement on why he should be mayor, "Why Are We in New York?" With few exceptions, the media loved the Jewish-Irish underdogs. "Vote the Rascals In" became as popular a campaign slogan as "No More Bullshit" and "I Would Sleep Better If Norman Mailer Were Mayor."

Mailer's second oldest child, Danielle, remembers the campaign well. She and her sister, Betsy, went to several events with their father. But most of the time when he was campaigning, the two girls were in school or with their mother. On weekends, however, they were usually at the Brooklyn apartment, where the maid, Hetty Diggs, was in charge when Mailer was away. One day an angry man showed up at the door. He had a gun, and said he was going to shoot Mailer. Hetty said, "Mr. Norman isn't home," and the man said, "Where the fuck is he?" She said she didn't know. Danielle and Betsy remained silent and he left. When they told their father, he said calmly, "Oh, I wonder who he was." But Mailer installed an intercom system, and no one could enter the building without being buzzed in.

The campaign had one near-ruinous evening followed a few weeks later by a day of redemption. On May 7, when Flaherty was convinced that enough nomination signatures had been gathered, a party was scheduled for the Village Gate, a large jazz nightclub. It had two purposes: raise campaign funds and give the hardworking staff a night off to meet the candidate, who had just signed his $1,000 Pulitzer Prize check over to the campaign. The momentum was positive and everyone was feeling good. Mailer sat at a "booze-laden table" with Bill Walker, recently out of prison and now his bodyguard. After Newfield and

Breslin spoke, Mailer came to the stage carrying a glass of whiskey. Speaking in his southern accent, he began to berate the campaign staff, calling them "a bunch of spoiled pigs," whose egos were undermining the campaign with "dull little vanities." When he was interrupted, he shouted back, "Fuck You." Mailer's half-drunken harangue put the staff in shock. As Mailer was concluding, Flaherty saw Breslin heading for the exit. Mailer didn't notice. He thought his speech had been a success and went home to bed. At four A.M., Breslin called Newfield on the telephone and asked, "Why didn't you tell me I was running with Ezra Pound?" The next morning Flaherty went to Brooklyn to confront Mailer. He carried the morning *Times*, which contained a damning account of the evening.

Flaherty told him that he had been "genuinely scary" the night before, and that staff members were dismayed; a few had quit. As Flaherty quietly criticized his performance, Beverly entered the room, and Mailer said, "This guy is bullying me to death." She replied, "I'm with him." Then Flaherty asked why he had called the staff a bunch of spoiled pigs. "He looked unbelieving: 'Did I say that?' " Beverly indicated that he had. "Tears welled up in his eyes, and he turned his head and buried it in the couch." Flaherty told him that the staff could survive one bad night. Mailer visited headquarters that afternoon and was a "portrait of repentance." For the rest of the campaign, Flaherty wrote, the candidate worked fourteen-hour days during a long hot spell, shaking hands at subways and speaking at synagogues, social clubs, and street fairs. "Like the girl with the curl," Flaherty said, "when he was good he was very, very good." Mailer also cut back on the bourbon, imbibing only after the day's work was done.

Perhaps the finest moment of the campaign came on Memorial Day. Like Breslin, Flaherty loved horse races, and the two of them put together a plan for the ticket to meet the crowd of seventy thousand gathered at Aqueduct for the Metropolitan Handicap. Mailer, dressed in a blue blazer, "his head a full-blown mass of curls, looked like the gentleman plunger," with "a radiant Beverly" at his side. Breslin wore a bright pink shirt and a huge speckled tie. The threesome worked the festive crowd and got perhaps the best reception of the entire campaign. Flaherty had put together a single-sheet flyer with the "Railbird's Picks . . . The Mayoral Handicap," and it was given to every reporter in attendance. On it, former mayor Wagner, "a gelding" who "knows the track," was the favorite, going off at 8–5. Ranged against him were the conservative city comptroller, Mario Procaccino, "Bronx Ridgling [a colt with undescended testicles], By Fear—Out of Law and Order," Congressman James Scheuer and Bronx Borough President Herman Badillo, both "By Liberal—Out of Loser." Going off at 20–1 was long-shot Mailer, "By Amateur—Out of Statehood, First-time starter, Good Barn." Railbird listed him as "Best Bet." In the actual horse race, the favorite was a three-year-old named Arts and Letters. "Such an omen," Flaherty wrote, "was not lost on Mailer the Magician," who put down a $90 bet and watched the chestnut colt come from behind to win. When Mailer saw him in the lead, he said to himself, "Maybe, maybe."

Writing about the campaign later that year, Mailer said that he had awakened "on many a morning with the clear and present certainty that he was going to win." Feeling guilty about sins that he does not name, he decided that he ought to be elected "as a fit and proper punishment." On primary day, June 17, Breslin got 66,000 votes for City Council president and lost to Francis X. Smith; Mailer got 41,000. The Democratic mayoral race was won by the law-and-order candidate, Procaccino, with 33 percent of the vote. Wagner was second with 29 percent; Badillo was third with 28 percent; Mailer was fourth with 5 percent; Scheuer also had 5 percent but two thousand fewer votes. In the Republican primary, John Lindsay lost to conservative Congressman John Marchi by a few thousand votes, after which Lindsay decided to run in the general election as a liberal-independent in a three-way race against Marchi and Procaccino. As liberal a Republican as can be conceived, Lindsay proceeded to defeat the two conservatives, getting 42 percent of the vote. It has been argued that if Mailer had not run, his votes might have gone to Badillo, who then could have defeated Procaccino. By keeping the liberal Badillo out of the general election, Mailer may have enabled Lindsay to win. Flaherty asks in his epilogue, "Did Mailer save the city for liberalism?" Inclined to say no, he nevertheless leaves the door ajar on the question of whether the two rascals kept the nation's largest city out of conservative hands.

Perhaps more important than the help provided Lindsay was the fact that Mailer and Breslin tried to change the nature of political debate. Theodore H. White, author of *The Making of the President* series, who was living in New York during the election, said that while he didn't vote for Mailer, he felt his campaign to be "considered and thoughtful, the beginning of an attempt to apply ideas to a political situation. The job of intellectuals is to come up with ideas, and all we've been producing is footnotes."

MAILER HAD BEEN prepared to give up writing and work an elected official's long days for the rest of his life, as he says in the opening pages of *Of a Fire on the Moon*, his third consecutive book written in the third person personal. "He would never write again if he were Mayor (the job would doubtless strain his talent to extinction) but he would have his hand on the rump of history, and Norman was not without such lust." But he lacked "any apocalyptic ability to rustle up huge numbers of votes." His foray into politics, like his filmmaking, confirmed that writing was his métier—not that he had given up on *Maidstone*, far from it. But he had to separate himself from filmmaking for a time, and in late June he traveled to Houston to begin work on the moon shot book. He hardly had time to say goodbye to his wife.

Beverly appears several times, briefly, in *Managing Mailer*, usually in the role of supportive spouse. In the one place that Flaherty characterizes her, he says she was "an earthy woman who, like Breslin's wife, would rather tend to the privacy of her home and children than get involved in the public limelight." But according to Mailer, the limelight was precisely what Beverly sought. "In the early days, she was marvelous," he said. "She made a home for my boys, and earlier, for my girls." But after a few years, he continued, "It turned south." The chief reason was that "she gave up acting too soon. And it ate at her, it ate at her, it ate at her. We did okay for a while; we used to have wonderful parties and stuff like that. It wasn't enough for her. And I didn't know what to do." He arrived in Texas with the impending breakup of his marriage on his mind. "It was impossible to believe," he wrote in *Fire on the Moon*, "but they each knew—they were coming to an end. They could not believe it for they loved their two sons as once they had loved each other, but now everything was wrong. It was sad." Aquarius and Pisces—as he referred to himself and Beverly—had met on a night when the moon was full.

> She was extraordinarily sensitive to its effects; she was at best uneasy and at worst unreachable when the moon was full. Through

the years of their marriage Aquarius had felt the fullness of the moon in his own dread, his intimations of what full criminality he might possess, had felt the moon in the cowardice not to go out on certain nights, felt the moon when it was high and full and he was occasionally on the side of the brave. And she was worse. Call her Pisces for the neatness of the scheme. Beverly born of Pisces. She was an actress who now did not work. An actress who does not work is a maddened beast. His lovely Pisces, subtle at her loveliest as silver, would scream on nights of the full moon with a voice so loud she sounded like an animal in torment.

Aquarius and Pisces communicated poorly over the next two months as he moved through his journalistic chores at the NASA Manned Space Center in Houston, the Marshall Space Flight Center in Huntsville, Alabama, and the Kennedy Space Center at Cape Kennedy, formerly Cape Canaveral, Florida. When they spoke on the telephone, one or the other often hung up in the middle of a heated conversation. Aquarius, a political also-ran suffering through an all-but-concluded marriage, had a diminished sense of self, despite his recent accolades and prizes. He likened himself to a "disembodied spirit." It was, however, the perfect condition—"detached from the imperial demands of his ego"—to puzzle out an approach for writing about the huge, audacious program to put a man on the moon. Mailer found Apollo 11 to be a "spooky" enterprise, apparently transparent, but ultimately mysterious.

Shortly after he signed contracts for his account of the moon shot, an article appeared in the *New York Times* under the headline, "Million Advance for Mailer Seen." The seven-figure number was a gross exaggeration by his agent, and Mailer was upset. He was distressed about having such huge attention drawn to a book he hadn't yet figured out how to write. In actuality, *Life* would pay $100,000 for three installments; Little, Brown, his new publisher, guaranteed $150,000 for the hardcover version; New American Library matched this amount for the right to publish the paperback. Scott Meredith was quoted as being "quite positive" that foreign and subsidiary rights would bring the figure to $1 million by the time the book was published in January or February 1970. He was wrong about the sum and the date, but from then on Mailer was known as a million-dollar writer. The article also stated, correctly, that he would begin the book in July, and would again use his own participation. It noted that he would describe the July 16 launch and would also include "a chapter on the philosophical and technological implications of the moon landing." As it turned out, the exploration of these implications would comprise the better part of the 180,000-word book, Mailer's longest since *Naked and the Dead.*

If Mailer had the advantage of an engineering degree to help him understand the physics of rocket science, he also faced obstacles that other reporters did not, all self-imposed. Most of the reporters covering the moon shot would be there for a few weeks, write their reports using NASA handouts and quotations from controlled interviews with the astronauts, and move on to another assignment. For Mailer-Aquarius, it was a matter of professional pride: "if you're gonna be paid a huge sum for it, you've gotta come back with something." The book also gave him the chance to explore his obsession with the "disease of technology," one of his major themes since *Cannibals and Christians.* Consequently, soon after his arrival in Houston, although he was "tempted to take a shortcut," he saw that he could not merely write about the hoopla of blast-off and provide folksy tidbits about the astronauts. "That would have been a cheat," he said. His mission was to write about "certain metaphysical problems" associated with the "technological sacrilege" of rocketing humans to the surface of a dead moon, a surface beneath which no humans were buried.

Everyone in the country knew the names and faces of the three astronauts, Neil Armstrong, Michael Collins, and Edwin "Buzz" Aldrin, but little more of consequence. *Life*'s editor, Thomas Griffith, had agreed to arrange for Mailer to be given access to them but, as Mailer recalled, NASA refused because it was "afraid he would write harsh things" about them. Mailer then wrote a letter to the astronauts saying, "You wouldn't let a commercial pilot fly Apollo, why not let someone who is recognized as one of the better journalists in the world meet you in order to write about you?" Armstrong wrote back and said, "Your argument is lucid and convincing but the answer is no." Through the magazine's Houston connections, he was able to spend an evening with Charles "Pete" Conrad, who would command Apollo 12 on the next moon mission. Conrad said that although Mailer had a reputation of being on the left, while he himself flew "right wing for Attila the Hun," they got along, helped by the better part of a bottle of scotch.

His time with Conrad and another unnamed astronaut made him see that they were "not dull people," and "not all of a piece." The Apollo 11 trio, however, remained off limits except for carefully orchestrated appearances. Consequently, Mailer's portraits of the three men may be the weakest part of the book. He demonstrated that he could repackage official biographies, quotes from staged events, and cursory interviews with the three national celebrities behind a glass wall as adroitly as any talented reporter. But not much better. He admitted years later that he was unhappy with what he had written about the trio: "I tended to lean too heavily on the few times I saw them in interviews with other writers," he said. "I saw them for a total of perhaps about three hours, and on that I attempted to understand them to write a book, and it got me into great trouble. I would have been better off if I'd never met them." There is a tendency if you meet someone for a little while, he said, "to see all of their personality as being similar to the little bit you glimpsed." Mailer spent his first days in Houston with the herd of reporters, all of them cramming.

Before he began to write the first installment for *Life*, Mailer told his new editor at Little, Brown, Ned Bradford, that he didn't know "how to locate myself in reference to it," and he had to figure it out because "one's stance determines one's style." He had a similar conversation with Willie Morris, who wanted Mailer to write about the moon shot for *Harper's* but could not match the offer from *Life*. Remembering that the writing he had done for *Harper's* required him to participate, more or less, in the events in question, Mailer asked, "How can I participate in a landing on the moon?" It was not entirely a rhetorical question. "God dammit," he told Morris, "I really would like to go to the moon," and said that he would get into good physical shape if he could get a seat on the rocket. In early 1971 shortly after *Fire on the Moon* was published, he was asked if he would have liked to make the trip himself. He said, "If I could have gone up it would have made a better book. I keep thinking I'm going to spend all my life pleading with NASA to send me to the moon, and then they'll finally decide to send John Updike." Mailer interviewed NASA officials, read technical manuals, and pondered his approach to the event.

During the summer, Beverly embarked on a love affair and traveled to Mexico. The unraveling of the marriage drove Mailer deeper into his work, and may even have aided it. He said many times that some of his best work was done when he was depressed. *Life*'s deadline for the first installment was in early August. The editors were expecting under ten thousand words, but as he said in some prefatory comments to his piece, "I can't write anything in 5,000 words, and 10,000 words is just for poker money." Working eight to ten hours a day for a fifteen-day stretch, he completed his thirty-thousand-word account of the Saturn V launch on schedule. "The pleasures you get writing," he said, "are the pleasures of the marathon runner." *Life* was mainly a pictorial magazine, although it occasionally published long prose works—Hemingway's *The Old Man and the Sea*, for example. The editors were not accustomed, however, to huge slabs of marbled prose in a nonfiction report. When it appeared in the August 29 magazine, his 26,000-word report—he cut it slightly—was by far the longest nonfiction piece the magazine had published in a single issue.

Mailer's description of the Saturn V rocket, as long and heavy as a U.S. Navy destroyer, seen from the press grandstand three and a half miles away, is the best thing in the installment. The influence of *Moby-Dick* (especially "The Whiteness of the Whale"), which years later Mailer admitted to be "enormous," is evident, especially when he compares the innards of the rocket to the innards of a whale—miles of tubes and massive tanks. Mailer had already stood in awe of the rocket as it was being readied for flight in the Vehicle Assembly Building, the largest building on the planet. The sight encouraged him "to release the string of the balloon and let his ego float off." He recognized that "a Leviathan was most certainly ready to ascend the heavens—whether for good or ill he might never know." Saturn was a furnace filled with a million gallons of varied fuels—kerosene and liquid oxygen and hydrogen. At blast-off, the flames sluiced away on each side for two hundred feet, "and in the midst of it, white as a ghost, white as the white of Melville's Moby Dick, white as the shrine of the Madonna in half the churches of the world, this slim angelic mysterious ship of stages rose without sound out of its incarnation of flame and began to ascend slowly into the sky, slow as Melville's Leviathan might swim, slowly as we might swim upward in a dream looking for air. And still no sound." When the noise of blast-off does come, it is with "the sharp and furious bark of a million drops of oil crackling suddenly into combustion." The wooden bleachers begin to shake, and he hears himself saying over and over, "Oh, my God!" Then he has "a moment of vertigo at the thought that man now had something with which to speak to God."

After the launch, he flew back to Houston to watch the four-day trip to the moon, the walk on its surface, and the flight back to earth. The astronauts' capsule splashed down in the Pacific on July 24, after eight days in space. By then Mailer had returned to Provincetown, where he watched the capsule being fished out of the water by the crew of the aircraft carrier, USS *Hornet* (CV 12). He wrote his *Life* articles, and then commenced work on the book. Beverly was gone, and Carol Stevens, who had visited Mailer in Houston, joined him. He rented an apartment for her nearby. She met his children, his father, and Uncle Louis, Barney's brother, who was visiting from South Africa. "Barney was adorable," she recalled, "greeting me with, 'Oh, what a beautiful girlie,' in an accent hard to repeat. A mix of Jewish and South African, unlike any accent I have ever heard. Uncle Louie was charming and persuasive, urging me to join them. He said jokingly that he was ready to leave Moos [his wife] for me, and Norman agreed we would make a perfect pair."

Later, Carol met Mailer's mother, who, she said, was not quite as friendly. In the fall of 1970 when she was pregnant with Mailer's fifth daughter, Maggie, Fan "lectured me on the merits of her genius son, explaining how unusual he was, and how he needed more love than other men. I would have to 'be more, give more, find more love, time, energy, devotion, for HIM.' That he 'needed more love than other men' was a line I obviously never forgot. I guess she was right on about that." Meeting the children that summer, Carol said, was also difficult. "The girls were young and fragile. They were obviously upset and frightened, more so, it seemed than Michael or Stephen. They were probably afraid to speak. They all acted like terrified little orphans. I think the boys were three and five when I met them."

In the fall of 1969, he wrote a brief note to Ginsberg about the "Call to War Tax Resistance" project they were both supporting. He added that the moon shot book, "keeps opening like a string one follows through the caves. So I hardly know where it will lead me." He had already written about the eight-day round-trip of Apollo 11, the human adventure, in Part I of the account. Now, in Part II, he was exploring obdurate material: the physics of liquefied gases, combustion and thrust, gravity and weightlessness, electricity and magnetism, orbits and the dark side of the moon. Drawing on his Harvard engineering knowledge, he presents superb expositions of these matters as they relate to Apollo 11, viewing them as mysteries to be probed, rather than complexities to be rendered. Few newspaper feature writers covering the moon shot, nor those who wrote full-length books about the event, entered into discussions of this kind. Few could. Nor did many commentators on the moon shot find it necessary to link the Apollo 11 mission with the inflamed state of race relations in the United States. Mailer had begun writing about the situation of American blacks in "The White Negro," and then did not address it substantively until 1968. He commented favorably on Black Power in a *Partisan Review* symposium in 1968, and again a year later in an essay in *Look*, "Looking for the Meat and Potatoes—Thoughts on Black Power."

In between these two pieces came his comments in *Miami and the Siege of Chicago*, which reveal a new ripple in his thinking about race, one that reflected a shift in the national mood in the late 1960s. Irritated that Rev. Ralph D. Abernathy, one of the late Dr. King's closest associates, was "scandalously late" for a press conference at the GOP convention in Miami, Mailer realized that "he was getting tired of Negroes and their rights." This leads him to a seven-page reverie on "how to divide the guilt" for black misery and disenfranchisement. On the one side, blacks had burned neighborhoods and threatened "Whitey" in half the major cities in the country over the previous four years. On the other, there were countless incidents of police breaking black heads with impunity, and unforgivable illegal discrimination. An "ugly thought" comes to him as he waits. However much the wealth and well-being of America was dependent on the underpaid or unpaid labor of blacks, "still the stew of the Black revolution had brought the worst to surface with the best, and if the Black did not police his own house, he would be destroyed and some of the best of the white men with him." Mailer wondered why only five of his fifty friendships with blacks over the past decade continued with any warmth. Who was to blame?

Although his admiration for black élan continued unabated, he was now "heartily sick of listening to the tyranny of soul music," and "bored with Negroes triumphantly late for appointments." Waiting with the other reporters for close to an hour, he became more and more peeved with Abernathy for making him wait "while the secret stuff of his brain was disclosed to his mind." Mailer's admissions are candid. He does not mention, however, that his current distaste for black arrogance, his weariness with "the smell of booze and pot and used-up hope in bloodshot eyes of Negroes bombed at noon" that he observes in the subways of New York, is squarely at odds with his praise for the dangerous life of blacks in "The White Negro." There he notes that the Negro knows "in the cells of his existence that life was war, nothing but war," and he admires how blacks "subsisted for Saturday night kicks."

His views on blacks shifted again the day after the astronauts walked on the moon. He ran into a black professor at a party in Houston. The two had met several times in the past, and were friendly. The unnamed professor, much admired on his Ivy League campus, has the "impressive voice and deliberative manner of a leader." Mailer observes that he has been drinking heavily, perhaps for several days, "as if he were looking to coagulate some floor between the pit of his feelings at boil and the grave courtesies of his heavy Black manner." As they talk, he recognizes that his friend is drinking because two white men have landed on the moon and are now flying back, an accomplishment of the "White superstructure which had been strangling the possibilities of his own Black people for years." Mailer and the professor agree that blacks are "possessed of a potential genius which was greater than whites." This genius is based not on numbers, but magic and telepathy. There are no black astronauts, the professor observes. No Jews either, Mailer replies. The victory of WASP culture relied on numbers and computers. If there was ever to be a great black civilization, he predicts, "magic would be at its heart. For they lived with the wonders of magic as the Whites lived with technology." The professor had good reason to drink, he observes. Technology was winning on all fronts, and NASA had scant interest in race relations or, for that matter, Mailer's hypothesis about the existence of the Thanatosphere, a ring around the moon where the souls of the departed rose after death, waiting, presumably, to be reincarnated. Mailer's magic side was worried that Apollo 11 might interfere with this celestial holding pattern, but the engineering side took some pleasure in what NASA had accomplished. His deepest loyalty, however, was for magic. Apollo 11, Mailer said later, was either "the greatest achievement of man," or "the most sacrilegious act that man ever committed." His navigator would keep him on a track away from technology to the end of his life.

THROUGH THE FALL of 1969 and the first four months of 1970, living in Provincetown with Carol Stevens, Mailer immersed himself completely in *Of a Fire on the Moon*, seldom traveling. Money was tight, as he was now supporting six children, plus Adele, Beverly, and, in part, Carol, who still worked professionally as a singer. He did make a trip to Chicago in January 1970, where he testified at the trial of seven men, including Jerry Rubin and Abbie Hoffman, who were accused of inciting a riot at the 1968 Chicago Democratic convention. The trial went on for months and was widely seen as polarizing. The seven were convicted, but the verdict was overturned on appeal.

Mailer complained to Harvey Breit's son, Luke, who had worked on his campaign staff, that *Fire on the Moon* was going to take nine months, all told, and he had hoped to complete it in three. But it appears that he had an almost complete draft in hand by the latter part of March because he spent a day answering a huge pile of mail. In his letter to Luke Breit, he describes his quiet writing days.

> It's like doing a benevolent stretch in stir. The meals are good, the prisoner gets his fresh air and walks, but can't drink or go out at night for fear of losing the next day's work. So gray Provincetown winter days go by and nothing happens and not much inner life and all that work until you begin to get the same kind of quiet self-pity that a lifer has. You're condemned to work at a species of literature for your natural life and it all began with the power of imagination.

The manuscript was nearly complete when he flew to Washington to serve the remainder of his sentence for disorderly behavior at the March on the Pentagon. The U.S. Supreme Court refused to hear his appeal, and on May 5 he entered the Alexandria city jail for the last three days of his sentence. His jail time was "near agreeable," he said. "I'm a believer in the rules of the game," he told reporters after he was released, and "if you cross that line you get arrested." New antiwar protests were scheduled for Washington the following day, and Mailer cautioned the protesters to avoid violence: "A winning hand this weekend is to have no violence. The point to be made is it's the administration shedding blood—not the New Left." At Kent State University in Ohio, four students had just been shot dead by national guardsmen. Mailer said that when President Nixon had called protesting students "bums," it gave the guardsmen "an out to pull the trigger." Nixon's comments about the United States not losing its first war, he continued, "are the babblings of a Chekhovian character." For good measure, he also called the president a "cathedral of hypocrisy," and compared him to Dickens's unctuous villain Uriah Heep. Mailer was driven to the airport by Rip Torn, with whom he was now reconciled.

The final manuscript of *Of a Fire on the Moon* went to Little, Brown shortly after he returned from Washington, and he spent the next two months shuttling between Provincetown and New York, where he worked on *Maidstone*, which now ended with Torn's attack. He and Carol relaxed before the summer season. In early June, they spent a few days at one of the dune shacks of the national seashore outside Provincetown. The shacks, a dozen or more, are sprinkled across miles of dunes and can be reached only by jeep or a long walk. There is no sound but the wind and the waves. "There are few places on the Eastern Seaboard where one could bury a man as easily and leave one's chances so to nature," Mailer had written. The shacks have neither electricity nor running water. According to Carol, it seemed certain to them that a child had been created while they were there. Maggie Alexandra was born a little more than nine months later.

Ever since his first visit to Maine in 1948, Mailer had wanted to return. In late June 1970, he left Provincetown for Mount Desert Island, where he rented a house for the summer. Acadia National Park is on the island, and within the park is Cadillac Mountain (elev. 1,528 ft.), where the morning sun first hits the continental United States during the fall and winter. The Mailer clan would explore the park on many an outing over the next dozen summers. Mailer would draw heavily on his summers in Maine for his 1991 novel, *Harlot's Ghost*. "Fortune Rock," the house that he rented, is a spacious modern structure built by Wells Fargo heiress Clara Fargo Thomas in the late 1930s. It stands at the end of Somes Sound, a fjord that runs nine miles to the ocean. The tide shifts are over ten feet in this part of Maine, and at high tide the water was about twenty feet below the house's cantilevered living room. At low tide, there is nothing but rocks and sand below. Carol remembers that Mailer was always testing himself, and at one point began walking on the narrow railings outside the living room. "He could have killed himself," she said.

Carol and all of his children—save Susan, who was in Europe—

joined him there, as did his sister, who came to help for two weeks. "It was," he later wrote, "not an unhappy summer, and he ended with the knowledge that he could run a decent home and sleep without a turn of guilt, knew he could run a home without screaming at children and be as a result thus mind-empty at night that solitaire pleased him." Danielle, Betsy, and Kate, thirteen, eleven, and eight, helped with Michael and Stephen, six and four. The boys, Mailer recalled, were "small powers out of doors. Inside, on rainy afternoons, their whining gave a hint of the whistle in the pipes of a maniac." The summer experiment in housekeeping and family excursions—which Mailer referred to as "the paving blocks at the crossroads of existence"—made him ponder parental roles: "He knew at last what a woman meant when she said her hair smelled of grease." He realized that, with help, he could handle a large family day to day, but he also believed that by doing so "the most interesting part of his mind and heart" would shrivel.

Until the end of her pregnancy, Carol traveled regularly with Mailer. She was three months pregnant in late August, when they went to Italy for the showing of *Maidstone.* Prior to their arrival in Venice, a friend had made arrangements for them to visit Ezra Pound and his companion, the violinist Olga Rudge. Carol remembers that Pound "was in a period of silence, but did say something to Norman." The old poet, she said, had "the most intense, penetrating blue eyes." A year after their visit, an American journalist visited Pound. He noticed a copy of Mailer's book of poems, *Deaths for the Ladies*, on a bookshelf and asked how it got there. Rudge said that Mailer had given them a copy. She added, "I had heard this Mailer was a wild man and I was a little afraid, but he was on his best behavior. Butter wouldn't melt in his mouth." At this point, Pound interrupted: "Mailer? Nice . . . young . . . fella." Rudge said that she read his poems to Pound and then turned to him: "And you liked some of them. Do you remember any?" Her thin, frail companion answered, "All of 'em!" Mailer later wrote of Pound, "The funny thing is that my poetry in *Deaths for the Ladies* while having unfortunately little of the sensuous quality of his work does subscribe to a few of his poetic principles." The difference, he said, is that "I have no talent—not for poetry but the prose is awfully good."

STOCK MARKET LOSSES plus a "staggering" income tax bill on the horizon led him to consider a proposal from Willie Morris to write an essay on the Women's Liberation Movement. He had hoped to begin another "big book"—the Egyptian novel, as it came to be called—but had to work his way out of his financial hole first. Earlier, in the summer of 1970, he received a call from *Time* editor Henry Grunwald as Mailer recalled in his essay, "The Prisoner of Sex" (republished unchanged as a book five months later). The magazine wanted to interview him. Mailer was interested because a cover story might help him find a distributor for *Maidstone*, but he demurred largely because the idea of his five children "cavorting for *Time*'s still camera did not make him happy." In addition, Stevens, to whom he dedicated *The Prisoner of Sex*, was present and she was "too proper to be photographed, too proud to be passed over." Grunwald said he was not proposing a cover story; rather, he wanted Mailer's opinions on the women's liberation movement, which was the burning topic of the day. Grunwald told him that he was the movement's "major ideological opposition." This announcement surprised and tempted Mailer: "To be the center of any situation was, he sometimes thought, the real marrow of his bone—better to expire as a devil in the fire than an angel in the wings." His strong suit was to "mobilize on the instant" with sharp remarks about "the ladies of the Liberation." But, finally, he said no: "Only a fool would throw serious remarks into the hopper at *Time*." Pithy statements for magazine readers came best from wits like Gore Vidal, he said.

Mailer had learned again about *Time*'s proclivity for unfairly condensing one's statements, most recently at a press conference in Venice. Asked by reporters to comment on the charge that his depiction of a brothel for female customers in *Maidstone* contributed to the exploitation of women, he went on for five minutes in a fairly complex fashion to discuss Women's Liberation. *Time* boiled his commentary down to this: "Exploitation of women? But it is impossible to exploit her because she has magic powers. I am against the emancipation of women just because I respect them." Mailer complained about what he believed to be unfair treatment by the magazine in a letter that it printed, but these three sentences do, in fact, encapsulate one of the major arguments of his *Harper*'s essay "The Prisoner of Sex" on gender, sex, procreation, and women's rights.

"There was a tissue of communion between the children and himself" that summer, he wrote, but by Labor Day the children had returned to their respective mothers to prepare for school and Mailer and Carol returned alone to Provincetown. He continued to worry about *Maidstone*, awaited the publication of *Fire on the Moon* in January, and worked on his "big, fat discursive piece" for Willie Morris. At the beginning of November, a copy of *Women's Wear Daily* containing a profile of Vidal came his way. Amidst a stream of remarks, Vidal noted that he was in unison with the Women's Liberation Movement on the lack of substantial difference between the sexes. He was different in this regard, he continued, from his colleague Norman Mailer, who "often sounds like the deranged commander of an American Legion post, particularly about women, whom he doesn't like very much. He has made politics out of sex." Vidal himself, as he explained, held that everyone is bisexual, although "not everyone practices it." Mailer read this as an endorsement of unisex, which he considered an abomination. He sent a letter to the paper a week later saying that Vidal's comments should be seen in the light of some statistical evidence: "marriages, Vidal-0, Mailer-4; children, Vidal-0, Mailer-6; daughters, Vidal-0, Mailer-4." While these figures were not conclusive, he continued, one might conclude that "Gore neither wed nor bothered to sire because he put womankind in such high regard that he did not wish to injure their tender flesh with his sharp tongue." The exchange was the beginning of a small war between the two that went on for more than fifteen years.

This flurry of activity on the topic of Women's Liberation was the direct result of the publication of a fierce attack on male chauvinism by Kate Millett, an apologist for feminism whose stated goal was "enlarging human freedom." Written originally as a Columbia University thesis, *Sexual Politics* was published in August 1970, exactly fifty years after the ratification of the Nineteenth Amendment to the Constitution that gave women the vote. "There was a great wave of feminism building," that summer, Millett wrote, and her book rode the crest. She appeared on the cover of the August 30 *Time*, and every literate person in the country, it seemed, had an opinion about her polemic. Mailer ordered a copy and was soon plowing through what he called "Kate Millett's hard clay." Although he commented on a score of feminist works (including Germaine Greer's *The Female Eunuch*, also published that year), *The Prisoner of Sex* was a concerted attempt to rebut and discredit Millett.

Mailer wrote to a friend that "the first inkling I ever had of woman's liberation" was when he heard his sister speak passionately about *The Second Sex*, Simone de Beauvoir's groundbreaking exploration of the ways that women had been marginalized through the ages. Betty Friedan's 1963 book, *The Feminine Mystique*, was also a powerful influence, and is often credited with initiating the "second wave" of feminism in the United States after the reverses that had followed the achievement of suffrage. Its "fundamental argument," as distilled by *New Yorker* writer Louis Menand, "is that there is no such thing as women's essential nature. The belief that women are biologically destined to be domestic and subordinate, is just a construct, constructed by psychologists and social scientists." Mailer never argued that women should be homebound cooks and babysitters, but he did believe that they shared an immutable biological identity.

The Women's Liberation Movement gained momentum all through the 1960s, aided by governmental action—President Kennedy's National Commission on the Status of Women in 1961 and the Equal Pay Act of 1963, for example—and the formation of innumerable organizations supporting women's rights—Friedan and other women and men founded the National Organization for Women in 1966—and reached its full flowering with the publication of Millett's *Sexual Politics*. She attacked the positions of a wide range of male thinkers in her study, including Freud, Reich, and Erik Erikson, but her three chief targets are D. H. Lawrence, Henry Miller, and Mailer.

In late December, he received his advance copies of *Of a Fire on the Moon*, which reproduced as cover art René Magritte's painting of a huge rock and the sea, *Le Monde Invisible*. The official publication date was January 11, 1971, and the major reviews came out that month. They were generally positive, but less glowing than those for *Armies of the Night* and *Miami and the Siege of Chicago*. The old pattern of evenly divided reviews repeated and would continue until the end of the 1970s. Benjamin DeMott's review in *Saturday Review* straddled the extremes. He complained of Mailer's "unremitting self-involvement and self-regard," but also argued that the author's narcissism "blesses him as an enthusiast," one who writes "pages that physically breathe with the vitality of the writer's will to pack in the whole, nail the kit complete—all two million functioning parts, every sensation, every fear, every lucked-out crisis" of the Apollo 11 mission. So it went through the rest of the reviews: encomiums for Mailer's ability to drill through NASA's layers of bureaucracy with his diamond-hard ego, and protest against the revelation of his personal life and theology, especially his "Manichean ox-team—his God and Devil in harness pulling on the universe in opposite directions," as Christopher Lehmann-Haupt described it in his *New York Times* review. The book's length put off some reviewers; others were troubled by what Morris Dickstein in *The New York Times Book Review* called "a certain slackness of execution" in some of the technical descriptions, paralleling the tedious parts of the cetology chapters in *Moby-Dick*. But these lapses are small, Dickstein argued, and Mailer's attempt, not just to bridge science and the humanities, "to leap over and back, to reclaim the event for mystery, romance and human dread," made the book exemplary.

Little, Brown pressed Mailer to do some publicity for *Fire*, and he agreed, but with no joy. In late January, he made appearances in New York, including *The David Frost Show*, and later traveled to Houston, Miami, and Los Angeles. At almost every stop, the crowd and reporters seemed more interested in his views on Women's Lib, as it was popularly called, than in *Fire on the Moon*. He wrote to Aldridge about how much he disliked the publicity grind: "I'm caught these days in the low hope that perhaps the book won't do too well and so prove my thesis that TV does not sell books." Mailer never entirely gave up this thesis, even after numerous appearances on television talk shows. What he was looking forward to at the time was the March 8 championship bout between Muhammad Ali and Joe Frazier at Madison Square Garden. It would prove to be the first of three epic boxing matches between the two men, both then undefeated. Ralph Graves, a *Life* editor, asked Mailer if he could write a five-thousand-word report for *Life* on what was being called "the fight of the century." The magazine's publication schedule meant he would have to submit the piece two days after the fight.

Working from seven in the morning until seven at night, he met the deadline and produced a 9,500-word essay. "I never wrote so fast in my life," he told Knox. "Ego: The Ali-Frazier Fight," is one of the best depictions of a prizefight ever written. Accompanied by nine color photographs taken by Frank Sinatra (one of many celebrities attending), it was *Life*'s March 19, 1971, cover story. The piece marks a subtle change in Mailer's self-referencing. In much of his writing from *Advertisements for Myself* on, he had used the incidents of his life willy-nilly to illumine whatever topic was at hand. But in "Ego," he began talking intently about *the artist* as an exemplary type, comparing, for example, Picasso and Joyce to the boxers with the most powerful egos, heavyweight champions such as Rocky Marciano and Muhammad Ali. "Boxing is a rapid debate between two sets of intelligence," he said, likening a championship bout to his public debate with William Buckley. Prizefighting is a language of the body, he argues, one that is "as detached, subtle and comprehensive in its intelligence as any exercise of mind." From this point onward, he would return again and again to the artist as archetype (with Norman Mailer as the unmistakable signature), using himself as a species of divining rod to explore the psychic depths of personalities as disparate as Marilyn Monroe, Henry Miller, Gary Gilmore, Lee Harvey Oswald, Picasso, Christ, and Hitler. In retrospect, "Ego" can be seen as the beginning of a major phase in his writing career: Mailer as biographer.

"Ego," however, was published in the shadow of "The Prisoner of Sex" a few weeks earlier. Willie Morris bought a ten-by-fifteen ad in *The New York Times* on publication day featuring the cover of the *Harper's* issue under this tag: "The Favorite Target of Women's Lib Chooses His Weapon. Harper's Magazine." At the bottom of the page was further enticement: "Pick Up a Copy. Before Your Newsstand Is Picketed." The ad, aided by Mailer's incendiary comments in various interviews, worked. Ideologues on both sides weighed in, columnists and pundits gleefully reported the battle between the sexes, and nine days after the magazine arrived on newsstands, it had sold out, if not entirely to his admirers. He was now booed and heckled at some public appearances, mainly by women. The badgering, he felt, was unjust, even though he abetted it. One of the few women who gave him public succor was Joan Didion. Mailer's position "strikes me as exactly right," she said. "I think sex is a lot darker than Kate Millett does. I think there is a lot more going on than meets her eye." Didion defended the sex scenes in *An American Dream*, for example.

Making matters worse was a comment he had made to Orson Welles the previous June on *The Mike Douglas Show.* Welles was "being pious for a moment about women," Mailer recalled, and he jumped in: "Oh, come on, Orson, women are sloppy beasts, they should be kept in cages." This pronouncement "poured ice cubes down everyone's back," Mailer said. Welles then got solemn, even after Mailer tried to take the edge off his pronouncement by saying that he did not hate women, adding, "Orson, we respect the lions in the zoo, but we want them kept in cages, don't we?" Years later, he said that he had made the remark "for fun and idiocy" and failed to realize "how intense the anger, fury and frustration, which I had caused, had become. I meant the remark as a joke, but I will admit that it was the wrong remark at the wrong time." The women's revolution was nearing its apogee and Mailer became its piñata. His *Harper's* essay merely confirmed for feminists, whether they read it or not, that Mailer was a male chauvinist. Later, while on a speaking tour for the book that grew out of the essay, he complained to a *Miami Herald* columnist that although he'd "spent my life writing about men and women and their enormously complicated relationship," the feminists were "killing my wallet, my ego, my reputation." New, young movements, he said, have to "kill someone symbolically. But that person has to have value." He never stopped believing that he was that scapegoat.

If the impetus to *The Prisoner of Sex* was Millett's twenty-five-page attack on him in *Sexual Politics*, Mailer immediately realized in writing it that he was addressing all the major issues of his life, as listed by one enthusiastic reviewer, the *Times*'s Anatole Broyard: "revolution, tradition, sex, the family, the child, the shape of the future, technology, the ethics of the critic, the male mystique, and the rights of minorities." The framework for Mailer's argument, as another reviewer, the novelist David Lodge, explained, was how he equated "the technological destruction of nature with the ideological destruction of male-female differentiation, likening Kate Millett to a 'technologist who drains all the swamps only to discover that the ecological balance has been savaged.' " The end result of freeing woman from her reproductive role, Mailer warned, would be "coitus-free conception monitored by the state," and the death of heterosexual romance. Forty years after his dire warnings, we can observe that sex differentiation is decidedly less clear-cut, but heterosexual romance survives. If he exaggerated the possibility of Big Sister supervising the embryo assembly line, some of the literature he surveyed for the essay looked forward to it. The SCUM Manifesto, written by Valerie Solanas, who shot Andy Warhol, proposed a program to "overthrow the government, eliminate the money system, institute complete automation, and destroy the male sex." Her manifesto was reprinted in *Sisterhood Is Powerful*, a bestselling anthology. Solanas's program "while extreme, even extreme of the extreme," he argued, "is nonetheless a magnetic north for Women's Lib." Technology could win.

Mailer's passionate if somewhat tendentious brief against such a world is built on a biological fact about women and an assertion about men: A woman possesses a "mysterious space within," while a man is "simple meat," a creature of unrest "who proceeded to become unmasculine whenever he ceased to strive." The "purse of flesh" that was the womb, contained

> psychic tendrils, waves of communication to some conceivable source of life, some manifest of life come into human beings from a beyond which persisted in remaining most stubbornly beyond. Women, like men, were human beings, but they were a step, or a stage, or a move or a leap nearer the creation of existence, they were—given man's powerful sense of the present—his indispensable and only connection to the future.

If women wished to enter the male occupations and professions, he argued, "go to work with a lunch pail and a cigar" (sarcasm was not off limits), wear a uniform, and die of male diseases, what would happen to their link to the infinite? He said that he would assent to every feminist demand for equality, certainly all their economic demands; he would "agree with everything they asked but to quit the womb." But in 1970 it was no longer a simple either/or decision for women (if it ever had been), and in the years since then it became clear that women, while still lagging in paycheck size, have achieved parity in many though not all professions. Equilibrium for women between child rearing and work was possible, but no one would claim it was easy.

Millett unfairly truncated some of the quotations she took from the work of Henry Miller and D. H. Lawrence, or as Mailer put it, "the bloody ground steamed with the limbs of every amputated quote." He restored the severed parts as carefully as Isis reconstructed the body of Osiris, then situated the sexual investigations of Miller on the ridgeline between love and lust "where the light is first luminous, then blinding, and the ground remains unknown. Henry, a hairy prospector, red eye full of lust, has wandered these ridgelines for the years of his literary life." Mailer's admiration for Miller's pioneering explorations of the ways in which lust "can alter to love or be as suddenly sealed from love," is obvious. Miller read the essay and wrote him a warm letter from Big Sur, his last retreat. In 1976, Mailer would publish a full-scale examination of Miller's work, *Genius and Lust*. The finest chapter in *The Prisoner of Sex*, however, is Mailer's discussion of D. H. Lawrence, arguably his most incisive piece of literary criticism.

For Mailer, Lawrence's literary and personal life stood as clear evidence "that a firm erection on a delicate fellow was the adventurous juncture of ego and courage." Successful coitus was an achievement, but loving sex was harder, yet Lawrence believed in it with all the passion of the last romantic: the love affairs he depicted in a half dozen novels—*Lady Chatterley's Lover* was Mailer's favorite—"come in like winds off Wuthering Heights—but never had a male novelist written more intimately about women—heart, contradiction, and soul; never had a novelist loved them more, been so comfortable in the tides of their sentiment, and so ready to see them murdered." Like Mailer, he was spoiled, "and could not have commanded two infantrymen to follow him, yet he was still a great writer, for he contained a cauldron of boiling opposites—he was on the one hand a Hitler in a teapot, on the other he was the blessed breast of tender love, he knew what it was to love a woman from her hair to her toes." The parallels with Mailer—recall Lindner calling him "a pint-sized Hitler"—are obvious, and when we hear that Lawrence's incompatibles were intensified by an "intellectual ambition sufficient to desire the overthrow of European civilization," it is clear that he identifies with Lawrence as much as with Hemingway, and owes him a deeper debt. "Lawrence's point, which he refines over and over, is that the deepest messages of sex cannot be heard by taking a stance on the side of the bank, announcing one is in love, and then proceeding to fish in the waters of love with a breadbasket full of ego. No, he is saying again and again, people can win at love only when they are ready to lose everything they bring to it." Mailer elaborates masterfully on Lawrence's derision of "meaningless fucking . . . that was the privilege of the healthy," and his celebration of genuine sexual love as "the only nostrum which could heal," but only when the partners were without what Lawrence called "reserves or defenses."

The son of a mother who loved him "outrageously," and a father who despised him, Lawrence was a sickly youth, "bone and blood of the classic family stuff out of which homosexuals are made," Mailer avers, and became masculine only by willpower. Lawrence stole Frieda von

Richthofen, a German baron's daughter, from her husband. She left him and her three children, risking everything for a poor miner's son from Nottingham. The love of Lawrence's mother and that of Frieda empowered Lawrence psychologically even as he was slowly dying of tuberculosis. He was dead at forty-four. Mailer says he was "possessed of a mind which did not believe any man on earth had a mind more important than his own," a mind that created a novelistic manifest for heterosexual love as the saving power of humanity. Mailer compares him to a general, deploying his words as battle troops. Reading Mailer's forty pages on Lawrence, a brilliant interpretation of Lawrence's profound belief in erotic instinct and risk, reinforced by a close reading of a dozen key passages (restored from Millett's truncations), one cannot escape the conclusion, as one critic put it, that Mailer's books—"through their familiar litany of concern with love, sex, inhibitive society, and modern mechanization—appear like a karmic reformulation of Lawrence's own most prominent preoccupations." In a 1985 letter to another Lawrence scholar Mailer said, "*Lady Chatterley* changed my life."

BOTH OF A *Fire on the Moon* and *The Prisoner of Sex* were nominated for the National Book Award in 1972, the former in the sciences, and the latter in contemporary affairs. Neither won, but the publicity helped sales and eased his financial burden somewhat. *Prisoner* brought in just under $200,000 in royalties, and *Fire* earned nearly $500,000. In late 1974, he would begin to receive advances from Little, Brown for a trilogy of unwritten novels. Rivers of money flowed in, rivers of money flowed out. While his needs were great, the sums he was earning would have been sufficient had it not been for the amount he spent on filmmaking and play production—close to $400,000. These projects put him in a deep hole, and the IRS began dunning him. He began taking on more and more lecturing, flying around the country to pick up a few thousand here and there, shoveling honoraria against the tide of debt. Ultimately, he was forced to get loans from Scott Meredith ($185,000) and from his mother ($90,000, her life savings) to keep solvent.

Shortly after *The Prisoner of Sex* appeared, Willie Morris resigned from *Harper's* under pressure from the publisher, William S. Blair, and the chairman of the magazine's board, John Cowles Jr. He had been summoned to a corporate meeting in Minneapolis where the centerpiece was the magazine's balance sheet. It had not made a profit in three years, and Morris's editorial boldness was very much on the minds of the financial stakeholders. Over his four-year tenure, he had published not only Mailer's lengthy pieces, but a big chunk of Styron's *The Confessions of Nat Turner*, an excerpt from James Jones's novel *The Merry Month of May*, and Seymour Hersh's exposé of the 1968 My Lai massacre in Vietnam. Editorially, the magazine tilted to the left; the Cowles family tilted the other way. One board member at the meeting said to Morris, "No wonder it's such a failure. Who are you editing this magazine for? A bunch of hippies?" "The money men won," Morris said. The entire editorial staff resigned, save a young editor, Lewis Lapham, who at a last-ditch staff meeting with Cowles agreed with him (according to Morris) and stayed behind when the rest walked out. He was later appointed editor and remained in the position for thirty years.

In his resignation letter, Morris said that "The Prisoner of Sex" had "deeply disturbed the magazine's owners. Mailer is a great writer. His work matters to our civilization." It was widely believed, as *Time* reported, that Morris's downfall "was precipitated in large degree by a prominently displayed, controversial article by Norman Mailer." Asked if this was true, Mailer said that he suspected "a strong connection, at least." He called the resignation "the most depressing event in American letters in many a year. Under Willie's editorship, *Harper's* has been the boldest and most adventurous magazine in America." Later, in his memoir, *New York Days*, Morris admitted that Mailer's essay "was not central to the issue, only part of it," he wrote, "less at that moment substantive than symbolic." But at that moment, Morris felt impelled to make Mailer the heroic artist arrayed against the benighted forces of Midwest plutocracy. For some time, the media had shown a tendency to drag Mailer from the margins to the center of events. When it was clear that Morris was out, Mailer said he would never write for the magazine again, and kept his word, as did many other important contributors—Styron, James Jones, David Halberstam, and playwright and novelist Larry L. King.

Meredith had negotiated a million-dollar deal for a trilogy of novels by Mailer, "the highest known payment agreed to for a single unpublished work of fiction," according to what New York publishing executives told *The New York Times*. Mailer would be paid in installments, however, and would not receive the full amount until he had completed the 600,000-word work that would, according to Meredith, "encompass the entire history of a human family from ancient times to the world of the future." After he finished *The Prisoner of Sex* and "Ego," he began assembling a library of books on ancient Egypt, where the first novel of the trilogy would commence. He and Carol had moved to her East 54th Street apartment to await the arrival of the baby, due in early March. After Carol delivered, they planned to go to either Maine or Vermont, where he would begin writing.

Maggie Alexandra was late, born on March 21, 1971, Earth Day, at Beth Israel Hospital in Manhattan. Carol remembered the day: "My water broke and suddenly we were in a panic. I was surprised by Norman's behavior. He was the most anxious of all." In the lobby of the hospital, people asked for his autograph as the couple waited for the elevator. "We hadn't a minute to spare as baby presented herself feet first, cord wrapped around her neck," she said. Mailer described Maggie (safely delivered) to Knox: she has "my mother's nose, bless her, but when she looks the strongest, you would think you were staring at the bust of a Roman emperor or a big man in the Mafia. Tough!" Shortly after the birth, Mailer rented a house in South Londonderry, Vermont, not far from the New York border. Before leaving New York, he had to fulfill a commitment. He had agreed to be the moderator at a meeting sponsored by New York University and the Theatre for Ideas, "A Dialogue on Women's Liberation," to be held at Town Hall, on West 43rd Street.

Diana Trilling, one of the four women panelists at the event, writing about her experience, said: "It would be difficult to exaggerate the disorder of the evening: the raucousness, the extreme of polemic, invective, obscenity." It seemed perfectly clear to the audience that Mailer's challenge to Women's Liberation in his *Harper's* essay made it incumbent upon him to take his turn on the ducking stool. The *New York Times* reporter opened his account of the evening by saying, "For a while last night it seemed like Norman Mailer against the world." Three of the four panelists attacked "The Prisoner of Sex"; the fourth, Jill Johnston, a columnist for *The Village Voice*, gave a prepared speech in a kind of singsong chant, beginning: "All women are lesbians, except those who don't know it, naturally," and "all men are homosexuals." Another of the four panelists, Germaine Greer, called the evening "Town Bloody Hall."

Among the luminaries in the audience were four writers, Betty Freidan, Susan Sontag, Cynthia Ozick, and Elizabeth Hardwick, all of whom threw barbs barely disguised as questions at the moderator. There were plenty of men in the packed auditorium, including two Normans, Rosten and Podhoretz, neither of whom rose to defend Mailer. The *Times* book reviewer Anatole Broyard tried to frame a question about the nature of heterosexual sex after the women's revolution, but Greer told him his "unreasonable question" was out of order. The first panelist to speak was Jacqueline Ceballos, the president of the National Organization for Women. She said that it was women's lib—"not the civil rights movement, the anti-war movement or the environmental movement"—that was addressing the root problem of the country. Mailer, she said, had been "sincerely trying to understand" the movement in his essay, but missed the distorted way women were depicted in our culture. In commercials, she said, the woman "gets an orgasm when she gets a shiny floor." Mailer, unimpressed, asked sarcastically, "Is there anything in your program that would give men the notion that life would not be as boring as it is today?" The tone for the night was set by this exchange.

Greer began by suggesting that the masculine artist figure is "more a killer than a creator." Throughout the evening, she came back to this theme, calling for a return to the anonymous artists of the past such as those who built Chartres cathedral. Greer, who had wanted to meet Mailer and go to bed with him, was quite solicitous toward him during the evening, and passed him a number of notes. To men, she said, "We were either low sloppy creatures or menials, or we were goddesses, or worst of all we were meant to be both, which meant that we broke our hearts to keep our aprons clean."

Diana Trilling, the final speaker, was the most cogent and the most sympathetic to the situation of her old friend, whom she referred to in her speech as "the most important writer of our time." He had been "under most intemperate assault" (she wrote in her later account), and she was therefore happy that he struck back; she did not want to be part of "a symbolical slaughter." Trilling was a Lawrence scholar, and her partial agreement with *The Prisoner of Sex* was based on her admiration for the "poetry of biology" in the work of Lawrence and Mailer. Both novelists, and Henry Miller (she said in her speech), believed in "the body as the gateway to heaven." While avowedly a feminist, she couldn't join Mailer's female attackers because she preferred "even an irresponsibly poeticized biology to the no-biology-at-all of my spirited sisters." Someone called out "traitor" when she made this comment.

Mailer said that he was in agreement with some of what Trilling and her colleagues said, but he saw no reciprocity. The movement seemed to overlook the fact that "men's lives are also difficult." He conceded, however, that "Women's Lib has raised the deepest questions facing us," and ended by thanking everyone present "for an incredible evening." Rarely is Mailer given any credit for writing a treatise that lays out such an array of arguments—shrewd, skewed, impassioned, and crazy (for example, contraception leads to overpopulation)—on every aspect of human sexuality and gender identity, publishing it in a popular magazine, and then taking a stage to debate his ideas with all comers. He had, in effect, put himself into the clutches of his detractors and offered them a bully pulpit to attack his ideas. At the end of the section on Miller in *Prisoner of Sex*, he notes that Henry Miller's male readers were not ready to stand with him in any debate with women, no, "the men moving silently in all retreat pass the prophet by." Few stood with Mailer either. The righteous ire of women was too strong.

Not long after the Town Hall debate, he ran into Dotson Rader and Germaine Greer at a party. She was "tracking Norman like a bounty hunter," Rader said. After a good deal of drinking, the three left in a cab. They had a "terrible row" on the ride, Rader said, because she wanted Mailer to return to her hotel with her, and he refused. Mailer yelled, "Stop the fucking cab," and he and Rader got out. Greer told him to go fuck himself. Rader and Mailer went to a bar.

The reviews for *The Prisoner of Sex* were significantly less positive than for his previous five books. Because almost every female reviewer attacked the book, as did at least half the males, the ratio of favorable to unfavorable reviews enjoyed by *Of a Fire on the Moon* was reversed. Brigid Brophy's conclusion in the *Times Book Review* that Mailer's essay "is modeled on a dribble: long and barely continuous" is closer to the tone of the majority than Anatole Broyard's comment that it was "Mailer's best book." *Prisoner* was a Book-of-the-Month Club selection and sold fairly well, but soon it was viewed more as the fruit of a benighted mind than a fair response to Women's Lib. Proud of "his ability to apprehend what lived on the other side of the hill," Mailer may have sensed the coming avalanche. He told Vance Bourjaily that he was in "a stinking depression" during its composition.

Joyce Carol Oates is one of the few female reviewers who showed some sympathy for Mailer's essay. She called him "a visionary, a poet, a mystic—he is shameless in his passion for women, and one is led to believe anything he says because he says it so well." Her admiration is qualified, however, by a counterargument to which Mailer gives short shrift: "Sexual identity is the least significant aspect of our lives," Oates says. She speaks for herself; her primary identity, like Mailer's, is as an artist. But many women, perhaps most women, have aspirations that equal or exceed the one that he says is paramount: "to find the best mate possible . . . and conceive children who will improve the species." Mailer detested all technology that sought to supplant or undermine natural procreation—the pill, the diaphragm ("corporate rubbery obstruction"), test-tube babies, extrauterine gestation. In the long term, he believed that technology's tendency was to homogenize nature, eliminate gender distinctions, and leach out individual differences. He was thinking a century ahead; women were remembering the suffering of the ages.

Oates argues that for all of human time on the planet "women have been machines for the production of babies," and until this function is ameliorated or abrogated, women's full potential will not be realized. "Once we are freed from the machine of our bodies, perhaps we will become truly spiritual." This is the crux of the issue Mailer confronted: was childbearing a function that could be assumed by technology, freeing women to be more than sacred vessels, or was it an inevitably harrowing but heroic destiny, one that elicits male adoration of women, itself biologically destined? Or both? Oates calls it "a difficult question." For insisting on women's procreative destiny, he drew "the rage of Women's Liberation," she says. "And we understand slowly that what is being liberated is really hatred. *Hatred of men.* Women have always been forbidden hatred." Mailer stepped freely to the center of the target, and Women's Liberation was pleased to see him pinned and wriggling. Danielle, then fourteen, was present at the Town Hall debate, along with her younger sister Betsy, and her older sister, Susan. Norman's sister and mother were also there. Danielle recalled being "devastated by the abuse" of her father. Susan was similarly upset, but kept asking herself why her father kept egging the women on. When she saw a film of the event years later, she realized that he was being playfully provocative, something often missed in his encounters with feminists. Mailer said it was the night his hair turned white.

WHEN SCHOOL WAS out, Mailer's six eldest children joined him, Carol, and the baby at a farm they rented in Vermont. Myrtle Bennett, a nanny from Honduras who would become virtually a member of the family, joined them to help with Maggie. It was a huge spread, 470 acres, and they had six horses, three ponies, and several cats. The summer was hot and the bugs plentiful, but it was peaceful. "I haven't felt as collected in a long time," he wrote to Knox.

José and Ramona Torres visited in June and July, and rented a house nearby. Mailer had hung boxing bags in the barn and he and José boxed three two-minute rounds daily. He said later that if he learned anything from Torres in Vermont, it was defense. "He was a marvelous teacher for that because he would tap me with a jab, let's say, and if I made the same mistake he'd tap me a little harder." With the encouragement of Pete Hamill, Torres had started writing boxing articles for the Spanish-language newspaper *El Diario*. He asked Mailer to help him improve his English writing skills, and for over a month, every day, he would bring his new pages to Mailer, who gave him "a fatherly hand with verb tenses." Mailer said that the book that came out of that summer's work, *Sting Like a Bee: The Muhammad Ali Story*, was a "modest phenomenon," because it offered "a view of boxing which comes for the first time, genuinely and authentically from the inside." He swore that it was Torres's book.

When Selden Rodman, the poet and art collector, came for a visit, Mailer showed him the book he had used as a guide, *Fasting Can Save Your Life*. He explained that by the fourth day of eating nothing and drinking only water, you lose your appetite, and "all your poisons are coming out as sweat." The regimen was soothing, he said. "I began to get actually *calm*! No temper, no fighting anymore." This clarity of mind made him think fasting might be beneficial for schizophrenics. Rodman watched Mailer spar, and he jogged along with him. At lunch one day,

Carol told Rodman about the time Mailer had rushed to get his rifle to shoot a pesky raccoon, but then hesitated. "I, the great *macho*," Mailer added, couldn't pull the trigger.

He did no writing that summer, although he did begin to assemble his magazine work of the previous five years into a collection titled *Existential Errands*. Over 125,000 words in length, it contains "Ego," essays on filmmaking, theater, and bullfighting, and a sampling of reviews and interviews. Departing from his method in the earlier miscellanies, he made no attempt to write a set of prefaces. He told Yamanishi that he "just lay fallow like an old field. But now I feel the stirrings of literary work. It would be nice if the time has come to begin a long book." That summer he made some forays into Egyptian history and mythology. The two books that led him in this direction were André Schwarz-Bart's novel *The Last of the Just* (especially the first thirty pages), and Will Durant's chapter on ancient Egypt in *The Story of Civilization*. In early 1972, he would begin "the Egyptian novel," and continue work on it for the next ten years, breaking away only when unable to resist some contemporary phenomenon. He would be forty-eight in January 1971, and was more than ready to begin.

After the children left, Mailer intended to get to work, but two public depictions of him, one comic and one not, made him too angry to write. The September 1971 issue of *Esquire* contained "My Mailer Problem," Germaine Greer's account of her various interactions with him. The cover bothered him more than her essay. Given his generally raspy, sometimes flirtatious relationship with Greer, it seems to have been almost inevitable that they would clash. Mailer, decked out in a gorilla suit, holds a miniature Greer, smiling seraphically, in his simian hands: King Kong Mailer and Fay Wray Greer. A year earlier, Harold Hayes had written to Mailer apologizing for the way *Esquire* had treated him, and promised "empathetic treatment" in the future. In his reply, Mailer recounted a recent conversation with an *Esquire* editor about a possible article on Fidel Castro. Mailer told the editor what would happen if he took the assignment.

> I would spend two months getting ready to do the piece and a lot of time in Cuba and then I would work at writing the piece for another few months and maybe it would be the best thing I'd ever done and then *Esquire* would print a picture of Fidel Castro on the cover

> with Richard Nixon's asshole installed on his forehead. And the kid said, "Do you really think *Esquire* would do that?" And I said, "Don't you?"

He ended his letter by saying that there was a "philosophical gulf" between him and Hayes. The gulf widened after the King Kong cover appeared, and Mailer appeared in *Esquire* only a few times over the next twenty years. His allegiance was transferred to *Playboy.*

THE OTHER, MUCH more painful, depiction was a work by Vidal. In a July 1971 review of *Patriarchal Attitudes* by Eva Figes, Vidal linked Mailer with Henry Miller and Charles Manson, who had recently been convicted of masterminding the murders of nine people in California, including pregnant actress Sharon Tate. Vidal's stated contention is that men hate women, and the three named men are emblematic of this loathing: "The Miller-Mailer-Manson man (or M3 for short) has been conditioned to think of women as, at best, breeders of sons; at worst, objects to be poked, humiliated, killed." During the Puritan era, "M3 was born, migrated to America, killed Indians, enslaved blacks, conned women." In an interview the year before, Vidal had called Mailer a "deranged" American Legion commander; now he likened him to a "VFW commander in heartland America" who sees women "as a creature to be used for breeding." Mailer seethed; he said he felt something blow in his brain. Instead of attempting to show that there were "startling and frightening similarities" between Mailer and Manson, he said, Vidal spoke of M3 as if it were an established fact. Mailer looked forward to engaging his erstwhile friend.

Torres's book was to be published on October 15, and Mailer came up with the idea of a televised boxing exhibition to promote it. He contacted Dick Cavett and it was agreed that a prizefight ring would be created for Cavett's program. On the program, aired October 7, he tried hard to hit Torres, a great defensive boxer, with a telling blow, and failing, took more than he gave, which was his boxing style. At one point, Torres was concerned that he had hurt Mailer with a punch, and paused, but his opponent was okay. Later, Torres called his former manager, Cus D'Amato, and told him, "Cus, I hit him hard in the stomach and he didn't go down. Not *hard*, but hard." Mailer wrote to his Uncle

Louis and Aunt Moos that he had "boxed three moderately confident two-minute rounds with him, and I hope my enemies and detractors gnash their teeth. I know my friends did." For many friends and foes, the exhibition seemed to be an attempt to link himself with Hemingway, which it certainly was, in part. But Mailer's deeper view, as noted in his comments on Hemingway's suicide, was that Papa was not particularly brave; rather, "the truth of his long odyssey is that he struggled with his cowardice." So did Mailer, who saw the match with Torres as another rung on the ladder out of his fears. He wrote the following about Hemingway's boxing: "There are two kinds of brave men: those who are brave by the grace of nature, and those who are brave by an act of will." Hemingway was the latter, he said.

Mailer did not do a great deal of writing in 1971, but he published more titles than in any other year of his career: *Of a Fire on the Moon* had come out in January; *King of the Hill* (a paperback edition of "Ego" with photographs) in April; *The Prisoner of Sex* in May; *Sting Like a Bee*, with his preface, in September; *Maidstone* in early October; *The Long Patrol*, a 739-page collection of selections from twelve Mailer books, edited by Bob Lucid, appeared at the end of October; and in December, a paperback edition of *Deaths for the Ladies*, with a new introduction. Lucid's edited collection of critical essays, *Norman Mailer: The Man and His Work*, which opened the floodgate of comment on his work, was also published in 1971. Mailer especially liked Lucid's comment that although Mailer had yet to write a single work that would put him in the company of Faulkner or Hemingway, "he has accumulated a body of work which can be taken to have an overall unity—Mailer himself has often remarked on this unity—and which so considered is fine enough to be called an actual realization of Mailer's soaring aspiration." What remained to be accomplished, Lucid concluded, was "a huge novel, vast as his imagination is demonstrably vast."

Twice more before the end of the year, he found himself in the public eye. Dotson Rader asked him to participate in a "Remember the War" benefit rally at the Cathedral of Saint John the Divine in New York. The Episcopal bishop, Paul Moore Jr., welcomed the antiwar coalition. Rader, who was a close friend of Tennessee Williams's, had also convinced the playwright to take part. Mailer decided to stage his one-act play, *D.J.*, adapted from *Why Are We in Vietnam?* For this performance, Rip Torn, Beverly Bentley, and her boyfriend, Paul Guilfoyle, played the key roles. Six thousand people packed the church, and Mailer's play followed speeches by Gloria Steinem and Williams. "It was a disaster," Rader wrote. "Tennessee walked out halfway through the play's performance, furious at hearing such filthy language profaning a great Christian house of worship." Mailer was pleased with the event and told the crowd that it was "the first time in my life that students, a peace movement, ever succeeded in shifting a major empire from its military aims."

According to Rader, the bishop almost lost his job as outraged Episcopalians around the country complained about what they regarded as a sacrilege. "It was intense," the bishop said. "They wanted my head." Williams was so distraught by the situation that he never appeared at a political event again. Mailer wrote to Rader after the event to ask "why Tennessee acted like a ruptured dingleberry that night and give my regards to the Bishop, who is a gentleman." But a few weeks later, he wrote a mea culpa letter to the bishop, saying, "I should have had the wit to recognize that the humor would be lost in the caverns of a public address system and that each word would quiver like a psychotic animal." Years later, Rader visited Moore when he was dying, and the bishop asked about Mailer. He told Moore he would send him Mailer's novel *The Gospel According to the Son*, which he said was "the best book I've ever read about Jesus." Moore answered, "I know. I read it."

His other moment in the public eye was his public debate with Gore Vidal on *The Dick Cavett Show.* The December 1, 1971, program was his most memorable television appearance, one that challenged the rules of the talk show. Appearing with him and Vidal was Janet Flanner, the *New Yorker*'s longtime Paris correspondent, who was seventy-nine at the time. Before the show, Mailer had had several drinks at a publication party and was well oiled as he waited in the Green Room. Vidal caressed the back of Mailer's neck and got a slap to the cheek, which Vidal returned. Then Mailer head-butted him "between half and three-quarter throttle," after which Vidal called him crazy and left the room. Mailer came on stage after Vidal and Flanner. Cavett described his entrance: "His hands were fists and carried high, and he had the tousled look of having visited a favorite bar or two en route. His suit was disheveled, his bow to Miss Flanner courtly, and his refusal to shake Vidal's extended hand caused a murmuring in the audience." Mailer's plan was to confront Vidal about the review, but he undercut himself by passing a copy of the magazine to Vidal and ordering him to "read what you wrote." Vidal demurred, and then Flanner leaned over to whisper something to him. Mailer complained about this breach of decorum.

> MAILER: Hey, Miss Flanner, are you workin' as the referee or as Mr. Vidal's manager? [laughter] I'm perfectly willing to accept you in either role . . . my mind is fragile, and I find it very hard to think, and if you're muttering in the background, it's difficult.
>
> FLANNER: I made only the slightest mutter. [laughter] You must be very easily put off center.
>
> MAILER: It's true, you made only the slightest mutter.
>
> FLANNER: A tiny mutter.
>
> MAILER: Yes, yes, but I listen to you spellbound.
>
> FLANNER: I won't bother you anymore. [laughter]

Mailer reported later, according to Cavett, that after this exchange "he began to wonder whether anything he did was going to work, and that he made a small vow never to drink again before going on TV."

Louis Menand summed up the situation at this juncture: "Mailer was entitled to think that he had wrestled with the questions raised by the women's movement honorably, and that Vidal was high-handedly slandering him; but he was unable, in the condition in which he had entered the ring, to lay a glove on his opponent. Vidal feigned perplexity at Mailer's distress, joined forces with Flanner (who clearly found him *très gentil*), and made Mailer look ridiculous the way a cat makes a dog look ridiculous." At this point, Mailer went after Cavett.

> MAILER: Why don't you look at your question sheet and ask a question?
>
> CAVETT: Why don't you fold it five ways and put it where the moon don't shine.
>
> [Following this exchange, wild, sustained laughter. Mailer, eager to reply, can only stab the air with his finger until it subsides.]
>
> MAILER: Mr. Cavett, on your word of honor, did you just make that up, or have you had it canned for years, and you were waiting for the best moment to use it?
>
> CAVETT: I have to tell you a quote from Tolstoy?
>
> [Mailer turns his chair away from the others and to the audience.]

MAILER: Are you all really, truly idiots or is it me?
[A chorus replies, (You!) Then applause.]

The rules of talk shows at that time were as strict as the codes of a Cistercian monastery, and as the television audience watched in amazement, Mailer flouted them, pushing the genre in a new direction. He assumes, or tries to assume, the host's position as moderator, punctures the format's drawing-room civility, brings in private quarrels, and roundly insults the other guests. "Finally," as one television historian has pointed out, "Mailer also challenges the studio audience. He refuses to let it play its role as an invisible surrogate for the audience at home, an unquestioned presence and responsive but essentially silent chorus to the talk on the stage. Mailer forces the audience to articulate its own position." He was booed more than once.

Writing to a friend a few weeks after the show, Mailer said that he had "never received so many letters on any single thing in my life, and well-written or pretty poorly, sympathetic or critical, what gets me is that they are penetrating." As one correspondent wrote to him: "The studio audience was not aware (monitors notwithstanding) of the stark terror in Vidal's eye and your own basilisk glance. And, if they had read his article in *The New York Review* they would have noted his woeful sense of wrong-doing." Mailer said he had been charged up that night "to meet any one of ten people (like Germaine Greer, you know, who has been putting ice-picks in my wax doll all summer) and Gore happened to be the one; but I think I would have commenced an ulcer in my stomach that night if I had found myself on the show playing ping-pong with Gore." Television critics, for the most part, raved about the show. The *New York Post* critic said the program was "the kind of plain-spoken talk-show that all three networks should be carrying, free of the incessant stars plugging plays and movies and records with inconsequential small-talk. Call the Cavett show with Vidal and Mailer nothing less than honest." Mailer wouldn't see Vidal again until 1977.

"PROVINCETOWN IS BEAUTIFUL now: grey days with lights of pearl and sunlight with pink and blue of diamonds," he wrote to his Cape Cod friend Eddie Bonetti, adding that he and Carol would spend the winter there. "It is five years since I tried fiction," he said. "Who knows if the steam is there?" If there was no economic pressure, "I wouldn't write for another two years." He had to produce 100,000 words to get another payment from Little, Brown. To bring in some money in the meantime, he had come to an understanding with *Life* about writing about the upcoming political conventions. He also contracted with a professional agency to arrange speaking engagements at various colleges and universities, where he was much sought after. Underwriting *Maidstone* (in part by selling most of his *Village Voice* shares) had proven to be the worst financial mistake of his life. "I was looking for fuck you money," he told his cousin Basil Mailer (son of Uncle Louis and Aunt Moos) "and was ready to gamble my all on my ability to make a million dollars profit." What he also disliked about the ordeal ahead was that writing "is so bad for your vanity. You get fat; you get soft; you get out of condition; and it takes you a number of drinks at a party before you feel even moderately agreeable." A small wave of self-pity came over him as he commenced writing.

In another letter, he gave a clue to the kind of book he was embarking on. "I have come to a place where I think it is almost impossible to go on with a novel unless one can transcend the domination of actual events—invariably more extraordinary and interesting than fiction." Accordingly, the locus Mailer chose for his new novel is the reign of Ramses IX, an obscure pharaoh, who ruled from 1123 to 1104 B.C. As Lucid argued in 1986, Mailer was "following his navigator toward a novel that he himself found bewildering: a novel set so far back in time as to be out of history altogether." Moving back over three thousand years gave him the freedom to create a society unfettered by the ruling beliefs of Western culture—Judaic monotheism, Christian compassion, Faustian progress, romantic love, and Freudian guilt. He knew it was time to write the novel of his life, or give it up and be satisfied with the primacy first accorded him by Robert Lowell: the nation's finest journalist.

Another prompting, a bit more than a nudge, came from a new critical study by Richard Poirier, who had already given Mailer's work high praise in an essay in his collection *The Performing Self*. Mailer had liked it well enough to write to Poirier's publisher in April 1971 to say he was "on his way to becoming America's first authoritative critic in many a year." By then, Poirier was writing a critical study of Mailer, and shortly afterward sent him the manuscript for his response, which Mailer provided, prompting Poirier to thank him for the "detailed usefulness of your comments." He ended his letter by saying that when Mailer was "writing or talking about writing there's no one alive who is better." This mutual esteem notwithstanding, Mailer undoubtedly read a troubling summative statement in Poirier's book, *Norman Mailer*, published in 1972. Despite the merit of his hugely varied books, Poirier says, "Mailer now is like Melville without *Moby-Dick*, George Eliot without *Middlemarch*, Mark Twain without *Huckleberry Finn*." In Mailer's recent work—*Of a Fire on the Moon* and *The Prisoner of Sex*—Poirier said, he seems locked into a system of dualisms and needs to escape. He could escape, Poirier says, because he is an inveterate critic of his past efforts, and so "is always implicitly proposing for himself some fresh start in the future." Mailer later acknowledged to Poirier that he got this message, but there would be no departure from his system. It was at age 49 a permanent reflection of his double selves.

After only five weeks of work, Mailer broke away from the novel. Over the next three weeks, he spoke at two dozen universities. He showed *Maidstone* at almost every stop, and also got into some heated discussions about Women's Liberation. The crowds were large, and he felt like "a carpetbagger because each day you pick up a fat lecture fee." Mailer told Lucid that he felt something was wrong with his approach to college audiences. Lucid wrote back to say that unlike the students of the 1960s, who were sympathetic to the new order promoted by Abbie Hoffman, Jerry Rubin, and the SDS, their younger brothers and sisters were more worried about graduating with marketable skills and were less interested in drugs than careers. Writing about ancient Egypt was not a bad idea at this juncture, Lucid said.

Sparring with Torres the previous summer had led to a detached retina, and on April 7 he went to a Boston hospital for an operation. Carol recalled that when she entered his darkened room, "I felt his pain. It was intense. I sat down next to him and in a few minutes, he turned to me and said, 'I know what you are doing. It's working. The pain is leaving my body, but be careful. You can hurt yourself.' I was astounded that he immediately knew that I was working to take away his pain." Mailer attributed psychic powers to Carol and said her singing could cure cancer. He called her a white witch. After the operation he wrote to Yamanishi about the difficulty of writing a novel "with very little tradition or precedent to help one along." His plan was to continue on the novel until the Democratic convention in Miami Beach in July, write his account over a two-week period, and do the same at the end of September for the Republican convention, also in Miami Beach. By this time he had written sixty thousand words on the Egyptian novel. Just before he left, he wrote to Lucid, inviting him to come to Maine to read the opening chapters. "I promise you, the new book is going to take the top of your head off," he said. "These pioneer works are pissers." Lucid, with the help of Fan Mailer, had recently begun organizing and storing Mailer's papers and putting them in storage, and their friendship had deepened. He would be one of the first to read Mailer's new work for the next thirty-five years.

THE UPCOMING ELECTIONS, Mailer believed, would be "the most exciting American election in my memory." He told Yamanishi, "There is a new mood in America these days," he said, and while Nixon was strong, "McGovern will prove no Goldwater and easily could win." His victory would "carry the disease to a higher level," for the right would mobilize against the idealistic and radical elements in his politics. He was wrong about the Johnson-Goldwater race in 1964, and just as wrong about the Nixon-McGovern race in 1972. Goldwater had won six states; McGovern won only Massachusetts and the District of Columbia. He was defeated by 18 million votes, the worst popular vote defeat in any presidential election. There was indeed a new mood in America, but it was not radical. Assassinations and antiwar activism, and some of the excesses of the Woodstock Generation, as it was now called, had moved the nation toward conservatism, although the pendulum would swing the other way after the Watergate scandal. While Mailer would continue to prognosticate, he never felt in touch with the 1970s. At the beginning of the decade, he had written to Allen Ginsberg that he was constantly being asked what he thought it would be like. "I don't have the remotest idea," he said. "We were sure of what would happen in the 60's and we weren't far from wrong. The 70's are just a fearful blank to me."

In early June he, Carol, and Maggie drove to Maine from Provincetown, again renting the Thomas house on Somes Sound. The children arrived when school was out. Right after the July 4th weekend, Mailer left for the Democratic National Convention in Miami Beach. He had begun an affair with Suzanne Nye, a young woman who had done secretarial work for him, and it had moved beyond casual. She joined him in Miami. Compared to its predecessor, the 1972 convention was a subdued affair. At the end of July, *Life* published "The Evil in the Room," the first part of his report on the conventions.

This report, while full of keen-eyed portraits of notable Democrats at the convention, is hobbled by the lack of any real convention drama. Some of McGovern's supporters tried to pass platform planks supporting in various ways drug users, draft evaders, and women's reproductive rights—"acid, amnesty and abortion," as the platform was crudely described—but these were easily defeated, despite the energies of Jerry Rubin and Abbie Hoffman and others who feared the coming of a corporate, technocratic world. The Democratic Party was weak; fissiparous forces were afoot. And the nation itself was also divided. "Out in America, far beyond Miami, lived a dull damp *wad* of the electorate," Mailer wrote. "They often did not vote. It took no ordinary issue to fire their seat." But they would stand strong against unsanctioned sex, proscribe marijuana, condemn welfare, and look with disfavor upon concessions to Black Power. They were against much and for little, and perhaps could only hold hands on the flag, the family, and the nation's military. They were the Silent Majority of Richard Nixon.

Most of the remainder of his account of the conventions—published in book form by New American Library as *St. George and the Godfather*—is devoted to the unrepentant chicanery of President Nixon, the ultimate, brilliant, political puppeteer, and his consummate control of the Republican convention. This portion of the book was published in *The New York Review of Books* under the title "The Genius," accompanied by a David Levine ink sketch of Nixon scrubbing up in a bathtub full of blood, the caricaturist's response to the savage bombings of Cambodia and Laos. Nearly five million were killed, wounded, or became refugees under Nixon—a million more than under Johnson. Mailer likens the U.S. bombing to the irrationality of "a man who walks across his home town to defecate each night on the lawn of a stranger—it is the same stranger each night." Yet the president retained the support of a majority.

> Nixon was the artist who had discovered the laws of vibration in all the frozen congelations of the mediocre. Other politicians obviously made their crude appeal to the lowest instinct of the wad, and

> once in a while a music man like George C. Wallace could get them to dance, but only Nixon had thought to look for the harmonics of the mediocre, the miniscule dynamic in the overbearing static, the discovery that this inert lump which resided in the bend of the duodenum of the great American political river was more than just an indigestible political mass suspended between stomach and bowel but had indeed its own capacity to quiver and creep and crawl and bestir itself to vote if worked upon with unremitting care and no relaxation of control.

He finished writing *St. George and the Godfather* in late August, just in time to move to a shingled, three-story house on five acres in Stockbridge, Massachusetts. He paid $75,000 ($60,000 mortgage) for the large rambling place. Carol did not like the house and begged him not to close on it. "The house had negative vibrations," she said. Later, she learned that a number of couples who had lived in the house had gotten divorced. But Mailer was adamant. There was room enough for all of his children, and it was not a long drive to New York in his Porsche. He now owned three homes: 565 Commercial Street in Provincetown, where Beverly lived most of the time with the two boys, 142 Columbia Heights, and the new place in the Berkshires.

The only way for *St. George and the Godfather* to influence the election was for it to be published in paperback. Mailer agreed, hoping it could appear in mid-October, at the latest, three weeks before election day on November 7. In late September he left on a thirty-day, twenty-college speaking tour to publicize the new book and earn approximately $50,000 to stanch his financial bleeding. He complained more than once during the tour about the delay in getting the book to bookstores. "Book publishers are all Democrats," he said, "and distributors all Republicans." It finally appeared at the end of October.

At every college, his audience brought up his opposition to Women's Liberation. When he felt feisty, he brought it up first. He usually stated, as he did at Towson State in Baltimore, that he agreed with "the body of demands that ask for equity," but disagreed with the movement's "sexual ideals." He also complained that women would not enter into a dialogue with him, which he called "potentially totalitarian." This college tour went west, with stops at San Francisco State (where he saw Lois Wilson), and the University of California, Berkeley. At this stop, Mailer began by asking the feminists in the audience to hiss. When they did, he said, "Obedient little bitches," which drew laughs and more hisses. He then went on, according to a news report, to deliver an electrifying speech, "dumping poisonous invective on just about every aspect of the feminist movement and gleefully one-upping most of the epithets that his audience snarled back at him." In the course of the speech, he said that "a little bit of rape is good for a man's soul." Whatever the context, the line was widely reported and cemented his position as the bête noir of Women's Liberation. *Time* ran it, unadorned, as the beginning of its "People" squib on the speech in the November 6 issue. He wrote a letter, complaining as he had in the past, about being quoted out of context. But he had said it and the damage was done.

Barney had been treated for cancer for several months, and on October 12, when Mailer was speaking in New Orleans, he died. Suzanne Nye was with him when he got the news. He came back for the funeral service and interment at the cemetery in Long Branch where Fan's parents were buried. Shortly after the funeral, an elderly woman showed up at Fan's apartment in Brooklyn Heights. She had a signed note from the secretive Barney, notarized, for $26,000 that he owed. Mailer recalled discussing it with his mother. "I think we have to pay it," he said. "My mother didn't altogether want to pay it. He just charmed her [the woman]; I just know it." The family paid. Mailer had made Barney the dedicatee of *St. George and the Godfather.* His father, eighty-one, died two weeks before Mailer could put a copy in his hands.

TEN
THE TURN TO BIOGRAPHY

When Mailer was in New York, he often ate and socialized at Elaine's, an Upper East Side restaurant popular with people in the arts. Plimpton, Talese, and other writers had made the place a sort of clubhouse. Celebrities such as Jacqueline Kennedy Onassis dined there; Woody Allen had his own table (no. 8), and might give you a glance as you passed it on the way to the restrooms, or to "Siberia," the back dining room where tourists were exiled. During a visit to the city in November 1972, Mailer had dinner there with Jeanne Campbell and Frank Crowther, a *Paris Review* editor and freelance publicity agent. They suggested that he organize some sort of bash for his fiftieth birthday. Mailer was opposed, saying, "Another ego trip. Who needs it?"

A short time later, he was at another dinner at another favorite restaurant, Vincent Rao's on 114th Street in East Harlem, with independent filmmaker John Cassavetes and Larry Schiller, a journalist and media entrepreneur. Schiller had agreed to pay Mailer $50,000 to write a preface to a collection of photographs of Marilyn Monroe that he had assembled for an exhibition earlier that year. Mailer brought up the birthday party idea and mentioned his huge alimony and child care expenses. A few days later Schiller called to propose that Mailer charge admission as a way of generating some income. It was the first of many financial schemes he would suggest to Mailer over the next thirty-five years. Mailer liked the suggestion. Celebrities typically pay for attendance at such events with their presence. Members of the Fourth Estate wouldn't pay on principle. For this party, everyone, even his ex-wives, had to purchase a ticket—$30 a person, $50 a couple. Some friends—Kurt Vonnegut and Rip Torn, for example—refused to pay and stayed home. Fan Mailer said to Larry Schiller, "All these people are paying to see my son. I see him all the time for nothing."

Mailer called the project the Fifth Estate, but gave no details, promising to make "an announcement of national importance (major)" at the event. In December five thousand invitations were mailed out for the February 5 party at the Four Seasons restaurant on Park Avenue. Working out of a rented office at the Algonquin Hotel, Campbell and Crowther made all the arrangements. Crowther described the event as "a family and literary event—a night for the written word," which only increased speculation. Would Mailer make a serious proposal, or was it a ploy to raise money for alimony, or to send his children to college? Perhaps it was Mailer's answer to Capote's Black and White Ball (Capote didn't attend Mailer's party). Arthur Schlesinger Jr. suggested that Mailer was going to announce his vasectomy. As the night of the party neared, interest surged and there was a last-minute run on tickets. Calls came in asking what to wear—the invitation said "finery." Mailer's new secretary, Molly Malone Cook, bought an ankle-length pink gown and dyed her prematurely white hair black. She and her partner, poet Mary Oliver, also in a gown, drove in from Provincetown. Later, "in a rare tender moment," Oliver recalled, Mailer told them how touched he was by their thoughtfulness. Mailer and Carol drove down from Stockbridge, arriving at noon. The party began at ten P.M. and almost everyone came on time.

Close to six hundred people attended, including Senator Jacob and Marion Javits and Senator Eugene McCarthy; Jack Lemmon, Shirley MacLaine, and Rod Steiger were part of the Hollywood contingent; Larry L. King, Larry McMurtry, and Jessica Mitford were three of the many writers. Dotson Rader came with Princess Diane von Furstenberg; Elaine Kaufman, owner of Elaine's, was there; Plimpton, Andy Warhol, and cabaret singer Bobby Short. The major gossip columnists and reporters showed up, grudgingly in some cases. Dorothy Schiff, owner of the *New York Post*, came, but Gloria Steinem did not. She called and left a message for Mailer: "Tell Norman it's been a breathless 10 years." The Mailer family was represented by Fan, Al, and Barbara, Mailer's four eldest daughters, ex-wives Jeanne and Adele, and current partner, Carol, whom Mailer was now calling his fifth wife although they weren't married. His assistant, Suzanne Nye, in a low-cut satin dress, was at his side during the evening. Everyone drank and nibbled for close to two hours. The *Voice*'s reporter watched the swirling crowd: "At its center was sure to be Norman Mailer, in the flesh, feet wide planted, drink in hand, finger jabbing chests or tits or air, sterling silver Brillo pad hair bobbing up and down to the rhythm of the crowd he had drawn, pink face-a-pulsing, vibrating jigsaw puzzle impossible to assemble without first killing the man, making him quiet and still." At midnight, Jimmy Breslin introduced Mailer as "one of the half dozen original thinkers of this century."

Mailer began with a dirty joke concerning the respective lengths and depths of male and female genitalia. He began to lose the audience. He maundered. He was, as he said the next day, "a hint too drunk." Finally, the announcement: the Fifth Estate would be a people's organization to track and publish the activities of the FBI and the CIA in the wake of the emerging Watergate scandal—the burglary of the Democratic National Headquarters in Washington, D.C., the previous June. "If we have a democratic secret police keeping tabs on Washington's secret police, which is not democratic but bureaucratic, we will see how far paranoia is justified." Sally Quinn, the *Washington Post*'s reporter, summarized what followed: "He digressed, with a few attacks on the press. He used words like 'totalitarianism,' 'plots,' 'Kennedy assassination,' 'J. Edgar Hoover,' 'sober organization,' 'bugging.' A few people began hissing and walking out."

There were some shouted questions and catcalls as he warned of the nation's drift toward totalitarianism, but the crowd was ebbing away. Adele shouted, "You blew it, Norman." He ended by saying that he planned to form a steering committee in the near future, and left the podium saying he would return in thirty minutes for discussion. Applause was light. Crowther told him to save his remarks for the press conference at the Algonquin Hotel the following day. Mailer acquiesced. At 2:30 in the morning, he was drunk and disconsolate: "I have a demon inside me," he said. The next day, the Algonquin was packed with TV cameras and reporters.

Mailer had a hangover. It was a "terrible mistake" to call the Fifth Estate "a democratic secret police," he told the media. What he was really proposing, he explained, was an organization like the American Civil Liberties Union. He wanted it to be staffed by "the best literary, scholarly and detective minds," and serve as a kind of national ombudsman in a "morally dastardly" country, one that should take a long, hard look at the events of the recent past to determine if government conspiracies existed. He had no desire to head the organization, but would like to have "an umbilical relationship with it." After expenses, the party netted only $600.

A year earlier, Wilfrid Sheed, a novelist and essayist, had written a magazine piece titled "Norman Mailer: Genius or Nothing," which argued that Mailer "has caught every fashion at its crest." He ended the essay: "He gives himself unstintingly, opening his lungs to experience with a romantic willingness that comes close to being noble . . . a weather vane with that kind of accuracy is something to prize. Watch Mailer: if he turns to contemplation, buy a prayer mat; if he stays with politics, expect huge voter turnouts. As Mailer goes, so goes the nation. That is the form his genius takes." But after the embarrassing failure of the birthday party, and despite his sober and reasoned explanation of the Fifth Estate idea the next day, it seemed as if he had lost his bellwether status. Even some of his friends piled on. Pete Hamill said that "the best writer in America was reduced to the role of a nightclub comic"; Shirley MacLaine called the party "a disaster," although she felt Mailer's concerns were on target. John Leonard, editor of *The New York Times Book Review*, said that as proposed, Mailer's idea was "just another vigilante group." Like MacLaine, Rader also felt Mailer was on to something, but after the party, he said, "there was a general feeling around New York that Norman Mailer was nuts, and getting nuttier, poor old Norman, he shouldn't drink so much . . . the journalists I talked to put Mailer down, some of them viciously, and most of them said Watergate was nothing, it would blow away."

On February 7, the day after Mailer's press conference, the Senate voted to create the Select Committee on Presidential Campaign Activities, chaired by Sam Ervin, a Democrat from North Carolina, and co-chaired by Howard Baker, Republican of Tennessee, to investigate the Watergate burglary. This action was prompted in large part by the reporting in *The Washington Post* of Carl Bernstein and Bob Woodward. On the same day some of President Nixon's officials met to cover up the forthcoming investigation, as later revealed by White House counsel John Dean. By the third week in April, Dean and Attorney General John Mitchell were implicated in the cover-up, and slowly but thoroughly the cover-up was exposed. Nixon writhed and prevaricated, but on August 9, 1974, he became the first U.S. president to resign. As these events unfolded, Mailer's warnings were reevaluated.

Crowther revisited the matter in a July 12, 1973, *Village Voice* article. He contacted all of Mailer's detractors, and most of them ate some crow. Jimmy Breslin said that Mailer had been right, "and the asshole dilettantes who laughed didn't know what they were talking about, as usual. The only two guys who should have been at the party were Woodward and Bernstein, but they couldn't come because they were too busy." Mailer, writing to Poirier about the party, said, "I have rarely behaved with less éclat." But as Crowther reported, Mailer still saw merit in the Fifth Estate idea. "I still think there's a function for it, when Watergate is over," he said. "A continuing investigation can break a powerful institution, with extraordinary results." Mailer helped establish the fledgling organization and was pleased when in March 1974 it merged with CARIC, the Committee for Action/Research on the Intelligence Community. It soon faded away, however. In an article in *Counter-Spy*, the magazine published by the new organization, he characterized its role as "homeopathic medicine—one small drop for a large disease." He was vindicated by events, but his time at the pinnacle of celebrity was ending. *Time* now referred to him as "the grand middle-aged man of American letters." What Gloria Steinem called the "breathless 10 years" were over.

BACK IN STOCKBRIDGE after the party, Mailer picked up where he had left off with the preface to the Monroe photographs from the Schiller exhibition, 111 of them by twenty-four photographers. With the help of Schiller and Robert Markel, editor in chief at Grosset and Dunlap, Mailer obtained copies of twenty-four of her thirty films and watched them. Before that, he read *Norma Jean* by Fred Lawrence Guiles and *Marilyn Monroe* by Maurice Zolotow. He read a few more books, including *Marilyn: An Untold Story* by his Brooklyn pal Norman Rosten, who shared it with him in manuscript. He also consulted a series of gossip-crammed articles by Ben Hecht. Because he had only two months to write his piece, he interviewed—"in modest depth"—only fourteen people who had known her, including two of her ex-husbands, Jim Daugherty and Arthur Miller, several coworkers and friends. Pat Newcomb, Monroe's publicist, lent him a nine-hour tape of Monroe talking informally, which Mailer said was "no small bonus." He learned that Monroe's favorite perfume was Chanel No. 5, and bought a bottle to experience the scent. His research agenda was modest but sufficient, he thought, for a preface of 25,000 words.

As he wrote, he got "so excited" that the preface kept growing. "Let it be the longest preface ever written," he thought. At some point, he realized that he was embarking on a biography. "I wanted to say to everyone," he told a *Time* interviewer, "that I know how to write about a woman." He would rely on Guiles and Zolotow for the basic facts, add new ones obtained from the interviews, and draw on his own experience: "I know an awful lot about living with one's legend," he said later. "And I know an awful lot, as a result, about the sort of separation of mind that goes on. I know what it's like to live a little bit on the edge of schizophrenia." His film work had given him insight into the sensibilities of actors, and his sports writing, especially his profile of Muhammad Ali, gave him a sense of how the ego of Monroe's husband Joe DiMaggio might function. His Brooklyn roots were a factor, he said, not merely because Arthur Miller came from there, but because Monroe "had the basic stuff out of which Brooklyn dream girls are made." For everything else, he said, "I speculated."

Beneath her celebrity, her comic ability, her beauty, and her sexuality ("the sugar of sex came up from her like a resonance of sound in the clearest grain of a violin"), was her divided self. He believed that he shared "existential similarities" with her. Monroe was both sweetly vulnerable and a strong-minded careerist. Depending on whom you listened to, she was either sexually voracious or frigid. Lacking much formal education, she was intellectually ambitious and read Freud, Whitman, Edna St. Vincent Millay, and *Ulysses*. She was brave, she was timid. Most appealing to Mailer was her determination to be a great movie star. His description of her intense desire to succeed recalls his own.

> She'd finally laid down a directive for herself. She'd become the instrument of her will. And her will said: you will succeed. Whenever anyone does that, they take everything that's weak in them and they submerge it, very often for years. All hegemony is given to the strength. There'll be a much weaker personality travelling with that strong personality which has its own habits, its own demands, and it will become more and more inflamed. At the first success there's a tendency to relax just that little bit.

He had done the same after *Naked*, engaging in what he called the "ego-gobblings" of celebrity.

The manuscript was due on March 1, and as he approached the deadline, he saw that there was much he would not be able to write about, including an "indelible" impression he had of Monroe. In 1961 or early 1962, he had sat behind her at an Actors Studio performance. "She just looked like a tired blonde. She had a red nose and straw hair . . . really a great mound of straw hair wedged under a black babushka . . . all hair and big dark glasses in a forlorn little huddle. She had this sort of off-beat laugh, an irritating giggle not unlike the buzz of a bee or a wasp, an incredible sound." The other thing he lacked time to investigate fully was her death, and when he was interviewed on *60 Minutes* by his old adversary Mike Wallace just before publication, this fact would cause him grief.

Mailer had seen many of the photographs that would be in the Monroe book, but hadn't given much thought to how they would appear. But for Schiller, the layout of photographs by world-famous photographers such as Richard Avedon, Cecil Beaton, and Bert Stern was the main event; the text was secondary. Dyslexic and blind in one eye from a childhood accident, Schiller was not much of a reader; he had to lock himself in the bathroom and concentrate just to read a newspaper article. He said that when he was working on *Marilyn* he could count on one hand all the books he had read in his life. Despite this, he saw "The Legend and the Truth" exhibition of Monroe photographs he had assembled as the heart of an iconic book. He hired a leading book designer, Allen Hurlburt, and, initially gave as much thought to Mailer's text as Mailer gave to the photographs. It was Mailer's name and what he stood for that he wanted. "We're laying out the book to make it exciting," he said, "to make it lovable, huggable, and fuckable, you know, and so it doesn't matter who the writer is, as long as the text is controversial." All Schiller wanted, Mailer said, was "some nice grey matter between the photographs." When Schiller went to Stockbridge at Mailer's invitation, he discovered their opposed conceptions.

Schiller was a bit nervous, remembering Mailer's reputation as a brawler. "I expected somebody like the Hulk," he said, but he found his host to be "very polite, overly courteous." The evening started well. Mailer told Schiller that his wife was a jazz singer—"You're going to love her," he said—and for the first hour of his visit they listened to her

▲ 19 Two of Mailer's best friends, Mickey Knox (*left*) and James Jones, with Adele and Mailer in 1953.

▲ 20 Rhoda Lazare Wolf (Barbara Mailer's best friend), and her husband, Dan Wolf, one of the co-founders of *The Village Voice*.

◂ 21 Lady Jeanne Campbell, Mailer's third wife, late 1950s.

▴ 22 Mailer in his Triumph convertible with Jeanne Campbell shortly after their May 1962 marriage. Tibo is in the back seat.

▸ 23 Mailer and his secretary, Anne Barry, 1963.

▴ 24 José Torres, light heavyweight champion in the mid-1960s, traded boxing lessons for writing lessons with Mailer.

▲ 25 Mailer and Beverly Bentley, his fourth wife, March 1964.

▲ 26 A photo for an *Esquire* essay on his contemporaries, taken in the Gramercy Gym in New York, 1963.

▲ 27 A still from Mailer's 1968 film, *Beyond the Law,* in which his friend Eddie Bonetti played an ax murderer, and Mailer an Irish-American police lieutenant.

▲ 28 Mailer speaking at a demonstration against the Vietnam War, Central Park, New York, March 1966.

▲ 29 Mailer campaigning for mayor of New York City on Wall Street in May 1969.

▲ 30 Joe Flaherty, Mailer's campaign manager, discusses strategy with his candidate.

▲ 31 Germaine Greer and Mailer on a panel discussion about Women's Liberation, Town Hall, New York City, April 1971.

▲ 32 Mailer and his sister, Barbara, with their parents at their 50th wedding anniversary celebration in 1972.

◂ 33 Mailer and Carol Stevens, his fifth wife, with their daughter, Maggie, 1973.

▴ 34 Eileen Fredrickson, who had a long affair with Mailer, beginning in 1979.

◂ 35 Gary Gilmore shortly before his execution by firing squad on January 17, 1977.

▲ 36 Norris Church Mailer, Mailer's sixth wife, during her years as a fashion model in the mid-1970s.

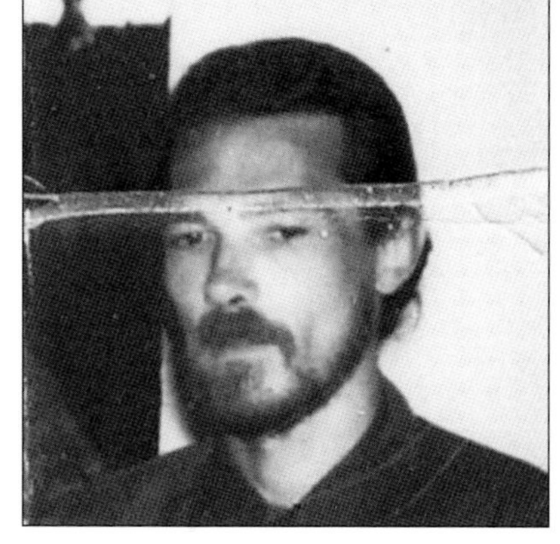

▶ 37 Norris Mailer's Polaroid photo of Jack Abbott, taken shortly after his 1981 release from prison.

▲ 38 Mailer as the architect and playboy Stanford White in Milos Forman's 1981 film, *Ragtime*. Norris played his girlfriend in the scene where White is murdered.

◂ 39 Bernard "Buzz" Farbar and Mailer in the early 1980s.

▴ 40 Mailer's close friend the writer and former drug dealer Richard Stratton.

◂ 41 Mailer on the set of the 1987 film he directed, *Tough Guys Don't Dance*, based on his novel of the same name.

▲ 42 Mailer and Fidel Castro in Cuba, 1989.

▲ 43 Marina Oswald and Mailer in Dallas, June 1993.

▲ 44 The Mailer clan gathered for the 1993 wedding of Kate and Guy Lancaster in Vermont. *Back row:* Matthew Mailer, Michael Moschen (Danielle's first husband), Danielle Mailer, Norris Church Mailer, Valentina Colodro (Susan Mailer's eldest), Isabella Moschen, Antonia Colodro, Christina Nastasi and her mother, Betsy Mailer; *front row:* John Buffalo Mailer, Peter Alson, Norman Mailer, Susan Mailer, Barbara Mailer Wasserman, Maggie Mailer; sitting before his father, Michael Mailer.

▲ 45 Six Mailer siblings in the 1990s: Stephen, Kate, John Buffalo, Matthew, Michael and Danielle.

◂ 46 Jean Malaquais, approximately fifty years after meeting Mailer in Paris. Mailer called him his intellectual mentor.

▴ 47 Lawrence Schiller, Mailer's collaborator on several books (including *The Executioner's Song*) and film projects, in Washington, D.C., in 1994.

▲ 48 Muhammad Ali with Mailer and his Random House editor, Jason Epstein, at the 1998 publication party for *The Time of Our Time*.

◄ 49 Al and Barbara Wasserman in 1998.

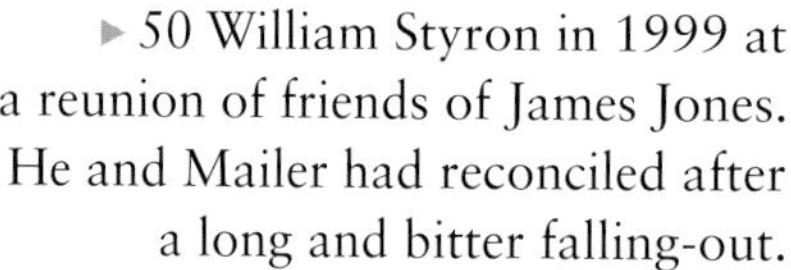

► 50 William Styron in 1999 at a reunion of friends of James Jones. He and Mailer had reconciled after a long and bitter falling-out.

◀ 51 Mailer and Gore Vidal in Provincetown after their appearance in *Don Juan in Hell,* October 2002. Mailer's sister, Barbara, is in background. Mailer and Vidal were also reconciling after years of enmity.

▲ 52 J. Michael Lennon and Robert F. Lucid at the 2005 Mailer Society conference in Provincetown.

▲ 53 The Mailer family at the Norman Mailer Center Gala, 2009: Norris, John Buffalo, Matthew, Betsy, Peter Alson, Michael, Maggie, Barbara, Stephen, Susan, Danielle and Kate.

of such a love affair, or the depth of the incapacity to love anyone else, except as a servant to one's dream of glamour.

Laid bare here is what Mailer believed to be the mainspring of Monroe's psychology, and with some qualifications, his own as well. He was no orphan, but his narcissism, born of early spectacular success, parallels hers. He uses the same word—"Napoleonic"—to describe her desire to capture the attention of the world that he often used in connection with his own. "She is her career, and her career is herself," he says, and this shoe fits him as well, if not quite as snugly. Like him, she is an actor with many faces: "No one can be certain whether she was playing an old role, experimenting with a new one, or even being nothing less than the *true self* (which she had spent her life trying to discover)."

The trying on of faces by great actors, Mailer continues, is the desperate search for an identity. "It is no ordinary identity that will suit them, and no ordinary desperation can drive them. The force that propels a great actor in his youth is insane ambition." Monroe's quicksilver nature can only be captured by a novelist, he says. His biography must be seen, therefore, as "a *species* of novel ready to play by the rules of biography." He puts it another way: "Set a thief to catch a thief, and put an artist on an artist." Great actors (Monroe, Brando), like great politicians (Kennedy, Nixon), great poets (Lowell, Ginsberg), and great boxers (Torres, Ali) are best grasped by the handles of identity and ambition. Novelists are best equipped to do the grasping, and great novelists have the surest hands.

His largest regret about the book was the cover of *Time*, which he felt had hurt his reputation as a serious writer. Schiller recalled that shortly after the magazine appeared, Mailer either called him or saw him in person. "I remember him saying very strongly, 'With that fucking *Time* magazine cover, I'm never going to win the Nobel Prize for Literature.' And he did say that to me just in those words." Schiller wasn't particularly bothered at first, but later "I remember it haunting me a lot of times," he said. "I had not perceived how something could really hurt somebody who was very, very important." Over the years, he said, "those words just ring in my ears, all the time." Mailer's memory is somewhat different, but not contradictory. Asked about Schiller's recollection, he said, "I don't recall saying that," but admitted he might have had the thought. "I can promise you there are a good many things that are going to keep me from winning the Nobel Prize," he said, "and that might be one of them, but that's one item in a prime list of fifty or sixty items."

Mailer described his working relationship with Schiller on *Marilyn* with a Yiddish word, *shidduch*, a matchmaking or engagement. But "a *shidduch* made in Hell is the way it felt. Neither of us was very happy with the other, not at all." Schiller felt the same. "I was done with Norman Mailer. He had fucked me over," he said. They didn't speak for over a year. Nevertheless, the collaboration set each of them on a new path. Schiller got into publishing in a big way. The following year, two books that he "produced" appeared: *Ladies and Gentlemen, Lenny Bruce!* by Albert Goldman, and *Muhammad Ali: A Portrait in Words and Photographs*. For Mailer, *Marilyn* provided a way to use his experience less directly than he had in *The Armies of the Night*, while undertaking a life study on a larger scale than in his political and boxing profiles. Looking back a decade later he said, "All through the 1970s I just sort of staggered along feeling very confused." Turning to *Marilyn* was useful, he said. "If you write a book about one person, it helps to focus what you think." Over the next decade, he would write four more books of a biographical nature, all the while plowing ahead on the Egyptian novel.

DURING THE SUMMER of 1973, Mailer spent several weeks in a rented house in Sorrento, Maine. Carol and all of the children were there, save Susan, who was in Mexico studying to become a psychoanalyst. Danielle recalled the routine of those summers: "We'd be in our bunks and Dad would come down with his army bugle and he would blow it a few times and he would say, 'Drop your cocks, pick up your socks, now get out of your fart sacks, you bastards!' And we'd get up and we'd have this elaborate choreography of tuna fish sandwiches and lemonade. All of us would be in gear and ready to sail. We'd go out in our Luders 16 and often would sit in irons for half the day." She also remembered summer activities in Provincetown: "There was always some drama, something a little scary, something unpredictable. We used to take rides in the dunes in his Land Rover. We'd go up cliffs and do things that were really dangerous. Afterwards, we'd be shaking with fear, and Dad would say, 'But don't you feel virtuous having looked the Devil in the eye?' " He was also testing himself, Danielle said.

Betsy recalled that at times her father was urging them "to do things that were challenging and scary and difficult and out of our comfort zone. And I would balk at that and complain and be angry at him and be scared. But in retrospect, and quite quickly after the fact, I would realize how invigorating it was that he pushed us to go out on the Luders boat, two or three of us." He helped us "overcome our apprehensions and our sense of fear," she said.

In addition to the physical challenges, there were psychological ones, Michael Mailer recalled.

> We were away from our mothers; we didn't have that sort of protective shield. If Dad pushed us too hard, we didn't have somebody to fall back on to protect us, so to speak. I think that for him it was a way to test his child-rearing philosophies. From my standpoint, we got a lot out of it. It pushed me through my fears—I was a very fearful child and he knew that. He wasn't always correct in his methodologies, but by and large, I think those summers allowed me to transcend those fears.

Speaking at her father's memorial in 2008, Kate added another dimension: She recalled the summer artistic pursuits: "One summer he gave us all movie cameras, to film, splice and edit our own creations. Another summer we were to work on scenes from *A Streetcar Named Desire*, cast and directed by him." Her father said that all these pursuits were undertaken for the purpose of "improving our souls by going beyond what we thought we were good at." All nine Mailer children have similar memories of summers in Maine.

Earlier in the year, when Carol Stevens told him that she was uneasy about their relationship, he bought her a Tiffany wide gold band and gave it to her under a full moon. They considered themselves to be married, although he was not yet ready to start divorce proceedings against Beverly. He knew they would be difficult. Carol accompanied him to accept the MacDowell Medal at the writers colony of the same name in Peterborough, New Hampshire. Suzanne Nye, traveling separately, also came, and Carol began to suspect that she was more than an assistant. On the drive back to Maine, she confronted him. He admitted the affair. "As long as you didn't know about her, everything was fine between us," he said, which only made matters worse as far as she was concerned. "I had had it and wanted out," Carol recalled, but the family was waiting for them in Maine, he was contrite, and she relented. Still angry, she flushed her gold ring down the toilet, but tied a string to it. Mailer fished it out and put it on his dresser.

AT THE END of 1973 when *The New York Times* surveyed him and other celebrities on their New Year's resolutions, Mailer's reply was: "To work on a novel . . . just those five words, to work on a novel." To aid him in re-creating the Egypt of three millennia past, Mailer turned to books on Egypt. One of his chief sources was E. A. Wallis Budge's edition of *The Egyptian Book of the Dead*, a collection of spells and prayers placed in the coffins of wealthy Egyptians. Mailer was gripped by the specifics of Egyptian embalming and burial customs, and their ideas of the afterlife. He was especially interested in the perilous journey that all souls had to make through a horrific underworld where monsters and demons threatened them as they made their way to final judgment by the dog god Anubis, who weighed each person's heart. Those heavy with sin and crime were eaten by Ammit, a female demon, part lion, part hippopotamus, part crocodile. The good went on to heaven. He found Egyptian myths and customs to be a relief from American culture and saturated himself in all their gruesome complexity. He wrote to Richard Poirier in early March to say that after all the speed writing he had done over the previous decade, he was finding that "novel writing is *hard*—I move so cautiously." He said that the novel was different "from anything I've done before, in style, matter, stance, nitty gritty. I think you'll love it." He was doing push-ups every other day, fifty to sixty sit-ups daily, and was planning to jog when the weather got warmer. Fasts, exercise, and less drinking (he gave up bourbon almost entirely) enabled him to get down to 165 pounds.

Financial problems were still worrying him. "These days I pant after money in one heat after another," he said. When he received an advance or large royalty check, he rarely escrowed a portion for taxes. The money went out immediately for mortgages, tuition payments, alimony, and child care. Consequently, he was always in arrears with the IRS. What made it worse was that someone in Scott Meredith's office had spread the word about his deal with Little, Brown. "Now everybody thinks of me as a no-good rat-fuck millionaire," he wrote in a long, complaining letter to Mickey Knox. He continued, saying that there were a dozen or more American writers making more than him—"I must include Mr. Vidal on this list"—but a perception was growing that he was "Mailer the radical who sold out." Knox's divorce and separation from his children led Mailer to comment on the damage to his own children from divorce. "There's no kidding oneself," he said, "something always gets lost in them, some little pinching off of some of their higher possibilities." The only consolation is that children do grow up, he wrote. Remembering the troubled marriage of his own parents, he said that he had finally comprehended why his mother had never left his father: "It was as if it would interfere with the largest particular work of her life, which happened to be me." More marital problems, and the concomitant toll on the children, were on the near-horizon.

After Molly Cook came to work for Mailer in 1972, she found herself dealing with "a lot of personal stuff, especially with Beverly Bentley, who was always fighting with Norman," as her partner, Mary Oliver, who also worked for him, recalled. "Molly was always busy. Generally, she kept a bank account and kept records of what was paid out, 'took care' of the wives, made travel arrangements, took many phone calls asking what the caller wanted, then reporting to Norman." There were calls from editors, journalists, and one of Scott Meredith's chief associates, Jack Scovil, Mailer's contact at the agency for many years. Oliver also recalled hearing from a range of celebrities: "Jackie O, Dick and Doris Goodwin, Plimpton, Lillian Hellman, Tennessee Williams, and so on." As time passed, Mailer asked Cook to take on more and more. She established an excellent filing system for his correspondence and manuscripts, and dealt with fans, friends, and family. She and Mailer had some "terrible tiffs," Oliver said, but established a close working relationship. Working for him was "very heavy duty." He could be "brutal," but he was also "a bright, tender, funny guy." Oliver mainly typed his manuscripts (including parts of *The Executioner's Song* and *Ancient Evenings*) and letters. Once, when he asked her to take on an onerous task, she said, "Deliver your own shit." When Molly drove the kids to Stockbridge (smoking her pipe "incessantly" in the car, Michael remembers), Mary always came along. "I was backup," she said.

Sometime in February or March 1974, Larry Schiller called to say that he had a collection of interesting photographs of New York graffiti artists and needed some text. He offered Mailer $50,000 for an essay to accompany the photographs of Jon Naar, in a book designed by Mervyn Kurlansky. The book would be published as *The Faith of Graffiti* and in England as *Watching My Name Go By*. Mailer agreed to write a ten-to-fifteen-thousand-word essay for the book, which was to be published in early May, with a long excerpt appearing simultaneously in *Esquire* (Mailer said he allowed it to be printed there because Harold Hayes had left the magazine). He and Schiller "hardly spoke," Mailer recalled, "not because we were cold, but because there was just nothing to talk about. It was understood that I'd write my piece . . . he could do what he wanted with the pictures." They had little contact, Mailer said, but "we cooperated completely, almost as if to say, 'This is really like a shakedown cruise for future material.' " Schiller remembered the situation the same way: "The ice had been broken for *The Executioner's Song*."

The Faith of Graffiti may be Mailer's least cogent major essay. He gives two chief reasons for admiring the work of the teenagers with spray cans, several of whom he interviewed briefly. First, their "masterpieces in letters six feet high on the side of walls and subway cars" are acts of transgression. Urban graffiti is another battle "in the long war of the will against the power of taboo." To bolster his argument, he refers to Giotto, Raphael, Van Gogh, Jackson Pollock, and ten other major artists, but makes no substantive connection between the graffitists and any of them. He admires the boldness of the young men from the ghetto who risk beatings from the transit police if caught with a spray can. The second reason for his esteem, like the first, begs the question of whether nicknames ("tags") scrawled on public surfaces have any intrinsic merit or beauty. If their work had not been painted over as soon as time allowed, he speculates, then the face of New York "might have been transformed, and the interlapping of names and colors, those wavelets of ego forever reverberating on one another, could have risen like a flood to cover the monstrosities of abstract empty techno-architectural twentieth-century walls where no design ever predominated" over the lust for profit. Most did not agree, New York Mayor John Lindsay for one. When Mailer interviewed him, Lindsay made it clear that he was "the implacable enemy" of graffiti writers, not only because of the cost of effacing it, but because seeing new subway cars marked up inside and out "depressed people terribly," Lindsay said. But Mailer's faith in the essay never wavered.

WHILE LIVING IN Stockbridge, Mailer and Carol got friendly with a local couple, the biographer Anne Edwards and her husband, Stephen Citron, who ran an inn called Orpheus Ascending. Carol had not done much singing for a few years, and when they invited her to sing on Friday nights, her "enormous black eyes which are deep and compassionate," as Edwards put it, opened wide with anticipation. In her memoir, *The Inn and Us*, Edwards described Carol's opening night. Mailer was sitting next to two loud, boisterous couples. When Carol began her first number, Mailer asked the man nearest him to lower the volume. The man paid no attention. Mailer began to get angry.

> Halfway through Carol's third number, the man nearest Norman turned away from his companions and called out, "Is that broad stacked!" "Be quiet," Norman ordered. "Sex-y!" the man continued. With that Norman turned to face the stranger, grabbed him by the ears and in a split moment had butted his own head so hard against the man's head that there was a resounding *craaaaack!* The stranger was holding his head and moaning. Norman had turned back to watch Carol. She was a ghostly sight, unable to conceal the fear in her eyes as she raised the decibel level of her voice.

The music stopped. A melee was in the offing. Carol told Mailer that if that happened she would never forgive him. Mailer and the man went outside. Carol was worried that the man might have a knife. She and Edwards waited, and then walked into the bar, where most of the patrons were gathered. "Standing in the center were Norman and the stranger, no longer a stranger, bear-hugging, toasting each other. 'You have a hard head,' Norman said admiringly." The evening, just another night out for Mailer, ended happily.

Sometimes Beverly, Michael, and Stephen would visit, occasionally staying overnight. Fan was also a regular visitor. One weekend when Fan, Beverly, and the boys were at the house, Carol was singing at another local nightspot, and Beverly stayed for her performance. According to Carol, there was a good deal of drinking, and when Mailer introduced Carol as Mrs. Mailer (as he always did), Beverly declaimed to the crowd that Carol was not Mailer's wife; she was. Carol was mortified. Later, back at the house, Carol and Mailer had a fight, "the only big one we ever had." Mailer, Beverly, and some of the local crowd were going to a late night party and Carol refused to go. As he was making a drink, he squeezed a lemon in her face and then shoved her. She fell down and banged her head. Fan heard the noise and came down from her bedroom. "She stepped right over me to see if Norman was all right," Carol recalled. Mailer left to join Beverly and the others; Carol went to bed and locked the bedroom door. He was furious when he returned home and found it locked, and they did not speak to each other for a week.

Another visitor to Stockbridge in the spring of 1974 was Richard Stratton, then an aspiring writer. Their conversations, which began then and continued through the summer in Maine, eventually became one of Mailer's most important interviews, appearing in two consecutive issues of *Rolling Stone* the following January. They had met three years earlier in Provincetown when Stratton was a writing fellow at the Provincetown Fine Arts Work Center, and doing carpentry on the side. He had read a lot of Mailer's work, and it "changed my life," he said.

> When I read "The White Negro," I felt like Norman was writing about me. Because that whole thing of being brought up in the suburbs in a kind of air-conditioned nightmare . . . the malls, the malling of America, and the mediocrity of that life. I was rebelling against that from the earliest age. I went to reform school at 14; I was a juvenile delinquent. But I didn't understand it until I read Mailer. I was rebelling against the aridity of that life, the blandness, and not taking risks. I was living it, and I think when Norman met me, he saw that.

On the spring night in 1971 that they met, Mailer was forty-eight, Stratton twenty-five. They watched a football game, drank Scotch and cognac, and stayed up until dawn talking about writing. Stratton recalled that Mailer told him that writing was a blessing, and that "the real joy is to discover some shard of truth on the page at the end of the pen." He hired Stratton to build wooden tables for his son's model trains, and gave him the keys to his Provincetown house so Stratton could keep an eye on it when he and Carol were traveling. Their friendship and frank conversations continued for the next thirty-five years.

Stratton's two-part *Rolling Stone* interview, accompanied by photographs by Annie Leibovitz, stands out for the breadth of matters discussed. Mailer comments on Capote's *In Cold Blood*, praising its "elegiac tone," but criticizing its lack of penetration into the minds of the two murderers, Perry Smith and Richard Hickock. And then, in a demonstration of his own abilities in this line, he provides an analysis of Charles Manson (the interview notes that Mailer and Stratton made a trip to the site of the Spahn Ranch that was Manson's headquarters in California). Mailer saw something extraordinary in him: "If Manson had become an intellectual, he would have been most interesting"; he had "bold ideas, and he carried them out." His personality was "Dostoyevskian" because he was "more psychopath than just about any psychopath and more of a hustler than any average hustler that's come along." To see him only as "an example of pure evil, unrestrained psychopathy," he argues, is to miss the "Napoleonic" dimensions of his psyche. Vicious mass murderer, yes, but utterly devoid of worthy qualities, no. Reading this in 1975, a reader might have wondered if Mailer could even discover some humanity in Adolf Hitler.

The interview also contains his first public comments of any length on the Egyptian novel, made to correct Scott Meredith's remark that the novel would follow a Jewish family for a few thousand years. "Some early scenes in the book may take place in Egypt," Mailer said, "but that's not to say that the book begins there and inches along chronologically." Actually, he had no settled idea of the novel's structure at the time. The country was moving into "apathetic hippie beatdom," he told Stratton, and it was time for him to "look for some ground on which to rally." In the late summer of that year, he found it in Africa.

MUHAMMAD ALI WAS twenty-five years old, undefeated, and perhaps the fastest heavyweight champion of all time when he refused, after being drafted in 1967, to enter the army. "I ain't got no quarrel with the Viet Cong. No Viet Cong ever called me nigger," he said, a comment treasured by antiwar activists. He almost went to prison, was stripped of his title, and forbidden to box. In 1970, he regained the right to box, and over the next four years won and lost some major bouts—including the

1971 bout with Joe Frazier that Mailer wrote about in "Ego." By 1974, he had earned the right to challenge the current champion, George Foreman, who had destroyed Frazier, knocking him down six times in their match. Foreman was twenty-five, seven years younger than Ali. The fight was scheduled for the end of September 1974 in Kinshasa, the capital of Zaire. The publicity buildup was massive; some said that Ali was the most famous man in the world. Early that summer, Mailer was unable to resist a ringside seat at what promised to be one of the greatest prizefights in history. So he put Scott Meredith to work selling a magazine deal so he could obtain press credentials. In the meantime, there was time "to think over the peculiarities of a passion for boxing which could take a man away from his work for months and more," and time to ponder the depth of his loyalty to Ali.

He made the decision in early July, just about the time he wrote to Crowther to say that he hoped to see him in New York. I want to explain "the transformations of the Egyptian gods," he said. "To fuck a lady of their choice they were ready to become a hippopotamus, baboon, a reptile or a beetle. Anything to get in," he said. "Those daimons knew how to live." He also responded to a friendly invitation from Kate Millett (who, he had learned, was one of Susan's instructors at Columbia) to have a drink. "Only the Irish could invite you so pleasantly to have a drink," he wrote, although he was in New York too briefly to get together with her or Crowther. He flew to Cairo from New York in early September. Before he left, he learned that *Playboy* would publish his account of what would be called "The Rumble in the Jungle."

Mailer had never been to the Middle East and "was hardly a Zionist," but his week-long visit to Cairo made him feel more sympathy for Israel. The Ramadan–Yom Kippur War had taken place the previous year and the city had not recovered. He was repelled by "the collision of overflowing new wealth and scabrous poverty, teeming inefficiency, frantic traffic and cripples walking on sores." The opening of *Ancient Evenings* takes place inside the Pyramid of Khufu, and Mailer wanted to see it. A guide drove him there at six A.M. and they began the illegal climb. "I always thought when I got up to the top of the pyramids I would have an epiphany, but just as I got to the top, heaving and panting, my vision blurred, there were the smoke plumes of the police coming through the desert." He got down just as the police arrived. Later, he realized that "I could do my book only if I didn't go back there." He left the next day for Kinshasa, arriving on the day that the fight was postponed. Foreman had been cut over his eye while sparring, and the fight was rescheduled for October 30.

He remained in Zaire for "three miserable days," then flew back to New York. Along the way, he picked up some kind of undulant fever and stayed in bed for ten days. He wrote his army friend, Fig Gwaltney, when he was recovered that he was worried about getting sick again, but he couldn't afford *not* to go back; he needed the money. "I'm beginning to think that part of Hemingway's genius was that he knew how to keep from getting the Turistas, as simple as that." At the end of October, he flew back to Kinshasa.

As a fight reporter with *Playboy* credentials, Mailer had access to both Foreman and Ali, especially the latter, as they were more than just acquaintances. He observed their training regimens, their friends and flunkies. He also walked the streets of Kinshasa, and noticed that "the black crowds moved about him with an indifference to his presence that succeeded in niggering him; he knew what it was to be looked upon as invisible," like Ralph Ellison's protagonist. Initially, this revived the resentment toward blacks that he recorded in *Of a Fire on the Moon*, but this feeling passed as he perceived the "tragic magnetic sense of self" in the slim, tall Zairois. All at once, he felt the uniqueness of Africa: "even if Kinshasa was to the rain forest as Hoboken to Big Sur—yes impossible not to sense what everyone had been trying to say about Africa for a hundred years, big Papa first on line: the place was so fucking sensitive! No horror failed to stir its echo a thousand miles away, no sneeze was ever free of the leaf that fell on the other side of the hill." The book that helped him to fathom this quality was *Bantu Philosophy* by a Belgian priest, Placide Tempels.

The gist of the book is that the Zairois see humans not as beings, but as forces. People are more than the sum of their parts; they are the vectors of the energies that possess them, emanating from the living and the dead. A man, in Mailer's extrapolation, is not merely "a human with his own psyche but a part of the resonance, sympathetic or unsympathetic, of every root and thing (and witch) about him." Without ever having said so in as many words, he recognizes it as something he had always believed. The boxing match Mailer would watch and then retell would be presented as the battle of two men wielding their ever-changing *n'golo* (the Congolese word for life force). It would be a bout enveloped in "the messages, the curses, and the loyalties of the dead."

HE MET FOREMAN in the lobby of a Kinshasa hotel. When they were introduced, the champion made a generous comment about Mailer, who greeted him and held out his hand. "Excuse me for not shaking hands with you," Foreman answered softly, "but you see I'm keeping my hands in my pockets." This tautological remark made Mailer remember his week of work at the mental hospital thirty years earlier, and the catatonic who remained motionless for hours, "only to erupt with a sudden punch that broke the jaw of a passing attendant." Foreman practiced a similar discipline: "One did not allow violence to dissipate; one stored it." The champ wanted no unnecessary contact. Ali was the hero of Africa, and Foreman's "concentration would become the ocean of his protection against Africa." When Mailer saw Foreman training he realized how much power was there.

Hitting the heavy bag is a daily task, and it is hard work. Foreman's eighty-pound bag (some are heavier) hung from a chain, and it was held to keep it from swinging wildly. Foreman hit it 150 times in 3 minutes, took 30 seconds off, and did it again, four times altogether, 600 hits in less than 15 minutes. His punches, Mailer wrote, "were probably the heaviest cumulative series of punches any boxing writer had ever seen. Each of these blows was enough to smash an average athlete's ribs; anybody with poor stomach muscles would have a broken spine." As he worked, his sweat formed a circle about his feet; the bag developed "a hollow as deep as his head." Foreman's strategy was palpable in the purest sense of the word. When Ali got tired in the late rounds and could no longer slip punches, or absorb them on his arms, then Foreman would hammer him as he did the bag.

Foreman reappears in the book before the account of the fight, but briefly. There are nineteen chapters in the book, and Ali dominates most of them. We meet his team, watch him train, and follow him as he circulates through the country, press corps in his wake, collecting accolades from his fans, and absorbing *n'golo* as he can. Mailer and Ali had known each other since Las Vegas in 1963, well enough for Mailer to go jogging with him. Mailer had done no exercise to speak of for two months. The run starts at three A.M. and Mailer does not sleep beforehand. He runs a mile and a half and then has to drop out. Ali commends him for doing so well in his fifty-second year. On the walk back to Ali's villa, Mailer hears a lion roar. It was "no small sound, more like thunder," the same sound described by Hemingway in his Africa stories. He begins running, impelled by the thought of death by carnivore. His only solace is that such an end would all but guarantee ensconcement in the canon of American literature. "To be eaten by a lion on the banks of the Congo—who could fail to notice that it was Hemingway's own lion waiting down the years for the flesh of Ernest until an appropriate substitute had at last arrived." When he tells Ali's retinue the story, they laugh. The lion lives in the nearby zoo.

Every move Mailer makes before the fight is calibrated to help Ali defeat Foreman, whether by inveigling his body around a partition separating his seven-story balcony from the balcony of the adjacent room (done while "good and drunk"), accepting derision for telling the lion story, or happily losing at the casino as a way of gaining compensatory *n'golo*. Spin and reverse spin. By doing these magical things (even as he is "furious at the vanity" of thinking that he can affect the outcome), he is acting out of conviction: if Ali wins, Mailer ardently believes, it would be "a triumph for everything which did not fit into the computer: for audacity, inventiveness, even art." Ali's victory would demonstrate how an artist can regenerate his powers. "What could be of more importance to Norman?" he asks.

The fight ends in the eighth round. Ali comes off the ropes and throws a combination of punches ending with a hard right that knocks Foreman down. But the final punches Ali threw were effective only because of the amazing innovations of the previous rounds. Possessed of exceptional reach (eighty inches), and one of the greatest left jabs of all time, Ali threw straight right-hand punches in the first round. Right-hand leads are usually reserved for the later rounds, and Foreman is shocked by them. Ali also had the fastest feet of any heavyweight fighter, and bragged about his ability to "dance," but in the second round, he retreated to the ropes and let Foreman pound him. No one had ever seen what Ali later called his "rope-a-dope" tactic; it seemed insane to let the hardest puncher alive hit you at will. "For as long as Foreman had strength," Mailer wrote, "the ropes would prove about as safe as riding a unicycle on a parapet. Still what is genius but balance on the edge of the impossible?" Ali covered his head with his hands, his belly with his elbows, and leaned back on the ropes (which had been loosened just before the match by Ali's team), forcing Foreman almost to fall on him. "Blows seem to pass through him as if he is indeed a leaf spring built to take shock." Ali taunts Foreman. "Can't you hit," he says. "You can't hit, you push." His scorn maddens Foreman, who overextends himself.

The rope-a-dope is a stupendous success. Foreman has a good round in the fifth, but after that tires quickly and begins to look "like a drunk, or rather a somnambulist, in a dance marathon." Mailer avails himself of every weapon in his metaphoric armory to capture the stages of the champion's disintegration: "Foreman was becoming reminiscent of the computer Hal in *2001* as his units were removed one by one, malfunctions were showing and spastic lapses." By the seventh round he was moving as "slow as a man walking up a hill of pillows." On the occasions when he was able to put together a flurry, Ali would reach over the barrage and "give a prod now and again to Foreman's neck like a housewife sticking a toothpick in a cake to see if it is ready." After Ali hits him with the winning combination in the eighth, Foreman "went over like a six-foot sixty-year-old butler who has just heard tragic news, yes, fell over all of a long collapsing two seconds, down came the champion in sections." Guile bested force; art defeated power.

He began work on his account right away, as *Playboy* had scheduled it for the May issue. As usual, he gave them far more than they were expecting, approximately 54,000 words, which they published in two parts in May and June. When it appeared in book form in late July, it had grown to 67,000 words, but was still divided in two parts, "The Dead Are Dying of Thirst" and "N'golo." It is perhaps the most detailed, certainly the most dramatic, and arguably the most engrossing description of a major prizefight ever written, as well as a demonstration that professional boxing, brutal, sleazy, and corrupt as it often is, can be the locus of artistry of the highest order. As Mailer said later, it is "a book about a genius." But pleased as he was to depict Ali's abilities and applaud his against-the-odds comeback, he had doubts about continuing to write this kind of nonfiction.

He states this baldly in *The Fight*, speaking of himself: "He was no longer so pleased with his presence. His daily reactions bored him. They were becoming like everyone else's. His mind, he noticed, was beginning to spin its wheels." He could continue chasing events, writing a book every year, but he was having some doubts about his ability to read the river of American life. His reputation "had been burning low in the literary cathedral these last few years," he admitted. The reviews of *The Fight* were generally positive, but were few in number. It could be argued that Mailer's fecundity in the late 1960s and early 1970s irked the literary world, especially after the story appeared about his million-dollar advance for a novel, the "descendant of *Moby-Dick*," promised in *Advertisements for Myself*. "Let us see this masterwork" was the unspoken sentiment.

Seymour Krim, one of his most devoted admirers, was discouraged, as he noted at the end of his generally favorable review: "These reportorial books after a while become something of a sham, a waste, a kind of John Barrymore exhibition for the cash no matter how much fine skill goes into the performance." When this line was read to him, Mailer said, "I think it's legitimate," adding that he had "mixed feelings" about the book. "Maybe I have ten years left to write," he said, "maybe I have 20." He had spent a half year on *The Fight* and he wondered aloud, "was that right, was it sensible?" Looking back now at what is generally considered a masterpiece of sports biography, one could justly conclude that the expenditure of effort was worthwhile.

IN EARLY 1975, Mailer was in a state of what must be called anomie. Dogged by debt, caught in a web of romantic relationships, displeased with recent work, and uncertain of his ability to deliver his promised big novel, he wanted change on every front. He had to agree with reviewers who were getting weary of him as a lens, a protagonist, an autobiographer, and a self-described "Nijinsky of ambivalence," and without announcing it he concluded that the participatory journalism phase of his career was over. He would occasionally describe himself in the third person again, but only in short pieces. For the remainder of his writing life—he had 30 more years, not 20—he would move back and forth between the novel and biography of various kinds, sometimes combining the two. But at this point, he knew that he had to heed the message from his navigator, two words repeated over and over: "big novel . . . big novel." He wanted it and his fans wanted it (his publisher expected it), and so for the next three years he would be faithful, after his fashion, to the Egyptian novel, which he referred to as a forgiving wife, a lady always ready to welcome him home from the fleshpots of other genres.

The actual lady he was living with, Carol Stevens, showed less forbearance. She suspected that his affair with Suzanne Nye was continuing. Matters came to a head in late 1974. Carol said that they agreed to sit down and have a formal discussion of the situation. "He had tears streaming down his cheeks and I suddenly felt sorry for him. We talked for some time and when I asked him if he wanted to be with her or hold on to what we had, he said he would leave her. We agreed on a six-month period where he would remain faithful. I really believed that he meant it." He may have. For three or four months, he stayed close to home and worked on *The Fight*. When it was finished, he went on another college speaking tour. After speaking in New Orleans, he flew to Arkansas in early April to spend a few days with Fig and Ecey.

The Gwaltneys threw a party for him, attended by Fig's colleagues and friends at Arkansas Tech. One of the people he met was a former student of Fig's, a stunning redheaded schoolteacher named Barbara (née Davis) Norris. When she learned Mailer would be visiting, she got herself invited to the party so she could get her copy of *Marilyn* signed. Divorced and the mother of a young boy, she was a tall drink of water, five foot ten. That day she wore platform shoes that made her an inch or two over six feet. She said, "How are you, Mr. Mailer," and shook his hand. He turned and walked out of the room. "The *last* thing I had on my mind was romance," she wrote years later in her memoir, although she changed her mind later that night. Mailer had a favorite French expression, force majeure. Norris Church, as she would soon sign her name, was such a force for him, and would be his last great love. It was the same with her.

She was about to leave the party when he returned. She remembered "the intensity of his blue eyes, and his charisma" (which she compared to those of Bill Clinton, a former lover), and the way he "radiated energy like a little steam heater. He couldn't sit still." When he discovered that they had the same birthday, born one minute (and 26 years) apart, he got quite excited. She did as well, being as skeptical as he was about coincidences being accidental. At the dinner party, Mailer told her how beautiful she was, something he would repeat to her often in their thirty-three years together. He borrowed Fig's car and followed her home, where she offered him a glass of Boone Farm apple wine. They made love on the living room rug, but it was uncomfortable because her son, Matthew, was sleeping in the next room.

That night, he explained his obligations: three homes, seven children, three ex-wives, an estranged wife, Beverly, and Carol, the woman to whom he was currently married (except in the eyes of the law). All told, he was sole supporter of fourteen people. "It was all rather overwhelming," Norris wrote, "but I appreciated his honesty." She did not want to become part of his harem, however. Maybe it was just an "interlude on his lecture tour," she thought. Getting married again didn't interest her. Nevertheless, they agreed to think about a meeting in late May when he would be on the road again. He promised to send her a box of his books, as she had read only part of *Marilyn*, and she sent him a photograph to the address he gave her, a post office box in Lee, Massachusetts, a small town a few miles from Stockbridge. Mailer used it for correspondence with his girlfriends.

He saw her a couple of months later in Little Rock, where Norris had reserved a room at the Sheraton. Fig and Ecey were not told of the visit. He bought her a ring that she didn't take off for a long time. With Matthew, age three and a half, staying overnight with her parents, Norris felt uninhibited; she was drawn to a man unlike anyone she had ever met. It wasn't just physical; she admired his running commentary on everything under the sun. But the sexual connection was strong. "Through the years, no matter the circumstances of our passions and rages, our boredoms, angers, and betrayals large and small, sex was the cord that bound us together," she later wrote. They both realized after the two nights they spent together in Little Rock that their interlude could develop into a full-blown relationship.

Norris was twenty-six, exactly half his age. An Arkansas Tech graduate in art and English, she had worked in a pickle factory, as a bookkeeper, and as a high school teacher. Married at twenty to her college boyfriend, Larry Norris, she was divorced at twenty-five. She had never been away from home. In her memoir, *A Ticket to the Circus*, she lists the "firsts" she achieved while getting to know Mailer: flying in an airplane, riding in a cab, drinking red wine, hearing live jazz, eating real Chinese food, and seeing Chicago and New York. She savored it all, although she was a bit intimidated at times, especially by her first visit to a jazz club. Carol was a well-known jazz artist and when Mailer introduced Norris to saxophonist Sonny Stitt, she felt like "an interloper" in Carol's world. But with her height, high cheekbones, and cascading red hair, the former Little Miss Little Rock was usually the most beautiful woman in the room. "I instinctively knew that Norman needed a strong, confident woman, and that was what I was determined to be," she wrote.

Scott Fitzgerald said that the sign of a first-rate intelligence is the ability to function while holding opposed ideas in mind. By this measure, Mailer was a genius. After he became involved with Norris, he had to balance more irreconcilables—in love, family, and work—than ever before. His private life, he wrote to Susan, "has erupted all over the place." Half of him was exhilarated by the challenges; the other half was in the dumps. Smitten by Norris, he felt a deep attachment to Carol, but was not quite ready to break off with Suzanne. There were other women as well: Lois Wilson; Shari Rothe, a flight attendant; and Carol Holmes, a former student of Bob Lucid's he was seeing in New York. He had also had a brief affair with Barbara Probst Solomon, a dear old friend of his and his sister's. He had made a good start on the Egyptian novel, but was enamored of several new projects and not merely for financial reasons. All the while, he had the children with him at the Thomas house in Maine, as well as Carol (still in the dark about Norris), his mother, and nanny Myrtle Bennett, who helped keep the household running. He was appearing on talk shows, giving interviews, and doing readings to promote *The Fight*. Molly Cook and Mary Oliver were running his business affairs from Provincetown, and he was on the telephone with them constantly. His relations with Beverly were "harrowing," he told Knox, and he stopped talking to her on the phone because "she'd end up shrieking." To call Norris or Suzanne, he had to go to a phone booth. His situation during the summer of 1975 might be compared to his analogy for Ali on the ropes: riding a unicycle on a parapet.

NOT LONG AFTER Mailer met Norris, Barney Rosset of Grove Press contacted him about doing an anthology of Henry Miller's work. Mailer, ever in need of ready money, jumped at the advance of $50,000, to be divided with Miller. For all of that summer, whenever he wasn't hiking or sailing with the kids, or entertaining guests, or keeping peace among his far-flung harem, he was rereading Miller's books, beginning with *Tropic of Cancer.* Another project was editing a collection of his essays on political conventions, entitled *Some Honorable Men*, which would be published the following year. He swore that when he completed work on the collection and the Miller book, he would return to the novel "before its spirit begins to expire." Despite this promise, he began talking to director Peter Bogdanovich about making a movie based on *An American Dream.* He wanted Cybill Shepherd, who had been in Bogdanovich's *The Last Picture Show* and *Daisy Miller*, to play Cherry. The lure of film remained strong, but the project died aborning.

In mid-1975, the IRS began putting levies on his income to satisfy back taxes of $60,000. His other debts amounted to $140,000. He still had some shares in *The Village Voice*, but had been unable to find a buyer. When the paper was sold to Clay Felker, Mailer got exactly enough from the proceeds, he thought, to pay off the government. "So I'm half breathing now, which is to say I got one lung back," he wrote to Larry L. King in July, adding that he would like to declare bankruptcy. "The only trouble is that the people I owe the money to I happen to be real fond of—like my mother." Then, about six weeks later, he learned that he owed another $100,000 in taxes. This was a heavy blow, because he was living on what came in each month. "I'm really going to have to change my life style from top to bottom," he wrote to Knox, and "it's depressing because I have no habits for worrying about money." A big score was needed.

Norris knew nothing of her lover's finances. His letters to her were vague about everything except his passionate feelings. Memories of their last tryst and plans for the next one filled pages. "For the first time in my life I don't want to possess my woman's soul," he wrote at the end of July after she had made her first trip to New York. "I want to have all of you, and we've gone so far already, but only at your rate." But after he had said goodbye to her, he got depressed, he wrote, by "the heavy and crossed responsibilities of my life."

> I knew all we needed was twelve hours of sleep and we would be ready to explore into one another again for another week, and instead I was going to be throwing all the switches and working and playing with the children—that special species of work—and being considerate to Carol and missing you, missing your redheaded an-

> gelic insanity and your tender sense of the next move—little Miss I Ching of Spring meeting Old Hard-Heart's Ice, yes, it is new air to breathe when one is around you, and then I always hate good-byes in airports.

Norris's letters matched his for ardor.

> I at last have found someone who is just a little tougher than I am, smarter than I am, and who can love with a passion and tenderness equal (at least) to everything I have to give. I love you. I believe with everything in me that we would be happy together. We feed each other—the monstrous egos that ride both our backs—the hot sexual needs that rise a little hotter each time we meet—the tenderness and love that is given and taken and in the process grows double its size. We are good for each other.

As the relationship grew, Mailer recommended that Norris (Mailer always called her Barbara) read D. H. Lawrence's *The Rainbow*, with its frank examination of sexual relationships. His vision of the love he hoped to achieve with her owed something to the dynamics of Lawrence's. "So often," he wrote, "one finds love, and then looks for a cave where one can feast on it—soon such love grows stale." He didn't want that; he wanted a love that they each deserved, a love that would put "every demand on us—because for once, I want to be in love without guilt, and want a woman to love me without guilt." She was in love with a man who had two selves, he wrote, and they corresponded to her own two. The first he called Cinnamon Brown.

> That's your other female, the tall jaunty slightly mysterious woman who can't walk into a bar without turning it on since there's a sexual voltage comes off you then which you may even be unaware, and it says, "I want to fuck. I want to fuck the most exciting man in the house, whoever he is, because that is the most natural expression for whatever peculiar reason I'm here," and that lady, of course, is a distance away from Barbara who is looking to have one love till she dies and wants to make an art of that love so that she gives strength and gains strength and tenderness passes forward and back. And I, of course, love those ladies because there's one of them for each

> of me, Barbara for Norman since he is probably as tender as she is (that is saying a lot) and as much in love with the religion of love which is to make it with one's mate and thereby come out to a place very few people visit and you can be true to that idea of love; then another side not so different from Cinnamon, a cold creation full of lust who might just as well have a name like Ace or Duke or some such hard-cock name far from Norman—and yet not a bad side, no worse than Cinnamon, for so much of the action is there, even an instinct for some of the better adventures.
>
> I used to be that way when I was twenty-six; I still am. One past needs to be in love—the other can remain in love only so long as the love keeps changing, and so if it is the same woman, the ante keeps rising. There has to be more and more. Of course one cannot always name what *more* might be—it is rather that one has to believe it is possible. Then the two sides of my nature come together.

He invited Norris to come to New York, to "try it for a while," and sent her a plane ticket. No promises; it was an experiment. Matthew would remain with her parents for a few months until she got a job. Norris, an only child, said that her mother cried and then asked what kind of woman she was "to turn from all the people who love her?" Her father, a heavy equipment operator just a year older than Mailer, took it better, but "deep down he is very hurt," she said. Norris told her parents that she would be living in an apartment near Mailer's, "which would give Mother and Daddy the illusion that I wasn't living in sin, although I certainly would be." The cover story for Mailer's family was that Norris was Fig's niece and was looking for a modeling job in New York, which was half true. She arrived in mid-August, and he came down from Maine for a week to help her get settled. A couple of months later, Norris rented a small apartment in Fan's building on Willow Street, a five-minute walk from 142 Columbia Heights.

Remembering Norris's first months in New York, Barbara said, "I always tried to be totally nonjudgmental about Norman's newest woman; I didn't want to not like them." In Norris's case, she had no reservations. "It was absolutely extraordinary that one could be that beautiful and that nice." The arrival of Norris on the scene changed things, she explained. "She had that wonderful joie de vivre, really. She just loved the family; she made everybody feel life was fun. She was enjoying herself. And she was tough. For instance, the relationship between Michael, Stephen, and Matt [Norris's son] was very difficult at first, but she managed to cope with it." It was easier with the girls, she said. "They got along famously—a lot of girl stuff." Fan also hit it off with Norris. "I'm sure they had a lot of questions," Norris recalled, "but refrained from asking them." She continued her masquerade as a country girl looking for a job. "No one mentioned his wife," she recalled.

In Maine, he continued work on the Miller book, which he thought would present no problems. When he did encounter trouble, he wrote to Norris, it made him remember what Ali had told him: "There are no easy fights. The easy ones become the tough ones." Miller's work, in Mailer's view, was radically uneven, and exasperatingly difficult to characterize. But as he told Norris, except for the lost time, he didn't mind the effort, because Miller "is the ideal subject whenever I become too in love with love, for he's in love with cunt—a healthy corrective: I start thinking of Big Red and her Arkansas gold." He continued work on the Miller book through the summer.

In the fall, he had the difficult conversation with Carol. He told her that he was in love with Norris and wanted to move from Stockbridge at the end of 1975. According to Mary Oliver, it was Molly Cook who made the difficult call to Suzanne Nye.

A few months before he died, Mailer spoke of the reasons for his breakup with Carol. He said that part of it was Stockbridge. The town is the home of the Tanglewood festivals, and many of the locals were musical, not literary. Mailer said he didn't know anything about classical music and "found them a dull gang, essentially." There was more, as he explained.

> I was bored due to the fact that my life was dwindling into less and less, or so it seemed. Carol had no interest in a social life, so that was the beginning of the heart of inactivity to me in the marriage. It would have kept us together, and sexually we were fine, too, so it was a lovely marriage in that one way and that was enough for a long time because as the years went by, it built and built. But, finally, when I met Norris, there was no question that I wanted to move, and did. This was the one marriage that broke up that I'd say that I broke up—that I felt bad about. Felt bad about leaving

> Maggie, felt bad about deserting Carol, who had never done me any harm.

There was another element, he said. "As a novelist, I thought, 'I'm not learning anything. If I don't learn anything, I'll dry up.' That was terribly important. And, of course, Norris just filled it all up. And was beautiful as well." In addition, she "loved" the social life in New York, and had been a successful schoolteacher, so "to take care of six of my kids was nothing." Carol said that she never stopped loving Mailer, and after a time, began seeing him again, just as she had when he was living with Beverly.

He divided his time between Stockbridge and New York. Now that Carol knew about Norris, Mailer began to introduce her to his children. Stephen remembers meeting her in Provincetown. He was nine and Michael was eleven. "We were at Ciro's and Sal's for dinner and she walked in with Molly and Mary and my Dad. He might have introduced her as a friend of theirs. I thought she was great. She was beautiful, and a lot of fun. She was wearing a great hat." Danielle remembers that at that time she and her sister "were very jagged and spinning out of control," and Norris was very calm. We were "overly analytical and second-guessing. I don't think she had that fault. She was very direct."

The relationship with Norris was difficult for Susan. "She [Norris] was so young and beautiful. Dad and I always had this thing with looks. I think I look most like him in many ways—in terms of physical appearance, my height, my eyes," and her father, she said, "was always finding fault with the way I looked. That's what I felt. I didn't dress well; I wasn't chic; I wasn't this, I wasn't that, my hair, my friends. So in walks this beautiful model and I had a shit fit." It was more of a shock for her than for her siblings, she said, because she and Norris were the same age. At first, she thought it might be just "another of Dad's love affairs," but then, over a couple of months, she changed her mind. "Norris was really nice. There was something very sweet and earnest about her. She really tried hard; she reached out, and so I got to know her."

NORRIS WAS PLEASED when Mailer asked her to go with him to the Philippines for the third and final match—"The Thrilla in Manila"—between Ali and Frazier, on October 1. He was uncertain about writing about it, but the chance to see the landscape where he had fought three decades earlier appealed to him. After a twenty-two-hour flight, they arrived. Norris remembers that her clothes were rumpled. The first person they saw as they walked into the airport was Larry Schiller, who was photographing the fight for *Time.* Schiller had just changed money, and offered them a stack of Philippine pesos for dollars. Mailer, always wary of Schiller's schemes, hesitated, but then exchanged the money (and later learned it was a fair deal). Schiller was surprised to see him with a new woman. "Lo and behold, there's Norman with this knockout chick who's taller than him. He's got this chick on his arm." Mailer introduced her, "Here's my girl," Schiller recalled, and "the way he says it is like, 'What do you think?' You know? And I say to myself, 'What a pair of legs.' " Schiller, Norris wrote in her memoir, "would figure in our lives over and over throughout the years."

Mailer wanted to try to find the village outside Manila where he had spent time during the war, and they took the highway south out of Manila and drove until there was no road. "There was like a little pig trail that went through the jungle," Norris recalled. "We were in this huge limousine going through this jungle with the leaves slapping on each side of the car and there's all these huts with reed ceilings and fronds and a village store." He thought he recognized a large tree in the center of a field where his unit had bivouacked in 1945, and "in the spirit of the occasion, we pulled out a picnic basket, spread a cloth on the grass, and had a picnic under the tree that once had (maybe) sheltered a young Norman Mailer when he was hatching the plot for *The Naked and the Dead.*" They spent a week in the Philippines, and saw Ali retain his crown in a bruising fifteen-round fight. Mailer decided not to write about it; he had to finish his book on Miller.

The original title was *Mailer on Miller*, but he decided against foregrounding himself—another sign of his diminishing self-interest—and changed it to *Genius and Lust: A Journey Through the Major Writings of Henry Miller.* He completed it shortly after he returned. Because of difficulties obtaining permissions for the excerpts for the collection, the Miller book did not appear until the fall of 1976. He had hoped to get back to the Egyptian novel, but he had agreed to write a film script, his maiden effort in the genre. It had to be written rapidly, and in Italy.

In late October, he and Norris flew to Rome. Knox had recommended Mailer to Sergio Leone, the maestro of spaghetti westerns, as the perfect person to adapt a novel by Harry Grey, *The Hoods*, about Prohibition-era Jewish gangsters in New York. Leone offered him $75,000, a sum that would pay off most of his IRS bill. He thought he could write it in a month. During the day, he worked at Leone's office while Norris explored the city. They spent evenings with Mickey Knox. He introduced them to a fashion designer, Angelo Litrico, who made Mailer a beautiful blue velvet suit. Midway through their stay, Leone said that he wanted enough material for two films, the first one to be called *Once Upon a Time in America*. Mailer made the necessary adjustments and two weeks later turned in a script of two-hundred-plus pages. He thought the script contained "some of my best dialogue," but Leone was unimpressed.

A master of the close-up, Leone could also film haunting images of lonely desert places, but as Knox explained, "Mailer's screenplay gave Leone a dish he couldn't possibly eat; it had serious social content." Shortly afterward, the Italian magazine *Express* ran a spurious account of Mailer's time in Rome. The article quoted Leone's partner, Alberto Grimaldi, who said that Mailer had been living in a hotel room with an eighteen-year-old girl and had written the script on toilet paper. It was so poorly done, Grimaldi said, that no payment was warranted. Knox was furious and grilled Grimaldi, who insisted that the magazine had made up the story. The matter ended in a standoff, and Mailer and Norris flew home. Peter Bogdanovich and another director, William Friedkin, read the script at Mailer's request and pronounced it worthy, whereupon Mailer sued for payment. Several years later, the Italians were ordered to pay, but much of the money went to lawyers. With the help of several writers, Leone came up with a new script, and with Robert De Niro in the lead role *Once Upon a Time in America*, Leone's last film, was released in 1984.

THROUGH MAILER, NORRIS had become friendly with the wife of fashion photographer Milton Greene, who ran a Manhattan beauty shop. Amy Greene told her that if she lost fifteen pounds and got a portfolio of photographs together, she would introduce her to Wilhelmina Cooper, who ran one of the leading model agencies in New York. Norris dutifully brought her weight down and went for an interview. "Trying not to look like a girl from Arkansas, full of foreboding about being turned down," she presented her portfolio of head shots taken in Rome, along with others by Milton Greene, who had been one of Marilyn Monroe's favorite photographers. She was accepted and began modeling right away. Mailer was pleased that she had stopped talking about going for an MFA and had started a new career.

It was Mailer who came up with the professional name Norris Church. She first used it in a letter to him in August 1975 when she went back to Arkansas to sell her house and furniture. Later, with his help, she wrote an article for *Cosmopolitan* about how she had gotten started. He liked her new name, she wrote in her memoir, and was "thrilled" that his "Henry Higgins strategy was paying off." Even with the new income, Norris had to take money from him for expenses, especially after Matt began living with her. "In the beginning I pretended it was a loan I would pay back, but he just laughed and said don't worry about it. That was one thing about Norman, he was generous to a fault. Not only with me but with all the kids and exes." In December, Mailer wrote to Aunt Moos to tell her about "a tall lovely red-haired model whom you would find divine." The affair was over; a long-term relationship was now under way.

Through the fall, he shuttled between Stockbridge and Brooklyn. He explained to Carol that he had promised Norris that he would move permanently by New Year's Eve. He spent Christmas in Stockbridge, and most of the children visited. A few days later, he said goodbye. He told her that the relationship with her was the deepest he had ever had, but he wanted to be with Norris. "Let me have my starlet," he said. He left Carol his Porsche and borrowed her larger car. With all the children, including Maggie, (Nannie) Myrtle and the dog, he drove off, leaving her alone in the big house on the hill. At the beginning of the year, Norris moved into Mailer's apartment. Carol was stricken. She remembered taking long drives in the country and crying.

He now worked steadily on the Egyptian novel. He found it easy to reengage, partly because of his excitement in writing about the ancient civilization's carnal spirituality, partly because there was ample space for his imagination to wander among the dynasties, and partly because he was distressed with American culture. As he told Aunt Moos, the still unnamed book "is like a good wife and I am like a drunken sea captain on a three-year cruise." His metaphor may also reflect the thinking he was doing, now that Norris had moved in, about marriage and fidelity.

He wrote to another correspondent about how he was meditating on "the possibility of committing oneself to one mate, taking the good with the bad." He had wondered if his newfound fidelity was part of a reaction to "an entire era of narcissism which began after World War II." His early years with Norris were his most monogamous since his early years with Bea. As long as he was working on *Ancient Evenings*, he was faithful—mainly. Norris always said it was her favorite book. She loved its exoticism, and it was written during the happiest time of their marriage. While she cleaned and redecorated the apartment, he worked, often in a small aerie twenty feet above.

In late February 1976, Mailer received the Gold Medal for Literature from the National Arts Club, where he was extolled by Bob Lucid and Steven Marcus. In his acceptance remarks, he lamented the difficulties of fiction writing at present. "The nature of existence cannot be felt anymore," he said. "As novelists, we cannot locate our center of values." He echoed these remarks two months later at the National Book Awards ceremony. William Gaddis won the fiction award in 1976 for his novel *JR*, a brilliant, nearly formless work described by one critic as a novel of "waste, flux and chaos," much in the mode of Thomas Pynchon's *Gravity's Rainbow*, which had won the NBA three years earlier. Entropy is abundant in both novels, and Mailer loathed it. (A few years later when he was asked about Pynchon, he said he was "either a genius or vastly overrated.") The "psychological demeanment" and "gloom" and "corruption of self" a writer must face, he said to the NBA audience, comes from maintaining that one's "vision will possess illimitable value." Art is the product of struggle, and great art comes from titanic struggle.

Mailer wanted his books to be the literary equivalent of Stravinsky's *The Rite of Spring,* or Picasso's *Guernica,* works that would alter the course of artistic history. In the early decades, he was pushing into unexplored territory—sex, violence, revolution—but in later years he was upping the aesthetic ante, trying to reshape narrative forms in both fiction and nonfiction, while delivering to the country a deeper vision of itself. This is one of the reasons he was always unable to complete volume two of the several multinovel schemes he laid out for himself. He conceived of vast projects that would shift consciousness, change lives, revamp narrative modes. Consequently, when the first novel in a sequence was not all he hoped it would be, he abandoned the scheme and sought a new one. For the Egyptian novel he created the largest expectations, raised the bar to its highest, and for a decade advertised his forthcoming leap.

WITHOUT MAILER'S KNOWLEDGE, an excerpt from his commentary in *Genius and Lust* was published in the *Los Angeles Times* at the end of March, and Miller wrote to him with thanks. The French think they are marvelous critics, Miller said, "but believe me, none that I read ever came near you for originality, muscularity or wind power." He encouraged Mailer to keep writing, not about movie stars and boxers, but "just about yourself, *Life*." Mailer thanked him and said that whenever he was down on himself as a novelist, he concluded, "ruefully," that his last career may be literary critic. His commentary on Miller's oeuvre, eighty-eight pages of a 576-page book, is as much biography as it is literary commentary, but this is as it should be in discussing Miller, a writer who saw no distinction between fiction and memoir and was usually the central character of his own books.

Miller's self-assurance impressed Mailer. "He has such an extravagant sense of mission that his presence is palpable," and what is on his mind at any moment is "vastly more real than any of the people who come and go in his life," a comment that could be applied to Mailer, who was similarly enraptured. Miller's lack of qualms, guilt, and doubts about his genius, and his escape from his puritanical family, were the foundation of his power, although Mailer must have swallowed hard when he wrote this line: "One had to go back to Melville to find a rhetoric which could prove as noble under full sail." Yet, when one reads the passages Mailer chose from ten of Miller's books (for example, the opening of *Tropic of Cancer*, and his description in *Sexus* of the first time he met "Mona," his second wife, June Edith Smith), the following celebration of Miller's prose does not seem exaggerated.

> Miller at his best wrote a prose grander than Faulkner's, and wilder—the good reader is revolved in a farrago of light with words heavy as velvet, brilliant as gems, eruptions of thought cover the page. You could be in the vortex of one of Turner's oceanic holocausts when the sun shines in the very center of the storm. No, there is nothing like Henry Miller when he gets rolling. Men with literary styles as full as Hawthorne's appear by comparison stripped of their

> rich language, stripped as an AP style book; one has to take the English language back to Marlowe and Shakespeare before encountering a wealth of imagery equal in intensity.

Mailer posed this literary test: what would happen if Miller, Hemingway, and Henry James had to write about a character who "entered a town house, removed his hat, and found crap on his head?" James would have been paralyzed, Mailer says, unlike Stendhal, Tolstoy, or Dostoyevsky, and "Hemingway would have been bothered more than he liked," whereas "Miller bounces in the stink." If Hemingway thrived, for a time, in an earlier world of "individual effort, liquor, and tragic wounds," Miller was at home in a later one, "the big-city garbage can of bruises, migraines, static, mood chemicals, amnesia, absurd relations and cancer. Down in the sewers of existence where the cancer was being cooked, Miller was cavorting." Mailer found such cockroach vitality to be "inestimable."

When he looks at the narcissism of Miller and June, there are echoes of his "Cinnamon Brown" letter to Norris, the one in which he foresees their double selves in an upward spiral of excitation and challenge. Miller is the first American, he says, to explore "the uncharted negotiations of the psyche when two narcissists take the vow of love." The key passage not only demystifies Miller's 1,600-page, three-decker novel (*Sexus, Nexus*, and *Plexus*) about his obsessive love for June, it is also an excellent précis of Mailer's "Lipton's Journal" that tells us as much about Mailer's own inner life as anything he ever wrote.

> The narcissist suffers from too much inner dialogue. The eye of one's consciousness is forever looking at one's own action. Yet these words turn us away from the psychic reality. The narcissist is not self-absorbed so much as one self is absorbed in studying the other. The narcissist is the scientist and the experiment in one. Other people exist for their ability to excite one presence or another in oneself. And are valued for that. Are even loved for that. Of course, they are loved as an actor loves an audience. Since the amount of stimulation we may offer ourselves is obviously limited, the underlying problem of the narcissist is boredom. So there are feverish and/or violent attempts to shift the given, to alter the context in which one self is forever regarding the other. It is a reason why narcissists are forever

> falling in and out of love, jobs, places and addictions. Promiscuity is the happy opportunity to try a new role. Vanity is the antidote to claustrophobia.

For June, "every day is a scenario," and the question of whether she loves Miller is moot; if there is a part for a lover in that day's script, she might. None of her lives are "more real to her than last year's role for an actor." Her repertoire kept Miller on the balls of his feet for thirty years, trying to understand and to play opposite. "To be living as a detective one day and as a criminal the next is to keep one's interest in one's own personality alive."

Mailer was looking for something close to this in his relationship with Norris. The repertoire of roles is much different, given the life circumstances and ambitions of the two couples, but the dynamics of the two relationships are congruent, or so he hoped. This is what Mailer meant in the letter where he tells her that he loves the two ladies ensconced in her, "because there's one of them for each of me." It will be easier, of course, if Norris develops new identities to match the mutations he will doubtless undergo. If they can make it, perhaps he will not feel compelled to improve his image in his books, at least not as much as before they fell in love. Norris did change, and over the years of their marriage made serious and successful attempts at modeling, acting, painting and writing, and this versatility is one of the most important reasons why she was, as she always said when asked, the *last* Mrs. Norman Mailer. But there are other reasons, all to be explored. He probably wrote his letter to Norris before writing the narcissism passage, but we can't say for sure. It is possible that he had not even read *The Rosy Crucifixion* trilogy by that time. But it doesn't matter. He had these ideas long before he took on Miller. Meeting Norris and reading Miller were double confirmation, always the best kind for him.

Mailer told Miller that he expected to be attacked by Miller's supporters and rightly so for "putting much of myself into you. It is the technique by which I work and I've never pretended to hide it. When I wrote about Marilyn Monroe I tried to understand her with that part of her I felt was similar to myself. I've made the same attempt with you," he said, and thought he had come even closer, given their Brooklyn background, his appreciation of Miller's style, and even the similar ways their names were spelled. He added some comments about his own writing, saying he was "guessing what Egypt conceivably might be like, and for that I have a few clues," one of them being the similarity of Egyptian theology and his own. On the day of his letter, May 25, 1976, he had written 130,000 words, and had, he told Miller, 350,000 to 400,000 to go.

For sixteen years, since 1960, Mailer had written about the quadrennial political conventions, but he lacked enthusiasm to do this in 1976. The advances from Little, Brown, he calculated, would exceed anything he could earn in piecemeal journalism, and he saw "a path through my financial difficulties." He had written one piece that spring, "A Harlot High and Low," which holds up for puzzled scrutiny shards of evidence pointing to the CIA's involvement in the Watergate break-in. But the piece, published in *New York*, never coheres, and resembles a pile of research notes. There were far too many tendrils of fact, rumor, and supposition surrounding Watergate than could be dealt with in a twenty-page magazine article. He saw that fathoming the CIA's role in American life could only be addressed in a longer work, and he already had one massive narrative on his hands. Another reason to step away from journalism was his growing confidence about the novel. After writing hundreds of pages about Egypt, "I've finally come to a place where I think I understand what I'm up to," he told Yamanishi.

FOR HIS FIRST summer with Norris and the children, Mailer rented a place in Wellfleet, a short drive from Provincetown. The house was in a salt marsh on Lieutenant Island and could be reached only at low tide, which required planning. Danielle, Betsy, and Kate, who by this time, Norris said, saw her "as something between a girlfriend and an older sister," helped with the cooking and laundry. Michael and Stephen "were normal rowdy boys who half loved me and half were wary of me," Norris wrote, "now that I was the figure of authority. The kids really knew after that summer that the guard had changed." The family took long hikes, went swimming and canoeing, and occasionally went into P-Town for dinner. Carol was scheduled to visit the house and Norris was nervous. Mailer had "talked about her constantly," Norris said, "and she had achieved epic status in my imagination. I knew she was a great beauty." When she arrived, Norris thought she resembled Elizabeth Taylor. They liked each other, and although there was mutual jealousy for some years, they eventually settled into a warm friendship.

That summer, Jimmy Carter of Georgia won the Democratic nomination for president. Shortly after the July convention, *The New York Times Magazine* asked Mailer to profile Carter, and he accepted, traveling to Plains, Georgia. The resulting profile, which he wrote in "a towering depression," was published in the *Times* on September 26. Mailer had only a few hours with the candidate, and wasted a lot of it "haranguing a future president" about "the insuperable complexities of moral examination opened by Kierkegaard," the putative benefits of the sexual revolution, and whether Carter had given much thought to "the possibility that Satanism was loose in the twentieth century." Carter smiled at these questions; he wanted to talk about politics and programs, not the affairs of the universe. Mailer left the interview with "the twice dull sense that he liked Carter more than Carter had any reason to like him." He wrote to Knox that the piece had elicited warm congratulations from many New Yorkers, and he said that the piece had helped elect Carter. Later, he thought less of it and did not include it in his next collection of essays, *Pieces and Pontifications*.

Genius and Lust was generally ignored, especially after William Gass in the *Times Book Review* called Mailer's judgments on Miller "romantically overblown." There was little advertising and only a modest publication party. Norris turned heads at the event.

In December he and Norris threw a party at the Columbia Heights apartment to mark the first wedding anniversary of Dick and Doris Kearns Goodwin. Norris described the party in *A Ticket to the Circus*: "The room was so packed that nobody could move. Drinks were passed overhead through the crowd, and the guests had to link arms to get their drinks to their mouths." She made a massive bowl of coleslaw, along with ham and beans and corn muffins, but most of it was untouched; drink flowed. Jacqueline Onassis, a friend of the Goodwins, came, as did Pat Kennedy Lawford, Arthur and Alexandra Schlesinger, Dick Cavett and his wife, Carrie Nye, and a number of writers, including Kurt Vonnegut and his wife, photographer Jill Krementz. Bob Dylan arrived with an entourage but kept to himself, as Mailer later remembered. Hunter Thompson was one of the last to leave, but returned at six A.M. and asked Norris to make him eggs and bacon. She said he looked "as if his very life hinged on those eggs and bacon," and she cooked for him. He then fell asleep in the hammock under the skylight until mid-afternoon. It was, in effect, Norris's coming out party in New York, and she made several friendships that lasted for years.

AT THE END of the year, Herbert Mitgang profiled Mailer for *The New York Times*. Mailer told him that he was writing a multipart novel about Egypt as he conceived it might have been three millennia earlier, and his aspiration in writing it was "to go beyond one's reach." But he had to take on other work fairly regularly, he said. "You have to keep the bread coming in." In December alone, three of his smaller pieces were published: an interview with one of Nixon's top aides, John Ehrlichman, who was serving a prison term for his complicity in the Watergate cover-up; a preface to the memoir of Hemingway's son Gregory; and a screenplay, "Trial of the Warlock," based on Joris-Karl Huysmans's 1891 novel *Lá-Bas*. Mailer's editor at Little, Brown was also interviewed for the Mitgang piece. He reported that Mailer was working "systematically" on the novel and had written more than 175,000 words.

Saul Bellow won the Nobel Prize in Literature that fall, shortly after the publication of *Humboldt's Gift*, and Mailer sent him a telegram of congratulations. "To my surprise," he told Mitgang, "I felt good about Saul getting it, because he deserved it." When Meyer Levin, an old friend and the author of several long novels about Jewish-Americans, asked if Bellow was his favorite author, Mailer said no, but his congratulations had been genuine, adding, "Obviously, others also deserved it. [Henry] Miller, Nabokov, Mailer, even old rat-fuck Meyer Levin." Bellow's Nobel was another spur to his commitment to the Egyptian novel. He wrote to Knox that he was "resisting intensely" excursions from it. "Can it be that I have at last turned a little serious?" he asked.

Robert Gorham Davis, Mailer's Harvard instructor, read the Mitgang piece and wrote to ask if it were true that he was writing about the 19th Dynasty and the obscure pharaoh Ramses IX. Yes, Mailer replied; he had picked this pharaoh because of "the total inventive freedom" it provided. But as Mailer's research continued, he got caught up in the life of another pharaoh, Ramses II, the most powerful and longest ruling (sixty-seven years) of all pharaohs, and his astounding victory over the Hittites at the Battle of Kadesh, fought in 1274 B.C. on the banks of the Orontes River in what is now Syria. He decided to write about Ramses IX, but to accommodate his enthusiasm for the earlier Ramses (who sired over 150 children and created the colossal sculpted figures at Abu Simbel), Mailer was forced to resort to an awkward flashback, jumping back in time 150 years from the reign of Ramses IX to that of Ramses II. The bridge figure was a general of Ramses II, Menenhetet I, who had learned from a Hebrew slave how to procreate himself again and again, allowing him to know both pharaohs. The scheme created narrative lesions that weakened the novel, but it was the only way he could find to link the two pharaohs. He also told Davis that he planned to include a chapter on Moses, who purportedly lived in the reign of Ramses II (as depicted in the film *The Ten Commandments*, with Charlton Heston as a muscular Moses and Yul Brynner as an august Ramses), although few historians believe it.

The IRS still hounded him, and in a letter he told Susan that his best hope for getting out of debt was writing a book on Gary Gilmore, who was executed in Utah on January 17, 1977, the first legal execution in the United States in ten years. There are "plenty of pitfalls" to such a project, he said, but a large advance and the opportunity to write about Gilmore, a man who "fascinates me out of sight," led him away from the novel once again. In retrospect, the repeated breaking of his resolve seems comic, but as he said more than once, the navigator embraced surprises.

ELEVEN
DEATH WISHES: GILMORE AND ABBOTT

Gary Gilmore was in the news at the end of 1976. The Utah double murderer had not merely acquiesced in his death sentence. Speaking to the judge at a subsequent hearing, he said, "You sentenced me to die. Unless it's a joke or something, I want to go ahead and do it." His determination created consternation among those opposed to capital punishment, and cultish fascination among his admirers. He received over forty thousand letters during his final months, and his face was everywhere, including the cover of *Newsweek*, under the caption "Death Wish." Mailer, like half the nation, was following the story. He recalled being struck by how handsome Gilmore was in photographs. "It was an arresting face, particularly that one shot, the famous one, of the long face," he said. Legal maneuvers followed for months, and Gilmore tried twice to commit suicide. One of these attempts led to a memorable radio report: "Dr. L. Grant Christensen said Gilmore can leave the hospital and return to Death Row if he continues to improve." His first suicide attempt was in tandem with that of a young woman, Nicole Baker Barrett. "Nicole and I have known and loved each other for thousands of years," Gilmore said. She was young, beautiful, and devoted to him. Mailer found the story becoming more engrossing.

On the day of Gilmore's execution, January 17, Mailer saw Larry Schiller on the evening news. "I could see he was going through something," Mailer said. Two days later, Molly Cook told him that Schiller had called and "wants you to do some writing for him." Schiller had already done interviews with many of those involved, including over thirty hours with Gilmore, to whom he paid $60,000 for exclusive access. In February, he sent Mailer an interview that he and Barry Farrell had done with Gilmore. It appeared in *Playboy* and was the longest interview that magazine had ever published. Mailer thought it might "be the best single interview of its sort I've ever read." On March 4, he and Schiller signed a contract with Warner Books for their third collaboration. It called for eighty thousand words on "the life and death of Gary Gilmore," to be submitted no later than March 1978.

The $500,000 advance for a paperback edition, divided 50-50 with Mailer, was negotiated by Schiller with Howard Kaminsky, editor in chief at Warner Books, which had published the paperback edition of *Marilyn*. This money, coupled with the proceeds from the pending sale of the lower floors of 142 Columbia Heights, gave Mailer the wherewithal to take another sabbatical from the Egyptian novel. He made plans to go to Utah. Little, Brown could not have been pleased about this turn of events, not given the amount of money the firm had invested in *Ancient Evenings*. The lurid media frenzy that had surrounded Gilmore—his execution was featured on the front page of the *National Enquirer*—did little to convince Arthur H. Thornhill, Little, Brown's president, of the story's literary merits, and at first the firm turned it down. As Schiller put it in a letter to Mailer, "I do not believe that Little, Brown took the book very seriously," at least not initially. But Mailer was enthusiastic and ultimately the firm agreed to publish the hardcover version of the book.

The book was Schiller's idea and he would not only provide the majority of the raw material, he would also have a hand in marketing the book. Meredith had told him that it would be difficult to convince publishers that Mailer could and would write a narrative. None of his recent books explored large swaths of society such as found in Theodore Dreiser's 1925 novel *An American Tragedy*, a book that would become one of Mailer's models for *The Executioner's Song*. "All he does is write these 30,000-word articles for *Life* and everybody else and then turns them into books," Meredith told Schiller. "And some of them are good books, but he's not writing narratives. They're really big essays." Schiller said, "I was lost—I don't even know the difference." But he was quick to grasp it and was careful to tell Kaminsky that Mailer intended to write a narrative, and thus the deal was struck. Mailer was unaware of this promise, and at the time had no sense of how he was going to structure the book, nor its tone, style, or length. He thought he could finish it in six months.

At first, he wanted to call the book "The Saint and the Psychopath." Gilmore fit both roles perfectly, he thought. On the one hand he possessed "a deep vein of what's commonly called criminality," but he was not "an ordinary thug," Mailer said. No, he had "a quality that was almost saintly." His ability to rise above his situation and regard it with detachment was "extraordinary." Initially, he thought he'd write a twenty-thousand-word essay and "cover the biography skimpily," focusing on Gilmore's belief in karma and reincarnation. He "embodied many of the themes I'd been living with all my life," Mailer said, and "was the perfect character for me." He planned to scrutinize Gilmore's choices: be executed and bolster his chance for reincarnation, or molder for thirty or forty years in prison and feel his soul slowly shrivel.

Schiller had been interviewing everyone who knew Gilmore and Nicole, and then sending the interviews to Mailer. "I'm inundating him with more and more interviews," Schiller said. "I'm going on and on and I remember one time he does say to me, 'Stop, stop, I've got enough to write a book!' And I say, 'No, we don't have enough to tell the whole story.' " When Mailer did dig into the interviews, he recalled years later, he was "aghast because the material that was there was so rich and so deep and so full of a kind of American life that I knew only in passing from the Army, but didn't really know, and there it was." The book would have to be considerably different, and longer, than he had thought.

In late March of 1977, Nicole flew to New York with Schiller to meet Mailer. She had never been out of Utah, and they took her to Trader Vic's for lunch. Then they all went ice skating in Central Park. From the start, Mailer had seen Gilmore as "a man who was quintessentially American and yet worthy of Dostoyevsky," but when he met Nicole he saw that there was another dimension to the story, one vying for importance with Gilmore's dead-serious insistence on execution. He explained her appeal to a *Washington Post* writer: "She's been injured so much by life, and at the same time she's so strong. I thought that she had such a life-force in her in a way, while at the same time such despair. To me, she's a heroine in the old sense. She's a protagonist." Nicole recounted her life in many long interviews. She was "probably the most open person I've ever spoken with," Schiller said, and was particularly frank about her sexual experiences with Gilmore and others. She was sexually abused when she was not yet a teenager and was the mother of two children before she was nineteen. She did not open up immediately, however. Schiller was patient.

After Gilmore's execution, Schiller got Nicole released from a mental facility and moved her, along with her children and her mother, to a beach house in Malibu. He bought her a Great Dane puppy and paid her $25,000 for the rights to her story. Schiller's wife, Stephanie, spent time with her and built a relationship. Then Schiller used the same method with her that he used with all the important characters in the book: he created what he called "a dictionary" of her life. "I listen more than I ask," he explained. "When someone starts a sentence, let them finish the sentence, let them finish the paragraph. Never interrupt." Everyone has their story, but nobody cares to listen. Except Schiller, as Mailer explained.

> Very often an hour would go by before he would ask the first question about Gary Gilmore. These people had never been interviewed before in their lives, and they were having this incredible experience of talking about themselves, and having someone truly interested, or so it seemed, in everything they had to say. And so they went on and on and on, and by the time Larry got to Gary Gilmore, they were wide open, they were ready to tell all.

Mailer knew he had to get to Utah and get the feel of the local culture and the landscape, and sit in on interviews. He also wanted to visit the Oregon prison where Gilmore had done time. His March visit to Oregon State Prison and discussions with the warden, Wyatt Cupp, was the first of a number of visits to the place where Gilmore spent many years, and it enhanced Mailer's understanding of prison life. In late May, he returned again for three weeks and met members of Gilmore's and Nicole's families. He stayed in the motel room where Gilmore had spent the night with Nicole's sister, April, and met Gilmore's uncle, Vern Damico, and Vern's daughter, Brenda Nicol, who befriended Gilmore after his release from prison in April 1976 (he had served fifteen years for many crimes, including armed robbery). Norris went along with Mailer on some of his early visits to Utah, and he took her skiing. Never particularly athletic but always game, she managed, "not prettily," to get down the slopes on her first try. They had now been living together for almost a year and a half, and the Mailer clan had accepted her and her son, Matt, whom Mailer treated as one of his own. "Our life was coalescing," Norris said.

Confirmation can be seen in a letter he wrote to Carol Holmes, one of his former girlfriends. She had written him about a rumor, first reported in the *New York Post*, that Norris was pregnant. Mailer wrote an angry letter to the editor denying the report, and the *Post* printed a retraction. Mailer explained all this to Holmes and added that she might not be hearing from him in the near future, but "you need not take it amiss. I certainly liked the way you looked the last time I saw you. These however are odd years for me. I'm interested at last in the most difficult venture of all, fidelity."

By this time, Norris wrote, she was handling "the minutiae" of Mailer's daily life, as well as being a stepmother for however many children were living with them. As her best friend, Aurora Huston, said, "She was his practical side. He had no idea of the needs of the kids, problems with neighbors. She would tell him, 'Norman, this or that has got to be done.' She could put her foot down when she had to." She had also begun to take over the finances. Norris and Molly Cook had not hit it off, and Mailer had become progressively unhappy with Cook. The sum of their differences finally led to what he called "a bloody rupture." Norris took over the family finances for the remainder of their long relationship. In her memoir, she tells a story about needing something from Mailer one day early in their relationship. He was then working in a studio he had begun renting, an unfurnished third floor apartment about a block away from their apartment.

> At the time I thought it was important, so I went and knocked on his door. He was not pleased. He said, "When I'm writing, pretend I have gone to South America. What would you do if I was in South America? You have a brain. You can deal with whatever comes up." I apologized and said, "Okay," and I never knocked on his door again. I realized then that he would never be a partner for me, like a lot of marriages were.

As she put it in a 2009 interview, "Norman and I had a deal. He wrote, and I did everything else."

ON AUGUST 4, 1976, the family left for Maine, Norris's first visit. She had heard about the overhanging deck at the Thomas house, and the family lore about the twenty-foot plunge into Somes Sound. A few years before, Stephen had been the first one to take it, followed by Mailer, and the following summer, Michael. Norris took a look when she arrived at the Thomas house and, "pretending to be bolder and more athletic than I was," jumped in. It was "terrifying," she said, and not just because of the height. The water temperature is shockingly cold and takes one's breath away. Remembering the moment many years later, Mailer said, "When I saw that long-legged creature jump in, I knew I'd have to go," and "I dove in like a sack of potatoes." Norris said she earned many brownie points that day. A week or so later, she told him she was pregnant. He was "thrilled," she said.

Work on the Gilmore book went slowly. Plowing through a hundred-plus interviews containing "tons of scintillating details" was "a work of digestion, not erection," he told Knox. As a break from his labors that summer, Mailer began work on a baseball betting scheme. "At some point," Danielle recalled, "he said, 'I think I have a foolproof method of guaranteeing a windfall. I think there's a correlation between the performance of players and their biorhythms.' " The fundamental (and much derided) idea of biorhythms is that all humans experience high and low points of physical, emotional, and intellectual achievement, cycles that last from twenty-three to thirty-three days, pulsing up and down like a roller coaster. When the three cycles of a big league pitcher crest on the same day that he is on the mound, Mailer reasoned, an extraordinary performance is likely. Bet on the team that has the greatest number of players whose cycles are peaking. So he bought baseball magazines with birth dates, Danielle said. "We would sit with our little No. 2 pencils and we would mark down in columns these numbers. And then he would pull out his calculator and do this complicated calculation and come up with a prediction of who would win the game. I think he was paying us like $10 an hour—we made a lot of money. But he didn't win much." Nephew Peter Alson also remembered working on the project, and Stephen recalled that Mailer extended it to basketball and football. "He was a terrible gambler," Peter said.

> It was the engineer in him, he loved systems and he believed that there were ways to predict wins. I sort of loved that quality of his and got caught up in some of his more convoluted schemes. At his core, he had betting genes and he liked to gamble and devising a sys-

> tem gave him a rationale for doing so. The biggest flaw in his system was the calculator, which he found in a mail order catalogue. There might have been something to the theory of biorhythms, but we were using a device that was little more than a novelty item. It was the equivalent of using a toy telescope to practice astronomy.

In a 1989 interview, Mailer explained his error: "Finally, what came to me was the realization that these guys were not bound by the past. What makes a man a good professional is he can do his work on a bad day." The scheme "was a joke."

WORKING "LIKE A lawyer preparing briefs" through the early fall in Provincetown, Mailer accumulated over two thousand pages of notes on Schiller's interviews. He also traveled again to Utah to do more interviews. On some of these trips, he and Schiller went again to Oregon to learn more about Gilmore's time in prison there. Bessie Gilmore, Gary's mother, lived in a trailer in Milwaukie, south of Portland, and he and Schiller knocked on her door several times, but she refused to let them in. "No, no, no, don't bother me, you don't need me," she told them. The last time they tried, it was pouring rain, Schiller recalled.

> And Norman's sitting in the car. He's mad at me, and I said, "Norman, we got to do this." I go knock on the door—same response. I say, "It's raining Bessie, we're out here in the goddamn rain. Norman just wants to sit and talk to you." "No, no, no." And if my memory serves me right, I said, "Bessie, Norman's got to go to the bathroom. You know, he's not a young man anymore." "All right," she says, "if he has to go to the bathroom." She opens the door. And I make the decision not to go in. I'm not trying to make myself a hero. He's writing the book.

While Schiller sat in the car, Bessie and Mailer had a long talk, the only face-to-face interview she gave, although she spoke many times on the telephone to both men. That day, Mailer asked her about the story that Harry Houdini was related to her husband, Frank, but her knowledge was "second-hand and rather fanciful," Mailer said, "and all I could conclude was that Houdini being the father of Gary Gilmore's father was a *psychological* reality in that family." Gilmore's father, who was much older than his mother, had been in show business for a time, but there was no hard evidence of a blood relationship with Houdini. The fact that she would discuss this with Mailer during the visit supports Schiller's observation that "She loved Norman."

Arranging to interview the widows of the men Gilmore killed, Colleen Jensen and Debbie Bushnell, was a challenge. Schiller didn't want to contact them until it was known that Mailer was writing the book "because I knew that the Mormons might look upon me as a negative person—the guy who paid Gilmore's family money, who's going to make a hero out of him." When Mailer's participation became public, Schiller set up a reception in Salt Lake City for the attorney general, Mormon church officials, and other leaders. Mailer was the star attraction. After that, and probably because of it, the lawyers for the victims informed Schiller that the widows had agreed to be interviewed.

Looking back, Schiller said that he was nervous, as it was the first time he and Mailer were conducting interviews as a team. But as they prepared, he saw that Mailer respected his methods enough to have him take the lead. Mailer would give a sign when he wished to ask a question; otherwise, Schiller would run the interview. The separate interviews with the widows, delicate and emotion-laden, were each four hours long. When Mailer did ask a question, Schiller said, "it was so perfect and important—a question I could not have conceived of." In their later collaborations, they often fought, but for *The Executioner's Song*, at least in the early going, they worked together as smoothly as Holmes and Watson.

The interviews continued through the first half of 1978. All told, Mailer states in an afterword to the book, there were over three hundred separate interview sessions with over one hundred people. Some interviews went on for weeks. This total includes a number with lawyers involved in the case, which were conducted by Judith McNally, Molly Cook's replacement, who would work for Mailer for the next twenty-five years. All together, the collected transcripts came to over fifteen thousand pages. Mailer had more material to work with than on any previous book. In a 1980 interview with John Aldridge, Mailer said that after leaving an interview with a woman, they were driving along, "and suddenly, Schiller, who has a passion for verification, started pounding the wheel and said, 'She's lying, she's goddamn lying!' Part of figuring out what happened was living with these interviews long enough to compare them to other interviews until you felt you could decide what probably did occur in a given situation."

Schiller had always collaborated with other writers, providing raw material. But he retained the final say, and this had led to a falling out with a previous collaborator, Albert Goldman, who worked with him on the Lenny Bruce biography. Goldman called him a "voyeur" interested in "the *most* lurid, the *most* gross, the *most* hideous" things imaginable. In return for giving an interview, Schiller often insisted that negative comments like Goldman's be balanced by a positive. For example, he invariably asked that the book he published by celebrated photographer W. Eugene Smith, *Minamata: Words and Photos*, be cited. Smith had been attacked and almost blinded by thugs hired by the Japanese chemical company that had discharged methyl mercury via wastewater into Minamata Harbor. Schiller became Smith's angel and provided financial support and professional assistance so he could finish the book, one of the first photographic records of industrial pollution.

Producer David Susskind offered Gilmore $150,000 for the rights to his story, an offer that far exceeded Schiller's $60,000, and he also offered to share profits in the film he planned to make. But Schiller had made it a point to send Gilmore telegrams and books, and to meet with members of his family, including, most importantly, Vern Damico, Gilmore's uncle and appointed agent. Schiller spent time with Vern and his wife, Ida, and their daughters, Brenda Nicol and Toni Gurney, sat in their living rooms, and listened to their stories. He purposely made several spelling errors in a telegram to Gilmore, which allowed the convict to feel slightly superior to him, as he took justifiable pride in his language skills. Susskind was peppering Gilmore and Damico with telephone calls from New York, and at one point said to Damico, "Any contest between me and Mr. Schiller would be like the Dallas Cowboys playing the local high school." When Schiller heard Damico repeat this line, he said, "Susskind is right, he is the Dallas Cowboys. But I'm suited up, I'm here on the playing field and ready to play. Where is David Susskind? I don't even see him in the stadium." Schiller won the rights. But Schiller also insisted that the victims' families be compensated. Gilmore agreed, and they received $40,000 of his $60,000.

Mailer said that Schiller reminded him of Harold Hecht, the Hollywood agent and producer who had tried and failed to make a film out of *The Naked and the Dead*: "He wanted to do good work—wanted to raise himself in the estimate of the world, not be seen as an opportunist and an operator." Mailer needed Schiller's organizational abilities, his deal-making chutzpah—he called him in a later letter "one of the great wheeler-dealers of all time"—and his bottomless energy. "I owe him more than a little, because *The Executioner's Song* would never have been nearly as big, and perhaps not as good as it is, if it hadn't been for his skill in interviewing." Schiller's omnivorous information-gathering operation changed Mailer's way of writing to some degree. He had always been proud of discovering truth at the tip of his pencil, but now saw that it would not be sufficient for capturing Gilmore and Nicole. He began to see that literary imagining could be more than just scouring his innards for original insights and waiting for prompts from the navigator. It could be exercised in other ways. Smelting a story from a mountain of facts, factoids, perceptions, hunches, and lies was one. Selecting the right narrative voice, or rediscovering one that had lain dormant for thirty years, was another.

ONE OF THE last of Gordon Lish's accomplishments as fiction editor at *Esquire* (1969–76) was to convince Mailer to write a piece on television, "Of a Small and Modest Malignancy, Wicked and Bristling with Dots." The essay sorted through Mailer's experiences on programs going back to Mike Wallace's *Night Beat* in the late 1950s. Mailer's fight with Vidal on the Cavett show is the memoir's focal point, although Mailer also discusses a number of other programs. *Esquire* was on the newsstands in mid-October 1977, about a week before Mailer attended a dinner party for visiting British publisher George Weidenfeld, the publisher of six of his books. Jason Epstein, editorial director at Random House, asked if Vidal, one of the firm's authors, and his partner, Howard Austen, could join them after dinner, and the hostess, journalist and biographer Lally Weymouth, said of course.

In her column describing the party, Liz Smith called it "one of the grandest private parties ever tossed in Manhattan." Weymouth, the daughter of *Washington Post* publisher Katharine Graham, invited about two dozen for dinner at her East 72nd Street apartment, and fifty for drinks afterward. Her mother came, and some good friends: CBS board chairman William Paley; Jacqueline Onassis, accompanied by architect John Warnecke; Pete Hamill; Barbara Walters; Clay Felker and his date, Gail Sheehy; and lawyer–literary agent Mort Janklow. Rose and Bill Styron were there, as were Lillian Hellman and Susan Sontag. Governor Jerry Brown of California came, as did some West Coast film people, including producer Sam Spiegel. British ambassador Peter Jay, a friend of Weidenfeld's, was also present.

Before dinner, Mrs. Onassis asked Mailer some questions about fighting, according to Warnecke. "Norman, who has a theory about everything, began to expound on the subject. He said, 'You must keep ice-cool.' " After dinner Vidal arrived as the guests were talking and drinking in the crowded living room. Mailer was in the kitchen, again in conversation with Onassis, when Norris told him of Vidal's arrival. He went immediately to the living room and as soon as he saw Vidal, Janklow said, "he charged." Mailer told a *Washington Post* reporter that he had "been looking for Gore for six years and last night I finally found him. When I saw Gore, I just felt like butting him in the head, so I did." Accounts vary, but it seems that Mailer threw a gin-and-tonic in Vidal's face and bounced the glass off his head. Mailer didn't remember throwing a punch, but Vidal later told columnist Liz Smith, "Then came the tiny fist!" Janklow, who was talking to Hamill and Felker, said that Vidal "just stood there kind of frozen." Then they scuffled, with Vidal grabbing Mailer's lapels, and Mailer gripping Vidal's arm so tightly that bruise marks remained for weeks. About this time, the hostess walked in from the kitchen, unhappy to see a fight at her party. "God, this is awful; somebody do something," she yelled. Clay Felker, at ringside, said, "Shut up, this fight is making your party."

Janklow grabbed Mailer, who was "flustered and genuinely angry. My interest," Janklow said, "was to separate them so it didn't degenerate into a brawl. Gore was stunned and his glasses askew. Then Gore's companion, Howard Austen, started screaming and hollering, 'Norman, you are nothing!' Norman came forward again—he's potentially dangerous—but I held him back. Gore didn't say anything." Sam Spiegel tried to quiet Mailer, and Vidal sat down on the couch at the other end of the room and used someone's handkerchief to clean his bloody lip. Barbara Walters said, "To me the most interesting thing was that Mailer's girlfriend, slim and tall and wearing a Grecian dress, stood there like a white obelisk with no expression on her face and said nothing." Mrs. Onassis watched from the kitchen doorway. According to Warnecke, Mailer looked much the same, "taut and unruffled." At this point, Mailer said, "Howard [Austen] came up to me and said he would fight for Gore. I said, 'My fourteen-year-old son could take you.' Howard never forgave me for that remark." Shortly afterward, Mailer approached Weymouth and said, "Either he goes or I go." Faced with a Hobson's choice, she did nothing and Mailer got ready to leave. As he and Norris were walking out, Epstein said, "Norman, grow up." Vidal stayed and "held court," as one guest described it.

The following day both men gave postmortems. Mailer said that Vidal "was nothing but a mouth." Vidal told a reporter, "I actually feel sorry for him. After all, it's not easy being a failure like Norman." Not long after the Weymouth party, Norris went alone to another dinner party as Mailer was in Utah. Someone rose and gave a toast to Mailer, after which record executive Ahmet Ertegun gave a toast to Vidal, who was also absent. As one of the dinner guests recalled, "Norris stood up and doused him with a whole glassful of wine right in his face. Ahmet's wife was there and they both laughed. I was surprised, honestly, because if someone other than Norris had done it, they wouldn't have stood for it."

Mailer explained to Gordon Lish that even after he had excoriated Vidal in his *Esquire* essay on television, he was still angry when he ran into him at Weymouth's. "Nothing mattered. I just had to trash him. I think I'd a taken a dive into cancer gulch that night if I hadn't." For her part, Norris wrote, she had been "horrified and helpless" watching the altercation. She and Mailer never could figure out why Vidal had compared Mailer to Charles Manson, she wrote, which was the root cause of the animosity. "We were never invited to Lally Weymouth's again," she said, adding that Weymouth said later that the party "probably had made her reputation as a hostess." Vidal passed over the incident in his memoir, *Palimpsest.* When he included the essay that had started the feud, retitled "Feminism and Its Discontents," in his 1993 collection, *United States: Essays, 1952–1992*, he dropped the comparison of Mailer to Manson.

AS 1977 ENDED, Mailer was ready, after eight months of research and several trips to Utah, to begin writing. He was still weighing titles and listed several in his early notes: "Let's Do It" [Gilmore's final words], "American Virtue," and "Violence in America: A Novel in the Life of Gary Gilmore." His titles all point to his search for Gilmore's humanity, the praiseworthy but recessive character traits—the minority within—that offset his banality and violent crimes. Shortly after the book was published, Mailer said that Gilmore was "a kind of litmus test for compassion" because he was "on the one hand despicable and detestable and, on the other, he's admirable. How are you going to swallow that?" He wanted the story to "force people to look at how narrow our concepts of human nature are."

For the book that he would eventually title *The Executioner's Song*, Mailer returned to methods used in *The Naked and the Dead*. Both are told by anonymous, omniscient narrators who wheel their perspective through a large cast of characters, range freely in time and space, and knit two major and several minor plot strands into a huge social tapestry. Given these similarities, it might seem that his decision to revert to this perspective, even after thirty years, was not unduly complicated. Yet it was. The materials for the story, covering the nine-month period from Gilmore's release from prison to his execution, were in hand. But Mailer was at a loss as to how to approach the story, which seemed to consist of alternating layers of complexity and simplicity, and a chain of contingencies running back a hundred years, as revealed in the final sentence of the first chapter, in which Gilmore's cousin Brenda reflects on Gary flying home to Utah from St. Louis, after being released from federal prison.

> With all the excitement, Brenda was hardly taking into account that it was practically the same route their Mormon great-grandfather took when he jumped off from Missouri with a handcart near to a hundred years ago, and pushed west with all he owned over the prairies, and the passes of the Rockies, to come to rest at Provo in the Mormon Kingdom of Deseret just fifty miles below Salt Lake.

Achieving this laconic, ungarnished style—Mailer described it as "a gentle voice that seems to come in from over the hill"—was no easy matter, and during his first month of writing, from mid-January to mid-February 1978, he was paralyzed, he said. His first attempt was to begin the narrative at one remove.

He created a character named Staunchman, "a middle-aged movie-writer whose marriage had broken up and he was living in Paris and he was miserable, just a big ungainly man with two huge suitcases, sort of a figure in the Latin Quarter and everybody would wonder, 'What is this man with the two huge suitcases doing?' " His baggage is filled with all the interviews with Gilmore and company, and he was charged with writing a novel-length treatment for a famous director, someone like Francis Ford Coppola, who said to him, "Put everything in, don't leave anything out; I want to know all about this man Gilmore before I make the movie." But Mailer did not immediately see that placing Staunchman between the reader and the Gilmore story, using him as a sort of impresario of the voices of the characters, would be a problem. He was enamored of his "baroque" style, he recalled, and uneasy about making the switch to something simpler. It had been "so difficult," he said, "for me to arrive at my own style—after all I'd been a public writer for 10 to 12 years before I felt I'd come into my own style as such [with *Advertisements for Myself*]—I didn't start with an identity. I forged an identity." Achieving this style was a matter of some pride because "it's not easy to master. It's not supple. It does not adapt to everything that comes up." Indeed. For a 1,000-page saga with approximately 300 characters, half of whom have speaking parts, the baroque style was a dull tool.

Finally, he decided to drop Staunchman and adopt "the shifting point of view used in the 19th-century when people believed in God and the novelist could play at being the All Knowing Supreme Deity." He had to take the leap but he felt, as he said later, as if he'd "violated the fundamental integrity of the novel." The modern novel, it should be said. Dickens and Balzac would not object. Whatever the offense to the ghosts of Conrad and James, he concluded that he had to "get myself knuckled down to the simple point of telling that story flatly, blankly, in the third person," returning to the omniscient point of view last used in his first novel.

"The deity," reviewer Ted Morgan notes, "orchestrates the voices, but does not join the song." Gone are the hallmarks of Mailer's rococo style, "the existential musings, the outrageous ideas, the over-characterizing." In earlier years, Mailer said, he would have been unable to relegate himself to being "nothing but a transmission belt." It was hard to silence the subjunctive selves who had voiced his anticipations, intimations, fears, and, occasionally, hopes, as Mailer made clear after the fact. He surprised himself by this departure, and astounded the literary world. Habituated to his refractive presence in the nonfiction narratives of the previous dozen years, almost every one of the numerous reviewers of *The Executioner's Song* remarked on his conspicuous absence, one "so pronounced," reviewer Richard Stern noted, "that it dominates the book like an empty chair at a family dinner." He calls *The Executioner's Song* "unremittingly unmailerian," and "an act of literary suicide." Stern was almost alone in this view, however. The overwhelming majority of the book's reviewers agreed that Mailer's decision to tell the story of Gilmore's final months and execution in a quiet voice from the other side of the hill demonstrated "narrative technique of real genius."

THE ONLY THING he published in 1978 was a preface to his 1944 novel, *A Transit to Narcissus*, brought out in a limited facsimile edition by his friend Howard Fertig. He accepted few speaking engagements, and none at colleges save a brief talk at his thirty-fifth Harvard reunion, where he was introduced as "the folk hero of our class and nation." In February, he attended a huge party in New York with friends and admirers of James Jones, who had died of congestive heart disease the previous May. The party celebrated the posthumous publication of the concluding novel of Jones's World War II trilogy, *Whistle*, published by Doubleday, where Gloria Jones was an editor. Jacqueline Onassis, also a Doubleday editor, attended the party and was quoted as saying that *Whistle* was her favorite novel by Jones. Mailer, wearing his (now tight-fitting) Angelo Litrico velvet suit, was photographed countless times during his conversation with Mrs. Onassis. Norris, who accompanied him, told reporters that she would give birth to their child in April, via natural childbirth, "and Norman plans to be in the delivery room."

Mailer had seen Gloria Jones only a few times since the late 1950s, and until that night had never met Jones's daughter, Kaylie, who would become a novelist after college. Kaylie does not mention the book party in *Lies My Mother Never Told Me*, her graceful and frank memoir of her struggle to give up alcohol and become a writer, but provides an account of another meeting with Mailer in 1989. It took place at the apartment of Jean Stein, editor of the literary journal *Grand Street*, who was a good friend of Mailer's. "He turned to me," she wrote, "and said simply, 'I loved your father. He was the best friend I ever had, and I've missed him every day of my life. Losing him was one of the worst things that ever happened to me.' " Kaylie was taken aback: "This was the tough-talking, wheedling, arrogant son of a bitch my father was so angry at all through my childhood?" Mailer went on to say that he deeply regretted his last conversation with Jones, which had taken place in Elaine's a few months before Jones died. Jones was sitting alone at the bar when Mailer walked in and said to him, half seriously, "Let's settle this thing once and for all, Jim. Let's go outside and fight it out," which was his time-tested way of cementing a friendship, win or lose. But Jones was not up to it. "I can't Norman, I'm sick. I've got a bum heart." Mailer described to Kaylie the way Jones said it: "There was no bravado, no self-pity, no anger in his words. Just a fact, and the total exhaustion in his eyes." Mailer felt bad, and regretted his challenge. To the end of his life, he remembered this final meeting, and repeated to others that his friendship with Jones was the most intense of his life. Mailer told Kaylie that he would like to help her if he could. Gloria immediately proposed that he give a blurb to Kaylie's forthcoming novel about Russia, *Quite the Other Way*, and offered to give him a blowjob for his endorsement. Norris, who was listening to the conversation, burst out laughing, as did everyone else at the party. Kaylie got the blurb, gratis. Mailer knew he owed something to the memory of the man he said later had "the wisdom of an elegant redneck."

IN MID-FEBRUARY 1978, Mailer received a letter from a convict named Jack Abbott, who would play a small role in the composition of *The Executioner's Song*. Abbott was in the same prison that Gilmore was paroled from in 1976, the U.S. Penitentiary in Marion, Illinois, built to replace Alcatraz. Abbott had read that Mailer was working on a book about Gary Gilmore, and offered to tell him what life was like in maximum security prisons. Like Gilmore, he had also done time in the Utah State Prison (and held the distinction of being the only person to escape from it) and, through the convict grapevine, had learned a few things about Gilmore. Mailer wrote back to thank him for his insights into "the psychology of violence inculcated in one after fifteen years in jail that is not easily communicable and not necessarily obliging to the works of the imagination." He asked Abbott to tell him stories of prison life, and Abbott did. None of Mailer's many correspondents mailed him more words than did Jack Henry Abbott, a convicted forger, bank robber, and murderer, serving an intermediate term of up to nineteen years for his crimes. Over the next three years, Abbott wrote Mailer over two thousand pages.

His first letter "was intense, direct, unadorned, and detached." His voice was unique, Mailer said, and he had "an eye for the continuation of his thought that was like the line a racing-car driver takes around a turn." He was also "an intellectual, a radical, a potential leader with a vision of more elevated human relations in a better world that revolution could forge."

> So he has a mind like no other I have encountered. It speaks from the nineteenth century as clearly as from the twentieth. There are moments when the voice that enters your mind is the clear descendant of Marx and Lenin untouched by any intervention of history. Indeed, Abbott, who is half Irish and half Chinese, even bears a small but definite resemblance to Lenin, and the tone of Vladimir Ilyich Ulyanov rises out of some of these pages. . . . Freedom and justice are oxygen to Abbott.

These words came three years later as part of Mailer's introduction to Abbott's prison letters, which he helped to have published. During their early correspondence, however, Mailer was too preoccupied with Gilmore to see Abbott as more than just a fairly interesting informant.

From January to early May, he worked almost every day in the office on the floor below his apartment. Mounds of transcripts and notes took up most of the floor space in the eight-by-twelve room with a single window overlooking the Brooklyn Heights promenade, the East River, and lower Manhattan. Trucks on the Brooklyn-Queens Expressway under the Promenade rattled the windows day and night. The radiator hissed and clanked. The confined space reminded him of a prison cell, he said, and over the months of ten- and twelve-hour days he came to understand Gilmore "as well as I know some of my ex-wives." When he came up for air to write some letters on May 10, he had six hundred pages of typescript. One letter was to Abbott, who was the first correspondent to learn that Norris had given birth to a son on April 16. "We're calling him John Buffalo—don't ask me why, I just like the name," he wrote.

In a letter to Uncle Louis and Aunt Moos, Mailer wrote that the book would have "as many characters and situations and clarity of purpose, I hope, as 'The Naked and the Dead.' " What he was aiming for, he went on, was the deep psychology of the murderer, "which has never been touched by anyone, except for that author sitting next to God himself, old Dostoyevsky." This letter, and several others written that day, show that Mailer had now firmly decided on most of the narrative key episodes, selected his post of observation, found his voice, and chosen a title. But knowing the full story, he said later, was "a hazard." When writing novels, he didn't want to know how things were going to turn out, preferring to learn as he proceeded. He wanted *The Executioner's Song* to read the same way, and was purposely inattentive to anything but that portion of the story under construction. Being overly conversant with its future events, he said later, "would make me curve what was happening to my characters at the place where I had them." Having made the key decisions, he was now ready to pick up the pace, and not merely because of his confirmed sense of direction; he needed a new infusion of cash. He planned to work double shifts for the next three months in order to have a 1,200-page manuscript by August 1. He told Morton Yanow, a California writer with whom he had struck up a correspondence, that *Song* would be "not unlike 'In Cold Blood' except, of course, vastly different in tone but the same essential technique," that is, nothing would be imagined, but it "reads in the form of a novel." He hoped that the similarities ended there because it would be "tedious" if his book was compared to Capote's in every review.

Mailer stayed in New York in June and July and worked. To help their financial situation Norris was doing portraits on commission and also teaching art classes at St. Ann's School, where Matthew attended. On weekends some of the other children visited. Mailer told Louis and Moos that it is "truly a menagerie come Saturday and Sunday—the great irony is that I was never cut out for fatherhood at all." Norris handled whatever came up with the children and was "a splendid mother," he said. She also read the manuscript as it was typed by one of a half dozen typists, including Martha Thomases, who became a valued helper and good friend. Judith McNally was also proving to be a fine assistant. She did research for the book while handling Mailer's literary affairs and correspondence, and like his other secretaries pitched in to help with household chores. Within a year or two, she would sign his name to letters, although she never achieved a good facsimile of his inelegant, but serviceable handwriting.

Another assistant was Jere Herzenberg, who came to work for him at about the same time as Judith McNally. A musicologist working on a graduate degree, she told Mailer biographer Carl Rollyson, "he dictated just about everything into a tape recorder to get the accent and the rhythm down. I would go over the transcriptions of the tape checking for grammar and punctuation, and then he would edit the transcripts." He wanted everything to be scrupulously documented, and he also wanted to capture, as far as possible, the idiolects of his huge cast of characters. As Herzenberg put it, Mailer wanted the book to be "in the voice of the people of Utah."

Before he left for Maine he wrote again to Yanow about his progress. "The manuscript will probably go on to 1400 or 1500 pages," he said. Looking ahead to the publicity he would be doing for the book, he said, "God, will I get tired of the question, 'Why did you spend so much time and space on such a man?' " This prediction was accurate; it was often the first question he was asked. To Abbott, who was deluging him with descriptions of prison life, he revealed that he would run out of money by the end of September, but did not feel sorry for himself because it was a situation "entirely of my own making as I was warned often enough en route as I kept getting married and divorced." He said he needed a minimum of $250,000 a year to support his establishment. "I thought I'd be able to do the book on Gilmore in six months and gain a half year on myself." Now he predicted that it would take him until January 1979 to complete it.

Mailer took off three weeks in August and then returned to work. He wrote no letters and did little else except write the book. In Maine, he jogged three times a week, but back in Brooklyn he got little exercise—he sparred with Torres, his son Michael, and other friends once a week—and his weight blew up to two hundred. He had learned over the years that it was impossible to write and keep in shape at the same time. He summed up his situation in a letter to a writer friend, Mary Breasted:

> I work six or seven days a week don't go out, and curse my primal verbosity of mind. The worst of it is that all the people who like my other books will probably not like this one. It's not searching, but panoramic and descriptive, almost pedestrian. The materials are so godawful strong I didn't know any other way to do it. Just put it there and take people through the waxworks. It's incredible stuff, really.

He continued working through the fall, and on December 6 delivered a rough draft of 1,969 double-spaced pages, as he announced to Gilmore's cousin Brenda, whom he counted on to spread the word to her family.

NORRIS HAD GOTTEN pregnant with John Buffalo in the summer of 1977 when she and Mailer were living in Provincetown. Mailer, Norris, and the children drove to Hartford one night to see Beverly perform. Norris was getting along fairly well with her at the time, but after her pregnancy was revealed, things changed. Toward the end of the year, he called Beverly in Provincetown and asked her to come to Brooklyn for a talk. He had been putting off asking for a divorce, but with a second child to be born out of wedlock, and obvious pressure from Norris, he was ready. Norris states in her memoir that "Beverly totally flipped out" when she was told of the pregnancy. Mailer was leaning in the window of her car on the street outside 142 Columbia Heights when she floored the gas pedal. "He said he'd pulled his head out of the car just in time to keep from being decapitated." Beverly sued for divorce in Massachusetts in October 1978; as Norris wrote, "that started a legal battle that lasted for nearly three years."

Money was the chief contention at the trial. Both pointed to fights, lapses, indignities, and infidelities, but Beverly stated publicly that Mailer was a good father, and the boys moved back and forth between the parents, eventually dividing their time between the two when they were teenagers. Mailer had been giving her $400 a month and paying the mortgage and taxes on their Provincetown house, but Beverly planned to move to New York to renew her acting career and wanted more support. She argued that she had supported his career for six years, 1963 to 1969, during which time he had published eight major books (four of them dedicated to her), and won several major awards. Now it was her turn. She asked for $1,000 a week, child support, the house in Provincetown (valued at $135,000), and $10,000 a year for a New York apartment. "Listen," she told *People*, "he said he was broke when I met him, and it's the same story now. Norman is a corporation. He's screaming poverty, but he makes $347,000 a year." His response was that she was asking for $120,000 in annual pretax dollars, an impossible sum, as he currently owed a total of $400,000 to Scott Meredith, his mother, and the IRS, and was making regular payments to Adele, Jeanne Campbell, and Carol Stevens, whom he called "my fifth wife." When asked by Beverly's lawyer if he was feeling "a sense of obligation" toward Stevens, he said, "If feelings of loyalty and tenderness are obligation, then I felt an obligation," adding, "She is a fine, unselfish woman . . . an artist in her field," who "is not built for rough living." He was at a loss trying to explain how various advances had been spent, or what he had done with the money from the sale of his *Village Voice* stock. "His affairs are a holy mess," Mailer's lawyer, Monroe Inker, told the judge. Mailer added, "My talent is making money, not managing it."

The trial, a miserable affair, went on for months. Unpleasant details of the marriage were reported in the *Boston Herald* and other papers. Perhaps the only moment of humor came when Mailer told the *Herald* that his fourth wife was a talented actress. "In fact," he said, "after she testified in the divorce case I went up and spoke to her for the first time in a year. I said, 'I want to congratulate you on a fine performance. Of course, you could use somebody to write your dialogue.' " The divorce was granted on March 21, 1980, under existing Massachusetts law as a *decree nisi*, a provisional judgment. A six-month waiting period was required.

Judge Shirley R. Lewis granted Beverly a lump sum of $7,500 from the pending sale of a farm in Philips, Maine, that Mailer owned with Dick Goodwin, and awarded her $575 a week in alimony for seven years, plus $200 a week in child support. He was also required to pay their tuition at the private schools they were attending and for four years of college, and to keep up health care benefits for all three. Finally, he was required to pay the premium on a $50,000 life insurance policy on his life. But the waterfront house in Provincetown, which contained so many memories for the Mailers, was lost. Despite various attempts to save it, it was sold by the IRS for $65,000. After a long legal struggle, Beverly was evicted.

A month after Judge Lewis's decree, Beverly decided to contest the divorce. Her lawyer said she was unhappy with the settlement terms and wanted to relitigate the matter in a New York court. Judge Lewis rejected her appeal on September 25, and Inker told Mailer he was free to marry. His plan was to marry Carol, divorce her posthaste, and marry Norris. When Norris saw him leave on the evening of November 7 for the ceremony with Carol, she put on a "brave face," but knew "he was on his way to marry a woman he still had feeling for. (He would always have feeling for her. It was something I lived with, like arthritis)." He married Carol in the chambers of Judge Shirley Fingerhood, a friend of his sister's. As Norris noted, "They had written down their vows, which were on the order of, 'I want to honor the years we have spent together and the love that created this beautiful child, Maggie.' " She lay awake that night wondering if Carol would decide to remain married "and let me stew, as she had stewed for ten plus years while he was married to Beverly." Her fears were for naught; Carol signed the papers. The next day Mailer flew to Haiti for a weekend divorce. On the morning of his second marriage in four days, November 11, 1980, he was distraught when he awoke. He said, "All my life, all I have ever wanted was to be free and alone in Paris." Norris said to him:

> Look, sweetie. What would happen if you were free and alone in Paris? You'd be walking down one of the boulevards and you'd sit at a sidewalk café to have a cup of espresso. A pretty girl would walk by and you would give her one of your twenty-five cent smiles. She would smile back and stop to talk. You would invite her to sit and buy her a cup of coffee. You'd go to a museum, and then take her out to dinner. Soon she would be living with you, and then she would get pregnant, and you wouldn't be free and alone in Paris anymore, would you?

Mailer laughed, and as John Buffalo jumped into their bed, he said, "Okay. Let's go get married and legitimize this little bugger."

Calls were made to friends for the ceremony that afternoon. Pat Kennedy Lawford came with a case of champagne, and the maid of honor, Norris's friend, Jan Cushing Olympitis, brought a wedding cake. Mayor Ed Koch attended with his deputy Dan Wolf (Mailer's old friend), as did future mayor David Dinkins, who was the city clerk at the time and had signed their marriage license. Susan, Michael, and Maggie couldn't make it, but Matt and John Buffalo, Betsy, Danielle, and Kate were there, as was Stephen, the best man. Rabbi David Glazer performed the ceremony. A few others attended: Barbara and Al, Fan, Dotson Rader, José and Ramona Torres, Jean Stein, and the Goodwins (who drove down from Massachusetts) among them. Mailer's boxing friend, Jeffrey Michelson, said that Mailer said his vows "with great theatrical diction and when he gets to the part about 'fidelity,' he drops half an octave lower, drawls the word with precision and looks Norris in the eye with conviction bordering on a glare. Not a threatening glare, but a drop-dead serious, I-swear-to-God, strike-me-dead glare." Norris's parents couldn't attend but were very happy that their daughter was legally wed. "I was no longer the tootsie; I was the wife," she recalled.

Undeterred by the weddings, Beverly continued her appeals. Her lawyer, Gerald L. Nissenbaum, accused Mailer of committing bigamy. "And I call it trigamy," he said, "because he's gotten married twice since his divorce" from Beverly, which because of appeals was not final, he argued. Eventually, the case went to the Supreme Judicial Court of Massachusetts, which in September 1982 decided against the fourth Mrs. Mailer in a ruling that overturned previous rulings that had allowed many divorce cases to go on interminably. It ruled that once a probate judge grants a divorce, the party seeking the divorce cannot seek dismissal merely to seek a better settlement—"forum shopping"—in another venue. The decision, in effect, rewrote the state's divorce laws going back to 1933. *The New York Times*, in a brief editorial titled "Mailer's Ring Cycle," praised him for reminding the world of the merits of marriage at a time when the institution was in question. "Call the novelist a matrimoniac, or call him a mensch. We call Norman Mailer a still point in a turning world." Mailer's lawyer put his own seal on the situation: "Norman Mailer won't get married again. And you can quote me on that." He was correct: Norris and Norman lived together as man and wife for one day short of twenty-seven years.

WHILE THE DIVORCE case was dragging on, he was making final changes to *The Executioner's Song*. By the end of March the revisions were completed and the manuscript whittled down to 1,681 pages. As soon as it was in the hands of Ned Bradford at Little, Brown, Mailer composed a form letter to the hundreds of people to whom he owed letters. After the salutation—"Friends, Penpals, Champions, Calumniators, and Occasional Correspondents"—he went on to announce his divorce case and the submission of a manuscript "a little short of 400,000 words." He added that it was "as long as The Brothers Karamazov and one-quarter as good."

He told Mort Yanow that it had been enjoyable in the past "to explore the states of your own feeling," but all he had done recently was "a lot of slogging." The book's completion, made him feel like "a con who's counting the days since he stepped through the gate" to freedom. Louis and Moos got only a few words on the book—he told them "it reads as easily as greased peanuts. You can't stop." He also talked about John Buffalo, who had just turned one: "He's sturdy as hell," with "a glint of pure intelligence in his eye." Mailer was 55 when John was born, and had more opportunity and inclination to observe his qualities and quirks than any of his other children. John later called his father "my best friend." Mailer would never call John his favorite, but the bond with his youngest child was strong. Mailer had also grown close to John's half-brother Matthew, who had decided a few years later to change his last name to Mailer.

Mailer's favorite correspondent during this period was Jack Abbott; he made his most extensive epistolary comments on *Executioner's Song* in a long letter to the convict. He said he had considered incorporating some of Abbott's experience into Gilmore, but didn't because he wanted to exclude anything he was not certain Gilmore had felt or said. Also, he said, Gilmore did not share Abbott's Marxist-Leninist thinking. He was "a profoundly religious man with an unshakable conviction of karma" who was "softer" than Abbott, and gave "much more parley to what you would consider the enemy," that is, the prison administration. For many years, Mailer told Abbott, he had been a disciple of Jean Malaquais, but "turned away from his thought because I found it—and this word will infuriate you—unendurably arid." Entering into a genuine dialogue with Abbott, he said, would depend on openness to each other's arguments. But he sensed the same granitic intellection in Abbott that he saw in Malaquais, who had harangued him the previous evening. "He said the same thing he was saying to me for twenty years," he said. Finally, his old mentor began to irritate him and he said: "You are like a monkey who's lost his arms and lost his legs and clings to the top branch with his teeth. You're so afraid that if you fall into the pit below, you might have to accept one spooky or divine notion of existence." Malaquais' mind was fully formed and impermeable to new ideas, Mailer believed. They remained friends, but engaged in fewer deep discussions.

Abbott told Mailer that Israel was the puppet of the capitalist democracies. Mailer replied that he was "no automatic Zionist hardon," a partisan who had the same question for all propositions: "Is this good for Israel?" Abbott also kept reminding Mailer that he didn't understand what a long-term convict's experience was like, and Mailer came back strong.

> You the fuck don't know what it is to be a Jew. You don't know what it is to have six million of your people killed when there are only twelve million of them on earth. You don't know the profound and fundamental stunting of existence that got into the blood cells of every Jew after Hitler had done his work. It's easy for you, it's contemptuous, you say "There's Israel doing the lackey's work for the U.S. against the bold, brave Arab nations"—who, as you know full well, have the most hideous prisons in the history of civilized existence. Yet you have your kneejerk reflexes, and one of them is up the Arabs down the Israelis.

Mailer's stance on his Jewish identity throughout this remarkable letter is similar to Bellow's, who gave a talk in 1988 about his identity as a writer, a nonobservant Jew, and an American. Like Mailer, Bellow found it neither possible nor desirable to escape from "the Jewish past—not only its often heroic suffering but also the high significance of the meaning of Jewish history." Watching the 1945 newsreels of army bulldozers pushing piles of bodies into burial pits had given Bellow "a deeply troubling sense of disgrace or human demotion," his version of the "profound and fundamental stunting of existence" he felt when he and Adele had visited Buchenwald.

In later letters to Abbott, Mailer brought up the Jewish experience several times, and encouraged him to read Heinrich Graetz's *History of the Jews*, and the Talmud. Mailer owned the six volumes of the former and twenty-six volumes of the Soncino edition of the latter. He offered to send Abbott a single volume of the Talmud, saying it would take him two years to read it properly. Some years later, Abbott converted to Judaism.

A GOOD DEAL of Mailer's time during this period was spent in Boston going over the manuscript of *Executioner's Song* with Little, Brown's lawyer, John Taylor "Ike" Williams. Because of the large number of living people who speak or are spoken about in *Executioner's Song*, there were multiple legal issues to deal with: privacy, defamation of character, copyright, and the legality of the releases Schiller had obtained from scores of people in Utah. Williams had met Mailer once before in 1963 (at a rowdy New York party where Williams punched him in the nose—both were drunk), but he did not know Schiller. As Williams recalled:

> So, here is this heavy guy with all those cameras around his neck. This was at Haussermann, Davison & Shattuck, Little, Brown's law firm. We were in this conference room which we had to ourselves for weeks. My job was to legally vet the manuscript with Norman. This guy was always popping in and out and taking pictures, and I said, "Who the fuck is that?" Norman said, "That's Larry Schiller. There wouldn't be any book without him." He explained that Larry was the one who went out to Utah early on, got the rights from the Gilmore family tied up, and gathered up interviews. And Larry was the one who attended the execution. When Larry approached Norman, he already had this enormous body of material. He said to Norman, "I just don't know how to write the narrative on this spectacular material." I didn't really have an idea then about how important Larry was to the book. It was deserved, but at that point for Little, Brown this was Norman's book. Norman never said, "You'll have to ask Larry." Larry never sat with us. Norman had mastered the material and felt it was his book.

Ned Bradford died on May 12, 1979, and another Little, Brown editor, Roger Donald, began working with Mailer. Shortly before Bradford's death, Mailer and Schiller met with him to talk about the marketing of *Song*, which had been announced as a forthcoming nonfiction book. Schiller was worried that it would be reviewed in tandem with a forthcoming crime narrative about another real-life murderer, Charles Sobhraj, in Thomas Thompson's *Serpentine*. Tom Wolfe's book about the Mercury astronauts, *The Right Stuff*, was also to be published at the end of the year, and Wolfe, like Mailer, was writing it as a straight narrative, excluding himself. Schiller saw these developments as potentially "devastating." He told several people—not including Mailer—that if nothing changed, Mailer might be throwing away a Pulitzer. Schiller recalled the meeting: "I'm sitting with Norman and Ned Bradford at Little, Brown, and Norman says, 'Well, Ned, I'm not going to put this on the nonfiction list. It's going to go on the fiction list and I'm going to call it a true life novel.' And of course I immediately inside myself say, 'Thank God, because a novel is never reviewed in tandem with a nonfiction book.' " Asked if Bradford or anyone else at the firm objected, Schiller said, "No. Ned needed a little explanation by Norman; he didn't understand it for a few moments. Norman explained to him that there are areas in which he had extrapolated. Between A and C he'd written B. I personally believe he never would have won the Pulitzer if it was on the nonfiction list." Schiller may have been correct. To win in nonfiction, *Executioner's Song* would have to have beaten Douglas Hofstadter's *Gödel, Escher, Bach: An Eternal Golden Braid*, a classic study of cognitive science and creativity in three geniuses (which did win the Pulitzer). In fiction, the other two contenders were Philip Roth's *The Ghost Writer* and William Wharton's *Birdy*, important books, but less distinguished than *The Executioner's Song*, which is indisputably one of Mailer's finest works, perhaps his greatest.

Mailer describes *Song* in his afterword as "a factual account," one which is "as accurate as one can make it." Given the fact that the material from the transcripts, legal documents, media, and psychiatric reports was not altered in any significant way, and that no one came forward later to complain that words had been put in their mouth (as they had with Capote's *In Cold Blood*), the obvious question is how could he call the book a fiction, a "true life novel," as the dust jacket says. When asked this question by a *New York Times* reporter, Mailer admitted that his decision had caused some confusion, but defended it by noting that "nonfiction provides answers and novels illumine questions. I think my book does the latter." Readers a century from now, he continued, people who know nothing of Gilmore or Mailer, "would say,

'That's a good novel.' " He wanted the book "to read like a novel, feel like a novel, to smell like a novel."

> If you feel like you're in the room with people, the events have taken place before you and you don't know what is going to happen next, and you want to know what happens next, then you're in the presence of a novel. I thought that this is what the true definition of whether something is fiction or non-fiction. I think that non-fiction bears the same relationship to life as vitamin pills bear to food. In non-fiction, there's a tendency to digest the material, absorb it, and return it to you as vitamin pills. The essence is gotten out of the various experiences, compressed and delivered to the reader. The reader can then digest the non-fiction and convert it back to fiction, convert it back to reality.

Mailer wanted it both ways: accrue every benefit of factuality and historicity—"this really happened"—while adding fictional immediacy and interiority. No one made too much of a fuss about his generic claim, and Mailer was fairly successful in distinguishing his "true life novel" from *In Cold Blood*, Capote's "nonfiction novel."

Schiller remembered Mailer and Capote meeting several months before *Executioner's Song* was published. He and Mailer walked into the bar at the Hotel Bel-Air in Los Angeles. "Sitting there all alone at the bar is Truman Capote. Norman doesn't even notice him, but I do. And being my normal bold self I say, 'Mr. Capote, I'm a friend of Mr. Mailer's. Would you like to join us for a drink?' And he gets this twinkle in his eye and a little smile and says, 'Of course.' "

> He sits down next to Norman, and says—I'm paraphrasing all this—"Norman, about this book you've written, it's awfully long isn't it? I hear it's very, very good. But awfully long, isn't it? It'd be nice if every once in a while you could condense something a little." Norman says something like, "I don't think you've ever understood anything I've written." And Capote says, "How could I understand it? I get lost because it's so long." At which point there was a bit of pleasant conversation, and then Truman said, "I've got to go. It's so delightful to see you, Norman." I forget exactly how he said it, but definitely that word—delightful.

In a 1983 interview with Lawrence Grobel, Capote recalled that in the introduction to his 1980 collection, *Music for Chameleons*, he had pointed out that Mailer had won several prizes and earned a great deal from his nonfiction books, "although he has always been careful never to describe them as 'nonfiction novels.' No matter; he is a good writer and a fine fellow and I'm grateful to have been of some small service to him." During a subsequent television interview with Grobel, Mailer said he didn't mention his debt to *In Cold Blood* because it "was so famous that you didn't have to give credit to it." Capote saw this program and was angry. He said he had "no respect" for Mailer's book because "he didn't live through it day by day," as Capote had with his murderers, Perry Smith and Dick Hickock. "He didn't know Utah, he didn't know Gary Gilmore, he never even *met* Gary Gilmore," he said. Mailer's book "just really *annoyed* me." As for him calling Mailer a copycat, "Well, Norman *has* been copying me for years."

Mailer had another reason to be upset. Capote had warned Norris that it would be a mistake for her to marry Mailer. "That was the measure of his vanity," Mailer told George Plimpton. "I wasn't even furious. I was amused. I thought, 'My God! He sure doesn't understand Norris!' It reminded me of that joke: What's the epitome of vanity? Answer: It's a guy floating downstream on his back with a hard-on. He approaches a drawbridge and yells that it's got to be raised." In September 1984, two weeks after Capote died, Mailer was asked again about their tiff about acknowledging influence. He said, "I think he was terribly hurt that I didn't have some sort of dedication page in *The Executioner's Song*, which went on the order of 'If not for *In Cold Blood* . . . ' " Mailer went on: "But this is all nonsense, I mean, we can't stand around giving credit to each other all the time." Perhaps. Yet it would have been gracious for Mailer to have included a nod to Capote in his afterword to *Executioner's Song*, as he had for Abbott.

Both writers acknowledged Lillian Ross's nonfiction narrative *Picture: A Story About Hollywood*, an account of the making of *The Red Badge of Courage*. Her 1952 book is fictive, if not fiction, and uses several novelistic techniques. This debt aside, the books of Mailer and Capote are different in several ways. First, Capote's murderers were not seasoned convicts who had served long terms like Gilmore. Second, they were inarticulate by comparison. Capote tried to make Perry Smith into a litterateur, but his essential banality is apparent. Mailer said many times that the best writing in *Executioner's Song* was not his, but is found in Gilmore's letters to Nicole. He wrote her ten or twenty pages a day for months, about 1,500 pages all told. Mailer includes all or part of fifty-eight of them, including this one:

> Nothing in my experience, prepared me for the kind of honest open love you gave me. I'm so used to bullshit and hostility, deceit and pettiness, evil and hatred. Those things are my natural habitat. They have shaped me. I look at the world through eyes that suspect, doubt, fear, hate, cheat, mock, are selfish and vain. All things unacceptable, I see them as natural and have even come to accept them as such. I look around the ugly vile cell and know that I truly belong in a place this dank and dirty, for where else should I be? There's water all over the floor from the fucking toilet that don't flush right. The shower is filthy and the thin mattress they gave me is almost black, it's so old. I have no pillow. There are dead cockroaches in the corners. At nite there are mosquitos and the lite is very dim. I'm alone here with my thoughts and I can feel the oldness. Remember I told you about The Oldness? and you told me how ugly it was—the oldness, the oldness. I can hear the tumbrel wheels creek. So fucking ugly and coming so close to me. When I was a child . . . I had a nightmare about being beheaded. But it was more than just a dream. More like a memory. It brought me right out of my bed. And it was sort of a turning point in my life. . . . Recently it has begun to make a little sense. I owe a debt, from a long time ago.

Mailer parcels out the love letters carefully over eight hundred pages, from Gilmore's arrest to the day before his death. Their star-crossed love-and-death affair—few commentators fail to note the similarities to the tragedy of Romeo and Juliet—is one of the story's two keels; the other is the fierce legal struggle that dominates the second half of the book, one side trying to halt the execution, the other trying to hasten it.

"Real life," Ivy Compton-Burnett once observed, "seems to have no plots." But as Mailer stated several times, nonfiction was much easier for him to write than fiction because journalists and historians do have some sort of a record and usually know beforehand their characters, settings, and themes; they have documents, witnesses, artifacts. Sometimes there is too little information; occasionally, there is too much. In the case of the Gilmore saga, Mailer was initially bewildered by "trying to put people and events together. I really had to work it out. Try encountering a hundred names at once. It's like looking at the laid-out pieces of a clock." Even after mastering the huge cast, Mailer faced another problem. On one of their plane rides, he said to Schiller, "I have a problem with the book." After their suicide attempt, Gilmore goes back to prison and Nicole is sent to a mental institution. "Who's the character that ties these two people together?" Mailer asked. Schiller had two suggestions. The first was Tamera Smith, the *Deseret News* reporter who befriended Nicole and obtained copies of Gilmore's letters to her. But she had no personal contact with Gilmore. The second was Earl Dorius, the chief assistant to the attorney general of Utah. Mailer went to lunch with Dorius, who was then dealing with the legal situations of both Gilmore and Nicole, and then called Schiller up: "Oh, wonderful, nice guy, but he doesn't work. You don't know anything about writing books." A short while later, showing that he did know a thing or two, Schiller pointed out to Mailer that the only other person significantly involved with both Gilmore and Nicole after the suicide attempt was none other than Larry Schiller.

Mailer could have cut out most of the legal and media exertions detailed in Part Two, "Eastern Voices." The first five hundred pages of the book cover the period from Gilmore's release to the day that he insists that his sentence be carried out, November 1, 1976. "By that time," we are told, "Gary Gilmore was a household name to half of America." Even allowing extra space for the execution and autopsy, Mailer could have covered the final ten weeks of his life in two hundred pages, bringing in the book at a hefty but manageable seven hundred pages. But after his conversation with Schiller, he realized that Gilmore's story could not be dissevered from the stories of those who helped assemble it—Schiller and his team. Schiller "might be the only one with a realistic notion of what could happen when you died in public," as Schiller's associate Barry Farrell observed.

"Eastern Voices" moves deftly among the huge cast: from Gilmore to those who seek to aid or impede his effort to die, to Nicole, friends and families, prisoners, and to various members of the media—Farrell, Tamera Smith, and national figures like Jimmy Breslin, Bill Moyers, David Susskind, and, at the end, Geraldo Rivera and Rupert Murdoch. At the center is Schiller, frantically seeking to record everything. Schiller "had to obtain this story," Mailer wrote. "That was fundamental. He wanted this story from his spinal cord out." He was Gilmore's chief interviewer (they met five times in person), as well as his advisor, paymaster, salesman, media spokesman, witness to his execution, literary executor and distributor of his ashes. Over three hundred people have speaking parts in *The Executioner's Song*, and Schiller had dealings with 99 percent of them.

Mailer's abilities were put to the test by "Eastern Voices," not only by the increased size of his cast (169 new characters are mentioned by name) but by the nature of their relations—supportive, manipulative, parasitical, obliquely and directly opposed—with each other and with Gilmore, Nicole, and Schiller. In "Eastern Voices" Mailer not only carries the story to its grim conclusion, he also doubles back, recounting Schiller's efforts to collect the information. Approximately 125 of the final five hundred pages of the book consist of documentary material. Mailer wisely chose to include this material, without which Gilmore's legal battles and love affair would be opaque.

But his decision to extend the ambit of his narrative and present a full portrait of Schiller was dictated not only by Schiller's centrality, but also by Mailer's desire to give the reader something that Capote purposely omits: the story of the story. The interviews with George Plimpton and others that Capote gave on both his personal involvement with the killers and his methods of research and reconstruction are at least half again as interesting as *In Cold Blood* itself and would have been a welcome addition to the book. He cannot be criticized for leaving out what the nineteenth century called "the love interest"—unlike Mailer, he had none—but any careful comparison of his book and Mailer's should fault the lack of reference to Capote's emotional and extended involvement with Hickock and, especially, Smith. Mailer recognized that half of his story was the sharp-elbowed maneuvers of the media to gain access to Gilmore and his legal struggle—which he won by losing his life—and that this vicious, tawdry, but equally fascinating part of the story could best be seen from the centrifugal vantage point occupied by ringmaster Schiller. As Gilmore's chief observer, he provided Mailer not only with his observations of Gilmore, but with a privileged view of himself observing Gilmore. "Do you *really* want to have this story in the book?" Mailer asked Schiller, who replied, "Do what you want." As he states in his afterword, "Schiller stood for his portrait, and drew maps to his faults," exposing not only "the stuff of his visions but the logic of his base schemes."

Schiller realized, he said later, that by giving enough unedited material to Mailer, "I will never fucking have to worry about somebody saying that I hired Norman Mailer to write this book and he whitewashed Larry Schiller and cleaned up all the things that he was being criticized for doing to get this story." Mailer interviewed Schiller a number of times. "I held back very, very little," Schiller said. "I knew I'd be helping the project." Schiller's self-scrutiny is roughly equivalent to Mailer's sometimes comic, sometimes somber, generally unsparing self-portrait in *The Armies of the Night*. Schiller was critical to the success of the book in more ways than one and became Mailer's most important collaborator until Mailer's death. Real life does have plots, if you have the wit to see them.

The Executioner's Song was published on October 15, and Mailer embarked on a publicity tour, traveling to Boston, Washington, D.C., Chicago, Ann Arbor, Salt Lake City, Los Angeles, not to mention several appearances in New York. He appeared on William Buckley's *Firing Line*, and did a two-part interview with Dick Cavett on PBS. *Executioner's Song* appeared in England on November 5, and Mailer flew over for three days of meetings with reporters, who seemed as interested in his divorce case as the book. He told one British reporter that he felt it was a mistake to have called his book a "true life novel," and should have called it a "true crime novel." In later years, Mailer said more than once that he wished he had eschewed a subtitle altogether.

James Atlas's long profile of Mailer was the cover story in *The New York Times Magazine* a few weeks before *Executioner's Song* was published. It was the longest biographical piece on him since Brock Brower's 1965 profile in *Life*. The cover photo of Mailer in an open-necked blue work shirt was a good one. He had lost weight after finishing the book and looked trim. The camera angle was kind to his big ears. Mailer had to like this photograph, as well as the others accompanying the profile, one of which showed him standing with Norris, looking beautiful, and John Buffalo on the rocky, low-tide shore below the Thomas house in Maine. But he hated the profile, calling it, with some justice, "a defile." Atlas is vinegary throughout. He sets the tone with his opening description of what he felt was Mailer's boring reading at Harvard in the spring of 1979—there is no mention of any successful readings or talks at his alma mater or elsewhere—and continues with a catalogue of gaffes and blunders. Less attention is given to his achievements. Atlas gives a fairly brief description of *Executioner's Song*—presumably the profile's raison d'être—and makes only a few evaluative comments. He grants that Mailer "made eloquent the sprawling cast of inarticulate characters" in the story, but says it is flawed by "his addiction to the grandiose." He dislikes the "Homeric" description of Larry Schiller, and says the book is "far too long." Atlas returns relentlessly to the question—a fair one—of whether Mailer will make good on his early promise to write the great American novel. He is not hopeful and cites the "shrinkage of his literary reputation" and how he "cultivates a prurient reputation." Like Jean-Jacques Rousseau, he says, Mailer is "garrulous, vain, paranoid, vengeful, incessantly self-reflective." Two weeks after the profile appeared, Mailer responded to a reporter at *New York* magazine.

Atlas, he said, "merely pretended great friendship and sympathy during months of interviewing," and then went on to write a "mean-spirited" piece. He was upset with Atlas's suggestion that the only reason he had classified *Executioner's Song* as a novel was "to compensate for his failure to produce the definitive work of fiction he used to boast of so tirelessly." But what angered him most was the quote he included from William Styron, who said Mailer had become "a figure of pathos." Atlas passed over their long-running feud, and Mailer cried foul. Many years later, when a friend showed him a copy of the profile, Mailer said that he believed that Atlas (whom Mailer now liked) might have been given editorial direction to rough him up. Norris was still angry about Atlas saying that Mailer bored the Harvard audience. She was there, she said, and it was "not true." She recalled how she got back at him. At a party at the home of Jean Stein, not long after the profile appeared, Stein brought Atlas over to meet Norris, who was several inches taller than him. She looked right over his head and said, "Oh yes, where is he?"

MAILER OWED A book to the British publisher of *Marilyn*, Hodder and Stoughton, and within a week of turning in the final draft of *Executioner's Song*, he began work on *Of Women and Their Elegance*, which he later described as a "fantasy autobiography" of Marilyn Monroe. Having been preoccupied with matters of veracity and documentation for over two years, Mailer was ready to give his imagination a workout, and the short novel invents several improbable episodes—some quite salacious—in Monroe's life during the period she was married to Arthur Miller. He would later transform the novel into a play, *Strawhead*, which was performed at Actors Studio. The book grew out of Mailer's interaction with Milton Greene, who had taken photographs of Marilyn Monroe, as well as many other celebrities such as Gene Kelly, Marlene Dietrich, and Jimmy Durante. Mailer agreed to write a text on the photos but he didn't want to interview models. "I wanted to write about Marilyn," he said. The novella received few reviews, the majority negative, and was overshadowed by *The Executioner's Song*, which was a paperback bestseller through the end of 1980.

When he was finished with the fifty-thousand-word Monroe book, he went off to Maine with Norris and the children. The summer of 1979 was their last at the Thomas house. While there he wrote to Susan and said he had "a nice feeling" being with all the kids, especially now that he was done writing. He had written so much, he said, that "I don't even squeeze words out of my dick no more, they come out through my elbows, and I'm probably capable of writing with my nose." He had to take some time off, he said, or "I was going to go squeak." Susan was about to marry Marco Colodro, a Chilean economist, and he offered to have a party for her at the Brooklyn apartment. He relaxed, did a series of interviews with James Atlas for a *New York Times* profile, and caught up with his correspondence.

Abbott wrote to Mailer for help; he wanted to be paroled. Mailer asked Abbott what he should say, noting that the authorities would be unlikely to believe anything he might say about "your good character, sterling deportment" since it was obvious that they had never met. "I could, however, write glowingly about your literary possibilities. I did as much for [Eldridge] Cleaver years ago and it was one of the factors contributing to his release." Abbott was still nearly two years from his release, and Mailer kept up a stream of encouraging letters.

With *Executioner's Song* on its way to the printer, he felt relaxed enough to compose a faux obituary, which he published in *Boston* magazine. "Novelist Shelved" is a comic offshoot of the divorce follies in which he was engaged. "Norman Mailer passed away yesterday," it begins, "after celebrating his fifteenth divorce and sixteenth wedding. 'I just don't feel the old vim,' complained the writer recently." The piece contained a number of brief tributes from notables: Capote ("He was always so butch"); Vidal ("He had the taste of a Snopes"); Gloria Steinem ("A pity. He was getting ready to see the light"); and Warhol ("I always thought Norman kept such a low profile"). President Jimmy Carter lauded him for advancing "American book-writing and reading," and regretted that he and his wife "never did get to invite Norman Miller [*sic*] to the White House." Family members were not quoted, but it was reported that around the deathbed were "eleven of his fifteen ex-wives, twenty-two of his twenty-four children, and five of his seven grandchildren, of whom four are older than six of their uncles and aunts." The piece became a family favorite, and John Buffalo read it at the Carnegie Hall memorial for his father twenty-nine years later.

IN AN INTERVIEW with John Aldridge about *Executioner's Song*, Mailer said that for years he had been interpreting the American scene, and felt that he had "used up my audience." Now, he said, "I want another audience. I want those people who think I'm difficult to read." So in the period between turning in the manuscript and publication day, he began to cast about for representatives of this new readership. Martha Thomases, who had helped type *Executioner's Song*, introduced him to twenty-three-year-old Legs McNeil, one of the founders of *Punk* magazine, and perhaps the first to use the word "punk" to describe the mid-1970s hard-edged rock 'n' roll. *Punk* also took swipes at the establishment, left and right. After Gilmore's death, his final words, "Let's do it," appeared on punk musicians' T-shirts. McNeil was associated with the major early punk group the Ramones, and was the manager of another, Shrapnel. He admired Mailer's writing and considered himself to be "representative of the new audience Norman hoped to reach."

According to McNeil, his outspoken manner had been compared to Mailer's in a *Village Voice* story, and people were watching when they met in Martha Thomases's kitchen. "I'm sure you've never read anything I've written, and I've never read anything you've written, so, just to set the record straight, we're even." Mailer laughed at this bluster. McNeil invited him to come to CBGB, a music club in the Village where Shrapnel was doing a benefit to buy bulletproof vests for the police. He was surprised when Mailer showed up a few nights later with "a scorching redhead," Norris. It was smoky and loud, but Mailer seemed to enjoy the scene, and later he and Norris went to a party with McNeil at Joey Ramone's loft. Thomases recalled Mailer saying that the musicians reminded him of young boxers. Mailer took McNeil aside for a talk, and told him that "he was the Godfather and I had to listen to him because I was just like him." Two days later McNeil came to Brooklyn to interview Mailer.

When he showed up, Mailer challenged him to walk across the narrow catwalks twenty feet above the apartment floor. McNeil, who had a hangover, declined, saying, "I haven't got anything to prove." After a quick tour, they sat down for the interview, which was published in the marijuana magazine *High Times*. Mailer touched on many topics in the interview, including Hemingway and the Women's Liberation Movement, at the time staples in all of his interviews, but made scant comment on drugs for an interview in a magazine devoted to the topic. He did say that he liked punk music more than he thought he would. Perhaps the most interesting comment is when McNeil asks him about cancer, which Mailer calls "schizophrenia of the cells." He explains that when people are in a crux—he uses the example of being in a bad place while rock climbing—"I think we get driven very near this insanity of the mind or the flesh." He repeated what he had said many times before: some people under great stress "opt for letting the mind go, other people opt for letting the body go." He would present such a situation a few years later in *Tough Guys Don't Dance*.

Shrapnel was invited to play at the engagement party for Susan and Marco Colodro at the Mailer apartment. She remembers a huge crowd, including Woody Allen and Kurt Vonnegut. The band set up in the loft above and played while the guests danced to tunes such as "I Lost My Baby at the Siegfried Line." "Damn good song," Vonnegut said to the guitarist, "lots of feeling." Mailer got into a head-butting contest with Glen Buxton, another rocker, and later got into a wrestling match with McNeil. As the band was leaving, Mailer pressed bottles of Scotch on them. One of them said, "Norman, we don't know how to drink Scotch yet." Mailer replied, "Well, you'll learn, you'll learn." Shrapnel played at the house a few more times, but Mailer soon drained what meanings he could from punk rock. McNeil would become a family friend, but there would be fewer such hijinks as the decade went forward.

THE EXECUTIONER'S SONG was reviewed as widely and as warmly as *The Naked and the Dead* and *The Armies of the Night.* With the exception of negative reviews by Diane Johnson in the *NYRB* and Germaine Greer in *The Hollywood Reporter*, all the major reviews were enthusiastic. The book reached number three on the *New York Times* bestseller list and spent longer—twenty-five weeks—on it than any of his other books, excepting *Naked and the Dead.* Mailer maintained the approval of his old admirers and gained the attention of a new audience. He was awarded his second Pulitzer for *Executioner's Song* (which gave him "an emotional boost," Norris recalled), and was a finalist for both the American Book Award and the National Book Critics Circle Award. It has never gone out of print and is probably the Mailer book most often taught in college classes—English, journalism, American studies, and criminology.

There was disagreement over the relative merits of the book's halves. Partly because of Schiller's recording of the final moments of criminals and celebrities, partly because of the media's disinclination to read about its own avidity for the sensational, and partly because of the force of "Western Voices," "Eastern Voices" was generally less admired. As a character, Schiller failed to impress everyone. One reviewer said, "When Mailer has Schiller thinking of Gilmore's letters to Nicole, 'must be tons of meat and potatoes in those envelopes,' we know Mailer isn't writing about Francis of Assisi." But another reviewer, John Cheever, notes that Schiller "is offered a large sum of money for an exclusive account of the execution [$125,000 from one of Rupert Murdoch's editors, who called him repeatedly], but he refuses money for the first time in his career and contributes a sense of decency and fitness to the narrative that is shared by the other principals." Christopher Lehmann-Haupt found the book's finest achievement to be "a stunningly candid report on the complex, ambiguous and often-disturbing relationship that increasingly exists among the news, the newsmakers, and the reporters."

Joan Didion's review, in *The New York Times Book Review* stands with Kazin's on *Armies* as one of the finest and most influential appreciations of Mailer's work. She points out that the dominant speakers in "Western Voices" are those of women, and that "Eastern Voices" is largely comprised of stories by men: "Men tend to shoot, get shot, push off, move on. Women pass down stories." She quotes what Bessie Gilmore says after she learns that Gary is under arrest for murder: "I am the granddaughter and great-granddaughter of pioneers on both sides. If they could live through it, I can live through it." Didion calls this "the exact litany which expresses faith in God west of the 100th meridian." Her key perception, however, is that the first half of the book, because its strongest speakers are women, is "a fatalistic drift, a tension, an overwhelming and passive rush toward the inevitable events that will end in Gary Gilmore's death." These western women do not generally "believe that events can be influenced. A kind of desolate wind seems to blow through the lives of these women." Conversely, the men of "Eastern Voices," the lawyers and reporters and prison administrators, "move in the larger world and believe that they can influence events." The contrast, she says, gives the book its immutable form, a symphony in two movements. She concludes her review: "This is an absolutely astonishing book."

Discussing Didion's characterizations of the two parts of the book, Mailer said, "Yes, she's absolutely right." But he didn't see it at the time. When he was writing "Western Voices" he was thinking of cowboy movies, and for "Eastern Voices" he had a vision of media hordes coming from New York. "I saw the first half of the book as masculine and the second half as feminine." After reading her review, however, he realized the opposite was also correct—"women playing a masculine role in the first half of the book and men playing a feminine role in the second half." It was not done intentionally, he said. "If it emerges out of something you haven't thought about, out of the unconscious preoccupations of your mind, where you sort of half-see what you're doing and someone else sees the other half, that's always the ideal." Years later, he offered another metaphor for what he often referred to as the navigator, which reinforces his comments on the composition of *Executioner's Song*: "What I found as a writer is that signals from the unconscious are faint. It's as if you are on an outpost in the North Pole and your radio is weak and you can barely hear what people are saying."

TWO WEEKS AFTER *Executioner's Song* was published, Mailer flew to Illinois to give Jack Abbott a copy. He traveled via Chicago, and stayed at the Drake Hotel on Lake Michigan. When he checked in, the front desk receptionist, an attractive middle-aged woman named Eileen Fredrickson, recognized him. She asked if he would sign her copy of *Naked and* *the Dead*, and he agreed to do so the next day when she brought it to work. The next morning, she told him that she had forgotten the book. He asked where she lived and said he'd be happy to take a cab there to sign it when she was off work. They set a time, and Eileen, who was excited, called her sister to tell her. "Be careful, he stabbed his wife," she was told, but Eileen said she wasn't worried. Mailer came and stayed the night. In the morning, she recalled, "I took him back to the Drake about seven-thirty in the morning in my car. I said to him, 'Norman, just consider it a one-night stand.' The next day he called me and said, 'If I came over again it wouldn't be a one-night stand, would it?' And I said, 'No.' " The relationship they started would continue until the year he died. He called her often, sent her autographed copies of his books, and got together with her when he was in Chicago.

J. Michael Lennon, a young professor at the University of Illinois–Springfield, had been working with Mailer to put together his latest essays and interviews for what would become *Pieces and Pontifications*, and when Mailer told him that he was coming to see Abbott, he offered to pick him up at the airport. His brother, Peter, who was familiar with southern Illinois, came along, and on November 3, 1979, they drove Mailer to the prison. Peter recalled the visit.

> Over breakfast, he talked at some length about *Apocalypse Now* and how Brando personified evil in it. He said the atmosphere and combat scenes in it were the best he'd ever seen. He said he was keeping an epistolary promise by visiting Abbott. He seemed eager—not nervous, but curious about the visit. It was a half hour drive through a dense, leafless forest to the isolated maximum security Marion Federal Penitentiary. After Norman announced our arrival (by speaking into a mechanical device a few hundred yards from the walls, at which point you are surveyed from the guard towers), we parked and walked to the main entrance. Norman remarked that everything, the sky, landscape, razor wire and walls were grey and, in fact, colorless. No one liked it. Michael and I were confined to the outer hallway alongside a guard station. Norman had one hour and it was just noon. At precisely one he was back out—book in hand.

Over drinks later, Mailer said that he liked Abbott and felt that in a few years, he might get out. Abbott deserved a chance, he said.

Upon his return, Mailer wrote a long letter to Abbott telling him that Cy Rembar had agreed to be his literary lawyer, and would not charge him anything "until you make some real money." He said that he would find a way to get Abbott a copy of the book (advance permission was required), adding that he wished the situation had occurred when he was still writing *Executioner's Song*. "It would have given me more understanding of Gilmore's vast rage at the regulations," he wrote. "Somehow I think that the human soul is built to encounter major injustice with more equanimity than the penny varieties." The meeting in Marion was "terrific," he continued, "and if you like me, that's great, 'cause I dug you." The rest of the letter is devoted to a discussion of Abbott's writing. He said it was natural for him to write about "the journey of your soul."

> It is the kind of writing which is very hard to read over long stretches when written by anyone smaller in stature than Nietzsche or Kierkegaard. And while I'd never say you cannot end up ultimately as good as them the odds are obviously not in your favor. Guys like that come along once or twice a century. In any event, I have no hesitation in suggesting, nay, recommending the following because even if it never takes hold and you don't do much with it, I think it will enrich your writing in general. And that is, I would attempt if I were you to try other forms of writing as exercises, literary exercises, and build up your skills—that is probably anathema to you—in a way parallel to the way some work out to build up their bodies.

Mailer said he suspected that Abbott would have a flair for drama. In 1987, Abbott proved him to be correct about his dramatic abilities. He wrote and published a play, *The Death of Tragedy*, which seeks to exonerate him for the crime that returned him to prison three months after he was paroled.

Abbott finally got a copy of *Executioner's Song*, and at the end of November sent Mailer a fifty-six-page letter of commentary. Mailer wrote back to say that while he did not agree with everything, he found it to be "fascinating," especially the parallels Abbott made between *Song* and Stendhal's *The Red and the Black*. He was at some pains to defend why he had not taken a position on various matters in the book. "It's the first book I've written," he wrote, "without a clear sense of what I thought and what I wanted to teach others." Abbott felt that Brenda had betrayed her cousin Gary by setting up his arrest. Mailer responded by noting that while Brenda loved Gilmore, he had killed two innocent people in two days.

> She is thinking of the neighbors as well as her family. Gary could shoot the cop, Toby, her neighbor. Hurrah, say you. Horrors, says Brenda. It isn't necessarily all cowardice on her part although you will think so, and Gary as well. But she lives on the surface of society where you breathe the advantageous air. In that place, the loyalties are on the surface, to one's neighbors, to society, to the team. Horseshit, you say. And, horseshit, say I, but faintly. Because I don't know for sure anymore.

Mailer would soon find himself in a bind similar to Brenda's, torn between supporting a friend and condemning him for a senseless crime.

With *Executioner's Song* selling briskly, Scott Meredith had been able to renegotiate the contract with Little, Brown. He would now "receive $30,000 a month" against the royalties for the projected three-volume novel, and by the fall of that year he had been paid close to $1.5 million, which allowed him to pay off his loans to Meredith and his mother, and finally get even with his taxes. For the first time in a decade, he had enough money coming in to focus all of his energies on the novel. "I leave it for two years and come back," he told his biographer Hilary Mills, "and it says, 'Oh you look tired, you've been away, here let me wash your feet.' " But he saw that the patience of this good wife of a novel was not bottomless. "I think," he said, "I've finally got to finish the Egyptian novel." By the end of January, he had eight hundred pages of manuscript.

His focus was intense enough that he forgot to write a second letter for Abbott, supplying some details left out of an earlier one, to the Utah Board of Pardons. He apologized in an April 11 letter, and told Abbott not to read any "psychological substrata into all this." During a two-month burst of writing, he had failed to write a number of important letters. "I'm just not mentally coordinated enough to put a really big show on the road," he said. He had delegated to Judith McNally the task of assembling Abbott's letters into a piece that might be sold to a magazine, buttressing Mailer's testimonial to the board about Abbott's literary skills. Mailer had told Robert Silvers, coeditor of *The New York Review of Books*, about Abbott, and on June 26 the letters were published there. In his introduction, Mailer explained how he had become friendly with Abbott, recounted his decades in federal prisons, which he said had been Abbott's "secondary school, his university, his family, his culture."

HE RETURNED TO Provincetown in July of 1980, his first summer visit there in three years. In August the family traveled to Maine, renting for the first time a sprawling old farmhouse on the water that belonged to the Putnam family, descendants of Rufus Griswold, the scurrilous nineteenth-century editor and anthologist who created the false legend of Edgar Allan Poe as a dipsomaniac and drug addict. Even with a household full of guests, Mailer worked a few days a week on *Ancient Evenings*. He sometimes tricked new visitors into jumping off the dock into the bone-chilling water. "Come on in; it's perfect," he yelled to them. Mailer loved the water and tried to swim daily in the summer.

In the fall, back in Brooklyn, he wrote to Larry L. King about their abstemious situation—both he and King had quit drinking.

> By temperament, I'm a manic-depressive, which means I enjoy the depressions if they're deep, rich, mahogany, and melancholy, almost as much as the highs. My idea how to live is to feel in one hour that one is the best damned zapped fucker in the U.S. and then spend the next day mourning the tragic depths of one's profound incompetence. I've always looked upon that as living. Now here I am, trimmed-down Norm, down to 170 from 200, able to jog two miles a day at a peppy clip, brisk and birdlike in my manner to all and sundry who greet me, slightly reminiscent of a Democratic-party equivalent to George [H. W.] Bush, you know, peppy.

His moods did not alternate much, he said.

> I keep telling myself it's the dues I must pay, that maybe a year must go by, or two years, before the epiphanies ring in my ears once more. I don't know, Larry. You've had it a lot tougher than me, because

> you're a born hell-to-leather drinker, and I was just a nice Jewboy from Brooklyn who acquired the habit, but I console myself ultimately with the thought that it's curious and interesting to be without booze this long. I find my relations to everyone are as altered as they were during the period when I ran for mayor and found myself shaking hands with individuals whose eyes I would not normally have deigned to spit into. I'm sort of tolerant and bland and can't stand myself these days, but on the other hand, I boxed three three-minute rounds a couple of Saturdays ago.

One of the reasons Mailer stopped drinking for eighteen months was to channel all his energy into *Ancient Evenings*, which could no longer be shunted to a siding while he took on journalism assignments. He now had the time, strength, cash, and patience to complete it. Based on numerous comments he had made in interviews, the literary world half believed he would actually deliver it in the near future. A few hangovers a month would impede the steady progress he was making, not to mention the loss of brain cells. He said more than once that a night of heavy drinking cost him a lot more than boxing three rounds. Sparring once a week during the years 1978 to 1982 was one of Mailer's distinct pleasures, and a welcome break from writing all day in a tiny room.

"By the time I was born," John Buffalo wrote, "boxing had become the family sport. My father and his friends, my brothers and their friends, and my cousin and his friends went to the Gramercy Gym every Saturday morning." Michael and Stephen had been boxing for years with their father, as had their cousin Peter Alson (Barbara's son), who was a decade older. From the age of three, John went along with them to the gym, where they were joined by a group of friends, including Jeffrey Michelson, editor of a porn magazine, *Puritan*, and Sal Cetrano, a poet and high school English teacher. José Torres, who had trained at Gramercy under Cus D'Amato, had a set of keys to the grimy third floor walk-up on East 14th Street. During the week professionals and Golden Glove contenders trained there, but on weekends it was locked. Torres let them in and often stayed to give free tutorials to "the raging Jews," as Mailer's amateurs called themselves. Among the group, John Buffalo wrote, there was an understanding: "They were not there to beat the piss out of each other, but to learn a little about themselves."

Torres was the boxing advisor on a movie titled *The Main Event*, starring Ryan O'Neal and Barbra Streisand, then being filmed in New York. O'Neal was an excellent boxer, a former Golden Gloves fighter, and Torres started bringing him to the gym on Saturdays. At first O'Neal boxed with Torres, but as time passed he began to spar serially with the Mailer crowd. Michael, who would box in Golden Gloves tournaments a couple of years later, was sixteen at the time, and much lighter than O'Neal, but got in the ring with him a number of times. "He was very good and technically proficient," Michael recalled, "although like a true Irish boxer, he enjoyed taking a punch. I used to hit him at will and marveled at how easy it was to connect on him, but he would punch back and it stung." His father also liked mixing it up with O'Neal; it was a chance "to get extended in the ring," Mailer wrote in a boxing memoir, because "Ryan could be as mean as cat piss." On one occasion, O'Neal broke Cetrano's jaw. On another Saturday, as Mailer described it, O'Neal threw "cruel left hooks to the stomach until the editor [Michelson] collapsed, still conscious, in the middle of the second round, wholly unable to go on." Mailer, who was next up against him, saw that O'Neal had turned "angelic," a bit ashamed of what he had unleashed on Michelson, "a sweet guy, extraordinarily optimistic about life." "Feeling like an avenger," Mailer hit O'Neal with several straight rights. In their first clinch, O'Neal said, "You punch harder than anyone here." Mailer replied, "Go fuck yourself." He and O'Neal continued to box, and Mailer relished their exchanges: "It was as close as it ever came for me to gain some knowledge of how a professional might feel in a real bout for money with a hard-hearted crowd out there and the spirit of electricity in the ring lights."

Boxing, Mailer said, is as close to chess as to football, all three requiring "discipline and intelligence and restraint." As does writing, which he often compared to boxing. In an interview shortly after Mailer's death, the British novelist Ian McEwan said of him: "Boxing and writing were wonderfully confused in his mind." But while Mailer compared the two, he knew how different they were. Take the matter of discipline. Writers and boxers who are professionals must be formidably disciplined to achieve their goals, but in one sense writing requires more discipline because, as Mailer pointed out, "boxing has objective correlatives." Invariably, one boxer dominates the other, he continued, but with writing, "you can't tell if it's good on a given day, and you almost don't want to know." Over long years, a writer may develop the instinct to see that something is quite well done, but the chance of delusion is considerable.

There is another large difference between the two pursuits, as Mailer had explained to Torres in the summer of 1973 when they traded writing and boxing lessons. Mailer, Torres recalled, said that writing was about truth but "boxing was the opposite. It's about cheating and deceiving and lying," and Mailer predicted that it would be hard for him to learn to write well after years in the ring "cheating with a jab." Writing is also a form of mendacity, it could be argued, but beneath these differences Mailer believed, was one "huge similarity," which is "this battle with yourself that goes on constantly, and this demand to get the maximum out of yourself." Both boxers and writers "have to call up something deep down in themselves in order to continue." An ambitious boxer wants his victory to be remembered for years, decades, while a writer who is serious seeks "to make a change in the history of one's time." In both boxers and writers, there is an inner struggle, an *intestinum bellum*, between courage and resignation. Great boxers and writers, Mailer said, "become aware that the main bout is with themselves."

Also, the bodily toll, he believed, was much the same for professionals in the two fields, as he said in an interview with his friend Barry Leeds. Writing a novel is hell, he said.

> It's an unnatural physical activity to sit at a desk and squeeze words out of yourself. It means that you secrete various kinds of fatigues and poisons through your system that you don't get rid of easily. As you get older, it's worse. . . . One of the things that characterizes almost every older fighter I've ever seen training for a fight is the depression that hangs over him and his camp because the only thing good that can come out of it is money. The rest is all a foregone conclusion. Even if he wins the fight—even if he wins it well—he's not going to get a new purchase on life out of the fight the way a young writer can by a decisive victory. And that's true of writing. Writers will often make grave decisions—am I going to write this book or not? And at a certain point you have to believe that the book can be enormously important or you won't suffer that kind of self-destruction.

Consequently, both writers and fighters are often hypochondriacs. "It goes with the territory," he said.

A headache was the usual result of a day at Gramercy for Mailer, but overall it was a welcome respite from the physical inactivity of writing. Psychologically, it brought his two selves, or at least his "two systems of anxiety," as he put it, into some kind of "quiet balance." A couple of years later, when his knees started to go, "I gave it up, I eased out of it," he said, "and have never felt as virtuous since." Michelson remembers getting into the ring with Mailer just before he hung up his gloves. "I don't remember who it was," he said, "but someone at the gym asked Norman on his fifty-ninth birthday just how good a boxer he considered himself to be, and Norman came back with: 'I'm better than any other 59-year-old novelist.' "

IMMEDIATELY AFTER THEIR marriage, the Mailers left for England. He had been offered a minor role in *Ragtime*, based on E. L. Doctorow's novel and directed by Milos Forman, with whom he had become friendly. Mailer played Stanford White, the flamboyant nineteenth-century architect who designed, among many other structures, Madison Square Garden. A socialite and womanizer, he had a serious affair with actress Evelyn Nesbit, perhaps the most famous beauty of her day, when she was sixteen and he was in his mid-forties. Nesbit's jealous husband, the railroad magnate Harry K. Thaw, shot and killed him in the roof garden of Madison Square Garden in 1906. Norris got a bit part in the film as White's date, sitting next to her husband when he is shot.

The John Lennon tragedy occurred shortly after Mailer finished his stint on the film, and, retrospectively, it changed the experience for him. "The killing of John Lennon," he said, altered everything: I no longer took my movie death seriously; I had the shock of a real death going through my system. Like fifty million other people I cared about Lennon; my own concerns were put into proportion." A few years earlier Lennon and Yoko Ono had responded to Mailer's request for financial help for a Canadian drug dealer, Robert Rowbotham, a friend of Richard Stratton's, who had received an unconscionably long sentence for selling marijuana. Mailer testified at his trial. Lennon and Ono had also attended Susan and Marco's engagement party in Brooklyn earlier in the year.

Forman had offered Mailer the role because he had the same kind of status in New York in 1980 that White had in 1900. "They both had an aura of accomplishment in art and social life," Forman said. "Besides, I thought it might help me get invited to his parties." Mailer said he took the role "to satisfy my curiosity." He wanted to compare the experience of making experimental films with being in a $20 million commercial film, this one produced for Paramount Pictures by Dino De Laurentiis. "I thought it must be wonderful being a screen actor. Much easier than staring at blank sheets of paper. I was wrong. It wasn't easy at all." But he did get to meet his boyhood idol Jimmy Cagney, who played the police commissioner in the film. He and Norris also had their honeymoon during their week in London. When Michelson asked her what sights she saw during her visit, she answered, "The ceiling of my hotel room."

The national moratorium on executions ended with Gilmore's death, which opened a national debate on the morality of capital punishment. It was not surprising, therefore, that Walter Anderson, the new editor of *Parade* magazine, the Sunday supplement with a readership of 40 million, would contact Mailer about writing a piece on the topic. Anderson, a thirty-four-year-old ex-Marine sergeant who had done a tour in Vietnam, was a bit apprehensive, however, because Mailer had once described involvement with the magazine as "stepping in shit." But Anderson was changing the gravitas of *Parade* by publishing writers such as Studs Terkel, David Halberstam, and John Cheever. Mailer had questions: "Norman wrote to me about the capital punishment essay," Anderson recalled, "and said, 'You may not be comfortable with what I produce.' " Anderson replied that whatever Mailer wrote would "set the benchmark on what people will argue against." Anderson, who became a close friend and reader of Mailer's manuscripts, said the piece was "brilliantly written."

"Until Dead: Thoughts on Capital Punishment," could have been the appendage Mailer once considered putting at the end of *The Executioner's Song*. It explores the pros and cons in detail, noting that Gilmore's insistence on being shot to death had underlined the issue "in royal purple ink." He first considers the deterrence claim and finds it to be specious. Most murders, he argues, are committed by psychopaths "in need of quick gratification. Patience is not part of their powers." Those who commit atrocities "are usually poor, raddled wretches so schizophrenic in their inmost wheels that psychiatry itself is disturbed by a look into their minds." Retribution from society is not something that necessarily occurs to them. Conversely, there are crimes that "make one sick with rage"—innocent children killed in acts of mayhem, old ladies raped and tortured. Such crimes call forth "the instinct to flush it out," find a scapegoat. "Living amid all the blank walls of technology, we require a death now and again, we need to stir that foul pot." Perhaps, he says, "we need the official bloodbath to restore ourselves to the idea that society is not only reasonable, but godlike," a point of view he immediately dubs as "cynical reasoning" and "vastly offensive." Yet, he concludes that the primitive instinct that supports capital punishment "may be one of our last defenses against the oncoming wave of the computer universe."

Anderson said that the magazine received thousands of letters on the essay. The response was so large, he believes, because Mailer's reason for supporting *some* executions "is neither vengeance nor justice. Capital punishment is a safety valve." Mailer's ambivalence on the matter, a manifestation of the clash between his left-radical and conservative selves, is instructive, and sharpens the debate. But soon Jack Abbott would commit a crime that would add another layer of complexity to the question.

HE MIGHT HAVE completed *Ancient Evenings* in the summer of 1981, but Abbott was paroled on June 5, 1981. Jack Henry Abbott had been born out of wedlock in January 1944 (the month Mailer received his induction notice) at Camp Skeel, an army base in Michigan, to Mattie Jung, a prostitute of Chinese descent from Salt Lake City, who later committed suicide. His father was Rufus Abbott, an Irish-American soldier from Texas, reputed to have been a "short-tempered alcoholic." Young Abbott grew up in foster homes and detention centers, and began a run of sentences as a teenager that kept him behind bars for all but nine months of his life until age thirty-seven. His crimes included passing bad checks, robbing a bank, and killing another inmate in a prison fight. Abbott was proud, violent, intransigent, and consequently spent a lot of time in solitary—fourteen years. An intelligent and voracious reader with an extensive vocabulary, he was unable to pronounce many words that he had never heard spoken. He called himself a "state-raised convict," and wrote that he had "high esteem" for violence. For the good convict, violence is a tool that "makes us *effective*, men whose judgment impinges on others, on the world: Dangerous killers who act alone and *without* emotion, who act with calculation and principles, to avenge themselves." But outside prison walls, he promised, it would be different. Thomas Harrison, the parole chairman, asked him: "What we're interested in is your potential for hurting somebody. You say there is no such potential, is that right?" Abbott replied "No, no. . . . There won't be nothing like that."

Abbott's anger was not unusual. He had been beaten, drugged, and humiliated any number of times. In the months before he was paroled, there was a prison strike at Marion, which began when an inmate threw a tray of food from his cell. Then, as alleged in a U.S. District Court suit filed by prisoners, Marion guards took prisoners one at a time, hands manacled, to a special room where they were beaten with three-foot wooden clubs. Abbott was the last one. After that, he told his sister, he expected to be killed and became paranoid about his situation. A lawyer he knew later told a reporter, "He had become deathly afraid of ending up in a cemetery plot there." It was at this point that he gave authorities the names of the strike leaders and implicated some defense lawyers in giving drugs to inmates, which led to his release.

Mailer, Scott Meredith, Robert Silvers, of the *NYRB*, and Erroll McDonald, a young editor at Random House, wrote letters to the Utah Board of Pardons at Abbott's request attesting to Abbott's extraordinary literary abilities (because Abbott had escaped from the Utah State Prison, he had to return there in order to be paroled). In his letter, Mailer said, "I am aware of the responsibility of what I propose," adding that "Abbott is in need of a special solution that can reach out to his special abilities." Mailer later told a friend, "I didn't see how I could not help." He became Abbott's most devoted champion, although McDonald and Mailer's wife, Norris, spent more time with him, and Silvers was generous to him in several ways. Random House gave Abbott a book contract and a $12,500 advance. Mailer picked up Abbott at the airport, and insisted on carrying his bags. Then he brought him home for dinner. Norris looked down as they climbed the stairs and saw him for the first time.

> He was wearing a dark blue pin-striped suit with a vest, a white shirt, and red tie, and little round glasses. It was a color Xerox of

> what Norman wore all the time. He came up to the door, smiled, and stuck out his hand. "I'm Jack," he said. He was about as tall as I am, slim, neat, and nervous. I couldn't tell what his ethnicity was. He had a slightly exotic look, with tan skin, and was much more attractive than I had anticipated. I wasn't afraid of him at all. In fact, there was something moving about him, dressed up in his Norman suit with those little glasses.

John Buffalo showed Abbott his G.I. Joe toys and then sat down with him, Matt, and their parents for a dinner of roast chicken and mashed potatoes. Abbott had seconds and said it was the best meal of his life. Norris was saddened when she realized that what he said was probably not flattery.

For the next few weeks, Abbott came to dinner two or three times a week. He thought Norris was marvelous. Silvers recalled Abbott telling him, "She's great, she's great! She understands." He confided in her, told her about his mother and how he had bought a new stone for her grave in Salt Lake City. Almost every day he would call her on the telephone. Mailer was at his studio down the street most of the day working on *Ancient Evenings*. Abbott asked Norris for advice on matters such as where to buy toothpaste or stamps. According to Robert Sam Anson, who wrote a long, detailed piece about him for *Life*, Abbott told her about his hopes and fears, including some unnamed women he said "were after me." Norris said, "Don't worry, Jack. I'm not after your body; I'm after your mind," and Abbott laughed, which was "something rare for him." Norris also took him shopping at Macy's. Buying a pair of jeans was a major operation.

> "Is there someone who issues them to you?" he said, eyes wide, looking at the stacks and racks of clothes.
>
> "No. You just find your size in something you like and go try them on. Over there, in the dressing rooms."
>
> "You mean they let you take and try these on? With nobody watching?"

"It was a concept he could hardly grasp," Norris said. She hesitated to get too involved with him, "but Norman had little time or inclination to go shopping with Jack, or answer his questions—there were so many."

Mailer did bring Abbott to the Salvation Army halfway house on East 3rd Street in the Bowery, where he was required to live until August 25. On another day, he took him to the New York Public Library and showed him the *Denkmäler aus Aegypten und Aethiopien* (*Monuments of Egypt and Ethiopia*), twelve massive folio volumes created in the second half of the nineteenth century by one of the fathers of Egyptology, Karl Richard Lepsius. It is likely that he showed him Volume III, containing drawings of bas-reliefs of Ramses II at the Battle of Kadesh, a key episode in the yet unpublished *Ancient Evenings*. Jill Krementz took a photo, published in *People*, of Mailer and Abbott examining one of the folios.

Erroll McDonald had regular meetings with Abbott about the upcoming publication of *In the Belly of the Beast* (a series of letters to Mailer about prison life) and was one of the few people who saw how frazzled Abbott was, especially in new social situations. As he and Abbott were about to enter the Metropolitan Museum of Art, Abbott almost lost his temper when a guard ordered him to put out his cigarette. He put it out, but glared at the guard. There were other such incidents. When Mailer appeared on the Cavett show several months later, he explained the psychology of state-raised convicts. "When you're in a jail cell, the only way you keep your head intact is to make constructions with that head, every day of your life." Creating scenarios to explain all that you observe is a critical survival tool, he said. Compounding this sense of menace is the noise in prisons. "The din is constant," Mailer said.

> In prison, every little moment is of significance. The guard who walks by who's been friendly to you every other day and suddenly he frowns at you; that means the warden has gotten down on your case. Or that some powerful prisoner is having thoughts about you. And the guard is associated with that powerful prisoner and you're getting the message. Now whether these things are true or not, it's the way people in prison tend to think, because they have nothing to divert themselves.

If there is agreement about any aspect of the Abbott story, it is that the Bowery halfway house was one of the worst places imaginable for him to have been sent. It wasn't prison, but it was noisy, filled with parolees, and located in a tough neighborhood. There were rules and regulations to be followed, including daily face-to-face checks. Later, Mailer would testify that Abbott loathed living there. "Instead of unwinding him, it was tightening him up." When someone lifted a pair of his shoes, Abbott called Norris and said he was going to kill the thief. Not much later, his blue pin-striped suit was missing, and when he called Norris, she got "the feeling of lava boiling down inside Jack." As it turned out, the director of the house had put the suit away so it would not be stolen.

One night after Abbott had been in New York for about two weeks, the Mailers had a dinner party for him, inviting four close friends: Jean Malaquais and his daughter, Dominique, Dotson Rader, and Pat Kennedy Lawford. Abbott was uneasy. Rader described him as "the repairman who came to fix the fridge and then was asked to stay for dinner." But Abbott knew Malaquais and agreed with his radical politics, and he had also read some of Rader's books about the anti–Vietnam War movement, so he was able to carry on a conversation. The evening fell apart, however, when Malaquais began criticizing the United States as an imperialist country. "Abbott ratcheted it up a notch," Norris wrote, "calling America a fascist hellhole run by pigs." Mailer was getting nervous, especially after Pat Lawford, the sister of a martyred president, got into it with Abbott. She asked him why, if he hated the country so unreservedly, he didn't leave it. He answered he would like to go to Cuba. That was sufficient, Norris said, to unhinge Mrs. Lawford, who replied, "*Cuba!* Splendid, I'll buy you a ticket. *One way!*" Then she and Rader left. On the way home, she told him that Abbott had a killer's eyes.

At the end of June, the Mailers went to Provincetown where they were renting a large house in the East End for a month. Abbott was invited for a long weekend. He had his own room on the water, and gazed out for hours. He had never seen the ocean before and didn't know how to swim. They showed him around town, and he had his first ice cream cone in thirty years. Over lunch with Norris at an outdoor café on Commercial Street, he explained to her how to kill someone with a knife. "He said it should be a sharp knife, and you should put the tip between the person's second and third shirt buttons and push hard, one quick thrust. That sends the knife right into the heart, and it's over immediately." Abbott seemed to think that he was providing her with a valuable tip, she said.

Danielle was there during Abbott's visit, and her father asked her to go to the movies with him. "It never occurred to any of us that we should be afraid of him," Norris said. Danielle, twenty-four at the time, said she would never dream of defying her father. "He was always certain of the value of unusual experience." She and Abbott, whom she described as "extremely handsome with chiseled features," walked over a mile to the theater. He was "socially unskilled, but very respectful," she said, and "seemed like a caged animal." Abbott got up four or five times during the show, and when he came back, "he was sniffing and snorting like he had taken cocaine." On the long, dark walk back to the East End, he talked a bit about prison, but was generally reserved. The whole experience was "unnerving," she said.

A letter from a Marion inmate, Garrett Trapnell, to novelist Peter Matthiessen had been passed on to Mailer by Bob Silvers. It stated that Abbott had given a 116-page deposition to an assistant U.S. attorney about lawyers sneaking in drugs to prisoners in Marion, and also that he had informed on others, breaking the code of convict solidarity. That deposition had made Abbott immediately eligible for parole. The letters of Mailer and others played only a minor role. The Utah Board of Pardons chairman was quoted in *The New York Times* as saying that "Mr. Abbott had been given psychological tests and that the results were 'consistent' with his being released." When he was in Provincetown, Anson wrote, Abbott was concerned about how Mailer now felt about him, given the information that he was a snitch. He denied, however, informing on fellow convicts, admitting only to implicating the lawyers. Mailer said he couldn't judge him. "I don't know what I would have done. I never had to spend 25 years in prison."

Abbott took a bus back to New York, and a week or so later the Mailers drove in to attend a celebratory dinner at a Greenwich Village restaurant, hosted by Jason Epstein, editorial director at Random House. Attending the event beside the Mailers were Silvers, Erroll McDonald, and novelist Jerzy Kosinski. Abbott had corresponded with Kosinski starting in 1973 when he was president of the American chapter of PEN, and asked that he be invited to the dinner. They embraced passionately like long-lost friends. "Abbott was sort of bewildered by all this," Silvers recalled. "He was like walking in a dream, and he didn't know quite how to cope." At the end of the dinner, Epstein offered a toast to Abbott's literary success. On the telephone, Abbott told his sister, "These people *really* like me," and after a pause, "That's never happened to me before."

Norris was worried about Abbott in the heat of the city, a place "where everyone was testy, a bad combination for someone as paranoid as Jack." He called her on the phone in a state of agitation and said, "I'm going to blow, I'm going to blow." She told him to stay cool; his book would be published on July 18, and good things were in store. When David Rothenberg, executive director of the Fortune Society, which helps released prisoners, saw Abbott and Mailer on *Good Morning America,* he immediately called Random House and urged them "to go slow with him on the interviews. He has to learn how to walk." Rothenberg invited Abbott to come by for help, but Abbott turned him down. Richard Stratton, who had met a few criminals in his day, advised Mailer not to get involved with Abbott. Mailer answered, "You know, that's one of the things I like about our friendship. We don't have to agree." Like everyone else, Mailer was also counting on good reviews and sales for Abbott's book to level Abbott out. He and Abbott discussed the possibility of getting him a residency at the MacDowell Colony in New Hampshire. Norris later summed it up, "Boy, were we naïve."

The early reviews of *In the Belly of the Beast* were enthusiastic. Abbie Hoffman, in a *Soho News* review, compared Abbott with two other writers who had taken on the prison systems of their countries, Russia's Aleksandr Solzhenitsyn and Argentina's Jacobo Timerman (Mailer had recently written a letter to New York officials supporting a lesser sentence on a drug charge for Hoffman, who had been on the lam for seven years). Writing in *The New York Times Book Review*, Terrence Des Pres also summoned up the Russian gulags, describing the maximum security prisons where Abbott had grown up as "an archipelago of the damned." Des Pres, who had written an important work on the Holocaust death camps, described Abbott's book as "the most fiercely visionary book of its kind in the American repertoire of prison literature. *In the Belly of the Beast* is awesome, brilliant, perversely ingenuous; its impact is indelible, and as an articulation of penal nightmare it is completely compelling." Mailer spoke to Abbott on the telephone on July 17, a Friday, and told him that the Sunday review from Des Pres was going to make him a star. When Abbott went out to celebrate that night, he must have felt like Jay Gatsby when he first saw the green light on Daisy's dock. But only a day before the Sunday *Times* containing the rave review appeared, Abbott got into a violent disagreement outside a twenty-four-hour restaurant, the Binibon, on the corner of Second Avenue and East 5th Street, just two blocks from the halfway house.

On the evening of July 17 Abbott went dancing at a German beer hall with two young women, Veronique de St. Andre from France, and Susan Roxas, a Barnard College student from the Philippines, whom he had met in an East Village bar. Roxas later testified that she had seen a knife sticking out of Abbott's belt, and asked him about it. "This is a bad neighborhood," he said. After the beer hall he took them for an early morning snack at the Binibon, walking in with one on each arm at around five A.M. He had eaten there before, although there is no evidence that he knew Richard Adan, the night manager and their waiter. A twenty-two-year-old Cuban-born actor and aspiring playwright, Adan was the son-in-law of the restaurant's owner, Henry Howard, himself an actor. Abbott ordered some food, and while the women were looking over their menus they noticed that Abbott was having an argument with the waiter. Then he was gone.

It is not clear why Abbott and Adan then went outside, but they argued about the rest room. Apparently, Adan said that the bathroom was for staff use only, citing insurance concerns, and Abbott didn't like the answer. It is possible that Abbott invited him outside to argue, or fight, or that Adan went out to try to calm him down, something he knew how to do, according to Bill Majeski, the New York detective who would soon become involved. Adan may also have been showing Abbott where he could relieve himself behind a dumpster located next to a wall mural honoring the slain John Lennon. An eyewitness at Abbott's trial, Wayne Larsen, said Abbott lunged at a conciliatory Adan, who was backing away, "with terrific velocity because his hair [Abbott's] sprung back from his head." Abbott stabbed him in the chest with a knife with a four-inch blade. Larsen, a Marine veteran of Vietnam, said the blow "made a resounding impact," and then, "for emphasis," Larsen "thumped his chest with both hands, which shook visibly during his testimony." Abbott then stepped back and screamed at Adan, who was trying to stanch a "canal of blood" flowing from his chest, "Motherfucker, do you still want to continue this?" Adan screamed back, "God, no. I already told you I don't." Then he walked a few steps along Second Avenue and fell, bouncing on the pavement "like a Ping-Pong ball." He died within minutes. Roxas testified that Abbott came to the door of the restaurant and shouted to her and her friend, "Let's get out of here! I just killed a man." They went outside and Abbott said, "You don't know me." Then he ran.

"By the time I got there," Majeski recalled,

> there were about twenty people standing around. When I walked up to the scene the overnight detective squad was just arriving. I saw a kid lying in the street and he had this angelic look on his face. So many years later I can still see that look on his face. My first impression was, "This is not a bad guy." Clearly he was a kid. There was a flow of blood that emanated from his chest because he was stabbed in the heart. Apparently, there was a lot of blood pumped out very quickly, and there was a stream running from the middle of the sidewalk down the curb and then into the street itself, a pool of blood in the street.

At six A.M. Abbott called Mailer in Provincetown. Mailer was groggy, and Abbott said he'd call back. Abbott returned to the halfway house, where a security guard saw him in the lobby. Next, he went to Erroll McDonald's apartment, but McDonald didn't answer—he had a feeling it was Abbott. At eleven, Abbott kept a brunch date at the Upper East Side apartment of Jean Malaquais. "He was extremely subdued and talked, as always, about literature and his projects," Malaquais recalled. Abbott left at noon.

At Port Authority Bus Terminal in Midtown, he caught a bus and for the next nine weeks eluded capture. He went south, via Chicago and Texas, to Mexico and the Guatemala border, and then to the oil fields near New Orleans. Majeski said, "I had a lot of conversations with Richard Adan's mother early on, and with his father-in-law. I kind of found myself promising the both of them, independent of each other; I promised them that I would get him. Once I made that commitment, to myself, then I couldn't let it go." He read *In the Belly of the Beast* and realized it was well written, but saw that Abbott "was not well-informed about life on the outside." He concluded that eventually Abbott would ask for help from people he knew, as he had only $200 when he fled. Majeski spoke to Mailer briefly on the telephone the next day, but knew he needed to meet him in person. He called Judith McNally, Mailer's secretary, who told him it was impossible for Mailer to come to New York. "You know how Judith could be—very standoffish. I said, 'Unless you arrange a meeting with him I will show up and I will arrest him.' She was saying, 'You can't do that, you just can't do that.' I wasn't going to do it, but that's how I got to him." The first meeting did not go well, but Majeski was persistent and kept calling Mailer and others.

> Anytime I got a new lead or a suspicion as to where he was I would call them and say, "Listen I've got information that Jack was seen in Chicago and I understand that he was trying to get in touch with you." They'd say, "Oh no, he's not trying to get in touch with me." But a couple days later I'd talk to that same person, "I heard he was reaching out to you." And they say, "Ah . . . oh no, no he didn't call." So I knew he was. I believed that Norman was going to get contacted by Jack and he was. And later Norman did tell me he was contacted by Jack, but he didn't tell him where he was. Norman was probably the least cooperative of all—maybe not least, but less than most, although there was mutual respect from the beginning. He was not a big help in telling me things verbally, but he still fell into that category of *not* telling me information. And that's fine. If Norman knew Jack was in Texas, I could still pick that up from him just like I could from all the other people. Every conversation with the people I called ended with me saying, "Tell Jack Majeski's right behind him." And when I finally met Abbott in the courthouse corridor, he knew immediately who I was. "You're Majeski," he said.

One of the people Abbott was calling was Scott Meredith, his agent. Meredith had the phone records. "Abbott was calling him," Majeski said, "to find out how his fucking book was selling."

Ultimately, Majeski was able not only to tell Louisiana authorities where Abbott was working, but also the alias he was using: Jack Eastman—Abbott kept his first name because it was tattooed on the fingers of his left hand. On September 23, he was captured in the oil fields. He was charged with murder upon his return, and immediately retained Ivan Fisher, a New York criminal defense lawyer recommended by Mailer. Abbott was put in twenty-four-hour lockdown, solitary, because Fisher was afraid someone would kill him. Majeski and Fisher got to know each other at the ensuing trial, and they both became lifelong friends with Mailer. During the time Abbott was on the run, his book went through five printings, and the following year the paperback became a bestseller. He earned approximately $100,000 in royalties while he was in Louisiana loading and unloading trucks for $4 an hour.

ON JULY 16, two days before the events at the Binibon, Barbara Probst Solomon flew to Provincetown to do an interview with Mailer about *Ancient Evenings*, which Mailer was determined to finish that summer. She hoped to publish her interview in *The New York Times Magazine*. In recalling the visit, she explained her relationship with him, which went back to the fall of 1947 when she had met him in Paris. "I knew him from the time I was a young high school graduate and he was not yet THE Norman Mailer." Her husband had died in 1967, and shortly after that, she continued, "at a time when Mailer had broken up with Beverly, Norman and I sought each other in a more intimate way. But that was temporary. I would characterize what we had over those many years as simply a profound friendship." As they were talking in Mailer's studio on Bradford Street Saturday the 18th, someone—a friend or perhaps one of the older children—came in and said that Jack Abbott had killed someone in New York.

> It was the first time I ever saw Norman cry. He broke down, he cried, at that moment—cried for the dead student. This is not a side he often revealed. "This is the worst thing," he said. By the worst thing he meant he felt in some way responsible for the murder. And then the *Times* said to me, "Well, put Abbott in your interview." But my interview had been a literary interview. It actually was completed before we knew of the murder. So I said, "Abbott happened after. You'll see when you look at it. This was a literary interview. We finished it." The *Times* then said no. I called up Bob Silvers of the *New York Review*, and he said, "Oh, this is not the time for a literary in-

terview with Mailer." So it was published in the *Boston Review* and *Pieces and Pontifications*, and other places. When I told Mailer, he said, "Well, I'm in the outfield now."

Writing to Professor Mike Lennon on July 29, Mailer said, "I've been in a state of shock from Black Friday, i.e., early Saturday A.M. I can still hardly believe Jack did it. Your relative V. I. Lenin once said 'Whom?' as a test to ask 'who benefits?' when you can't figure something out. I reckon it was the devil." Norris believed that their telephones in Provincetown and Brooklyn were tapped, but Majeski said this was not the case. During this period, Mailer had nothing to say to the press. In early August they went to Maine with the family. Danielle remembers that he was "extremely depressed." Unable to reach Mailer, frustrated reporters pestered Scott Meredith for a statement. Mailer's agent said that he had met Abbott "a few times after his release and he seemed a gentle, kind person." As far as Mailer was concerned, Meredith said, he was "still unwilling to talk about it. I think that unwillingness will be permanent. He's just heartsick." His first public statement came when Abbott was caught: "Jack Abbott has had one of the toughest lives I've ever encountered, and the next stage is not going to be any easier." From start to finish, Mailer did nothing to distance himself from Abbott.

Norris first met Ivan Fisher when she and Mailer went to his office to discuss the upcoming trial. Fisher, who stands about six foot five and speaks in a booming voice, said, "We're going to have Jack back out on the streets before you know it. Don't worry about a thing." Norris was "flabbergasted," and replied that Abbott "is going to do this again and again if he gets out," and should be locked up permanently. "Norris was morally offended, deeply, that I actually wanted to win an acquittal for Abbott," Fisher recalled. "This set us apart instantly." Mailer, "the constant voyeur," moved his chair back, so to speak, to watch the exchange. "He loved the notion," Fisher said, "that there I was, you know, the complete counterpoint to the soul of the woman he loved most in the world."

The trial began in mid-January 1982. Fisher mounted a strong defense, reading from Abbott's book about prison-induced paranoia, and speaking emotionally about how Abbott's worldview was the result of a twenty-five-year prison education. Pounding on a table and speaking in loud tones, he said, "He went from the belly of his mother to the belly of the beast." The prosecution had a dozen witnesses who either saw Abbott stab Adan or placed him in the restaurant that morning. Abbott's claim that Adan pulled a knife, which would have made his act self-defense, convinced no one. Naomi Zack, a philosophy professor who later married Abbott, said that long after he had been convicted Abbott still asked friends to search for Adan's knife in the alley. It was "the holy grail" for him, she said. Needless to say, it was never found.

Mailer testified for twenty minutes on January 18, and described how he and Abbott had corresponded, and the letter he wrote in support of his parole. His testimony merited only a few lines in news reports. But after the proceedings were over that day, reporters surrounded him and he got into an impromptu discussion with them in the courthouse press room. It was a terrific mistake to take on thirty-five reporters, but he had no calculation in his bones. He admitted that he had missed Abbott's capacity for violence, that he didn't "pay enough attention to the little warnings he gave me in a quiet little voice about how that halfway house was really getting him ready to blow." Asked what he felt about Adan's death, he said, "Richard Adan's death is an absolute tragedy. Who's pretending that it isn't? It's a hideous waste, it's a horror. The fact that Richard Adan is killed is something that the people who are closest to Abbott are going to have to live with for the rest of their lives. I mean, you can't have my blood unless you go for it, but you can have my psychic blood, because naturally, I, like many other people are upset about the death of Richard Adan." The mood shifted when Mailer said he was opposed to a lengthy sentence for Abbott. "Adan has already been destroyed," he said, "at least let Abbott become a writer." Further pressed, he said, "Putting people in prison and turning the key on them, and forgetting about them, that is the cellar, that's the ground floor of fascism. A democracy involves taking risks." This enraged the reporters. Paul Montgomery of *The New York Times* said that in his twenty-five years as a reporter, Mailer's press conference "was the worst New York press gang bang I've ever seen. Everybody went crazy at once, pushing forward."

Norris said, "Norman was never cool under pressure, and tended to get angry and say stupid things when goaded, and the press are expert in goading." If Abbott was freed again, Mailer was asked, wouldn't he kill again? He replied, "I'm saying culture is worth a little risk, that's what I'm saying over and over for 30 years." Mike Pearl of the *New*

York Post came back sharply: "Which elements are you willing to gamble with? Cubans? Waiters? What?" Mailer repeated himself: "Society has got to take certain risks," adding that he felt "very responsible" for what had happened. Things got raucous at this point, and the volume went up; insults were traded. Mailer used the phrase "scumbag journalism," and shortly after the news conference dissolved in acrimony.

The jury was divided between those who wanted to come in with a murder verdict and those who wanted manslaughter. After fifteen hours of deliberation, those favoring manslaughter won. At the courthouse, Adan's father-in-law, Henry Howard, called the verdict "ridiculous"; Mailer called it "fair." The sentence was fifteen years to life. Abbott, who had spent the previous five months in solitary reading *The Golden Bough*, Sir James George Frazer's massive compilation of religious myths and practices—Mailer owned a twelve-volume set and had sent him a reprint—received the verdict with resignation. Mailer called Abbott after the verdict, and they talked about the problems state-raised convicts faced when they get out. Their conclusion was that such men "are both too strong and too weak to handle the world." When told, after the verdict, that Henry Howard had said that his son-in-law's blood was on his hands, Mailer said, "I think he's right," and walked away.

Norris ended her account of these painful events in her memoir by discussing how Mailer had "analyzed violence, studied it his whole life, played with it in his imagination." She puts his fascination with violence in the context of his writing, especially "The White Negro," and also the stabbing of Adele. From the stories he told her, she concluded that the 1960 stabbing had been a crucible, and that "he had gone through the fire and come out cleaner and forged of greater steel." She concluded, "Norman always had a huge ego; he believed he could change the course of a river by the strength of his personality." He thought Abbott could do the same, failing to understand, as she observed, that not everyone was like him.

Mailer had pretty much been given a pass for "The Trouble"—the stabbing of Adele—although not by himself, nor by Adele, and he knew that there would be a never-ending cost to his children, especially Danielle and Betsy. But in their comments on the "Abbott business," most reporters and editorial writers, pundits, and writers of letters to the editor, abetted by Mailer's ill-considered and inflammatory statements about culture and risk, were righteous. Noting Mailer's own earlier stabbing was de rigueur. The pieties of law and order were fingered like rosaries by op-ed writers, and Mailer was pilloried for romanticizing violence. *The New Republic* ran a color cover depicting him and Abbott sitting at a restaurant table on which lay a bloody knife and an open handcuff. On the wall, there is a portrait of the ex-con Jean Genet and his champion Jean-Paul Sartre. Inside the magazine, James Atlas called Abbott's book "a hectic screed full of shrill political jargon," adding that it was "irresponsible" of Mailer to say that Abbott could earn a living as a writer. Lewis Lapham, still at *Harper's* after his colleagues had resigned en masse, stated in the *Chicago Tribune* that "Mailer now endorses sociopathic killers instead of prize fighters." Lance Morrow of *Time* complained of the soft sentence Abbott had received and suggested that Abbott and Mailer "be shackled together with molybdenum chains." In a front-page essay in the *Times Book Review*, Michiko Kakutani wrote a thoughtful, balanced piece that explored the Mailer-Abbott relationship. There was a myth at work, she wrote.

> It was the myth, as Mailer puts it in his introduction, whereby "the boldness of the juvenile delinquent grows into the audacity of the self-made intellectual." It was the wishful impulse to see Mr. Abbott's life as a story not just of crime and punishment, but of crime and punishment and redemption; and it was the fervently held belief that talent somehow redeems, that art confers respectability, that the act of writing can somehow transform a violent man into a philosopher of violence.

Kakutani, who would later become Mailer's critical bête noire, came closer than anyone else to articulating Mailer's unspoken assumptions about Abbott. Mailer never stopped believing that art can ennoble, and that it is possible to rise above one's errors and crimes, but the "Abbott business" challenged his deepest beliefs about human nature. It forced him to recognize the folly of believing that sinners and criminals could *invariably* be saved by art, could move forward into greater humanity rather than retreating into less.

The majority of those who attacked Mailer for his advocacy of Abbott made the assumption that his letter to the Utah Board of Pardons was the linchpin of his release. Mailer never disputed this, even when it was convincingly shown that his testimony was only one factor, and far from the most important, in the board's decision. But even after friends pointed to his limited culpability, Mailer insisted it was greater. Malaquais, Torres, Lucid, and others all tried to convince him otherwise, to no avail. Appearing on the Dick Cavett show after Abbott's conviction, he said, "I'm not trying to hide behind others. Or say that I wasn't the only one who got him out. I certainly was one of the two or three people who were finally instrumental in getting him out." Mailer's idea of retributive balance, karmic debt, made him take more blame than he was due, according to his daughter Danielle. On some level he may have believed that he was atoning for his stabbing of Adele twenty-one years earlier. But it was only a down payment on that huge debt.

At a Fortune Society meeting shortly after Abbott's conviction, William Styron stood up for Mailer, saying, "My heart goes out to him. I have an Abbott in my life." Styron had aided a prisoner, Benjamin Reid, who later raped a woman while on parole. Styron repeated his defense of Mailer at a PEN conference, and in an essay, where he said, "Remembering one's own Elysian childhood in juxtaposition with that of Reid and Abbott, I think it is fair to say that a concern for either of those wretched felons has less to do with romanticism than with a sense of justice, and the need for seeking restitution for other men's lost childhoods." Styron's gesture led Mailer to write him a letter, his first to him since 1958. He wrote, "I just wanted to say that it was gracious of you and generous and kind of gutty to speak up for me the way you did about the Abbott business." Mailer and Styron's friendship was rekindled, perhaps the only happy outcome of their separate attempts to help "wretched felons."

TWELVE
PHARAOHS AND TOUGH GUYS

"I had to go to Yugoslavia for some reason," Schiller said, "but on the way to Yugoslavia, I stop to see Norman in London." This was not happenstance. Schiller had purposely flown via London instead of Frankfurt so that he could see Mailer, who was there acting in Milos Forman's *Ragtime*. Five months earlier, in July 1980, NBC had signed an agreement with Schiller to produce and direct a television miniseries based on *The Executioner's Song* and had insisted that he sign Tracy Keenan Wynn to write the script. Wynn had many film and television credits, and a few years earlier had won an Emmy for his adaptation of Ernest Gaines's novel *The Autobiography of Miss Jane Pittman*. "Take your four million dollars," the executives told Schiller, "and go make your film." Schiller had a problem, however.

Mailer had been his first choice to write the screenplay, but both CBS and ABC, where Schiller had good relationships, didn't want Mailer because he had never had a script produced. Schiller then went to movie studios, and they accepted Mailer as the first draft writer (mainly because all screenplays are rewritten), but they didn't think Schiller had the requisite experience to direct a feature film. "I realized then that, you know, no way was this deal ever going to be made with both of us together," Schiller said. Next, he tried NBC where the new president of the entertainment division, Brandon Tartikoff, was revamping programming and taking chances. He liked the proposed miniseries. Nick Nolte was the first choice to play Gilmore, and Priscilla Presley as Nicole; (ultimately the roles went to Tommy Lee Jones and Rosanna Arquette). Schiller called Mailer and told him that he was going with Wynn and NBC. "You've written the book and won your Pulitzer, and now it's time for me to tell the story my way." Mailer didn't argue, Schiller said.

At lunch with Mailer and Norris in London in December, Schiller knew Mailer would ask about Wynn's script. Schiller said that it was a fine adaptation, but not exciting. Not much else was said, and Schiller left for Yugoslavia. In February 1981, Schiller received a script in the mail from Mailer, written on spec. Schiller liked it enough to send it to NBC. It seemed nearly the same as Wynn's, but there were subtle changes, lines shuffled or dropped, and some additions. Schiller explained.

> With every single character in Mailer's version, the dialogue defines the character. I just couldn't believe it. "I don't give a shit about your pants"—that line defines Brenda right off the bat. In Mailer's scene that was the first line. Tracy used the same thing, but it was the third line in his scene. By the time you got to that line, its power was dissipated.

NBC also liked the script. "It was just different," an NBC vice president stated. "It had a different tone." Schiller had already paid Wynn, and when NBC accepted Mailer's version, he had to pay Mailer $250,000.

The question of who should get the screen credit was contested and went to the Writers Guild for arbitration. Mailer had not read Wynn's script, and wrote a brief letter to the guild that attempted to prove it. His argument was that anyone who wrote a script based on the book would have to depict the same key events and characters. He explained it this way.

> If two people are driving from San Luis Obispo to San Francisco following the coastal road, they're likely to stop at the same road-houses en route, they're likely to sleep at the same inns and so forth and so forth and so forth. And that book had a clearly marked line of narrative, if ever a book did and, therefore, if you're going to do a script with it, you'd be following the book. So we each were following the book very closely. The difference was that I felt that I knew the book in a way that no one else did.

The guild's judgment was based on reading the two scripts with the writers' names coded, Writer A and Writer B. Besides the subtleties of characterization, Mailer's script also contained, according to Schiller, new scenes drawn from the original interviews and research, material not used in the book. His familiarity with this material was an obvious advantage, and the guild awarded him sole screenplay credit. Wynn accepted the ruling. Mailer, rankled by the rejection of his screenplay by Sergio Leone five years earlier, felt vindicated.

He was also working intermittently on *Strawhead*, his play about Marilyn Monroe. *Ancient Evenings* was still a long way from completion, but first he had to finish work on his new collection, divided into a dozen essays and prefaces (*Pieces*) and twenty interviews (*Pontifications*). His reflections on television, "Of a Small and Modest Malignancy," his comic memoir of *The Harvard Advocate*, "Our Man at Harvard," and his essay on Watergate, "A Harlot High and Low," were the key writings. The interview section included a 1975 interview with Laura Adams on reincarnation and magic. This interview, one of Mailer's most important, contains a long discussion of his belief in magic, something he was exploring in *Ancient Evenings*. The four-hundred-page collection, which he dedicated to his sister, appeared on June 21, 1982, not long after Abbott was sentenced. The timing did not help the book's reception, which was quiet and mixed.

Pieces and Pontifications, Mailer's fifth miscellany, is a product of the 1970s, when he "was much out of step." Besides dropping the third person personal and shifting focus away from himself, he had withdrawn from politics to a great extent after the 1972 election. Lucid put his finger on Mailer's malaise in the decade: he spent his first twenty years as a writer "envisioning and anticipating moments of climactic crisis," in his personal life, in politics and culture, and sometimes all three, overlapping. "But always the crisis was *about* to happen. Always our situation was *before*. The 1970s represented *after*. The counterculture was over. The war in Vietnam was over." One world was dying and a new one had not yet been born.

He ends his review by noting that *The Executioner's Song* was "the first child" of the new time, the first reimagining. While the film version (broadcast in November 1982) did not enjoy the huge popularity of the book, it was deemed a success by the critics and the television audience, garnering the highest rating for an NBC program in fifteen months. It was nominated for five Emmys, including one for Mailer's adaptation. It won two, one for sound production and one for Tommy Lee Jones as best actor. The film led to a directorial career for Schiller and was a breakthrough for Jones. Mailer's achievement whetted his desire to write more screenplays and to try his hand again as director.

THROUGH ALL THIS period, from the publication of *Executioner's Song*, through his divorces and marriage to Norris, Abbott's release and Adan's death, work on *Strawhead, Pieces and Pontifications*, and the teleplay of *Song*, Mailer had slighted his patient literary spouse, the Egyptian novel, working on it only sporadically. But in the summer of 1982, Little, Brown was pressing him. As he wrote to a writer friend, the prospect of trying to write several hundred more pages of *Ancient Evenings* in a short period was "a perfect expression of my character: work ten years with great care on something, and then arrange matters so that I have to sprint at the end." He worked all summer in Provincetown and Maine. Barbara and Al visited, and Susan came with his first grandchild, Valentina. Unlike previous summers, several of the children were either traveling or working and the house was not always full. In the fall he finally finished the novel, completing the last revision of the galleys in early December. He announced the end in a long letter to his old friend Richard Stratton. "I really need another year to get this behemoth into classic shape for the ages," he said, but further delay was out of the question. He felt he had realized his goal of re-creating for the reader

> some possible Egyptian society, full of its pagan, sacramental sophistication, a world without Moses or Jesus, but stacked with acquisitive and elegant society—quite a trick, I tell you—for eleven years I've been fumbling around in it, but now, going over it for this last time, I begin to recognize how much of me is in it and in ways too deep for even me to understand. My sister after reading it laughed and said, "You know, in a funny way, this is the best argument for karma I've ever come across." How could [you] ever know all this stuff if you didn't live then was what she said finally by implication.

Little, Brown set publication for April 4, 1983, to be followed by the novel's appearance in England in late May.

Mailer's letter to Stratton reached him in Portland, Maine, where he was awaiting trial on charges of drug smuggling. A raid by an American-Canadian drug enforcement team in March 1982, "Operation Rose," led to the arrest of Stratton and fourteen others in Maine, Quebec, and Toronto. The drugs, smuggled in from Beirut, had a street value of $30 million, and Canadian authorities said the thirty-six-year-old Stratton was the boss of "the largest hashish and marijuana smuggling ring ever to be broken" in that country. Stratton denied the charges, stating that he was researching a book about the international drug trade. The end point for the drugs—2,500 pounds were seized—was Robert Rowbotham, a friend of Stratton's whom Mailer had testified for at an earlier drug trial in Toronto. (Rowbotham was running his drug operation from prison). Stratton admitted receiving approximately $200,000 from Rowbotham, which he said was payment for a biography of the marijuana guru, nicknamed "Rosie."

A few days after telling Stratton that he would be a character witness for him at his upcoming trial, Mailer got a call from Buzz Farbar, who had been working as a money courier for Stratton, to set up a lunch date. On December 9, Mailer met him at a Brooklyn restaurant, Armando's, on Montague Street. He had no way of knowing that three weeks earlier Farbar had been arrested at gunpoint for paying $24,000 for a kilo of what he thought was cocaine from an undercover DEA agent, Martin McGuire. Within ten minutes of his arrest at his New York apartment, McGuire said to him, "We know your friend Mailer is involved." The feds had "a serious hard-on" for Mailer, Stratton said. "After Mailer had testified at the Rowbotham trial, up in Canada," Stratton recalled, "they broke into Norman's place in Brooklyn and rifled through his stuff, found a couple of ounces of pot, and left it right in the middle of the bed as a kind of sign or warning. *We're watching you, Mailer.*"

It was Farbar who, unwittingly, had made Mailer a DEA target. In 1981, he had organized a dinner party for "my heavy connections in Beirut," as Stratton described them, and the Mailers. "Buzz was showing off," Stratton said. As Stratton was to learn, the Lebanese were cooperating with American authorities, and his arrest, and later Farbar's, resulted from information they had provided. The DEA busted Farbar, but they wanted Mailer, Stratton said.

> It was a time when John DeLorean had been set up in that sting operation in Los Angeles. John Lennon had been busted. They were making drug cases against famous people to discredit them. It was propaganda in the war on drugs. They figured that Mailer's scalp would've been great to have on somebody's belt. He was already a government target for a lot of other reasons, because he was so vocally critical of the government. And people listened to Norman, particularly a generation of young people who were already fed up with the lies our government was telling us about Vietnam, pot, and what have you.

The DEA had given Farbar a lie detector test and asked him if Mailer had invested in the hashish deal. He denied it. "We know you've been lying," he was told. "You have a family on the one hand, and Mailer on the other. One will have to go." Knowing that Mailer was innocent, Farbar agreed to wear a recorder at his lunch with him. As instructed, Farbar brought up Stratton's hashish smuggling. Mailer indicated that he didn't want to talk about it. Farbar persisted and an irritated Mailer told him to stop. "I'm possibly going to be testifying at Richard's trial as a character witness, and I certainly don't want to get into a situation where I'm going to be in jeopardy of perjury." He went on to say that Stratton was a great friend, but he didn't know much about his background; he knew him as a writer. Farbar kept pressing. "I've never had anything to do with the drug business," Mailer said. "I don't want to hear nothing about Richard, all right?" Farbar said that he had brought up the subject out of concern for Mailer. "I'll worry about my own ass in my own way," Mailer replied. When the DEA agents heard the recording, they said the conversation appeared to have been rehearsed, and Farbar was convicted and sentenced to six years for hashish smuggling, a harsh sentence for a first offender.

Dick and Doris Kearns Goodwin were old friends of Stratton's, and they attended his trial. She and Mailer testified to his literary abilities. But he was convicted and sentenced to fifteen years in federal prison. Stratton was on his way to the penitentiary, ready to do his time. But the federal drug prosecutors hadn't given up on nailing Mailer. They pulled Stratton off the bus in New York and told him they were going to try him under the continuing criminal enterprise, or "Kingpin," statute. He met the prosecutor, who, according to Stratton, said in effect, Give us

Mailer, and you'll walk. They were also interested in Hunter Thompson, a noted drug user, and a few other high-profile figures. "I refused to cooperate with the government. I figured, I did this, let me pay for it." Mailer was not permitted by Judge Constance Baker Motley to testify at Stratton's trial. She sentenced Stratton to an additional ten years with no possibility of parole, basing this extraordinarily long sentence on his refusal to cooperate. Stratton later wrote his own appeal, which argued that individuals can only be sentenced for their crimes, not for refusing to implicate others. The courts agreed with his appeal, and he was released after eight years. Farbar got out after forty-six months.

To the surprise of some of Mailer's friends, he did not break with Farbar. "I figure some dealer was throwing my name around in an attempt to impress people," Mailer said. "The feds must have heard it on somebody's wiretap. You could smell their lust from here to Laos." Asked if he was angry at Farbar, he said, "There was a squeeze on Buzz of a horrendous sort. He was trying to protect his family. If I had been in the same situation, what would I have done?" He visited Farbar and Stratton in prison, and wrote to them regularly.

He did not visit Abbott, but he continued to write to him for several years, and sent him books, as did Robert Silvers. Mailer encouraged Abbott to write, sending him some of William Burroughs's novels. He put others in touch with Abbott, including his friend, Mashey Bernstein, who corresponded with Abbott about Judaism. The biggest obstacle you face, Mailer wrote Abbott, "is that the past draws you back like a magnet and you get so sorrowful and so enraged and so bilious, so incoherent with rage, and so vengeful and so mournful and so contrite and so proud and so much this and so much that that you can't think straight." His own troubles, Mailer said, "are on the other side. With rare exceptions, the past has lost its vividness for me, so I feel these days as if I'm writing with an empty gut."

Fig Gwaltney, the army buddy at whose house he had met Norris, had died a year earlier. Mailer had promised his wife, Ecey, that he would come to Arkansas in March 1983, give a talk, and donate the honorarium to a scholarship in his memory. Fig was his oldest friend, and although they had not seen each other recently, Mailer remembered his loyalty. A few days after writing Ecey, he turned sixty. He said, "Fifty caused a long, continuous woe. Fifty had an awful sound to it. Worse than 60. Sixty feels all right. Forty felt great. Thirty felt lousy. Maybe

I've just got something against odd numbers. Maybe at 70 I'll go into a tailspin." In fact, his next decade, while not free of difficulties, would be one of his happiest.

HE HAD BEEN paid handsomely for *Ancient Evenings*, but the money was gone and he was again in arrears to the IRS. In mid-January he flew to Boston to try to renegotiate his contract with Little, Brown. He had already received $1.4 million, and the contract called for an additional $2.5 million for the final two novels of the trilogy, but the executives were not eager to advance much of this sum until they knew the sales of *Ancient Evenings*. They were fearful, Mailer said, of losing three quarters of what had already been advanced. The contract also called for a short novel to be delivered in the fall of 1983. Having pushed back deadline after deadline for him over the past decade, Little, Brown was insistent that he meet this one. But before he could begin thinking seriously about this new novel, he had to go on a very demanding tour for the current one. Mailer had stated publicly that the Egyptian novel was his masterwork, and he intended to take every opportunity to hold forth on its merits.

His first big outing for the book was at the Lotos Club in New York on January 28, a luncheon meeting with six out-of-town book editors. Mailer was expansive on his research for the book, citing Budge's edition of *The Egyptian Book of the Dead*, a collection of prayers belonging "to an infinitely remote and primeval time." These prayers were painted and inscribed on the tomb walls and sarcophagi of the wealthy, written on papyri placed in their coffins, and also on the narrow linen bandages that swathed the remains. "Properly uttered," Budge wrote, these prayers "enabled the deceased to overcome every foe and to attain the life of the perfected soul" in Aaru, the abode of the blessed. Those souls virtuous enough to traverse the Land of the Dead, the Duad, would enjoy unspeakable eternal happiness in the company of numerous gods and goddesses, and ride in the Boat of Ra pulling the sun through the heavens. There is no definitive version of *The Egyptian Book of the Dead*, or even complete agreement about the nature of the Duad and Aaru. The possibility of the soul expiring after the body, however, was accepted dogma. The Egyptian belief in a possible second death "had huge interest for me," Mailer said, "because I'd really been writing about that in one way or another for a long time." Gary Gilmore's desire to protect his soul by sacrificing his body is one instance. Rojack's similar fear in *An American Dream* is another. At the luncheon Mailer also mentioned Flinders Petrie, a pioneering Egyptologist, who in 1896 discovered a stele or monument stone, on which a pharaonic victory over a tribe from Israel is recorded, the first mention of that nation in an ancient Egyptian record. Moses's revolt in Egypt is noted in passing in the novel. Using a dictionary compiled by Budge, Mailer began learning hieroglyphics, but found it too difficult. What fascinated him was its dialectical nature, how "words often reverse themselves in different contexts," an existential language.

The editors asked if he had read Vidal's novel *Creation*, about ancient Greece and Persia, and he said no. "Gore and I are always working in terribly different directions." Vidal is a rationalist and an atheist, he said, and comparatively speaking, I am "a diabolist and mystic." Mailer's protagonist, Menenhetet I, is a magus who seeks the links between the high and the low, excelsior and excrement. As Robert Begiebing notes in his study of the novel, in Menenhetet's Egypt, "there is no clear division between the sacred and the secular, no desacralization of the world." For the Egyptians, "death is risky and adventurous," he says, and "the debts and wastes of one's life carry significance beyond earthly existence." The appeal of such a belief system to Mailer was powerful. He had also avoided Vidal's novel because he wanted to keep his rational side on short rations during the Egyptian excursion. "Gore is not the worst writer in the world," Mailer told the editors. "He can even be delightful and he can be seductive." His anger with Vidal appeared to be subsiding.

The editors also asked if he was making oblique statements about American imperialism or American class structure in the new novel. "I've spent my writing life trying to understand America," he said, and this novel was an attempt "to try and get some idea of what life was like before anything we know," before the Judeo-Christian tradition. Over and over during the book tour he was asked if he had allegorical or symbolic intentions linking ancient Egypt and contemporary America. "Piety and snobbery," Mailer said, are the only traits that existed in both ancient Egypt and the modern world. Going to Egypt, he said, was "pure escapism." More than one critic compared *Ancient Evenings* to *Salammbô*, Flaubert's novel set in third century B.C. Carthage. Both are bloody, bawdy, and exotic, and both were published shortly after works of excruciating realism—*Madame Bovary* and *The Executioner's Song*.

One of the earliest inspirations for the novel, he said, was André Schwarz-Bart's novel *The Last of the Just*, which begins with the Crusades and ends in the Nazi death camps. He was impressed by how the novel moved swiftly through a dozen or more Jewish cultures. "I thought that I would take a character, start in Egypt, have him reborn in Greece, then Rome, then somewhere in the Middle Ages, and so forth," following Schwarz-Bart's example. But Mailer was unable to make the leap after he got enmeshed in the fascinating beliefs and practices of the ancient Egyptians. He was, for example, deeply attentive to the fact that a dung beetle had been deified as Khepera, the god who propelled the Boat of Ra out of the Duad in the morning, and pushed it below the horizon at night. For decades he had been fascinated with magic and had read widely in works such as Sir James George Frazer's *The Golden Bough* and Lynn Thorndike's eight-volume *History of Magic and Experimental Science*, both of which he owned. Ancient Egypt, a culture saturated in magic for thousands of years, was the perfect place for him to explore his interests. He was fascinated, he said, by "the substitution of magic for technology" in Egyptian life. "As you start getting into it, the problems they solved with their magic were about as cock-eyed and absurd as the problems we solve with our technology." When asked what *Ancient Evenings* was about, he often said, it's "a novel about magic."

He followed his sources with modest rigor. Professor David B. O'Connor, an Egyptologist at the University of Pennsylvania, said that he enjoyed the novel because "Mailer had so well grasped the cultural and historical thrust of ancient Egypt," despite a few errors. The largest of these, as Mailer readily admitted, the practice of telepathy, was never part of Egyptian belief. Several of his characters send and receive mental messages, and Mailer argued later that at some point in the distant past, before the Egyptians, humans had the power of telepathy. But in modern times, he speculated, "the amount of electromagnetic disturbance all our machines make, particularly our communication machines, has polluted whatever that ring is around the earth that transmits messages." He based this belief, in part, on the fact that dogs never watch television. "I think," he said (remembering the clairvoyant Tibo), "they live in so complete a telepathic framework that the set communicates nothing to them." Such were the wrinkles in the mind of the novelist at sixty.

The earliest excerpt (published in *The Paris Review*, four months before the novel was released) is also the one he read to audiences for decades. It comes from the first book (of seven) in the novel, "The Book of One Man Dead," and is a description of the embalming of Menenhetet's great-grandson Menenhetet II (called Meni), who died in a drunken brawl at the age of twenty-one. All the sensuous particularities of the embalming process, including the removal of the inner organs, which are sealed in canopic jars and accompany the Remains, the Sekhu, on their final journey, are rendered by Meni himself, the embalmee.

> Somewhere in those first few days they made an incision in the side of my belly with a sharp flint knife—I know how sharp for even with the few senses my Remains could still employ, a sense of sharpness went through me like a plow breaking ground, but sharper, as if I were a snake cut in two by a chariot wheel, and then began the most detailed searching. It is hard to describe, for it did not hurt but I was ready in those hours to think of the inside of my torso as common to a forest in a grove, and one by one trees were removed, their roots disturbing veins of rock, their leaves murmuring. I had dreams of cities floating down the Nile like floating islands. Yet when the work was done, I felt larger, as if my senses now lived in a larger space.

The embalming tent was "no bloody abattoir," Meni recalls, but a "herb kitchen" where his body cavity is cleansed and soothed.

Over time, Meni's senses become confused; he hears odors, smells colors—synesthesia—and then his consciousness dims as his Sekhu, held down by weights, renders up its moisture in a bath of natron, a salt mixture found in the dry lake beds of Egypt. After seventy days, "I became hard as the wood of a hull, then hard as the rock of the earth, and felt the last of me depart to join my Ka, my Ba, and my fearsome Khaibit." His aural faculty, the last to go, finally departs, and his Sekhu changes into something rich and strange, "like one of those spiraled chambers of the sea that is thrown up on the beach, yet contain the roar of waters when you hold them to your ear." Entombed, his Sekhu becomes "part of the universe of the dumb." The remaining six parts of his being, borrowed mainly from Budge, are: Ka (double); Ba (essential personality); Ren (secret name); Sekhem (soul or vital energy); Khu (guardian angel); and Khaibit (shadow). Mailer introduced these "lights and forces" of the Soul at the beginning of the novel to show the complexity of Egyptian belief, using the terms in the conversations of his major characters, sophisticated and wealthy Egyptians versed in magic and religion—two sides of the same coin for them.

Those of his friends and family who heard him read the embalming scene more than a few times became familiar with the characteristics he would repeat. His secretary, Judith McNally, who typed large portions of the novel and is thanked in the acknowledgments, knew Egyptian myth and lore nearly as well as her boss. An adherent of Wicca, Judith had a black cat named Khaibit.

Experts have not found fault with Mailer's religious explications nor his vivid retelling of the foundational myth—the story of Osiris and Isis. Told in the gloom of the tomb by the Ka of Menenhetet to the Ka of Meni in the novel's second book, "The Book of the Gods," it derives in uncertain percentages from various accounts of this magnificent story of the Egyptian gods in their primal years. "In this telling," reviewer Benjamin DeMott said, the myth "is made utterly new." Mailer combines episodes from different sources, adds flourishes of his own, and allows Meni to ask his great-grandfather questions that clarify, heighten interest, and provide breathing spaces. The interaction of teller and tale adds immeasurably to the richness of the telling, allowing the reader to share the thrill of discovery felt by Meni.

DURING THE YEARS he spent writing *Ancient Evenings*, 1972–82, Mailer gave several important print interviews, but he also turned down many and was chary about talking about his novel in progress. But in the months before and after the novel appeared, his reticence ended. He gave more than fifty interviews in 1983. The media campaign for the novel exceeded those for all his earlier books, but he told one interviewer that too much visibility is worse than too little. Authors who have good sales "get very little personal publicity. We don't read much about Saul Bellow, John Updike." He admitted that he had lost the battle with those who carved nasty messages on the sarcophagus of his legend. "So I've just said the hell with it." He often likened his clip file to the tail of a dinosaur. Collectively, the reviews for *Ancient Evenings* were worse than those received by any of his books since the 1950s. In *The New York Times Book Review*, DeMott called the novel "a disaster." Several reviewers—notably Vance Bourjaily, Richard Poirier, Barry Leeds, Christopher Ricks, Anthony Burgess, Christopher Lehmann-Haupt, and his former Harvard professor Robert Gorham Davis—reviewed *Ancient Evenings* positively but, with the exception of Ricks, seasoned their admiration with reservations and puzzlements. The words "audacious," "paradoxical," "demanding," and "risky" recur in these reviews, as well as a general lack of enthusiasm for the novel's many anal, fecal, and incestuous events, and the swarm of olfactory clues that accompany them—*Ancient Evenings* rivals *An American Dream* in this regard. Menenhetet supping on a paste made from bat dung to learn its healing powers is noted by many reviewers; it emerges as the touchstone of Mailer's outré preoccupations. To fully understand the deadly contest of Ahab and the White Whale, one must labor through the cetology chapters of *Moby-Dick*; to completely grasp the meanings of Menenhetet's and Meni's harrowing journeys in the afterlife, one must be immersed in its abominations.

Those reviewers who liked parts of the novel almost always point to the retelling of the Osiris-Isis myth, which Mailer believed could be published as a separate narrative. The Battle of Kadesh, another favorite, could also stand alone. The defeat of the Hittites and their mercenaries by the invading army of Ramses II takes up all of "The Book of the Charioteer," a 150-page tour de force that is the narrative heart of the novel. The barge trip down the Nile to Memphis in northern Egypt, composed, no doubt, with Shakespeare's *Antony and Cleopatra* at hand, is also cited as one of the novel's most splendidly imagined passages. But it is the chariot battle that stands out.

Commentators often point to the complicated way the story is narrated. It is not told by an anonymous narrator as in *The Executioner's Song*, but by the Ka of Meni, who, while conversing with his great-grandfather's Ka in the Great Pyramid, remembers a night fifteen years earlier, a night of dusk-to-dawn storytelling. Menenhetet, however, is the chief storyteller, and most of that ancient evening (and most of the novel) is given to his recounting of his extraordinarily long life, or lives—he has lived four—as they recline in the pharaoh's sumptuous garden lit by thousands of captured fireflies. Meni is clairvoyant and when Menenhetet pauses in his tale, or holds something back, Meni knows it, and also knows what others are thinking as well. His mother and great-grandfather share this ability. It is the voice of Menenhetet, however, that we hear most, relayed to us by Meni. As Poirier noted, Mailer had "a felt need to justify in some way the telling of story," and resorted to this awkward provenance. The overlay of voices is strained and confusing—Mailer said later that "the transitions of the narrator's voice were the hardest" challenge he faced—but he was wed from the outset to his nested voices.

Menenhetet is sixty when he tells his stories in the pharaoh's garden, the same age as Mailer when the novel was published. He denied, repeatedly and unconvincingly, that he was writing about himself in any important way. When his sister told him that it was his most autobiographical novel but couldn't decide whether he was Menenhetet or Ramses, "he said with uncustomary modesty, 'More like Ramses IX.' " He did not deny, however, that his protagonist's many careers—charioteer, harem master, high priest, tomb robber, brothel keeper, papyrus merchant, speculator in necropolis sites, wealthy noble, and pharmacist-magus—were of special interest. They were. For example, the research of Menenhetet into bat dung aligns with Mailer's homeopathic explorations in "The Metaphysics of the Belly," his long self-interview from 1962.

In the last three brief chapters we learn the Menenhetet's attempts to gain a fifth life have failed. After his Sekhu is buried in his great-grandson's tomb, their Kas proceed into the Duad. They observe with horror the punishments of those with impure hearts, many of which recall the sufferings of lost souls in Dante's *Inferno*—boiling lakes, for example. After his great-grandfather's Ka, unbidden, merges with his, Meni feels hope. He begins to ascend the "ladder of lights" (as described in the *Book of the Dead*) "where one might gaze like Osiris upon the portents of all that is ahead." He receives a message that "purity and goodness were worth less to Osiris than strength" (a restatement of Rojack's belief that "God is not love but courage"), and Meni has an abundance of it, it seems, for he is welcomed into the Boat of Ra. But then he feels a great pain coming, followed by "the scream of the earth exploding." The knowledge comes to him that his destiny is to "enter the power of the word," and to be born again as a storyteller. Ra's Boat, "washed by the swells of time," sails away and the novel ends as "past and future come together."

Mailer intended that "The Boat of Ra," the second novel of his planned trilogy, would begin with the explosion that concludes *Ancient Evenings*. In "The Last Night," his 1963 short story, a lone spaceship is propelled out beyond the sun's gravity by a series of planned nuclear detonations that destroy the earth, sending "a scream of anguish, jubilation, desperation, terror, ecstasy" across the heavens. Aboard are eighty humans and some animals seeking a new home in distant galaxies. Most of the novel, beginning with this story, would take place aboard the ship. Meni will be aboard, reincarnated in one of the survivors of earth, which has been ravaged by corruption, plagues, and wars. Humans may have been "mismated with earth," and "the beauty that first gave speech to our tongues commands us to go out and find another world," one where the power of the word will have primacy. Mailer's short story ends with "a glimpse of the spaceship, a silver minnow of light, streaming into the oceans of mystery, and the darkness beyond." A decade later in the mid-1990s, he and Norris would collaborate on several versions of a screenplay based on this story, the last attempt to salvage something of the unwritten trilogy.

The final novel of the three, "Of Modern Times," would introduce a last reincarnation of Menenhetet-Meni, now known as "Norman Mailer." After the account of his conception and early years (taken from "The Book of the First-Born"), he would grow into the writer who would write *Ancient Evenings*, thus completing the circle. Mailer saw that it would be a vainglorious mistake to lay this out when the first novel was published, to reveal that Menenhetet was a fictional forebear or that Meni would fulfill "the power of the word" aboard the spaceship. He also didn't know if he could pull it off, and as we now know, he could not.

Poirier was astute in ending his review by stating that what undergirded *Ancient Evenings* was "the desire, once and for all, to claim some ultimate spiritual and cultural status for the teller of tales, the Writer." Poirier calls it "his most audacious book." Ricks also found it to be a terrifically risky book, but endorsed Mailer's gamble by quoting a passage from T. S. Eliot about another risk taker, Harry Crosby, the sun-worshipping American writer and editor who died in a murder-suicide pact in 1929: "Of course one can 'go too far' and except in directions in which we can go too far there is no interest in going at all; and only those who will risk going too far can possibly find out just how far one can go."

Upon publication the novel jumped onto the bestseller list and stayed there for seventeen weeks before dropping off in mid-August. Without having read it, a Swedish publisher paid $100,000 for rights. It went for $120,000 in England. Other foreign editions brought in another half million. The paperback—sold to Warner for $501,000—did even better, reaching number two on the bestseller list the following spring. When income from foreign and subsidiary rights—over $750,000—is added to U.S. sales, the novel "earned out," recouped its hefty advance.

Mailer's pride was injured enough by the negative reviews for him to strike back at the novel's detractors. He assembled negative excerpts from reviews of four of his novel's major detractors and added to them ripe snippets from rotten reviews of four classic works: *Moby-Dick, Anna Karenina, Les Fleurs Du Mal*, and *Leaves of Grass*. Printed on poster board under the headline HIDEOUS REVIEWS, the assemblage was distributed to major bookstores as a counter display. A sampling: Captain Ahab is "a monstrous bore"; Tolstoy's masterpiece is "sentimental rubbish"; Baudelaire's poems are "filth and horror"; *Leaves of Grass* is "a mass of stupid filth." For *Ancient Evenings*, he selected Benjamin DeMott's pronouncement that the novel is a "disaster," followed by James Wolcott's "a muddle of incest and strange oaths . . . reducing everything to lewd, godly, bestial grunts"; Rhoda Koenig's condemnation of "the vanity that permeates the entire work"; and Eliot Fremont-Smith's summary: "holistic poop."

The novel's flaws—a tortured point of view, massive digressions, and the curtailed depiction of Menenhetet's later lives—are balanced by its strengths, most notably the heroic ethos of the early reign of Ramses II and the story of Isis regenerating Osiris, which prefigures Ramses' victory at Kadesh. Obscured by the narrative clutter is any clear sense of what critic Robert Begiebing, the novel's finest interpreter, says is Mailer's chief theme and "the deepest structural principle" of the novel: "the tragic conflict between vitality and entropy." Ramses II does not share his victory at Kadesh with his generals, builds monument after monument to his personal glory (Ramses is Ozymandias to the Greeks), and treats his comrade-at-arms, Menenhetet, shamefully. Evil begets evil.

"Ramses II," Begiebing says in summation, "fails to maintain his earlier power as an Osirian king of fertility and civilization whose lands, people, and political systems all depend on him for continuous productivity and harmony." Except for the brief final chapters, the novel ends bleakly. But *Ancient Evenings* was only the first phase of the dialectic for Mailer; Purgatorio precedes Paradiso. It seems likely that he planned to demonstrate counterpoint and resolution in the next two novels. We do know, however, that the "The Boat of Ra" would begin at the lowest point of entropy—the destruction of the planet—after which a saving remnant would re-create human life on a new planet. The final novel, "Of Modern Times," we can speculate, would depict a return to Osirian harmony and vitality.

A year after the novel appeared, Philip Bufithis sent Mailer an essay he had published praising aspects and parts of the novel, especially the opening where Mailer displays a consciousness "not met with in any other fiction. The reader is pulled into the Ka's strange cares and yearnings as it painfully orients itself to the shock of its nonmortal existence and meets the grim, awesome Ka of Menenhetet." Bufithis takes reviewers to task for deciding that *Ancient Evenings* is a study of decadence, instead of recognizing that Mailer is "inveighing against American parochialism" by writing what might be "the most olfactory novel ever written." It was "his way of assailing America's ongoing obsession with sanitizing nature out of more and more areas of life." But he finds fault with the lack of "richness, radiance, and imagination" in many of Mailer's metaphors, and sees other weaknesses, the most important of which is characterization: "Its people are insufficiently people. They are not felt presences. Their emotions, therefore, seem empty. Graphic and frequent, for example, as the novel's sexual episodes are, they remain tepid."

Given Mailer's belief in the primacy of character over plot in fiction, the essay, coming from Bob Lucid's former graduate student, must have been painful to read. He wrote back to Bufithis right away, and said that his criticism "is, I fear, all too good. I confess it's close to my own evaluation of the book when I feel depressed at all. I failed to ignite in every corner of the conception." Mailer's candor about a work that he described on publication as "the best book I've ever written" may seem extraordinary, but he was keeping faith with the pledge he made forty years earlier in his Harvard journal to probe for and admit to his sins and failures. His views shifted somewhat, however, especially after reading Begiebing's laudatory essay on the novel, published in 1989. He wrote to him to say that it was "the best thing I've read so far on that weighty tome and I was pleased at the thoroughness and insight, and—dare I say it?—the understanding you brought to it." In later years, when asked to name his best books, as he did on several occasions, *Ancient Evenings* was usually on the list, along with *The Naked and the Dead, An American Dream, The Armies of the Night, The Executioner's Song*, and *Harlot's Ghost.*

HOWEVER HAMPERED BY the first person point of view in *Ancient Evenings*, Mailer was not ready to abandon it. He used the same perspective—minus the telepathy exercised by Meni—in his next novel, *Tough Guys Don't Dance*, a murder mystery set in contemporary Provincetown. It is narrated by Tim Madden, a thirty-eight-year-old bartender with literary ambitions who spent three years in prison for selling cocaine. As Mailer explained after completing the novel, the first person was amenable because a good novel, he said, "can come out of the simplicity of an interesting, intelligent voice, full of unexpected turns and agreeable perceptions." Madden's colloquial American is welcome after the orotund locutions of Menenhetet. Conversant with literary and philosophical topics, Madden is well traveled on both sides of the tracks. He attends séances, collects coincidences, and is sensitive to the stark beauty of the Provincetown Spit, which he describes as "the fine filigree tip of the Cape [that] curls around itself like the toe of a medieval slipper." All of his senses are unsheathed, especially his olfactory abilities, which come close to matching those of Menenhetet. His vision is sharp enough to distinguish among the dozen shades of dun in the winter woods of the Cape; and his ears subtle enough to discern "the rustle along the beach that comes with the turning of the tide." He lives on the water side of Commercial Street in the quiet East End of town (near, therefore, to 627 Commercial Street, the three-story brick house Mailer rented from 1970 to 1972 and purchased in the early 1980s). The house is owned by Madden's wealthy wife, Patty Lareine, who on the "drear" November morning on which the novel opens, has been gone for twenty-four days. She has left him for a tall, powerful black man, a sexual athlete named Bolo.

Provincetown has a summer crowd of tourists, artists, college kids, a large LGBT contingent, and assorted eccentrics. It's a party town, but it also has some real history, and its colonial roots are impeccable since the Pilgrims spent three miserable weeks on the dunes near Race Point before settling in Plymouth. They made landfall on November 11, 1620, the Mailers' wedding day 360 years later. He liked to give lectures on the town's history to visiting friends, sometimes while standing before the observation window at the top of the Pilgrim Monument, a 252-foot stone tower that resembles the one at the Palazzo della Signoria in Florence. Dotson Rader recalled hearing such a lecture a few years before Mailer died.

> He climbed, I mean he literally pulled himself up the steps, and we stood on this platform that overlooks the cape. I was very excited listening to a spiel that he had given probably five hundred times to other people that had been up there. He was very proud of Provincetown. And he was going on about this thing, and he was making this point. He was making this very strong, almost angry, point, a very emphatic point that Provincetown was the first place they landed. That the whole Pilgrim story was wrong, and that somehow Provincetown had been robbed of its true place in American history. And I thought listening to him, "Norman always had gripes, but this really hits home to him." It's the first time, after all the time I knew Norman, that it suddenly occurred to me that Brooklyn wasn't really home to him emotionally anymore. Home to him was Provincetown.

The oldest art colony in the United States, Provincetown also has white gabled houses and dune shacks, a dozen fine fish-and-chowder restaurants, and a huge harbor running the length of the town. There is also a sizable community of Portuguese fishermen, many of whom Mailer had known for years and drank with in local watering holes. In the fall, as the weather changed, people stayed indoors, as Madden explains,

> with everyone gone, the town revealed its other presence. Now the population did not boil up daily from thirty thousand to sixty, but settled down to its honest sentiment, three thousand souls, and on empty weekday afternoons you might have said the true number of

> inhabitants must be thirty men and women, all hiding. There could be no other town like it. If you were sensitive to crowds, you might expire in summer from human propinquity. On the other hand, if you were unable to endure loneliness, the vessel of your person could fill with dread during the long winter.

All that remains are some year-rounders, including a clutch of burnt-out cases. One of these is Madden, who drinks alone every night at the bar of a local restaurant, the Widow's Walk. Christopher Ricks compares him to the hero-villains of Jacobean tragedy who have been "in complicity with evil. Like them he has wit and humour and courage, and a little grain of conscience keeps him sour." Distraught but not despairing, he sips bourbon, writes in his notebook, and recalls how twenty years earlier, "held in the grip of an imperative larger than myself," he tried to climb the side of the monument. Near the top, he froze and had to be rescued by the fire department. The effort buoyed his spirit, however, and he slept better afterward. "The importance of the journey must be estimated by my dread of doing it," he concludes. Risk taking is the engine of *Tough Guys Don't Dance*, which Mailer often referred to as an "entertainment."

Locked into what he calls "the dungeon of my massive self-absorption," Madden stumbles through day 24. In the early evening he returns to the Widow's Walk. There, while brooding over his decamped blond wife, he meets another blonde, Laurel Oakwode, and her escort, a bisexual lawyer named Lonnie Pangborn, in town to look at real estate. They drink, Oakwode and Madden flirt, and all three leave together. The next morning, Madden finds himself with a ferocious hangover, a splintered memory of seeing his wife the night before, another of Oakwode, an erection premised on it, and a new, crusty, tattoo on his arm—a heart enclosing "Laurel." The telephone rings and Police Chief Alvin Luther Regency, a macho Vietnam veteran who collects guns and knives, tells him to clean up the passenger seat of his car. Madden finds it covered with blood. At a meeting with Regency—who describes himself as half enforcer, half maniac—the chief suggests that he check his marijuana cache buried in a burrow in the woods of nearby Truro. He does and is terrified to find a plastic bag containing the severed head of a woman, a blonde. Unable to look at the face, he reburies it. The next time he checks, it is gone. When he checks again, there are two blond heads.

The situation at this juncture is compelling, worthy of novels by Raymond Chandler or Dashiell Hammett, which he read before beginning *Tough Guys*. Madden has many questions: Did he have sex with Oakwode? Did Pangborn, who has gone missing, kill Laurel after watching them have sex? Did Regency, who somehow knew the burrow's location, kill Laurel or both women? The darkest possibility is that Madden himself is responsible. He can't remember. As he sorts through the possibilities, he finds that his mind "is a book where pages are missing—no, worse, two books, each with its own gaps." One part of him wants to solve the crime, one doesn't.

The first person point of view works smoothly for the novel's first hundred pages, as Madden provides backstory—a tissue of coincidences—and ponders the identity of the decapitator(s). But from that point on Mailer runs into the same problem he encountered in *The Deer Park*: first person narrators can't be everywhere at once—unless they possess the clairvoyance of Meni. Because Madden was not present at many key events, Mailer was forced to use long conversations between him and several of the principal characters to get answers to his questions, along with detailed descriptions of their sexual activities. "The book is interested," Mailer said, in "the spectrum of male behavior," and hetero-, homo-, and bisexuality are explored more thoroughly in *Tough Guys* than anywhere else in his work. In an interview in 1983 Mailer said that his plots never came easy. "I have to work them out bit by bit, and eke them out." In this novel, the plot is the weakest element. The last third, he admitted, "drifts heavily and ponderously from revelation to revelation."

There was no time for meaningful revision. "I had been trying to start all year and I hadn't been able to get near it," he said. "And it was as if suddenly my mind cleared. It was one of those joke situations where they give Popeye the can of spinach. It took 61 days." With the exception of a day off to bring Michael to Harvard for his freshman year, he worked from eleven to nine every day through the late summer of 1983. During this time, his relationship with Little, Brown began to fray, and before he was done with the novel, he had severed his ties, quite amiably, with the firm he had been with for fifteen years and seven books. As he explained in one of his regular letters to Jack Abbott, Little, Brown had suggested that he find a new publisher. The arrangement "was too rich for their blood," he said, "and in more ways than one."

Scott Meredith said that Mailer felt that having a New York–based publisher (Little, Brown was in Boston) was desirable.

In early August, Mailer signed a four-novel deal with Random House, reported in the *New York Times* to be $4 million. His new editor, Jason Epstein, said, "I don't know where that figure came from, certainly not from us," and called it "Mailer's agent's advertisement for himself." But he acknowledged that Mailer could make over $3 million, all told, from the four novels—nonfiction books would require separate negotiations. The key provision of the contract, continued from Little, Brown, called for a $30,000 monthly advance against royalties. Mailer would collect it from Random House, his last publisher, for twenty-four years. When annual income from other projects—essays and screenplays, readings and lectures—was added, he would finally be able to pay his debts and support his family, although he carried sizable mortgages on his homes to the end of his life. "Money," Madden says, "was the game other people played that I tried to avoid by having just enough not to play it." The same was true for Mailer.

A few months later, Little, Brown told Mailer that they were not happy with the manuscript of *Tough Guys*. Meredith put a good face on it by issuing a statement: "We told Little, Brown we would count it a great courtesy if they would release the book so that it could be published with great fanfare instead of a swan song." Mailer said later, "I was shocked that they didn't like it," and surprised that they did not recognize its sales potential. Random House agreed to make the four-book deal a five-book deal, and the shift of publishers was complete. His new publisher advertised the book extensively, and published a first edition of 150,000 copies. The paperback edition went through at least fifteen printings.

Loyal to his clients, Meredith lent them money (at 8 percent) when they were in need. According to Jack Scovil, who worked for Meredith for decades, Mailer borrowed regularly and ran up large balances. "If you knew Scott," Scovil recalled, "and his love of money, and his hatred of letting any dime slip past his grasp, the fact that he had lent somebody $120,000, even Norman Mailer, I'm sure gave him many sleepless nights. But it all came back eventually." The two men were unfailingly loyal to each other. "They admired and respected each other," Scovil said, "and their intellectual talents. Scott was not an educated man. But nevertheless he was a very bright man, and one could even say brilliant in many aspects of his life. And he could parley with Norman quite well." Mailer said Meredith had "a supple brain."

At the time the Meredith agency had an impressive client list: P. G. Wodehouse, Margaret Truman, Garry Wills, Mickey Spillane, Spiro Agnew, Carl Sagan, and JFK's mistress Judith Campbell Exner (she received an $800,000 advance), to name a few. Mailer, Scovil explained, "was *the* prime client of the agency. There's no question about that, no question in Scott's mind. Norman was the number one client for, I think, both personal reasons but also for very pragmatic reasons as well. He was a name figure. He drew all kinds of people to the agency, simply by being there." The relationship had begun in 1963, when Mailer called Meredith on the phone.

> "I hear you're the guy who gets the money," said Mailer.
>
> "That's what I hear too," said Meredith.
>
> "Well, I need money," Mailer replied.

Meredith negotiated the lucrative deal for *An American Dream*, got Mailer out of a financial hole, and became his agent for the next thirty years. "Before Norman, Scott was a scruffy kind of agent," Scovil said, who "was looked down on by the literary establishment." After Mailer came aboard, Meredith picked up many major clients. Mailer "legitimized the agency in the eyes of the outside world," Scovil said, although he was never the agency's biggest moneymaker.

Part salesman, part banker and part counselor, Meredith bailed them out of jail and listened to their marital problems, but he did not spend much time reading their work. He left that to his able associates, Scovil and Russell Galen, who, after Meredith's death in 1993, started their own agency. They wrote detailed reports for Scott's meetings with Mailer. "To the best of my knowledge," Scovil said,

> Scott Meredith never read a word that Norman wrote. And I don't think Norman ever knew that, of course. The reason for the reports was to enable Scott to have his meeting, his dinner, there were always "dinner meetings" after a manuscript was delivered. I don't think Norman was actually expecting any criticism in the sense of "should I change this," or "should I change that," I don't think there was any question of that. But he did want to know what Scott's

> reaction was and Scott's reaction was based on how we were telling him to react. For the most part, if I remember correctly, the reports were quite lavish and laudatory.

Various people complained to Mailer about Meredith over the years, but their strong bond persisted. *Tough Guys Don't Dance* is dedicated to him.

Reviews of the novel were somewhat better than for *Ancient Evenings*, and it reached number four on the bestseller list, his third book in five years to make it. Singled out for praise in even some of the unfavorable reviews was Madden's father, Dougy, another in the long line of male mentor figures in Mailer's fiction. Madden senior arrives in Provincetown the morning after his son has retrieved the heads from the Truro burrow. In his prime, a large, strong man (six foot three, 280 pounds), he is now weak from chemotherapy and, disgusted with the nausea that accompanies the treatment, has decided to give it up. Bourbon is his new medicine. Tim Madden is half Irish, one quarter Jewish, and one quarter Protestant, a "sensitive Irishman." But his father is a "pure ethnic," Mailer said, "I wanted him to be a real Irishman marked by that special kind of probity that they can possess, along with powerful, murderous emotions."

During another gray P-town day, father and son pass the bottle and discuss cancer, courage, and the disposal of body parts. Statistics, Dougy says, indicate that people in mental institutions get cancer at a much lower rate than the general population. "I figure it this way," he says, passing on one of Mailer's favorite dualisms, "cancer is the cure for schizophrenia. Schizophrenia is the cure for cancer." But he discovers another cure: dirty jobs. The more horrible, the better. Dougy secures baling wire to an anchor, ties it to spikes he has driven through the eye sockets of the two heads he retrieved from the woods, and plummets them some fathoms down. Later, he gives sea burials to the bodies of the two women, as well as others, among them Regency, who is killed after he has a mental breakdown and a stroke. "Crazy people in serious places had to be executed," Madden says. A short time later, Dougy reaps the homeopathic benefit of his grisly work when his cancer goes into remission. "Maybe I was in the wrong occupation all this time," he tells his son.

The mayhem is hugger-mugger, very much as in Jacobean revenge tragedy, and motives are moot. Greed, blood, and terror engulf everyone, save the Maddens. Everyone is guilty to some degree. The last chapter of the novel tries and fails to explain how so many people could have disappeared without repercussions of any sort. What makes *Tough Guys Don't Dance* worth reading is not the tangled plot nor the missing links between motivation and deed, but Mailer's horrid crew of miscreants, who are as lovingly and convincingly drawn as any in his novels. The other quality that lifts the novel above its flaws is the tense, melancholy mood created by Tim Madden. The objective correlative for the damp, drizzly November in his soul is the half-deserted, haunted town at the edge of America, the place Mailer loved more than any other.

ABOUT SIX WEEKS before his concentrated effort on *Tough Guys*, Mailer completed an adaptation of Henry Miller's trilogy *Sexus, Nexus, Plexus*, known as *The Rosy Crucifixion*. The opportunity to write his third screenplay came from a young editor at *The Village Voice*, Rudy Langlais. He wanted to use Miller's masterwork as the basis for "the first classy X-rated Hollywood film." After he read *Genius and Lust*, he knew that Mailer was the screenwriter he wanted. Langlais pitched Mailer the story of Miller's profound love for his second wife, June Edith Smith (Mona in the novel), and her affair with Anastasia, who lived with them for a time: "Boy meets girl, boy loses girl to girl, boy gets girl back." Mailer was enthusiastic and went to work. Langlais, a novice in the film world, began the search for funding, and eventually gained the support of the head of Twentieth Century-Fox films, Joe Wizan. Mailer was paid $250,000.

After he finished the screenplay, he sent it to Langlais, who found that Mailer had followed the story line they had agreed on, but had added a framing character: "Old Henry," Miller as an eighty-year-old codger, who breaks into the action to make observations about himself as a younger man, played by a second actor. Mailer's desire for narrative provenance was again in play. Langlais felt that "Old Henry" was unnecessary, and with some trepidation began a cut-and-paste operation. He took the edited version to Mailer's Brooklyn apartment when he was done, but Mailer didn't want to read it. He wanted to drink, and they proceeded to put away several bottles of Frenesi, the white wine Mailer was currently favoring, as they discussed the affairs of the universe. Langlais left as the sun was coming up. Later that day, Mailer called him up, and said: "How dare you, how *dare* you . . . be right!"

Before this occurred, however, the studio executives insisted that Mailer come to Los Angeles to close the deal. Langlais picked him up at the airport, and while driving him to the hotel told him how much he had enjoyed *The Fight*, especially the description of Mailer climbing from one seventh floor balcony to another at his hotel in Kinshasa. When they walked into Mailer's room on the fifteenth floor of the Century Plaza Hotel, a stunned Langlais watched as he climbed to the railing of the balcony, and said, "I know what you're thinking: 'There goes my movie deal.' " Relief and laughter followed when Mailer climbed down.

The next day—April Fool's Day 1983—they met with Wizan and a squadron of VPs eager to meet Mailer, who came in feinting and jabbing. The executives were pleased. As they were leaving, one of them said he was so happy that a film would be made about Arthur Miller and his wife, Marilyn Monroe. Henry Miller was unknown to them, and they obviously had not read *The Rosy Crucifixion*. Like so many film projects, it slowly collapsed over the next year. It remains on the shelf at the studio. Langlais remained a good friend and later brokered another screenplay deal for him with Universal Studios—"Havana," the story of Meyer Lansky running racetracks and casinos for Cuban dictator Fulgencio Batista in the 1940s and 1950s. It also remains unproduced.

MAILER OFTEN SENT the manuscripts of friends to Meredith. He also used him to funnel money to people. Sometime in the mid-1980s, Mailer asked him to send money to a new mistress, Carole Mallory, a former cover model for major magazines like *New York* and *Cosmopolitan* who also had small roles in a few films in the 1970s, including *Take This Job and Shove It*. A large poster (which she gave Mailer) for this film, depicting a curvaceous Mallory in a bikini bottom and torn, scanty T-shirt, rivaled sales of Farrah Fawcett's famous swimsuit poster. Jack Scovil, who handled the transfer of funds, said that he was "surprised that Norman would get involved with someone like that," referring to Mallory's reputation as a star seducer. In several interviews, numerous gossip column snippets, and a 2009 memoir, Mallory lists the men that she had "picked up," including Clint Eastwood, Robert De Niro, Warren Beatty, Richard Gere, Sean Connery, Anthony Hopkins, Peter Sellers—she said Brits were "more fun than the Americans"—and Dodi Fayed, the Egyptian playboy who died in the car crash with Princess Diana. Plus a few rock stars. She was also engaged to Picasso's son Claude during the 1970s—he jilted her—and claims to have turned down propositions from Albert Finney and Jack Nicholson.

Buzz Farbar had introduced Mallory to Mailer at Elaine's. A few weeks later, in January 1984, she read that he would be speaking at a showing of his films at the Thalia Theater in Manhattan. When the event was over, she slipped him a note asking to meet the following day at a coffee shop. She wanted to get his opinion of a memoir of her years with Claude Picasso. They met, he read some of the manuscript—a chapter describing her night with Beatty—and she left some lipstick on his face as well as her telephone number in Los Angeles. That summer, when he was in Los Angeles doing publicity for *Tough Guys Don't Dance*, they had their first tryst at the Bel Air Hotel. Soon, she was seeing him when he was in L.A. and was in love. She loved his fame, his wit, his sexual equipment, his detailed writing advice. "I longed for an affair with a genius," she said. During their time together, she said, "I noticed that he used words like oxymoron, swath, and sententious. Hearing him speak was an education." She also loved the money he gave her. But at one point, her $200-a-week stipend ceased, as Scovil recalled.

> Scott would never authorize giving Carole money unless Norman had authorized it. And there was a point where Norman wanted to cut her off and Carole had come up to the office and caused a great scene. She was crying and she was screaming and she was doing all kinds of things, saying all kinds of things, and that she deserved the money.

Another way of helping Mallory financially was to give her interviews, which he did on several occasions. Through him, she also met other writers and celebrities. Joseph Heller, Erica Jong, Isabella Rossellini, and Kurt Vonnegut are some of the interviewees she mentions in her memoir. One of her interviews with Mailer included Vidal, and was the cover feature in the May 1991 *Esquire* (he and Mailer had made up by this time), but Mailer said it was a weak piece, even after he had tweaked it. He edited her interviews with him before they were published, with the exception of the last two, which she refused, in the name of honesty, she said, to let him review or change. Mallory was unaware that some famous people insisted on the right to do this. She believed that it was "his way of hiding the truth." By revising his comments, she said, "he controlled his image for history." Norris eventually learned about Mallory, who was not timid about showing up at Mailer events, but the affair was fairly quiet until Mallory moved to New York.

Among Mailer's close friends, the affair caused consternation, but he waved off every warning. The relationship was based on passion, according to Mailer's lawyer, Ivan Fisher. "It was a huge part of his being. And a huge part of his passion was sex. And his relationship with Mallory was 100 percent sexual. Period. There wasn't the teeniest, tiniest nanogram of anything other than sex involved there. If you are looking for an idea, read her book . . . *Flash*, yes. And you'll know exactly what this affair was about. It wound up causing [Norris] enormous pain." *Flash* is Mallory's 1988 novel about an alcoholic, sexaholic, drug-abusing female flasher. "Mallory packs her story with down-and-dirty sexual details," said one reviewer. Mailer gave it a blurb, as did Gloria Steinem. By the time the book was published, Norris realized that Mallory, unlike Mailer's other mistresses, lacked discretion, but not determination. She wanted to become the seventh Mrs. Mailer. The protagonist of her novel is trying, after an affair with a French millionaire, to win a major role in a film via the casting couch. Her true passion, however, is for Sacha Sachtel, a sixty-year-old producer, the "King of Kink," modeled on Mailer.

Gay Talese, who knew Mallory from Elaine's, recalls being at a literary event in the late 1980s where he was approached by Norris. "Mailer was somewhere [else], I don't know, but it was a big event, maybe something for PEN," he recalled. "Anyway, she came to me and said, 'I'm going to leave Norman.' And I said, 'Why?' 'Because he's fucking around,' she said. 'He's having affairs.' I'm surprised because I thought it was still a relatively new marriage. She was quite gorgeous. I knew he was having affairs, but I said, 'You know, you shouldn't do that. With Mailer, it's just a little adventure, none of them means anything.'

She was pretty pissed off." She was not angry enough to leave him, however.

Barbara met Mallory through her brother. "He sicced her on me when I was working at Simon and Schuster," she recalled. "I didn't ask any questions, but I guessed he was trying to buy her off because she presented me with a couple of manuscripts which were just ghastly." She realized that there was nothing she could do with Mallory's work. "I wished I could because I figured this would be one way to help him—one of the manuscripts was about all the men she had slept with. Norman was not in it. I figured maybe he had asked her to keep him out of it." When asked about her motives in 2006, Mailer said, "She was totally on the make." Fisher's interpretation notwithstanding, Mailer had more than one reason for continuing his relationship.

In a 1973 interview with Buzz Farbar, Mailer described the four stages of knowing a woman.

> First, there's living together. It's often thought equal to marriage. Not by half. You can live with a woman and never begin to comprehend her at all, not until you get married to her. Once you do that, you're in the next stage. The third, obviously, is children. Once again your woman is different. Say it's analogous to a culture going through major transformations. The fourth stage is knowing a woman once you're divorced. Then, indeed, you come to know something at last. So if it weren't for the fact that there are children, there would be something agreeable about moving from marriage to marriage, just as there is something exciting about spending five years in England and five in France. But there are children, and that's the vortex of all postmarital pain, which is always so surprisingly huge. Because finally the children come out of a vision in the marriage.

He does not mention the stage of a relationship that precedes living together: an affair. Besides Mallory, he was still seeing Carol Stevens, and whenever he visited Chicago, Eileen Fredrickson. He called her regularly. When he was on the West Coast, he rarely failed to spend time with Lois Wilson. They had a long correspondence. With these very different women, he never felt beleaguered and enjoyed friendship, sexual intimacy, dining out, and conversation. No strings. There were other affairs, but these were the most important.

One way to understand Mailer's relationship with Carole Mallory is to see it as part of his lust for experience, which he once defined as "the church—if the word may be allowed—of one's acquired knowledge." Experience was holy. His sister remembers him telling her, in so many words, that "experience was more valuable when you felt that you could, you know, turn it into art. Otherwise, there wasn't much point to it." Women were of inexhaustible interest to him—mysterious, dangerous, of infinite variety. Mallory was unlike anyone he had known before. He was fascinated by her crassness and amazed by her promiscuity, which seemed to match his own. There was so much to learn. When he was asked by *Cosmopolitan* his opinion of a woman if "she sleeps with you too soon," he replied: "No woman has ever slept with me too soon. I don't pretend I'm typical, but I've always found promiscuous women interesting. I suspect I would have been promiscuous if I'd been a woman. I certainly have been as a man. So I don't make judgments. The faster a woman would sleep with me, the more I liked her."

Mallory says that she was in love with him and not merely interested in what he could do for her. Perhaps she was. She knew him but superficially, however. Convinced that he was an alcoholic, she took him to one of her AA meetings. He went out of curiosity. He invited her to see a gay porn movie, and she took this as evidence that he was bisexual. Mailer once took Norris to such a film at the Adonis Theater in Manhattan, a well-known gay porn outlet. When the woman selling tickets said to Norris, "Honey, do you know what kind of shows we have here?" Norris, said, "Yes, ma'am, I certainly do." Dotson Rader was in the balcony when the Mailers came in, and was astounded to see them. He recalled his conversation with Mailer about gay sex.

> When I was very, very young and in New York I knew people like Parker Tyler and Glenway Wescott, Ginsberg and Auden. They were all gay guys older than me.... One of the things I was continuously warned about, by Tennessee and others, was homophobia. Norman was on the list. I was warned that he was homophobic. I knew Norman quite well and I never had a sense of that, quite the opposite. I feel he was fascinated, intrigued, by homosexuals and homosexuality. He would go into the very specific, raunchy details, and to me

> very embarrassing details, about exactly what physically you did as a gay person. And he wanted the moist specifics about the encounter. Sometimes I provided them, sometimes I would get my back up and say this is too much.

As Mailer explained more than once, when he had two motives, good and bad, for doing something, he felt a surge of energy. He attributed this to God and the Devil, or their minions, who, for their own reasons, agreed on the desirability of the action. He was not singled out for these nudges; he believed that all humans received them, often unknowingly. Later on, he would feel guilt or even self-loathing, but this did not negate his choice, not entirely. Much depended on the results, the fruits, of the action. He told Mike Lennon that he learned something about venality from Mallory and used it in the creation of Chloe, the sexy waitress in the opening chapters of *Harlot's Ghost*. "But," as he told Farbar, "the idea that people can be promiscuous without exploiting their own sensitivity is impossible." Promiscuity is a trade-off, and while you might gain knowledge, you also "take in waste from the other person's system." He continued, saying, "You pay for every last thing you get out of life."

> Years ago, Calder Willingham told me a story about a situation where he tried every trick to make a woman leave him. Finally she began going with another man. Then he discovered he was jealous. He told this story on himself with great humor, and looked at me and said, "Norman, you can't cheat life." He said this in his inimitable Georgia accent. It's not a remark one hasn't heard before. But there's such a thing as hearing a maxim at just the right moment for oneself. Then it goes all the way in. So that remark stayed with me. Whenever I'm trying to work out some sort of moral balance for myself, I find the thought useful.

Mailer found some kind of moral balance in regard to Mallory, enough to continue with her for almost eight years. Like Faust, he was greedy for knowledge and ready to trade punishment to gain it. "The more prohibited the act, the greater the lure for Mailer," according to Rader. "He wanted to know everything."

IN EARLY 1984 Mailer went alone to Russia on a *Parade* assignment, traveling there for two weeks in mid-March. He went first to Lithuania, and traveled by train from Kaunas to Vilnius, not far from the towns where his parents were born almost a century earlier. From there he traveled to Leningrad and Moscow. Everywhere he went, he saw the vestiges of World War II's destruction. Buildings were crumbling, the people looked battered. "It's a sad place," he wrote in the *Parade* piece, "A Country, Not a Scenario." "I felt as if I were back on the Lower East Side of New York 100 years ago. I could have been watching my grandparents walking by."

Schiller, who was in Russia filming *Peter the Great*, opened some doors for Mailer in Moscow. Mailer wanted to be relatively anonymous, so Schiller got him a room in the massive Rossiya Hotel, near Red Square. His tiny room had a sink and toilet but no bath or shower. Hot water was unreliable. The toilet paper was cut-up newspaper. With the aid of a bottle of vodka, Mailer persisted for three days, but when he could no longer endure the bad food, sandpaper towels, and rock-like soap, he called Schiller. "Get me out of here." Schiller got him into the majestic National Hotel, overlooking the Kremlin. Built in 1903, the hotel hosted Russian royalty as well as famous artists. What impressed Mailer was that its guests had included Trotsky, Lenin, and Felix Dzerzhinsky, the first head of the Russian secret police. In his year of study under Malaquais, Mailer had learned of the critical role played by Dzerzhinsky's organization, the Cheka, forerunner of the KGB. He would later write about Dzerzhinsky, an "evil artist" of counterespionage. Schiller got him booked into Room 107, where Lenin had stayed.

Mailer spent most of his time discovering the capital on his own, but Schiller introduced him to Vladimir Posner, the son of a Russian spy and a spokesperson for the Soviet Union in the 1980s. He also met Genrikh Borovik, a former KGB agent and journalist, who spent many years in the United States as head of Russian news agencies and wrote a book on Soviet double agent Kim Philby. Through them, Mailer met a number of Soviet intelligence figures who explained the structure and operation of the country's competing spy agencies. The *Parade* essay contains his initial observations on the KGB and the surveillance of citizens. Russia was much less of a police state than he expected, and he walked around Moscow unimpeded for several hours every day for a week. He met dissidents and questioned them about the reign of terror under the previous regimes. Glasnost, the open and frank discussion of the past, was about to commence under Mikhail Gorbachev, who became general secretary of the Communist Party in 1985. In June, he returned to Russia, this time with Norris, and they spent three weeks touring.

In a letter to Abbott after they returned, Mailer said that he was "lying around and thinking, wondering whether a new book is starting in me." That summer in Provincetown he did no writing. He gave interviews for *Tough Guys Don't Dance*, spent time with his children, swam, relaxed, and spent a month deciding what he would write next. He told a reporter that he had narrowed the field to three possibilities. "The Boat of Ra," promised to Random House, was the first. Learning enough science to make the intergalactic voyage of a spaceship credible worried him, however. He felt that an understanding of astrophysics, a fast-changing and complex field, would be essential, but giving some realistic notion of traveling at the speed of light would be a challenge.

The second novel he was considering was "The Castle in the Forest." It opens in 1945 when a U.S. Army unit arrives at a German castle used as a concentration camp. "The leading characters," according to Scott Meredith, "are an American Jewish doctor and a German doctor who confront each other and clash over contending philosophies." In 1954, Mailer had made a false start on this novel, which he then called "The City of God." The third possibility was a CIA novel. The Russian trips and the end to the Cold War influenced his decision, as did his 1973 essay on Watergate, "A Harlot High and Low." His continuing obsession with the assassination of JFK played a part, as well as his own opposed identities: family man and philanderer, Left-conservative, activist and observer, rationalist and transcendentalist, to name the most important. All these coalesced in his decision to embark on a huge circumambient novel of the Cold War and the bifurcated lives of spies. His title, *Harlot's Ghost*, came later.

In July, he appeared at the tenth anniversary celebration of the Naropa Institute in Boulder, Colorado, a Buddhist-inspired educational center. He was invited by Allen Ginsberg, one of the founders, to appear with William Burroughs. A few months earlier Mailer had sent a contribution to a *Festschrift* for the poet's sixtieth birthday.

> Years ago I wrote a poem about Allen which went something like—I quote from memory—
>
> Sometimes I think, "That ugly kike,
> That four-eyed faggot,
> Is the bravest man in America."
>
> Well, over the years, Allen's gotten considerably better looking and has doubtless earned that most curious position of being a major and near to elder statesman in homosexual ranks and his poetry, bless it, goes on forever.

Mailer and Ginsberg had become close when both of them were on the antiwar ramparts, but their friendship had begun tentatively. "Ginsberg and I met in a strange way," Mailer said. "Like scientists who are each working on the same problem—far apart in every other way." But now, he continued, "I have a lot of respect for him. He is truly one of the few honorable men I have known in the literary world." He also respected Burroughs, whom he called "the shyest man in the world." They did not have a close relationship, however. After Burroughs's death in 1997, Mailer said that he had spent perhaps the equivalent of six evenings with Burroughs, all told. At Naropa, the three men took part in a discussion titled "American Soul? What Is It?" Mailer had warm memories of the session: "We had the damnedest time out in Colorado," he said. "Being on with Burroughs is like being with W. C. Fields. He is one of the funniest men alive. He can say, 'It is eighty degrees today in Kansas,' and the audience is wiped out." He added that he still admired *Naked Lunch*.

Shortly after returning from Colorado, he went to a meeting of the American chapter of PEN, the international association of writers. He had served on the organization's executive board from 1968 to 1973. On July 25, he was elected president for a two-year term, and would preside over the 1986 International Congress in New York. "I always wanted to be president of something," Mailer said. For the next eighteen months, he would help plan the world congress, mostly by raising the money to underwrite it.

THE PEN PRESIDENCY forced Mailer to shelve his writing projects so that he could preside over committee meetings, twist the arms of potential givers, give speeches, and deal with media. One reason he accepted the job was that "men like myself in small towns who've been reprobates all their lives go into church work" when they reach sixty. After several years of monkish work, Mailer looked forward to the interactions that went along with the presidency.

Just as he was beginning his PEN presidency he was elected to the American Academy and National Institute of Arts and Letters, a group of 250 distinguished creators in literature, music, art, and architecture. He was installed on December 7, taking the seat of Tennessee Williams, who had recently died. He said he was glad to have Williams's seat and hoped some of his talent would rub off. Coming on the heels of his election as PEN president, the honor was recognition of his status as "one of the giants—if at times a wounded giant—of our age," as Arthur Schlesinger said in the official academy citation. He began it by noting that Mailer had "a career of living dangerously." There would be more risk taking over the remaining twenty-three years of his life. Now, however, Mailer was on the brink of becoming a senior citizen. His knees were sore, his breath getting short. He said that during his first trip to Russia, while crossing Red Square, he saw that everyone was passing him, yet he was walking as fast as he could.

His oldest children—Susan, Danielle, Betsy, and Kate—had all finished college, Michael was a sophomore and Stephen was in prep school; Maggie and Matt were in high school, and John Buffalo, the youngest, was in first grade. For the first time in twenty years, there were no babies crawling around the floor of 142 Columbia Heights—except when the grandchildren from Chile were visiting. Susan and Marco had their second child, Alejandro, in 1985. Norris now had more time and was doing a lot of painting, including several commissioned portraits. She had several shows, including her first in Little Rock. She introduced Mailer to Hillary and Bill Clinton—now governor of Arkansas—and they got a private tour of the governor's mansion. Dotson Rader and Pat Kennedy Lawford flew in for Norris's show and like everyone else were impressed when the Clintons attended the reception at the gallery. Lawford and Mailer saw Clinton as a potential presidential candidate. Hillary also impressed him. Later, he said, "That might be the brightest woman I ever met."

Through the spring of 1985, he worked on fundraising for the January 1986 PEN congress. Over two hundred distinguished writers from eighty-five countries were invited, plus eight hundred writers from the United States. Paying for the expenses of the foreign writers was the largest item on the budget. Mailer came up with the idea for a series of readings to be held in the fall of 1985, two writers a week at a Broadway theater that was dark on Sunday evenings. A series ticket would sell for $1,000, and if 1,000 people subscribed, the gross would be $1 million. Even after expenses, the budget for the congress would be covered. Selecting and pairing the writers, all from the United States, would require diplomatic skills of a high order. Mailer began writing letters and making calls.

There was no way not to include Gore Vidal, whose literary reputation was at its peak. His masterful novel *Lincoln*, the second volume of a heptalogy covering American history from the founding of the republic through the 1950s, was a bestseller for the latter half of 1984. Mailer had not seen Vidal since their fight at Lally Weymouth's party seven years earlier and knew that inviting him would require a sensitive rapprochement. Instead of making direct contact, he asked Mickey Knox to speak with him during one of Vidal's visits to Rome from his home in Rapallo. Find out, he told Knox, "whether his hatred for me is still essentially one of his first passions." Mailer now shared an editor, Jason Epstein, with Vidal, and Mailer thought Epstein "for his own self-interest, if nothing other, would like the feud to end." He asked him to float the idea to Vidal about appearing at one of the fundraisers. A month later, Mailer wrote to Vidal. "Our feud, whatever its roots for each of us, has become a luxury," he said. "It's possible in years to come that we'll both have to be manning the same sinking boat at the same time. Apart from that, I'd still like to make up. An element in me, absolutely immune to weather and tides, runs independently fond of you." Mailer gave him the roster of eleven writers who had already agreed to appear: Joan Didion, Susan Sontag, Kurt Vonnegut, William Styron, John Updike, I. B. Singer, John Irving, William F. Buckley, Tom Wolfe, Arthur Miller, and himself. He offered Vidal a solo night, or a joint appearance. Vidal accepted.

Next he turned to the notoriously prickly Saul Bellow. Mailer's sharp criticisms of his work had not been forgotten, as he had learned the last time he had seen him in 1975. Bob Cromie was interviewing them, back to back, on his Chicago radio show and raved to Mailer about

Bellow's new novel, *Humboldt's Gift*. Mailer recalled how he had tried to compliment the immaculately dressed Bellow when he bumped into him in the hallway. "Well, Saul," he said, "I hear you've written a terrific novel." Bellow looked up and down at the rumpled Mailer, paused two beats, and said, "Well, Norman, why not?" Then he strode off, Mailer said, "looking like an Italian count." Mailer wrote to Bellow about the purposes of the upcoming congress, and offered him a solo evening if he preferred. Bellow wrote back to say that the invitation, and the urging of Vonnegut, had made him decide, reluctantly, to give a reading, even though he was "not strong on civility." Mailer was pleased, as he wrote back to Bellow, but because of theater costs he could no longer give him an evening to himself. Four more writers had been added—Woody Allen, Alice Walker, Vidal, and Eudora Welty—and "I shudder to think of the matchmaking maneuvers that will ensue, but rush to offer you, esteemed colleague, your private pick of stablemate" from the list of fifteen.

Mailer gave Vidal the same perk of choosing his partner. Vidal had told him that he didn't think the audience would like what he had to say. Mailer replied, "Fine. Be lugubrious, be scalding and appalling, be larger than Jeremiah." He also gave him a choice of dates, and Vidal selected November 17, and for a partner, Mailer. The "PEN Celebrations" would take place on eight Sunday evenings from September 22 to December 15, 1985. Bellow and Welty would open, Allen and Updike would close, and Mailer and Vidal would appear in the middle. The sixteen writers were, arguably, the most impressive assemblage of literary talent ever gathered in the United States. Mailer did not pull it off singlehandedly; many others were involved—Sontag, Styron, Talese, and Vonnegut, in particular—but Mailer did have good enough relations with most of the roster, save Arthur Miller (still unhappy with him about *Marilyn*), Welty, and Walker (neither of whom he knew), to get everyone he wanted. He said that the pressure to raise $500,000 over the next year left him feeling "brusque and jagged."

He had continued writing to Abbott and encouraged several people to write to him, including Malaquais. Abbott didn't like Mailer's recent books and wrote him a ten-page letter, which ended, "Do you want to end our friendship?" It was clearly falling apart, as was Abbott's relationship with Malaquais. In Mailer's reply he said that Abbott, like

Malaquais, didn't like to lose an argument. "I would just as soon lose a discussion as win it," Mailer said, because

> it's the ones you lose that teach you more, and change your ideas, and I don't like living with the same idea too long because it gives me the feeling I'm inhabiting a subway. Anyway, I did my best to ponder it more and more, and finally could come to only one conclusion: guys who hate to lose arguments as much as you and Jean Malaquais must have some deep, unconscious conviction that their karma will be permanently altered if they do. Jack, if anyone wants to end our friendship it's you. That's your right. You can end it anytime you want. But don't put the onus on me.

It must be added that few individuals who argued with Mailer felt that he welcomed rejoinders. Sometimes he did; sometimes he sought them, but he could also be immodestly self-assured and dismissive. Endlessly curious, he was also terribly opinionated. Susan, his eldest, commented on this trait a few years after he died.

> If I had a problem and needed to talk to Dad about anything personal he was always ready to listen and on many occasions surprised me with his insights. But if we happened to discuss say, politics, religion or psychoanalysis, it was tough because he easily got impatient. I don't think he was really interested in what I had to say; he wanted to talk and be heard. Many times I didn't agree with him, but he expressed himself with such force my voice usually got lost along the way. Once in a while I'd surprise him with a fast rejoinder or a smart-ass remark, but usually our conversations turned into lengthy monologues. He had the same attitude with all my siblings. I'd watch him with his friends, with Norris; same thing. So I lost interest and I'm very sorry about this. If you ask me what I regret, I'd say the lost opportunities are close to the top of my list.

If Mailer could hear these words, he might respond by saying he came on strong with his children and friends to keep the dialectic supple, to encourage a strong response. "It's through opposition that creative possibilities rise," he maintained. A tension between being open-minded and being overbearing was characteristic of Mailer from his mid- to late thirties and on. He knew it, and explained it in a letter to a writer friend, Peter Arthurs.

> We're all divided between the moralists in ourselves and the novelist. The moralist is full of platitudes and mother's milk, always telling others how to live. The novelist, who always has an eye like a pair of tweezers, never fails to pick up a detail. The novelist is amoral, witty, private, and there to be followed in each of us. What I mean is if one relaxes the moral, authoritative side of one's nature and gets over the idea that one has to say something with one's novel, and merely allows one's characters to take their turns, and is, indeed, even surprised by the turns these characters take, as if they do in some fashion have life of their own, then marvelous things can come out of it.

During 1985, Mailer's correspondence burgeoned, as it usually did when he was not writing on deadline. He kept up with all his regular correspondents—Abbott, Stratton, Knox, Don Carpenter (west coast friend), Farbar (like Stratton, still incarcerated), and another writer, Bruce Dexter, as well as to people unknown to him who wrote with questions. To the editor of *The American Spectator*, R. Emmett Tyrrell, who had inquired about his current reading, Mailer said that John Cheever's collected stories was "the discovery" of the year, and that he regretted that he had never had a good discussion with him when he was alive—Cheever died in 1982. The other book he named was M. R. James's *Ghost Stories of an Antiquary.* He made no comment on it, but it clearly influenced the opening of *Harlot's Ghost*, which he would soon begin. In his letter to Dexter, he repeated something that he had announced to friends more than once: "I am a phenomenon to myself." He told Dexter that "no one to my knowledge has ever had the same apercu about me that you had." Dexter had seen clearly that

> I always was my own experiment, and that is such a simple way to live, and no one could ever comprehend it. I don't even think it took great guts, just my intense scientific curiosity about one's subject, myself and the bizarre phenomenon of myself. At any rate, those years are behind me now. I'm tempted to say alas. Once you lose the power to experiment on yourself, you lose half your ideas as well.

FAN MAILER, NOW in her nineties and failing, spent the summer of 1985 with her family. Barbara and Al were renting an apartment in Provincetown, and all of the children came to town as well. Fan spent most of her time in bed in the front bedroom overlooking Commercial Street. The local tour bus came by daily and Fan could hear the driver pointing out "the home of the famous writer Norman Mailer." Norris recalled that she and all five of Mailer's daughters, as well as Barbara, took turns sitting by her bed to keep her company. A woman named Eva, hired by the family, was almost always there. In late August, Fan and Eva were back in Brooklyn. When Barbara visited, she was disturbed when she saw that Fan was having difficulty swallowing. "The motor of the family," as Mailer called her, was shutting down. On August 28, Susan's birthday, Fan died. Eva called Provincetown. Mailer was out for a swim when the call came. Stephen recalled that he and Michael swam out to where their father was snorkeling to give him the news. "The three of us then, solemnly, walked back to the house with weighty, unspoken remorse." Fan was buried in the family plot in Long Branch next to Barney. Born (probably) the same year, 1891, she outlived him by almost thirteen years.

In a letter to Stratton, Mailer told him how at the end his mother "could no longer see, she could barely walk, she was bent over from arthritis, the forefront of her memory was gone, so that conversations with her consisted of her asking you the time, like clockwork, every twelve and a half seconds." But she was still feisty on occasion.

> Once, maybe a month before the end, she was complaining to her companion, a Jamaican lady [Eva] who took care of her, about how miserable she felt, and said, "I just wish I was dead," whereupon the Jamaican lady, who was probably fed up with her—she was not the world's greatest fun to take care of—said to her, "Would you like me to help you?" At that point, my mother drew herself up as well as she could with her bent back, and glaring at the woman with her sightless eyes said, "Drop dead." That was my mom.

The fall of the year was given over to fundraising and arrangements for the eight PEN Celebrations. Richard Snyder, the head of Simon &

Schuster, Tina Brown, editor of *Vanity Fair*, Gay Talese, and "takeover baron" Saul Steinberg and his wife, Gayfryd, were some of the key people who worked with Mailer to secure contributions from publishers and philanthropists for the congress. Talese was instrumental in convincing Donald Trump to donate two hundred hotel rooms for visiting writers. Added to the income from the PEN Celebrations, the total from major givers was more than sufficient to meet the budget. Talese, who headed the planning committee for the congress, said that without Mailer "and his fund-raising efforts, we would not be having an international congress." His eagerly anticipated evening with Vidal on November 17 drew a sell-out crowd, but the event was a dud. Both men criticized American imperial ambitions but with no special insights or revealing disagreements. Mailer's sister recalled that Vidal was the better speaker that night. Before introducing Allen and Updike at the final Sunday event in December, Mailer apologized for his appearance with Vidal, calling it "a meeting of two toothless tigers." As best he could during this hectic period, Mailer kept working on the new novel, and by the end of 1985 had four hundred pages of manuscript that he was describing to friends as "a spy novel."

In the midst of the PEN events, he learned from his doctor, as he told his boxing friend, Jeffrey Michelson, in early October, "I don't have a bad heart, but I don't have a good one either." Boxing was over for him he said, because of his wind. "It got to be sheer, simple hell just to get through a round," he said. "My chest used to feel like it was going to explode." He said he planned to eat a more healthy diet and asked Michelson to keep his condition confidential.

The news about his health came about the same time that he was selected by *McCall's* magazine as one of the ten sexiest American men over sixty, along with Paul Newman, Cary Grant, Joe DiMaggio, and President Reagan. Meredith was asked for comment on Mailer and declined. When told, Mailer said that he would have given a quote: "At long last, love." He told Knox, "It's all such marvelous crap." Confirming his confused status in the public eye, a few months later the Feminist Writers' Guild made him the "Guest of Dishonor" at their ninth annual meeting, where those present played a game called "Pin the tail on Norman Mailer," a protest against "his antifeminist writings." Mailer had no comment. He received one other award, on November 20, the Lord & Taylor Rose Award made annually to "a person of public accomplishment." Previous recipients included Lillian Hellman, Walter Cronkite, and Ella Fitzgerald. Michael Mailer was the master of ceremonies, and Liz Smith, Plimpton, Buckley, and Milos Forman spoke. Mailer was among friends. When he got to the lectern, he said just that morning he had been talking to his wife about the award. "I said to her how nice it was that Lord & Taylor is honoring me on my 60th birthday. She smiled at me and said, 'You're 62 and it's not your birthday.' "

THE 48TH INTERNATIONAL PEN Congress opened on January 12, 1986, at the New York Public Library with welcoming remarks by Secretary of State George Shultz. The majority of the conferees from both the United States and foreign countries were left-leaning and Shultz was not received warmly, even though he condemned censorship. Mailer had invited him at the suggestion of John Kenneth Galbraith, but without consulting the Executive Board—a blunder that he later apologized for—and there was significant opposition, given the unpopularity of the Reagan administration among liberals. Mailer said he thought it was appropriate to have the nation's top diplomat welcome the international delegates. E. L. Doctorow wrote an op-ed piece saying that Mailer's action had put PEN "at the feet of the most ideologically right-wing Administration this country has seen," and sixty-five of the seven-hundred-plus delegates signed a petition opposing it. Things improved slightly after the opening day furor, but the sour mood never dissipated. One commentator described the conference as "a week of petitions and statements and strategy meetings, of walkouts and protests and confrontations." Aesthetics withered in the ideological heat.

The theme of the conference, the brainchild of novelist Donald Barthelme and poet and translator Richard Howard, was "The Imagination of the State," intended to generate a discussion of two kinds of imagination, artistic and governmental. But many argued that states don't have imaginations, just the opposite; states have agendas, narrow sets of self-serving goals rarely lubricated by literature. Shultz, many believed, was the servant of an administration that had no imagination, not even a brain. It was Mailer, after all, who said later that the first precept of President Reagan was: "Be as shallow as spit on a rock and you will prevail." The conference theme was echoed in many of the titles of the panels: "How Does the State Imagine?" "Censorship in the U.S.," and

"Alienation in the State." Susan Sontag chaired one of these and led off by stating that she didn't understand the theme to be discussed. Mailer, who was in the audience, reminded Sontag that the panel themes "had been around for six months," and said, "Couldn't you have picked up the phone and asked?" Sontag, it was later revealed, was a member of PEN's program committee. "I was livid," he said.

On the fifth day of the conference, Mailer was attacked again, this time for the underrepresentation of women. A petition was presented to Mailer noting disproportions in the number of women involved in the Congress—there were only twenty-odd women out of 140 on conference panels. Earlier, when Betty Friedan confronted Mailer on the issue, he answered, "Oh, who's counting?" Friedan, joined by Grace Paley, Erica Jong, Margaret Atwood, and several others, was counting, and they wanted an explanation and a public apology. Mailer pointed out that at least two dozen important women writers had declined invitations, including Mary McCarthy, Iris Murdoch, Diana Trilling, Joan Didion, Barbara Tuchman, Mavis Gallant, Ann Beattie, Nathalie Sarraute, and Marguerite Yourcenar. His answer did not mollify the protesters, and the atmosphere worsened, especially after he said it was a bad idea to construct literary panels based on gender balance, adding that in many countries "there are no good women writers" because of the ingrained sexism of the culture that feminists deplored. Mailer started to dig himself into a deeper hole with comments about the mistake of stirring affirmative action into the literary pot, and some in the audience wondered if he would escape with his skin. Only after Gay Talese whispered some words of advice in Mailer's ear did he promise that the petitions would be addressed, and shortly afterward closed down the discussion. An ad hoc committee, headed by Grace Paley, was established afterward to examine the demands of the protesters. Vonnegut, another PEN official, said at the time that if he had been in the president's position he would have constituted the panels almost exactly the way Mailer had, given the roster of conferees from which to choose.

In point of fact, Mailer had little to do with selecting panel members, as he explained to novelist Mary Lee Settle, who wondered why she hadn't been chosen for one. "I stayed away from that," he wrote to her. "If I had started picking too many people, charges of nepotism, or whatever the word is, would damage us all." Most of his effort had gone into fundraising. The participation petition called for PEN to "include women in the decision-making roles." In a postmortem with *The New York Times*, Mailer said that the issue had not received much previous attention because "we have so many women in positions of such power." At the time of the congress, women headed six of the eight permanent committees and occupied three of the six vice presidencies. Half of the seven-hundred-plus individuals that attended the conference were women. "What are people who are calling for change going to change?" Mailer asked. But given the paucity of women panelists, Friedan's credentials, the backing of major figures such as Grace Paley, Erica Jong, and Nadine Gordimer, not to mention the feminist bull's-eye on his back, the protest could have been foreseen. The "brilliant end run," as *Time* called it, of inviting Shultz didn't help him, and continuing anger over the final defeat of the Equal Rights Amendment a few years earlier may also have contributed, although Mailer was on record as supporting it. He continued with PEN until mid-1986 when his term was up, and stayed on the board for a time, but felt bruised by his treatment at the congress. When asked in later years about PEN, all he could say was "cannibals."

The congress was not given over entirely to squabbling. There were lively receptions in the Egyptian wing of the Metropolitan Museum of Art; at Gracie Mansion, hosted by Mayor Ed Koch; at the New York Times Building, hosted by publisher Arthur Ochs "Punch" Sulzberger Sr. Nearby coffee shops, restaurants, and the bars of the two hotels where most of the panels and readings took place, the St. Moritz (Trump's hotel) and the Essex House, were crowded with writers in conversation. Mailer enjoyed the many dinners and cocktail parties, although the presence of Carole Mallory in the same room as Norris gave him no happiness.

Two months before the congress, Mailer asked Thomas Pynchon to take part and offered to have a drink with him. Pynchon wrote back with thanks and an apology, saying he would be away when the congress took place. "With luck, however, we may surface together in the same piece of space/time," he said, making it sound as if some sort of psychic rendezvous was in the cards. He said he would enjoy having a drink with Mailer, although his would have to be "something like Ovaltine." Mailer wrote back and gave Pynchon his telephone number for the next time he was in New York. The call never came, however.

The Crying of Lot 49 was the only Pynchon novel that Mailer ever finished, and he deplored it as an extended shaggy dog story. What might have been said if the entropist and the existentialist had clinked mugs of Ovaltine across the table, across the abyss?

Mailer's feelings about postmodern fiction surfaced in a letter he wrote to Gordon Lish a few months before the congress. Lish had edited some of his *Esquire* essays in the 1970s and had stayed in touch with him, sending him the books he was editing at Knopf, and his own fiction. One of these was *Peru*, an "obsessively circular novel," as one reviewer put it. The novel (which might be a memoir, or so it hints) is about the memories the narrator, Gordon, has of a boy he killed in a sandbox by gashing his skull with a toy hoe. The boys are six. Little by little, memory byte by memory byte, Gordon remembers the gory details but with no emotion. Mailer liked Lish but detested his book.

Lish admired the work of Gertrude Stein, but this earned him no points with Mailer. "I whisper to you that I don't really care in my secret heart whether Gertrude Stein lives forever or perishes tomorrow in Parnassus," Mailer wrote. "You have the perfect right to go in your direction"—Stein's direction—"just as I have to go in mine, but the directions are profoundly opposed."

> What your work catches is everything I detest about modern life. The entropy first, the breakdown of syntax, of concentration, mobility, all the murky tides that wash at our sensibilities. You capture that perfectly until my teeth are ready to grind. I feel as if literature is beleaguered, and that we must no longer study the disease but erect baroque monuments to stand against it, even if they're no more meaningful than sand castles against the filthy dull polluted tide. I want literature that has more syntax, more concentration, more in the way of symbols, and not that damned torturous undertow [words illegible] deterioration of forms, pervasive indefinable dread, and anomie.

He ends his condemnation of postmodernism by saying that he hesitated to write this kind of letter, but remaining silent would only "subject us both to the dirty and mucky tide." The letter was written just at the point when he was about to break from his spy novel and take up his rainmaking chores at PEN, and it is fair to surmise that his comments to Lish reminded him of the kind of novel he had begun, which he would devote himself to for the next five years. It would be his longest stretch of uninterrupted novel writing in forty years—almost uninterrupted, that is.

THIRTEEN
AN UNFINISHED CATHEDRAL: *HARLOT'S GHOST*

"You can no longer write an all-encompassing novel about America," Mailer said after *Ancient Evenings* was published. "It can't be done." For the eight years following its publication, he published nothing but *Tough Guys,* a few short pieces and a collection of his interviews. The period of focused effort ended with the publication of *Harlot's Ghost* in the fall of 1991. Mailer's tenth novel cannot justly be called all-encompassing, yet it does provide a privileged perspective on some of the most cataclysmic events and fabled figures of American life in the twenty years after World War II. Like a long freight train, Mailer's story of WASP intelligence agents in war and peace snakes through upper-class American life (Mount Desert, Yale, the "21" Club), picks up speed as it moves through international intrigues in Europe, slows to a crawl in Uruguay, and then accelerates rapidly as it moves through the CIA's attempts to poison Castro, its failed invasion at the Bay of Pigs, and the Cuban Missile Crisis. Some of JFK's extramarital love affairs comprise another strand of the novel's loosely braided narrative of deception, loyalty, betrayal, and heroism.

Shortly before it was published, a friend pointed out to him that the book's length could be a record in American publishing, surpassing James Jones's *Some Came Running* (1,266 pages). Mailer, a longtime communicant in the church of organic form, shrugged. The bound galleys of his novel came in at 1,334 pages. He said that Random House would add one line to every page to reduce the published volume to 1,310 pages. Longer and more detailed than any of Mailer's other fictions, the novel's several lines of action never really coalesce. The novel could be likened to a magnificent, half-finished cathedral, to borrow a metaphor he used to suggest the dimensions of his personality in *The*

Armies of the Night. "Plot is the enemy of the great novel," he said. "I'm interested in plots that do not have a resolution. Life is like that." *Harlot's Ghost* ends with these words: "TO BE CONTINUED"—a promise he would break. His greatest regret, he said the year before he died, was "the memory of the books I promised to write and didn't." Even as it stands, unfinished and abandoned, it may be his finest novelistic achievement, one of the last high peaks of his writing life, and the summa of his knowledge of postwar America, as seen through the eyes of two generations of CIA agents.

ANCIENT EVENINGS TOOK eleven years to complete, but Mailer left it for years at a time and wrote a half dozen other books in the interstices of its composition. Measured by clock hours, *Harlot's Ghost* took longer to write than any of his other works. He departed from it only twice, once, briefly, to direct *Strawhead* and a second, longer, period to write a screenplay based on *Tough Guys Don't Dance*, and then direct the film. He was prepared to postpone the novel if either of these projects was successful. But the play never got beyond short runs at Actors Studio, and the film, while not without its virtues, did not lead to a career change. There was a short-lived third project, a film version of *King Lear* based on Mailer's "Don Learo" screenplay, directed by the great director Jean-Luc Godard. Mailer said that "writing a screenplay for Godard is like putting a message in a bottle and sending it out to sea," but he completed it and sent it on for consideration. He was supposed to play Lear and his daughter Kate was to play Cordelia. Godard, however, wasn't the least interested in Mailer's screenplay, or Shakespeare's play, and appears in the film as a nutty professor. Godard wanted Mailer to play Mailer and utter lines such as: "Ah! At last I am done. What joy!" After only one day on the set, he and Kate left Switzerland where the film was being shot, and flew home. The experience was "a true horror tale," Mailer said. *King Lear*, called "a late Godardian practical joke" by critic Vincent Canby, was released in 1987 by Cannon Films. It baffled its small audiences.

In January 1986, several months before going to Switzerland with her father, Kate played Marilyn Monroe in *Strawhead* at Actors Studio, and got excellent reviews. Working with her father "brought me closer to him," she said, adding that she was not particularly awed working with him. "You're doing the work," she said. "It's a play." Bert Stern, the fashion photographer who photographed Marilyn for his book *The Last Sitting* six weeks before her death, took pictures of Kate for an April 1986 *Vanity Fair* article on the play. "No one has played Marilyn better, except Marilyn," Stern said, adding that he had seen many people imitate Monroe, "but only Kate has caught her vulnerability and sensitivity." Mailer told a friend, half seriously, that he sometimes wondered if Monroe had been reincarnated in Kate. James Atlas described Kate's performance in the *Vanity Fair* story, performing before "a select audience" that included Dustin Hoffman, Tina Brown, Al Pacino, Robert De Niro, and Elia Kazan. "Young Kate Mailer," he wrote, "amazingly *became* Monroe. She whimpered and flirted, was seductive and coy; she babbled to herself in a nervous, breathy, voice; she emanated sex."

Kate was "incredible" in the production, Mailer told Malaquais, and added,

> Perhaps in a year we will actually do the play Off-Broadway. I tell you, Jean, I was startled with her talent. She created a Marilyn who was lovely and vulnerable and sensitive and totally fucked-up, but restrained with instinctive taste to protect herself from her own ignorance. It was a lovely creation. People who know Marilyn came back to me afterward shaking their heads, telling me it was spooky, no one in the family can believe it.

Remembering the excitement surrounding *The Deer Park*'s four-month run in 1967, Mailer looked forward to returning to off-Broadway. But when the time came, Kate declined. Norris recalled the situation: "It was just a little complicated because of her dad directing her, and she didn't want anyone to know for a long time that she was his daughter, and [initially] called herself Kate Cailean, which is her middle name. And people didn't know for a long time that this actress was Norman's daughter. But, it was problematic for her. It's too complicated for me to talk about, but she just didn't want to make her career as being Marilyn Monroe, with her dad." Kate continued to act, and after *Strawhead* had roles in several plays, including Peter Brook's production of Chekhov's *The Cherry Orchard* and the film *A Matter of Degrees*.

With the exception of Susan, a practicing psychoanalyst and faculty member of the Chilean Institute for Psychoanalysis, all of the Mailer siblings went into the arts.

Mailer was not the easiest of fathers. He lectured his children vociferously, harangued them with the line "the good is the enemy of the great," and fought with them. He and Stephen had several memorable clashes, some in public, but they always reconciled. Mailer was stalwart, however, in encouraging them in their careers. In addition to directing Kate in *Strawhead,* he worked with and advised Michael on several film projects, read and praised Betsy's novel in progress, debated with Susan about psychoanalysis, and took pride in the elaborate, life-size horror figures that Matthew constructed, as well as his screenplay for "The Greatest Thing in the World." Stephen, whom Mailer praised for his "physical agility on stage and his sensitivity to character," said that his father "was very supportive because he is an artist." Maggie compared the houses where they summered in Maine and Provincetown to an artists colony. "I think we were lucky," she said.

> I felt encouraged and I think if Dad had not been always trying to impart the importance of being an artist, perhaps we would have rebelled and become bankers. But I always felt that he was interested in what I was doing, and sometimes too interested. I mean, his standards were so much higher than anything I could conceive of. You know, when I was a teenager, it was laughable. He once said something like "Once you've become recognized as a leader in your community and in your college, then you'll understand what I'm talking about." He just took it for granted that that would happen. So I think he expected all the kids to be artists. I remember at one point saying I didn't think I was up for that life, and he said, "Look, you have to do whatever you want, you know, and my love for you is there regardless."

He hung the paintings of his two artist daughters, Danielle and Maggie, on the walls of his two homes, and was pleased and proud when they had a joint show with Norris at the Berta Walker Gallery in Provincetown in 2007. Danielle, who describes her work as being "part autobiographical, part mythological and spiritual," painted a subtle self-portrait titled *The Good Daughter.* She is asleep in a chair holding a copy of *Ancient Evenings*, recognizable by the color drawing on the back jacket of an Egyptian head. She finished the painting, a tribute from one artist to another, the day before her father died.

He was aware of the pitfalls surrounding parental advice. He and Mickey Knox discussed the matter several times in their correspondence. In 1992, Mailer wrote:

> I agree with you: forget about giving advice to your children. It can't be done unless you have a special relation to them, and unless they have a true need for your knowledge from their own point of view. Otherwise, it's just a power trip to them and they are trying to establish their own power center, and won't accept anything from a parent. . . . So who the fuck am I to steer someone else's life? I would say just assume they'll mellow out toward you as they get older. In the meantime, give them a little of the green and stop complaining. What else do we have to spend it on, after all?

Mailer was financially generous with his children, as he was with his friends. He made many loans and gifts, and few people who dined out with him ever beat him to the check.

THE DEAL THAT called for Mailer to write "Don Learo" grew out of a luncheon meeting between Godard and Israeli film producer Menahem Golan at the Cannes Film Festival in May 1985. Golan, who ran Cannon Films with his cousin Yoram Globus, offered Godard $1 million for a film based on *King Lear.* They signed the deal on a napkin, which Golan framed and hung in his office. Working with Godard was a departure for Cannon, which heretofore had mainly churned out low-budget, high-violence films. During its peak year, 1986, Cannon made forty-three films. But Golan and Globus also aspired to produce high art films, which helps explain the deal with Godard. Tom Luddy, a producer at American Zoetrope Films, which for over thirty years has made films of the caliber of *The Godfather: Part II, Mishima*, and the restored version of Abel Gance's 1927 classic, *Napoleon*, had close ties with Godard. Golan wanted "a normal American movie," Luddy recalled, and therefore put in writing that Godard must use a screenplay approved by Cannon Films. Mailer's name was suggested by Godard as the screenwriter and added to the napkin contract as "pre-approved" to write it. Golan tracked Luddy down at the festival, and asked him to enlist Mailer.

Mailer said no. "I knew I would have 30,000 Shakespeareans out to slaughter me," he said. But Luddy knew that Mailer wanted to see *Tough Guys Don't Dance* made into a film, and hoped to direct it. At a September 1985 meeting at a Midtown New York restaurant, Luddy sold him on the idea of a two-picture deal. "Tell Golan," Mailer said, "that if he'll do *Tough Guys*, I'll do *Lear.*" Luddy called Golan in Los Angeles and put him on with Mailer. "Mr. Mailer, I'm happy to agree with you on a two-picture contract," Golan said. Luddy agreed to be the film's executive producer. Four months after the PEN congress ended, Mailer began working on both screenplays. *Tough Guys* had taken him two months to write; the screenplay went through five drafts and took six months. Work on *Harlot's Ghost* all but ceased.

The biggest hurdle that he faced with the *Tough Guys* screenplay was that much of the novel takes place in Madden's head. A second problem was that the plot depended on actions and situations that took place months and years, even decades earlier. Somehow, this backstory had to be presented, or adroitly deleted. He eliminated some minor characters, enlarged the roles of others, wrote several flashback scenes, and flashbacks within flashbacks—one of them showed Madden in prison talking to his cell mate, played by Mailer's Provincetown friend Eddie Bonetti. He also planned to intimate Madden's half-crazy, tremulous state by using music and "subtly sinister" images of Outer Cape Cod in late fall. The sum of all these changes streamlined the story somewhat, but problems remained. He wrote most of it in Provincetown, living alone until the summer, when Matt and John were out of school and joined him there with their mother. Mailer wrote to Bruce Dexter in late April about the translation process. Being a screenwriter, he told Dexter,

> for a particular novel is, if it is not your own work, very much like being a first year medical student, and doing a long, detailed autopsy where you get to know the inside of the body you're studying conceivably better than God, who might have less time. I did a screenplay once of *The Rosy Crucifixion* and it's possible that I ended up knowing in a few small ways more of the work than Henry Miller. In working with *Tough Guys*, I can see the book on the table, all its

virtues, all the places where it is not so virtuous, and it is the oddest book. The people, reduced to the tight net of a screenplay, are by the measure of anyone looking for a little cheer about human nature, a negative lot. All the while I was writing the book I was in love with them for their charms—monsters with charm have always appealed to me—and something of that, I hope, is still in the screenplay.

IN A LETTER to Abbott, Mailer said he would like to send him the "Don Learo" screenplay to get his reaction to the Mafia characters, "where you think it's real, where you think it's phony." Abbott had written a new book, *My Return*, in collaboration with Naomi Zack, the young woman who had taken up his cause. Zack, who had earned a Ph.D. in philosophy at Columbia, was convinced at the time that Abbott "was unfairly convicted by an outraged public opinion inflamed by sensational treatment in the media." *My Return* consists of a play, "The Death Tragedy," depicting the murder of Adan with diagrams of the killing knife thrust, several appendices on the trial and the legal issues, and philosophical-polemical letters to Mailer, Styron, Silvers, Jerzy Kosinski, Mailer's friend Mashey Bernstein, and several others. Abbott maintains his innocence throughout, and uses as an epigraph the last words of Melville's Billy Budd before he is hanged—"God bless Cap'n Vere"—the implication being that Abbott stabbed Adan just as Budd had killed Claggart, out of instinct not malice, which may have been true.

Zack, who had begun a documentary film on Abbott, moved in 1985 to Plattsburgh, New York, near the correctional facility where Abbott was confined. For a nine-month period in 1985–86 she visited him every day. Zack was "bringing him books, conveying his messages, typing his writing. Of her relationship, she said: 'All I can say is my main purpose is Jack needs and wants a new trial. As for his intellectual work, I take it very seriously.' " (She and Abbott would marry in 1990, while he was still in prison.) At the time, Abbott was trying, he said, "to behave like a 'real' intellectual." Zack wrote to Mailer asking if he would write an afterword to their book. Mailer replied to Abbott: "You are so associated with me and people are so pissed off at me now after the P.E.N. Congress that it would result in your being taken less seriously." He offered to write a blurb for *My Return*—"if I like it." Abbott was convinced that a cabal was persecuting him, and Mailer was tired of his paranoia. "There are not legions lying awake every night trying to figure out how to thwart you," he told him. Ultimately, he declined to write the afterword, or give a blurb, and their correspondence ended.

Zack and Abbott would divorce after two years of marriage. "I am lucky to have survived it," she said. "I began to see that there was something wrong with all these women visiting prisoners." Even after she broke off contact with Abbott, she continued to send him $50 to $100 a month until his death. "Jack had no remorse," she said, adding that he "was proud of having been told by Mailer about [the birth of] his son, John Buffalo. I also think that he was well aware of the value of the world Mailer had taken him into, however briefly. Without Mailer, Jack would not have been a literary figure."

MAILER CONTINUED TO work on the novel, but with no real energy. He finished "Havana," a screenplay for Martin Starger at Universal Studios, and "Don Learo" before he and Kate went to Switzerland in August, and the final draft of *Tough Guys* shortly before filming began in Provincetown on October 27. In between, there were consultations about the cast and locations for the film with Tom Luddy, cinematographer John Bailey, and casting director Bonnie Timmermann. Even the 350th anniversary of the founding of Harvard in September didn't pull him away. He was asked to be "an official representative" at the commemorative celebration, but does not seem to have responded to the formal invitation, even after he was depicted with fifteen other outstanding "Sons of Harvard" in a painting on the cover of the July 20 *New York Times Magazine*. The sixteen men, grouped as if for a photo on the lawn of Harvard Yard, included five U.S. presidents—John Adams, John Quincy Adams, Teddy Roosevelt, FDR, and JFK. Mailer, in his pinstripe suit and loosened red tie, is pictured with Leonard Bernstein on either side of a seated T. S. Eliot, the two Jews crouching on either side of the ultimate WASP, as if ready to go into the game.

There were sixty-five locales used in the film, most of them in Provincetown but several in Truro and other nearby towns. Some of Mailer's favorite places—the Old Colony, Pepe's, the Red Inn, and Front Street restaurant—were filmed, and the Mailers' home at 627 Commercial became the novel's waterfront house. It was given a complete makeover to demonstrate Patty Lareine's gaudy idea of wealth and the decor remained for more than a decade until Norris redecorated.

Before filming began, there was a casting call at one of the local art galleries. Some extras came from Boston, and some from Provincetown, including Chris Busa, the publisher of *Provincetown Arts* magazine, several local artists and two retired firemen in their 80s. "I wanted to use townspeople for extras," Mailer said, "because the making of the movie had much more to do with Provincetown than the final results will." Seeing the actors in the local A & P, or walking along the town's narrow lanes, was the topic of conversation in the town. Ryan O'Neal was accessible, but Isabelle Rossellini kept to herself, eating her meals in her trailer. Mailer admired her acting in David Lynch's dark mystery, *Blue Velvet*, and sought the same mood for his film. Angelo Badalamenti, who scored the music for Lynch's film, was hired for Mailer's.

Mailer worked with sound designer Leslie Shatz to capture the sound of a punch to the face, as Shatz recalled at a twenty-year reunion of the cast and crew. According to Mailer, "the sounds of punches in movies are all phony." So he began hitting himself "at least twenty times in the face and the chest until we got it right." Shatz recorded the sound and used it in many movies afterward. "I always tell the other directors, 'You hear that? That's Norman Mailer punching himself. He's in your movie.' " Mailer's professionalism was something that Menahem Golan had taken for granted, but before the start of filming he did some checking and got a different picture of his director. Luddy recalled getting a five A.M. call from the Israeli, who said, "Tom, my knife is at your throat. Tom, you've given me Norman Mailer as a director. I've been talking to people in Hollywood, and they tell me he's crazy." But he proved himself to be completely disciplined, and was "adored" by the cast and crew. Working with a $5 million budget and a crew of ninety-seven, he brought the film in under budget and ahead of schedule.

There was some friction during the filming. O'Neal, who played Tim Madden, thought some of the dialogue "would come off as laughable," Tom Luddy recalled, and Lawrence Tierney, a notoriously difficult actor, who played Dougy Madden, did things his own way, sometimes ignoring direction. As producer, Luddy said he thought the screenplay "had a lot of problems." He wrote a memo listing eleven problems in the script, and Mailer agreed with most of them. But he had solutions only for a few, and ignored the rest. If he could relive the entire project, Luddy said, "I would get another writer to adapt the book and convince Norman to focus on directing it." Mailer hoped to solve his plot problems in the editing process.

In a letter written to the still-jailed Richard Stratton shortly after the production was completed in mid-December, Mailer described the experience of directing.

> I always felt as if I were in jail when I was writing a novel. A perfectly pleasant but subtly deadening spiritual jail. And directing the movie I found out why. Suddenly I could use my real talents: more superficial, perhaps than my developed talent as a writer, but with me all my life and dying to be honed: to wit, my practical side. Directing a movie, you contemplate 40 different categories of problem in a day, and you get an appetite for it. It becomes the best life you can have. I've been feeling logy for the last few years but on the film where we're working 15 hours a day, 6 days a week, and I had more energy, or let's say, as much energy as I've ever had.

Over and over in interviews, he compared writing and directing, in every instance grumbling about the former and exalting the latter. "*Anything*'s easier than writing," and novel writing is the hardest, he said. It is "an excruciating activity; when I'm in the middle of one I often feel like a monk in the wrong monastery." But directing, he said, made him feel like a general in "an ideal war" with no blood. "It is like a campaign: you eat outside standing up; everybody starts the day having breakfast together; it's a communal exercise. You move to different places every day; the campaign moves here, moves there; it's going to be over in forty-two days. It's like hunting with a camera in Africa."

When filming was done, Mailer wrote to his two imprisoned friends, and made plans to visit. He promised to visit Farbar in late January when he was in Pittsburgh to see Stephen in a play. After telling Stratton that he would definitely visit him in early spring, he went on to say that he had been relaxed during filming but was now feeling nervous because he owed Random House "a million dollars in advance royalties they've already paid me over the last three years for a book which is only half done." His plan was to edit the film half the time and write half the time, and this is what he did, more or less, for all of 1987. At this point, he had high hopes for the film. John Bailey's imaginative cinematography captured the bleakness of Cape Cod in the late fall, and the dailies that Mailer had seen were exceptional. He apologized to Mickey Knox for not finding a role for him in the film, but "if this picture hits, then I think I'll command larger budgets." Then Knox could be given roles. "At that time," he said, "I won't have to listen to you saying, 'But, Norman, you know nothing about directing a movie.' " One commercial film, he said, means that you're a director. "Indeed, I'm even a member of the Directors' Guild. How's that for news?" Mailer remained a member for the rest of his life but never got another chance to direct, to his great regret.

After enjoying Stephen's performance in Pittsburgh with Norris and John, Mailer went on alone to Altoona, where Farbar was incarcerated. They spent an hour and a half together catching up, discussing what kind of work Farbar might do after his release. He knew his friend might have trouble decompressing when he got out and tried to buck him up. "I respect the psychological work you've done on yourself," he said. But Farbar seemed more and more bitter.

IN THE SPRING of 1987 Mailer asked Carol Stevens to meet him for a few days in San Francisco, where he was doing postproduction sound work at Russian Hill Recording Studios. He recorded her doing the voice of one of the two witches who laugh and gibber at the end of *Tough Guys*, another attempt to give the film a haunted quality. He spent a month there in April, and had a romantic reunion with her for a few days while working on the soundtrack of the film. He also saw Lois Wilson. Cannon had given Mailer control over the final cut of the film, and he was trying to find a way to clarify the plot. As he began editing, the dimensions of the problem began to emerge. In the end, Mailer had no choice but to use voice-overs to explain the tangle of relationships and reveal who killed whom. His screenplay departed somewhat from the novel, but ultimately was too respectful of it.

He finished editing in time for the fortieth annual Cannes Film Festival in early May. He was asked to serve on the nine-member jury, headed by Yves Montand. Godard was there with *King Lear*, but he and Mailer don't seem to have met. Because he was a jurist, *Tough Guys* was screened out of competition. Mailer watched twenty-four films in twelve days, and met with other jurors to compare notes and vote.

Tough Guys was shown twice, once for the press and once for a general audience. The somewhat stilted dialogue, which sounded, as Roger Ebert put it, "as if everyone in the film had learned everything they knew from watching old crime movies," went over well with the press for the most part, although it got a sprinkling of boos. Vincent Canby, who had liked *Beyond the Law,* praised *Tough Guys*, calling it "a wonderfully exaggerated film noir story." Menahem Golan had several films in competition and threw a large dinner to honor Mailer. *Tough Guys* was screened after dinner and received a standing ovation.

Upon his return Mailer made some final changes to the film, then got to work on the novel, breaking away only to see rehearsals of Norris's play at the Actors Studio in June. For some time, she had been a member of the Actors Studio, writing both plays and screenplays, and directing. *Go See,* her two-character, two-act play about an erotic dancer and an anthropology professor was staged there in May or June of 1987, with Norris and Rip Torn acting the roles. Mailer was enthusiastic about her abilities and wrote to Farbar with praise. "All my life, as you know, I've wanted to be a successful playwright and simply don't have the knack for it," he said. Watching her staged reading, he said to himself, "My God, she's a better playwright than I am." He was always impressed with the effortless way his wife moved from one pursuit to another—model, actress (she played a drug dealer for six months on the television soap opera *All My Children*), playwright, and novelist, all while running the household. The Mailers were also leading a busy social life now that most of the children were adults. "Norman and Norris," she wrote, "became almost one word in the social columns." They dined at Elaine's, Nicola's, and Indochine, but Mortimer's, at Lexington Avenue and East 75th Street, where they met with Arthur and Alexandra Schlesinger, Diane and Ivan Fisher, Dotson Rader, and other friends, was their favorite Manhattan restaurant in the late 1980s.

AFTER JULY IN Provincetown, he and Norris went to Maine, and the family climbed mile-high Mount Katahdin, which stands at the northern end of the Appalachian Trail. The most well-known and difficult path to the summit lies across the Knife Edge. Several people have died in falls from this path, which is a mile long, but in places only three feet wide. In the afternoon, when descending the north slope, one is left in deep shadow.

Mailer made the climb—six hours each way—three or four times. Kate recalled one of these at her father's memorial. When they reached the Knife Edge, she announced she was going back down the mountain. He answered by saying that crossing it would enable her to grow and change in unforeseen ways. "It will be good for your karma," he said. She hollered back:

> My karma, my karma? I don't care about my karma. You might care about your karma. You're fifty-five years old. You have lived! You've written thirty books, You've had six wives and soon to be nine children, I am sixteen years old and I have never even been kissed! I have never even had a boyfriend! I DON'T WANT TO DIE. I WANT TO HAVE SEX!

Mailer told her that she would have an even better boyfriend if she crossed. "The man's will and charm were no match for mine," she said, and she made the transit. She felt better, but did not admit it. Looking back, she said that eventually she got "the best boyfriend who then became the best husband anyone could ever dream of, and I think sometimes it had something to do with Dad and the mountain, courage, and will."

That summer he was writing ninety pages a month and feeling good enough about his progress to say that the novel was "about the CIA." But his publisher was unhappy; he was a year past his due date. He had written a bestseller, *Tough Guys Don't Dance*, in sixty-one days, and Random House hoped that he would repeat this every year or so.

The film premiered on September 16, 1987, at Loew's Twin on Second Avenue and East 66th Street. It was a warm, lovely evening, and a big crowd mingled on the sidewalk before the doors were opened. The guest list shows that many of the Mailers' friends attended—the Fishers, Pat Kennedy Lawford, Bob Lucid, Legs McNeil, Jeff Michelson, the Schlesingers, Gay and Nan Talese, Jimmy and Rosemary Breslin, Mashey Bernstein, Jason Epstein, and Paul Newman. Most of the family was there. Judith McNally, his assistant, and Myrtle Bennett, the nanny for the younger children, both of whom rarely went to Mailer social events, also came. Tom Luddy, John Bailey, and most of the crew came, as did several of the actors. Carol Holmes, Mailer's former girlfriend, and Carole Mallory, his current one, were invited and showed up.

Mailer had recommended Mallory for a small role in the film, but casting director Bonnie Timmermann and producer Tom Luddy turned her down. Luddy recalled that Mallory had visited the set in Provincetown and interviewed Mailer.

In an interview with Roger Ebert during filming, he explained that as he grew older he had changed his ways. "I stopped drinking for a year and a half," he said, and "when I went back, I didn't enjoy the hangovers so much, so now I drink in moderation, of all damn things." He went on to say, "a man who says he is happily married is a fool, but I will take a chance and say that I am. I stopped getting into trouble years ago." In fact, Mailer's liaison with Mallory and other relationships continued. Despite some occasional suspicions, Norris was not to learn the extent of his infidelities until he had completed *Harlot's Ghost* in 1991. He insisted that she was the love of his life and valued the way she had become a second mother to his oldest seven children. When he did finally explain the root cause of his infidelities, he said that they really intensified about the time he began work on *Harlot's Ghost*, as Norris wrote in her memoir.

> He said his double life started when he began researching that book, and I suppose it could even be true. The timing was about right. All the clandestine talking on pay phones, making secret plans, hiding and sneaking around, were perfect spy maneuvers. He said he needed to live that kind of double life to know what his characters were going through. (It was an imaginative excuse. I do give him credit for that.)
>
> He said he had been totally true to me, except for one or two tiny one-night stands with old girlfriends when he was on lecture tours, for eight years after we got together, which might even be mostly true. It was his grand experiment in monogamy, and I had believed him. While it could hardly be said the experiment was a total success, it was the longest he had been true (more or less) to a woman in his life. His nature was to be a philanderer.

Mailer did attempt to be faithful to Norris during the early years of his marriage. If, in his confession to her, he smudged the facts about how many times he had fallen off the monogamy wagon, he was being entirely truthful about his motives for being unfaithful. He had two related reasons, one narcissistic, selfish, and sensual, the other bold, experiential, and to his mind completely necessary. His incessant affairs gave him purchase on the duplicity of intelligence agents and fed his narcissism. For Mailer, that it took a thief to catch a thief was an article of faith.

Before and after the premiere, he spent twenty days doing interviews for the film, and said it had received enough publicity "to float the Queen Mary." But the reviews, with a few exceptions, were mixed, and the box office figures paltry (the film eventually broke even). After looking at all the early reviews, which were with few exceptions either mixed or negative, Luddy told Mailer that, overall, they were not going to help him. "It's as if you opened a restaurant," he said, "and got two reviews. One said, 'This food is crazy, wild, and interesting,' and the other one said, 'Three people I know got food poisoning after our meal.' " The restaurant—the film—was doomed, Luddy said. Mailer reluctantly accepted this analysis.

He had told Susan that after the satisfaction he got from directing, the only way he would go back to writing "with any real happiness" was if there were no other way he could make a living. Cannon had hinted that he would give him another film to direct, but this was no longer in the cards, especially after the film was nominated for Golden Raspberry Awards in seven categories: worst picture, director, screenplay, actor and actress, supporting actress, and new star. Mailer tied for worst director with Elaine May, who had directed the monumental flop *Ishtar.* Conversely, the film was nominated for the Independent Spirit Award in four categories: best film, cinematography, female lead, and supporting male role. The fact that the film was nominated for best and worst film of the year by different groups confirmed Mailer's belief that his works would continue to receive polar receptions. *Tough Guys* eventually became a minor cult classic, praised for its "amusing vagueness" about its fundamental genre: mystery thriller or black comedy, horror film or comedy of manners. Luddy summed up the film as "Tarantino before its time," which he described as "long florid dialogue punctuated by grotesque violence." Whatever the case, it was clear that Mailer's film career was over. As he said in another letter, "Writing is the farm and movie-making is Paree." He was going home.

AT THE END of 1986 Danielle married Michael Moschen, a professional juggler. Mailer invited them to live in Provincetown during their first year of marriage. For the greater part of 1987, Danielle painted in Norris's studio, Moschen practiced his routines in the basement, and Mailer wrote in the attic studio. Norris was in New York with Matt and John and came up every other weekend. Danielle, her husband, and her father shared the chores, and enjoyed long quiet meals and discussions. "It was one of the best years I spent with my father," she said. But after a time, Mailer yearned for the city. In January 1988, he wrote to Farbar to say he was getting tired of working in Provincetown and planned to move back to Brooklyn for a stretch. He was still following his usual country-city alternation, moving whenever one or the other became "a species of spiritual incarceration," as he wrote Farbar about P-town. Mailer was paying some of his friend's legal bills, and much of their correspondence was given over to Farbar's various attempts to get his sentence commuted. These attempts failed, and Farbar became increasingly depressed. A year after his release he committed suicide.

His correspondence with Stratton was more literary. In Mailer's letters and visits, he encouraged him to complete his novel, *Smack Goddess.* Mailer read drafts of it, made suggestions, and with Meredith's help it was published in 1990. Mailer and Dick Goodwin gave it blurbs. Mailer was impressed with how Stratton had used his prison time to "look for some needed dimension" in his character. His comment on Stratton's "moral grit" revealed something about his own ideas of moral growth.

> That you're physically strong is one thing; that can be a gift. But the other side of you you built out of yourself. But the other side of anyone, moral strength that is, is a construction. For if that were given by God, there'd be no logic to anything. We would all be dealt unequal hands, and that doesn't feel right to accept. (Before we get too far in this, I don't mean the real stark ends of the scale, morally speaking, but I believe we all have the same ability to improve or coarsen our spiritual nature.)

This letter, like almost all of Mailer's letters since the late 1950s, was dictated, and he was sometimes slightly opaque. What he seems to be endorsing is the principle of spiritual growth and/or decay, while holding out for the possibility that saints and monsters have been shaped, at least in part, by divine or demonic intervention. This idea would be further developed in his final novel, *The Castle in the Forest.*

In the eighty or ninety letters that he wrote in mid-January, his tone is valedictory. He admits that his commercial film career is over and that his experimental films are a footnote. In one letter he said he was pleased that Jonas Mekas, a leading light in experimental cinema, was showing *Beyond the Law* and *Maidstone* in Manhattan. He was satisfied to be considered "a distinguished minor artist" in cinema history. He reacquainted himself with *Harlot's Ghost* and settled down for a long stretch of writing. "It's like going back to a wife," he told Stratton, and not particularly easy, "but oh, what fun when you begin to hold hands again."

Harlot's Ghost has great geopolitical sweep, looking back to World War II and forward to the Vietnam War, and is full of vivid portraits, divided between historical and fictional figures—he liked the idea of mixing them up in the same way E. L. Doctorow did in *Ragtime.* Of the former, the most notable are JFK and his brother Robert, their in-house nemesis J. Edgar Buddha (as everyone in the novel calls FBI Director Hoover), CIA director Allen Dulles, Uruguay station chief Howard Hunt (of later Watergate infamy), British double agent Kim Philby, Frank Sinatra, Mafia chieftain Sam Giancana, Fidel Castro, and William King "Bill" Harvey, Berlin base chief. Harvey is the most memorably drawn historical figure, matched only by the fictional Hugh Tremont Montague, a high CIA counterintelligence official, code name, Harlot. The narrator is Herrick "Harry" Hubbard, a young agent who goes into intelligence work in 1955 after graduation from Yale, following his father "Cal" Hubbard, an OSS officer in World War II. Cal's best friend is Harlot, who is also Harry's godfather and mentor. There are two major women characters: Harlot's wife, Hadley Kittredge Gardiner Montague, who is part of the agency's brain-trust, and Modene Murphy, a fictional stand-in for Judith Campbell Exner, the lover of JFK, Giancana, Sinatra, and young Hubbard.

It is no wonder that Mailer gave up his plan to chronicle the voyage of the spaceship-ark in favor of a novel of sharply etched character studies, none more so than Montague's, a master spy modeled on the legendary CIA counterintelligence chief James Jesus Angleton (himself a minor character in the book), a poet who corresponded with Pound and Eliot, collaborated during World War II with cardinals, ex-fascists, Mafia *capodecinas,* and Kim Philby, and worked for seven successive CIA directors. It was Angleton who came up with the "wilderness of mirrors" theory to explain how Soviet intelligence might be manipulating the agency. Mailer's Montague is just as fiercely determined to root out Russian moles as his model, or so it seems—with Montague, there is always a deeper layer, and his deepest loyalties are a mystery.

The novel begins in 1983 just before his body is found near his boat in Chesapeake Bay with most of the head blown off by a shotgun (Hemingway is one of the novel's presiding spirits), and the fingertips nibbled off by fish. A filling in one of the remaining two teeth corresponds "astonishingly well," to the Xrays in Harlot's dental file. Is it Harlot or a corpse of similar dimensions tricked up to deceive? Harry disappears himself and goes to Russia to find the answer. He carries with him the "Alpha manuscript," subtitled "The Game," a 1,000-page memoir of his life in the CIA from 1955 to the mid-1960s. As he reads his microfilm copy of the memoir with a flashlight on the wall of his room in the Hotel Metropole, we read along with him. Down the street is Lubyanka Square, dominated by a gigantic statue of "Iron" Felix Dzerzhinsky, the founder of the Russian secret police and one of the most dazzling twentieth-century practitioners of counterintelligence. Harlot gives seminars on Dzerzhinsky's techniques.

In his appended "Author's Note," to the novel, Mailer said his intention was to present "a large and detailed mural of a social organism moving through some real historical events," as well as through imagined ones, his claim being that novelists "can create superior histories out of an enhancement of the real." To accomplish this, massive research was necessary. His bibliography lists 130 books. When it got to the point that an easily consulted overview was needed, he turned to Judith, who was reading the source materials right along with him. Using three twenty-eight-by-twenty-two-inch pieces of heavy stock, Judith created an event timeline, running from 1940 to 1980. Across the top, she listed seventeen different people (Angleton, Harvey, Hoover, Hunt, Philby, Allen Dulles, and other top CIA operatives, Lee Harvey Oswald, Marilyn Monroe, Sam Giancana and his colleagues, and several Russian spies and/or counterspies), and five event categories (Watergate, Cuba, Vietnam, CIA Mind Control, and World Events). Mailer's scrawled additions, corrections, and notes on the charts are easily distinguished from her elegant script. Later, a further consolidation was made on a fourth chart, clustering some of the key events of the novel. Characteristically, he saw the novel more in terms of the characters and their actions, fair and foul, than from the perspective of events.

The timeline charts, which were taped together and propped up near Mailer's desk for easy reference, show that he planned the novel to cover the four decades from the beginning of World War II—the first events noted are the assassination of Leon Trotsky in August 1940 and the start of the German bombing of London a few weeks later—to the beginning of the end of the Cold War—the last event noted is the signing of the Strategic Arms Limitation Treaty II by President Carter in June 1979. But Mailer never reached the later events on his timelines, and the novel effectively ends with the Cuban Missile Crisis of 1962. The assassination of JFK takes place offstage, as it were, and while the novel continues to 1966, it barely does so.

He worked deliberately all through 1988 and by the end of the year had 1,300 pages of manuscript. His routine was to work four to six days at his New York studio, pack up his books and the timelines, drive to Provincetown for a week, and then return. One of the few breaks he took was for the ecumenical wedding ceremony of his daughter Betsy, who married Frank Nastasi in New York on February 14, 1988, and the large reception he and Norris hosted at 142 Columbia Heights. He also found time to go to two big fights. After Muhammad Ali's retirement, Mike Tyson was arguably the most impressive heavyweight boxer, and in 1988 was the undisputed world champion at the peak of his career. Tyson's first match was against former champion Larry Holmes, who came out of retirement for the bout. Mailer and Norris flew from the West Side of Manhattan to Atlantic City on one of Donald Trump's black helicopters. Mailer sat in the back row with Jack Nicholson where they discussed *Prizzi's Honor*, a film about a hit man and hit woman who fall in love. He told Nicholson that "if two people are equally murderous, they could really be in love." Tyson demolished Holmes and won the fight with a TKO in the fourth. In June, Mailer took his son Michael with him to Atlantic City to watch Tyson knock out Michael Spinks in the first round. He wrote about Tyson's amazing punching power in a September essay in *Spin* magazine, his last report on a professional bout.

Except for two advance excerpts from *Harlot's Ghost*, one in *Es-*

quire and the other in *Playboy*, the only other piece Mailer published in 1988 was an endorsement of Rev. Jesse Jackson for the Democratic nomination for president. It was Jackson's second run for the nomination and, for a short period, he led the eventual candidate, Governor Michael Dukakis of Massachusetts, in delegates. His endorsement appeared on the *New York Times* op-ed page the day before the April 19 primary. New York Mayor Ed Koch had said that any Jew who voted for Jackson was "crazy." Mailer took exception, and deplored Koch's statement as an example of small-minded political self-interest.

Although centuries of ghetto life had engendered in the Jews "a noble spirit alive in enough of us to permit the feeling that we were the first children of the Enlightenment," Mailer wrote, the "fearful curse" of Nazism was "still there to poison one's finer moral substance." The destruction of half the Jews in the world had created "an imperative to survive at all costs." The Holocaust "left us smaller, greedier, narrower, preternaturally touchy, and self-seeking." Politics for the Jews, he argued, too often boiled down to the question: "Is this good for the Jews?"

> It takes no great insight to recognize that oppression of the spirit is the meanest poverty of them all. We have descended from Shakespeare's parlous defense of the Jew as being able to bleed to Ed Koch's inaccurate assumption—I hope it is inaccurate—that we are, by now, conditioned reflexes—that is, machines, buttons for a politician to press. If-any-Jew-who-votes-for-Jackson-is-crazy proves to be a useful political button, then I say we Jews have become machines and can no longer look at serious matters by their true merits, or face up to fundamental problems.

Mailer's greatest concern was that the country would not be able to solve "any of our worst problems in organic fashion until a black man does become president." Jackson, he concluded, was the best candidate to bring out "the potential love of black and white for each other." Nationally, Jackson came in second to Dukakis, and lost to him in New York state, but in New York City Jackson defeated him by a few thousand votes. Mailer's endorsement may have been a factor, especially in Manhattan.

Mailer returned to *Harlot's Ghost* with few interruptions for the rest of the year. When Joyce Carol Oates sent him a story she had published, he said he would have to defer the pleasure of reading it, and gave an explanation he used on several occasions: "Reading good work when you're writing something of your own is like watching a marvelous Ferrari drive by while you have the parts of your own car spread over the garage floor. So I don't read good writers while I'm working."

There were exceptions to this rule, however. Mailer admired Don DeLillo and read his novel about Lee Harvey Oswald, *Libra*, when it was published in August. They had met a few years earlier when Mailer had invited him to a reading at the Actors Studio. DeLillo had no idea that Mailer knew of him and his work, and was surprised to receive the invitation. He recalled that in 1959 when he was a struggling young writer, he found a copy of *Advertisements for Myself* in a desk drawer at the advertising agency where he worked.

> I found it and I started reading it. I don't think I owned a single hardcover book, and now I had one, except for old school textbooks. I thought it was terrific. I still have that copy. I just ingested it. I read it at home and every subject one might try to explore had been explored by Mailer in this book—speaking, writing, arguing.

Before the reading at the Actors Studio, the two novelists chatted a bit, DeLillo said, and "in my awkwardness I found myself saying something I would never have said under another circumstance. I told him I was writing a novel about Lee Harvey Oswald, and it had an effect on him. I saw this in his face, obviously." After Mailer read *Libra*, he wrote to DeLillo with praise.

> What a terrific book. I have to tell you that I read it against the grain. I've got an awfully long novel going on the CIA, and of course it overlapped just enough that I kept saying, "this son of a bitch is playing my music," but I was impressed, damned impressed, which I very rarely am. I think we keep ourselves writing by allowing the core of our vanity never to be scratched if we can help it, but I didn't get away scot-free this time. Wonderful virtuoso stuff all over the place, and, what is more, I think you're fulfilling the task we've just about all forgotten, which is that we're here to change the American obsessions—those black holes in space—into mantras that we can

> live with. What you've given us [is] a comprehensible, believable, vision of what Oswald was like, and what Ruby was like, one that could conceivably have happened. Whether history will find you more wrong than right is hardly to the point: what counts is that you brought life back to a place in our imagination that has been surviving all these years like scorched earth, that is, just about. It's so rare when novel writing offers us this deep purpose and I swear, Don, I salute you for it.

A few years later, after he had finished *Harlot's Ghost*, Mailer told DeLillo that *Libra* had saved him five hundred pages, presumably by allowing him to leave out any exploration of the motives and actions of Oswald. He had been given one more year to turn in the final manuscript. Random House, he said, "has been damn decent to me, and I'd like to return the favor," so he was stripping down his life to the "essentials of a fighter's camp" to meet the deadline.

FOR SEVERAL YEARS, Mailer had been corresponding with a writer from Providence, an English professor named Edward McAlice who had an Irish flair for language. They met only a couple of times, but wrote regularly. Mailer read McAlice's manuscripts for over twenty years, offering advice and encouragement, and also enlisted Judith McNally to give him feedback. McAlice was one of scores of aspiring writers that he helped. Writing to him in early February 1989, Mailer lauded one of his phrases—"all the steaming shit and foul midden pools," noting that he had "said the same thing about this and that condition a hundred times, but never as well." He also praised his "power to characterize people in four or five lines," which he compared to that of Gabriel García Márquez. "Me," he said, "I can't get someone through a door without blowing a thousand words." Mailer was feeling bogged down. "The wind had better be breezing up," he told McAlice, because he was only half done with a novel that was due in a year.

At that time, he was writing about his narrator, Harry Hubbard, a young CIA agent posted to Uruguay, where Howard Hunt was the CIA station chief. Mailer could have sent Hubbard anywhere, but assigned him to this obscure post in order to contrast intelligence work in this backwater with the fast-paced, dangerous work of Harvey and his associates in Berlin, and to establish Hunt in preparation for using him when he got to Watergate. On Mailer's timeline charts, Hunt had his own column, with entries running from his OSS service in World War II, through Watergate and the suspicious death of his wife Dorothy (also a CIA agent), to Hunt's 1973 conviction. His plan, we can surmise, was to use Uruguay as a breathing space between the more dramatic events in Berlin in the early 1950s, and Cuba in the early 1960s.

But once Mailer got into the small-bore espionage of Hunt and Hubbard in Uruguay, he had difficulty extricating himself. Part Four of the novel, "Montevideo, 1956–1959," is the length of a good-sized novel, 266 pages, and while it has some bright spots, they are few. Hubbard could have described his time with Hunt in memoir fashion, but he chose to depict it in the correspondence between Hubbard and Montague's wife, Kittredge, then living in Washington. Mailer wanted to keep Kittredge before us because Hubbard will marry her 16 years later. And he also wanted to create a major woman character who is an intellectual. Kittredge is a "characterological theoretician," and the originator of the Alpha-Omega personality theory, an elaboration of his belief that we house two separate personalities. The first difficulty with understanding her theory, she tells Hubbard, is that everyone who has heard of schizophrenia or split personality assumes that Alpha and Omega are equivalent to two satchels in the psyche; one part lives, one part observes and interprets. Not so, she says, we are two people, both are "as complex and wholly elaborated as what we usually think of as a complete personality." Nevertheless, Alpha and Omega can be characterized: Omega "originates in the ovum and so knows more about mysteries":

> Conception, birth, death, night, the moon, eternity, karma, ghosts, divinities, myths, magic, our primitive past, so on. The other, Alpha, creature of forward-swimming energies of sperm, ambitious, blind to all but its own purpose, tends of course, to be more oriented toward enterprise, technology, grinding the corn, repairing the mill building, building the bridges between money and power, *und so weiter.*

Each self can borrow properties from the other, and do, because they are wed "like the corporal lobes of the brain." Marriage is one model for the relationship, she says, another possibility is Czarists and Bolsheviks. Kittredge's theory mirrors Mailer's ideas stretching back to "Lipton's" in the mid-1950s. It tells us more about Mailer, however, than Kittredge, who appears to have been willed into existence to satisfy the perception that he could not create a female character who is both passionate and intellectual. She is perhaps the least convincing major fictional character in his work. At the end of "Montevideo," not much of consequence has happened, while doubts and dissimulations have piled up.

As one plows through the Uruguay years, an expectation is created that the Alpha-Omega scheme will somehow be integrated into the plot. This does not happen, and the disputed theory's only real value, as Kittredge puts it, is to suggest "how spies are able to live with the tension of their incredible life-situations." Mailer flogs the theory, reinforcing the criticism that his worst sin, as Jonathan Franzen has argued, is redundancy. This tendency, along with the unbelievable ways by which Hubbard and Kittredge carry on their plain language correspondence about all kinds of classified operations—by regular mail and by diplomatic pouch—seriously damages the novel.

AS MAILER WAS working on "Montevideo," he was drawn into the controversy surrounding Salman Rushdie's novel *The Satanic Verses*, published in the fall of 1988. On February 14, 1989, the supreme leader of Iran, Ayatollah Ruhollah Khomeini, issued a fatwa, or religious decree, stating that Rushdie's novel was blasphemous and that he and his publishers should be killed. A Radio Tehran announcer read Khomeini's words: "I call on all zealous Muslims to execute them quickly, wherever they find them, so that no one will dare to insult the Islamic sanctions. Whoever is killed on this path will be regarded as a martyr, God willing." The next day an Iranian imam announced a $2.6 million award for any Iranian who carried out the fatwa, and $1 million for anyone else who did it. These amounts were doubled shortly afterward. Some devout Muslims were troubled by sections of the novel that suggested that the Prophet Muhammad had distorted some of the revelations—which comprise the Koran—given to him by Allah, and also by scenes depicting the Prophet's wives in brothels. There were riots and book burnings all over the Muslim world, including in sections of England with large immigrant Muslim populations. Two of the novel's translators were stabbed to death, and many died in the rioting. What saddened Rushdie was the fact that the novel (which was short-listed for England's Booker Prize), was intended "to give voice and fictional flesh to the immigrant culture of which I am myself a member," yet opposition was fierce among these very people, especially in England. Rushdie, born a Muslim in Mumbai, was offered protection by Prime Minister Margaret Thatcher and went into hiding.

A week later, the PEN American Center organized a rally of support for Rushdie, who had many friends in the United States. Gay Talese was one of the principal organizers, along with Mailer, Sontag, Doctorow, and Robert Stone. The rally took place in downtown Manhattan at the White Columns building, co-sponsored by the Authors Guild and Article 19, an international anticensorship organization. Joining these writers at the rally were DeLillo, Didion, Edward Said, Robert K. Massie (president of the Authors Guild), Robert Caro, Christopher Hitchens, Diana Trilling, Frances Fitzgerald, and Larry McMurtry, among others. Hitchens was applauded loudly when he borrowed Shelley's description of King George III to describe Khomeini: an "old, mad, blind, despised and dying king." The rally took place shortly after many bookstores pulled the novel from their shelves, citing fear of violence. DeLillo recalled that there was an anti-Rushdie demonstration going on outside the building when he and the other writers "took our seats and waited to be called to the rostrum—*all except Mailer.* He entered at some later point, dramatically, and spoke with Maileresque heat." He blasted the booksellers and said that Ayatollah Khomeini "wished to show the great length of the whip he can crack, the whip whose secret name is found in our bottomless pit of terrorism." The fatwa will make writers learn whether they are willing "to die for the idea that serious literature, in a world of dwindling uncertainties and choked-up ecologies, is the absolute we have to defend." He called on other writers to join him in a vow to open up "all literary meetings with a reading of the critical pages of *The Satanic Verses.*"

Rushdie was still in hiding three years later when Article 19 published a collection of letters to him from twenty-seven writers. In his letter, Mailer said that he had begun writing as a young man "with the inner temerity" that if he kept on eventually he would "outrage something fundamental in the world" and endanger his life. Rushdie had done just this and now was in "a living prison of contained paranoia."

> It is hard enough to write at one's best without bearing a hundred pounds on one's back each day, but such is your condition, and if I were a man who believed that prayer was productive of results, I might wish to send some sort of vigour and encouragement to you, for if you can transcend this situation, more difficult than any of us have ever known, if you can come up with a major piece of literary work, then you will rejuvenate all of us, and literature to that degree, will flower. So my best to you, old man, wherever you are ensconced, and may the muses embrace you.

JUST BEFORE THE controversy, he wrote to congratulate Styron on receiving the MacDowell Medal. Mailer, a past winner, had been on the committee that selected him and wrote to say it was "great fun" the day he was voted in. "I think I can whisper to you that the finalists were Styron and Bellow and you won out." Styron sent Mailer an article about the ceremony, which included a George Plimpton speech in which he described a trip Styron had made.

> A number of years ago, on a trip up the Amazon, Bill persuaded a group of tribal youths that the English word for "good morning" was "Norman Mailer," intoned in a curious sing-song rhythm, and to be delivered with a bright smile. He got them doing this in unison—fifteen or twenty of them "Nor-man Mai-ler!" My mother, who is 87, is thinking of taking a trip up the Amazon, and I have warned her about this—so that she can take it in stride if a row of semi-clad, spear-carrying tribesmen appear at the water's edge and call across the water: "Norman Mailer!"

Mailer told Styron that the Amazon story had given him a good laugh, which he needed because *Harlot's Ghost* was "in the doldrums."

In April he wrote to daughter Kate, who was touring with *The Cherry Orchard* in Russia, to say the novel was "now approaching the 1,500 page mark in manuscript, and God knows who will ever read it other than scattered members in the family, which is not large enough, I fear, to support me." He wrote a few more letters, and then stopped his correspondence completely for the next six months in an attempt to wrestle with what he called "a 300-lb greased beast." He used a more carnal metaphor in a letter to Mickey Knox, "I'm still staggering along with the novel. I tell anyone who's willing to listen that it's like fucking an elephant. Sometimes I believe I'm really in and working away, only to discover to my horror I'm out—I'm not in at all, I've merely been screwing a wrinkle in the hide." He worked steadily for the rest of 1989, taking some time off for July and August in Provincetown when the family came in shifts, but taking no trips and publishing nothing until November of 1989.

In that month's issue *Esquire* published a two-page restatement of his theological ideas. It is notable for its discussion of God's gender: "It has occurred to me, despite my reputation as a male chauvinist, that God may be referred to as 'She' as legitimately (for all we know) as 'He,' or, even better, as 'They,' if one can conceive of divinity as marriage between a godlike Male and Female." It seems likely that the piece might have been intended for the novel, which is rife with theological speculation. Harlot, like Angleton, is a profoundly religious Cold War warrior who believes that "Communism is the entropy of Christ." He repeats Mailer's belief that when Christ said, "Forgive the sons for the sins of the fathers," sanction for the scientific method was given, that is, once fathers knew that their children would not suffer, they were free to experiment, probe nature's secrets. "That," Harlot says, "was the beginning of the technological sleigh ride which may destroy us yet." Harlot also repeats a thought from Milton's *Paradise Lost* that Mailer learned from his Chicago friend Paul Carroll: "The Devil, you must never forget, is the most beautiful creature God ever made." He would repeat it several years later when he depicted Satan in *The Gospel According to the Son*. All through the fall he wrote rapidly and nothing interfered with his routine.

IN THE QUIET months of the off-season in P-town as he labored on the novel, the Mailers occasionally dined with a local contractor, Fred Ambrose, and his wife, Nancy. John Buffalo was the same age as their oldest son, David, and the two six-year-olds enjoyed each other's company. Ambrose was first invited to the Commercial Street house in the early 1980s to discuss various renovation projects, and he and Mailer hit it off immediately. Ambrose had spent a year in his twenties as secretary to Alan Dugan, the Pulitzer Prize–winning poet who lived in nearby

Truro, and knew his way around literature. He had read and admired several of Mailer's books, but their relationship was not a literary one. "We never really talked literature," Ambrose said. "Norman, from what I could gather—and maybe this is a broad statement—Norman liked people who were involved in real time and liked what they did, whether they were plumbers or politicians."

> I stayed with current events and, you know, I'd read, so Norman and I were able to really banter for 25 years over current topics, and if I disagreed with him I was usually able to support my position with a point and he'd get upset, so I knew I was gaining some footage. I'd never win, of course, but it was sort of like a boxing match. Norman liked to punch hard on an idea. He didn't want just a fluffy answer, he liked facts. He wanted the foundation of your argument, your premise, what your premise was. Norman was the Grand Inquisitor.

Ambrose was hired to replace a large window, the defining feature of the dining room, where Mailer spent most of his time when away from his study. It was an important job, Ambrose said, because views were important to Mailer. Besides the window in the dining room, there was a similar one in his third floor studio.

> It spanned the width of his oak desk, which was very plain; there was nothing up there. I was designing upstairs and I was very intimate with his workspace, and it was very sparse. There was a yellow pad, and pencils, a couple of Hemingway books, a dictionary, and a few odds and ends, and that was pretty much what I witnessed of the writing room. There was a cot on one side. The big window looked out to the west of Provincetown and down through the harbor. If you look at his apartment in Brooklyn, again Norman had these views. Norman always had to have a big pane of glass, and he had to have something really intricate to look at, whether it was Lower Manhattan, or he looked out at the stark view out of the dining room; it just went way out on the bay. The window upstairs in the study was much more complicated and it looked out onto the pier, and then some houses to the right, and then the boats in the harbor.

The six-by-six multi-paned dining room window had caught the spindrift for years, and was falling apart. When Ambrose redesigned it, he eliminated the small panes. "Norman had a fit," Ambrose said. "We had this heated conversation. I said, 'Norman, you got a world-class view out there. You live here because of your view. Live with it for thirty days. If you're not happy, we'll put the panes in.' Norman was really mumbling to himself and not happy." Mailer's tastes, Ambrose said, were Edwardian and neoclassical. "After about three months, Norman warmed up to the window and we never heard anything more about it. To this day the window is there."

Ambrose is also an inventor and holds a number of patents. Mailer was fascinated, he said, with inventing things. He came up with an idea for a hat that would shield his weak eyes. He had always been quite nearsighted, and in his late sixties developed cataracts. Driving in bright sunlight was difficult. "He wanted me to get involved in producing this bright orange baseball cap. He had taken brass wire and bent it and shaped it and put it under the brim of the hat. And he built this elaborate sliding mechanism under the bill. You could move it left and right and block the sun without impairing your vision. He just loved his invention." With Ambrose's help, Mailer built a working model. "In the marketplace, I don't think it would've gone far," Ambrose said. "I never told him to stick to his writing and stay out of the invention business. The amount of work he put into that hat was a testimony." Ambrose still has the model.

When he was tired of work, Mailer liked to go with Ambrose to local bars, where he knew many of the patrons. "There was a lot of respect for Norman," he said.

> The thing that Norman liked about Provincetown is that it's a very visceral town. People wear their hearts on their sleeves, and they think with their emotions. Whereas in the city people are calculating; they're guarded. In Provincetown people are either carpenters, or fishermen, or people very close to the trades, and they didn't have great secrets to keep so they were very open, and the recourse against them for speaking publicly was virtually nil. So Norman went out and talked to people and if they wanted to chew his ear off—and Norman liked to talk and sit with people—fine, it was

> always an open, candid conversation. People knew who they were talking with, but that would fade very quickly, and that's about it. Norman was just a regular person on the street. You have to understand, Provincetown's a walking town. You don't drive much. You can get pretty shitfaced in the center of town, and the golden rule was you didn't get flagged unless you fell off your stool. So you could do a lot of serious drinking and, you know, if you wanted to crawl home that was your business. There was a lot of freedom in Provincetown, and a lot of acceptance. I think it was the freedom that Norman liked in Provincetown.

Chris Busa grew up in Provincetown where his father, Peter, an important modernist painter, lived for many years. Father and son were both friendly with Mailer, who rented a studio from Peter. The younger Busa gave tennis lessons to Mailer's sister, Norris, and some of his children, and later sat in on Mailer's Texas hold 'em games. Mailer was featured twice on the cover of the annual *Provincetown Arts*, which Busa published and edited, and sometimes Mailer attended the annual July publication party. A year-round resident, Busa wrote that he "took comfort in walking by Mailer's house and seeing his light burning in the window of the attic, knowing he was working. He was some kind of power in the neighborhood, an engine that seemed to move the leaves as I walked down the street." Busa recalled an exchange Mailer had with Eddie Bonetti, one that characterizes the kind of P-Town frankness that Ambrose described.

> Norman and Eddie were at a cocktail party one summer afternoon in August. They were standing at the bar, enjoying the company and laughter and stuff, and Eddie says, "You know, Norman, I like you in spite of your celebrity." And Norman said, "Eddie, how would you like it if I said I liked you in spite of your obscurity?" You know, that's the kind of verbal play Mailer could always use to equalize the playing field.

WHEN HE TOOK a break in mid-March 1990 to address the stack of mail that had accumulated, *Harlot's Ghost* was only three hundred pages longer than it had been the previous April. Mailer had been backtracking, trying to bring coherence to his sprawling manuscript. That spring, he dictated over 130 letters, most of them notes. He told Knox that "my elephant" will be "two-thirds as long as 'Remembrance of Things Past' and half as good."

The novel opens in March of 1983 as Hubbard is driving up the icy coast roads of Maine to see Kittredge, his wife of ten years. In a magnificent ninety-page burst, Hubbard spins out in sharp flashbacks and reveries the central characters and events of the previous three decades. These backward glances, comprised of brief vignettes and brisk character sketches, alternate with his depiction of the spooky events on the night he arrives at the ancient, ghost-ridden, Hubbard family home. Shortly after Hubbard arrives, he learns of Harlot's possible death and confronts the ghost of Augustus Farr, a piratical sea captain, in the vault beneath the house, after which it burns down and Kittredge flees with another agent, a muscular, bisexual masochist named Dix Butler, with whom she is having an affair.

Harlot's hypothesis that the Watergate burglary was an attempt to tap the secrets of the Federal Reserve Bank, located on the next floor up, is also presented in this opening section, "Omega" (the last comes first), and we get our first taste of Kittredge's Alpha-Omega theory. The deaths of JFK, Monroe, and Dorothy Hunt (wife of Howard Hunt, one of the engineers of the Watergate break-in) Hubbard suggests, may be related, as well as Oswald's. There are also allusions to Castro and the Cuban Missile Crisis. Mailer was preparing to connect the dots between some of the most vexing mysteries of postwar American life, possibly by laying blame at the feet of Richard Nixon, whose crimes and resignation would have to be presented—in some fashion—in the second volume. We don't know much about Mailer's plan for the sequel, but there is a clue in one of his notes, which states that the affair of Hubbard and Kittredge was "P[oly] M[orphous] perverse in its early stages, cut off by K after [the rock-climbing] accident." Given his druthers, it's likely that Mailer intended to present all the details of their intimacies.

Mailer provides glimpses of Hubbard's early life, his tours in Berlin, Uruguay, Miami, and Vietnam, and we learn of his two writing projects, *The Imagination of the State* (an incomplete and abandoned study of the KGB), and a detailed memoir of his work in the agency since 1955. We never see the first study, but the memoir, "The Game," comprises the bulk of the novel. Hubbard also asks the questions that the reader will ponder for the next one thousand pages: Is Harlot dead? If so, by his own hand or another's? Was he a true-blue patriot and seeker of the Russian mole who has infiltrated the agency, or is he the mole?

There is another possibility: Harlot might have gone deeper into the wilderness of mirrors, switching sides and going to Moscow as a fake turncoat, or triple agent. Mailer's provisional plan for the sequel (to be titled "Harlot's Grave") was for Hubbard to find Harlot in Russia. He has gone there, according to his notes, because the general degradation he feels "convinces him that his life, reputation, career, and sense of inner status can be redeemed only if he sacrifices himself," exactly how Mailer does not say. But in another note he says, "Watergate operated by Harlot to fuck Nixon since he will make peace with Russians." Harlot, like Angleton, does not trust the Russians, does not want the Cold War to end, and does not want the CIA's power to shrivel. Many of the actions of the CIA's hierarchy are calculated to overestimate Russia's strength. Mailer later publicly criticized President Reagan for such fearmongering.

Random House had given him an extension until the end of June 1990, and when he missed this deadline, it was moved to the end of July. When dates are proposed, he said, "I nod my head and agree." He knew his manuscript would have to grow. One of his models was Thomas Wolfe, who "qualified as great on several counts, and one of them was the great length of his novel. You knew you were reading something important when you picked up 'Of Time and the River.' " Nowadays, he continued, mass booksellers want authors to write eighty-page books so "everyone can make more money, sell more product." Wolfe's manuscript, it should be noted, while enormous, was cut severely by Maxwell Perkins. Mailer dismissed most of the suggestions made by Jason Epstein on major excisions, but was always attentive to his editing. *Harlot's Ghost* is dedicated to him.

If he could reach 2,500 pages, Mailer wrote to an admirer, "we can nail half the book to the mast and call it a flag." Then, he assumed, Random House would give him two more years for the sequel. He worked through the summer in Provincetown, where he went on the assumption that with fewer interruptions, he could "write ten to twenty percent faster." There were few family excursions and no trip to Maine—he would never summer there again. Deadlines came and went as pages piled up in Provincetown and, in the fall, back in New York.

Mailer did not socialize. Around mid-December, he was done, and announced the completion in several letters. In one he called it "a fairly ambitious book—it may, in fact, be my most ambitious." For the next three months, he worked on the 2,700-page manuscript with Epstein, his secretary, Judith (a doughty grammarian), and the Random House copy editor.

Veronica Windholz, Mailer's copy editor on several of his subsequent books, described her first meeting with him. She was expecting to meet an "egomaniac" but, instead, "met a curious, gregarious, deeply intelligent, knowledgeable, jocular, voluble man," who was "generous and big-hearted, but he was also all business." Mailer hated semicolons, she soon learned, and would rewrite an entire paragraph to avoid using one. "He wrote with ease, fast, fluently, and with a smile of satisfaction when he was finished. He loved to write—he loved the challenge of expressing himself just so."

> Especially in the beginning, before he was familiar with my work, any query or small change I had made would cause him to reread the entire passage—and sometimes, if he found something in his own writing that he didn't like, a whole page. He'd take the paper in both his hands, lean back in his chair, and recite the prose to himself, rocking back and forth as he said the words out loud. He listened to—and for—the rhythms of his language as if he were composing music. If something was off by even a fraction of a beat, he knew it immediately.

Everything in his prose, Windholz said, "was subservient to style." Mailer was not a grammarian of note and had his own rules about punctuation—insisting, for example, that "So" at the beginning of a sentence be followed by a comma. "The heavy lifting" in his prose was handled by cadence, she said. Mailer couldn't carry a tune, but he was a master of English prose rhythms.

BOUND GALLEYS WERE sent to reviewers in May, and October 2, 1991, was set as the formal publication date, giving reviewers the summer months to digest Mailer's behemoth—a couple of reviewers quoted what Hollywood mogul Jack Warner said when asked if he had read Hervey Allen's 1,224-page novel *Anthony Adverse*: "Read it? I can't even lift it." Waiting for the reviews, he wrote a review of Bret Easton Ellis's novel of contemporary consumerism and sadism *American Psycho*. It was his first assignment as Writer-in-Residence at *Vanity Fair*, where Tina Brown had been editor in chief since 1984. Mailer had developed a warm relationship with her after she published two long excerpts from *Tough Guys Don't Dance* in the magazine, and helped him raise funds for the PEN congress. They had become good enough friends for her to request a letter endorsing her application for a green card (she was a British citizen). He said she had lifted *Vanity Fair* out of a "bog-ridden beginning," making it a magazine of "distinction and high style." He would write four more essays for the magazine over the next year, and continue his relationship with her when she became editor of *The New Yorker* in 1992.

Mailer did not review many books over his career; they can be counted on two hands. Some special circumstance had to entice him. In Ellis's case, it was the outcry from editorial writers and women's groups over the detailed descriptions of mutilation, torture, and dismemberment of innocents committed by the novel's protagonist, Patrick Bateman, a serial murderer and obsessive consumer of state-of-the-art commodities. Ellis had received a $300,000 advance from Simon & Schuster, but on November 15 the firm canceled the book just before copies were to be shipped to bookstores, a response to editorials condemning scenes of "unmitigated torture" in the novel—in one, a half-starved rat is introduced into the vagina of a half-slaughtered woman. Bateman, Mailer wrote, "kills man, woman, child, or dog, and disposes of the body by any variety of casual means." Ellis's goal: "to shock the unshockable." The novel was picked up by Vintage and published on "a tidal wave of bad cess," in Mailer's words, that made it a paperback bestseller.

Mailer found the novel's violence, after the first few shudders, to be repetitive and boring. "Murder is now a lumbermill where humans can be treated with the same lack of respect as trees." After torturing women, Bateman enjoys some yuppie delicacy—"swordfish meatloaf with kiwi mustard"—and then admires his girlfriend's "silk satin D'Orsay pumps from Manolo Blahnik." Is there any good reason, Mailer asks, for readers to tolerate the novel's endless catalogues of luxury goods and its many "acts of machicolated butchery"? His answer is that art will tolerate almost any extreme if something new and valuable is learned.

> Fiction can serve as our reconnaissance into all those jungles and up those precipices of human behavior that psychology, history, theology, and sociology are too intellectually encumbered to try. Fiction is indeed supposed to bring it back alive—all that forbidden and/or unavailable experience. Fiction can conceive of a woman's or a man's last thoughts where medicine would offer a terminal sedative.

Ellis intimates that Bateman resembles Raskolnikov sufficiently to use an epigraph from Dostoyevsky, but Mailer concludes that the snobbish yuppie is a cipher. "Bateman is driven, we gather, but we never learn from what." If Ellis hoped to reveal something new about the links between gratuitous violence and American materialism, then he had "to have something new to say about the outer limits of the deranged" in his chief character. "In the wake of the Holocaust," he says, it is legitimate for a novelist to seek an understanding of extreme acts of violence, but when we have finished with *American Psycho* "we know no more about Bateman's need to dismember others than we know about the inner workings in the mind of a wooden-faced actor who swings a broadax in an exploitation film. It's grunts all the way down." He ends by saying he cannot forgive Ellis for forcing the reader to go unnecessarily through his chamber of horrors.

In contrast, the reviews of *Harlot's Ghost* were better than any Mailer had received since *The Executioner's Song*, but there was little sympathy for its length and a division of opinion about the words he placed at the end: "TO BE CONTINUED." Some said the sequel could not come too quickly; others felt enough was enough and that the sequel would not be missed any more than the unwritten parts of other gargantuan works—Spenser's *The Fairie Queene* comes to mind. The tersest summation of the reviews is captured by Don DeLillo's comment: "extremely impressive if only he'd forgotten Uruguay." Except for Kittredge, Mailer's characters, both historical and fictional, were generally praised, especially Montague and Harvey, with Hunt and Modene Murphy not far behind. Christopher Lehmann-Haupt, like most reviewers, found Kittredge to be "unbelievable and inconceivable as a character until one begins to think of her as Norman Mailer." She acts so much like him, Lehmann-Haupt argues, and is so obviously a mouthpiece for his ideas that her effectiveness is sorely diminished. When she speaks, we hear her creator's characteristic locutions: "Vanity is the abominable conceit that one could run the world if only one weren't so weak."

We last see Harvey in the spring of 1966 in Rome, where he is chief of station. He has bungled relations with Italian intelligence, and Hubbard has been sent to tell him that he is being recalled. By this time Harvey is a dead-end alcoholic, and is recovering from a heart attack. Drawing on David C. Martin's account in *Wilderness of Mirrors*, Mailer ends "The Game" with an account of Hubbard's all-night meeting with Harvey over two bottles of bourbon. Harvey tells Hubbard, "I am ready to return in the first body-bag that can be passed through a pig's asshole." As they get drunk, Harvey keeps taking out his pistol and pointing it at Hubbard's forehead. He complains that he has been refused access to the Italian agents that Montague cultivated in World War II, and calls Montague his worst enemy, one he would shoot if he were in the room. After hours of fascinating rambling about JFK's assassination, Oswald and Castro (foreshadowing "Harlot's Grave"), Harvey tells Hubbard that when he fingered Kim Philby, he suspected that the Russians blew the Brit's cover to protect someone else, "*Someone* larger." He doesn't name the person, but he doesn't have to: "One part of my brain," Hubbard said, "was singed forever with the fear that it was Harlot." As he is departing with Harvey's promise to resign, Harvey head-butts Hubbard, Mailer-style, an unmistakable tap of approval from the author.

After a brief coda situating Hubbard in his Moscow hotel room in March 1984, the novel ends with the three words of Mailer's now famous broken promise. It is worth noting that March 1984 was when Mailer first arrived in Moscow, and checked into a hotel not far from Lubyanka Prison. If Hubbard's suspicion is correct, it would be the likely residence of the defector, Hugh "Harlot" Montague.

The generally positive response Mailer received from reviewers about his portraits of Harvey and Harlot was matched by equally warm comments about the portions of the novel which cover the years 1960 to 1963, from the preparations for the Bay of Pigs debacle in Cuba and the ensuing missile crisis through the unsuccessful assassination attempts on Castro (under Harvey, with Hunt, Sinatra, and Giancana as players) to the successful assassination of JFK. John Simon, writing in the *New York Times Book Review*, said that "Mailer really comes into his own and vividly evokes the internecine intrigues among the C.I.A., the F.B.I., the Pentagon and the State Department" in these adventures, a view echoed in other reviews. He has special praise for his depiction of the invasion—"a clandestine nocturnal operation by sea and land against Cuba is a gem any novelist could be proud of"—but goes on to rail against the novel's "lopsided" shape and the many exfoliations of the Alpha-Omega theory. He was not alone in making such complaints. Both John Aldridge and Christopher Hitchens found fault with the Uruguay section (as did almost every other reviewer), although they did not see the novel's defects to be as serious as Simon did. Aldridge says that the South American operation moves "at the pace of a paraplegic snail," but calls the novel Mailer's "best written," an accomplishment showing that "he possesses the largest mind and imagination at work in American literature today." (Mailer circled the passage for use in ads for the novel.) Hitchens sees merit in the "continuous emphasis . . . placed on the concept of 'doubling' and division," and says he has personally known and read of many CIA men who had the same "bipolar mentality" of Mailer's agents.

Simon's review infuriated Mailer—not what he had said, but that he had said it at all. Not only had Simon panned *Marilyn*, he had been one of only a very few critics who gave a negative review to *The Armies of the Night*, calling it "a demented Waring blender churning away at sexual, political, and literary power fantasies, sadomasochistic day-dreams." Given these reviews, why did the *Book Review* editor, Rebecca Sinkler, give Simon the job of reviewing Mailer's magnum opus? Mailer contacted *Times* publisher Punch Sulzberger, whom he knew slightly, to ask for a meeting with Sinkler. He got it, and asked her for space to write a rebuttal to the review. Sinkler, now in a somewhat defensive position in that she had not dug out the negative review of *Armies*, only the slam of *Marilyn*, told Mailer that Simon had read both advance excerpts from *Harlot's Ghost* in *Rolling Stone*. He liked them, she said. Simon's approval of the excerpts, coupled with his assurance that he could write a fair review convinced her to give him the assignment, which four others had turned down. The last thing Mailer laid on the table at the meeting was Simon's disapproval of Kate Mailer's 1988 performance in *The Cherry Orchard*. After he had read it in *New York* magazine, where Simon was the drama critic, Mailer put out the word to everyone who knew Simon: "Tell him," went the message, "not to get into the same room with me."

This last complaint added no luster to his request for a rebuttal, but the overlooked review of *Armies* apparently did, and Sinkler gave Mailer space for his piece. In it, Mailer repeated every bad thing Simon had said about him and suggested that the bad review of Kate's performance was really a barb at him. Simon was given space for a counter-rebuttal, and pointed out that Mailer made no attempt to refute anything in his review, so what was the big deal? His chief complaint about the novel, he repeated, was its "prolixity." In her concluding note, Sinkler said that in her judgment Simon had written "a fair and balanced review that met the standards of this newspaper," but also admitted that the editors had not been aware of the negative review of *Armies*, a tentative mea culpa.

Letters taking sides poured in over the next few weeks and the *Times* published twenty of them, about evenly divided. Sinkler said she took satisfaction in the fact that "in the long run readers got the last word." She said she still stood behind Simon's review, while adding that Mailer had been a "pussycat" at the meeting and after the episode "has never been rude or unpleasant." She and her colleagues "often chuckled," she said, "about how we got 1,600 words out of Norman Mailer without paying a cent." The dustup kept the novel in the public eye through the end of the year. Despite its high price—it was the first trade edition of an American novel to sell for $30—and weight of four pounds, it made the bestseller list for four weeks, his ninth book to do so.

One other review requires mention, that of Howard Hunt, who spent thirty-two months in federal prison for his part in Watergate. He recalled meeting Mailer and Jeanne Campbell at a dinner party given by Bill Buckley (a former CIA man recruited by Hunt), but says that the meeting was "what in espionage jargon is called a 'brush contact.' " Being included as a major character was an "unwanted distinction," he says, although he found no fault with his portrait. Hunt's generally favorable review ends the speculation that Mailer, once properly trained, might have joined the ranks of the CIA-backed Congress of Cultural Freedom back in 1949–50, an organization that sent its members—including Robert Lowell, Mary McCarthy, and Arthur Schlesinger—to challenge Mailer when he spoke at the 1949 Waldorf Conference. It is, therefore, unlikely that Mailer would have joined the agency. But he would have been tempted.

In the novel, Hunt proposes another qualification for a good CIA man, and he passes it on to Hubbard: "I will suggest that if anyone ever inquires why you think you're qualified to be in espionage, the only proper response is to look them in the eye, and say, 'Any man who has ever cheated on his wife and gotten away with it, is qualified.' " Mailer certainly had this qualification, and believed it was indispensable to his novelistic understanding of the CIA. His working principle, as stated by Lenny Bruce (when Hubbard, Harlot, and Kittredge see him perform) was: "Never tell your wife the truth. Because biologically it has been proven. Women's ears are not constructed to hear the truth. They will slaughter you if you tell it like it is. So, lie your ass off."

Mailer did. He continued his affairs for the length of time it had taken to write *Harlot's Ghost*. Not long after it was completed, Norris confronted him, and he faced the third great crisis of his life.

FOURTEEN
A MERRY LIFE AND A MARRIED ONE

In the seven years after *Harlot's Ghost*, Mailer published four books—three varieties of biography and a mammoth anthology of his work—and more political commentary and journalism than in any period since the 1963–72 outpouring. He covered the political campaigns and conventions of 1992 and 1996, traveling around the country with other political reporters on buses and planes. The oldest reporter on the campaign trail, he was referred to as "the Dean." He took pleasure in his ability to keep up with the younger reporters, and to write books on figures as disparate as Oswald, Picasso, and Jesus Christ. But he was deeply unhappy with his inability to begin the sequel to *Harlot's Ghost.* This failure in the creative realm was matched if not eclipsed by a near-disaster in the domestic one.

In the fall of 1991, Mailer's secret life all but ended. He was forced to break off, or drastically alter, relationships with several women in order to save his marriage. The crisis in his relationship with Norris continued for over a year, and for a time they separated. It was a private struggle; few people outside the immediate family realized how close the marriage had come to foundering. In public, they went through the motions, in private they fought. After much pain, they reaffirmed their commitment to each other, although Norris did not trust him completely for several years, if ever. His work was affected for a time, especially after Norris learned the full extent of his infidelity. But "he was still able to compartmentalize," she wrote in her memoir, and kept working all through this period.

As the situation unfolded, he took on a variety of small tasks. Some of these were related to the novel—the selection of excerpts from *Harlot's Ghost* for several different publications, including three long ones in *Rolling Stone*, a U.S. book tour (thirty-five interviews over two weeks), and another in England—and some were more enjoyable activities. Governor Mario Cuomo, upon the recommendation of a committee chaired by Albany novelist William Kennedy, appointed Mailer to a two-year term as New York State Author, an honor that came with a $10,000 stipend and few duties. Mailer also began organizing a dramatic reading of George Bernard Shaw's *Don Juan in Hell* with Gay Talese, Susan Sontag, and Gore Vidal, a benefit for the Actors Studio, where he was still involved. At the request of John Updike, he agreed to write a chapter in the official history of the National Institute of Arts and Letters and the American Academy of Arts and Letters, *A Century of Arts & Letters*. After it was clear that Bill Clinton had the Democratic presidential nomination wrapped up, Mailer wrote Hillary Clinton a long letter recommending that her husband focus on racial tensions in his acceptance speech at the 1992 convention, hoping that it might gain him some sort of role as an unofficial advisor. Continuing as *Vanity Fair*'s Writer-in-Residence, he published several more pieces in the magazine. His report on the Republican convention of 1992 was published in *The New Republic*. The companion piece on the Democratic convention was written but never published. Mailer felt that it was too obviously approving of Bill Clinton.

He continued to state in interviews and letters that he was on the cusp of beginning "Harlot's Grave," and many of his efforts during this period were connected to JFK's assassination, which he had handled obliquely and briefly in the novel. He planned to remedy this in the sequel. For example, when Updike proposed that Mailer write the chapter on the 1960s for the history of the American Academy, he accepted immediately, seizing an opportunity to revisit his favorite decade. For a *Vanity Fair* piece, he tried to arrange an interview with Castro, who was coming to New York for a U.N. meeting. Mailer sent his request to Castro via the Cuban U.N. delegation, and also asked Gabriel García Márquez, a close friend of the Cuban dictator's, to intercede. "I can promise," he wrote to Castro, "that your ideas will receive an honest display" in Tina Brown's fast-growing magazine, and gain related attention in other media. Castro's reflections on the assassination, presumably, would have been an asset for the sequel.

If Castro responded to Mailer's request, no record of it has surfaced. But Mailer was able to speculate on the assassination in two of his published *Vanity Fair* pieces. One was a review of Oliver Stone's 1991 film, *JFK*. Mailer praised the film, which won two Oscars, for presenting a controversial hypothesis about the assassination that rejected the conclusion of the Warren Commission that Oswald was the sole assassin. Mailer called it "the worst of the great movies," and applauded Stone for stirring the pot in an imaginative way. The other piece was a one-act play, "Earl and Lyndon: An Imaginary Conversation," which depicts, quite humorously, the arm-twisting techniques—lofty, carnal, and threatening—employed by a manipulative President Johnson to convince Chief Justice Earl Warren to head the commission investigating JFK's death.

Mailer also continued to meet with a group of writers who called themselves, with false bluster, the Dynamite Club. It came into being in 1989 as a forum for the examination of various conspiracy speculations about the assassinations of the 1960s, Watergate, and other mysteries. The group met in Washington and New York, often at Mailer's apartment. It included Jim Hougan, a writer and magazine editor; Dick Russell, a freelance investigative writer; and Edward Jay Epstein, author of a shelf full of books about the JFK assassination, Oswald, and the CIA. DeLillo also attended a few meetings, and recalls learning at one of them that Mailer had met and head-butted one of the Watergate burglars, although he could not recall which one. Finally, he wrote a short preface to *The JFK Assassination: The Facts and the Theories*, written by Carl Oglesby, one of the founders of a group called the Assassination Information Bureau. Mailer lauded the book for clarifying his thinking and praised Oglesby's efforts to keep the mysteries surrounding the assassination before the public eye and on the agenda of Congress.

THE CRISIS IN the Mailers' marriage, long simmering, came to a boil in August of 1991. His appetite for "a merry life and a married one," as he once described it, had become too blatant to ignore. Norris had been suspicious for some time, but whenever she asked questions about his hastily scheduled, unaccompanied trips, he got angry, and when he did try to explain, his excuses were flimsy. But now she had evidence: long-distance phone call bills and motel and restaurant credit card charges. "It all made sense now," Norris said. "I had been a complete and total fool. For years." One afternoon in Provincetown, she confronted him in front of his sister, as Barbara recalled.

> I remember I was sitting with Norman in the bar and Norris came down in a fury. She presented him with some stuff she found, I think, on the computer or something. I don't know where she found it because he'd been denying it. And then she left. I remember looking at him and asking him, "Why did you do it?" And he said, "Life was getting too safe."

Later, Mailer admitted to Norris that he had spent a night in Chicago with "an old girlfriend," Eileen Fredrickson, but swore it was the only time and promised it would never happen again. Norris was devastated and incredulous, especially when he kept changing the details of his account. For the next two weeks she peppered him with accusations, getting so angry that "I physically attacked him a time or two, hitting him with my fists like a child, him promising again and again that it was a one-time thing that was over." In late August, she returned to New York with John, thirteen, and Matt, nineteen, who was beginning college at NYU. Mailer stayed behind to do some writing.

Before she left, he gave her the keys to his studio and asked if she would drop off a small box of books there. She found this odd, because she had ventured up the three flights of stairs to the studio only once before. He called it his *querencia*, his lair or retreat. When she entered, she saw that it had never been swept and trash was piled in corners. Mailer had a high tolerance for mess. She went to his desk and found a collection of love letters. He had always said that women pursued him for his celebrity and that's why he received cards and letters with endearments and lipstick on them. This was certainly true. As anyone who spent much time with him in public can testify, women never stopped buzzing around him, even when he was over eighty. He had told Norris that she was the love of his life, which was also true, but that was hard for her to believe after digging through a desk crammed with billets-doux, photographs, and mementos. It seemed to her that he wanted his secrets to be found. "This other life," Norris wrote, "as he said over and over, willing me to understand, had nothing to do with me. Except, of course, it did." She went home and wrote him a long letter.

In it, she told what she had found, including a signed note from Carole Mallory, dated December 1, 1989, in which she promised not to ask Mailer for any money for three months. Then, Norris got to the nub:

"Are you in a dilemma as to whether or not you will risk our marriage to feed the beast?"

> After more than sixteen years I feel like I'm living with a stranger. Incredibly, insanely, the sex has been better with you these last two weeks than it has ever been, and I'm remembering the early years. You are all consuming to me now. I only want, more than anything, to go on with you in the life we have. I want us to continue to love our children and have the home life we perhaps have taken for granted all these years. But if you are truly dissatisfied—even a small part of you—and you really need other women in your life to make you complete, then I won't stay with you. I don't want to end up a bitter wife, searching phone bills and Visa receipts for clues of infidelity, dying inside when you take a trip; not believing you when you say in that flat voice, "I love you." I deserve better than that.

Mailer returned to Brooklyn the day he received the letter in the mail.

Norris had a small studio on nearby Hicks Street, and they walked there to have it out. "I'm going to tell you everything," he said, "but there will be no divorce. I don't want this to break us up. You are my life, and I won't let you leave me." Norris said she was making no promises. He opened up, detailing affairs, naming women, on and on, "like he was vomiting up a bad meal, and had to get it all out." Norris listened, wept, and then attacked him, hitting and scratching. He buttoned up, deflecting what blows he could and absorbing the rest, using an old club fighter's defensive skills. When he had told everything, Norris wrote, "We went back to the apartment, where we went to bed, totally exhausted, fell into each other's arms, and had wild sex. Go figure."

Norris confided in her close friends, and Susan, Danielle, Betsy, and Kate. Danielle recalls talking with her on the telephone.

> I was concerned that she was sharing all this with me, and I felt divided. On the one hand, I was angry with my father, and felt empathy for Norris, but I also felt loyal to my dad, and didn't want to get caught in the middle. So, I was very careful about what I said. I listened and was sympathetic, but I didn't want to be disloyal to my father. Another part of me was weary: here we go again,

dad is changing partners. My intuition was that Norris would not leave him.

The confessions continued, as he recalled brief affairs and one-night stands from years before, spitting out memories whenever they came to him—once in the back of a taxi. Norris told the driver to pull over and got out, and he chased after her. In front of others, they smiled and pretended, and somehow continued with work, family events, and black-tie social affairs. When they were alone, she said, their conversations were blunt, scathing, and brutal. When *Harlot's Ghost* was published, there were several book events in New York. At the Random House party at the "21" Club (scene of Cal and Harry Hubbard's memorable lunch in the novel), hosted by publisher Harry Evans on October 31, Carole Mallory showed up. She was "shockingly brazen," Norris said, and kept bringing photographers over to take her picture with Mailer. She seemed to be taunting Norris, or seeking to create a scene or a physical altercation. Norris ignored her, and then told her quietly that she might as well enjoy herself because "she had gotten the last nickel she was going to get out of Norman."

Norris was correct: Mallory lost her sugar daddy. In fact, Mailer had already broken with her. Their last tryst took place in June 1991 at the Hotel Bel-Air in Los Angeles. In mid-September, shortly after his confession in Norris's studio, Mailer called Mallory and told her he was severing relations. She threatened to go to the media with the story of their eight-year affair. According to Mallory, Mailer said that if she went public, her pain would be far worse than his. When she brought up his conscience, he said, "My conscience is my business. And so is my marriage. I love Norris." After a few recriminations, the call was over and except for the book party at the "21" Club and one chance meeting a few years later, they never saw each other again. In her 2009 memoir Mallory said she finally realized that Mailer needed Norris "to feel whole."

Lois Wilson had a far different relationship with Mailer, and a longer one. They first met at a Stanford University party in 1949. She was an unusual woman, as her daughter and only child, Erin Cressida Wilson, explained. Growing up very poor in Kentucky, Montana, and Ohio, she was "desperate to get out." At nineteen, she already had her master's degree, and received her Ph.D. from Stanford only a few years later. Married at twenty-four to another English professor, Graham

Wilson, she had a long, happy, and complex marriage. He died in 2005 at the age of eighty-nine. Their relationship, according to their daughter, "was deep and mysterious." Recalling her mother, she said:

> Lois had many lovers. Norman was her first, and the relationship lasted the longest. The rest of the men largely and eventually became good friends. One of them was Alberto Moravia [Mailer introduced them] who fell madly in love with Lois and begged her to come live with him in Rome. She did come to him on a Fulbright at the University of Rome (without leaving the relationship with Graham), but was never willing to leave Graham—or her life as a professor at San Francisco State—for Alberto. She desired freedom, even from her lovers.
>
> The relationship with Norman was almost the same length as the marriage—Graham and Norman died around the same time. Thus, the marriage with Graham and the relationship with Norman were both sixty years. There were many instances in which Norman socialized with Lois and Graham at the same time. Norman and Lois were sexually compatible—yes—but they were also good friends who didn't ask one another to hand over money, power, prestige, or family in return. They had somewhat of a pure relationship—one of fun, sex, secrecy, and endless talks into the night, lying next to one another. Lois was married to one man the entire time, and only had one child. Norman had many wives and many children during this time. They both knew that they had mates and other lovers, and there doesn't seem to have ever been an ounce of jealousy or possession.

Lois Wilson and Mailer met in hotel rooms two or three times a year for an intense day or two, not unlike the way the two lovers meet in Bernard Slade's play *Same Time, Next Year.* But while their meetings continued after he met Norris, their sexual intimacy ceased. Lois Wilson recalled:

> Everything changed when he met Norris. I could see that she was a good person for him. And that he loved her and that she loved him. And I thought I'd better lay off. She has a right to her own modus operandi. So, I would hear quite a bit about her because he liked to

> talk about her; he truly was very much taken with her and she made a life for him that he couldn't have made otherwise.

Wilson believes that she and Norris would have liked each other if they had met. But Mailer never brought them together, fearing Norris's jealousy. "Yes, she was jealous," Wilson said. "But she had no reason to be with me after a certain point. I was on her side."

Eileen Fredrickson's relationship with Mailer began thirty years after Wilson's, but it was similar. An avid reader who spoke fluent Japanese, acted in commercials, films, and television programs, she had a number of careers, including modeling, bartending, and hosting her own radio news program. Like Wilson, she sought nothing from Mailer except his presence, and saw him only when he was in Chicago. He called her weekly for many years, and sent her inscribed copies of his books. In early October 1991, just before he went on the book tour for *Harlot's Ghost*, he called to tell her that Norris had found her letters. Fredrickson recalled the conversation.

> Judith got suspicious about the bills from Chicago, and she told Norris that there was something going on. Norris, at that time, knew about Carole Mallory, and she put her foot down and said she was going to divorce him if he didn't vow, on his children, not to see me anymore. So he called me and told me that Norris had found out. He asked me to sit down, and then told me he had to take a vow on his children not to see me again. So from about 1991 or '92 he wasn't supposed to see me, but he called me all the time, and he did come to see me a couple of times.

Asked why he was involved with so many women, she said, "He just couldn't help himself. He should have been a Mormon."

Norris had stopped going on book tours with Mailer in the mid-1980s. She was tired of being ignored and disrespected by pushy fans and photographers. But she went along with him on the tour for *Harlot's Ghost*, traveling with him to Boston, Chicago, the West Coast, and Washington, D.C. He wanted her to accompany him, insisted on it, she said. Her chief motive was to keep an eye on him. His was to reassure her that he was a changed man, as several of his comments indicate. For example, when asked if there was anything he wanted to do that he hadn't, he said: "I'm too happily married to answer that." Reporters referred to him as "a mellower Mailer" and "a softer Mailer," and noted his "attestedly happy 11 years of marriage to Norris Church." With Norris sitting next to him in an ABC studio where he was waiting to be interviewed, he said he was "a more content man" than in the past. "I think you have to round out or round off after a certain age or you'll go crazy. You have to give up certain ideas of yourself. I gave up some of my crazier ambitions." He said he had followed "his inner voice" all his life, "sometimes as a clown or a fool."

His longest interview during the book tour was with David Frost. Frost led off by asking Mailer about the comic obituary he had written in 1979, which began with a report that he had passed away after his fifteenth divorce and sixteenth wedding. Frost wondered if he could write such a piece today.

> MAILER: Oh, I wouldn't dare. I'm married to a young, lively, proud and slightly—as she grows into imperiousness every year—woman. So, she wouldn't, she'd not look lightly on that.
>
> FROST: That's right. No fifteen divorces. No sixteen weddings. Number six looks as though it's going to last forever.
>
> MAILER: Oh, I think so. I think so.

He had no desire to see marriage number six end, but he wasn't sure that Norris felt the same. She held the cards.

In Chicago, the Mailers' driver and guide (hired by Random House) was none other than Eileen Fredrickson, whom he had helped get a job driving visiting writers around town. Norris was astonished, and thought Mailer was being cruel. As they drove, Norris saw that Fredrickson "obviously adored him." Fredrickson said that while it was a terribly awkward situation, Norris was "very gracious." Mailer invited her to a reception for him that night, and she attended but was the first person to leave. "Even though I was an adulteress," she said, "I was still a lady." The situation repeated itself in Los Angeles, where Mailer pointed out another old girlfriend (possibly Lois Wilson) in the audience. The fact that they were much older than she gave Norris no solace. "These women took over my life, I couldn't think of anything else; we couldn't seem to talk about anything else." Norris wasn't sure what to do; she prayed at night. It was the worst of times.

When they returned, Sam Donaldson and an ABC television crew came to their apartment for an interview with both Mailers about *Harlot's Ghost.* It was not Norris's favorite book, especially after she learned that Mallory was the model for the sluttish Maine waitress, Chloe. Norris liked Donaldson's "devilish air," and they got on well. With the camera rolling, he asked what it was like to live with Norman Mailer. She shot back her answer: "Well, Sam, it's kind of like living in the zoo. One day Norman is a lion; the next he's a monkey. Occasionally he's a lamb, and a large part of the time he's a jackass." Donaldson laughed; Mailer looked shocked. When the segment aired, Norris's answer was retained.

An old boyfriend, a bachelor surgeon in Atlanta, called her with concern after he saw the show, and she told him that she was thinking of leaving Mailer. The doctor invited her to visit. She declined and decided instead to go to Arkansas and see her parents and best friend, Aurora Huston. It was now late in the year, and Norman went skiing with Stephen and John. Norris enjoyed seeing her family, and then she, Aurora, and Aurora's husband, Phil, drove to Florida, where they met another old friend. "I was on the brink of totally changing my life and was giddy with possibilities," she said. But she was also worried. She had a comfortable life, loved all of Mailer's family, enjoyed their two homes and many friends, and the freedom she had to write and paint and act. She and her two friends talked over the situation at length.

While Norris was away, Mailer called up a friend, filmmaker James Toback, and asked him to meet him for dinner at Nicola's. They enjoyed one-on-one dinners, and shared what Toback called "extremely intense personal conversations" of the kind not to be repeated. He had witnessed Mailer's complicated relationships with several wives and mistresses, and watched him move from one to another. "There was never any notion, certainly in my observation, and I think in his, that he would ever find someone who would be the last." But when he listened to the way Mailer talked about Norris, he saw that the "endless cycle" had come to an end. Mailer told him why he had asked him to dinner.

> "Listen, the real reason I had to see you tonight is that I have a hole at the center of my being. I've never felt anything like it." I said, "Why is that?" And he said, "Well, Norris has left and I don't know if she's going to come back." He went on saying, "I did certain things

> and she confronted me and I confessed. Part of me wanted to lie. I felt if I lied I could get away with it, but I just couldn't get myself to lie, so I confessed. And that was it and she left." He said, "I don't regret having told the truth, but I don't know what to do with this feeling; it's the worst feeling I've ever had."
>
> So I volunteered, because I felt that's what he was looking for me to do. I said, "I've had that feeling on many occasions and I call it a bad abscessed tooth ache of the soul." And he said, "You can come up with something better than that."

A short time later, Mailer called Toback and said. "Well, she's back and I'm not going to do anything to cause her to leave again."

Norris had a brief encounter with the Atlanta surgeon although it "felt desperately wrong," she said. But the one-night stand had nevertheless enhanced her sense of self and made her ask herself: "Why had I been consumed by this old, fat, bombastic, lying little dynamo?" They went to dinner at a local restaurant, where Norris told him about the surgeon, more to hurt him than to be forgiven, and then announced that she was leaving him. Calmly, without tears, she began to discuss living arrangements after the marriage ended. He'd been through this with his other wives; it was an old routine for him. But he recoiled, slapped the table, his invariable reflex: "No, no, no, no, no," he barked. "We are not breaking up." Everyone in the restaurant was watching.

Norris realized that she didn't want it to end. "I loved our life, I even loved him," she later wrote, and she didn't want the family, especially John, the only one of his children who had lived continuously with his father past age six, to suffer. But there had to be trust; it was the sine qua non for continuing the marriage. Mailer started talking, using "all his talents and abilities, which were considerable," and before the meal was finished, he had convinced her of his love; she would be the last Mrs. Norman Mailer. The family was relieved that the crisis was over; they all loved Norris. But the confessions and fights had taken a toll. "I somehow had taken a step away from him in my heart," she said. It was a necessary step, flowing from her clear-eyed recognition that it might be impossible for him to control his roving eye and promiscuous penis. But he was slowing down, and she hoped he was ready to try monogamy again. He did try, and would be notably, if not perfectly, successful, at least by his own standards. He still loved several women—Carol Stevens, Lois Wilson, and Eileen Fredrickson. Perhaps others. Norris was philosophical: "It was better to be that little bit less in love and not care quite as much," she wrote.

In an interview two months after Norris died on November 10, 2011, Aurora Huston said that she believed that her best friend and Mailer "were both naive, in their own ways. There was always an innocence about Norris, always." Aurora and Norris called or e-mailed almost every day. They were utterly frank with each other. Aurora recalled her first meeting with Mailer, and gave her views on their marriage.

> The first time I saw them together, I knew they were real partners. Not just in a physical sense or even as a unified public entity. More than anything they were bound together in some deeply rooted corpus that they created together. Unfortunately, the very thing they created and loved was made from bits and pieces of their very souls. Norman was a hard man to love. His genius was also his folly. He thought himself right in every thought, word, and action. Norris, however much she loved him, was not going to let him get away with his foolishness. I do believe they loved each other until the very end, but they tore at the flesh of their relationship. Norris, in my opinion, humanized Norman and made him see the damage caused by his reckless behavior. Norman had too large an ego to look into the mirror and accept his reflection. He needed to be adored; he needed to be lustfully adventurous with careless bravado. The very traits that made her fall madly in love with him, made him alarmingly, ferociously, untamable. Nothing happened to their love, in truth, though both will swear differently. Life happened along the way. Disappointment, waves of illness and old age. Wherever they are, the undisputed truth is that they loved each other.

Norris also had a brief affair with someone she had known for years, and it confirmed her belief that she could also be happy with someone else. But her life, she wrote, was bound up with Norman, "that crazy wild man," and the affair, her last, was short-lived. "I knew that if I left him I would wonder the rest of my life what he was up to, and be sorry I wasn't with him." Slowly, as Mailer was covering the political conventions in the summer of 1992, their marriage began to heal.

The inscription in Norris's copy of *Harlot's Ghost*, dated October 1991, reflects the tensions of their marriage at that moment.

> To my baby wife alias the wise woman who is my dear lady and a hoyden heart mean as piss on rare occasions and lovely as a forest clearing when all is still, namely princess, I adore you Norman

In 1995, after their marriage had settled back into an easy groove, he dedicated *Oswald's Tale* to her.

> To Norris, my wife, for this book and for the other seven that have been written through these warm years, these warm twenty years we have been together.

IN EARLY 1992, Mailer began work on a short biography of Picasso. Even in the most trying times of the crisis, he went to his studio almost every day to write. His plan was to knock it off in six months, and then turn to "Harlot's Grave." Whatever might happen to his marriage, his literary activities would continue. He had first gotten interested in Picasso's work in his senior year at Harvard when he had taken a modern art course, which he said was the most enjoyable course he had taken in all four years—he got an A. He had always been interested in the way that Picasso's style kept changing, much as his own did. "I could've written under several different names," he said, "and gotten away with it." In the spring of 1962, he had signed a contract with Macmillan to write the biography and spent "eight happy weeks" at the Museum of Modern Art leafing through fifteen thousand reproductions of the great artist's work. "I think if you have a sensibility and you spend two intense months with Picasso the way I did, it just sits inside of you like a time bomb." But he shelved the project.

Thirty years later, he tried again. All through the first half of 1992 he worked on what would eventually be called *Portrait of Picasso as a Young Man*, completing it in September. The biography is 125,000 words in length, contains over two hundred illustrations, and takes Picasso from his birth through the Cubist period, ending in the early years of World War I. It is not a scholarly biography but an interpretive one that tries to explain the complexities of Picasso's character. Mailer borrowed freely and heavily from the work of a score of biographers, memoirists, and art critics. His most important borrowings are from the memoir of Picasso's mistress Fernande Olivier, and from the first volume of the authorized biography by John Richardson. "Nothing, of course, can equal the scholarship of John Richardson's book," Mailer said, "but I think mine may give a closer sense of what it would have been like if one had known Picasso personally as a young man." The book is dedicated to Judith McNally, who did invaluable research for it.

Jeanne Campbell had introduced Mailer to Richardson and his partner, Douglas Cooper, in the summer of 1962 in the south of France. Mailer recalled getting drunk with them. He had hoped that Richardson would introduce him to Picasso, but for whatever reason this did not occur. In 1991, Richardson published the first volume of his biography, covering the years 1881 to 1906, just before Mailer began work on his. Mailer read it, quoted extensively from it, some eight thousand words; there was a good deal of paraphrasing as well. Jason Epstein, also Richardson's editor, found himself in a difficult situation. Richardson's second volume, *The Painter of Modern Life*, which would take Picasso up to 1916, was well under way, and the prospect of two Random House biographies covering the same period and being published at the same time was awkward. "I was apprehensive," Epstein said, "and told Mailer there might be a problem." But in the late summer of 1992, before the problem came to a head, Mailer got a call from Larry Schiller.

SCHILLER HAD DEVELOPED extensive contacts with Russian high officials, including members of the KGB. His translator (and later his wife), Ludmilla Peresvetova, introduced him to the head of the KGB, Vadim Bakatin, and through him he was introduced to the top KGB official in Minsk, Aleksandr Sharkovsky. Schiller was informed that the KGB was interested in exploring the possibility of giving him access to its file on Lee Harvey Oswald, who had lived in Minsk in 1960–62. This file had been sealed since 1963, and everyone who had known Oswald had been warned to remain silent. But under glasnost life had changed, and the KGB realized that it possessed a property that could be monetized. Schiller explained the situation to Mailer, whom he wanted as a collaborator on the project, and found him to be "very interested, eager." Next, Schiller went to see Epstein, who agreed to fund additional trips to

Moscow and Minsk. Epstein did not reveal, according to Schiller, that investigative reporter Gerald Posner was already working on a book on the assassination for Random House. At that time the two books didn't seem to have much in common, less, in fact, than the biographies of Picasso by Richardson and Mailer.

Mailer loved to drop everything, mobilize his energies, and launch in a new direction. Metaphorically speaking, he always kept a bag packed on the chance he would hear the train whistle of a new adventure, which could lead to new energy, new success. At this point in his life, the Oswald-KGB project had immense appeal. "I had a double motive," he said. First, he wanted to learn about the KGB's exhaustive scrutiny of Oswald for the new book. He and Schiller would be in the front rank of what he called "the virtual Oklahoma land grab" for long-sealed records. Second, the KGB, he surmised, might have much to tell him about JFK's assassination, even if Oswald was not involved. Information on how the agency functioned in the old Soviet Union, now dismembering, and how it responded to the assassination, would "get me beefed up for the second volume of *Harlot's Ghost.*" There was a further incentive: the project would take him out of temptation's way and allow the recriminatory air between him and his wife to clear. He had no idea of the shape of the book he would write, but that didn't concern him. "Oswald's Years in Russia" was the working title that Schiller had given Epstein. Beyond that, it was all guesswork. Like Holmes and Watson, if you will, Mailer and Schiller were going on a long journey to solve a mystery.

From September of 1992 through the spring of 1993, Mailer spent the bulk of his time in Minsk and Moscow, even celebrating, quietly, his seventieth birthday in the Russian capital. Schiller, recently divorced from his second wife, was in one or the other city almost continuously through this period. Mailer flew back and forth several times for various reasons, including a trip to Dallas to meet Oswald's widow, Marina, arranged by Bill Majeski, the New York City detective responsible for Abbott's arrest. They also traced Oswald's footsteps around Dallas after the assassination, and made a one-day trip to New Orleans, where Oswald had also lived. He also came back for his appearance in *Don Juan in Hell* at Carnegie Hall on February 15. But for most of this eight-month period, he was in Minsk. Norris was worried that he might be "schtupping fat, old, ugly Russian women in babushkas," but Mailer was faithful and focused on Oswald.

Living conditions in Minsk were uncomfortable, especially once winter arrived. It was bitter cold. The sun, rarely visible through the endless snow, set in mid-afternoon. "I doubt if there were 10 sunny days," Mailer recalled. "Nothing to do but work. No night life." Mailer wrote to Knox about the food.

> It doesn't matter how rich you are, you cannot buy yourself a decent restaurant meal in Minsk, so the biggest gastronomic sensations in the last five months while living there are the scrambled eggs I make myself, or the borscht, or once or twice, the tuna with cabbage. It's a sad place, and I'll tell you about it when I see you, for it made me realize how Russian I am, even though Minsk is in Belarus (White Russia rather than Russia itself, and a separate country now) but it doesn't matter—one gets a sense of what life was like in the old Soviet Union.

He was exaggerating a bit, because Schiller, ever the dealmaker, soon came up with a way to get good food. After they had established relations with the KGB, he gave various officials (including Marina Oswald's aunt, Valya Prusakova, whose late husband had been a colonel in counterintelligence) cash to buy food on the black market. Then, the two overweight Americans were invited for lunch or dinner a few times a week; if they had borscht for lunch, they might have lamb for dinner, and some caviar. When Norris came for a two-week visit, she scrounged through the markets, buying beets and carrots, chunks of gristly beef rolled in newspaper, and "small hard eggs that came in a plastic sack of twenty, eggs squeezed from the butts of sturdy little chickens that continually pecked the frozen ground in search of an insect or a worm, scratching out a living like everybody else." Schiller didn't cook, and Mailer had a limited repertoire (including some decent pasta), so they ate better during Norris's stay. The visit was good for the marriage. After Norris returned, she told her last lover that she was staying with Mailer. "I'm not sorry we had our little fling," she told the lover. "It made me see that I really loved Norman, for better or worse."

Mailer and Schiller were shown the tiny apartment where Oswald and Marina lived, and the one above that the KGB used as a listening post. They met the Soviet rifle expert who attempted to duplicate Oswald's marksmanship, and they had several desultory meetings with Sharkovsky and his staff. All that they had been told of any consequence was that the Soviet Union had no hand in the murder of JFK. The officials were leery about receiving cash payments, but there was one thing they ardently desired: shoes. Schiller was given a list of sizes and types and arranged for a truckload of expensive footwear to be driven in from Austria and unloaded at KGB headquarters. He was also busy making arrangements for food and gifts—for example, getting Aunt Valya's television set fixed by a black market repairman—and getting his technology set up. He brought in expensive optical scanning and duplicating equipment (plus toner and paper), and made arrangements to send material out daily via Sprint satellite data transfer. When Mailer wasn't doing interviews with Schiller—they interviewed fifty or sixty people, all told—Mailer spent his time reading the Warren Commission Report. His eyesight wasn't good, so Schiller arranged to have excerpts from the twenty-six volumes blown up to double size.

One night in his overheated apartment, Mailer was cooking pasta for Schiller. Just the two of them were there, Schiller recalled. Mailer, standing over the stove in a sleeveless undershirt, pointed out that something Schiller had just said or written was jumbled. As they discussed the matter, Mailer said, lowering his voice a little, "Larry, I think you may be dyslexic," and then explained that he knew about dyslexia from one of his children. Schiller had heard of the disorder, but never thought he might have it. Mailer was always patient with him when he made spelling and grammar mistakes, Schiller said, defining words and giving him short grammar lessons now and then. There was never any condescension. When Schiller flew home for Thanksgiving—as did Mailer—he was tested and found that Mailer was correct. Schiller was fifty-six years old, and until then had not been diagnosed with this disability. Mailer's hunch helped Schiller understand and deal with his long-standing insecurities about reading and writing.

In their first months in Minsk, they spoke to people who had known Oswald and Marina: relatives and former friends of Marina, Oswald's coworkers at the radio factory where he had worked, neighbors and acquaintances. They had also been given access to the KGB library and some relatively unimportant files. But they still had not been shown the Oswald files. Finally, Schiller's instincts told him that it was time to force the situation, and he asked his translator, Ludmilla, to set up a luncheon meeting with Sharkovsky and his top staff at KGB headquarters. He pondered what he would say, but wrote nothing down, trusting his spontaneity. Mailer had no speaking role; he was to play the great writer and sit in august silence. In a brief biography written for the KGB by Schiller and Ludmilla, he was described as the American equivalent of Tolstoy.

After the elaborate lunch, Schiller began to speak, with Ludmilla translating. He said that if the Oswald files were given to the media, it would be disputed or forgotten. "But," he continued, "if you give it to a writer, such as Mr. Mailer, whose works are on the shelves of every library in the world, including your own KGB library, you are giving the information to history. You're preserving it with an independent voice that will establish the credibility of the fact that the Soviet Union was not involved in President Kennedy's assassination." He had their attention, and went on to say that Mailer ranked with Boris Pasternak and Aleksandr Solzhenitsyn. Ludmilla, "being as brilliant as she was," Schiller said, did not repeat this comparison, but substituted this: "You give it to a writer who, under his photograph in the Soviet encyclopedia, says Mr. Mailer is 'a writer who dares write what he thinks.' " After he concluded, Sharkovsky said no, he would not give them the files outright. He would, however, rent them an office in the KGB building, "and every time you ask a question, we'll bring you that part of the files that answers your question. If you stay long enough, and if you're smart enough to ask the right questions, you will learn much."

They rented the office for $1,000 a week and went to work. It was a laborious process and much time was spent in discussions about the wording and sequencing of questions. For weeks they spent five hours a day copying material in Russian from the Oswald file, which consisted of numerous bound volumes kept in potato sacks. Then it was translated into English and sent out daily by satellite.

They worked on through the darkest days in winter, accumulating more and more material. They learned that not long after Oswald arrived in Minsk, the KGB suspected that he had been sent to blow up a new hotel there where Premier Nikita Khrushchev was about to visit. They followed him from store to store as he purchased what looked like the parts for a wireless radio, but it turned out to be a toy he was making for a friend's child. Another possibility the Soviets considered was that he was a new kind of mole, one who would lie low for decades and then be activated at some critical time. The Soviets had sent similar moles to the United States (ten would be arrested in 2010 after living in the United States for several years). After five months Schiller and Mailer had accumulated eleven thousand pages, including their transcripts of the interviews with people who had known Oswald and Marina.

On several occasions, Mailer and Schiller had major disagreements about how to pursue a line of questioning. One of the biggest fights was about Marina's virginity when she married Oswald. Was Oswald faking it when he brought a piece of bloody sheet into the radio factory after his wedding night, the traditional Russian proof of deflowering? Some of Marina's former friends intimated that she had lost her virginity in Leningrad a few years earlier, after which, to get her away from the nightlife, she was sent to Minsk to live with Aunt Valya. There would be other arguments when Schiller, the lead interviewer (as he had been for *The Executioner's Song*) would ask a question and Mailer would object and want to ask something different. As Schiller recalled:

> Of course, the subject being interviewed didn't know what we were saying, because they didn't speak English, and sometimes he [Mailer] would get up and walk out of the room, saying, "You go finish the goddam interview yourself then." Or sometimes we would both go outside, sometimes Ludmilla would turn around and scream at us, saying, "What are you guys doing? Why are you fighting in front of somebody?"

Toward the end of their stay, Schiller came to the conclusion that they would need copies of large portions of the original files in order to have credibility with the media in the United States. Without such copies, Schiller asked himself, how can we prove that we're quoting from actual KGB reports? He concluded that they could not leave Minsk without copies of all the bugging reports.

Mailer wasn't worried in the least about credibility, Schiller said. He felt that his own name and voice carried sufficient weight. When Schiller told him he planned to give Sharkovsky's assistant $10,000 for three sets of copies of the reports, "Norman went ballistic." He was worried that they would be arrested for bribing high officials. Shoes were one thing; $10,000 in American money was another. They got into a loud argument in the stairwell outside Mailer's apartment, wrestling and pushing each other down the steps. "It was really an altercation," Schiller said. "He finally understood that I was not going to retreat." For a few weeks they weren't speaking, and then Schiller told him that he had paid the bribe. Now Mailer had to listen. Schiller's plan was for Mailer, himself, and Ludmilla (now married to Schiller) to leave from three different airports. Each would have a set of the reports. "If one of us was arrested," he said, "that made the drama, made the book more important because we would be taking out something that the West was unable to get their hands on. And that was my final argument to him: that if we were stopped at customs, we would actually be promoting the book. Mailer's answer was, 'Fine, as long as I am not the one who is arrested.' " Schiller told him that on the contrary he would be the most desirable person to be caught with the files. It would be a major story in the media worldwide, which could only help the book. Mailer saw his point.

Schiller would leave from Moscow, Ludmilla from Leningrad, and Mailer from Minsk. "We were worried," Schiller said. "I remember the night before I left I had bad cramps in my legs and I had to lie in the bathtub in the hotel." But their fears were unfounded. They were working with the KGB, paying them rent every week, and no one paid any attention to them at the airports. Their suitcases weren't even opened. The fix was in.

BACK IN THE States in the spring of 1993, John Aldridge noted in passing to Mailer that Judith was not terribly forthcoming when he asked for information on the telephone. Mailer, who had ceded a great deal of control over his public life—and some of his private—to his assistant, responded by noting that "Judith still treats me like an undergraduate and, for the record, whatever my talents, they do not include training Judith. Like Gore Vidal, she's untrainable; comes to you fully developed and you thank god for what you've got and put up with what you're not going to get." Mailer dictated this letter, and as usual Judith typed it, which added to the comic dimensions of their relationship. She could hold her own in repartee with him, and never hesitated to point out, wryly, the dangers of various rash ideas he had. Mailer valued her verbal skills, research abilities, and wit. They spoke on the telephone daily, sometimes several times, and when Mailer was in Provincetown he faxed whatever he had written to her for typing. A lot of material passed between them in this way. The fax machine is one of the few pieces of recent technology that Mailer deigned to use. Even so, he was ham-handed and broke several of them.

Mailer also told Aldridge about his research for "a book on Oswald in Minsk," one of his few comments on it in a letter. "Oswald," he said, "is a man of parts," and he hoped to depict "a character who's worthy, to some little degree, of the size that history has given him. At least he won't be a stick figure in a CIA/KGB set of scenarios." One of the ways he hoped to demonstrate that Oswald was worthy of a full-scale portrait was through the memories and insights of his widow, now remarried and living in Texas. Schiller had interviewed Marina earlier for an ABC-TV docudrama on Oswald. For the new project, he offered her $15,000 for five days of interviews in June of 1993.

During his earlier visit with Bill Majeski, Mailer had interviewed Marina for a few hours. But, now, with the Minsk interviews in hand, he and Schiller had many more questions and needed to conduct extended interviews with her. Schiller had a friendly relationship with her, but nevertheless had to use all his resources to convince her. Mailer, who once noted that "Larry Schiller makes Baron Von Munchausen look like George Washington," described his collaborator's methods. "Larry can be utterly unscrupulous," he said, "so he went around telling everyone with whom we wanted to do interviews, I was the American Tolstoy, and they owed it to history to be interviewed by us. He also succeeded in getting Marina Oswald to sit down with us for a few days and talk." She came with a friend to the sessions in a Dallas hotel, but for the interviews—three hours in the morning, three in the afternoon, and two in the evening—Marina would be alone with Mailer, Schiller, and a Russian-English dictionary.

The interviews started off well with questions about noncontroversial matters—the date she moved to Minsk, relationships with Aunt Valya and Uncle Ilya, where she worked, and so forth. They also asked more general questions: Did she and Oswald live as a couple in the United States about the same way as in Minsk? Had she understood that he would not be guaranteed a job in the United States as he had been in the Soviet Union? What did she remember about the time before the assassination when Oswald tried to shoot General Edwin Walker? She had gone over this ground before with the FBI; much of this material was in the Warren Commission Report. Mailer and Schiller also had a wealth of information from people in Leningrad and Minsk, so when they moved into more difficult territory, they could cross-check her replies.

On the third day, the questioning got tougher. As Schiller put it, "We started with Vaseline, but we knew we were going to end up with vinegar." They began asking about the time her uncle locked the door when she was out late with a boyfriend and she had to sleep on the landing. "She looked at me with real hatred in her eyes," and began screaming: "You're worse than the Secret Service; you're worse than the FBI." Schiller used the same tactic he had used on Nicole Baker for *The Executioner's Song*. "What do you have to hide?" he asked. Marina could have walked out at any time; Schiller had given her a cashier's check on the first day. "That is my modus operandi," he said. "I always want to take a little bit of the high road. I don't know if it produces something good or not, but you know she showed up every day." Mailer was interested in her early sexuality and particularly eager to learn how the blood got on the sheet that Oswald displayed to his coworkers. Eventually, she opened up and told them that she was not a virgin when she married Oswald, but she never explained how she deceived him on their wedding night. She called Schiller a liar when he brought up the story of the bloody sheet. "You can't use your capitalistic tricks on me," she screamed.

Marina felt betrayed, Schiller said, because she had assumed their relationship was personal, not adversarial. Her awe of Mailer had evaporated. On the final day, relations soured entirely. "Every single word out of her mouth was said with venom," said Schiller. They had pressed her hard, and all bridges were burned. The next morning, she and her friend drove away. No goodbyes, no hugs. Two years later Schiller sent an advance excerpt from the first part of the book to Marina. "We had a moral obligation, not a legal obligation, to let her know beforehand what Norman Mailer thought and was writing of her," Schiller said. She wrote back an angry letter to Schiller criticizing Mailer. "Tolstoy, he's not!" she said.

Mailer began writing in Provincetown in the summer of 1993, planning, as usual, to be done long before he was. He told one friend that he would be done by the end of the year "or my publishers will be in misery." Most of his correspondents got Xerox copies of one of his drawings, doodles, and cartoons, and faces made of numbers, an idea he says he got from Picasso, who as a boy thought the number seven was an upside-down nose. He would continue to send out these drawings—most had captions—to the end of his life, often with a handwritten note. One of the few letters he did write in the second half of the year was to Peter Balbert, a professor at Trinity University who had hosted Mailer when he spoke there.

> I hope eventually this book will have offshoots that prove interesting for the second volume of Harlot's Ghost. For now it's been an experience of some interest. I can tell you that I never disliked Ronald Reagan more than when I was in Russia and Belarus (Minsk) for whatever the old Soviet Union was, you can't call it an evil empire. A depressed, oppressive third-world country but an evil empire that would take over the world? Never.

He ended by noting that his Picasso book, which was "not at all a major effort," was almost done. Picasso "comes alive" in it, he said, and he had "more honest things to say about Cubism than the artistic establishmentarians."

THE REASON THAT the Picasso book had not yet gone to press was the opposition of these establishmentarians, none more so than John Richardson. Earlier in the year, Epstein had sent a manuscript copy of Mailer's book to Richardson. He wrote back, called it a "scissors-and-paste job," and turned down Mailer's request to quote from his biography. He and Mailer, hitherto friendly, began sniping at each other in the media. When Richardson read about a Provincetown exhibit of Mailer's drawings, "Guys and Droons," Richardson told the *New York Observer*, "He's not just writing about Picasso now, he's even trying to draw like Picasso." Mailer said that while he had no artistic ability, he had merely "let my hand, in a sense, lead me—that is, draw without preconception. There must have been some wholly unconscious message I'd gotten from Picasso." Told of Richardson's disdain for his drawings, he said, "I hope the poor boy is not too disappointed," and quoted the André Gide epigraph in *The Deer Park*: "Please do not understand me too quickly." Richardson went further, accusing Mailer of writing the book as a way of funding his alimony and child care payments.

Another Picasso scholar, William Rubin, sided with Richardson. Director emeritus of painting and sculpture at the Museum of Modern Art in New York, Rubin had recently published a major study, *Picasso and Braque: Pioneering Cubism*, from which Mailer had drawn extensively. Rubin refused permission for Mailer to quote from his work. "Obviously, Richardson sicced him on me," Mailer said. He was now in an unhappy situation that would interfere with his work on the Oswald book. Lacking the ability to quote from Richardson and Rubin, and possibly from the memoirs of Fernande Olivier (whose heirs were initially unresponsive), he would have to rewrite the book. And he would have to find another publisher. His first thought was Nan Talese, wife of his good friend, Gay, who had her own imprint at Doubleday. He had known her socially for years.

"As I understood it," she recalled, "Norman said to Jason, 'Would it be helpful if I go find another publisher just for this book?' And I think Jason said yes because it took the pressure off of him. So Norman asked me to read it and publish it. And I said, 'I'll publish it.' And he said, 'No, no, I think you should read it first.' " She read the book and was impressed. "I loved the book because I felt if there was anyone who could get inside Picasso's spirit and sense of self-importance, it was Norman." She saw this ability in his descriptions of the young Picasso, which seemed "as if he was associating his own feelings as a young writer with Picasso as a young artist." She had some editorial suggestions, and Mailer sat down with her and the manuscript. "What was wonderful was when I asked him a question either about motive or meaning or something like that, he immediately addressed it. He didn't say let me think about it; he had a pencil and would go over it."

Richardson said he would sue if Talese published Mailer's book. "Well, this is just my guess," she said, but his "underlying motive" might have been Mailer's discussion of Cubism. "That was going to be part of Richardson's next book." She said, "Norman had a theory of why Picasso was attracted to Cubism, and I think he was jumping the tracks" on Richardson's second volume, which was forthcoming. At this point she was still determined to publish and called Random House president Harry Evans. "I said, 'Harry, could you get John to just pull back so we can go ahead with this book?' And he did." Richardson relented and gave permission to quote, although William Rubin did not—he was not quoted in the draft Talese read. But Talese's boss decided not to publish because he feared that "John Richardson has spoiled everything, and this book is going to be trashed, and we're not going to make our money back on it."

Mailer had yet to sign a contract with Doubleday, and when Talese called him with the bad news, he was understanding. He asked if she could not go ahead on her own and publish it, and she explained that she could, but she wouldn't get any marketing money, and "it's not fair to the book." It was published instead by Grove/Atlantic.

GERALD POSNER'S *CASE CLOSED* was published just a few weeks before Mailer was the keynote speaker at the third annual Assassination Symposium on John F. Kennedy (ASK) in Dallas, November 18–22, 1993. Posner, after extensive research, concluded that Oswald had acted alone. His view, generally embraced by the media, cast a slight pall on the conference. Mailer, long a supporter of conspiracy theories, did not mention Posner's book, but he had read it, and in his speech seemed to be moving closer to Posner's position, a stance not appreciated by the symposiasts, the great majority of whom were ferocious opponents of the single assassin interpretation. Mailer said that we want to believe that Oswald was a tool of some intelligence agency because we don't like to be lied to, and neither the CIA nor the FBI was willing to open their Oswald files. This stonewalling encouraged conspiracy proponents. But Mailer was now uncertain and told the audience that they had become intoxicated by the "vertigo and fog that accompanies study of the conspiracy."

By the time of the symposium, he had been working for several months on the story of Oswald and Marina in Minsk, but before he was done he decided that he did not want the book to end there. He was more and more intrigued by Oswald's personality, which he felt had not been understood, and less and less convinced that Oswald was either a tool of the KGB, or a scapegoat for Mafia dons who had had JFK murdered. These theories, and countless others, were dissected at the symposium, and Mailer was growing weary of them. Like Don DeLillo (also a conspiratorialist), he wanted to dissect Oswald with the tools of a novelist, demonstrate that Oswald was not a monstrous nobody, but an understandable character with grandiose ambitions and courage. "The sudden death of a man as large in his possibilities as John Fitzgerald Kennedy," he wrote, "is more tolerable if we can perceive his killer as tragic rather than absurd."

Mailer called the assassination "the largest mountain of mystery in the Twentieth Century." Yet until *Oswald's Tale*, as the book Schiller and he conceived was called, he had never dealt with it head-on, only obliquely via its endless reverberations in the nation's psyche. In book after book, essay after essay, he alluded to it, adding rings of scaffolding around it, as if it could only be approached but not addressed. He planned to make the assassination the opening episode of "Harlot's Grave." Reading chunks of the Warren Commission Report through the long Russian winter was the precipitating event. He likened the report to "a dead whale decomposing on the beach," fascinating, pungent, and mysterious. "Every morning I'd read these juicy testimonies, and every afternoon and evening we'd have these interviews, and soon I was struck by how desperate Oswald was, how focused he was on a belief in himself, however delusional."

Back home in the spring of 1993, he went to work on "Oswald and Marina in Minsk." As he was completing it, he decided to add a hundred-page epilogue about Oswald in America. He told his publishers, and they said, "Oh, don't make it too long," and he replied, "Of course not." But when he completed the epilogue, it had become the biggest part of the book, 444 pages, compared to 347 for the Minsk portion. "I started with one book and ended with another," he said. After thirty years, he had finally found a way to write about that dark day in Dallas, "a huge and hideous event, in which the gods warred and a god fell," as he described it. At Random House, no one was happy. "You've got a rose," Harry Evans told him, "why put all that greenery around it." Epstein felt the same way.

Schiller thought Mailer was "out of his mind," and told him so. "We haven't done any research in the U.S.," he said. "There's no new information. I told him it was total insanity." But Mailer had been reading the Warren Commission Report, and saw a wealth of material. "All you're doing is a cut-and-paste job," Schiller said. "There isn't anything new in what you're doing." Mailer's old friend was making the same accusation that Richardson had made about Mailer's Picasso biography. "He got real mad at me, you know, really mad," Schiller said. "I was treading on his creativity." Mailer deferred to Schiller when it came to collecting information, but deferred to no one when it came to interpreting information. He believed he could extract the same kind of compelling story out of the vast corpus of inert material assembled by the Warren Commission as he had out of the trove of interviews and documents on Gary Gilmore that Schiller had collected. The second half of *Oswald's Tale* is a much abbreviated and expertly parsed redaction of the Warren Commission Report.

Posner's *Case Closed* was another factor. If it had not been published, Schiller said, "I would have insisted that we go out and do research for the second part of the book." But Posner had already picked the bones fairly clean. Schiller said it made no difference to him which side of the controversy Mailer came down on; his concern was the freshness of the material. In Gilmore's case, the material he and Mailer had collected was pristine, and the same was true of the Minsk material. This was not the case with the assassination. Whatever the Warren Commission had missed had been located by Posner, Edward Jay Epstein, and other investigators, including Priscilla Johnson McMillan, the author of *Marina and Lee*, one of the best studies of Oswald's psychology. Mailer cited all three in his bibliography, and relied heavily on McMillan, although the Warren Commission Report was his chief source.

Schiller wanted Mailer to write a book that made news, something he had always strived for, and continued with books about O. J. Simpson, JonBenét Ramsey, and the Russian spy Robert Hanssen. He valued Mailer's interpretive and storytelling skills, but he wanted their collaborations to be the first draft of history, and the second half of *Oswald's Tale* is a twice- or thrice-told tale, however intelligently deployed. Getting a story on the front page of newspapers, or on network news, was always Schiller's goal. As he said later about *Oswald's Tale*, "We can talk about a book that's well written and we can talk about a book that's well written that's going to sell well. Norman had long passed the point of caring whether his books sold or not. I believe that." Mailer had told Schiller that he wrote *Ancient Evenings* for people who had not been born, readers a century hence. Schiller conceded, however, that there is "brilliance" in parts of "Oswald in America," and the concluding section on Oswald's wife and mother "stands alone. No question." There Mailer describes Oswald and Marina's last night together.

Marina had put off Oswald when he wanted to make love the night before the assassination, Mailer wrote. She was angry with him and wanted to "discipline him."

> Afterward, she had to think, What if he really wanted to be close to me? What if I put him in a bad mood? It torments her. What if they had made love that last night? But she is the wrong person to talk about this, she would say, because she is not a sexual person. Sensuous but not sensual. She didn't like sex, she would say. She was not expert, nor could she tell you how grandiose something had been, because she had never experienced that. No Beethoven or Tchaikovsky for her, not in bed, no grand finale.

Remarried after Oswald's murder, Marina was smoking four packs of cigarettes a day. She didn't want to die, although her suffering was palpable.

> She sits in a chair, a tiny woman in her early fifties, her thin shoulders hunched forward in such pain of spirit under such a mass of guilt that one would comfort her as one would hug a child. What is left of what was once her beauty are her extraordinary eyes, blue as diamonds, and they blaze with light as if, in divine compensation for the dead weight of all that will not cease to haunt her, she has been granted a spark from the hour of an apocalypse others have not seen. Perhaps it is the light offered to victims who have suffered like the gods.

Marina's mother-in-law has her own burden, and it is "difficult not to feel some guarded sympathy for Marguerite Claverie Oswald. As with Lee, the internal workings of her psyche were always condemned to hard labor, and so much of what she tried, and with the best intentions, would fail." Asked by the interviewers of the Warren Commission if she had any family with her, she answered: "I have no family, period. I brought three children into the world, and I have sisters, I have nieces, I have nephews. I have grandchildren, and I'm all alone. That answers that question and I don't want to hear another word about it." She would die alone, riddled with cancer and guilt. Mailer imagines that when Mrs. Oswald reached the Bureau of Karmic Reassignment, she probably argued with the bureaucrats, "dissatisfied with the low station, by her lights, of her next placement. 'I gave birth to one of the most famous and important Americans who ever lived!' she will tell the clerk-angel who is recording her story."

> There she stands with her outrageous ego, and her self-deceit, her bold loneliness, and cold bones, those endless humiliations that burn like sores. Yet, she is worthy of Dickens. Marguerite Oswald can stand for literary office with Micawber and Uriah Heep. No word she utters will be false to her character; her stamp will be on every phrase. Few people without a literary motive would seek her company for long, but a novelist can esteem Marguerite. She does all his work for him.

IN LATE SPRING 1994, as the Oswald book was nearing completion, he accepted an assignment from *Esquire* to write a profile of Madonna. It came in the wake of her appearance on the *Late Show with David Letterman*. She had said "fuck" several times on the live show, and "the results," Mailer wrote, "produced a two-day Kristallnacht in the media." She was called sick, sordid, outrageous, and stupid for using the F-word, which CBS had adroitly bleeped every time. But Letterman had, of course, encouraged her, and Mailer was on Madonna's side. "Letterman," he said, "would not be caught dead offering one indication of how to conduct your life. Keep it meaningless and we'll all get along." Mailer mentioned his support to Liz Smith, the gossip columnist, and she wrote about it. This led to a call to his new agent, Andrew Wylie (Scott Meredith had died in 1991), from the editor of *Esquire*. The offer was made more attractive by the challenge of writing about someone with "an ego even larger than his own." He opens the piece by describing her as "a pint-size Italian American with a heart she hopes is built out of the cast-iron balls of the *paisans* in generations before her." Mailer reverted to the third person personal in "Norman Mailer on Madonna: Like a Lady," which is half conversation and half profile.

The piece covers predictable territory: obscenity, sexuality, censorship, the women's movement, AIDS, birth control, the loneliness of celebrity, and the sensuality of Catholicism. Mailer brings in Warren Beatty, Marilyn Monroe, and Andy Warhol as points of reference. He praises Madonna's ability "to take her kinks to the public."

> She offers no balm to sweet, sore places; she is the stern instructor who shows us how difficult it all is, especially sex in its consummation. Yet she gives us something Marilyn never could, something less attractive but equally valuable: she dramatizes for us how dangerous is any human's truth once we dare to explore it; she reminds us that the joys of life bed down on broken glass.

He ends this reverie with a line used by Dougy Madden in *Tough Guys Don't Dance*, one Mailer had taken to repeating whenever he was confronted by any depiction of humanity out of touch with the brute facts of existence, the answer, so to speak, of Caliban to Ariel: "*Inter faeces et urinam, nascimur*, she is always telling us, even if she never heard of Saint Odo of Cluny, but indeed it is true. 'Between piss and shit are we born.' " The piece holds interest, but it never soars. Madonna presents the same frank, quirky persona that can be seen in her music videos, and Mailer deals from his existential-excremental deck of cards. He does, however, make two comments that tell us a bit more about his dalliances and reveal the state of his relationship with Norris. The first is made to encourage Madonna to open up more. "Confessions—in good society—breed confessions," so he tells her that:

> Certain people cannot live without promiscuity. There have been years of my life when I was young when that was absolutely true. I had this feeling that something was near death in me . . . that something was trapped, and it was symbolized by the word *cancer.* To break out of this trap, I had to take on many roles, because every time you make love with someone else, you are in a new role, you are a new person.

Promiscuity for the young Mailer was health; like Rousseau he equated the satisfying of his sexual urges with both health and freedom, although unlike the Enlightenment philosophes, there was always a guilty edge to his adventures. The older Mailer is ready for limits and quid pro quos, as his second comment shows. The assigned photographer attempted to get a shot of Madonna sitting on Mailer's lap. Madonna was willing, but Mailer, at five foot seven, two hundred pounds, wearing a black dinner jacket that made him resemble "a barrel wrapped in velvet," said no.

> He had a mate who was all too proficient at bringing up old scores for the thrice-weekly bickerfest. So he certainly didn't want a photograph of himself sitting in a chair, girded in his black dinner jacket, while Madonna in a green gown was perched on his lap, one breast exposed. It is interesting to note that ten years ago, Mailer would have said to himself, "Damn the torpedoes; full speed ahead—Madonna on my lap!" What we are witnessing is the action of the female mind upon male flesh, otherwise known as the cumulative effect of being pussy-whipped over the course of twenty years by a strong, beautiful, redheaded wife.

A couple of months later, at the end of August, Mailer said that he had "finally met a woman who knows how to dominate me, a fate I've been trying to avoid all my life. Of course, like all girls she squeaks and squeals and claims it's I who dominate her. How smart they are!"

BY SEPTEMBER HE had a complete manuscript of 1,700 pages, a book of 1,000 pages, more or less. Two months later he had it down to 1,400 manuscript pages, which resulted in the published book of 828 pages. *The New Yorker*, now edited by Tina Brown, who had moved over from *Vanity Fair*, published a forty-five-page excerpt, including six pages of striking photos of Oswald in Minsk. It was his first (and last) major piece in the magazine, and he was pleased. Another excerpt, in *Parade*, builds to Mailer's conclusion: "Every insight we have gained of him suggests the solitary nature of his act. Besides, it is too difficult, no matter how one searches for a viable scenario, to believe that others could have chosen him to be the rifleman in a conspiracy." Mailer said he was 75 percent certain that Oswald acted alone.

Oswald's Tale was published on May 12, 1995. The reviews were generally positive, the best he had received since *The Executioner's Song*. Among the major reviewers, only Michiko Kakutani writing in *The New York Times* three weeks before the book's publication date, was dismissive, calling the book "boring and presumptuous, derivative and solipsistic." The British reviews were even better (it was published in England on September 7). A quartet of major literary figures—Martin Amis, Christopher Hitchens, Allan Massie, and Andrew O'Hagan—was enthusiastic in praise of how Mailer, as O'Hagan put it, recognized "Oswald's struggle to become a man—to become an important and effective male character—as the foundation of much of his adult distress." Massie found the portrait of Oswald to be "utterly convincing, partly because it contains so many contradictions." He was an idealist and a liar, "fiercely independent and emotionally dependent; this one day and the opposite the next. His Oswald is both likable and repulsive; to be pitied and feared. He is in many ways, as Mailer insists, like the young Hitler revealed in *Mein Kampf*."

When he went to Minsk, Mailer said, "I hoped there would be a smoking gun." Hitchens observes that Mailer's "natural writerly prejudice in favour of meaning and pattern over sordid random coincidence," his desire to find incontrovertible evidence of a conspiracy, made it difficult for him "to come to a conclusion that lies athwart his prejudices." Amis makes essentially the same point: "Everything in Mailer rebels against" the view that JFK "had his brains blown out by a malevolent Charlie Chaplin with a wonky rifle and a couple of Big Ideas." If Oswald was a lone wolf, Amis says, "All we are left with is absurdity, more garbage, more randomness and rot." There were only two ways for Mailer to get out of the dilemma: "Either Oswald wasn't acting alone—or he wasn't a nonentity." Confronted by what he learned in Minsk, reinforced by all that he had read, he chose the latter course: no conspiracy, and a complex Oswald; a man dealt a bad hand, in no way heroic, but bold, idealistic in a twisted way, and sympathetic. "What is never taken seriously enough in Oswald," Mailer said, "is the force of his confidence that he has the makings of a great leader."

Epstein faxed Mailer an unsigned review that appeared in *The Economist*. It seems in hindsight that Epstein was correct to call it "the most sensible review yet." The reviewer said that Mailer, writing thirty years after the event, faced "a doubly ungrateful audience: those who no longer care, and those whose minds are already made up." Nevertheless, those who could suspend their judgment would see that "Mr. Mailer has produced a masterpiece." The reviewer notes Mailer's touch in providing "tiny novelistic details."

> Thus Oswald sits lovingly polishing his rifle for hours; on the evening before the assassination, out in the garden, he tried to catch a butterfly with his baby daughter; when he goes off to work the next morning at the Book Depository in Dallas, he leaves behind a residue of instant coffee in a paper cup and, in a delicate flowered cup on the dresser, his wedding ring.

The details are historically accurate, but in his anatomy of Oswald's character, the reviewer says, Mailer is unable to resist making Oswald more likable, more tortured, and more substantial than he was. "What Mr. Mailer forgets is that he has told us so much about Oswald that we know just how thin any layer of nobility must be." In his laudatory review in *The New York Times Book Review*, Thomas Powers echoes the *Economist* reviewer—as do a majority of the other reviewers. "I admire Mailer for his effort to understand Oswald, but at some level I feel invited to place a sympathetic arm around the killer's shoulder," Powers wrote, and "I'm not about to do it." The Tolstoyan compassion Mailer sought to create for wretches like Oswald—Powers calls him "an insect" who "brought pain to many and happiness to none"—was unpalatable in 1995 and remains so. *Oswald's Tale*, like *Ancient Evenings*, is another of Mailer's books for readers a century hence, readers removed from the pain of one of the greatest tragedies of twentieth-century American life.

PORTRAIT OF PICASSO *as a Young Man* finally appeared on October 15, about three years after it was completed. The fact that it was Mailer's second published book in five months probably hurt sales. Morgan Entrekin, the Grove/Atlantic publisher, was quoted as saying he was cutting the first printing from 100,000 to 50,000 for this reason. He also said that he hoped book review editors would assign "literary types, rather than more exacting art critics to assess Mailer's view of another eminence." His hope was dashed; most of the major reviews were by professionals in the art world, some of whom had written extensively about Picasso. Writing in *The New York Times Book Review* (Michael Kimmelman), *The Nation* (Eunice Lipton), and *The New York Review of Books* (Roger Shattuck), three art critics were unanimous in their opinion that Mailer was "poaching on the turf of taste makers and scholars," as Robert Taylor (*Boston Globe*) put it. Kimmelman called the book "clumsy and disappointing" and chided him for missing the influence of the large, robust women in the works of Renoir and Maillol. Shattuck, an old acquaintance of Mailer's, lectured him on a variety of sins. Mailer's "most grievous failure" was failing to explain how "Kandinsky in Munich, Malevich in Russia, Mondrian in Holland, and Kupka and Delaunay in Paris crossed the line into non-figurative or 'abstract' painting" in his discussion of Cubism. Lipton criticized Mailer for leaving out the estimable views of William Rubin, unaware that he refused to be quoted. Mailer's speculations on Picassos's inner life were passed over, for the most part.

Mailer is no art critic; his descriptions of Picasso's work are solid but unexceptional. He does make a contribution by translating and then quoting adroitly from the memoir of Fernande Olivier, the woman who lived with Picasso from his years of obscurity to his early successes. Mailer's commentary on their relationship—both were narcissists—is one of the best things in the biography and an addition to Picasso scholarship. But art criticism was not his purpose. His announced goal was "to make Picasso as real as any good character in life or in art." To show the agonies and ecstasies of Picasso's early years, he drew on his own. Despite the usual denials, Mailer in more than one interview admitted to traits he shared with Picasso. "At a much higher level," he told Pete Hamill, "he had the same sort of restlessness in his mind that I have in mine." Both were short, stocky men possessed of huge energy, large libido, vast ambition, and an unshakable belief in the importance of their artistic missions. Both tried on a variety of masks as they moved from wife to wife, lover to lover. "I don't mean to compare myself to him," he said, "but there are certain large similarities."

> He grew up in a family filled with women; my mother had a number of sisters too. He was a spoiled darling. There are people who would say the same about me. Everything that went on in his life seemed to add up for me. Not that I was writing about myself—we're enor-

mously different. What's fun is to find someone you understand very well in one way, and have to explore in another.

In an interview with Barbara Probst Solomon, Mailer repeats his comment about Picasso being spoiled: "He was the center of the family. He was king. King at home. Then he would go out in the street. And he was little. And kids would push him around." It is obvious that he believed that Norman Kingsley Mailer and Pablo Picasso shared similar experiences. He continued: "Well, my mother and aunts did adore me. And I was short. Yes, I can imagine what he was feeling."

Picasso's life before thirty, when he "gambled on his ability to reach into mysteries of existence that no one else had even perceived," corresponds closely to Mailer's. After that, their experiences diverge. Mailer said he had no desire to write about Picasso's later life. "After Cubism," he said, "he lost his navigator; there's no narrative thread to his life after 1917." He does comment briefly on Picasso's final years, however, when their experiences are again similar. His insights into Picasso in his seventies and eighties vibrate with fellow feeling. He was "doomed," Mailer wrote, "to relive his obsessions through all ninety-one years of life," to continue painting until the end "as if work itself could hold death off." Mailer wrote furiously until just before his own death, and never gave up believing that he had more to accomplish. His comradely biography is summed up nicely by an unnamed reviewer in the *Atlantic Monthly*: "This is a biography constructed with a fiction writer's liberty of psychological insight and a fascinated observer's freedom of personal opinion." It is not one of his most important books, but it is one of his most readable and autobiographical.

The reviews, Mailer said, were "the worst I've ever gotten for a book." That is a slight exaggeration; they are almost as negative as those given to *Barbary Shore*. Kakutani again was in the lead, publishing her review two weeks before the book's publication date. Echoing Richardson, she called it "an old-fashioned cut-and-paste job," and criticized Mailer for promoting "the notion that art redeems, that the sins of a great artist can be rationalized, excused or glossed over." Mailer does find heroic qualities in Picasso, but saying that he overlooks his faults reveals a cursory reading. Mailer takes pains to criticize Picasso for his betrayals of friends and mistresses. Two days after Kakutani's review appeared, Mailer fired off a letter to the editor of the *Times*, complaining that she had rushed her negative review into print.

> That does the job. If the first notice we see on anyone's work is atrocious, it usually takes more than one good review to change a potential reader's mind. Since Ms. Kakutani's pieces are nationally syndicated, the damage is increased—and particularly for those small-city newspapers where she is the only reviewer some people will see. . . . Enough is enough. I would not wish to think that Ms. Kakutani has become personally if negatively addicted to my work, but there are signs.

Kakutani's record on Mailer's books is consistent. She panned his next three books, making it five consecutive negative reviews, four of them published before their publication dates. Mailer was riled.

IN NOVEMBER 1994 he flew to London for meetings with his publisher, and then went on to Paris to meet with the French publisher of *Portrait of Picasso*. He appeared with Jean Malaquais on ARTE, a French-German cultural television network. Their conversation, broadcast soon after, led to a serious breach between them. Malaquais sternly accused him of abandoning his ambition to be a history-changing writer and becoming "just a commodity," a television celebrity. Seven months after the program aired all over Europe, Mailer's oldest friend wrote to him dismissing the program as "poor," but not apologizing for or retracting his comments. Mailer replied in June 1995, calling Malaquais' letter "incomprehensible."

> You know perfectly well there's unfinished business between you and me concerning that occasion. It's one thing to say something insulting as you said in private. Then we can argue between us man to man. To announce it to the world, however, which in this case is somewhere between 100,000 to a few million people you've never met, who don't know you and who don't know me, and to do it at large in what was virtually a temper tantrum, I find damaging to the idea of friendship itself.

The comments Malaquais had made on the program were especially searing, coming, as they did, just after Mailer had acknowledged his debt to his mentor. He described him as "the last of his species," and said he had "learned more from him than anybody I know." We have been friends for forty-seven years, he said, "and love each other dearly." He referred to Malaquais, warmly, as "an old goat," and said that at their meetings "we argue back and forth but get nowhere, but have a fine time doing it." Then it was Malaquais' turn.

"You wanted to be a literary hero. What did you mean by hero?" Mailer replied that he was one of a group of writers who wanted to emulate engaged artists such as André Malraux. "We wanted to change the nature of American life," he said, but "none of us ended up as heroes; we ended up as celebrities." People know who I am, he said, mainly through television.

MALAQUAIS: Being a celebrity is your infantile malady.

MAILER: I would say that your insistence on keeping to a point that has no particular relevance to the discussion is a sign of your premature senility.

MALAQUAIS: There are no heroes in American life, just celebrities, and they are immediately transferred to television.

MAILER: You ask why do I go on television. The answer is it's the only game in town.

MALAQUAIS: Television is unchristian, untrue, distorting, decelebrating. You participate in this de-celebration of people.

Mailer tried to change the subject, but Malaquais resumed the attack.

MALAQUAIS: There was a time when intellectuals were, so to speak, in opposition, in ideological opposition. Some of them were revolutionaries. All of them, you included, sold out.

MAILER: We didn't sell out, sold out to what?

MALAQUAIS: To the establishment. You belong to the establishment. In France, all the former extreme leftists, the Maoists, all of them became pillars of society.

MAILER: Well, I'd hardly call myself a pillar of American society. To this day I'm seen in America as a bizarre creature who doesn't

> fit categories comfortably. But when you say I sold out, that's personally very insulting. I could say that you have sold out by being relatively inactive all these years and never doing anything but complain, but I'm not going to get into this. But saying one has sold out is the single most insulting thing you can say to someone.
>
> MALAQUAIS: But I wanted to be insulting.

This thrust went deep. It all but ended the conversation, which sputtered along for a few minutes to its conclusion.

Mailer wrote to two friends of Malaquais', Michael Seiler and Jean-Pierre Catherine, who had set up the ARTE conversation and told them his assessment of the program. "The general tone is somewhat unpleasant—fat, 72-year-old bully shuts up 86-year-old man for 45 minutes whereupon battered old fellow (whom I must say looks very good on the TV) strikes back and they have an unhappy exchange in which each denigrates the other. I was essentially charmless throughout." The experience made him conclude, he wrote, that a long documentary about him that Seiler and Catherine had proposed was a bad idea. After countless television appearances over a forty-year span, he wrote, "There's no desire to have still one more film made about me." Seiler and Catherine were persistent, however, and two years later Mailer agreed to the documentary.

Malaquais' second wife, Elisabeth, who had known Mailer since the 1960s, rebuked her husband for his public chastisement of Mailer during their television appearance. "To this day," she said in 2010, "the ARTE show gives me goose pimples." She felt that her husband was entitled to comment on "Norman's confusion between heroism and celebrity," but not publicly. Malaquais told her that he was sorry for the pain he had "apparently" caused, but was not ready to apologize. "Was it not the truth?" he asked. Realizing her husband's "inflexibility," she wrote to Mailer seeking a rapprochement. She argued that Mailer's letter had hurt Malaquais, and Malaquais' comments had hurt Mailer; the two injuries, therefore, canceling out each other. "There's no equality in the deeds," Mailer said in his reply. "Mine was a personal letter to my oldest friend, chilly as could be, with intent to wound, but finally, it was personal." Malaquais' "denunciation" was seen by a million people. He concluded his letter to Elisabeth:

> Finally, for Jean's own health (if I may presume to be a physician, and after all, why not? Do physicians know more than old friends?) he's going, for the sake of his soul, which I believe he has even if he doesn't, he's going to have to apologize to someone or something or just once in his life say: I did something stupid and wrong and bad and I'm sorry. If he can't do that, I really don't want to see him anymore.

After Mailer's death, Elisabeth provided a shrewd analysis of the relationship of Mailer and her husband, who died in 1998.

> Norman had become a celebrity, feted and listened to, maligned also, all too often. Jean, who stayed in the shadows, then provided him with a mainstay: no competition to fear from him, a foreign writer, save of an intellectual kind (though Norman never was one to like losing an argument!), no underhand meanness, above all total frankness, especially when it came to the overall passion of them both: writing. The years passed. Norman never missed an opportunity to remind the public of his own existence; his "stunts" often irked Jean and, at times, amused him, when they did not cause him considerable anguish (the Adele episode) or downright anger (the political posturing), for instance. I cannot recall any sign ever of indifference on Jean's part. Jean thought of Norman as a genuinely warm and kind man, demonstrably generous (not only vis-à-vis his friends) and incredibly attuned to the life of his country, intellectually of course, but emotionally in particular.

The two old friends resolved their differences less than a year after their public fight. Mailer "overcame his anger," she said, and "was generous and to the end showed Jean much affection." He and Norris visited Elisabeth and Jean in Geneva, where they were living, in 1996 and 1997. A short time after Malaquais' passing, his novel, *Planet Without Visa*, was reissued and Mailer attended the book party. "I was extremely touched," she said, "by the public homage he paid to his friend posthumously at the party given by Jean's publisher, Phébus, on the occasion."

AS HIS RELATIONSHIP with Malaquais sank to its nadir, Mailer saw the sales of *Oswald's Tale* trail off badly. He had hoped for a modestly strong showing, but the book failed to reach the bestseller list. He attributed its weak sales to its $30 price, its length, dislike of the "insect" Oswald, and the recently concluded trial of O. J. Simpson. Mailer said that the trial and Simpson's not guilty verdict had satisfied America's interest in forensics. He assumed that *Picasso*'s sales would be worse, and this proved to be the case. Added to these disappointments was the anxiety produced by the protracted contract negotiations with Random House conducted by his new agent, Andrew Wylie. At this inopportune time, Carole Mallory nudged her way back into his life.

In the summer of 1995, she contacted the "Page Six" gossip columnists of the *New York Post* to announce that she was almost done with a memoir of her affair with Mailer. At Norris's insistence, Mailer called a score of close friends and family members to tell them about the *Post* story before they heard about it. After summarizing the item, he intoned gravely, "You pay for your sins; you pay for your sins." He then explained that his affair with Mallory had been over for several years—his family knew this, but not all his friends—and that he and Norris were thoroughly and happily reconciled. His merry life was over, he said.

The situation at Random House was more complicated. He owed the firm over $3 million, and the sequel to *Harlot's Ghost*. For the first time in his career, he said, his fate was mainly in the hands of "suits," corporate people who didn't see him as a writer but as an asset, a commodity. Epstein and Evans could put in a good word for him, but they had no real say in the matter. Alberto Vitale, a former banker who was then CEO at Random House, had the final say on major author contracts. If, Mailer explained, Wylie was able to get him only a one-book deal (nullifying the contract negotiated by the late Scott Meredith), he would leave Random House and the firm would lose the possibly large returns from the books he wrote after the sequel. The possibilities he was considering included an anthology made up of excerpts from many of his books and some uncollected essays, two volumes of autobiography, and another novel. But signing him to a multi-book contract was also a gamble, given his age and health. By this time, he said, Random House had sunk over $1 million into *Oswald's Tale*, $30,000 a month for over three years. In some years, he earned $750,000, but after paying his agent, alimony, college tuitions (at one point six of his children were in college), mortgages on two homes, and rent for two studios, to name the major expenses, he needed every penny of it. He had no retirement fund.

According to Harry Evans, it was S. I. Newhouse, the chairman of Advance Publications (which included Random House and the Condé Nast magazines *The New Yorker, Vogue*, and *Vanity Fair*), who ultimately struck the deal with Wylie and his associates. (Mailer later described them as "my keen and formidable agents.") Evans said that Newhouse believed that it was important to keep Random House's major writers happy. The new contract called for him to continue to receive $30,000 a month for the rest of his life, in return for which all of his royalties from all of his publishers would go to Random House until the monthly payments had been covered. If, at his death, the monthly stipends totaled more than the grand total of his royalty income, the debt would be canceled. But to maintain his household, he needed another $300,000 a year. For each of the next twelve years he would earn approximately that amount from a combination of fees for magazine pieces, consultations, speeches, and screenplays.

The new contract meant that Mailer needed to focus on the sequel to *Harlot's Ghost.* But the enormity of the task and the reception of *Portrait of Picasso* and *Oswald's Tale* weighed on him, dulling his resolve. He was also dubious about the literary choices he had made over the past four years. John Aldridge, one of his most stalwart supporters, had written a middling review of the Oswald book, and Mailer wrote back saying it was obvious that Aldridge thought it was not the sort of book he should have written at this point in his life. "And in truth," he said, "and this is between us, I don't know that I disagree with you." In a letter to his daughter Susan, he said he was "angry and bruised" by the reception of *Picasso*. "What irks the hell out of me is that it's really a nice book and I really think it will last, at least if any of my books do. When you read it, let me know what you think. If your reaction is negative, dare to tell me so," adding that this was a "safe offer" because he recalled that she had liked the book in manuscript. The only other thing he had to report was that he was "trying to build up the intellectual capital and the energy to start the second volume of *Harlot's Ghost*, and in the meantime I look for distractions, do a piece about this, do a piece about that, whatever comes through. I truly know how old fighters feel when they want to avoid championship bouts." He ended this gloomy dispatch by sending love and noting that "all is relatively OK here." But it wasn't. He would be seventy-three in two months, and needed a victory.

One of the pieces he took on was a conversation with his son Michael about the recently concluded murder trial of O. J. Simpson, sometimes described as "the trial of the century." On October 3, 1995, Simpson was found not guilty of the murders of his wife, Nicole Brown, and her friend Ronald Goldman. Two weeks later, the conversation, titled "Black and White Justice," appeared in *New York* magazine. Mailer's conclusions centered on the anger felt about the verdict. Many believed that the jury (nine blacks, one Hispanic, two whites) ignored the evidence presented, but whites, Mailer said, "are not taking account of the attitude of most blacks toward American justice. Blacks see it as white justice; therefore it's not justice. It's a game waged by players, sometimes very skillful players." Blacks are usually represented by court-appointed defenders. "So they see it as a game they usually lose." O.J. had top talent, and he won, and blacks generally approved.

In a commencement address several weeks later, on May 27, 1995, Mailer was more upbeat. Speaking at Wilkes University in Wilkes-Barre, Pennsylvania, he spoke of the end of the Cold War. "Looking back on it, we were like magnetic filings in the power of a huge electromagnet, the Cold War, and almost all of us pointed in the same direction." But when Communism collapsed, "the great switch on this great electromagnet was released and now all the fragments went in all directions." Those who built their lives under the overhang of the Cold War "are now superannuated; myself among the others," and many Americans "don't have a clear sense of the future." But this dislocation had an upside, he told the graduates. "You will go forth in the rare position of being—in the spiritual sense—of being pioneers because you are going into a new and undiscovered frontier," a place where "all the guide rules of the 19th and 20th century have been used up." Perhaps, he concluded, you can regain the dream on which the nation was founded. "If you believe that there is more good than evil in the sum of humanity, then democracy can prevail," a sentiment that could be traced back a half-century to "The White Negro." For the future, he said, "exciting and fearful and incredible days and years await you." Mailer had already begun thinking about a book that would speak to the new millennium.

DURING THE WEEK in Paris when Mailer had his unhappy conversation with Malaquais, he stayed at the George V, one of his favorite hotels. Norris was not with him, and one night, unable to sleep, he found a Gideon Bible in English in the night table and began to read the New Testament. It was the first time he had looked at it for many years, although he had read parts of it in college. "I couldn't make head or tail of it," he said, adding that he was "a stranger to Christianity." This was not a result of overt anti-Semitism of the kind faced by his mother, who was called "sheeny" and "Christ killer" by Irish kids in Long Branch (an experience that made her wonder how her son could have so many Irish friends). Rather, he felt "subtly excluded."

> Christmas is not for you, and you don't know anything about Jesus Christ. You haven't grown up with him. When I was a kid, it was almost as if Christ was the enemy, the renegade Jew, the one who brought all the trouble down on the Jews. At least that was the mentality of the immigrant first-generation and second-generation Jews I grew up with. And then, of course, later in life one became sophisticated about it; Christ was certainly not the enemy, but he was still very much a stranger.

A few years earlier, he and Norris were visiting her family in Atkins, Arkansas. On this occasion, Norris's father, James Davis, a deacon at the local Freewill Baptist Church, invited Mailer to attend the adult Sunday School. "To my knowledge, no other Jew had ever come to that Sunday school," he recalled, adding that he had also been the first Jew that Norris had ever met. "They were so excited," he said, "because they'd been reading about Jesus the Jew for thirty, forty, fifty years. They'd been living with it. And they'd never seen a Jew. And now there was one among them. So they approached me with the most curious kind of respect." He felt the welcome was particularly warm. As he learned, they assumed that he might be better equipped to interpret some difficult lines in the Old Testament concerning Abraham and his son Isaac. Mailer did his best, and afterward kept pondering "this odd moment, where they felt that being Jewish gave me an authority in relation to the Bible." Perhaps, he thought, he might also have something to say about the New Testament.

Another experience that heightened his interest in the Bible had come in 1994 when he read *Crossing the Threshold of Hope* by Pope John Paul II. Written in the form of an interview, it deals with a range of topics, including the relationship of Christianity to other faiths. He read it because he remembered John Paul's 1987 encyclical *On Social Concerns*, which had impressed him enough to recommend that PEN offer the pope an honorary membership (which was opposed by Sontag, who succeeded Mailer as president), although it was never voted on. Mailer admired its analysis of the Cold War and the two superpowers, America and Russia (the former representing, as John Paul put it, "the power of greed," and the latter "the power of oppression"), and the poor in the Third World, as well as the underprivileged in the superpowers. The pope kept mentioning the Gospel of John, and this prompted Mailer to read it. "I was curious now," he said, and after reading John he read the synoptic gospels of Matthew, Mark, and Luke, first in Paris, and then several times in the United States.

He then realized "how good a story it was" and called it "the spiritual or psychological keel of Western civilization." But while Jesus' unique voice and profound sayings are "at the least worthy of Shakespeare," he found the story as a whole "not well written." The prophetic voice of John is memorable, but the narratives of the other three evangelists, who carry the burden of linking the early life of Jesus with his death and resurrection, are filled with clumsy transitions and vague descriptions. "I wanted to retell it the way all writers want to retell a classic story," he said. "There are easily one hundred writers who could do a better job, and I'm one of them." Ignoring his promises to Random House about "Harlot's Grave," and telling no one save Epstein, Norris, and Judith, in early 1995 he began working on his version of the New Testament, told in the first person by Jesus, speaking long after the events he describes.

Asked what motivated him to write it, Mailer said, "If suddenly I had picked up a copy of *The Iliad* and said I wanted to do a new version of it, people would have understood." But this was not the case with the New Testament; people "have stronger feelings about it," and a Jew rewriting the central story of Christianity was likely to be seen as a poacher, as he had been with Picasso. When he told Norris his intention "to write a book that her father would read," she told him he was crazy. Initially, Epstein was also against the idea. "I remember arguing with him at length about his book about Jesus," he recalled, "which I thought was simply not for him, and probably not for me either." Mailer was not moved. He described his attraction as "almost animal-like—the way an animal knows it's time to come out of hibernation, so it digs its way up to the surface whether or not it has a clear take on what the weather might be."

He did some research, reading two books by Elaine Pagels, *The Gnostic Gospels* and *The Origin of Satan*. Mainly, however, he relied on various versions of the New Testament and his own sense of Jesus' inner life. "Celebrities," Mailer told Charlie Rose, "are used to living with two personalities." The first is the "at-home personality; when you're brushing your teeth you're like everyone else." The other personality "has power in the world" and "people virtually p-e-e in their pants when they meet you." He said he felt he had "a small insight into what it was like to have a double nature since I've lived with it all my life since I was 25." He hastened to add that being a celebrity was far, far different from being a half-divine person. He was confident that he could make reasonable surmises about Jesus' dual nature by reference to his own. He continued working on it off and on through the first half of 1996, and then put it aside during the summer so he could attend the political conventions.

He wrote two pieces on the political campaigns for *George*, a new political magazine, but first published in *Esquire* an article on Pat Buchanan, a conservative political commentator and advisor to Republican presidents. Like his 1994 Madonna piece, it is half profile, half interview. He had discovered that Buchanan, who had just been defeated in the GOP presidential primaries by Senator Bob Dole, had qualities that he admired. Buchanan, a Reagan Republican, was critical of American corporations, angry that they loved their profit margins enough to send American jobs overseas. Mailer had thought that he was the only "Left-conservative" in the country, but now recognized that Buchanan had similar credentials. His growing admiration for Buchanan was based, in part, on his growing disillusion with the president. Mailer had met Clinton a few times, and he and Norris had visited him in the White House, but their conversations had never gotten beyond pleasantries and he had little hope of becoming a Clinton counselor or intimate. Still, he tried. In late 1994, he had asked for an interview. Clinton aides wrote back and asked for a list of the topics to be explored. Mailer declined to be specific (except for promising to bring up a matter on which they would disagree—the Cuban situation) and instead proposed that Clinton give him carte blanche to poke around in the presidential psyche: "I think you owe it to yourself to have one of our best American writers—myself humbly nominated—to take a shot at interpreting your presidency and yourself. My feeling, and it's paramount, is that the public needs a fresh look." Let us discuss, he continued, "your more intense concerns, your preferences, your biases." He offered his piece on Madonna as proof of his ability "to see you as a human being rather than as a public servant and/or politician." His letter was not as thoughtless as his 1961 letter to Mrs. Kennedy in which he spoke of the "odd strong honor" of the Marquis de Sade, but it was high-handed enough to earn the same response: silence.

Mailer was unhappy with Clinton for not making civil rights a larger theme of his presidency and for practicing what Mailer called "boutique politics"—providing a morsel for every interest group, but not being willing to risk political death for any large idea or policy. Mailer was so angry with what was going on in the country that he actually, seriously, thought about running in the primaries against Clinton. At one point, he said that he was thinking of running as Eugene McCarthy's second, and had spoken to him about it, but they decided against it. He knew he would lose, but he hoped his campaign might introduce intriguing ideas that would irritate Clinton. When Norris got wind of this quixotic venture, she replied, he said, in "the quiet tones he had come to know all too well—the steel in the voice of a soft-spoken southern woman is as palpable as the cutting edge of a Damascene blade"—that she would leave him if he dared to declare. She was particularly scornful of the speech he planned to give to the media: "I've been married six times. I committed a felonious assault against my second wife. I've been untrue to every woman I've cared about. Gentlemen and ladies of the press: Do your worst! I've broken through the media barrier. There's nothing to ransack in the closet." His wife, he concluded, was right again: "he was no recognizable grade of presidential timber." It would be a disaster. "It was the American presidency, after all. As soon could the Marquis de Sade have proposed himself for the papacy." Yet, at the time, he had been dead serious.

The two *George* reports—the first on the conventions, and the second on the subsequent campaigns—never enter deep waters. They provide overviews and samples of the speeches, platforms, and debates, and juicy details of political scandals. Dole is compared to various movie stars: "Seen up close, Dole looked tall and spare like a movie man, a leading man. Cowboy roles. Not Randolph Scott, exactly, not Gary Cooper or Clint Eastwood, but a casting director would put him in the file that said: HUMPHREY BOGART ON A HORSE." Clinton is held up to a range of movie stars and athletes, from Muhammad Ali to Warren Beatty, as well as to Ramses II and J. R. Ewing, the lead character in the television program *Dallas*. Both pieces are competent, as is the Buchanan profile-interview, but they are devoid of the drama and insight of his earlier political narratives. He was temporizing, running in place, instead of writing the sequel he had put off for over five years. He had long planned to begin it with the assassination of JFK, a fact he could not have failed to recall when he sat down to discuss his articles with the editor of *George*, the only son and namesake of the slain president.

WITH THE JESUS novel completed in early 1997, Mailer was happy to be given the opportunity to direct another feature film. His son Michael, who had launched a successful career as a movie producer, enlisted him for a proposed movie about an Irish-American boxer, "Ringside," which Michael and two colleagues had written. "It's the story of a street fighter who finds redemption through his relationships in and outside the ring," the younger Mailer said. Filming was scheduled to begin in April 1997. "The only trouble," Mailer said to a friend, "is I also want to get back to *Harlot's Ghost*, second volume, and so am suffering from the best dilemma of them all; there are two good things I want to do."

He was excited about the script. "Boxing," he said, "is a wonderful culture, a genre with edges that are rarely explored, and I would like to try my hand at directing one more time." He told Michael his only condition was that Knox be given a role. But shortly after preproduction work got under way, the backers pulled the plug. "*Tough Guys Don't Dance* was an interesting film, but not a commercially viable one," Michael recalled, and for that reason the backers were "nervous" about Mailer directing the new film. Another factor was that the two leading actors—Halle Berry and Brendan Fraser—were still relatively unknown. "My dad had the reputation of a man who was untested in the arena of Hollywood," Michael said.

Michael told his father that the money, $3.5 million, had been raised, the actors signed up, but then, for no announced reason, the backers stopped taking his phone calls. "Either they had found another property they wanted to work with more, or they simply didn't have the funds and couldn't face us," the elder Mailer said in a letter. Michael said that he was trying to find new backers. "Lord, I hope he succeeds," his father said. None of this was true. Michael had decided not to tell his father that the backers had insisted that he find another director, and he had shown them his middle finger. "To this day," Michael said, 'it's my most heartbreaking experience in the filmmaking business." Norman Mailer's directorial career was over.

Salving his disappointment over the cancellation of "Ringside" was the reception of the long-delayed documentary about the 1974 Ali-Foreman championship bout, *When We Were Kings*. Along with George Plimpton and Spike Lee, Mailer was recruited to give retrospective commentary on "The Rumble in the Jungle." He focused on the way Ali used the rope-a-dope to confuse and tire Foreman, recalling both the nuances and psychology of Ali's ringmanship. Released in February 1997, the film won several awards, including the Academy Award for best documentary. It is generally thought to be the finest documentary ever made on boxing and is linked permanently with Mailer's *The Fight*, often named as the best nonfiction narrative on a prizefight.

Kakutani was again the first major reviewer to comment on *The Gospel According to the Son*. Her early negative review in *The New York Times* drums on the theme of celebrity. Mailer is fascinated by it, she says, because he is one. His book, therefore, is "a sort of novelized 'Jesus Christ Superstar' starring Jesus as an ambivalent pop star and guru: a silly, self-important and inadvertently comical book that reads like a combination of 'Godspell,' Nikos Kazantzakis' 'Last Temptation of Christ' and one of those dumbed-down Bible translations, all seasoned with Mr. Mailer's eccentric views on God." Saving graces: none. Despite Kakutani's pan the novel was his tenth bestseller, and reached number seven on the list.

Besides his novelistic abilities, Mailer pointed to two assets he had for writing the novel. His celebrity had been of some help, as he noted in his conversation with Charlie Rose. But his Jewishness, he said, was "an inestimable advantage, because I tend to believe there is virtually a Jewish psychology." Jesus was "extremely Jewish. He worries all the time, he anticipates, he broods upon what's going on, there's an immense sense of responsibility." In writing the novel, "I began to realize for the first time in many, many years how Jewish I am." Another trait he shared with Jesus was the notion that you pay a price for everything you get. "That conviction," he said,

> is at the very center of Jewish belief, as opposed to Christian belief, where God takes mercy on you, and you're lifted and you're saved. The Jews tend to believe that you never get it without paying something in return. So it is delightful to contemplate these miracles once you recognize that you can use yourself up—indeed the angels whisper to Jesus at a certain point, and say in effect, "Don't overdo it."

Critic Frank Kermode, writing in the *NYRB*, praises the subtle way Mailer demonstrates how "God-given power in a man can be wasted or exhausted." The drain of healing power is "a major theme" in the novel, Kermode says, even if it meant that he was "infusing Jesus with a strong dose of Mailer."

Kermode finds Mailer's book to be daring, a "clever" addition to the apocrypha surrounding the Jesus story, and "the first, so far as I know, to be attributed to Jesus himself, a gospel-autobiography, no less, of the son of God." Mailer's midrash, his extensions of the Gospels (Jesus brooding on Herod's slaughter of the innocents for example), and his theological speculations are not what interest Kermode. "The writer's powerful mind works in a specialized way, not by theological argumentation, but by telling or retelling story." This was what Mailer set himself to do, Kermode concludes, and having "accepted the dare, Mailer can make a fair claim to have come honorably close to winning it."

Jesus' voice is the novel's largest achievement. Mailer was pleased to present both the spoken words of Jesus and his imagined thoughts. It was a gamble, but as Epstein noted, "Norman's more of a risk-taker than most of his contemporaries." Two novelists who reviewed the book, Reynolds Price and John Updike, commented favorably on Jesus' voice. Mailer's decision to provide access to "not only His mental weather, but the motives that underlay His titanic claims and actions," Price says, gives Mailer "powerful moments of invention," allowing him to "speculate with a welcome freshness on the secrets of Jesus' nature." Updike praises "the quiet ghostly voice of Jesus," rendered in "direct, rather relaxed English that has yet an eerie, neo-Biblical dignity." In its first draft, the locutions of Jesus were closer to those of the King James Bible, but Epstein objected to the overuse of words like "didst" and "mayhap," "penny" instead of "coin," and Mailer toned it down to the final, more modernized vocabulary. He was pleased when his father-in-law told him that he enjoyed the passages that presented the language of Jesus' thoughts.

Overall, *The Gospel According to the Son*'s reviews were better than those for *Portrait of Picasso as a Young Man*, worse than those for *Oswald's Tale*. The harshest review was in *The New Republic*. James Wood followed Kakutani in lashing Mailer for saying that his experience of celebrity aided him in understanding Jesus. But Wood's chief criticism was the first person perspective, which he found to be absurd, and the language, which he called "a spastic simulacrum of biblical style." However unhappy Mailer may have been with the review by Wood, an important critic, he was furious about the magazine's cover, which carried a cartoon portrait of Mailer with a crown of thorns on his head under the title of Wood's review, "He Is Finished." A few months after the review appeared, in the summer of 1997, Mailer ran into the magazine's publisher, Martin Peretz, outside a Provincetown restaurant. He had known Peretz since the mid-1960s when Peretz invited Mailer to speak at a Harvard rally against the Vietnam War. "If he'd just said, 'Hello Norman,' it would have been all right," Mailer said. "But he had this huge smile on his face. So I punched him." Then Peretz went in and told everyone that Mailer had hit him twice. "I guess it was a kind of badge of honor," Mailer said. Peretz said that Mailer's punches were "flabby." Mailer told friends he had hit him "hard, but not *hard*."

IN MANY OF the interviews he gave when doing publicity for *The Gospel*, he was asked about his promise to write a sequel to *Harlot's Ghost*. He often brought the issue up himself. But the fiftieth anniversary of *The Naked and the Dead* was less than a year away, and he had promised to write a new introduction for the anniversary edition. It occurred to him that the date, May 6, 1998, would also be a good time for a retrospective anthology. He would turn seventy-five a few months earlier, and the two celebrations could be combined. The editing job would not be particularly difficult, he assumed, and completing a new book only a year after the last would buy him goodwill from Random House, vital if he were to finish the sequel. Such a collection had been on his mind ever since Vidal had published his own retrospective collection in 1993. *United States: Essays, 1952–1992* is 1,295 pages long and contains the great majority of Vidal's literary and political-historical essays, but none of his fiction. Mailer decided that his book would also be long, and would include excerpts from virtually all his works.

As he worked through the spring and summer on the anthology, Mailer wrote a series of commiserative letters to his writer friend, Bruce Dexter, who was depressed about not getting published. He also tried, unsuccessfully, to get various agents and editors interested in his work. An excerpt from a letter to Dexter, who was recovering from a stroke, gives a sense of his own mood. He recalled the lecture he had heard in 1947 about the catastrophe theory of history: "Suddenly a catastrophe occurred and that was a form of history that the Jews knew all too well."

> I expect on the personal level a stroke has that quality, and I know I have an uneasiness about it that probably causes me more slight but actual psychic or spiritual discomfort than the thought of death itself. Death is as large and as final a transmogrification as one could ever find, but we spend our lives thinking about death, or trying to, whereas a stroke shunts us off to a siding. So from the above you can understand that I commiserate with you.

Reading in his seventy-fifth year almost everything that he had published in book form over the previous half century produced contrary emotions. He enjoyed passages of his writing that he had forgotten, but he also realized how much his powers had diminished. The result was melancholy. Another cause for gloom was his eyesight. He had cataracts, but the doctor told him he should wait until the fall to have them removed. "It's a little like Vaseline has been rubbed over the lens," he told his Providence friend Ed McAlice. Mike Lennon, who was helping Mailer assemble the collection, sent him over two thousand pages culled from his books, all of them blown up 100 percent, from which to make his selections. Mailer expected and accepted that the anthology would be seen as a farewell gesture.

The volume, now titled *The Time of Our Time* (an echo of his 1958 short story "The Time of Her Time") was finished around Labor Day

1997. Writing to an old friend, Edith Atkin, he said that the new book would be "a commemorative work. It isn't enough that I advertise myself, now I'm going to 'commemorate' me! Awful!" In a Random House Q and A to herald *TOOT*, as Mailer took to calling it, and maintain interest in *GATT*, his nickname for *The Gospel According to the Son*, Mailer said that "one extremely famous person" he'd like to read *GATT* was President Clinton, "in the wan hope it will remind him that we are not necessarily put on earth to aid and abet the rich in further enriching themselves." He also named *U.S.A.* by John Dos Passos as his model for *TOOT*, as he said in the acknowledgments and appreciations statement to the book: "Occasionally, since this had become an out-of-category volume influenced by one of the most monumental works of American literature, nothing less than *U.S.A.*, by John Dos Passos, I even took the liberty of improving old sentences." The most common improvement was to substitute "that" for "which" in numerous places, correcting an inveterate grammatical error that Random House copy editor Veronica Windholz had helped him to recognize. But he also revised many passages, usually cutting more than he added.

Dissatisfied with a topical organization ("equal to a row of potted plants"), as well as one based on order of publication ("useful presentation for a biographer" but of no interest to most readers), Mailer was at an impasse in his first months of work on the anthology. Eventually, he found a solution: with two notable exceptions, the 130-odd episodes from thirty of his books were arrayed along a chronological line from 1929 to 1996 because he decided to place each piece according to the date of the events depicted. "Boxing with Hemingway," the opening piece (a review of Morley Callaghan's *That Summer in Paris*) was published in 1963, but it depicts a 1929 event. The exceptions were excerpts from *Ancient Evenings* and *The Gospel According to the Son*, which were tacked on at the end.

World War II is the collection's armature. The great majority of the episodes demonstrate its direct or indirect influence on events, from the founding of the CIA, the Cold War, rocket technology, Cuba, the Vietnam War, and the assassination of JFK. Commenting on similarities between the film *Saving Private Ryan* and *The Naked and the Dead*, Mailer said, "The Second World War was a watershed. Everything is of it, before it or after it. It's a point of reference. It's still my point of reference." Dos Passos's point of reference, of course, was the First

World War. Mailer's unspoken intention was for *The Time of Our Time* to continue the narrative begun by Dos Passos, employing many of the narrative tactics, and doing for the second half of the twentieth century what his predecessor did for the first. In his foreword, he says, "There is little in this book, even when it comes under the formal category of non-fiction or argument, that has not derived, then, from my understanding of how one writes fiction." While Mailer did not go so far as to call his anthology a novel, it is in scope, structure, variety, voice, and "feel" congruent with Dos Passos's three-volume masterpiece.

The two books are of a size: Mailer's at 1,286 pages and Dos Passos's at 1,449. Both use many storytelling modes and handle equally well rapid shifts of narrative focus. Film and journalistic techniques are adapted by both writers, from the "camera eye" of movies to interpolated newspaper articles and headlines, as well as capsule biographies of the great figures of the age. Dos Passos includes profiles of J. P. Morgan, John Reed, and FDR, and Mailer gives sketches of Marilyn Monroe, Abbie Hoffman, and JFK. Various points of view are used, and both books have several touchstone characters. When an interviewer pointed out to Mailer that his collection reminded her of *U.S.A.*, he said he was following Dos Passos's lead with "the idea of certain characters reappearing in somewhat different circumstances, 30, 40, 200 pages down the road. For example, Gene McCarthy reappears three or four times. Nixon does, Castro does. And some of the fictional characters reappear and reappear. And what I like about it was the nearness of fictional characters to real characters. Of course, Dos Passos was doing that." Mailer and Dos Passos were the chief novelistic chroniclers of what Henry Luce called the "American Century," incontestably.

The reception of *TOOT* was better than for any of his books going back to *The Executioner's Song*. Even Kakutani had some kind words and her review appeared two days *after* the publication date, perhaps in response to Mailer's letter of complaint. She praised his "quick, observant eye, his gift for the cameo portrait, his radar for atmosphere and mood" in his nonfiction, and called *The Executioner's Song*, a "masterpiece." His novels she summed up as "jerry-built constructions" festooned with obsessive ideas that are "adolescent, irresponsible or just plain flaky." She concludes that "in the end, he remains his own most intriguing creation." Harold Bloom made precisely the same point in his warm review of *TOOT*, saying that Mailer "is above all the author of 'Norman Mailer,' his most persuasive fiction." His remarks about the collection are warmer, however. Very few other writers of the previous fifty years, Bloom states, have been "so endlessly sensitive to the phantasmagoria that is American reality," an achievement based on Mailer's love of country, "passionate sincerity," and an ability to fuse "acute sensibility and intensity with his public concerns."

One of the most perceptive reviews of the collection is entwined with a profile, which records a visit to Mailer in his third floor study in Provincetown. David Denby had read all or most of Mailer's books and it is clear that he enjoyed the man and admired the writer, but this side idolatry. Near the beginning of his twelve-page piece in *The New Yorker*, he gives a sketch of him at seventy-five.

> Mailer is looking well. His hearing has faded slightly, and he has some arthritic trouble with his knees. Using a cane, he sways on Provincetown's streets like a retired sea captain. But he's lost weight—he's down to about a hundred and eighty pounds from the rotund two hundred of a few years ago; the loss is partly the result of a complicated diet that commences with a nearly indigestible cabbage soup. ("The elements fight against one another so hard," he tells me, "that the cells exhaust themselves, and you lose weight." Mailer is a vitalist in all things, even in weight reduction.) His hair is thinning but snowy white, his forearms are strong, his voice is full; all in all, he still has the look of a barrel-chested elder Jewish sage which he achieved about fifteen years ago. David Ben-Gurion striding through some brave kibbutz gave off a similar robust glow.

The portrait, and other glimpses he gives of Mailer at ease with family and friends and giving a tour of the town, prepares us for an appraisal of the book that transcends the usual reviews.

Denby praises *TOOT*, saying that no one of Mailer's generation "could match the book's variety, its manic energy, its spiritual violence and striving." It is both "daunting," he says, and "eccentric," referring to the book's unusual organizational principle. He asked Mailer if using the normal method—date of composition—might not have been a better strategy because it would present readers with "a clear spiritual autobiography of Norman Mailer." Mailer answered with a sigh. "I've been waiting to write an autobiographical novel all these years, but I've been waiting to become the hero of my own life in order to write it. I have never become the hero of my own life." One clear reflection of his answer to Denby's question is the way Mailer limited his presence in *TOOT.* He excludes most of the self-portraits in his work, especially the nonfiction narratives of 1968–75, *The Armies of the Night* to *The Fight*. There is self-reference, but a reasonable quantity. "The main good motive behind this book was my desire to let people separate my work from myself," he said.

Mailer becomes just another character in the American cavalcade he presents, taking his turn along with Sergeant Croft and McLeod; Monroe and DiMaggio; Herman Teppis and Lulu Meyers; Rojack and Ruta; John and Jacqueline Kennedy; the astronauts; Oswald, his mother, and wife, Marina; Gene McCarthy; Gary and Nicole; Harry Hubbard, Hugh and Kittredge Montague, Modene Murphy; and Sinatra, Nixon, Ali, and Madonna. The glue that holds *TOOT* together, as Denby points out, is "Mailer's imagination of history," and one of the great things about the book is that we "forget which realm we are in—nonfiction or fiction, reality or fantasy—or why any of these categories matter." As James Campbell has noted, Mailer, like Didion, Vidal, and Baldwin, is a "two-hander," that is, "adept at both fact and fiction." His version of the history of the country from World War II to the century's end, in Denby's fine metaphor, is "a long, long night in which movie stars, Presidents, intelligence operatives, and gangsters meet in that ideal Mailer after-hours spot where only grownups are allowed to gather and where the music is always insinuating and sweet." The endless critical discussion about primacy among Mailer's fiction, history, biography, and journalism gets a one-word answer from *TOOT*: moot.

Random House threw a large celebratory party at the Rainbow Room in Rockefeller Center on May 6, 1998. Most family members were in attendance, as well as a number of friends: Plimpton, Styron, Vonnegut, S. I. Newhouse, Lillian Ross (who wrote about the party in *The New Yorker*), Schiller, Toback, and Lucid. Some younger writers were there, Jay McInerney and Bret Easton Ellis, who said he came because "there will never be another Norman Mailer." The surprise guests were Muhammad and Lonnie Ali. A hush came over the room when Ali was spotted, and the waiters rushed to get his autograph. He and Mailer mugged for the camera and traded fake jabs. Ali did some magic tricks, and when introduced to people, Lennon recalled, leaned in and said with a smile, "You're not as dumb as you look."

For the summer, Mailer planned to see his family and do a lot of reading: Cormac McCarthy's novels, DeLillo's latest, *Underworld*, and as soon as it was available, Tom Wolfe's *A Man in Full*, which he had agreed to review for the *NYRB*. He'd also been reading a lot of Jung, including Barbara Hannah's *C. G. Jung: His Life and Work*. He intended to stay on in Provincetown for the rest of the year. "In winter, it's wonderful to wake up and you don't feel sorry for yourself that you're missing anything, because nothing is happening," he said.

His major commitment was the sequel. "I've been waiting seven years to be visited by the muse for this second volume. She's been silent. I've been waiting. But now she's come back. What happened is that I got a major idea. So now, we'll see." The idea, he said later, was to make Hugh Montague a Jungian and open the sequel with him living secretly in Moscow. He was considering how he might use Jung's ideas as a way to avoid writing about the event-crammed 1960s and 1970s, especially the Vietnam War. But by the end of 1998, he still had not written a word of "Harlot's Grave."

FIFTEEN
OLD FREIGHTER, UNCERTAIN SEA

The first years of the new millennium were a time of contraction and consolidation for Mailer. He had a new right hip installed in February 2000, and his doctors told him that he should get knee replacements, but he kept putting off the operation. He wore dual hearing aids (and was forever losing them), and walked with two canes to make the dependencies equal, and for "the illusion that you are going in for cross country skiing and poling along." His waistline was again expanding and his eyesight dimming. After his cataract surgery, he learned that he had the beginnings of macular degeneration. He took nitroglycerin tablets for angina. The sum of these ailments "leaves me cheerful and chirpy, however," he wrote to Lois Wilson. "I figure the daily pains enable me to pay off my bad karma on the installment plan. Rest assured—you are a part of the good karma." He had taken to describing himself as an "old guy with slits in his sneakers," more of a geezer than a hipster. Norman Mailer had grown old.

His health problems were age-related and not immediately threatening; his wife's were more severe. In 1999 she had a hysterectomy, but the doctor removed only one of her fallopian tubes, and she soon learned that there were cancerous tumors on the other. Several operations and both chemotherapy and radiation treatments followed. When she went on a book tour for her first novel in 2000, she wore a wig, having lost all her beautiful red hair. For the next ten years, as the tumors spread, Norris battled cascading illnesses, and did so with stoic grace and a dash of gallows humor.

Windchill Summer, her coming-of-age murder mystery novel, was written before she met Mailer. She described it as "a story about boys going to Vietnam and the toll it took on them and everyone close to them." She began it at Arkansas Tech shortly after her husband, Larry

Norris, shipped out for Vietnam. Mailer had not been complimentary about it when he read the manuscript shortly after they began living together. In the late 1990s, having learned a good deal about the craft, Norris began an entirely new version.

She had a studio adjacent to his on the third floor of their Provincetown home, and to communicate with him, one would e-mail her, and she would walk ten steps into his space with the message. Otherwise, they worked separately, he writing, and she painting or handling the family finances. But after she began writing, she talked to him about technical matters, and then asked if he would read her unfinished manuscript. He said no. "I told her that if I read it, and she didn't finish it she would never forgive me. And she nodded. She's fairly tough-minded." When the page proofs arrived, he said that perhaps it was time to take a look at it, and she agreed.

After an hour of reading, he handed her his initial edits. Amazed to see that he was line editing her novel, she bridled. "No. You can't edit this book. I have to be able to say that I wrote the whole thing myself. I don't want you to edit it," she said. "Our styles are too different." When asked, "Do we influence each other?" he said:

> Not all that much. We are both very stubborn. She's got a whole set of attitudes and values that don't match with mine at all. When it comes to literature, particularly, we are very far apart. She wouldn't read Proust if I put a gun to her head! She loves bestsellers. And I hate bestsellers. My favorite writer is Tolstoy. I don't mind these differences. By now I know that you never get the woman of your dreams. Nor is there a dream man. But as long as there is a balance, it may work. Of course it's difficult to be married to a writer. Writers are as egocentric as any artists. Because the more talented the artist, the more he is in love with something else than the woman: his work.

Norris's self-assessment in regard to literature matches Mailer's. She said more than once that she preferred *People* magazine to *The New York Review of Books*. The primacy of his work was obvious to her, and the entire family.

Mailer told her that if he couldn't edit her novel as he went along, then he couldn't read it. "Fine," she replied. "Then you'll either read it when it comes out or you won't read it." He handed her back the proofs. "I never even looked at what he had done. I know there were a lot of people who would have given three years of their lives if Norman Mailer would have edited their manuscripts, but I was not one of them." When asked how he'd have edited the novel, he said, "I could have made it about five percent better. That's all though. The book was essentially there." Norris had made her point. Her novel was a modest success, with generally warm reviews, good sales, and a paperback edition. It is dedicated to her husband and two sons.

ABOUT THE SAME time that *Windchill Summer* appeared, Tom Wolfe published *Hooking Up*, an essay collection. It included a full-throated attack on three novelists who had found fault with his 1998 novel, *A Man in Full*. Titled "My Three Stooges," the essay accuses Mailer, Updike, and John Irving of wasting their careers by pursuing private obsessions instead of exploring "the rich material of an amazing country at a fabulous moment in history." Wolfe's long-held contention was that the American novel had fallen into a "weak, pale, tabescent condition"—a view for which Mailer had some sympathy—that could be remedied only by sending "a brigade of Zolas" out to document the raw life of a fast-changing, unpredictable country. He was happy to present himself as the American Zola and label the three novelists as "old lions" who had "retreated, shielding their eyes against the light, and turned inward." The unspoken, root cause of their criticisms of him, Wolfe argued, was his success—*A Man in Full* was a number one bestseller for ten weeks—and the three "old piles of bones" were "shaken," fearful of becoming "effete and irrelevant." Mailer (*NYRB*) and Updike (*New Yorker*) had written longish reviews of Wolfe's novel; Irving made his comments on a television talk show.

The media loved all this nastiness. Some commentators pointed out that the three old lions were hardly uninterested in the riptides of American culture, as even a cursory look at their numerous and notably realistic books demonstrated, for example, Irving's *The World According to Garp*, Updike's Rabbit Angstrom tetralogy, and *The Executioner's Song*. Wolfe's demeaning of Mailer's book seemed especially trumped up. Asked how he could call Mailer inward-looking in the face of the immensely detailed societal portrait given in his Pulitzer Prize–winning narrative, Wolfe said that Mailer owed it all to "a remarkable Santa Claus named Lawrence Schiller," and proceeded to imply that Mailer had sat at home while his friend did all the research. Schiller did wear out a lot of shoe leather, but Mailer did his share of interviewing, before transforming fifteen thousand pages of research into an unforgettable thousand-page story. Wolfe conceded nothing, however.

The three novelists held hands on one aspect of Wolfe's novel: the flatness of his characters. Irving called him a journalist who "can't create a character." Updike said that Wolfe's story is smothered by set pieces and subplots, "spreading like kudzu, sending eager tendrils everywhere," and that he makes his laborious narrative too cluttered "for sustaining suspense and characters we can care about." The hero, a sixty-year-old Atlanta multimillionaire named Charlie Croker, "is a specimen under glass," and the novel is "a provincial curiosity." Updike's summary judgment: *A Man in Full* "amounts to entertainment, not literature, even literature in a modest aspirant form." Mailer was no kinder.

Echoing Updike, he said that Wolfe's general strategy, whenever he reached an impasse, was "to cook up new ingredients and excursions for his plot." Some of it is excellent, but his plots are a way of covering up "an endemic inability to look into the depth of his characters with more than a consummate journalist's eye." When he enters the minds of his chief characters, as he must to establish motivation, the interior monologues "are surprisingly routine and insist on telling us what we know already. There is almost no signature quality of mind." Wolfe, Mailer said, has the talent to write a major novel, but also possesses the ability to write a mega-bestseller and was unable to decide which he was writing. Mailer delivered the coup de grâce at the close of his review, calling Wolfe "certainly the most gifted best-seller writer to come along since Margaret Mitchell," a barb that helps to explain Wolfe's defensive, twenty-six-page-long rejoinder. Mailer punctuated the exchanges when he responded to a British journalist's question about being called a jealous old bag of bones. "It's true that I'm a bag of bones," he said, "but if I'm going to be jealous, it will be of Tolstoy."

RON ROSENBAUM'S 1998 study, *Explaining Hitler: The Search for the Origins of His Evil* intrigued Mailer when he read it. A novelist and journalist of wide experience and interests, Rosenbaum had spent ten years off and on interviewing Hitler experts in the United States and Europe. The book turned Mailer's head. "Long after the details had faded from my mind the feeling of the book remained," he said, and just as he was settling on his plan for the sequel to *Harlot's Ghost*, "this little muse appeared in an apse of the literary church," he recalled, "and wiggled her finger at me." Until then, "I was absolutely intrigued with the idea of Montague as a Jungian," intending to have him surface in Russia with "some mad notion" of converting the nation to a polity based on Jungian principles. But then the idea of a Hitler novel came to him. All through 1999 he researched, eventually deciding to write about Hitler's childhood. "There were only a few good books. Just three or four really counted, and none of them of course could do more than satisfy a little bit." In addition to Rosenbaum's study, Mailer drew heavily on August Kubizek's *The Young Hitler I Knew* and Franz Jetzinger's *Hitler's Youth*. He also read several books on apiary science. Beekeeping would play an important part in the novel that he would write over the next seven years.

As he continued to read and take notes, he also began another project with Schiller, a teleplay based on a number one bestseller that Schiller and James Willwerth had written about the highly controversial O. J. Simpson murder trial. Schiller paid him $250,000 for reshaping *American Tragedy: The Uncensored Story of the Simpson Defense* into a four-hour miniseries. Initially, Mailer had been uninterested in the trial, but he thoroughly enjoyed the Schiller-Willwerth book. "My old friend and colleague has come up with a book that is impossible to put down," he said. He finished the teleplay in July 2000, and it was broadcast in mid-November. Simpson went to court to try to block the miniseries, claiming that Schiller had violated an agreement with him in which Simpson had the right to review the screenplay, but his claim was rejected and the program was aired as scheduled. It received fairly strong ratings.

Meanwhile, Mailer did research for the Hitler novel secretly, as he explained to one of his admirers, Morton Yanow.

> I have not told anyone what the private idea of it is, not even my wife or Judith, both of whom, being excellent private detectives, are trying to find out but will not necessarily know until I begin the

> writing. The reason I don't want to talk about it is I think it would spook this work and would be even more dangerous than the usual pitfall of talking a book away. So I wrap silence around me and austerity, as if I were a grand old man, which for better and for worse, I am not.

Judith typed this letter and soon learned the secret. She did, after all, order books for him, and she and Norris surmised what the novel would be about. The specifics—the portion of Hitler's life to be depicted, the point of view, beekeeping, and life in rural Bavaria—were still evolving. Mailer ended his letter to Yanow with a metaphor about his condition that reveals his weakening health, his determination, and his self-dramatizing imagination.

> The pleasure of writing a long letter to an old friend is no longer mine, and I don't regret it since as you get older, the analogy of one's own mind and body, one's working corpus, comes closer and closer to the notion of a heavy old freighter, seriously overloaded, in an uncertain sea, and therefore, discarding ballast as it goes. You are at least 20 years from that, but I want to tell you, it's not a gloomy situation, since one is pleased with all the clarity of mind that is left and that takes care of one's mood.

With the help of a German-speaking friend, Elke Rosthal, Mailer began studying German, aided by his memory of the Yiddish his parents spoke at home. His reading was not limited to books about Hitler and World War II; he also read German philosophy (Herder, Schopenhauer, and Nietzsche) and poetry (Goethe, Heine, and Rilke). He particularly enjoyed *Conversations of Goethe with Johann Peter Ekermann*, and saw parallels between himself and the German polymath. Both he and Goethe, he said, essayed a variety of literary forms, were interested in science, politics, government, and led active social lives. The Faust myth was something else that connected them. "I'm raising the bar higher than ever before," he said about the new novel. "It will contain every idea I ever had." It would have "some of the magical aura" of the Egyptian novel, but it would also be more documentary, historical, objective—less so than *Oswald's Tale* and *The Executioner's Song*, however. After he completed the Simpson script, he was ready to begin.

He wanted a different location to begin writing, a place completely free of interruptions. A few years earlier, Lennon and his wife Donna had purchased a condo about half a mile from the Mailer home. Mailer knew the area well and called it P-Town's suburbs, a place atop a modest hill away from the noise of the town's center. He liked the view of the monument and the harbor from the third floor studio. The condo was vacant except on some weekends and its owners were happy to give Mailer a key. In mid-December 2000, Norris dropped him off there with his notes, a ream of paper, and a fistful of pencils, and he began writing. If the weather was bad, she would drive him back and forth; otherwise he walked four or five days a week and, if the condo was free, also on weekends. He could do a mile with his canes, one third of a mile without them. By the beginning of April, when he returned to his study at home, he had written 150 typescript pages.

This was Mailer's writing routine, taken from Lennon's "Mailer Log" for July 15, 2005:

> When I first spent a lot of time with him, in the 80s, he had dinner at a reasonable hour—around 7:30. But then he began working later and later, often not coming down from his study until close to 9 P.M., while his family and guests waited and starved. But he has changed his pattern now and does not work much after 6 P.M. "It was just too hard," he told me a couple of months ago, "so I am working shorter periods." He normally gets up between eight and nine, but takes a long time to get downstairs. Then he has his breakfast, often two poached eggs and dry white toast, sometimes fruit and oatmeal. Hearty breakfast with o.j. and coffee. He reads the papers as he eats—the *Boston Globe* and the *New York Times*, and does the *Times* crossword puzzle every day, until they get really difficult on Friday. The *Globe* publishes a daily epigram by Dr. Johnson or Emerson, Montaigne, etc., and NM often writes a rejoinder to them (a collection of these is now in the hands of his agent). He goes to the loo around 11 and sits on the can reading for a long time. His last act before going up to his study is to play a couple of hands of solitaire—"combing my mind," he calls it. Then, somewhere between 11 and 12, he climbs slowly up the two flights to his study and begins to work. He has a late lunch, around 2:30 or 3:00, and then takes a nap. He has always pushed himself, and rarely broke

routine unless he was traveling to promote a book, speak, or be on a panel, etc. When he isn't working, he told me, he gets into trouble. True.

NM always sits in the same chair at the dining room table—the center of all activity at the Mailer home—with his back to the living room and facing a wall, not the glare from the sun and sea to his right. Visitors will often sit to his left at the head of the long wood table that seats ten. The table is full of the day's projects: piles of mail, manuscripts, books and magazines, photographs and piles of newspapers. When it gets too cluttered, the papers are thrown away and the rest moved to the six-foot wide, three-foot deep shelf before the Oriel window. When the shelf is packed a foot or two high, the stuff is shunted to the basement. It is fascinating to go through this stuff; last week I saw the following: letters from other writers or editors seeking endorsements of a ms., books to be signed for fans, copies of newly published editions of NM's work from around the globe, contracts for film and literary work, letters and cards and drawings from old friends, *Poetry* magazine, *Nation, Stop Smiling, American Conservative, New York Review of Books, Provincetown Arts*, as well as the black box containing poker chips and cards for the nightly Texas hold 'em game. A green felt poker board, folded up into sections, leans on the wall near the window. A lot of this stuff spills into the bar, which adjoins the dining room. From the telephone there, NM speaks to Judith several times a day. In the afternoon after lunch, he goes through the mail, makes phone calls to Judith, and usually to a few of his nine kids. Hardly a day goes by without some of them calling.

THE SPAT WITH Tom Wolfe brought Mailer into closer contact with John Irving. Mailer admired *The World According to Garp*, but had met Irving only a few times. In March 2001, Irving wrote to ask if he and Norris would do a benefit reading for a private school in Manchester, Vermont. He suggested A. R. Gurney's *Love Letters*, in which a man and a woman read aloud their fifty-year correspondence. Mailer didn't think it was a role he could do well, and Norris thought perhaps that George Plimpton might substitute. When Mailer called him, Plimpton came up with a different play, *Zelda, Scott, & Ernest,* which he and Tom Quinn had written, based on the letters of the Fitzgeralds and Hemingway, as well as excerpts from Hemingway's *A Moveable Feast* and Zelda's novel, *Save Me the Waltz*. "Norris can be Zelda," Plimpton said. "She's an actress and from the South." Mailer, who would of course play Hemingway, read the script and liked it. Over the next eighteen months, Plimpton and the Mailers would perform the play more than a dozen times, beginning in Vermont. In the summer and fall of 2002, the trio performed it in seven European cities, beginning in Paris and ending in London.

All of their performances drew sell-out crowds. After the first one in Vermont, a man in the audience yelled out. "This should be in every high school and college in the country." Mailer wore khaki pants and a safari shirt, Plimpton a sport coat and a Princeton tie, and Norris tied on a flapper head scarf. The play could have been commercially successful, but the estates of the writers would permit it to be done only as a fundraiser for not-for-profits. "In other words," Mailer said, "I'm safe from becoming James Tyrone," the character in Eugene O'Neill's *Long Day's Journey into Night* (based on O'Neill's father) who played the same role thousands of times. Mailer found the role to be "damn interesting. As I'm doing it I'm thinking of the ways that Hemingway is Hemingway and I am not, and the ways in which there are similarities." Physically, he said, "we each have spindly legs and we're barrel-chested." Mailer said Papa was a writer who

> changed the ways in which we perceived things, and he changed the way in which we write. That's two pretty powerful jobs. Either one is enough to make you a great writer. What he lacks—all great writers lack something—is a certain charity of mind. He was very narrow-minded, and that shows in his work. But on the other hand, it also gives that intensity, that luster, that patina that you think of when you read Hemingway's prose. So it's a delight to read him. In George's play, the speeches are all terrific. You can't go wrong.

Norris was less enthusiastic about her role. She had the fewest lines and interacts only with Scott, not Hemingway. She was also miffed about being given less notice in reviews of the play and in joint interviews with Mailer. "I'm not much like Zelda in temperament or mind or anything else, but our situation is the same," she said. "I'm married to a famous writer, and I'm trying to be a writer herself"—she had begun work on a sequel to *Windchill Summer.* Mailer interrupted the conversation at this point. "So far I haven't stolen any of your stuff," he said. "No, you haven't stolen my stuff," she answered. "Scott lifted Zelda's diary. He lifted whole passages of her work and put it in his work and didn't attribute it to her." You're exaggerating, Mailer said, adding that since Zelda was in a mental hospital when he took the passages, and Fitzgerald "was thinking she's never going to do it, so I might as well use it." Norris pushed back: "Well, you'd be above stealing my work?" His reply: "Well, I hope I would be." Ever since the crisis in their marriage, and especially after the publication of her first novel, Norris was less willing to act merely as the dutiful domestic manager of the household and more eager to present herself as a writer. They jousted more now in public.

But one thing was clear, Norris said, her husband "always made me feel terribly important." She told Larry Shainberg, a Cape Cod friend who accompanied them on part of the European tour, that some of the dialogue between Scott and Zelda "makes you want to cry. Part of it, of course, is the era. Women didn't have the vote. They were totally subjugated to men." For the last eighteen years of her life Zelda was in and out of mental hospitals, and then died when a fire burned down the institution where she was confined. Zelda told Scott that being in a mental hospital was better than being with him because at least they allowed her to write. "It was as if she had no right to her own life," she told Shainberg. "Their life together was Scott's material. 'I'm the writer,' he said. 'How dare you use the name Fitzgerald?' " Her own life was nothing like this, Norris said. "Norman has been completely supportive. He's never held me back at all. He's not that kind of person." She agreed that he had made some dumb statements about feminists, but also felt that feminists had unfairly made him into a punching bag. "He's no enemy of women," she said.

Shainberg spent many evenings with the Mailers in Provincetown, especially during the gray winter months, and observed their exchanges, which he said were "sometimes nasty, sometimes playful, often both, as if testing each other's tolerance and patience and, together, how near they can get to the edge of the cliff without going over." Norris said, "He wins a few, I win a few." Mailer said, "Marriage is an excrementitious relationship. One can take all that's bad in oneself and throw it at one's mate. She throws it back at you and you both shake hands and go on with your business—you can't do that when you're out in the world." Mailer often said that people overlooked his playfulness, missed his wink, and Shainberg noted that "even when he's angry, it's not clear how much he means to be taken seriously."

Riding in a limo in Vienna with the Mailers before a performance of *Zelda, Scott, & Ernest,* Shainberg heard Mailer serve up another metaphor for their verbal tussles: "Norris and I are like two old gym rats. Fighting is our hobby." He paused a moment, and then gave a demonstration.

> "When you're my age and you've been married as long as I have, your wife can have half your IQ and twice your rage and you still argue like equals."
>
> "Did you say half?"
>
> "Maybe 55%."
>
> "Fuck you, Norman."
>
> "Fuck you too, baby. You act like my older sister. Christ, I've got to be the only 80-year-old in the world who's treated like a six-year old. When I leave you, I'll say it's 'cause you have frustrated my late adolescence."
>
> "If you leave me, who'll arrange for your wheelchair at the airport?"

Shainberg became concerned, but then an expression—half grin, half scowl—appeared on Mailer's face.

What happened to wild man Mailer, the gent who butted heads in bars and got into boisterous scrapes on television? "Well," Mailer said, "he finally ran into a woman who was exactly his equal, which I think is very important. People only get domesticated when they meet their equals."

BETWEEN PERFORMANCES OF the play, he continued working on the Hitler novel, as well as working on still another Schiller project. In February 2001 Robert Hanssen, a longtime FBI agent with an unblemished record, was arrested for passing classified information to the Russians in exchange for cash and jewels. He was only the third FBI agent to be accused of spying. Hanssen was a devout Catholic and member of Opus Dei, a conservative institution for rank-and-file members of the Church. The father of six who brought his family to Sunday Mass at the same church attended by FBI director Louis Freeh, Hanssen had been passing secrets to the Russians for fifteen years. What made the situation of larger interest was the fact that Hanssen's job at the FBI was counterintelligence, and one of his responsibilities was to design a plan to ensnare a suspected mole inside the FBI—himself. Mailer could hardly ignore the story of a man who gave the following description of his secret life to his Russian handlers: "I am either insanely brave or quite insane. I'd answer neither. I'd say, insanely loyal. Take your pick. There is insanity in all the answers."

Schiller asked Mailer to write the script for a miniseries, but unlike the O. J. Simpson teleplay, where he had worked from Schiller's book, the Hanssen project required travel and research. In the months following the arrest, Mailer and Schiller again took to the road, this time to interview people associated with the man responsible for what former FBI director William Webster described as "possibly the worst intelligence disaster in U.S. history." They traveled around the United States and to London and Moscow to speak with family members, Russian and U.S. intelligence agents who had worked with Hanssen, his closest friends (including Catholic priests), and one of the psychiatrists who interviewed him after his arrest. The two people they most wanted to interview were Hanssen and his wife, Bonnie. Mailer wrote to her in April.

> No one can understand what you have had to contend with these past days, and I recognize that this letter is one more imposition. Nonetheless, I believe I have acquired some understanding of the complexity of the human spirit over the years, and I have learned not to sit in quick judgment. As matters now stand, I will be writing a screenplay for CBS. It will not be cheap or sensational. By all the accounts of the people to whom we have spoken already, your husband possesses a mind that is complicated and second in intelligence to few others. That is the way I will present him in the teleplay.

He ended by saying that he would do his best to protect her privacy, and would not "go at the story like a journalist who has a deadline to meet and so lives with the temptation to distort the material in order to excite his reader's attention." Because both Hanssens later signed plea bargain agreements with the Justice Department, Mailer and Schiller were unable to interview either.

On September 11, 2001, Mailer was in Provincetown working on the teleplay when his daughter Maggie, who was staying at his Brooklyn apartment with a clear view of the World Trade Center, called him about the attack. Like millions of others, she was "terribly affected," he said. For the next few days, he watched television constantly. "That only happens a few times in your life," he said. "Jack Kennedy, Bobby Kennedy. Martin Luther King. Maybe ten times." His first reaction was to feel left out: "Being up in Provincetown, 300 miles away, the bit of blood that's still journalistic felt wistful."

Right after the disaster, in a telephone interview, Mailer called the World Trade Center "an architectural monstrosity" and offered the opinion that if no one had been killed "a lot of people would have cheered to see the towers destroyed." He went on to say that the terrorists who carried out the attack were "brilliant." To do such a thing required courage, but most Americans were convinced that the act was carried out by "blind, mad fanatics who didn't know what they were doing." It was time to "take a calm look" in order to understand what motivated a mission of such horrific destruction. In a second telephone interview, he said that most Americans didn't understand that in many countries, Americans were seen as "cultural oppressors" who erect "high rise buildings until the meanest, scummiest capital in the world will nonetheless have a ring of high-rise hotels and buildings around their airports. A lot of people resent it profoundly." If the United States did not recognize the damage caused by its "huge, profit-making way of life," he concluded, "we are going to be the most hated nation on earth."

A few months later when he was in Vienna, he was awarded the Honorary Cross for Science and Art, First Class, the highest honor Austria can give to an artist. The speaker on the occasion, Günther Nenning, one of the founders of Austria's Green Party, pointed to the merits of Mailer's brand of patriotism.

> We small Austrians have a very clear position towards your great America. We are always for America and always against America. Always for America because we want to be protected and because, in the global clash of civilizations, we belong after all to the West.

> Always against America because in our central European souls, there is a lot of arrogance coupled with anger and envy. It is therefore a great relief when Mailer shoulders our anti-American burden because you can't be more anti-American than this great American. Norman Mailer has a European concept of patriotism: he loves his country not how it is but how it should be.

The 9/11 attack, and then President George W. Bush's decision to launch the Iraq War, revitalized Mailer's energies as a Jeremiah after his interest in national issues had flagged during the Clinton years. He would publish two polemical books focused on the arrogance of American wealth and imperialistic ambitions: *Why Are We at War?* in 2003, and *The Big Empty* (with his son John Buffalo) in 2006.

The Hanssen teleplay was completed by November, at which time Schiller decided to write a nonfiction narrative based on Mailer's script, adding more information from other sources. It was published the following May as *Into the Mirror: The Life of Master Spy Robert P. Hanssen*, and was another bestseller for Schiller. The miniseries, which was well received, was broadcast on CBS in two parts on November 10 and 17, with William Hurt as Hanssen and Mary-Louise Parker as his wife. Mailer was paid $250,000 for the teleplay, and the income enabled him to keep up with his huge monthly expenses, approximately $50,000. The Hitler novel was years away and Mailer felt obliged to come up with a book for Random House—it had been four years since *The Time of Our Time*. In early 2002, he began to think seriously about a project Lennon suggested. Mailer's insights and anecdotes about the craft of writing were scattered in several of his books, in various collections, uncollected interviews, transcripts of television programs and in talks he had given. "Presented with the cache," Mailer wrote in the acknowledgments to the resulting book, "I began to see that the form of a legitimate work was present, barely visible, but with the unmistakable heft of a book." In early February 2002, he began to delineate the contents of what would be *The Spooky Art: Some Thoughts on Writing*.

On February 10, just as he was beginning, he received word that Jack Abbott, who had been denied parole in 2001, had committed suicide. Michael Kuzma, who had advised Abbott in a lawsuit against the state of New York about a beating he had received in prison two years earlier, said that he was not satisfied that Abbott had killed himself. Abbott had told him that he was worried about his safety. He was discovered hanging from a sheet and a shoelace in his cell. Bill Majeski, the detective responsible for his capture, questioned whether it was suicide. "Everybody hated him," he said. Abbott's sister, Frances Amador, also doubted it was suicide. "But it's not something you can prove," she said. Abbott's ex-wife, Naomi Zack, noted that Abbott's eye disease and dental problems may have been factors. He tried to kill himself at least twice before, she said. Henry Howard, the father-in-law of Richard Adan, said, "That's the third person he murdered, and he got the right one."

When informed of Abbott's death, Adan's widow said, "I am happy he will not kill again." In a 1990 law suit, she had been awarded $7.5 million in damages, to be paid out of Abbott's royalties from his two books. She received approximately $115,000. Mailer, who had not corresponded with Abbott since 1986, issued a statement: "His life was tragic from beginning to end. I never knew a man who had a worse life. What made it doubly awful is that he brought a deadly tragedy down on one young man full of promise and left a bomb-crater of lost possibilities for many, including most especially himself." Abbott left a suicide note, but its contents have never been disclosed.

NORRIS'S FATHER HAD a heart condition, and in the spring of 2002 began to decline. She flew to Arkansas several times to help her mother, usually accompanied by either Matt or John. On July 21, after a long hospital stay, James Davis died. After the funeral, Norris tried to convince her eighty-three-year-old mother to move to Provincetown, but Gaynell refused. She had diabetes and didn't drive; she had never written a check, and was afraid to be alone at night. After Gaynell broke her ankle four months later, Norris got her to agree, after considerable cajoling, to move to Provincetown. Norris was now driving her husband, her mother, and herself to doctors' appointments in Boston and Hyannis, as well as shopping, cooking, and running the house. Mailer, who would be eighty in a few months, rarely drove anymore. Gaynell was miserable and wanted to return to Arkansas. She and her son-in-law were usually cordial, but it was "like they were from different planets," Norris said. Depressed and lonely, Norris's mother, a devout Baptist, found almost everything on television sinful and repugnant and "did nothing all day except sit and read in a chair tucked into a small room off the living room, the black ink of her mood seeping out all around her."

Added to Norris's load was a nonpaying position as artistic director of the Provincetown Repertory Theater, which she enjoyed but was able to handle only with the help of her production manager, David Fortuna. Mailer, remembering the successful reading of *Don Juan in Hell* they had done nine years earlier, proposed a benefit performance to aid the always needy theater. He contacted Vidal and asked him to reprise his role as the Devil. Norris would take the part of Doña Ana, Don Juan's former paramour; Lennon would play her father, the Commodore; and Mailer would be Don Juan, and direct. Vidal accepted immediately and flew in from his home in Rapallo, Italy, for rehearsals. Norris thought that Vidal got involved to make up to Mailer for his Charles Manson remark years earlier.

Vidal stayed at a nearby guesthouse, but came to the Mailers' every morning for breakfast. Norris recalled the "wild and wooly week" in her memoir: "Rehearsal all day, some kind of lunch, and dinner, ending with a late night of drinking and verbal sparring between Norman and Gore in our bar. I didn't for the life of me see how Gore was making it so well. He had more energy than all of us combined. We were all exhausted." Lennon recalls dropping off Vidal at the White Horse in Provincetown, watching him pour himself a Scotch nightcap, and then returning in the morning to find him lying fully dressed on his bed with the glass still in his hand. The seventy-seven-year-old Vidal popped up and went right back to work.

Don Juan in Hell is a ninety-minute dream sequence in the third act of Shaw's *Man and Superman*. It is often cut from productions of the play, one of Shaw's greatest, and performed separately. Mailer trimmed *Don Juan* to sixty minutes and made further refinements during rehearsal. Vidal knew his part almost by heart and while he listened politely to Mailer's suggestions, played the role his own way. On the night of the performance, October 12, Vidal, wearing his jacket with the dark red lining, told Mailer, "Norman, when I walk on that stage, you are going to hear a roar of applause the likes of which you have never heard." Vidal flashed the lining as he walked on stage, and the applause was indeed loud. A reviewer said, "the reading flowed and had sparks of brilliance," especially in the Devil's arguments for the superiority of his abode over the dull place above. The four dissect with every weapon of wit and rhetoric the great philosophical questions, culminating in a masterful set of exchanges between Don Juan and the Devil on the merits of the Life Force. It is brilliant dialogue, perhaps Shaw's finest. "If you were scoring the bout, it would go to Vidal," said the reviewer, who called Vidal's portrayal "flawless." Mailer agreed that Vidal was terrific, "almost as good as Charles Laughton in playing that role."

About the same time as the *Don Juan in Hell* performance, Mailer submitted the final manuscript of *The Spooky Art*. A party was planned for publication day, which would also be a joint birthday celebration, and invitations went out to over two hundred friends.

"The portals of eternity," to use Mailer's phrase, were on his mind, and he spoke more and more about his grave, his will, his epitaph, and his physical deterioration. In a letter to his boxing pal Sal Cetrano, he brought up the question of organ transplants. If modern science could provide us with a new liver, he wrote, "after we'd corrupted the juice out of the old one, then who was going to benefit? Some of the worst and lousiest and richest people on earth, tyrants, tycoons and so forth." There would be no opportunity to "look forward to some horrible old bastard dying." One's approaching death should lead to "the most serious meditation one could ever engage in," a process that would be disrupted by the possibility of "popping in new organs."

> I tell you, Sal, I get nervous about the possibilities of human nature even making it through the next century. We're just too fucked up, too determined to take over the savvy, the realm of genius of the Creator. I expect it's because we're prodigiously dissatisfied after the 20th Century with His or Her inability to come to our aid in times of terrible historic stress, but then, none of these liberals out there ever seem to recognize that the Devil may be just as powerful as God, and you can't lay blame on the first party who is probably doing the best He or She can do under these dreadfully parlous circumstances.

Showing the powers of the Evil One (as the Devil is referred to in *The Castle in the Forest*) as he and other evil spirits wander through the world seeking the ruin of souls—Hitler's especially—would be one of the chief preoccupations of the novel he was writing, and Mailer was perfectly willing to believe that organ transplants were a demonic activity. He was making good progress on the novel, losing only a few months to assemble *The Spooky Art*. In between performances of *Zelda, Scott, & Ernest* in the fall of 2002, he and Norris had driven across Germany to Vienna, accompanied by their Austrian friends Hans and Freidl Janitschek, stopping to see the Dachau concentration camp, Hitler's Berchtesgaden retreat, and locales in Upper Austria where he had lived as a boy, which would be the main setting of the novel.

Several weeks after they returned, Norris learned that her cancer had recurred. The birthday party was canceled. The new tumors were removed surgically, and a port was implanted in her abdomen. A strong drug was dripped into the port and she rolled over and over in her bed so that it would bathe her intestines. This went on for several weeks and exhausted her. Her sons and friends helped her, but her husband, she said, "pretty much left me to myself."

> Cancer had always been Norman's metaphor for evil, and now here was his wife, suffused with it. Was it his fault? Had he given it to me? It weighed on him, tormented him, and caused him to stay away from me. He moved into the bedroom down the hall, which hurt me at first, but the luxury of having my own bathroom and my own TV compensated.

Her weight dropped to 103, and for a time she had to wear a colostomy bag. She joked about it, telling her friends that she was going to "design a 'Bag Bag,' in all different colors and fabrics, so people could wear them outside their clothing," instead of hiding them. Mailer helped by doing some of the cooking. He was having chest pains, but refused to see his doctor in Boston, and began "popping nitroglycerine tablets like they were candy." Gaynell was still in a slough of despond, especially when she realized that she would not be returning to Arkansas. Aurora Huston came for a week, as did Christina Pabst, a friend from the Actors Studio, and the children helped whenever they could. Finally, the Mailers decided to hire a waiter from a local restaurant, Dwayne Raymond, whom they found to be both congenial and bright. He would work as cook, personal assistant, and a bit later, typist and researcher. Raymond would also become one of Norris's confidants. He worked for the family until Mailer died four years later.

THE RECEPTION FOR *The Spooky Art* was surprisingly warm, given the fact that it is an omnium-gatherum containing little original writing. Some slack, perhaps, was given to the old lion on his eightieth birthday. There was some debate about how skillfully Mailer had cobbled together cuttings from over two hundred different sources, but most reviewers found the book to be a thoughtful analysis of the psychological aspects of the writing life. Michiko Kakutani, again reviewing the book before almost everyone else, praised the sections on craft—point of view choices and the struggle to create a style—and Mailer's "keenly perceptive" comments on the weaknesses of his own books, but overall she found the book to be "startlingly" uneven. She compared it to the blather of a "garrulous raconteur" next to you on a long bus ride, sometimes compelling but also benumbing in his "self-absorption, his defensiveness, his capacity for wacky mumbo jumbo." Her summation: "Such ridiculous, self-indulgent nattering is just the sort of thing that won Mr. Mailer a reputation as a 'criminally egomaniacal' writer in his heyday, and distracted attention from his better work." For Kakutani, self-effacement stands near the summit of writerly virtue.

Mailer, characteristically, was of two minds about the merits of detachment. Kakutani quotes approvingly his negative stance on the question: "Writers aren't taken seriously anymore, and a large part of the blame must go to the writers of my generation, most certainly including myself. We haven't written the books that should have been written. We've spent too much time exploring ourselves. We haven't done the imaginative work that could have helped define America, and as a result, our average citizen does not grow in self-understanding."

Other reviews found merit in Mailer's self-spelunking. Both James Campbell (*The New York Times Book Review*) and Ron Rosenbaum (*New York Observer*) found introspection to be one of the collection's virtues. Echoing the judgments of Harold Bloom and Alfred Kazin, Campbell says that readers go to Mailer's books chiefly "for his alertness to 'every intimation about himself,' which he has expressed with greater vivacity than any contemporary." Rosenbaum says that in

Advertisements for Myself Mailer "broke ground for every memoirist who's put pen to paper since," and lauds him for "finding a way—in *Armies of the Night* to write about the personal and the metaphysical, the personal and the ideological, and even the personal and the *theological.*" Years earlier in his review of *Armies of the Night,* Alfred Kazin remarked that Walt Whitman was just as "outrageous an egoist and actor as Mailer." Like Whitman, Mailer had bouts of narcissism, but then got bored with himself. Then the cycle repeated. The salutary effect of this alternation, which runs through Mailer's work from the late 1950s on, is often overlooked. His self-promotion and his self-effacement, his blather and his brilliance, cannot be separated. As Walter Goodman, a *Times* colleague of Kakutani's, said of Mailer, "At his most engaging, he manages to be off the wall and on the mark at the same time."

Mailer wrote another letter to the publisher of the *New York Times*, with copies to Kakutani and fourteen other *Times* writers and editors, complaining about her consistently early reviews and asking for a meeting with her. He also pointed out that she was in error when she said in her review that dates for items in the book were not supplied, since the main text is followed by ten closely printed pages of source notes. The *Times* acknowledged this error in its corrections column, but Kakutani did not reply to Mailer's request for a meeting. A few weeks later, he said in an interview that he had a female literary enemy at the *Times* whom he described as "a posterior aperture." He would continue to up the ante.

In the same interview, he named his other enemy: President George W. Bush. The invasion of Iraq was imminent and Mailer was stoked up in opposition in a way not seen in the previous decade, a period when "I really didn't have anything to say about America." His uncertainties disappeared with the 9/11 attacks. The nation's guilt over what he called "economic gluttony," and its growing imperial ambitions had been smoldering for years; the 9/11 attacks lit the flame. Mailer put aside the Hitler novel, and began giving speeches and interviews and writing a series of antiwar, anti-Bush essays. "I know I'm going to have to pay for it," he said, and using a typical Mailer analogy added, "but if you don't use freedom of speech, it's like an unused dick. It tends to dwindle."

Invited to address the Commonwealth Club of California, Mailer carefully prepared a speech, and told his sister the occasion was a great opportunity. He drew on some of the rhetoric of *Cannibals and Christians* for his address, titled "Only in America," and also displayed the same empathy for the poor described in *The Gospel According to the Son*. He opened with an indictment of the "manic money-grab" of the 1990s, something that God did not approve of, he surmised.

> For certain, Jesus did not. You weren't supposed to pile up a mountain of moolah. You were obligated to spend your life in altruistic acts. That was one half of the good American psyche. The other half, pure American, was, as always: beat everybody. One can offer a cruel, but conceivably accurate remark: To be a mainstream American is to live as an oxymoron.

Despite the contrived evidence of Saddam Hussein's weapons of mass destruction, and lack of proof of his collusion with Osama bin Laden, the fears generated by 9/11 were powerful enough for Bush to declare war against evil, a word he used "as a narcotic for that part of the American public which feels most distressed," Mailer said. Saddam Hussein was an excuse, Mailer argued, for establishing an overwhelming American military presence in the oil-rich Middle East, an essential first step in the inevitable struggle for world dominance. "Flag conservatives truly believe America is not only fit to run the world, but we must. Without a commitment to Empire, the country will go down the drain." Mailer was not alone in his analysis. Vidal wrote his own short book on American imperialism, and numerous foreign affairs commentators issued the same warnings. Mailer quoted one of them, Paul Brookman, who said that after the fall of the Soviet Union in 1992, a document came out of the Defense Department that "envisioned the United States as 'a Colossus astride the world, imposing its will and keeping world peace though military and economic power.'"

With a few refinements, "Only in America," was reprinted in *The New York Review of Books* at the end of March and, combined with excerpts from his interview with Dotson Rader on 9/11 and another interview on the dangers of empire from *American Conservative*, appeared as a 111-page paperback in April 2003. *Why Are We at War?* was reviewed along with Vidal's collection of essays *Dreaming War: Blood for Oil and the Cheney-Bush Junta*, which came out a few months earlier. Both books make many of the same arguments. Both were well received, at least on the left-liberal side, and Mailer's made the paperback bestseller list. After witnessing the president's triumphant arrival via navy jet on the deck of an aircraft carrier where he announced, prematurely, the end of major combat operations in Iraq, Mailer shifted from a geopolitical to a psycho-political stance in his attacks on Bush.

In his *NYRB* essay titled "The White Man Unburdened" (nod to "The White Negro"), Mailer points to white male insecurity as one of the buttresses of Bush's war. A successful effort in Iraq would provide "psychic rejuvenation" to those white males who were "spiritually wounded" by 9/11, he wrote. White males had been taking "a daily drubbing over the last thirty years. For better or worse, the women's movement has had its breakthrough successes and the old, easy white male ego has withered in the glare." Rooting for white sports heroes was no longer the same, unless you were a fan of tennis, ice hockey, skiing, and a few other sports. "Black genius now prevailed" in football, basketball, boxing and a lot of baseball, "and the Hispanics were coming up fast; even the Asians were beginning to make their mark." But white Americans could still root for "an extraordinarily good, if essentially untested, group of armed forces, a skilled, disciplined, well-motivated military." The military could prove to be "quintessential morale-builders to a core element of American life"—the average American male who "had very little to nourish his morale since the job market had gone bad." If watching your favorite sports teams was not what it used to be, then tune in to the war—"sanitized but terrific." Mailer's invective had not been as good since he went after LBJ.

"I'm still trying to keep on working on a big novel," he wrote in August 2003. "The worst thing about Bush at times—from my point of view—is how much time he consumes writing about him and his gang." Giving interviews, writing op-ed essays and letters to the editor kept Mailer occupied through much of 2003. He and Norris also did a third benefit for the Provincetown Theater, a staged reading of excerpts from *Long Day's Journey into Night* at the Provincetown Town Hall. Mailer was James Tyrone, an actor famous for playing the leading role in *The Count of Monte Cristo*, an adaptation of the Dumas novel. He enjoyed being the overbearing father who spoke with "a touch of the very edge of an Irish accent." He was joined by Norris as Tyrone's wife, Mary, a morphine addict, with Stephen and John Buffalo as the Tyrone brothers, Jamie and Edmund, and Kate as the maid Cathleen. The one-night performance on August 15 went off flawlessly—although Stephen, an accomplished actor, had some boisterous disagreements with his father about the way Mailer cut the play—and the Mailers raised another slug of money for the theater. Norris resigned as artistic director after the performance in order to work on *Cheap Diamonds*, the sequel to *Windchill Summer*, in which her heroine moves to New York City and begins a modeling career.

Another project was a collection of approximately one hundred captioned head drawings, "droons," which were interspersed with poems from his 1962 collection, *Deaths for the Ladies*, and a few new ones. Mailer kept his assistant, Dwayne Raymond, busy for three months printing out various page layouts and cover designs for the softbound volume of 276 pages, titled *Modest Gifts: Poems and Drawings*. The cover consisted of the title and a five-stroke sketch of Norris's features, which also could be seen as birds in flight. Mailer often studied the formation flying of a flock of pigeons swooping around his house and over the harbor. He remarked more than once that its movements were so acrobatically precise that the pigeons must be inhabited by the spirits of departed Army Air Force pilots. He insisted that there be no publicity campaign for the collection, published on October 23, and it was hardly noticed.

Mailer also agreed to a series of conversations with Lennon about his theological ideas and beliefs, and during the last half of 2003, they taped three of them. His only proviso was that he not be given questions beforehand so that his answers could be spontaneous. "Improvisational," he said, "is still my favorite word." The interviews would continue every few months until mid-2005 when they had exhausted the subject. Mailer thought it might be a good book to appear after he "got on the bus," the euphemism used by family and friends to refer to his death. But he would change his mind as boarding time neared.

In September, George Plimpton died. Mailer spoke at the memorial at St. John the Divine in Manhattan. Philip Roth also attended and later transferred his memory of Mailer's eulogy to a character in his novel *Exit Ghost*.

> Guy's eighty now, both knees shot, walks with two canes, can't take a stride of more than six inches alone, but he refuses help going up to the pulpit, won't even use one of the canes. Climbs this tall pulpit all by himself. Everybody pulling for him step by step. The

> conquistador is here and the high drama begins. The Twilight of the Gods. He surveys the assemblage. Looks down the length of the nave and out to Amsterdam Avenue and across the U.S. to the Pacific. Reminds me of Father Mapple in *Moby-Dick*. I expected him to begin "Shipmates!" and preach upon the lesson Jonah teaches. But no, he too speaks very simply about George. This is no longer Mailer in quest of a quarrel, yet his thumbprint is on every word. He speaks about a friendship with George that flourished only in recent years—tells us how the two of them and their wives had traveled together to wherever they were performing a play they'd written together, and of how close the two couples had become, and I'm thinking, Well, it's been a long time coming, America, but there on the pulpit is Norman Mailer speaking as a husband in praise of coupledom. Fundamentalist creeps, you have met your match.

After the service, Mailer headed for the men's room. "Urination had become one of my preoccupations," he said. As he was cranking along on his canes he saw Roth, with whom he'd had "an edgy relationship for thirty or forty years." Roth asked him where he was going in such a hurry. Mailer told him, and added, "Let me warn you, when you get to my age, you're going to be looking around for telephone booths in which you can relieve yourself." That time had already arrived, Roth informed him. "Well, Phil," he said, "you always were precocious." It was the only time they had ever laughed together, Mailer said. He attributed the warm moment to Plimpton's spirit. He had liked George enormously, admiring the way he moved with ease through such a range of projects and pursuits while managing to edit a leading literary quarterly for a half century. After the memorial he wondered aloud about how much time he still had, considering all his ailments, if someone with George's vigor could die at seventy-six.

EVERY YEAR, THE Mailers spent less time in New York and more in Provincetown, and the children, grandchildren, and friends visited there in all seasons, not just the summer as in earlier years. By the summer of 2003 five of Mailer's children had married (Susan, Danielle, Betsy, Kate, and Stephen), and produced eight grandchildren. They all visited regularly, as did Al and Barbara, her son, Peter, and other members of the family. The increase in visits was prompted to some extent by the fact that Mailer was eighty and had a weakening heart. Susan recalled her father during this period.

> He was in dire need of care, felt lonely, but was too proud to acknowledge it. During that period he made more phone calls than he ever had, he who hated speaking on the phone! He actually asked us to visit him, two or three times, when he called us in Chile. As I write this I'm sad Marco and I didn't visit more often. Those last four years, his overall mood changed, he had more time for his children, and especially, was more in need of us, something he'd kept well hidden before. We, his older children, have commented among us how he finally became the gentle, accessible dad we had wanted in our childhood. He told me many times during this period that he now enjoyed being with his kids and having family dinners almost more than anything else.

The Mailers also opened their home to his friends in the Norman Mailer Society (founded in 2003), which met in Provincetown from 2004 to 2007. The Mailers invited the keynote speakers for lunch every year. Neil Abercrombie, a Democratic congressman from Hawaii (now governor), spoke in 2004. He had written his Ph.D. thesis on Mailer, and they had been friends for decades. Ed Doctorow, who was one of the editors of *An American Dream*, was the 2005 speaker, and William Kennedy spoke in 2006. Mailer thought it would be gauche to listen to speeches and panels about him and his work, so he had never attended any of the conference events, but hosted the closing party. Kennedy had met Mailer in 1968 when he was editing *Maidstone*, and written a warm review of *Beyond the Law.* They saw each other many times in the 1980s—at PEN meetings, fundraisers at the New York Public Library, and at the Actors Studio. Mailer introduced him to Paul Newman, who wanted to play Francis Phelan in the film version of Kennedy's Pulitzer Prize–winning novel, *Ironweed*, but Jack Nicholson already had sewn up the role. Newman was a bit too cerebral for Phelan, Kennedy said, "and he didn't look like a bum. Jack had a magical way of transforming himself into the slouch of a bum." Nicholson was nominated for an Oscar for his portrayal, which Mailer admired. The Kennedys and Mailers enjoyed each other's company.

For his keynote, Kennedy wrote a half-comic, half-serious dialogue among him, his uncle "Billy," an unnamed interviewer, and Mailer. When he learned that the Mailers didn't plan to be at the luncheon where he would read it, he quickly cajoled them into attending. Mailer said it would be like Huck Finn listening to the eulogies at his own funeral, but Kennedy told him he would regret missing the jokes. The Mailers came and laughed as hard as everyone else at Kennedy's piece, "Norman Mailer as Occasional Commentator in a Self-Interview and Memoir." Toward the end of the dialogue, Mailer notes that American novelists have failed to do the imaginative work of defining America, and Kennedy responds, using Mailer's published words.

> KENNEDY: I soon realized I wasn't up to the task and throttled down to the individual, for instance in a novel about a pool hustler very like my favorite uncle. I called him Billy Phelan and he comes to a crisis during a political kidnapping when he refuses to be an informer. If I may, I'd like to invite Billy into this conversation, buy him a drink. Will you have a drink, Billy?
>
> BILLY PHELAN: The last time I refused a drink I didn't understand the question.
>
> INTERVIEWER: I think we should get back to the serious novel.
>
> NORMAN: The serious novel begins from a fixed philosophical point—the desire to discover reality—and it goes to search for that reality in society, or else must embark on a trip up the upper Amazon of the inner eye.
>
> KENNEDY: What I take home from that remark is that the novel's choices are scope versus self. Norman also says Hemingway and Faulkner both gave up scope.
>
> NORMAN: Their vision was partial, determinedly so; they saw that as the first condition for trying to be great—that one must not try to save. Not souls, and not the nation. The desire for majesty was the bitch that licked at the literary loins of Hemingway and Faulkner: The country could be damned. Let it take care of itself.
>
> KENNEDY: I remember a critic panning a self-absorbed novelist and saying rather neatly that literature wasn't about the self, but what came home to the self through experience. Norman has written

> extensively about the *self*, about *writing*, about the self, and *against* writing about the self. Norman seems to have written about every choice a human being can make. . . .
>
> INTERVIEWER: Norman has Hitler as a character in his new novel. No narcissism there.

A year later, at the Institute for Writers at the State University of New York—Albany, Mailer read from the Hitler novel, *The Castle in the Forest*, and engaged in a dialogue with the audience. During the visit, the Kennedys hosted a reception for Mailer, as described in Lennon's "Mailer Log."

> Kennedy was a great host and hosted a cocktail party at his city house, the Albany row house where Legs Diamond was shot in 1931. NM talked about the problems of writing the sequel to *Castle*, the largest being the vast amount of material to be covered. He wants to write about Hitler as a struggling student-artist in Vienna, about his affair with his cousin and her mysterious death, about the events after the 1933 seizure of power when Hitler, and of course the war, the concentration camps and his suicide in the bunker. He offered one possibility for handling all this and more: move the story to Russia and Rasputin for a time to avoid chronicling every major milestone in Hitler's life. He explained that he thought of doing something like this with Montague in the unwritten sequel to *Harlot's Ghost.*

Mailer was reading biographies of Grigory Efimovich Rasputin, Czarina Alexandra's confidant, and had become fascinated with the divisions in his psyche. Asked what the good-evil split was in the Mad Monk, he said, "Fifty-fifty, and that is why he is so interesting to me."

Dick and Doris Kearns Goodwin were also regular visitors to Provincetown. Whenever either of the Mailers had to go to Boston for medical work, they invariably stayed at the Goodwins' home in Concord, twenty miles outside Boston. The Goodwins are dinner conversationalists of some repute, and the Mailers loved Dick's memories of the Kennedy White House, Castro, and Che Guevara, and Doris's tales of interviewing LBJ at his Texas ranch in his final years. Mailer's opinion of Johnson improved after reading her book *Lyndon Johnson and the American Dream*, based on her extensive interviews with the former president. Mailer relished her account of how LBJ carried on long conversations with "delicate Kennedyites" while sitting on the toilet.

Goodwin said she loved talking to Mailer. "I felt he respected women. One time he gave me the nicest compliment in the world. He said, 'You're not the smartest person I ever met; you're not the nicest person I ever met, but you're the smartest nicest person I ever met.' I thought it was great." She likes to tell the story of one memorable visit. In the morning when they sat down for breakfast, Mailer informed his hosts that there was a problem with the toilet in the guest suite. When Doris Goodwin asked what it was, he said, "The water level is high, and when you get old, your balls hang low." If she wanted him to return, she'd have to get it adjusted. The story always brought laughter, even when she told it at Mailer's funeral in Provincetown. "He genuinely liked women," she said. "And he was also a sensual guy. You felt a physical strain that came from him." As for his numerous affairs:

> All these women he had the affairs with still care. I think the answer is, perhaps serially, the fact that he loved them. You can't fake that. Women know if you're just using them and I think he never did. He had to fall for someone to be really interested in them. Maybe I'm being too overly positive toward him, but my guess would be it's one thing to have a whole series of love affairs, whether it's three days or sixty years, versus just using women for sex. I don't think he did that; at least that would not be the man I knew. He might have done that earlier. He just loved women and that's what is so bad about the rap he got from some of the writing that he did. I felt to the contrary that he totally respected my opinions and feelings on things. He would ask me, often at dinner, what I thought about this or that. There was never a sense of, a moment of, condescension.

Mailer was a fan of Goodwin's new book about Lincoln, *Team of Rivals,* and talked about it with Lennon, as he wrote in his "Mailer Log."

> NM and NCM have both read Doris' book about Lincoln, *Team of Rivals.* He told me how much he likes the language, written and spoken, of the time. When I asked if he liked Abe's homespun

metaphors, he said no, not particularly. It is the high rhetoric of statesmanship and congressional debate, the speeches and passionate letters about abolitionism that he enjoys. This made me remember that many years ago I asked him what he thought of the Elizabethan Age, with its cast of daring, dashing players: Essex, Raleigh, Marlowe and so on. He said that he much preferred the Victorian Age with ladies in layers of petticoats and corsets, and men in vests and cravats, and went on with glee about the efforts needed to undress and possess the beauties of that time. NM relishes formal (if humorous) rhetoric, long, rolling, Melvillean sentences. He also admires Carlyle and has been compared to him, as well as to Spengler, Emerson, Edmund Burke. This love of slightly pompous, slightly humorous, somewhat ponderous prose is just one side of his linguistic identity, but it is perhaps the dominant one.

IN 2004 AND early 2005, working in Provincetown, he made steady progress on *The Castle in the Forest.* He had no desire to travel, but he needed the speaking fees. Norris was not strong enough to travel with him, and so either one of his sons or Lennon accompanied him. He was still fuming about Bush and the Iraq War, now in its second year, and wrote a number of additional pieces on American arrogance and greed. Three of them, one each in *Playboy, New York*, and *Stop Smiling*, were conversations with John Buffalo, who came up with the idea of enlarging them into a book that would examine a range of topics: politics, sex, God, boxing, morality, poker, George W. Bush, and the war.

John Buffalo and Michael accompanied their father to Toronto, where he was a boxing consultant on the film *Cinderella Man*, based on the career of James Braddock, the heavyweight champ in the mid-1930s. Before the trip Mailer read up on Braddock, played by Russell Crowe, and watched old footage of his fights. Ron Howard, the film's director, listened to his analysis of Braddock's bout with Max Baer, whom he defeated for the championship in June 1935 at Madison Square Garden. A 10–1 underdog, Braddock won a unanimous decision. "Baer got spoiled," Mailer said, "he wasn't used to getting hit." For the film, Crowe trained hard for a year in Australia, boxing and weight lifting, to get ready for the role. He and Mailer, according to Michael, got along well. After completing one scene, Crowe was sweating and took off a black fleece vest that had the name of Crowe's training camp on it. He gave it to Mailer, who brought it home. He wore it with dark sweatpants and Uggs, Australian sheepskin boots with fleece on the inside that were comfortable and required no socks—one fewer time waster, he remarked. Mailer liked Crowe, who reminded him of Brando. "He's suspicious and mercurial, but genuine," he said.

He was paid $100,000 for his advice, but it was a stopgap. Mailer was still locked in what he called "the bowels of cash flow," and needed a new paying project every few months. In the fall of 2004, he agreed to appear with Stephen on an episode of *The Gilmore Girls*, a long-running comedy series about a single mother and her daughter living in Connecticut. Stephen was cast as a reporter, and his father played "Norman Mailer." A few years earlier, he and Stephen appeared in the pilot for a series called *Street Time*, directed by his friend Richard Stratton. Mailer was "Saul (Two Canes) Cahan," a Jewish mobster just released from twenty-seven years in prison who has to report regularly to his parole officer, played by Stephen. One cast member said that Mailer was convincing because "he has a certain rough kind of look about him—his voice, his mannerisms." Mailer loved playing an old wiseguy and slipped into the role easily. He would put on his sunglasses, look you up and down slowly, and say in a leathery voice, "Who the fug are you?"

Financial relief arrived in the spring of 2005 when the Harry Ransom Center at the University of Texas–Austin agreed to purchase Mailer's archive. The deal was brokered by Glenn Horowitz, a New York rare book dealer who got Mailer $2.5 million for his papers, to be paid over six years. The delivered archive contained five hundred cubic feet of material, including manuscripts and personal papers from Mailer's childhood through the early 2000s, and approximately 45,000 letters. It is the largest author collection in the center's extensive holdings. Mailer became friendly with the center's longtime director, Tom Staley, and made two trips to Austin in connection with the transfer. In addition to the price, Mailer said he liked the idea of his papers being in Texas because of his wartime service with the 112th Cavalry.

As the deal sending his papers to the Ransom Center was nearing completion, the Mailers were visited by John Hemingway, grandson of Ernest and son of Gregory, whom Mailer had met on several occasions.

John Hemingway wanted to talk about a book he was writing about his family. Mailer and John got along famously, and the wine flowed that evening. In a letter to Anne Barry about the evening, Mailer said, "The sad truth is I'm still at my best when half loaded." He said he over-served himself with Grappa, a very strong Italian brandy that they drank "in honor of Hemingway."

> I said to Norris the next day, "If you ever see me go near Grappa again, just pick up the nearest heavy object and knock me out with it because the effect will be the same and at least it will save my digestion from having to deal with Senor Grappa again." Anyway, my sense of the ridiculous as you can see remains firm and complete. Only an eighty-two-year-old would tell drinking stories about his own drinking.

He ended his letter by noting that after nearly five years of work, he had completed seven hundred pages of *The Castle in the Forest.* He had interrupted work on it several times, but he also wrote much more slowly than in the past. "I used to pride myself on the white heat of my first drafts," he said. But now they took more time as he trimmed and polished. "I work them over in return for losing that early speed and smoke and flash and dash. The moment a sentence disappoints me slightly I start looking at what's wrong with it." He was continuing to work with John on the collection, which they were calling *The Big Empty*, and also continuing the theology interviews with Lennon.

During his first visit to the University of Texas in late April 2005, Mailer met Douglas Brinkley, a prolific young historian and editor. Brinkley wrote a story in *The New York Times* about the sale of Mailer's papers and followed up a few months later with a long profile in *Rolling Stone.* Brinkley used the occasion of Mailer's April speech at the university attacking Bush and the Iraq War—a "steppingstone to taking over the rest of the world"—to write his brisk overview of Mailer's career. The day after Mailer's speech they went to lunch and after disposing of Bush, yet again, Mailer talked about literature. He said that Kerouac's *On the Road* was a classic that "captured something hard about late adolescence—the thing about being free enough to travel and take your adventures where they come." And he talked about his old antiwar comrade the late Allen Ginsberg. In 1979, Mailer was at a National Arts

Club event where Ginsberg was the speaker. "He was a little nutty," Mailer said. "You never knew when Allen the Hun would take over."

A discussion followed of Kakutani's review of *The Gospel According to the Son*, which led Mailer to say of her that she can't be fired because "she's a threefer." Brinkley asked him to clarify. "Asiatic, feminist and, ah, what's the third? Well . . . let's just call her a twofer. They get two for one. She is a token. And deep down, she probably knows it." Brinkley was amazed. "Why make a quasi-racist remark about the most powerful book critic in America?" Mailer says that one benefit of being over eighty is that "you can say what you think."

Kakutani and the *Times* made no comment, but Esther Wu, the president of the Asian American Journalists Association, wrote a letter of protest to Jann Wenner, publisher and editor of *Rolling Stone*. She noted that "Asiatic" and "Oriental" were offensive terms to describe Asians and Asian Americans, and lambasted Mailer's remarks because he "diminishes the accomplishments of all women and journalists of color." The tabloids jumped into the dispute, and Mailer obliged them, telling the New York *Daily News* that Wu's letter was "an excellent example of high-octane political correctness." Wu countered by saying, "Perhaps if Mr. Mailer were a little more politically correct, he would not be making such racist remarks." Mailer foolishly persisted.

To friends at dinner over the Fourth of July weekend, Mailer said that he had "walked right into it" with his remarks, and acknowledged that his words were poorly chosen. He also said that Steve Erlanger, the *Times* cultural editor, had given him a commitment that Kakutani would not rush her next review of one of his books into print, but Mailer still intended to keep the pressure on. She may be a power unto herself, but "the *Times* must choose," he said, "between reining her in and pissing off Norman Mailer."

He decided to begin compiling Kakutani's reviews of other white male authors, looking for a pattern. Asked if he would include reviews of some younger writers—Dave Eggers and David Foster Wallace, for example, he said, "WR," or waiting room. In his mind, their literary stature remained to be determined. Over the next several months, he assembled "The Kakutani File," a collection of thirty-nine reviews of books by ten writers (Bellow, DeLillo, Doctorow, Irving, Mailer, Cormac McCarthy, Roth, Robert Stone, Updike, and Wolfe) over a twelve-year period, 1994–2006. By his count, twenty-two of the reviews had been published four or more days before the books' publication days, and ten were fifteen to thirty days early. His books got the worst reviews, with Wolfe, Stone, Irving, and Updike doing somewhat better, and Bellow, DeLillo, McCarthy, and Roth getting the best reviews. There was no correlation between the warmth of the review and the date of a book's publication—early reviews were just as likely to be negative as later ones. But it was clear that Kakutani did like to be out there first. Mailer was uncertain if he should use this survey, and how.

AFTER A REGULAR heart test on July 13 at Mass General Hospital, Mailer was told he needed an operation. His response: "After I finish the novel." He detested the thought of dying on the operating table and believed that his status in the hereafter might be enhanced if he was lucid and sharp when he got on the bus. Asked why one's state of mind at death was so important, he said, "It's our point of departure, our angle of flight, if you will."

> I think at the moment we die, we are the sum of all the good and bad we've done, all the courage and cowardice we've exercised. And so, for example, if we die with a desire to be reborn, I think it means a great deal to God. If you will, it's like reaching into a litter to select a pup, and there's one who catches our eye because he wants us. He is the one we choose to take home. Using that crude analogy, I would say it's important to be ready. After all, that is the one situation we can't simulate, can't preempt.

AFTER A MONTH of nagging by Norris and the family, he agreed to bypass surgery, and it was scheduled for September 8, 2005. The decision to have the operation, he said, made him "automatically five years older" because his ongoing efforts "to stave off old age" were now moot.

John Buffalo was around for most of the summer and he and his father finished work on *The Big Empty*, and turned in the manuscript to Nation Books for publication in February 2006. John challenged his father in some of their exchanges, gently but firmly, and this gave the book some narrative tension as they worked their way through issues of dissent, politics, and the psychology of boxing and poker.

Before the surgery, he had written three fourths of *The Castle in the Forest*, enough, he said, for it to be published if he died. In the month before the operation, he wrote about a hundred pages of notes outlining the so-called emergency ending. If he didn't make it through surgery, he hoped his notes could be appended to what he had completed. He wanted the novel to end shortly after the death of Hitler's father in 1903, with some additional material on Russia and the dislocations there during World War I. He had already written about the 1896 coronation of Czar Nicholas II at some length, which moved the narrative away from the Hitler family for several chapters. This was done in preparation for Rasputin becoming a major figure in the next volume of what he hoped would be a series of three novels. He said that Rasputin had considerable presence and was loved by many for his healing powers. Indeed, Rasputin is the perfect Mailer character: charismatic and drunken, soulful and carnal, a demonic-saintly figure who moved easily from Gypsy debauch to the czar's court.

Mailer had been taking two nitro tablets a day, and his recognition that he could not keep increasing the dosage was one more reason to agree to the operation. But he still had reservations. "Having my blood pumped out of me and sloshing around in a machine, running through loops of plastic is an unhappy prospect," he said. The plastic, he believed, might be the reason that Tom Wolfe and Larry McMurtry had become depressed after bypass surgery. Told that surgery depression passes after a time, he said, "Yes, but when you're 83 you don't want to lose six months; it's not worth it."

Mailer's quadruple bypass operation was successful and the doctor reported that he had the heart of a forty-year-old. After two weeks in the ICU, he was moved to a rehabilitation facility on Cape Cod. From there he was able to talk by telephone. Speaking in a hoarse, excited voice, he said that a tremendous number of new ideas had come to him, especially about spiritual matters. "I'd like to talk about them now," he said, "but talking gets me too excited. I'd only be scraping the rim of the can." The experience had brought him closer to Norris, he said, and he was troubled by how much she worried about him. Two days later, he said that he had gotten into too many bad habits. "I feel like Scrooge, all my previous life revealed in a flash, along with a desire to change." In October, he went home. His favorite journey used to be the sight of the Brooklyn Bridge after dinner in Manhattan, but now it was "the sight of Provincetown as one rides up over the last rise and there is the Pilgrim Monument in all its subtle presence." The vista always gave him a lift. Still short of breath, he had to blow into some sort of plastic device—which he loathed—to test his wind. He was counting on the salt air to strengthen his breathing and energize his psyche.

He told friends visiting him in mid-October that while recovering in the hospital, he got into conversations with the staff, especially the nurses. He liked one Irish-American nurse in particular because she didn't keep telling him he was looking better. She said that his recovery was "on the slow side." He told her that he had been married to Norris for thirty years, and the nurse replied that it was probably high time for a "treaty" with his wife, or as she explained it, an agreement to avoid certain sore subjects and so making life less antagonistic. "When we fight," he said, "it gets personal right away." Norris liked the idea of not discussing certain matters. For example, if he would not make any comments about women's lib, then she would not challenge his literary judgments. At some point they "signed" such a pact. As he was discussing the treaty with friends, he said, "Look at me, proud, semi-helpless, and opinionated." And then he laughed. His self-depictions were often sardonic.

While he was still in rehab, he learned that the National Book Foundation would award him the 2005 Medal for Distinguished Contribution to American Letters on November 16. He said it was coming at the appropriate time, that is, after Bellow, Roth, and Updike, who in his mind were less controversial. His acceptance speech would be the first thing he would write after he had recovered. For the rest of the year, he intended to rest and read, and did not expect to get back to *The Castle in the Forest* until the new year.

Recovery was slow. He spent a lot of time on the deck napping and watching the pigeons and gulls maneuver over the low tide flats. He read a piece in *The Atlantic* by Bernard-Henri Lévy, a French writer and public intellectual, who had spent a year traveling around the United States, following the footsteps of Tocqueville. Shortly before he returned to France, Lévy visited Provincetown and interviewed Mailer. In the profile, he made several errors, the most important of which was calling Mailer "the most secular of American novelists." When this and other errors were pointed out to Mailer, he was unfazed. It wasn't important, he said, and "Lévy did catch something about me: that I have my mind on eternity." The old Mailer would have snapped out a letter to the editor pointing out his long-standing theological interests, a friend said. Mailer waved it off. "I'm thinking of eternity," he repeated.

A few weeks later he felt strong enough to give a reading from his work at the Mailer Society conference, along with Norris, Stephen, and John. He was pleased that Judith McNally attended, her first visit to Provincetown. And on November 11, he and Norris celebrated twenty-five years of marriage with a dinner with John Buffalo at Front Street, one of their favorite Provincetown restaurants. His breathing had improved somewhat, and he began talking about getting back to work. On November 16, he went to New York to receive the National Book Award medal from Toni Morrison and give a short speech on the decline of interest in serious novels. "Rarely are good novels good page-turners," he said.

Jason Epstein had retired, and his new editor, David Ebershoff, came to Provincetown to discuss *The Castle in the Forest.* Ebershoff recalled that Mailer wanted to see the book published, but showed "a little bit of uneasiness about whether he could finish. He didn't say that, but I sensed it." Random House wanted him to extend it at least to 1903, bringing Hitler up to his late teens. Mailer had long planned to do this, but he said to Ebershoff with false indignation, "You realize what you've just told me is going to give me nine to twelve more months of work?" Ebershoff laughed and said, "Yeah, I do." A more delicate issue was the Russian section.

Ebershoff and others who had read the manuscript found the long description of the courtship of Nicholas and Alexandra, and other events leading up to Nicholas's coronation, to be problematic. The narrator, a fallen angel named Dieter, or D.T., leaves young Hitler and spends a hundred book pages fomenting confusion in the imperial Russian court. Norris, Lucid, and others compared the Russian excursion to the bloated Uruguayan episode in *Harlot's Ghost.* Mailer seemed to be repeating his mistake. Ebershoff found it to be "incredibly digressive." In early 2006 in New York, Gina Centrello, the president and publisher of Random House, agreed on the need to cut back the Russian section. At one meeting with Mailer, she and Ebershoff listed all the qualities of the novel that they admired. Then they told him that there was a section that needed "a little work," which she explained was "a publisher's euphemism for, 'This section needs to be cut.' "

> I barely got the sentence out before Norman jumped in, "You don't like the Nicholas II section, do you? I know the critics will hate it," he said.
>
> I nodded sheepishly.
>
> "If I delete it, the book will be more of a page-turner," said Norman.
>
> Feeling encouraged, I responded, "That's right, Norman, it would be much more of a page-turner."
>
> Then, with a twinkle in his blue eyes, he announced, "Gina, I hate page-turners."

Mailer did trim the section, including many of the love notes exchanged between Nicholas and Alexandra during their courtship. But when he turned in the final manuscript in the spring of 2006, the bulk of the Russian material was still there. He thought it was critical to show how Dieter, a leading minion of the Evil One, created the disaster after the coronation at Khodynskoye Pole, a meadow where celebrating peasants were gathered to receive gifts from the Czar. Over 1,300 people were trampled to death, which destroyed the festivities. Ebershoff recalled that Centrello still felt strongly that the Russian material had to go. She joined him for a final editorial meeting with Mailer. "We went to see him in Brooklyn Heights, for lunch," Ebershoff recalled,

> and we were talking about the book's publication, but also the Russian section in particular. He said that he had been hearing this, obviously, from me and Norris, and it's been going on for a while, and he knew what we were saying had some merit. And right at the table he said, "I know what I'm going to do. I'll dare the reader to skip over it. I'll just tell them just turn to page X," and he said, "Make sure the copy editor figures out what the page numbers will be, and Adolf Hitler's story will pick up again right there." It was brilliant. I saw that he immediately understood what he was doing, not only in terms of the narrative, but the way people might talk about it, and that it could be controversial, and some people would

love it because it's kind of a wink. Other people would be infuriated. I thought it was so clever.

He also extended the novel to 1905, two years after the death of Adolf's father, Alois, making it a 477-page book, a relatively modest length for him. Publication was set for January 31, 2007, his eighty-fourth birthday. He dedicated it to his grandchildren, his grandniece, and his godchildren.

THE BIG EMPTY was published on January 24, and while not reviewed widely, it received generally warm notices with a few complaints about some of the conversations being recycled. It also got kudos for the range of topics covered and the easy back-and-forth between father and son. One of the themes undergirding their conversations is the comparisons, elicited by John, between the post–World War II Zeitgeist and that of the period after 9/11. Mailer contrasts the altruism of the earlier generation who created the Marshall Plan to rebuild Europe with the greed of global capitalists who are blind to "the real spirit of Jesus." John rarely disagrees with his father, except about the effects of marijuana, but nudges him deftly to expatiate on various matters, including the merits of civil protest.

Another theme woven through the dialogues is a contrast he made in his 2004 Nieman Fellows lecture at Harvard, titled "Myth Versus Hypothesis." The lecture is a careful demolition of the premises for the Iraq War, and the myths that sustained it. President Bush and Vice President Dick Cheney enunciated the myths: "We must war against the invisible kingdom of Satan," now manifested in Islamic monsters opposed to all that America, God's favored nation, holds sacred. Therefore, "Good will overcome a dark enemy." Opposed to the simplisms of American exceptionalism is the art of hypothesis employed by novelists: "A good novel," Mailer says, is "an attack on the nature of reality," a reality that is always changing: "The honor, the value, of a serious novel rests on the assumption that the explanations our culture has given us on profound questions are not profound. Working on a novel, one feels oneself getting closer to new questions, better ones, questions that are harder to answer." There is no assertion that novelists capture reality completely—"unless you are Charles Dickens and are writing *A Christ-*

mas Carol." Novelists *approach* reality; certainties are few and surmises abound. He placed the lecture near the beginning of *The Big Empty*, and the dialectic it endorses sets the tone for the conversations.

In an interview after publication, Mailer spoke of his relationship with John: "As a father of nine, I've tried not to have a favorite, but John endangers that position. I'm close to all of my children, but the two of us are extra-close." Because of his age—more than six years younger than Matthew—John had "the insularity of the single child," but also had the advantages of a big family. John made the same point in 2012, but went further.

> Since the folks have passed, it has become clearer to me that being both an only child, and being the youngest of nine have each played an equal role in my understanding of what the word 'family' means. In my estimate, I easily got the best of my dad because he had mellowed some by the time I came around. He was more interested than ever in dedicating time to being a parent. Not that I think he wasn't a great parent to all nine of us, although some of my siblings may disagree with me. It's undeniable that he had something different with my mother than he had with his previous wives, and I think it boils down to stability.

ON MAY 4, shortly after the final manuscript of *Castle in the Forest* was in the hands of Mailer's editor, Judith McNally died. A heavy smoker who resisted all entreaties to quit, she had not felt well for a few months. An extraordinarily intelligent person, she nevertheless persisted in the belief that smoke killed germs and was good for her plants. When her friend took her cat from her apartment after her death, it went into withdrawal and the vet had to put on a nicotine patch. Mailer wrote to his Providence friend, Ed McAlice, whose manuscripts Judith had read and critiqued for years, about her passing. McAlice himself was ill with emphysema, and becoming depressed. Mailer commiserated.

> Growing old without cracking may be the subtlest of the art forms. Incidentally, while we're on these sad and sour subjects, let me tell you that Judith McNally died over a month ago. We never knew quite of what, she hid her illnesses, but I believe she had cancer of

> the lungs and cancer of the liver. As you can imagine she left quite a gap behind her. Indeed we had a memorial service for her at my apartment in Brooklyn. I still find it hard to believe. . . . She, like me, despite her intense and often harsh criticisms of your work, had a very high opinion of your talent and thought the real stuff was there. So do I.

Norris was in and out of the hospital during this period. Mailer wrote to a cousin about her, and said, "She has lost so much weight she looks again as she did many years ago when she was a model and is, if a touch weak, strikingly elegant and fun to look at." Sometimes she and Mailer would drive to Boston together for their medical problems. Stephen also became ill and had surgery for a bleeding colon just before the Mailers went to New York for Judith's memorial. He came through all right, but his father and Norris were worried. The night before the surgery, Mailer called Stephen in the hospital. He was in too much pain to talk much, so Mailer just said, "I love you." When he got off, he told Norris that Stephen had said the same thing to him. Their relationship was strained at times but the love was always there.

The Castle in the Forest was Mailer's first family novel, and he planned to make this point in prepublication interviews. The interstices of family life, the grudges and anxieties and hidden agendas, all that nitty-gritty, are carefully delineated in the novel. The death—euthanasia, really—of the household dog, Luther, brings out the cross-currents in the family, and Adolf's mother, Klara's mistaken belief that Alois is part Jewish is even richer in its presentation and implications. All this gave Mailer hope of good reviews. But every Mailer book is tested against his announced aspirations and accomplishments over a half century, and some reviewers want notches on their guns. He was also concerned about how the novel would be received in Germany. Would it be read "for exculpation" or would it be regarded as one more finger pointing at the German psyche. He didn't like any of the initial dust jacket designs and sketched out a new one that became the basis for the final jacket. For the German edition, and those in other European countries, the swastika over the entrance of a castle was removed, as it violated the EU law.

With the novel put to bed, Mailer immersed himself in poker. There was a game three or four nights a week, and during the day he read the pile of poker books he had collected. He believed that Texas hold 'em was so popular because it enabled players to exercise buried paranoiac and anti-paranoiac tendencies. When a player surmises that another is bluffing, the former trait is put into play; the latter is a counterforce, akin to cold sober reasoning. He saw the game as a way of toning underused psychic muscles. Asked if Alpha and Omega were also a factor, he said it was too complicated to contemplate because A and O could have both paranoiac and counter-paranoiac tendencies.

When she wasn't too tired, Norris liked to sit in, as did his sister and the Lennons. Neighbors Astrid Berg, Chris Busa and Marty Michaelson also played, as did a local journalist, Anne Wood, and a retired telephone operator, Pat Doyle, whose wry wit Mailer enjoyed. Most of his children played when they were visiting, and some of their spouses. All guests were encouraged to play. It was an open game with a $20 buy-in so it was rare when someone lost or won $100. When Mailer's nephew Peter, who played professionally and wrote a book about participating in the World Series of Poker, *Take Me to the River*, showed up for a game, some players groaned. A superb player, he usually walked out as a winner.

In July, a magazine editor heard about Mailer's interest in poker and contacted him about doing a piece on the World Series of Poker depicting tournament highlights and characters, and presenting his ideas about the lure of the game. "I feel that there is a big poker novel to be written," he said. If he had been younger and healthier, there is little doubt that he would have taken the assignment. When someone said that it would be a shame if he dropped the Hitler series, he nodded his head in agreement. "I've been abandoning novels like wives for many years, and I'd like to continue this one."

MAILER HAD GOTTEN heavier in the early 2000s. Now not much more than five foot five, he weighed about 220 before the surgery. But afterwards he began to shed pounds as his appetite waned. Walking had become increasingly difficult, and traversing the quarter of a mile to Michael Shay's, his favorite restaurant, was hard going. He loved the oysters they served, and ate there several nights a week, especially when Norris was back in New York. Her two sons and most of her stepchildren were there and she wanted to move her mother there. It was a touchy subject. Michael had gotten married in 2004, and Matthew and nephew Peter the following year. The number of grandchildren continued to grow. Only John Buffalo and Maggie hadn't yet married. Norris loved spending time with the Mailer clan and her many New York friends, and took special delight in Mattie James, the daughter of Matthew and Salina Sais, but felt guilty about being away from her husband, who much preferred Provincetown. She drove back and forth, six hours each way.

The loss of one's upper teeth, Mailer said, was a blow to manhood. He made many trips to the dentist for complicated implant procedures, and for treatment of an infection. He received a huge bill from a New York periodontist but had to put off payment until he cashed the first check from the University of Texas. He rarely spoke of his health problems in any detail, but couldn't resist occasionally dramatizing his situation, as in this letter to Jim Blake, an architect with whom he had struck up a long-distance friendship.

> The feet can go, the knees, the hips—not that they're all gone yet, but they're going—the eyesight, the hearing, the sense of taste, the screwing. I take pleasure in announcing to friends that once I could boast of a seven and a half inch column of silver dollars, but now I'm down to half a roll of dimes. This, believe it or not, inspires my pleasure. It's a wan expression of audacity but it's still my own. Anyway, I tell you this not to feel sorry for me—I've had a reasonably interesting life—but to present this as preface to the one solid benefit of old age, which is you come to know at last who the hell you are. And so you are at peace with what you did and what you failed to do. And even the envy and competitiveness that kept one driving and working is moderated to the point where your heart does not turn black if a fellow novelist of high proportions has written a good book.

One of the things that cheered him up was a box of business-size cards that a friend of John's had printed up. Each card carried a color photograph of a sailboat going before the wind beneath a bright sun, a greeting card scene. Three large letters were printed across the scene: G F Y. Mailer gave them out to everyone for months. He would pull one out of his shirt pocket, and hand it mysteriously to arriving guests. Then he would slap the table (as Barney used to), and laugh. At one point he got the idea of copyrighting the card and making money on it, enough to buy a large ranch out west where all the Mailers would have their own houses and follow their separate pursuits of writing, painting, and so forth. He eventually saw the folly of the notion, but as Norris wrote, "he got a million dollars' worth of fun" from the cards.

Old friends were another pleasure. Hans Janitschek, loud, funny and irrepressible, always buoyed him up. In early October, Mailer went to lunch with him and the Lennons at a seafood restaurant in nearby Wellfleet, as recorded in the "Mailer Log":

> We got a table and ordered a drink as the rain came down on the saltwater lagoon outside. NM wanted oysters, the famous Wellfleet oysters; so did Hans. We got a table right in the middle of the room, which held about 25 other diners, mainly older Wellfleeters. While we waited for our meals, NM told a story about a dinner meeting with the British publisher, George Weidenfeld, in the late 1960s. Joining them was K, a beautiful blonde heiress who was attracted to him, he said, and who he lusted after. But after three hours together, she said, "Goodnight Norman," and went off with the publisher. Hans said that Weidenfeld was famously endowed; his member had a valuable twist. NM: "An S-shape?" Hans: "No, sort of a half moon." Hans went on in his blustery voice to explain—with most of the restaurant listening—that Americans mispronounce "penis." "They call it pee-NUS," he said loudly, and then repeated the mispronunciation three times for emphasis. NM laughed at this and his teeth loosened. He took them out, wiped them with his napkin, and then pulled out a tube of glue or paste and applied it. He said he usually does this in the restroom, but "what the hell." The Wellfleet locals, all of whom recognized NM, enjoyed the show.

Whenever Mailer had oysters, which was often, he examined the shell, and half the time found a face there, in relief. The waitress at Michael Shay's with whom he flirted asked him at the end of every meal which pile he was bringing home and boxed them up. He cleaned them and then put them out on his deck to bleach. On each shell he saw the suggestion of one, a Greek warrior, or a long-dead beauty. He had Norris touch up the features with paint and photograph them. He thought they might make an interesting book.

ADVANCE REVIEW COPIES of *The Castle in the Forest* were in the hands of reviewers by late October 2006, and Mailer was scheduled for a round of interviews in New York the following month. He glanced through the Kakutani file, and read again her review of *Oswald's Tale*, which she had called "ultimately superfluous." In an upcoming *Esquire* interview he thought he might say something about her, and perhaps at a large meeting of book reviewers at a Manhattan restaurant. "I want the maximum of focus on her," he said, "so that when she picks up my book her hand is shaking with hate." He was also considering sending a copy of his analysis to the top editors at *The New York Times*, but did not. When anyone brought up the wisdom of his questioning Kakutani's motives, he bristled.

He didn't mention her at the luncheon with twenty-odd book editors at Keens Steakhouse on West 36th Street. He said afterward that he'd made "a tactical decision." But in his interview with Tom Junod, the literary editor of *Esquire*, he did. He was going through the likely responses to the novel: from the left (they will hate it because they are "essentially rationalistic" and don't want the Devil taken seriously); the right (Mailer's God is not all-powerful, a sacrilegious idea); the Jews (unhappy to see German responsibility for Hitler undermined); and Kakutani, "Princess of the cookie cutter" because she eviscerates all his books. Why she has "a hair up her immortal Japanese ass is beyond me," he said, unable yet again to resist attacking her.

Back in Provincetown, he was feeling more optimistic about the novel's chances. He said that he had three things going for him: 1) Hitler, about whom there is always interest; 2) the ten-year gap since his last novel, which would make readers curious; and 3) Dieter, his demonic first person narrator, who is intermittently omniscient. Limiting his power are the Cudgels, God's angels, who can shield the consciousness of certain people—Nicholas II, for example—so that Dieter cannot enter the person's mind. But he can follow young Hitler's thoughts easily, and can also use "dream-etchings" to suggest nefarious actions to his charge. Using a celestial figure as narrator allowed Mailer to retain the intimacy of the first person voice while not being bound by its limitations, a perspectival sleight-of-hand that parallels the clairvoyance of Meni in *Ancient Evenings.*

With no interviews scheduled until the new year, he began to think about a new dramatic version of *The Deer Park*. Michael had been visiting and talking with his father about filming a staged reading of the play. Stephan Morrow, who had played Stoodie in *Tough Guys Don't Dance*, had directed and acted in a staged reading of the play the previous year, which Mailer saw and liked. He invited Morrow to codirect, if the money could be raised, about $200,000 Michael estimated. Mailer wanted to do it at the Provincetown Theater with professional actors but no audience. Michael thought he could sell it to cable television. As Mailer was working on a new version of the play, a work that had engaged him, off and on, for a half century, word came that Bob Lucid had died of a heart attack on December 12.

Mailer agreed to speak at the memorial service for his old friend at the University of Pennsylvania in April. He had also agreed to speak at the Boston memorial for Bill Styron, who had died a month earlier at the age of eighty-one. On December 14 he made the two-and-a-half-hour drive from Provincetown to Boston, making several pit stops, some on the shoulder of the busy highway—Mailer was unfazed about public urination. He slept through a lot of the trip, but talked about both Lucid and Styron. He said he generally hated funerals because "people say all the wrong things." He was one of the last speakers at the event, which was held at the Boston Public Library. Impatient and bored, he could hear little of what was said. But when he got behind the microphone, he was fully in charge, bantering with the audience, laughing at his own infirmities. He opened by saying, "On top of everything, I'm deaf," and dominating the room. He told a funny story about playing croquet in Connecticut with Bill and Rose Styron and Howard Fertig. Rose was sitting in the front row and laughed heartily. Four months later, when the time came for Lucid's memorial, he felt too weak to attend, and his remarks were read by Lennon.

To what extent Mailer's complaints registered at the *Times* is unknown, but Janet Maslin, longtime *Times* film and then literary reviewer judged *The Castle in the Forest.* Maslin's blows are glancing; her tone is respectful. She almost seems to like Mailer's extensive research on Hitler's incestuous heritage, but turns up her nose at the excremental and apiary investigations, the former as too exhaustive, and the latter too obvious. Two days later, Lee Siegel, in a 6,200-word essay in the *Times Book Review*, thoughtfully examines Mailer's entire career before giving unalloyed praise to the novel, which he calls "an utterly strange work of naked, wild empathy." Mailer, he said, is "an immensely disciplined craftsman and stylist who has spent the larger portion of his life at the writer's trade." The *Times*, Mailer noted, had not pissed him off; indeed, Siegel's review certainly helped Mailer's novel become a bestseller. Nor was he displeased with J. M. Coetzee's conclusion in *The New York Review of Books*: "Keeping the paradox *infernal-banal* alive in all its anguishing inscrutability may be the ultimate achievement of this very considerable contribution to historical fiction."

A majority of the other reviews praised the subtlety of Mailer's insights into Hitler's diseased psyche, and the story's singular provenance. Many reviewers found Alois, Hitler's father, to be a more compelling figure than his son, much as the father figures in his earlier novels were so judged. According to Ebershoff, early sales were strong. Second and third printings were ordered, bringing the number of hardcovers in print to over 100,000. Mailer enjoyed following the novel's sales figures as they rose and fell with reviews and public appearances. After appearing on Charlie Rose's show on February 3, he saw the novel's ranking at Amazon and Barnes & Noble jump the next day. *The Castle in the Forest* made the bestseller list for three weeks, reaching number five on February 11, 2007, just after Mailer's eighty-fourth birthday. It was his eleventh bestseller. He had now had at least one in each of seven decades, 1948 to 2007.

DURING HIS WEST Coast swing for *Castle in the Forest*, Mailer, accompanied by John Buffalo, arranged to meet Lois Wilson for dinner at his hotel on the Embarcadero waterfront in San Francisco. After John Buffalo was introduced, he left them sitting in a booth. "We had the end section of the restaurant," Wilson recalled in a conversation with her daughter. "It was very dark. And we talked and talked." They had trouble seeing the menu, she said. "They turned the lights way down, and we had sweeping curtains around, and he talked about how he was so sick."

> They pulled all his teeth because they were afraid his mouth would get infected and that was something that wasn't necessary, but it made a big difference. He said, "Did you ever know anybody who lost his teeth?" [Lois getting very emotional here, having trouble breathing and talking] And I said, "Yes," and he said, "What was their reaction?" and I said, "Desolation." [Lois very upset and serious during this part of interview] That was my father. He was so proud of himself—handsome—and they pulled his teeth and they never fit and they moved around in his mouth, and so I said, "No, I know it's terrible." And Norman said, "It sure is," and he'd had a lot of his vital parts operated on, I don't know what's what, and the same thing happened to Norris. So, then he said, "How would you characterize me?" I didn't say a word.

A little later, he asked her the same question, but she still couldn't come up with anything. At the end of the meal he got up on his two canes and said, "Would you like to come up to the room?" She said, "If I come up, I'll fall asleep." He replied that he would too, and walked her to the lobby to get a cab. "Norman and I exchanged, at a distance, noisy kisses [she makes a smack noise], like one does with one's husband." She went home alone, "kind of drunk."

The next day, February 5, she called him on his cell phone.

> I got him at KQED about to be interviewed by Mike Krasny. And he said, "I'll call you in an hour." And he did, exactly in an hour. And I said, "I'll never see you again." I knew that that was it. And he said, "Yes, I'll be here, I'll be back here in a year. I will have finished the next book and I'll be talking to Mike Krasny about it." And I said, "That's good, I look forward to it." And that was that [long silence]. I'm not sure I have anything else to say about Norman. I tried to think of a way of characterizing him in a word or two, but you know, I can't. That's not how you go about Norman. He's very—he's magnificent and rare. Nothing else like him.

Shortly after Mailer returned from the West Coast, Norris told him that she was going to move to Brooklyn. They had talked earlier about selling the Provincetown house and buying a place in Connecticut to be near family and New York doctors, but nothing came of it. By the spring of 2007, Mailer had lost over fifty pounds, and his breathing was as bad as before the bypass surgery, perhaps worse. His doctor prescribed asthma medicine, but Norris suspected it was something else. He believed the sea air was sustaining him, and refused to go to the city.

Norris was insistent about her move. She told friends that she was tired of "rattling around in this big house while Norman rattles around in his head." She told Raymond, "People are going to think I'm just the worst," but eventually her absence would make him "understand how much more sensible it is for us to be in Brooklyn." On March 9, with the help of friends she packed her clothes, books, the manuscript of her new novel, and her computer—a sign that the move was not temporary—and left with her mother for New York in a rental car. He made no fuss but was clearly sad, and had a tear in his eye. She was tearful but firm. When Lennon arrived the next evening to take him to dinner, Mailer was sitting alone in the dark. At Michael Shay's, nearly deserted, he ate sixteen oysters, and as usual pondered the shell faces. Back at the house for a nightcap, he said that his eyes were going from macular degeneration and that he could be blind in eighteen months. "I'm not worried about it," he said. Norris e-mailed friends that she was as happy as she had been for a long time. Mailer said he would like her to spend at least ten days a month with him.

Norris left their Toyota sedan in case he needed it, but Raymond or friends usually drove him wherever he needed to go. But on April 17, he announced to Raymond that he was taking a day off from working on the revision of *The Deer Park—A Play*, and going to lunch at the Wicked Oyster in Wellfleet. Raymond was a bit worried about his boss driving and offered to accompany him, but Mailer said he preferred to go alone. As soon as Mailer left, Raymond called Norris in Brooklyn, and she said there was nothing to be done. Raymond drove by the house at 7:45 P.M., but the car wasn't there. He learned later that Mailer had gotten home safely, after dinner at the Lobster Pot, the big tourist restaurant. He'd left the Toyota when he had trouble starting it, and taken a cab home. Norris e-mailed Raymond that she was proud of Norman, "and you can tell him that for me."

The next day, Mailer told Raymond about his lunch in Wellfleet, and how he'd driven around the country roads in Truro before going to the Lobster Pot for dinner, and then a final drink at the Old Colony. Mailer had done all this, but not alone. He had been saying goodbye to another old friend. Eileen Fredrickson had flown in from Chicago for a two-day visit, and Mailer had picked her up at her motel and squired her around. After she returned to Chicago, Fredrickson recalled, Mailer called her and told her it was "a perfect visit." He called her again a few days later and told her that he loved her and talked of another visit in October. It was to be their last conversation.

Norris came to Provincetown regularly in the spring, and Mailer traveled to New York for a few events—to receive the Hadada Award from *The Paris Review* on April 23, presented by E. L. Doctorow, and on June 27 to appear in conversation with Günter Grass and Andrew O'Hagan at the New York Public Library. He had lost more weight, and was subsisting on oysters, red wine mixed with orange juice, and Dove Bars. "He couldn't walk more than a few steps, even with two canes, without resting," Norris wrote. "He could hardly breathe. The audience gasped when he walked out on stage at the Public Library." When Kate saw her father looking like King Lear at the promised end, she said, "We shouldn't let Dad do this. We have to take him to the hospital right now." But when he got on stage and began talking, Norris said, "He was astounding in his clarity and scope of thought." Barbara, sitting next to Norris, said, "If we can keep him on stage, he'll live forever."

Grass had just published a memoir, *Peeling the Onion*, in which he revealed that as a teenager in wartime Germany he had been a member of the Waffen-SS. He had been criticized for hiding this affiliation for sixty years, and O'Hagan was pressing him on the matter. Mailer rose to his defense, saying "How many of us would have the courage at age seventeen to go against the reigning government and fight it alone? Especially one as brutal as the Nazis?" Grass's situation, he said, had caused him to reflect on something that "I have held on to for a long, long time, and never written about"—the stabbing of Adele. He said he now knew that he never would. "I'm happy to be here tonight with him, and I honor the man," Mailer said. Grass was visibly moved by his statement.

Mailer told the audience at the beginning of the program that this would probably be his last public appearance. But he would travel back to New York for one more event, a showing of *Tough Guys Don't Dance* and *Maidstone* at Lincoln Center on July 22. In between the films there was a discussion on stage with film critic Michael Chaiken, Lincoln Center programmer Kent Jones, and Lennon. "He spoke powerfully and eloquently about his years directing," Chaiken recalled, "the pleasure it had brought him, and the seriousness with which he endeavored to make" his films. After the discussion, *Maidstone* was shown. Mailer said that the second half was "repetitive and self-indulgent," with too much histrionic foreshadowing. In the Green Room afterward, a number of friends and admirers stopped by. He knew that this was his last public outing, and drew out his conversations.

Back in Provincetown, Mailer was up and down—weak and dispirited one day, feisty and grumpy the next. There was talk of him getting an electroshock treatment. He said that if it didn't help, "I will be an invalid for the rest of my life." He continued to work. The success of Christopher Hitchens's *God Is Not Great* was a key factor in his decision not to postpone the theology conversations book. Random House was eager to publish it as soon as it was edited. After much discussion, he approved the title: *On God: An Uncommon Conversation.* It was scheduled for publication on October 16.

Norris returned to Provincetown for the summer, and all the children sensing this could be his last summer, visited. On August 1, Norris left on a three-week promotional tour for her new novel, traveling to Atlanta, Chicago, and the West Coast. She planned to return in time for the September wedding of Maggie and John Wendling on the low-tide flats behind the house. For an hour or two a day, Mailer went over the final changes and jacket design for *On God.* He also read and was impressed with Andrew O'Hagan's review of Don DeLillo's new novel about 9/11, *Falling Man.* He said that perhaps it would be DeLillo who replaced him as the writer who takes on all the big themes and events in American life. He went on to say, "There was a time when I felt completely secure in tackling all the big topics. I was totally confident." In 2010 DeLillo said that it was Mailer's "ambition, risk, broad vision, wide range—aspects of the American tradition—that put me on the path I've been following all these years."

On Norris's instructions, Mailer's three upcoming speaking engagements were canceled. He was angry that this was done without his knowledge, but admitted that he wasn't up to long trips anymore. He still planned, however, to go ahead with the filming of *The Deer Park—A Play* in November. Michael hadn't yet raised the necessary production money, so Mailer planned to use the next big check from the University of Texas. Norris didn't know of his plan, and he knew she would be furious when she learned. One obvious reason that he continued to take on new projects was to keep the adrenaline flowing. But he was realistic enough to know that he probably wouldn't be able to write the next Hitler novel.

He wrote his last letter on August 3 to help honor an old friend. "James Jones is one of the few major American novelists to emerge here since the Second World War. He was immensely talented and I think it is a splendid idea to endow a chair in his name at Eastern Illinois University. He would have grumbled, but I think it would have given him true pleasure." He wanted to begin the sequel to *Castle*. "It's all there," he said, pointing to his head, "a helluva novel. Hitler was so human, and I'd love to cook him to a turn." Now he was only functioning five or six hours a day, sleeping the rest. In mid-August, he stopped climbing to his study, and worked sporadically at the dining room table.

His breathing continued to get worse and he went to Massachusetts General Hospital for an exam. One lung was partially collapsed and there was fluid in the other. There were other problems, including some sort of lesion on his pancreas. The doctors thought it might be best to keep him in Boston, which meant missing Maggie's wedding on September 8. Norris asked the doctors to tell him the seriousness of his condition. "He is going down; it's just a question of when," she said to friends. Against medical advice, he came home two days before the wedding, after eight days in the hospital. The afternoon he arrived he got into a conversation with Susan and Lennon about the way elderly Eskimos and Indians wandered into the woods so they would not be a burden.

Mailer asked, "But how would they die?"

"By not eating or drinking," Lennon said.

"Or eaten by a wild beast," Susan said.

"That would be the way to go," he said, "fighting a wild animal. I am whipped by time."

Norris, sad and worried, wanted to bring him to Brooklyn, where he would be near a hospital, but he resisted.

Carol Stevens, the bride's mother, attended the wedding, with about a hundred others. Norris and Carol had become good friends—"almost like sisters," Carol said—and e-mailed each other almost every day, but Mailer had seen her only a few times in the past few years. He spent a few minutes in a quiet conversation with her. Mailer's sons got him down to the beach for the brief ceremony. He looked wretched sitting in the brisk wind on the flats with a flower in his lapel. Afterward, he had a glass of champagne, posed for photos with the newly married couple, and then went upstairs to lie down.

A few days later when Lennon stopped by, Mailer said he had an epiphany at three A.M. and almost called him. He explained that he wanted to do another book of conversations, this one on cancer. It would explore the idea that besides stress, trauma, repression, and guilt, cancer is caused by boredom. His plan was to have someone read the obituaries of corporate leaders in *The New York Times* over a one-year period to see how many died of cancer, his idea being that it kills a disproportionate number. Challenged over long, busy lives, executives get bored after retirement and succumb to cancer. He wanted Lennon to assemble all the references to cancer in his interviews and writings on the topic. He went on for forty-five minutes and then said he wanted to sleep. Before he lay down, he said that his doctor told him that if he didn't start eating he would die. He said he was trying hard, eating steak and eggs in the morning, soup, more chocolate and ice cream and fish at night.

William and Dana Kennedy visited him, as did his Chicago friends Gene and Sarah Kennedy, and many others. On September 19, Bill Majeski came, and there was poker for several nights running, Mailer's last games. On the 22nd, Danielle and her (second) husband, Peter McEachern, drove him to Brooklyn. Norris had finally convinced him. They made numerous pit stops on the six-hour drive. He now weighed less than a hundred, and Peter was able to carry him up the four flights of stairs to the apartment. His plan was to return to Provincetown in a month for the Mailer Society meeting.

Matthew recalled seeing his father in Brooklyn.

> I was in denial as to how bad off he was. He was losing weight and didn't look good. I brought Salina and Mattie over for a visit. He'd just gotten up from his nap; he was sleeping a lot at that time. Got to the table and I learned he was planning on going to the hospital. It dawned on me that this could be it. I asked him, "Are you afraid? Do you think this is going to be it?" And he said, "Look, I've had a great life, I just don't want a bad end. I finished my novel, I'd like to write another book but I don't have that burning desire to write another one, it's just not there." There was this dark cloud over him.

Mom took a picture of us sitting there—I think it was the last picture ever taken, come to think of it.

On October 3, he checked into Mount Sinai Hospital on the Upper East Side of Manhattan. Copies of *On God* arrived that day, and he signed a few. Surgery was scheduled for 7:30 the next morning. At one P.M., the surgeon told those waiting that the operation was successful. Larry Schiller and his then-wife, Kathy Amerman, had just flown in from the West Coast and joined everyone in the waiting area. The doctor said that she had drained and inflated Mailer's lung, and that his heart was strong through the operation. Family and friends were allowed in a few at a time to see him later in the afternoon. When they went in, they saw right away that he was still feeling the painkillers. He was ranting. He had a dream that Schiller was the Devil and he was God and they made a pact to rid the world of technology. He flirted with the twenty-nine-year-old nurse, who took it with good humor. He told her that she should write a novel and use her meeting with a famous author as the first chapter. Later, he had her write a vignette about a weekend with her boyfriend and promised to critique it.

The next day, more family members and friends arrived. The doctors said that the lack of oxygen in his blood had all but destroyed his appetite. The prognosis was good. He was in a private room where the lights could be lowered and he had a full-time nurse. Everyone was optimistic. Norris was feeling wonderful. She gave a bravura reading at a Barnes & Noble in Manhattan on the day after the surgery, and answered questions about her book and her husband's health.

But a few days later, everything changed. On October 9, he came down with pneumonia, and the doctors found that he had lymphoma of the stomach—cancer—and this had been the cause of his weight loss. These problems could be treated with drugs, but Mailer was pessimistic. He told Norris to get him transferred to the Hyannis hospital on Cape Cod and from there he would sneak home. "He wants to die," she said. She was worn down by the long daily trip from Brooklyn to see him, as well as visiting her mother in assisted living.

The media was eager for information, and e-mailed and called friends and family. So many people, some of them crazy, were trying to visit him in the hospital that finally a guard had to be posted to screen visitors. He looked somewhat better toward the end of the month, but he wanted to pull out all his tubes and wires. For obscure reasons, he had a tracheotomy, and so could only mouth words, and write notes, most of them illegible. He wrote a note to Donna Lennon, and then pointed to the word "P-town," and then to himself, indicating that he wanted to go there. The family discussed getting him there, but the risks were too great. On October 29, he was operated on for an infection in a vein in his groin. He told his nephew Peter, "My ass feels like Iraq." Seeing one of the most ferocious, intense communicators of the last hundred years, the man who had written forty books and been interviewed a thousand times, locked into silence by his ailments was heartbreaking. The look in his eyes was woeful. He was angry and very frustrated that no one could read his chicken scratches.

He was cheered a bit when *New York* published excerpts from *On God*. The cover of the magazine had a head shot of him, white hair flowing, with clouds behind him as if he were a celestial being. He nodded his head in approval, and enjoyed the sections Norris read to him. Earlier when he could still talk, he saw Norris crying and said, "You must really love me." She answered, "Of course I love you, you silly old coot! Why else do you think I've stuck around all this time?" Peter McEachern, knowing that Mailer missed the ocean, drove to Provincetown and taped the sound of waves from the master bedroom window, complete with an occasional groan from the Long Point fog horn. He played the tape, on a loop, in Mailer's room.

During the second week in November, he began sinking. Family members took turns sitting with him. At one point, the phone rang. It was Michael, who had an idea: a last drink for the old man. Peter went through a drink list with him, and Mailer nodded his head yes for rum and orange juice. Peter told the story at Mailer's memorial some months later.

> Michael finally returned with a bottle of rum and a container of orange juice. But all we had was a plastic cup, which if you knew my uncle, was worse than no cup at all. So Michael went to the nurses' station and managed to get a real glass, and we started to mix the drink. Norman took over at this point, indicating the correct proportions for water, orange juice, and rum. One last problem: how to give it to him. Because of the breathing tube in his throat, he wasn't supposed to drink; he could choke. Sacrilege, but we gave him the

> drink on one of those lollipop-shaped sponge-on-a-stick thingies. I dipped the sponge in the glass then put it in his mouth. He gave a look of utter exasperation. Then he grabbed the glass out of my hand. I looked to Michael. He shrugged. We all watched Norman put the glass to his lips and take a nice long sip. Then another. He was going to drink that drink the way it was supposed to be drunk even if it killed him. After a few sips, he allowed himself a smile. We all did. Norman held up the drink and pointed at each of us. He wanted us to share the drink with him. So we passed the glass and we each took a sip.

A few hours later there was a conference with the doctors, who said that he would go quickly if all the tubes were removed. The family agreed that this would be done in the morning. Stephen, who had just flown back from the West Coast where he was in a play, said he would stay the night with his father, and everyone else went home.

"About five A.M.," Barbara wrote in a memoir,

> the telephone rang and woke me. It was Norris, who had just received word from the hospital that Norman had died. Sue and Marco were staying with me. We threw on some clothes and grabbed a cab. Stephen was there, of course, with his tale of how the bells and whistles Norman was attached to had awakened him and that as he stood at the foot of the bed, Norman sat up, gave him a beatific smile, and then fell back. A medical team came into the room and pronounced him dead. We sat in the room with Norman's body for several hours until the usual arrangements could be made. The family began to arrive. We were pretty quiet and grim to begin with. I think at one point Betsy went over to the bed and held Norman's hand. And Marco got a copy of the Hebrew prayer, Kaddish, from the hospital rabbi, and he and Michael and Stephen read it, and we all said "Amen." But as others began to arrive, the usual Mailer élan revived, and we were all talking at once. Leading to a moment of ghoulish comedy. A young doctor, probably an intern or resident, opened the door and entered the room.
>
> "Well," she said cheerfully, "you seem to have a nice party going. But I have to give Mr. Mailer an injection." There was stunned silence until someone blurted, "But he's dead."

Oops. She was out the door. She fled so fast we couldn't help ourselves. We burst out laughing.

I hope Norman's spirit was still there. It was a moment he would have relished.

The official time of death was 4:28 A.M., November 10, 2007. The cause on the death certificate was acute renal failure.

Laudatory tributes appeared within forty-eight hours on the front pages of newspapers around the world. Kakutani's was among the most thoughtful.

> Mr. Mailer used his copious talents—quick skewering eye; a gift for the cameo portrait; bat-quality radar for atmosphere and mood; and blustering, bellicose prose—to capture the American spirit as it lurched from the civil rights and antiwar demonstrations of the '60s into the Watergate era of the '70s. In his best work Mr. Mailer made America his subject, and in tackling everything from politics to boxing to Hollywood, from astronauts to actresses to art, he depicted—or tried to depict—the country's contradictions: its moralistic prudery and grasping fascination with celebrity and sex and power; the outsize, outlaw past of its frontier; and its current descent into "corporation land," filled with cheap consumer blandishments and the siren call of fame.

About two hundred people paid respects at McHoul's funeral home in P-Town, mainly locals. Several of his children and friends spoke at the grave the next day. Stephen sang. Everyone threw handfuls of sand on his coffin. Norris was poised and serene throughout. She posed for photos for the flock of reporters who were there, and answered a few questions. After that, she invited everyone back to the house for food and drink, including two ex-wives, Beverly and Carol.

Before the coffin was closed, John Buffalo put the ace of spades in one of his father's pockets; his poker friend Pat Doyle slipped in another card, and Donna Lennon a white poker chip. His grandson Alejandro contributed a handcrafted piece of orgonite. Matthew placed a photograph of the family taken in Maine on his father's chest. Norris added a note. Norman Mailer, singular, unprecedented and irreplaceable, was prepared for his next voyage.

APPRECIATIONS

First on line is Mailer himself, who asked me to write this biography. Beginning in the late 1970s, I worked with him on various projects, served as his archivist, and edited several books by and about him. In December 2006, after the death of his close friend and authorized biographer, Robert F. Lucid, Mailer asked me to take over. I had been working for several years on an edition of his letters (still in progress), while filling the role of biographer understudy. Lucid had covered Mailer's life only to 1951, and our perspectives and styles differed considerably, so with Mailer's blessing I decided to make a fresh start. In his final years we completed over twenty interviews focused largely on his personal life and beliefs. My wife and I had purchased a condo in Provincetown in 1997, and during the last thirty months of Mailer's life I stopped by almost every day and when he was in the mood drew him out in conversation. Even as his health declined, he insisted on detailing people and events from every period of his life, for example, devoting an interview to each of his six wives. These interviews and my notes on our conversations ("Mailer Log") are one of my most important sources, surpassed only by his massive correspondence, more than 45,000 letters over sixty-eight years. While always his own best lawyer, Mailer never hinted at how he wished to be portrayed, nor did he ask my intentions. He answered all my questions candidly and with much good humor, enjoining me to "put everything in." I had full access to his papers, library, and correspondence. Few biographers have had a more cooperative subject.

Mailer's last wife, the late Norris Church Mailer, his sister, Barbara Wasserman, and the rest of the family were invariably helpful, patient, and bighearted. Not only did all of them stand for interviews and answer follow-up questions, they provided documents, read portions of the manuscript, and made corrections and suggestions. Barbara read all my chapters as I wrote them, edited them with care and irreplaceable knowledge, and helped me understand her brother, the Mailer family, his circle of friends, and the spirit of his times. Her confidence and editorial acumen have been sustaining. Barbara and Norris (until her death in November 2010) also fed and housed me on my regular trips to New York. My deepest thanks go to them. I am also grateful to Mailer's cousin Sam Radin; his nine children, and Barbara's son, Peter, and their spouses: Susan Mailer and Marco Colodro, Peter Alson and Alice O'Neill, Danielle Mailer and Peter McEachern, Elizabeth Ann (Betsy) Mailer and Frank Nastasi, Kate Mailer and Guy Lancaster, Michael Mailer and Sasha Lazard, Stephen Mailer and Elizabeth Rainer, Matthew Mailer and Salina Sais, Maggie Mailer and John Wendling, John Buffalo Mailer and his girlfriend Katrina Eugenia. Four of Mailer's ex-wives are living, and they answered my questions and/or provided copies of their correspondence with him. Thanks to Beatrice Silverman, Adele Morales, Beverly Bentley, and, especially, Carol Stevens, who spoke to me at length many times over several years.

From the time my wife, Donna Pedro, took a photograph of me reading my first letter from Norman Mailer in January 1972 to the present, she has shared my interest in his life and work, and supported me with steady counsel and advice. Like Barbara, she read every chapter upon completion, provided shrewd feedback on matters of style and substance, and ran the household single-handedly for four years. My sons and their spouses, Stephen M. and Lauren B. Lennon, Joseph A. Lennon and Marika Beneventi, and James C. Lennon, read and commented on portions of the manuscript, and helped in uncounted and unselfish ways. My siblings, Peter Lennon, Kathleen Arruda, and Maureen Macedo, were similarly supportive. Peter read the entire manuscript, made many useful comments and corrections, and also passed on innumerable pertinent reviews, essays, and contextual material. Thanks also to my uncle, Hugh Lennon, for sending me Mailer clippings for more than thirty years.

Four other people read the entire manuscript, all the while making hortative utterances that buoyed me up. Robert Heaman, my colleague at Wilkes University, read the chapters as they emerged and did an extremely thorough line edit. With me from the start has been my agent, John T. "Ike" Williams, who provided astute counsel and perceptive commentary on a regular basis. Robert Bender, my editor at Simon & Schuster, guided me over the three-plus years of composition, and helped bring the manuscript into its final form with his masterful ability to see every stitch in the tapestry, and the full tapestry as well. Fred Chase copyedited the manuscript and improved it considerably, ferreting out errors and tightening continuity. Elisa Rivlin, Simon & Schuster legal counsel, gave me detailed and thoughtful advice on a number of difficult issues. I am happy to acknowledge with a cheer the steady and careful assistance of the staff at Simon & Schuster, especially Maureen Cole, Gypsy da Silva, and Johanna Li. I must also salute Nancy Potter, my mentor at the University of Rhode Island, who has been a steadfast and wise presence in my life for many years. She read portions of the manuscript and made a number of subtle suggestions. I owe a large debt to all these good people.

Several graduate students in the Wilkes University graduate Creative Writing Program did research on various aspects of Mailer's life. Matthew Hinton was my graduate assistant for two semesters and created a regularly consulted event timeline. The following individuals spent a semester doing excellent research on aspects of Mailer's life and thought: Amber Barron, the late Allen Boone Barton, Rachael Goetzke, Maureen O'Neill Hooker, Bill Lowenburg, Nancy Slowikowski, and Michael Suppa. I am indebted to them for their able assistance.

I was aided in conducting interviews by four people: my brother Peter, who interviewed Eileen Fredrickson and Richard G. Stern; John Buffalo Mailer, who interviewed Edwin Fancher and Anne Barry; Michael Chaiken, who spoke with James Toback; and Erin Cressida Wilson, who interviewed her mother, Lois Mayfield Wilson. Lawrence Schiller provided copies of interviews with him conducted by Lawrence Grobel, and also several that Grobel did with Mailer. I am beholden to the two Larrys. Beginning in 2007, I interviewed over 80 people (see accompanying list), a number of them several times. The interviews were transcribed by my wife, with the exception of a few early ones done by Julia Overlin.

Several others require special thanks. The late Robert F. Lucid, my friend and mentor and the dean of Mailer scholarship, was my first guide to Mailer's life and work, and discussed them with me for thirty years. Instrumental in creating Mailer's archive, he instructed me on its contents and importance. My debt to him is tremendous. Six colleagues, Robert Begiebing, Philip Bufithis, Morris Dickstein, Barry H. Leeds, Phillip Sipiora, and John Whalen-Bridge, have written and/or edited important studies of Mailer's work, and have engaged and enlightened me on Mailer's place in the American canon. Mashey Bernstein helped me get a richer sense of Mailer's deep Jewish roots; Stephen Borkowski, chair of the Provincetown Art Commission, cheerfully helped on numerous research and logistical matters, and been a knowledgeable and reliable consultant; Fred and Nancy Ambrose, and Christopher Busa, editor of *Provincetown Arts* magazine, carefully delineated Mailer's Provincetown history; Sal Cetrano, Ron Fried, Michael Mailer, and Jeffrey Michelson provided vivid accounts of Mailer's boxing exploits; Michael Chaiken was my guide to the American film scene in the 1960s; Ivan Fisher, William Majeski, Barbara Probst Solomon, and Naomi Zack helped me re-create the Jack Abbott affair; Mark Olshaker, president of the Mailer Society, has been inordinately generous with his time and knowledge; and Richard Stratton illumined Mailer's temperament with candor and intelligence. I owe much to Eileen Fredrickson and the late Lois Mayfield Wilson, who magnanimously contributed candid and detailed memories of their long, intimate relationships with Mailer. Finally, Lawrence Schiller, Mailer's most important collaborator, has been unstinting. He kindly opened his archives, shared his memories of his friend and their several joint projects, and provided thoughtful feedback on my manuscript. I would also like to thank my colleagues at Wilkes University for their interest and warm encouragement, especially those who commented on parts of my manuscript: John Bowers, Philip Brady, Jason Carney, Bonnie Culver, Jaclyn Fowler, Kaylie Jones, Nancy McKinley, and Robert Mooney.

Dean John C. Stachacz and the staff of the E. S. Farley Library at Wilkes University have my gratitude for assistance over many years, with special thanks going to Brian R. Sacolic, who cut through many a bibliographic knot for me. I am grateful for the fellowship awarded by the Harry Ransom Center at the University of Texas–Austin where Mailer's papers are housed, and am happy to acknowledge the creative and tireless help of Director Thomas F. Staley and his staff, including Patrice F. Fox, Robert Fulton, Molly Hardy, Jennifer Hecker, Cathy Henderson, Kathryn Hill, Steve C. Mielke, Richard W. Oram, Gabriela Redwine, Molly Schwartzburg, Joan Sibley, Apryl Sullivan, and Richard Workman. Thanks also to my friends and colleagues in the James Jones Literary Society, the Norman Mailer Society, and the Norman Mailer Center, whose good fellowship and enthusiasm have been of huge value to my work. Let me also salute the countless friends who listened patiently to me on Mailer matters over the decades.

Following is a list of others who have commented on portions of the manuscript and/or enabled me in various thoughtful ways: Chester Aaron, Neil Abercrombie, Rashidah Ismaili Abubakr, Steve Adams, Allen and Patricia Ahearn, Joyce Anzalone, Layle Armstrong, Peter Balbert, Anne Barry, Margaret Bay, Jim Blake, Larsen and Jeanette Bowker, Leo Braudy, Douglas Brinkley, Linda and Tom Bushar, Martha Campbell, Luceil Carroll, Jack Chielli, Vasundhra Choudhry, Antonia Colodro, Joseph Comprone, Harold Cox, Gerald H. Crown, Greg Curtis, B. H. Custer, Essy Davidowitz, Ann and Cullom Davis, Hope Denenkamp, Nicole DePolo, Patrick and Robin Dickson, Carol Dine, Robert M. Dowling, Michael Downend, Laura Adams Dunham, David Ebershoff, Ray Elliott, Judith Everson, Mia Feroleto, Diane Fisher, Thomas H. Fiske, Katherine Flynn, Dick Fontaine, the late B. H. Friedman, Russell and Betty Gaudreau, Laurel Guadanzo, Shawn Hatten, Tom Hayes, Wilbur Hayes, Patricia Heaman, John Hemingway, William Heyen, Alexander Hicks, Beverly and Harry Hiscox, Immy Humes, Mark James, Sheldon Kaplan, Donald Kaufmann, Dana and William Kennedy, Eugene Kennedy, Robert Klaus, Ross Klavan, Albert LaFarge, Dawn Leas, Michael Lee, David and Susan Light, Michael Lindgren, Laurie Loewenstein, Barbara Lounsberry, Jerome Loving, Gerald R. Lucas (my talented webmaster), Townsend Ludington, Melania Lumia, Jan Maluf, David Margolick, Jay and Robbin Martinelli, Deborah Martinson, Annette and Warren Mason, Lori A. May, Vicki Mayk, Colum McCann, Tim McCarthy, Maggie McKinley, Louis Menand, Martin Michaelson, Jonathan Middlebrook, Michael and Jane Millgate, Lee Moore, Laura Moran, Carolyn Olshaker, Christina Pabst, Dean and Denise Pappas, Mary C. Pedro, Paul Pedro, Kathy Perutz, Taylor Polites, Tom Quinn, Pam Radin, Dwayne Raymond, Christopher Ricks, Dana Riguette, Anna Schnur-Fishman, Maureen Seeberg, Lawrence Shainberg, Larry Shiner, David Sokosh, Claire Sprague, Barbara and Robert Springer, Charles Strozier, Anne Taylor, Marc Triplett, Ken Vose, Nina Wiener, and Guy Wolf.

I quote from Mailer's letters approximately seven hundred times; his correspondence and interviews with him, his family, friends, and associates are my key sources, along with his writings. I thank the Mailer Estate for allowing me to quote from his published and unpublished work. I also benefited greatly from the work of the four Mailer biographers who preceded me. Thanks especially to Hilary Mills (the first one of us into the quarry), and Mary Dearborn, Peter Manso, and Carl Rollyson. Their books and my other sources are noted in my bibliography and source notes. I should add that *The Mailer Review,* a joint publication of the Mailer Society and the University of South Florida, has been an indispensable resource. I am indebted to all of these sources and individuals for insight and information; errors and oversights are my sole responsibility. Thanks to all, remembered or, alas, forgotten, who helped me research and write this biography.

BOOKS BY NORMAN MAILER

The Naked and the Dead. NY: Rinehart, 1948.
Barbary Shore. NY: Rinehart, 1951.
The Deer Park. NY: Putnam's, 1955.
The White Negro. San Francisco: City Lights, 1959.
Advertisements for Myself. NY: Putnam's, 1959.
Deaths for the Ladies (and Other Disasters). NY: Putnam's, 1962.
The Presidential Papers. NY: Putnam's, 1963.
An American Dream. NY: Dial, 1965.
Cannibals and Christians. NY: Dial, 1966.
The Short Fiction of Norman Mailer. NY: Dell, 1967.
The Deer Park: A Play. NY: Dial, 1967.
Why Are We in Vietnam? NY: Putnam's, 1967.
The Bullfight. NY: CBS Legacy, 1967.
The Armies of the Night. NY: New American Library, 1968.
Miami and the Siege of Chicago. NY: New American Library, 1968.
Of a Fire on the Moon. Boston: Little, Brown, 1971.
King of the Hill. NY: New American Library, 1971.
The Prisoner of Sex. Boston: Little, Brown, 1971.
Maidstone: A Mystery. NY: New American Library, 1971.
The Long Patrol: 25 Years of Writing from the Work of Norman Mailer. Ed. Robert F. Lucid. NY: World, 1971.
Existential Errands. Boston: Little, Brown, 1972.
St. George and the Godfather. NY: New American Library, 1972.
Marilyn: A Biography. NY: Grosset & Dunlap, 1973.
The Faith of Graffiti. Documented by Mervyn Kurlansky and Jon Naar. Prepared by Lawrence Schiller. NY: Praeger, 1974.
The Fight. Boston: Little, Brown, 1975.
Genius and Lust: A Journey Through the Major Writings of Henry Miller. NY: Grove, 1976.

A Transit to Narcissus. NY: Howard Fertig, 1978.

The Executioner's Song. Boston: Little, Brown, 1979.

Of Women and Their Elegance. NY: Simon & Schuster, 1980.

Pieces and Pontifications. Ed. J. Michael Lennon. Boston: Little, Brown, 1982.

Ancient Evenings. Boston: Little, Brown, 1983.

Tough Guys Don't Dance. NY: Random House, 1984.

Conversations with Norman Mailer. Ed. J. Michael Lennon. Jackson: University Press of Mississippi, 1988.

Harlot's Ghost. NY: Random House, 1991.

Oswald's Tale: An American Mystery. NY: Random House, 1995.

Portrait of Picasso as a Young Man: An Interpretive Biography. NY: Atlantic Monthly Press, 1995.

The Gospel According to the Son. NY: Random House, 1997.

The Time of Our Time. NY: Random House, 1998.

The Spooky Art: Some Thoughts on Writing. Ed. J. Michael Lennon. NY: Random House, 2003.

Why Are We at War? NY: Random House, 2003.

Modest Gifts: Poems and Drawings. NY: Random House, 2003.

The Big Empty: Dialogues on Politics, Sex, God, Boxing, Morality, Myth, Poker and Bad Conscience in America. Coauthor, John Buffalo Mailer. NY: Nation Books, 2006.

The Castle in the Forest. NY: Random House, 2007.

On God: An Uncommon Conversation. With Michael Lennon. NY: Random House, 2007.

NOTES

In addition to the Appreciations, I would like to reiterate my profound thanks to the Mailer Estate for permitting me to quote freely from Mailer's published and unpublished work, the latter housed in the Mailer Archive of the Harry Ransom Center at the University of Texas–Austin. Permission to quote from these materials, especially Mailer's letters, has allowed me to reveal his inner life as never before. Over the past seven years, the Mailer family and the staff of the Ransom Center have provided encouragement and cheerfully acceded to my every request for information or documents.

In the source notes that follow, I have cited where I have obtained the quotations and facts used in the book. There are three exceptions, namely my interviews, conversations, and e-mail exchanges with the late Norman Mailer, his sister, Barbara Mailer Wasserman, and Lawrence Schiller. Because of the number of conversations with these three key sources over many years—in Mailer's case going back to the early 1970s—I have not tried to date quotations from them unless their comments have been published. The dates of my conversations with the more than eighty other individuals I have interviewed are given in the source notes.

AUTHOR'S INTERVIEWS

Anna Lou Humes Aldrich, 12-17-10; Peter Alson, 8-19-08, 4-23-12, 9-19-12; Fred Ambrose, 8-16-09; Nancy Ambrose, 8-16-09; Walter Anderson, 4-20-11; John Bailey, 4-15-12; Anne Barry, 5-4-11, 5-8-12, 11-23-12, 11-24-12; Adele Becker, 1-21-07, 4-8-09; Robert Begiebing, 3-3-12; Beverly Bentley, 5-26-11; Mashey Bernstein, 5-24-09; John Bowers, 3-23-10; Brock Brower, 12-30-10; Millicent Brower, 5-14-09; Tina Brown, 5-31-12; Philip Bufithis, 5-17-11; Christopher Busa, 3-14-09; Sal Cetrano, 10-?-12; Michael Chaiken, 4-19-11; Don DeLillo, 3-29-10;

Laura Adams Dunham, 1-24-12; David Ebershoff, 3-26-10; Jason Epstein, 6-25-03, 11-6-08; Harry Evans, 5-31-12; Edwin Fancher, 10-18-10; Mia Feroleto, 8-?-12; Eileen Geist Finletter, 4-15-10; Ivan Fisher, 4-14-09; Eileen Fredrickson, 10-15-11, 12-12-11, 5-19-12; Aaron Goldman, fall, 2004; Doris Kearns Goodwin, 12-14-11; Richard Goodwin, 12-14-11; Thomas Heffernan, 5-24-10; Carol Holmes, 4-14-09, 11-29-11; Margo Howard, 5-24-10; Aurora Huston, 1-17-12, 2-10-12; William Kennedy, 8-4-11, 8-5-11; Mickey Knox, 9-15-08, 9-16-08, 9-17-08; Rudy Langlais, 3-1-12; Barry Leeds, 9-27-10; Peter Lennon, 3-14-11; Robert J. Lifton, 9-14-10; Tom Luddy, 3-?-12; Danielle Mailer, 8-20-08, 8-3-11, 10-19-11, 1-11-12, 4-17-12, 5-21-12, 4-17-13; Elizabeth (Betsy) Mailer, 11-29-11; Kate Mailer, 3-11-13; John Buffalo Mailer, 1-29-09, 10-16-10, 4-24-12; Maggie Mailer, 3-27-09; Matthew Mailer, 8-21-08, 12-28-11, 9-5-12; Michael Mailer, 11-1-03, 8-21-08, 12-28-11; Norris Church Mailer, 5-13-08, 11-17-08, 4-15-09, 1-30-09, 3-28-10, 10-16-10; Stephen Mailer, 11-5-08, 11-20-11, 3-22-12; Susan Mailer, 9-5-07, 10-29-10, 5-13-11, 8-18-11, 11-03-11, 1-23-12, 4-18-13; William Majeski, 4-23-12, 6-4-12; Elisabeth Malaquais, 6-10-10; Clifford Maskovsky, 2-5-10; Peter McEachern, 8-22-12; Legs McNeil, 7-19-12; Jeffrey Michelson, 7-24-11, 12-31-11; Adele Morales, 4-?-12; Adeline Lubell Naiman, 8-21-07; Mary Oliver, 9-20-11; Dotson Rader, 3-25-10, 3-8-12; Sam Radin, 5-23-10; Jack Richardson, 4-6-11; Lee Roscoe, summer, 2010; Carol Schneider, 3-24-10; Jack Scovil, 3-24-10; Irwin Shaw, 6-?-83; Robert Silvers, 4-15-09; Barbara Probst Solomon, 5-13-09, 3-26-10, 4-23-10; Richard G. Stern, 12-14-10; Carol Stevens, 3-28-09, 5-15-11, 6-13-11, 6-18-11, 9-21-11, 4-12-12; Richard Stratton, 4-15-09; Gay Talese, 1-23-11; Nan A. Talese, 10-19-10; Bonnie Timmerman, 5-28-12; James Toback, 8-14-10; John T. "Ike" Williams, 10-23-11; Erin Cressida Wilson, 11-15-11, 5-15-12, 4-21-13; Lois Mayfield Wilson, 11-15-11; Veronica Windholz, 3-25-10; Rhoda Wolf, 1-30-09, 5-11-12; Naomi Zack, 1-2-12, 1-3-12.

ABBREVIATIONS

Titles of books by and about Mailer cited in the Notes are abbreviated as follows:

AAD *An American Dream*
AE *Ancient Evenings*

AFM	*Advertisements for Myself*
AON	*The Armies of the Night*
BE	*The Big Empty*
BS	*Barbary Shore*
CAC	*Cannibals and Christians*
CIF	*The Castle in the Forest*
CNM	*Conversations with Norman Mailer*
DFL	*Deaths for the Ladies (and Other Disasters)*
DP	*The Deer Park*
EE	*Existential Errands*
ES	*The Executioner's Song*
FIG	*The Fight*
GAL	*Genius and Lust: A Journey Through the Major Writings of Henry Miller*
HG	*Harlot's Ghost*
LNM	*The Lives of Norman Mailer* (Carl Rollyson)
MAR	*Marilyn: A Biography*
MBD	*Mailer: A Biography* (Mary Dearborn)
MBM	*Mailer: A Biography* (Hilary Mills)
MG	*Modest Gifts: Poems and Drawings*
MLT	*Mailer: His Life and Times* (Peter Manso)
MM	*Maidstone: A Mystery*
MSC	*Miami and the Siege of Chicago*
NAD	*The Naked and the Dead*
OFM	*Of a Fire on the Moon*
OG	*On God: An Uncommon Conversation*
OT	*Oswald's Tale*
PAP	*Pieces and Pontifications*
POP	*Portrait of Picasso as a Young Man*
POS	*The Prisoner of Sex*
PP	*The Presidential Papers*
SA	*The Spooky Art*
TC	*A Ticket to the Circus* (Norris Church Mailer)
TGD	*Tough Guys Don't Dance*
TOT	*The Time of Our Time*
WN	*The White Negro*
WVN	*Why Are We in Vietnam?*

Publications and names cited in the Notes are abbreviated as follows:

MR	Mailer Review
NYRB	New York Review of Books
NYT	New York Times
NYTBR	New York Times Book Review
NYTM	New York Times Magazine
PR	Partisan Review
VV	Village Voice
AM	Adele Mailer
BW	Barbara Wasserman
EY	Eiichi Yamanishi
FG	Francis I. Gwaltney
FM	Fan Mailer
HJ	Harvard Journal (Mailer)
HN	Harvard Notebook (Mailer)
HRC	Harry Ransom Center
IBM	Isaac Barnett Mailer
JM	Jean Malaquais
JML	J. Michael Lennon
MK	Mickey Knox
NCM	Norris Church Mailer
NM	Norman Mailer

PROLOGUE: THE RIPTIDES OF FAME: JUNE 1948

NM's letters are located at the HRC.

Page

1 *"Pourquoi Paris?":* Stanley Karnow: *Paris in the Fifties* (NY: Times Books, 1997), 3.

1 *drove to Italy in a small Peugeot:* Unless otherwise noted, descriptions of the trip are from BW's letter to Robert F. Lucid, 1-12-98.

2 The Little Foxes: Hellman's play premiered at the National Theatre in New York on 2-15-39 and ran for 410 performances.

2 *"a lot of respect":* NM to William Raney, 6-7-48.

2 *"batches of reviews":* NM to Jenny Silverman (mother-in-law), 5-12-48. He said he'd received more mail that week "than ever in my life."

2 *"The thing I've got to get down":* NM, "Journal May 27 [1948]" (HRC).

4 *New York editor:* Robert N. Linscott, Random House.

4 *"It was the luckiest timing":* Bob Minzesheimer, "To Mailer, A Good Soldier Puts Words on Paper," *USA Today*, 4-10-03, 7D.

4 *"caught in a riptide":* Margo Hammond, "Norman Mailer on the Media and the Message," *Book Babes*, Poynter Institute, 2-6-04, www.poynter.org.

4 *"I used to feel that I didn't":* Michael Lee, "A Conversation with Norman Mailer," *Cape Cod Voice*, 8-2-01, 12.

4 *"an acquired appetite":* Alastair McKay, "Still Stormin'," *Scotsman*, 7-22-00, S2.

4 *"was the last time Norman":* James Atlas, "Life with Mailer," *NYTM*, 9-9-79, 88.

5 *"felt kind of blue":* Louise Levitas, "*The Naked* Are Fanatics *and the Dead* Don't Care," *New York Star*, 8-22-48; rpt., CNM, 6.

ONE: LONG BRANCH AND BROOKLYN

In addition to the sources identified below, the following were drawn on: Fan Mailer's "Fan's Memoir"; BW's "In Search of Mother's Age"; Adele Becker's (NM's cousin) "The Schneider Family"; JML's "Mailer Log," a record of the last thirty months of NM's life; Robert F. Lucid's 1989 interview with NM; JML's unpublished interviews with NM and BW. NM's letters are located at the HRC.

Page

7 *The Mailers and the Schneiders:* NM believed his last name had been anglicized. In "The Book of the First-Born," an unpublished autobiographical novel fragment (HRC), he gives his grandfather Mailer the name Ivan Mirilovicz.

7 *three towns:* Libau and Daugavpils in Latvia are also possible cities of origin.

7 *"placed madness next to practicality":* PP, 190–91. NM's column in *Commentary*, titled "Responses and Reactions," was devoted mainly to elucidations of Martin Buber's *Tales of the Hasidim*, published in two volumes, *The Early Masters; The Later Masters (Ten Rungs: Hasidic Sayings)* (NY: Schocken, 1947–48); rpt., foreword by Chaim Potok, Schocken, 1991. The *Commentary* columns appeared every other month from December 1962 to October 1963, and were collected, in part, in PP and CAC.

8 *"Inside there is a narrow marble counter":* NAD, 481.

9 *"his maternal grandfather":* Brock Brower, "Norman," *Other Loyalties: A Politics of Personality* (NY: Atheneum, 1968), 132. Charles "Cy" Rembar, Beck's son, preceded NM at Harvard and Bertram, Joe's son, followed him.

9 *"That's where all the brains":* MLT, 13.

11 *"dapper," "fussy," and "punctilious":* Robert Begiebing, "Twelfth Round: An Interview with Norman Mailer," *Harvard Magazine* 85 (1983); rpt., CNM, 316.

11 *"elegant impoverished figure":* Marie Brenner, "Mailer Goes Egyptian," *New York*, 3-28-83, 36.

11 *"was very English":* Begiebing, "Twelfth Round," CNM, 316–17.

12 *"I. B. from Brooklyn":* Jimmy Breslin's friend Fat Thomas was I. B. Mailer's bookie. Jimmy Breslin, *I Want to Thank My Brain for Remembering Me* (Boston: Little, Brown, 1996), 31.

12 *born in this country:* Barney also lied about his country of birth, claiming on his U.S. visa application in 1919 that he was born in South Africa (HRC). NM thought this was the case until the early 1960s.

13 *"As time goes by":* NM to IBM, 5-21-44.

13 *"My mother":* Carole Mallory, "Norman Mailer," *Elle*, January 1986, 38.

14 *"very, very upset":* Toby Thompson, "Mailer's Alpha and Omega," *Vanity Fair*, October 1991, 158.

15 *Barbara quickly recognized:* Adele Becker notes this in her memoir and BW confirmed it.

15 *"She was observant":* Bill Broadway, "Norman Mailer: New Advertisements for Himself," *New Millennium Writings*, 3, Spring/Summer 1998, 18.

15 *"The Adventures of Bob and Paul":* HRC.

15 *"Boxing Lessons":* HRC.

16 *"The Martian Invasion":* HRC; the first chapter appeared in *First Words: Earliest Writing from Favorite Contemporary Authors*, ed. Paul Mandelbaum (Chapel Hill, NC: Algonquin, 1993).

16 *"This novel filled":* Steven Marcus, "Norman Mailer: An Interview," *Paris Review*, Winter/Spring, 1964; rpt., CNM, 78.

16 *On his application to Harvard:* HRC.

16 *"a quiet section":* Levitas, CNM, 9.

16 *"in those days":* Robert Begiebing, "Twelfth Round," CNM, 308.

16 *"had to make certain basic distinctions":* Christopher Hitchens, "Interview with Norman Mailer," *New Left Review*, March/April 1997, 117.

17 *"I was a physical coward":* AFM, 22.

17 *never got into fistfights:* Transcript of *The Phil Donahue Show*, WGN-TV Chicago, 11-21-79.

17 *"He seemed to be on a shorter leash":* MLT, 27.

17 *"was very proper":* Ibid., 29.

17 *"an ego that was lopsided":* Ramona Koval, "Norman Mailer Interview," 9-1-00, www.abc.net.ay/arts/new/arts_01092000.htm.

19 *"We also had a sense":* Eugene Kennedy, "The Essential Mailer," *Chicago Tribune Magazine*, 9-9-84, rpt., CNM, 333.

20 *"Very intense":* Toby Thompson, "Mailer's Alpha and Omega," 154.

20 *"the most fabulous kid":* Ibid.

20 *"I'd been frightened":* Ibid., 156.

20 *felt he knew Humphrey Bogart:* "I always felt that Humphrey Bogart was an uncle of mine, and I never met him. But he had the same intensity in my psychic life as a strong uncle I once had." Transcript of *Mailer's America* (French documentary, 1998), Tape 11, 2.

20 *"I worshipped him":* Quoted in introduction, Charles Rembar, *The End of*

Obscenity: The Trials of Lady Chatterley, Tropic of Cancer and Fanny Hill (NY: Bantam, 1969), vi.

21 *"He loved to teach":* BW, "Growing Up with Norman," *MR* 1 (2007), 176.

21 *the candy store:* MLT, 30.

21 *bar mitzvah speech:* HRC.

21 *"the rabbi looked very pale":* Marie Brenner, "Mailer Goes Egyptian," *New York*, 37.

21 *"MAYOFIS JEW":* According to Yiddist Michael Wex, author of *Born to Kvetch* (NY: St. Martin's, 2005), a Mayofis Jew is "the Jewish counterpart of an Uncle Tom: servile, dancing for the goyim and saying 'yassuh.' "

21 *"Hitler has been in my mind":* JML, "*The Castle in the Forest*: A Conversation with Norman Mailer," *MR* (2008), 424.

22 *"I felt straddled":* Begiebing, CNM, 309.

22 *"When launched":* Edward Pell, "His Childhood Was a Happy Time," *Daily Register* (Red Bank, NJ), 12-12-66, 1.

23 *"too many crystals":* Michael Lee, "A Conversation with Norman Mailer," *Cape Cod Voice.* In 1992, NM said, "I've never written about Brooklyn in any real way. There's a lot of things I haven't written about. I think they're probably crystals." Gregory Feeley, "Waiting for Mailer's Big One," *Million: The Magazine About Popular Fiction*, January/February 1992, 13.

23 *Crystals, as he explained:* NM discussed memory crystals with Christopher Busa, "An Interview with Norman Mailer," *Provincetown Arts* (1999), 27.

23 *"I don't feel joy":* Anthony Haden-Guest, "The Life of Norman," *Harpers & Queen*, October 1997, 192.

23 *student at Boys High:* NM's high school records are at the HRC.

23 *vaulting over the horse:* MBM, 49.

23 *"In Brooklyn I was always":* Begiebing, CNM, 311.

24 *One scheme dreamed up:* MLT, 28.

24 *"I could keep beat":* Ibid.

24 *"High school's that place":* Lawrence Grobel, "Norman Mailer: Stupidity Brings Out Violence in Me," *Endangered Species: Writers Talk About Their Craft, Their Visions, Their Lives* (Cambridge, MA: Da Capo, 2001), 294.

24 *"quiet, studious and inconsequential":* "Vital Statistics," *Parade*, 12-16-84, 7.

24 *"when I said I might go to Harvard":* Ramona Koval, "Norman Mailer Interview."

TWO: HARVARD

In addition to the sources identified below, the following were drawn on: JML's "Mailer Log"; NM's untitled, handwritten, forty-nine-page journal, kept at Harvard from December 13, 1941, to May of 1942 (hereafter HJ); NM's pocket notebook, begun circa February 1941 (hereafter HN); JML's unpublished interviews with NM and BW. HN, HJ, and all of NM's Harvard papers are located in the HRC, as are his letters.

Page

25 *"white men, gray men":* Theodore H. White, "Harvard Lies at the End of the Subway," *The Harvard Book: Selections from Three Centuries*, ed. William Bentinck-Smith (Cambridge: Harvard University Press, 1982), 293. The class structure White described persisted after he graduated. A *Life* (5-5-41) article on Harvard, "Harvard: America's Great University Now Leads World," describes commuter students as "the lowest undergraduate social stratum, once derided as 'untouchables' and long neglected by the administration."

26 *"had solved more delicate social situations":* Begiebing, CNM, 310.

26 *four out of five of his friends:* NM's comments on his social circle and his new clothes are from ibid., 310–11.

26 *"a young man going":* NM to Lobos Jurik, 2-3-89.

26 *"Unformed" is the word:* HJ.

26 *"a smiler":* MLT, 40.

27 *We know that one of them was a George Petty:* NM to FM, IBM, 10-8-39, 10-25-39.

27 *When the band had appeared:* JML interview with Millicent Brower, 5-14-09.

27 *English A:* See NM's preface to Hallie and Whit Burnett's *Fiction Writer's Handbook* (NY: Barnes & Noble, 1975).

27 *"about the dullest":* NM to FM, IBM, 10-25-39.

27 *"Before I was seventeen":* AFM, 27.

28 *"the monotony and the boredom":* "Interview: Norman Mailer," 7-12-04, Academy of Achievement, www.achievement.org/autodoc/page/mai0int-1.

28 *"Suddenly I realized you could write":* Steven Marcus, CNM, 79.

28 *"the bitterest blow":* Begiebing, CNM, 314.

28 *home for the Christmas holiday:* HN.

28 *"I threw down my pen":* Ramona Koval, "Norman Mailer Interview."

28 *"I can't write humorously":* NM to FM, IBM, 2-18-40.

29 *he accepted an invitation:* NM to FM, IBM, 2-28-40.

29 *an anecdote from his friend Larry Weiss:* MBM, 47.

30 *"There's no use in making it":* NM to FM, IBM, 2-28-40.

30 *A week later he wrote home:* NM to FM, IBM, 3-7-40.

30 *For the last paper of the year:* Frederick Christian, "The Talent and the Torment," *Cosmopolitan*, August 1963, 66. See also Weinberg's version, MBM, 45.

31 *"as a finality": The 1943 Harvard Album*, 12–13.

31 *"We are frankly determined":* Richard Norton Smith, *The Harvard Century: The Making of a University to a Nation* (NY: Simon & Schuster, 1986), 138–39.

31 *"The forces of violence":* Ibid., 138.

31 *"We were going through the barbed-wire":* AFM, 391.

31 *Swing bands were the rage:* Richard Norton Smith, *The Harvard Century*, 138.

31 *A member of the class of 1942:* John T. Bethell, *Harvard Observed: An Illustrated History of the University in the Twentieth Century* (Cambridge: Harvard University Press, 1998), 130.

31 *In a May 1940 poll:* Conducted by the *Christian Science Monitor*, in Richard Norton Smith, *The Harvard Century*, 141.

31 *A good part of student reluctance:* Richard Norton Smith, *The Harvard Century*, 138–39.

31 *The leader of Harvard's noninterventionists:* Kathleen Schaeper, *Rhodes Scholars, Oxford, and the Creation of an American Elite*, rev. ed. (NY: Berghahn, 2007), 126.

31 *Mailer heard him lecture:* Begiebing, CNM, 313.

32 *Arthur Schlesinger Jr.: Our Harvard: Reflections on College Life by Twenty-two Distinguished Graduates*, ed. Jeffrey L. Lant (NY: Taplinger, 1982), 112.

32 *He even wrote an essay: The 1943 Harvard Album*, 30–37.

32 *"crap":* MBM, 42.

32 *During his sophomore year:* NM to Jeffrey Meyers, 1-17-85.

33 *Victorian ark:* Henrik Ibsen made a similar comment, not located.

35 *An active communist:* Davis's obituary, *NYT*, 7-17-98.

35 *"I can't tell you how my back":* SA, 11–12.

35 *"made the biggest dent":* HJ.

35 *Sy Breslow said that Mailer:* MBM, 48.

35 *Along the way with his friend:* Ibid., 49–50.

36 *"I weighed 135 pounds":* NM to Edward McAlice, 3-7-95.

36 *"accepted Lawrence's thesis":* NM to Jeffrey Meyers, 1-17-85.

36 *Harold Marantz:* HJ.

36 Portrait of Jennie: (NY: Knopf, 1940); it was made into a 1948 film by David O. Selznick.

37 *and he was awarded a $150 scholarship:* NM was notified that he would receive a Lillie A. Ridgway scholarship in a 12-18-40 letter from the Harvard Committee on Scholarships (HRC).

37 *The* Advocate *informed Mailer:* NM to FM, IBM, 3-2-41.

37 *"I simply can't stand":* NM to FM, IBM, 3-9-41.

37 *"they're a bunch of snobs":* NM to FM, IBM, 3-16-41.

37 *"supernova of eccentricity":* Andrew McLaren, "Bowden Broadwater, 1920–2005," *St. Bernard's Newsletter*, Summer 2006, 1. NM said, "Bowden had more style than anyone I'd ever met. He dominated the *Advocate*, his personality. . . . I remember when I read *Brideshead Revisited*, I kept clucking as I read it. It wasn't that Bowden looked in any way like Sebastian Flyte or that we were close friends. On the contrary, we were on opposite sides. There were two factions." Begiebing, CNM, 313.

37 *A week later Mailer was invited:* Undated invitation from *Advocate* secretary, Holmes H. Welch, mid-March 1941 (HRC).

37 *Goethals as Martha Gets-Horned:* MLT, 52.

37 *only a playbill survives:* HRC.
38 *Mailer's first review: Harvard Crimson*, 4-21-41, 2.
38 *"It's all happening too easy":* NM to FM, IBM, 4-13-41.
38 *"Please tell your friend":* NM to Millicent Brower, 5-11-41.
38 *major story on Harvard in* Life*:* "Harvard: America's Great University Now Leads World."
38 *"The nice Jewish boy":* AON, 152.
38 *On May 7, he was informed:* John Holabird to NM, 5-7-41.
39 *sketch parodying Hemingway:* HRC.
39 *recent* Life *article:* "The Hemingways in Sun Valley: The Novelist Takes a Wife," *Life*, 1-6-41, 49–57.
39 *He always had great admiration:* See PP, 149–50; SA, 167, 260–64.
39 *That night he met Roy E. Larsen:* NM to FM, IBM, 5-14-41. Given the fact that NM feuded with Henry Luce's *Time* magazine for decades, it is no small irony that Larsen, one of the magazine's cofounders, helped launch his career. Larsen was impressed by NAD, but after that said he gave up reading NM's works altogether (Frederick Christian, "The Talent and the Torment," *Cosmopolitan*, 64).
39 *First, Professor Davis wrote to him:* Fan pasted all of these communications into her scrapbook (HRC).
39 *It was followed a few days later:* Crockett wrote: "Norman, the enclosed letter arrived at the Advocate house yesterday along with one to Marvin. It seems like a good market for your novel. Have a good summer. So long, Jack Crockett."
40 *"Probably nothing has happened":* AFM, 70.
40 *Before he arrived, he had written 45,000 words:* NM to FM, IBM, 5-17-41.
40 *"How is the writing coming":* FM to NM, 6-25-41.
40 *But this comes at the end:* NM to FM, late July 1941.
41 *much like Barney Kelly:* Like Sherman Wexler, Kelly lives in a penthouse, has a spoiled daughter, and is powerful and corrupt. Unlike Wexler, he wants to murder his son-in-law, and almost does.
41 *Going on the road:* MLT, 55–56; MBM, 54.
41 *He said the idea came from Dos Passos:* HJ.
41 *He told his friends:* MBM, 54.
42 *The completed novel went off to Amussen:* NM to FM, IBM, late September 1941; Amussen wrote to NM, 9-26-09, to say he had read the last two parts of the novel with "keen interest."
42 *He wrote home:* NM to FM, IBM, 10-?-41.
42 *Amussen arranged to meet Mailer:* Amussen to NM, 9-26-09.
42 *Anne and Dave Kessler, whose support:* NM said that Dave Kessler and his mother disagreed on who really paid for his Harvard education. "For him it was the money he did not take out of the Sunlight Oil Company and for her it was the hours she put in and the work that made it successful and profitable in a way that someone he hired would not make it profitable."

43 *They were followed by a letter from Burnett:* Whit Burnett to NM, 10-21-41.
43 *"shows brilliance":* Amussen to NM, late November 1941.
43 *"the writing and psychology":* Burnett to NM, 1-28-42.
43 *President Conant called a mass meeting:* Richard Norton Smith, *The Harvard Century*, 150–51.
43 *The campus was transformed:* A majority of the class of 1944 graduated with NM in June 1943; his yearbook contains the photographs and activities of both classes.
43 *"would feed the novel":* MBM, 60.
43 *"I may as well confess":* AFM, 28.
43 *"didn't know his ass":* MBM, 66.
44 *In a psychological profile of her:* "Cova, and Her Case," submitted to Dr. Henry A. Murray's Psychology class, 12-14-42 (HRC). Cova was NM's pseudonym for Silverman. He used the name again for a character in *A Calculus to Heaven.*
45 *Barton invited Mailer:* HJ.
45 *"The Bodily Function Blues":* Complete lyrics published in *MR* (2008), 221–23.
45 *"listener" or "monotone":* As described in "Music Teachers I Have Known and Loved," submitted in English 3-A (HRC).
45 *"triangle" of influence:* "Interview: Norman Mailer," Academy of Achievement.
46 *"Modern American Literature":* Begiebing, CNM, 315.
46 *Proust, Mann, and Joyce:* MLT, 50.
46 *eighteenth-century British poetry:* MLT, 61.
46 *Milton:* See HG, passim.
46 *especially the French:* NM to Pierre Brodin, 10-16-63: "The French novel has always been more congenial to me than the English"; rpt., *Présences: Contemporaines Écrivains Amérains D'Aujourd* (Nouvelles Editions Debresse, 1964), 205.
46 *"I'd like to be another Malraux":* AFM, 29.
46 *"struck at once":* Frederick Christian, "The Talent and the Torment," *Cosmopolitan*, 66. Morrison added that he wasn't in complete sympathy "with all the uses to which he put his talent."
46 *Pete Barton, Mailer wrote home:* NM to FM, IBM, 2-12-42.
47 *"haunted degeneracy":* Bernard James McMahon Jr., "On the Shelf: the Harvard Advocate, May 1942," *Harvard Crimson*, 5-25-42.
47 *"Maybe Next Year":* AFM, 84.
47 *corresponding with Whit Burnett:* NM to Burnett, 2-11-42, 3-15-42; Burnett to NM, 2-18-42, 4-6-42.
47 *time to drop condoms:* Howard M. Spiro, "The Optimist: Saintliness and Sanity," *Science & Medicine*, September/October, 1998, 2.
47 *"incredibly self-disciplined":* MBM, 58.
47 *"had suspended himself":* "Our Man at Harvard," PAP, 1–5. On the table of contents page of a copy of the anniversary issue, NM wrote: "Being a

little memorabilia compounded of the vices and pederasties of one T. John Crockett (stolen from the *Advocate* Sanctum in October, 1942)."

47 *"smart-alecky":* MBM, 62.
48 The New Yorker *was turned down:* NM to FM, IBM, 4-12-42.
48 *not selected in the MGM competition:* Kenneth MacKenna to NM, 6-18-42.
48 *nursed the Chevy:* NM to FM, IBM, 5-3-42.
49 *Boston State Hospital:* NM to FM, IBM, 6-5-42.
49 *assigned to the violent ward:* Brock Brower, *Other Loyalties,* 120.
49 *"very hard, very horrible":* NM to FM, IBM, 6-21-42. In 1975, NM remembered the catatonics he worked with and how they "would not make a gesture from one meal to the next" (FIG, 46).
49 *"The Darndest Thing":* Not located.
49 *soda fountain job:* NM to FM, IBM, 6-23-42.
50 *"the work is congenial":* NM to FM, IBM, 7-29-42.
50 *cast of* Othello: Dramatic Society invitation to NM, 8-8-42.
50 *liked Bea very much:* NM to FM, 8-31-42.
50 *"Fear, for Norman":* Robert F. Lucid, "Boston State Hospital: The Summer of 1942," *MR* (2007), 32.
50 *"fear ladder":* NAD, 176.
51 *It took him fifteen days:* The dates of composition, August 31–September 14, 1942, are given on the last page of the 113-page manuscript, which NM typed (HRC).
51 *he submitted the play:* NM to FM, IBM, 9-29-42.
51 *suite with Harold Katz:* NM to FM, IBM, 9-25-42.
51 *Harvard draft advisor:* NM to FM, IBM, 9-28-42, 9-29-42.
52 *"Man Chasm," was "a dark horse": Harvard Crimson*, 2-25-43.
52 *"All that men": Man's Fate* (NY: Modern Library, 1961), 190.
52 *Southern Mortuary:* To view the corpses at the Southern Mortuary morgue on Albany Street, NM and Bea had to walk down a set of stairs guarded by a pair of sphinxes, a descent that offers the possibility that the seed of AE was sown that day. Andrew Ryan, "Old Morgue Finds New Life as Clinic for Homeless," www.boston.com/new/local/articles/2008/05/31/08/old_morgue_finds_new_life_as/clinic_for_homeless.
52 *safe in Dunster:* NM to FM, IBM, 11-29-42.
52 *"He remembered the burnt body":* AFM, 59.
53 *"Yes, sometimes you want":* AFM, 70.
54 A Calculus at Heaven *was the best:* Amussen to NM, 3-23-42.
54 *Mailer reported to Millie Brower:* NM to Millicent Brower, 4-10-43.
54 *"You say, Mother":* NM to FM, IBM, 4-10-43.
55 *Uncle Dave came up:* NM to FM, IBM, 4-18-43.
55 *"Lord knows you've waited":* NM to FM, IBM, 4-25-43.
55 *a new work, another novel:* NM to FM, IBM, 4-18-43.
55 *"but what importance do my masks":* Undated postcard to FM, IBM, late April 1943.

55 *Cape Cod, Provincetown:* According to NM, he had never heard of Provincetown until Bea told him it was an interesting place.

55 *Winston Churchill:* Churchill finally received his honorary LLD at a special convocation, 9-6-43, after which he gave a radio address where he praised those opposing Nazism, "a generation that terror could not conquer and brutal violence could not enslave" (John Bethel, *Harvard Observed,* 154–56).

THREE: THE ARMY

In addition to the sources identified below, the following were drawn on: NM's Harvard Journal (HJ, at HRC); JML's "Mailer Log"; JML's unpublished interviews with NM and BW. NM's letters are located at the HRC.

Page

56 *"unearthly" beauty:* Tim McCarthy, "Norman Mailer Gets Moral," *Life in Provincetown*, 8-14-03, 10.

56 *"the feel of 1790":* Joseph P. Kahn, "Our Town," *Boston Globe Magazine*, 6-22-03, 19.

56 *inn on Standish Street:* Christopher Busa, "An Interview with Norman Mailer," *Provincetown Arts* (1999), 24. NM told Busa that he came by train with Bea in July of 1942 and stayed three days but, in fact, they arrived by ferry from Boston on 6-9-43 and stayed for a week. He sent postcards to his parents describing Provincetown, but not mentioning Bea, on June 9 and 11, 1943. Busa's interview contains NM's longest and richest evocation of Provincetown outside of his fictional depictions.

56 *he told George Goethals:* Raymond Karl Suess II, "Tom Sawyer, Horatio Alger and Sammy Glick: A Biography of Young Mailer," St. Louis University dissertation, 1973, 83.

56 *request that Stanley Rinehart:* Amussen to NM, 7-9-43.

56 *"I was a little frightened":* Introduction to *A Transit to Narcissus: A Facsimile of the Original Typescript* (NY: Howard Fertig, 1978), viii.

57 *"I was as lonely":* Ibid.

57 *Edwin Seaver wrote:* Seaver to NM, 8-27-43. Seaver's comments on NM's "remarkable performance for one so young" can be found in his memoir, *So Far, So Good: Recollections of a Life in Publishing* (Westport, CT: Lawrence Hill, 1986), 146.

57 Cross-Section: Ed., Edwin Seaver (NY: L. B. Fischer, 1944).

57 *lawyer named Riorden:* Perhaps the most intriguing character in the novel, Riorden has the polished manners and Jesuitical subtlety later seen in General Cummings in NAD and Barney Kelly in AAD.

58 *"was a devastating":* LNM, 34.

58 *"ponderosities":* Introduction, *A Transit to Narcissus,* ix.

58 *ski trip:* NM to FM, IBM, 12-20-43.

58 *"Yeah, and suddenly I felt":* Bea's version is that NM "needed an anchor on the home front" (MBM, 75).

58 *Berta Kaslow:* Kaslow to NM, 12-14-43.
58 *"occasions [in] me a great deal":* NM to Seaver, 1-11-44.
58 *Mailer responded:* NM to Martha Keller, Chief Clerk, Local Board 317, Brooklyn, 1-19-44.
59 *"Fanny," she said, "just didn't want":* MBM, 75.
59 *"Neither Barbara nor I":* NM to FM, 10-29-44.
59 *IQ test:* NM to FM, IBM, 4-1-44.
59 *"potentially very important writer":* Kaslow to NM, 4-4-44.
60 *salute before they had sex:* MBM, 75.
60 *burned out:* Marcus, CNM, 97.
60 *"THE war novel":* Levitas, CNM, 3.
60 *instead of keeping a journal:* NM to FM, IBM, 4-12-44.
60 *lexicon of military slang:* NM to FM, IBM, 4-30-44.
60 *"Mailer never felt more":* AON, 58–59.
61 *"He wasn't that good":* MLT, 76. Details of NM's basic training are drawn from MLT, 74–78, and JML interview with Clifford Maskovsky, 2-5-10.
61 *"When it came to taking care":* AFM, 91.
61 The New York Times Book Review: Marjorie Farber reviewed *A Calculus at Heaven* in the *NYT*, 5-28-44; Thomas Lyle Collins reviewed it for the *Herald Tribune* on the same day. Anticipating the consistently sharp division of opinion on all but a few of NM's books, the reviewers disagreed: Farber said "the writer's imagination . . . fails him," while Collins says the novella is "a remarkable achievement for so young a writer."
61 *"with my lip buttoned":* AFM, 91.
61 *first extended piece:* NM to Bea, 5-26-44.
61 *tableaux of sodden GIs:* NAD, 93-104.
61 *patch of observation:* NM to Bea, 6-6-44.
61 *"one of the best novelists":* NM to FM, BW, 7-9-44.
61 *"stinker":* NM to Bea, 6-6-44.
61 *"a twenty volume Transit":* NM to Bea, 4-15-45.
61 *He scheduled the reunion:* NM to Bea, 7-13-44.
62 *"my first reaction was of disappointment":* NM to Bea, 6-8-44.
62 *"a feeling for the culture":* AFM, 28.
62 The Young Lions: (NY: Random House, 1948). NM later admitted that "the European war would have been too much for me. I realized that when I read *The Young Lions* and saw how much more Shaw knew about Europe than I did." Interview with Eric James Schroeder, *Vietnam, We've All Been There*, ed. Schroeder (Westport, CT: Praeger, 1992), 91.
62 *"considerable merits":* AFM, 28.
62 *Shaw landed at Normandy:* JML interview with Irwin Shaw, June 1983.
62 *"I can understand that":* NM to Bea, 8-22-44.
63 *Mailer is often described:* The most solemn asseveration of NM as an urban writer is Martin Green's essay "Norman Mailer and the City of New York: Faustian Radicalism," a chapter in his *Cities of Light and Sons of the Morning* (Boston: Little, Brown, 1972), 58–89. It contains a

double-page photo of NM leaning on an uncertain rest superimposed over the New York skyline.

63 *"The most dramatic moments":* Diana Trilling, "The Moral Radicalism of Norman Mailer," *Claremont Essays* (NY: Harcourt, Brace & World, 1964), 184.

63 *"That sad deep sweet beauteous":* WVN, 205.

63 *He told his ever anxious mother:* NM to FM, IBM, 9-10-44.

63 The Führer: NM lists Heider's study in the bibliography of CIF.

63 *reading Oswald Spengler's:* NM to BW, 10-24-44.

64 *"mind is peculiarly violable":* Trilling, "The Moral Radicalism of Norman Mailer," 184. Trilling was the first critic to point to D. H. Lawrence as NM's "predecessor in the line of literary minds dedicated to the renovation of society by means of a revolution in the individual consciousness" (179).

64 *the past as an organism: The Decline of the West*, Vol. I, *Form and Actuality* (NY: Knopf, 1926), 45. In 1975, NM wrote that he was "overpowered" in his youth by Spengler's idea that "history is an organism, and reveals a sense of style, a divine stroke of the pen to every era" (FIG, 221).

64 *"a ridge or peak as symbol":* NM to Bea, 10-5-44.

64 *cast his first vote:* NM to FM, 11-4-44.

65 *"Without you":* NM to Bea, late December 1944.

65 *112th Cavalry:* The unit's history is drawn largely from *We Ain't No Heroes: The 112th Cavalry in World War II*, ed. Glenn T. Johnston and compiled by Heather Dalton, Craig Johnston, Glenn Johnston, Alex McQuade, Alayna Payne, Chelsea Payne, and Elisabeth Schmiedel (Denton: University of North Texas Press, 2005). NM was one of several veterans of the unit interviewed for the project. The other major source is *The War in the Pacific: Triumph in the Philippines* by Robert Ross-Smith (Washington, DC: Center of Military History, U.S. Army, 1993).

65 *"the aristocracy of the outfit":* William McDonald, "An Evening with Norman Mailer," *Lone Star Review* (*Dallas Times Herald*), 4-?-81, 1, 3.

65 *"a Texas regiment":* Johnston, ed., *We Ain't No Heroes*, 4.

66 *"So, the infantry replacements":* Ibid., 254.

66 *he had a typing assignment:* NM to Bea, 4-25-45. His other option was to become part of a reconnaissance platoon attached to Headquarters Company, which is where he ended up three months later.

67 *Julian W. Cunningham:* NM to Bea, 2-14-45. NM used Cunningham, in part, as a model for General Cummings in NAD. Both were strong disciplinarians and zealous about improving bivouac areas. See Johnston, ed., *We Ain't No Heroes*, 233, and NAD, 106.

67 *interpreting aerial photographs:* NM to Bea, 3-11-45. NM was also hospitalized with jaundice for several days while assigned to Headquarters. NM to Bea, 2-16-45.

67 *"galling at times":* NM to Bea, 3-18-45. NM repeated this sentiment in a 3-29-45 letter to Bea, saying, "when I'm not with you . . . I often wonder if I'm really worth anything much at all."

67 *building a shower:* NM to Bea, 3-25-45.
67 *"Variety, darling":* Ibid.
67 *"It had a little bit":* NM to Bea, 2-24-45.
67 *used in Chapter 7:* See NAD, 211.
68 *Benton's anthology:* NM to Bea, 4-11-45.
68 *Strachey's* Eminent Victorians*:* NM to Bea, 4-20-45.
68 *"an unguent for the psyche":* NM to Bea, 2-1-45.
68 *"any better than he should be": Up at the Villa* (NY: Random House, 2000), 29.
68 *"perpetual oscillation":* NM to Bea, 2-1-45.
69 *an elaborate clock:* DP, 99. In 2000, NM said that his view of life was founded on Maugham's line. "I think you should be a little better than you ought to be. That's what manhood's all about." See Alastair McKay, "Still Stormin'," *Scotsman*, 7-22-00, 2.
69 *"there's a wonderful quality":* NM to FM, 2-19-45.
69 *The unit had 192 casualties:* Glenn T. Johnston, "Interview with Norman Mailer" (8-25-04), University of North Texas Oral History Collection, No. 1560, 39. In 1965, NM said that he had "the feeling you're going to be killed—I became emotionally convinced of it, and didn't care much anymore what happened." Brock Brower, *Other Loyalties*, 109.
69 *Combat Infantryman's Badge:* NM's army records (HRC). NM was given a new badge for Christmas 2004. Notoriously difficult to buy a gift for, he liked the gift and recalled how proud he had been to wear it.
69 *"been in a little combat":* NM to Bea, 4-11-45.
70 *"You must make him realize":* NM to Bea, 4-20-45.
70 *mythic eight-day patrol:* Johnston, "Interview with Norman Mailer," University of North Texas, 21.
70 *"birth allegory":* NM to Bea, 4-18-45.
71 *"quixotic":* NM to Bea, 4-25-45.
71 *"A part of me":* Marcus, CNM, 83.
71 *"none of us had the slightest":* AFM, 390.
71 *"Good, I don't see none either":* Melvyn Bragg, "Norman Mailer Talks to Melvyn Bragg," *Listener*, 12-20-73, CNM, 197.
71 *"fifteen miles older":* AFM, 389.
72 *the Hukbalahap or Huks:* NM to Bea, 5-18-45.
72 *"The gun had a detestable odor":* AFM, 143.
72 *"crack Japanese marines":* Johnston, "Interview with Norman Mailer," University of North Texas, 33.
72 *"The most intense ecstasy":* NM to Bea, 5-14-45.
73 *"No other writer on war":* Eric Homberger, *The Second World War in Fiction*, ed. Holger Klein, John Flower, and Eric Homberger (London: Macmillan, 1984), 177.
73 *"What the hell did Horton mean":* Johnston interview, 25.
73 *"black halo, black stockings":* NM to Bea, 5-10-45.
74 *"I gave up writing":* Levitas, CNM, 8. BW recalled that during the war when her brother and Bea were writing, she felt that Bea had the best

chance to write a bestseller. NM told Amussen that Bea's novel about the *Waves* "wasn't bad" (MBM, 94), but apparently Amussen's response was too negative for her to revise it.

74 *"a very intense Somerset Maugham":* NM to Bea, 5-17-45.

74 *"Remember that awful priest":* Jeffrey Michelson and Sarah Stone, "Ethics and Pornography," PAP, 108.

74 *Seaver was turning down:* Seaver to Kaslow, 6-22-45.

74 *He told Bea that this novel:* NM to Bea, 5-20-45.

75 *Francis Irby Gwaltney:* NM first mentions Fig in a letter to Bea, 6-9-45.

75 *"You can't talk that way":* Johnston interview, 31.

75 *"a brave soldier":* Brock Brower, *Other Loyalties,* 109.

75 *He sent Bea a few comments:* NM to Bea, 7-25-45.

75 *"soft-spoken, sly":* NM to Bea, 10-3-45.

76 *"If there is a God":* NM to Bea, 10-5-45.

76 *But he began with real soldiers:* "I think the thing that gave *The Naked and the Dead* its sense of absolute realism . . . is that the characters were good. . . . I had lived among these soldiers for two years and I knew a lot about them." Academy of Achievement, "Interview: Norman Mailer."

76 *"I studied engineering":* Marcus, CNM, 84.

76 *He is the novel's titular hero:* Lieutenant Hearn, a default liberal, is often named as the protagonist of NAD because he opposes both General Cummings and Sergeant Croft, but NM told Bea (10-20-45) that his "ridge novel" would not focus on a particular character. NM did not consciously select Croft as the protagonist of NAD, but he is undoubtedly the most realized character in the novel, with the possible exception of Cummings.

76 *Mailer was in garrison:* NM to Bea, 7-16-45.

76 *GI Bill:* NM to Bea, 7-21-45.

76 *graduate courses at Harvard:* NM to FM, IBM, 2-26-45.

77 *Tateyama Naval Airdrome:* Johnston, ed., *We Ain't No Heroes,* 267–71.

77 *"We would have been massacred":* Takaaki Mizuno, "Flag-Waving U.S. Shows Signs of Totalitarianism," *Asahi Shimbun,* 9-14-06.

77 *"pathological":* NM to Bea, 8-8-45.

77 *"The White Negro":* NM's essay on urban hipsters, blacks, jazz, and marijuana was first published in *Dissent* 4, Summer 1957, and reprinted in AFM, 337–58.

77 *"starved, grinning, irritatingly polite":* NM to Bea, 9-1-45.

77 *"milestones":* Ibid.

78 *"many summers that had gone by":* NM to Bea, 8-16-45.

78 *His ship was with the assembled fleet:* NM, Bill Garbo, and J. C. Lay, Johnston, ed., *We Ain't No Heroes,* 266–68.

78 *"The commentator said":* NM to FM, IBM, Dave and Anne Kessler, 9-4-45.

78 *Tateyama was on the lip:* Johnston, ed., *We Ain't No Heroes,* 269–70.

78 *Mailer volunteered to be a cook:* NM to Bea, 10-1-45.

78 *"Chorus: The Chow Line":* NAD, 86–87.

79 *The mess sergeant liked him:* NM to Bea, 10-1-45.

79 *Eric Ambler's spy novels:* NM to Bea, several letters, June through December 1945.

79 *"Their goodness had no radiation":* NM to Bea, 10-20-45.

80 *"reminds us that life":* SA, 23.

80 *"the language of knee":* NM to Bea, 10-21-45.

80 *Cooking for 160 men:* NM's 1951 short story "The Language of Men" follows NM's experiences more closely than anything else he wrote in fiction. It was his first piece in *Esquire*, April 1953; rpt., AFM, 122–32.

80 *Mailer was suspicious:* NM to Bea, 11-8-45.

80 *"I feel very strong":* NM to Bea, 10-21-45.

80 *promoted to sergeant:* NM to FM, 2-4-46.

80 *"a peon in a fascist organization":* NM to FM, IBM, 11-14-45. However corrupt and inefficient the army seemed to NM, it kept offering him new experiences. In late November 1945, he was asked to teach an American history course to ten GIs. He began the course, but an officer soon took it over, as he told Bea, 11-23-45.

80 *"vision sergeant":* NM to Bea, 12-22-45.

81 *"He died happy":* NM to Bea, 11-22-45.

81 *"He was efficient and strong":* NAD, 156.

81 *Mailer's buddies had discovered:* NM's 1951 short story "The Paper House" examines the relations of GIs and geishas; rpt., AFM, 109–22.

81 *"the time-honored American purchase":* NM to Bea, 11-25-45. NM later wrote her a second letter (seven pages, undated), analyzing his feelings in great detail; he said doing so made him "feel at ease with myself and purged." Around the same time, NM concluded that masturbation was wrong and stopped, permanently, as he later explained to JML.

82 *kind of portable typewriter:* NM to FM, IBM, 12-16-45.

82 *asked Bea to separate out:* NM to Bea, 3-3-46.

82 *North Conway:* NM to Bea, 11-12-45. At the end of January, NM, his captain, and a Japanese mess boy climbed a mountain about fifteen miles inland from Onahama. NM to Bea, 1-27-46.

82 *Provincetown in the summer:* NM to Bea, 1-11-46.

82 *"a great humanist":* NM to Bea, 12-8-45.

82 *names of 161 soldiers:* NM to Bea, 1-12-46.

82 *thirty to forty soldiers:* NM to FM, IBM, 1-14-46.

83 *fourteen enlisted men as significant characters:* NM to Bea, undated fragment, February or March 1946.

83 *"insights into the weakly Evil":* NM to Bea, undated fragment, January or February 1946.

83 *"I don't know if its Harvard":* NM to Bea, 1-25-46.

83 *"He also enjoyed writing "Sgt.":* NM to Bea, 4-4-46.

83 *"chickenshit son-of-a-bitch":* NM to Bea, 4-4-46. NM gave his parents a slightly sanitized version in a 4-7-46 letter.

84 *"was when the keel":* Brock Brower, *Other Loyalties*, 109.

84 *His immediate response:* NM to Bea, 4-9-46.

84 *"Whose ass did you kiss":* JML interview with Clifford Maskovsky, 2-5-10.

85 *worst experience of his life:* JML, "A Conversation with Norman Mailer," *New England Review*, Summer 1999, 138–48.

85 *"the third lousiest guy":* Levitas, CNM, 3. See Christopher Hitchens, "Interview with Norman Mailer," *New Left Review*, 119, where NM says that in a squad of twelve he was "third or fourth from the bottom, I was mediocre at best."

85 *"You know really my only decent function":* NM to Bea, 7-11-45. The "and/or" is prescient, as for many years of his life NM could not decide which activity was paramount.

85 *"Through most of the Great Wet Boot":* AFM, 29.

86 *"It was the only book":* Bob Minzesheimer, "To Mailer, a Good Soldier Puts Words on Paper," *USA Today.*

86 *"the Norman legend":* NM to Bea, 2-7-46.

86 *asked if she could see* Transit*:* Adeline Naiman to NM, 1-24-46.

86 *badly flawed work:* NM summed up his feelings about *A Transit to Narcissus* in 1955 when he called it "a romantic, morbid, twisted, and heavily tortured work." "Mailer, Norman," *Twentieth Century Authors*, First Supplement, ed. Stanley J. Kunitz (NY: H. W. Wilson, 1955), 628.

86 *if no changes were requested:* NM to Bea, 2-7-46.

86 *"who wasn't dashingly articulate":* JML interview with Adeline Naiman, 8-21-07.

86 *Crow's Nest Cottages:* Christopher Busa, "An Interview with Norman Mailer, *Provincetown Arts*, 26. See also Robert F. Lucid's detailed account, "Crow's Nest Cottages, North Truro, 1946," *Provincetown Arts* (1999), 32–33.

87 *Mailer was writing an ensemble novel:* NM told JML in 1981, "In a lot of those reviews of the time, I remember, I kept exclaiming in amazement, 'This work has no hero.' And I don't see why a work has to have a hero. You know if you can write a book without a hero, well, all to the good."

87 *"love of planning & chess":* NAD notes, HRC.

87 *"The truth is, Robert":* NAD, 182.

87 *Mailer makes Cummings a homosexual:* AFM, 223.

88 *"Time Machine" flashbacks:* In his 8-29-55 letter to Mr. Broich, NM said, "There is no doubt at all that the Time Machines in *The Naked and the Dead* were influenced directly by the poetic biographies in *U.S.A.*"

88 *"bi-functional":* NM to Bea, late September 1946.

88 *"One was the product":* SA, 237.

88 *"show something of the turn":* Marcus, CNM, 81.

89 *"is going to be the greatest novel":* A. Lubell [Naiman], "Trade Editorial Report, Little, Brown & Company: The Naked and the Dead, 9-18-46" (HRC). Naiman sent a copy sub rosa to NM, and his father carried it around in his wallet for the rest of his life, as she later explained in "How I Discovered Norman Mailer" (HRC).

89 *"the author's marvelous sense":* Untitled assessment, HRC. Naiman

recalled that she may have predicted a sale of only 3,700 in JML interview, 8-21-07.

89 *"a piece of realism":* NM to Naiman, 9-25-46.

90 *"a mystic kick":* Harvey Breit, "Talk with Norman Mailer," *NYT*, 6-3-51; rpt., CNM, 15.

90 *"it is certain to be prosecuted":* Bernard DeVoto critique, HRC.

90 *"DeVoto's criticism is essentially sound":* NM to Naiman, late October 1946. NM was just as certain of his potential in a 10-24-46 letter to BW about the Little, Brown imbroglio: "As far as I'm concerned Barbara I'm going to be the greatest writer of this decade, and while Little, Brown may not share my enthusiasm, they're damn fools."

91 *"We you* coming-to-get*":* The forty typescript pages NM refers to begin with one of the most memorable exertions in the novel, the platoon muscling 37mm guns over a muddy jungle trail, which leads up to the attack at the river (NAD, 121–55).

92 *Cummings's demonic underling:* The definitive examination of Melville's influence on NAD is Bernard Horn, "Ahab and Ishmael at War: The Presence of *Moby-Dick* in *The Naked and the Dead*," *American Quarterly* 34, Fall 1982, 379–95.

92 *"I hate everything":* NAD, 164.

92 *"hard, isolate, stoic":* Robert Ehrlich, *Norman Mailer: The Radical as Hipster* (Metuchen, NJ: Scarecrow, 1978), 26. Lawrence's line is from *Studies in Classic American Literature* (NY: Thomas Seltzer, 1923), 92.

92 *"the most secret admiration":* Paul Krassner, "An Impolite Interview," PP, 136.

92 *"Killing and being killed":* Alfred Kazin, *Bright Book of Life: American Storytellers from Hemingway to Mailer* (Boston: Little, Brown, 1973), 77.

92 *"crude unformed vision":* NAD, 156.

92 *"a limit to his hunger":* Ibid., 701.

92 *"missed some tantalizing revelation":* Ibid., 709.

92 *This locus provides:* My comments on the confined setting of the novel are based on those of Peter G. Jones, *War and the Novelist* (Columbia: University of Missouri Press, 1976), 88–89.

93 *"General Cummings articulates":* Levitas, CNM, 4.

93 *"Iron Curtain" speech:* Given at Westminster College, Fulton, Missouri, 3-5-46. The sole member of President Truman's cabinet who did not favor a strong response to Russian expansionism was Secretary of Commerce Henry Wallace. His stance appealed to NM, who later worked in his 1948 presidential campaign.

93 *"people in our government":* Levitas, CNM, 4.

93 *Norman Rosten:* Ten years older than NM, Rosten was the first writer NM knew who lived by his pen. Their paths crossed often in Brooklyn, where Rosten served as poet laureate from 1979 to his death in 1995. In their correspondence, Rosten always addressed Mailer as "Norm I"; he was "Norm II."

93 *"We would talk":* Christopher Bigsby, "Alarm Calls for American

Dreamers," *Independent*, 2-9-02, 10. In his autobiography, Miller says that the first time he met NM he had just seen Miller's play, *All My Sons*, and told Miller that he could write a play like that. "It was so obtusely flat an assertion that I began to laugh, but he was completely serious. . . . Mailer struck me as someone who seemed to want to make converts rather than friends, so our impulses, essentially similar, could hardly mesh." *Timebends: A Life* (NY: Grove, 1987), 139.

94 *"If you give me a contract":* Frederick Christian, "The Talent and the Torment," *Cosmopolitan*, 66.

94 *"damn fool if you don't":* MBM, 92. See also MLT, 104–5.

94 *profanity conference:* MBM, 92, MLT, 104–5.

94 *"the irreducible minimum":* Levitas, CNM, 8.

94 *"fug":* MLT, 105–6, MBM, 93. NM was never able to beat back the rumors about why and when he first used "fug." Some of the blame can be laid at the feet of Tallulah Bankhead or, more likely, her press agent. She was quoted as saying that shortly after *Naked* was published, she met him and said, "Are you the young man who doesn't know how to spell fuck?" Bankhead admitted later that the incident was apocryphal (*Tallulah, Darling* by Denis Brian [NY: Macmillan, 1980], 17), but the story never died. NM told *Newsweek* (12-23-68, 7), "I had decided to use the word fug before the book was even begun." In the same magazine thirty years later (6-28-99, 49), he was still trying: "I started with 'fug.' . . . What bothered me was that people said, 'Oh, Mailer was using f— and the publisher said he had to use fug so he gave in.' It never happened that way." When NM finally did meet Bankhead, many years later, Brian reports, they just nodded and smiled. Confusion about the word's origin has been complicated by the comments of several people. Theodore Amussen, Mailer's first Rinehart editor, told Hilary Mills that NM had invented fug *after* the novel was accepted by Rinehart (Mills, 93), and Mailer's cousin and lawyer, Cy Rembar, told Peter Manso that he himself had come up with the term during a meeting with NM, a statement that NM refuted (MLT, 105–06). Both Amussen and Rembar are in error. The drafts of the manuscript at the HRC confirm NM's statement that he used the word from the beginning, as does his mention of "fug" in a letter to Angus Cameron of Little, Brown in October 1946, when he had only written 184 pages. NM later told Edward de Grazia that fug was chosen because "there wasn't any way in the world you could use 'fuck,' you just couldn't get near it" (*Girls Lean Back Everywhere: The Law of Obscenity and the Assault on Genius* [NY: Random House, 1995], 520). Despite NM's repeated denials of the Bankhead story, Jesse Sheidlower perpetuated the canard in *The F Word* (NY: Random House, 1995), and compounded it by attributing the misspelling story to Dorothy Parker, while passing over entirely Mailer's denials. Although Mailer corrected Sheidlower in print (see Brad Weiner's "Dysfunctionally Literate," *San Francisco Bay Guardian*, December 1995, 3), the 2009 reprint of *The F Word* repeats the story, and says Mailer was "required by his publishers to use the euphemism" fug.

94 *placate Rinehart's mother:* MBM, 93.
94 *"A saturnine Irishman":* JML, "Literary Ambitions," PAP, 165.
95 *Mailer hired him:* MLT, 107.
95 *"sometimes cruel in his criticism":* MLT, 107.
95 *"Oh, for the good old days":* NM to Devlin, 11-19-53.
95 *"the Shah of Brat-mah-phur":* NM to Basil Mailer, 11-17-54.
95 *"a bonus":* Marcus, CNM, 80.
95 *the "crawfish" scene:* Ginny Dougary, "The Norman Conquests," *Sunday Independent*, 6-26-00, 6L.
95 *"would have been considered":* Marcus, CNM, 80.
96 *few pages of* Anna Karenina*:* SA, 22. NM expanded on his influences, saying that NAD "had been written out of what I could learn from reading James T. Farrell and John Dos Passos, with good doses of Thomas Wolfe and Tolstoy, plus homeopathic tinctures from Hemingway, Fitzgerald, Faulkner, Melville and Dostoyevsky" (SA, 74).
96 *Jackie Robinson:* NM to Joe Mac, 5-7-97.
96 *apartment of Millie Brower:* Brower e-mail to JML, 7-15-09.
96 *He hired Millie's husband:* JML interview with Millicent Brower, 5-14-09.
96 *seemed to me at the time:* MLT, 108.
96 *Fritz Lang's classic films:* In an unpublished short story, "The Thalian Adventure," NM wrote about going to see these films with his parents and his Aunt Rose and Uncle Harry Paley. The older generation was unimpressed (HRC).
96 Blood of the Poet: BW remembers NM attending the screenings of surrealist films at the Museum of Modern Art in the 1940s.
96 *Mailer and Harvey Anhalt:* NM to Adelaide A. Scherer, 5-10-48.
96 *"several in-camera tricks":* JML interview with Michael Chaiken, 4-19-11. In 2008, with a grant from the National Film Preservation Board, Chaiken worked with the HRC and the Harvard Film Archive to help restore the film, which has the working title "Millie's Dream." Millicent Brower and NCM attended a screening of the restoration at the New York Film Festival on 8-4-09.
96 *"I think we Jews":* NM to Bruce Dexter, 5-6-97. The professor NM heard lecture is unknown, but it is possible that he was drawing on the historical ideas of both Henry Adams and/or Walter Benjamin. See F. J. Teggart, *Theory of History* (New Haven: Yale University Press, 1925).
97 *"Actually, it offers":* Lillian Ross, "Rugged Times," *New Yorker*, 10-23-48; rpt., CNM, 14.
97 *"War may be the ultimate purpose":* Kazin, *Bright Book of Life*, 74.

FOUR: PARIS AND HOLLYWOOD: PROMINENT AND EMPTY

In addition to the sources identified below, the following were drawn on: "Fan's Memoir"; JML's "Mailer Log"; Ph.D. dissertation of Raymond Karl Suess II, "Tom Sawyer, Horatio Alger and Sammy Glick: A Biography of Young Mailer" (St. Louis University, 1974), for letters from Francis I. "Fig" Gwaltney to NM; Robert W. Rosen's interview with Jean Malaquais, and for historical context;

JML's unpublished interviews with NM and BW. NM's letters are located at the HRC.

Page

98 *The Mailers shivered:* NM, Robert F. Lucid, and Richard Wilbur, "Postwar Paris: Chronicles of Literary Life," *Paris Review*, Spring 1999, 273.

98 Cours de Civilisation Française: Although it has been reported otherwise, NM completed the course. On his final examination, he scored 23 out of a possible 40 points ("assez bien"), and was awarded a Certificate de Langue Française, dated 2-28-48 (HRC).

98 *"You get to longing":* NM to FG, 11-11-47.

99 *critical study of Melville: Herman Melville: The Tragic Vision and the Heroic Ideal* (Cambridge: Harvard University Press, 1939).

99 *"ennobled":* NM, Lucid, and Wilbur, "Postwar Paris," *Paris Review*, 279.

99 *"the commission of acts of force":* Truman's Executive Order 9835 remained in force until the mid-1960s when the Supreme Court struck it down on grounds of vagueness and undue breadth.

99 *"I've gone quite a bit to the Left":* NM to FG, 10-7-48.

100 *introduced to Jean Malaquais:* Suess, "Young Mailer," 131; MBM, 95.

100 *Malaquais' background:* James Kirkup, "Obituary: Jean Malaquais," *Independent*, January 6, 1999, independent.co.uk/arts-entertainment/obituary-jean-malaquais-1045270; Nick Heath, "Malaquais, Jean, 1908–1998," 12-18-06, libcom.org/hist_org/malaquais-jean-1908-1988; NM, preface to Jean Malaquais, *The Joker* (NY: Warner, 1974); rpt., in part, PAP, 97–105.

100 *"Morally and intellectually":* Kirkup. "Obituary," *Independent*.

100 *"Malaquais loathed formula":* NM, preface, *The Joker*, 15.

101 *"had more influence":* Ibid., 11.

101 *"a boy scout":* Robert W. Rosen, interview with Jean Malaquais, 8-23-71, in Suess, "Young Mailer," 133.

101 *"exploit him":* Raymond M. Sokolov, "Flying High with Mailer," *Newsweek*, 12-9-68, 84–88.

101 *"disliked me":* Ibid.

101 *"long leaky French winter":* AFM, 91.

101 *"I have never heard":* NM to IBM, 12-6-47.

101 *He came back with two ideas:* NM's "Journal January '48" (HRC).

102 *"a collective novel":* NM to IBM, 11-1-47.

102 *"Maybe I'm not scared":* NM to IBM, 11-8-48.

102 *"If my past":* AFM, 93–94.

102 *E. M. Forster's novels:* NM read *The Longest Journey* (1907) before he completed NAD and said the unexpected death of Gerald, the rugby player, near the beginning, gave him the idea for the similarly surprising death of Hearn in NAD. He says in the Bill Broadway interview ("Norman Mailer: New Advertisements for Himself," *New Millennium Writing*, Spring/Summer 1998, 13), that killing "a very interesting character" is tricky, but "one of the most powerful techniques you could ever use in a novel."

102 *work by Jean-Paul Sartre:* NM did not read Sartre's philosophical works until the mid-1950s. In Paris, he may have read *The Age of Reason* (NY: Knopf, 1947).

102 The Red and the Black: Stendhal's novel was a touchstone for NM; he admired the audacity of Julien Sorel, the archetypal young man from the provinces. See his comment in Charles Monaghan, "Portrait of a Man Reading," *Washington Post Book World*, 7-11-71; rpt., CNM, 189.

102 *"That English fairy":* NM to FG, 1-?-48.

102 Goodbye to Berlin: Christopher Isherwood, *Goodbye to Berlin* (NY: Random House, 1939). See Marcus, CNM, 81, for NM's comment on Sally Bowles.

102 *"emasculation":* NM to Raney, 1-23-48, 1-24-48.

103 *"howls and sulks":* NM to Raney, 2-7-48.

103 *Raney's upcoming visit:* Raney arrived sometime in the latter half of April. His consultation with NM seems to have gone well. See NM, Lucid, and Wilbur, "Postwar Paris," *Paris Review*, 279.

103 *"It is a tone":* NM to Raney, 2-7-48.

104 *a sentimental, Ernie Pyle version:* Ernie Pyle (1900–45), a Pulitzer Prize–winning war correspondent for the Scripps Howard newspaper chain killed in combat near Okinawa, was much revered for his reports on individual soldiers written in homey, nonjournalistic prose.

104 *"no bitch":* NM to Raney, 3-1-48.

104 *"Around dusk":* NM to FM, BW, 3-17-48.

105 *An American-owned car:* Barbara Wasserman, "Spain, 1948—A Memoir," *Hudson Review*, Autumn, 2000, 365.

105 *"In a large bare room":* POP, 15.

106 *"thrilled":* BW to Robert F. Lucid, 1-12-98. This five-page letter and BW's memoir were invaluable in establishing the chronology, events, and atmospheric details of the spring and early summer of 1948.

106 *"What pleased me":* Barbara Probst Solomon, "A Long Friendship," *MR* (2008), 186.

106 *mission was scary:* The story of rescuing the political prisoners is also told in Barbara Probst Solomon, *Arriving Where We Started* (NY: Harper & Row, 1972).

106 *work on a screen treatment:* NM to Adelaide Scherer, 5-10-48.

106 *"a courageous piece of publishing":* John Dos Passos to Stanley Rinehart, 5-6-48.

107 "U.S.A. *meant more":* JML, "A Conversation with Norman Mailer," *New England Review*, 141.

107 *"Norman was flush":* MLT, 114.

107 *Gore Vidal and Tennessee Williams:* Gore Vidal, "Some Memories of the Glorious Bird and an Earlier Self," *Matters of Fact and of Fiction (Essays, 1973–1976)* (NY: Random House, 1977), 142.

107 *"I remember thinking meanly":* Gore Vidal, "Norman Mailer's Self-Advertisements," *United States: Essays, 1952–1992* (NY: Random House, 1993), 31.

107 *"All they could do was choke":* NM to FG, 5-21-48.
108 *"I have no worries":* NM to Raney, 6-7-48.
108 *"a tough baby":* NM to FM, IBM, 8-4-48.
108 *"what the French would call":* Philip Schopper, interview with NM for *American Masters* documentary on Lillian Hellman, 8-7-98.
108 *"truly formidable bare breast":* NM, Joan Mellon, *Hellman and Hammett* (NY: HarperCollins, 1996), 258.
108 *"What is a carbine?":* Lillian Hellman file, HRC.
108 *visit with Sinclair Lewis:* Interview with Sylvia B. Richmond, *Chelsea* (Massachusetts) *Record*, 10-2-48, 50.
109 The Naked and the Dead *reached first place:* NAD remained on the list until 7-24-49, a total of sixty-two weeks. It was in the top five for forty-three weeks.
109 Times, Cue, *the* New York Star, *and* The New Yorker*'s:* These appeared in 1948 on 8-15, 8-21, 8-22, and 10-23, respectively.
109 *"Getting your mug":* Ross, CNM, 13.
109 *"a novelist to re-create":* "Fiction in the U.S.," *Life*, 8-16-48, 24.
109 *"insidious slime":* "From Here to Obscenity," *Life*, 4-16-51, 40.
110 *"both vulgar and innocent":* FG to Karl Suess, 3-9-73, "Young Mailer."
110 *"all but the tough-skinned":* Rinehart postcard, spring 1948 (HRC).
110 *"Everyone was both startled and shocked":* MBM, 99.
110 The New Yorker, New York Times, Newsweek, New York Herald Tribune Book Review: The reviews appeared in 1948 on 5-15, 5-9, 5-10, and 5-9, respectively.
110 *"more explicitly vile speech":* Orville Prescott, "Books of the Times," *NYT*, 5-7-48, 21.
110 *"I think I suffered":* "Norman Mailer on *An American Dream*," *New York Post*, 3-25-65; rpt., CNM, 100-03.
110 *made over thirty:* Ross, CNM, 12.
110 *associated with the Progressive Party's:* Cedric Belfrage and James Aronson, *Something to Guard: The Stormy Life of the National Guardian, 1948–1967* (NY: Columbia University Press, 1978), 24. NM wrote "A Credo for the Living" for the paper (10-18-48), railing against "anti-Russian hysteria" and calling for Wallace's election. He describes himself in the piece as "an ignorant Marxist" because he had yet to read the basic works of Marxist theory.
111 *2,500-word feature article:* "Do Professors Have Rights," *New York Post*, 10-8-48, 5, 34.
111 *"Everyone who was anyone":* Shelley Winters, *Shelley II: The Middle of My Century* (NY: Simon & Schuster, 1989), 69.
111 *"unintentionally eloquent":* NM, Lucid, and Wilbur, "Postwar Paris," *Paris Review*, 281.
111 *"unbeknownst to us":* Farley Granger, *Include Me Out: My Life from Goldwyn to Broadway* (NY: St. Martin's, 2007), 94–95.
112 *two hundred other writers:* AP wire story, 10-9-48.
112 *"Ballots vs. Book Burning":* "Speech for Writers for Wallace" (HRC).

112 *"Communists are the closest thing":* Bonnie K. Goodman, www.presiden tialcampaignselectionsreference.wordpress.com/overviews/20th–century/ 1948–overview/.
112 *"When I met Norman":* MBM, 98.
112 Report of Court Proceedings: Moscow: People's Commission of Justice in the U.S.S.R., 1938. NM's battered copy is still in his library.
113 Stalin: A Critical Survey of Bolshevism: London: Longmans, Green, 1939. It is likely that NM also read Trotsky's three-volume *History of the Russian Revolution* (NY: Simon & Schuster, 1937).
113 Dissent: NM wrote a number of articles for the socialist journal founded by Howe, and served on its board from its founding until the mid-1980s.
113 War Diary: (NY: Doubleday, Doran, 1944).
113 *"opinionated, cocksure":* MLT, 129.
113 World Without Visa: (NY: Doubleday, 1948).
113 *"it was a disaster":* Philip Schopper interview.
113 *"unrelenting":* MK, *The Good, the Bad, and the Dolce Vita: The Adventures of an Actor in Hollywood, Paris, and Rome* (NY: Nation Books, 2004), 70.
113 *"a thoroughly constipated Stalinist hack":* Malaquais, Rosen interview in Suess, 165.
113 *"child's play":* MBM, 112.
113 *"There were times":* PAP, 160.
114 *"You're 25":* Transcript of *The Phil Donahue Show*, 11-21-79, 8.
114 *"Celebrity was great":* Alastair McKay, "Still Stormin'," *Scotsman*, 2. See also NM's comment on his sudden fame in his January 1968 *Playboy* interview with Paul Carroll: "Of course I dug it. I had to dig it. . . . It enabled me to get girls I would not otherwise have gotten" (rpt. PAP, 32–45).
114 *"cauterizes a lot":* Anthony Haden-Guest, "The Life of Norman," *Harpers & Queen*, 192.
114 *"a lobotomy to my past":* AFM, 93.
114 *"Once I had been":* Ibid., 92–93.
114 *"I was a dependable pain":* SA, 116.
114 *"a big fat one":* NM to Sinclair Lewis, 11-15-48.
115 *"The Devil's Advocate":* HRC.
115 *"a damn thing about labor unions":* Marcus, CNM, 81.
115 *"Full of second-novel panic":* Ibid.
115 *Waldorf conference:* The following were drawn on: AFM, 408–10; Neil Jumonville, *Critical Crossings: The New York Intellectuals in Postwar America* (Berkeley: University of California Press, 1991), 1–48; Dwight Macdonald, "The Waldorf Conference," *Politics*, Winter 1949, 32A–32C; Freda Kirchwey, "Battle of the Waldorf," *Nation*, 4-2-49, 377–78; Tom O'Connor, "News Tailored to Fit," *Nation*, 4-16-49, 438–40; Joseph P. Lash, "Weekend at the Waldorf," *New Republic*, 4-18-49, 10–14; Cedric Belfrage, "Guardian Reports on the Peace Conference Panels," *National Guardian*, 4-4-49, 9; "The Russians Get a Big Hand from U.S. Friends," *Life*, 4-4-49, 39–43; reports in the *NYT*, March 24–28, 1949; Diana

Trilling, "An Interview with Dwight Macdonald," *Partisan Review: The Fiftieth Anniversary Edition* (NY: Stein & Day, 1984), 312–32; Michael Macdonald's unpublished interview with NM, 7-9-98 (HRC), MLT, 134–37; MBM, 112–13.

115 *"out of the dream"*: AFM, 408.

116 *"Dupes and Fellow Travelers"*: *Life*, 4-4-49.

116 *Trojan horse:* NM, "The Only Way for Writers," *Speaking of Peace: An Edited Report of the Cultural and Scientific Conference for World Peace*, ed. Daniel S. Gillmor (NY: National Council of the Arts, Sciences and Professions, 1949), 82–83.

116 *"melancholy debauch"*: NM to Muriel? 5-3-49.

116 *"both Russia and America"*: NM, "The Only Way for Writers," *Speaking of Peace*, 83.

116 *"must always work"*: Norman Podhoretz, "Norman Mailer: The Embattled Vision," *Doings and Undoings: The Fifties and After in American Writing* (NY: Farrar, Straus & Giroux, 1964), 187.

117 *"living more closely"*: Marcus, CNM, 85.

117 *"felt like a rodent"*: AFM, 409–10.

117 *"I was immediately able"*: MBM, 114.

117 *Macdonald came up:* Michael Macdonald interview (HRC).

117 *"stay incognito"*: NM to FG, 1-1-49.

118 *"the theoretical and empirical"*: NM to Larry Weiss, 11-16-48.

118 *"an adult fairy tale"*: NM to FG, 1-1-49.

118 *"a good flair for plots"*: NM to Cy Rembar, 4-26-49.

118 *"You're going back"*: MLT, 120.

119 *"the ugliest city"*: NM to FG, 11-16-48.

119 *"reap the wind"*: NM to JM, 7-3-49.

119 *"incredibly foul and beastly"*: (London) *Sunday Times*, 5-1-49, 1.

119 *"is like a bell ringing"*: Transcript of NM's conversation with AP, 5-?-49 (HRC).

119 *"foul, lewd and revolting"*: Sir Hartley Shawcross, *Evening Standard*, 5-23-49.

120 *"respectable society"*: V. S. Pritchett, "Kinsey's Army," *New Statesman and Nation*, 5-14-49.

120 *"the best war book"*: George Orwell to David Astor, 1-21-50, *Why Orwell Matters*, ed. Christopher Hitchens (NY: Basic Books, 2002), 113.

120 *"profoundly prophetic"*: NM, "Light on Orwell," *Listener*, 2-4-71, 144.

120 *"combine the political essay"*: AFM, 186.

120 *"Lotus Land"*: NM to Hellman, 8-8-49.

120 *Lancaster was slated:* MK, *The Good, the Bad, and the Dolce Vita*, 71.

120 *war clouds over Korea:* "There was no way then," NM said, "of making a fairly serious movie of the book." David Thompson, "Mailer by the Bay," *California*, August 1987, 68.

120 *Shelley Winters asked for his help:* Winters gave her version in *Shelley, Also Known as Shirley* (NY: Morrow, 1980), 253–56. NM gave his in an

interview with Andrew O'Hagan, "Norman Mailer: The Art of Fiction," *Paris Review Interviews* III (NY: Picador, 2008), 407–8.

121 *"looked like a prize fighter":* NM to FM, IBM, 9-1-49.
121 *"running to the hospital":* NM to FG, 9-?-49, 1949.
122 *"high comedy":* MLT, 138.
122 *"The day after the contract":* Ibid.
122 *"The Character of the Victim":* Final script, George Landy Agency (HRC).
122 *"He wanted it changed":* MBM, 119.
122 *They refused and retained:* NM to FM, IBM, 11-27-49.
122 *"stank":* "Novels Are Easy," *Esquire*, April 1953; rpt., CNM, 19.
122 *"treated me well":* Letter to the Editor, *NYTBR*, 4-30-89, 24.
123 *"I want you to give me":* IBM to NM, 11-21-49.
123 *"If I ever had any doubt":* NM to IBM, 11-24-49.
124 *Mailer used a similarly indignant tone:* NCM, *A Ticket to the Circus* (NY: Random House, 2010), 315–16.
124 *the last lodes:* NM specifically mentions violence in this connection in the O'Hagan interview, 415–16, *Paris Review Interviews III.* His reputation as a pioneer in sexual exploration began with *The Deer Park* (1955), and was solidified with his 1959 short story in AFM, "The Time of Her Time."
125 *"a sponger":* MLT, 148.
125 *"I even fell a little":* MBM, 118.
125 *"was the unhappiest woman":* MLT, 148.
125 *Christmas party description:* MBM, 121; MLT, 149–50; Rosen interview, in Suess, "Young Mailer," 187; *Shelley, Also Known as Shirley*, 296–99; NM to JML, 7-17-07; Darwin Porter, *Brando Unzipped* (NY: Blood Moon Productions, 2006), 289–94.
125 *"Look, Mr. Chaplin":* Rosen interview, in Suess, "Young Mailer," 187.
125 *"Norman, what the fuck": Shelley, Also Known as Shirley*, 298.
126 *"Norman had an enormous reputation":* MBM, 121.
126 *landed a job at Twentieth Century-Fox:* NM to FM, IBM, 11-27-49.
126 *"the whole Hollywood venture":* NM to FM, IBM, 3-31-50.
126 *"Hollywood stinks":* NM to FG, early spring 1950.
126 *police lineup:* NM to George Lea, 3-26-58.
126 *"is the best novel written in America":* NM to BW, 6-18-50.
127 *"The house Marion purchased":* AFM, 519. NM's evocations of Provincetown are collected in *Norman Mailer's Provincetown: The Wild West of the East*, ed. JML (Provincetown Arts Press, 2005).
128 *"almost drove me nuts":* NM to Adeline Naiman, 7-28-50.
128 *"fulfills none of the qualifications":* NM to BW, 6-18-50.
128 *"If a writer really wants":* Breit, CNM, 16.
128 *"To own something!":* NM to Adeline Naiman, 7-28-50.
128 *"not writing the book myself":* Marcus, CNM, 82.
129 *"brazen, touchy, touching":* Philip H. Bufithis, *Norman Mailer* (NY: Ungar, 1978), 37.
129 *hard to miss:* MLT, 156.
129 *"quinine tongue":* BS, 249.

129 *"Malaquais's philosophy in Devlin's body"*: MLT, 158.
129 *"the biggest whang"*: BS, 62.
130 *"would have been a precursor to Women's Liberation"*: Jeffrey Michelson and Sarah Stone, "Ethics and Pornography," PAP, 123.
130 *"Here I was"*: MBM, 123.
130 *"was a very strong woman"*: Michelson, PAP, 123.
130 *"she was perfectly prepared"*: "I never started drinking until it [*Naked*] came out." Frederick Christian, "The Talent and the Torment," *Cosmopolitan*, 67.
131 *"Norman was making"*: Brock Brower, *Other Loyalties*, 126.
131 *"He listened inside himself"*: *The Last Tycoon: An Unfinished Novel* (NY: Scribner's, 1941), 95.
131 *"How could I know"*: AM, *The Last Party: Scenes from My Life with Norman Mailer* (NY: Barricade, 1997), 61.
131 *"A thriller, a western"*: NM to George Landy, 10-29-50.
132 *"It knocked me down"*: Unpublished interview with JML, 10-14-83, excerpted in JML and George Plimpton, "Glimpses: James Jones, 1921–1977," *Paris Review*, Summer 1987, 205–36. NM told Barry H. Leeds in 1987, "I always thought that *Eternity* was a bigger book." Barry H. Leeds, "A Conversation with Norman Mailer," *The Enduring Vision of Norman Mailer* (Bainbridge Island, WA: Pleasure Boat Studio, 2002); rpt., CNM, 374.
132 *"It's a big fist"*: NM to Burroughs Mitchell, 12-21-50.
132 *"It always gave me a boost"*: AFM, 463.
132 *"So in a certain sense"*: JML and George Plimpton, "Glimpses: James Jones," *Paris Review*, 213.
132 *"incredible explosion"*: AM, *The Last Party*, 68.
133 *"What I gave"*: Ibid., 71.
133 *"The Meaning of Western Defense"*: "Originally titled "The Defence of the Compass," it appeared in *The Western Defences*, ed. Sir John George Smythe (London: Wingate, 1951); rpt., AFM, 204–13.
133 *"the third-rate Eighteenth Brumaire"*: NM to Dwight Macdonald, 2-20-51.
133 *"Western Defense has the ultimate"*: AFM, 204.
133 *"the particular equipment"*: NM to Warren Allen Smith, 2-20-51.
134 *"We had a good marriage"*: NM to Dave and Anne Kessler, 4-19-51.
134 *"liking you immensely"*: NM to Lois Wilson, spring 1951.
134 *"small-beer* Nineteen Eighty-Four*"*: "Last of the Leftists," *Time*, 5-28-51, 110.
134 *"a monolithic, flawless badness"*: Anthony West, "East Meets West, Author Meets Allegory," *New Yorker*, 6-9-51, 108; Irving Howe, "Some Political Novels," *Nation*, 6-16-51, 568–69; Harvey Swados, "Fiction Parade," *New Republic*, 6-18-51; 20–21.
134 *"the most interesting American"*: V. S. Pritchett, *Bookman*, January 1952.
135 *"a party of two"*: Hitchens, "Interview with Norman Mailer," *New Left Review*, 119.
135 *"It's a political tract"*: MBM, 126.

135 *"But I rather suspect":* NM to JM, 7-20-51.
135 *consider other occupations:* NM thought about becoming a psychoanalyst, going into business or working with his hands (AFM 108–9).
135 *"an underlying anger":* AM, *The Last Party*, 85.
136 *Palm Springs:* MK, *The Good, the Bad, and the Dolce Vita*, 92.
136 *"Later, he told me":* AM, *The Last Party*, 88, 93.
136 *loft party description:* MBM, 132–34; MLT, 171–75; AFM, 237; NM to FG, 9-?-1951; AM, *The Last Party*, 107–9.
136 *"a mingling of personalities":* AM, *The Last Party*, 108.
137 *Provincetown Art Association panel: Provincetown Advocate*, 8-16-51, 10.
137 *"was the nearest thing to Jehovah":* O'Hagan, *Paris Review Interviews III*, 429.
137 Humboldt's Gift: (NY: Viking, 1975). Macdonald was Bellow's model for the ineffectual intellectual, Orlando Higgins; Humboldt is based loosely on the poet Delmore Schwartz.
137 *"the sight of paunchy, aging bodies":* AM, *The Last Party*, 130.
137 *"grim apartment":* AFM, 154.
137 *Vance Bourjaily:* Another multitalented World War II veteran, Bourjaily (1922–2010) was friendly with many of NM's crowd in the 1950s. He wrote a number of novels, including *Brill Among the Ruins* (1970), which was nominated for a National Book Award.
137 After the Lost Generation: (NY: McGraw-Hill, 1951; rpt., NY: Arbor House, 1985).
138 *"The reviews were depressing":* NM to Bourjaily, 9-5-51.
138 *"In those days":* NM to Andrew Spear, Christopher Joyal, April 1999.
139 *film of* From Here to Eternity*:* MBM, 132.
139 *"the worst writing":* AFM, 107.
139 *turned out three stories:* Collected in AFM.
139 *"I move ahead":* AFM, 108.
139 *"The Notebook": The Berkley Book of Writing, 3*, ed. William Phillips and Philip Rahv (NY: Berkley, 1956); rpt., AFM, 150–53.
139 *"You were just watching":* AM, *The Last Party*, 110.
140 *an untitled journal:* Unpaginated, approximately twenty pages (HRC).
140 *Ross had promised:* NM to Dave Kessler, 1-7-52.
140 *"journeyman":* Introduction, *The Short Fiction of Norman Mailer* (NY: Dell, 1967), 9. He adds that he does not "have the gift to write great stories, or perhaps even very good ones."
141 *"an intense need to play Pygmalion":* AM, *The Last Party*, 102–3.
141 *"Ah, to live indignant":* Emile Zola, quoted in Philo M. Buck, *The World's Great Age: The Story of a Century's Search for a Philosophy of Life* (NY: Macmillan, 1936).

FIVE: *THE DEER PARK*

In addition to the sources identified below, the following were drawn on: "Fan's Memoir"; NM's untitled 1952 journal; JML's "Mailer Log"; JML's unpublished interviews with NM and BW. NM's letters are located in the HRC.

Page

145 *"dreams or conceives":* AFM, 154.

145 *"exercises in imagination-isometrics":* Robert F. Lucid, introduction, *Norman Mailer: The Man and His Work*, ed. Lucid (Boston: Little, Brown, 1971).

145 *"a small frustrated man":* AFM, 154.

145 *With encouragement:* AFM, 156.

145 *"The Man Who Studied Yoga":* First published in a collection with the work of others, *New Short Novels*, 2 (NY: Ballantine, 1956), the story was reprinted in AFM, 157–85.

145 *"I would introduce myself":* AFM, 157.

145 *"lies foundered":* AFM, 183, 185.

146 *epigraph to Mailer's pleasure novel:* The quotation, which concerns "the evil of this dreadful place" of "depravity, debauchery and all the vices," is taken from Mouffle D'Angerville's *Vie Privée De Louis XV* (London: Leyton, 1781). NM first learned of the king's brothel in an unnamed book about the Marquis de Sade, as he told Walter Kahnert in a letter, 11-20-53.

146 *Mailer wrote to congratulate:* NM to Bea, 4-22-52.

146 *"agony":* NM to FG, 4-22-52.

146 *"quiet, witty, sad":* NM to Adeline Naiman, late May 1952.

147 *"Our Country and Our Culture": PR*, May/June 1952, rpt., AFM, 187–90.

147 *"I think I ought to declare":* Ibid., 187, 188, 190.

147 *work within the Democratic Party: Twenty-five Years of* Dissent: *An American Tradition*, ed. Irving Howe (NY: Methuen, 1979), xiv–xv.

147 *published three pieces:* "The Meaning of Western Defense," Spring 1954; "In Re: Sidney Hook," Summer 1954; "David Riesman Reconsidered," Autumn 1954.

147 *"We did a prodigious amount":* Styron, foreword, *To Reach Eternity: The Letters of James Jones*, ed. George Hendrick (NY: Random House, 1989), viii–x.

148 *"At the last bar":* MK, *The Good, the Bad, and the Dolce Vita*, 89–90.

148 *"joyously announcing":* Ibid., 89.

148 *"Moving about":* Styron, foreword, *To Reach Eternity*, x.

148 *"I seem unable":* NM to Bea, 6-18-52.

148 *"seriously fagged":* Ibid.

149 *"The Paper House": New World Writing: Second Mentor Collection* (NY: New American Library, November 1952); rpt., AFM, 109–22.

149 *"The Language of Men": Esquire*, April 1953; rpt., AFM, 122–32.

149 *"The Dead Gook": Discovery*, 1 (NY: Pocket Books, 1952); rpt., AFM, 132–49.

149 *"inoffensively general": Discovery* editorial statement, JML files.

149 *"I've been meaning":* NM to Styron, 2-23-53.

149 *Styron wrote back:* Styron to NM, 3-4-53, *Selected Letters of William Styron*, ed. Rose Styron, with R. Blakeslee Gilpin (NY: Random House, 2012), 170–71.

150 The Old Man and the Sea: *Life*, 9-1-52, and in book form from Scribner's, 9-8-52.
150 *"but I just can't bear his prose":* NM to Lillian Ross, 9-2-52.
150 *"make his personality enrich":* AFM, 21.
150 *"one of the few writers":* AFM, 265.
150 *41 First Avenue:* AM, *The Last Party*, 100–101; MLT, 167–68; NM to Bea, 10-7-52; NM to Natalie? 11-18-52.
151 *"I don't think Norman":* AM, *The Last Party*, 101.
151 *"overall scheme is so grandiose":* NM to Graham Watson, 9-2-52.
151 *entertaining Susan:* NM to Bea, Steve, 11-17-52.
151 *some large reservations:* NM to Bea, Steve, 12-13-52.
152 *"So I wrote the report":* MBM, 145-46.
152 *seventy-six-year-old grandmother:* MBM, 146, 153.
152 *"You have hardly acted":* NM to John W. Aldridge, 1-12-53.
153 *"reasonable doubt":* The story of the Civil Service Commission allegation and NM's response is told by his cousin, Charles Rembar, *The Law of the Land: The Evolution of Our Legal System* (NY: Simon & Schuster, 1980), 370–75.
154 *flurry of letters:* NM to Walter Kahnert, 1-12-53; FG, 1-15-53, 2-12-53, 4-15-53; NM to Dave and Anne Kessler, 2-5-53; NM to Bea, 3-7-53, 4-24-53, 5-22-53; NM to Lindner, 4-15-53; NM to EY, 4-15-53, 5-22-53; NM to Styron, 4-24-52; NM to Tobias Schneebaum, 5-22-53.
154 *"precisely the courage":* NM to Bea, 2-5-53.
154 *"top to bottom":* NM to FG, 2-12-53.
154 *"some sort of evil genius":* Marcus, CNM, 92.
155 *"common pimp":* "Manners and Morals: A Boy Who Likes Girls," *Time*, 8-25-52.
155 *"steeped in filth":* Thomas P. Ronan, "Ban at Jelke Trial Upheld by Jurist," *NYT*, 2-18-53.
155 *"evil genius":* Marcus, CNM, 92. According to Mia Feroleto, NM may have gotten the name Marion Faye from her mother, Marion Fay, with whom he socialized in the early 1950s. Feroleto said that her mother's mother had some of the same life experiences as Faye's mother, Dorothea O'Faye, who was modeled after MK's friend Lois Andrews.
155 *"I've been rushing":* NM to Styron, 4-24-53.
156 *"boudoir Pygmalion":* DP, 12.
156 *"fundamental poverty of imagination":* NM to Styron, 7-24-53.
156 *"The most powerful leverage":* AFM, 238.
156 *copy, word for word:* JML and George Plimpton, "Glimpses: James Jones," *Paris Review*, 215.
157 Some Came Running: (NY: Scribner's, 1958). Jones was forced to abridge the novel for the 1959 New American Library paperback edition because the technology of the day did not allow for such a huge novel.
157 *"Lowney Handy and Jones":* NM to Styron, 7-24-53.
157 *"the beautiful, raven-haired woman":* John Bowers, *The Colony* (NY: Dutton, 1971), 190, 187.

158 *in "as little as possible":* AM, *The Last Party*, 143.
158 *"the music ripped":* Ibid., 147. See also NM's comments on the New Orleans trip in Mark Binelli, "Norman Mailer," *Rolling Stone*, 5-3-07, 69.
158 *"deep down":* NM to Dan Wolf, 7-28-53.
159 *"as boffing huts":* NM to Styron, 7-24-53.
159 *"what with the income tax":* NM to Cy Rembar, 8-22-53.
159 *"My experience":* NM to Vance Bourjaily, 9-26-53.
161 *Susan remembers sitting:* JML interview with Susan Mailer, 9-5-07.
161 *"I'm sick of writing it":* NM to Irving Howe, 10-20-53.
161 *"Ladders to Heaven": New World Writing*, 4 (1953); rpt., as "Novelists and Critics of the 1940s," *Homage to Daniel Shays: Collected Essays* (NY: Random House, 1972).
161 *"We don't even get mentioned":* NM to Styron, 10-23-53.
161 *"that talentless, self-promoting":* Styron to NM, 11-15-53, *Selected Letters*, 195.
161 *"I've got you":* Gore Vidal, *Palimpsest: A Memoir* (NY: Viking, 1995), 238.
161 *"gornisht":* JML interview with Millicent Brower, 5-14-09.
162 Don Juan in Hell: In the 2-15-93 reading at Carnegie Hall, Susan Sontag played Doña Ana, NM was the Commodore, and Gay Talese was Don Juan.
162 *"fifty pages in the middle":* NM to Charles Devlin, 11-19-53.
162 *"half third draft":* NM to Chester Aaron, 11-19-53.
162 *probably marry:* NM to Adeline Naiman, 11-19-53.
162 *"I go off dreaming":* NM to Devlin, 11-19-53.
162 *"Norman found that if you":* MBM, 134. Descriptions of White Horse gatherings are from MBM, 134–38.
163 *"I was so pleased":* MBM, 137.
163 *sharp critique:* Robert Lindner, *Prescription to Rebellion* (NY: Rinehart, 1952), 67–74.
164 *"become axiomatic":* Ibid., 73.
164 *"A way has to be found":* Ibid., 144.
164 *"The alternative to adjustment":* Ibid., 218.
164 *"surely right":* Charles Rycroft, *Wilhelm Reich* (NY: Viking, 1972), 27.
165 *never gone into analysis:* Hitchens, "Interview with Norman Mailer," *New Left Review*, 119.
165 *"The Psychodynamics of Gambling":* Robert Lindner, "The Psychodynamics of Gambling," *Annals of the American Academy of Political Science and Social Science* 269 (May 1950).
165 *"While I read your monograph":* NM to Lindner, 4-15-53.
166 *"renowned* toreros de salon*":* NM to Lew Allen, 11-20-53.
166 *"always dependent":* NM to Nat Halper, 10-20-53.
166 *only four or five weeks away:* NM to Jonathan Cape, 1-6-54.
166 *"evil principle":* NM repeats Lindner's words in NM to Lindner, 1-19-54.
167 *"The experience was just fantastic":* NM to Chester Aaron, 2-1-54.
168 *"I didn't exactly nag":* AM, *The Last Party*, 175.

168 *"after all, I was"*: Ibid., 179.
168 *"Well, Mrs. Mailer"*: Ibid., 180.
169 *"happy because I was Mrs. Norman Mailer"*: Ibid., 183.
169 The Caine Mutiny Court-Martial: The play ran from 1-20-54 to 1-22-55.
169 *"an extraordinary story of the Marines"*: NM to Devlin, 2-23-54.
169 *"by dint of pushing"*: NM to Chester Aaron, 4-30-54.
170 *"they" liked it:* NM to FG, 4-29-54.
170 *"Life with Jonesie"*: NM to Allen, 4-30-54.
170 *"John Phillips"*: pen name of novelist John P. Marquand, Jr. (1923–1995).
170 *"Something in the sex"*: NM to Devlin, 5-26-54.
171 *"a lousy liver"*: NM to FG, 5-28-54.
171 *"the shits"*: AFM, 19.
171 *"fancy indiscretions"*: Lois Wilson to NM, 5-19-54.
171 *"as the years go by"*: NM to Lois Wilson, 5-29-54.
171 *"I took the descriptive edge"*: NM to Lindner, 6-12-54.
171 *"Tentatively, she reached"*: AFM, 260.
172 *"Things at Rinehart"*: NM to Lindner, 7-16-54.
172 *"a bright spot"*: NM to Lindner, 7-18-54.
172 *"an uneasy feeling"*: NM to Bill and Rose Styron, 7-16-54.
172 *"honest and brilliant"*: Styron to NM, 7-19-54, *Selected Letters*, 202–5.
172 *"truly appreciated"*: NM to Styron, 8-18-54.
173 *write a preface:* NM repeats Lindner's offer in his 12-15-54 letter.
173 *review in* The Village Voice: Published 11-9-55.
173 *"Because I loved him"*: AM, *The Last Party*, 134.
173 *In August, reports appeared:* Thomas M. Pryor, "Gregory Acquires 'Naked and Dead,' " *NYT*, 8-20-54; Irene Thirer, " 'Naked and Dead' Movie Scheduled," *New York Post*, 8-20-54.
173 *private printing of* The Deer Park: NM to MK, 11-30-54; NM to Lindner, 12-15-54.
174 *"by the cartload"*: NM to BW, 8-23-54.
174 *I found it impressive:* NM to Styron, 10-7-54.
174 *"My pride was that"*: AFM, 221.
174 *"maggots like [Walter] Winchell"*: NM to Mr. Lambert, 9-7-54. Winchell (1897–1972), a New York gossip columnist, was a right-wing syndicated columnist for the *New York Daily Mirror*; Mortimer (1904–63) was a muckraking columnist for the *New-York Mirror* and coauthor with Jack Lait of *U.S.A. Confidential* (1952), and similar books about prostitution and gambling.
174 *"the way to me"*: AFM, 221.
175 *"The Homosexual Villain"*: The essay appeared in *One*, January 1955; rpt., AFM, 222–27.
175 *"I had been acting"*: AFM, 225.
175 *"unpleasant, ridiculous, or sinister"*: Ibid., 223.
175 *"I had no conscious"*: Ibid., 226.
175 *"So when I was first with Norman"*: JML interview with Dotson Rader, 3-25-10.

175 *"under control":* Amussen to NM, 10-7-54.
175 *wrote to Styron:* NM to Styron, 10-7-54.
176 *$110,000:* NM to MK, 11-16-54.
176 *three or four more books:* NM to MK, 10-10-54.

SIX: GENERAL MARIJUANA AND THE NAVIGATOR

In addition to the sources identified below, the following were drawn on: NM's "Lipton's Journal"; JML's "Mailer Log"; JML's unpublished interviews with NM and BW. NM's letters are located at the HRC.

Page

178 *"Calculation never made":* John Henry Cardinal Newman, *An Essay on the Development of Christian Doctrine*, 1845.
178 *"He wished to live":* NM to Bourjailys, 11-29-54.
178 *"a certain spirituality":* NM to Gregory, 11-1-54.
178 *cited continental writers:* NM to Mr. Cole, 11-16-54; NM to William Phillips, 11-16-54.
178 *"it meant something":* NM to Louis Mailer, 11-17-54.
178 *Rinehart halted production:* AFM, 229.
179 *"The Mind of an Outlaw": Esquire*, November 1959; rpt., AFM, 228–67, as "The Last Draft of the Deer Park."
179 *"the most accurate account":* MLT, 216.
179 *"cliques, fashions, vogues":* AFM, 233.
179 *Hiram Haydn:* AFM, 230.
179 *"gray and dreary":* Hiram Haydn, *Words & Faces* (NY: Harcourt Brace Jovanovich, 1974), 263.
179 *"a pretty bad book":* Jones to NM, 3-31-56, *To Reach Eternity*, 243.
179 *"I took out sentence after sentence":* NM to Lindner, 12-20-54.
180 *"eager":* Unpublished Alfred Knopf memoir (HRC).
180 *"hard cash":* NM to Knopf, 10-8-55.
180 *"no reason to care":* Alfred Knopf to NM, 10-?-55.
180 *"just sit staring":* AM, *The Last Party*, 214.
180 *"as a stage-struck mother":* AFM, 232.
180 *"The Crack-Up": Esquire*, February, 1936; rpt., *The Crack-Up*, ed. Edmund Wilson (NY: New Directions, 1945). *Time* was perhaps the first to make the connection between the two essays, titling its review of AFM (11-2-59) "The Crack-Up," and attacking NM's "fascination with Hip—that freemasonry of the beard and the weird."
180 *Exaggerated descriptions:* NM to Lindner, 12-20-54; NM to the Bourjailys, 12-28-54.
181 *costly legal effort:* AFM, 232.
181 *"The City of God":* Only a fragment exists in the HRC. NM's setting was a Soviet concentration camp; he changed it to a German camp when he revived the idea in CIF.
181 *"drove a spike":* AFM, 232–33.
181 *"the best novel":* MBM, 157.

181 *savoring his anger:* NM to Lindner, 1-20-55.
181 *"intricate music":* Hitchens, "Interview with Norman Mailer," *New Left Review*, 127.
181 *"I do not know":* AFM, 234.
182 *"As was evident":* "Lipton's Journal," (HRC).
183 *incontestable that two people:* In addition to several reiterations of this idea in "Lipton's Journal," NM refers to it in a 1-20-55 letter to Lindner, saying that his disappointment about Putnam's accepting DP "proves what a saint-psychopath I am at bottom."
187 *"And this is Tolstoi": Phoenix II: Uncollected Writings of D. H. Lawrence*, ed. Warren Roberts and Harry T. Moore (NY: Viking, 1970), 421.
188 *"I never felt pushed":* AM, *The Last Party*, 187.
188 *telephone numbers:* Ibid., 190.
188 *he slapped her:* Ibid., 204.
188 *"nagging voice":* Ibid., 188.
189 *"Rocky Marciano":* Ibid.
189 *"The White Negro":* The essay was reprinted in the first major anthology of Beat writers, *The Beat Generation and the Angry Young Men*, ed. Gene Feldman and Max Gartenberg (NY: Citadel Press, 1958); it was reprinted as a pamphlet in 1959 by Lawrence Ferlinghetti's City Lights Press, where it went through many subsequent printings. NM reprinted it in AFM, 337–71, along with a point-counterpoint follow-up with Malaquais and Beat writer Ned Polsky, which first appeared in *Dissent*, Winter 1958. Since then, it has been reprinted many times in the United States and abroad as a pamphlet and in anthologies.
189 *"Probably, we will never":* AFM, 338–39.
189 *Lyle Stuart:* NM explains the circumstances of Stuart circulating his ideas on "Southern rage" in his prefatory comments to WN, AFM, 331–36.
190 *rotating his crops:* SA, 106.
191 *"You* believe *in that?":* Laura Adams, "Existential Aesthetics: An Interview with Norman Mailer," *PR* 42 (1975); rpt., CNM, 218.
191 *"terrified":* OFM, 468.
192 *corrected galleys was April 15:* NM to Kahnert, 3-7-55.
192 *"He gave me a marvelous":* NM to Elsa Lanchester, 4-15-68.
192 *"Hiroshige and Hokusai":* Utagawa Hiroshige (1797–1858) and Katsushika Hokusai (1760–1849) were acclaimed Japanese woodblock printmakers.
192 *return of the galleys:* NM to Laughton, 3-25-55.
193 *"ripping up the silk":* AFM, 237.
193 *"an implicit portrait":* Ibid., 238.
193 *"Bombed and sapped":* Ibid., 243.
193 *drove up to Provincetown:* NM to the Kesslers, 8-24-55.
194 *"lowered* The Deer Park*":* AFM, 245.
194 *"think of Sex":* DP, 375.
194 *"Truly Bob":* NM to Lindner, 8-25-55.

194 *novel's ending:* AFM, 245.
194 *Writing to Uncle Dave:* NM to Kesslers, 8-24-55.
194 *close to speaking:* See NM's comments on canine intelligence, OG, 140–41.
194 *Laughton had lost interest:* NM to MK, 8-25-55.
194 *1955 financial statement:* HRC.
195 *30 percent share:* Kevin McAuliffe, *The Great American Newspaper: The Rise and Fall of the* Village Voice (NY: Scribner's, 1978), 13–14.
195 *inventing the name:* AFM, 277; McAuliffe, *The Great American Newspaper*, 13.
195 *inscribed copies:* AFM, 265–67.
195 *Brando got a copy:* NM to Brando, 8-25-55.
195 *best wishes to Vidal:* NM to MK, 8-25-55.
195 *"I could not keep myself":* AFM, 265–66.
196 *"was inevitably imitative":* DP, 353.
196 *"If you want to come on":* AFM, 266.
196 *urging of George Plimpton:* See Plimpton's account in his *Shadow Box* (NY: Putnam's, 1977), 259–64, corroborated by Hemingway's letter to Plimpton, 1-17-61, *Ernest Hemingway: Selected Letters, 1917–1961*, ed. Carlos Baker (NY: Scribner's, 1981), 912.
196 *"shitty reviews":* Hemingway to NM, 8-12-59 (HRC); see Hemingway's full letter in *MR* (2010), 15–18.
196 *"ended in fiasco":* AFM, 267.
196 *"usual qualities of vitality":* Moravia to NM, 10-30-55.
197 *MacGregor interview:* Only NM's copy of the typescript has been located; it probably appeared in the *Post* sometime in November 1955.
197 *"with a couple of drinks":* AFM notes (HRC).
197 *climbed to number six:* DP reached number six on November 13 and spent a total of fifteen weeks on the list, falling off on 2-12-56.
197 *"a very personal faith":* Lyle Stuart, "An Intimate Interview with Norman Mailer," *Exposé*, December 1955; rpt., CNM, 24.
197 *"Marxian anarchist":* Ibid., 22–23.
197 *"a really great writer":* Ibid., 27–28.
197 *positive reviews with negative:* Such an ad ran in the *NYTBR*, 10-30-55.
197 *"a thoroughly nasty book":* Orville Prescott, *NYT*, 10-14-55.
197 *Malcolm Cowley:* A friend of Lost Generation writers, Cowley (1898–1989), wrote an important memoir of his expatriate years in Paris, *Exile's Return* (NY: Norton, 1934).
197 *"the serious and reckless novel":* Cowley's endorsement of NM's novel is contained in a 9-23-55 letter to Paul S. Eriksson of Putnam's. He also gave it a positive review in the *New York Herald Tribune Book Review*, 10-23-55.
198 *$10,000 on advertising:* John Tebbel, *Between Covers: The Rise and Transformation of Book Publishing in America* (NY: Oxford, 1987), 398.
198 *half-page ad:* NM reproduces it in AFM, 249.
198 *"that I no longer gave a dog's drop":* AFM, 249.

198 *"Our generation":* Dan Wakefield, *New York in the Fifties* (Boston: Houghton Mifflin, 1992), 121.

198 *"to feel the empty winds":* AFM, 277.

199 *the third person:* Mary Dearborn may have been the first to comment on NM's use of the third person personal in his *VV* columns (MBD 113).

199 *"Drawing upon hash":* Ibid., 278.

200 *appeal to several publics:* JML questions for Edwin Fancher, 10-8-10, conducted by John Buffalo Mailer. For accounts of the *VV* start-up, see McAuliffe, *The Great American Newspaper*, and J. Kirk Sale, "The Village Voice: You've Come a Long Way Baby, but You Got Stuck There," *Evergreen Review*, December 1969, 25–27, 61–67; and Louis Menand, "It Took a Village," *New Yorker*, 1-5-09, 36–45. Also valuable is *The Village Voice Reader*, ed. Daniel Wolf and Edwin Fancher (NY: Doubleday, 1962).

200 *"radical and abrasive":* MBM, 167.

200 *"what with* épater le bourgeois*":* NM to Chester Aaron, 3-23–56.

200 *"I really had the notion":* Notes for AFM, HRC.

200 *The first column:* All quotes from and about "Quickly" and letters from readers are from AFM, 279–318.

202 Must You Conform?: (NY: Rinehart, 1956).

203 *"The psychopath knows instinctively":* AFM, 346.

203 *European and American existentialism:* I draw heavily here on Robert Solotaroff's comprehensive and penetrating examination of NM's existentialism in his study, *Down Mailer's Way* (Urbana: University of Illinois Press, 1975), 82–123.

203 *"had a dialectical mind":* PP, 273.

203 *"alienated beyond alienation":* AFM, 341.

203 *"its enormous teleological sense":* AFM, 38.

204 *"WHY DON'T YOU":* McAuliffe, *The Great American Newspaper,* 30, 34.

204 *"For a socialist":* MBM, 170.

204 *"should be very radical":* MBM, 166.

205 *"I had mad ideas":* Sokolov, "Flying High with Mailer," *Newsweek,* 12-9-68, 87.

205 *"when I have to crack up":* NM to MK, 2-29-56.

205 *trip to Europe:* NM to Malaquais, 4-5-56.

205 *orgasmic struggles:* Originally titled "Sergius and Denise," the composition of "The Time of Her Time" cannot be dated precisely, but it was conceived, if not written, shortly after he resigned from the *VV.*

205 *"on the philosophy of the hipster":* NM to Irving Howe, 5-3-56.

206 Waiting for Godot: Premiered in Paris in January 1953; New York premiere, 4-19-56.

206 *"So I doubt if I will like it":* AFM, 316.

206 *"Baby, you fucked up":* Ibid., 319.

206 *"finally putting together":* Ibid.

206 *"A Public Notice":* *VV*, 5-9-56; rpt., AFM, 320–25.

206 *"in the bends of marijuana":* OFM, 468.
206 *"consciously or unconsciously":* AFM, 324.
206 *"riding the electric rail":* From the first of NM's six bimonthly columns discussing the *Tales*, "Responses and Reactions I," *Commentary*, December 1962, 505.
207 *"hulled":* Buber's preface to 1991 edition, *Tales of the Hasidim*, xxi.
207 zaddikim: Description of Hasidic leaders from Buber's preface and Chaim Potok's foreword.
207 *"The Fear of God":* Zusya's Tale, "Responses and Reactions V," *Commentary*, August 1963, 164.
207 *"for a small intellectual raid": Commentary*, December 1962, 506.
207 *"angry impotence":* AFM, 325.
207 *"the whispers of a new time":* AFM, 324.
208 *relaxed on the crossing:* AM, *The Last Party*, 225.
208 *"Jimmy had an absolutely":* James Campbell, *Talking at the Gates: A Life of James Baldwin* (NY: Viking, 1991), 140.
208 *"Two lean cats":* James Baldwin, "The Black Boy Looks at the White Boy," *Nobody Knows My Name: More Notes of a Native Son* (NY: Dial, 1961), 218.
209 *"to be an American":* Ibid., 217.
209 *"myth of the sexuality":* Ibid., 220–21.
209 *"Norman—confident":* Ibid.
209 *"wandered through Paris":* Ibid., 224.
209 *"A Wandering in Prose":* PP, 309–10.
209 *"still reeling":* AM, *The Last Party*, 228.
210 *"Norman laughed":* Ibid., 229–30.
210 *"never learned to disentangle":* Ibid., 235.
210 *"How I wish":* Ibid.
210 *offering to review:* NM to Francis Brown, 8-16-56.
210 *carbon of his letter:* NM to Baldwin, 8-16-56.
210 *"very sweet thing":* Baldwin to NM, 9-?-56.
210 *"aware of a new and warm":* Baldwin, "The Black Boy Looks at the White Boy," *Nobody Knows My Name*, 220.
211 *"a partner":* Campbell, *Talking at the Gates*, 141.
211 *"The house is old":* NM to JM, 11-22-56.
211 *"hoodlums":* NM to JM, 10-13-56.
212 *working up the nerve:* NM to Baldwin, 10-17-56.
212 *"Phone calls":* NM to JM, 10-13-56.
212 *"in a perpetual stagefright":* MBD, 109.
212 *Satan and his wife:* NM to Chester Aaron, 3-23-56.
212 *"inhuman city":* NM to JM, 10-13-56.
212 *"writing a fucking column":* Jones to NM, 3-31-56.
213 *"Dear Jim":* NM to Jones, summer 1956.
213 *second, toned-down draft:* Jones told NM this in his 3-31-56 letter.
213 *note to Styron:* NM to Styron, 11-8-56.
213 *"boiling mad":* MLT, 236–37.

213 *"because he permitted":* Gay Talese, *A Writer's Life* (NY: Random House, 2006), 175.
214 *"Anything that dealt openly":* Wakefield, *New York in the Fifties*, 147.
214 *orgone box:* NM's plywood carpeted box, about the size of a small phone booth, was a fixture in all of his New York studios until a few years before his death. He junked it when he gave up his last studio in the DUMBO area of Brooklyn in the early 2000s.
214 *"scream and snort":* NM to MK, 2-29-56.
214 *polished wooden egg:* MBM, 190.
214 *curl up, and be rocked:* AM, *The Last Party*, 261.
214 *bongo board:* MBM, 180.
214 *"Norman was ready":* MBM, 181.
214 *turned to handball:* Bill Gallo, www.handballcity.com/boxersplay.htm.
215 *"Hiya champ":* AM, *The Last Party*, 265.
215 *"Norman sat up":* Ibid., 267.
215 *"all-purpose expression":* Marie Brenner, "Mailer Goes Egyptian," *New York*, 31.
215 *"I started as a generous":* AFM, 22.
216 *"You're not a publisher":* MBM, 181.
216 *"Violence and pain":* Ibid., 180.
216 *one of the first novels about hipsters: Who Walks in Darkness* (NY: New Directions, 1952).
216 *"beginning to see himself":* NM to Dachine Rainier, 12-11-56.
217 *"She looked splendid":* PAP, 28–29.
217 *"in the elevator":* Ibid., 30–31. See also *Mike Wallace Asks: Highlights from 46 Controversial Interviews* (NY: Simon & Schuster, 1958), 26–27, and NM's account of his *Night Beat* appearance in AFM, 406–10.
218 *Leslie, according to Danielle:* JML interview with Danielle Mailer, 8-3-11.
218 *Mailer made a fuss:* AM, *The Last Party*, 250–51.
218 *"a fantastic experience":* NM to MK, 3-27-57.
218 *"Norman always loomed":* Phyllis Silverman Ott-Toltz, with Barbara Bamberger Scott, *Love Bade Me Welcome: The Life of Phyllis Ott* (Lake Forest, CA: Behler, 2006), 39–40.
218 *"what I thought would be a new life":* AM, *The Last Party*, 251.
218 *"he smashes the living shit":* NM to MK, 3-27-57.
219 *beginning of April:* NM to Howe, 4-29-57.
219 *"Each moment fills":* Joseph Wenke, *Mailer's America* (Hanover, NH: University Press of New England, 1987), 81.
220 *"too elliptic":* NM to Bourjaily, 2-25-58.
220 *"rarely bothers to distinguish":* Morris Dickstein, *Leopards in the Temple: The Transformation of American Fiction, 1945–70* (Cambridge: Harvard University Press, 2002), 151.
220 *"a changing reality":* AFM, 354.
220 *"God is energy":* Ibid., 351.
220 *"ready to go":* Ibid., 350.
220 *"downright impenetrable":* Baldwin, *Nobody Knows My Name*, 229.

220 *City Lights edition:* Francis Ferlinghetti's City Lights Press, which published Allen Ginsberg's *Howl* in 1956, published the first printing (1,500 copies) of WN in the late spring of 1959. It carried no publication date, and is usually and erroneously dated 1957. At least five printings followed over the next dozen years.

220 *rumored at the time to be Paul Newman:* The photo was of photojournalist Harry Redl. See Sarah Bishop, "The Life and Death of the Celebrity Author in Maidstone," *MR* (2012), 288–308.

221 *"is an attempt to impose":* Alfred Kazin, *Contemporaries* (Boston: Little, Brown, 1962), 364.

221 *"two strong eighteen-year-old hoodlums":* AFM, 347.

221 *"If one wants a better world":* Ibid., 357.

221 *"a momentous shift":* Dickstein, *Leopards in the Temple*, 151.

222 *"a kindergarten":* AM, *The Last Party*, 254.

222 *"swapping stories":* Ibid., 254.

222 *"an air of smug":* Ibid., 238.

222 *"were intense and stimulating":* James L. W. West III, *William Styron: A Life* (NY: Random House, 1998), 286–87.

223 *"was originally king":* MLT, 243.

223 *"going on and on":* AM, *The Last Party*, 259.

223 *Howe was excited:* MBM, 186–87.

223 *Beats had their reservations:* MLT, 258.

223 *"acceptable":* MLT, 256.

223 *"a good illustration of a swiftly":* Jones to NM, 3-18-58, in *To Reach Eternity*, 260.

223 *"like coughing up blood":* West, *William Styron*, 288.

224 *"fascinated by it nonetheless":* Ibid.

224 *race-gender-power debates:* See, for example, Andrew Hoberek, "Liberal Antiliberalism: Mailer, O'Connor, and the Gender Politics of Middle-Class *Ressentiment*"; and Frederick Whiting, "Stronger, Smarter and Less Queer: 'The White Negro' and Mailer's Third Man," both in *Women's Studies Quarterly* 33, Fall/Winter 2005.

224 *"a new way to think":* NM to MK, 8-8-57.

224 *"emboldened":* MLT, 254.

224 *"my writing about sex":* NM to Chandler Brossard, 5-18-57.

224 *"one of the four or five":* NM to MK, 8-8-57.

224 *"it's better than Death":* NM to Bea, 8-8-57.

224 *"so bold":* NM to JM, 8-8-57.

225 *"dream cast":* NM to Monica McCall, 8-8-57.

225 *product of O'Shaugnessy's memory: The Deer Park: A Play* (NY: Dial, 1967), 33.

225 *"a rather incredible hell":* NM to MK, 10-23-57.

225 *showing the play:* Louis Calta, "Mailer Finishes First Stage Work," *NYT*, 12-5-57.

225 *"the mysteries of murder":* AFM, 107.

225 *"a bad play":* NM to JM, 12-30-57.

225 *"side work":* NM to MK, 9-25-57.
225 *"with a medium gruesome":* NM to JM, 12-30-57.
225 *"this enormous novel":* Ibid.
225 Intimate Journals: Charles Baudelaire (1821–67) wrote most of the entries toward the end of his life. Christopher Isherwood translated it from the French (London: Blackamore, 1930).
225 *"Now there's a man":* NM to JM, 12-30-57.
225 *"If I had twice":* Ibid.
226 *Meyer Schapiro:* A Columbia professor and renowned art historian, Schapiro (1904–96) was admired by NM for the breadth of his learning.
226 *"An artist exists":* quoted in "The Invincibles," *TLS*, 5-5-13, 20.
226 *Actors Studio:* MK, *The Good, the Bad, and the Dolce Vita*, 178; AM, *The Last Party*, 252–54.
226 *Frank Corsaro, staged some readings:* MLT, 249–52.
226 *recast several of his novels:* Dramatic and/or film versions of the following were attempted/completed by NM or others: NAD, BS, DP, AAD, WVN, ES, AE, TGD, as well as short stories "The Greatest Thing in the World" and "The Time of Her Time."
226 *"Norman's anger":* AM, *The Last Party*, 262.
227 *"I handled it":* Ibid., 269.
227 *Believe it or not:* Ibid., 272.
227 *"The Know-Nothing Barbarians":* First published in *Partisan Review*, Spring 1959; rpt., *Doings and Undoings* (NY: Farrar, Straus, 1964), 143–58.
227 *"sheer intellectual":* Norman Podhoretz, *Ex-Friends* (NY: Free Press, 1999), 186–89.
227 *"suggest a major novelist":* "Norman Mailer: The Embattled Vision," *PR*, Summer 1959; rpt., *Doings and Undoings*, 179.
228 *"And how about you":* Diana Trilling, *The Beginning of the Journey: The Marriage of Diana and Lionel Trilling* (NY: Harcourt, Brace, 1993), 353.
228 *highbrow, popular, and Beat:* For a comprehensive, annotated record of NM's periodical appearances and interviews, as well as a life chronology and secondary bibliography, see JML and Donna Pedro Lennon, *Norman Mailer: Works and Days*, preface by NM (Shavertown, PA: Sligo, 2000).
229 *"conspicuous success":* Charles A. Fenton, "The Writers Who Came Out of the War," *Saturday Review*, 8-3-57, 6.
229 *"the promising talent":* Edmund Fuller, "The New Compassion in the American Novel," *American Scholar*, Spring 1957, 162.
229 *"I value Mailer":* Dwight Macdonald, "The Bright Young Men of the Arts," *Esquire*, September 1958, 39.
229 *"Lousy people":* NM to Chester Aaron, 2-11-58.
229 *"Styron's Style":* HRC.
229 *"would laugh along":* CAC, 109–10.
230 *"Bill, I've been told":* NM to Styron, 3-12-58.
231 *"astonished":* West, *William Styron*, 294.
231 *"Bill was scared":* MBM, 192.
231 *"warped and perverted":* West, *William Styron*, 294.

231 *"profoundly upsetting"*: LNM, 116.
232 *"probably bragged"*: AM, *The Last Party*, 261.
232 The Pistol: NY: Scribner's 1958.
232 *"contains a perfect"*: NM to Jones, 2-25-58.
232 *"emotional sword-twirling"*: Jones to NM, 3-18-58, in *To Reach Eternity*, 260.
233 *"Norman: Your letter was*: Styron to NM, 3-17-58, in *Selected Letters*, 250.
233 *"Parasites"*: NM to Jones, 3-20-58.
234 *"I just got back"*: NM to Styron, 3-27-58.
235 *"beautifully written and intellectually alive"*: NM to Baldwin, 3-20-58.
235 *"Writing ties me into knots"*: NM to MK, 3-20-58.
235 *fragment about Faye being raped*: HRC.
235 *"on the edge"*: NM to Philip Rahv, 2-27-58.
235 *"need to be shocked"*: Rahv to NM, 3-4-58.
235 *"damn-the-torpedoes"*: NM to Rahv, 3-20-58.
235 *Rahv selected "Way Out"*: "Advertisements for Myself on the Way Out," *PR*, Fall 1958; rpt., AFM, 512–32.
235 *"awkward," "muddled," "cloying"*: See, respectively, Jennifer Bailey, *Norman Mailer: Quick-Change Artist* (London: Macmillan, 1979), 69; Wenke, *Mailer's America*, 230; Solotaroff, *Down Mailer's Way*, 87.
235 *"my name eludes me"*: AFM, 512.
235 *"ghost,* geist, *demiurge"*: Ibid., 520.
236 *"yes, God is like me"*: Ibid., 532.
236 *"climactic party"*: Ibid., 515.
236 *"in the history of our republic"*: Ibid., 530.
236 *"Brave murder"*: Ibid., 526.
237 *"between the stirrup and the ground"*: Ibid., 532.
237 *University of Chicago*: Morton D. Zabel invited NM to Chicago, 2-11-58.
237 *Richard G. Stern*: Novelist and longtime professor at University of Chicago, Stern (1928–2013) corresponded with NM over the next decade and wrote about him in his collection, *One Person and Another: On Writers and Writing* (Dallas: Baskerville, 1993).
237 *"enjoyed the sheer"*: NM to MK, 6-18-58.
237 *"series of questions"*: NM to Zabel, 2-11-58.
237 *thanked Stern*: NM to Stern, 6-6-58.
237 *Paul Carroll*: A Chicago poet and teacher, Carroll (1927–96) was the editor of the Beat magazine *Big Table*, where NM would publish an excerpt from AFM.
237 *"the only big city"*: NM to George Lea, 10-29-58.
238 *"rushing into a confession"*: AFM, 376.
238 *"Hip, Hell, and the Navigator"*: It first appeared in *Western Review* 23, Winter 1958; rpt., AFM, 376–86.
238 *"a pitch of excited engagement"*: AFM, 378.
238 *"anti-expressionism"*: Ibid., 379.
238 *"a fantastic assertion"*: Ibid., 380.

238 *"Stern: This is really something":* Ibid., 381.
239 *"consciously makes decisions":* Ibid., 386.
239 *"has an enormous teleological sense":* See NM's oblique answer to a question about the fallibility of the unconscious, JML, "Writers and Boxers, PAP, 158–59.
239 "Partisan *is the most important":* NM to FM, 7-9-58.
239 *"much discussed":* NM to EY, 6-18-58.
239 On the Road: (NY: Viking, 1957). The novel spent five weeks on the bestseller list; sales of later printings have been huge.
239 *major publications, and* Life: The Luce publications ran several negative articles on the Beats; the most disapproving was by Paul O'Neil, "The Only Rebellion Around: But the Shabby Beats Bungle the Job in Arguing, Sulking and Bad Poetry," 11-30-59. See also John Clellon Holmes, "The Philosophy of the Beat Generation," *Esquire*, February 1958; and Jack Kerouac, "Origins of the Beat Generation," *Playboy*, June 1959. Ann Charters is the leading scholar of the movement. She wrote *Kerouac: A Biography* (San Francisco: Straight Arrow, 1973), and edited the most important anthology, *The Portable Beat Reader* (NY: Viking Penguin, 1992), which has an extensive bibliography. Bill Morgan is to Ginsberg what Charters is to Kerouac; see his *I Celebrate Myself: The Somewhat Private Life of Allen Ginsberg* (NY: Viking, 2006).
239 *"the most venturesome intellect":* John Clellon Holmes, *Passionate Opinions: The Cultural Essays* (Fayetteville: University of Arkansas Press, 1988), 86–87.
239 Notes from the Underground: Dostoyevsky's 1864 novel of anger and irrationality is ultimately a celebration of free will and is often called the first existential novel.
240 *associate member of The Family:* As noted by Bruce Cook in *The Beat Generation* (NY: Scribner's, 1971), 17. His study contains important interviews with NM and the major Beat figures.
240 *dismissal of the Beats:* Standing shoulder to shoulder with Podhoretz's "The Know-Nothing Bohemians" is Diana Trilling's "The Other Night at Columbia," *Claremont Essays*, 153–73.
240 *"solitary Bartlebies":* Charters, ed. *Portable Beat Reader*, xviii.
240 *"ecstatic flux":* AFM, 466.
240 *"Beat still has no center":* "Ten Words from the Dean," *Wagner Literary Magazine*, Spring 1959, 26–27.
240 *"All that green": The Diaries of Dawn Powell, 1931–1965* (South Royalton, VT: Steerforth, 1995), 387.
240 *film version of* Naked: Produced by Paul Gregory for RKO, directed by Raoul Walsh, and distributed by Warner Brothers, the film was shot in Panama. It premiered in New York on 8-6-58. Raymond Massey played General Cummings and Cliff Robertson was Lieutenant Hearn. It cost $1 million to make and earned a profit, although the reviews were middling to poor.

240 *"the disembowelling naked greed":* Untitled eleven-page response to the film (HRC).
240 *"the worst movie":* "Norman Mailer," interview with Joseph Gelmis, *The Film Director as Superstar* (Garden City, NY: Doubleday, 1970), rpt., CNM, 172.
241 *"Nor could the novelist":* NM, *Marilyn: A Biography* (NY: Grosset & Dunlap, 1973), 19–20.
241 *"The bastard":* AM, *The Last Party*, 246.
241 *"might make good company":* Miller, *Timebends*, 532–33.
241 *"too impressed by power":* W. J. Weatherby, *Squaring Off, Mailer vs. Baldwin* (NY: Mason/Charter, 1977), 125.
242 *"terrible tragedy":* Bragg, CNM, 203.
242 *Ginsberg-Mailer-Kerouac meeting:* MLT, 256–62.
242 *"more than I would have thought":* AFM, 466.
242 *"In Buddhist terms":* MLT, 257.
242 tikkun olam: I owe this insight to Mashey Bernstein.
242 *"a sense of brotherhood":* MLT, 260.
242 *"the most intelligent":* Ibid.
242 *Mailer saw Kerouac:* AM, *The Last Party*, 286.
242 *"influence the history":* Stuart, CNM, 20.
243 *"the artist should be": Selected Letters: Gustave Flaubert*, ed. Geoffrey Wall (NY: Penguin, 1998), 217.
243 *"much better when people":* Ross, CNM, 13.
243 *"a little desperate":* NM to George Lea, 10-29-58.
243 *"shit work":* Ibid.
243 *"detested":* NM to William Phillips, 11-15-58.
243 *a provisional plan:* NM to Walter Minton, 12-9-58.
244 *"to jiggle his Self":* AFM, 17–18.
244 *"five or ten years":* NM to EY, 1-7-59.
244 *"my half-vanished techniques":* NM to MK, 1-8-59.
244 *"important theological document":* NM to Stern, 2-18-59.
244 *"intensely curious":* PAP, 37.
244 *"in a dry little voice":* Ibid.
244 *"When it comes to personality":* NM, "The Capote Perplex," *Rolling Stone*, 7-19-73, 8.
244 *"a hint bewildered":* PAP, 39.
245 *"Oh, man, did Truman":* Ibid., 40.
245 *"young-old face":* Ibid., 41.
245 *"Nothing like it":* NM, "The Capote Perplex," 8.
245 *"entirely new":* Janet Winn, "Capote, Mailer and Miss Parker," *New Republic*, 2-9-59, 27–28.
245 *"None of these people":* Ibid., 27.
245 *"two-thirds for Jack's virtues":* PAP, 38.
245 *"demolished Mr. Mailer's":* Janet Winn, "Capote, Mailer and Miss Parker," 28.

246 *"out of the way":* NM to George Lea, 2-19-59.
246 *"to make the scene":* Ibid.
246 *"a thoroughgoing autobiography":* AFM, 10.
246 *"the only writer of my generation":* AFM drafts (HRC).
247 *"assassin to myself":* NM to Richard G. Stern, 3-31-59.
247 *"Evaluation: Quick and Expensive Comments on the Talent in the Room":* AFM, 463–73.
247 *"know about the intense":* Doug Ford, "How Yeats Did It," *NYRB*, 4-3-08.
247 *"The confession is over":* AFM, 336.
248 *"at its worst it was a travelogue":* Ibid., 466–67.
249 *"Of all the writers":* Ibid., 467.
249 *"is everyone's favorite":* Ibid.
249 *"the first figure":* Ibid., 465–66.
249 *"Truman Capote I do not know well":* Ibid., 465.
249 *"is essentially a hateful":* Ibid., 471.
249 *"The early work of Mary McCarthy":* Ibid., 472.
249 *"I happened to grow up":* Zoë Heller, "Yes, I Misbehaved Sometimes," *Daily Telegraph*, 3-3-03, 19.
250 *bitterly* intoned: See Francine Prose, "Scent of a Woman's Ink: Are Women Writers Really Inferior," *Harper's*, June 1998, 61–70; Joanna Scott, "Male Writers vs. Female Writers: Beyond the Preconceptions," www.salon.com/media/1998/07/03media.html; Dasee Starr, "Norman Mailer," www.daseestarr.blogstop.com/2010/01/look-up-words-you-don't-know.html.
250 *"ridden with faults":* AFM, 463–64.
250 *"the prettiest novel":* Ibid., 464–65.
250 *"sense of moral nuance":* Ibid., 471–72.
251 *"more arresting":* Ibid., 472.
251 *200,000 words:* NM to EY, 4-25-59.
251 *"The Mind of an Outlaw" appeared in* Esquire*:* Harold Hayes accepted all of NM's conditions for publication in the November 1959 issue. The two most important were that no changes could be made to the text, and his name and the title would appear above any other that appeared on the cover—"top billing," as Cy Rembar put it in a letter (7-1-59) to Hayes. From the start, NM's relations with *Esquire* editors were contentious and legalistic.
251 *"Buddies": VV*, 9-16-59; rpt., AFM, 412–21.
251 *"Quick and Expensive": Big Table* 3, Autumn/Winter 1959; rpt., AFM, 463–73.
251 *two scenes:* "Scenes from 'The Deer Park,' " *PR*, Fall 1959; rpt., AFM, 442–60.
251 *"overground":* Hilary Mills's interview with Harold Hayes, 1982 (HRC).
251 *"an indifferent caretaker":* AFM, 477.
252 *"I remember I received":* Andrew O'Hagan, "Norman Mailer: The Art of Fiction," *Paris Review Interviews III* (NY: Picador, 2008), 432–33. The actual inscription reads: "To my most feared friend, to my most beloved enemy. Jim."

252 *letters to thirteen literary critics:* The letter to Macdonald is dated 5-5-59; the rest are dated 5-11-59.
252 *supportive reviews:* F. W. Dupee, "The American Norman Mailer," *Commentary*, February 1960; Leslie Fiedler, "Antic Mailer—Portrait of a Middle-Aged Artist," *New Leader*, 6-25-60; Irving Howe, "A Quest for Peril," *PR*, Winter 1960; Alfred Kazin, "How Good Is Norman Mailer?," *Reporter*, 11-26-59.
252 *"the avenger":* AFM, 488.
253 *"proud, aggressive":* Ibid., 494.
253 *"Sergius is the hipster":* Andrew Gordon, *An American Dreamer: A Psychoanalytic Study of the Fiction of Norman Mailer* (Rutherford, NJ: Fairleigh Dickinson University Press, 1980), 113–28.
253 *"You dirty little Jew":* AFM, 502.
253 *"whole life is a lie":* Ibid.
253 *"literary seriousness":* Alfred Kazin to NM, 5-21-59.
253 *"the single most unattractive":* NM to Kazin, 5-26-59.
254 *"a fantastically courageous book":* Diana Trilling to NM, 9-2-59.
254 *"is a bit obsessed with Hemingway":* NM to Diana Trilling, 9-23-59.
255 *"A man is nothing":* NM to Lois Wilson, 5-4-59.
255 *wrote to a New York hotel:* NM to Hotel Taft, 5-29-59.
255 *"once in a while I think":* NM to Wilson, 6-26-59.
255 *"was very much a Mailer":* NM to Dave Kessler, 10-5-59.
256 *"Dear Lady (with the light)":* NM to Lois Wilson, 11-6-59.
256 *notably strong reviews:* See earlier list of supportive reviews and Harry T. Moore, "The Targets Are Square," *NYTBR*, 11-1-58; Kenneth Tynan, untitled review of AFM, *VV*, 11-18-59; "The Crack-Up," *Time*, 11-2-59.
257 *The insight Mailer remembered:* In 1964, NM quoted Kazin's "very funny" remark, and said the tendency he noted came from trying to compensate for "a certain flatness" in his style (Marcus, CNM, 89).
257 *"was forged":* Preface, *Advertisements for Myself* (NY: Berkley, 1976), v–vii.
258 *"a fun evening":* MK, *The Good, the Bad, and the Dolce Vita*, 143.
258 *"in a kind of drunken":* Baldwin, "The Black Boy Looks at the White Boy," *Nobody Knows My Name*, 234.
258 *"a surrogate for Norman":* MBM, 201.
258 *"Styron wrote the prettiest":* MK, *The Good, the Bad, and the Dolce Vita*, 144.
258 *"started twitching":* MBM, 201.
258 *"kept a copy":* Ibid.
258 *"First Mailer came out":* Ibid., 202.
258 *"Well, if this was going":* Baldwin, "The Black Boy Looks at the White Boy," 236.
259 *"I think I–probably":* MBM, 203.
259 *"because it dramatizes":* John Aldridge to NM, 11-15-59.
259 *"the particular lucidity":* NM to John Aldridge, 12-1-59.

259 *persistent detractors:* See Aldridge's essay "William Styron and the Derivative Imagination," *Time to Murder and Create: The Contemporary Novel in Crisis* (NY: McKay, 1966), 30–51.
259 *"You call him":* Plimpton, *Shadow Box*, 260.
260 *"We're pretending":* Ibid., 263.
260 *"both scared and excited":* Ibid., 264.
260 *"because I've been talking":* NM to Lucid, 12-29-59.
260 *writing blurbs:* NM wrote approximately 150 blurbs over the course of his life. See Matthew Hinton, "Advertisements for Others: The Blurbs of Norman Mailer," *MR* (2010), 452–61.
260 *"entirely possible":* Alfred Kazin, "The Jew as Modern American Writer," Introduction, *The Commentary Reader*, ed. Norman Podhoretz (NY: Atheneum, 1966), xxiv.

SEVEN: A FELONIOUS ASSAULT AND *AN AMERICAN DREAM*

In addition to sources noted below, the following were drawn on: "Fan's Memoir"; JML's "Mailer Log"; JML's unpublished interviews with NM and BW. NM's letters are located at the HRC.

Page

261 *"Superman Comes to the Supermarket": Esquire*, November 1960; rpt., PP, 25–57. *Esquire* publisher Arnold Gingrich changed the last word of the essay's title to "Supermart," angering Mailer. The original was restored when it was reprinted in PP.
261 *Gore Vidal's review:* "The Norman Mailer Syndrome," *Nation*, 1-2-60; rpt., Vidal, *United States: Essays, 1952–1992*, 31–40.
261 *"honorable":* Ibid., 40.
261 *"Great Golfer":* Ibid., 31.
261 *"a Bolingbroke":* Ibid., 39.
261 *"create not arguments":* Ibid., 38.
261 *"a born cocktail-party":* Ibid., 34.
262 *"a swelling, throbbing":* Ibid., 36.
262 *"the American president":* Ibid., 39.
262 *"His drive seems":* Ibid., 35.
262 *"very dangerous":* Ibid., 34.
262 *some mild rejoinders:* NM, "The Shiny Enemies," letter to the editor, *Nation*, 1-30-60, 2.
262 *"I think he was having":* AM, *The Last Party*, 282.
262 *garnet crucifix:* Ibid., 285.
263 *"since I came on":* Ibid., 293.
263 *"steadily digging the grave":* Ibid., 294.
263 *"Norman glared at me":* Ibid.
263 *"lead in the direction":* NM to Yamanishi, 3-13-60.
263 *full-page advertisement:* "What is Really Happening in Cuba?," *NYT*, 4-6-60, L33.
264 *"the first and greatest":* PP, 67–68.

264 *met in Cuba:* NM and NCM visited Cuba in 1989 and had a private meeting with Castro.
264 *"An Open Letter to Fidel Castro":* Mailer added a letter to Kennedy, and changed the title to "An Open Letter to JFK and Fidel Castro" when it was published in the *VV*, 4-27-61; rpt., PP, 63–79.
264 *"Back in December":* PP, 67.
264 *"I met him once":* Notes for AON (HRC).
265 *"very astute":* MBM, 207.
265 *"exploding all ever":* Ibid., 20.
265 *"I had read his pronouncement":* Ibid., 208.
265 *senators, were actively challenging:* See early chapters of Robert Caro's *Lyndon Johnson: The Passage of Power* (NY: Knopf, 2012).
265 *"a well-to-do":* Oriana Fallaci, *The Egoists: Sixteen Surprising Interviews* (Chicago: Regnery, 1968), 1–18.
266 *"characteristic quality":* PP, 48.
266 *essay on Picasso:* "An Eye on Picasso," *Provincetown Annual*, August 1960; rpt., AFM, 461–62, and *Beat Coast East: An Anthology of Rebellion*, ed. Stanley Fisher (NY: Excelsior, 1960).
266 *Seymour Krim:* An important essayist and editor, Krim (1922–1989) is often linked with the beat movement. NM wrote the foreword to his first collection, *Views of a Nearsighted Cannoneer* (NY: Excelsior, 1961).
266 *summers of the early 1960s:* AM, *The Last Party*, 307–20; MLT, 290–99; Tim McCarthy, "Mailer Gets Moral," *Life in Provincetown*, 8-14-03, 10; Joseph P. Kahn, "Our Town," *Boston Globe Magazine.*
266 *"wild, absolutely wild":* Tim McCarthy, "Mailer Gets Moral," *Life in Provincetown.*
266 *"At least ten times":* Joseph Kahn, "Our Town," *Boston Globe Magazine.*
267 *Roger Donoghue:* Douglas Martin, "Roger Donoghue, 75, Boxer and Brando's 'Waterfront' Trainer, Dies," *NYT*, 8-25-06, C10.
267 *"I sometimes thought":* AM, *The Last Party*, 314.
267 *"I've always loved the Irish":* Vincent Canby, "When Irish Eyes Are Smiling, It's Norman Mailer," *NYT*, 10-27-68; rpt., CNM, 139–44.
267 *"a drinker with writing problems":* Gerry Coughlan and Martin Hughes, *Irish Language and Culture* (Australia: Lonely Planet, 2007), 116.
267 *"blessed":* AON, 47.
267 *arriving at the apartment with Behan:* JML interview with Susan Mailer, 9-5-07.
267 *"taxi, taxi":* Dwight Macdonald wrote the best account: "Massachusetts vs. Mailer," *Discriminations: Essays & Afterthoughts*, introduction by NM (Cambridge, MA: Da Capo, 1985), 194–209.
267 *"I was afraid":* "A Letter from Provincetown," *New York Post Magazine*, 7-3-60, 5.
268 *"The only political writing":* MBM, 209.
268 *"The Democrats fascinated him":* Ibid., 208.
268 *"I know how":* Ibid., 209.
268 *"the day I saw":* Ibid.

268 *"I had an epiphany":* MLT, 305.
268 *"prefabricated politics":* Transcript of *Mailer's America* (French documentary, 1998), 9-29-09, Tape 4, 4.
268 *"deliberate political intention":* Auchincloss and Lynch, CNM, 50.
269 *"It was much better":* MBM, 209.
269 *"Sweating like a goat":* PP, 84–85.
269 *Accompanied by Gore Vidal:* Vidal, *Palimpsest*, 374–78.
270 *"altogether meaningful":* PP, 46–47.
270 *"at that time in his life":* MBM, 210–11.
270 *"After I saw the Kennedys":* PP, 87.
270 *"When it came out":* MBM, 213.
270 *"It made an enormous":* Ibid.
270 *"set the tone":* Ibid.
270 *"a vague memory":* MLT, 303.
270 *"I never dreamed":* Jacqueline Kennedy to NM, 10-24-60.
271 *"The Kennedy cortege":* PP, 37–38.
272 *"Sergius O'Shaugnessy born rich":* PP, 44.
272 *a great many Irish:* Sean Abbott, "Mailer Goes to the Mountain," *At Random*, Spring/Summer 1997, 50.
272 *"Since the First World War":* PP, 38.
272 *"The night Kennedy":* Ibid., 60–61.
273 *"cool conclusion":* Ibid., 88–89.
273 *"sober, the apotheosis":* Ibid., 59.
273 *"I hate you":* NM to Capote, 8-11-60.
273 *Harold L. "Doc" Humes:* Harold L. Humes Wikipedia entry.
273 The Underground City: (NY: Random House, 1958).
273 *Citizens' Emergency Committee:* MLT, 306–8.
273 *Richard "Lord" Buckley:* Lord Buckley Wikipedia entry.
274 *"one of the few people":* NM, quoted in *Doc* (2008), an Independent Lens documentary about Humes, made by his daughter, Immy Humes.
274 *made him fantasize:* PP, 87.
274 *"I wanted to be an advisor":* Transcript, (French documentary) *Mailer's America*, 9-29-99, Tape 4, 5.
274 *"some drinks and dinner":* Joseph Roddy, "The Latest Model Mailer," *Look*, 5-27-69; rpt., CNM, 148.
274 *"was grim-faced":* MBM, 219.
274 *"this insane, cruel, rapacious":* NM, foreword, Seymour Krim, *Views of a Nearsighted Cannoneer*, 6.
274 *"I think he even described":* MLT, 309.
275 *instructed Rembar:* NM to Rembar, 10-18-60.
275 *"You print nice stuff":* NM, "A Farewell to His Honor," *Esquire*, January 1961, 15.
275 *flurry of letters:* NM to Allen, 10-28-60; NM to Kempton, 10-26-60; NM to Krim, 10-26-60; NM to Edd, 10-28-60.
275 *"it is necessary":* NM to Walter Kahnert, 10-28-60.
275 "Naked Lunch *is a book":* NM to Ginsberg, 10-28-60.

276 *"tragic":* NM to Arthur Schlesinger Jr., 10-28-60.

276 *"Kennedy's Wagnerian vision":* NM to John L. Saltonstall Jr., 10-28-60.

276 *In undated letters:* The letters to Brosnan, Cheever, Spender, and Eliot can be dated contextually to the beginning of November 1960.

276 *Jim Brosnan:* A major league pitcher from 1954 to 1963, Brosnan (b. 1929), wrote several baseball memoirs, the most important being *The Long Season* (NY: Harper's, 1960).

276 *John Cheever:* One of the greatest American short story writers, Cheever (1912–82) also wrote several major novels, including *The Wapshot Chronicle* (1958), which won the National Book Award. "The Death of Justina" was collected in *The Stories of John Cheever* (NY: Knopf, 1978). NM did not meet him until 1963.

276 *Stephen Spender:* British poet, essayist, and editor, Spender (1909–95), was literary editor of *Encounter* from 1953 to 1966.

276 *T. S. Eliot:* NM never met Eliot (1888–1965), who was at the pinnacle of his international fame in the 1960s, but was familiar with his poetry.

277 *"There's a man":* NM to Jacqueline Kennedy, 11-3-60.

277 *"a fair climax":* PP, 87–88.

277 *"smashed the limits":* Ibid., 88.

278 *Mailer called a meeting:* "MINUTES OF MEETING WITH 'DISSENT' PEOPLE, 11/5/60, ON RUNNING MAILER FOR MAYOR ON A NEW PARTY IN NEW YORK." The note taker of this five-page typed document is not identified (HRC).

278 *"What's the matter":* AM, *The Last Party*, 340–41.

278 *"I thought I was unique":* Irma Kurtz, "Mailer: I've Always Been an Apostle of Freedom," *Nova Magazine* (March 1969), 107.

278 *arrested at Birdland:* "Norman Mailer in Tiff," *NYT*, 11-15-60.

279 *"terribly philosophical":* Auchincloss and Lynch, CNM, 43.

279 *occasional toke:* Ibid., 47.

279 *"I think he's going to last":* Ibid., 49.

279 *rough diary:* "Sequence from Tuesday—2 days before Providence," NM's seventeen-page typed account based on handwritten notes taken during the period (HRC).

279 *Noel Parmentel Jr.:* Parmentel (b. 1927) was a clever satirist who wrote for both the left-wing *Nation* and the right-wing *National Review.* His books include *Folk Songs for Conservatives*, with Marshall J. Dodge III (NY: Unicorn, 1964). NM remained friendly with him through the 1960s.

279 *reading at Brown:* Richard Holbrooke (1941–2010), later President Obama's special envoy to Afghanistan and Pakistan, wrote "Mailer Directs Group Tour of Mailer World," *Brown Daily Herald*, 11-18-60, 1, 4. Ellen Shaffer wrote a story on NM's visit for the *Brown Daily*, and sent a copy to Norman Podhoretz, who passed it on to NM. Her published article has not been located.

279 *"I thought I had God's message":* "PPA Press Conference," *Publishers Weekly*, 3-22-65, 44.

280 *the party, stabbing, and Bellevue:* The following were drawn on: PP,

63–64; TOT, 384–85; MG, 257–63; NM, "Sequence from Tuesday"; JML's "Mailer Log"; JML interviews with NM, BW, MK, Jason Epstein, Robert Silvers, Susan Mailer, Danielle Mailer, Betsy Mailer, and Anna Lou Humes; AM, *The Last Party*, 348–63; MK, *The Good, the Bad, and the Dolce Vita*, 178–81; Podhoretz, *Ex-Friends*, 200–203; LNM, 135–44; MBM, 215–32, MLT, 310–35; Brock Brower, *Other Loyalties*, 110–13, 128–29; James Atlas, "Life with Mailer," *NYTM*; Benjamin DeMott, "Docket No. 15883," *American Scholar* 30, Spring 1961, 232–37; "Of Time and the Rebel," *Time*, 12-5-60, 16–17; brief articles in *NYT, New York Post, New York Herald Tribune*, New York *Daily News*, AP, and UPI, and summaries of many of the newspaper stories in NM's FBI file (HRC).

280 *"he was truly":* MLT, 311–12.

281 *"was in a strange zone":* MK, *The Good, the Bad, and the Dolce Vita,* 179.

281 *"It was a spooky evening":* MBM, 221.

281 *"To my eternal shame":* MLT, 314.

281 *"I don't know anything":* MBM., 221–22.

281 *"There was a lot of bad":* Ibid., 222.

282 *"It has been quite apparent":* "The Lyons Den," *New York Post*, 11-23-60, 27.

282 *"I wish you'd hit me":* Brock Brower, *Other Loyalties*, 110.

282 "Aja toro, aja": AM, *The Last Party*, 349.

283 *Evelyn Waugh:* Mark Amory, the editor of *The Letters of Evelyn Waugh* (London: Hodder & Stoughton, 1980), wrote to NM in August 1978 to check on the veracity of Waugh's claim that NM had tried to cut his wife's throat.

283 *George Plimpton:* Plimpton told Peter Manso that NM used a kitchen knife (MLT, 313).

283 *alleged that scissors:* Oliver Burkeman, in his profile of NM (*Guardian*, 2-5-02), stated that NM used scissors.

283 *claimed Mailer had shot her:* The anonymous writer of "Norman Conquest: Norman Mailer Takes on Picasso" (*St. Paul Pioneer Press*, 11-4-95) states that NM shot Adele.

283 *"always a take-charge guy":* JML interview with Anna Lou Humes Aldrich, 12-17-10.

284 *"zombielike" state:* MLT, 315.

284 *"He didn't say anything":* "Of Time and the Rebel," *Time*, 12-5-60, 16.

285 *"He looked haggard":* AM, *The Last Party*, 356–57.

285 *"That first unmanageable cell":* The poem appeared in DFL, no pagination; rpt., MG, 85.

285 *"Christ, I thought":* MK, *The Good, the Bad, and the Dolce Vita*, 179–80.

286 *"The knife to a juvenile":* MBM, 224.

286 *"In my opinion Norman Mailer":* "Norman Mailer Sent to Bellevue," *NYT*, 11-23-60, 26.

286 *"I refuse to answer":* Leeds Moberly, "Hold Norman Mailer in Stabbing of Wife," New York *Daily News,* 11-23-60.

287 *Kemp, a young man: Eat of Me, I Am the Savior* (NY: Morrow, 1972). NM called it "a bold novel which takes many chances and succeeds."
288 *"So long/as/you/use/a/knife"*: The poem appeared twice in DFL, but NM chose not to reprint it in MG. Many commentators assume that NM was writing about the stabbing of Adele, yet in PP (145), he states that "I wasn't trying to reveal my private life in that poem. I was trying to crystallize a paradox." In his January 1968 *Playboy* interview with Paul Carroll, he says, "I was really thinking about a long conversation I had with a man who stabbed his brother. . . . Once something crystallizes, you have to be ruthless about presenting it; it doesn't matter who gets hurt, starting with yourself."
288 *"not psychotic"*: "Norman Mailer Is Found Sane," *NYT*, 12-10-60.
288 *"My husband and I"*: Benjamin DeMott, "Docket No. 15883," *American Scholar*, 232.
289 *"I really couldn't say"*: Normand Poirier, "Mailer: 'I Don't Worry About It,' " *New York Post*, 1-31-61.
289 *"because he feared"*: "Norman Mailer Admits Guilt in Stabbing of Wife," *NYT*, 3-10-61, 56.
289 *"I gamble on human beings"*: "Judge Gives Mailer a Break," *New York Mirror*, 5-11-61, 5.
289 *Signed by eight writers:* "Letters: Norman Mailer," *Time*, 12-12-60.
289 *"a fine thing to do"*: Christopher Hitchens, "Interview with Norman Mailer," *New Left Review*, 122–23.
289 *"I walked into the room"*: Marie Brenner, "Mailer Goes Egyptian," *New York*, 32–33.
290 *"the bosom"*: AM, *The Last Party*, 372.
290 *"a lousy wife"*: Jones to Burroughs Mitchell, 12-19-60, in *To Reach Eternity*, 293.
290 *"Letter written in psycho ward"*: MLT, 329.
290 *"My boy's a genius"*: not located.
290 *"I saved his neck"*: AM, *The Last Party*, 369–74.
290 *"It affected me"*: JML interview with Susan Mailer, 9-5-07.
291 *"I was maybe four or five"*: JML interview with Danielle Mailer, 8-20-08.
291 *I let God down:* JML in conversation with Betsy Mailer, 9-20-05.
291 *I think there was:* JML interview with Betsy Mailer, 11-29-11.
291 *"comes from the fact"*: Andrew O'Hagan and E. J. Camp, "The Martyrdom of Mailer," *Guardian Weekend*, 8-30-97, 14.
292 *"One got out of Bellevue"*: PP, 64.
292 *"Through the years"*: TOT, 384–85.
292 *"I lost any central"*: Brock Brower, *Other Loyalties*, 111.
292 *"a good deal"*: Ibid., 111–12.
292 *"A decade's anger"*: James Atlas, "Life with Mailer," *NYTM*, 94.
293 *"damaged in a lot"*: JML interview with Danielle Mailer, 8-20-08.
293 *"You know, my mother"*: JML interview with Betsy Mailer, 11-29-11.
293 *"I was trapped"*: AM, *The Last Party*, 376.
293 *"I want my book"*: Anne Kingston, *The Meaning of Wife: A Provocative*

Look at Women and Marriage in the Twenty-first Century (Toronto: HarperCollins, 2003), 180.

293 *"reduced his drinking":* "Norman Mailer Goes Free in Knifing Case," *NYT*, 11-14-61, 45.

293 *"explosively":* Introduction, *Deaths for the Ladies (and Other Disasters)* (NY: New American Library, 1971), no pagination. The introduction did not appear in the first, hardcover edition of the collection (NY: Putnam's, 1962), the source for all the poems in this chapter. NM reprinted the introduction in EE, 198–204.

294 *few reviews: Time*, 3-30-62, 84. Simon: *Hudson Review*, Autumn 1962; Swenson: *Poetry*, May 1963, 124–25; Lanham: *VV*, 7-5-62; Rodman: *NYTBR*, 7-8-62; Macdonald: *Commentary*, August 1962, 169–72.

294 *an interlude:* "Two Bucks—20 Dances," *Newsweek*, 3-12-62, 104.

294 *"way of digging myself":* Introduction, DFL.

294 *Vidal's apartment:* Fred Kaplan, *Gore Vidal: A Biography* (NY: Doubleday, 1999), 548.

294 *"The night I met him":* MBM, 237.

295 *Jeanne Louise Campbell's background:* Alan Brinkley, *The Publisher: Henry Luce and His American Century* (NY: Knopf, 2010); Anne Chisholm and Michael Davie, *Lord Beaverbrook: A Life* (NY: Knopf, 1993); Janet Aitken Kidd, *The Beaverbrook Girl* (London: Collins, 1987); Rosemary Mahoney, "Powerful Attractions," *NYTM*, 12-30-07, 26; Jeanne Campbell, "Jeanne Campbell Interviews Her Former Husband," *London Evening Standard*, 10-19-70, 17.

295 *"very attractive":* Kaplan, *Gore Vidal*, 549.

295 *"some idea of possibly":* Ibid.

295 *"I had never gone":* Ibid.

296 *"the hate book":* Rosemary Mahoney, "Powerful Attractions," *NYTM*, 26.

296 *her reaction to her background:* JML interview with Kate Mailer, 3-11-13.

297 *"The Lady and I":* NM to MK, 5-17-61.

297 *different magazines:* "Gourmandise" and "Eternities," *New Yorker*, 9-16-61, 11-11-61, respectively; five poems appeared in *Atlantic*, January 1962; *PR* turned down sixteen poems he submitted; several appeared in *VV*.

297 *"Some of the best":* NM to Don Carpenter, 5-12-61.

297 *"We had both been extremists":* Jeanne Campbell, "Jeanne Campbell Interviews Her Former Husband," *London Evening Standard*, 17.

298 *"one full heart-clot":* OFM, 3.

298 *"Hemingway constituted":* Ibid., 4.

298 *the father of modern:* Barbara Probst Solomon, "A Conversation with Norman Mailer," *Horse-Trading and Ecstasy* (NY: North Point, 1989), 145.

298 *"I keep thinking of John Gardner's":* SA, 120.

298 *"doubly depressing":* Alfred G. Aronowitz and Peter Hamill, *Ernest Hemingway: The Life and Death of a Man* (NY: Lancer, 1961), 20.

298 *"the most difficult death":* PP, 103. Except for the comparison with Saint

Thomas (AON, 105), NM's comments on Hemingway, including on his style, are taken from SA and CNM, both of which are indexed.

299 *"damn depressing":* Alfred G. Aronowitz and Peter Hamill, *Ernest Hemingway*, 20.

299 *"There is a no-man's":* PP, 104–5.

300 *"so articulate":* Leslie Fiedler, "An Almost Imaginary Interview: Hemingway in Ketchum," *PR* (September 1962); rpt., *A Fiedler Reader* (NY: Stein & Day, 1977), 162.

300 *"The Big Bite":* NM's *Esquire* column ran from November 1962 through December 1963.

300 *"The Metaphysics of the Belly":* First published in PP, 277–302; rpt., CAC, 262–305. Two other self-interviews, "The Political Economy of Time" and "The First Day's Interview," appeared in tandem with "The Metaphysics of the Belly" in CAC. The latter was first published in *Paris Review*, Summer/Fall 1961, NM's first piece there, and was also reprinted in part in PP, 245–60.

300 *"an introductory chapter":* Michael Mailer, "Mailer on Mailer," *Time Out*, 10-11-95, 20–23.

300 *Mailer: Postulate a modern:* CAC, 269–71.

302 *"the Beast":* AON, 21–22.

302 *publication in England:* AFM's British publication date was 10-29-61.

302 *accept the evisceration:* The full text was restored in the 1968 Panther paperback edition.

302 *"this draping of breasts":* NM to Deutsch, 5-6-61.

302 *sipping Scotch:* "Peter Underwood Meets Norman Mailer," *British Books*, November 1961, 12–15.

303 *"a combination of Brendan Behan":* W. J. Weatherby, "The Pursuit of Experience," *Manchester Guardian*, 9-28-61, 14.

303 *"hotch-potch":* W. G. Smith, "Young American Rebel: An Interview with Norman Mailer," *Books and Bookmen*, November 1961, 28.

303 *Richard Wollheim:* A major figure in the study of philosophical aesthetics, Wollheim (1923–2003) coined the term "minimal art." In his interview, "Living Like Heroes" (*New Statesman*, 9-29-61; rpt., CNM, 65–68), he draws out NM on violence as well as anyone ever has.

303 *"can literally recreate himself":* Wollheim, CNM, 65.

303 *"had killed 500,000":* Ibid., 66.

303 *"There's a psychic poverty":* Ibid., 68.

304 *millennial promise:* See Wenke's *Mailer's America*, 237–39 and passim for a thoughtful discussion of NM's focus on this lapsed ideal.

304 *"Mrs. Kidd's Ball":* Evelyn Waugh to Ann Fleming, 9-23-61, in Mark Amory, ed., *The Letters of Evelyn Waugh*, 572.

304 *"The horse did bite":* NM to Amory, 9-5-78.

305 *"a detestation of all":* Transcript: "Colin MacInnes Interviewing Norman Mailer" (HRC).

305 Time *reported:* "Customs: Instant Fad," *Time*, 10-20-61.

305 *"a nice knife job":* NM to Don Carpenter, 10-23-61.

305 *house in Bucks County:* NM to MK, 11-11-61.
305 *"I always suffer":* NM to Don Carpenter, 12-9-61.
305 *"lucky":* NM to Grant, 12-9-61.
305 *"I suppose I suffer":* NM to William Watson, 8-5-61.
306 *"I wonder how it is":* http://bernews.com/2010/12/historical/photos/president/kennedy-in-bermuda/.
306 *"I'll be a bachelor":* NM to MK, 12-9-61.
306 *book on Castro:* NM to Emile Capouya, 11-7-61.
306 *"old honey bun":* NM to Randolph Churchill, 1-2 (?)-62.
306 *"are still together":* NM to MK, 1-8-62.
306 *Felker contacted him:* NM to A. C. Spectorsky, 8-10-62.
306 *end his feud:* PP, 92.
306 *harsh critique:* "The Devolution of Democracy," *Dissent*, Winter 1962, 6–22.
306 *Paul Goodman:* In AON (33), NM noted his admiration for *Growing Up Absurd* (NY: Random House, 1969), and the generally positive influence of Goodman (1911–72) on college students.
307 *"because his style": "A COMMENT BY NORMAN MAILER"* was written in early January 1962.
307 *"delivered exactly to the jugular":* AON, 32.
307 *as he said in the essay:* "An Evening with Jackie Kennedy," *Esquire*, July 1962; rpt., PP, 81–98, with a new title, "The Existential Heroine: An Evening with Jackie Kennedy, or, The Wild West of the East"—not "Wild Witch" as it has been mistakenly titled.
307 *"One's presence was not":* PP, 92.
308 *"surprisingly thin":* Ibid., 86.
308 *"attack on the flag":* Ibid., 81.
308 *"And I could see": George, Being George*, ed. Nelson Aldrich Jr. (NY: Random House, 2008), 181–82.
308 *asked Richard Goodwin:* Podhoretz, *Ex-Friends*, 208.
308 *"So, Norman":* MLT, 475.
309 *"Because my father":* Jerry Tallmer, "At Home with Lady Jean [*sic*] Campbell," *New York Post Magazine*, 4-8-72, 33.
309 *"Grandfather and Norman":* Ibid.
309 *"As I was saying goodbye":* Anne Chisholm and Michael Davie, *Lord Beaverbrook*, 488–89.
309 *"by a Black woman":* Jeanne Campbell, "Jeanne Campbell Interviews Her Former Husband," *London Evening Standard*, 17.
310 *"so arduous":* NM to EY, 5-1-63.
310 *"Jews have a bad head":* Irma Kurtz, "Mailer: I've Always Been an Apostle of Freedom," *Nova* (London), March 1969, 107.
310 *"making separate starts":* NM to FG, 4-14-62.
310 *"The novel sits":* Notes for "big novel" (HRC).
310 *"Truth and Being; Nothing and Time": Evergreen Review*, September/October 1962; rpt., PP, 271–77.
310 *"an odd, even exceptional":* NM to William Phillips, 1-22-62.

310 *"archbishop of the New"*: PP, 274.
311 *"a rebellion of the cells"*: Ibid., 272.
311 *"the final executor"*: Ibid., 273.
311 *"expel the exquisite"*: Ibid., 275.
311 *"the state of Being"*: Ibid., 276.
311 *"Egypt is fertile"*: Anthony Burgess, "Magical Droppings," *Observer*, 6-5-83, 30.
311 *"It is characteristic"*: PP, 274.
311 *"Some of the best"*: Ibid.
312 *"we could empty a room"*: Rosemary Mahoney, "Powerful Attractions," *NYTM*, 26.
312 *immerse yourself*: NM to Harry G., 4-14-62.
312 *marvelous idea:* Sonia Brownell to NM, 5-14-62.
312 *"whirled round the nightspots"*: Janet Aitken Kidd, *The Beaverbrook Girl*, 213.
312 *Jeanne and her mother urged:* Transcript of "Norman Mailer's New Year Message," 12-30-62, Canadian TV program with Nathan Cohen (HRC).
312 *announcement of Kate's birth:* Margaret Drabble, *Angus Wilson: A Biography* (NY: St. Martin's, 1996), 310.
312 *Roman circus:* "Future of Novel Discussed at Writers' Conference," *Times* (London), 8-25-62, 8; see also James Campbell, "Let's Do It," *TLS*, 8-17-12, 36.
312 *"A nice touch"*: "Authors' Meeting Breaks Up with Song," *Times* (London), 8-22-62, 6.
313 *French delegation:* Raymond Walters Jr., "In and Out of Books: Circus," *NYTBR*, 9-16-62, 8.
313 *"a bit of a public figure"*: Transcript of "Norman Mailer's New Year Message," with Nathan Cohen (HRC).
313 *"This man Mailer"*: Magnus Magnusson, "Writers' Conference Is Growing in Stature," *Scotsman*, 8-24-62.
313 *"was felt to be the pap"*: Transcript, International Writers Conference, August 1962, part four.
314 *"It is all of a piece"*: EE, 262–63.
314 *"leaned over"*: Transcript of *Mailer on Miller*, 1975 television program, 21.
314 *"The method"*: Transcript, International Writers Conference, part five.
314 *"he spoke to his friends"*: Peter O. Whitmer with Bruce VanWyngarden, *Aquarius Revisited* (NY: Macmillan, 1987), 64.
314 *"Edinburgh had very many"*: Alastair McKay, "On the Town with Norman and Sam," *Scotsman*, 12-8-01.
315 *"He told me to let go"*: "edinburgh book festival footnotes"; *Sunday Herald*, The.FindArticles.com. 30 Dec, 2010, http://findarticles.com/p/articles/mi_qn4156/is_20010715/ ai_n13961293/. See also James Campbell, "Let's Do It," *TLS*.
315 *"the most important conservative"*: NM to EY, 9-12-62.
315 *"frighteningly bright"*: NM to Sonia Brownell, 11-28-62.

315 *"moved and excited":* Graham Greene to NM, 7-2-62.
315 *Anne Barry:* MBM, 262–63.
316 *"He was a particularly":* "First Meeting with Norman, March, 1962," Anne Barry files.
316 *Barry-Mailer relationship:* MLT, 346–49; MBM, 262–63.
316 *"a very funny man":* MLT, 347.
316 *"Mrs. Mark Twain":* MLT, 349.
317 *"a stuck-up little":* NM to Don Carpenter, 10-5-64.
317 *take care of Sadie:* JML interview with Anne Barry, 5-9-12.
317 *"freedom, his humor":* MBM, 263.
317 *"The Real Meaning of the Right Wing in America":* The speeches of NM and Buckley were published in *Playboy*, January 1963, and the ensuing debate in February issue. NM reprinted his speech in PP, 161–74; Buckley reprinted his in *Rumbles Left and Right* (NY: Putnam's, 1963), 71–84.
317 *"Let communism come":* PP, 171.
317 *"The airports look":* PP, 166.
317 *Rachel Carson's* Silent Spring*:* Serialized in *The New Yorker* in June 1962, it was published by Houghton Mifflin on 9-27-62.
317 *"I don't care":* "Reading from Left to Right," *Playboy*, April 1963, 8.
318 *"Dread has been loose":* PP, 161.
318 *"Metaphysics disappears":* Ibid., 167.
318 *"in the openness of Being":* Heidegger, "The Quest for Being," Walter Kaufmann, ed., *Existentialism from Dostoyevsky to Sartre* (NY: World, 1956), 272.
318 *"a repetition of infantile":* PP, 151.
318 *during his seventeen-day stay:* NM to Don Carpenter, 1-13-61; CNM, 57–58.
318 *"For believe me":* Nietzsche, "Live Dangerously," Walter Kaufmann, ed., *Existentialism from Dostoyevsky to Sartre*, 127.
318 The Concept of Dread: First published in 1844; rpt., as *Kierkegaard's Concept of Dread*, translated by Walter Lowrie (Princeton: Princeton University Press, 1957).
319 *"the saint and the psychopath":* EE, 210.
319 *"in secret union":* Heidegger, "The Quest for Being," Walter Kaufmann, ed., *Existentialism from Dostoyevsky to Sartre*, 253.
319 *"put iron":* DFL introduction, EE, 204.
319 *"a clever jabber":* Gay Talese, "Mailer Debates William Buckley; Chicago Political Bout a Draw," *NYT*, 9-24-62, L31.
319 *"a summer weight suit":* JML interview with Gay Talese, 10-19-10.
320 *"The crowd was high partisan":* PP, 174.
320 *Roger Donoghue, Mailer's second:* Pete Hamill, "Mailer vs. Buckley: Good Fight, No Decision," *New York Post*, 9-24-62, 70.
320 *"I was full":* PP, 227.
320 *"Ten Thousand Words a Minute": Esquire*, February 1962, rpt., PP, 213–67.
320 *"Paret got trapped":* PP, 244.

321 *"Have any of you":* Ibid., 216–17.
321 *"Heavy types, bouncers":* Ibid., 223.
322 *"He had stopped":* Ibid., 228.
322 *"plot-ridden, romantic,":* Ibid., 261.
322 *widely reported:* A. J. Liebling, *New Yorker*, 10-6-62; Red Smith, *New York Herald Tribune*, 9-27–62; Leonard Shecter, *New York Post*, 9-27-62; Stan Isaacs, *Newsday*, 9-27-62.
322 *"some ghost of Don Quixote":* PP, 266.
322 *"a* mélange de genres*":* NM to EY, 11-28-62.
323 *"Go to Oxford, Mississippi":* NM telegram to Robert F. Kennedy, 9-28-62.
324 *Carnegie Hall:* See Millicent Brower, "The Novelist Comes to Carnegie Hall, *VV*, 5-30-63, 1, 6–7, 18.
324 Cosmopolitan *interviewed him:* Frederick Christian, "The Talent and the Torment," August 1963.
324 *"Jeanne and I":* NM to Adeline Naiman, 1-15-63.
325 *"indications":* NM to MK, 6-13-63.
325 *"Part of the absolute funk":* NM to Harvey Breit, 6-13-63.
325 *"She's got a will":* NM to Moos Mailer, 6-15-63.
326 *"dare a bold stroke":* NM to André Deutsch, 10-15-63.
326 *"to do my big book":* NM to FG, 11-9-63.
326 *"Norman Mailer Versus Nine Writers": Esquire*, July 1963; rpt., CAC, 104–40; *The Thin Red Line* (NY: Scribner's, 1962); *Set This House on Fire* (NY: Random House, 1960); *Another Country* (NY: Dial, 1962); *Naked Lunch* (NY: Grove Press, 1959); *Catch-22* (NY: Simon & Schuster, 1962); *Rabbit, Run* (NY: Knopf, 1960); *Letting Go* (NY: Random House, 1963); *Franny and Zooey* (Boston: Little, Brown, 1961) and *Raise High the Roof Beam, Carpenters and Seymour: An Introduction* (Boston: Little, Brown, 1963); *Henderson the Rain King* (NY: Viking, 1959).
326 *"Well, one might as well":* CAC, 126–27.
327 *Sitting with Bentley:* JML interview with Beverly Bentley, 5-26-11.
327 *Hemingway's birthday party in Málaga:* A photo in A. E. Hotchner's *Papa Hemingway* (NY: Random House, 1966) shows Beverly and Hemingway wearing fireman's hats and holding drinks. See also Valerie Danby-Smith, *Running with the Bulls: My Years with the Hemingways* (Waterville, ME: Thorndike, 2004), 81–86; Jennifer Hagar, "Beverly Bentley: A Life in the Theater of Our Times," *P'Town Women* (1998), 41.
328 *"I wanted a home":* MBM, 271.
328 *relationship with jazz trumpeter Miles Davis:* John Szwed, *So What: The Life of Miles Davis* (NY: Simon & Schuster, 2002), 145–49.
328 *Associated Press Photo:* "Stand-In," *New York Post*, 4-7 (?)-63.
328 *"seeing what the mood is":* NM to MK, 6-13-63.
329 *"a man who takes": New York Post*, 6-?-63.
329 *"My darling let us":* Jeanne Campbell to NM, 6-2-63.
329 *tested for pregnancy:* MBD, 195–96.
329 *"lustful and proud":* AAD, 266–67.
330 *"Cancer":* (HRC).

330 *neurobiologists conclusively established:* Maureen O'Neill Hooker, "Norman Mailer: From Orgone Accumulator to Cancer Protection for Schizophrenics," *MR* (2010), 445–51.

330 *beginning the new novel:* See Robert F. Lucid, Introduction to Laura Adams, *Norman Mailer: A Comprehensive Bibliography* (Metuchen, NJ: Scarecrow, 1974), xiv–xv.

331 *"I used the sense":* Brock Brower, *Other Loyalties*, 102.

331 *Las Vegas and Harold Conrad:* MLT, 377–78.

331 *telegram from Arkansas:* MBD, 194.

331 *late night drive:* MLT, 379.

331 *San Francisco visit:* MLT, 379–81.

331 *narrow ledges:* NM to Helene Caprari, introduction, *Norman Mailer's Letters on An American Dream, 1963–69*, ed. JML (Shavertown, PA: Sligo, 2004), 12.

332 *Rojack's harrowing minutes:* AAD, 256–60.

332 *"an ex-Southern master-sergeant":* NM to FG, 9-10-63.

332 *Scott Meredith:* NM's agent for almost forty years, Meredith (1923–1993) was a hard-driving dealmaker who popularized literary auctions and other innovations. He supplanted Cy Rembar as NM's agent, although Rembar remained involved in NM's affairs.

332 *convinced Walter Minton:* NM to Deutsch, 10-15-63.

332 *sold the idea:* MLT, 386–87.

332 *"great interest in the suicidal nature":* MBM, 276.

332 *"was much like Hollywood":* NM to Alan Earney, 10-15-63.

332 *"a fantastic advance royalty":* NM to EY, 10-16-63.

332 *"It seems":* NM to Adeline Naiman, 11-5-63.

333 *"one hundred thousand finished words":* NM to FG, 10-15-64.

333 *in early November: The Presidential Papers* (NY: Putnam's) was published on 11-8-63.

333 *"The Last Night": Esquire*, December 1963; rpt., CAC, 380–97.

333 *"The early installments":* "The Big Bite," *Esquire*, December 1963, 26.

334 *"has me more or less pissing":* NM to Don Carpenter, 1-15-64.

333 *"one of the more Dostoevskian novels":* Nancy Weber, "Norman Mailer's 'American Dream': Superman Returns," *Books* (*New York Post*), March 1965, 14.

333 *"I met Jack Kennedy":* "An American Dream: A New Novel Serialized Exclusively in Esquire by Norman Mailer Installment One: The Harbors of the Moon," *Esquire*, January 1964, 77.

333 *Rojack's retelling of events:* NM's chronology problem is carefully examined in Hershel Parker's "Mailer's Revision of *An American Dream*," *Flawed Texts and Verbal Icons* (Evanston, IL: Northwestern University Press, 1984), 181–212. He argues strenuously that the assassination "wrecked" the novel's time scheme, but few have even noticed the problem.

333 *"The Kennedy thing":* NM to MK, 12-17-63.

335 *"At any rate, I have no desire":* NM to EY, 12-15-63.

335 *"an intellectual adventurer":* PP, 114.

336 *accurate, if spiteful:* NM to MK, 12-17-63.

336 *open poem:* "Open Poem to John Fitzgerald Kennedy," *VV*, 11-23-61, 4.

336 *"because his nature":* Nancy Weber, "Norman Mailer's 'American Dream': Superman Returns," *Books* (*New York Post*), 17.

336 *"A holocaust of a love":* Jeanne Campbell, "Jeanne Campbell Interviews Her Former Husband," *London Evening Standard*, 17.

336 *"A remarkable girl":* Rosemary Mahoney, "Powerful Attractions," *NYTM*, 26.

337 *"I was crazy about her":* Frederick Christian, "The Talent and the Torment," *Cosmopolitan*, 66; Campbell later married John Cram, and in 1968 had a second daughter, Cusi.

337 *"playing ten-second chess":* NM to FG, 12-20-63.

337 *"Years ago, Theodore Reik":* NM to Bourjaily, 1-16-64.

337 *Theodore Reik:* An American psychologist, Reik (1888–1969) was an early and brilliant acolyte of Freud.

337 *tribute to Kennedy:* "The Fate of the Union: Kennedy and After," *NYRB* (12-26-63), 6.

337 *Vincent Scully:* "Mailer vs. Scully," *Architectural Forum*, April 1964, 96–97.

337 *"The Killer": Evergreen Review*, April/May 1964; rpt., CAC, 222–27.

337 *"you are a magnetic":* Paul Gardner, "Mailer and Buckley Talk on 'Open End,' " *NYT*, 2-3-64.

337 *young heavyweight:* NM to Don Carpenter, 3-24-64.

338 *postpone an installment:* Carol Polsgrove, *It Wasn't Pretty, Folks, but Didn't We Have Fun? Esquire in the Sixties* (NY: Norton, 1995), 112.

338 *"Rojack is still considerably":* "Norman Mailer on *An American Dream*," CNM, 102.

338 *"a huge mass":* AAD, 19–20.

338 *"high private pleasure":* AAD, 44.

338 *"a pruning job":* Carol Polsgrove, *It Wasn't Pretty, but Didn't We Have Fun?* 112.

338 *new problem:* Ibid., 111–14.

338 *"I've been down":* NM to Harvey Breit, 2-11-64.

339 *ad in* The New York Times*: NYT*, 4-22-64, L48.

339 *"It's the only great":* NM to MK, 2-17-64.

339 *"banging away":* NM to Vahan Gregory, 3-16-64.

339 *"feeling wrung out":* NM to Martin Peretz, 3-17-64.

339 *"looks more like his mother":* NM to Louis and Moos Mailer, 4-17-64.

339 *"not up to the first four":* NM to MK, 4-19-64.

339 *"A good writer feels":* Fern Marja Eckman, "The New Moral Climate: The Writers and Poets," *New York Post*, 6-26-64, 39.

339 *"If psychic coincidences":* CAC, 173.

340 *"The Executioner's Song": Fuck You: A Magazine of the Arts* 7, September 1964, ed. Ed Sanders, one of the founders of the rock group the Fugs. NM later used the poem's title for chapter 15 of FIG, and as the title of ES; rpt., CAC, 131–32.

341 *"from imminent alcoholism":* Leeds, *The Enduring Vision of Norman Mailer*, 77.
341 *"died and was in the antechamber":* AAD, 206–07.
342 *"I'll never write that well":* NM in Conversation with JML, 12-28-05.
342 *"a canopy encrusted":* AAD, 234.
342 *"a solicitor for the Devil":* Ibid., 236.
342 *balcony of the thirty-eighth-floor:* Margaret H. Bay of the real estate firm of Brown Harris Stevens confirmed information about the balcony of the thirty-eighth-floor apartment, which NM probably visited in the early 1960s.
342 *"something like sane":* AAD, 270.
342 *"What a murderous":* NM to MK, 6-2-64.
343 *"usually fought a speech":* CAC, 30.
343 *"looked like a handsome":* Ibid., 31.
343 *"a pleasant urbane":* Ibid., 15.
343 *"Talking in a soft":* Ibid., 23.
343 *"smelled like formaldehyde":* Jeffrey Michelson and Sarah Stone, "Norman Mailer: The Interview," *Puritan Quarterly Journal Number* 7 (1981), 32.
344 *"giving off the barbaric":* CAC, 25.
344 *"Acute disease is cure":* PP, 7.
344 *"like millions of other whites":* CAC, 26.
344 *"If we are ill":* PP, 104.
344 *"One worried":* CAC, 26.
344 *"In the Red Light: A History of the Republican Convention in 1964":* *Esquire*, November 1964; rpt., CAC, 6–45.
344 *"until you can't stand it":* NM to Kemp, 9-30-64.
345 *"hard stick-'em-up":* NM to Deutsch, 9-14-64.
345 *$70,000:* George Frazier, "Literary Loot," *Boston Herald*, 5-12-64.
345 *"had a face":* CAC, 57–58.
345 *"It is even not impossible":* CAC, 69.
346 *"hard, greedy, exceptionally":* Ibid., 48–49.
346 *"a city of the future":* NM to Tina Bourjaily, 12-23-64.
346 *Vertical City:* "Cities Higher than Mountains," *NYTM*, 1-31-65; rpt., CAC, 233–37.
346 *"feel flat and dead":* NM to Don Carpenter, 1-27-65.
346 *"He catches the beauty":* Edward de Grazia, *Girls Lean Back Everywhere: The Law of Obscenity and the Assault on Genius* (NY: Random House, 1992), 486.
346 *"changed the literary history":* Ibid., 495.
346 *"for the days of oppression":* Ibid.
347 *"the golden islands":* Preface, *Works and Days*.
347 *Gravel, was a friend:* Mike Gravel to NM, 2-8-65; NM to Mike Gravel, 2-20-65.
347 *Edmund Skellings:* NM to Edmund Skellings, 2-18-65; NM to Donald Kaufmann, 4-20-65.
347 *Alaska trip:* Donald Kaufmann's "Norman Mailer in 'God's Attic,'" *MR*

(2008), 298–312, is the best account of NM's visit, written by Skellings's Alaska colleague.

347 *National Book Award events:* "PPA Press Conference," 44.

347 *"our rebels":* Thorpe Menn, "But Without the Golden Age, There Is No Waste Land," *Kansas City Star*, 3-21-64, L39.

347 *"the apocalyptic romanticism":* Nina A. Steers, " 'Successor' to Faulkner: An Interview with Saul Bellow," *Show*, September 1964, 37–38.

348 *"But we moral nihilists":* Thorpe Menn, "But Without the Golden Age, There Is No Waste Land," *Kansas City Star*, L39.

348 *"hostess of the intellectual":* P. Albert Duhamel, "Book Awards Bespeak a Return to Relevancy," *Boston Herald*, 3-14-65.

348 *"flirting with Beverly":* MBM, 285.

348 *"I didn't want to hit":* Ibid.

348 *"fairly drunk":* Ibid.

348 *"was absolutely catatonic":* Ibid.

349 *"a small round girl":* Ibid., 286.

349 *"wearing an old trench coat":* Ibid., 287.

349 *Phillips, sent the review:* Phillips to NM, 3-25-65.

349 "An American Dream *has received":* "A Small Public Notice by Norman Mailer," *PR*, Spring 1965, 180–81.

349 *the division of opinion:* Hardwick: *PR*, Spring 1965; Hicks: *Saturday Review*, 3-20-65; Rahv: *NYRB*, 3-25-65; Shattuck: *VV*, 5-13-65; Hyman: *New Leader*, 3-15-65; Wolfe: *Book Week*, 3-14-65; Aldridge: *Life*, 3-19-65; Bersani: *PR*, Fall 1965; Rhodes: *Kansas City Star*, 3-14-65; Didion: *National Review*, 4-20-65; Pickrel: *Harper's*, April 1965; Poirier: *Commentary*, June 1965; *Chicago Tribune*: Paul R. Jackson, 3-14-65; *Time*: 3-19-65; *Newsweek*: 3-15-65.

350 *"Congratulations on a nearly":* Buckley to NM, 4-7-65.

350 *"nicest":* NM to Buckley, 4-20-65.

350 *"an extraordinary piece of crap":* NM to Diana Trilling, 6-8-65.

350 *"because no vice":* NM to Diana Trilling, 3-25-65.

EIGHT: THIRD PERSON PERSONAL: *ARMIES* AND AFTER

In addition to the sources identified below, the following were drawn on: "Fan's Memoir"; JML's "Mailer Log"; JML's unpublished interviews with NM and BW. NM's letters are located at the HRC.

Page

352 *offered to lend him money:* MBM, 292.

352 *"greeted the new champ":* Brock Brower, *Other Loyalties*, 115.

352 *"Where's that tough guy":* Donald Kaufmann, "Norman Mailer in 'God's Attic,' " MR (2008), 302.

353 *"I can breathe here":* Tim Bradner, "Mailer on Alaska," *Alaska Living (Anchorage Daily News)*, 6-30-68, 3.

353 *"The future of this state":* Donald Kaufmann, "Norman Mailer in 'God's Attic,'" *MR*, 305.

353 *"All the messages":* Tim Bradner, "Mailer on Alaska," *Alaska Living*, 3.
353 *"For twenty long minutes":* Donald Kaufman, "Norman Mailer in 'God's Attic,'" *MR*, 310–11.
354 *"Now what I'd like":* NM to Diana Trilling, 3-25-65.
354 *"adored":* Diana Trilling to NM, 5-17-65.
354 *"in what must be called":* Marcus, CNM, 77.
354 *"Being around Norman":* JML interview with Peter Alson, 8-29-12.
355 *teach-in at Berkeley:* Louis Menashe, editor and compiler, wrote the notes accompanying speech excerpts (including NM's) on two LPs, *Berkeley Teach-In: Vietnam*, Folkway Records, No. FD5765, 1966; NM's speech was first published in *Realist*, June 1965; rpt., *We Accuse*, ed. James Petras (Berkeley: Diablo, 1965), and CAC, 67–82.
355 *the largest audience:* NM to EY, 6-3-65.
355 *"buried unvoiced faith":* CAC, 71.
355 *"shedding the blood":* Ibid., 79.
356 *"bully with an Air Force":* Ibid., 81.
356 *"close to insanity":* Ibid., 77–78.
356 *"You, Lyndon Johnson":* Ibid., 82.
356 *"a standing ovation":* NM to EY, 6-3-65.
356 *Fig and Ecey:* NM to FG, 3-31-65.
356 *Al Wasserman:* An Academy Award–winning documentary filmmaker, Wasserman (1921–2005) was also the founding producer of NBC's *White Paper* programs, and from 1976 to 1986 was a producer for *60 Minutes* on CBS. He directed a 1973 NBC documentary based on Theodore White's book *The Making of the President, 1972*. See Christopher Lehmann-Haupt, "Al Wasserman Dies at 84," *NYT*, 4-10-05.
356 *Harvard's Sanders Theatre:* W. J. McCarthy, "2,000 Hear 'Teachers-In' Demand LBJ Resignation," *Boston Herald*, 7-15-65; "President Assailed by Norman Mailer," *NYT*, 7-16-65.
356 *"Three cheers, lads":* "On Vietnam," *PR*, Fall 1965, 620–56; NM's contribution; rpt., CAC, 83–90.
357 *intellectual precursor:* Robert Freidman, "Clay, Mailer in 'Draw,'" *San Juan Sunday Star*, 8-1-65.
357 *interviewed several times:* JML interview with Brock Brower, 3-17-11.
357 *"We would each become":* NM to Brock Brower, 8-19-65.
357 *"final confirmation":* "'Life' Goes to Norman Mailer," *National Review*, 11-2-65.
358 *"What the hell":* NM to Buckley, 10-18-65.
358 *"his flair for arch":* Richard Witkin, quoted in Sewell Chan, "Remembering Buckley's 1965 Run for Mayor," *NYT*, 2-27-08.
358 *"majestically unsuited":* "Norman Mailer on Lindsay and the City," *VV*, 10-28-65; rpt., CAC, 63.
358 *"was genuinely pissed off":* Richard Kluger to NM, 3-16-65.
359 *"bawled the hell":* Kluger to NM, 6-22-65.
359 *results of the poll: Book Week*'s 9-26-65 issue, titled "American Fiction:

The Postwar Years, 1945–65," was devoted to the poll, including excerpts from the comments of forty-five of the respondents (excluding NM's).

359 *"Just think when Time":* NM to Kluger, 7-14-65.

359 *new miscellany:* NM to EY, 10-8-65.

359 *"the ghosts of the Nazis":* CAC, 3–4.

359 *"the minority within":* The final chapter of Poirier's critical study of NM, *Norman Mailer* (NY: Viking, 1972), titled "The Minority Within," is a brilliant examination of this formulation, which he defines as an element that "has somehow been repressed or stifled by conformity to system" (112).

359 *"is quite unable":* Ibid., 114.

359 *"two huge types":* CAC, 3.

360 *"The Book of the First-Born":* Various drafts are at the HRC. NM sent Scott Meredith (9-6-74) a list of the separate fictional pieces that he was considering incorporating into AE, including "The Book of the First-Born."

360 Tristram Shandy: *The Life and Opinions of Tristram Shandy, Gentleman,* published in several volumes from 1759 to 1769, is a masterpiece of comic digression.

361 *"Good fucks make good babies":* POS, 191.

361 The Prisoner of Sex: First published in *Harper's* in March 1971, this fifty-thousand-word essay was reprinted in book form by Little, Brown in 1971.

361 *"the saga of the Mailer family":* Gregory Feeley, "Waiting for Mailer's Big One," *Million*, 40.

362 *"a writer of the period":* John Whalen-Bridge, "The Karma of Words: Mailer Since *Executioner's Song*," *Journal of Modern Literature* 30, Fall 2006, 9.

362 *"so many years":* NM to EY, 12-9-65.

362 *Lucid, had organized:* "American Calendar," *American Quarterly* 18, Spring 1966, 118–20.

362 *audience of approximately two thousand:* James Yuenger, "What Norman Means," *Chicago Tribune Magazine*, 2-6-66, 50, 52.

363 *"Mailer, in a fine blue suit":* Richard G. Stern, "Report from the MLA," *NYRB*, 2-17-66, 26.

363 *"a phenomenon never before":* "Modes and Mutations: Quick Comments on the Modern American Novel," *Commentary*, March 1966; rpt., as "The Argument Reinvigorated," CAC, 96.

363 *"like a weed":* Ibid., 99.

363 *"clarify a nation's vision":* Ibid., 98.

363 *"of the deepest":* Ibid., 103.

363 *"thundered applause":* Ibid., 28.

364 *Poetry Center: Program, The Poetry Center, 1965–66.*

364 *traveling to Japan:* NM to EY, 3-23-66.

364 *"to explain":* Ibid.

364 *"a 19th century novelist":* NM to David Madden, 3-24-66.

364 *waterfront house:* NM to Don Carpenter, 4-16-66.
364 *wrote to Eldridge Cleaver:* NM to Cleaver, 4-26-66.
365 *"prophetic and penetrating":* Eldridge Cleaver, "Notes on a Native Son," *Ramparts*, June 1966.
365 *"so odd and horrible":* Preface to a paperback reprint of *Why Are We in Vietnam?* (NY: Berkley, 1977), v; rpt., as "Are We in Vietnam?" PAP, 9–12. NM also intended to draw on accounts of the 1959 murder and dismemberment of four women by a Provincetown man, Tony Costa, and did draw on descriptions of Costa's marijuana cache in the Truro woods in TGD, as detailed in an unpublished paper by Christopher Busa, "Mailer's Tough Guys: Novelist Invites His Characters to Dance," delivered at the October 2012 Mailer Society conference.
365 *"I was, as I say":* NM, preface, *Why Are We in Vietnam?*, viii.
366 *"bonuses, gifts":* "Mr. Mailer Interviews Himself," *NYTBR*, 9-17-66; rpt., CNM, 107.
366 *"a mystique":* MBM, 296.
366 *long letter from her:* Trilling to NM, 5-6-66.
366 *"an unhappy question":* NM to Trilling, 6-?-66.
367 *"These McLuhans, these Pinchens* [sic] *and Jeremy Larners":* Marshall McLuhan (1911–1980), communication theory guru and author of *Understanding Media* (NY: McGraw-Hill, 1964); Thomas Pynchon (b. 1937), reclusive author of complex novels about, among other things, paranoia and technology. NM may have been responding to the buzz surrounding the publication of Pynchon's postmodern novel *The Crying of Lot 49* (Philadelphia: Lippincott, 1966); Jeremy Larner (b. 1937), novelist, teacher, and screenplay writer, published a novel about a college basketball star, *Drive, He Said* (NY: Delacorte, 1964).
367 *"I carry my ideas":* NM to EY, 4-24-66.
367 *"adventurers, rebels":* "Our Argument at Last Presented," CAC, 307.
368 *"Modern science may prove":* Ibid., 308.
368 *Eliot Fremont-Smith:* "A Nobel for Norman," *NYT*, 8-22-66, 31.
368 *A. Alvarez:* "Dr Mailer, I Presume," *Observer*, 10-15-67, 27.
368 *"to position himself":* John Wain, "Mailer's America," *New Republic*, 10-1-66, 19–20.
368 *anthology devoted to the Beats:* Feldman and Gartenberg, eds., *The Beat Generation and The Angry Young Men* (NY: Citadel, 1958).
368 *Leo Garen:* A television and film writer and director of off-Broadway theater, Garen (1936–2006) met NM in Provincetown and later worked with him on MM.
369 *"white with fury":* MBM, 295.
369 *"When I was pregnant":* Ibid., 305.
369 *Carol Stevens:* Born in 1930, Stevens cannot recall the month in 1962 that she met NM.
369 *Stevens was on a date:* JML interview with Carol Stevens, 3-28-09.
369 *"Norman never held her down":* MBM, 305.
369 *"he doesn't want to share":* Ibid., 296.

369 *"We did it up here":* NM to Louis and Moos, 9-25-66.
370 *"to running the (at times enormous)":* MBD, 272.
370 *"Norman's career":* William Wolf, "Mrs. Mailer Describes Life with Mailer," *Asbury Park Sunday Press*, 3-19-67, 25.
370 *"I began to feel":* MBD, 272.
370 *"all the lard":* NM to MK, 8-3-66.
370 *Theatre de Lys:* NM to EY, 12-14-66.
370 *"At least I'll be done":* NM to Breit, 9-24-66.
370 *review of* Rush to Judgment: "The Great American Mystery," *Book Week*, 8-28-66; rpt., EE, 269–83.
370 *"had no intention":* EE, 272.
370 *"literary commission":* Ibid., 282.
370 *"The game is not over":* Ibid., 273.
370 *social event of the year:* Madeline Belkin (NM's secretary) to Elizabeth Davies, 10-14-66.
370 *Black and White Ball:* Gerald Clarke, *Capote: A Biography* (NY: Simon & Schuster, 1988), 369–80; George Plimpton, *Truman Capote: In Which Various Friends, Enemies, Acquaintances, and Detractors Recall His Turbulent Career* (NY: Nan A. Talese/Doubleday, 1997), 247–78; Phillip Schopper interview for *American Masters* documentary on Lillian Hellman; www.flickr.com/photos/52207413@NO2/5472186684/.
371 *"dirty gabardine raincoat":* George Plimpton, *Truman Capote*, 276.
371 *"Everything felt anointed":* Ibid., 277.
371 *"I was dissolute":* Ibid., 269.
372 *paid him $20,000:* NM to Deutsch, 12-1-66.
372 *"ten stunning":* Introduction, *The Deer Park: A Play* (NY: Dial, 1967), 7–32.
372 *"perhaps the dearest":* DPP, 11–12.
372 *"a twin tower":* Richard Gilman, "Big Red Heart," *Newsweek*, 2-13-67, 109.
372 *shameless vice figure:* Walter Kerr, "Evil: Plainly a Fun Thing," *NYT*, 2-12-67, 1.
372 *interviews to* The Village Voice *and the* New York Post*:* Stephanie Harrington, "Norman Mailer's 'Deer Park': Countdown Drama," *VV*, 1-5-67, 1, 23; Jerry Tallmer, "Norman Mailer: Playwright," *New York Post Magazine*, 2-11-67.
372 *"A Statement of Aims":* *VV*, 1-5-67.
373 *a long essay:* "Mr. Mailer Passes Out the Cigars," *NYT*, 1-22-67.
373 *"I wanted the critics":* Dick Schaap, "Opening Night at the Theater," *New York Post*, 2-2-67, 29.
373 *"I think we've got":* Ibid.
373 *ad in the* Times*:* *NYT*, 4-26-67, 4D.
373 *"host a Village":* Stephanie Harrington, "Mailer's Street Scene: Renewal on Sunday," *VV*, 5-4-67, 1, 21.
373 *"his own drum":* Wilfrid Sheed, "Another Word from the Sponsor," *Life*, 2-24-67, 8.

373 *"the complicated story":* Michael Smith, "Theatre Journal," *VV*, 2-9-67, 23.
373 *"Mailer is a moralist":* Walter Kerr, "Evil: Plainly a Fun Thing," *NYT*, 1.
374 *"spout philosophy":* Wilfrid Sheed, "Another Word from the Sponsor," *Life*, 8.
374 *"I hold on":* NM to MK, 5-2-67.
374 *lost $60,000:* NM to JM, 5-3-67.
374 *short stories: The Short Fiction of Norman Mailer* (NY: Dell, 1967).
374 Why Are We in Vietnam?: (NY: Putnam's, 1967).
374 The Bullfight: Subtitled *A Photographic Narrative with Text by Norman Mailer* (NY: CBS Legacy Books/Macmillan, 1967); NM's essay first appeared in *Playboy*, October 1967, as "The Crazy One"; rpt., EE, 37–60; Lorca poem, *The Poetry Bag*, Winter 1967–68; rpt., EE, 236–42.
374 *"reluctance":* NM to Felicia Geffen, 3-2-67.
375 *antiwar speeches:* "Mailer Says U.S. Dangerously Split," *Dallas Morning News*, 3-29-67; Lee Coppola, "Mailer—Man of Fevered Words," *Buffalo Evening News*, 4-1-67; "Mailer Speaks for City TNT," *Goucher Weekly*, 4-14-67.
375 *"We had absolutely fantastic":* "Norman Mailer," Interview with Joseph Gelmis, CNM, 158.
375 *"Norman suggested to Buzz":* MK, *The Good, the Bad, and the Dolce Vita*, 256.
375 *"a gestalt of galoot":* Michael Chaiken, "The Master's Mercurial Mistress: How Norman Mailer Courted Chaos 24 Frames per Second," *Film Comment*, July/August 2007, 38.
376 *"had the horror":* Gelmis, CNM, 164.
376 *"almost unendurable":* Canby, CNM, 141.
376 *"usual narcissistic fog":* NM to Harvey Breit, 6-13-63.
376 *"sounds as if* everybody*":* Canby, CNM, 141.
376 *"I just loved cutting":* Gelmis, CNM, 159.
376 *"the worst movie":* "Celebrities Make Spectacles of Themselves," *New Yorker*, 1-20-68.
376 *"I thought I was going":* Canby, CNM, 141.
376 *$450,000 advance:* MBM, 301.
376 *"Jewish experience":* Ibid., 302.
376 *"was going to follow":* Ibid.
376 *Mailer wrote back:* NM to Bill Walker, 7-15-67.
377 *"far too concerned":* NM to Don Carpenter, 7-14-67.
377 *"fallen on dull, chilly days":* NM to MK, 5-2-67.
377 *publishing a major new novel: The Confessions of Nat Turner* (NY: Random House, 1967).
377 *"putting out peace feelers":* NM to MK, 7-21-67.
377 Go to the Widow-Maker: (NY: Delacorte, 1967).
377 *"paranoia, megalomania":* NM to MK, 4-7-67.
377 *"an extraordinary idea":* NM to JM, 5-3-67.
377 *mailed him his review:* NM to JM, 9-9-67.

377 Playboy *interview:* rpt., in part, PAP, 32–45.
377 *"metaphorical" and "elliptical":* NM to Nat Lehrman, 7-5-67.
378 Making It: (NY: Random House, 1967).
378 *one of Mailer's literary executors:* NM to Rembar, 5-25-64.
378 *a copy to Provincetown:* Podhoretz, *Ex-Friends*, 215.
378 *reviews of* Why Are We in Vietnam?*:* John W. Aldridge, "From Vietnam to Obscenity," *Harper's*, February 1968, 91–97; Eugene Glenn, *VV*, 9-28-67, 6–7, 41; Eliot Fremont-Smith, "Norman Mailer's Cherry Pie," *NYT*, 9-8-67, 41M; Jack Kroll, "The Scrambler," *Newsweek*, 9-18-67, 103–5; Denis Donoghue, "Sweepstakes," *NYRB*, 9-28-67, 5–6; Granville Hicks, "Lark in the Race for Presidency," *Saturday Review*, 9-16-67, 39–40; Christopher Nichols, "Psychedelic Freakout," *National Review*, 10-31-67, 1216–17; "Hot Damn," *Time*, 9-8-67, D12–13.
378 *"Disc Jockey":* WVN, 24.
378 *"genius brain":* Ibid., 27.
378 *"The fact of the matter":* Ibid., 23.
379 *"a taste of fish":* Ibid., 69.
379 *"There were two eyes":* Ibid., 70–71.
379 *"Write from experience":* Henry James, "The Art of Fiction" (1884); rpt., *Henry James: Essays on Literature, American Writers, English Writers* (NY: Library of America, 1984), 53.
380 *"intensity of this process":* AON, 152–53.
380 *The cast included: Evergreen Scorecard* 2, no. 3, November/December 1968.
380 *young woman named Lee Roscoe:* JML interview with Lee Roscoe, Summer 2010.
380 *"He's not only convinced":* Roger Ebert, review of *Beyond the Law, Chicago Sun-Times*, 11-4-69.
380 *"slightly manic":* Canby, "Norman Mailer Offers 'Beyond the Law,'" *NYT*, 9-30-68.
381 *"a real course in filmmaking":* MBD, 234.
381 *"lugubrious conscience":* AON, 16–17.
381 *"are not in focus":* Ibid., 19.
382 *compared to Joyce:* Christopher Lehmann-Haupt: "Norman Mailer as Joycean Punster and Manipulator of Language," *Commonweal*, 12-8-67, 338–39.
382 *outrageous theories:* Richard Gilman, "Big Red Heart," *Newsweek*, 109.
382 *made his daughter Susan:* AON, 13.
382 *"endless blendings":* Ibid., 74–75.
382 *"He had in fact learned":* Ibid., 13–14.
383 *"leisurely twilight":* Ibid., 21.
383 *"the exploratory personal":* Werner Berthoff, "Witness and Testament," *Aspects of Narrative*, ed. J. Hillis Miller (NY: Columbia University Press, 1971), 189.
383 *"as a piece of material":* Canby, CNM, 142.
384 *architecture of ancient Egypt:* AON, 178.

384 *"the architecture of his personality":* Ibid., 26.
384 *"serves willy-nilly":* Ibid., 66.
384 *"half-heroic":* JML, "An Author's Identity," PAP, 153.
384 *"Curious, when you're with X":* Lowell, quoted in Macdonald's review of *The Armies of the Night* in *Esquire*, May 1968; rpt., Macdonald, *Discriminations*, 210–16.
385 *"finest journalist":* AON, 30–31.
386 *"The eye is the first circle":* "Circles," *Ralph Waldo Emerson: Essays and Lectures* (NY: Library of America, 1983), 403.
386 *"sound-as-brickwork":* AON, 99.
387 *"marked the move":* Sandy Vogelgesang, *The Long Dark Night of the Soul: The American Intellectual Left and the Vietnam War* (NY: Harper & Row, 1974), 134.
387 *"Future historians":* Ibid., 131.
387 *"for the war spoke":* AON, 108.
387 *"to be able to enjoy":* Ibid., 91–92.
388 *"as if finally":* Ibid., 129.
388 *"It was as if the air":* Ibid., 147.
388 *"feeling like the people's":* Ibid., 225.
388 *"had every promise":* Ibid., 98.
389 *"No, in fact":* Donald Newlove, "Dinner at the Lowells'," *Esquire*, September 1969, 178.
389 *"I've been trying":* Lowell to NM, 3-13-68.
389 *"a Quixote":* Ian Hamilton, "A Conversation with Robert Lowell," *The Review* (London), 1971; rpt., *American Poetry Review*, September/October 1978, 26; Robert Lowell, *Notebook, 1967–68* (NY: Farrar, Straus & Giroux, 1969).
389 *"For Norman Mailer":* Ibid., 183.
389 *"the form of the book":* Ian Hamilton, "A Conversation with Robert Lowell," *The Review*, 26.
389 *"Prince of Bourbon":* AON, 42.
389 *"the expression on his face":* Ibid., 43.
389 *"fatally vulgar":* Ibid., 54.
390 *"a blending so dramatic":* Ibid., 50–51.
390 *"What a good short story":* Matthew Grace and Steve Roday, "Mailer on Mailer: An Interview," *New Orleans Review* 3, no. 3 (1973), 231.
390 *"was an astronomical figure":* MBM, 321.
391 *"crouched like a boxer":* Ibid.
391 *"No book I wrote":* SA, 141.
391 *"isolated and bored":* MBM, 322.
391 *"going off in a new":* Christopher Bollen, "Norman Mailer, Writer," *V* magazine, January/February 2003, 7.
391 *"A Shaky Start":* *Time*, 10-27-67, 25.
391 *"really tied the thing together":* MBM, 316.
391 *"The average reporter":* AON, 78.
391 *"Now we may leave":* Ibid., 12.

391 *read a long chapter:* SA, 99.
392 The Education of Henry Adams: Published by Houghton Mifflin in 1918. Using the third person personal as effectively as the major writers who had employed it both before him and after him (Thucydides, Julius Caesar, Gertrude Stein), he writes about the huge changes, especially in technology, that he observed over his long life. The grandson of John Quincy Adams, the sixth president, Henry Adams (1838–1918), was also acquainted with Albert Einstein, as well as many major American political figures and artists of England and the United States.
392 *"It's as if I":* SA, 99.
392 *"damned odd":* Ibid., 127.
392 *"part of the ego":* Ibid., 86.
392 *"already laid out":* MBM, 321.
392 *forty thousand words:* NM to EY, 11-20-67.
392 *"I was stunned":* MBM, 322.
392 *"I think we should":* Willie Morris, *New York Days* (Boston: Little, Brown, 1993), 217.
393 *Beverly cooked:* Ibid., 218.
393 *"On one especially":* Ibid.
393 *"frizzy hair": North Toward Home* (Boston: Houghton Mifflin, 1967), 358.
393 *"The Steps of the Pentagon": Harper's*, March 1968, 47–103; rpt., in revised form as Book I of *The Armies of the Night* (NY: New American Library, 1968).
393 *"Look, I wish":* Morris, *New York Days,* 218.
393 *"I said,* 'Umbashrien' *":* MLT, 471.
394 *"History as a Novel":* Published as "The Battle of the Pentagon," *Commentary*, April 1968; rpt., as Book II of AON.
394 *"only an afterthought":* Morris, *New York Days*, 219.
394 *"old dear great":* "Up the Family Tree" (review of *Making It*), *PR*, Spring 1968; rpt., EE, 171–97.
394 *Beverly was searching:* Morris, *New York Days*, 219.
394 *"dirty little secret":* Podhoretz, *Making It*, xvi–xvii.
394 *"Mailer-like bid":* Ibid., 356.
394 *"very nasty indeed":* Norman Podhoretz, *Breaking Ranks* (NY: Harper & Row, 1979), 221.
394 *"agreeable variety":* EE, 176.
395 *"squalid yard":* EE, 172.
395 *"Here I was":* MLT, 473.
395 *"himself as a* literary *character":* EE, 180.
395 *"One is advancing":* Ibid., 181.
396 *"forced to jog":* Ibid., 189.
396 *"muted limited account":* Ibid., 187–88.
396 *"Podhoretz apes":* Robert Kirsch, "Hang-ups of Podhoretz in Aping Mailer," *Los Angeles Times*, 1-14-68.
396 *"invariably as attractive":* EE, 187.
396 *"deserted his possibilities":* EE, 189.

396 *"was probably too cruel":* Andrew O'Hagan, "Norman Mailer: The Art of Fiction," *The Paris Review Interviews III*, 425.
396 *"probably would dislike":* Podhoretz, *Ex-Friends*, 214.
397 *Among the major reviews:* John Simon, "Mailer on the March," *Hudson Review*, Autumn 1968, 541–45; Mario Puzo, "Generalissimo Mailer: Hero of His Own Dispatches," *Book World* (*Chicago Tribune*), 4-28-68; "First Person Singular," *Time*, 2-23-68, 81.
397 *"Willie, if I ever":* NM to Willie Morris, 3-7-69.
397 *"diary-essay-tract-sermon":* Alfred Kazin, "The Trouble He's Seen," *NYTBR*, 5-5-68; rpt., JML, *Critical Essays on Norman Mailer*, 62.
397 *"the best American writers":* Ibid., 64–65.
397 Death in Life: (NY: Random House, 1967).
397 *"He immediately took BJ":* JML interview with Robert J. Lifton, 9-14-10. Lifton repeats the story in his memoir, *Witness to an Extreme Century* (NY: Free Press, 2011), 355–56.
398 *"Your speaker is here":* "Accepting the National Book Award," EE, 254–55.
398 *"pleasant":* NM to MK, 3-4-68.
399 *"the movies are not there":* Gelmis, CNM, 167.
399 *"the horror of life":* Ibid., 168.
399 *"Making movies is a religious":* Ibid., 172.
399 *over $70,000:* Ibid., 158.
399 *"below the reality":* Ibid., 160.
399 *"people were pegged":* Michael Chaiken, "The Master's Mercurial Mistress," 38–39.
399 *Jack Newfield:* A well-known leftist journalist who wrote for *VV* and other newspapers, Newfield (1938–2004) was a friend of Robert F. Kennedy's and wrote *Robert Kennedy: A Memoir* (NY: Nation Books, 2003), and several books about New York City politics.
399 *Newfield wrote a piece:* "On the Steps of a Zeitgeist," *VV*, 5-30-68; rpt., JML, *Critical Essays on Norman Mailer* (Boston: G. K. Hall, 1986), 99–103.
399 *"Norman Mailer, novelist, counterpuncher":* Ibid., 100.
400 *"I want a guarantee":* Ibid., 101.
400 *"they are an active":* Ibid., 102.
400 *"Norman Mailer is one":* Ibid.
400 *"with every stimulus":* "A Course in Filmmaking," *New American Review*, August 1971; rpt., *Maidstone: A Mystery* (NY: New American Library, 1971), 157. Criterion Films (Eclipse Series 35) reissued remastered versions of *Maidstone, Wild 90*, and *Beyond the Law* in 2012, with notes by Michael Chaiken.
400 *"there had not been a President":* AON, 135.
401 *"unbelievably paranoiac":* JML interview with Carol Stevens, 7-5-11.
401 *James Toback:* Writer and in some cases also the director of several important films, Toback (b. 1944), was a longtime friend of NM's, and also

worked with his son Michael on film projects, including *Two Girls and Guy* (1997).

401 *"There was a fair amount":* JML's questions for James Toback, 8-14-10, interview conducted by Michael Chaiken.

402 *"tacitly understood":* MM, 159.

402 *"a bunch of enforced existentialists":* Ibid., 139.

402 *"You crazy fool":* MM, 121. See Michael Mailer's account, "Over-Exposed—My First Taste of Filmmaking," *PlumHamptons*, June 2011, 209.

402 *"all too unhappily":* MM, 177.

403 *Toback's* Esquire *article:* "At Play in the Fields of the Bored," *Esquire*, December 1968; rpt., MM, 8–21.

403 *"When we discussed it":* JML's questions for James Toback, 8-14-10, conducted by Michael Chaiken.

403 *"they're part of a certain":* JML interview with Michael Chaiken, 4-19-11.

404 *"We came here":* AP, "Mailer at Venice with Film Aiming to Be Memorable," *NYT*, 8-31-70, 21.

404 *"drew more than anybody":* NM to MK, 10-21-70.

404 Guy Domville: The story is best told in the novelized version of the event by David Lodge, *Author, Author* (NY: Viking, 2004).

404 *"came under the head*[*ing*]*":* John M. Lee, "Mailer, in London, Trades Jabs with Audience over Film," *NYT*, 10-17-70, 21.

404 *"my failed cinematic masterpiece":* SA, 198.

404 *spending $125,000:* NM to MK, 7-28-68.

404 *shares in* The Village Voice: MM, 156.

405 *"the Republic hovered": Miami and the Siege of Chicago* (NY: New American Library, 1968), 14.

405 *"God may have withdrawn":* Not located.

405 *"There had never been":* MSC, 46.

405 *"inner debate":* Ibid., 44.

406 *"Most of them were ill-proportioned":* Ibid., 34–35.

406 *"he had the presence":* Ibid., 71–72.

407 *"body armoring":* See Theodore P. Wolfe's translation of Reich's 1933 study, *Character Analysis* (NY: Farrar, Straus & Giroux, 1970).

407 *spent ten days:* NM to EY, 9-30-68.

407 *"The reporter was sentimental":* MSC, 85–86.

407 *"police riot":* The phrase was used in "The Walker Report," formally titled *Rights in Conflict* (Chicago: National Commission on the Causes and Prevention of Violence, 1968).

407 *"people whose ancestors":* MSC, 104.

407 *"Gestapo tactics":* Ibid., 180.

408 *"It seemed to him":* Ibid., 185.

408 *"had allowed him to write":* Ibid., 187.

408 *"potential militancy":* Ibid., 188.

408 *"Write good, baby":* Ibid., 190.

409 *By August 21:* NM to Susan Mailer, 8-21-68.
409 *fifty thousand words:* NM to EY, 9-30-68.
409 *"more conventional":* Eliot Fremont-Smith, "Family Report," *NYT*, 10-28-68, 45.
409 *"to unfold":* Jack Richardson, "The Aesthetics of Norman Mailer," *NYRB*, 5-8-69, 3–4.
409 *"holds up better":* Frank Rich, "Introduction," *Miami and the Siege of Chicago* (NY: New York Review of Books, 2008), vii–xi.

NINE: POLITICIAN TO PRISONER

In addition to the sources identified below, the following were drawn on: JML's "Mailer Log"; JML's unpublished interviews with NM and BW. NM's letters are located at the HRC.

Page

410 *articles for* Life: NM to EY, 3-17-69.
410 *"the real had become":* OFM, 141.
410 *suggestions from three writer friends:* Michael Gross, "Norman Mailer: The Writer as Candidate," *New York*, 4-6-98.
410 *Gloria Steinem:* One of the most celebrated American feminists, Steinem (b. 1934), is a distinguished journalist and the author of several books, including a biography of Marilyn Monroe, *Marilyn: Norma Jeane* (NY: Henry Holt, 1986).
410 *"bring them whole":* AON, 135.
411 *"with the heart":* William Inge to NM, 5-29-68.
411 *"the disease of the 20th century":* NM to Inge, 6-15-68.
411 *"One key, one solution": Emerson: Essays and Lectures*, 966.
411 *honor guard:* MSC, 203–4.
411 *Weidenfeld and Nicolson:* AON was the first of NM's books published by this firm; later it published DPP, WVN, MSC, OFM, and POS.
411 *Harvard Board of Overseers:* Thomas Nagel to NM, 7-24-68.
411 *"comic, philosophical":* NM to Nagel, 8-2-68; see also Robert M. Smith, "Mailer and a Member of S.D.S. Seeking Posts on Harvard's Board of Overseers," *NYT*, 4-21-69, 37.
411 *"an auspicious moment":* Grunwald to NM, 9-26-68; NM to Grunwald, 9-30-68.
412 Newsweek *beat it:* Raymond Sokolov, "Flying High with Mailer," 12-9-68.
412 *"the poorest part":* MSC, 203.
412 *"the awful cry":* Ibid., 221.
412 *"balance every moment":* Ibid., 93.
412 *"enjoying a dalliance":* Ibid., 94.
412 *"illimitable funds":* Ibid.
412 *honorary degree:* Honorary Doctor of Letters degree on 6-4-69.
412 *"feeling a little tired":* NM, form letter, early 1969.
412 *Carolyn Mason, invite:* Joe Flaherty, *Managing Mailer* (NY: Coward-McCann, 1970), 15.

413 *Jimmy Breslin:* A Pulitzer Prize–winning newspaper columnist who writes from the perspective of ordinary people, Breslin (b. 1930), is also an accomplished novelist and investigative reporter.
413 *"street smarts":* Flaherty, *Managing Mailer*, 18.
413 *"could be matched":* Ibid.
413 *"hip left-right coalition":* Ibid., 80.
413 *"Electoral politics":* Ibid., 20.
413 *"Do you know something":* Ibid., 23.
413 *full-page ad: VV*, 4-17-69, 13.
413 *ticket as comptroller:* See "Gloria Steinem Remembers Norman Mailer," *NYT*, 11-12-07.
413 *"either because of fatigue":* Carolyn G. Heilbrun, *The Education of a Woman: The Life of Gloria Steinem* (NY: Dial, 1995), 178.
414 *"You're a half hour late":* Flaherty, *Managing Mailer*, 32.
414 *staff was hired:* Unless otherwise noted, campaign information comes from Flaherty, *Managing Mailer.*
414 *Giuliani was quoted:* Sam Roberts, "Ideas and Trends; A City Asks for a Return on Its Dollar," *NYT*, 1-15-95.
414 *"Well, those farmers":* Flaherty, *Managing Mailer*, 43.
415 *"for five years":* Ibid., 48.
415 *"Mailer was after all":* Ibid., 49.
415 *"swore to Christ":* Ibid., 50.
415 *several other campaign ideas:* See *Running Against the Machine: A Grass Roots Race for the New York Mayoralty* by Norman Mailer, Jimmy Breslin, Peter Maas, Gloria Steinem, and others, ed. Peter Manso (Garden City, NY: Doubleday, 1969), a compilation of material concerning the campaign; and NM's "Letter from Norman Mailer to the Voting Democrats of New York," *NYT*, 6-15-68, Sec. E, 7.
415 *"real people": Managing Mailer*, 52–53.
416 *"I'd piss on it":* Flaherty, *Managing Mailer*, 58.
415 *"Where are the pigs":* Ibid., 61.
415 *"candidates had become":* Ibid., 66.
415 *"would not deal":* Ibid., 67.
415 *"obviously had been":* Ibid.
417 *disproportionate amount of coverage:* See JML and Donna Pedro Lennon, *Norman Mailer: Works and Days*, 67–74, for a list of media stories on the campaign.
417 *"The press was horny":* Flaherty, *Managing Mailer*, 130.
417 *"the grace of the Doge": Women's Wear Daily*, 5-2-69, 12.
417 *"Why Are We in New York?": NYTM*, 5-18-69; rpt., EE, 322–38.
417 *angry man showed up:* JML interview with Danielle Mailer, 10-19-11.
417 *"booze-laden table":* Flaherty, *Managing Mailer*, 106.
418 *"a bunch of spoiled pigs":* Ibid., 113.
418 *"Why didn't you tell me":* Ibid., 119.
418 *damning account:* Sidney E. Zion, "Mailer Plays a Nightclub Date in Mayoral Quest," *NYT*, 5-9-69, 24.

418 *"genuinely scary":* Flaherty, *Managing Mailer*, 121.
418 *"This guy is bullying me":* Ibid., 122.
418 *"portrait of repentance":* Ibid., 123.
418 *"Like the girl with the curl":* Ibid., 161.
418 *"his head a full-blown mass":* Ibid., 182.
418 *"Railbird's Picks":* Ibid., 183.
419 *"Maybe, maybe":* Ibid., 184.
419 *"on many a morning":* OFM, 5.
419 *election vote totals:* "New York City Mayoral Elections," Wikipedia entry.
419 *"Did Mailer save":* Flaherty, *Managing Mailer*, 219.
419 *"considered and thoughtful":* Theodore White, quoted in Flaherty, *Managing Mailer*, 220.
420 *"He would never write":* OFM, 5.
420 *"an earthy woman":* Flaherty, *Managing Mailer*, 64.
420 *"It was impossible":* OFM, 436–37.
421 *"disembodied spirit":* Ibid., 6.
421 *an article appeared:* Henry Raymont, "Million Advance for Mailer Seen," *NYT*, 5-13-69, 44.
422 *"if you're gonna be paid":* Ron Rosenbaum, "The Siege of Mailer: Hero to Historian," *VV*, 1-21-71; rpt., CNM, 180.
422 *"disease of technology":* NM to EY, 3-17-69.
422 *"tempted to take a shortcut":* Matthew Grace and Steve Roday, "Mailer on Mailer: An Interview," *New Orleans Review* 3 (1973), 232.
422 *"afraid he would write":* MBM, 349.
422 *"You wouldn't let a commercial":* Barbara A. Bannon, "Authors and Editors: Norman Mailer," *Publishers Weekly*, 1-25-71, 178.
422 *"right wing for Attila":* MBM, 351.
423 *"not dull people":* Matthew Grace and Steve Roday, "Mailer on Mailer," *New Orleans Review*, 233.
423 *"how to locate myself":* NM to Ned Bradford, 4-12-69.
423 *"How can I participate":* MBM, 347.
423 *"If I could have gone":* Barbara A. Bannon, "Authors and Editors," *Publishers Weekly*, 179.
423 *Beverly embarked:* MBM, 356, and Tom Sullivan and Harold Banks, "Mailer Capers . . . His n' Hers in Divorce Ditty," *Boston Herald*, late October 1979.
424 *"I can't write anything":* Ralph Graves, "Norman Mailer at the Typewriter," *Life*, 8-29-69.
424 *The influence of* Moby-Dick*:* NM to JML, 5-30-90.
424 *innards of the rocket:* This comparison originates with John P. Sisk, "Aquarius Rising," *Commentary*, May 1971, 83.
424 *"to release the string":* OFM, 55.
424 *"and in the midst":* Ibid., 100.
425 *"Barney was adorable":* JML interview with Carol Stevens, 6-13-11.
425 *"lectured me on the merits":* Ibid.
425 *"keeps opening like a string":* NM to Ginsberg, 12-9-69.

426 PR *symposium:* "Black Power: A Discussion," *PR*, Spring 1968; rpt., EE, 305–9.
426 *essay in* Look*:* "Looking for the Meat and Potatoes—Thoughts on Black Power," *Look*, 1-7-69; rpt., EE, 287–304.
426 *"scandalously late":* MSC, 51–52.
426 *"heartily sick":* Ibid., 53.
427 *"in the cells of his existence":* AFM, 341.
427 *"impressive voice":* OFM, 134.
427 *"as if he were looking":* Ibid., 136–37.
427 *"magic would be at its heart":* Ibid., 139.
427 *Thanatosphere:* Ibid., 109, and "What Apollo Has Meant to Mankind," *Christian Science Monitor*, 1-3-73, 13.
427 *"the greatest achievement":* Leticia Kent, "The Rape of the Moon: Norman Mailer Talks About Sexual Lunacy and the WASP," *Vogue*, February 1971, 135.
428 *"It's like doing a benevolent":* NM to Luke Breit, 3-?-70.
428 *"near agreeable":* NM to Larry L. King, 9-8-70.
428 *"I'm a believer":* Myra MacPherson, "The Nonviolent Norman Mailer," *Washington Post*, 5-8-70, B1.
428 *"bums":* Nancy Scannell, "Norman Mailer to Serve Sentence," *Washington Post*, 5-6-70.
429 *"are the babblings":* Myra MacPherson, "The Nonviolent Norman Mailer," B2.
429 *"cathedral of hypocrisy":* Nancy Scannel, "Norman Mailer to Serve Sentence."
429 *"There are few places":* AFM, 518.
429 *According to Carol:* JML interview with Carol Stevens, 3-28-09.
429 *"He could have killed":* JML interview with Carol Stevens, 3-28-09.
430 *"It was":* POS, 11–12.
430 *"was in a period":* JML interview with Carol Stevens, 6-18-11.
430 *"I had heard":* Alan Levy, "Ezra Pound's Voice of Silence," *NYTM*, 1-9-72, 68.
430 *"The funny thing":* NM to Mary Jane Matz, 12-3-70.
431 *"staggering":* NM to R. W. B. Lewis, 9-21-70.
431 *"cavorting for* Time's*":* POS, 15–16.
431 *"too proper":* Ibid., 16.
431 *"major ideological":* Ibid.
431 *"Only a fool":* Ibid., 16–17.
431 *exploitation of women:* "People," *Time*, 9-14-70.
432 *"There was a tissue":* POS, 17.
432 *"big, fat discursive piece":* NM to Anne Barry, 9-21-70.
432 *"often sounds like":* Hector Arce, "Vidal Statistics," *Women's Wear Daily*, 11-2-70.
432 *"marriages, Vidal-0":* NM to *Women's Wear Daily*, 11-12-70.
432 *"enlarging human freedom":* Introduction to Touchstone edition of *Sexual Politics* (NY: Simon & Schuster, 1990), xviii.

432 Sexual Politics: (NY: Doubleday, 1970), ibid.
432 *"There was a great wave":* Introduction to Touchstone edition of *Sexual Politics.*
432 *August 30* Time*:* "The Liberation of Kate Millett," *Time*, 8-30-70.
432 *"Kate Millett's hard clay":* NM to Bourjaily, 10-21-70.
433 *"the first inkling":* NM to Selden Rodman, 9-11-71.
433 The Second Sex: Translated by H. M. Parshley (NY: Knopf, 1953).
433 The Feminine Mystique: (NY: Norton, 1963).
433 *"fundamental argument":* Louis Menand, "Books as Bombs," *New Yorker*, 1-24-11.
433 Of a Fire on the Moon: (Boston: Little, Brown, 1971).
433 *"unremitting self-involvement":* Benjamin DeMott, "Inside Apollo 11 with Aquarius Mailer," *Saturday Review*, 1-16-71, 25–27, 57–58.
434 *"Manichean ox-team":* Christopher Lehmann-Haupt, "Mailer's Dream of the Moon—I," *NYT*, 1-7-71, 33.
434 *"a certain slackness":* Morris Dickstein, "A Trip to Inner and Outer Space," *NYTBR*, 1-10-71, 1, 42–45.
434 The David Frost Show: See Rosenbaum, CNM, 180–86.
434 *"I'm caught these days":* NM to Aldridge, 1-24-71.
434 *appearances on television:* See JML, "Mailer's Sarcophagus: The Artist, the Media and the 'Wad,' " *Modern Fiction Studies* 23, Summer 1977, 179–87.
434 *"I never wrote so fast":* NM to MK, 4-21-70.
434 *"Ego: The Ali-Frazier Fight": Life*, 3-19-71; rpt., *King of the Hill: Norman Mailer on the Fight of the Century* (NY: New American Library, 1971), and EE, 3-36.
435 the artist *as an exemplary type:* See Robert F. Lucid, "The Artist as Fantasy Figure," *Massachusetts Review* 15, Autumn 1974, 581–95.
435 *"Boxing is a rapid":* EE, 6–7.
435 *ad in the* New York Times*:* 1–16, 71.
435 *columnists and pundits:* See, for example, Digby Diehl, "Norman Mailer Crosses Swords with Women's Lib," *Los Angeles Times Calendar*, 2-14-71, and Lynn Sherr, "Manly Mailer Strikes Out," Associated Press, 3-?-71.
435 *"strikes me as exactly right":* Trudy Owett, "Three Interviews: Joan Didion," *New York*, 3-15-71, 41.
435 *"being pious":* "Norman Mailer on Women, Love, Sex, Politics, and All That!," *Cosmopolitan*, May 1976, 184.
435 *"poured ice cubes":* POS, 28–29.
436 *"for fun and idiocy":* Transcript of interview with Marie-Louise von der Leyen, "Norman Mailer on Anger and Love," October 2004; translated into German, the interview was published in *Lifelines: Unusual Characters Tell Their Story* (Munich: Piper Verlag, 2006).
436 *"spent my life":* Janet Chusmire, "Mailer's on Tour, Recouping," *Miami Herald*, 2-7-72, 16A.
436 *"revolution, tradition, sex":* Anatole Broyard, "Norman Writes a Dithyramb," *NYT*, 5-27-71, 41.

436 *"the technological destruction":* David Lodge, "Male, Mailer, Female," *New Blackfriars*, December 1971, 561.
436 *"coitus-free conception":* POS, 192.
436 *"overthrow the government":* Valerie Solanas, "Excerpts from the SCUM (Society for Cutting Up Men) Manifesto," in *Sisterhood Is Powerful*, ed. Robin Parker (NY: Random House, 1970), 514.
437 *"while extreme":* POS, 47.
437 *"mysterious space within":* Ibid., 59–60.
437 *"go to work":* Ibid., 233.
437 *have achieved parity:* Department of Professional Employees, AFL-CIO, "Fact Sheet 2010: Professional Woman Vital Statistics."
437 *"the bloody ground":* POS, 95.
437 *"where the light":* Ibid., 110.
438 Genius and Lust: Subtitled *A Journey Through the Major Writings of Henry Miller* (NY: Grove, 1976).
438 *"that a firm erection":* POS, 44–45.
438 *"come in like winds":* Ibid., 134.
438 *"and could not have commanded":* Ibid., 137–38.
438 *"Lawrence's point":* Ibid., 147.
438 *"meaningless fucking":* Ibid., 155.
438 *"the only nostrum":* Ibid., 148.
438 *"outrageously":* Ibid., 153–54.
439 *"possessed of a mind":* Ibid., 153.
439 *compares him to a general:* Ibid., 153.
439 *"through their familiar":* Peter Balbert, "From *Lady Chatterley's Lover* to *The Deer Park*: Lawrence, Mailer, and the Dialectic of Erotic Risk," in *Critical Views: Norman Mailer*, ed. Harold Bloom (Philadelphia: Chelsea House, 2003), 109–26.
439 "Lady Chatterley *changed":* NM to Jeffrey Meyers, in ibid., 115.
439 *Rivers of money:* Income figures taken from Scott Meredith's annual reports to NM (HRC).
439 *Morris resigned:* The two most complete accounts of the situation are found in Morris's memoir, *New York Days*, and Stuart Little, "What Happened at Harper's," *Saturday Review*, 4-10-71, 43–47.
440 *"No wonder it's such":* "Hang-Up at *Harper's*," *Time*, 3-15-71, 45.
440 *"The money men":* Alden Whitman, "Morris Resigns in Harper's Dispute," *NYT*, 3-5-71, L37.
440 *meeting with Cowles:* Morris, *New York Days*, 362.
440 *"deeply disturbed":* Barbara Trecker, "Mailer Tells Harper's—Me, Too," *New York Post*, 3-6-71.
440 *"was precipitated":* "Hang-Up at *Harper's, Time.*
440 *"a strong":* Ibid.
440 *"the most depressing":* Ibid.
440 *"was not central":* Morris, *New York Days*, 356.
440 *"the highest known payment":* Eric Pace, "Mailer Getting $1-Million for Next Novel," *NYT*, 2-21-71, C24.

441 *"encompass the entire history":* Scott Meredith, quoted in Warner Bros. press release, 4-15-74.
441 *"My water broke":* JML interview with Carol Stevens, 6-18-11.
441 *"my mother's nose":* NM to MK, 4-21-71.
441 *"It would be difficult":* Diana Trilling, "The Prisoner of Sex," in Trilling, *We Must March My Darlings: A Critical Decade* (NY: Harcourt Brace Jovanovich, 1977), 200.
441 *"For a while":* Israel Shenker, "Norman Mailer Vs. Women's Lib," *NYT*, 5-1-71, L19.
441 *"All women are lesbians":* Jill Johnston, *Town Bloody Hall*, a documentary by Chris Hegedus and D. A. Pennebaker, 1979. Unless otherwise noted, all participant quotes are taken from the film.
442 *Greer, who had wanted to meet Mailer:* According to Diana Trilling, *We Must March My Darlings*, 200.
442 *"under most intemperate assault":* Diana Trilling, *We Must March My Darlings*, 200.
442 *Lawrence scholar:* Diana Trilling, ed., *The Selected Letters of D. H. Lawrence* (NY: Farrar, Straus & Cudhay, 1958).
443 *"the men moving silently":* POS, 125.
443 *Few stood with Mailer:* In addition to Broyard and Lodge, NM got positive notices from Eugene Kennedy, "Do You Have a Scar on Your Scrotum?," *Critic*, November 1971, 69–73; V. S. Pritchett, "With Norman Mailer at the Sex Circus," *Atlantic*, July 1971, 40–42; Garry Wills, "Norman Mailer vs. Woman," *Book World* (*Washington Post*), 7-11-71, 1–2.
443 *"tracking Norman":* Dotson Rader, "The Bishop and Norman Mailer," *MR* (2008), 175–76.
443 *"is modeled on a dribble":* Brigid Brophy, "Meditations on Norman Mailer, by Norman Mailer, Against the Day a Norman Mailest Comes Along," *NYTBR*, 5-23-71, 41.
443 *"Mailer's best book":* Anatole Broyard, "Norman Writes a Dithyramb," *NYT*, 5-27-71, 41.
443 *"his ability to apprehend":* POS, 6.
444 *"a stinking depression":* NM to Bourjaily, 3-26-71.
444 *"a visionary":* Joyce Carol Oates, "Out of the Machine," *Atlantic*, July 1971, 42–44.
444 *to find the best:* POS, 188.
444 *"corporate rubbery obstruction":* AAD, 127.
444 *"women have been machines":* Oates.
444 *"devastated":* JML interview with Danielle Mailer, 8-3-11.
445 *Susan was similarly:* JML interview with Susan Mailer, 8-18-11.
445 *hair turned white:* MBM, 371.
445 *"I haven't felt":* NM to MK, 6-20-71.
445 *"He was a marvelous":* Jessica Blue and Legs McNeil, "The Mailer Side of Mailer," *Details* (1984), 86.

445 *"a fatherly hand":* NM, preface to Torres's *Sting Like a Bee: The Muhammad Ali Story* (NY: Abelard-Schuman, 1971), x.

445 *"modest phenomenon":* Ibid., xi.

445 Fasting Can Save Your Life: Herbert M. Shelton (Chicago: Natural Hygiene Press, 1965).

445 *all your poisons:* Selden Rodman, *Tongues of Fallen Angels* (NY: New Directions, 1974), 172.

446 *I, the great* macho: Ibid., 178.

446 *assemble his magazine work:* NM to Ned Bradford, 8-15-71.

446 *"just lay fallow":* NM to EY, 9-21-71.

446 *The two books that led him:* NM, in Marie Brenner "Mailer Goes Egyptian," *New York*, 37.

446 The Last of the Just: (NY: Atheneum House, 1960).

446 The Story of Civilization: Vol. I, *Our Oriental Heritage* (NY: Simon & Schuster, 1963).

446 *"empathetic treatment":* Harold Hayes to NM, 6-?-71.

446 *"I would spend":* NM to Hayes, 6-12-70.

447 *His allegiance was transferred to* Playboy: Large excerpts from FIG, ES, and AE appeared in *Playboy* in 1975, 1979, and 1982, respectively.

447 *review of* Patriarchal Attitudes: Vidal, "Women's Liberation Meets Miller-Mailer-Manson Man," *NYRB*, 7-22-71; rpt., *Homage to Daniel Shays: Collected Essays, 1952–1972* (NY: Vintage, 1973), 389–402.

447 *"startling and frightening":* "Of a Small and Modest Malignancy," PAP, 57.

447 *"Cus, I hit him":* Torres, in Jeff Silverman, ed., *The Greatest Boxing Stories Ever Told* (NY: Lyons, 2002), 18.

447 *"boxed three moderately":* NM to Louis and Moos, 10-18-71.

448 *"the truth of his long":* "Punching Papa," *NYRB*, February 1963; rpt., TOT, 4. On NM and boxing, see Barry H. Leeds, "Boxing as a Moral Paradigm in Mailer's Work," in Leeds, *The Enduring Vision of Norman Mailer*, 57–74, and Bill Lowenburg, "Hooking Off the Jab: Norman Mailer, Ernest Hemingway and Boxing," *MR* (2010), 105–22.

448 The Long Patrol: subtitled: *25 Years of Writing from the Work of Norman Mailer* (NY: World, 1971).

448 *liked Lucid's comment:* NM to Ned Chase, 11-30-71.

448 *"he has accumulated":* Lucid, ed., *The Long Patrol*, xxv–xxvi.

448 D.J.: Published as "A Fragment from *Vietnam*," EE, 223–35.

449 *"It was a disaster":* Dotson Rader, "The Bishop and Norman Mailer," *MR*, 177; see also Rader's longer account, "The Day the Movement Died," *Esquire*, November 1972, 130–35, 194–204.

449 *"the first time":* "People," *Time*, 12-20-71, 45.

449 *"It was intense":* Dotson Rader, "The Bishop and Norman Mailer," *MR*, 177.

449 *"why Tennessee":* NM to Dotson Rader, 1-31-72.

449 *"I should have had":* NM to Paul Moore, 2-?-72.

449 *"the best book":* Dotson Rader, "The Bishop," 181.

449 *"between half and three-quarter throttle":* "Of a Small and Modest Malignancy," PAP, 61.
449 *"His hands were fists":* Dick Cavett, "In This Corner, Norman Mailer," *NYT*, 11-14-07.
449 *"read what you wrote":* transcript of 12-1-71 *The Dick Cavett Show*, Daphne Productions, 1971.
450 *"he began to wonder":* Dick Cavett, "In This Corner, Norman Mailer."
450 *"Mailer was entitled":* Louis Menand, "Talk Story," *New Yorker*, 11-22-10, 130.
450 *"Mailer: Why don't you":* Dick Cavett, "In This Corner, Norman Mailer."
451 *The rules of talk shows:* Analysis and the ending quote about the studio audience are both from Bernard M. Timberg, *Television Talk: A History of the TV Talk Show* (Austin: University of Texas Press, 2002), 83.
451 *"never received":* NM to Marshall Frady, 12-24-71.
451 *"The studio audience":* JML to NM, 12-22-71.
451 *"to meet any one":* NM to Earl and Sharon Perry, 12-30-11.
451 *"the kind of plain-spoken":* Bob Williams, "On the Air," *New York Post*, 12-2-71, 87.
451 *"Provincetown is beautiful":* NM to Eddie Bonetti, 12-30-71.
452 *understanding with* Life: NM to John Leonard, 12-30-71.
452 *"I was looking":* NM to Basil Mailer, 1-1-72.
452 *"I have come":* NM to JML, 1-30-72.
452 *"following his navigator":* Robert F. Lucid, "Prolegomenon to a Biography of Mailer," in JML, ed., *Critical Essays on Norman Mailer,* 181.
452 The Performing Self: Subtitled *Compositions and Decompositions in the Languages of Contemporary Life* (NY: Oxford, 1971).
452 *"on his way":* NM to John R. B. Brett-Smith, 4-2-71.
453 *"detailed usefulness":* Poirier to NM, 1-9-72.
453 *"Mailer now is like":* Poirier, *Norman Mailer*, 3.
453 *got this message:* NM to Poirier, 2-2-74.
453 *"a carpetbagger":* NM to Bill Walker, 3-7-72.
453 *"I felt his pain":* JML interview with Carol Stevens, 6-18-11.
453 *"with very little tradition":* NM to EY, 4-2-72.
454 *"I promise you":* NM to Lucid, 5-31-72.
454 *"the most exciting":* NM to EY, 5-31-72.
454 *"I don't have the remotest:* NM to Ginsberg, 12-9-69.
455 *"The Evil in the Room": Life*, 7-28-72; excerpted from SGG.
455 *"acid, amnesty and abortion":* Paul F. Boller, *Presidential Campaigns* (NY: Oxford University Press, 1984), 339.
455 *Jerry Rubin and Abbie Hoffman:* SGG, 30.
455 *"Out in America":* Ibid., 53.
455 *"The Genius": NYRB*, 11-2-72, 16–20.
455 *"a man who walks":* SGG, 155.
455 *"Nixon was the artist":* Ibid., 138.
456 *paid $75,000:* MBM, 386.
456 *"The house had negative":* JML interview with Carol Stevens, 6-18-11.

456 *thirty-day, twenty-college:* JML, "Norman Mailer in Illinois," *Sunrise* (Macomb, IL), November 1972, 24–26.
456 *"Book publishers":* Randi Henderson, "Norman Mailer Talks Politics at Towson," *Baltimore Sun*, 10-9-72, 1.
456 *"the body of demands":* Ibid.
457 *"Obedient little bitches":* "People," *Time*, 11-6-72.
457 *"dumping poisonous invective":* William Moore, "Norman Mailer in Full Cry," *San Francisco Chronicle*, 10-26-72, 7.
457 *cemented his position:* Ten years later, *Ms.* magazine quoted the line: "They Speak for Themselves," *Ms.*, July/August, 1982, 46.
457 *He wrote a letter:* "Moral Superiority," *Time*, 12-11-72, 9.
457 *"I think we have to pay it":* NM, interview with Robert F. Lucid, 1-17-89 (HRC).

TEN: THE TURN TO BIOGRAPHY

In addition to the sources identified below, the following were drawn on: JML's "Mailer Log"; JML's and Lawrence Grobel's unpublished interviews with NM and Lawrence Schiller; JML's unpublished interviews with BW. NM's letters are located at the HRC.

Page

458 *Frank Crowther:* The manager of NM's fiftieth birthday party, Crowther (1932–76) committed suicide and was eulogized by NM in *The Paris Review*, Fall 1976; rpt., PAP, 82–88.
458 *fiftieth birthday:* Mel Gussow, "Mailer's Guests ($50 a Couple) Hear His Plan on 'Secret Police,' " *NYT*, 2-6-73, 23; Patricia Bosworth, "Fifth Estate at the Four Seasons," *Saturday Review*, March 1973, 5–7; Sally Quinn, "Norman Mailer Turns 50," *Washington Post*, 2-7-73, B1, B7; Lucian K. Truscott IV, "Mailer's Birthday," *VV*, 2-8-73, 1, 24–26; Linda Franke, "A Half Century of Mailer," *Newsweek*, 2-19-73, 78; Jan Hodenfield, "A Party Scripted by Norman Mailer, Age 50," *New York Post*, 2-6-73, 2, 74; Frank Crowther, "Mailer's 5th Estate: Who's Paranoid Now?", *VV*, 7-12-73, 1, 10-13; LNM, 249–51; MBD, 1–10; MLT, 532–34; MBM, 388–93.
458 *"Another ego trip":* NM, in Mel Gussow, "Mailer's Guests," *NYT*.
459 *"an announcement of national importance":* Birthday party invitation.
459 *"a family and literary event":* Mel Gussow, "Mailer's Guests," *NYT*, 23.
459 *Mailer's answer to Capote's:* MBD, 2.
459 *"in a rare tender":* JML interview with Mary Oliver, 9-1-11.
459 *"Tell Norman":* Sally Quinn, "Norman Mailer Turns 50," *Washington Post*, B7.
459 *fifth wife:* Patricia Bosworth, "Fifth Estate at the Four Seasons," *Saturday Review*, 7.
459 *"At its center":* Lucian Truscott, "Mailer's Birthday," *VV*, 24.
460 *"one of the half dozen original thinkers":* Linda Franke, "A Half Century of Mailer," *Newsweek*, 78.

460 *"a hint too drunk":* Sally Quinn, "Norman Mailer Turns 50," *Washington Post*, B7.
460 *"If we have a democratic secret police":* Patricia Bosworth, "Fifth Estate at the Four Seasons," *Saturday Review*, 7.
460 *"He digressed":* Sally Quinn, "Norman Mailer Turns 50," *Washington Post*, B7.
460 *"You blew it":* As recalled in JML interview with Carol Stevens, 3-28-09.
460 *"I have a demon":* Patricia Bosworth, "Fifth Estate at the Four Seasons," *Saturday Review*, B7.
460 *"terrible mistake":* Sally Quinn, "Norman Mailer Turns 50," *Washington Post*, B7.
460 *"morally dastardly":* Mel Gussow, "Mailer's Guests," *NYT*, 23.
461 *only $600:* Patricia Bosworth, "Fifth Estate at the Four Seasons," *Saturday Review*, 7.
461 *"Norman Mailer: Genius or Nothing": The Morning After: Selected Essays and Reviews* (NY: Farrar, Straus & Giroux, 1971), 9–17.
461 *"has caught every fashion":* Ibid., 10.
461 *"He gives himself":* Ibid., 17.
461 *"the best writer":* Frank Crowther, "Mailer's 5th Estate," *VV*, 1.
461 *"a disaster":* Sally Quinn, "Norman Mailer Turns 50," *Washington Post*, B1.
461 *"just another vigilante group":* Frank Crowther, "Mailer's 5th Estate," *VV*, 12.
461 *"there was a general":* Ibid.
462 *"and the asshole dilettantes":* Ibid., 12.
462 *"I have rarely":* NM to Poirier, 2-2-74.
462 *"I still think":* Frank Crowther, "Mailer's 5th Estate," *VV*, 13.
462 *merged with CARIC:* Louise Lague, "Mailer Headlines Counter-Spy Pitch," *Washington Star-News*, 3-25-74, D1.
462 *"homeopathic medicine":* "The CIA vs. Democracy," *Counter-Spy* 2, Spring/Summer 1975, 40.
462 *"the grand middle-aged man":* Stefan Kanfer, "Two Myths Converge: NM Discovers MM," *Time*, 7-16-73, 63.
462 *he read:* Fred Lawrence Guiles, *Norma Jean: The Life of Marilyn Monroe* (NY: McGraw-Hill, 1969); Maurice Zolotow, *Marilyn Monroe* (NY: Harcourt Brace, 1960); Norman Rosten, *Marilyn: An Untold Story* (NY: New American Library, 1973).
462 *Ben Hecht: Empire News*, 5-9-54 to 8-1-54.
462 *"in modest depth":* MAR, 259.
463 *"so excited":* William McDonald, "An Evening with Norman Mailer," *Lone Star Review*, 3.
463 *"Let it be the longest":* Bragg, CNM, 194.
463 *"I wanted to say":* Stefan Kanfer, "Two Myths Converge," *Time*, 60.
463 *"had the basic stuff":* Ibid., 64.
463 *"I speculated":* Bragg, CNM, 195. See LNM, 255–59, for a convincing analysis of how NM melded fact and speculation in MAR.

463 *"the sugar of sex":* MAR, 15.
463 *"existential similarities":* Stefan Kanfer, "Two Myths Converge," *Time*, 60.
463 *"She'd finally laid down":* Bragg, CNM, 202.
464 *"ego-gobblings":* AFM, 93.
464 *due on March 1:* "The Monroe Doctrine," *New York*, 2-26-73, 59.
464 *"indelible":* Walter Robinson, "Mailer on Mailer on Monroe," *Sunday Times Magazine* (London), 9-9-73, 22.
466 *"There was a monumental":* MBM, 398.
466 Life *cover story:* "For Marilyn, a Look Back in Adoration," *Life*, 8-19-72; 71–74.
466 *accused Mailer of plagiarism:* "Publisher Stays New Mailer Book," *NYT*, 6-22-73, 21.
466 *"No one is going":* Eric Pace, "Mailer Denies He Plagiarized," *NYT*, 6-27-73, 68.
466 *exceeded the limits:* "War of Marilyn Bios Erupts Again: Zolotow Suing Mailer," *Hollywood Reporter*, 7-3-73, 1, 9.
466 *$6 million:* "Zolotow Files $6-Million Suit Over Mailer's Book 'Marilyn,' " *NYT*, 8-4-73.
466 *"the literary heist of the century":* Zolotow letter of apology, *NYTBR*, 12-8-73, 15.
466 *paid to Zolotow and Guiles:* Maurice Duke, "Too Many Facts Are Missing in Norman Mailer's 'Marilyn,' " *Richmond Times-Dispatch*, 7-29-73; NM, "Mailer's Side," *Arkansas Times*, 7-7-94, 6.
467 60 Minutes: NM interview, aired 7-13-73; all quotes from program taken from CBS-TV transcript.
467 *Murray later recanted:* Eunice Murray Wikipedia entry.
468 *biography was a cover story: Atlantic*, August 1973, contained an excerpt, as did *NYRB*, 8-9-73, and two in *Ladies' Home Journal*, July and August 1973; four weekly excerpts from the biography ran in the *Sunday Times Magazine* (London) beginning 9-16-73.
468 *400,000 copies:* "Marilyn by Norman Mailer," Grosset & Dunlap summary, August 1973 (HRC).
468 *600,000 copies:* Advertisement in *Publishers Weekly*, 5-13-75.
468 *"a new genre called":* John Simon, "Mailer's Mystic Marriage," *New Leader*, 9-17-73, 21–23.
468 *"is great as only a great":* Pauline Kael, "A Rip-off with Genius," *NYTBR*, 7-22-73, 1–3.
468 *"creating too wan":* MAR, 37.
469 *"Napoleonic":* Ibid., 23.
469 *"She is her career":* Ibid., 102.
469 *"No one can be certain":* Ibid., 18.
469 *"It is no ordinary":* Ibid., 22.
469 *"a* species *of novel":* Ibid., 20. I am indebted to Carl Rollyson for enriching my discussion of MAR. See LNM, 251–61. See also Rollyson's discussion of MAR in *Female Icons: Marilyn Monroe to Susan Sontag* (iUniverse, 2005).

470 *two books that he "produced": Ladies and Gentlemen, Lenny Bruce!* (NY: Random House, 1974); *Muhammad Ali: A Portrait in Words and Photographs* (NY: Alskog/Crowell, 1974).
470 *"All through the 1970s":* William McDonald, "An Evening with Norman Mailer," *Lone Star Review*, 3.
470 *Sorrento, Maine:* NM to Mary Bancroft, 9-21-73.
470 *"We'd be in our bunks":* JML interview with Danielle Mailer, 8-20-08.
471 *"to do things":* JML interview with Betsy Mailer, 11-29-11.
471 *"We were away":* JML interview with Michael Mailer, 8-21-08.
471 *One summer he gave us:* Kate Mailer, "The Knife's Edge," *MR* (2008), 35.
471 *Tiffany wide gold band:* JML interview with Carol Stevens, 5-15-11.
472 *"To work on a novel":* Deirdre Carmody, "The Rich, Famous, Talented and Powerful Resolve," *NYT*, 1-1-74, C1.
472 The Egyptian Book of the Dead: Originally published by the British Museum in two volumes, 1894–95, it was reissued as a Dover Press paperback in 1967, which NM used.
472 *"novel writing is* hard*":* NM to Poirier, 3-6-74.
472 *doing push-ups:* NM to Neil Abercrombie, 3-25-74.
472 *down to 165:* NM to Cus D'Amato, 6-15-73.
472 *"These days I pant":* NM to Rust Hills, 11-19-73.
473 *"Now everybody thinks":* NM to MK, 3-25-73.
473 *"a lot of personal stuff":* JML interview with Mary Oliver, 9-1-11.
474 *The book would be published: Watching My Name Go By.* Documented by Mervyn Kurlansky and Jon Naar, Prepared by Lawrence Schiller (London: Mathews, Miller, Dunbar, 1974); *The Faith of Graffiti* (NY: Praeger, 1974); rpt., PAP, 134–58.
474 *simultaneously in* Esquire*:* May 1974.
474 *Hayes had left:* NM to Ed Meadows, 5-12-74.
474 *The ice had been broken:* MLT, 559.
474 *"masterpieces in letters":* PAP, 140.
474 *"might have been transformed":* Ibid., 142.
474 *"the implacable enemy":* Ibid., 149–50.
475 *"enormous black eyes":* Anne Edwards and Stephen Citron, *The Inn and Us* (NY: Random House, 1976), 76.
475 *"Halfway through":* Ibid., 77–78.
475 *"Standing in the center":* Ibid., 79.
476 *"the only big one":* JML interview with Carol Stevens, 5-15-11.
476 *consecutive issues of* Rolling Stone*:* "Aquarius Hustling," 1-2-75, 41–47, 71; "Sympathy for the Devil," 1-16-75, 42–47, 56–57.
476 *"changed my life":* Richard Stratton, "Meeting Mailer," *MR* (2008), 314.
477 *"elegiac tone":* "Aquarius Hustling," 46.
477 *"If Manson had become":* Ibid., 45.
477 *"Dostoyevskian":* Ibid., 46.
477 *"Napoleonic":* Ibid., 71.
477 *"Some early scenes":* "Sympathy for the Devil," 45.
477 *"apathetic hippie beatdom":* "Aquarius Hustling," 42.

478 *most famous man:* Terrence Doody, "Two Heroes: Mailer and Ali," *Houston Chronicle*, 7-27-75.
478 *"to think over":* FIG, 161.
478 *"the transformations":* NM to Crowther, 7-11-74.
478 *Only the Irish:* NM to Kate Millett, 7-16-74. Denise Pappas referred me to an interview in which Millett recalled having a drink with NM in Provincetown, and he was "friendly but condescending." www.eastvillage.Thelocal.nytimes.com/2012/06/06/35371.
478 *"was hardly a Zionist":* FIG, 161.
478 *"I always thought":* Marie Brenner, "Mailer Goes Egyptian," *New York*, 3-28-83, 38.
479 *"I could do my book":* George Plimpton, "Unbloodied by the Critical Pounding, Norman Mailer Defends the Egyptian Novel," *People*, 5-30-83; rpt., CNM, 305.
479 *"three miserable days":* FIG, 20.
479 *undulant fever:* NM to MK, 10-9-74.
479 *"I'm beginning to think":* NM to FG, 10-9-74.
479 *"the black crowds":* FIG, 36.
479 Bantu Philosophy: (Paris: Presence Africaine, 1959).
479 *"a human with his own psyche":* FIG, 38–39.
480 *"Excuse me for not shaking":* Ibid., 45–46.
480 *"concentration would become":* Ibid., 48.
480 *"were probably the heaviest":* Ibid., 61.
481 *"no small sound":* Ibid., 91–92.
481 *"good and drunk":* Ibid., 124.
481 *"a triumph for everything":* Ibid., 162.
481 *"For as long as Foreman":* Ibid., 185.
482 *"Blows seem to pass":* Ibid., 186.
482 *"like a drunk":* Ibid., 201.
482 *"Foreman was becoming":* Ibid., 204.
482 *"slow as a man":* Ibid., 204–5.
482 *"give a prod":* Ibid., 197.
482 *"went over like":* Ibid., 208.
482 *He began work:* NM to MK, 2-18-75.
482 *appeared in book form: The Fight* was published by Little, Brown on 7-21-75.
482 *"a book about a genius":* Stan Isaacs, "Norman Mailer: 'I'm Like a Minor Champ,' " *LI: Newsday Magazine*, 9-21-75, 22.
482 *"He was no longer":* FIG, 31.
483 *"had been burning":* Ibid., 34.
483 *"These reportorial books":* Seymour Krim, review of FIG, *Newsday*, 7-28-75.
483 *"I think it's legitimate":* Stan Isaacs, "Norman Mailer," *LI: Newsday Magazine*, 22.
483 *"Nijinsky of ambivalence":* OFM, 472.
484 *"He had tears":* JML interview with Carol Stevens, 6-18-11.

484 *"How are you, Mr. Mailer":* Judy Klemesrud, "Life with Mailer: After Four Years, So Far, So Good," *NYT*, 4-16-79, B13.
484 *"The* last *thing":* TC, 83.
484 *"the intensity of his blue":* Ibid., 85.
485 *"It was all rather overwhelming":* Ibid., 88.
485 *"Through the years":* Ibid., 98–99.
486 *"an interloper":* Ibid., 105.
486 *"I instinctively knew":* Ibid.
486 *a first-rate intelligence: The Crack-Up*, 69.
486 *"has erupted":* NM to Susan Mailer, 10-22-75.
486 *"harrowing":* NM to MK, 7-7-75.
486 *anthology of Henry Miller's work:* MBM, 417–18.
487 Some Honorable Men: The collection contains excerpts from PP, CAC, MSC, and SGG; it was published by Little, Brown in October 1976.
487 *"before its spirit":* NM to Peter Bogdanovich, 8-8-75.
487 *IRS began putting levies:* NM to MK, 5-9-75.
487 *When the paper was sold:* Felker and his partners took over *VV* in June 1974, but NM did not receive any money until the following spring.
487 *"So I'm half breathing":* NM to Larry L. King, 7-7-75.
487 *"I'm really going":* NM to MK, 8-28-75.
487 *"For the first time":* NM to NCM, 7-30-75.
488 *"I at last have found":* NCM to NM, 7-?-75.
488 *read D. H. Lawrence's* The Rainbow: NM to NCM, 9-12-75.
488 The Rainbow: (London: Methuen, 1915).
488 *"So often one finds":* NM to NCM, 6-5-75.
488 *Cinnamon Brown:* NM to NCM, 7-3-75.
489 *"try it for a while":* TC, 120.
489 *"to turn from all":* NCM to NM, 8-?-75.
489 *"which would give Mother":* TC, 123.
490 *"I'm sure they had":* Ibid., 120.
490 *"There are no easy fights":* NM to NCM, 8-?-75; 5.
490 *call to Suzanne Nye:* JML interview with Mary Oliver, 9-1-11.
491 *she never stopped loving Mailer:* JML interview with Carol Stevens, 5-15-11.
491 *"We were at Ciro's":* JML interview with Stephen Mailer, 10-24-09.
491 *"were very jagged":* JML interview with Danielle Mailer, 8-20-08.
491 *"She was so young":* JML interview with Susan Mailer, 9-5-07.
492 *her clothes were rumpled:* TC, 159.
492 *"would figure":* Ibid.
492 *"There was like a little pig":* JML interview with NCM, 1-30-09.
492 *"in the spirit":* TC, 162.
492 *Sergio Leone:* Best remembered for his western trilogy from the mid-1960s starring Clint Eastwood, *A Fistful of Dollars, For a Few Dollars More*, and *The Good, the Bad and the Ugly*, Leone (1929–89) hired MK to help dub the last of these films into English.
493 The Hoods: (NY: Crown, 1952).

493 *"some of my best dialogue":* NM to Moos, 12-5-75.
493 *"Mailer's screenplay gave Leone":* MK, *The Good, the Bad, and the Dolce Vita,* 301–2.
493 *Bogdanovich and another:* TC, 181.
493 *introduce her to Wilhelmina Cooper:* Ibid., 183–85.
493 *"Trying not to look":* Norris Church, "Getting My Book Together," *Cosmopolitan*, August 1977, 130–38.
494 *letter to him:* NCM to NM, 8-?-75.
494 *"thrilled":* TC, 185.
494 *"In the beginning":* Ibid., 193.
494 *"a tall lovely red-haired":* NM to Moos, 12-5-75.
494 *"Let me have my starlet":* JML interview with Carol Stevens, 6-18-11.
494 *"is like a good wife":* NM to Moos, 12-5-75.
495 *"the possibility of committing":* NM to Luke Breit, 12-5-75.
495 *"The nature of existence":* "Book Ends," *NYTBR*, 3-14-76, 37.
495 JR: (NY: Knopf, 1975).
495 *"waste, flux and chaos":* Susan Strehle, *Fiction in a Quantum Universe* (Chapel Hill: University of North Carolina Press, 1992), 97.
495 Gravity's Rainbow: (NY: Viking, 1973).
495 *"either a genius":* JML, "An Author's Identity," PAP, 157.
495 *"psychological demeanment":* Eliot Fremont-Smith, "Do Writers Ride in Cadillacs?," *VV*, 5-3-76.
496 *published in the* Los Angeles Times: "Henry Miller: Celebrating a Cause Celebre," *Los Angeles Times Book Review*, 3-28-76, 1, 3.
496 *"but believe me":* Henry Miller to NM, 3-28-76.
496 *"ruefully":* NM to Henry Miller, 4-13-76.
496 *"He has such":* GAL, xiv.
496 *"One had to go back":* Ibid., 4.
496 *"Miller at his best":* Ibid.
497 *"entered a town house":* Ibid., 15–17.
497 *"inestimable":* Ibid., 17.
497 *"the uncharted negotiations":* Ibid., 186.
497 *"The narcissist suffers":* Ibid., 187–88.
498 *"To be living":* Ibid., 189.
498 *"putting much of myself":* NM to Henry Miller, 5-25-76.
499 *"a path through my financial difficulties":* NM to EY, 4-13-76.
499 *piece, published in* New York: "A Harlot High and Low: Reconnoitering the Secret Government," *New York*, 8-16-76, 22–46.
499 *"I've finally come":* NM to EY, 4-13-76.
499 *"as something between a girlfriend":* TC, 204–5.
499 *"talked about her":* Ibid.
500 *"a towering depression":* NM to Lucid, 11-23-76.
500 *published in the* Times: "The Search for Carter," *NYTM*, 9-26-76; rpt., in part, TOT, 948–59.
500 *"haranguing a future president":* TOT, 955.
500 *"the possibility that Satanism":* Ibid., 956.

500 *"the twice dull sense":* Ibid., 959.
500 *wrote to Knox:* NM to MK, 11-25-76.
500 *"romantically overblown":* William Gass, "The Essential Henry Miller, According to Norman Mailer," *NYTBR*, 10-24-76, 1–2.
500 *"The room was so packed":* TC, 200.
500 *Jacqueline Onassis:* Guest list from Charlotte Curtis, "The Fashionable Armies of the Night," *NYT*, 12-20-76, C14.
500 *"as if his very life":* TC, 201.
501 *"to go beyond one's reach":* Herbert Mitgang, "Mailer Takes on the Heavyweight Novel," *NYT*, 12-10-76, C24.
501 *John Ehrlichman:* "A Conversation Between Norman Mailer and John Ehrlichman," *Chic* 2, December 1976, 16–40, 70, 88–92.
501 *memoir of Hemingway's son:* Preface to *Papa: A Personal Memoir* (Boston: Houghton Mifflin, 1976).
501 *a screenplay:* "Trial of the Warlock," *Playboy*, December 1976, 121–32, 235–56.
501 *"To my surprise":* Herbert Mitgang, "Mailer Takes on the Heavyweight Novel," *NYT*, C24.
501 *"Obviously, others also deserved":* NM to Meyer Levin, 1-6-77.
501 *"resisting intensely":* NM to MK, 1-14-77.
501 *Harvard instructor:* Robert Gorham Davis to NM, 12-14-76.
501 *"the total inventive freedom":* NM to Davis, 1-7-77.
502 *"plenty of pitfalls":* NM to Susan Mailer, 3-14-77.

ELEVEN: DEATH WISHES: GILMORE AND ABBOTT

In addition to the sources identified below, the following were drawn on: JML's "Mailer Log"; JML's and Lawrence Grobel's unpublished interviews with NM and Lawrence Schiller; JML's unpublished interviews with BW. NM's letters are located at the HRC.

Page

503 *"You sentenced me":* ES, 492.
503 *cover of* Newsweek*:* 11-29-76.
503 *"It was an arresting":* Kevin Bezner, "Mailer on Gilmore," *Washington Book Review*, January/February 1980. 4.
503 *"Dr. L. Grant Christensen":* Barry Farrell, "Merchandising Gary Gilmore's Dance of Death," *New West Magazine*, December 1976; rpt., Barry Farrell, *How I Got to Be This Hip: The Collected Works of One of America's Preeminent Journalists*, ed. Steve Hawk (NY: Washington Square Press, 1999), 118.
503 *"Nicole and I":* Barry Farrell and Lawrence Schiller, "Playboy Interview: Gary Gilmore," *Playboy*, April 1977, 77.
503 *"I could see he":* "Norman Mailer," *Publishers Weekly*, 10-8-79, 8.
503 *$60,000:* Grace Lichtenstein, "Gilmore's Agent an Entrepreneur Who Specializes in the Sensational," *NYT*, 1-20-77.

504 *contract with Warner Books:* The contract, which specifies that NM and Schiller share the copyright, is in the HRC.
504 *$500,000:* MBM, 425–26.
504 *front page of the* National Enquirer*:* Dennis D'Antonio and Thomas Kuncl, "173 Death Cell Letters Take You Inside the Mind of Gary Gilmore," *National Enquirer*, 1-11-77, 1, 32–33.
504 *"I do not believe":* Schiller to NM, 12-3-79.
504 An American Tragedy*:* (NY: Boni & Liveright, 1925). NM said that Dreiser's novel was a model for ES; see SA, 90.
504 *"All he does":* Jeffrey Severs, "The Untold Story Behind *The Executioner's Song*: A Conversation with Lawrence Schiller," *MR* (2007), 100.
504 *six months:* NM to Jack Abbott, 8-5-78.
504 *"The Saint and the Psychopath":* As noted in a draft of a contract with Bantam that Schiller attempted to negotiate (HRC).
505 *a quality that was almost saintly:* John W. Aldridge, "An Interview with Norman Mailer," *PR*, July 1980; rpt., CNM, 264.
505 *Trader Vic's:* Jeffrey Severs, "The Untold Story," *MR*, 97.
505 *"a man who was quintessentially American":* Aldridge, CNM, 270.
505 *"She's been injured":* Kevin Bezner, "Mailer on Gilmore," *Washington Book Review*, 6.
505 *"probably the most open":* Jeffrey Severs, "The Untold Story," *MR*, 98.
506 *Malibu:* Ibid., 97.
506 *$25,000:* Grace Lichtenstein, "Gilmore's Agent an Entrepreneur," *NYT*, 1-20-77.
506 *"a dictionary":* Jeffrey Severs, "The Untold Story," *MR*, 82.
506 *"not prettily":* TC, 232.
506 *"Our life was coalescing":* Ibid., 210.
507 *angry letter to the editor:* NM to Robert Spitzler, 12-9-76.
507 *"you need not take it":* NM to Carol Holmes, 4-20-77.
507 *"the minutiae":* TC, 233.
507 *"She was his practical":* JML interview with Aurora Huston, 1-15-12.
507 *"a bloody rupture":* NM to JML, 12-22-77.
507 *"At the time":* TC, 190.
507 *"Norman and I had":* JML interview with NCM, 1-30-09.
508 *"pretending to be bolder":* TC, 219.
508 *"thrilled":* Ibid., 218.
508 *"tons of scintillating":* NM to MK, 8-2-77.
508 *"At some point":* JML interview with Danielle Mailer, 7-29-09.
508 *Stephen recalled that Mailer:* JML interview with Stephen Mailer, 11-20-11.
508 *"He was a terrible gambler":* JML interview with Peter Alson, 4-23-12.
509 *"like a lawyer preparing briefs":* NM to Gordon Lish, 11-15-77.
509 *"No, no, no":* Jeffrey Severs, "The Untold Story," *MR*, 104.
509 *"second-hand and rather fanciful":* NM to Jonathan Silverman, 10-4-93.
510 *"because I knew that the Mormons":* Jeffrey Severs, "The Untold Story," *MR*, 103.

510 *fifteen thousand pages:* "An Afterword," ES, 1051.
510 *"and suddenly, Schiller":* Aldridge, CNM, 268.
511 *voyeur:* Robert Friedman, "Hell's Agent," *Esquire*, October 1978, 77.
511 Minamata: Words and Photos: (NY: Alskog-Sensorium and Holt Rinehart Winston, 1975).
511 *"Any contest between me":* Barry Farrell, "Merchandising Gary Gilmore's Dance of Death," *How I Got to Be This Hip*, 117.
511 *"I'm suited up":* Jeffrey Severs, "The Untold Story," *MR*, 90.
511 *$40,000:* Grace Lichtenstein.
512 *"He wanted to do":* David Thompson, "Mailer by the Bay," *California*, August 1987, 68.
512 *"one of the great wheeler-dealers":* NM to Bonnie B., 3-28-99. NM also called Schiller "you falloozeling genius."
512 *Gordon Lish:* Mailer had a warm relationship with Lish (b. 1934), aka Captain Fiction, who was known for his valiant efforts on behalf of emerging writers such as Raymond Carver and Amy Hempel.
512 *"Of a Small and Modest Malignancy":* *Esquire*, November 1977; rpt., PAP, 13–81.
512 *Mailer-Vidal fight at Lally Weymouth's:* Drawn from the following: Liz Smith, "There's Always a Morning After," New York *Daily News*, 10-27-77; Liz Smith, "Vidal Plus Mailer: Pow," *Chicago Tribune*, 10-30-77; "Still Feuding After All These Years, Gore and Norman Stage Fight Night at Lally's," *People*, 11-14-77, 42–43; Nancy Collins, " 'The Fight,' Starring Mailer and Vidal," *Washington Post*, 10-28-77; "Newsmakers," *Newsweek*, 11-7-77, 67, 69; MBM, 418–19; MLT, 604–5; Kaplan, *Vidal: A Biography*, 708–11.
514 *Norris stood up:* MBM, 419.
514 *"Nothing mattered":* NM to Lish, 11-15-77.
514 *"horrified and helpless":* TC, 239.
514 *1993 collection: United States: Essays, 1952–1992.*
514 *weighing titles:* ES files (HRC).
515 *"a kind of litmus test":* Jan Herman, "Raising the Ante as He Appraises His Holdings," *Providence Journal*, 10-29-80, H16.
515 *"With all the excitement":* ES, 10.
515 *"a gentle voice":* Joseph McElroy, "A Little on Novel-Writing," *Columbia: A Magazine of Poetry and Prose*, 6 (1981); rpt., PAP, 172.
516 *"a middle-aged movie-writer":* William F. Buckley and Jeff Greenfield, "Crime and Punishment: Gary Gilmore," transcript of *Firing Line*, 10-11-79; rpt., CNM, 251.
516 *"Put everything in":* ES files (HRC).
516 *"baroque":* Jan Herman, "Raising the Ante as He Appraises His Holdings," *Providence Sunday Journal Arts and Travel*, H16.
516 *"so difficult":* Hilary Mills, "Creators on Creating: Norman Mailer," *Saturday Review*, January 1981, 53.
516 *"it's not easy":* Herman.

516 *"the shifting point of view":* Ted Morgan, "Last Rights," *Saturday Review*, 11-10-79, 57–58.
516 *"violated the fundamental integrity":* McElroy, PAP, 177–78.
516 *"The deity":* Ted Morgan, "Last Rights," *Saturday Review*, 57.
517 *"so pronounced":* Richard G. Stern, "Where Is That Self-Mocking Literary Imp?," *Chicago*, January 1980, 108.
517 *"narrative technique of real genius":* Frank McConnell, review of ES, *Saturday Review*, 10-27-79, 30.
517 *1944 novel: A Transit to Narcissus* was published on March 29.
517 *"the folk hero":* William Hamilton, "Mom Mailer's Advice, and Other Things," *Boston Globe*, 6-8-78.
517 *"and Norman plans":* Judy Klemesrud, "Party Hails Publication of Jones's Last Novel," *NYT*, 2-23-78, C15.
517 *"He turned to me":* Kaylie Jones, *Lies My Mother Never Told Me* (NY: Morrow, 2009), 229–30.
518 *repeated to others:* In a conversation with JML, 5-26-95.
518 Quite the Other Way: NM gave a blurb to the 1989 Fawcett edition of Kaylie Jones's novel.
518 *"the wisdom of an elegant redneck":* NM, *James Jones Literary Society Newsletter*, Spring 1999.
518 *"the psychology of violence":* NM to Abbott, 2-23-78.
519 *"was intense, direct, unadorned":* NM, introduction to Jack Henry Abbott, *In the Belly of the Beast: Letters from Prison* (NY: Random House, 1981), x–xi.
519 *"So he has a mind":* Ibid., xv.
519 *"as well as I know": Publishers Weekly*, 1-8-79, 9.
520 *"We're calling him John":* NM to Abbott, 5-10-78.
520 *"as many characters":* NM to Louis and Moos Mailer, 5-17-78.
520 *"a hazard":* McElroy, 175.
520 *work double shifts:* NM to John Wisner, 5-10-78.
520 *"not unlike 'In Cold Blood' ":* NM to Morton Yanow, 5-10-78.
520 *doing portraits:* MBD, 345.
520 *"truly a menagerie":* NM to Louis and Moos, 5-17-78.
521 *"he dictated":* LNM, 288.
521 *"in the voice":* Ibid.
521 *"The manuscript will probably":* NM to Yanow, 7-17-78.
521 *"entirely of my own":* NM to Abbott, 8-5-78.
521 *jogged three times:* NM to Peter Arthurs, 5-17-78.
522 *"I work six or seven":* NM to Mary Breasted, 7-17-78.
522 *delivered a rough draft:* NM to Brenda Nicol, 12-13-78.
522 *see Beverly perform:* MBD, 345; TC, 148.
522 *"Beverly totally flipped out":* Ibid., 230–31.
522 *a good father:* Martha Smilgis, "Once Norman's Conquest, the Fourth Mrs. Mailer Fights Her Final Marital Battle," *People*, 2-26-79, 24–26.

523 *$1,000 a week:* Tom Sullivan and Harold Banks, "Mailer Story Has It All: Love, Hate, Sex, Drama," *Boston Herald American*, 11-30-78.
523 *"Listen":* Smilgis.
523 *total of $400,000:* Robert Garrett, "Mailer's P-Town Pad Put on Block Too," *Boston Globe*, 4-1-79.
523 *"my fifth wife":* Peggy Eastman, "Mailer Pays $1,000 to Former Mistresses, Testimony Reveals," *Cape Cod Times*, 1-24-79, 3.
523 *"His affairs are a holy":* Sullivan and Banks, "Mailer's Real-Life Escapades Outdo Fiction," *Boston Herald American*, 12-10-78, A3.
523 *"My talent":* "People-Talk: That's How His Money Goes," *Providence Bulletin*, 1-26-79, C43.
523 *Unpleasant details:* Sullivan and Banks, 11-30-78.
523 *"In fact":* Ibid.
523 *lump sum of $7,500:* Tom Sullivan, "Mailer: Unjust Law Delays His 5th Marriage," *Boston Herald American*, 5-21-80.
524 *sold by the IRS:* UPI, "IRS Takes Over Mailer's House," *Chicago Tribune*, 4-29-79.
524 *Beverly was evicted:* Edward Quill, "Mailer's Former Wife Evicted from Provincetown Home," *Boston Globe*, 10-1-81, 27.
524 *contest the divorce:* Tom Sullivan, "Mailer: Unjust Law Delays His Fifth Marriage," *Boston Herald American*, 5-21-80.
524 *free to marry:* "Appealing Wife Clouds Mailer's Weddings," *Boston Herald American*, 11-2-80.
524 *"brave face":* TC, 251–53.
525 *"with great theatrical diction":* Jeffrey Michelson and Laura Bradley, *Laura Meets Jeffrey: Both Sides of an Erotic Memoir* (Lehigh Valley, PA: New Blue Books, 2012), 97.
525 *"I was no longer":* TC, 256.
525 *"And I call it trigamy":* UPI, "Norman Mailer Weds Twice, Divorces Twice," *Fall River Herald News*, 12-?-80.
525 *Supreme Judicial Court:* Harold Banks, "Novelist Rewrites State's Divorce Laws," *Boston Herald American*, 9-1-82.
525 *"Mailer's Ring Cycle": NYT*, 10-19-80.
525 *"Norman Mailer won't get":* "Marriage a La Mode," *Boston Herald American*, 12-18-80.
526 *"Friends, Penpals":* NM to many correspondents, 4-79.
526 *"to explore the states":* NM to Mort Yanow, 4-9-79.
526 *"a con who's counting":* NM to Luke Breit, 4-10-79.
526 *greased peanuts:* NM to Louis and Moos, 4-20-79.
526 *"my best friend":* Marcus Warren, "Another Rogue Mailer," http://cannabisnews.com/news/17/thread17904.shtml.
526 *"a profoundly religious":* NM to Abbott, 4-18-79; rpt., *NYRB*, 3-12-09, 26–27.
527 *"no automatic Zionist hardon":* NM to Abbott, 4-18-79.
527 *"the Jewish past":* Saul Bellow, "A Jewish Writer in America—II," *NYRB*, 11-10-79, 28–29.

527 History of the Jews: NM to Abbott, 4-26-84.
528 *John Taylor "Ike" Williams:* A leading publishing lawyer and literary agent who represents Schiller, JML, and the estate of NCM, among others, Williams (b. 1938) is a longtime friend of and advisor to the Mailer family.
528 *punched him:* NM did not remember Williams, but he remembered the punch.
528 *"So, here is this heavy guy":* JML interview with John T. Williams, 10-23-11.
528 *Bradford died:* NM thanked his editor of ten years in the afterword to ES, calling him "that good, fine, and devoted man of literature."
528 *Roger Donald:* NM's editor at Little, Brown until 1984.
529 Serpentine: (NY: Doubleday, 1979).
529 The Right Stuff: (NY: Farrar, Straus & Giroux, 1979).
529 *"I'm sitting with Norman":* Severs.
529 Gödel, Escher, Bach: (NY: Basic Books, 1979).
529 The Ghost Writer: (NY: Farrar, Straus & Giroux, 1979).
529 Birdy: (NY: Knopf, 1979).
529 *"a factual account":* ES, 1051–52.
529 *complain that words:* Phillip K. Tomkins ("In Cold Fact," *Esquire*, June 1966, 166–71) presents the testimony of several people who say Capote misquoted them or invented things they said, including Detective Alvin Dewey, who apprehended Hickock and Smith, and Josephine Meier, the wife of Undersheriff Wendle Meier, who fed Smith his meals.
529 *"nonfiction provides answers":* Tony Schwartz, "Is New Mailer Book Fiction, in Fact?," *NYT*, 10-26-79, C24.
530 *"to read like a novel":* Kevin Bezner, "Mailer on Gilmore," *Washington Book Review*, 6.
531 *Capote recalled:* Lawrence Grobel, *Conversations with Capote* (NY: New American Library, 1985), 112–14.
531 *"although he has always": Music for Chameleons* (NY: Random House, 1980), xvi.
531 *"was so famous":* Grobel, *Conversations with Capote*, 113–14.
531 *"no respect":* Grobel, Ibid., 112.
531 *"That was the measure":* Plimpton, *Truman Capote*, 153–54.
531 *"I think he was terribly":* Radio interview with Milt Rosenberg, *Extension 720*, WGN, 9-6-84.
531 *nod to Capote:* NM did note his debt to Capote in several interviews, with Milt Rosenberg, and with William Buckley and Jeff Greenfield on *Firing Line*, for example.
531 *acknowledged Lillian Ross's:* Capote in Grobel, *Conversations with Capote*, 114; Mailer in Plimpton, *Truman Capote*, 214.
531 *Ross's nonfiction narrative: Picture* (NY: Rinehart, 1952).
532 *"Nothing in my experience":* ES, 305.
532 *Romeo and Juliet:* See, for example, http://www.crimenarrative.com/2010.02/book-review-executioners-song-by-norman.html.

532 *"Real life":* Ivy Compton-Burnett, "A Conversation Between I. Compton-Burnett and M. Jourdain," Rosamund Lehmann et al. (eds.), *Orion 2: A Miscellany* (London: Nicholson & Watson, 1945), 2.
533 *"trying to put people":* Aldridge, CNM, 267.
533 *"I have a problem":* Jeffrey Severs, "The Untold Story," *MR*, 105.
533 *could have cut out:* NM said as much to Paul A. Attanasio, "Talking with Mailer," *Harvard Crimson Fall Book Supplement*, October 1979, 23.
533 *"By that time":* ES, 503.
533 *"might be the only":* ES, 639.
534 *"had to obtain this story":* ES, 619.
534 *three hundred people have speaking parts:* A careful count reveals that ES has 317 characters mentioned by name who are significantly involved with one of the principals—Gilmore, Nicole, and Schiller. Part I presents 148; Part II introduces 169 *new* characters. Of the total of 317, 140 have speaking parts, that is, their words are in quotation marks in the main narrative, not counting the fifty-one media reports, fifty-eight Gilmore letters, and sixty-five other documents (court and psychiatric reports, for example), that are quoted from or interpolated entirely.
534 *interviews with George Plimpton:* Plimpton's interviews and several others are collected in Irving Malin's *Capote's* In Cold Blood: *A Critical Handbook* (Belmont, CA: Wadsworth, 1968).
534 *"Do you* really *want":* Philippa Toomey, "Mailer and a Monument to Death," *The Times* (London), 11-17-79, 14.
534 *"Schiller stood":* ES, 1053.
535 *"I will never":* Jeffrey Severs, "The Untold Story," *MR*, 106.
535 *embarked on a publicity tour:* See JML and Donna Pedro Lennon, *Norman Mailer*, 114–18.
535 *Buckley's* Firing Line*:* 11-11-79.
535 *interview with Dick Cavett:* Broadcast on November 21 and 22, 1979.
535 *appeared in England:* On 11-5-79 by Hutchinson.
535 *"true life novel":* Adrienne Blue, "Death, Taxes and Norman Mailer," *Time Out* (London), 12-7-79, 14–16.
535 *"a defile":* Paul A. Attanasio, 23.
536 *"made eloquent":* James Atlas, "Life with Mailer," *NYTM*, 53–55.
536 *"garrulous, vain, paranoid":* Ibid., 96.
536 *"merely pretended":* "'Times' Irks Mailer, Atlas Shrugs," *New York*, 9-24-79, 8.
536 *when a friend showed him a copy:* JML, 7-22-05.
536 *"not true":* NCM to JML, 7-22-05.
536 Of Women and Their Elegance: (NY: Simon & Schuster, 1980; London: Hodder & Stoughton, 1980).
536 *"fantasy autobiography":* "Norman Mailer Writes a New 'Fantasy Autobiography' of Marilyn Monroe," advance excerpt in *Ladies' Home Journal*, September 1980, 93–95, 154–64.
537 Strawhead: Unpublished (HRC), except for "Strawhead: An Extract from Act One," *Vanity Fair*, April 1986, 63–66.

537 *I wanted to write:* Beverly Beyette, "Mailer on Mailer," *Pantagraph News* (Illinois), 12-14-80, C1.
537 *"a nice feeling":* NM to Susan Mailer, 8-25-79.
537 *"your good character":* NM to Abbott, 6-3-79.
537 *faux obituary:* "Novelist Shelved," *Boston*, September 1979, 91.
538 *"used up my audience":* Aldridge, CNM, 266.
538 *Martha Thomases:* Legs McNeil, "Norman Mailer: The Champ of American Letters," *High Times*, September 1979, 43.
538 *"Let's do it":* MBD, 352.
538 *"I'm sure you've never":* Legs McNeil, "Norman Mailer," *High Times*, 44.
539 *young boxers:* MBD, 353.
539 *"I haven't got":* MBD, 353.
539 *"schizophrenia of the cells":* Legs McNeil, "Norman Mailer," *High Times*, 43–44.
539 *"Damn good song":* "Random Notes," *Rolling Stone*, 4-17-80, 34.
539 *"Norman, we don't":* Ibid.
540 *negative reviews:* Diane Johnson, "Death for Sale," *NYRB*, 12-6-79, 3–6; Germaine Greer, "The Book Page," *Hollywood Reporter*, 12-7-79, 38.
540 *"an emotional boost":* TC, 249.
540 *most often taught:* A surmise based on observation, and the fact that in 1999, thirty-six judges working under the aegis of New York University's Journalism Department ranked ES number seventy-two on a list of the top one hundred works of journalism of the twentieth century. See Felicity Barringer, "Journalism's Greatest Hits: Two Lists of a Century's Top Stories," *NYT*, 3-1-99.
540 *"When Mailer has Schiller":* John Garvey, "Of Several Minds," *Commonweal*, 3-14-80, 134–35.
540 *"is offered a large sum":* John Cheever, "A 'True Life Novel' of a Murderer Transfigured by Death," *Chicago Tribune*, 10-7-79.
540 *"a stunningly candid":* Christopher Lehmann-Haupt, "Existential Gunslinger," *NYT*, 9-24-79.
540 *"Men tend to shoot":* Joan Didion, "I Want to Go Ahead and Do It," *NYTBR*, 10-7-79, 1, 26–27; rpt., JML, *Critical Essays on Norman Mailer*, 80–81.
541 *"This is an absolutely":* Ibid., 82.
541 *"Yes, she's absolutely right":* Kevin Bezner, "Mailer on Gilmore," *Washington Post Book World*, 5–6.
541 *"What I found":* Christopher Bollen, "Norman Mailer Writer," *V* magazine, 7.
542 *"Be careful, he stabbed":* JML questions for Eileen Fredrickson, 12-22-11, conducted by Peter Lennon.
542 Pieces and Pontifications: (Boston: Little, Brown, 1982). JML edited the second half of this collection, containing twenty interviews, mainly from the 1970s and early 1980s. Each half is numbered from page one on; *Pieces* contains twelve essays, all from the 1970s.
542 *"Over breakfast, he talked":* Peter Lennon to Robert F. Lucid, 7-28-86.

543 *"until you make":* NM to Abbott, 11-5-79.
543 *"The Death of Tragedy":* Contained in a collection Abbott assembled with Naomi Zack, *My Return* (Buffalo, NY: Prometheus, 1987).
543 *"fascinating":* NM to Abbott, 11-26-79.
544 *"receive $30,000 a month":* MBM, 432.
544 *"I leave it":* Hilary Mills, "Creators on Creating," *Saturday Review*, 52.
544 *eight hundred pages:* NM to Diana Trilling, 1-28-80.
544 *"psychological substrata":* NM to Abbott, 4-11-80.
545 *Mailer had told Robert Silvers:* JML interview with Robert Silvers, 4-15-09.
545 *letters were published:* "In Prison," *NYRB*, 6-26-80, 34–37.
545 *"By temperament":* NM to Larry L. King, 10-25-80.
546 *"By the time":* NM and John Buffalo Mailer, *The Big Empty: Dialogues on Politics, Sex, God, Boxing, Morality, Myth, Poker and Bad Conscience in America* (NY: Nation Books, 2006), 173.
547 The Main Event: Produced by First Artists/ Barwood Films; directed by Howard Zieff, 1979.
547 *"He was very good":* JML interview with Michael Mailer, 12-28-11.
547 *"to get extended":* "The Best Move Lies Close to the Worst," *Esquire*, October 1993; rpt., TOT, 1049–50.
547 *"It was as close":* Ibid., 1051.
547 *"discipline and intelligence and restraint":* BE, 185.
547 *"Boxing and writing":* Deborah Solomon, "A Sinner's Tale: Questions for Ian McEwan," *NYT*, 12-2-07.
547 *"boxing has objective correlatives":* Jessica Blue and Legs McNeil, "The Maler Side of Mailer," *Details* (1984), 87.
548 *"boxing was the opposite":* Ibid., 85.
548 *"huge similarity":* BE, 89.
548 *"Great boxers and writers":* Herbert Mitgang, "Mailer Takes on the Heavyweight Novel," *NYT*, C24.
548 *"It's an unnatural":* Leeds, CNM, 375–76.
549 *"two systems of anxiety":* "The Best Move Lies Close to the Worst," TOT, 1050.
549 *"I don't remember":* JML interview with Jeffrey Michelson, 12-13-11.
549 *"The killing of John Lennon":* Joan Juliet Buck, "Ragtime: Dreaming America," *Vogue*, November 1981, 492.
549 *Robert Rowbotham:* Transcript of NM's testimony, "On Weed and Karma," *Stone Age* 1, Winter 1978, 28–29.
550 *"They both had an aura":* Joan Juliet Buck, "Ragtime," *Vogue*, 492.
550 *"Besides, I thought":* William Borders, "Mailer, Dying for a Part in 'Ragtime,' " *NYT*, 12-17-80, C25.
550 *"I thought it must":* Roderick Mann, "Mailer Writes Off Acting . . . Too Hard," *Los Angeles Times*, 12-?-81.
550 *"The ceiling":* JML interview with Jeffrey Michelson, 7-24-11.
550 *"stepping in shit":* JML interview with Walter Anderson, 4-20-11.
550 *in royal purple ink:* "Until Dead: Thoughts on Capital Punishment," *Parade*, 2-8-81, 8–9.

551 *"make one sick":* Ibid., 11.
551 *"is neither vengeance":* Ibid.
551 *"short-tempered alcoholic":* Paul L. Montgomery, "Abbott Tells Trial of His Life in Foster Homes and Prisons," *NYT*, 1-15-82, B3.
552 *"state-raised convict":* Abbott, *In the Belly of the Beast*, 13.
552 *"What we're interested in":* Robert Sam Anson, "The Brief and Violent Freedom of Jack Abbott," *Life*, November 1981, 124.
552 *"He had become deathly afraid":* Ibid., 123.
552 *"I am aware":* Ibid., 123–24.
552 *"I didn't see":* Ibid.
553 *"He was wearing":* TC, 264–65.
553 *"She's great, she's great!":* JML interview with Robert Silvers, 4-15-09.
553 *"were after me":* Robert Sam Anson, "The Brief and Violent Freedom of Jack Abbott," *Life*, 126.
553 *"Is there someone":* TC, 265–66.
554 *showed him the* Denkmäler: "How 1981 Treated Some Personalities Since We Saw Them Last," *People*, 12-28-81.
554 *enter the Metropolitan Museum of Art:* Robert Sam Anson, "The Brief and Violent Freedom of Jack Abbott," *Life*, 126.
554 *"When you're in a jail cell":* Transcript of *The Dick Cavett Show*, 2-24 and 2-25, 1982.
555 *"Instead of unwinding":* Mark Gado, "Jack Abbott: From the Belly of the Beast," http://www.trutv.com/library/crime/index.html.
555 *"the feeling of lava boiling":* TC, 267.
555 *"the repairman who came":* Ibid., 267–68.
555 *"Abbott ratcheted it up":* Ibid.
556 *first ice cream cone:* Robert Sam Anson, "The Brief and Violent Freedom of Jack Abbott," *Life*, 128.
556 *"He said it should":* TC, 269.
556 *"It never occurred":* Ibid.
556 *"He was always certain":* JML interview with Danielle Mailer, 1-11-12.
556 *A letter from a Marion inmate:* Robert Sam Anson, "The Brief and Violent Freedom of Jack Abbott," *Life*, 126.
556 *"Mr. Abbott had been given":* M. A. Farber, "A Killing at Dawn Beclouds Ex-Convict Writer's New Life," *NYT*, 7-26-81.
556 *"I don't know":* Anson, 126.
557 *corresponded with Kosinski: Conversations with Jerzy Kosinski*, ed. Tom Teichholz (Oxford: University Press of Mississippi), 205.
557 *"Abbott was sort of bewildered":* JML interview with Robert Silvers, 4-15-09.
557 *"These people* really *like me":* Robert Sam Anson, "The Brief and Violent Freedom of Jack Abbott," *Life*, 128.
557 *"where everyone was testy":* TC, 269.
557 *"to go slow with him":* "Prose and Cons: Abbott, Mailer and the Real Crimes of Romance," *Soho News*, 2-2-82, 10–11.
557 *come by for help:* Bell Gale Chevigny, *Doing Time: Twenty-five Years of Prison Writing* (NY: Arcade, 1999), xx.

557 *"You know, that's one"*: JML interview with Richard Stratton, 4-15-09.
557 *"Boy, were we naïve"*: TC, 270.
557 Soho News: Quoted in *The Nation*; see Lee Bernstein, *America Is the Prison: Arts and Politics in Prison in the 1970s* (Chapel Hill: University of North Carolina Press, 2010), 158.
557 *"an archipelago of the damned"*: Terrence Des Pres, "A Child of the State," *NYTBR*, 7-19-81.
558 *Holocaust death camps: The Survivor: An Anatomy of Life in the Death Camps* (NY: Oxford University Press, 1976).
558 *Mailer spoke to Abbott:* UPI, "Defense Alters Plan in Murder Trial of Author Jack Abbott," *Reading Eagle*, 1-14-82, 29.
558 *"This is a bad neighborhood"*: Ruth Landa, AP, "Witness Describes Knife Convict-Author Carried," *Gettysburg Times*, 1-14-82, 6.
558 *slain John Lennon:* M. A. Farber, "A Killing at Dawn Beclouds Ex-Convict Writer's New Life," *NYT*, 7-26-81.
558 *"with terrific velocity"*: UPI, "Defense Alters Plan."
559 *"like a Ping-Pong ball"*: M. A. Farber, "A Killing at Dawn Beclouds Ex-Convict Writer's New Life," *NYT*, 7-26-81.
559 *"Let's get out of here"*: Ruth Landa, "Witness Describes Knife," *Gettysburg Times*, 6.
559 *"By the time I got there"*: JML interview with William Majeski, 6-4-12.
559 *Abbott called Mailer:* Dean Brelis, "In New York: Tracking a Murder Suspect," *Time*, 10-26-81.
559 *went to Erroll McDonald's apartment:* Robert Sam Anson, "The Brief and Violent Freedom of Jack Abbott," *Life*, 130.
559 *"He was extremely subdued"*: M. A. Farber, "A Killing at Dawn Beclouds Ex-Convict Writer's New Life," *NYT*, 7-26-81.
559 *"I had a lot of conversations"*: This quotation, and those following up to "how his fucking book was selling" are from JML interview with William Majeski, 6-4-12.
561 *On September 23, he was captured:* Wendell Rawls Jr., "Convict-Author Eluded Police for Month," *NYT*, 9-25-81, 16.
561 *afraid someone would kill him:* Michael Coakley, "Convict Author Back in 'Belly of the Beast,' " *Chicago Tribune*, 10-25-81, Sec. 3, 10.
561 *$100,000 in royalties:* Michael Reese, Holly Morris, and Susan Argest, "Back in the Belly of the Beast," *Newsweek*, 9-28-81, 31.
561 *"I knew him from the time"*: JML interview with Barbara Probst Solomon, 4-23-10.
561 *"It was the first time"*: JML interview with Barbara Probst Solomon, 5-3-09.
562 *"I've been in"*: NM to JML, 7-29-81.
562 *telephones in Provincetown:* TC, 279.
562 *"extremely depressed"*: JML interview with Danielle Mailer, 1-11-12.
562 *"a few times after"*: "Convict Author Is Sought by Police in Stabbing Death," *Publishers Weekly*, 7-31-81.
562 *"still unwilling to talk"*: Rick Hampson, AP, "Mailer's Ex-Con Protege Now a Fugitive," *Chicago Sun-Times*, 8-18(?)-81.

562 *"Jack Abbott has had":* Michael Reese, Holly Morris, and Susan Argest, "Back in the Belly of the Beast," *Newsweek*, 9-28-81, 31.
562 *"We're going to have Jack":* JML interview with Ivan Fisher, 4-14-09.
562 *"flabbergasted":* TC, 271.
563 *"He went from the belly":* Paul L. Montgomery, "Abbott Rejects Account of Him as Violent Man," *NYT*, 1-19-82, B3.
563 *"the holy grail":* JML interview with Naomi Zack, 1-3-12.
563 *Mailer testified:* Thomas Hanrahan and Stuart Marques, "Abbott Jurors Hear His Text on Knife-Killing," New York *Daily News*, 1-19-82, 4, 17.
563 *"pay enough attention":* Transcript of NM press conference, Manhattan courthouse, 1-21-81 (JML files).
563 *"was the worst New York press gang bang":* MBM, 16.
563 *"Norman was never cool":* TC, 272.
564 *"I'm saying culture":* Transcript of NM press conference.
564 *"scumbag journalism":* Mike Pearl and Cynthia R. Fagen, "Mailer: I Would Risk Freeing Killer," *New York Post*, 1-19-82, 3.
564 *jury was divided:* Mike Pearl, Cynthia Fagen, and Philip Messing, "Inside the Jury Room," *New York Post*, 1-22-82, 5, 31.
564 *"ridiculous"; "fair":* Murray Weiss and Stuart Marques, "Victim's Kin Gives His Verdict," New York *Daily News,* 1-22-82, 3, 18.
564 *Fifteen years to life:* AP, "Abbott Given Prison Term of 15 Years to Life," *Springfield State Journal-Register*, 4-16-82.
564 *"are both too strong":* Thomas Hanrahan and Don Singleton, "Might Help Again, Mailer Says," New York *Daily News*, 1-23-82.
564 *"I think he's right":* Murray Weiss and Stuart Marques, "Victim's Kin Gives His Verdict," New York *Daily News*, 18.
564 *"analyzed violence":* TC, 272–73.
565 *color cover depicting him: New Republic*, 9-9-81.
565 *"a hectic screed":* James Atlas, "The Literary Life of Crime," *New Republic*, 9-9-81, 21–23.
565 *"Mailer now endorses":* Lewis Lapham, "Mailer Asks Us to Take the Risk," *Chicago Tribune*, 2-26-82.
565 *"be shackled together":* Lance Morrow, "The Poetic License to Kill," *Time*, 2-1-82, 82.
565 *"It was the myth":* Michiko Kakutani, "The Strange Case of the Writer and the Criminal," *NYTBR*, 9-20-81, 1, 36–39.
566 *limited culpability:* MBM, 34–35.
566 *"I'm not trying":* Transcript of *The Dick Cavett Show*, 2-24 and 2-25, 1982.
566 *according to his daughter Danielle:* JML interview with Danielle Mailer, 1-11-12.
566 *"My heart goes out":* James L. W. West III, *William Styron*, 429.
566 *"Remembering one's own Elysian":* "Aftermath of 'Aftermath,' " *This Quiet Dust and Other Writings* (NY: Random House, 1982), 141.
566 *"I just wanted to say":* James L. W. West III, *William Styron*, 429. NM and Styron had spoken as early as 1972. See photo in *NYRB*, 1-10-13, 33.

TWELVE: PHARAOHS AND TOUGH GUYS

In addition to the sources identified below, the following were drawn on: JML's "Mailer Log"; JML's and Lawrence Grobel's unpublished interviews with NM and Lawrence Schiller; JML's unpublished interviews with BW. NM's letters are located at the HRC.

Page

567 *I had to go:* Jeffrey Severs, "The Untold Story," *MR*, 111.

567 *liked the proposed miniseries:* Aljean Harmetz, "Tracy Wynn Fighting to Get TV-Series Credit," *NYT*, 1-15-82.

567 *At lunch with Mailer:* Jeffrey Severs, "The Untold Story," *MR*, 11–12.

568 *written on spec:* Aljean Harmetz. "Tracy Wynn Fighting to Get TV-Series Credit," *NYT.*

568 *"With every single character":* Jeffrey Severs, "The Untold Story," *MR*, 112.

568 *"It was just different":* Aljean Harmetz, "Tracy Wynn Fighting to Get TV-Series Credit," *NYT.*

568 *The guild's judgment:* Aljean Harmetz, "Wynn Loses 'Song' TV Credit Case," *NYT*, 1-16-82.

569 *1975 interview with Laura Adams:* "Existential Aesthetics: An Interview with Norman Mailer," *PR*, Spring 1975; rpt., CNM, 207–27.

569 *"was much out of step":* Preface, PAP, x.

569 *"envisioning and anticipating":* Robert F. Lucid, "Mailer's Latest Is a Career Signpost," *Philadelphia Inquirer*, 6-20-82, 7.

569 *"the first child":* Ibid. The film version of ES, 157 minutes in length, was broadcast in two parts, November 28 and 29, 1982. The later, theatrical version, is ninety-seven minutes and contains several new scenes.

570 *"a perfect expression":* NM to Bruce Dexter, 7-2-81.

570 *"I really need":* NM to Richard Stratton, 12-6-82.

571 *"the largest hashish and marijuana":* Colin Nickerson, "Drug Smuggler or Budding Author?," *Boston Globe*, 12-19-82, 53, 68.

571 *"We know your friend":* Jerry Capeci, "Feds Tried to Trap Mailer," *New York Post*, 10-14-83, 3.

571 *"a serious hard-on":* JML interview with Richard Stratton, 4-15-09.

571 *"my heavy connections":* Ibid.

572 *"It was a time":* Ibid.

572 *"We know you've been lying":* Jerry Capeci, "Feds Tried to Trap Mailer," *New York Post*, 3.

573 *Give us Mailer:* JML interview with Richard Stratton, 4-15-09.

573 *"I figure some dealer":* Andrea Chambers, "Crime and Puzzlement: The Real-Life Mystery Behind Norman Mailer's New Thriller," *People*, 9-10-84, 42–45.

573 *as did Robert Silvers:* JML interview with Robert Silvers, 4-15-09.

573 *William Burroughs's novels:* NM to Abbott, 2-24-84.

573 *Mashey Bernstein:* Born in Dublin in 1946, Bernstein has taught writing

and film at University of California, Santa Barbara since 1971. He met NM in a New York bar in 1978, and remained friends with him. In 1991, he conducted a Passover Seder at NM's Brooklyn apartment.

573 *"the past draws you back":* NM to Abbott, 1-17-83.

573 *promised his wife:* NM to Ecey Gwaltney, 1-29-83.

573 *"Fifty caused a long":* Raymond G. Cushing, "Outspoken in the '60s, Mailer Mellows in His 60s," *Minneapolis Star and Tribune*, 4-25-83, 1C.

574 *losing three quarters:* NM to Richard Stratton, 1-18-83.

574 *Budge:* Translator of *The Egyptian Book of the Dead*, E. A. Wallis Budge (1857–1934) was one of the great Egyptologists, and is primarily responsible for building the Near Eastern antiquities collection of the British Museum. He discovered several manuscripts, including *The Papyrus of Ani*, the chief source for *The Egyptian Book of the Dead.*

574 *"to an infinitely remote": The Egyptian Book of the Dead: The Papyrus of Ani*, translated and compiled by E. A. Wallis Budge (1895; NY: Dover, 1967), xii.

574 *"Properly uttered":* Ibid., xxx.

574 *Duad:* Usually spelled "Duat"; Mailer made numerous small orthographic changes.

575 *"had huge interest for me":* William F. Ryan, "Norman Mailer's Ancient Magic," *Virginia Country*, October 1983, 34–39, 88.

575 *Flinders Petrie:* Another giant of Egyptology, Petrie (1853–1942), the chair of Egyptology at University College London, donated his head for study by the Royal College of Surgeons.

575 Creation: (NY: Random House, 1981).

575 *"Gore and I":* William Robertson, "Mailer Hits 60," *Miami Herald*, 2-6-83, 1G–2G.

575 *As Robert Begiebing notes:* Robert Begiebing, *Toward a New Synthesis: John Fowles, John Gardner, Norman Mailer* (Ann Arbor: UMI Research Press, 1989), 99–101.

575 *"Gore is not the worst":* William Robertson, "Mailer Hits 60," 2G.

575 *"I've spent my writing life":* William Robertson, "Mailer Hits 60," *Miami Herald*, 1G.

575 *"pure escapism":* Robert Taylor, "Mailer Says Best Is Yet to Come with 'Ancient Evenings,' " *Chicago Sun-Times*, 2-10-83, 82.

575 Ancient Evenings *to* Salammbô*:* Harold Bloom, introduction, *Bloom's Modern Critical Views: Norman Mailer* (Philadelphia: Chelsea House, 2003), 2.

576 *"I thought that I would":* Digby Diehl.

576 The Golden Bough: NM owned the twelve-volume set published by Macmillan in 1930.

576 History of Magic and Experimental Science: (NY: Columbia University Press, 1923).

576 *"the substitution of magic":* William Ryan, "Norman Mailer's Ancient Magic," 37.

576 *"a novel about magic":* Begiebing, CNM, 326.
576 *"Mailer had so well":* Marshall Ledger, "The Surreal Professor," *Pennsylvania Gazette*, May 1983, 22.
576 *"the amount of electromagnetic":* William Ryan, "Norman Mailer's Ancient Magic," 37.
577 *The earliest excerpt:* "From a Work in Progress," *Paris Review*, Winter 1982, 10–14.
577 *"Somewhere in those":* AE, 27–28.
577 *synesthesia:* See Maureen Seaberg, *Tasting the Universe: A Spiritual and Scientific Exploration of Synesthesia* (Pompton Plains, NJ: New Page, 2011), 107–14, for a discussion of synesthesia in AE and MAR.
577 *"I became hard":* AE, 29.
578 *"lights and forces":* Used by NM as a covering phrase in a headnote to the excerpt in *The Paris Review.*
578 *"In this telling":* Benjamin DeMott, "Norman Mailer's Egyptian Novel," *NYTBR*, 4-10-83, 1.
578 *more than fifty interviews:* The most important include: Begiebing, CNM, 306–29; Marie Brenner: "Mailer Goes Egyptian," *New York*; Eugene Kennedy, "Mailer's Long Pursuit of His 'Murky Unconscious,' " *Detroit News*, 4-24-83, 1E, 2E; George Plimpton, "Unbloodied by the Critical Pounding," *People*; William Ryan, "Norman Mailer's Ancient Magic," 34–39. James Campbell, "Making Ends Meet: James Campbell Meets Norman Mailer," *Literary Review*, July 1983, 28–31.
578 *"get very little":* Begiebing, CNM, 318.
578 *tail of a dinosaur:* Chuck Pfeifer, "Norman Mailer," *Interview*, August 1984, 60.
579 *"a disaster":* Benjamin DeMott, "Norman Mailer's Egyptian Novel," *NYTBR*, 34.
579 *friendly reviewers:* Vance Bourjaily, "Return of the Ancient Mailer," *Esquire*, April 1983, 116–17; Richard Poirier, "In Pyramid and Palace," *Times Literary Supplement*, 6-10-83; rpt., JML, ed., *Critical Essays on Norman Mailer*, 82–89; Barry Leeds, "Mailer's Latest Worth the Wait," *Hartford Courant*, 4-24-83; Christopher Ricks, "Mailer's Primal Words," *Grand Street*, Autumn 1983, 161–72; Anthony Burgess, "Magical Droppings," *Observer*, 6-5-83, 30; Christopher Lehmann-Haupt, "Books of the Times," *NYT*, 4-4-83; Robert Gorham Davis, "Excess Without End," *New Leader*, 5-16-83, 14–15.
580 *"a felt need to justify":* Richard Poirier, "In Pyramid and Palace," *Times Literary Supplement*, *Critical Essays on Norman Mailer,* 87.
580 *"the transitions":* Eugene Kennedy, "Mailer's Long Pursuit," *Detroit News*, 2E.
580 *He denied, repeatedly:* See, for example, Brenner, 31.
580 *ladder of lights:* AE, 708–09.
580 *as described in the* Book of the Dead: Budge, lxx–lxxi.
581 *"a scream of anguish":* CAC, 394–97.
581 *"the desire":* Poirier, 89.

582 *Swedish publisher:* Jinny St. Goar, "Mailer in Swedish," *Forbes*, 8-15-83, 90–92.
582 *$120,000 in England:* Dick Lochte, "Book Notes," *Los Angeles Times*, 9-6-81.
582 *Other foreign editions:* Edwin McDowell, "Mailer and Random House Sign a $4 Million Contract," *NYT*, 8-2-83.
582 *HIDEOUS REVIEWS:* HRC.
582 *Wolcott's "a muddle of incest":* "Enter the Mummy," *Harper's*, May 1983, 81–83.
582 *Koenig's condemnation:* " 'Give Me Your Obelisk,' " *New York*, 4-25-83, 71–72.
582 *Fremont-Smith's summary:* Appeared in *VV*, probably in spring 1983.
582 *"the deepest structural principle":* Begiebing, *Toward a New Synthesis*, 109.
582 *Ramses II:* Ibid., 112.
583 *Bufithis sent Mailer an essay:* "Norman Mailer," *Dictionary of Literary Biography, 1983* (Detroit: Gale, 1984), 162–66.
583 *"not met with in any other":* Ibid., 163.
583 *"inveighing against American":* Ibid., 165.
583 *"richness, radiance":* Ibid., 166.
583 *Lucid's former graduate student:* Bufithis wrote his Ph.D. dissertation under Lucid at the University of Pennsylvania.
583 *"is, I fear":* NM to Bufithis, 6-25-84.
583 *"the best book":* Julie Rubenstein and Greg Tobin, "Behind the Lines," *Literary Guild Magazine*, June 1983, 5.
584 *"the best thing I've read":* NM to Begiebing, 4-19-89.
584 Tough Guys Don't Dance: Published by Random House, 8-20-84.
584 *"can come out":* NM to Bruce Dexter, 4-5-89.
584 *"the fine filigree tip":* TGD, 17.
584 *"the rustle along the beach":* Ibid., 101.
584 *"drear":* Ibid., 3.
585 *"He climbed":* JML interview with Dotson Rader, 3-25-10.
585 *"with everyone gone":* TGD, 6. NM named this passage as his favorite depiction of place in his work: *Three Minutes or Less: Life Lessons from America's Greatest Writers* (NY: Bloomsbury/PEN/Faulkner, 2000), 221.
586 *"in complicity with evil":* Christopher Ricks, "Rectum," *London Review of Books*, 10-18-84, 15.
586 *"held in the grip":* TGD, 81–82. NM knew that Jonathan Thomas, husband of Sandy Charlebois Thomas, his secretary in the late 1960s, almost made it to the monument's peak in 1959. See "To Fellows and Friends," *Provincetown Advocate*, 7-23-59.
586 *"the dungeon":* TGD, 12.
587 *"is a book":* Ibid., 25.
587 *"The book is interested":* Peter E. Howard, "Mailer: Tough Guy at Ease in P'town," *Cape Cod Times*, 8-12-84, 1, 12.

587 *"I have to work":* James Campbell, "Making Ends Meet," *Literary Review*, 29.
587 *"drifts heavily":* Edwin McDowell, "Publishing: Mailer Talks About His New Thriller," *NYT*, 6-8-84.
587 *"I had been trying":* Dermot Purgavie, "Thoughts of a Tough Guy," *Mail on Sunday Magazine*, 10-14-84, 78.
587 *worked from eleven to nine:* NM to Stephen Mailer, 8-29-83.
587 *"too rich":* NM to JA, 10-11-83.
588 *New York–based publisher:* Edwin McDowell, "Mailer and Random House Sign a $4 Million Contract," *NYT*, 8-2-83.
588 *"I don't know where":* Ibid.
588 *"Mailer's agent's advertisement":* John Blades, "Mailer Presides over a Novel Launching," *Chicago Tribune*, 5-31-84, Sec. 5, 9.
588 *"Money," Madden says:* TGD, 104.
588 *"We told Little, Brown":* "Little, Brown Releases Mailer Novel to RH," *Publishers Weekly*, 10-21-83.
588 *"I was shocked":* John Blades, "Mailer Presides over a Novel Launching," *Chicago Tribune*.
588 *lent them money:* Tom Dunkel, "Great Scott," *United Airlines Magazine*, September 1985.
588 *"If you knew Scott":* JML interview with Jack Scovil, 3-23-10.
589 *"a supple brain":* Paul D. Zimmerman, "Literary Hustler," *Newsweek*, 3-1-76, 76.
589 *"was* the *prime client":* JML interview with Jack Scovil, 3-23-10.
589 *"I hear you're the guy":* Tom Dunkel, "Great Scott," *United Airlines Magazine*.
589 *Before Norman:* JML interview with Jack Scovil, 3-23-10.
589 *Part salesman, part banker:* Alan D. Hass, "Great Scott! It's Meredith," *Book Views*, October 1977.
589 *"To the best of my knowledge":* JML interview with Jack Scovil, 3-23-10.
590 *"sensitive Irishman":* Eugene Kennedy, CNM, 333.
590 *"I figure it this way":* TGD, 159.
590 *"Crazy people":* Ibid., 227.
590 *"Maybe I was":* Ibid.
591 *Rudy Langlais:* A film producer, whose credits include *Who Killed Atlanta's Children* (2000), Langlais began his film career working with NM.
591 *"the first classy X-rated":* JML interview with Rudy Langlais, 3-1-12.
592 *"How dare you":* Ibid.
592 *"I know what":* Ibid.
592 *"surprised that Norman":* JML interview with Jack Scovil, 3-23-10.
592 *gossip column snippets, and a 2009 memoir:* "Esquire Goes on a Date with Carole Mallory," *Esquire*, December 1980, 57–58; Ed Naha, "Mallory Labors on the 'Job,' " *New York Post*, 8-26-81; Carole Wagner Mallory, "My Story," *Parade*, 6-28-87, 4–6; Annette Witheridge, http://www.dailymail.co.uk/femail/article-563593/The-siren-conquered-Hollywood

-Socialite/index.html; Carole Mallory, *Loving Mailer* (Beverly Hills: Phoenix, 2009).

593 *"more fun than the Americans":* Annette Witheridge, "The Siren Conquered Hollywood," *Daily Mail.*

593 *films at the Thalia:* Nan Robertson, "Mailer Will Star with His Movies," *NYT*, 1-19-84, C17.

593 *"I longed for an affair":* Annette Witheridge, "The Siren Conquered Hollywood," *Daily Mail.*

593 *"I noticed that he used":* Mallory, *Loving Mailer*, 56.

593 *"Scott would never authorize":* JML interview with Jack Scovil, 3-23-10.

593 *with Mailer included Vidal:* Carole Mallory, "Mailer and Vidal: The Big Schmooze," *Esquire*, May 1991, 108–12.

594 *a weak piece:* NM to JML, 3-15-91.

594 *"his way of hiding the truth":* Mallory, *Loving Mailer*, 101.

594 *"It was a huge part":* JML interview with Ivan Fisher, 4-14-09.

594 Flash: Carole Mallory, *Flash* (NY: Poseidon, 1988).

594 *"Mallory packs her story":* *Kirkus* review, quoted before text of *Flash.*

594 *"Mailer was somewhere":* JML interview with Gay Talese, 1-23-11.

595 *"First, there's living together":* Buzz Farbar, "Marriage," PAP, 91.

596 *"the church":* PAP, v.

596 *"No woman has ever slept":* "A Doctor Is No Better than His Patient: An Interview with Norman Mailer," *Cosmopolitan*, May 1990, 332.

596 *"Honey, do you know":* JML interview with NCM, 11-17-08.

596 *"When I was very, very young":* JML interview with Dotson Rader, 3-25-10.

596 *Parker Tyler:* A poet, novelist, and film critic, Tyler (1904–74) wrote *Underground Film: A Critical History* (NY: Grove, 1969).

596 *Glenway Wescott:* A friend of Hemingway's and Gertrude Stein's as a member of the Paris expatriate community in the 1920s. Wescott (1901–87) was a novelist and essayist.

597 *something about venality:* NM to JML, 2-19-06.

597 *"But, the idea":* Buzz Farbar, "Marriage," PAP, 99, 95.

597 *greedy for knowledge:* NM says as much in AON, 135.

597 *"The more prohibited":* JML interview with Dotson Rader, 3-28-12.

598 *"It's a sad place":* "A Country, Not a Scenario," *Parade*, 8-19-84, 4.

598 *"evil artist":* HG, 441.

598 *Vladimir Posner:* A journalist and explainer of the Soviet system to Americans, Posner (b. 1934) lived in the United States for many years. His father was a Russian spy.

598 *Genrikh Borovik:* A Russian writer and filmmaker later active in the Soviet peace movement, Borovik (b. 1929) was reputed to have been a Russian spy. His son Artyom, an investigative reporter, died in a mysterious 2000 airplane crash in Moscow. NM was friendly with father and son.

598 *book on Kim Philby: The Philby Files: The Secret Life of Master Spy Kim Philby* (Boston: Little, Brown, 1994).

599 *"lying around and thinking":* NM to JA, 8-13-84.

599 *narrowed the field:* Peter Howard, "Mailer: Tough Guy at Ease in P'town," *Cape Cod Times*, 12.
599 *understanding of astrophysics:* Gregory Feeley, "Waiting for Mailer's Big One," *Million*, 38.
599 *"The leading characters":* Robert Taylor, "Little, Brown Loses Mailer to Random House," *Boston Globe*, 8-2-83, 57, 62.
599 Harlot's Ghost: NY: Random House, 1991.
600 *"Years ago I wrote":* NM to Bill Morgan, 3-22-84.
600 *"Ginsberg and I met":* Peter Whitmer, *Aquarius Revisited*, 64–65.
600 *elected president:* "Mailer Gets P.E.N. Post," *NYT*, 7-25-84.
600 *"I always wanted":* NM to Bellow, 1-15-85.
601 *"men like myself":* NM to Howard Fertig, 10-4-84.
601 *talent would rub off:* Herbert Mitgang, "Mailer and Caldwell Join Academy's Select 50," *NYT*, 12-8-84, 13.
601 *everyone was passing him:* Marie-Louise von der Leyen, "Norman Mailer on Anger and Love," in *Lifelines*.
601 *"That might be":* TC, 279.
601 *January 1986 PEN congress:* Madalynne Reuter, "1000 Writers to Meet in New York at PEN International Congress," *Publishers Weekly*, 1-8-85, 23–24.
602 Lincoln: (NY: Random House, 1984).
602 *"whether his hatred":* NM to MK, 10-23-84.
602 *"Our feud":* NM to Vidal, 11-20-84.
603 *Mailer wrote to Bellow:* NM to Bellow, 11-20-84.
603 *"not strong on civility":* Bellow to NM, 12-11-84.
603 *"I shudder to think":* NM to Bellow, 1-15-85.
603 *"Fine. Be lugubrious":* NM to Vidal, 1-15-85.
603 *eight Sunday evenings:* John Blades, "Mailer-Vidal Reading Highlights Series of Forums by 16 Famous U.S. Writers," *Chicago Tribune*, 9-1-85.
603 *"brusque and jagged":* NM to Howard Fertig, 1-29-85.
603 *"Do you want":* JA to NM, quoted by NM in his 1-29-85 letter to JA.
604 *I would just as soon:* Ibid.
604 *"If I had":* JML interview with Susan Mailer, 8-18-11.
604 *"It's through opposition":* Schroeder, *Vietnam, We've All Been There*, 101.
605 *Peter Arthurs:* NM corresponded for several years with Arthurs, the author of *With Brendan Behan: A Personal Memoir* (NY: St. Martin's, 1981).
605 *"We're all divided":* NM to Arthurs, 9-18-84.
605 *"the discovery":* NM to R. Emmett H. Tyrrell, 10-1-85.
605 *Cheever's collected stories: The Stories of John Cheever* (NY: Knopf, 1978) won the 1979 Pulitzer Prize for fiction.
605 *M. R. James:* Considered by many to be the finest ghost story writer of the twentieth century, James (1862–1936), was a medieval scholar at Cambridge University.
605 Ghost Stories of an Antiquary: (London: Arnold, 1931), reprinted in many paperback editions, including one from Dover (1971), which NM owned.
605 *"I am a phenomenon":* NM to Bruce Dexter, 6-13-85.

606 *all five of Mailer's daughters:* TC, 288.
606 *"The three of us":* JML interview with Stephen Mailer, 3-22-12.
606 *"could no longer see":* NM to Richard Stratton, 9-20-85.
607 *"takeover baron":* Tracy Daugherty, *Hiding Man: A Biography of Donald Barthelme* (NY: St. Martin's, 2009), 463.
607 *"and his fund-raising efforts":* Edwin McDowell, "Mailer Sparkplug for Writer's Congress," *Chicago Tribune*, 1-2-86.
607 *"a meeting of two toothless tigers":* "A Rampancy of Writers," *Time*, 1-13-86, 22.
607 *four hundred pages:* Edwin McDowell, "Mailer Sparkplug for Writer's Congress," *Chicago Tribune.*
607 *"I don't have a bad":* NM to Michelson, 10-11-85.
607 *ten sexiest American men:* Natalie Gittelson, "America's Ten Sexiest Men over 60," *McCall's*, October 1985.
607 *"At long last, love":* NM to MK, 10-1-85.
607 *"Guest of Dishonor":* John Blades, "Feminists Make Mailer Guest of Dishonor," *Chicago Tribune*, 7-10-86, C10.
607 *"a person of public accomplishment":* Fred Ferretti, "Celebrating Norman Mailer," *NYT*, 11-22-85.
608 *not received warmly:* Walter Goodman, "Shultz Opens PEN Assembly Amid Protests," *NYT*, 1-13-86, A1.
608 *"at the feet":* R. Z. Sheppard, "Independent States of Mind," *Time*, 1-27-86, 74.
608 *"a week of petitions":* Carol Iannone, "The Political-Literary Complex," *Commentary*, June 1986, 64.
608 *theme of the conference:* Edwin McDowell, "Mailer Sparkplug for Writer's Congress," *Chicago Tribune.*
608 *Donald Barthelme:* Author of *The Dead Father* (NY: Farrar, Straus & Giroux, 1975) and other postmodern fiction, Barthelme (1931–89) served on the PEN board with NM.
608 *Richard Howard:* Howard (b. 1929) won the National Book Award for his 1983 translation of *Les Fleurs du Mal.*
608 *"Be as shallow": How the Wimp Won the War* (Northridge, CA: Lord John Press, 1992), 5.
609 *"had been around":* Walter Goodman, "Norman Mailer Offers a PEN Post-Mortem," *NYT*, 1-27-86.
609 *disproportions in the number of women:* Edwin McDowell, "Women at PEN Caucus Demand a Greater Role," *NYT*, 1-17-86, C26.
609 *"there are no good":* Carol Iannone, "The Political-Literary Complex," *Commentary*, 64, 67.
609 *Vonnegut, another PEN official:* Miriam Schneir, "The Prisoner of Sexism," *Ms.*, April 1986, 83.
609 *"I stayed away":* NM to Mary Lee Settle, 2-13-86.
610 *"include women in the decision-making roles":* Edwin McDowell, "Women at PEN Caucus Demand a Greater Role," *NYT*, C26.
610 *"we have so many":* Walter Goodman, "Norman Mailer offers a PEN

Post-Mortem," *NYT*; see also Salman Rushdie, "The Pen and the Sword," *NYT*, 4-17-05.
610 *"brilliant end run":* R. Z. Sheppard, 74.
610 *"With luck, however":* Thomas Pynchon to NM, 1-8-86.
610 *Mailer wrote back:* NM to Pynchon, 2-13-86.
611 Peru: (NY: Dutton, 1986).
611 *"obsessively circular":* George Johnson, "New and Noteworthy," *NYT*, 1-10-88.
611 *"I whisper to you":* NM to Gordon Lish, 9-12-85.

THIRTEEN: AN UNFINISHED CATHEDRAL: *HARLOT'S GHOST*

In addition to the sources identified below, the following were drawn on: JML's "Mailer Log"; JML's unpublished interviews with NM and BW. NM's letters are located at the HRC.

Page

613 *"You can no longer write":* Michael Schumacher, "Modern Evenings: An Interview with Norman Mailer," *Writer's Digest*, October 1983, 34.
613 *collection of his interviews: Conversations with Norman Mailer*, ed. JML (Jackson: University Press of Mississippi, 1988); consists of thirty-four previously published interviews, three of them self-interviews.
613 *friend pointed out:* JML, "Mailer's America," *Chicago Tribune, The Arts*, 9-29-91, 18.
613 Some Came Running: (NY: Scribner's, 1957); Existing paperback technology was such that Jones was required to abridge the novel for the Signet edition published in 1958.
614 *"Plot is the enemy":* Christopher Bigsby, "Alarm Calls for American Dreamers," *Independent*, 2-9-02, 10.
614 *"the memory of the books":* Graydon Carter, ed., *Vanity Fair's Proust Questionnaire* (NY: Rodale, 2009), 132.
614 *"writing a screenplay for Godard":* Roger Ebert, "Tough Guy Mailer Shows He Can Dance with the Big Boys," *Chicago Sun-Times*, 1-23-86; rpt., CNM, 353.
614 *"Ah! At last":* NM to Vincent Canby, 2-4-88.
614 *"a late Godardian":* Vincent Canby, "Film: Godard in His Mafia 'King Lear,' " *NYT*, 1-22-88.
614 *It baffled its small audiences:* Godard's biographer, however, calls the film one of the director's "greatest artistic achievements." Richard Brody, *Everything Is Cinema: The Working Life of Jean-Luc Godard* (NY: Henry Holt, 2008), 492.
614 *"brought me closer":* David Lida, "Stage Daughters," *W* magazine, 2-8-88, 37.
615 The Last Sitting: (NY: Morrow, 1982).
615 *"No one has played Marilyn":* "Striking Pose Looks Familiar," *Boston Herald*, 3-26-86, 11.
615 *"but only Kate":* Tina Brown, "Editor's Letter," *Vanity Fair*, April 1986, 8.

615 *"a select audience":* James Atlas, "The First Sitting," *Vanity Fair*, April 1986, 58–63.

615 *"Perhaps in a year":* NM to JM, 4-23-86.

615 *"It was just a little":* JML interview with NCM, 4-15-09.

615 *Kate continued to act:* Atlas, "The First Sitting."

615 *Chekhov's* The Cherry Orchard*:* Kate played Dunyasha in Peter Brook's 1988 New York production of Chekhov's 1904 play.

615 A Matter of Degrees: Directed by W. T. Morgan, Backbeat Productions, 1990.

616 *Mailer siblings went into the arts:* Danielle is a visual artist whose work has been given many shows, and is the chair of the art department at a private school in Connecticut. Betsy is a writer, currently working on a novel and a memoir. Michael is a writer and independent film producer with more than twenty films to his credit. Stephen, a veteran stage and screen actor with credits going back to the 1980s, has also appeared in television, including an appearance on *The Gilmore Girls* with his father. Maggie, like her older sister, is a successful visual artist and the founder of the Storefront Artist Project in Pittsfield, Massachusetts. Matthew is a director and screenwriter who made his directorial debut in 1998 with a film he made with his brother Michael, *The Money Shot.* John Buffalo, the youngest of the nine siblings, is a playwright, actor, producer, and journalist. In 2006, he coauthored a book of conversations with his father, *The Big Empty.*

616 *"physical agility":* NM to Susan Mailer, 2-18-87.

616 *"was very supportive":* "Biography for Stephen Mailer—Trivia," IMDb.

616 *"I think we were lucky":* JML interview with Maggie Mailer, 3-27-09.

616 *"part autobiographical":* www.daniellemailer.com.

617 *"I agree with you":* NM to MK, 5-19-92.

617 *Tom Luddy:* A cofounder and one of the current directors of the Telluride Film Festival, Luddy (b. 1943) has been an executive at American Zoetrope since 1979, and has served on the juries of most major international film festivals, including Cannes and Berlin.

617 *"a normal American movie":* In his interview with JML (3-?-12), Luddy explained the deal that brought him, Mailer, Godard, and Cannon Films together.

618 *"I knew I would":* Dinitia Smith, "Tough Guys Make Movies," *New York*, 1-12-87, 34.

618 *"Mr. Mailer, I'm happy":* Transcript of NM's 9-22-87 interview with members of the Hollywood Foreign Press Association (HFPA), 17 pp., JML files.

618 *"subtly sinister":* Ibid.

618 *"for a particular":* NM to Bruce Dexter, 4-23-86.

619 *"where you think":* NM to JA, 4-24-86.

619 *"was unfairly convicted":* Catalogue description for *My Return*: http://www.prometheusbooks.com/index.

619 *"bringing him books":* Mark Muro, "Murder He Wrote, in a Bid for Freedom," *Boston Globe*, 9-13-87, C31, C34.

619 *"to behave":* Ibid.
619 *"You are so associated":* NM to JA, 4-24-86.
620 *"There are not legions":* NM to JA, 5-22-86.
620 *"I am lucky":* JML interview with Naomi Zack, 1-2-12.
620 *He finished "Havana":* NM to JA, 5-22-86. NM also discusses these screenplays in Todd McCarthy, "Mailer Gives Film Another Fling with 'Guys,' " *Variety*, 5-4-87, 2, 13-14.
620 *John Bailey:* An award-winning cinematographer and director, Bailey (b. 1942) has worked on scores of films, including *Mishima, As Good as It Gets* (1997), and *Groundhog Day* (1993).
620 *Bonnie Timmermann:* One of the most accomplished casting directors in the business.
620 *"an official representative":* Harvard's invitation was received sometime in early 1986.
620 *"Sons of Harvard":* The color painting is the work of Teresa Fasolino; it is unknown how the sixteen men were chosen.
620 *sixty-five locales: Tough Guys Don't Dance* Location Contact List, JML files.
620 *complete makeover:* Details from Dinitia Smith, "Tough Guys Make Movies," *New York*, 33; Daphne Merkin, "His Brilliant (New) Career?", *American Film*, October 1987, 42–49; and *Tough Guys Don't Dance* press kit, JML files.
621 *casting call:* Bonnie Barber and Gregory Katz, "Camera Angles: Reporters on the Set of 'Tough Guys,' " *Provincetown Arts*, summer 1987, 116.
621 Blue Velvet: David Lynch wrote the screenplay and directed the 1986 film.
621 *"sounds of punches":* Mark Singer, "The Pictures: Tough Guy," *New Yorker*, 5-21-07, 30–31.
621 *"Tom, my knife":* JML interview with Tom Luddy, 3-?-12.
621 *"adored":* Mark Singer, "The Pictures: Tough Guy," *New Yorker*, 30.
621 *"was way over the top":* Philip Sipiora, "Perspectives on Cinema: A Conversation with Tom Luddy," *MR* (2009), 568.
621 *"had a lot of problems":* Ibid.
622 *"I would get":* Ibid.
622 *"I always felt":* NM to Richard Stratton, 12-31-86.
622 "Anything*'s easier than writing":* Dinitia Smith, "Tough Guys Make Movies," *New York*, 33.
622 *"an excruciating activity":* Alan Richman, "No Longer Such a Tough Guy, Norman Mailer Frets over His Shaky Career as a Filmmaker," *People*, 10-5-87, 40.
622 *"an ideal war":* Bonnie Barber and Gregory Katz, "Camera Angles," *Provincetown Arts,* 21.
622 *promised to visit:* NM to Farbar, 12-31-86.
622 *"a million dollars in advance":* NM to Richard Stratton, 12-31-86.
623 *"if this picture hits":* NM to MK, 1-6-87.

623 *"I respect the psychological":* NM to Farbar, 2-19-87.
623 *twenty-four films in twelve days:* Tim Miller, " 'Proud Father': Mailer Pleased with Tough Guys," *Cape Cod Times*, 8-14-87.
624 *"as if everyone":* Roger Ebert, *Two Weeks in the Midday Sun: A Cannes Notebook* (NY: Andrews & McMeel, 1987), 146.
624 *"a wonderfully exaggerated":* Vincent Canby, "Pialat Film Gets Top Prize at Cannes," *NYT*, 5-20-87, C24.
624 *"All my life":* NM to Farbar, 6-15-87.
624 *"Norman and Norris":* TC, 286.
625 *"It will be good":* Kate Mailer, "The Knife's Edge," *MR,* 37.
625 *"the best boyfriend":* Kate married Guy Lancaster, a writer who grew up in Bermuda, in July 1993.
625 *ninety pages a month:* NM to Farbar, 6-15-87.
625 *"about the CIA":* The first public mention of the CIA may have been in Todd McCarthy, "Mailer Gives Film Another Fling," *Variety.*
625 *guest list:* JML files.
626 *"interviewed Mailer":* Carole Mallory, "An Interview with Norman Mailer," *L.A. Alive*, 9-18-87, 25.
626 *"I stopped drinking":* Ebert, CNM, 357–58.
626 *"He said his double life":* TC, 322.
627 *"to float the Queen Mary":* NM to JML, 10-15-87.
627 *"It's as if":* Ibid.
627 *"with any real happiness":* NM to Susan Mailer, 2-18-87.
627 *"amusing vagueness":* Mark Singer, "The Pictures: Tough Guy," *New Yorker*, 30.
627 *"Tarantino":* Ibid., 31.
627 *"Writing is the farm":* NM to Pat Smith, 2-18-97.
628 *"It was one of the best":* JML interview with Danielle Mailer, 4-17-12.
628 *"a species of spiritual incarceration":* NM to Farbar, 1-9-88. See NM's comments about Farbar's suicide, and speaking at his funeral: NM to Charles McGrath, *NYTBR*, 12-20-99.
628 Smack Goddess: (NY: Carol, 1990).
628 *"look for some needed":* NM to Richard Stratton, 11-25-87.
629 *"a distinguished minor artist":* NM to Luke Breit, 1-14-88.
629 *"It's like going back":* NM to Stratton, 11-25-87.
629 Ragtime: (NY: Random House, 1975). See PAP, 130.
629 *William King "Bill" Harvey:* An Indiana lawyer, Harvey (1915–76) began his government career with the FBI, but moved to the CIA in 1947. Stationed in Washington, D.C., in 1951, he uncovered British diplomat Kim Philby as a spy. In 1955 in Berlin, he tapped into Russian phone lines via a tunnel over a quarter of a mile long. King disliked the Ivy League graduates who dominated the CIA, as NM shows in HG. At the end of his career, he worked to try to topple Castro.
629 *fictional stand-in:* NM claimed in the "Author's Note" to HG that he "felt bound by the precise edge" of Exner's accounts of her life, and to have

greater freedom to invent, he substituted Modene Murphy. He was in the same situation with several other historical characters, and did not refrain from putting words in their mouths, as he notes. Potential legal issues may have made him take this course with Exner, who was still alive when HG was published.

629 *Judith Campbell Exner:* A controversial figure, Exner (1934–99) told the story (with Ovid Demaris) in *Judith Exner: My Story* (NY: Grove, 1977) of her involvement with JFK and others, but modified it in interviews years later.

630 *"wilderness of mirrors":* Angleton coined the phrase to describe the layered dissimulations of spies and counterspies, moles and defectors. In his author's note, NM singles out David C. Martin's *Wilderness of Mirrors* (NY: Harper & Row, 1980) as a key source for his portraits of Angleton and Harvey.

630 *"astonishingly well":* HG, 72.

630 *"a large and detailed mural":* "Author's Note," HG, 1288.

630 *event timeline:* JML files.

630 *fourth chart:* An image of this fourth chart is reproduced in an essay on the NM holdings at the HRC: Cathy Henderson, Richard W. Oram, Molly Schwartzburg, and Molly Hardy, "Mailer Takes on America: Images from the Ransom Center Archive," *MR* (2007), 141–75.

631 *four to six days:* NM to Farbar, 4-22-88.

631 *Trump's black helicopters:* Julie Baumgold, "Mr. Lucky and the Champs," *New York*, 2-15-88, 35–40.

631 *Atlantic City to watch Tyson:* "Mr. Peeper's Nights: Good Night Irene," *New York*, 7-11-88, 15.

631 *"if two people":* Ibid., 16.

631 *essay in* Spin*:* "Fury, Fear, Philosophy: Understanding Mike Tyson," *Spin*, September 1988, 40–44, 78.

631 *two advance excerpts:* "A Piece of *Harlot's Ghost*," *Esquire*, July 1988, 80–90; "The Changing of the Guard," *Playboy*, December 1988, 86–88, 196–98.

632 *His endorsement appeared:* "Jackson Is a Friend of Life's Victims," *NYT*, 4-18-88, 23.

633 *"Reading good work":* NM to Joyce Carol Oates, 7-27-88.

633 Libra: (NY: Viking, 1988).

633 *"I found it":* JML interview with Don DeLillo, 3-29-10.

633 *"What a terrific book":* NM to Don DeLillo, 8-25-88.

634 *"has been damn decent":* NM to Farbar, 10-14-88.

634 *"all the steaming shit":* NM to Edward McAlice, 2-1-89.

635 *suspicious death:* Dorothy Hunt died in a December 1972 plane crash in Chicago with $10,000 in her purse as the Watergate scandal was unfolding.

635 *"characterological theoretician":* HG, 446.

635 *"as complex and wholly":* HG, 498–99.

635 *"originates in the ovum":* Ibid.

635 *"like the corporal lobes"*: 499.
636 *"how spies are able"*: HG, 177.
636 *redundancy:* Jonathan Franzen, "I, Spy," *L.A. Times Book Review*, 9-29-91, 1, 8.
636 The Satanic Verses: (NY: Viking, 1988).
636 *"I call on all zealous"*: W. J. Weatherby, *Salman Rushdie: Sentenced to Death* (NY: Carroll & Graf, 1990), 154.
636 *"to give voice"*: Ibid., 133.
637 *went into hiding:* Sheila Rule, "Khomeini Urges Muslims to Kill Author of Novel," *NYT*, 2-15-89.
637 *rally of support:* Richard Bernstein, "Passages in Defense of a Colleague: Writers Read and Speak for Rushdie," *NYT*, 2-23-89.
637 *"took our seats"*: DeLillo to JML, 5-19-12.
637 *"wished to show"*: "A Folly Repeated," *Writer's Digest*, July 1989; rpt., TOT, 1059–62.
637 *"with the inner temerity"*: Steve MacDonogh, ed., *The Rushdie Letters: Freedom to Speak, Freedom to Write* (Lincoln: University of Nebraska Press, 1993), 73.
638 *"great fun"*: NM to Styron, 2-3-89.
638 *"A number of years ago"*: "Styron's Novels Have Tackled, Boldly and Yet Patiently, the Great Issues of Our Time," *MacDowell Colony News*, Fall/Winter 1988, 3.
638 *"In the doldrums"*: NM to William Styron, 2-3-89.
638 *"now approaching the 1500"*: NM to Kate Mailer, 4-18-89.
638 *"a 300-lb greased beast"*: NM to Jim Beattie, 4-22-88.
638 *"I'm still staggering"*: NM to MK, 5-17-88.
639 *restatement of his theological ideas:* "Cosmic Venture: A Meditation of God at War," *Esquire*, December 1989, 156–57.
639 *"Communism is the entropy"*: HG, 394.
639 *"Forgive the sons"*: Ibid., 157.
639 *"We never really talked"*: JML interview with Fred Ambrose, 8-16-09.
642 *twice on the cover: Provincetown Arts*, 1987 and 1999.
642 *"took comfort in walking"*: Christopher Busa, "This Is a Town Worth Digging In and Fighting For," *MR* (2008), 94.
642 *"my elephant"*: NM to MK, 3-15-90.
643 *"P[oly] M[orphus]"*: JML files.
644 *"convinces him that his life"*: Ibid.
644 *"I nod my head"*: NM to Bonnie B., 5-10-90.
644 *"we can nail"*: NM to Alex Hicks, 5-10-90.
644 *"write ten to twenty"*: NM to Gottfried and Renate Helnwein, 5-29-90.
644 *"a fairly ambitious book"*: NM to Tom Fiske, 12-13-90.
645 *"egomaniac"*: Veronica Windholz, "Reading Mailer in Brooklyn," *MR* (2008), 203–15.
645 *"Read it?"*: James Wolcott, "Happy Man Haunted by Papa," *Observer*, 10-13-91.
645 American Psycho: (NY: Vintage, 1991).

646 *"bog-ridden beginning":* "To Whom It May Concern" letter, appended to NM's letter to Tina Brown, 5-16-88.
646 *"unmitigated torture":* "Children of the Pied Piper," TOT, 1067.
646 *"kills man, woman":* Ibid., 1070.
646 *"to shock the unshockable":* Ibid., 1069.
646 *"a tidal wave":* Ibid., 1067.
646 *"Murder is now":* Ibid., 1073.
646 *"swordfish meatloaf":* Ibid., 1071.
646 *"silk satin D'Orsay":* Ibid., 1069.
646 *"acts of machicolated butchery":* Ibid., 1075.
646 *"Fiction can serve":* Ibid., 1073.
647 *"Bateman is driven":* Ibid., 1075.
647 *"to have something new":* Ibid.
647 *"In the wake":* Ibid.
647 *"we know no more":* Ibid., 1076.
647 *"extremely impressive":* JML interview with Don DeLillo, 3-29-10.
647 *"unbelievable and inconceivable":* Christopher Lehmann-Haupt, "The Alpha and the Omega of Norman Mailer," *NYT*, 9-26-91, C15, C20.
647 *"Vanity is the abominable":* HG, 1054.
648 *"I am ready":* Ibid., 1272.
648 "Someone *larger":* Ibid., 1277.
648 *"Mailer really comes":* John Simon, "The Company They Keep," *NYT*, 9-29-91.
649 *"at the pace":* John W. Aldridge, "Mailer Spies on the CIA," *Chicago Tribune Sunday Books*, 9-29-91, 1, 4.
649 *"continuous emphasis":* Christopher Hitchens, "On the Imagining of Conspiracy," *London Review of Books*, 11-7-91, 6–10.
649 *"a demented Waring blender":* John Simon, "Mailer on the March," *Hudson Review*, Autumn 2000, 541–45.
649 *Mailer contacted* Times *publisher:* NM to Aldridge, 1-2-92.
649 *"Tell him," went the message:* Quoted in NM's reply to Simon, "A Critic with Balance: A Letter from Norman Mailer," *NYTBR*, 11-17-91, 7.
650 *"prolixity":* Simon, comments appended to "A Critic with Balance."
650 *"a fair and balanced":* Rebecca Sinkler, comments appended to "A Critic with Balance."
650 *"in the long run":* Rebecca Sinkler, "Picks, Pans and Fragile Egos," *Civilization*, July/August 1991, 48–53.
650 *"what in espionage":* E. Howard Hunt, "Hocus Bogus," *GQ*, November 1991, 246.
650 *"I will suggest":* HG, 726.
650 *"Never tell your wife":* Ibid., 437.

FOURTEEN: A MERRY LIFE AND A MARRIED ONE

In addition to the sources identified below, the following were drawn on: JML's "Mailer Log"; JML's unpublished interviews with NM and BW. NM's letters are located at the HRC.

Page

652 *"he was still able"*: TC, 318.

652 *excerpts from* Harlot's Ghost: Appeared in the following: *Esquire*, July 1988; *Playboy*, December 1988; *Story*, Autumn 1989; *Rolling Stone*, 7-11, 8-8, 8-22-91; *Paris Review*, Fall 1991; *PR*, Fall 1991; *New York*, 9-23-91; *NYRB*, 9-26-91; *NYTBR*, 9-29-91; *Cosmopolitan*, March 1992.

653 *New York State Author:* Appointed 11-13-91; see AP, "Mailer Dubbed Big Apple's Author," 11-14-91.

653 Don Juan in Hell: Presented at Weill Recital Hall, Carnegie Hall, 2-15-93.

653 A Century of Arts & Letters: (NY: Columbia University Press, 1998).

653 *wrote Hillary Clinton a long letter:* NM to Hillary Clinton, 6-26-92.

653 *report on the Republican convention:* "By Heaven Inspired," *New Republic*, 10-12-92; rpt., TOT, 1092–1113.

653 *beginning "Harlot's Grave":* Charles Trueheart, "Norman Mailer, Company Man," *Washington Post*, 9-23-91, C1, C4; Bruce Cook, "Mailer Muzzles His Mouthpiece," *L.A. Life*, 10-22-91, 18–19; NM to Alex Hicks, 1-2-92; NM to MK, 5-19-92.

653 *asked Gabriel García Márquez:* NM to Márquez, 6-20-91.

653 *"I can promise":* NM to Castro, 6-20-91.

653 *review of Oliver Stone's:* "Footfalls in the Crypt," *Vanity Fair*, February 1992, 124–29, 171.

654 JFK: Warner Brothers; directed by Oliver Stone.

654 *"Earl and Lyndon": Vanity Fair*, April 1992, 200–6.

654 *Dynamite Club:* Scott Spencer, "The Old Man and the Novel," *NYTM*, 9-22-91, 40.

654 *Jim Hougan:* Perhaps his most important book is *Secret Agenda: Watergate, Deep Throat, and the CIA* (NY: Random House, 1984).

654 *Dick Russell:* He wrote *The Man Who Knew Too Much: Hired to Kill Oswald and Prevent the Assassination of JFK: Richard Case Nagell* (NY: Carroll & Graf, 1993), and collaborated with Jesse Ventura on *American Conspiracies* (NY: Skyhorse, 2010).

654 *Edward Jay Epstein:* His writings about JFK's assassination have been collected into one volume: *The Assassination Chronicles* (NY: Carroll & Graf, 1992).

654 *Mailer had met and head-butted:* JML interview with Don DeLillo, 3-29-10.

654 The JFK Assassination: (NY: Signet, 1992).

654 *"a merry life and a married one":* MSC, 94.

654 *"It all made sense":* TC, 316.

655 *"an old girlfriend":* Ibid., 315–16.

655 *"This other life":* Ibid., 318.

656 *"Are you in a dilemma":* Ibid., 320–21.

656 *"I'm going to tell you":* Ibid., 323.

656 *"I was concerned":* JML interview with Danielle Mailer, 5-21-12.

657 *"shockingly brazen":* TC, 324.

657 *last tryst:* Mallory, *Loving Mailer*, 177.
657 *"My conscience":* Ibid., 186.
657 *"to feel whole":* Ibid., 199.
657 *"desperate to get out":* JML interview with Erin Cressida Wilson, 11-15-11.
658 *"Everything changed when he met Norris":* JML questions for Lois Wilson, conducted by Erin Cressida Wilson, 11-15-11.
659 *"Judith got suspicious":* JML questions for Eileen Fredrickson, 10-15-11, conducted by Peter Lennon.
660 *"I'm too happily married":* Dana Kennedy, "Norman Mailer: Back in the Ring at 68," *Boston Globe*, 10-31-91, E4.
660 *"a mellower Mailer":* Maureen O'Brien, "On the Publicity Trail with Norman Mailer," *Publishers Weekly*, 10-25-91.
660 *"a softer Mailer":* Tim Warren, "The Softer Norman Mailer," *Baltimore Sun*, 9-29-91.
660 *"attestedly happy":* Peter Stothard, "Soft Spots in a Tough Disguise," *Times Saturday Review* (London), 10-12-91, 16–17.
660 *"a more content man":* Maureen O'Brien, "On the Publicity Trail with Norman Mailer," *Publishers Weekly*.
660 *"his inner voice":* Julia Braun Kessler, "Mailer's Many Lives," *Life: The World and I*, January 1992, 335.
660 *"Mailer: Oh, I wouldn't dare":* Transcript of *Talking with David Frost*, 1-24-92.
660 *"obviously adored him":* TC, 324.
660 *"very gracious":* JML questions for Eileen Fredrickson, 10-15-11, conducted by Peter Lennon.
660 *"These women took over":* TC, 325.
661 *"devilish air":* Ibid., 326.
661 *"Well, Sam":* Ibid.
661 *"I was on the brink":* Ibid., 327.
661 *"extremely intense personal":* James Toback, speaking at the Norris Church Mailer tribute, 4-22-12, http:/vimeo.com/43772583.
662 *"felt desperately wrong":* TC, 328–31.
662 *"I loved our life":* Ibid., 331–34.
663 *"were both naive":* JML interview with Aurora Huston, 1-17-12.
663 *"that crazy wild man":* TC, 335.
664 *most enjoyable course:* Pete Hamill, "Kindred Spirits," *Art News*, November 1995, 210.
664 *"I could've written":* John Baron, "Self Propelled: Mailer—with Ego Intact—Looks at Picasso's Early Years," *Chicago Sun-Times*, 11-26-95, B70.
664 *"eight happy weeks":* POP, xi.
664 *"I think if you":* Hamilton Kahn, "Chapter Two," *Cape Cod Times*, 7-23-93, C3.
665 *Fernande Olivier: Souvenirs Intimes*, ed. Gilbert Krill (Paris: Calmann-Lévy, 1988).

665 *authorized biography: A Life of Picasso: The Prodigy, 1881–1906* (NY: Random House, 1991).
665 *"Nothing, of course, can equal"*: NM to Jacques?, 6-25-92.
665 *introduced Mailer to Richardson:* Barbara Probst Solomon, "Callow Young Genius," *New York*, 9-11-95, 81; Rebecca Ascher-Walsh, "Norman Conquest," *Entertainment*, 11-10-9.
665 *eight thousand words:* Doris Athineos, "Picasso Biographer in a Blue Period: Has Mailer Painted Him into a Corner?," *New York Observer*, 9-6-93; *The Cubist Rebel* (NY: Random House, 1996).
665 *"I was apprehensive"*: Doris Athineos, "Picasso Biographer in a Blue Period," *New York Observer.*
665 *"very interested, eager"*: JML, "Long Legs, the American Tolstoy, Oswald and the KGB: A Conversation with Lawrence Schiller," *MR* (2009), 32.
666 *investigative reporter Gerald Posner:* The author of investigative books on Hitler, the Mafia, 9/11, and several other subjects, Posner (b. 1954) published in 1993 perhaps his most important book, *Case Closed: Lee Harvey Oswald and the Assassination of JFK.*
666 *"I had a double motive"*: Wil Haygood, "Mailer Obsessed," *Boston Globe*, 5-2-95, 59.
666 *"the virtual Oklahoma land grab"*: Peter DePree, "Oswald's Ghost: An Interview with Norman Mailer," *Bloomsbury Review*, March/April 1996, 3; and in slightly different wording in OT, 349.
666 *"get me beefed up"*: Sean Abbott, "America's Obsessions: Norman Mailer Talks About Lee Harvey Oswald, JFK, the KGB, O. J. Simpson, and the Nasty Nineties," *At Random*, Summer 1995, 14.
667 *"schtupping fat, old"*: TC, 335.
667 *"I doubt if there were"*: Wil Haygood, "Mailer Obsessed," *Boston Globe*, 68.
667 *"It doesn't matter"*: NM to MK, 3-8-93.
667 *"small hard eggs"*: TC, 336.
667 *"I'm not sorry"*: Ibid., 339.
668 *shown the tiny apartment:* JML, "Long Legs, the American Tolstoy, Oswald and the KGB," *MR*, 34. Descriptions of the Minsk operation, unless otherwise noted, are taken from ibid.
668 *interviews with Schiller:* Patricia Holt, "Norman Mailer Tells 'Oswald's Tale,' " *San Francisco Chronicle*, 5-1-95, E2.
669 *"But if you give it"*: JML, "Long Legs, the American Tolstoy, Oswald and the KGB," *MR*, 43–44.
670 *"Of course, the subject"*: Ibid., 46.
671 *"Norman went ballistic"*: Ibid., 56–57.
671 *"We were worried"*: Ibid., 57.
671 *"Judith still treats me"*: NM to Aldridge, 3-8-93.
672 *"a book on Oswald in Minsk"*: Ibid.
672 *ABC-TV docudrama:* Schiller produced *The Trial of Lee Harvey Oswald* for ABC-TV, broadcast in 1976.

672 *"Larry Schiller makes Baron":* Liz Smith column, quoted by Andrew O'Hagan, "Oswaldworld," *London Review of Books*, 12-4-95.
672 *"Larry can be utterly":* NM to Bonnie B., 3-28-99.
673 *"We started with Vaseline":* JML, "Long Legs, the American Tolstoy, Oswald and the KGB," *MR*, 60–62.
673 *"Every single word":* Ibid., 65.
673 *advance excerpt from the first part:* "Oswald in the U.S.S.R.," *New Yorker*, 4-10-95, 56–99.
674 *"or my publishers":* NM to Swanee Hunt, 7-7-93.
674 *"I hope eventually":* NM to Peter Balbert, 10-4-93.
674 *"scissors-and-paste job":* Doris Athineos, "Picasso Biographer in a Blue Period," *New York Observer.*
674 *When Richardson read:* One likely source is Robert Taylor, "Mailer's Latest Lines," *Boston Globe*, 7-23-93, 39, 49.
674 *"Guys and Droons":* NM's drawings were on display at the Berta Walker Gallery in Provincetown, 7-23 to 8-4-93; NM defined a droon as "an oddball, someone who's seriously skewed."
674 *"He's not just":* Doris Athineos, "Picasso Biographer in a Blue Period," *New York Observer.*
674 *"let my hand":* Ibid.
675 *"I hope":* Ibid.
675 *"Obviously, Richardson sicced him":* Ibid.
675 *"As I understood it":* JML interview with Nan Talese, 10-19-10.
675 *"Well, this is just":* Ibid.
676 *"it's not fair":* Ibid.
676 *"vertigo and fog":* Doug Smith, "Big Dealy," *New Republic*, 12-13-93, 11–12.
677 *also a conspiratorialist:* NM later told DeLillo that he now doubted the single assassin theory.
677 *"The sudden death":* OT, 198.
677 *"the largest mountain":* "A Special Message for the First Edition from Norman Mailer," *Oswald's Tale: An American Mystery* (Franklin Center, PA: Franklin Library, 1995), unpaginated.
677 Oswald's Tale: The first edition was published by Random House on 5-12-95.
677 *"a dead whale decomposing":* OT, 351.
677 *"Every morning I'd read":* Patricia Holt, "Norman Mailer Tells 'Oswald's Tale,'" *San Francisco Chronicle*, E2.
677 *add a hundred-page epilogue:* Holt.
677 *"Oh, don't make it":* Joseph Cummins, "Interview with Norman Mailer," *BOMC Insights*, May 1995, 1.
677 *"I started with one book":* "No Ordinary Secret Agent," *Newsweek*, 4-24-95, 60.
677 *"a huge and hideous":* William Grimes, "What Debt Does Hollywood Owe to Truth?," *NYT*, 3-5-92.
677 *"You've got a rose":* JML interview with Harry Evans, 5-31-12.

677 *Epstein felt the same way:* JML interview with Jason Epstein, 11-06-08.
677 *"out of his mind":* JML, "Long Legs, The American Tolstoy, Oswald and the KGB," *MR*, 49–51.
678 *"I would have insisted":* Ibid., 51.
678 Marina and Lee: (NY: Harper & Row, 1977).
678 *O. J. Simpson, JonBenét Ramsey, Robert Hanssen: American Tragedy: The Uncensored Story of the Simpson Defense* (NY: Random House, 1996), written with James Willwerth; *Perfect Murder, Perfect Town: JonBenét and the City of Boulder* (NY: HarperCollins, 1997); *Into the Mirror: The Life of Master Spy Robert P. Hanssen* (NY: HarperCollins, 2002).
678 *"We can talk":* JML, "Long Legs, The American Tolstoy, Oswald and the KGB," *MR*, 52.
678 *"brilliance":* Ibid., 55.
679 *"discipline him":* OT, 786–88.
679 *"difficult not to feel":* Ibid., 789–90.
680 *"the results":* "Norman Mailer on Madonna: Like a Lady," *Esquire*, August 1994; rpt., TOT, 1115.
680 *mentioned his support to Liz Smith:* Liz Smith, "Rumors Put Pfeiffer Onscreen as Evita," *Toledo Blade*, 6-1-94, 19.
680 *"an ego even larger":* TOT, 1117.
680 *"a pint-size Italian American":* Ibid., 1114.
681 *"to take her kinks":* Ibid., 1113.
681 *"Confessions—in good society":* Ibid., 1133–34.
682 *"a barrel wrapped in velvet":* Ibid., 1118.
682 *"finally met a woman":* NM to Graham ?, 9-23-94.
682 *1,700 pages:* NM to Tom Fiske, 9-23-94.
682 *down to 1,400:* NM to Alex Hicks, 11-23-94.
682 *forty-five-page excerpt:* "Oswald in the U.S.S.R.," *New Yorker.*
682 *"Every insight":* "What American Haunts Us More?," *Parade*, 5-14-95.
682 *75 percent certain:* Wil Haygood, "Mailer Obsessed," *Boston Globe*, 68.
683 *"boring and . . . derivative":* Michiko Kakutani, "Oswald and Mailer: The Eternal Basic Questions," *NYT*, 4-25-95.
683 *"Oswald's struggle":* Andrew O'Hagan, "Oswaldworld," *London Review of Books.*
683 *"utterly convincing":* Allan Massie, "The Road from Minsk to Dallas," *Daily Telegraph*, 9-2-95.
683 *"I hoped there would":* Philip Martin, "American Psycho," *Arkansas Democrat-Gazette*, 7-7-95.
683 *"natural writerly prejudice":* Christopher Hitchens, "The Man Who Killed JFK," *Financial Times*, 9-2-95.
683 *"Everything in Mailer":* Martin Amis, "Fatally Flawed," *Sunday Times*, 9-10-95, 1–2.
683 *"What is never taken":* Andrew O'Hagan, "Oswaldworld," *London Review of Books.*
683 *an unsigned review:* "The Russian Connection," *Economist*, 7-10-95, 111–12.

683 *"the most sensible review":* Jason Epstein to NM, 7-16-95.
684 *"I admire Mailer":* Thomas Powers, "The Mind of an Assassin," *NYTBR*, 4-30-95, 33.
684 *"literary types":* "Norman Mailer's *Picasso*," *Publishers Weekly*, 3-4-96, S14.
684 *major reviews:* Michael Kimmelman, "Tough Guys Don't Paint," *NYTBR*, 10-15-95; Eunice Lipton, "Cubism Was a Guy Thing," *Nation*, 11-6-95, 543–44; Roger Shattuck, "Brinkmanship," *NYRB*, 1-11-96, 4–8.
685 *"poaching on the turf":* Robert Taylor, "Mailer Conjures a Mailer-Like Picasso," *Boston Globe*, 10-25-95.
685 *"to make Picasso as real":* POP, xii.
685 *"At a much higher":* Pete Hamill, "Kindred Spirits," *Art News*, 213.
685 *"I don't mean to compare":* Bruce Barcott, "Picasso Couldn't Box," *Seattle Weekly*, 10-25-95, 19.
686 *"He was the center":* Barbara Probst Solomon, "Callow Young Genius," *New York*, 82.
686 *"gambled on his ability":* POP, 357.
686 *"After Cubism":* M. R. Montgomery, "Mailer vs. Picasso at Harvard," *Boston Globe*, 11-14-95, 82.
686 *"doomed to relive his obsessions":* POP, 352.
686 *"as if work itself":* Ibid., 367.
686 *"This is a biography":* "Portrait of Picasso as a Young Man," *Atlantic*, November 1995, 145–46.
686 *"the worst I've ever gotten":* M. R. Montgomery.
686 *"an old-fashioned cut-and-paste job":* Michiko Kakutani, "Egos and Outlaws: Like Attracts Like," *NYT*, 9-29-95, CI, C29.
687 *"That does the job":* "Why Picasso Biography Quotes So Fully," *NYT*, 10-3-95.
687 *"just a commodity":* "Entretien: Norman Mailer and Jean Malaquais": taped in late November or early December 1994, and broadcast on the ARTE network in early 1995; all quotations are from the transcript of the program.
687 *"incomprehensible":* NM to JM, 6-28-95.
689 *"The general tone":* NM to Jean-Pierre Catherine and Michael Seiler, 3-7-95.
689 *"To this day":* JML interview with Elisabeth Malaquais, 6-10-10.
689 *"There's no equality":* NM to Elisabeth Malaquais, 9-8-95.
690 *"Norman had become":* JML interview with Elisabeth Malaquais, 6-10-10.
690 *"overcame his anger":* Ibid.
690 Planet Without Visa: *Planéte sans Visa* (Paris: Phébus, 1999).
691 *satisfied America's interest:* NM to Don Carpenter, 7-21-95.
691 *contacted the "Page Six":* Richard Johnson, "Mailer's Ex-Lover Writes It Down," *New York Post*, 9-15-95, 6.
692 *According to Harry Evans:* JML interview with Harry Evans, 5-31-12.
692 *"my keen and formidable agents":* CIF, acknowledgments page.

692 *middling review:* John W. Aldridge, "Documents as Narrative," *Atlantic*, May 1995.
692 *"And in truth":* NM to Aldridge, 1-24-96.
692 *"angry and bruised":* NM to Susan Mailer, 11-29-95.
693 *"are not taking account":* "Black and White Justice," *New York*, 10-16-95, 29.
693 *commencement address:* NM received an honorary Doctor of Humane Letters degree from Wilkes University, and gave the commencement address, 5-27-95.
694 *found a Gideon Bible:* Thomas Curwen, "The Art of Faith," *Los Angeles Times*, 2-22-04.
694 *"I couldn't make":* Sean Abbott, "Mailer Goes to the Mountain," *At Random*, 50.
694 *"To my knowledge":* Sean Abbott, Ibid., 51.
694 *"this odd moment":* Bill Broadway, "Norman Mailer: New Advertisements for Himself," *New Millennium Writings*, 14.
695 Crossing the Threshold of Hope: (NY: Knopf, 1994).
695 On Social Concern: (Boston: Pauline Books and Media, 1987).
695 *offer the Pope:* Walter Goodman, "No, PEN Decides It Won't Invite the Pope to Join," *NYT*, 5-17-88, C20.
695 *"the power of greed":* Sean Abbott, "Mailer Goes to the Mountain," *At Random*, 50.
695 *"I was curious":* Ibid.
695 *"how good a story":* Donn Fry, "Mailer's Literary Touch Backed by Audacity," *Seattle Times*, 1-26-97.
695 *"the spiritual or psychological keel":* Bruce Weber, "The Gospel According to Mailer," *NYT*, 4-24-97, B1–B2.
695 *"at the least worthy":* Thomas Curwen, "The Art of Faith," *Los Angeles Times*, 2-22-04.
695 *"I wanted to retell":* Bill Broadway, "Why Mailer Decided to Play Jesus," *Washington Post*, 5-10-97.
695 *"If suddenly I had":* Donn Fry, "Mailer's Literary Touch Backed by Audacity," *Seattle Times*.
695 *"to write a book":* Andrew O'Hagan, "The Martyrdom of Mailer," *Guardian Weekend*, 8-30-97, T10.
695 *"I remember arguing":* JML interview with Jason Epstein, 6-25-03.
696 *"almost animal-like":* Sean Abbott, "Mailer Goes to the Mountain," *At Random*, 50.
696 *He did some research:* Ibid., 54; Bob Minzesheimer, "Mailer Retells the Greatest Story Ever," *USA Today*, 4-24-97.
696 *Elaine Pagels: The Gnostic Gospels* (NY: Random House, 1979); *The Origin of Satan* (NY: Random House, 1995).
696 *"Celebrities":* Transcript of *Charlie Rose*, 4-22-97.
696 *two pieces on the political campaigns:* "War of the Oxymorons," *George*, November 1996, 6–24; "How the Pharaoh Beat Bogey," *George*, January 1997, 54–60, 82–86.

696 *article on Pat Buchanan:* "Searching for Deliverance," *Esquire*, August 1996, 54–61, 118–27.
696 *Clinton aides wrote back:* Bill Clinton to NM, 12-6-94.
697 *"I think you owe it":* NM to Bill Clinton, 12-28-94.
697 *"boutique politics":* "Searching for Deliverance," *Esquire*, 54.
697 *"the quiet tones":* Ibid., 55.
697 *"I've been married":* Ibid.
698 *"Seen up close":* "How the Pharaoh Beat Bogey," *George*, 59.
698 *"It's the story":* JML interview with Michael Mailer, 11-1-03.
698 *Filming was scheduled:* Andrew Hindes and Chris Petrikin, "In This Corner, Mailer Helming 'Ringside,' " *Variety*, 3-2-97.
698 *"The only trouble":* NM to Bruce Dexter, 5-6-97.
698 *"Boxing":* Ibid.
698 "Tough Guys Don't Dance *was":* JML interview with Michael Mailer, 11-1-03.
699 *"Either they had found":* NM to Dexter, 5-6-97.
699 *"To this day":* Michael Mailer interview.
699 When We Were Kings: Produced by Das Films/Sonenberg/Polygram, directed by Leon Gast.
699 *"a sort of novelized":* Michiko Kakutani, "Norman Mailer's Perception of Jesus," *NYT*, 4-14-97, B7.
699 *"an inestimable advantage":* Sean Abbott, "Mailer Goes to the Mountain," *At Random*, 54.
699 *"extremely Jewish":* Bill Broadway, "Norman Mailer: New Advertisements for Himself," *New Millennium Writings*, 14.
700 *"I began to realize":* Ibid.
700 *"That conviction":* Sean Abbott, "Mailer Goes to the Mountain," *At Random*, 54.
700 *"God-given power":* Frank Kermode, "Advertisements for Himself," *NYRB*, 5-15-97.
700 *"Norman's more":* Dinitia Smith, "Narrator of Mailer's Next Novel: Jesus," *NYT*, 4-4-97.
700 *"not only His mental":* Reynolds Price, "Mailer, Mark, Luke and John," *NYTBR*, 5-4-97, 9.
700 *"the quiet ghostly voice":* John Updike, "Stones into Bread," *New Yorker*, 5-12-97.
701 *King James Bible:* Maureen Conlan, "Mailer's Jesus Is Remote, But Language Shines," *Cincinnati Post*, 6-7-97.
701 *his father-in-law told him:* Ray Waddle, "Mailer Stresses Jesus as a Man in Rewrite of Gospels," *The Tennessean*, 6-15-97, 1B, 2B.
701 *"a spastic simulacrum":* James Wood, "He Is Finished," *New Republic*, 5-12-97.
701 *"If he'd just said":* Mick Brown, " 'He Smiled, So I Punched Him,' " *Daily Telegraph*, 9-25-97, 26.
701 *"I guess it was":* "Norman Mailer's Gut Reaction," *New York*, 7-29-98.
701 *"flabby":* Ibid.

701 *promise to write a sequel:* Bob Minzesheimer, "Mailer Retells the Greatest Story Ever Told," *USA Today.*

701 *anniversary edition: The Naked and the Dead, Fiftieth Anniversary Edition, with a New Introduction by the Author* (NY: Henry Holt, 1998).

702 *"Suddenly a catastrophe":* NM to Bruce Dexter, 2-16-97.

702 *"It's a little like":* NM to Edward McAlice, 3-26-97.

703 *"a commemorative work":* NM to Edith Atkin, 9-9-97.

703 *"one extremely famous person":* "Meet the Author: Norman Mailer," Random House publicity sheet, 9-97.

703 *"Occasionally, since this had": The Time of Our Time* (NY: Random House, 1998), xi.

703 *"equal to a row":* Ibid., vii.

703 *"The Second World War":* Martin Arnold, " 'Private Ryan' Revives a Genre," *NYT*, 7-30-98, E3.

704 *"There is little":* TOT, ix.

704 *"the idea of certain":* Elizabeth Taylor, "Fine Distinctions," *Chicago Tribune, Books*, 5-24-98, 3.

704 *"quick observant eye":* Michiko Kakutani, "Self-Portrait of an Artist with Customary Élan," *NYT*, 5-4-98.

704 *"is above all":* Harold Bloom, "Norman Mailer's Testament," *Washington Post Book World*, 5-24-98, 1, 10.

705 *"Mailer is looking well":* David Denby, "The Contender," *New Yorker*, 4-20-98, 63–64.

705 *"could match the book's variety":* Ibid., 62.

705 *"a clear spiritual autobiography":* Ibid., 64–65.

706 *"The main good motive":* Sean Abbott, "Norman Mailer on Literary Instincts and Ambitions," *At Random*, 4-27-98.

706 *"Mailer's imagination of history":* David Denby, "The Contender," *New Yorker*, 64.

706 *"two-hander":* James Campbell, "Seeking Susan," *NYTBR*, 6-24-12, 15.

706 *"a long, long night":* David Denby, "The Contender," *New Yorker*, 64.

706 *The endless critical discussion:* See JML, "Norman Mailer: Novelist, Journalist, or Historian," *Journal of Modern Literature*, Fall 2006, 91–103.

706 *who wrote about the party:* Lillian Ross, "Ink," *New Yorker*, 5-18-98, 31.

706 *"there will never be another":* George Rush and Joanna Molloy, "Mailer's a Knockout," New York *Daily News*, 5-8-98, 14.

707 *a lot of reading:* Rick Lyman, "After Half a Century, Still Writing, Still Questing," *NYT*, 5-7-98, E1, E8.

707 Underworld: (NY: Scribner's, 1997).

707 *a lot of Jung:* Rick Lyman, "After Half a Century, Still Writing, Still Questing," *NYT.*

707 C. G. Jung: His Life and Work: (Boston: Shambhala, 1991); originally published in 1977, the Shambhala edition is in NM's library.

707 *"In winter, it's wonderful:"* Rick Lyman, "After Half a Century, Still Writing, Still Questing," *NYT.*

707 *"I've been waiting":* Ibid.

FIFTEEN: OLD FREIGHTER, UNCERTAIN SEA

In addition to the sources identified below, the following were drawn on: JML's "Mailer Log"; JML's unpublished interviews with NM and BW. NM's letters are located at the HRC.

Page

708 *hearing aids:* At the urging of Tom Luddy, who saw that Mailer could not hear what members of the film crew were saying, NM began wearing one during the 1987 filming of *Tough Guys Don't Dance.*

708 *"the illusion that you":* NM to Emmerich Kusztrich, 1-26-05.

708 *"leaves me cheerful":* NM to Lois Wilson, 11-22-02.

708 *"old guy with slits":* Hillel Italie, "The Greatest American Writer," *Chicago Tribune*, 7-5-99, 3C.

708 *more of a geezer:* Tim Warren, "The Softer Norman Mailer," *Baltimore Sun,* 9-29-91.

708 *Several operations:* TC, 350–54.

708 Windchill Summer: (NY: Random House, 2000).

708 *"a story about boys":* TC, 55.

709 *"I told her":* Carolyn T. Hughes, "Norman Mailer: A Literary Lion Roars," *Poets and Writers*, March/April 2001, 45.

709 *"No. You can't edit":* TC, 345.

709 *"Do we influence":* Marie-Louise von der Leyen, "Norman Mailer on Anger and Love," in *Lifelines.*

709 *"Fine":* TC, 345–46.

710 *"I could have made it":* Carolyn Hughes, "Norman Mailer: A Literary Lion Roars," *Poets and Writers*, 45.

710 Hooking Up: (NY: Farrar, Straus & Giroux, 2000).

710 *"My Three Stooges": Hooking Up*, 145–71.

710 *"the rich material":* Ibid., 156.

710 *"weak, pale":* Ibid., 147.

710 *"old lions":* Ibid., 156.

710 *"old piles of bones":* Ibid., 152.

710 *"shaken":* Ibid., 154.

710 The World According to Garp: (NY: Dutton, 1978).

710 Angstrom tetralogy: Published by Knopf in 1960, 1971, 1981, 1990, respectively.

711 *"a remarkable Santa Claus": Hooking Up,* 156.

711 *"can't create a character":* Irving, quoted on a Canadian Broadcasting Corporation program hosted by Evan Solomon, *Hot Type*, 12-17-99.

711 *"spreading like kudzu":* John Updike, "Awriiiighhhhhhhht!," *New Yorker*, 11-9-98.

711 *"to cook up":* "A Man Half Full," TOT, 1292.

711 *"certainly the most gifted":* Ibid., 1299.

711 *"It's true that I'm":* Ginny Dougary, "The Norman Conquests," *Sunday Independent*, 6-25-00.

711 Explaining Hitler: (NY: Random House, 1998).
712 *"Long after the details":* Ron Rosenbaum, "Oh, the Devil He Knows," *Moment*, June 2007, 34.
712 *"this little muse":* Ibid., 60.
712 *"I was absolutely":* Ibid., 34.
712 *"There were only":* Ibid., 60.
712 The Young Hitler I Knew: (Boston: Houghton Mifflin, 1954).
712 Hitler's Youth: Translated by Lawrence Wilson (London: Hutchinson, 1958).
712 *books on apiary science:* Karl von Frisch, *Bees: Their Vision, Chemical Senses, and Language* (Ithaca: Cornell University Press, 1950); Maurice Maeterlinck, *The Life of the Bee* (NY: Dodd, Mead, 1919).
712 American Tragedy: (NY: Random House, 1996).
712 *a four-hour miniseries:* Produced by Lawrence Schiller and Lyn Raynor; directed by Schiller; broadcast on 11-15-00.
712 *"My old friend":* Blurb on jacket of *American Tragedy.*
712 *Simpson went to court:* Jason Gay, "Norman Mailer to CBS: You Blew It!," *New York Observer*, 11-27-00.
712 *"I have not told":* NM to Morton Yanow, 3-24-99.
713 *"The pleasure of writing":* Ibid.
713 Conversations of Goethe with Johann Peter Ekermann: (San Francisco: North Point, 1984).
714 *a collection of these:* NM abandoned this project when his publisher said the contents had no unifying theme.
715 Love Letters: (NY: Plume, 1990).
715 Zelda, Scott, & Ernest: Unpublished.
716 A Moveable Feast: (NY: Scribner's, 1964).
716 Save Me the Waltz: (NY: Scribner's, 1932).
716 *"Norris can be Zelda":* Michael Lee, "The Lost Generation Will Be Found in Provincetown," *Cape Cod Voice*, 9-27-01, 43.
716 *"This should be":* Ibid., 43.
716 *"I'm safe from becoming":* Sue Harrison, "Norman & Norris Are Acting Up," *Provincetown Banner*, 9-20-01.
716 *"damn interesting":* Debbie Forman, "Norman and Norris Seem Letter Perfect for Roles of Literary Legends Who Lived Large," *Cape Cod Times*, 9-15-01.
716 *"I'm not much like":* Sue Harrison, "Norman & Norris Are Acting Up," *Provincetown Banner.*
717 *"always made me feel":* Debbie Forman, "Norman and Norris Seem Letter Perfect," *Cape Cod Times.*
717 *"makes you want to cry":* Lawrence Shainberg, "History Looking at Itself: On the Road with the Mailers and George Plimpton," *Norman Mailer's Later Fictions:* Ancient Evenings *Through* Castle in the Forest, ed. John Whalen-Bridge (Basingstoke, England: Palgrave Macmillan, 2010), 166.
717 *"sometimes nasty":* Ibid., 167.

718 *"Norris and I"*: Ibid., 169.
718 *"Well, he finally"*: Sean Abbott, "Norman Mailer on Literary Instincts and Ambitions," *At Random*.
718 *third FBI agent:* ABC News, February 20, 2001.
719 *"I am either insanely"*: Schiller, *Into the Mirror*, xv.
719 *"possibly the worst intelligence":* Elaine Shannon, "More Questions about the FBI's Hanssen Homework," *Time*, 5-7-02.
719 *"No one can understand"*: NM to Bonnie Hanssen, 4-5-02.
720 *"terribly affected"*: NM and Dotson Rader, "The Devil's Big Day," *Sunday Times Magazine* (London), 9-08-02, 40.
720 *"That only happens"*: Ann Treneman, " 'Ruin More Beautiful than the Building,' " *Times* (London), 9-13-01.
720 *"Being up in Provincetown"*: NM and Dotson Rader, "The Devil's Big Day," *Sunday Times Magazine* (London), 40.
720 *"an architectural monstrosity"*: Ibn Warraq, "The Assassination of President John F. Kennedy, 9/11 and the Apologists of Islamic Terrorism," *New English Review*, March 2009.
720 *"cultural oppressors"*: Ann Treneman, "Ruin More Beautiful than the Building," *Times* (London).
720 *"We small Austrians"*: Shainberg, 163–4.
721 Why Are We at War?: (NY: Random House, 2003).
721 *"Presented with the cache"*: SA, 309.
721 The Spooky Art: (NY: Random House, 2003).
721 *Kuzma, who had advised Abbott:* Robert F. Worth, "Jailhouse Author Helped by Mailer Is Found Dead," *NYT*, 2-11-02.
722 *"Everybody hated him"*: JML interview with William Majeski, 4-23-12.
722 *"But it's not something"*: Robert F. Worth, "Jailhouse Author Helped by Mailer Is Found Dead," *NYT*.
722 *"That's the third person"*: Bill Hutchinson, "Killer-Author Hangs Himself in Upstate Jail," New York *Daily News*, 2-11-02.
722 *"I am happy"*: Robert F. Worth, "Jailhouse Author Helped by Mailer Is Found Dead," *NYT*.
722 *"His life was tragic"*: Ibid.
722 *"like they were from different"*: TC, 366.
723 *Norris thought that Vidal:* Ibid.
723 *"wild and wooly week"*: Ibid., 368.
723 Man and Superman: Shaw's play was first staged in London in 1905, but it was not performed in its entirety until 1915.
723 *"Norman, when I walk"*: TC, 368–69.
723 *"the reading flowed"*: Carol Beggy, "Mailer and Vidal Reunite Harmoniously at a Provincetown Benefit Reading," *Boston Globe*, 10-14-02.
724 *"almost as good"*: Barbara Lane interview, *Commonwealth*, 4-15-03, 22. The interview accompanies Mailer's speech to the Commonwealth Club, "Only in America."
724 *his grave, his will his epitaph:* NM wanted to be buried in Provincetown;

had his will made; and gave Michael Lee two possible epitaphs: "He may have been a fool, but he did his best and that can't be said of all fools"; and Gide's line: "Please do not understand me too quickly." Lee, "A Conversation with Norman Mailer." His family decided on the following quote from DP for his gravestone: "There is that law of life, so cruel and so just, that one must grow or pay more for remaining the same."

724 *"after we'd corrupted":* NM to Sal Cetrano, 4-22-02.

724 The Castle in the Forest: Published by Random House, January 23, 2007.

725 *losing only a few months:* Christopher Bollen, "Norman Mailer, Writer," *V* magazine, 7.

725 *"pretty much left me":* TC, 172–73.

725 *"popping nitroglycerine":* TC, 373.

726 *"keenly perceptive":* Michiko Kakutani, "Quoting Himself on His Lofty Dream," *NYT*, 1-22-03, EI, E9.

726 *"Writers aren't taken seriously":* SA, 163.

726 *"for his alertness":* James Campbell, "Don't Put Your Wife in a Novel," *NYTBR*, 2-23-03, 8.

727 *"broke ground for every memoirist":* Ron Rosenbaum, "Mailer Was the Rage," *New York Observer*, 2-10-03, 1, 8.

727 *"outrageous an egoist":* Alfred Kazin, "The Trouble He's Seen," *NYTBR*, 5-5-68; rpt., JML, ed., *Critical Essays on Norman Mailer*, 60–65.

727 *"At his most engaging":* Walter Goodman, "Mailer Plugs Himself Instead of His Book," *NYT*, 1-24-92, C28.

727 *letter to the publisher:* NM to Arthur Ochs Sulzberger Jr., 3-24-03.

727 *The* Times *acknowledged this error: NYT*, Metropolitan Desk/Corrections, 4-9-03.

727 *"a posterior aperture":* Barbara Lane, interview with NM, *Commonwealth* 22.

727 *"I really didn't have":* Christopher Bigsby, "Alarm Calls for American Dreamers," *Independent*, 10.

727 *"economic gluttony":* NM, Speech at Commonwealth Club, "Only in America," 15.

727 *"I know I'm going":* Christopher Bigsby, 10.

728 *"manic money-grab":* "Only in America," 15–16.

728 *"envisioned the United States":* Ibid., 17.

728 *dangers of empire:* Taki Theocoracopolos, Kara Hopkins, and Scott McConnell, "I Am Not for World Empire," *American Conservative*, 12-2-02, 8–18.

728 Dreaming War: (NY: Thunder's Mouth Press/Nation Books, 2002).

728 *triumphant arrival:* President Bush landed on the deck of the USS *Abraham Lincoln* (CVN 72) on 5-1-03.

729 *"The White Man Unburdened": NYRB*, 7-17-03, 4–6.

729 *"I'm still trying":* NM to Thomas de Zengotita, 8-4-03.

729 *Giving interviews:* NM was interviewed on Bush and Iraq in June 2003 by Gabriel Contreras for *Lateral*, a Spanish literary magazine (not located);

and on 11-15-02 by Mark Olshaker on the occasion of receiving the John P. McGovern Medal in Literature by the Cosmos Club Foundation in Washington, D.C.

729 *"a touch of the very edge":* Yvonne Shafer, "The Mailers and *Long Day's Journey into Night*," www.eoneill.com/reviews/journey_provincetown_shafer.htm.

730 Cheap Diamonds: (NY: Random House, 2007).

730 *busy for three months:* Dwayne Raymond, *Mornings with Mailer* (NY: Harper Perennial, 2010), 53.

730 Modest Gifts: (NY: Random House, 2003).

730 *"Guy's eighty now":* Philip Roth, *Exit Ghost* (Boston: Houghton Mifflin, 2007), 255.

731 *"Urination had become":* Nelson Aldrich Jr., *George, Being George* (NY: Random House, 2008), 374–75.

732 *"He was in dire need":* JML interview with Susan Mailer, 8-18-11.

732 *Norman Mailer Society:* Ron Rosenbaum was the keynote speaker at the first society meeting in Brooklyn, 11-1-03, followed by a party at NM's apartment.

732 *review of* Beyond the Law: William Kennedy, "Mailer Is onto Something with His Second Film," *Albany Times-Union*, 10-1-68, 20.

732 *"and he didn't look like a bum":* JML interview with William Kennedy, 8-5-11.

733 *"Kennedy: I soon realized":* "Norman Mailer as Occasional Commentator": *MR* (2007), 23–26.

734 *read from the Hitler novel:* NM read on, 5-1-07.

734 *"Legs Diamond": Legs* (NY: Coward, McCann & Geoghegan, 1975) was the first volume of William Kennedy's Albany series.

734 *biographies of Grigory:* The first and most important is René Fülöp-Miller, *Rasputin: The Holy Devil* (NY: Viking, 1928); after Mailer finished CIF, he was also impressed with Brian Moynahan, *Rasputin: The Saint Who Sinned* (NY: Random House, 1997).

735 *"delicate Kennedyites":* Doris Kearns Goodwin, *Lyndon Johnson and the American Dream*: (NY: Harper & Row, 1976), 223.

735 *"I felt he respected":* JML interview with Doris Kearns and Richard Goodwin, 12-14-11.

735 *book about Lincoln:* Goodwin, *Team of Rivals: The Political Genius of Abraham Lincoln* (NY: Simon & Schuster, 2005).

736 *number of additional pieces:* "Reflections on Courage, Morality and Sexual Pleasure," *Playboy*, December 2004, 86–88, 98, 190–98; "Father to Son: What I've Learned About Rage," *New York*, 8-9-04, 28–35; "Mailer vs. Mailer," *Stop Smiling*, 4-15-05, 38–43, 91.

736 *Ron Howard, the film's director:* www.thoroughlyrussellcrowe.com.onthisdayin/dec/dec25.html.

736 *"Baer got spoiled":* "Story Notes for *Cinderella Man*," www.amctv.com/movie-blog/2012/05/story-notes-trivia-cinderella-man.php.

737 *"he has a certain":* Jason Gay, "Norman Mailer Does Street Time," *New York Observer*, 1-22-01.

737 *Tom Staley:* Director of the Harry Ransom Center for a quarter of a century, Staley is also a Joyce scholar.

738 *"The sad truth":* NM to Anne Barry, 3-24-05.

738 *"I used to pride myself":* James Toback, "A Certain Grim Pleasure," *V Life*, December/January 2005, 114.

738 *Douglas Brinkley:* A history professor at Rice University, Brinkley (b. 1960) recently published *Cronkite* (NY: Harper, 2012).

738 *sale of Mailer's papers:* Douglas Brinkley, "Mailer's Miscellany," *NYT*, 4-25-05.

738 *long profile:* Douglas Brinkley, "The Last Buccaneer," *Rolling Stone*, 6-30-05, 84–95, 162, 166.

738 *"captured something hard":* Ibid., 90.

739 *"she's a threefer":* Ibid., 94.

739 *"Asiatic" and "Oriental":* Esther Wu to Jann Wenner, 6-25-05; rpt., Lloyd Grove and Hudson Morgan, "Ethnic Group Is Stormin' over Norman," New York *Daily News*, 6-30-05.

739 *"an excellent example":* Ibid.

740 *"It's our point of departure":* OG, 97–98.

742 *"the sight of Provincetown":* Graydon Carter, ed., *Vanity Fair Proust Questionnaire*, 131.

742 *married to Norris for thirty years:* Actually they were married almost twenty-five, but both had taken to adding on the five years they lived together.

742 *read a piece in* The Atlantic: Bernard-Henri Lévy, "In the Footsteps of Tocqueville," *Atlantic*, November 2005; excerpted from *American Vertigo: Travelling America in the Footsteps of Tocqueville* (NY: Random House, 2006).

742 *several errors:* See JML, "BHL," Letters to the Editor, *Atlantic*, February 2006, 24.

743 *"Rarely are good novels":* www.nationalbook.org/nbaacceptspeech_nmailer06.html.

743 *David Ebershoff:* NM's editor for his last four books.

743 *"a little bit of uneasiness":* JML interview with David Ebershoff, 3-26-10.

743 *"incredibly digressive":* Ibid.

744 *"a little work":* Gina Centrello, "Remembering Norman Mailer," *MR* (2008), 13–14.

744 *Khodynskoye Pole:* See Stephen Borkowski, "A Tear Shed into a Cup of Sorrow," *MR* (2011), 367–69.

744 *"We went to see him":* JML interview with David Ebershoff, 3-26-10.

745 *grandchildren:* Valentina, Alejandro, and Antonia Colodro (Susan and Marco Colodro); Isabella Moschen (Danielle and Michael Moschen); Christina Marie Nastasi (Betsy and Frank Nastasi), Callan and Theodore

Mailer (Stephen and Lindsay Marx); Natasha Lancaster (Kate and Guy Lancaster); Mattie James (Matthew and Salina Sais); Cyrus Force Mailer (Michael and Sasha Lazard); two more grandchildren, Jackson Kingsley Mailer (Matthew and Salina) and Nicholas Maxwell Mailer Wendling (Maggie and John Wendling) were born after NM died.

745 *grandniece:* Eden River Alson (Peter Alson and Alice O'Neill).

745 *godchildren:* Kittredge and Clay Fisher (Ivan and Diane Fisher); Sebastian and Julian Rosthal (Elke Rosthal).

745 *"the real spirit of Jesus":* BE, 81.

745 *"We must war against":* Ibid., 74–75.

745 *"A good novel":* Ibid., 68–69.

746 *"As a father":* "Relative Values: Norman Mailer and His Son John," 11-19-06, www.timesonline.co.uk/printfriendly/0,,1-531-2458074-531,00.html.

746 *"Since the folks have passed":* JML interview with John Buffalo Mailer, 4-24-12.

746 *"Growing old without cracking":* NM to Ed McAlice, 6-22-06.

747 *"She has lost":* NM to Gillie Mailer, 6-15-06.

748 Take Me to the River: (NY: Simon & Schuster, 2007).

749 *Michael had gotten married:* To Sasha Lazard; Matthew to Salina Sais; Peter to Alice O'Neill; Stephen married Elizabeth Rainer in 2010.

749 *"The feet can go":* NM to Jim Blake, 6-22-06.

750 *"he got a million":* TC, 376.

751 *"essentially rationalistic":* Tom Junod, "The Last Man Standing," *Esquire*, January 2007, 131.

752 *Stephan Morrow:* He recounts his involvement with the play in "Norman Mailer: A Requiem," *MR* (2008), 149–54.

752 *Maslin's blows:* "Putting Hitler on the Couch, and Finding Bees," *NYT*, 1-19-07.

753 *"an utterly strange work":* Lee Siegel, "Maestro of the Human Ego," *NTYBR*, 1-21-07.

753 *"Keeping the paradox":* J. M. Coetzee, "Portrait of the Monster as a Young Artist," *NYRB*, 2-15-07.

753 *eleventh best seller:* JML, "Norman Mailer's Best Sellers," *MR* (2008), 270–71.

753 *"We had the end section":* JML questions for Lois Wilson, 11-15-11, conducted by Erin Cressida Wilson.

755 *"People are going to think":* Raymond, *Mornings with Mailer*, 150.

755 *taking a day off:* Ibid., 270–71.

755 *Raymond called Norris:* Ibid., 272–74.

755 *"and you can tell him":* Ibid., 275.

755 *Mailer told Raymond:* Ibid.

756 *"a perfect visit":* JML questions for Eileen Fredrickson, conducted by Peter Lennon, 10-15-11.

756 *Hadada Award:* www.parisreview.org/audio/5767/presentation-of-the-2007-hadada-award-to-norman-mailer-e-l-doctorow.

756 *"He couldn't walk"*: TC, 386.
756 *"We shouldn't let Dad"*: Ibid.
756 Peeling the Onion: (NY: Harcourt, 2007).
756 *"How many of us"*: TC, 386.
756 *"I have held on to"*: Timothy Garton Ash, "The Road from Danzig," *NYRB*, 8-16-07.
756 *"I'm happy"*: Ibid.
757 God Is Not Great: (NY: Twelve, 2007).
757 *Andrew O'Hagan's review:* "Racing Against Reality," *NYRB*, 6-28-07.
757 Falling Man: (NY: Scribner's, 2007).
757 *"ambition, risk, broad vision"*: Don DeLillo to JML, 4-15-10.
758 *"James Jones is one"*: NM to Ray Elliott, 8-3-07.
759 *"I was in denial"*: JML interview with Matthew Mailer, 8-21-08.
761 *"You must really love me"*: TC, 389.
761 On God: (NY: Random House, 2007).
761 *"Michael finally returned"*: Peter Alson, "One More for the Road," *MR* (2008), 26–27.
763 *"Mr. Mailer used his copious talents"*: Michiko Kakutani, "A Novelist's Nonfiction Captured the American Spirit," *NYT*, 11-11-07.

SELECT BIBLIOGRAPHY

Abbott, Jack Henry. *In the Belly of the Beast: Letters from Prison.* Introduction by Norman Mailer. NY: Random House, 1981.

Abbott, Jack Henry, and Naomi Zack. *My Return.* Buffalo, NY: Prometheus, 1987.

Adams, Henry. *The Education of Henry Adams.* NY: Modern Library, 1931.

Adams, Laura. *Norman Mailer: A Comprehensive Bibliography.* Introduction by Robert F. Lucid. Metuchen, NJ: Scarecrow, 1974.

———, ed. *Will the Real Norman Mailer Please Stand Up.* Port Washington, NY: Kennikat, 1976.

Aldrich, Nelson, Jr., ed. *George, Being George.* NY: Random House, 2008.

Aldridge, John. *After the Lost Generation.* NY: McGraw Hill, 1951; rpt., Introduction by Norman Mailer. NY: Arbor House, 1985.

———. *Time to Murder and Create: The Contemporary Novel in Crisis.* NY: McKay, 1966.

Alson, Peter. *Take Me to the River.* NY: Simon & Schuster, 2007.

Aronson, Judith. *Likenesses: With the Sitters Writing About One Another.* Manchester, UK: Lintott, 2010.

Bailey, Jennifer. *Norman Mailer: Quick-Change Artist.* London: Macmillan, 1979.

Baldwin, James. *Nobody Knows My Name: More Notes of a Native Son.* NY: Dial, 1961.

Beauvoir, Simone de. *The Second Sex.* Trans. H. M. Parshley. NY: Knopf, 1953.

Begiebing, Robert. *Acts of Regeneration: Allegory and Archetype in the Works of Norman Mailer.* Columbia: University of Missouri Press, 1980.

———. *Toward a New Synthesis: John Fowler, John Gardner, Norman Mailer.* Ann Arbor: UMI Research Press, 1989.

Bloom, Harold, ed. *Critical Views: Norman Mailer.* Philadelphia: Chelsea House, 2003.

Bowers, John. *The Colony.* NY: Dutton, 1971.

Braudy, Leo. *Norman Mailer: A Collection of Critical Essays.* Englewood Cliffs, NJ: Prentice Hall, 1972.

Brower, Brock. *Other Loyalties: A Politics of Personality.* NY: Atheneum, 1968.

Buber, Martin. *Tales of the Hasidim; The Early Masters; The Later Masters (Ten Rungs) Hasidic Sayings.* Vols. 1–2. NY: Schocken, 1947–48.

Buckley, William F., Jr. *Rumbles Left and Right.* NY: Putnam's, 1963.

Budge, E. Wallis. *The Egyptian Book of the Dead.* NY: Dover, 1967.

Bufithis, Philip H. *Norman Mailer.* NY: Ungar, 1978.

———. "Norman Mailer." *Dictionary of Literary Biography, 1983.* Ed. Matthew Bruccoli. Detroit: Gale, 1984.

Burnett, Hallie and Whit. *Fiction Writer's Handbook.* Preface by Norman Mailer. NY: Barnes & Noble. 1975.

Campbell, James. *Talking at the Gates: A Life of James Baldwin.* NY: Viking, 1991.

Chaiken, Michael, and Jason Altman. Producers. DVD. *Maidstone and Other Films by Norman Mailer.* NY: Eclipse from the Criterion Collection, 2012.

Charters, Ann, ed. *The Portable Beat Reader.* NY: Viking Penguin, 1992.

Clarke, Gerald. *Capote: A Biography.* NY: Simon & Schuster, 1988.

Dearborn, Mary. *Mailer: A Biography.* NY: Houghton Mifflin, 1999.

de Grazia, Edward. *Girls Lean Back Everywhere: The Law of Obscenity and the Assault on Genius.* NY: Random House, 1992.

DeLillo, Don. *Falling Man.* NY: Scribner, 2007.

———. *Libra.* NY: Viking, 1988.

Dickstein, Morris. *Leopards in the Temple: The Transformation of American Fiction, 1945–70.* Cambridge: Harvard University Press, 2002.

Doctorow, E. L. *Ragtime.* NY: Random House, 1975.

Dreiser, Theodore. *An American Tragedy.* NY: Boni & Liveright, 1925.

Ehrlich, Robert. *Norman Mailer: The Radical as Hipster.* Metuchen, NJ: Scarecrow, 1978.

Ellis, Bret Easton. *American Psycho.* NY: Vintage, 1991.

Feldman, Gene, and Max Gartenberg, eds. *The Beat Generation and the Angry Young Men.* NY: Citadel, 1958.

Fiedler, Leslie. *A Fiedler Reader.* NY: Stein & Day, 1977.

Fitzgerald, F. Scott. *The Crack-up.* Ed. Edmund Wilson. NY: New Directions, 1945.

Flaherty, Joe. *Managing Mailer.* NY: Coward-McCann, 1970.

Friedan, Betty. *The Feminine Mystique.* NY: Norton, 1963.

Fülöp-Miller, René. *Rasputin: The Holy Devil.* NY: Viking, 1928.

Gelmis, Joseph, ed. *The Film Director as Superstar.* Garden City, NY: Doubleday, 1970.

Gillmor, Daniel S., ed. *Speaking of Peace: An Edited Report of the Cultural and Scientific Conference for World Peace.* NY: National Council of the Arts, Sciences and Professions, 1949.

Glenday, Michael K. *Norman Mailer.* NY: St. Martin's, 1995.

Goodwin, Doris Kearns. *Lyndon Johnson and the American Dream.* NY: Harper & Row, 1976.

Gordon, Andrew. *An American Dreamer: A Psychoanalytic Study of the Fiction of Norman Mailer.* Rutherford, NJ: Fairleigh Dickinson University Press, 1980.

Green, Martin. *Cities of Light and Sons of the Morning.* Boston: Little, Brown, 1972.

Greer, Germaine. *The Madwoman's Underclothes: Essays and Occasional Writings.* NY: Atlantic Monthly Press, 1987.

Grobel, Lawrence. *Conversations with Capote.* NY: New American Library, 1985.

———. *Endangered Species: Writers Talk About Their Craft, Their Visions, Their Lives.* Cambridge, MA: Da Capo, 2001.

Guiles, Fred Lawrence. *Norma Jean: The Life of Marilyn Monroe.* NY: McGraw-Hill, 1969.

Gwaltney, Francis Irby. *The Day the Century Ended.* NY: Rinehart, 1955.

Hamill, Pete. "Norman Mailer." *American Rebels.* Ed. Jack Newfield. NY: Nation Books, 2003.

Hemingway, Ernest. *Selected Letters, 1917–1961.* Ed. Carlos Baker. NY: Scribner's, 1981.

Hemingway, Gregory. *Papa: A Personal Memoir.* Preface by Norman Mailer. Boston: Houghton Mifflin, 1976.

Holmes, John Clellon. *Passionate Opinions: The Cultural Essays.* Fayetteville: University of Arkansas Press, 1988.

Johnston, Glenn T., ed. *We Ain't No Heroes: The 112th Cavalry in World War II.* Denton: University of North Texas Press, 2005.

Jones, James. *From Here to Eternity.* NY: Scribner's, 1951.

———. *The Pistol.* NY: Scribner's, 1958.

———. *To Reach Eternity: The Letters of James Jones.* Ed. George Hendrick. NY: Random House, 1989.

———. *Some Came Running.* NY: Scribner's, 1958.

Jones, Kaylie. *Lies My Mother Never Told Me.* NY: Morrow, 2009.

Jones, Peter G. *War and the Novelist.* Columbia: University of Missouri Press, 1976.

Jumonville, Neil. *Critical Crossings: The New York Intellectuals in Postwar America.* Berkeley: University of California Press, 1991.

Kaplan, Fred. *Gore Vidal: A Biography.* NY: Doubleday, 1999.

Kaufmann, Walter, ed. *Existentialism from Dostoyevsky to Sartre.* NY: World, 1956.

Kazin, Alfred. *Bright Book of Life: American Storytellers from Hemingway to Mailer.* Boston: Little Brown, 1973.

———. *Contemporaries.* Boston: Little, Brown, 1962.

Kidd, Janet Aitken. *The Beaverbrook Girl.* London: Collins, 1987.

Kierkegaard, Søren. *Kierkegaard's Concept of Dread.* Trans. Walter Lowrie. Princeton: Princeton University Press, 1957.

Knox, Mickey. *The Good, the Bad, and the Dolce Vita: The Adventures of an Actor in Hollywood, Paris, and Rome.* Preface by Norman Mailer. NY: Nation Books, 2004.

Leeds, Barry H. *The Enduring Vision of Norman Mailer.* Bainbridge Island, WA: Pleasure Boat Studio, 2002.

Lennon, J. Michael, ed. *Critical Essays on Norman Mailer.* Boston: G. K. Hall, 1986.

———. *Norman Mailer's Provincetown: The Wild West of the East.* Provincetown Arts Press, 2005.

Lennon, J. Michael, and Donna Pedro Lennon. *Norman Mailer: Works and Days.* Preface by Norman Mailer. Shavertown, PA: Sligo, 2000.

Lifton, Robert. *Witness to an Extreme Century.* NY: Free Press, 2011.

Lindner, Robert. *Prescription for Rebellion.* NY: Rinehart, 1952.

Lowell, Robert. *Notebook, 1967–68*. NY: Farrar, Straus and Giroux, 1969.

Lucid, Robert F., ed. *Norman Mailer: The Man and His Work*. Boston: Little, Brown, 1971.

Macdonald, Dwight. *Discriminations: Essays and Afterthoughts*. Introduction by Norman Mailer. Cambridge, MA: Da Capo, 1985.

MacDonogh, Steve, ed. *The Rushdie Letters: Freedom to Speak, Freedom to Write*. Lincoln: University of Nebraska Press, 1993.

Mailer, Adele. *The Last Party: Scenes from My Life with Norman Mailer*. NY: Barricade, 1997.

Mailer, Norris Church. *Cheap Diamonds*. NY: Random House, 2007.

———. *A Ticket to the Circus*. NY: Random House, 2010.

———. *Windchill Summer*. NY: Random House, 2000.

Malaquais, Jean. *The Joker*. Preface by Norman Mailer. NY: Warner, 1974.

———. *World Without Visa*. NY: Doubleday, 1948.

Mallory, Carole. *Loving Mailer*. Beverly Hills: Phoenix, 2009.

Malraux, André. *Man's Fate*. NY: Modern Library, 1961.

Manso, Peter. *Mailer: His Life and Times*. NY: Simon & Schuster, 1985.

Manso, Peter, ed. *Running Against the Machine*. Garden City, NY: Doubleday, 1969.

Martin, David C. *Wilderness of Mirrors*. NY: Harper & Row, 1980.

Martinson, Deborah. *Lillian Hellman: A Life with Foxes and Scoundrels*. Washington, D.C.: Counterpoint, 2005.

Maugham, W. Somerset, *Up at the Villa*. NY: Doubleday, Doran, 1941.

McAuliffe, Kevin. *The Great American Newspaper: The Rise and Fall of the* Village Voice. NY: Scribner's, 1978.

McMillan, Priscilla Johnson. *Marina and Lee*. NY: Harper & Row, 1977.

Menand, Louis. *The Metaphysical Club: A Story of Ideas in America* (NY: Farrar, Straus and Giroux, 2001).

Michelson, Jeffrey, and Laura Bradley. *Laura Meets Jeffrey: Both Sides of an Erotic Memoir*. Foreword by Norman Mailer. Lehigh Valley, PA: New Blue, 2012.

Miller, Arthur. *Timebends: A Life*. NY: Grove, 1987.

Millett, Kate. *Sexual Politics*. NY: Doubleday, 1970.

Mills, Hilary. *Mailer: A Biography*. NY: Empire, 1982.

Morris, Willie. *New York Days*. Boston: Little, Brown, 1993.

Olivier, Fernande. *Souvenirs Intimes*. Ed. Gilbert Krill. Paris: Calmann-Lévy, 1988.

Ott-Toltz, Phyllis Silverman, with Barbara Bamberger Scott. *Love Bade Me Welcome: The Life of Phyllis Ott*. Lake Forest, CA: Behler, 2006.

Pagels, Elaine. *The Gnostic Gospels*. NY: Random House, 1979.

———. *The Origin of Satan*. NY: Random House, 1995.

Plimpton, George. *Shadow Box*. NY: Putnam's, 1977.

———. *Truman Capote: In Which Various Friends, Enemies, Acquaintances, and Detractors Recall His Turbulent Career*. NY: Nan A. Talese/Doubleday, 1997.

Podhoretz, Norman. *Doings and Undoings: The Fifties and After in American Writing*. NY: Farrar, Straus and Giroux, 1964.

———. *Ex-Friends*. NY: Free Press, 1999.

———. *Making It*. NY: Random House, 1967.

Podhoretz, Norman, ed. *The Commentary Reader*. NY: Atheneum, 1966.

Poirier, Richard. *Norman Mailer*. NY: Viking, 1972.

Polsgrove, Carol. *It Wasn't Pretty, Folks, But Didn't We Have Fun? Esquire in the Sixties*. NY: Norton, 1995.

Posner, Gerald. *Case Closed: Lee Harvey Oswald and the Assassination of JFK*. NY: Random House, 1993.

Raymond, Dwayne. *Mornings with Mailer*. NY: Harper Perennial, 2010.

Reich, Wilhelm. *The Sexual Revolution: Toward a Self-Governing Character Structure*. Trans. Theodore P. Wolfe (NY: Orgone Institute Press, 1945).

Rembar, Charles. *The End of Obscenity: The Trials of Lady Chatterley, Tropic of Cancer and Fanny Hill*. Introduction by Norman Mailer. NY: Bantam, 1969.

Report of Court Proceedings: In the Case of the Anti-Soviet Bloc. Moscow: People's Commission of Justice in the U.S.S.R., 1938.

Richardson, John. *A Life of Picasso: The Prodigy, 1881–1906*. NY: Random House, 1991.

———. *A Life of Picasso: The Cubist Rebel*. NY: Random House, 1996.

Rollyson, Carl. *Female Icons: Marilyn Monroe to Susan Sontag*. iUniverse, 2005.

———. *The Lives of Norman Mailer*. NY: Paragon House, 1991.

Rosenbaum, Ron. *Explaining Hitler*. NY: Random House, 1998.

Ross, Lillian. *Picture*. NY: Rinehart, 1952.
Rosten, Norman. *Marilyn—An Untold Story.* NY: New American Library, 1973.
Roth, Philip. *Exit Ghost*. Boston: Houghton Mifflin, 2007.
Rushdie, Salman. *The Satanic Verses*. NY: Viking, 1988.
Schiller, Lawrence, and James Willwerth. *American Tragedy: The Uncensored Story of the Simpson Defense*. NY: Random House, 1996.
Schiller, Lawrence, with Norman Mailer. *Into the Mirror: The Life of Master Spy Robert P. Hanssen*. NY: HarperCollins, 2002.
Schroeder, Eric James, ed. *Vietnam, We've All Been There*. Westport, CT: Praeger, 1992.
Seaver, Edwin, ed. *Cross-Section: A Collection of New American Writing*. NY: L. B. Fischer, 1944.
Sipiora, Phillip, ed. *The Mailer Review*, Vols. 1–6 (2007–12).
Solomon, Barbara Probst. *Horse-Trading and Ecstasy.* NY: North Point, 1989.
Solotaroff, Robert. *Down Mailer's Way.* Urbana: University of Illinois Press, 1975.
Spengler, Oswald. *The Decline of the West; Form and Actuality*, Vol. 1. NY: Knopf, 1926.
Stern, Richard G. *One Person and Another: On Writers and Writing.* Dallas: Baskerville, 1993.
Styron, William. *Lie Down in Darkness*. Indianapolis: Bobbs-Merrill, 1951.
———. *Selected Letters of William Styron*. Ed. Rose Styron, with R. Blakeslee Gilpin. NY: Random House, 1989.
———. *This Quiet Dust and Other Writings*. NY: Random House, 1982.
Suess, Raymond Karl, II. "Tom Sawyer, Horatio Alger and Sammy Glick: A Biography of Young Mailer." Ph.D. diss., St. Louis University, 1974.
Szwed, John. *So What: The Life of Miles Davis*. NY: Simon & Schuster, 2002.
Talese, Gay. *A Writer's Life*. NY: Random House, 2006.
Tempels, Placide. *Bantu Philosophy.* Paris: Présence Africaine, 1959.
Timberg, Bernard M. *Television Talk: A History of the TV Talk Show.* Austin: University of Texas Press, 2002.
Trilling, Diana. *Claremont Essays*. NY: Harcourt, Brace & World, 1964.

———. *We Must March My Darlings: A Critical Decade.* NY: Harcourt Brace Jovanovich, 1977.

Trotsky, Leon. *History of the Russian Revolution.* NY: Simon & Schuster, 1937.

Vidal, Gore. *Dreaming War.* NY: Thunder's Mouth Press/Nation Books, 2002.

———. *Homage to Daniel Shays: Collected Essays, 1952–1972.* NY: Vintage, 1973.

———. *Matters of Fact and Fiction: Essays, 1973–1976.* NY: Random House, 1977.

———. *Palimpsest: A Memoir.* NY: Viking, 1995.

———. *Point to Point Navigation.* NY: Doubleday, 2006.

———. *United States: Essays, 1952–1992.* NY: Random House, 1993.

Vogelgesang, Sandy. *The Long Dark Night of the Soul: The American Intellectual Left and the Vietnam War.* NY: Harper & Row, 1974.

von der Leyen, Marie-Louise. *Lifelines: Unusual Characters Tell Their Story.* Munich: Piper Verlag, 2006.

Wakefield, Dan. *New York in the Fifties.* Boston: Houghton Mifflin, 1992.

Wasserman, Barbara. "Spain 1948." *Hudson Review*, Autumn 2000.

Wenke, Joseph. *Mailer's America.* Hanover, NH: University Press of New England, 1987.

West, James L. W., III. *William Styron: A Life.* NY: Random House, 1998.

Whalen-Bridge, John, ed. *Norman Mailer's Later Fictions:* Ancient Evenings *Through* Castle in the Forest. Basingstoke, England: Palgrave Macmillan, 2010.

Winters, Shelley. *Shelley, Also Known as Shirley.* NY: Morrow, 1980.

———. *Shelley II: The Middle of My Century.* NY: Simon & Schuster, 1989.

Wolf, Daniel, and Edwin Fancher, eds. *The Village Voice Reader.* NY: Doubleday, 1962.

Wolfe, Tom. *Hooking Up.* NY: Farrar, Straus and Giroux, 2000.

Zolotow, Maurice. *Marilyn Monroe.* NY: Harcourt Brace, 1960.

PHOTO CREDITS

1–12, 14, 17, 19, 25, 32, 39–40, 44–45: Courtesy of Barbara Mailer Wasserman. 13: U.S. Army Military History Institute. 15: Gerald Holton. Courtesy of Alaric Naiman. 16: Courtesy of Erin Cressida Wilson. 18: Udel Brothers/Rinehart and Co. 20: Courtesy of Rhoda Lazare Wolf. 21: Associated Newspapers/Solo Syndication. 22: Ivan Massar/Black Star. 23: Emily Barry Lovering. 26: Copyright © The Estate of Diane Arbus, LLC. Courtesy of Lawrence Schiller. 27, 41: Cannon Films. 28: Yvonne Hannemann. 29: Paul Schwartzman. Copyright © The Norman Mailer Estate. 30: Courtesy of Sheldon H. Ramsdell Estate. 31: Donn Pennebaker. 33: Courtesy of Carol Stevens. 34: Courtesy of Eileen Frederickson. 35, 43, 47: Copyright Polaris Communications, Inc. All rights reserved. 36, 42, 46, 51: Copyright © The Norman Mailer Estate. 37: Norris Church Mailer. Courtesy of Matthew Mailer. 38: Milos Forman/Dino De Laurentiis/Sunley Productions. 48: Copyright © Nancy Crampton. 49: Donna Pedro Lennon. 50: Warren Mason. 52, 53: Mark James. 54: Courtesy of the Norman Mailer Center. All rights reserved.

INDEX